HARCOURT HORIZONS

United States History

TEACHER'S EDITION

VOLUME 2

Initial	Last Name, First Name	B337674/2019	
B	Byrne, Terri		✓
Book Title		# of Items 4	
Harcourt Horizons 5th grade US History			Pickup
Gr/Subject OR Category			Item Number 0069
5th - Soc. Studies			
Condition			
Good			
Fri. Price $15.00	Sat. Price $7.50	518839	

Harcourt
SCHOOL PUBLISHERS

Orlando   Austin   New York   San Diego   Toronto   London

Visit *The Learning Site!*
www.harcourtschool.com

HARCOURT HORIZONS

Printed in the United States of America

ISBN 0-15-339633-4

2 3 4 5 6 7 8 9 10 030 10 09 08 07 06 05

Contents

Harcourt Horizons
Components

For content updates and additional information for teaching Harcourt Horizons, see The Learning Site: Social Studies Center at www.harcourtschool.com.

STUDENT SUPPORT MATERIALS	K	1	2	3	4	5	6
Pupil Editions*		●	●	●	●	●	●
Big Book*	●						
Unit Big Book*		●	●				
Activity Books*	●	●	●	●	●	●	●
Time for Kids Readers*	●	●	●	●	●	●	●

TEACHER SUPPORT MATERIAL	K	1	2	3	4	5	6
Teacher's Editions*	●	●	●	●	●	●	●
Activity Books, Teacher's Editions*				●	●	●	●
Assessment Programs*		●	●	●	●	●	●
Skills Transparencies*		●	●	●	●	●	●
Reading and Vocabulary Transparencies*		●	●	●	●	●	●
Audiotext Collections*	●	●	●	●	●	●	●

TECHNOLOGY	K	1	2	3	4	5	6
The Learning Site: Social Studies Center	●	●	●	●	●	●	●
GeoSkills CD-ROM*		●	●	●	●	●	●
Field Trip Videos*		●	●	●	●	●	●

* Available in Spanish

HARCOURT HORIZONS
United States History

Harcourt
SCHOOL PUBLISHERS

Orlando   Austin   New York   San Diego   Toronto   London

Visit *The Learning Site!*
www.harcourtschool.com

HARCOURT HORIZONS

UNITED STATES HISTORY

General Editor

Dr. Michael J. Berson
Associate Professor
Social Science Education
University of South Florida
Tampa, Florida

Contributing Authors

Dr. Robert P. Green, Jr.
Professor
School of Education
Clemson University
Clemson, South Carolina

Dr. Thomas M. McGowan
Chairperson and Professor
Center for Curriculum and Instruction
University of Nebraska
Lincoln, Nebraska

Dr. Linda Kerrigan Salvucci
Associate Professor
Department of History
Trinity University
San Antonio, Texas

Series Consultants

Dr. Robert Bednarz
Professor
Department of Geography
Texas A&M University
College Station, Texas

Dr. Asa Grant Hilliard III
Fuller E. Callaway Professor
  of Urban Education
Georgia State University
Atlanta, Georgia

Dr. Thomas M. McGowan
Chairperson and Professor
Center for Curriculum and Instruction
University of Nebraska
Lincoln, Nebraska

Dr. John J. Patrick
Professor of Education
Indiana University
Bloomington, Indiana

Dr. Philip VanFossen
Associate Professor,
  Social Studies Education,
  and Associate Director,
  Purdue Center for Economic Education
Purdue University
West Lafayette, Indiana

Dr. Hallie Kay Yopp
Professor
Department of Elementary, Bilingual, and
  Reading Education
California State University, Fullerton
Fullerton, California

Content Reviewers

United States Geography

Dr. Phillip Bacon
Professor Emeritus
Geography and Anthropology
University of Houston
Houston, Texas

Native Americans and European Exploration

Dr. Susan Deans-Smith
Associate Professor
Department of History
University of Texas at Austin
Austin, Texas

Dr. John Jeffries Martin
Professor
Department of History
Trinity University
San Antonio, Texas

Richard Nichols
President
Richard Nichols and Associates
Fairview, New Mexico

Early Settlement and the American Revolution

Dr. John W. Johnson
Professor and Head
Department of History
University of Northern Iowa
Cedar Falls, Iowa

Dr. John P. Kaminski
Director, Center for the Study of
  the American Constitution
Department of History
University of Wisconsin
Madison, Wisconsin

Dr. Elizabeth Mancke
Associate Professor of History
Department of History
University of Akron
Akron, Ohio

The Constitution and United States Government

Dr. James M. Banner, Jr.
Historian
Washington, D.C.

Carol Egbo
Social Studies Consultant
Waterford Schools
Waterford, Michigan

Dr. John P. Kaminski
Director, Center for the Study of
the American Constitution
Department of History
University of Wisconsin
Madison, Wisconsin

Dr. John J. Patrick
Professor of Education
Indiana University
Bloomington, Indiana

The National Period and Westward Expansion

Dr. Ross Frank
Professor
Department of Ethnic Studies
University of California at San Diego
La Jolla, California

Civil War and Reconstruction

Dr. Judith Giesburg
Assistant Professor
Department of History
Northern Arizona University
Flagstaff, Arizona

The United States in the Twentieth Century

Dr. Carol McKibben
Visiting Professor
Monterey Institute of International Studies
Monterey, California

Dr. Albert Raboteau
Henry W. Putnam Professor
Department of Religion
Princeton University
Princeton, New Jersey

Classroom Reviewers

Kathleen Arseneau
Teacher
St. Matthew's School
Kalispell, Montana

Portia F. Bohannon-Ramsey
Teacher and Social Studies Chair
James E. McDade Classical School
Chicago, Illinois

Anna Bordlee
Teacher
Bridge City Elementary School
Bridge City, Louisiana

Lucille Ferragamo
Teacher
A. C. Whelan Elementary School
Revere, Massachusetts

Barbara Haack
Teacher
Perkins Academy
Des Moines, Iowa

Kimberly Hillman
Teacher
Council Traditional Magnet School
Mobile, Alabama

Margaret Kennedy
Teacher
Jason Lee Elementary School
Portland, Oregon

Amy M. Krohn
Teacher
Tombaugh Elementary School
Las Cruces, New Mexico

Cindy Merchant
Teacher
Denver Place School
Wilmington, Ohio

Barbara Motzer
Teacher
General Wayne Elementary School
Malvern, Pennsylvania

Wendy Ogawa
Schoolwide Coordinator
Wheeler Elementary School
Wahiawa, Hawaii

Timothy C. Owens
Principal
Shore Acres Elementary School
St. Petersburg, Florida

Heather Skelton
Teacher
James I. Gibson Elementary School
Henderson, Nevada

Sandra Young
Teacher
Palm Lake Elementary School
Orlando, Florida

Maps
researched and prepared by
MAPQUEST.COM

Readers
written and designed by
TIME FOR KIDS

Take a Field Trip
video tour segments provided by

CNN Turner Le@rning

Printed in the United States of America

ISBN 0-15-339619-9

1 2 3 4 5 6 7 8 9 10 048 13 12 11 10 09 08 07 06 05 04

Contents

· UNIT ·

1

The Land and Early People

iv

 · UNIT ·

2

Time of Encounters

· UNIT ·
3

The English Colonies

· UNIT ·

4

The American Revolution

vii

· UNIT ·

5

A New Nation

viii

· UNIT ·

6

Civil War Times

· UNIT ·

7

The Twentieth Century

· UNIT ·

8

The United States and the World

Reference

Features You Can Use

Time Lines

Reading Your Textbook

Getting Started

Your textbook is divided into eight units.

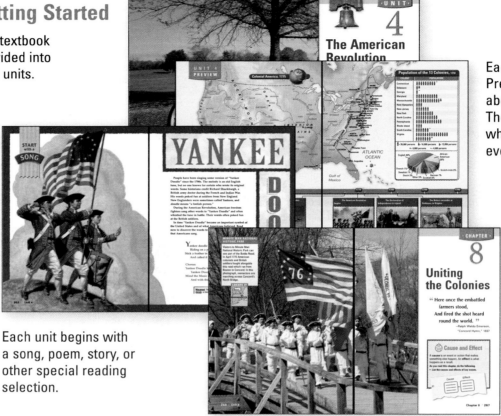

Each unit has a Unit Preview that gives facts about important events. The Preview also shows where and when those events took place.

Each unit begins with a song, poem, story, or other special reading selection.

Each unit is divided into chapters, and each chapter is divided into lessons.

The Parts of a Lesson

This statement gives you ideas to help you as you read the lesson.

This statement tells you why it is important to read the lesson.

These are the new vocabulary terms you will learn in the lesson.

Lesson title

This part of the time line shows the period when the events in the lesson took place.

Each new vocabulary term is highlighted in yellow and defined.

Each lesson is divided into several short sections.

Each lesson, like each chapter and each unit, ends with a review. There may be a Summary Time Line that shows the order of the events covered in the lesson. Questions and a performance activity help you check your understanding of the lesson.

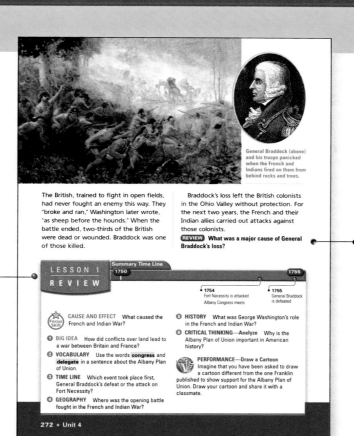

General Braddock (above) and his troops panicked when the French and Indians fired on them from behind rocks and trees.

The British, trained to fight in open fields, had never fought an enemy this way. They "broke and ran," Washington later wrote, "as sheep before the hounds." When the battle ended, two-thirds of the British were dead or wounded. Braddock was one of those killed.

Braddock's loss left the British colonists in the Ohio Valley without protection. For the next two years, the French and their Indian allies carried out attacks against those colonists.

REVIEW What was a major cause of General Braddock's loss?

Each short section ends with a **REVIEW** question that will help you check whether you understand what you have read. Be sure to answer this question before you continue reading the lesson.

LESSON 1 REVIEW

Summary Time Line
1750 · 1755

• 1754 Fort Necessity is attacked; Albany Congress meets
• 1755 General Braddock is defeated

Focus Skill — **CAUSE AND EFFECT** What caused the French and Indian War?

1 **BIG IDEA** How did conflicts over land lead to a war between Britain and France?

2 **VOCABULARY** Use the words **congress** and **delegate** in a sentence about the Albany Plan of Union.

3 **TIME LINE** Which event took place first, General Braddock's defeat or the attack on Fort Necessity?

4 **GEOGRAPHY** Where was the opening battle fought in the French and Indian War?

5 **HISTORY** What was George Washington's role in the French and Indian War?

6 **CRITICAL THINKING**—Analyze Why is the Albany Plan of Union important in American history?

PERFORMANCE—Draw a Cartoon Imagine that you have been asked to draw a cartoon different from the one Franklin published to show support for the Albany Plan of Union. Draw your cartoon and share it with a classmate.

272 • Unit 4

Skills

Your textbook has lessons that will help you build your reading, citizenship, chart and graph, and map and globe skills.

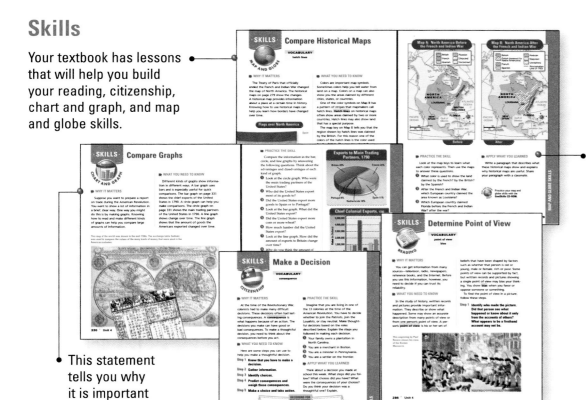

This statement tells you why it is important to learn the skill.

You will be able to practice and apply the skills you learn.

xvii

Special Features

The feature called Examine Primary Sources shows you ways to learn about different kinds of objects and documents.

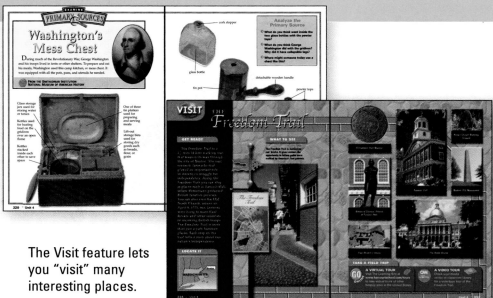

The Visit feature lets you "visit" many interesting places.

Atlas

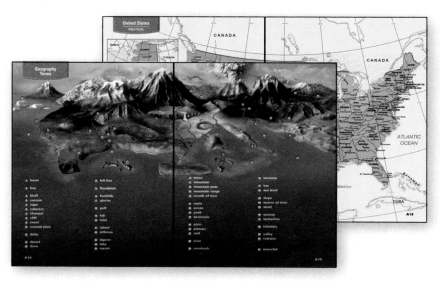

The Atlas provides maps and a list of geography terms with illustrations.

For Your Reference

At the back of your textbook, you will find the reference tools listed below.

- Almanac
- American Documents
- Biographical Dictionary
- Gazetteer
- Glossary
- Index

You can use these tools to look up words and to find information about people, places, and other topics.

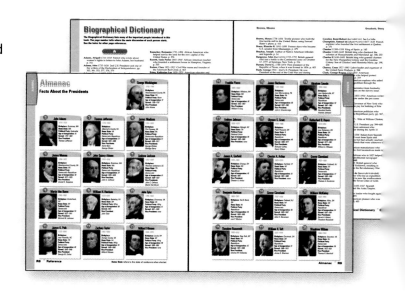

xviii

Atlas

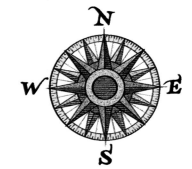

A1

Skill Lesson

OBJECTIVES

- Explain what a map is.
- Identify the parts of a map.
- Use a grid system to locate places.

Vocabulary

map title p. A2	compass rose
map key p. A2	p. A3
inset map p. A2	cardinal
grid system	directions p. A3
p. A3	intermediate
locator p. A3	directions p. A3
map scale p. A3	

WORD CARDS

See pp. V1–V2.

1 Motivate

Why It Matters

Discuss why reading maps is an important skill. Have students brainstorm ways they can use maps in social studies. Emphasize that maps help us learn more about the world.

·SKILLS· Read a Map

VOCABULARY

map title	grid system	compass rose
map key	locator	cardinal directions
inset map	map scale	intermediate directions

➡ WHY IT MATTERS

Maps provide many kinds of information about the world around you. Knowing how to read maps is an important social studies skill.

➡ WHAT YOU NEED TO KNOW

A map is a drawing that shows all of or part of the Earth on a flat surface. Mapmakers add certain features to most of the maps they draw.

Mapmakers sometimes need to show places marked on the map in greater detail or places that are beyond the area shown on the map. Find Alaska and Hawaii on the map of the United States on pages A10–A11. This map shows the location of those two states in relation to the rest of the country.

- A **map title** tells the subject of the map. It may also identify the kind of map.
  - Political maps show cities, states, and countries.
  - Physical maps show kinds of land and bodies of water.
  - Historical maps show parts of the world as they were in the past.
- A **map key**, or legend, explains the symbols used on a map. Symbols may be colors, patterns, lines, or other special marks.
- An **inset map** is a small map within a larger map.

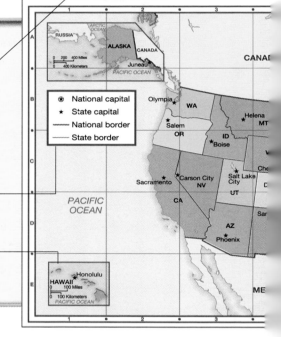

The United States

A2

BACKGROUND

Map Key Symbols Not all maps use the same symbols in the map key. However, a star is the most widely used symbol for national and state capital cities. The national capital is often represented with a bigger star than state capitals. In addition, the line for a national border is generally darker and thicker than the line for a state border.

Now find Alaska and Hawaii on the map below. To show this much detail for these states and the rest of the country on one map, the map would have to be much larger. Instead, Alaska and Hawaii are each shown in a separate **inset map**, or a small map within a larger map.

To help people find places on a map, mapmakers sometimes add lines that cross each other to form a pattern of squares called a **grid system**. Look at the map of the United States below. Around the grid are letters and numbers. The columns, which run up and down, have numbers. The rows, which run left and right, have letters. Each square on the map can be identified by its letter and number. For example, the

top row of squares in the map includes square A1, square A2, and square A3.

➡ **PRACTICE THE SKILL**

Use the map of the United States to answer the following questions.

1. What cities can be found in square B7?
2. In which direction would you travel to go from Phoenix, Arizona, to Columbia, South Carolina?
3. About how many miles is it from Austin, Texas, to Montgomery, Alabama?
4. Which two oceans border Alaska?

➡ **APPLY WHAT YOU LEARNED**

Choose one of the maps in the Atlas. With a partner, identify the parts of the map and discuss what the map tells you. Ask each other questions that can be answered by reading the map.

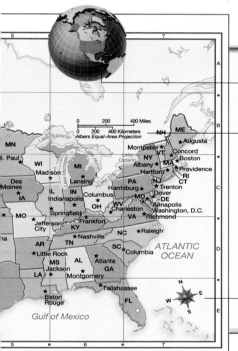

- A **locator** is a small map or picture of a globe that shows where the place on the main map is located.

- A **map scale** compares a distance on the map to a distance in the real world. It helps you find the real distance between places on a map.

- A **compass rose**, or direction marker, shows directions.
  - The **cardinal directions**, or main directions, are north, south, east, and west.
  - The **intermediate directions**, or directions between the cardinal directions, are northeast, northwest, southeast, and southwest.

MAP AND GLOBE SKILLS

A3

2 Teach

What You Need to Know

Ask students to read the labels describing the parts of a map. Point out to students that this is a political map. Discuss with students how the key, locator, scale, and compass rose make reading the map easier.

Q What besides bodies of water and the shape of land does this map show?

A capital cities, states, and countries

Practice the Skill—Answers

1. Phoenix
2. northeast
3. about 400 miles
4. Arctic Ocean and Pacific Ocean

3 Close

Apply What You Have Learned

Encourage students to reread the skill lesson if they are unable to identify parts of the map. You may wish to have students write down their questions and answers to share with the class.

ACTIVITY BOOK

Use ACTIVITY BOOK, p. 1, to give students additional practice using this skill.

TRANSPARENCY

Use SKILL TRANSPARENCY Atlas–1.

EXTEND AND ENRICH

Informative Writing Divide the class into small groups. Each group should write down as many uses for maps as they can think of. Then, ask groups to write an informative paragraph describing how maps influence and benefit people's lives.

RETEACH THE SKILL

Use the Map Scale Write four or five United States cities on the board. Have students use the map scale to estimate distances between the cities. Provide students with the correct distances. Direct students to compare their estimates with the true distances.

The World: Political

Set the Purpose

Main Idea Explain to students that a political map shows the names and borders of various political units, such as cities, states, provinces, and countries. This political map shows the names and borders of all the countries in the world.

Why It Matters Point out to students that this political map can be used to tell where a country is located and to see what size and shape that country is. The map can also be used to find out where a country is located in relation to other countries.

Visual Learning

Map Ask students how the map uses color to convey information. Guide them in recognizing that each country is a different color from the countries that surround it.

Also call students' attention to the map key. Tell students that a map key explains what the symbols used on a map stand for. This map key shows that gray lines indicate national borders.

Finally, point out the inset maps. Explain that inset maps are enlarged versions of a section of a map. Inset maps make it possible to show places in greater detail or to show places that are beyond the area shown on the main map.

Map Study

Geography Review latitude and longitude with students. Then ask them to identify the equator and the prime meridian.

Q If you were at a latitude of 20°N and a longitude of 100°W, in which country would you be?

A Mexico

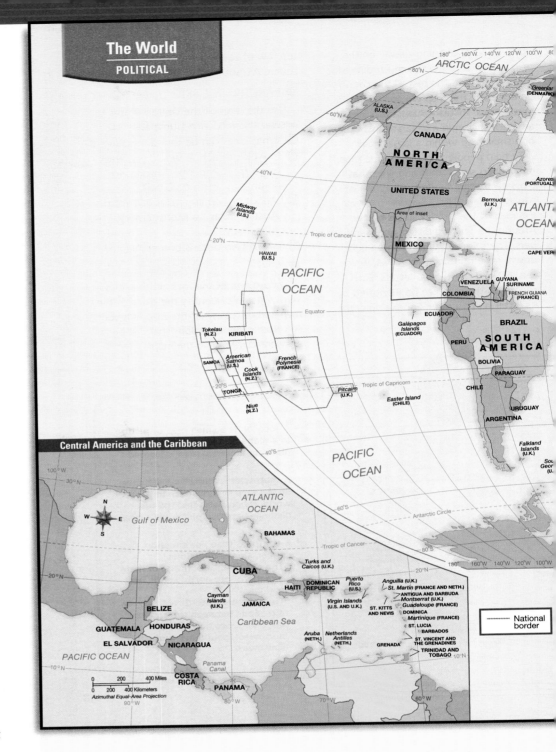

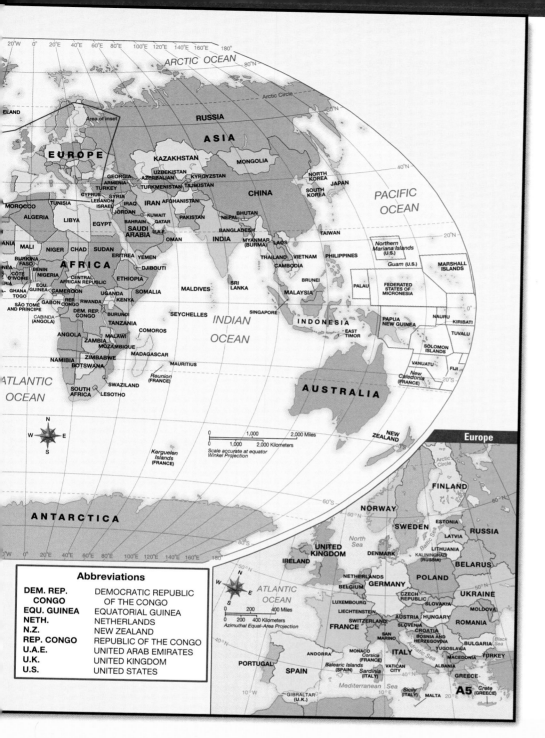

Abbreviations	
DEM. REP. CONGO	DEMOCRATIC REPUBLIC OF THE CONGO
EQU. GUINEA	EQUATORIAL GUINEA
NETH.	NETHERLANDS
N.Z.	NEW ZEALAND
REP. CONGO	REPUBLIC OF THE CONGO
U.A.E.	UNITED ARAB EMIRATES
U.K.	UNITED KINGDOM
U.S.	UNITED STATES

Map Study

Geography Review the concept of regions with students. Explain that regions are areas that have specific characteristics that set them apart from other areas. A region may be defined, for example, by its landforms, by its cultural or political characteristics, or by other characteristics such as economic activities or the language people speak. For example, Latin America is a large region that refers to Central and South America, Mexico, and the Caribbean Islands. The term refers to the languages spoken in the countries that make up this region: Spanish, Portuguese, and French, all of which are languages that are derived from Latin.

Geography Call students' attention to the compass rose on the main map. Remind students that a compass rose is used to determine direction. Compass roses are useful for explaining where a country is located in relation to another country.

Q What direction would you travel to get from Sri Lanka to India?

A north

CD-ROM

Explore GEOSKILLS CD-ROM to give students additional practice using map and globe skills.

MENTAL MAPPING

The Continent of North America You can use mental maps to judge students' level of knowledge and to correct any misconception students may have. Have students draw the continent of North America. They should label Canada, the United States, and Mexico. Have them include a compass rose on their drawings. After students have finished their drawings, have them compare their maps with an actual map of North America.

EXTEND AND ENRICH

Make a Political Map Scrapbook Organize students in groups of four or five and ask them to search discarded newspapers and magazines as well as online sources for examples of political maps. Have them find three or four good examples to paste onto sheets of paper. For each map, have them identify the political units shown on the map and write a caption describing how the map was used in its original context.

The World: Physical

Set the Purpose

Main Idea Explain that the map on this page is a physical map of the world. A physical map shows what the surface of Earth looks like.

Why It Matters Physical maps are useful for getting an overview of the key physical features of the area shown on the map. This map can be used to find out where the world's mountains, lakes, rivers, oceans, and other physical features are located.

Visual Learning

Map Emphasize that this map's primary purpose is to show physical features. Landforms and bodies of water are the main focus and are labeled. National borders are shown but are not labeled. Have students study the map key and note how the map uses color to show terrain and vegetation patterns. If necessary review terms such as *arid* and *tundra* with students.

Map Study

Geography Point out the compass rose, and ask a volunteer to describe its purpose. Be sure students understand the concept of both cardinal and intermediate directions.

Q If you traveled from North America to Europe, which direction would you be going?

A east

Geography Have students locate the Tropic of Cancer and the Tropic of Capricorn on the map. Explain that the area between these lines is known as the tropics and the weather there is usually warm.

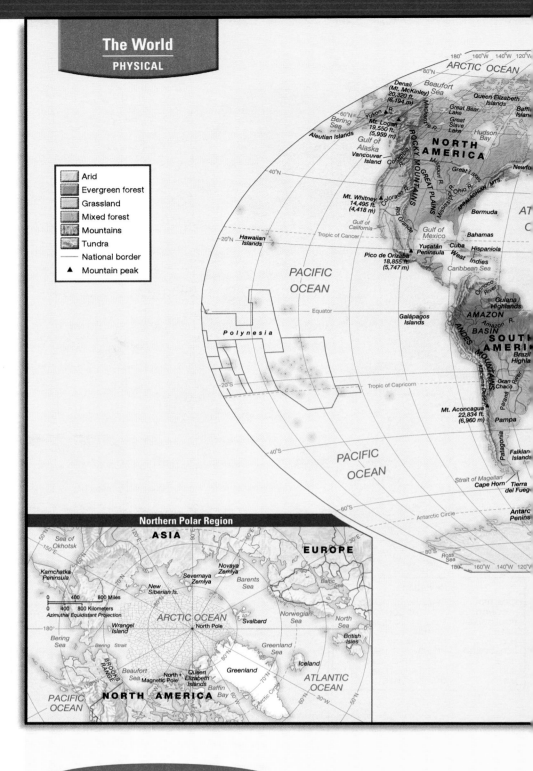

BACKGROUND

Map Projections Throughout history mapmakers have struggled with the difficulty of representing a spherical object—Earth—on a flat map. It is not possible to make a flat map completely accurate. The size and shape of some landmasses and areas become distorted, or changed.

Mapmakers must make compromises when they make flat maps. They use different projections, or ways of drawing Earth, depending on the main focus of the map. The main map on pages A6–A7, for example, is most accurate for the areas closest to the equator. Distortion increases as distance from the equator increases. The polar regions of the Arctic and Antarctic circles, for example, are quite distorted. Examine how different these two regions look on the inset maps, which use different projections to give a better representation.

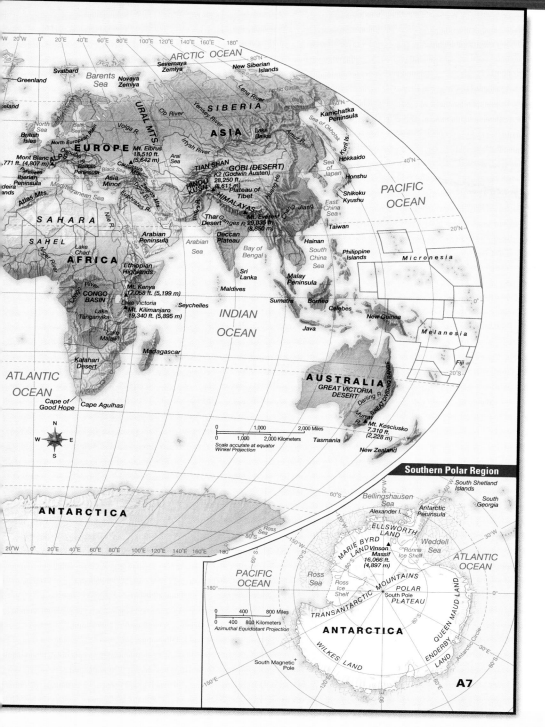

Southern Polar Region

A7

Map Study

Geography Invite students to use the map key and the compass rose to formulate descriptive sentences about key physical features of each continent. For example, for Africa students might come up with the following sentence: "The northern part of Africa is mainly arid, but the central part of the continent has more forests and is more mountainous."

Geography Call students' attention to the symbol used for a mountain peak.

Q What is the highest mountain shown on the map and on which continent is it found?

A Mt. Everest is in Asia

Geography Have students notice the different kinds of bodies of water shown on the map. You might mention that there are four oceans: the Pacific, Atlantic, Indian, and Arctic Oceans. Seas, bays, and gulfs are all parts of these oceans.

Q What body of water lies between Africa and Europe?

A the Mediterranean Sea

CD-ROM

Explore GEOSKILLS CD-ROM to give students additional practice using map and globe skills.

INTEGRATE MATHEMATICS

Measure Distances Have students use the map scale to measure the width of Australia from east to west along the Tropic of Capricorn. Ask them to first find the distance in miles and to then measure the distance in kilometers. The distance in miles is about 2,000. The distance in kilometers is about 3,200 kilometers.

REACH ALL LEARNERS

Advanced Learners Challenge students to find information to answer this question: How do internal and external forces change the physical makeup of Earth? To answer this question, suggest students research such physical phenomena as earthquakes, volcanoes, weathering, and erosion. Students may present their findings as an oral or written report.

EXTEND AND ENRICH

Create Physical Feature Factsheets Have students choose a landform or body of water shown on the map that they would like to visit. Ask them to research the feature. Then have them write a fact sheet (containing at least five facts) about the feature. Have students read their fact sheets to the rest of the class or post them on a bulletin board or wall map.

Western Hemisphere: Political

Set the Purpose

Main Idea Remind students that the equator divides Earth into the Northern and Southern Hemispheres and that the prime meridian divides Earth into the Eastern and Western Hemispheres. Explain that the map on page A8 is a political map of the Western Hemisphere.

Why It Matters A map that focuses on a single hemisphere is useful because it can show more detail than a world map. The map on page A8, for example, can be used to find the location of national capitals and major cities as well as nations and national borders.

Visual Learning

Map Remind students that a political map shows political units. In this case, the political units are countries, each of which is a different color from those that surround it. Remind students that the map key identifies symbols used on the map, the scale is used to determine distances, and the compass rose is used to determine direction.

Map Study

Geography Be sure students understand that although the map shows all the national capitals, it does not show every city in the Western Hemisphere. It shows only the major cities.

Q **What is the capital of Brazil?**

A Brasília

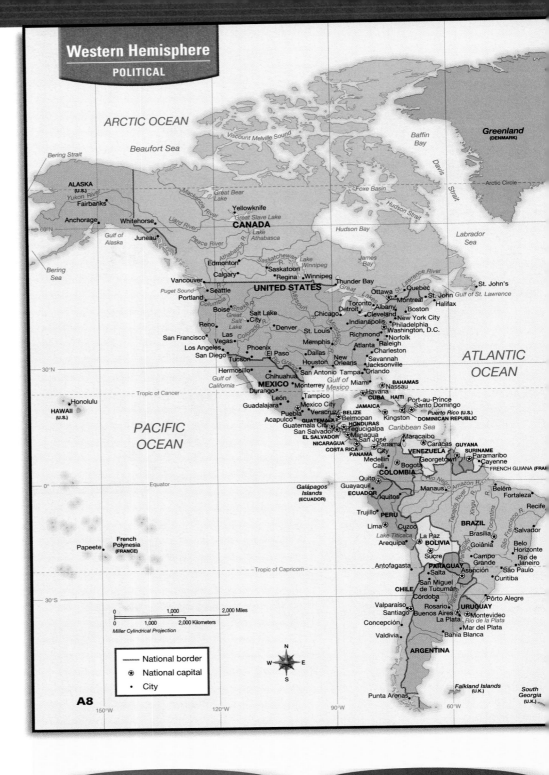

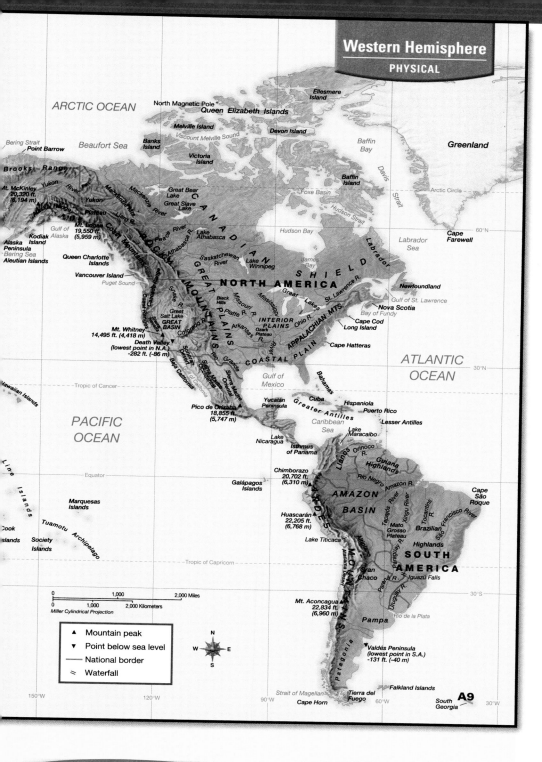

ARCTIC OCEAN

North Magnetic Pole
Queen Elizabeth Islands

Ellesmere Island

Melville Island
Devon Island

Viscount Melville Sound

Bering Strait
Point Barrow

Beaufort Sea

Banks Island

Victoria Island

Baffin Bay

Greenland

Brooks Range

Mt. McKinley 20,320 ft. (6,194 m)

Yukon

Baffin Island

Davis Strait

Arctic Circle   60°N

Yukon

Mackenzie Mts.

Great Bear Lake

Great Slave Lake

Foxe Basin

Mackenzie River

Peace River

Gulf of Alaska

Mt. Logan 19,550 ft. (5,959 m)

Kodiak Alaska Island

Alaska Peninsula

Bering Sea

Aleutian Islands

Queen Charlotte Islands

Vancouver Island
Puget Sound

Athabasca R.

Saskatchewan River

Lake Athabasca

Lake Winnipeg

Hudson Bay

Hudson Strait

James Bay

Labrador Sea

Labrador

Cape Farewell

SHIELD

CANADIAN

GREAT PLAINS

MOUNTAINS

ROCKY

NORTH AMERICA

Black Hills

Missouri R.

Platte R.

Great Lakes

St. Lawrence R.

Newfoundland

Gulf of St. Lawrence

Nova Scotia

Bay of Fundy

Cape Cod

Long Island

Great Salt Lake

GREAT BASIN

Colorado R.

INTERIOR PLAINS

Arkansas R.

Ohio R.

Ozark Plateau

APPALACHIAN MTS.

Mt. Whitney 14,495 ft. (4,418 m)

Snake R.

Death Valley (lowest point in N.A.) -282 ft. (-86 m)

Sierra Nevada

Rio Grande

COASTAL PLAIN

Cape Hatteras

ATLANTIC OCEAN   30°N

Gulf of California

Baja California

Sierra Madre Oriental

Gulf of Mexico

Bahamas

Hawaiian Islands

Tropic of Cancer

Yucatán Peninsula

Cuba
Greater Antilles

Hispaniola

Puerto Rico

Lesser Antilles

Pico de Orizaba 18,855 ft. (5,747 m)

PACIFIC OCEAN

Lake Nicaragua

Caribbean Sea

Lake Maracaibo

Isthmus of Panama

Orinoco R.

Llanos

Guiana Highlands

Line Islands

Equator

Galápagos Islands

Chimborazo 20,702 ft. (6,310 m)

Rio Negro

Amazon R.

Cape São Roque

Marquesas Islands

AMAZON BASIN

Huascarán 22,205 ft. (6,768 m)

Tapajós River

Xingu River

Tocantins R.

São Francisco River

Cook Islands

Tuamotu Archipelago

Society Islands

Lake Titicaca

Mato Grosso Plateau

Brazilian Highlands

ANDES

Tropic of Capricorn

Altiplano

Paraguay R.

SOUTH AMERICA

Gran Chaco

Iguazú Falls

MOUNTAINS

Paraná R.

Uruguay R.

30°S

0   1,000   2,000 Miles
0   1,000   2,000 Kilometers
Miller Cylindrical Projection

Mt. Aconcagua 22,834 ft. (6,960 m)

Pampa

Rio de la Plata

▲ Mountain peak
▼ Point below sea level
— National border
≈ Waterfall

N
W   E
S

Valdés Peninsula (lowest point in S.A.) -131 ft. (-40 m)

Patagonia

150°W   120°W   90°W

Strait of Magellan

Tierra del Fuego

Cape Horn   60°W

Falkland Islands

South Georgia   30°W

A9

Western Hemisphere: Physical

Set the Purpose

Main Idea Tell students that this map is a physical map of the Western Hemisphere. Remind students that a physical map's main purpose is to show what the surface of Earth looks like.

Why It Matters Because this is a map of the Western Hemisphere and not of the whole world, more detail about the Western Hemisphere's landforms and physical features can be shown.

Visual Learning

Map Allow students time to identify various kinds of physical features shown, such as mountains, lakes, rivers, highlands. Discuss how color and shading are used to distinguish these features. For example, rivers and bodies of water are shown in blue and mountains are shaded in a way that suggests the peaks and valleys of real mountains.

Map Study

Geography Point out the symbols in the map key. Ask students to identify the symbol that is used to show a mountain peak and the symbol used to show a point below sea level. Consider asking these questions:

- What is the lowest point in South America? the Valdés Peninsula
- What is the highest point in the Andes Mountains? Mt. Aconcagua

CD-ROM

Explore GEOSKILLS CD-ROM to give students additional practice using map and globe skills.

INTEGRATE SCIENCE

The North Poles Explain that the North Pole can be described in two ways. The geographic north pole is the place in the Northern Hemisphere where all the lines of longitude meet. There is also the north magnetic pole. Earth's rotation and its iron core create a magnetic field that, in fact, makes Earth act like a giant magnet. A compass needle aligns with the north magnetic pole, not the geographic north pole.

EXTEND AND ENRICH

Define Terms Ask students to use a geographical dictionary to find a description of each of the following physical features: altiplano, archipelago, highland, llano, pampas, point, range, strait, sierra, sound. Ask students to draw a picture of each feature and write a caption for it. Discuss the features with the class and then have students locate an example of each on the map.

United States Overview

Set the Purpose

Main Idea Explain to students that the map on these pages gives an overview, or general picture, of the United States. The map shows state borders, national borders, and major bodies of water that border the United States.

Why It Matters This map can be used to find the location of all the states in the United States and to see where they are located in relation to each other. The map is also helpful for identifying the countries that are the United States' closest neighbors.

Visual Learning

Map Point out to students that all parts of the United States are shown in pink and that each state is labeled with its name and the two-letter abbreviation used by the United States Postal Service.

Have students locate each of the 50 states as you call out state names.

Q Which state lies farthest north? farthest east?

A Alaska; Maine

Have students note that all other countries are simply labeled with their names. No internal borders, such as those of states or provinces, are shown for these other countries, as the focus of the map is the United States.

Map Study

Geography Have students identify the bodies of water that surround the United States.

Q Which ocean is located on the eastern border of Georgia?

A the Atlantic Ocean

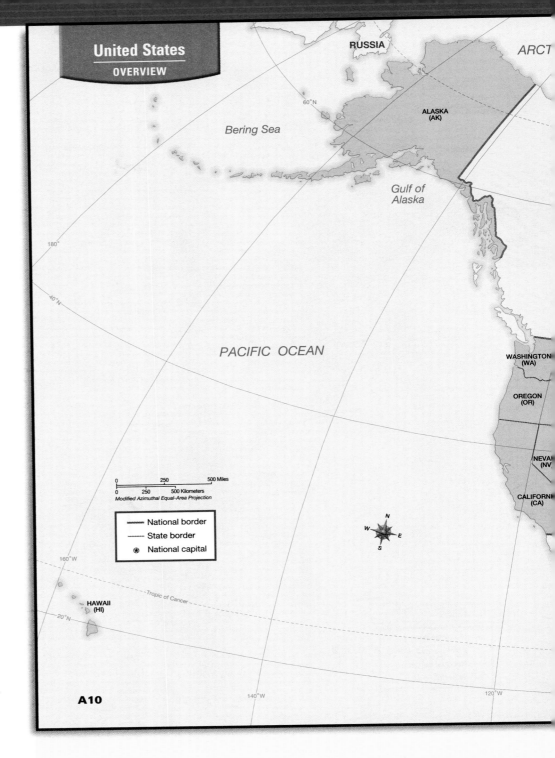

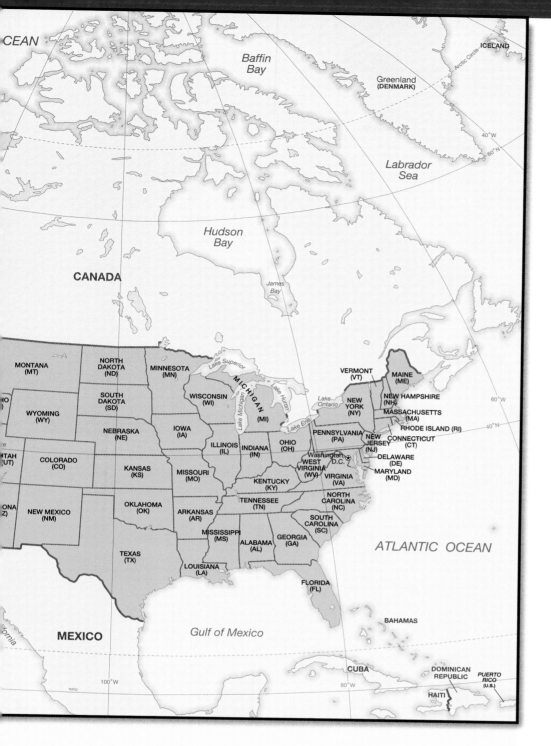

Geography Ask students to explain the purpose of a map scale. If necessary, review how to use the map scale to measure distances. Point out that the scale can be used to measure distances in miles or kilometers.

Q What is the distance in kilometers of the border between Arkansas and Louisiana?

A about 250 kilometers

Geography Discuss with students how borders for countries and states are decided. Point out that some national and state borders follow the paths of physical features such as rivers. Invite students to look at the state borders on the map and hypothesize which ones might follow a physical feature. Have students consult the physical map of the United States on pages A14–A15 to check their hypotheses.

CD-ROM

Explore GEOSKILLS CD-ROM to give students additional practice using map and globe skills.

BACKGROUND

Alaska Alaska is the largest state in the United States. When Alaska became a state in 1959, it increased the size of the country by 20 percent! At the time of its purchase from Russia in 1867, many Americans thought of the area as a vast frozen wasteland. They sneeringly referred to it as Seward's Folly—a reference to the United States Secretary of State William S. Seward, who pushed the deal through. Alaska, however, proved to have a wealth of natural resources.

EXTEND AND ENRICH

Have a Class Discussion Invite students to name other states they have visited. List the states on the board, and have students locate them on the map. Then ask students to share their impressions of the other states' climate, cities, plant life, and so forth. Discuss how the other states compare with your state and what it might be like to live in one of the other states.

United States: Political

Set the Purpose

Main Idea Explain to students that the map on these pages is a political map of the United States. It shows the borders of states as well as the borders of the United States. The map also divides the United States into four regions.

Why It Matters A political map of the United States can be used to find out where a state is located and to see what size and shape that state is. This map can also be used to identify regions of the United States, each state capital, and a number of major cities.

Visual Learning

Map Students will probably notice that one of the key features of this map is that it divides the United States into four regions. Point out the map key and the color coding used to identify these regions. Explain that these regions are geographic regions. In other words, each region consists of several states located in the same part of the country. In general, the states in each region have similar physical features. For example, the West has many mountainous areas while the Middle West is known for its vast expanses of plains.

Map Study

Geography Ask a volunteer to name each geographic region. Consider asking these questions:

- Which region appears to be the largest? the West
- In which region do you live? Students should correctly identify the region in which they live.

Geography Have students practice identifying the 50 states on a map and telling which states are part of each of the four geographical regions.

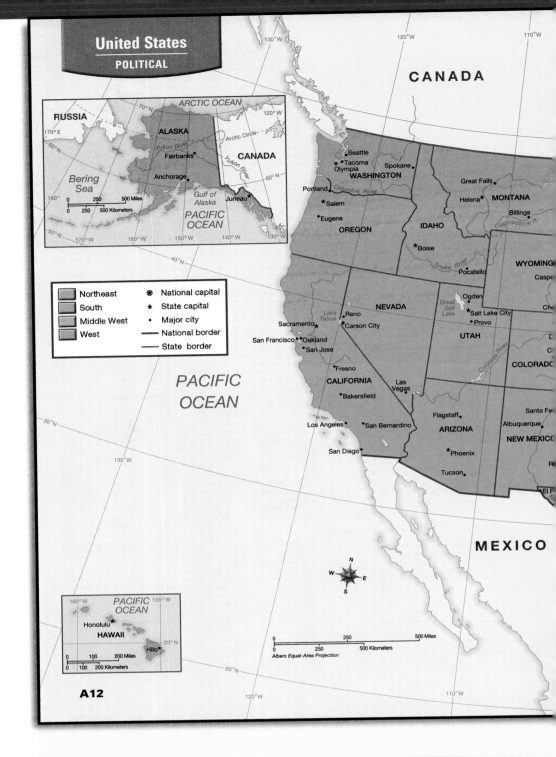

INTEGRATE LANGUAGE ARTS

Write a Short Story
Ask students to choose a region to research. Then ask them to write a short story that is set in that region. Encourage them to incorporate information about climate and weather, physical features, and the history and culture of the region into their stories to give their stories a sense of reality.

MAKE IT RELEVANT

At Home Have students interview adult relatives about what they like about the geographical location they live in. Encourage students to ask about any other regions the relatives have lived in and how they compare with the region they now live in. Invite volunteers to share their findings with the class and discuss what the results of the interviews reflect about the climate, economy, and location of the region.

CANADA

Lake of the Woods

NORTH DAKOTA   Grand Forks

Bismarck   Fargo   Duluth

MINNESOTA   Sault Sainte Marie

Lake Superior

MICHIGAN

Lake Huron

MAINE

Augusta

VERMONT   Portland

Burlington   **NEW HAMPSHIRE**

Montpelier   Concord

Lake Champlain

SOUTH DAKOTA   St. Paul   Minneapolis

WISCONSIN   Green Bay

Pierre   Madison

Sioux Falls

Lake Michigan

Grand Rapids   Flint

Milwaukee   Lansing   Detroit

Lake St. Clair

Lake Erie

Lake Ontario

NEW YORK   Manchester   Boston

Rochester   Albany   Worcester   **MASSACHUSETTS**

Buffalo   Providence   **RHODE ISLAND**

CONNECTICUT

Hartford   Bridgeport

Sioux City

IOWA   Cedar Rapids   Rockford   Chicago   South Bend   Toledo

Cleveland   **PENNSYLVANIA**

Harrisburg   **NEW JERSEY**

Newark   New York City

NEBRASKA   Omaha   Des Moines   Davenport   **ILLINOIS**   Gary   **OHIO**   Wheeling   Pittsburgh

Peoria   **INDIANA**   Columbus   Baltimore   Philadelphia

Platte River   Lincoln   Decatur   Dayton   Cincinnati   Wilmington   **DELAWARE**

Springfield   Indianapolis   Annapolis   Dover

WEST VIRGINIA   Washington, D.C.   **MARYLAND**

Ohio River   Charleston   **VIRGINIA**   Richmond

Topeka   Kansas City   St. Louis   Louisville   Frankfort   Lexington   Roanoke   Newport News   Norfolk

KANSAS   Missouri River   Jefferson City   Evansville   **KENTUCKY**

Wichita   **MISSOURI**   Springfield

Greensboro

Knoxville   Winston-Salem   Raleigh   **NORTH CAROLINA**

Nashville   Charlotte

OKLAHOMA   Tulsa   **ARKANSAS**   **TENNESSEE**   Chattanooga

Arkansas River   Memphis   Huntsville   **SOUTH CAROLINA**   Columbia

Oklahoma City   Fort Smith   Little Rock   Atlanta   Charleston

Red River   Lake Texoma   Birmingham   **GEORGIA**

Fort Worth   **MISSISSIPPI**   **ALABAMA**   Macon

Abilene   Dallas   Meridian   Montgomery   Columbus   Savannah

LOUISIANA   Jackson

TEXAS

Austin   Beaumont   Baton Rouge   Biloxi   Mobile   Tallahassee

Houston   Shreveport   New Orleans   **FLORIDA**

San Antonio   Orlando

Rio Grande   Tampa   West Palm Beach

Laredo   Corpus Christi   St. Petersburg   Lake Okeechobee

Miami

ATLANTIC OCEAN

BAHAMAS

Gulf of Mexico

CUBA

A13

Map Study

Geography Have students use the map key to find the symbol for the major cities. Then ask them what they think is meant by "major city." Guide them in understanding that major cities are those with large populations.

Geography Ask students to look at the map key and identify the symbol for the national capital.

Q In which region is the national capital?

A the South

Geography Call students' attention to the inset maps. Explain that in this case, the inset maps are used to show Alaska and Hawaii—places that are beyond the area shown on the main map.

CD-ROM

Explore GEOSKILLS CD-ROM to give students additional practice using map and globe skills.

Agriculture in the Middle West

Land use is another way of defining a region. The Middle West, for example, is one of the key agricultural regions of the United States. The region may be divided into subregions according to land use. Many of these subregions have nicknames. For example, a broad swath of land extending west from Ohio to South Dakota is often called the Corn Belt because so much of the land in the area is planted with corn.

Explore Regional Cooking

Discuss the link between foods and regions and how traditional regional dishes tend to depend on foods locally available or on the ethnic or cultural backgrounds of the people that live in the region. In the Northeast, which is close to the Atlantic Ocean, seafood figures prominently in typical regional dishes such as clam chowder. Have students choose a region and then use cookbooks or online recipe archives to research recipes traditionally associated with that region.

United States: Physical

Set the Purpose

Main Idea Tell students that the map on these pages is a physical map of the United States. It shows important landforms and bodies of water found in the United States.

Why It Matters This map can be used to learn the names and locations of important physical features in the United States.

Visual Learning

Map Refer students to the map key. Point out that the colors represent different kinds of terrain, vegetation, or plant life. Review any unfamiliar terms. Ask a volunteer to explain how the map shows where the land is flat and where it is mountainous.

Map Study

Geography Remind students that the United States may be divided into geographic regions—the Northeast, the Middle West, the South, and the West.

Q Which region has the most arid areas?

A the West

Geography Have students describe the relative locations of major physical features of the United States.

Q How would you describe the location of the Mojave Desert?

A Possible response: The Mojave Desert lies on the border of California and Nevada not far from Death Valley and Lake Mead. It is in the western part of the country.

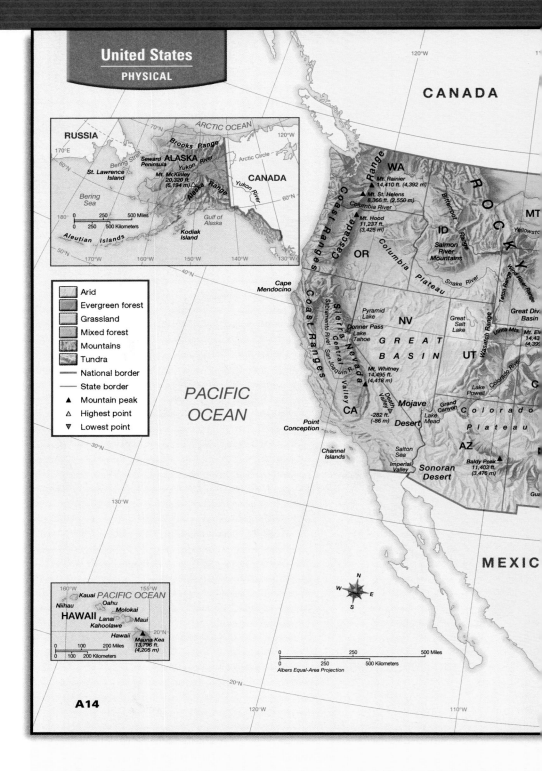

CANADA

100°W   90°W   80°W   70°W

50°N

40°N

70°W

30°N

100°W   90°W   80°W

Lake of the Woods

Upper Red Lake
Lower Red Lake
Mesabi Range
Isle Royale
Keweenaw Peninsula
Lake Superior
Upper Peninsula

Lake Sakakawea

ND

Leech Lake
Mille Lacs Lake

MN

WI

Lower Peninsula
Lake Michigan

MI

Lake St. Clair
Lake Huron

Lake Ontario
Niagara Falls
Lake Erie

Lake Oahe

SD

Missouri River
Mississippi River
Wisconsin River

Lake Winnebago

ME
Moosehead Lake
Mt. Katahdin 5,269 ft. (1,606 m)

Lake Champlain
VT
NY
Adirondack Mountains
Green Mts.
Connecticut R.
White Mts.
Mt. Washington 6,288 ft. (1,917 m)
NH
MA
Cape Ann
Cape Cod

Finger Lakes
Hudson R.
CT
RI

Long Island

Sand Hills

NE

Platte R.

IA

INTERIOR
PLAINS

Illinois River

IL

Wabash River

IN

CENTRAL PLAINS

OH

PA

Allegheny Mts.

NJ

Ohio River

WV

VA

Potomac R.
MD
DE
Delaware Bay

APPALACHIAN MOUNTAINS
PIEDMONT
COASTAL PLAIN

Cape Charles
Chesapeake Bay
Albemarle Sound

Smoky Hills

KS

Red Hills

Missouri River

MO

Lake of the Ozarks

Harry S. Truman Reservoir

Ozark Plateau

Mississippi River

Lake Barkley

Cumberland Gap

Cumberland R.

Mt. Mitchell 6,684 ft. (2,037 m)

KY

TN

James R.
Roanoke R.

NC

Cape Fear River

Cape Hatteras

OK

Canadian River

Arkansas River

Ouachita Mountains

Lake Texoma

AR

Red River

MS

Tombigbee R.

Alabama R.

Savannah River
Clark Hill Lake
Stone Mountain
Ocmulgee R.
Oconee R.

SC

GA

Cape Fear

ATLANTIC OCEAN

TX

Sabine River

Brazos River

Sam Rayburn Reservoir

Toledo Bend Reservoir

LA

COASTAL PLAIN

Lake Maurepas
Lake Pontchartrain

AL

Chattahoochee R.

Altamaha R.

Okefenokee Swamp

St. Johns River

Cape Canaveral

Edwards Plateau

Colorado River

Rio Grande

COASTAL PLAIN

Galveston Bay

Mississippi Delta

Mobile Bay

Tampa Bay

FL

Lake Okeechobee

BAHAMAS

Everglades
Cape Sable
Florida Keys
Straits of Florida

Gulf of Mexico

CUBA

A15

Map Study

Geography Allow students a few moments to identify the major mountain ranges in the United States. Call their attention to the map key and the symbol for mountain peaks.

Q **Are the tallest mountains found in the eastern or western mountain ranges?**

A the western mountain ranges

Geography Have students compare and contrast landforms and bodies of water in different parts of the country. You might ask questions like these:

- How is southern California different from northern California? Southern California is arid and northern California has evergreen forests.
- Which part of the United States is mostly flat grassland? the central part of the United States
- Which state has a large tundra area? Alaska

CD-ROM

Explore GEOSKILLS CD-ROM to give students additional practice using map and globe skills.

MENTAL MAPPING

The Mountain Ranges of the United States Invite students to draw a map of the United States. Ask them to draw in and identify at least two major mountain ranges. Evaluate students' efforts by checking the accuracy of the location and the length of the mountain ranges.

Rocky Mountains

Appalachian Mountains

EXTEND AND ENRICH

Take a Virtual Hike Have groups of students do online research on one of the following long-distance hiking trails in the United States: the Appalachian Trail, the American Discovery Trail, the Continental Divide Trail, the North Country National Scenic Trail, or the Pacific Crest Trail. Have students mark the route on an outline map of the United States and then give a presentation to the rest of the class about the trail.

Canada

Set the Purpose

Main Idea Explain to students that this map of Canada shows political units as well as some physical features. The map shows Canada's ten provinces and three territories.

Why It Matters This map can be used to find out where Canada's provinces are located and to compare their sizes and shapes. This map can also be used to identify key cities and capitals and a number of important physical features.

Visual Learning

Map Have students notice Canada's huge size. Mention to students that Canada is larger than the United States and is, in fact, one of the largest nations in the world. Only Russia has more territory than Canada. Point out each province and territory for students. Have them note the difference in size between the province of Prince Edward Island and the provinces of Quebec or Ontario.

Map Study

Geography Like the United States, Canada may be divided into geographic regions. Newfoundland and Labrador, Nova Scotia, New Brunswick, and Prince Edward Island are known as the Atlantic Provinces; Quebec and Ontario are often called the Central Provinces; Manitoba, Saskatchewan, Alberta, and British Columbia are known as the West; and the territories are referred to as the North.

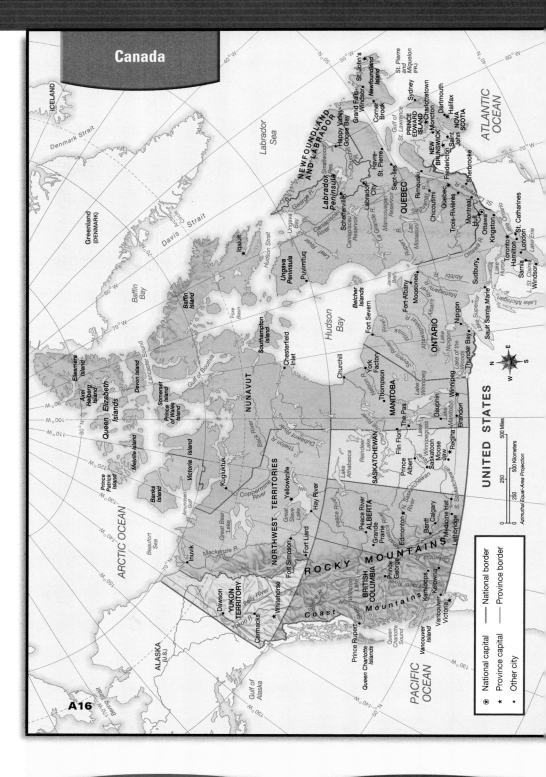

INTEGRATE LANGUAGE ARTS

Write a How-To Paragraph Have students imagine that they want to travel by boat from Banff to Winnipeg. Have them write a paragraph describing the route. Encourage them to give detailed instructions that include descriptions and names of physical features along the way, the names of provinces and cities they pass through or near, the direction they are traveling, and the names of rivers they cross.

EXTEND AND ENRICH

Find the Origins of Names Allow students a few minutes to study the names of Canada's provinces, territories, and major cities. Ask students to choose the name of a province, territory, or city and write down how they think it might have gotten its name. Then ask students to do some Internet research to find out the actual origin of the name. As a class, discuss the various origins of the names and how the names reflect the history, culture, or geography of the place.

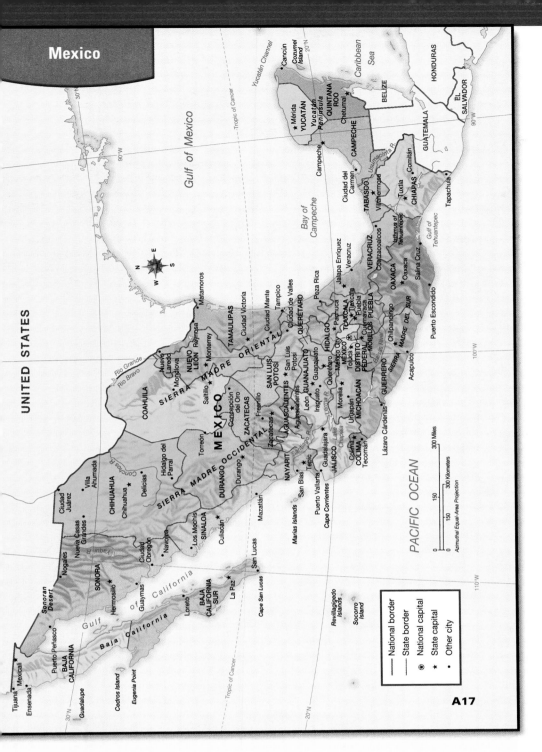

Mexico

Gulf of Mexico

UNITED STATES

PACIFIC OCEAN

Tropic of Cancer

Yucatán Channel

Cozumel Island

Cancún

Yucatán Peninsula

Caribbean Sea

HONDURAS

QUINTANA ROO

Mérida
YUCATÁN

Chetumal

BELIZE

CAMPECHE

Campeche

EL SALVADOR

GUATEMALA

Ciudad del Carmen

Comitán

TABASCO

Villahermosa

Tuxtla

CHIAPAS

Tapachula

Usumacinta R.

VERACRUZ

Coatzacoalcos

Isthmus of Tehuantepec

Gulf of Tehuantepec

Salina Cruz

Jalapa Enríquez

Veracruz

OAXACA

Oaxaca

Puerto Escondido

Bay of Campeche

Poza Rica

Pachuca

Tlaxcala

Puebla

HIDALGO

TLAXCALA

MEXICO City

Toluca

PUEBLA

DISTRITO FEDERAL

MORELOS

Cuernavaca

GUERRERO

Chilpancingo

SIERRA MADRE DEL SUR

Acapulco

Balsas River

Ciudad Mante

Ciudad de Valles

Tampico

QUERÉTARO

Querétaro

SAN LUIS POTOSÍ

San Luis Potosí

GUANAJUATO

Guanajuato

León

Irapuato

Morelia

MICHOACÁN

Uruapan

Lázaro Cárdenas

Lerma River

Chapala Lake

COLIMA

Colima

Tecomán

JALISCO

Guadalajara

NAYARIT

Tepic

San Blas

Puerto Vallarta

Cape Corrientes

Mazatlán

Marías Islands

Ciudad Victoria

TAMAULIPAS

Matamoros

Reynosa

Nuevo Laredo

NUEVO LEÓN

Monterrey

Monclova

SIERRA MADRE ORIENTAL

MEXICO

Concepción del Oro

ZACATECAS

Zacatecas

Fresnillo

Aguascalientes

AGUASCALIENTES

COAHUILA

Saltillo

Torreón

Hidalgo del Parral

DURANGO

Durango

SIERRA MADRE OCCIDENTAL

Rio Grande

Rio Bravo

Villa Ahumada

CHIHUAHUA

Chihuahua

Delicias

Ciudad Juárez

Conchos R.

Nueva Casas Grandes

Nogales

Yaqui R.

SONORA

Hermosillo

Guaymas

Ciudad Obregón

Navojoa

Los Mochis

SINALOA

Culiacán

San Lucas

Gulf of California

California

BAJA CALIFORNIA SUR

La Paz

Loreto

Cape San Lucas

San Lucas

Baja California

BAJA CALIFORNIA

Puerto Peñasco

Sonoran Desert

Mexicali

Tijuana

Ensenada

Guadalupe

Cedros Island

Eugenia Point

Revillagigedo Islands

Socorro Island

300 Miles
150
0

300 Kilometers
150
0

Azimuthal Equal-Area Projection

| National border |
| State border |
| ⊛ National capital |
| ★ State capital |
| • Other city |

A17

Set the Purpose

Main Idea Explain to students that this map of Mexico shows key physical features and the names and borders of Mexico's 31 states. The map also shows the national borders between Mexico and other countries.

Why It Matters This map can be used to find out where states in Mexico are located and to see the size and shape of each state. This map can also be used to identify all the state capitals and the major cities in each state.

Visual Learning

Map Point out that each state is a different color from the states that surround it. Then call students' attention to the map key. Ask them to describe the difference between a state border and a national border. Mention that the map also shows the locations of the national capital, state capitals, and major cities.

Map Study

Geography Ask a volunteer to identify Mexico's capital city. Have students notice that Mexico City is located in what is known as the *Distrito Federal*, or Federal District. Explain that the *Distrito Federal* is a separate administrative area—not a state—somewhat like the District of Columbia in the United States.

Geography Have students notice the bodies of water that surround Mexico and the countries that border it.

Q Which Mexican states border the United States?

A Baja California, Sonora, Chihuahua, Coahuila, Nuevo León, and Tamaulipas

CD-ROM

Explore GEOSKILLS CD-ROM to give students additional practice using map and globe skills.

REACH ALL LEARNERS

English as a Second Language Invite Spanish-speaking students to pronounce some of the names and terms used on the map so that other students can hear the proper pronunciation. If students feel comfortable translating, they may want to explain what some of the terms and names mean. For example, they might explain that *ciudad* means "city," or that *sierra* means "mountain range," or that *puerto* means "port."

EXTEND AND ENRICH

Create a Travel Brochure Have students choose one of the cities shown on the map to research in order to make a travel brochure. Suggest they devote about half of the brochure to an overview of the city that includes information about the city's history, economy, and population and focus the rest of the brochure on sightseeing activities related to landmarks and culture.

Geography Terms

1. **basin** bowl-shaped area of land surrounded by higher land

2. **bay** an inlet of the sea or some other body of water, usually smaller than a gulf

3. **bluff** high, steep face of rock or earth

4. **canyon** deep, narrow valley with steep sides

5. **cape** point of land that extends into water

6. **cataract** large waterfall

7. **channel** deepest part of a body of water

8. **cliff** high, steep face of rock or earth

9. **coast** land along a sea or ocean

10. **coastal plain** area of flat land along a sea or ocean

11. **delta** triangle-shaped area of land at the mouth of a river

12. **desert** dry land with few plants

13. **dune** hill of sand piled up by the wind

14. **fall line** area along which rivers form waterfalls or rapids as the rivers drop to lower land

15. **floodplain** flat land that is near the edges of a river and is formed by silt deposited by floods

16. **foothills** hilly area at the base of a mountain

17. **glacier** large ice mass that moves slowly down a mountain or across land

18. **gulf** part of a sea or ocean extending into the land, usually larger than a bay

19. **hill** land that rises above the land around it

20. **inlet** any area of water extending into the land from a larger body of water

21. **island** land that has water on all sides

22. **isthmus** narrow strip of land connecting two larger areas of land

23. **lagoon** body of shallow water

24. **lake** body of water with land on all sides

25. **marsh** lowland with moist soil and tall grasses

26	**mesa**	flat-topped mountain with steep sides	**40**	**savanna** area of grassland and scattered trees

26 **mesa** flat-topped mountain with steep sides

27 **mountain** highest kind of land

28 **mountain pass** gap between mountains

29 **mountain range** row of mountains

30 **mouth of river** place where a river empties into another body of water

31 **oasis** area of water and fertile land in a desert

32 **ocean** body of salt water larger than a sea

33 **peak** top of a mountain

34 **peninsula** land that is almost completely surrounded by water

35 **plain** area of flat or gently rolling low land

36 **plateau** area of high, mostly flat land

37 **reef** ridge of sand, rock, or coral that lies at or near the surface of a sea or ocean

38 **river** large stream of water that flows across the land

39 **riverbank** land along a river

40 **savanna** area of grassland and scattered trees

41 **sea** body of salt water smaller than an ocean

42 **sea level** the level of the surface of an ocean or a sea

43 **slope** side of a hill or mountain

44 **source of river** place where a river begins

45 **strait** narrow channel of water connecting two larger bodies of water

46 **swamp** area of low, wet land with trees

47 **timberline** line on a mountain above which it is too cold for trees to grow

48 **tributary** stream or river that flows into a larger stream or river

49 **valley** low land between hills or mountains

50 **volcano** opening in the earth, often raised, through which lava, rock, ashes, and gases are forced out

51 **waterfall** steep drop from a high place to a lower place in a stream or river

A19

A New Nation

Inkwell from the Assembly
Room at Independence Hall

Unit 5 Planning Guide A New Nation

Introduce	CONTENT	RESOURCES
pp. 339–343	**UNIT OPENER**, p. 339 **PREVIEW**, pp. 340–341 **START WITH A STORY** *Shh! We're Writing the Constitution*, pp. 342–343	Unit 5 Audiotext Unit 5 School-to-Home Newsletter, p. S9 🌐 Reading and Vocabulary Transparency, 5-1 Time for Kids Readers 💻 Internet Resources
Chapter 10		
The Constitution, pp. 344–381	**INTRODUCE THE CHAPTER**, pp. 344–345 **LESSON 1** The Confederation Period, pp. 346–350 **LESSON 2** The Constitutional Convention, pp. 351–357 **LESSON 3** Three Branches of Government, pp. 358–363 **CHART AND GRAPH SKILLS** Read a Flow Chart, pp. 364–365 **LESSON 4** Approval and the Bill of Rights, pp. 366–372 **CITIZENSHIP SKILLS** Act as a Responsible Citizen, p. 373 **LESSON 5** The New Government Begins, pp. 374–379 **CHAPTER REVIEW AND TEST PREPARATION**, pp. 380–381	Activity Book, pp. 94–102 ✓ Assessment Program, Chapter 10, pp. 77–80 🌐 Reading and Vocabulary Transparencies, 5-2, 5-3, 5-4, 5-5, 5-6, 5-7 🌐 Skills Transparencies, 5-1, 5-2 💻 Internet Resources
Chapter 11		
The Nation Grows, pp. 382–421	**INTRODUCE THE CHAPTER**, pp. 382–383 **LESSON 1** The Louisiana Purchase, pp. 384–388 **LESSON 2** The War of 1812, pp. 389–394 **LESSON 3** The Age of Jackson, pp. 395–399 **EXAMINE PRIMARY SOURCES** Audubon's Paintings, pp. 400–401 **LESSON 4** From Ocean to Ocean, pp. 402–409 **MAP AND GLOBE SKILLS** Identify Changing Borders, pp. 410–411 **LESSON 5** An Industrial Revolution, pp. 412–419 **CHAPTER REVIEW AND TEST PREPARATION**, pp. 420–421	Activity Book, pp. 103–111 ✓ Assessment Program, Chapter 11, pp. 81–84 🌐 Reading and Vocabulary Transparencies, 5-8, 5-9, 5-10, 5-11, 5-12, 5-13 🌐 Skills Transparency, 5-3 💻 Internet Resources 💿 GeoSkills CD-ROM
Wrap Up		
pp. 422–426	**VISIT** Old Ironsides, pp. 422–423 **UNIT REVIEW AND TEST PREPARATION**, pp. 424–426	💻 Internet Resources The Learning Site: Virtual Tours Take a Field Trip Video ✓ Assessment Program, Unit 5, pp. 85–93

4	WEEK 1	WEEK 2	WEEK 3	WEEK 4
WEEKS	Introduce the Unit	Chapter 10	Chapter 11	Wrap Up the Unit

Unit 5 Skills Path

Unit 5 features the reading skills of summarizing and drawing conclusions. It also highlights the social studies skills of reading a flow chart, acting as a responsible citizen, and identifying changing borders.

FOCUS SKILLS

CHAPTER 10 READING SKILL

 SUMMARIZE

- INTRODUCE p. 345
- APPLY pp. 347, 350, 352, 355, 357, 360, 363, 370, 371, 372, 378, 379

CHAPTER 11 READING SKILL

 DRAW CONCLUSIONS

- INTRODUCE p. 383
- APPLY pp. 385, 388, 393, 394, 396, 399, 403, 405, 409, 416, 419

READING SOCIAL STUDIES

- Graphic Organizer, pp. 347, 349, 359, 361, 363, 385, 388
- Anticipation Guide, pp. 352, 356
- Read Aloud, p. 366
- Personal Response, pp. 342, 343, 367, 372
- Study Questions, pp. 375, 379, 390, 394, 413, 419
- Prediction, pp. 396, 399
- K-W-L Chart, pp. 403, 409

CHART AND GRAPH SKILLS

READ A FLOW CHART

- INTRODUCE pp. 364–365
- APPLY p. 381

CITIZENSHIP SKILLS

ACT AS A RESPONSIBLE CITIZEN

- INTRODUCE p. 373
- APPLY p. 381

MAP AND GLOBE SKILLS

IDENTIFY CHANGING BORDERS

- INTRODUCE pp. 410–411
- APPLY pp. 421, 425

STUDY AND RESEARCH SKILLS

- Skimming and Scanning, pp. 351, 408
- Outlining, p. 356
- Using Reference Sources, p. 384
- Graphic Organizer, pp. 391, 413

Multimedia Resources

The Multimedia Resources can be used in a variety of ways. They can supplement core instruction in the classroom or extend and enrich student learning at home.

Independent Reading

Easy

Jakes, John. **Susanna of the Alamo.** Harcourt Brace, 1990. Story focuses on Susanna Dickinson and her infant daughter, who were the only survivors of the Alamo.

Lavender, David. **The Santa Fe Trail.** Holiday House, 1995. This book recounts the risks of traveling on the Santa Fe Trail.

Van Steenwyk, Elizabeth. **My Name Is York.** Northland Pub., 1997. The exploration and journey of Lewis and Clark as told through the eyes of Clark's slave, York, who traveled with the pair.

Average

Gregory, Kristiana. **Across the Wide and Lonesome Prairie: The Oregon Trail Diary of Hattie Campbell, 1847.** Scholastic Trade, 1997. The diary of 13-year-old Hattie describing the challenges and joys of her family's journey to Oregon in a covered wagon.

Karwoski, Gail Langer. **Seaman: The Dog Who Explored the West With Lewis and Clark.** Peachtree Publishers, 1999. Historical novel based on events from the journals of Lewis and Clark. Seaman is a Newfoundland dog that joins the expedition team.

Kroll, Steven. **By the Dawn's Early Light: The Story of the Star-Spangled Banner.** Scholastic, 1994. This book tells the tale of the events that inspired the writing of our national anthem.

Challenging

Beller, Susan Provost. **Woman of Independence: The Life of Abigail Adams.** Shoe Tree Press, 2000. A biography of John Adams's wife, whose outspoken nature made her a woman ahead of her time.

Collier, Christopher. **Creating the Constitution: 1787.** Benchmark Books, 1998. Focuses on early American politics and government.

Greenwood, Barbara. **Pioneer Sampler: The Daily Life of a Pioneer Family in 1840.** Houghton Mifflin Co., 1995. Although the family is fictitious, the history depicted in this story explains many factual aspects of pioneer life.

Computer Software

Becoming a Nation. Clearvue, 1996. Mac/Windows. Through interactive activities, the program examines the events that led to the creation of the national government.

The Oregon Trail, 5th Edition. The Learning Company, 1997. Real life decision-making and problem solving skills needed to survive life on the Oregon Trail.

Videos and DVDs

Railroads On the Frontier. Clearvue, 1992. Covers the history of railroad construction and how railroads shaped the nation.

The Presidency. Clearvue, 1993. Explains the executive branch and how the presidency has evolved throughout history.

Additional books also are recommended at point of use throughout the unit.
Note that information, while correct at time of publication, is subject to change.

ISBNs and other publisher information can be found at **www.harcourtschool.com**

The Learning Site: Social Studies Center

The Learning Site at www.harcourtschool.com offers a special Social Studies Center. The center provides a wide variety of activities, Internet links, and online references.

Here are just some of the HARCOURT Internet resources you'll find!

Multimedia Biographies
www.harcourtschool.com

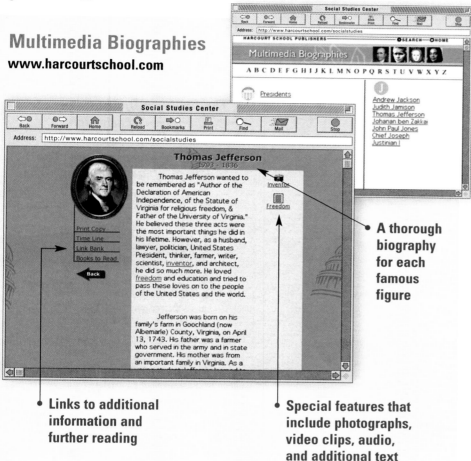

- A thorough biography for each famous figure

- Links to additional information and further reading

- Special features that include photographs, video clips, audio, and additional text

Primary Sources

- Artwork
- Clothing
- Diaries
- Government Documents
- Historical Documents
- Maps
- Tools

and more!
www.harcourtschool.com

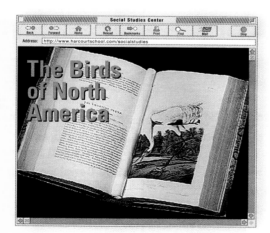

Virtual Tours

- Capitols and Government Buildings
- Cities
- Countries
- Historical Sites
- Museums
- Parks and Scenic Areas

and more!
www.harcourtschool.com

Integrate Learning Across the Curriculum

Use these topics to help you integrate social studies into your daily planning.
See the page numbers indicated for more information about each topic.

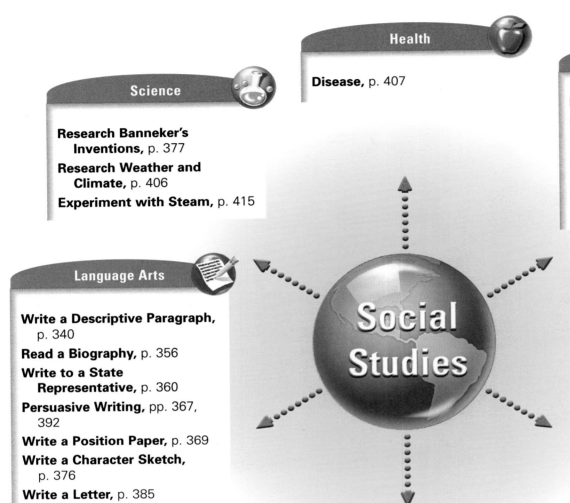

Health

Disease, p. 407

Reading/Literature

Read *The Federalist,* p. 368
Read a Biography, pp. 374, 396
The Santa Fe Trail, p. 426
By the Dawn's Early Light, p. 426
Woman of Independence: The Life of Abigail Adams, p. 426

Science

Research Banneker's Inventions, p. 377
Research Weather and Climate, p. 406
Experiment with Steam, p. 415

Language Arts

Write a Descriptive Paragraph, p. 340
Read a Biography, p. 356
Write to a State Representative, p. 360
Persuasive Writing, pp. 367, 392
Write a Position Paper, p. 369
Write a Character Sketch, p. 376
Write a Letter, p. 385

Languages

Research Spanish Place-Names, p. 403

Technology

GeoSkills CD-ROM, p. 411
Go Online, pp. 343, 353, 370, 391, 401, 404, 423
CNN Video, p. 423

Art

Draw Pictures, p. 353
Make a Bulletin Board Display, p. 362
Make a Collage, p. 370
Plan an Ad Campaign, p. 377
Weave, p. 416

Mathematics

Compare Populations, p. 340
Figuring the Cost of Inflation, p. 348
Figure Area, p. 349
Calculate Percentages, p. 353
Calculate the Number of Citizens Represented, p. 359
Computation, pp. 397, 413, 422
Calculate Averages, p. 406

Music

Perform a Song, p. 362
Draw Pictures for "The Star-Spangled Banner," p. 393
Erie Canal Song, p. 414

Reach All Learners

Use these activities to help individualize your instruction. Each activity has been developed to address a different level or type of learner.

English as a Second Language

Materials

- notebook paper
- textbook
- pens or pencils
- dictionary

PREVIEW THE UNIT Have students who are acquiring English scan Unit 5 titles and illustrations to preview its content.

- Organize students who are learning English into groups.
- Invite students to scan the lesson titles, illustrations, and vocabulary terms to preview the early years of the United States.
- Encourage group members to list unfamiliar vocabulary terms from the unit in their journals.
- Have students illustrate or write definitions for unfamiliar words as they complete the unit.

Below-Level Learners

Materials

- paper
- pens, markers, or pencils
- textbook

DRAW HISTORIC SCENES Have students work in pairs to research and create a storyboard for a historic event discussed in Unit 5.

- Allow pairs to review the unit and choose a key historic event or turning point, such as a battle or the adoption of the Constitution.
- Direct pairs to take notes on the events before and during the turning point, using a time line or flow chart organizer.

- Instruct pairs to draw at least three scenes that show the events leading up to the event they selected and the event itself. Students may use art supplies or find appropriate illustrations in books, newspapers, and magazines.

Advanced Learners

Materials

- paper
- pen or pencil
- textbook

SOLVE A HISTORIC PROBLEM Have advanced learners research a historic problem and think of a solution.

- Ask students to identify a historic problem discussed in Unit 5, such as the conflict between the United States government and the Cherokee Indians.
- Direct students to research the problem in their textbook and in other resources.
- Have students write a short paper that identifies the problem, possible solutions to the problem, and the solution that was chosen.
- Ask students to explain whether the chosen solution worked well. Challenge students to present alternative solutions.
- Have students present their ideas to the class.

Assessment Options

The Assessment Program gives all learners many opportunities to show what they know and can do. It also provides ongoing information about each student's understanding of social studies.

Formal Assessment

- **LESSON REVIEWS,** at ends of lessons
- **CHAPTER REVIEWS AND TEST PREPARATION,** pp. 380–381, pp. 420–421
- **CHAPTER TESTS**
  Assessment Program, pp. 77–80, pp. 81–84
- **UNIT REVIEWS AND TEST PREPARATION,** pp. 424–425
- **UNIT ASSESSMENT**
  STANDARD TEST,
    Assessment Program, pp. 85–91
  INDIVIDUAL PERFORMANCE TASK,
    Assessment Program, p. 92
  GROUP PERFORMANCE TASK,
    Assessment Program, p. 93

Student Self-Evaluation

- **ANALYZE PRIMARY SOURCES AND VISUALS** within lessons of Pupil Book
- **GEOGRAPHY THEME QUESTIONS** within lessons of Pupil Book
- **INDIVIDUAL END-OF-PROJECT SUMMARY** Assessment Program, p. viii
- **GROUP END-OF-PROJECT CHECKLIST** Assessment Program, p. ix
- **INDIVIDUAL END-OF-UNIT CHECKLIST** Assessment Program, p. x

Informal Assessment

- **ANALYZE THE LITERATURE,** p. 343
- **REVIEW QUESTIONS,** throughout lessons
- **EXAMINE PRIMARY SOURCES,** pp. 400–401
- **SOCIAL STUDIES SKILLS CHECKLIST** Assessment Program, p. iv
- **SKILLS**
  Practice the Skill, pp. 365, 373, 411
  Apply What You Learned, pp. 365, 373, 411

Performance Assessment

- **PERFORMANCE ACTIVITY** in Lesson Reviews
- **UNIT ACTIVITIES** p. 426
- **COMPLETE THE UNIT PROJECT,** p. 426
- **INDIVIDUAL PERFORMANCE TASK** Assessment Program, p. 92
- **GROUP PERFORMANCE TASK** Assessment Program, p. 93

Portfolio Assessment

STUDENT-SELECTED ITEMS MAY INCLUDE:
- **THINK AND WRITE,** pp. 380, 420
- **UNIT ACTIVITIES,** p. 426
- **COMPLETE THE UNIT PROJECT,** p. 426

TEACHER-SELECTED ITEMS MAY INCLUDE:
- **UNIT ASSESSMENT** Assessment Program, pp. 85–91
- **PORTFOLIO SUMMARY** Assessment Program, p. xv
- **GROUP END-OF-PROJECT CHECKLIST** Assessment Program, p. ix
- **INDIVIDUAL END-OF-UNIT CHECKLIST** Assessment Program, p. x

Unit 5 Test

STANDARD TEST

5 Test

Part One: Test Your Understanding

MULTIPLE CHOICE (2 points each)

Directions Circle the letter of the best answer.

1 Which of the following was **not** a problem Congress encountered under the Articles of Confederation?
A Representatives seldom agreed on issues.
B There was no set place to hold meetings.
C Decisions could be made with agreement from fewer than half of the representatives.
D States did not want to be under the control of Congress.

2 Under the Articles, which of the following led to inflation, or having to spend more money to buy the same goods?
F Congress printed too much money.
G Congress didn't print enough money.
H Congress did not have the authority to print money.
J Greedy merchants overcharged for goods and services.

3 Delegates to the Annapolis Convention decided that the country needed—
A stronger state governments.
B more individual rights for its citizens.
C to print more money.
D a strong national government.

4 Which of the following is **not** one of the three branches of government?
F legislative
G congressional
H executive
J judicial

5 Once Congress makes laws, it is the job of which branch of government to carry them out?
A the executive branch
B the judicial branch
C the legislative branch
D the federal branch

6 The group of the President's most important advisers is known as the—
F Supreme Court.
G Cabinet.
H Congress.
J House of Representatives.

(continued)

Unit 5 Test   Assessment Program ▪ 85

STANDARD TEST

Name _____ Date _____

7 The Bill of Rights is part of which of the following documents?
A the Declaration of Independence
B the Constitution
C the Magna Carta
D the Articles of Confederation

8 Which of the following was **not** a requirement for voters under the Constitution in 1788?
F male
G white
H property owner
J 18 years of age or older

9 Alexander Hamilton's followers formed a political party that wanted a strong national government. They were known as—
A Federalists.
B Republicans.
C Nationalists.
D Democrats.

10 The Louisiana Purchase significantly increased the size of the United States. By approximately what percent did the country grow?
F 50 percent
G 75 percent
H 100 percent
J 200 percent

11 Which of the following expeditions ended with many of the explorers being put in jail for trespassing on Spanish land?
A the Corps of Discovery
B the Lewis and Clark expedition
C the Pike expedition
D the Northwest Territory expedition

12 Which of the following was **not** a cause of Americans' anger with the British in the early 1800s?
F The British formed a trade alliance with the French against the Americans.
G The British helped the Native Americans fight off the settlers.
H The British stopped American ships at sea.
J The British forced American sailors to work on their ships.

13 Which of the following accurately describes the outcome of the War of 1812?
A The British were the clear winners.
B Neither side was clearly the winner.
C The Americans were the clear winners.
D The Native Americans were the winners.

14 Where did Brigham Young take his Mormon followers to practice their religion freely?
F the Oregon Country
G Texas
H the Great Basin
J the Gadsden Purchase area

15 A journey along the Oregon Trail could take as long as—
A six weeks
B six months
C six years
D six days

(continued)

86 ▪ Assessment Program   Unit 5 Test

STANDARD TEST

Name _____ Date _____

MATCHING (2 points each)

Directions Match the description on the left side with the correct name on the right. Write the letter of the correct name in the space provided.

16 __C__ the runner-up in the first presidential election who became the first Vice President

17 __A__ the nation's first secretary of state

18 __E__ the French leader who sold Louisiana to the United States

19 __D__ the writer of "The Star-Spangled Banner"

20 __B__ helped lead the first expedition through the Louisiana Purchase

21 __G__ was given the nickname "Old Hickory" while serving in the military

22 __F__ Tennessee native whose motto was "Be always sure you're right—then go ahead!"

23 __H__ the first commander of the army of the Republic of Texas

A. Thomas Jefferson

B. Meriwether Lewis

C. John Adams

D. Francis Scott Key

E. Napoleon Bonaparte

F. Davy Crockett

G. Andrew Jackson

H. Sam Houston

(continued)

Unit 5 Test   Assessment Program ▪ 87

STANDARD TEST

Name _____ Date _____

SHORT ANSWER (3 points each)

Directions Answer each question in the space provided.

24 Explain the causes of Shays's Rebellion in the 1780s.

Possible response: Poor farmers had to pay high taxes and many went into debt. The courts were taking away farms when the farmers could not pay, and Shays's Rebellion was an attempt to stop the courts from seizing any more farmers' property.

25 The delegates at the Constitutional Convention agreed to create a federal system. What is a federal system?

Possible response: In a federal system, the right to govern is shared by the national and state governments. The states give up some rights and the national government oversees things that affect the nation as a whole.

26 How did the Pike Expedition lead to economic changes in New Mexico?

Possible response: Pike found that the people of Santa Fe needed manufactured goods and soon traders were heading for New Mexico with their goods.

27 American borders were expanding rapidly in the early and mid-1800s, and the words "manifest destiny" were heard for the first time. What did those words mean?

Possible response: They referred to the belief, shared by many Americans, that the United States should one day stretch from the Atlantic to the Pacific.

28 What is mass production, and how did it affect prices in the 1800s?

Possible response: Mass production is a system of producing large amounts of goods at one time. When the supply of goods rose, prices fell.

(continued)

88 ▪ Assessment Program   Unit 5 Test

Unit 5 Test

STANDARD TEST

Name _____ Date _____

Part Two: Test Your Skills
IDENTIFY CHANGING BORDERS (20 points)

Directions Use the historical map to answer the following questions.

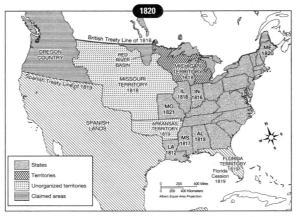

29 How many new states were added between 1812 and 1819? ____five____

30 What state bordered Spanish Lands in 1820? ____Louisiana____

31 What unorganized territories were established between 1818 and 1819?

The Arkansas Territory and Missouri Territory were established.

32 What state was added to the Union in 1820? ____Maine____

(continued)

STANDARD TEST

Name _____ Date _____

Part Three: Apply What You Have Learned

33 Compare and Contrast (9 points)

Use the Venn diagram to compare and contrast the United States government under the Articles of Confederation and the Constitution. Do the statements apply to the government under the Articles, the Constitution, or both? Write the statements below in the correct places on the Venn diagram.

- states print their own money
- states have power over their own affairs
- states make treaties with other countries
- states can tax citizens
- people elect representatives
- a President is elected
- has three branches of government

Articles of Confederation
states print their own money; states make treaties with other countries

Both
states have power over their own affairs; states can tax citizens; people elect representatives

Constitution
a President is elected; has three branches of government

(continued)

STANDARD TEST

Name _____ Date _____

34 ESSAY (10 points)

The Constitution describes three branches of government. Name and explain the duties of each branch. Why was the government of the United States set up this way?

Possible response: The branches of government are the legislative, executive, and judicial branches. The legislative branch is the lawmaking branch, responsible for making the nation's laws. It consists of two houses, the House of Representatives and the Senate. The executive branch is responsible for carrying out the laws. The President heads the executive branch and today is seen as the representative of all the people. The judicial branch decides if the laws are working fairly. It is made up of the court system. The reason for the three branches is that delegates at the Constitutional Convention did not want any one branch of the government to have too much power. This created a government in which one branch could check the power of another.

(continued)

NOTES

Name _____ Date _____

Individual Performance Task
A Journey Journal

Choose one of the expeditions listed below and create a journal as if you are a member of the expedition team. Start the journal on the night before you leave and record your thoughts, feelings, and fears. Include at least five entries in total. The last one should be written from your final destination.

- Lewis and Clark's expedition through the Louisiana Purchase
- the Pike expedition through the southwestern portion of the Louisiana Purchase
- a Christian missionary's trip to the Oregon Country
- the Mormon's journey to Utah
- a group of Forty-niners traveling by boat to take part in the gold rush

Start your project by rereading the information in the unit that is related to your subject. You may also want to do further research to gather additional information. In your journal entries, be sure to provide information about the following topics:

- initial thoughts before the journey
- why you are on the journey
- who you are traveling with
- climate
- sites of interest
- experiences you have along the way
- reaction when you arrive at your final destination

Give each of the entries in your journal a date from the correct time period. Be sure your details fit that time period. Be creative, but keep your journal entries true to history.

© Harcourt

(continued)

Name _____ Date _____

Group Performance Task
Role Play

Choose one of the following historical moments and create a 10-minute role-playing performance in which group members portray important historical figures who discuss their involvement in the event. The performance can take the form of a conversation or debate focusing on the event. Find information about your topic in your textbook, in a library, or on the Internet. Be creative, but stay true to history.

➡ **TOPIC 1** After months of debate, the Constitution is signed on Sept. 17, 1787. Historical figures to portray could include Benjamin Franklin and Patrick Henry.

➡ **TOPIC 2** The Louisiana Purchase is finalized. Possible historical figures to portray include Thomas Jefferson and Napoleon Bonaparte.

➡ **TOPIC 3** British troops invade Washington, D.C., in 1814. Possible historical figures to portray include First Lady Dolley Madison and Francis Scott Key.

➡ **TOPIC 4** James Marshall discovers gold in California in 1848. Possible historical figures to portray include James Marshall and John Sutter.

© Harcourt

(continued)

RUBRICS FOR SCORING

SCORING RUBRICS The rubrics below list the criteria for evaluating the tasks above. They also describe different levels of success in meeting those criteria.

INDIVIDUAL PERFORMANCE TASK

SCORE 4	SCORE 3	SCORE 2	SCORE 1
• Rich description is provided. • Details fit historical period strongly. • Journal entries are well organized. • Discussion is well developed.	• Some description is provided. • Details fit historical period. • Journal entries are somewhat organized. • Discussion is fairly well developed.	• Little description is provided. • Details fit historical period weakly. • Journal entries are poorly organized. • Discussion is minimally developed.	• No description is provided. • Details do not fit the historical period. • Journal entries are not organized. • Discussion is not developed.

GROUP PEFORMANCE TASK

SCORE 4	SCORE 3	SCORE 2	SCORE 1
• Performance shows excellent creativity. • Performance is historically accurate. • Performance is highly informative.	• Performance shows some creativity. • Performance is mostly historically accurate. • Performance is somewhat informative.	• Performance shows little creativity. • Performance is partially historically accurate. • Performance is minimally informative.	• Performance shows no creativity. • Performance is not historically accurate. • Performance is not informative.

Introduce the Unit

OBJECTIVES

- Use artifacts and primary sources to acquire information about the United States.
- Interpret information in visuals.

Access Prior Knowledge

Invite students to tell what they know about the colonial struggle for freedom. Lead the class in brainstorming a list of qualities that they might want in a new government. freedom of speech, freedom of assembly, representation, equality

Visual Learning

Picture The background image is Independence Hall in Philadelphia, Pennsylvania. Tell students that the United States Constitution was drafted at a convention in Philadelphia.

Independence Hall, Philadelphia, Pennsylvania

BACKGROUND

Inkwell at Independence Hall The first draft of the Constitution was not the only document penned at Independence Hall in Philadelphia, Pennsylvania. The Declaration of Independence was written there, too. Independence Hall was also the place that both documents were signed.

The Great Seal The designers of the Great Seal of the United States did more to celebrate the unification of the colonies than simply declare them as "one." There are multiple depictions on both sides of the seal that appear in numbers of thirteen. On the front there is a flag on the eagle's chest bearing 13 red and white stripes. There are thirteen stars encircling the eagle's head. The eagle holds a twig with thirteen leaves in its right claw and thirteen arrows in its left claw.

·UNIT· 5

A New Nation

" *E pluribus unum* "
(Out of many, one)

—Motto on the Seal of the United States,
adopted on June 20, 1782

Preview the Content

Read the title and the Big Idea for each lesson in the unit.
Then use what you have read to make a web for each chapter.
Write down words or phrases that will help you identify the main
topics to be covered in the unit.

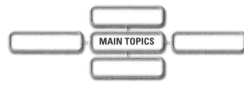

MAIN TOPICS

Preview the Vocabulary

Context Clues Context clues are words that can help you figure out the meaning of a word that is unfamiliar. Scan the unit
and find the terms **inflation**, **commerce**, and **investor**. Write a
sentence explaining how these words relate to one another.

Analyze Primary Sources

Inkwell Have students look closely at
the inkwell and describe what they
see. Then ask why they think that this
artifact is important to United States
history. Students may observe that
many important documents were
penned at it.

Quotation Have a volunteer read
aloud the quotation from the Great
Seal of the United States.

**Q Compare the message in this quo-
tation with the one on page 259.
How does it show that things have
changed?**

A Students may say that this quotation
states unification as a conclusion,
already achieved. The previous
quote suggested it as a useful
alternative.

AUDIOTEXT

Use the Unit 5 AUDIOTEXT for a
reading of the Unit narrative.

5

·Unit 5·

Preview the Content

Students' webs should be similar to the
one below.

Preview the Vocabulary

Make sure students understand that
these terms all have to do with
economics or money.

Preview the Unit

PAGES 340–341

OBJECTIVES

- Interpret information in data-bases and visuals.
- Use appropriate mathematical skills to interpret social studies information such as maps and graphs.

Access Prior Knowledge

Have students describe what they have already learned about the unification and westward expansion of the United States.

Visual Learning

Map Ask students to examine the map and discuss how the border of the United States changed during this period.

Time Line To help students prepare for their reading, have them work in pairs to ask and answer questions about the time line. For example, a student might ask:
- *By what year had people moved to California?* by 1849

Time Line Illustrations Ask students to speculate about the significance of the events shown on the time line.
- After much debate, a new Constitution was signed and ratified by all 13 states.
- After the Constitution was ratified, ten amendments known as the Bill of Rights were added to the Constitution.
- The Corps of Discovery, led by Lewis and Clark, set out to explore the Louisiana Purchase.
- At the Alamo, Texans fought for independence from Mexico.
- After a year of conflict, the United States defeated Mexico in the Mexican-American War.
- Thousands of people from the United States, Europe, and Asia rushed to California to mine gold.

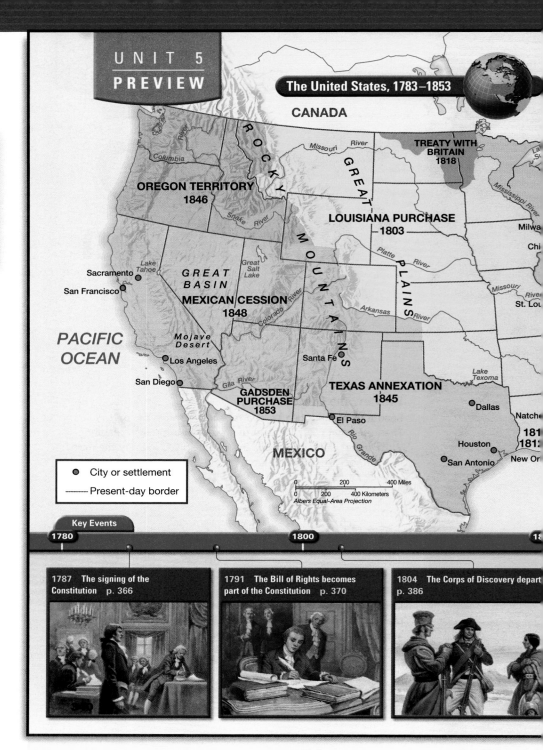

UNIT 5 PREVIEW

The United States, 1783–1853

CANADA

TREATY WITH BRITAIN 1818

OREGON TERRITORY 1846

LOUISIANA PURCHASE 1803

Milwa

Chi

St. Lou

GREAT BASIN

MEXICAN CESSION 1848

PACIFIC OCEAN

Mojave Desert

Los Angeles

Santa Fe

Lake Texoma

San Diego

TEXAS ANNEXATION 1845

Dallas

GADSDEN PURCHASE 1853

El Paso

Natch

181

MEXICO

Houston

181

San Antonio

New Or

- City or settlement
------- Present-day border

0   200   400 Miles
0   200   400 Kilometers
Albers Equal-Area Projection

Key Events

1780   1800   18

1787 The signing of the Constitution p. 366

1791 The Bill of Rights becomes part of the Constitution p. 370

1804 The Corps of Discovery depart p. 386

INTEGRATE LANGUAGE ARTS

Write a Descriptive Paragraph Tell students to write down the observations they have about the information on the map and graphs. Have them use these insights to write a paragraph describing an imaginary journey west that might have been taken at this time.

INTEGRATE MATHEMATICS

Compare Populations Have students work in pairs to write math problems based on the picture graph on page 341. Students' math problems should require the class to figure out the numerical value of cities' populations as well as to compare populations. Have partners quiz the class with their questions. Sample questions include: *What is Albany's population? (25,000 × 2 = 50,000 people)* or *How many more people did Brooklyn have than St. Louis? (100,000 − 80,000 = 20,000 more people)*

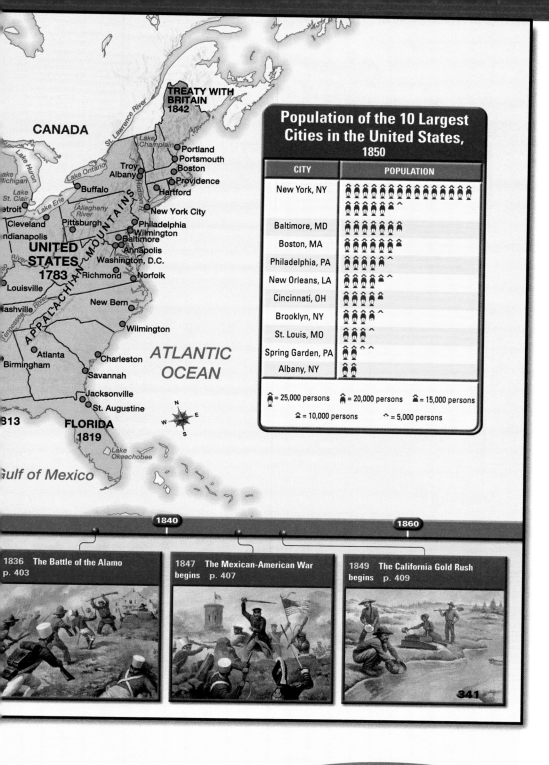

Population of the 10 Largest Cities in the United States, 1850

CITY	POPULATION
New York, NY	
Baltimore, MD	
Boston, MA	
Philadelphia, PA	
New Orleans, LA	
Cincinnati, OH	
Brooklyn, NY	
St. Louis, MO	
Spring Garden, PA	
Albany, NY	

= 25,000 persons   = 20,000 persons   = 15,000 persons

= 10,000 persons   = 5,000 persons

1840   1860

1836 The Battle of the Alamo p. 403

1847 The Mexican-American War begins p. 407

1849 The California Gold Rush begins p. 409

341

Visual Learning

Picture Graph Work with students to interpret the data presented in the picture graph. To assist them with understanding the information presented, you may want to ask these questions:
- *Which city had the largest population?* New York, NY
- *Did any of the cities have the same population?* No
- *Which cities have populations that are almost the same size?* New Orleans and Philadelphia, and New Orleans and Cincinnati.

Make Connections

Link Picture Graph and Map Ask students to use the information presented in the picture graph and the map to draw conclusions about the location of cities in the United States. Most of the cities are located in the eastern United States because most people live in this area. As more people move to the West, more Western cities will be built.

Link Map and Time Line Have students identify which events are related to the expansion of the United States. The Corps of Discovery departing, the Mexican-American War, and the California gold rush

5

SCHOOL TO HOME

Use the Unit 5 SCHOOL-TO-HOME NEWSLETTER on pages S9–S10 to introduce the unit to family members and suggest activities they can do at home.

OBJECTIVES

- Describe how most people felt about becoming one nation after the Revolutionary War.
- Identify leaders in the movement to unite the thirteen colonies as one country, such as George Washington.

Summary

Explain that many people did not want to be united after the Revolutionary War.

1 Motivate

Set the Purpose

Inform students that in colonial America, many people did not see the purpose in uniting as one nation.

Access Prior Knowledge

Discuss the kinds of characteristics that make different states unique.

READING SOCIAL STUDIES

Personal Response Have students who have played team sports discuss their experiences as members of a team. Tell students that the people chosen to create a new government for the United States had to think of themselves as citizens of a nation.

● USE READING AND VOCABULARY TRANSPARENCY 5-1.

5-1 TRANSPARENCY

2 Teach

Read and Respond

Understand the Story Have students discuss why people from different states poked fun at each other.

Shh! We're Writing the Constitution

by Jean Fritz
pictures by Tomie dePaola

The job of turning the 13 former British colonies into a new nation was not an easy one. The biggest problem was getting people to think of themselves as citizens of a country. Until this time most Americans thought of themselves as citizens of their states — Connecticut, Delaware, Georgia, Maryland, Massachusetts, New Hampshire, New Jersey, New York, North Carolina, Pennsylvania, Rhode Island, South Carolina, or Virginia.

———————☆———————

After the Revolutionary War most people in America were glad that they were no longer British. Still, they were not ready to call themselves Americans. The last thing they wanted was to become a nation. They were citizens of their own separate states, just as they had always been: each state different, each state proud of its own character, each state quick to poke fun at other states. To Southerners, New Englanders might be "no-account Yankees." To New Englanders, Pennsylvanians might be "lousy Buckskins." But to everyone the states themselves were all

342   Unit 5

REACH ALL LEARNERS

Kinesthetic Learners
Ask students to role-play George Washington's effort at convincing his troops to swear allegiance to the United States. Request that the troops provide reasons for why they do not feel comfortable swearing their allegiance to the United States.

BACKGROUND

State Constitutions In May 1776 the Second Continental Congress told the states to write state constitutions. Each state's constitution specified the powers and limits of its government and guaranteed the rights for all of its citizens.

AUDIOTEXT

Text of this story can be found on the Unit 5 AUDIOTEXT.

important. "Sovereign states," they called them. They loved the sound of "sovereign" because it meant that they were their own bosses.

George Washington, however, scoffed at the idea of "sovereign states." He knew that the states could not be truly independent for long and survive. Ever since the Declaration of Independence had been signed, people had referred to the country as the United States of America. It was about time, he thought, for them to act and feel united.

Once during the war Washington had decided it would be a good idea if his troops swore allegiance to the United States. As a start, he lined up some troops from New Jersey and asked them to take such an oath. They looked at Washington as if he'd taken leave of his senses. How could they do that? they cried. New Jersey was their country!

So Washington dropped the idea. In time, he hoped, the states would see that they needed to become one nation, united under a strong central government.

But that time would be long in coming.

Analyze the Literature

❶ Why was the idea of "sovereign states" important?

❷ How was George Washington's point of view about the nation different from that of most other Americans?

READ A BOOK

START THE UNIT PROJECT

A Growing Nation Time Line With your classmates, create an illustrated time line. As you read, make a list of the key events, people, and places you learn about. This list will help you decide which items to include on your time line.

USE TECHNOLOGY

GO ONLINE Visit The Learning Site at www.harcourtschool.com for additional activities, primary sources, and other resources to use in this unit.

Unit 5 343

Analyze the Literature
Answers

❶ Citizens considered the states to be very different from one another. This is why they believed that the independent states should govern themselves.

❷ Although most people believed the states should remain sovereign, George Washington believed that they should be unified as a single nation.

Use Technology

GO ONLINE **INTERNET RESOURCES**

THE LEARNING SITE Go to www.harcourtschool.com to view Internet resources for this unit.

TIME FOR KIDS Go to www.harcourtschool.com for the latest news in a student-friendly format.

---

3 Close

Summarize the Reading

- After the Revolutionary War, many people did not want the thirteen colonies to become a nation.
- George Washington favored the unification of thirteen colonies into one nation.

READING SOCIAL STUDIES

Personal Response Ask students to share how they felt about having to hold a position on the team and work interdependently with other team members.

● USE READING AND VOCABULARY TRANSPARENCY 5-1. **5-1 TRANSPARENCY**

Read a Book

Students may enjoy reading these leveled Independent Readers. Additional books are listed on pp. 339D–339E of this Teacher's Edition.

Easy *The Star-Spangled Banner* by Lisa deMauro. Students learn how and why Francis Scott Key penned the words of our national anthem.

Average *Wagons West* by Shirley Frederick. This book re-creates historical and present-day Oregon Trail journeys leaving from Independence, Missouri.

Challenging *Mr. Peale's Amazing Museum* by Terry Simon. Students visit the portrait gallery and museum of Charles Willson Peale, located inside Independence Hall.

Start the Unit Project

Hint Suggest that students list the key events, the dates they happened, and an idea for how to illustrate each event in the following table as they read.

Event	Date	Illustration Idea

Chapter 10 Planning Guide The Constitution

Introducing the Chapter, pp. 344–345

LESSON	PACING	OBJECTIVES	VOCABULARY
Introduce the Chapter pp. 344–345	1 Day	■ Summarize events that led to the creation of the United States Constitution. ■ Understand amendments to the United States Constitution, including the Bill of Rights.	**Word Work:** Preview Vocabulary, p. 345
1 The Confederation Period pp. 346–350	1 Day	■ Summarize the events that led to the creation of the Constitution. ■ Examine the role of governments in economic systems. ■ Identify the contributions of individuals to the democratic process. ■ Explain the Northwest Ordinance and its importance in governing the Northwest Territory.	**republic** **inflation** **arsenal** **territory** **ordinance** **Word Work:** Related Words, p. 346
2 The Constitutional Convention pp. 351–357	2 Days	■ Describe the events that led up to the Constitutional Convention. ■ Discuss the Constitutional Convention and its influence on the democratic process. ■ Identify the contributions of those who helped write the Constitution. ■ Explain the "Great Compromise" and its importance in representative government.	**convention** **commerce** **federal system** **bill**
3 Three Branches of Government pp. 358–363	1 Day	■ Explain the purpose of the Constitution as stated in the Preamble. ■ Identify the three branches of the federal government and understand their functions. ■ Explain checks and balances and the reasons for them.	**census** **electoral college** **veto** **impeach** **justice** **checks and balances** **Word Work:** Categorize Vocabulary, p. 358

READING	INTEGRATE LEARNING	REACH ALL LEARNERS	RESOURCES

Summarize, p. 345

Reading Social Studies:
Graphic Organizer, p. 347

Reading Social Studies:
Graphic Organizer Responses, p. 349

Mathematics
Figuring the Cost of Inflation, p. 348

Mathematics
Figure Area, p. 349

Advanced Learners, p. 346

Below-Level Learners, p. 347

Advanced Learners, p. 348

Extend and Enrich, p. 350

Reteach the Lesson, p. 350

Activity Book, p. 94

Reading and Vocabulary Transparency, 5-2

Reading Social Studies:
Anticipation Guide, p. 352

Summarize, p. 352

Reading Social Studies:
Anticipation Guide Responses, p. 356

Art
Draw Pictures, p. 353

Mathematics
Calculate Percentages, p. 353

Language Arts
Read a Biography, p. 356

Auditory Learners, p. 355

Extend and Enrich, p. 357

Reteach the Lesson, p. 357

Activity Book, p. 95

Reading and Vocabulary Transparency, 5-3

Internet Resources

Reading Social Studies:
Graphic Organizer, p. 359

Reading Social Studies:
Graphic Organizer, p. 361

Reading Social Studies:
Graphic Organizer Responses, p. 363

Mathematics
Calculate the Number of Citizens Represented, p. 359

Language Arts
Write to a State Representative, p. 360

Music
Perform a Song, p. 362

Art
Make a Bulletin Board Display, p. 362

Auditory Learners, p. 358

Extend and Enrich, p. 363

Reteach the Lesson, p. 363

Activity Book, p. 96

Reading and Vocabulary Transparency, 5-4

Internet Resources

Chapter 10 Planning Guide The Constitution

LESSON	PACING	OBJECTIVES	VOCABULARY
CHART AND GRAPH SKILLS **Read a Flow Chart** pp. 364–365	1 Day	■ Organize and interpret information from charts. ■ Create thematic charts representing various aspects of the United States.	**flow chart**
4 Approval and the Bill of Rights pp. 366–372	1 Day	■ Identify the struggle to ratify the Constitution. ■ Explain the role the Bill of Rights played in the approval process. ■ Explain the individual rights of every American citizen as guaranteed in the Bill of Rights.	**ratify** **Federalist** **Anti-Federalist** **amendment** **Magna Carta** **due process of law** **reserved powers**
CITIZENSHIP SKILLS **Act as a Responsible Citizen** p. 373	1 Day	■ Understand the importance of voluntary individual participation in the democratic process. ■ Summarize a historic compromise and peaceful resolution.	
5 The New Government Begins pp. 374–379	1 Day	■ Describe President Washington's decisions for the executive branch. ■ Identify individual members of the first presidential cabinet and their contributions. ■ Discuss the formation of the nation's first political parties. ■ Explain the significance of John Adams's election.	**Cabinet** **political party** **candidate** **Word Work:** Preview Vocabulary, p. 374
Chapter Review and Test Preparation pp. 380–381	1 Day		

READING	INTEGRATE LEARNING	REACH ALL LEARNERS	RESOURCES
		Advanced Learners, p. 364 **Extend and Enrich,** p. 365 **Reteach the Skill,** p. 365	**Activity Book,** p. 97 🌐 **Skill Transparency,** 5-1
Reading Social Studies: **Read Aloud,** p. 366 (Focus Skill) **Summarize,** p. 366 Reading Social Studies: **Personal Response,** p. 367 (Focus Skill) **Summarize,** p. 371 Reading Social Studies: **Personal Response,** p. 372	Language Arts **Persuasive Writing,** p. 367 Reading **Read** *The Federalist,* p. 368 Language Arts **Write a Position Paper,** p. 369 Art **Make a Collage,** p. 370	**Kinesthetic Learners,** p. 367 **Advanced and Auditory Learners,** p. 368 **Tactile Learners,** p. 369 **Extend and Enrich,** p. 371 **Reteach the Lesson,** p. 372	**Activity Book,** p. 98 🌐 **Reading and Vocabulary Transparency,** 5-5 💻 **Internet Resources**
		Extend and Enrich, p. 373 **Reteach the Skill,** p. 373	**Activity Book,** p. 99 🌐 **Skill Transparency,** 5-2
Reading Social Studies: **Study Questions,** p. 375 Reading Social Studies: **Study Question Responses,** p. 379	Reading **Read a Biography,** p. 374 Language Arts **Write a Character Sketch,** p. 376 Art **Plan an Ad Campaign,** p. 377 Science **Research Banneker's Inventions,** p. 377	**Auditory Learners,** p. 375 **Advanced Learners,** p. 378 **Extend and Enrich,** p. 379 **Reteach the Lesson,** p. 379	**Activity Book,** p. 100 🌐 **Reading and Vocabulary Transparency,** 5-6
		Test Preparation, p. 380	**Activity Book,** pp. 101–102 🌐 **Reading and Vocabulary Transparency,** 5-7 ✔ **Assessment Program, Chapter 10 Test,** pp. 77–80

Activity Book

LESSON 1

Name _____ Date _____

The Confederation Period

Directions Each statement below is false. For each sentence, cross out the wrong word. Then, in the blank at the end of the sentence, write the word that would make the sentence true.

1 After the war with Britain ended, Congress printed too much money, causing terrible ~~rebellion~~. _inflation_

2 A form of government in which people elect representatives to govern the country is called a ~~dictatorship~~. _republic_

3 Decision making required representation from at least ~~five~~ states. _nine_

4 Shays's Rebellion started over ~~army policy~~. _taxes_

5 Shays's Rebellion took place in ~~Virginia~~. _Massachusetts_

6 An arsenal is a place to store ~~food~~. _weapons_

7 A territory is land that belongs to the ~~state~~ government but is not represented in Congress. _national_

8 Congress passed an ~~arsenal~~, or set of laws, to measure the western lands. _ordinance_

9 The newly settled lands were called the ~~Southeast~~ Territory. _Northwest_

10 Townships were ~~8~~ miles on each side. _6_

11 The new lands were to offer ~~private~~ schools to everyone. _public_

LESSON 2

Name _____ Date _____

The Constitutional Convention

Directions Read the following list of issues debated at the Constitutional Convention. Match the resolution of each one with the correct issue. Write the letter of the correct resolution on the blank provided.

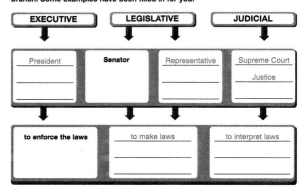

1 __B__ the relationship between the states and national government

2 __C__ representation of each state in Congress

3 __A__ the issue of enslaved African Americans

A. the Three-Fifths Compromise

B. a federal system of shared powers

C. a system of two houses of Congress

Directions Read each sentence below, and fill in the blank with the correct term. Use the words from the Word Bank.

George Read	George Washington	Roger Sherman
Rhode Island	Benjamin Franklin	

4 All the states except _Rhode Island_ sent delegates to Philadelphia.

5 The oldest member of the convention was _Benjamin Franklin_.

6 The delegates elected _George Washington_ president of the convention.

7 _George Read_ believed that states should be done away with altogether.

8 The Connecticut Compromise was created by _Roger Sherman_.

LESSON 3

Name _____ Date _____

The Three Branches of Government

Directions Read the list below of positions in the government. In the space provided, name the correct branch of government for each one. Then write a brief description of the qualifications and duties of the person holding that job.

1 President _Executive; serves for 4 years, must be at least 35 years old, must have been born in the United States or have parents who were born in the United States. A President has veto power, is commander in chief of the armed forces, and represents the country to other nations._

2 Supreme Court Justice _Judicial; appointed by the President for life, subject to Senate approval; tries cases dealing with the Constitution, national law, or treaties._

3 Representative _Legislative; serves for 2 years, must be at least 25 years old, must have been a citizen for 7 years, must live in the state he or she represents. Representatives can make laws, declare war, coin money, and originate tax bills._

SKILL PRACTICE

Name _____ Date _____

CHART AND GRAPH SKILL
Read a Flow Chart

Directions Fill in the flow chart to show the jobs in each of the three branches of government. In the second row, describe the main task of each branch. Some examples have been filled in for you.

EXECUTIVE	LEGISLATIVE		JUDICIAL
President	Senator	Representative	Supreme Court Justice
to enforce the laws	to make laws		to interpret laws

LESSON 4

Name _____ Date _____

Approval and the Bill of Rights

Directions Read the freedoms guaranteed by the Bill of Rights. Then read each statement that follows. If the statement is a fact, write *F* in the blank. If the statement is an opinion, write *O* in the blank.

1. People may follow any religion. The government cannot financially support or promote any religion. People have freedom to speak, to publish, and to hold meetings.

2. People may keep and bear weapons.

3. People do not have to board soldiers in their homes during peacetimes.

4. The government cannot search people's homes or remove their property without the permission of a judge.

5–8. People have the right to a fair trial by a jury. Defendants do not have to testify against themselves. They may have a lawyer represent them in court. They cannot be tried twice for the same crime.

9. People have other rights not specifically listed in the Constitution.

10. The federal government can do only what the Constitution gives it permission to do. All other powers belong to the states and to the people.

❶ __O__ It's not fair to have soldiers sleeping in your home at any time.

❷ __F__ People can hold public meetings to talk about their government.

❸ __O__ Newspapers should print only good news.

❹ __O__ The federal government has gotten too powerful.

❺ __F__ A person cannot be tried twice for the same crime.

❻ __O__ The individual states don't have enough power.

❼ __F__ People do not have to testify against themselves in court.

SKILL PRACTICE

Name _____ Date _____

 CITIZENSHIP SKILL
Act as a Responsible Citizen

Directions Citizens have responsibilities as well as rights and privileges. Read each statement below the picture. Then suggest how a responsible citizen might handle the situation.

❶ You notice that people are being careless about litter in your neighborhood. Answers will vary but may suggest picking up litter, organizing a group to monitor litter, or petitioning for more trash containers to be placed in public areas.

❷ Several dogs in your neighborhood are not on leashes. Answers will vary but may suggest creating or enforcing leash laws.

❸ Skateboarders in your neighborhood are practicing on sidewalks and in the street. Answers will vary but may suggest trying to persuade local officials to designate a skateboard park area.

❹ A local election is coming up. Answers will vary but should indicate that a responsible citizen would vote.

❺ A new law is coming up for discussion before being voted on. Some people disagree with the law. Answers will vary but may suggest writing a letter to the editor of a local newspaper or attending local political meetings to express opinions.

LESSON 5

Name _____ Date _____

The New Government Begins

Directions The two major political parties of the late eighteenth century differed in several ways. Fill out the chart below to show how they were different. One example has been given.

FEDERALIST	REPUBLICAN
Believed in a strong central government	Believed that the powers of the national government should be limited to those stated in the Constitution
Answers may include the following: Believed government should encourage manufacturing; Believed the United States should have close ties with Britain; Wanted a federal bank to issue paper money; Were followers of Hamilton	Answers may include the following: Believed the economy should depend on agriculture; Believed the United States should have close ties with France; Wanted little government; Were followers of Jefferson

---

CHAPTER 10 REVIEW

Name _____ Date _____

A New Form of Government

Directions Complete this graphic organizer by summarizing the facts about the writing and ratification of the United States Constitution.

TOPIC OR EVENT
The Constitutional Convention

→

IMPORTANT DETAILS

What?
A convention to discuss the Articles of Confederation

Who?
Delegates from 12 of the 13 United States

Where?
Philadelphia

How?
in secret

Why?
to discuss the many ideas delegates attending the convention had on how to improve the Articles of Confederation

→

SUMMARY
Delegates to the Philadelphia Convention met to discuss ways to improve upon the Articles of Confederation. Instead, the Convention delegates decided to do away with the Articles and create a new form of government.

· CHAPTER ·

Name _____ Date _____

10 Test Preparation

Directions Read each question and choose the best answer. Then fill in the circle for the answer you have chosen. Be sure to fill in the circle completely.

1 _____ was one good reason for changing the weak national government set up by the Articles of Confederation.
- Ⓐ The Northwest Ordinance
- Ⓑ The way Congress moved around
- ● Shays's Rebellion
- Ⓓ The ideas of James Madison

2 The Great Compromise established —
- Ⓕ how enslaved African Americans would be counted.
- Ⓖ who had the rights to tax.
- Ⓗ the balance between state and federal government.
- ● how states would be represented in Congress.

3 A President who does not perform the duties of the office can be —
- ● impeached by Congress.
- Ⓑ forced to leave town.
- Ⓒ tried before the Supreme Court.
- Ⓓ sent to a foreign country.

4 The Bill of Rights was influenced by the —
- Ⓕ Spanish constitution.
- ● British Magna Carta.
- Ⓗ Italian Bill of Rights.
- Ⓘ French political practice.

5 George Washington set an example for future Presidents by —
- Ⓐ riding a white horse.
- Ⓑ placing his friends in government positions.
- ● serving only two elected terms.
- Ⓓ naming the person to be the next President.

102 ▪ **Activity Book**   Use after reading Chapter 10, pages 344–379.

© Harcourt

COMMUNITY RESOURCES

Historical Societies
_____
_____
_____
_____
_____

Museums
_____
_____
_____
_____
_____

Experts in Government
_____
_____
_____
_____
_____

Area Government Buildings
_____
_____
_____
_____
_____

Chapter 10 Assessment

CONTENT / VOCABULARY

·CHAPTER·
Name _____ Date _____

10 Test

Part One: Test Your Understanding

MULTIPLE CHOICE (4 points each)

Directions Circle the letter of the best answer.

1 A form of government in which people elect representatives is called—
A a confederation.
B a republic.
C a congress.
D an ordinance.

2 Which of the following is **not** an accurate description of the government in 1781 under the Articles of Confederation?
F The states seldom agreed about anything.
G Congress could declare war and make treaties.
H Congress could regulate trade and collect taxes.
J The states had the right to have their own militias.

3 Daniel Shays led armed groups of farmers in attacks on courthouses in the hope of—
A stopping the courts from seizing any more of the farmers' property.
B allowing the states to form their own militias.
C collecting money to buy tools and seeds for planting.
D passing land ordinances to divide their land fairly.

4 As a result of Congress passing a land ordinance, western lands were divided into squares called—
F territories.
G arsenals.
H boundaries.
J townships.

5 The Northwest Ordinance, a plan for governing the Northwest Territory, included all of the following elements **except** that—
A Native Americans should be treated fairly.
B freedom of religion was promised.
C people could keep slaves.
D residents had the right to trial by jury.

6 Which of the following was true of money under the Articles of Confederation?
F States could not print their own money.
G States accepted money printed by other states.
H Money was printed by states and by the central government.
J Money was standard throughout the states.

(continued)

Chapter 10 Test   **Assessment Program ▪ 77**

CONTENT / VOCABULARY

Name _____ Date _____

7 Who was one of the first to arrive at the Philadelphia Convention and was elected president of the convention?
A Thomas Jefferson
B George Washington
C James Madison
D Benjamin Franklin

8 Which of the following groups was represented at the Philadelphia Convention?
F women
G Tories
H merchants
J Native Americans

9 Under the federal system, the states gave up some rights. Which of the following did they keep?
A the right to raise money by taxing citizens
B the right to raise armies and navies
C the right to make treaties with other countries
D the right to print money

10 The lawmaking branch of the government is known as the—
F executive branch.
G judicial branch.
H congressional branch.
J legislative branch.

FILL IN THE BLANK (4 points each)

Directions Fill in the blank with the correct word or words from the list below.

11 _____James Madison_____ is remembered as the Father of the Constitution.

12 When each side in a conflict gives up something it wants in order to come to an agreement, the result is called a _____compromise_____.

13 "The supreme law of the land," established by the delegates at the Philadelphia Convention, was called the _____Constitution_____ of the United States of America.

14 The highest court in the United States is known as the _____Supreme Court_____.

15 Those who favored the Constitution and wanted a strong national government were known as _____Federalists_____.

Supreme Court
Constitution
James Madison
Federalists
compromise

(continued)

78 ▪ Assessment Program   Chapter 10 Test

SKILLS

Name _____ Date _____

Part Two: Test Your Skills

READ A FLOW CHART (20 points)

Directions Use the flow chart to answer the questions below.

Matt's neighbor caused $1,000 worth of damage to Matt's garage. His neighbor refuses to pay him, so Matt is taking him to court in a civil trial.

Matt (the plaintiff) files a complaint with the court. He describes the damage and asks the court to make his neighbor pay for it.
↓
The neighbor (the defendant) receives a copy of the complaint.
↓
Matt and his neighbor provide information to each other about the case (discovery).
↓
The judge encourages them to settle their problem without going to trial.
↓ or ↓
The neighbor decides to pay Matt for the damage. | Matt and his neighbor go to trial. They both present their sides of the story in court.
↓
The judge makes a decision (verdict) that the neighbor should pay Matt.
↓ or ↓
The neighbor pays Matt for the damage. | The neighbor disagrees with the decision (appeals).

16 Once the complaint has been filed and discovery has taken place, Matt and his neighbor have two options. What are those options? They could agree to settle the problem or go to trial.

17 What must the judge do before the neighbor can appeal? The judge must make a decision (verdict) that the neighbor should pay Matt.

18 Which process involves more steps, settling in court or out of court? Why might this process take longer to complete? Possible response: Settling in court involves more steps and may take longer because there is an extra person involved who must hear the stories and make a decision.

(continued)

Chapter 10 Test   **Assessment Program ▪ 79**

APPLICATION / WRITING

Name _____ Date _____

Part Three: Apply What You Have Learned

19 COMPARE AND CONTRAST (10 points)

Almost as soon as the new government under the Constitution began, President Washington's top advisers, Alexander Hamilton and Thomas Jefferson, started to disagree about what was best for the United States. These arguments led to the formation of two political parties, the Federalists and the Jefferson Republicans. The two groups had very different views on the direction the country should take. In the chart below, briefly explain what the parties' opinions about the topics on the left would be.

Topic	Federalists' Opinion	Jeffersonian Republicans' Opinion
increased manufacturing	Possible response: would be in favor of this and would encourage increased trade as well	Possible response: would be against this because they thought the economy should depend on agriculture
decreased government power	Possible response: would be displeased because they supported a strong central government	Possible response: would be pleased because they wanted as little government as possible
increased international relationships	Possible response: in favor if relationship was with Britain, which had a large trading network	Possible response: in favor if relationship was with France, an ally of the United States in the Revolutionary War

20 ESSAY (10 points)

Under the Articles of Confederation, the central government was weak, referred to by George Washington as "a half-starved, limping government." Write a paragraph explaining some of the problems Congress faced under the Articles.

Possible response: Congress was often ineffective because either not enough members were present at meetings or the states could not agree. Congress had no place to hold meetings. Congress had limited powers, which did not include regulating trade or collecting taxes, two problem areas. While the government could print its own money, Congress printed too much, causing inflation. The difficulties Congress encountered led to economic problems for many Americans.

80 ▪ Assessment Program   Chapter 10 Test

Introduce the Chapter

OBJECTIVES

- Summarize events that led to the creation of the United States Constitution.
- Understand amendments to the United States Constitution, including the Bill of Rights.

Access Prior Knowledge

Ask students to think about a time when they were part of a committee or group working to accomplish a goal. Perhaps they were on a committee to plan a school event, or had to work as part of a group on a class project. What helped the group work together successfully? When are groups not effective? What personal skills are required to complete a task as part of a group?

Visual Learning

Picture Have students examine the photograph and the Locate It map. Have students describe the room and its location. Ask students what these images might reveal about the Constitution.

INDEPENDENCE NATIONAL HISTORIC PARK

Few places in the United States have been home to as many historic events as the Assembly Room of Independence Hall in Philadelphia. In this room, the Declaration of Independence was adopted, the design for the American flag was chosen, and the Constitution was debated and written.

LOCATE IT

PENNSYLVANIA
Philadelphia

344 ▪ Unit 5

BACKGROUND

Picture Discuss with students the arrangement of the Assembly Room in Independence Hall. Point out that the large tables surrounded by chairs suggests that the groups meeting here planned to work together to solve problems. Ask students to suggest reasons for the presence of the large fireplaces and numerous candles. These features were used before electricity for light and warmth. Independence Hall, or the Old State House, was one of the most important buildings in colonial America. The Liberty Bell was rung here, and George Washington was chosen to lead the Continental Army. Many other historic buildings surround Independence Hall.

BACKGROUND

Quotation The Constitutional Convention that met at Independence Hall in 1787 was a collection of colonial America's most accomplished leaders. Although the Constitution is considered a joint accomplishment of all 55 delegates, Gouverneur Morris, an attorney from New York, actually created the written draft that reflected the ideas of the convention.

10

The Constitution

" We the people of the United States . . . "

—Constitution of the United States,
Preamble, September 17, 1787

Focus Skill Summarize

When you **summarize**, you give a shortened version of what you have read.

After you read this chapter, be sure to do the following.

- Summarize the lessons about the Constitution and the early national government.

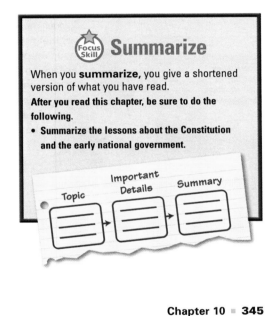

Topic → Important Details → Summary

Locate It Map Philadelphia is located on the Delaware River. During the Revolutionary War, it was the capital of the 13 colonies.

Read and Respond

Have students discuss what they think they will learn about the Constitution in this chapter.

Quotation Have a volunteer read the quotation aloud. Encourage students to discuss the importance of the language used.

Focus Skill Summarize

Have students create graphic organizers for each lesson to help them write their summaries.

- A blank graphic organizer appears on page 101 of the Activity Book.

- Point out that asking *Who? What? Where? When? How?* and *Why?* about each topic helps identify key facts.

- A completed graphic organizer for summarizing can be found on page 101 of the Activity Book, Teacher's Edition.

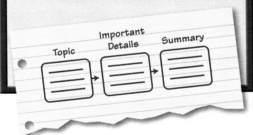

Topic → Important Details → Summary

WORD WORK

Preview Vocabulary Have students use a chart to record definitions of the lesson vocabulary terms. They should also write an original sentence using each term to illustrate its meaning.

Vocabulary Chart		
Word	Definition	Sentence

MAKE IT RELEVANT

Discussion Topics Use the following topics to discuss further the creation of the Constitution and the founding of the United States.

- Why do you think it was important for a group of people to write the Constitution?

- Can you think of any reasons why a colony would have decided *against* sending a delegate to the Constitutional Convention?

- If you were going to write a constitution for your school, what would you include in the document?

OBJECTIVES

- Summarize the events that led to the Constitution.
- Examine the role of governments in economic systems.
- Identify the contributions of individuals to the democratic process.
- Explain the Northwest Ordinance and its importance in governing the Northwest Territory.

 Summarize pp. 345, 346, 347, 350, 380

Vocabulary

SEE READING AND VOCABULARY TRANSPARENCY 5-2 OR THE WORD CARDS ON PP. V57–V58.

republic p. 346	**territory** p. 349
inflation p. 347	**ordinance**
arsenal p. 348	p. 349

 When Minutes Count

Have students scan the lesson to find the meaning of the lesson vocabulary terms. Then ask them to use the terms in sentences about the lesson.

Quick Summary

This lesson examines the factors behind the formation of a strong central government in the United States.

 Motivate

Set the Purpose

Big Idea Explain that United States leaders faced a series of challenges in forming a new government.

Access Prior Knowledge

Have students discuss what they know about the importance of groups becoming organized.

· LESSON ·

1

The Confederation Period

1780 1800 1820 1840 1860

1781–1787

SUMMARIZE
As you read, summarize the problems and successes of the new nation's first government.

BIG IDEA
The first government of the United States had many problems and successes.

VOCABULARY
republic
inflation
arsenal
territory
ordinance

In 1781, before the war with Britain had ended, the 13 former colonies—now independent states—approved the Articles of Confederation. This plan for a central government made the United States of America a republic. A **republic** is a form of government in which people elect representatives to govern the country. People hoped that under the Articles of Confederation, all 13 states could act together as one nation when needed. Under the Articles, however, the central government was weak. It was, as George Washington called it, "a half-starved, limping government."

Problems from the Start

Under the Articles of Confederation, the representatives met in a Congress. However, there often were not enough representatives present to allow Congress to take action. To make an important decision, representatives from at least 9 of the 13 states had to agree. Even when enough representatives were present, the states seldom agreed on anything. No state wanted to be under the control of the other states.

Nassau Hall in New Jersey was once a meeting place for Congress.

FAST FACT
Nassau Hall served as the United States capital for three months during the summer of 1783.

346 ■ Unit 5

REACH ALL LEARNERS

Advanced Learners
Discuss some of the problems associated with the Articles of Confederation. Organize students into pairs and have each pair research a particular problem of the Articles of Confederation, such as a weak national government. Encourage students to use the text to guide their research. Ask students to share their findings with the class.

WORD WORK

Related Words Ask students to work in pairs to develop a list of words that are related to the term *inflation*. inflate, deflate, deflation Discuss with the class any knowledge they have of those terms. For example, students may note that inflating something, such as a tire, means to enlarge it, and deflating something means to make it smaller.

Congress printed many paper bills known as Continentals. They had so little value that some Americans used the phrase *not worth a continental* to describe things that were worthless.

The new government had to face other challenges, too. Congress did not have a building of its own, so representatives had to hold meetings in many different cities and states. Also, the Articles limited the powers of the central government. For example, Congress could declare war, make treaties, and borrow money, but it could not collect taxes.

To get some of the money it needed, Congress asked each state to contribute money to help support the central government. Congress could not force the states to pay, though. State leaders could refuse to send money. They could also refuse to pay debts that they owed.

The central government could raise funds by printing and coining money. However, Congress caused inflation by printing too much money. **Inflation** occurs when the value of a government's money falls because there is too much of it. This meant that people needed more money to buy the same goods and services. During this time goods that used to cost two cents cost twenty dollars!

The Articles also stated that Congress could not raise a large army without the permission of the states. State leaders were afraid that a large army could be used to enforce unfair laws. This meant that raising an army to defend the nation against attack was difficult.

REVIEW What happened when Congress tried to print money to raise funds?

SUMMARIZE It printed too much money, which caused terrible inflation.

Shays's Rebellion

Economic problems during the 1780s made life difficult for many Americans. Some former soldiers still had not been paid for fighting during the Revolutionary War. Although they were poor, they had to pay high state taxes. To buy tools and seeds for planting, many farmers had to borrow money and go into debt.

Going into debt caused more problems for poor Americans. If people could not pay their debts or their taxes, the courts of some states would take away their farms. In 1786 and 1787, poor farmers protested by refusing to let the courts meet. Some of these protests, such as Shays's Rebellion in Massachusetts, turned violent.

The rebellion was named for Daniel Shays, a captain in the Continental army. During the fall of 1786, some farmers rebelled against the laws of Massachusetts.

Chapter 10 ■ 347

2 Teach

Problems from the Start

Read and Respond

Link Economics with Civics and Government Explain that under the Articles of Confederation, any state could override a national treaty. This is why British leaders in 1785 were reluctant to enter into a commerce treaty with the United States.

Shays's Rebellion

Read and Respond

Civics and Government Inform students that farmers and soldiers involved in Shays's Rebellion had originally tried to bring about change through the courts. Explain that they had asked the Massachusetts legislature to issue more currency or to slow the rate of foreclosures on people's farms. However, the legislature did not resolve these issues.

Q How might the legislature's response to the farmers' request have helped contribute to the rebellion?

A The farmers may have felt they had no alternative but to attack courthouses and march against the arsenal to bring attention to their cause.

Read and Respond

Link History with Civics and Government The uprising in Massachusetts was a demonstration against high taxes and harsh economic conditions. As a result of the rebellion, the Massachusetts legislature enacted laws to ease those conditions.

The Western Lands

Read and Respond

History Inform students that Thomas Jefferson first proposed an ordinance for western lands in 1784. In his plan he suggested splitting the region into states and also making slavery illegal there. This proposal was passed but never enacted. Explain that many of the ideas contained in this proposal were later reflected in the Northwest Ordinance.

Visual Learning

Map Direct students' attention to the map on page 349. Point out that states formed from the Northwest Territory were Michigan, Ohio, Indiana, Illinois, Wisconsin, and part of Minnesota.
CAPTION ANSWER: Settlers would be able to establish property boundaries and they would be close to a school.

Shays led the group in attacks against the courthouses. The farmers hoped that they could stop the courts from taking their land. Then, in January 1787, Shays led an attack on a United States arsenal located in Springfield, Massachusetts. An **arsenal** is a building that is used for storing weapons.

The arsenal at Springfield belonged to the central government, but Shays and his group attacked it anyway. Shays declared, "That crowd [the members of Congress] is too weak to act!" Congress did not have an army to defend the arsenal. Instead, the governor of Massachusetts called out state troops to stop Shays. During the fighting, four of Shays's followers died. Soon the rebellion had come to an end.

Shays's Rebellion showed that many Americans were unhappy with the state governments. Under the Articles of Confederation, Congress did not have an army to defend United States property. State governments had to defend their own lands. Americans feared that the states could not stop all the unrest.

REVIEW Why did Daniel Shays and other farmers rebel against the government?
They wanted to stop the courts from taking their farms.

The Western Lands

In spite of such problems, Congress was still responsible for many important decisions. One was about how to divide and govern the nation's new lands west of the Appalachians. In the years after the United States gained its independence, many settlers moved to the

The governor of Massachusetts issued the Proclamation of 1786 (below) to explain that acts such as Shays's Rebellion (left) would not be tolerated.

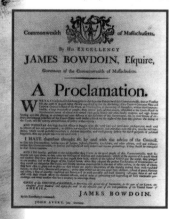

348 Unit 5

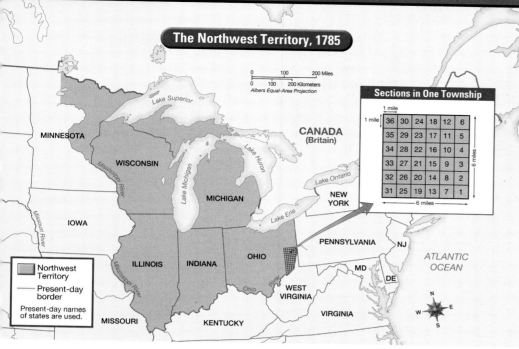

The Northwest Territory, 1785

Sections in One Township

36	30	24	18	12	6
35	29	23	17	11	5
34	28	22	16	10	4
33	27	21	15	9	3
32	26	20	14	8	2
31	25	19	13	7	1

Northwest Territory
Present-day border
Present-day names of states are used.

Regions This map shows how the Northwest Territory was divided into townships with many sections.

◈ How might the township system have helped settlers?

western lands. These lands had previously been set aside for Native Americans. Some of those settlers moved to lands north of the Ohio River, an area that had become known as the Northwest Territory. A **territory** is land that belongs to a national government but is not a state and is not represented in Congress. Over time, thousands of settlers followed the Ohio River west and settled there.

At first, there was no plan in place for how the land should be divided among the settlers. It was difficult to tell where each person's property ended. As a result, many boundary disputes occurred.

In 1785 Congress passed a land **ordinance**, or set of laws, that created

a system to survey, or measure, the western lands. The land was divided into squares that were called townships. A township measured 6 miles (10 km) long on each side, and its land was divided into 36 smaller squares, or sections. One of these sections was set aside for public schools. Then the central government sold the rest of the squares for at least one dollar per acre. This system was so successful that most of the land west of the Mississippi River was divided that way. Township and section lines are still used in many parts of the United States today.

Two years later, in 1787, Congress passed the Northwest Ordinance.

Chapter 10 ■ 349

Assess

Lesson 1 Review—Answers

 SUMMARIZE Shays's Rebellion occurred because people protested the government's seizure of property as payment for debts. Many of these farmers had been soldiers during the Revolutionary War, but had not been paid. Since they had little or no money but still had to pay taxes, many of these farmers went into debt.

① **BIG IDEA** Problems included a weak central government, few state representatives in Congress, no place to hold meetings, and high inflation. Successes included the land ordinance of 1785 and the Northwest Ordinance of 1787.

② **VOCABULARY** Possible answer: The government of the United States caused **inflation** by printing too much money.

③ **TIME LINE** the approval of the Articles of Confederation

④ **CIVICS AND GOVERNMENT** Patrick Henry feared a strong national government so he did not want to give Congress more power.

⑤ **CRITICAL THINKING—Analyze** He meant that Congress had no real strength and could not keep the confederation of states from breaking apart.

> **Performance Assessment Guidelines** Students' letters should be clearly written and should express their opinion about the time of unrest.

ACTIVITY BOOK

Use ACTIVITY BOOK, p. 94, to reinforce and extend student learning.

Members of Congress (above) discussed the possibility of a stronger central government.

This ordinance set up a plan for governing the Northwest Territory and for forming new states from the lands. It said that the Ohio River would form the southern boundary of the Northwest Territory. The ordinance also promised the settlers freedom of religion and it did not allow slavery. It showed that Congress could work to plan the growth of the nation.

REVIEW Which ordinance set up a plan for governing the Northwest Territory? the Northwest Ordinance

A Rope of Sand

Some people argued that Congress needed more power. James Madison, who represented Virginia, was the youngest member of Congress in 1780. Madison had studied ways of governing, and saw several weaknesses in the Articles of Confederation. He worried that Congress had become "a rope of sand."

Some others, such as John Adams and Thomas Jefferson, agreed with Madison. They believed that the nation needed a stronger central government. That was the only way, they said, to keep the states from breaking apart.

Others did not agree. Patrick Henry of Virginia was one of many who favored the Articles. Henry, like others, feared a strong central government. A rope made out of sand they said, was better than a rope made out of iron.

REVIEW Why did James Madison and others want a stronger central government? They believed that only a stronger central government could keep the states from breaking apart.

LESSON 1 REVIEW

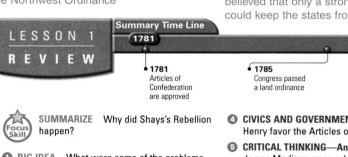

Summary Time Line

1781 — 1787

• **1781** Articles of Confederation are approved
• **1785** Congress passed a land ordinance
• **1786** Daniel Shays's rebellion starts

SUMMARIZE Why did Shays's Rebellion happen?

① **BIG IDEA** What were some of the problems and successes of the government under the Articles of Confederation?

② **VOCABULARY** Use the word **inflation** in a sentence about the powers of the central government during the 1780s.

③ **TIME LINE** Which event happened first, Shays's Rebellion or the approval of the Articles of Confederation?

④ **CIVICS AND GOVERNMENT** Why did Patrick Henry favor the Articles of Confederation?

⑤ **CRITICAL THINKING—Analyze** What did James Madison mean when he said that Congress had become "a rope of sand"?

PERFORMANCE—Write a Letter Imagine that you are living in Massachusetts during the time of Shays's Rebellion. Write a letter expressing your opinion about the unrest.

EXTEND AND ENRICH

Write a Children's Book Organize students into four groups and assign each group a section from this lesson. Have each group summarize the information in its section and use it to write part of a children's book. Inform students that they may have to simplify or explain some terms. When students have completed their writings, compile the sections into one book and share it with younger students.

RETEACH THE LESSON

Teach the Class Organize the class into four groups. Assign each group one section from this lesson. Ask students to prepare a lesson for the class based on the information provided in the section. Encourage students to use visual aids. Then have each group teach the class.

The Constitutional Convention

1780 1800 1820 1840 1860

1786–1787

Governing the country under the Articles of Confederation became very difficult. In 1786 some leaders called on the states to hold a **convention**, or an important meeting, to discuss trade among the states. It was held at Annapolis, Maryland, in September 1786.

The Annapolis Convention

Only five states—Delaware, New Jersey, New York, Pennsylvania, and Virginia—sent representatives in time to attend the Annapolis Convention. Chief among the delegates' concerns was **commerce**, or trade. Under the Articles, each state had the authority to print its own paper money. However, money from one state was usually not accepted in another state.

The delegates to the convention talked briefly before deciding that a stronger national government was needed in order to regulate commerce.

The Annapolis State House in Maryland is the oldest state capitol still in use. Shown below is an eight-dollar bank note from Massachusetts.

Chapter 10 351

SUMMARIZE

As you read, summarize the key events at the Constitutional Convention.

BIG IDEA

Leaders had to work together to decide on a new plan of government.

VOCABULARY

convention
commerce
federal system
bill

OBJECTIVES

- Describe the events that led up to the Constitutional Convention.
- Discuss the Constitutional Convention and its influence on the democratic process.
- Identify the contributions of those who helped write the Constitution.
- Explain the "Great Compromise" and its importance in representative government.

Summarize pp. 345, 351, 352, 355, 357, 380

Vocabulary

SEE READING AND VOCABULARY TRANSPARENCY 5-3 OR THE WORD CARDS ON PP. V57–V58.

convention p. 351	**federal system** p. 354
commerce p. 351	**bill** p. 356

When Minutes Count

Organize the class into four groups. Have each group study a different section. Then ask each group to share what the group learned.

Quick Summary

This lesson discusses how leaders compromised to create a new form of national government.

1 Motivate

Set the Purpose

Big Idea Explain that leaders debated various plans of government.

Access Prior Knowledge

Remind students that states held great power under the Articles of Confederation. Ask students why that made it difficult to govern.

BACKGROUND

Amending the Articles In the month preceding the Annapolis Convention, several proposals were made in Congress to update the Articles of Confederation. Proposals included revising the court system and increasing congressional power over trade. Adoption of such amendments required unanimous approval, which they did not receive.

STUDY/RESEARCH SKILLS

Skimming and Scanning Ask students to scan this subsection. Then have them turn to a partner and recall what they can about the topic. Ask students to write down any questions that they have about the material they are about to cover. Ask volunteers to share their questions with the class. Encourage students to write the answers to these questions as they cover the material in this subsection.

Anticipation Guide Ask students to predict which statements are true and which are false. Students may correct their predictions as they read.

1. The Annapolis delegates decided to revise the Articles of Confederation. FALSE

2. At the Philadelphia Convention, a new form of government was proposed. TRUE

3. The Great Compromise resolved the states' conflict. TRUE

● USE READING AND VOCABULARY TRANSPARENCY 5-3.

5-3 TRANSPARENCY

2 Teach

The Annapolis Convention

Read and Respond

Civics and Government Remind students that Rhode Island did not send delegates to the convention because its leaders feared a strong central government. Ask students to draw upon their knowledge of Rhode Island's history to infer why this was so. Students may respond that Rhode Island was founded upon religious freedom, and its leaders did not want to surrender that or any other freedoms to the government.

James Madison

Citizenship Encourage students to list examples of how James Madison reflected the character trait of citizenship. Students may indicate that Madison's actions included helping develop a government structure and serving in the public sector. Have students identify other actions that could exemplify good citizenship skills. voting, activism, volunteerism

This meant that the Articles of Confederation had to be changed. To change the Articles, however, all the states had to agree.

The delegates sent a letter to Congress, asking it to call another convention. Representatives from all the states could meet to discuss all their problems. They could also decide whether changing the Articles might help solve those problems.

At first Congress did not want to call a convention, but after Shays's Rebellion it agreed to participate. Each state was asked to send delegates to a convention to be held in Philadelphia in the spring of 1787. Rhode Island was the only state that refused to send a delegate. Its leaders feared a strong national government. They believed that such a government would be a threat to the rights of citizens.

REVIEW What decision did delegates reach at the Annapolis Convention? They decided that the United States needed a stronger national government.

The Philadelphia Convention

The delegates to the convention began to gather in Philadelphia in May 1787. One of the first to arrive was George Washington of Virginia. In 1787 Washington was 55 years old and the most highly honored hero of the Revolutionary War. The first action the delegates took was to elect Washington president of the convention.

Benjamin Franklin, representing Pennsylvania, made the most colorful entrance. Franklin was 81 years old, and he was unable to walk far or ride in a bumpy carriage. He arrived in a Chinese sedan chair carried by prisoners from the Philadelphia jail.

In all, 55 delegates from 12 of the states met in the Pennsylvania State House, which later became known as Independence Hall. The delegates were mostly lawyers, planters, and merchants. Some, such as Roger Sherman and

James Madison   1751–1836

Character Trait: Citizenship

James Madison's Virginia Plan provided the basic framework for the Constitution. Because of his efforts in planning the Constitution and winning its final approval, Madison is remembered as the Father of the Constitution. Madison, however, often dismissed this title by saying the Constitution was not "the off-spring of a single brain" but "the work of many heads and many hands." Madison later served as an official in the United States government. In 1808 he was elected fourth President of the United States.

MULTIMEDIA BIOGRAPHIES
Visit The Learning Site at www.harcourtschool.com
to learn about other famous people.

GO ONLINE

352 ■ Unit 5

Q Who were the Founding Fathers?

A A group of American delegates who worked to set up the foundations of the new United States government. They included Benjamin Franklin, Alexander Hamilton, and George Washington.

Summarize Organize students into pairs and have them review the main ideas of the first two subsections. Then have them use words and pictures to summarize what they have learned about the conventions. Ask pairs to share their summaries with the class.

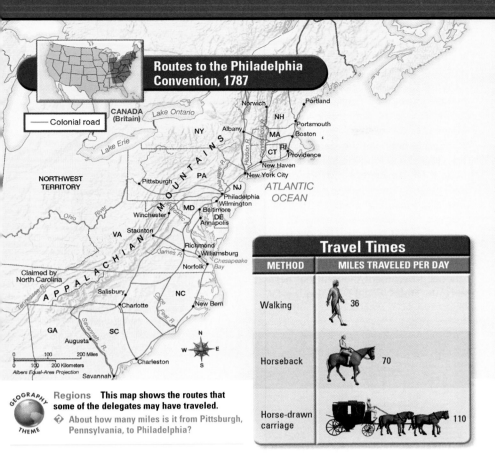

Routes to the Philadelphia Convention, 1787

— Colonial road

Travel Times

METHOD	MILES TRAVELED PER DAY
Walking	36
Horseback	70
Horse-drawn carriage	110

Regions This map shows the routes that some of the delegates may have traveled.
◆ About how many miles is it from Pittsburgh, Pennsylvania, to Philadelphia?

Benjamin Franklin, had been signers of the Declaration of Independence.

Some famous people were not delegates. Thomas Jefferson, who had written the Declaration of Independence, was in Paris as ambassador to France. John Adams was in London as ambassador to Britain. His cousin Samuel Adams was in ill health, and John Hancock was too busy as governor of Massachusetts to attend. Patrick Henry refused to take part because he did not believe that a stronger national government was a good idea.

REVIEW Who was elected president of the convention? *George Washington*

The Work Begins

From the beginning, the delegates agreed to conduct their meetings in secret. They believed that secret meetings would allow them to make the best decisions. Windows in the State House were covered, and guards stood at the doors.

As the convention began, some of the delegates offered ideas that they thought would improve the Articles of Confederation. Almost immediately, however, they reached a surprising decision. An entirely new plan of government—a new constitution—needed to be written.

Chapter 10 ■ 353

The Philadelphia Convention

Read and Respond

History Inform students that George Washington came out of retirement to preside over the convention. Explain that he declined to join the debates.

Q Why did Washington decline to join in the debates?

A As president of the convention, Washington believed he needed to remain impartial.

Culture and Society Explain that during this time, women, African Americans, and Native Americans had few rights. As such, they were not included at the conventions.

Q Since delegates were mostly educated men, did they represent the interests of all the people?

A No. The delegates likely did not represent women, African Americans, or Native Americans.

The Work Begins

Read and Respond

History Explain that the convention's events were kept secret for many years. Inform students that James Madison's notes about the convention were not published until 1840.

Visual Learning

Map Explain to students that some delegates began their journey weeks before the date of the convention. CAPTION ANSWER: about 250 miles

GO ONLINE Students might enjoy researching information about other historic maps. Have them visit The Learning Site at **www.harcourtschool.com**.

Chart Direct students' attention to the chart on page 353. Explain to students that distance and road conditions determined why some delegates might walk and others might ride.

Read and Respond

Civics and Government Review the powers that the states would retain and lose under the proposed federal system. They would retain the power over affairs of state, such as the power to make laws and hold elections. They would give up the power to print money, to raise armies and navies, and to make treaties.

Q **Why would states need to give up these powers under a federal system?**

A to avoid conflict with the federal government

Read and Respond

History Remind students that under a federal system, state and national governments share certain powers, such as taxing, spending for the public welfare, and borrowing money. Explain that James Madison referred to such an arrangement as a "compound republic."

Q **What did James Madison mean when he referred to the federal system as a "compound republic"?**

A He meant that the state and national governments would share certain powers.

Visual Learning

Chart Explain to students that under a federal system some powers are given to the national government, some are given to the state government, and others are shared.
CAPTION ANSWER: The national government controls trade, maintains armed forces, prints money, admits new states, declares war and makes peace, and makes laws for immigration and citizenship. State governments set up local governments, provide education, conduct elections, control state trade, enact marriage and divorce laws, and set qualifications for voting. Both governments have the power to collect taxes, set up courts, charter banks, borrow money, and make laws.

To do this, the delegates worked diligently for the next four months.

One of the first issues discussed by the delegates to the Constitutional Convention, as the Convention in Philadelphia became known, was the relationship between the states and the national government. Some delegates thought there should be a strong national government. Others believed that the state governments should be stronger.

Only a few delegates agreed with George Read of Delaware. He said that the states should be done away with. Even most of those who wanted a strong national government thought that getting rid of the states would be going too far.

Instead, the delegates agreed to create a **federal system**, one in which the right to govern would be shared by the national government and the state governments. The states would keep some rights, and share some rights with the national, or federal, government. The national government would keep all power over matters that affected the nation as a whole.

The states would keep power over their own affairs, set up state and local governments, make state laws, and conduct state and local elections. However, the states would no longer print money, raise armies and navies, or make treaties with other countries, as they had done under the Articles of Confederation.

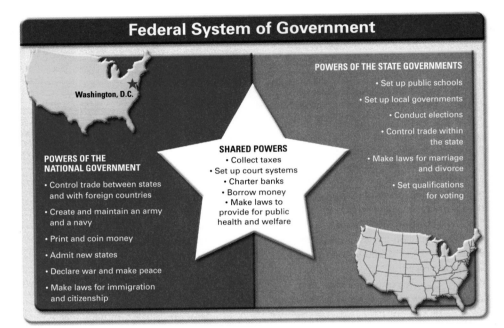

Federal System of Government

Washington, D.C.

POWERS OF THE NATIONAL GOVERNMENT
- Control trade between states and with foreign countries
- Create and maintain an army and a navy
- Print and coin money
- Admit new states
- Declare war and make peace
- Make laws for immigration and citizenship

SHARED POWERS
- Collect taxes
- Set up court systems
- Charter banks
- Borrow money
- Make laws to provide for public health and welfare

POWERS OF THE STATE GOVERNMENTS
- Set up public schools
- Set up local governments
- Conduct elections
- Control trade within the state
- Make laws for marriage and divorce
- Set qualifications for voting

Analyze Charts This chart illustrates the relationship between the national and state governments.
◆ Why do you think state governments need the power to create local governments?

In Your City Remind students that local governments are also created within states. Have students research some local government leaders and research what services those leaders provide for the community. Ask students to write their findings in a brief report.

Limited Government The United States has a limited form of government. This means that the power of each government leader is controlled by the rules of the Constitution. These laws protect the rights of American citizens. Other forms of government, such as dictatorships, do not have such limitations. Under an unlimited form of government, a nation's leaders can act in any way they please. In many cases, citizens can be arrested if they do not obey the will of their leaders.

Three delegates to the Constitutional Convention—Edmund Randolph of Virginia, Roger Sherman of Connecticut, and William Paterson of New Jersey—presented ideas for the new government that started great debate and compromise.

Both the states and the national government would be able to set up their own court systems and to raise money by taxing citizens. The delegates made it clear that, under this federal system, the new rules of government would be "the supreme law of the land." They called these new rules the Constitution of the United States of America.

REVIEW How is the power to govern shared in a federal system? 🔘 SUMMARIZE
Authority to govern is shared by the national government and the state governments.

Debate and Compromise

During their work, the delegates to the convention often failed to agree with one another. The new Constitution came into being only because the delegates were willing to agree to several compromises. The delegates often had to give up some of what they wanted in order to reach an agreement. As compromises were made, decisions were written down and the Constitution took shape.

One important compromise resolved the delegates' differences over how each state would be represented in the new Congress. Some people called this agreement the Great Compromise.

Edmund Randolph and the other Virginia delegates, including James Madison, thought the number of representatives that a state would have in the new Congress should be based on the number of people living in that state. Under this Virginia Plan, as it was called, states with more people would have more representatives and more votes in Congress. This plan would favor the large states of Virginia, Massachusetts, and Pennsylvania, which had many people.

"Not fair!" replied the delegates from the small states. William Paterson of New Jersey said that he would "rather submit to a monarch, to a despot [ruler with unlimited power], than to such a fate." Paterson then offered his own plan.

Chapter 10 ■ 355

Debate and Compromise

Read and Respond

Civics and Government Remind the class that the Virginia Plan and New Jersey Plan provided several new ideas used to form the federal government. The Virginia Plan proposed a two-house Congress, a central leader chosen by Congress, a national court, and a central council with veto powers. The New Jersey Plan included equal representation, the right for Congress to levy taxes and regulate foreign trade, and a national court.

Q **On which feature did proponents of the Virginia and New Jersey plans agree?**

A a national court

History Inform students that Roger Sherman's plan helped establish the basis of our present government. Explain that Sherman was an early supporter of American independence from Britain and that he helped draft the Articles of Confederation.

Q **Why did Roger Sherman create a new plan, instead of supporting either the Virginia or New Jersey plan?**

A He probably realized that neither plan had the broad appeal needed to become law, so he created one that did.

Analyze Primary Sources

Artifact Direct students' attention to the illustration on page 356. Explain that the Virginia Plan favored a new national government. Most of the small states sided with the New Jersey plan because it proposed equal rather than proportional representation of the states.

Read and Respond

History Explain that, although the delegates spent considerable time discussing the issue of slavery, the words *slave* and *slavery* do not appear in the Constitution. Ask students why they think this is so. Students may respond that slaves were not considered citizens.

Close

Summarize Key Content

- Because few delegates attended the Annapolis Convention, a second convention was held.
- George Washington was elected president of the Philadelphia Convention.
- At first, delegates considered improving the Articles of Confederation before deciding to write a new Constitution.
- The Great Compromise featured fair representation in government.
- The Three-fifths Compromise counted three-fifths of the total number of enslaved people as citizens.

READING SOCIAL STUDIES

Anticipation Guide Have students check their responses.

1. The Annapolis delegates decided to ~~revise the Articles of Confederation~~. ask Congress to call a new convention.

2. At the Philadelphia Convention, a new form of government was proposed.

3. The Great Compromise resolved the states' conflict.

● USE READING AND VOCABULARY TRANSPARENCY 5-3.

5-3 TRANSPARENCY

The Virginia Plan, supported by Edmund Randolph, called for representation based on population. The New Jersey Plan, offered by William Paterson, favored an equal number of representatives for each state.

Under this plan, called the New Jersey Plan, the new Congress would have one house, in which each state would be equally represented. This plan would give the small states the same number of representatives as the large states.

For weeks the delegates argued about how states should be represented in Congress. "We are now at a full stop," wrote Roger Sherman of Connecticut. The convention decided to set up a committee to work out a compromise.

In a committee meeting, Sherman presented a new plan, which became known as the Great Compromise. It was based on the idea of a two-house Congress. In one house, representation would be based on the population of each state, as in the Virginia Plan. In the other house, each state would be equally represented, as in the New Jersey Plan. Either house could present a **bill**, or an idea for a new law, but both had to approve it before it became a law.

Committee members from the large states did not like the compromise. They

356 ■ Unit 5

believed that it gave too much power to the small states. The committee added another idea. The house in which representation was based on population would have the sole authority to propose tax bills. In the end, the committee presented its plan to the whole convention. The delegates soon came to understand that if they did not agree to the Great Compromise, there would be no new plan of government.

Another compromise had to do with slavery. Delegates from the northern and southern states argued about whether enslaved African Americans should be counted when figuring each state's population. Population would affect a state's taxes and its representation in Congress.

Because the northern states had fewer enslaved African Americans than the southern states, the northern states did not want slaves to be counted for representation. After all, the delegates argued, slaves were not citizens under the Articles of Confederation and they would not become citizens under the Constitution. For tax purposes, however, the northern states did want slaves to be counted.

Delegates from the southern states wanted slaves to be counted for representation. That way they could count more

STUDY/RESEARCH SKILLS

Outlining Organize the class into groups of four. Ask each group to discuss the contents of this lesson. Have them identify the main ideas of each subsection and several supporting details. Encourage them to use an outline to present their information to the class.

INTEGRATE READING

Read a Biography
Encourage students to work with the school librarian to find a biography of Phillis Wheatley. Remind students that Wheatley was brought to Massachusetts as a slave and that she spoke out against slavery in the new nation. Urge students who read Wheatley's biography to present to the class some of her experiences and writings.

This painting by Thomas Coram shows slave quarters on a South Carolina plantation. The issue of slavery sparked heated debates among northern and southern delegates.

people and get more representatives in Congress. For tax purposes the southern states did not want slaves counted.

The delegates finally reached a compromise by counting three-fifths of the total number of slaves. This Three-fifths Compromise moved the delegates closer to forming a new government.

REVIEW What idea was called the Great Compromise? *the idea of a two-house Congress*

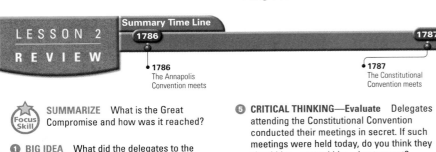

LESSON 2 REVIEW

Summary Time Line

1786 — 1787

1786
The Annapolis Convention meets

1787
The Constitutional Convention meets

 SUMMARIZE What is the Great Compromise and how was it reached?

1 BIG IDEA What did the delegates to the Constitutional Convention have to do before they could decide on a new plan of government?

2 VOCABULARY Explain the meaning of the term **federal system**.

3 TIME LINE Which event happened first, the Annapolis Convention or the Constitutional Convention?

4 CIVICS AND GOVERNMENT Under the new Constitution, what rights would the states keep?

5 CRITICAL THINKING—Evaluate Delegates attending the Constitutional Convention conducted their meetings in secret. If such meetings were held today, do you think they should be—or could be—kept secret? Explain your answer.

 PERFORMANCE—Write a News Story Imagine that you are a newspaper reporter in 1787. Write a brief news story about the Constitutional Convention and the decisions the delegates finally reached. Share your report with classmates.

Chapter 10 ■ 357

ACTIVITY BOOK

Use ACTIVITY BOOK, p. 95, to reinforce and extend student learning.

Assess

Lesson 2 Review—Answers

 SUMMARIZE The Great Compromise was reached by a committee. It created a two-house Congress. In one house each state would be represented based on its population. The other house would represent each state equally.

1 BIG IDEA They had to debate the issues and reach a compromise on them.

2 VOCABULARY Possible answer: A **federal system** is one in which the power to govern is shared by the national and state governments.

3 TIME LINE the Annapolis Convention

4 CIVICS AND GOVERNMENT The states would keep power over their own affairs, set up state and local governments, make state laws, and hold state and local elections.

5 CRITICAL THINKING—Evaluate Responses will vary, but could indicate that with today's media presence it would be difficult to keep such a meeting secret.

Performance Assessment Guidelines Students' news stories should mention the people who attended the convention, the issues, and their resolution.

EXTEND AND ENRICH

Make an Artifact Organize the class into four groups. Assign each group one subsection from this lesson. Have each group make an artifact for a class museum exhibit called "The Constitutional Convention." Guide students to make an artifact that reflects the main idea of their subsection. Groups also should write a paragraph explaining the artifact's meaning. Display items around the classroom for students to view.

RETEACH THE LESSON

Make It Relevant Have students make up a question about each subsection in this lesson. Then have them challenge a partner to correctly answer their questions. For example, *We went to Annapolis— who are we and what did we want?* delegates from Delaware, New Jersey, New York, Pennsylvania, and Virginia; we wanted a stronger national government.

OBJECTIVES

■ Explain the purpose of the Constitution as stated in the Preamble.

■ Identify the three branches of the federal government and understand their functions.

■ Explain checks and balances and the reasons for them.

Summarize pp. 345, 358, 360, 363, 380

Vocabulary

SEE READING AND VOCABULARY TRANSPARENCY 5-4 OR THE WORD CARDS ON PP. V57–V60.

census p. 359   **justice** p. 361

electoral college   **checks and**
  p. 360   **balances**

veto p. 361   p. 363

impeach p. 361

 When Minutes Count

Ask students to scan the lesson to find out the names of the three branches of the government.

Quick Summary

This lesson describes the contents of the Constitution. It explains the three branches of the government and how they work together.

1 Motivate

Set the Purpose

Big Idea Explain that the leaders of the United States divided power among three distinct branches.

Access Prior Knowledge

Review with students the various compromises made by the states in fashioning a new form of government.

SUMMARIZE
As you read, summarize the powers of the different branches of government.

BIG IDEA
Delegates created three branches for the United States government.

VOCABULARY
census
electoral college
veto
impeach
justice
checks and balances

Gouverneur Morris (right) was responsible for much of the wording of the Constitution (below).

3 Three Branches of Government

The delegates to the Constitutional Convention, wrote the Constitution with great care. Gouverneur (guh•ver•NIR) Morris of Pennsylvania spent long hours writing down and polishing each sentence. The delegates gave him the job of recording all the ideas that had been approved during the convention.

The Preamble

In the Preamble to the Constitution, Morris began with the words

❝ We the people of the United States . . . ❞

He had originally written "We the people of the States of New Hampshire, Massachusetts, . . ." Morris changed the words because he wanted the American people to know that the Constitution would make them citizens of a nation first and citizens of separate states second. This change also helped link the Constitution with the idea in the Declaration of Independence that a government should get its power from the consent of the people.

Morris went on to explain in the Preamble that the purpose of the Constitution was to create a better plan of government. This government would work

358 ■ Unit 5

WORD WORK

Categorize Vocabulary Instruct students to skim the lesson and read the definitions of the vocabulary terms. Then ask them to place each term into the appropriate category: *Executive, Legislative,* or *Judicial.* Point out that some terms may fit into all three categories. *Executive:* electoral college, veto, impeach, checks and balances; *Legislative:* repeal, impeach, checks and balances; *Judicial:* justice, impeach, checks and balances

REACH ALL LEARNERS

Auditory Learners
Organize students into a group and have them practice reading aloud the Preamble. Then ask them to perform a dramatic reading of the piece for the class. Discuss with students the ideas contained in the Preamble to ensure their understanding.

toward fairness and peace. It would allow the nation to defend itself and it would work toward the nation's well-being.

Morris also wrote that the Constitution would provide "the blessings of liberty" for the American people. These words let the citizens of the United States know that the Constitution would make sure that they remained a free people.

REVIEW Why did Gouverneur Morris change the wording in the Preamble to the Constitution? to let people know that the Constitution would make them citizens of a nation first

The Legislative Branch

In Article I of the Constitution, Gouverneur Morris described the law-making, or legislative, branch of the new government. The Congress could make laws, regulate commerce between states and with other countries and Indian tribes, and raise an army and a navy. It would also have power to declare war and coin money.

Congress would have two houses—the House of Representatives and the Senate. Either house could propose most bills, but tax bills could be proposed first only in the House of Representatives. For any bill to become law, the majority of those voting in each house would have to vote for it.

The number of members each state sent to the House of Representatives would depend on the state's population. A **census**, or population count, would be taken every ten years to find out the number of people in each state. Today the total number of members in the House of Representatives is limited to 435. That number is divided among the states, based on their populations. In the Senate each state has two senators.

For more than 200 years, the United States Capitol building has been home to the legislative branch of the federal government.

Graphic Organizer Have students copy this chart and fill it in as they read through this lesson.

Branch	Structure	Function
Executive		
Legislative		
Judicial		

● USE READING AND VOCABULARY TRANSPARENCY 5-4.

5-4 TRANSPARENCY

2 Teach

The Preamble

Read and Respond

History Share with students the text of the Preamble:

"We the People of the United States, in Order to form a more perfect Union, establish Justice, insure domestic Tranquility, provide for the common defence, promote the general Welfare, and secure the Blessings of Liberty to ourselves and our Posterity, do ordain and establish this Constitution for the United States of America."

Q Why are certain words in the Preamble capitalized?

A Students may respond that they were capitalized for greater emphasis.

The Legislative Branch

Read and Respond

Civics and Government Explain that Article I states that both houses are to set rules of procedure. These include dates they will adjourn and, for the House, the date it will convene.

In Your State Remind students that every state has its own legislature. Have students research the structure of their state legislature. Instruct them to write a report that includes details such as the number of districts as well as the location of each district. Encourage students to use charts and maps as visual aids.

Calculate the Number of Citizens Represented Ask students to research the number of national congressional representatives for their state. Then have them calculate the number of citizens served by each representative by dividing the state's population by the number of its representatives.

Read and Respond

Civics and Government Have students identify who their state representatives are, and how long they have been in office.

The Executive Branch

Read and Respond

Civics and Government Explain that James Wilson of Pennsylvania led the delegates who thought that one person should be chief executive. Wilson thought that a single executive would be more efficient than a committee. The electoral college was also Wilson's idea.

Read and Respond

History Inform students that the number of electoral votes, not popular votes, determines who wins the presidency. A candidate must receive 270 electoral votes to be elected President. Explain that on three occasions, a candidate has been elected President despite receiving fewer popular votes than his opponent. Inform students that this most recently occurred in 2000 when George W. Bush was elected President despite receiving about 500,000 fewer popular votes than Al Gore. Explain that George W. Bush was elected President with 271 electoral votes.

Read and Respond

Civics and Government Have students think about the leadership qualities needed to be a national leader in the United States. Then ask them to compare the leadership qualities of the President and the Vice President.

---

to make laws; control commerce; raise an army and a navy; declare war; and coin money

James Madison thought that the voters of each state should elect the members of both houses of Congress. Other delegates disagreed. Some felt that most citizens were not informed enough to have a say in government. After a long debate, the delegates agreed that citizens should vote directly for members of the House of Representatives. Senators would be selected by their state legislatures. Today, however, citizens vote directly for members of both houses of Congress.

In Article I, the delegates also outlined other rules for Congress that are still in effect. Members of the House of Representatives are elected to 2-year terms. They must be at least 25 years old, must have been citizens of the United States for at least 7 years, and must live in the state they represent. Senators are elected to 6-year terms. They must be at least 30 years old, must have been citizens of the United States for at least 9 years, and must live in the state they represent.

REVIEW What are the main responsibilities of Congress? **SUMMARIZE**

The Executive Branch

Once Congress makes the laws, it is the job of the executive branch, according to Article II of the Constitution, to carry them out. The delegates had many long arguments about whether this branch should be headed by one person or by a group of people. Some delegates believed that one person should be the chief executive, or leader. Others worried that a single executive would be too much like a monarch.

The delegates finally decided on a single chief executive called the President. The President is elected to a 4-year term. To be elected President, a person must be at least 35 years old and must have been born in the United States, or have parents who are United States citizens. The President must also have lived in the United States for 14 years.

The delegates decided that citizens would vote for electors, who, in turn, would vote for the President. This group of electors is called the **electoral college.**

The White House is the official residence of the President of the United States.

360

Housed in this building since 1935, the Supreme Court is the highest court in the United States.

The delegates also had long debates about how much power the President should have. They eventually decided that the President should be able to **veto**, or reject, bills that are passed by Congress.

The delegates decided that the President would represent the nation in dealing with other countries. The President would also be commander in chief of the military. The President's chief responsibility, however, would be to "take care that the laws be faithfully executed." If these duties were not carried out according to law, Congress could **impeach** the President, or accuse the President of crimes. The President could then be tried by the Senate and removed from office if found guilty.

REVIEW What is the President's main responsibility? to see that the laws of the United States are faithfully carried out

The Judicial Branch

Once laws are made and carried out, the judicial branch, according to Article III of the Constitution, must decide if they are working fairly. The judicial branch is the court system.

The states had always had their own courts. Now the delegates agreed on the need for a federal court system. These courts would decide cases that dealt with the Constitution, treaties, and national laws. They would also decide cases between states and between citizens of different states.

The delegates made most of their decisions about the highest court in the United States, which they called the Supreme Court. The delegates decided that the President would nominate the Supreme Court **justices**, or judges.

Chapter 10 ■ 361

The Branches Work Together

Read and Respond

Civics and Government Review with students the checks and balances within the federal government.

Q What recourse does Congress have if the President vetoes its legislation?

A Congress can override the President's veto with a two-thirds majority of votes in the Senate and House of Representatives.

Visual Learning

Diagram Direct students to use their finger to trace the arrows on the chart. Note that each branch can check or control the decisions of the other branches.

CAPTION ANSWER: The President can veto a bill passed by Congress.

3 Close

Summarize Key Content

- The Preamble expresses the unity of the American nation under a new government.
- The legislative branch makes the laws people live by.
- The executive branch consists of an elected President who has veto power over Congress.
- The judicial branch is made up of courts and judges who make sure laws are fair and that they agree with the United States Constitution.
- A system of checks and balances prevents any branch of the federal government from gaining too much power.

The Senate would vote whether to approve them. It was decided that a Supreme Court justice would stay in office for life. In this way, justices could make decisions without worrying about losing their jobs. No decision was made as to how many justices would be on the Supreme Court. Congress decided on that number later. At first there were six justices on the Supreme Court. Today there are nine.

REVIEW What are the duties of the federal courts? to decide cases having to do with the Constitution, treaties, and national laws, and cases between states or citizens of different states

The Branches Work Together

None of the delegates wanted any one branch of the new government to have too much power. So they gave each branch some ways to check, or limit, the power of the other two branches.

Congress, for example, can check the power of the President if two-thirds of each house votes to override, or cancel, the President's veto. If that happens, a bill

Analyze Diagrams This diagram shows the checks and balances within the three branches of the federal government.
◆ How can the President check the authority of Congress?

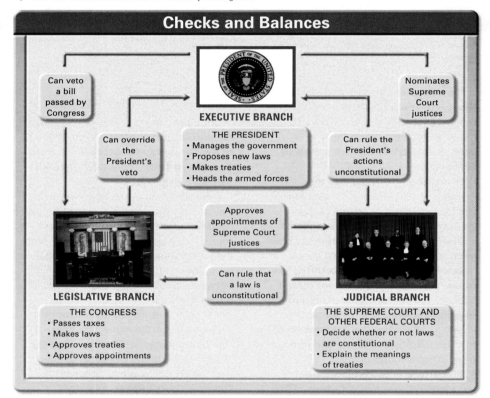

Checks and Balances

EXECUTIVE BRANCH
- Can veto a bill passed by Congress
- Nominates Supreme Court justices

THE PRESIDENT
- Manages the government
- Proposes new laws
- Makes treaties
- Heads the armed forces

- Can override the President's veto
- Can rule the President's actions unconstitutional

- Approves appointments of Supreme Court justices

- Can rule that a law is unconstitutional

LEGISLATIVE BRANCH
THE CONGRESS
- Passes taxes
- Makes laws
- Approves treaties
- Approves appointments

JUDICIAL BRANCH
THE SUPREME COURT AND OTHER FEDERAL COURTS
- Decide whether or not laws are constitutional
- Explain the meanings of treaties

INTEGRATE MUSIC

Perform a Song
Organize the class into small groups. Have each group write a song summarizing the main functions of each branch of government. Suggest that students write one stanza per branch and close with a verse about the branches working together. Allow groups to sing their songs to the class.

INTEGRATE ART

Make a Bulletin Board Display Have students make a bulletin board display that conveys their knowledge about the branches of the United States government. For example, students may wish to make an illustrated chart with annotations explaining how the branches work together.

Delegates to the Constitutional Convention set up a system of checks and balances so that no branch of the federal government would have too much power.

becomes a law even if the President objects. The Supreme Court can check the power of Congress by ruling that a law does not follow the Constitution.

The President can check the power of the Supreme Court by nominating its justices, and Congress can check the power of the President by either approving or not approving the President's choices. Congress can check the power of the Supreme Court by suggesting constitutional amendments, by

impeaching and convicting justices of wrongdoing, and removing them from the Court.

The delegates set up these checks to keep a balance of authority among the three branches. This system of **checks and balances** keeps any one branch from becoming too powerful or using its authority wrongly. It helps all three branches work together.

REVIEW **Why was the system of checks and balances outlined in the Constitution?** to keep any one branch from becoming too powerful or using its authority wrongly

LESSON 3 REVIEW

 SUMMARIZE Summarize the powers given to each branch of government.

1 BIG IDEA What are the three branches of the United States government?

2 VOCABULARY Explain how the terms **veto**, **impeach**, and **checks and balances** are related.

3 CIVICS AND GOVERNMENT How can the Supreme Court check the power of Congress?

4 CRITICAL THINKING—Analyze Why is the White House a symbol of the United States?

 PERFORMANCE—Draw a Chart Draw a large triangle on a sheet of paper. On each point of the triangle, write the name of one branch of the federal government. Beside each name, write what that branch does and who or what is the head of it. Add a title to your chart, and then compare your chart with those of classmates.

Chapter 10 ■ 363

EXTEND AND ENRICH

Role Play Organize the class into three groups. Assign each group the role of one of the three branches. Have each group decide which role each member will play in its branch. Ask each group to take turns appearing before the class and demonstrating the role its branch plays in the governing structure.

RETEACH THE LESSON

Make a Chart Have students make a chart demonstrating the three branches of the new government. Suggest that they include a few sentences explaining how the structure provides checks and balances among the branches.

Graphic Organizer Have students compare charts.

Branch	Structure	Function
Executive	President	Carries laws out for the nation
Legislative	Members of the House and the Senate	Makes the laws for the nation
Judicial	Supreme Court Justices	Hears and decides cases of national law

● USE READING AND VOCABULARY TRANSPARENCY 5-4.

5-4 TRANSPARENCY

Assess
Lesson 3 Review—Answers

 SUMMARIZE Legislative: makes laws, can impeach President, approves appointments; Executive: runs government, vetoes bills, appoints justices; Judicial: decides if laws are fair

1 BIG IDEA legislative, judicial, and executive

2 VOCABULARY Possible answer: The system of **checks and balances** keeps any one branch from becoming too powerful. The President can **veto** a bill passed in Congress and Congress can **impeach** the President.

3 CIVICS AND GOVERNMENT The Supreme Court can check the power of Congress by ruling that a law is unconstitutional.

4 CRITICAL THINKING—Analyze Possible answer: The President lives in the White House.

 Performance Assessment Guidelines Students' charts should clearly state what each branch of government does.

ACTIVITY BOOK

Use ACTIVITY BOOK, p. 96, to reinforce and extend student learning.

Skill Lesson
PAGES 364–365

OBJECTIVES

- Organize and interpret information from charts.
- Create thematic charts representing various aspects of the United States.

Vocabulary

flow chart p. 364

WORD CARDS

See pp. V59–V60.

1 Motivate

Why It Matters

Explain to students that it is sometimes easier to understand information when it is presented visually, such as in a flow chart.

2 Teach

What You Need to Know

Guide the class through the flow chart on page 365. Begin by identifying the first step in the lawmaking process. Point out to the class that it is located in the first, or top, box. Ask them to read silently through the remaining steps in the process. Then have volunteers summarize the process in their own words.

· SKILLS ·
CHART AND GRAPH

Read a Flow Chart

VOCABULARY
flow chart

▶ WHY IT MATTERS

Have you ever read something and had a difficult time understanding its meaning? Sometimes information is better understood when it is presented in a different way—as in a flow chart. A **flow chart** is a drawing that shows the order in which things happen. It uses arrows to help you to read the drawings, or steps, in the correct order.

▶ WHAT YOU NEED TO KNOW

The flow chart on page 365 shows how the federal government makes new laws for the United States. The top box on the flow chart shows the first step in the process of a bill becoming a law. In this step a member of the House of Representatives or Senate introduces a 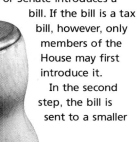 bill. If the bill is a tax bill, however, only members of the House may first introduce it.

In the second step, the bill is sent to a smaller

This early gavel was used in the Senate to open and close meetings.

group called a committee, where it is reviewed. This committee is made up of members of either the House of Representatives or the Senate. The committee members study the bill, and if they decide that the bill would make a good law, they tell the rest of the House and Senate. You can find out what happens next by reading the remaining steps shown on the flow chart.

▶ PRACTICE THE SKILL

Use the flow chart on page 365 to answer these questions.

1. What happens after both the House and the Senate approve the bill?
2. What happens if the President signs a bill?
3. Where does a bill go if the President vetoes it?
4. How can a bill become a law if the President vetoes it?

▶ APPLY WHAT YOU LEARNED

With a partner, make a flow chart that explains to your classmates how something works. Write each step on a strip of paper. When you have finished, glue the steps—in order—on a sheet of posterboard. Then connect the strips with arrows. Give your flow chart a title, and present it to your classmates.

364 ▪ Unit 5

MAKE IT RELEVANT

In Your School Explain to students that flow charts can contain various types of information. Ask students to make their own flow charts about an issue or activity at school. Have students include all relevant details in the proper order. Display flow charts in the classroom.

REACH ALL LEARNERS

Advanced Learners
Explain that a flow chart also can be written and interpreted horizontally, or from left to right. Have each student redraw the flow chart on this page as a horizontal flow chart. Then have students compare their work with a partner and correct any discrepancies.

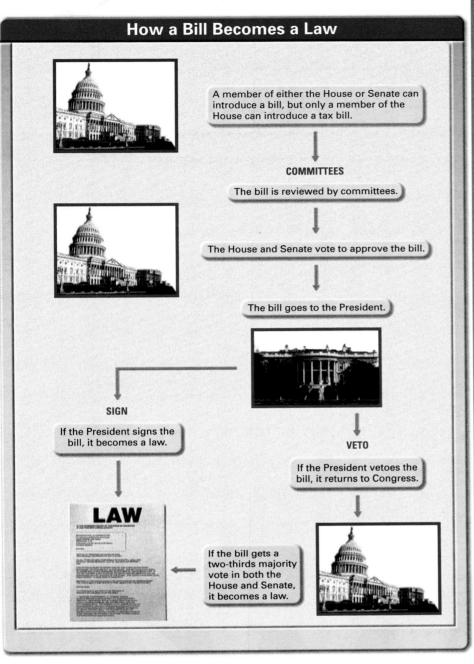

How a Bill Becomes a Law

A member of either the House or Senate can introduce a bill, but only a member of the House can introduce a tax bill.

COMMITTEES

The bill is reviewed by committees.

The House and Senate vote to approve the bill.

The bill goes to the President.

SIGN

If the President signs the bill, it becomes a law.

LAW

VETO

If the President vetoes the bill, it returns to Congress.

If the bill gets a two-thirds majority vote in both the House and Senate, it becomes a law.

CHART AND GRAPH SKILLS

Chapter 10 ■ 365

Practice the Skill—Answers

1. It is sent to the President.
2. The bill becomes law.
3. The bill returns to Congress.
4. It can become law if both the House and the Senate override the veto with a two-thirds majority vote.

3 Close

Apply What You Learned

Students' flow charts should show the correct steps in a process. The title should accurately reflect the contents of the chart.

ACTIVITY BOOK

Use ACTIVITY BOOK, p. 97, to give students additional practice using this skill.

TRANSPARENCY

Use SKILL TRANSPARENCY 5-1.

EXTEND AND ENRICH

Interpret a Flow Chart Ask students to locate flow charts on topics that are interesting to them. Then have students interpret the information or process described in the flow charts.

RETEACH THE SKILL

Write a Paragraph Ask students to convert the information in the flow chart on page 365 into a paragraph. Encourage students to compare their paragraphs with a partner to check for accuracy.

Lesson 4

OBJECTIVES

- Describe the struggle to ratify the Constitution.
- Explain the role the Bill of Rights played in the approval process.
- Explain the individual rights of every American citizen as guaranteed in the Bill of Rights.

 Summarize pp. 345, 366, 370, 371, 372, 380

Vocabulary

SEE READING AND VOCABULARY TRANSPARENCY 5-5 OR THE WORD CARDS ON PP. V59–V60.

ratify p. 366

Federalist p. 368

Anti-Federalist p. 368

amendment p. 370

Magna Carta p. 370

due process of law p. 372

reserved powers p. 372

 When Minutes Count

Have pairs of students work together to find the answers to the subsection review questions.

Quick Summary

This lesson describes the struggles encountered during the ratification of the Constitution.

1 Motivate

Set the Purpose

Big Idea Inform students that the Bill of Rights was added to the Constitution to ease conflicts that arose during the approval process.

Access Prior Knowledge

Review with the class the checks and balances included in the Constitution. Why might people have worried about individual freedoms with such a balance of power?

· LESSON · 4

Approval and the Bill of Rights

 SUMMARIZE
As you read, summarize facts about the Constitution and the Bill of Rights.

BIG IDEA
The Bill of Rights was added to the Constitution to protect the freedoms of people in the United States.

VOCABULARY
ratify
Federalist
Anti-Federalist
amendment
Magna Carta
due process of law
reserved powers

1780	1800	1820	1840	1860

1787–1791

On September 17, 1787, the Constitution was complete. There were 42 delegates still present at the Constitutional Convention, and all but 3 of them—Elbridge Gerry, George Mason, and Edmund Randolph—signed their approval. As delegates were signing the document, Benjamin Franklin spoke of the confidence he felt in the nation's future. During the convention, Franklin had often looked at the chair used by George Washington. Its high back had a carving of a sun on it. Franklin had not been able to decide if the sun shown was supposed to be rising or setting. Afterward, he said, "I have the happiness to know that it is a rising and not a setting sun."

A Struggle to Ratify

Despite Franklin's words, the Constitution that he and the other delegates had approved was not yet the law of the land. According to Article VII, 9 of the 13 states had to **ratify**, or approve, the Constitution before it would go into effect. After the document was signed, the Convention sent it to the Congress of the Confederation. Congress, in turn, sent copies to the states. In each state, voters elected delegates to a state convention.

This sun design is on the chair used by George Washington.

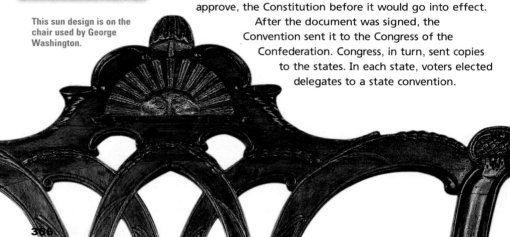

 366

This painting shows George Washington (standing at right) addressing the delegates.

These delegates would vote for or against the Constitution.

At the state conventions, arguments began again. Patrick Henry in Virginia and George Clinton in New York told their conventions that the new national government was too strong. Some delegates did not like the way the Preamble began with "We the people." They thought it should say "We the States."

There was one point, however, on which most delegates agreed. They felt the Constitution also should limit the power of the federal government and protect the basic rights of the people. The state delegates wanted to protect the freedoms they had won in the Revolutionary War. They feared unlimited government would have the power to limit freedoms, as the British government had done.

Many delegates to the state conventions said they would be more willing to approve the Constitution if a bill, or list, of rights were to be added. Supporters of the Constitution promised that after the Constitution was ratified, a bill of rights would be added.

REVIEW **What would adding a bill of rights to the Constitution do?** It would protect the powers of the states and the rights of the people.

The Vote

The first state to call for a vote on the Constitution was Delaware. In December 1787, all the Delaware state delegates voted to ratify the Constitution. Later that month, state delegates in Pennsylvania and New Jersey also voted to approve the Constitution. In January 1788, state delegates in Georgia and Connecticut voted to ratify. Still, eight states had not yet voted. Among those were the states of Virginia and New York. Citizens worried that the new government could not possibly work if some of the nation's largest states voted against it.

From January to June 1788, those who favored the Constitution and those against it both tried to get the backing of people in the states that had not yet voted.

2 Teach

A Struggle to Ratify

Read and Respond

Civics and Government Review the process of conflict resolution. Explain that several state legislatures used these skills in the ratification process. For example, Massachusetts, New Hampshire, and Virginia agreed to ratify the Constitution if they could submit proposed amendments with their votes.

The Vote

Read and Respond

Civics and Government Point out that the Anti-Federalists objected to the new Constitution because they feared that the proposed system of checks and balances would give too much power to the central government. They also were concerned about giving up control of certain activities, such as trade, to the national government. Many of the speeches and letters written by the Anti-Federalists were later organized into a book entitled *The Antifederalists Papers*.

Read and Respond

Civics and Government Tell students that *The Federalist* papers were written with the belief that people tend to need guidance. Explain that the writers of these papers thought that a strong government would help curb this instinct by guiding people to consider the needs of the nation, not just their individual needs. Ask students how *The Federalist* might have been different had the writers believed that people act selflessly. The papers might have been focused less on persuading people and more on applauding their actions.

POINTS OF VIEW
For or Against the Bill of Rights

Encourage students to analyze the two viewpoints to identify the differences in opinion.

Analyze the Viewpoints— Answers

❶ Thomas Jefferson supported the addition of a bill of rights; James Madison opposed it.

❷ because Jefferson believed that not having a bill of rights would make the national government too strong and Madison believed that a bill of rights would weaken the national government

❸ Ask volunteers to share occasions when their views changed on a subject. Ask them why their views changed.

Read and Respond

Civics and Government Explain that although the necessary nine states had ratified the Constitution by June 1788, neither New York nor Virginia had yet approved it. Inform students that some people believed that without the approval of New York and Virginia, the new Constitution could not succeed. Explain that both New York and Virginia soon narrowly approved the Constitution, and both North Carolina and Rhode Island eventually followed suit.

Those citizens who favored the constitution came to be called **Federalists**. Federalists wanted a strong national, or federal, government. Those who did not became known as **Anti-Federalists**. Because the Constitution did not yet contain a bill of rights, the Anti-Federalists feared the document made the national government too strong.

Throughout America the two sides used the newspapers to tell what they thought and why. In New York, Alexander Hamilton, James Madison, and John Jay wrote essays defending the Constitution. These essays were later published as a book called *The Federalist*.

Citizens who could read followed the argument in the newspapers. Others heard the arguments at community meetings and even at church services. Some people saw the Constitution as the work of "lawyers, and men of learning, and moneyed men that talk so finely . . . to make us poor, illiterate people swallow down the pill." Others thought that having a new government was a good idea. They also trusted the promise of a bill of rights.

No one was certain how all the arguing would affect the vote in the state conventions. In Massachusetts, however, the promise of changes to the Constitution

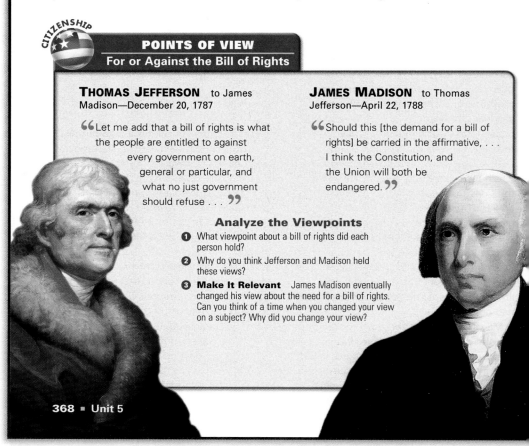

CITIZENSHIP
POINTS OF VIEW
For or Against the Bill of Rights

THOMAS JEFFERSON to James Madison—December 20, 1787

❝Let me add that a bill of rights is what the people are entitled to against every government on earth, general or particular, and what no just government should refuse . . .❞

JAMES MADISON to Thomas Jefferson—April 22, 1788

❝Should this [the demand for a bill of rights] be carried in the affirmative, . . . I think the Constitution, and the Union will both be endangered.❞

Analyze the Viewpoints

❶ What viewpoint about a bill of rights did each person hold?

❷ Why do you think Jefferson and Madison held these views?

❸ **Make It Relevant** James Madison eventually changed his view about the need for a bill of rights. Can you think of a time when you changed your view on a subject? Why did you change your view?

368 ▪ Unit 5

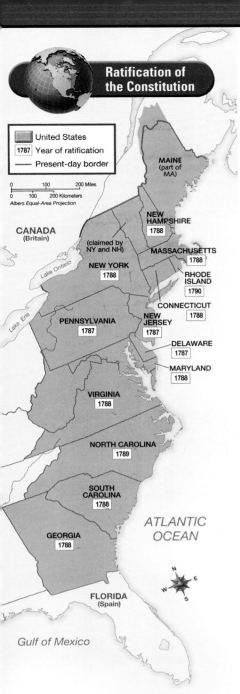

Ratification of the Constitution

	United States
1787	Year of ratification
—	Present-day border

0   100   200 Miles
0   100   200 Kilometers
Albers Equal-Area Projection

CANADA
(Britain)

MAINE
(part of MA)

NEW HAMPSHIRE
1788

(claimed by NY and NH)

MASSACHUSETTS
1788

NEW YORK
1788

RHODE ISLAND
1790

CONNECTICUT
1788

PENNSYLVANIA
1787

NEW JERSEY
1787

DELAWARE
1787

MARYLAND
1788

VIRGINIA
1788

NORTH CAROLINA
1789

SOUTH CAROLINA
1788

GEORGIA
1788

ATLANTIC OCEAN

Lake Ontario

Lake Erie

FLORIDA
(Spain)

Gulf of Mexico

helped change the minds of some very important people. Samuel Adams and John Hancock went to the state convention as Anti-Federalists. They returned home as Federalists. As a result, Massachusetts decided to ratify the Constitution in February 1788.

Maryland and South Carolina followed Massachusetts's example that spring. Then, on June 21, 1788, New Hampshire became the ninth state to ratify the Constitution. That was the number of states needed to put it into effect. Four days later Virginia ratified it, and New York followed in July. By the spring of 1789 the new government was at work.

Place The map and table show when the Constitution was ratified by each of the 13 states. The table also lists the number of votes for and against the Constitution.

❖ In which state was the vote closest to being a tie?

Constitution Ratification Vote

STATE	DATE	VOTES FOR	VOTES AGAINST
Delaware	Dec. 7, 1787	30	0
Pennsylvania	Dec. 12, 1787	46	23
New Jersey	Dec. 18, 1787	38	0
Georgia	Jan. 2, 1788	26	0
Connecticut	Jan. 9, 1788	128	40
Massachusetts	Feb. 6, 1788	187	168
Maryland	April 28, 1788	63	11
South Carolina	May 23, 1788	149	73
New Hampshire	June, 21, 1788	57	47
Virginia	June 25, 1788	89	79
New York	July 26, 1788	30	27
North Carolina	Nov. 21, 1789	194	77
Rhode Island	May 29, 1790	34	32

Source: Encyclopedia of American History

Chapter 10 ▪ 369

Read and Respond

Civics and Government Explain that leaders in Rhode Island at first refused to ratify the Constitution because it lacked a bill of rights. Explain that Congress passed the Bill of Rights in September 1789 and that Rhode Island ratified the Constitution the following spring, with the narrowest margin of any state—34 in favor, 32 against.

Visual Learning

Map Encourage students to study the map on page 369. Ask students to note the date when each state ratified the Constitution.

CAPTION ANSWER: Rhode Island

The Bill of Rights

Read and Respond

History Explain that a number of states followed Virginia's lead and incorporated some form of bill of rights in their state constitutions. Explain that by 1781—ten years before the Bill of Rights was added to the Constitution—the eight bills of rights adopted by various states contained a total of 90 different provisions. Some rights were state-specific, but most shared provisions such as freedom of speech and freedom of the press.

Q Why do you think the framers of the Constitution did not initially include a bill of rights?

A Most states already had one.

Civics and Government The Constitution has been in effect for more than 200 years. In that time, there have been only twenty-seven amendments to it—the first ten being the Bill of Rights. Ask students why they think the Constitution has undergone so few changes over time.

Answers may vary, but should reflect that the Constitution included a broad range of rights.

Read and Respond

History Explain that as originally written, the Bill of Rights included twelve amendments. Inform students that most states did not ratify the first two amendments, which concerned congressional seats and pay raises. Explain that these amendments were omitted and the original third article of the Bill of Rights became the First Amendment.

 Students might be interested in learning more about the Bill of Rights. Have them visit the Learning Site at **www.harcourtschool.com.**

Later that year North Carolina approved the Constitution. Rhode Island finally gave its approval in 1790.

REVIEW Why did the Federalists favor the Constitution and want a strong national government? **SUMMARIZE**
the Federalists wanted a new government in which all the nation's states worked together

The Bill of Rights

As promised, not long after the states had ratified the Constitution, ten **amendments**, or changes, were added to protect the rights of the people. These ten amendments, called the Bill of Rights, became part of the Constitution in 1791.

The Bill of Rights was influenced by the Magna Carta and the English Bill of Rights of 1689. The **Magna Carta** was a charter granted by the king of England in the year 1215. It listed the rights of the upper class and limited the power of the king. The English Bill of Rights listed the rights of English citizens.

The Virginia Declaration of Rights also had a major influence on the United States Bill of Rights. Written by George Mason, the Virginia Declaration of Rights had been adopted by Virginia's state constitutional convention in June 1776. It said that "all men are by nature equally free and independent and have certain inherent rights." These rights were "the enjoyment of life and liberty, with the means of acquiring and possessing property." The Declaration also protected some rights by name, including freedom of the press, freedom of religion, and trial by jury.

The First Amendment to the Constitution gives people the freedom to follow any religion they choose.

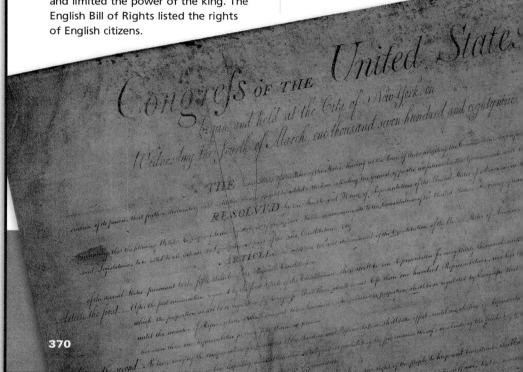
370

It also says the government cannot promote or financially support any religion.

Many people believe that the Virginia Statute for Religious Freedom influenced the First Amendment. This statute, written by Thomas Jefferson, supported complete religious freedom. It became law in Virginia in 1786, due in large part to the leadership and support of James Madison.

The First Amendment also protects freedom of speech and freedom of the press. It further says that people can hold meetings to discuss problems and they can petition, or ask, the government to correct the wrongs.

The Second Amendment protects people's right to carry arms or weapons. It says, "A well-regulated militia being necessary to the security of a free State, the right of the people to keep and bear arms shall not be infringed [taken away]."

The Third Amendment says that government cannot force citizens to quarter soldiers in peacetime. Before the Revolutionary War, many colonists had to house and feed British soldiers.

The Bill of Rights (left) lists the basic rights of the people. During the late 1700s, the printing press (below left) was the main tool for spreading news and opinions. The Seventh Amendment gives people accused of crimes the right to a trial by jury (right). The First Amendment allows people to publicly debate ideas (bottom).

Chapter 10 ■ 371

History Remind students that the United States was founded on religious freedom. Ask students why the First Amendment says that the government cannot promote or financially support any religion. Government support of any one religion would show unfair favor towards that religion.

Read and Respond

Civics and Government Remind students that the Fifth through Eighth Amendments concerned due process of law. Ask students to consider why these rights are so important to all citizens.

Q Why is it important that the right to an attorney is written into the Bill of Rights?

A Not every citizen can afford an attorney; therefore, if the right to an attorney was not guaranteed in the Bill of Rights, only those who could afford it would have legal counsel.

Civics and Government Ask students to describe each right listed in the Bill of Rights. Then have volunteers share their descriptions with the class.

3 Close

Summarize Key Content

- Many people believed that the Constitution should protect the powers of the states and the basic rights of the people.
- The Federalists supported the Constitution and the idea of a strong national government. The Anti-Federalists feared the loss of state and local power to a national government.
- The Bill of Rights was written to protect the rights of the people.

READING SKILL

Summarize Discuss with the class the amendments in the Bill of Rights. Then have students select the three that they think are most important. Ask students to summarize these using words or pictures.

EXTEND AND ENRICH

Research Ask students to find out more about the Constitutional Convention. Encourage them to use primary and secondary sources to gather information about the convention. Students should give a brief oral report about their findings.

READING SOCIAL STUDIES

Personal Response Discuss students' responses as a class. Responses will vary, but students should provide the reasoning for their answers.

● USE READING AND VOCABULARY TRANSPARENCY 5-5.

5-5 TRANSPARENCY

Assess

Lesson 4 Review—Answers

 SUMMARIZE Although five states quickly ratified the Constitution, the remaining eight needed assurances that a bill of rights would be added before they too would approve it.

❶ **BIG IDEA** Delegates to the state conventions were more willing to approve the Constitution if a bill of rights were added.

❷ **VOCABULARY** Possible answer: Those who favored the Constitution were called **Federalists**. Those who opposed the Constitution were known as the **Anti-Federalists**.

❸ **TIME LINE** 1791

❹ **CIVICS AND GOVERNMENT** Answers should include freedom of religion, freedom of speech, freedom of the press, the right to assemble, and the right to petition the government

❺ **CRITICAL THINKING—Evaluate** Students' responses should indicate that people feared the government might take away certain individual rights and liberties if they were not included in the Constitution.

Performance Assessment Guidelines Students' letters should state the contents of and reasoning for the new amendment. Letters should be correctly addressed to their state representative.

ACTIVITY BOOK

Use ACTIVITY BOOK, p. 98, to reinforce and extend student learning.

The bald eagle became a symbol of the United States in 1782.

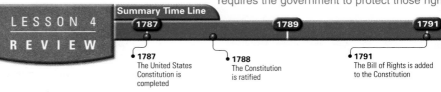

Under the Fourth Amendment, the government cannot search a person's home or take his or her property without that person's permission or the approval of a judge.

The Fifth through Eighth Amendments deal with **due process of law**. This means that people have the right to a fair public trial to be decided by a jury. They do not have to testify against themselves in court. They have the right to have a lawyer defend them. If they are found innocent of a crime they cannot be put on trial a second time for that same crime. They also cannot be sentenced to any cruel and unusual punishments.

The Ninth Amendment says that people have many other rights not specifically listed in the Constitution. These include the "unalienable rights" of "Life, Liberty and the pursuit of Happiness" described in the Declaration of Independence.

As a final protection for citizens, the Tenth Amendment says that the national government can do only what is listed in the Constitution. This means that all other authority, called the **reserved powers**, belongs to the states or to the people.

REVIEW Why is the Bill of Rights an important part of the Constitution? It protects the rights of every citizen of the United States, gives the government no power to limit those rights, and requires the government to protect those rights.

LESSON 4 REVIEW

Summary Time Line

1787 — 1789 — 1791

● 1787 The United States Constitution is completed
● 1788 The Constitution is ratified
● 1791 The Bill of Rights is added to the Constitution

 SUMMARIZE What events led to the Constitution being ratified?

❶ **BIG IDEA** Why was the Bill of Rights important in getting the Constitution approved?

❷ **VOCABULARY** What was the difference between a **Federalist** and an **Anti-Federalist**?

❸ **TIME LINE** When was the Bill of Rights added to the Constitution?

❹ **CIVICS AND GOVERNMENT** What rights does the Bill of Rights guarantee?

❺ **CRITICAL THINKING— Evaluate** Why do you think some delegates felt nervous about signing the Constitution without a bill of rights?

 PERFORMANCE—Write a Letter With your classmates or by yourself, think of an amendment you would like to see added to the Constitution. Write a letter to one of your state representatives explaining your idea and telling why you think it would benefit citizens.

372 ■ Unit 5

RETEACH THE LESSON

Make a Visual Summary
Organize the class into three groups. Assign each group one of the three subsections in this lesson. Then have each group make a series of drawings that depict the main ideas covered in their subsection. Ask each group to describe to the class the contents of its summary.

·SKILLS· CITIZENSHIP

Act as a Responsible Citizen

➡ WHY IT MATTERS

Responsible citizens know what is happening in their country, choose wise leaders, and take part in government. Citizens and leaders must also think about public service.

➡ WHAT YOU NEED TO KNOW

Before the Constitution could be ratified, citizens elected delegates to vote for or against the Constitution. Many of these delegates did not feel they could vote for a plan of government that did not protect the rights of the states and citizens. Here are some steps delegates may have used to act as responsible citizens:

Step 1 They learned about the problem—some of the rights of the states and of individuals might not be protected.

Step 2 They thought about ways to solve the problem that would be good for the whole country.

Step 3 They worked together to bring about change.

➡ PRACTICE THE SKILL

Imagine that you are a delegate to your state convention. Will you vote for the Constitution? Explain your decision and the steps you followed to act as a responsible citizen.

➡ APPLY WHAT YOU LEARNED

Some acts of citizenship, such as voting, can be done only by adults. Others can be done by citizens of almost any age. Use the steps above to decide on ways you might act as a responsible citizen of your school.

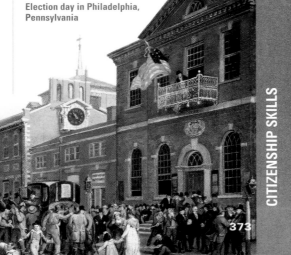

Election day in Philadelphia, Pennsylvania

CITIZENSHIP SKILLS

373

Lesson 5

PAGES 374–379

OBJECTIVES

- Describe President Washington's decisions for the executive branch.
- Identify individual members of the first presidential cabinet and their contributions.
- Discuss the formation of the nation's first political parties.
- Explain the significance of John Adams's election.

 Summarize pp. 345, 374, 378, 379, 380

Vocabulary

SEE READING AND VOCABULARY TRANSPARENCY 5-6 OR THE WORD CARDS ON PP. V59–V62.

Cabinet p. 375   **candidate** p. 378
political party
p. 377

 When Minutes Count

Have pairs of students read the lesson together. Then ask them to write a summary sentence for the lesson.

Quick Summary

This lesson describes how the nation's early leaders worked together to strengthen the United States.

1 Motivate

Set the Purpose

Big Idea Explain that leaders of the United States worked together to overcome their differences.

Access Prior Knowledge

Have students discuss what they know about the struggles between the Federalists and Anti-Federalists over the Constitution. How were these differences resolved?

5

 SUMMARIZE
As you read, summarize facts about new leaders and the new government.

BIG IDEA
The nation's new leaders worked together despite their growing differences.

VOCABULARY
Cabinet
political party
candidate

The New Government Begins

1780–1800

The first elections under the new Constitution began in 1788. Voters elected members of the United States House of Representatives. Each state legislature chose two senators for the United States Senate. They also chose people who would serve in the electoral college and elect the first president.

The New Leaders

In 1789 George Washington was elected as the nation's first President. John Adams became the first Vice President. His job was to help President Washington carry out his duties. When

Americans painted pictures and sewed samplers to pay tribute to their new President.

374 ▪ Unit 5

WORD WORK

Preview Vocabulary Have students make a three-column chart for the vocabulary words in this lesson. Students should write the vocabulary words in the first column and their definitions in the second column. In the third column, students should write clues to help them remember the meanings of the words.

INTEGRATE READING

 Read a Biography
Inform students that the lives of important historical figures, such as George Washington, usually are well-documented in biographies. Have students find and read a biography of George Washington and prepare reports about it for the class.

Washington was elected, Congress planned to meet in New York City. On April 30, 1789, George Washington stood on the balcony of Federal Hall in New York City. There he recited the President's oath of office, "I do solemnly swear (or affirm) that I will faithfully execute the office of President of the United States, and will, to the best of my ability, preserve, protect, and defend the Constitution of the United States."

One of Congress's first actions was to pass the Judiciary Act. This act set up the federal judicial branch and decided the number of Supreme Court justices. President Washington named John Jay of New York as the first chief justice.

President Washington also chose advisers to help him carry out the main responsibilities of the executive branch. These people would serve as the secretaries, or heads, of executive departments that included the State Department, the Treasury Department, and the War Department.

The President asked Thomas Jefferson to serve as the nation's first secretary of state. Jefferson helped the President deal with other countries such as Spain, France, and Britain. Washington also asked Alexander Hamilton to serve as secretary of the treasury. Hamilton worked to set up a new banking system and to pass new tax laws.

Henry Knox, who had been a general in the Revolutionary War, served as secretary of war. Knox began building a national army of 1,000 soldiers to defend the nation. Another important adviser was Edmund Randolph. He became the new President's legal adviser, now called the attorney general. He

The First President

Analyze Primary Sources

This print from 1789 celebrates George Washington and the new nation. Thirteen of the circles around Washington show the 13 state coats of arms. The top circle is the nation's Great Seal.

❶ The Great Seal of the United States.

❷ State coats of arms.

❸ President George Washington.

◈ Why do you think the artist placed the 13 state coats of arms in a circle around President Washington?

A DISPLAY of the UNITED STATES of AMERICA

explained the laws and the powers of the Constitution.

Together, Jefferson, Hamilton, Knox, and Randolph became known as the **Cabinet**, a group of the President's most important advisers. Every President since Washington has relied on such a group. Over time, however, the number of Cabinet members has grown.

REVIEW Who were the members of Washington's Cabinet? Thomas Jefferson, Alexander Hamilton, Henry Knox, and Edmund Randolph

Chapter 10 ▪ 375

Study Questions Have students answer these questions as they read the lesson.

1. What was the purpose of the Cabinet?

2. On what subject did Jefferson and Hamilton disagree?

3. Why did George Washington serve only two terms?

⬤ USE READING AND VOCABULARY TRANSPARENCY 5-6.

5-6 TRANSPARENCY

2 Teach

The New Leaders

Read and Respond

Civics and Government Inform students that George Washington was careful not to overstep the bounds of the executive branch. As a result, he was respectful of the legislative and judicial branches and their places in United States government.

Q Why do you think President Washington was careful not to overstep the bounds of the executive branch?

A Students may say that President Washington feared such acts could lead the country toward a system of monarchy, such as they had experienced under British rule.

Analyze Primary Source

Artifact When Washington became President, there was a national celebration. Prints such as this used state symbols and artwork to convey unity.

CAPTION ANSWER: Possible answer: The placement of the 13 state coats of arms indicated unity.

Political Parties

Read and Respond

History Inform students that arguments between Hamilton's and Jefferson's supporters in Congress led to the formation of the first political parties in the nation. Lead students to understand that Hamilton envisioned the government encouraging manufacturing. Jefferson thought the government should encourage agriculture.

Civics and Government Have students explain the meaning of *political party* and identify the viewpoints of the first two political parties.

Q **Why do people in politics organize into political parties?**

A to have the ideas they believe in carried out by the government; to join together in supporting or opposing certain laws

• BIOGRAPHY •

Benjamin Banneker

Inventiveness Have students describe ways in which Benjamin Banneker displayed the character trait of inventiveness. Ask them to name people today who exhibit that trait.

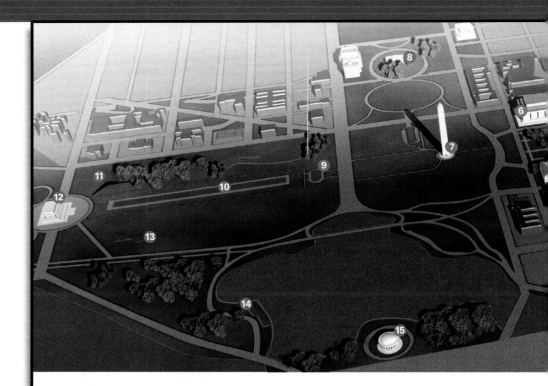

• BIOGRAPHY •

Benjamin Banneker
1731–1806
Character Trait: Inventiveness

Our nation's capital was built by the work of people such as Benjamin Banneker. In 1791 and 1792, he worked with Andrew Ellicott, the chief surveyor, to plan Washington, D.C. Banneker later became famous as the author of his own almanac, and he sent a copy to Thomas Jefferson. Banneker included a letter that asked Jefferson to help work for the rights of African Americans.

Banneker was also successful in other ways. He taught himself astronomy and mathematics. At a time when many African Americans were still enslaved, Banneker became a famous scientist.

MULTIMEDIA BIOGRAPHIES
Visit The Learning Site at **www.harcourtschool.com**
to learn about other famous people.

GO ONLINE

MAKE IT RELEVANT

In Your State Lead a discussion with students about the issues that led to the formation of early political parties. Have students find present-day newspaper and magazine articles about similar issues occurring today.

INTEGRATE LANGUAGE ARTS

Write a Character Sketch Organize the class into pairs and have each pair write a character sketch of both a Federalist and a Democratic-Republican. Suggest that students begin by listing qualities of both party members. Encourage students to include a sketch for use as a visual aid.

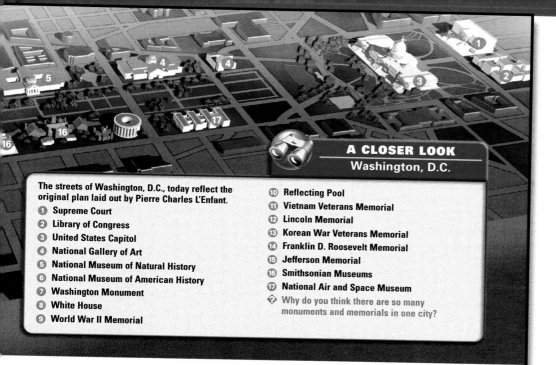

The streets of Washington, D.C., today reflect the original plan laid out by Pierre Charles L'Enfant.

1. Supreme Court
2. Library of Congress
3. United States Capitol
4. National Gallery of Art
5. National Museum of Natural History
6. National Museum of American History
7. Washington Monument
8. White House
9. World War II Memorial
10. Reflecting Pool
11. Vietnam Veterans Memorial
12. Lincoln Memorial
13. Korean War Veterans Memorial
14. Franklin D. Roosevelt Memorial
15. Jefferson Memorial
16. Smithsonian Museums
17. National Air and Space Museum

◇ Why do you think there are so many monuments and memorials in one city?

Political Parties

Before long, two of Washington's top advisers, Alexander Hamilton and Thomas Jefferson, began to argue about what was best for the United States. Hamilton wanted to have a strong national government. He favored setting up a national bank to be run by the central government. This bank would be responsible for issuing national money. Hamilton also wanted the United States to become friendly with Britain and to make use of Britain's large trading network.

Jefferson did not agree with these ideas. He thought that there should be as little central government as possible. He also believed that the United States should become friendly with France instead of with Britain. Jefferson argued that France had been an ally of the United States during the Revolutionary War.

From their disagreements, the nation's first political parties were formed. A **political party** is a group whose members try to elect government officials who share the party's point of view about many issues.

Hamilton's followers formed what became known as the Federalist party. It included people who had supported the Constitution during the state ratifying conventions. Like Hamilton, they were in favor of a strong national government. John Adams and Henry Knox became members of the Federalist party.

Chapter 10 ■ 377

Read and Respond

Civics and Government Explain that the two main political parties today are the Democrats and the Republicans. In time the donkey became a symbol of the Democratic Party and the elephant became a symbol for the Republican Party. Ask students to research these political symbols and explain why they were selected.

Civics and Government Ask students how people today participate in political parties. Student's responses should include that people join political parties and they vote for candidates in their party.

Ask students to examine the illustration of Washington, D.C., and answer the question in the caption. CAPTION ANSWER: Because Washington, D.C., is the nation's capital, it is an ideal place to build monuments and memorials to past leaders.

Ask students why they think most of the government buildings are in one section of the city. Probably to make it easier for the President and other members of the government to interact with each other.

INTEGRATE ART

Plan an Ad Campaign
Organize the class into groups. Have each group design an advertising campaign supporting either Federalist or Anti-Federalist ideas. Suggest that students include such elements as slogans, jingles, and propaganda devices.

INTEGRATE SCIENCE

Research Banneker's Inventions Ask students to research Benjamin Banneker's various innovations and select one to learn more about. Suggest that students make a visual display that illustrates their findings.

A Change in Leadership

Read and Respond

Civics and Government Remind students that the day John Adams took the oath of office marked one of the first times that a nation had changed leaders by peaceful election. Explain that this peaceful change has continued to the present day, even in times of severe crisis such as war and economic depression.

Q **How do you think voter participation in an election helps bring about a peaceful change of leaders?**

A The voting process allows voters to become involved in the selection of leaders. Voters understand that the candidate with the majority of votes will win the election.

History Remind students that in 1796 the presidential candidate with the most votes became President and the candidate with the second-most votes became Vice President. Explain that today, however, presidential and vice-presidential candidates run for office together as part of the same party.

3 Close

Summarize Key Content

- George Washington became the first President of the United States and selected a Cabinet of officials to assist him in governing the country.
- The Federalist Party and the Democratic-Republican Party resulted from disagreements among key leaders such as Alexander Hamilton and Thomas Jefferson.
- In 1796 John Adams succeeded George Washington as President of the United States.

Jefferson's supporters, such as James Madison and Patrick Henry formed the Democratic-Republican party. They believed that the powers of the national government should be limited to those listed in the Constitution. Members of the Democratic-Republican party were sometimes called the Jeffersonian Republicans. This political party, however, was not the same as today's Republican party.

In Congress, Jeffersonian Republicans and Federalists often had to compromise so that the laws could be passed. In one compromise, they agreed to build a national capital for the new government. George Washington chose the location for the capital city that came to carry his name. Both Maryland and Virginia agreed to give up some land to create the District of Columbia (D.C.).

REVIEW How can you summarize the disagreements between Alexander Hamilton and Thomas Jefferson? SUMMARIZE

A Change in Leadership

George Washington served as President for two terms, each of which was four years long. Many people wanted him to run for a third term, but Washington said that two terms were enough. His decision set an example for future presidents.

By 1796, however, the growth of political parties had changed the way the electoral college chose the President. Instead of making its own list of

Hamilton wanted a strong national government; Jefferson thought there should be as little central government as possible.

George Cooke painted this picture of the nation's capital in 1833. At that time, Washington, D.C., was a much smaller city than it is today.

REACH ALL LEARNERS

Advanced Learners
Organize these learners into groups and have each group research the growth of political parties in presidential elections from 1796 to the present. Have students make an annotated time line for use in presenting their findings.

BACKGROUND

Washington's Farewell Address When George Washington left office, he wrote a farewell address to the nation. In it, he suggested that the party system could lead to a dangerous split between the North and the South. He also warned leaders not to make any permanent alliances with other countries. He felt, instead, the nation should maintain its policy of neutrality and focus on domestic affairs in its early years.

candidates, or people to choose from, the electoral college was given a list by each political party. In the election of 1796, the Federalist party backed John Adams. The Jeffersonian Republican party backed Thomas Jefferson instead. When the votes were counted, Adams won by three votes. Jefferson became Vice President.

On March 4, 1797, John Adams became the second President of the United States. He took the oath of office at Congress Hall, in Philadelphia. This was an important day in history. It was the first time that the nation had changed leaders by means of a peaceful election.

When John Adams started his term as President, Congress met in Philadelphia. Three years later, in November 1800, the federal government moved to the District of Columbia. When John Adams and his family moved to the new capital city, they lived in a special house built for the President. At first it had many names, including the President's House and the

John Adams was the first President to live in what is now the White House. Abigail Adams, his wife, wrote that the house was "built for ages to come."

Executive Mansion. By the early 1900s, however, this building was known as the White House—the name by which it is known today.

REVIEW Why did John Adams's taking the oath of office mark an important day? It was the first time that the United States had changed leaders by means of a peaceful election.

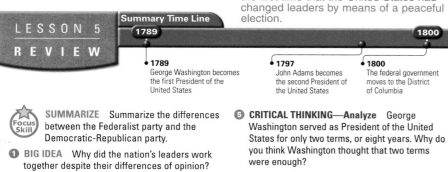

LESSON 5 REVIEW

Summary Time Line
1789 — 1800

- **1789** George Washington becomes the first President of the United States
- **1797** John Adams becomes the second President of the United States
- **1800** The federal government moves to the District of Columbia

SUMMARIZE Summarize the differences between the Federalist party and the Democratic-Republican party.

1 BIG IDEA Why did the nation's leaders work together despite their differences of opinion?

2 VOCABULARY Use the words **political party** and **candidate** in a sentence.

3 TIME LINE Who became President in 1797, John Adams or George Washington?

4 HISTORY What party did Thomas Jefferson support?

5 CRITICAL THINKING—Analyze George Washington served as President of the United States for only two terms, or eight years. Why do you think Washington thought that two terms were enough?

PERFORMANCE—Make a Chart Make a chart that shows what the Federalist party and the Democratic-Republican party believed in. Then explain the differences between the two parties to a classmate.

Chapter 10 ■ 379

EXTEND AND ENRICH

Write an Oral History Have students work in small groups to create oral histories about what they have learned in this subsection. Encourage students to write and memorize a part of the history from this time period. Ask groups to recite their oral histories to the class.

RETEACH THE LESSON

Write an Encyclopedia Entry Have students work in pairs to write a short summary of each subsection that could be used as an encyclopedia entry. Ask volunteers to read their entries to the class.

Assess

Lesson 5 Review—Answers

SUMMARIZE Federalists: a strong national government, an alliance with Britain, and a national bank; Democratic-Republicans: a government of limited powers, no national bank, and an alliance with France

1 BIG IDEA They felt they were best serving the interests of the country.

2 VOCABULARY Possible answers: Alexander Hamilton backed the **candidate** from the Federalist **political party**.

3 TIME LINE John Adams

4 HISTORY Democratic-Republican Party

5 CRITICAL THINKING—Analyze Students may respond that Washington may have felt that leaving after two terms would help maintain the democratic process.

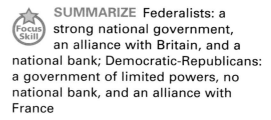

Performance Assessment Guidelines Charts should reflect students' understanding of the text.

ACTIVITY BOOK

Use ACTIVITY BOOK, p. 100, to reinforce and extend student learning.

Chapter 10 Review

 SUMMARIZE

Students may use the graphic organizer that appears on page 101 of the Activity Book. Answers appear in the Activity Book, Teacher's Edition.

Think & Write

Write a Conversation Students' conversations should include accurate references to the Virginia Plan, the New Jersey Plan, and the Great Compromise as mentioned in Lesson 2 of this chapter. Students should describe the issues involved in each of the plans as well as the result of the discussion that took place at the Constitutional Convention.

Write an Explanation Students' explanations should display an understanding of their selected right. Students also should provide logical reasons with adequate support for the choice of their particular right.

ACTIVITY BOOK

A copy of the graphic organizer appears in the ACTIVITY BOOK on page 101.

TRANSPARENCY

This graphic organizer appears on READING AND VOCABULARY TRANSPARENCY 5-7.

· CHAPTER ·

10 Review and Test Preparation

Summary Time Line
1780

1781
The Articles of Confederation are approved

1787
The Constitu Conven

 Summarize

Copy the following graphic organizer onto a separate sheet of paper. Use the information you have learned to summarize the facts about the writing and ratification of the United States Constitution.

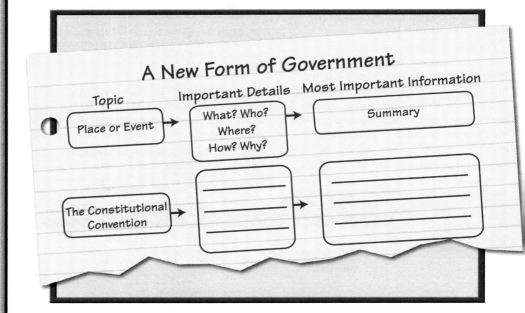

A New Form of Government

Topic	Important Details	Most Important Information
Place or Event	What? Who? Where? How? Why?	Summary
The Constitutional Convention		

THINK & WRITE

Write a Conversation Write a conversation that could have taken place between James Madison, William Paterson, and Roger Sherman during the Constitutional Convention. The three leaders should discuss the issue of representation.

Write an Explanation The Bill of Rights protects the individual freedoms of all Americans. Many people place a special value on certain rights. Choose one right from the Bill of Rights and explain why it is important to you.

380 ■ **Chapter 10**

TEST PREPARATION

Review these tips with students:

■ Read the directions before reading the questions.

■ Read each question twice, focusing the second time on all the possible answers.

■ Take the time to think about all the possible answers before deciding on an answer.

■ Move past questions that give you trouble, and answer the ones you know. Then return to the difficult items.

UNIT PROJECT

Progress Check Encourage students to make a chart to use as they study the material in this unit. Suggest that students list, on the left side of the chart, events related to the economic and territorial growth of the United States during the 1800s. Then students can use the right side of the chart to write a brief summary of each event.

Time Line

1790   1795   1800

1788
The United
States
Constitution
is ratified

1789
George Washington
is elected the first
President of the
United States

1791
The Bill of
Rights is
added to the
Constitution

1797
John Adams is
elected the
second President
of the United States

USE THE TIME LINE

Use the chapter summary time line to answer these questions.

1 When did the Constitutional Convention take place?

2 Was George Washington elected President before or after the Bill of Rights was added to the Constitution?

USE VOCABULARY

For each pair of terms, write a sentence that explains how the terms are related.

3 **veto** (p. 361), **checks and balances** (p. 363)

4 **amendment** (p. 370), **reserved powers** (p. 372)

5 **political party** (p. 377), **candidate** (p. 379)

RECALL FACTS

Answer these questions.

6 How did Roger Sherman contribute to the creation of the Constitution?

7 What is the purpose of the Constitution according to its preamble?

Write the letter of the best choice.

8 The main function of the legislative branch of the federal government is—
   A to carry out laws.
   B to decide whether or not laws follow the Constitution.
   C to make laws.
   D to select members of the Cabinet.

9 George Washington set an example for future American Presidents by—
   F greatly increasing taxes.
   G taking the President's oath of office in Philadelphia.
   H serving only two terms.
   J allowing Congress to select his Cabinet.

THINK CRITICALLY

10 What do you think was James Madison's greatest contribution to the creation of the Constitution?

11 How might representation have been different if African Americans had been counted the same way white citizens were counted?

APPLY SKILLS

Read a Flow Chart
Study the flow chart on page 365. Then answer the following questions.

12 What happens after a bill is introduced?

13 What happens if the President vetoes a bill?

14 What happens if the President signs the bill?

Act as a Responsible Citizen

15 Identify a person who you think is a responsible citizen. Write a paragraph explaining why you think that person is acting responsibly.

Chapter 10 ■ **381**

Think Critically

10 Responses may vary. Students may cite Madison's organization and leadership of the first convention or the Virginia Plan, which provided the basic framework for the Constitution.

11 The South would have had far greater populations and therefore more representatives in the House.

Apply Skills

Read a Flow Chart

12 The bill is reviewed by committees.

13 The bill returns to Congress.

14 The bill becomes a law.

Act as a Responsible Citizen

15 Students should explain clearly their reason for selecting the person they chose and provide adequate support for their reasoning.

ACTIVITY BOOK

Use the CHAPTER 10 TEST PREPARATION on page 102 of the Activity Book.

ASSESSMENT

Use the CHAPTER 10 TEST on pages 77–80 of the Assessment Program.

Use the Time Line

1 in 1787

2 before

Use Vocabulary

Possible responses:

3 Through a system of **checks and balances** a presidential **veto** of a congressional bill keeps Congress from becoming too powerful.

4 The Tenth **Amendment** states that all other powers not described in the Constitution are **reserved powers** that belong to the states and to the people.

5 Each **political party** nominates a **candidate** for President.

Recall Facts

6 He came up with the Great Compromise, which proposed a two-house Congress. (p. 356)

7 to create a better plan of government (pp. 358–359)

8 C (p. 359)

9 H (p. 378)

Chapter 11 Planning Guide The Nation Grows

Introducing the Chapter, pp. 382–383

LESSON	PACING	OBJECTIVES	VOCABULARY
Introduce the Chapter pp. 382–383	1 Day	■ Use visual clues to describe patterns of land use in the United States. ■ Use critical thinking skills to understand and interpret primary sources.	**Word Work:** Preview Vocabulary, p. 383
1 The Louisiana Purchase pp. 384–388	1 Day	■ Analyze how the United States expanded beyond the Mississippi River. ■ Identify lands included in the Louisiana Purchase. ■ Describe contributions made by explorers Meriwether Lewis, William Clark, and Zebulon Pike.	**inauguration** **pathfinder** **trespass**
2 The War of 1812 pp. 389–394	2 Days	■ Explain the reasons many Americans wanted to go to war with Britain a second time. ■ Describe the major battles of the War of 1812. ■ Analyze how nationalism swept over the United States after the War of 1812. ■ Explain the purpose of the Monroe Doctrine.	**impressment** **war hawk** **national anthem** **siege** **nationalism** **annex** **doctrine**
3 The Age of Jackson pp. 395–399	1 Day	■ Analyze the growth of democracy in the United States in the 1800s. ■ Describe major events in Andrew Jackson's presidency. ■ Explain the Indian Removal Act. ■ Analyze how the growth of the United States affected Native Americans.	**democracy** **ruling** **Word Work:** Word Origins, p. 395
EXAMINE PRIMARY SOURCES **Audubon's Paintings** pp. 400–401	1 Day	■ Identify paintings made by John James Audubon. ■ Explain the importance of Audubon's paintings to our understanding of several bird species.	

Draw Conclusions, p. 383

Reading Social Studies:
Graphic Organizer, p. 385

Reading Social Studies:
Graphic Organizer Responses, p. 388

Language Arts
Write a Letter, p. 385

Advanced Learners, p. 387
Extend and Enrich, p. 388
Reteach the Lesson, p. 388

Activity Book, p. 103
🌐 **Reading and Vocabulary Transparency, 5-8**

Reading Social Studies:
Study Questions, p. 390

Reading Social Studies:
Study Question Responses, p. 394

Language Arts
Persuasive Writing, p. 392

Music
Draw Pictures for "The Star-Spangled Banner," p. 393

Advanced Learners, p. 389
Extend and Enrich, p. 394
Reteach the Lesson, p. 394

Activity Book, pp. 104–105
🌐 **Reading and Vocabulary Transparency, 5-9**
💾 Internet Resources

Reading Social Studies:
Prediction, p. 396

Reading Social Studies:
Prediction Responses, p. 399

Reading
Read a Biography, p. 396

Mathematics
Computation, p. 397

Tactile Learners, p. 398
Extend and Enrich, p. 399
Reteach the Lesson, p. 399

Activity Book, p. 106
🌐 **Reading and Vocabulary Transparency, 5-10**

Extend and Enrich, p. 401
Reteach, p. 401

💾 Internet Resources

Chapter 11 Planning Guide The Nation Grows

LESSON	PACING	OBJECTIVES	VOCABULARY
4 **From Ocean to Ocean** pp. 402–409	1 Day	■ Analyze the westward expansion of the United States. ■ Describe Texas's fight for independence. ■ Identify routes used by settlers moving west. ■ Analyze reasons people moved west. ■ Explain the events leading to the Mexican Cession and the Gadsden Purchase. ■ Analyze the migration of people to California during the gold rush.	**manifest destiny** **dictator** **cession** **gold rush** **forty-niner** **Word Work:** Preview Vocabulary, p. 402
MAP AND GLOBE SKILLS **Identify Changing Borders** pp. 410–411	1 Day	■ Identify borders on a map. ■ Apply critical thinking skills to organize and use information from maps. ■ Use historical maps to collect data about the past.	
5 **An Industrial Revolution** pp. 412–419	1 Day	■ Analyze the changes in the United States brought about by the Industrial Revolution. ■ Analyze how the transportation of goods changed during the nineteenth century. ■ Analyze how mass production and interchangeable parts affected the economy of the United States.	**industrial revolution** **investor** **textile** **interchangeable parts** **mass production** **supply** **cotton gin** **demand** **patent**
Chapter Review and Test Preparation pp. 420–421	1 Day		

| --- | --- | --- | --- |
Reading Social Studies: **K-W-L Chart**, p. 403 (Focus Skill) **Draw Conclusions,** p. 403 **Reading Social Studies:** **K-W-L Chart Responses,** p. 409	**Languages** **Research Spanish Place-Names,** p. 403 **Science** **Research Weather and Climate,** p. 406 **Mathematics** **Calculate Averages,** p. 406 **Health** **Disease,** p. 407	**Advanced Learners,** p. 404 **Extend and Enrich,** p. 408 **Reteach the Lesson,** p. 409	**Activity Book,** p. 107 **Reading and Vocabulary Transparency,** 5-11 Internet Resources
		Advanced Learners, p. 410 **Extend and Enrich,** p. 411 **Reteach the Skill,** p. 411	**Activity Book,** p. 108 **Skill Transparency,** 5-3 **GeoSkills CD-ROM**
Reading Social Studies: **Study Questions,** p. 413 (Focus Skill) **Draw Conclusions,** p. 416 **Reading Social Studies:** **Study Question Responses,** p. 419	**Mathematics** **Computation,** p. 413 **Music** **Erie Canal Song,** p. 414 **Science** **Experiment with Steam,** p. 415 **Art** **Weave,** p. 416	**English as a Second Language,** p. 412 **Extend and Enrich,** p. 418 **Reteach the Lesson,** p. 419	**Activity Book,** p. 109 **Reading and Vocabulary Transparency,** 5-12
		Test Preparation, p. 420	**Activity Book,** pp. 110–111 **Reading and Vocabulary Transparency,** 5-13 **Assessment Program, Chapter 11 Test,** pp. 81–84

Activity Book

LESSON 1

Name _____ Date _____

The Louisiana Purchase

Directions Read each numbered item below. Fill in each blank with the name of the person or persons connected to the description. Use names from the Word Bank. You may use a name more than once.

Sacagawea	Thomas Jefferson	Meriwether Lewis	Zebulon Pike
York	William Clark	Napoleon Bonaparte	

1 hoped to revive French power in North America
Napoleon Bonaparte

2 wanted the United States to have a port on the lower Mississippi River
Thomas Jefferson

3 needed money to fight a war   Napoleon Bonaparte

4 leaders of the Corps of Discovery   Meriwether Lewis and William Clark

5 African American who helped the Corps of Discovery by hunting and fishing
York

6 helped the Corps of Discovery by guiding them through the land of the
Shoshones   Sacagawea

7 explored the southwestern portion of the Louisiana Purchase
Zebulon Pike

LESSON 2

Name _____ Date _____

The War of 1812

Directions Look at the time line below. Match the events with the correct date on the time line. Place the letter of the correct event in the blank provided.

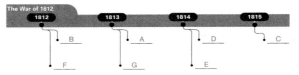

A. Battle of Lake Erie

B. United States declares war against Britain

C. Battle of New Orleans

D. British burn Washington, D.C.

E. Francis Scott Key writes "The Defense of Fort McHenry"

F. The warship *Constitution* defeats the British ship *Guerrière*.

G. Battle of the Thames

(continued)

LESSON 2

Name _____ Date _____

Directions Answer the questions below.

1 Give two reasons that the United States declared war on Britain.
The British in Canada supplied Native Americans with guns and impressed United States sailors.

2 What United States senator believed that the United States should "take the whole continent"?   Henry Clay

3 What was the nickname of the warship *Constitution*?   Old Ironsides

4 What Shawnee Indian leader was killed at the Battle of the Thames?
Tecumseh

5 What action did Dolley Madison take before leaving the White House?
She saved important government papers and a portrait of George Washington.

6 What did Francis Scott Key do after seeing the battle at Fort McHenry?
He wrote the poem that later became known as "The Star-Spangled Banner."

7 What years came to be known as the Era of Good Feelings?
1817–1825

8 Why was the Battle of New Orleans unnecessary?   A peace treaty between the British and the Americans had been signed two weeks before, on December 24, 1814.

LESSON 3

Name _____ Date _____

The Age of Jackson

Directions Read the paragraph below. Fill in the graphic organizer to show why the United States Supreme Court said the Cherokees could keep their land. Then answer the questions that follow.

United States Supreme Court Chief Justice John Marshall wrote the opinion of the Court in the case of *Worcester* v. *Georgia*. Marshall referred to Britain's past treaties with the Cherokee. He said the Cherokee had honored the treaties. That proved that the Cherokee were a nation able to govern themselves. He also argued that the laws of Georgia had no power over the Cherokee nation people because they were a "distinct community." Finally, Marshall said that the Native Americans had previous possession of the land. It was theirs. Unfortunately, President Andrew Jackson refused to accept the ruling. He said, "John Marshall has made his decision; now let him enforce it." Jackson then ordered federal troops to remove the Native Americans and take the land.

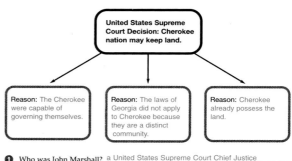

1 Who was John Marshall?   a United States Supreme Court Chief Justice

2 What did President Andrew Jackson say about Marshall's decision?
"John Marshall has made his decision; now let him enforce it."

3 What did Jackson then do?   President Jackson ordered federal troops to remove the Native Americans and take their land.

LESSON 4

Name _____ Date _____

From Ocean to Ocean

Directions Fill in the blanks in the paragraph below, using terms from the Word Bank.

Mormons	gold rush	dictator	forty-niners
Oregon	Cession	manifest destiny	

In the early 1800s many people began to believe that the United States should stretch from the Atlantic Ocean to the Pacific Ocean. This idea was known as _____manifest destiny_____. In time, this goal seemed possible. In 1834 when General Santa Anna took over the Mexican government and made himself _____dictator_____, Texas settlers were alarmed. After battles at the Alamo and San Jacinto, the settlers defeated Santa Anna and Texas became an independent republic. Several years later, Mexico and the United States again clashed over the Texas border. Mexico agreed to give up its claims in what was called the Mexican _____Cession_____. In addition, some people went west in search of religious freedom. The _____Mormons_____ settled in Utah after being driven from Illinois. Marcus and Narcissa Whitman went to the _____Oregon_____ Territory to set up missions. Finally, when gold was discovered in California, a _____gold rush_____ began. Those who went called themselves _____forty-niners_____ because many settlers moved there in 1849.

Use after reading Chapter 11, Lesson 4, pages 402–409.

Activity Book ■ 107

SKILL PRACTICE

Name _____ Date _____

MAP AND GLOBE SKILLS

Identifying Changing Borders

Directions Use the map below to answer the questions that follow.

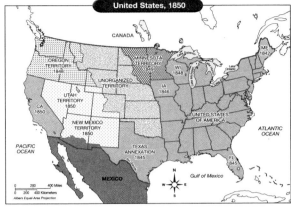

United States, 1850

❶ In what year did the United States gain control of the Utah Territory? _1850_

❷ What state was the farthest west in 1850? _California_

❸ What river eventually became the border between Mexico and the United States? _Rio Grande_

❹ By 1850 had the idea of manifest destiny been achieved? Explain.
Yes: Possible answer: By 1850 the United States had control of the Oregon Territory and had gained California as a state. The United States now stretched from the Atlantic to the Pacific Ocean.

108 ■ Activity Book

Use after reading Chapter 11, Skill Lesson, pages 410–411.

LESSON 5

Name _____ Date _____

An Industrial Revolution

Directions Tell how each invention listed below played a part in the Industrial Revolution. Write your answers on the blanks provided. Students' answers will vary; possible answers are given.

❶ The steam engine The steam engine was used in both boats and trains. It reduced the time and cost of travel and shipping.

❷ Cotton mills The machines to spin thread and weave cloth cut the time needed to make fabric. Mills were the first examples of large-scale manufacturing in the United States. People began working in factories instead of at home.

❸ Interchangeable parts This made mass production possible. The supply of manufactured goods increased.

❹ Cotton gin The cotton gin removed seeds from cotton faster than people could. This allowed cotton to be cleaned and prepared for market in less time.

❺ Mechanical reaper The reaper allowed farmers to harvest as much wheat in one day as they could in two weeks using hand tools.

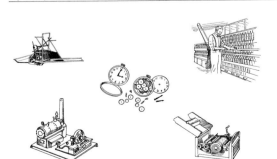

Use after reading Chapter 11, Lesson 5, pages 412–419.

Activity Book ■ 109

CHAPTER 11 REVIEW

Name _____ Date _____

America and the Industrial Revolution

Directions Complete this graphic organizer by drawing conclusions about the Industrial Revolution.

WHAT YOU KNOW	NEW FACTS	CONCLUSION
Student answers will vary. Sample answer: At the time, most Americans had never been anywhere outside of the United States.	Life was often difficult for Americans, especially those who chose to settle in unexplored lands.	The Industrial Revolution made the lives of most Americans much easier, improving the ways many people lived, traveled, and worked.
Student answers will vary. Sample answer: At one time, Americans did most farming work by hand.	With new inventions like the reaper, wheat that once took two weeks to cut could now be cut in one day.	
Student answers will vary. Sample answer: Traveling in the United States was once very difficult and took a great deal of time.	By the mid-1800s more than 88 thousand miles of road and 9 thousand miles of rail had been built in the United States.	

110 ■ Activity Book

Use after reading Chapter 11, pages 383–419.

CHAPTER

Name _____ Date _____

11 Test Preparation

Directions Read each question and choose the best answer. then fill in the circle for the answer you have chosen. Be sure to fill in the circle completely.

1 Napoleon was willing to sell Louisiana because —
- Ⓐ he knew he was too far away to control it.
- Ⓑ he had no use for the land.
- ● he needed money to fight a war.
- Ⓓ he was persuaded by Jefferson's representatives.

2 The years from 1817 to 1825 are called —
- Ⓕ the Age of Jackson.
- Ⓖ manifest destiny.
- Ⓗ the Monroe Doctrine.
- ● the Era of Good Feelings.

3 All of the following are reasons for Andrew Jackson's election *except* that
- Ⓐ he was a war hero.
- ● he had lots of money.
- Ⓒ for the first time all white men could vote.
- Ⓓ he was considered a common man.

4 _____ was the starting point for many travelers and was called the Gateway to the West.
- ● St. Louis
- Ⓖ Michigan
- Ⓗ the Santa Fe trail
- Ⓙ Cincinnati

5 *Tom Thumb* proved that
- Ⓐ steam-powered railroad engines were faster than horses.
- Ⓑ locomotives were undependable.
- ● steam-powered railroad cars had better pulling power than horses.
- Ⓓ trains needed much improvement to be practical.

© Harcourt

Use after reading Chapter 11, pages 382–421.

Activity Book ■ 111

COMMUNITY RESOURCES

Historical Societies

_____
_____
_____
_____
_____

Museums

_____
_____
_____
_____
_____

Experts in United States Expansion

_____
_____
_____
_____
_____

Historical Sites

_____
_____
_____
_____
_____

Chapter 11 Assessment

CONTENT / VOCABULARY

· CHAPTER ·

Name _____ Date _____

11 Test

Part One: Test Your Understanding

MULTIPLE CHOICE (4 points each)

Directions Circle the letter of the best answer.

1 In 1800, which one of the following places was still not a state—
A Vermont
B Ohio *(circled)*
C Kentucky
D Tennessee

2 Why did Jefferson purchase the Louisiana Territory from France?
F to keep Louisiana out of Spanish control
G to set up military headquarters
H to establish a port for farmers in the Northwest Territory *(circled)*
J to improve the United States's relationship with Spain

3 After traveling more than 3,000 miles from St. Louis, what landmark did Lewis and Clark reach?
A the Rocky Mountains
B the Shoshone lands
C the Caribbean
D the Pacific Ocean *(circled)*

4 Zebulon Pike's capture by the Spanish governor of New Mexico led to—
F an increase in the number of American traders traveling to New Mexico. *(circled)*
G war between Texas and New Mexico.
H a standoff between the United States and Spain in the Gulf of Mexico.
J Spanish control of the Louisiana Territory.

5 The British took American sailors off their ships and forced them to work on British ships, a practice known as—
A annexation.
B impressment. *(circled)*
C a siege.
D nationalism.

6 Who helped supply the Native Americans with guns to fight off the American settlers moving west?
F France
G Spain
H Britain *(circled)*
J Portugal

(continued)

Chapter 11 Test

CONTENT / VOCABULARY

Name _____ Date _____

7 Which of the following was **not** true of the War Hawks?
A They wanted to force the British out of North America
B They wanted to take over Florida.
C They wanted to capture Canada.
D They wanted to be allies with the Native Americans. *(circled)*

8 American Captain Oliver Hazard Perry defeated the British in what battle, which was an early turning point in the War of 1812?
F the Battle of Lake Erie *(circled)*
G the Battle of Nova Scotia
H the Battle of the Thames
J the Battle of New Orleans

9 What President issued a doctrine stating that European nations must stop colonizing lands in North America?
A Thomas Jefferson
B James Monroe *(circled)*
C James Madison
D John Quincy Adams

10 Which of the following was **not** true of President Andrew Jackson
F He was the first President elected from a western state.
G He was nicknamed "Old Hickory."
H He came from a wealthy Massachusetts family. *(circled)*
J He was a lawyer and judge.

TRUE OR FALSE

Directions Decide whether each of the following states are correct, and write True or False on the lines provided.

11 __T__ Meriwether Lewis and William Clark led the first expedition across the Louisiana Purchase.

12 __F__ Merchants strongly supported the War of 1812 as a way to increase trade partners.

13 __F__ Native Americans, angered by Tecumseh's death, increased their attacks on western settlers in 1813.

14 __T__ In a democracy, people are free to make choices about their lives and government.

15 __F__ President Jackson's strongest supporters were the wealthy land owners.

16 __F__ By signing the Treaty of Guadalupe Hidalgo, Mexico gave the United States two areas of land known as the Mexican Cession and the Oregon Territory.

(continued)

Chapter 11 Test

SKILLS

Name _____ Date _____

Part Two: Test Your Skills

IDENTIFY CHANGING BORDERS (5 points each)

Directions Use the historical maps of the western United States to answer the following questions.

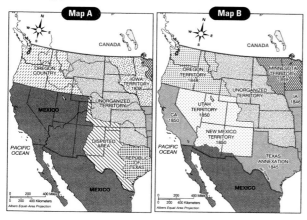

17 What country originally controlled most of what is now the western United States? _____Mexico_____

18 What states and territories were formed out of what was once part of Mexico?
_____California, Utah Territory, New Mexico Territory_____

19 How did Mexico's border change over time? _It moved much farther south._

20 What place is shown as a territory on Map A and a state on Map B?
_____Iowa_____

(continued)

Chapter 11 Test

APPLICATION / WRITING

Name _____ Date _____

Part Three: Apply What You Have Learned

21 PROBLEM-SOLUTION (6 points)

The Industrial Revolution changed the way people in the United States lived, traveled, and worked. Listed below in the right-hand column are innovations that solved problems during that period. Fill in the column on the left with the problem that made each solution necessary.

Problem	Solution
Possible response: Trade and transportation were difficult because most roads were dirt paths that turned into rivers when it rained.	The National Road
Possible response: Road travel was expensive and wagons had limited space. Boats and barges traveling along canals could carry more at a lower cost.	The Erie Canal
Possible response: Boats had been unable to travel easily upstream and horses had been pulling railroad cars. Neither the boats nor the trains were a very fast or powerful means of transportation.	Steam engine

22 ESSAY (10 points)

As ideas about democracy changed, more Americans were given the right to vote. Write an essay explaining the effect that giving the vote to all white men had on the type of people elected as public officials. Give an example of an official who was elected during this time.

Possible response: People elected as public officials were no longer always

wealthy landowners. Some were not very well educated. Those

who were elected now were more likely to represent ordinary citizens.

Davy Crockett and Andrew Jackson are both examples of ordinary citizens

who were elected to public office during this time period. Crockett even

admitted to never having read a newspaper in his life.

_____

Chapter 11 Test

Introduce the Chapter
PAGES 382–383

OBJECTIVES

- Use visual clues to describe patterns of land use in the United States.
- Use critical-thinking skills to understand and interpret primary sources.

Access Prior Knowledge

Ask students to think about an adventure they have had. Perhaps they have visited a new place or participated in a new hobby or sport. Ask students to describe how they felt at the time of their adventure.

Visual Learning

Picture Ask students to describe the landscape pictured on pages 382–383. Have them use this image to predict what the chapter is about.

Locate It Map The peak of Chimney Rock National Historic Site sits about 500 feet (153 m) above the North Platte River in western Nebraska. It is about 35 miles (56 km) from the Wyoming border.

CHIMNEY ROCK NATIONAL HISTORIC SITE

For settlers journeying on the Oregon Trail, Chimney Rock was an important landmark. It marked the place where the prairies ended and the ground became more rugged, heading west toward the Rocky Mountains. From 1812 to 1866, nearly half a million settlers passed Chimney Rock on their journey west.

LOCATE IT

NEBRASKA

Chimney Rock National Historic Site

382 ■ Unit 5

Picture Chimney Rock was a notable landmark on the Oregon Trail, one of the major land routes used by westward-moving settlers in the early nineteenth century. Missouri was the Oregon Trail's eastern starting point. People traveling along the 2,000-mile (3,219-km) route made their way through Nebraska and eventually followed the North Platte River through the western part of the state and into Wyoming. As they crossed what is now the state line, travelers would have seen Chimney Rock towering above the red soil. Ask students if they agree with an early explorer who described this area of western Nebraska as the "Great American Desert."

Quotation John Soule's exhortation for people to "go west" was first seen by readers of an Indiana newspaper, the *Terre Haute Express*. The migration on the Oregon Trail had begun in 1843, and by 1851, the mass movement westward was fully underway.

11
The Nation Grows

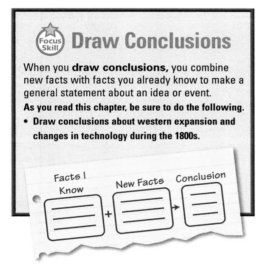

" Go west, young man,
go west. "

—John B. L. Soule, editorial in the
Terre Haute Express, 1851

Draw Conclusions

When you **draw conclusions,** you combine new facts with facts you already know to make a general statement about an idea or event.

As you read this chapter, be sure to do the following.

* Draw conclusions about western expansion and changes in technology during the 1800s.

Facts I Know + New Facts → Conclusion

Read and Respond

Ask students to think about what images people might have had of the West in the 1850s. Have students discuss what they expect to learn about the growth of the United States in this chapter.

Quotation Have a volunteer read the quotation aloud.

Q **Who do you think John Soule was addressing when he wrote this line?**

A Answers should reflect that he may have been directing his message at settlers seeking a better life or opportunity.

Draw Conclusions

Have students record in a graphic organizer what they already know, what they learn, and conclusions they draw about chapter topics Remind them that when they draw conclusions, they are making statements that were not provided in the text.

* A blank graphic organizer appears on page 110 of the Activity Book.

* A completed graphic organizer can be found on page 110 of the Activity Book, Teacher's Edition.

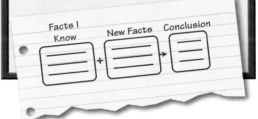

Facts I Know + New Facts → Conclusion

WORD WORK

Preview Vocabulary Organize students in groups and have them review the lesson vocabulary lists. Assign terms to various group members and have them skim the chapter for their meanings. Have members share their definitions and complete a group vocabulary chart.

Group Vocabulary Chart	
Term	**Definition**

MAKE IT RELEVANT

Discussion Questions These topics might provide useful opportunities for discussion as you teach this chapter.

■ Would you have been eager to travel west in the 1800s?

■ Are there any places that have not been settled yet in the United States?

■ Why do people leave their homelands today to settle in a different place?

Lesson 1

PAGES 384–388

1

The Louisiana Purchase

 Draw Conclusions pp. 383, 384, 385, 388, 420

OBJECTIVES

- Analyze how the United States expanded beyond the Mississippi River.
- Identify lands included in the Louisiana Purchase.
- Describe contributions made by explorers Meriwether Lewis, William Clark, and Zebulon Pike.

DRAW CONCLUSIONS
As you read, draw conclusions about why the Louisiana Purchase was important to the growth of the United States.

BIG IDEA
The United States grew west of the Mississippi River.

VOCABULARY
inauguration
pathfinder
trespass

Vocabulary

SEE READING AND VOCABULARY TRANSPARENCY 5-8 OR THE WORD CARDS ON PP. V63–V64.

inauguration p. 384
pathfinder p. 387
trespass p. 388

 When Minutes Count

Have students examine the map on page 385. Then use the map as a springboard to discuss the Big Idea of the lesson.

Quick Summary

This lesson describes the Louisiana Purchase and the westward expansion of the United States.

1800–1806

By 1800 Vermont, Kentucky, and Tennessee were added to the original 13 states, and the Northwest Territory was divided into the territories of Ohio and Indiana. Americans were moving west in greater numbers. Some Americans even began to look beyond the Mississippi to the land the French had named Louisiana. France had given Spain this huge region after France lost the French and Indian War in 1763. At this time Spain also controlled all the lands along the Gulf coast.

The Louisiana Purchase

On March 4, 1801, Thomas Jefferson became the third President of the United States. At his **inauguration** (ih•naw•gyuh•RAY•shuhn), or taking office, Jefferson spoke of his hopes for the young nation. He called the United States "a rising nation, spread over a wide and fruitful land." He knew, however, that the nation faced some serious problems.

The United States had no ports of its own on the Gulf of Mexico. Farmers who lived in Kentucky, Tennessee, and the Northwest Territory had to ship their goods down the Mississippi River to New Orleans. From there they could sell the goods to ships sailing for ports in Europe or along the Atlantic coast of the United States.

After the Louisiana Purchase, soldiers at the fort at New Orleans replaced the French flag with the United States flag. The French artist, who mistakenly added hills and cactus to the area, had probably never been to New Orleans.

384 ▪ Unit 5

1 Motivate

Set the Purpose

Big Idea Display a map of the United States, and discuss with students how much of the present-day United States is west of the Mississippi River.

Access Prior Knowledge

Ask students to think about what was happening in the United States in the early 1800s. Consider why people might want to move west. The East was becoming more crowded; land was becoming more expensive.

STUDY/RESEARCH SKILLS

Using Reference Sources
Direct students to use an encyclopedia and other reference materials to find out how American inauguration ceremonies have changed since their beginning. Ask students when Inauguration Day became officially known by that name in the United States. 1829

BACKGROUND

Inauguration Inform students that until 1933 the presidential inauguration was held on March 4 of the year following the presidential election. The Twentieth Amendment changed Inauguration Day to January 20 beginning in 1933.

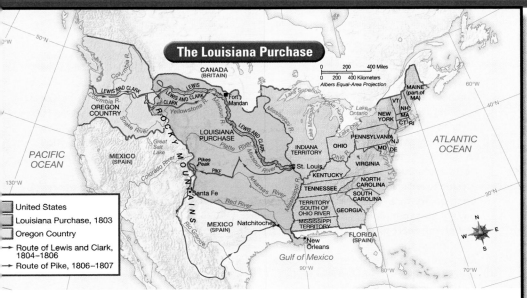

The Louisiana Purchase

United States

Louisiana Purchase, 1803

Oregon Country

→ Route of Lewis and Clark, 1804–1806

→ Route of Pike, 1806–1807

Place **The Louisiana Purchase doubled the size of the United States.**

❖ What natural features of the territory made it easy to explore?

Spain once had allowed American farmers to load and unload their goods free of charge at New Orleans. That changed, however, and it became more costly for farmers to sell their products. Jefferson worried that people in the western United States might not stay loyal to the government if they had no way to ship their products to market.

Soon after Jefferson became President, he learned that Spain had given Louisiana back to France. The French leader, Napoleon Bonaparte (nuh•POH•lee•uhn BOH•nuh•part), hoped to once again establish French power in North America. However, Jefferson knew that having the French in control of Louisiana could prevent the United States frontier from moving farther west.

Jefferson sent representatives to France to ask Bonaparte to sell the land along the east bank of the Mississippi River, including New Orleans, to the United States. With this land, the United States would have a port on the Gulf of Mexico.

At this time France was getting ready for war with Britain. People in the French colony of St. Domingue (SAN daw•MANG) in the Caribbean had also rebelled against French rule. Bonaparte needed money to fight two wars. He offered to sell *all* of Louisiana— more than 800,000 square miles (2,071,840 sq km)— to the United States for about $15 million.

The agreement to buy Louisiana was made on April 30, 1803. The sale of this huge territory became known as the Louisiana Purchase.

REVIEW Why did Jefferson want to buy the land along the east bank of the Mississippi?
  DRAW CONCLUSIONS
so the United States would have its own port on the Gulf of Mexico   **Chapter 11 ■ 385**

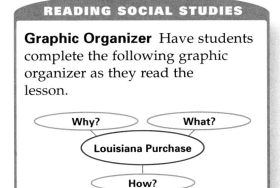

Graphic Organizer Have students complete the following graphic organizer as they read the lesson.

Why?   What?

Louisiana Purchase

How?

● USE READING AND VOCABULARY TRANSPARENCY 5-8.

5-8 TRANSPARENCY

2 Teach

The Louisiana Purchase

Read and Respond

Economics Discuss with students why the Mississippi River was the most economical route for farmers in what was then the western United States to use to get their products to market.

Q **Why did President Jefferson think possessing New Orleans and the surrounding area was so important?**

A The United States needed a port on the Gulf of Mexico so that western farmers could use rivers to ship their products to market.

Visual Learning

Map Direct students' attention to the map on page 385. Ask them how the amount of land acquired in the Louisiana Purchase compared with the size of the United States at the time. Encourage students to locate landmarks such as the Mississippi River and the Rocky Mountains.
CAPTION ANSWER: rivers

Lewis and Clark

Read and Respond

Civics and Government Explain that Congress approved the project that sent Lewis and Clark on an expedition that would become one of America's greatest stories of adventure. Congress approved $2,500 for the mission to explore the uncharted West and determine whether the Missouri River system connected to the Pacific Ocean.

Q Why was exploring the West important to Congress?

A Possible responses: Congress wanted to know more about the newly-acquired lands in the Louisiana Purchase; Congress wanted Americans to find a land route to the Pacific so that pioneers could settle the Pacific Coast.

Visual Learning

Map Refer students again to the map on page 385. Invite students to trace with their fingers the route of the Lewis and Clark expedition. Have them locate Fort Mandan.

Artifact Meriwether Lewis took two compasses on the journey. Ask students what direction the magnetic needle always points to. north

Read and Respond

History Remind students that Sacagawea's husband was the person originally hired by Lewis and Clark as an interpreter and guide. Tell students that Sacagawea and her infant son were allowed to go with her husband on the expedition. Explain that when the explorers reached the land of the Shoshones, they met a tribe of Shoshones led by Sacagawea's brother. Sacagawea was able to obtain from her brother needed supplies, such as horses and food.

Q How did Sacagawea and the Shoshones contribute to the Lewis and Clark expedition?

A Sacagawea contributed by guiding the expedition through the Shoshone land. The Shoshones helped by providing the expedition with horses and food.

Lewis and Clark

Few people in the United States knew much about the Louisiana Purchase. It was a huge region, reaching from the Mississippi River to the Rocky Mountains and from New Orleans north to Canada. Americans had never explored it, so President Jefferson asked Congress for money to pay for an expedition to find out more about it.

Jefferson then chose Meriwether Lewis to lead the expedition. Lewis had been an army officer and had served in the Northwest Territory. Jefferson also chose William Clark, a good friend of Lewis and brother of the Revolutionary War hero George Rogers Clark, to help lead the expedition.

Lewis and Clark put together a group of about 30 soldiers. They called their group the Corps of Discovery. One

William Clark used this compass in the expedition to the Louisiana Purchase.

member of the Corps of Discovery was York, William Clark's African American slave who was skilled in hunting and fishing.

In May 1804 the group left its camp near present-day St. Louis and traveled up the Missouri River by boat. By October the expedition had reached present-day North Dakota. With winter coming on, they built a small camp near a Mandan Indian village. They named their camp Fort Mandan.

At Fort Mandan, Lewis and Clark hired a French fur trader to interpret some Indian languages for them. The fur trader was married to a Shoshone (shoh•SHOH•nee) Indian woman named Sacagawea (sa•kuh•juh•WEE•uh). Sacagawea agreed

Meriwether Lewis (far right) and William Clark (right) led the Corps of Discovery through the Louisiana Purchase. The painting shows Sacagawea using sign language to communicate with the Chinooks during the expedition.

386 ■ Unit 5

BACKGROUND

The Trip Home When Lewis and Clark reached tidewater on the Columbia River, they met coastal Indians. Discovering that the Indians' speech was laced with expressions learned from English-speaking sailors, Lewis and Clark learned that trading vessels from New England often visited the Columbia. Lewis and Clark hoped that such a vessel might arrive to take them and their company home in relative comfort. However, no ship arrived for several months, so the expedition returned as it had come. Lewis took the water route across Montana, while Clark went overland to the Yellowstone River and floated down to its junction with the Missouri River. There he met up with Lewis. The expedition reached St. Louis on September 23, 1806, to the cheers of the city's people.

to guide the expedition when it reached the land of the Shoshones.

In the spring of 1805, the Lewis and Clark expedition set out again. They moved farther up the Missouri River toward the Rocky Mountains. With Sacagawea's help, the expedition got horses from the Shoshones and continued their journey through the mountain passes of the Rockies. Once over the mountains, the explorers built boats and rowed down the Clearwater, Snake, and Columbia Rivers toward the Pacific coast.

In November 1805, after traveling for more than a year and covering more than 3,000 miles (about 4,800 km), the Lewis and Clark expedition reached the Pacific Ocean. Clark wrote in his journal,

6 6 Great joy in camp. We are in view of the . . . great Pacific Octean [Ocean], which we have been so long anxious to see, and the roreing [roaring] or noise made by the waves brakeing [breaking] on the rockey [rocky] shores (as I may suppose) may be heard distinctly. 99

In March the Corps of Discovery began the long journey back to St. Louis. They reached the settlement in September 1806. The expedition had collected many facts about the Louisiana Purchase. They brought back seeds, plants, and even living animals. They could tell what the people and the land were like, and they had drawn maps to show where mountain passes and major rivers were. In later years the work of these pathfinders helped American settlers find their way to the Pacific coast. A **pathfinder** is someone who finds a way through an unknown region.

REVIEW Who led the first expedition to the Louisiana Purchase? Meriwether Lewis and William Clark

387

Analyze Primary Sources

Quotation Inform students that President Jefferson wanted to find a waterway to the Pacific Ocean for trading and commerce.

Read and Respond

Geography Ask students to speculate on the reasons for Jefferson's interest in accurate records of the geography, climate, people, plants, and animals in the lands of the Louisiana Purchase.

Q **Why were the journal and maps from the Lewis and Clark expedition important?**

A Students might speculate that they provided information to later pioneers who wanted to settle the Pacific Coast.

The Pike Expedition

Read and Respond

Civics and Government Discuss with students why Pike's expedition landed him in jail. Have students infer the Spanish governor's reason for asking whether the United States was planning to invade Spanish lands.

Q **Why would it have been economically beneficial for the Spanish to trade with the United States?**

A Students should indicate that goods would not have had to travel as far.

3 Close

Summarize Key Content

- The United States purchased Louisiana from France in 1803.
- Meriwether Lewis and William Clark explored the northern part of the Louisiana Purchase to the Pacific Ocean.
- Zebulon Pike explored the southwestern part of the Louisiana Purchase and helped promote trade between New Mexico and the United States.

Graphic Organizer Check students' graphic organizers against the one shown below.

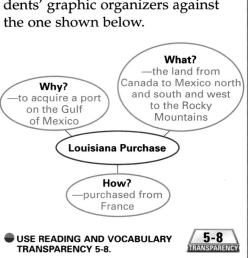

Why?
—to acquire a port on the Gulf of Mexico

What?
—the land from Canada to Mexico north and south and west to the Rocky Mountains

Louisiana Purchase

How?
—purchased from France

● USE READING AND VOCABULARY TRANSPARENCY 5-8.

5-8 TRANSPARENCY

Assess

Lesson 1 Review—Answers

DRAW CONCLUSIONS Possible response: Lewis and Clark wanted to show people some of the things they had seen.

❶ **BIG IDEA** because the United States bought Louisiana from France

❷ **VOCABULARY** one who finds a way through an unknown region

❸ **TIME LINE** 1803

❹ **GEOGRAPHY** from the Mississippi River to the Rocky Mountains and from New Orleans to Canada

❺ **CRITICAL THINKING—Evaluate** The explorers mapped the areas they traveled through and wrote detailed reports about what they had seen and encountered. Their work helped people find their way to the Pacific coast.

Performance Assessment Guidelines Students' maps should show the Louisiana Purchase and the route they wish to explore.

ACTIVITY BOOK

Use ACTIVITY BOOK, p.103, to reinforce and extend student learning.

The Pike Expedition

As the Lewis and Clark expedition made its way back to St. Louis in 1806, another expedition was exploring the southwestern part of the Louisiana Purchase. This small group of pathfinders was led by Captain Zebulon Pike.

By the winter of 1806, the Pike expedition had reached a huge prairie in present-day Kansas. As the expedition traveled farther west, Pike saw what he described as a "blue mountain" in the distance. Today that blue mountain is called Pikes Peak, for the explorer.

The expedition followed the Rocky Mountains south to what Pike thought was the Red River, one of the rivers that led into the Mississippi River. It was really the northern part of the Rio Grande. The expedition had wandered out of the Louisiana Purchase and into Spanish land.

Spanish soldiers soon reached the small fort that the Americans had built along the river. The soldiers took Pike and the others to Santa Fe, the capital of the Spanish colony of New Mexico. The explorers were put in jail for **trespassing**, or going onto someone else's property without asking. In Santa Fe the Spanish governor asked Zebulon Pike if the United States was getting ready to invade the Spanish lands. Pike answered no.

When the Spanish set him free several months later, Pike reported that the people of Santa Fe needed manufactured goods. Soon American traders were heading for New Mexico.

Zebulon Pike

REVIEW **Why did Spanish soldiers put Captain Zebulon Pike and the rest of his explorers in jail?** They were put in jail for trespassing on Spanish land.

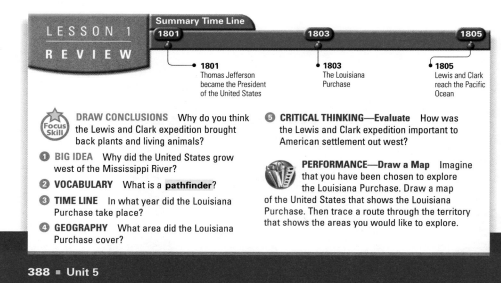

LESSON 1 REVIEW

Summary Time Line

1801 — 1803 — 1805

1801
Thomas Jefferson became the President of the United States

1803
The Louisiana Purchase

1805
Lewis and Clark reach the Pacific Ocean

DRAW CONCLUSIONS Why do you think the Lewis and Clark expedition brought back plants and living animals?

❶ **BIG IDEA** Why did the United States grow west of the Mississippi River?

❷ **VOCABULARY** What is a **pathfinder**?

❸ **TIME LINE** In what year did the Louisiana Purchase take place?

❹ **GEOGRAPHY** What area did the Louisiana Purchase cover?

❺ **CRITICAL THINKING—Evaluate** How was the Lewis and Clark expedition important to American settlement out west?

PERFORMANCE—Draw a Map Imagine that you have been chosen to explore the Louisiana Purchase. Draw a map of the United States that shows the Louisiana Purchase. Then trace a route through the territory that shows the areas you would like to explore.

388 ■ Unit 5

EXTEND AND ENRICH

Write a Journal Entry Challenge students to imagine that they are part of the Lewis and Clark expedition and that they have just reached the Pacific Ocean. Direct students to write journal entries about the relief they feel at finally reaching the ocean.

RETEACH THE LESSON

Graphic Organizer Have students fill in the following flow chart showing how ownership of Louisiana changed. Request that students write which countries acquired the land and how they did so.

France—claimed by France and named Louisiana

Spain—given Louisiana by the French

France—given Louisiana by the Spanish

United States—bought Louisiana from the French

The War of 1812

1780 1800 1820 1840 1860

1805–1825

As Meriwether Lewis, William Clark, and Zebulon Pike were exploring the Louisiana Purchase, American settlers were pushing the frontier farther and farther west. As settlers moved west, however, they ran into many angry Native Americans who tried to stop them from taking their lands. The Indians were helped by the British in Canada, who sold them guns and encouraged them to fight the Americans. Before long, troubles in the western lands helped push the United States into a second war with Britain—the War of 1812.

War Fever

Americans were angry with the British for other reasons, too. To stop Americans from trading with the French and other Europeans, the British navy stopped American merchant ships at sea. They even forced sailors off American merchant ships and put them to work on British navy ships. Taking workers against their will this way is called **impressment**.

This engraving shows impressment of American sailors by the British in Boston.

389

· LESSON ·

2

 DRAW CONCLUSIONS

As you read, draw conclusions about events during the War of 1812.

BIG IDEA

The United States once again found itself at war with Britain.

VOCABULARY

impressment
war hawk
national anthem
siege
nationalism
annex
doctrine

Lesson 2
PAGES 389–394

OBJECTIVES

- Explain the reasons many Americans wanted to go to war with Britain a second time.
- Describe the major battles of the War of 1812.
- Analyze how nationalism swept over the United States after the War of 1812.
- Explain the purpose of the Monroe Doctrine.

 Draw Conclusions pp. 383, 389, 393, 394, 420

Vocabulary

SEE READING AND VOCABULARY TRANSPARENCY 5-9 OR THE WORD CARDS ON PP. V63–V64.

impressment p. 389	**siege** p. 393
war hawk p. 390	**nationalism** p. 394
national anthem p. 393	**annex** p. 394
	doctrine p. 394

When Minutes Count

Have students read the paragraph about "The Star-Spangled Banner" on page 393. Then invite them to tell in their own words what they just read.

Quick Summary

This lesson examines the War of 1812.

1 Motivate

Set the Purpose

Big Idea Explain that the Revolutionary War was the first of two wars that the United States and Britain fought. The second one was the War of 1812.

Access Prior Knowledge

Request that students make a list of the reasons countries might go to war.

Study Questions Have students use the following questions as a guide for their reading.

1. How did the *Constitution* get the nickname Old Ironsides?

2. What was the Monroe Doctrine?

● USE READING AND VOCABULARY TRANSPARENCY 5-9.

5-9
TRANSPARENCY

2 Teach

War Fever

Read and Respond

Civics and Government Explain to students that the United States can declare war only by an act of Congress. Ask why the Constitution gives this power to Congress. so that no single person can send the United States to war

History Discuss some of the reasons why Americans were angry with Britain. Point out that the British in Canada supplied weapons to Native Americans and encouraged them to fight against American settlers. Explain that Britain's impressment of American sailors also angered many Americans.

Q Who were the war hawks?

A Americans who wanted the United States to go to war against Britain

Economics Explain that not every American wanted war. Many northern merchants had made a lot of money trading with the British, and they feared a war would end their trade.

Geography Have students locate where the battle between the *Constitution* and the *Guerrière* took place. off the coast of Nova Scotia Explain that most of the early fighting in the war took place in the Great Lakes region, which forms part of the border between the United States and Canada.

Members of Congress from Ohio, Kentucky, and Tennessee, as well as the southern states, wanted war with Britain. Those who wanted war became known as **war hawks**. The war hawks thought the way to deal with the British was simple—take over Canada and drive the British out of North America. Many war hawks also believed that the United States should take over Florida, which was held by Spain. Congress member Henry Clay of Kentucky, one of the best-known war hawks, said the United States should "take the whole continent."

The desire for war grew strong in much of the nation. In June 1812 President James Madison of the United States, asked Congress to declare war on Britain. Congress quickly voted for war.

As the fighting began, Britain had the strongest navy in the world. Yet the small United States Navy, with only 16 ships, won two important battles early in the war. One was on the Atlantic Ocean and the other on the Great Lakes.

On August 19, 1812, the United States warship *Constitution* fought the British ship *Guerrière* (gair•YAIR) off the coast of Nova Scotia and won. After the two ships had shot cannonballs at each other, the *Guerrière* was in bad shape. Cannonballs, however, could not pierce the hard oak sides of the *Constitution*. Legend has it that a crew member said, "Her sides are made of iron." After that, the *Constitution* was nicknamed Old Ironsides.

On September 10, 1813, the Battle of Lake Erie became an early turning point in the war. Ships commanded by American Captain Oliver Hazard Perry beat the British. This allowed General William Henry Harrison to lead 4,500 soldiers across Lake Erie into Canada. At the Battle of the Thames (TEMZ) on October 5, 1813, the American forces beat the British and their Indian allies. Among the dead was Tecumseh (tuh•KUHM•suh), the Shawnee leader of an Indian group that had tried to stop Americans from taking Indian lands. From that time on, settlers in the Northwest Territory were free of conflicts with Indians.

REVIEW What victory allowed General Harrison to lead his troops into Canada? The Battle of Lake Erie

The Battle of Lake Erie was a clash between American and British ships that lasted more than three hours.

390 • Unit 5

BACKGROUND

Henry Clay Inform students that Henry Clay served in the Kentucky legislature before being elected to the United States House of Representatives. He later served in the United States Senate. He ran unsuccessfully for President twice—1832 and 1844.

BACKGROUND

American Attempts to Invade Canada Soon after the war began in 1812, Brigadier General William Hull attempted to invade Canada from Detroit. After learning that the British army was marching toward Detroit, Hull retreated to Detroit and was later forced to surrender the fort to the British. That same year, the United States tried for a second time to invade Canada, this time along the Niagara frontier. The American militia, however, refused to cross into Canada.

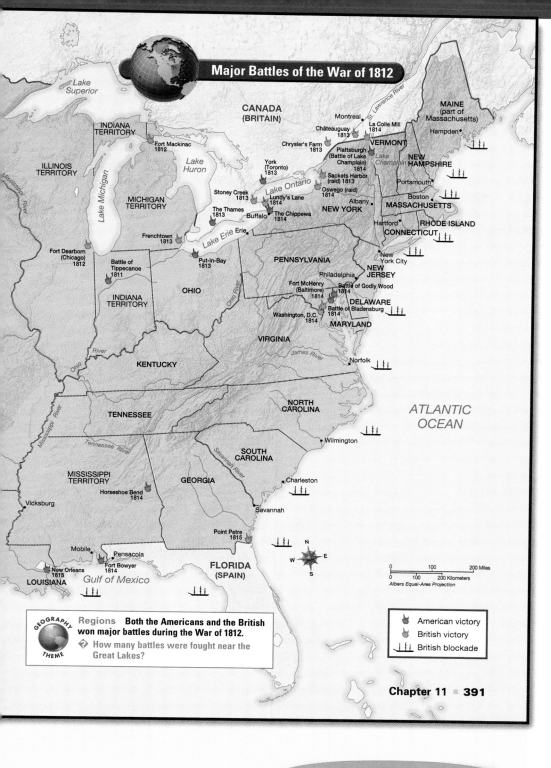

Major Battles of the War of 1812

Lake Superior

CANADA (BRITAIN)

INDIANA TERRITORY

Fort Mackinac 1812

Lake Huron

ILLINOIS TERRITORY

Lake Michigan

MICHIGAN TERRITORY

Montreal

St. Lawrence River

Châteauguay 1813

La Colle Mill 1814

MAINE (part of Massachusetts)

Hampden

Chrysler's Farm 1813

VERMONT

York (Toronto) 1813

Plattsburgh (Battle of Lake Champlain) 1814

NEW HAMPSHIRE

Lake Champlain

Lake Ontario

Sackets Harbor (raid) 1813

Oswego (raid) 1814

Portsmouth

Stoney Creek 1813

Lundy's Lane 1814

Albany

Boston

The Thames 1813

Buffalo

The Chippewa 1814

NEW YORK

MASSACHUSETTS

Frenchtown 1813

Lake Erie Erie

Hartford

RHODE ISLAND

CONNECTICUT

Fort Dearborn (Chicago) 1812

Put-in-Bay 1813

PENNSYLVANIA

New York City

Battle of Tippecanoe 1811

OHIO

Philadelphia

NEW JERSEY

INDIANA TERRITORY

Ohio River

Fort McHenry (Baltimore) 1814

Battle of Godly Wood 1814

DELAWARE

Washington, D.C. 1814

Battle of Bladensburg 1814

MARYLAND

VIRGINIA

James River

Norfolk

KENTUCKY

Mississippi River

TENNESSEE

Tennessee River

NORTH CAROLINA

ATLANTIC OCEAN

Wilmington

MISSISSIPPI TERRITORY

GEORGIA

SOUTH CAROLINA

Charleston

Horseshoe Bend 1814

Savannah River

Vicksburg

Savannah

Point Petre 1815

Mobile

Pensacola

New Orleans 1815

Fort Bowyer 1814

FLORIDA (SPAIN)

LOUISIANA

Gulf of Mexico

N W E S

0 100 200 Miles
0 100 200 Kilometers
Albers Equal-Area Projection

GEOGRAPHY THEME

Regions Both the Americans and the British won major battles during the War of 1812.

◈ How many battles were fought near the Great Lakes?

🔥 American victory
🔥 British victory
⚓ British blockade

Chapter 11 ▪ 391

Read and Respond

History Explain that even though American naval forces were smaller than those of the British, the United States was more successful at sea. This was primarily because the British were already involved in disputes elsewhere. When the War of 1812 began, the British were involved in the Napoleonic Wars in Europe. This enabled American warships to move about more freely.

Visual Learning

Illustration Direct students' attention to the illustration on page 390. Explain that after the Battle of Lake Erie, 28-year-old Captain Perry sent a message to headquarters: "We have met the enemy and they are ours." The victory put Lake Erie under United States control and forced the British to retreat farther north.

GO ONLINE Students might enjoy researching information about other historic sites in the United States. Have them visit The Learning Site at **www.harcourtschool.com.**

Map Have students study the map on page 391. Have students take turns pointing out battle sites on the map and indicating the victor in each battle.

Q How did the British attempt to stop trade in port cities in the United States?

A with blockades

CAPTION ANSWER: eleven

STUDY/RESEARCH SKILLS

Graphic Organizer Have students complete the following graphic organizer about the American naval victories in the War of 1812.

Battle	Where?	Who won?
Constitution vs. *Guerrière*	off the coast of Nova Scotia	the United States
Battle of Lake Erie	Lake Erie	the United States

British Raids

Read and Respond

Civics and Government Remind students that in 1814 Washington, D.C., was a very small city and that President Madison was only the third President to occupy the White House.

Q **Why do you think the British burned the White House?**

A to destroy a strong symbol of American government

History Remind students that there had been tension among the states when choosing a place to establish the nation's capital. Explain that after the White House was burned, once again there was talk of moving the capital to another location. However, President Madison urged Congress to rebuild Washington, D.C. Tell students that the new White House duplicated the one destroyed by the British.

Q **How would moving the capital have affected the United States?**

A Responses will vary. Students may mention that the land area of Maryland would have increased.

Culture and Society Explain to students that at the time of the War of 1812 the Library of Congress took up only one room in the Capitol. After the British burned the library, Congress rebuilt the collection with Thomas Jefferson's private library, which contained about 6,000 books.

This engraving shows the White House damaged by fire after the British attack on Washington, D.C., in August 1814.

British Raids

In August 1814 British soldiers marched toward Washington, D.C., a city of only 8,000 people at the time. Just 7 miles (about 11 km) away, American soldiers were fighting to defend the city from the British. As the noise of guns and cannons filled the air, First Lady Dolley Madison waited for news from her husband. President Madison had left the White House the day before to meet with the American soldiers.

With British soldiers quickly advancing, the First Lady gathered up important government papers. Having "pressed as many papers into trunks as to fill one carriage" she also collected valuable items from the White House. One of these items was a life-size portrait of George Washington. Because of the portrait's size, it was secured to the wall. This made it difficult to remove.

With the enemy nearly upon her, the First Lady had the portrait's frame smashed and the canvas rolled up. Only after everything was safe did Dolley Madison finally leave Washington. That evening the British burned many buildings, including the White House, the Capitol, and the Library of Congress.

With Washington in flames, the British sailed up Chesapeake Bay to Baltimore. Baltimore was protected by Fort McHenry. Although British ships bombed the fort for hours, the Americans would not give up. The sight of the huge American flag waving over the fort after the battle made Francis Scott Key very happy. He quickly wrote a poem that became the song "The Star-Spangled Banner." In 1931 it became our national

Dolley Madison rescued important items from the White House in the War of 1812.

392 ▪ Unit 5

BACKGROUND

The White House Throughout its history, the White House has been called the President's Palace, the President's House, and the Executive Mansion. President Theodore Roosevelt officially named it the White House in 1901.

INTEGRATE LANGUAGE ARTS

Persuasive Writing Challenge students to imagine that they are members of Congress during the War of 1812. Ask them to write persuasive letters to President James Madison, requesting that the nation's capital be moved from Washington, D.C. Direct them to choose where they would like the capital to be. Emphasize the need to include strong reasons that support their arguments.

anthem. A **national anthem** is a song of praise for a country that is recognized as the official song of that country.

When they could not beat the Americans at Baltimore, the British sailed south to New Orleans. American soldiers under the command of General Andrew Jackson were waiting for them there. Earlier that year, with the help of the Cherokees, Jackson had defeated the Creeks at the Battle of Horseshoe Bend in present-day Alabama. The Creeks were allies of the British.

When word came to General Jackson that the British might attack New Orleans, his troops hurried to defend the city. There they lived through a 10-day siege by British soldiers. A **siege** is a long-lasting attack. After fierce fighting, Jackson's soldiers finally forced the British out. Upon learning this, Jackson said, "By the Eternal, they shall not sleep on our soil!"

Americans would later learn that the Battle of New Orleans had not been necessary. On December 24, 1814—two weeks *before* the battle—the British and Americans had signed a peace treaty in Europe. Because news traveled so slowly at that time, word that the war was over had not reached New Orleans in time.

REVIEW Why was Francis Scott Key inspired to write "The Star-Spangled Banner"?

🔵 DRAW CONCLUSIONS

• HERITAGE •

"The Star-Spangled Banner"

Originally a poem titled "The Defense of Fort McHenry" the song known today as our national anthem was first performed in October of 1814. Quickly renamed, the song was issued as a handbill, or flyer, and soon became a favorite of American troops. By 1904 American military bases were required to perform the song every time the national flag was raised or lowered. In 1931 Congress voted to officially make "The Star-Spangled Banner" the national anthem of the United States.

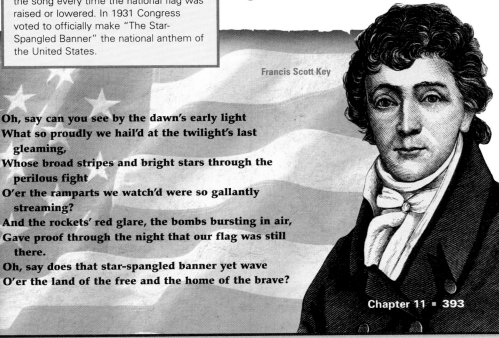

Francis Scott Key

Oh, say can you see by the dawn's early light
What so proudly we hail'd at the twilight's last
   gleaming,
Whose broad stripes and bright stars through the
   perilous fight
O'er the ramparts we watch'd were so gallantly
   streaming?
And the rockets' red glare, the bombs bursting in air,
Gave proof through the night that our flag was still
   there.
Oh, say does that star-spangled banner yet wave
O'er the land of the free and the home of the brave?

Chapter 11 ■ 393

The Era of Good Feelings

Read and Respond

Culture and Society Remind students that the United States has always been made up of people from many different countries who have brought their traditions and cultures with them. Explain that after the War of 1812, Americans felt united.

🄠 **How did the wave of nationalism that swept the country help to make the government strong?**

🅐 The government had the support of many of the people and was able to make confident decisions.

3 Close

Summarize Key Content

- In 1812 the United States declared war on Britain because the British supported Native Americans in opposing westward expansion and they impressed American sailors.
- Americans were victorious in key battles at sea against the British.
- In 1814 the British burned the White House, the Capitol, and many other buildings in Washington, D.C.
- Following the War of 1812, nationalism swept the United States and the Monroe Doctrine closed the Western Hemisphere to future colonization by European countries.

INTEGRATE MUSIC

Draw Pictures for "The Star-Spangled Banner"
Play a recording of "The Star-Spangled Banner," and have students recite or sing the words. Play the recording again, and have students draw pictures of the scene the song describes. Display students' pictures on a classroom wall.

QUESTIONS KIDS ASK

🄠 **Why did neither side win the War of 1812?**

🅐 Neither side was able to force the other out of its territory. Instead of continuing a war that no one was winning, leaders signed a peace treaty to end the fighting.

Assess

Lesson 2 Review—Answers

 DRAW CONCLUSIONS because they were angry with Britain for supplying arms to Native Americans

❶ **BIG IDEA** because the British supported the Native Americans in opposing westward expansion and were impressing American sailors

❷ **VOCABULARY** Students may suggest that the word *national* in **nationalism** can help them remember that nationalism is pride in a nation.

❸ **TIME LINE** in 1813

❹ **HISTORY** so the United States could keep growing without interference

❺ **CRITICAL THINKING—Evaluate** because many war hawks wanted the United States to have the entire North American continent

 Performance Assessment Guidelines Students' research should include new facts that they have learned about the War of 1812.

ACTIVITY BOOK

Use Activity Book, pp. 104–105, to reinforce and extend student learning.

The Era of Good Feelings

Neither side was clearly the winner in the War of 1812. However, Americans were proud that the United States had stood up to Britain. After the war a wave of **nationalism**, or pride in the country, swept over the land. For this reason the years from 1817 to 1825 have been called the Era of Good Feelings.

National pride could be seen in the strong way the government acted with other countries. James Monroe, the fifth President of the United States, negotiated a new boundary line between the United States and British Canada. He also got Spain to give up its claims to West Florida, which had been **annexed**, or added on, to the United States earlier. In another treaty, Spain agreed to sell East Florida to the United States, too.

President Monroe knew that if the United States wanted to keep growing, it had to stop the growth of Spanish,

He issued the Monroe Doctrine, which closed the Western Hemisphere to future European colonization.

French, Russian, and British colonies in the Americas. So on December 2, 1823, President Monroe announced a **doctrine**, or government plan of action. It came to be called the Monroe Doctrine.

In the Monroe Doctrine, President Monroe acknowledged Europe's colonies in the Western Hemisphere. However, the doctrine closed the hemisphere to any future colonization by European countries.

REVIEW What did President Monroe do to stop the growth of European colonies in the Americas?

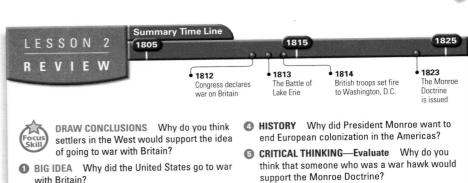

President Monroe sent a strong warning to European nations that had interests in the Western Hemisphere.

LESSON 2 REVIEW

Summary Time Line

1805 — 1815 — 1825

• 1812 Congress declares war on Britain

• 1813 The Battle of Lake Erie

• 1814 British troops set fire to Washington, D.C.

• 1823 The Monroe Doctrine is issued

 DRAW CONCLUSIONS Why do you think settlers in the West would support the idea of going to war with Britain?

❶ **BIG IDEA** Why did the United States go to war with Britain?

❷ **VOCABULARY** What clues can you use to remember the meaning of **nationalism**?

❸ **TIME LINE** When was the Battle of Lake Erie?

❹ **HISTORY** Why did President Monroe want to end European colonization in the Americas?

❺ **CRITICAL THINKING—Evaluate** Why do you think that someone who was a war hawk would support the Monroe Doctrine?

PERFORMANCE—Use the Internet Research the War of 1812 on the Internet to gain more information about it. Then share what you learned with your classmates.

394 ▪ Unit 5

The Age of Jackson

1780 1800 1820 1840 1860

The year 1826 marked the fiftieth anniversary of the Declaration of Independence. In that time the country had grown from the original 13 states to 24 states. Its land area had more than doubled in size. Ideas about democracy also were growing with the nation. In a **democracy** the people rule, and they are free to make choices about their lives and government.

Democracy Grows

In the early days of the country, voting was usually limited to property owners. In most of the new western states, such as Kentucky and Tennessee, this changed. Those states gave the vote to all white men, not just to those who owned property. This practice soon spread to all states. No other country in the world was so democratic, even though women and most free African Americans could not vote and Native Americans were not counted as citizens.

Once all white men could vote, there was a change in the kind of person elected. People elected as public officials were no longer always wealthy, well-educated men who owned property. Some, in fact, had little money or schooling. Davy Crockett, from Tennessee, was an example of this new kind of leader. Many people felt the frontier spirit of the United States was reflected in Davy Crockett's motto.

Davy Crockett started his political career in Lawrence County, Tennessee. The sketch shows the office he had there.

Chapter 11 ■ 395

DRAW CONCLUSIONS

As you read, draw conclusions about how the right of people to make decisions about government changed.

BIG IDEA
Important events took place while Andrew Jackson was President.

VOCABULARY
democracy
ruling

OBJECTIVES

■ Analyze the growth of democracy in the United States in the 1800s.

■ Describe major events in Andrew Jackson's presidency.

■ Explain the Indian Removal Act.

■ Analyze how the growth of the United States affected Native Americans.

 Draw Conclusions pp. 383, 395, 396, 399, 420

Vocabulary

SEE READING AND VOCABULARY TRANSPARENCY 5-10 OR THE WORD CARDS ON PP. V63–V64.

democracy p. 395
ruling p. 398

 When Minutes Count

Model for students how to turn headings into questions.

Heading–Democracy Grows

Question–How did democracy grow?

Then have pairs of students work together to write questions and answer them.

Quick Summary

This lesson describes the changes that took place in the United States during the presidency of Andrew Jackson.

1 Motivate

Set the Purpose

Big Idea Point out to students that when Andrew Jackson was President, the United States was still very young.

Access Prior Knowledge

Remind students that at this time the right to vote was limited to white males who owned property.

WORD WORK

Word Origins Have students find the word *democracy* in a dictionary. Ask them to look for the origin of the word. Students should find that *democracy* comes from the Greek word *demos*, meaning "the people."

BACKGROUND

The Right to Vote Inform students that the Fifteenth Amendment to the Constitution gave men of all races the right to vote in 1870. However, the right of African Americans to vote was not truly enforced until the 1960s. The Nineteenth Amendment gave women the right to vote in 1920.

Prediction Have students predict how people's idea of democracy changed during this period of time. Have students record their predictions and read the lesson to confirm whether or not their predictions are accurate.

● USE READING AND VOCABULARY TRANSPARENCY 5-10.

5-10
TRANSPARENCY

2 Teach

Democracy Grows

Read and Respond

Civics and Government Discuss with students why the type of people being elected to office changed when all white men were given the right to vote. Emphasize that people are often likely to vote for people like themselves. Ask students why this might be so. People might think that people like themselves will better represent their interests.

The Election of Andrew Jackson

Read and Respond

Geography Ask students to locate Tennessee and South Carolina on a map of the United States. Discuss why Tennessee was considered a western state in 1828. Next, ask students to locate Massachusetts and Virginia on the map. Emphasize that all of the Presidents before Andrew Jackson had come from those two states. Ask students to explain why this happened. Presidents probably came from these states because Massachusetts and Virginia had established governments and experienced leaders.

His motto was "Be always sure you're right—then go ahead!"

Davy Crockett held several local and state offices in Tennessee before winning a seat in the House of Representatives. When Crockett first ran for office, he had to say he knew nothing about government. "I had never read even a newspaper in my life," he said. Crockett learned about government by being part of it.

Andrew Jackson

REVIEW How did government change once all white men could vote?

🌎 **DRAW CONCLUSIONS** The men elected to public office were no longer always wealthy, well-educated property owners.

The Election of Andrew Jackson

In 1828 Andrew Jackson of Tennessee was elected the seventh President of the United States. The six Presidents before him had all come from families from either Massachusetts or Virginia. Now for the first time a person from a western state had been elected. It was also the first election in which all white American men could vote. Many of the new voters liked Jackson because they felt he was a "common man," like them.

Jackson was born in the backcountry of South Carolina to a poor family living in a log cabin. Tough and stubborn, Jackson taught himself law by reading books. In time he became a successful lawyer and later a judge.

While serving in the military, Jackson got the nickname "Old Hickory"—hickory being a very hard wood. "He's tough," said his soldiers, "tough as hickory." As a general during the War of 1812, Jackson

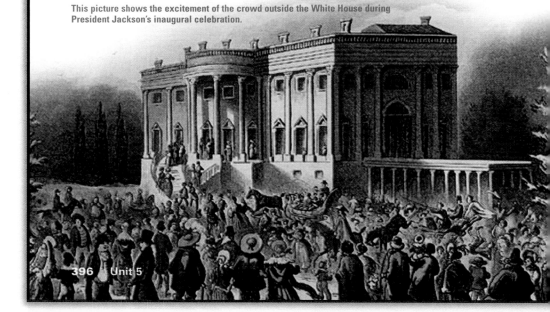

This picture shows the excitement of the crowd outside the White House during President Jackson's inaugural celebration.

396 Unit 5

Davy Crockett Davy Crockett served with General Andrew Jackson in the struggle with the Creek Nation in 1813. Historians think this experience broadened Crockett's view and led him to seek public office. Crockett served in the Tennessee legislature before entering Congress. He was defeated in his first bid for reelection to Congress but won again two years later. After his next defeat at the polls, Crockett went to Texas where he fought and died at the Alamo.

INTEGRATE READING

Read a Biography Encourage students to work with a librarian to find a biography of Davy Crockett at their reading level. Invite students to share what they learn from the biography with the class.

became a national hero after his troops beat the British at the Battle of New Orleans.

When Jackson became President on March 4, 1829, his followers were overjoyed. Thousands had streamed into Washington, D.C., for the inauguration. Many of them later showed up at the White House for the party that followed. Rough-and-tumble people from the frontier stood in their muddy boots on the satin-covered chairs to get a look at their hero. To keep from being crushed by the crowd, Jackson had to escape by a back door.

As President, Andrew Jackson continued to be both tough and stubborn. His view of politics soon came to be known as "Jacksonian democracy." According to Jackson, all American citizens needed to play a greater role in government. He did not believe that wealthy landowners should control the actions of the federal government. Many people living in new Western settlements agreed with Jackson's ideas. They believed that men who did not own property should be able to vote. Some wealthy people did not like Andrew Jackson because they feared he would work to end their power.

Andrew Jackson also fought to bring about an end to the Second Bank of the United States. In Jackson's eyes the bank

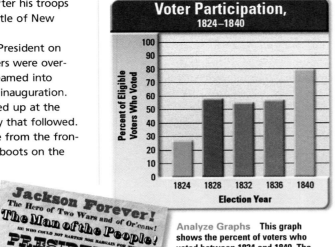

Voter Participation, 1824–1840

Percent of Eligible Voters Who Voted (y-axis: 0–100)
Election Year (x-axis: 1824, 1828, 1832, 1836, 1840)

Analyze Graphs This graph shows the percent of voters who voted between 1824 and 1840. The poster (left) helped persuade people to vote for Andrew Jackson.

◈ About what percent of voters voted in the election of 1828?

was a "hydra of corruption." A *hydra* is a many-headed monster from Greek mythology. The troubled First Bank of the United States, created while George Washington was President, had closed after the War of 1812. The Second Bank of the United States was started in 1816.

In spite of its success, Jackson believed the bank was too powerful. It controlled one-fifth of all the bank notes in the United States and one-third of all the nation's gold. Jackson argued that the bank put too much money power in the hands of the wealthy bank owners and a few rich customers and did not care about the needs of the general public.

REVIEW How did Andrew Jackson differ from earlier Presidents of the United States?
Before Jackson, all Presidents had come from families from either Massachusetts or Virginia; he was the first President from a western state.

Chapter 11 ■ 397

BACKGROUND

Jacksonian Democracy Many changes took place during Andrew Jackson's two terms as President. These changes created great regional and national tensions. Many people living in the West and in the nation's growing cities agreed with Jackson's policy of equal political power for all. Many people living in the South did not agree with the principles of Jacksonian democracy. Even Vice President John C. Calhoun disagreed with the President over new tariffs that affected Calhoun's home state of South Carolina.

INTEGRATE MATHEMATICS

Computation Ask students to calculate the length of time the Second Bank of the United States was in operation. The bank was started in 1816 and its charter expired in 1836. $1836 - 1816 = 20$ years

---

Visual Learning

Bar Graph Direct students' attention to the graph on page 397. Have students speculate why the percentage of voters rose significantly in 1828. Jackson was the popular choice for President, and this was the first time all white American men could vote. CAPTION ANSWER: about 58%

Analyze Primary Sources

Quotation Explain to students that President Jackson had very strong opinions about the Second Bank of the United States. Tell students to read the words of Andrew Jackson on page 397. Jackson was determined that a private monopolistic bank, independent of government regulation, should not be entrusted with public finances.

Q **What did Jackson mean when he called the bank a "hydra"?**

A A hydra is a many-headed monster from Greek mythology.

Read and Respond

Economics Explain to students that the closing of the Second Bank of the United States created many economic problems. The United States was struggling to find a stable currency. Point out that without a national banking system in place, a stable currency was difficult to maintain. Tell students that the 30 years after the Second Bank of the United States closed are referred to as the "dark decades of American banking" because people did not follow sound banking practices. During this period, it was easy for counterfeiters and speculators to take advantage of people.

Q **Why did President Jackson want the Second Bank to close?**

A President Jackson thought the bank was too powerful.

Indian Removal

Read and Respond

Civics and Government Discuss with students why President Jackson was able to ignore Justice John Marshall's ruling. Emphasize that Jackson had great support from the people who wanted to settle the frontier.

Q Why did Jackson ignore the Supreme Court's ruling?

A He had popular opinion and the Army on his side.

Visual Learning

Map Ask students to use their finger to trace the Trail of Tears. Encourage students to use the scale to calculate the distance of the journey.
CAPTION ANSWER: The Trail of Tears led to the Indian Territory in what is now the state of Oklahoma.

Read and Respond

Culture and Society Have students research some of the contributions made by Cherokees. Students may respond that the Cherokee built New Echota, they started schools and businesses, and the Cherokee leader Sequoyah created a Cherokee writing system. They also started a newspaper that was printed in both English and Cherokee.

3 Close

Summarize Key Content

- Most new western states gave all white men the right to vote, a practice that soon spread to all states.
- In 1828, Andrew Jackson became the first person from a western state to be elected President.
- President Jackson closed the Second Bank of the United States and forced many Native Americans to move west of the Mississippi River.

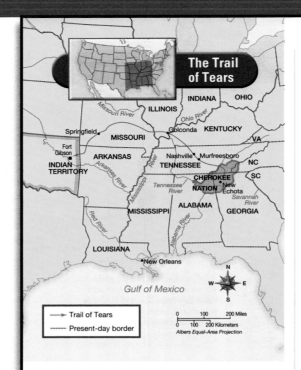

The Trail of Tears

Movement **This map shows the route that the Cherokees were forced to take.**
To where did the Trail of Tears lead?

Indian Removal

Jackson's toughness also meant harsh and unfair treatment of the Native Americans who lived east of the Mississippi River. In 1830 Congress passed the Indian Removal Act. It had been Jackson's idea. This act said that all Indians east of the Mississippi had to leave their lands and move west to the Indian Territory. This area spread across most of what is now the state of Oklahoma.

Many tribes refused to leave their homelands. Instead, some chose to stay and fight against the soldiers sent to remove them. Led by Chief Black Hawk,

the Sauk and Fox Indians in the Great Lakes region fought United States troops and Illinois militia in the Black Hawk War. In the southeastern United States, the Seminoles of Florida, led by Osceola and helped by runaway slaves, also fought United States troops. In both wars, many Native Americans were either killed or forced to leave their homeland.

Instead of fighting on the battlefield, the Cherokee nation chose to fight for its homeland in the United States courts. Led by Chief John Ross, the Cherokees were one of the richest tribes in the United States. They had many towns and villages throughout the Southeast, including New Echota (ih•KOH•tuh), Georgia, the capital of the Cherokee nation.

In a treaty signed in 1791, the United States government had recognized the Cherokee nation's independence. In 1828, however, the state of Georgia said that Cherokee laws were no longer in effect. As a result, when gold was discovered on Cherokee lands a year later, settlers were free to pour in and stake their claims.

By 1832 the Cherokees' case had gone all the way to the United States Supreme Court. There Chief Justice John Marshall gave the Court's **ruling**, or decision. He said that Georgia had no say over the Cherokee lands. The Court's ruling, however, was ignored, and federal troops were ordered to remove the Cherokees.

In late 1838 federal troops forced the last large group of Cherokees to leave their lands. They traveled from North Carolina and Georgia through Tennessee, Kentucky, Illinois, Missouri, and Arkansas—more than 800 miles (about 1,300 km)—to the Indian

BACKGROUND

New Echota, Georgia By the 1830s New Echota, the capital of the Cherokee republic, was a city like any other city in the United States. It had churches, businesses, and schools. It also had its own newspaper, the *Cherokee Phoenix*, which was printed in both English and Cherokee. Although spoken for hundreds of years, the Cherokee language was not written until 1821. In that year a Cherokee leader named Sequoyah (sih•KWOY•uh) created a writing system for it.

REACH ALL LEARNERS

Tactile Learners Some students may not be able to visualize the movement of Native Americans to the Indian Territory. Suggest that these students look at a map of the United States and trace the approximate routes taken by the Sauk and Fox, Seminole, and Cherokee Indians to the Indian Territory (Oklahoma).

This painting by Cherokee artist Troy Anderson shows a group of Cherokees on the Trail of Tears. The Cherokees were forced to walk a great distance to the Indian Territory during the cold winter months.

Territory. By the time their journey ended in March 1839, more than 4,000 Cherokees had died of cold, disease, and lack of food. The Cherokees called their long journey the "Trail Where They Cried." It later became known as the Trail of Tears.

REVIEW How was the way in which the Cherokees fought the loss of their land different from that of other Indian tribes?
The Cherokees fought for their lands in the courts instead of on the battlefield.

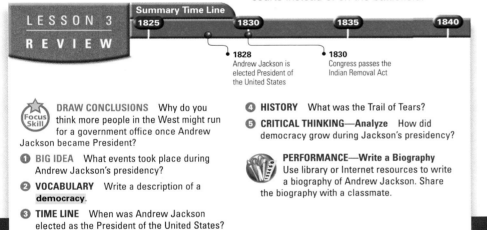

LESSON 3 REVIEW

Summary Time Line

1825 — 1830 — 1835 — 1840

- 1828 Andrew Jackson is elected President of the United States
- 1830 Congress passes the Indian Removal Act

 DRAW CONCLUSIONS Why do you think more people in the West might run for a government office once Andrew Jackson became President?

❶ **BIG IDEA** What events took place during Andrew Jackson's presidency?

❷ **VOCABULARY** Write a description of a **democracy**.

❸ **TIME LINE** When was Andrew Jackson elected as the President of the United States?

❹ **HISTORY** What was the Trail of Tears?

❺ **CRITICAL THINKING—Analyze** How did democracy grow during Jackson's presidency?

PERFORMANCE—Write a Biography Use library or Internet resources to write a biography of Andrew Jackson. Share the biography with a classmate.

Chapter 11 ▪ 399

EXTEND AND ENRICH

Research Indian Tribes Divide the class into small groups. Tell students that each group will select an Indian tribe of the Southeast to research. Groups may select from the following: Cherokees, Seminoles, Choctaws, Chickasaws, and Creeks. Tell each group to find information about its tribe's culture, history, and contributions. Have each group share its information with the class.

RETEACH THE LESSON

Graphic Organizer Have students complete the following chart, listing major events of Andrew Jackson's presidency.

Indian Removal Act

Andrew Jackson's presidency

Closed the Second Bank of the United States

Prediction Have students recall their predictions from the beginning of the lesson, and allow time for them to correct their predictions, if needed. Students should note that people's idea of democracy changed during this period of time as states gave the vote to all white men and new kinds of leaders were elected.

● USE READING AND VOCABULARY TRANSPARENCY 5-10.

5-10 TRANSPARENCY

Assess

Lesson 3 Review—Answers

 DRAW CONCLUSIONS Andrew Jackson was from the West and probably inspired people from that area to become involved in government.

❶ **BIG IDEA** Andrew Jackson closed the Second Bank of the United States and Congress passed the Indian Removal Act.

❷ **VOCABULARY** A **democracy** is a representative form of government in which the people rule.

❸ **TIME LINE** 1828.

❹ **HISTORY** The Trail of Tears is the name given to the Cherokees' journey from Georgia to the Indian Territory.

❺ **CRITICAL THINKING—Analyze** During Jackson's presidency more "common" people became involved in government, helping democracy grow.

Performance Assessment Guidelines Students' biographies of Andrew Jackson should be clearly written and include the major events in his life. Students' work should include a bibliography.

ACTIVITY BOOK

Use ACTIVITY BOOK, p.106, to reinforce and extend student learning.

Examine Primary Sources

PAGES 400–401

OBJECTIVES

- Identify paintings made by John James Audubon.
- Explain the importance of Audubon's paintings to our understanding of several bird species.

1 Motivate

Set the Purpose

John James Audubon helped document birds in North America by traveling the land and painting hundreds of pictures of them in their natural habitats. By studying the Audubon paintings pictured on these pages, students will better understand North American birds.

Access Prior Knowledge

Remind students that extinct animals are species that no longer have any living members. Have students identify animals they know to be extinct. Answers may include dinosaurs and other prehistoric species.

2 Teach

Read and Respond

Have students study each of the four species of birds pictured on pages 400–401. Ask volunteers to compare each kind of bird with the others.

EXAMINE
PRIMARY SOURCES
Audubon's Paintings

John James Audubon was a gifted artist born in 1785 in what is now Haiti. During his life, Audubon observed and painted hundreds of pictures of birds and other wildlife. Some, such as those pictured on these pages, are now extinct. Audubon's attention to detail gives people today the opportunity to see animals they can no longer find in North America. Audubon's work inspired George Bird Grinnell to establish the National Audubon Society in 1886. The society works to conserve nature.

FROM THE EWELL SALE STEWART LIBRARY AND THE ACADEMY OF NATURAL SCIENCES

John James Audubon

Carolina Parrot
Because they were used as a source for feathers to decorate hats, Carolina parrots were extinct by 1920.

400 ■ Unit 5

BACKGROUND

More About the Time At one time, passenger pigeons were among the most numerous birds in eastern North America. Scientists think that their total population may have reached as many as 5 billion. Several factors, including increased hunting of the species, led to the extinction of the passenger pigeon.

In addition, people cut down the great oak and beech forests where the passenger pigeons nested. The last passenger pigeon, a bird named Martha, died at the Cincinnati Zoo on September 1, 1914, at approximately 1:00 P.M. This may be the only species whose exact time of extinction is known.

Pied Duck
The last recorded sighting of a pied, or labrador, duck was in 1878 in Elmira, New York.

Passenger Pigeon
Hunted for food, the last passenger pigeon died in 1914.

ACTIVITY

Compare and Contrast Keep a journal for one week of the kinds of birds that you notice in your yard or on the schoolgrounds. Write or draw details that are unique to each kind of bird you see. Share your observations with the class. How are your observations alike? How are they different?

Audubon kept drawings in this box.

Analyze the Primary Source

❶ What do the paintings tell you about the environment in which each bird lived? Look at the bills of each of the birds shown here. Why might different birds need bills that are suited for their different environments?

❷ Why do you think people chose to use the feathers from the Carolina Parrot?

❸ Why do you think people might be interested in studying Audubon's bird paintings?

Great Auk
The Great Auk was the last flightless seabird of the Northern Hemisphere. The last two confirmed adults were killed in 1844.

RESEARCH

 Visit The Learning Site at **www.harcourtschool.com** to research other primary sources.

Chapter 11 ▪ 401

Analyze the Primary Source
Answers

❶ Some birds lived by the water, others lived in trees or forests. Birds eat different kinds of foods in different environments; their bills help them eat foods unique to their environments.

❷ They might have used the feathers because they were full or colorful.

❸ By studying Audubon's bird paintings, people can learn more about birds of the past.

3 Close

Activity

Compare and Contrast Ask students to identify the names of the birds on their lists, while a volunteer adds each name to a master list on the board. Then, for each name, ask students to raise their hands if that name appears on their lists, too. Have the volunteer count the hands, then list by the name the total number of students who saw that bird in the past week. When the master list is complete, ask students to identify the most common birds in their neighborhood, based on the number of sightings.

Research

Students will find a variety of paintings at The Learning Site at **www.harcourtschool.com.**

Ask students to select one of the paintings displayed at the site. Have them study the painting, then ask them to describe what the painting depicts.

INTERNET RESOURCES

THE LEARNING SITE Go to **www.harcourtschool.com** for a DIRECTORY OF PRIMARY SOURCES.

Lesson 4

OBJECTIVES

- Analyze the westward expansion of the United States.
- Describe Texas's fight for independence.
- Identify routes used by settlers moving west.
- Analyze reasons people moved west.
- Explain the events leading to the Mexican Cession and the Gadsden Purchase.
- Analyze the migration of people to California during the gold rush.

 Draw Conclusions pp. 383, 402, 403, 405, 409, 420

Vocabulary

SEE READING AND VOCABULARY TRANSPARENCY 5-11 OR THE WORD CARDS ON PP. V65–V66.

manifest destiny p. 402	**gold rush** p. 409
dictator p. 402	**forty-niner** p. 409
cession p. 407	

 When Minutes Count

Ask students to write down the lesson vocabulary terms and their definitions. Then read aloud the Big Idea statement. Ask volunteers to explain how each term relates to the Big Idea of the lesson.

Quick Summary

This lesson examines how the United States grew to reach from the Atlantic Ocean to the Pacific Ocean in the 1800s.

 **Motivate**

Set the Purpose

Big Idea Discuss ways in which a country can expand its borders.

 DRAW CONCLUSIONS
As you read, draw conclusions about why Americans settled new lands.

BIG IDEA
The United States expanded its borders westward in the 1800s.

VOCABULARY
manifest destiny
dictator
cession
gold rush
forty-niner

From Ocean to Ocean

1780	1800	1820	1840	1860

1820–1850

Americans in the early 1800s began to push beyond the nation's borders. They looked to the Spanish colony of Texas, to the Oregon Country in the Pacific Northwest, and to other western lands. In 1845 the words **manifest destiny** were heard for the first time. These words referred to the belief shared by many Americans that the United States should one day stretch from the Atlantic Ocean to the Pacific Ocean.

Americans in Early Texas

In 1820 a Missouri businessperson named Moses Austin asked Spanish leaders in Mexico to let him start a colony in Texas so that people from the United States could settle there. The Spanish leaders agreed to let Austin start a colony, but he died before he could carry out his plan. Stephen F. Austin, Moses Austin's son, took up his father's plan and started the colony. He chose an area between the Brazos and Colorado Rivers. Americans began to settle there in 1821.

That same year Mexico won its independence from Spain. At first the new Mexican government left the Americans alone. As more Americans arrived in Texas, however, the Mexican government became worried. In 1830 it passed a law stopping more Americans from settling in Texas. Mexican leaders also insisted that settlers already in Texas obey Mexico's laws and pay more taxes. This made the Americans angry.

In 1834 General Antonio López de Santa Anna took over the Mexican government and made himself **dictator**, a leader who has complete control of the government. Santa Anna sent troops to Texas to enforce Mexican laws. The American settlers, called Anglos, and many Tejanos (tay•HAH•nohs)—the

Stephen F. Austin started the first American colony in Texas. In the colony's early years, he served as leader, lawmaker, judge, and commander of the military. Present-day Austin, Texas, was named for him.

402 ■ Unit 5

WORD WORK

Preview Vocabulary Ask volunteers to define each vocabulary term. If students are unable to define a term, encourage them to use the term's context in the lesson to decipher the meaning. Tell students that some terms, such as *manifest destiny,* are used only to describe certain events in history.

BACKGROUND

Manifest Destiny Explain that the term *manifest destiny* was originally coined by John L. O'Sullivan, a New York City journalist. In 1845 he wrote, "Our manifest destiny is to overspread the continent allotted by Providence for the free development of our yearly multiplying millions."

settlers from Mexico who lived in Texas—were angered by Santa Anna's actions. As a result, fighting broke out. Both groups living in Texas revolted against the Mexican government.

On November 3, 1835, Texas leaders met to organize a temporary government. They wanted to drive out Santa Anna's army, so they ordered Texas soldiers to attack the Mexican troops at San Antonio on December 5, 1835. After four days of fighting, the Mexican troops gave up. Santa Anna was so angry that he marched to San Antonio himself with thousands of soldiers to take back the city.

Texans in San Antonio took shelter behind the walls of a Spanish mission called the Alamo. Among them were Americans who had come to Texas to help them in their fight for freedom. They included James Bowie, Davy Crockett, and their commander, William B. Travis.

Santa Anna's forces attacked the Alamo on February 23, 1836. When it finally fell on March 6, all 189 Texans and their supporters had been killed. Only women and children survived.

On March 2, as the battle at the Alamo raged on, Texas leaders met to declare their independence and set up the Republic of Texas. They chose David G. Burnet as president of the new nation and Sam Houston as commander of the army.

On April 21, 1836, Houston's army took the Mexicans by surprise at the Battle of San Jacinto (hah•SEEN•toh). With the battle cry "Remember the Alamo!" the Texans beat the Mexican army and captured Santa Anna. In return for their sparing his life, Santa Anna agreed to grant Texas its independence. Texas remained an independent republic until it became part of the United States in 1845.

REVIEW When did Texas become a republic? on March 2, 1836

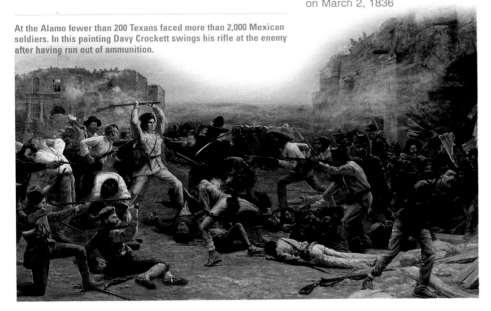
At the Alamo fewer than 200 Texans faced more than 2,000 Mexican soldiers. In this painting Davy Crockett swings his rifle at the enemy after having run out of ammunition.

READING SKILL

Draw Conclusions Ask students to answer the following questions after they have read the subsection Americans in Early Texas.

1. **Why was the Mexican government worried about more Americans settling in Texas?** because strong ties to the United States would conflict with their allegiance to Mexico

2. **Why were the Texas settlers angry about having to obey Mexico's laws?** They did not want to be ruled by Mexico or pay taxes to Mexico.

INTEGRATE LANGUAGES

Research Spanish Place-Names Ask students to research how strong the influence of Spanish is on place-names in Texas. Have them develop lists of Spanish place-names and, where possible, give the English equivalent of these names.

Access Prior Knowledge

Ask students to suggest reasons why Americans moved west. Students may respond that they wanted land or new opportunities.

READING SOCIAL STUDIES

K-W-L Chart Have students fill in a K-W-L chart before they begin reading and then add to it as they read the lesson.

What I Know	What I Want to Know	What I Learned
People moved west to find land and gold.	Where did they find gold?	

● USE READING AND VOCABULARY TRANSPARENCY 5-11.

5-11 TRANSPARENCY

2 Teach

Americans in Early Texas

Read and Respond

Geography Ask students to look at a map of Texas and find the Colorado and Brazos Rivers. Point out that Stephen F. Austin chose a site between these rivers for his colony.

History Discuss the events that led to Texas independence. Explain that the Mexican army occupied the Alamo before Texas soldiers drove the army from San Antonio in December 1835. The Texans then occupied the former mission and strengthened its defenses prior to their battle with Santa Anna. Have students conclude why the Alamo inspired other settlers to continue to fight for independence rather than give up.

Q What does the fight at the Alamo tell you about the Americans who settled Texas?

A They were probably fiercely independent and determined.

Visual Learning

Map Have students trace the routes of Santa Anna and Sam Houston on the map. Challenge them to draw conclusions about why Santa Anna wanted to keep that territory for Mexico.

Q Did the Republic of Texas include the same land area as the state of Texas does today?

A no, only a portion of it
CAPTION ANSWER: Gonzales, San Jacinto

Read and Respond

Civics and Government Inform students that after Texas gained its independence, many Texans wanted Texas to be annexed by the United States. Explain that the United States was reluctant to accept Texas as a state because it would be a slave state and because the annexation of Texas could start a war with Mexico.

History Have students do research to locate and differentiate between primary and secondary sources to acquire more information about Texas and its history. Encourage students to use both primary sources and secondary sources, such as computer software; interviews; biographies; artifacts; and oral, print, and visual materials.

 Students might also enjoy going online to learn more about Texas and its history, landmarks, and people. Have them visit The Learning Site at **www.harcourtschool.com**.

Trails West

Read and Respond

Geography and Economics Tell students that the Santa Fe Trail split—the main trail followed the Arkansas River to La Junta, Colorado, and then to Santa Fe, and the other one cut across the Cimarron Desert to Santa Fe. Explain that the route through the desert was shorter but more dangerous. Ask students why some traders took the shorter route despite the risks. They wanted the economic advantage of being first.

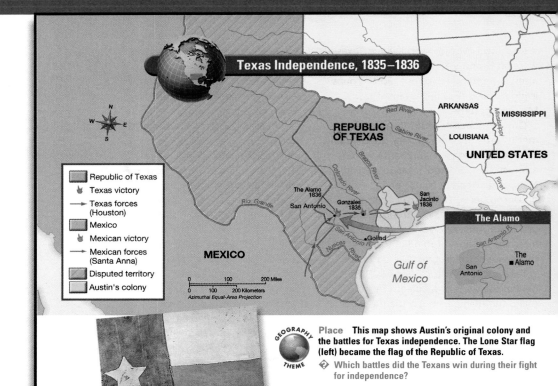

Texas Independence, 1835–1836

Republic of Texas
Texas victory
Texas forces (Houston)
Mexico
Mexican victory
Mexican forces (Santa Anna)
Disputed territory
Austin's colony

The Alamo

Place This map shows Austin's original colony and the battles for Texas independence. The Lone Star flag (left) became the flag of the Republic of Texas.

◇ Which battles did the Texans win during their fight for independence?

Trails West

The same year that the first settlers from the United States traveled to Texas, a Missouri trader named William Becknell opened the Santa Fe Trail. This trail ran from Independence, Missouri, to the city of Santa Fe in New Mexico and covered a distance of 780 miles (1,255 km). By the 1850s, many people were using the trail to travel west. A new part of the trail, called the Old Spanish Trail, linked Santa Fe to Los Angeles in California.

In 1834 Christian missionaries pushed into the Oregon Country. This region in the Pacific Northwest was claimed by both the United States and Britain. It included what are now Oregon, Washington, Idaho, western Montana, and western Wyoming.

Travelers in the West wrote about the new lands. One settler named Narcissa Whitman wrote letters about the beautiful valleys and rich soil of the Oregon Country. Her letters were later published, and by 1842 they had attracted a large group of settlers to the region. An explorer named John C. Fremont also wrote about his travels with a guide named Kit Carson. Many people read Fremont's writings about Oregon and California.

MENTAL MAPPING

State Location Challenge students to identify the five states that were once part of Oregon Country by completing the following graphic organizer.

Washington		Montana
	Idaho	
Oregon		Wyoming

REACH ALL LEARNERS

Advanced Learners Have students choose a settlement in the Oregon Country to research. Ask them to make posters showing what the settlement looked like, who lived there, and what the people did. Invite students to share their posters with the class.

Travelers to the Oregon Country usually gathered in St. Louis, Missouri. From St. Louis they traveled up the Missouri River to Independence, Missouri. In Independence they joined wagon trains to cross the Great Plains and the Rocky Mountains.

The route they followed came to be called the Oregon Trail. It led northwest from Independence to the Platte River. From the Platte, it cut through the Rocky Mountains and crossed the Continental Divide. Then the trail followed the Snake and Columbia Rivers and ended at the Willamette (wuh•LA•muht) Valley in present-day Oregon.

The Oregon Trail was more than 2,000 miles (about 3,200 km) long. The journey could take as long as six months, and there were many hardships along the way. Yet many reached Oregon, and settlements there grew quickly.

The United States wanted to set up a clear border between itself and British Canada. For a long time, it looked as if arguments over the Oregon Country

This painting shows settlers gathered in St. Louis, Missouri, which came to be called the Gateway to the West.

might cause yet another war between the United States and Britain. Finally, in 1846, President James K. Polk agreed to divide the Oregon Country with Britain and signed a treaty fixing the 49th parallel as the dividing border.

REVIEW Why might settlers have been eager to travel along the Oregon Trail?

DRAW CONCLUSIONS in order to reach new lands and begin settlements

• BIOGRAPHY •

Narcissa Prentiss Whitman 1808–1847

Character Trait: Courage

Narcissa Whitman was one of the first white women to travel west along what would become the Oregon Trail. While on her travels, she began to write her family a series of letters describing her new life. The letters, covering a span of 11 years, told of Narcissa's adventures—both good and bad—living in the American West. Upon her death these letters were published, inspiring young women across America to make the journey on the Oregon Trail.

GO ONLINE MULTIMEDIA BIOGRAPHIES
Visit The Learning Site at www.harcourtschool.com to learn about other famous people.

Chapter 11   405

Mormons Settle Utah

Visual Learning

Map Ask students to find the Platte and Arkansas Rivers on the map. Explain that often rivers were used as transportation.

Q **What other reason would make settlers want to be near water?**

A Drinking water is necessary for people and animals.

CAPTION ANSWER: California Trail

Read and Respond

Culture and Society Explain that many people were opposed to the Mormons because of their beliefs. Others opposed them because they were afraid of the economic competition that could come from such a large, united group. Have students discuss other groups of people, both historical and contemporary, whose beliefs have made them the target of discrimination.

Q **How did the Mormons turn a negative experience into a positive one?**

A Although they lost their leader, they quickly found a new one. They found a new place to live where no one would bother them and, sustained by their faith, they turned a desert into a garden.

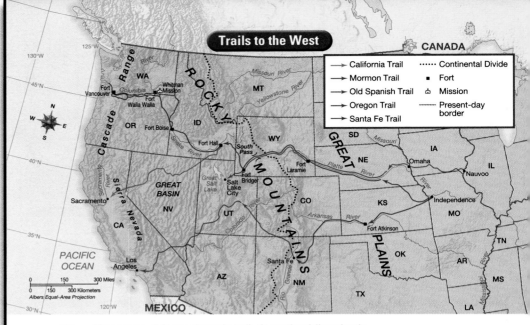

Trails to the West

Legend:
- → California Trail
- → Mormon Trail
- → Old Spanish Trail
- → Oregon Trail
- → Santa Fe Trail
- ······ Continental Divide
- ■ Fort
- ⌂ Mission
- ---- Present-day border

GEOGRAPHY THEME

Movement This map shows the trails that settlers followed to the West.

❖ Which trail led to Sacramento, California?

Mormons Settle Utah

In the 1840s the Mormons, or members of the Church of Jesus Christ of Latter-day Saints, joined the many Americans traveling west. The Mormons and their leader, Joseph Smith, had settled in the town of Nauvoo (naw•VOO), Illinois. Their beliefs caused problems with other settlers, however, and in 1844 an angry crowd killed Joseph Smith.

When Brigham Young became the new leader of the Mormons, he decided that they should move to a place where no one would bother them. In 1846 Young and the first group of

Mormons set out for the Rocky Mountains. In July 1847 the Mormons reached the Great Salt Lake in the Great Basin. Young said, "This is the place!"

The Great Basin was such a harsh land that Brigham Young thought no other settlers would want it. He used words from the Bible to tell his followers, "We will make this desert blossom as the rose." To do so, one of the first things the Mormons did was build irrigation canals. The canals brought water from the surrounding mountains and made the dry land suitable for farming.

Brigham Young

406 ■ Unit 5

BACKGROUND

The Mormons The Mormon settlement in Nauvoo, Illinois, maintained its own militia and its own laws. By 1842 it was the largest town in Illinois. The Mormons in Nauvoo prospered, but they deliberately isolated themselves from their neighbors in the town. After Joseph Smith's death, Brigham Young led a group of Mormons to the Great Salt Lake valley in present-day Utah. Utah was admitted as a state in 1896.

INTEGRATE SCIENCE

Research Weather and Climate Remind students that Brigham Young believed that Salt Lake City was the right place for the Mormons because its inhospitable climate would not attract many other settlers. Have students research the climate and weather in Salt Lake City. Discuss with students whether they would like to live in a place with that type of climate.

INTEGRATE MATHEMATICS

Calculate Averages Present students with the following information, and have them answer the question. In 1848 there were 2,000 Mormons living in Utah. Over the next 12 years, 38,000 more Mormons came to settle there. What was the average number of newcomers each year from 1849 to 1860? approximately 3,167 people

The Great Salt Lake region grew fast. It soon became known as the Utah Territory. Brigham Young became the territory's first governor.

REVIEW What was one of the first things the Mormons did once they settled in the Great Basin? They built irrigation canals.

War with Mexico

The land the Mormons settled and the rest of the lands west of Texas belonged to Mexico. Only a few months later, most of those places would become part of the United States.

The United States and Mexico did not agree on where the border between Texas and Mexico was. The United States wanted the Rio Grande as the border, but Mexico believed its lands went farther north. When Mexican troops crossed the Rio Grande in April 1846 and fought with an American patrol, President James K. Polk asked Congress to declare war on Mexico.

The United States invaded Mexico in 1847. Federal troops led by General Winfield Scott captured Mexico City.

After more than a year of fighting, the United States won the war.

In February 1848 the United States and Mexico formally ended the war by signing the Treaty of Guadalupe Hidalgo (gwah•dah•LOO•pay ee•DAHL•goh). Under the treaty's terms, Mexico had to give up all claims to southern Texas and give the United States a huge region known as the Mexican Cession. A **cession**, or concession, is something given up. The Mexican Cession included all of present-day California, Nevada, and Utah and parts of Arizona, Colorado, New Mexico, and Wyoming. In return, the United States paid Mexico $15 million.

In 1853 James Gadsden, the United States minister to Mexico, arranged to buy more of Arizona and New Mexico. This land became known as the Gadsden Purchase. The Gadsden Purchase brought the continental United States, or the part of the United States between Canada and Mexico, to its present size. It also set the current border between the United States and Mexico.

REVIEW How did the United States benefit from the Treaty of Guadalupe Hidalgo?

During the Mexican-American War, American forces captured the Spanish town of Monterey, California.

Mexico had to surrender all claims to southern Texas and give to the United States the huge region known as the Mexican Cession.

Chapter 11 ■ 407

War with Mexico

Read and Respond

History Explain that President Polk's desire to extend the United States to the Pacific Ocean was an important element leading to war with Mexico. So was the disputed Texas border. Have students complete the following graphic organizer about the Mexican-American War.

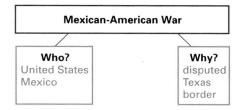

Mexican-American War	
Who? United States Mexico	**Why?** disputed Texas border

Geography Have students look at a map of the United States. Ask them to locate the following states that were acquired as part of the Mexican Cession: California, Nevada, Utah, and parts of Arizona, Colorado, New Mexico, and Wyoming.

Q How do you think the American settlers felt about the American victory in the war with Mexico?

A relieved and excited about acquiring new lands for the United States

Next, have students locate the areas that were acquired in the Gadsden Purchase: southern Arizona and southern New Mexico. Remind students that the United States paid $0.33 per acre for the land in the Mexican Cession.

BACKGROUND

New Mexico Before the lands in the North American West became part of the United States, their governance often changed. For example, the Spanish claimed the area of New Mexico in 1539, but were driven out by Native Americans in 1680. In 1692, the Spanish returned, but by 1821 the region became a province of Mexico. Just twenty years later the area was taken over by the independent country of Texas. It was not until 1850 that the United States Congress claimed New Mexico as a territory.

INTEGRATE HEALTH

Disease Tell students that during the war with Mexico, the United States lost 12,000 soldiers, but fewer than 1,800 of them died in battle. Ask students to brainstorm how the other 10,000 may have died. Inform students that they were killed in accidents, by execution, or by disease and illness. Point out that an outbreak of smallpox was responsible for many deaths.

The California Gold Rush

Read and Respond

Geography Have students use a map or globe to locate Cape Horn on the tip of South America. Discuss why people in a hurry traveled around Cape Horn rather than across the western lands.

3 | Close

Summarize Key Content

- Texas gained independence from Mexico on April 21, 1836.
- Thousands of settlers followed the Santa Fe and Oregon Trails westward.
- The Mormons settled at the Great Salt Lake in the Great Basin in 1847.
- The Mexican-American War led to the Mexican Cession by which the United States acquired from Mexico most of the land in the present-day southwestern United States.
- More than 80,000 gold seekers arrived in California in 1849.

• GEOGRAPHY •

Marshall Gold Discovery State Historic Park

Understanding Places and Regions

While building a sawmill in the winter of 1848, James Marshall discovered gold in a nearby riverbed. By 1849, Marshall's find set off one of the largest migrations in history—the California gold rush of 1849. People came from all over the United States in wagons. Some even sailed around the southern tip of South America to reach California.

In time, people from all over the world knew of Marshall's discovery, moving to California with the hope of striking it rich. Today, the site of Marshall's discovery is located inside the Marshall Gold Discovery State Historic Park in Coloma, California.

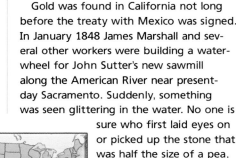

The California Gold Rush

In the 1840s California was a land of large ranches and a few small towns, such as Monterey and Los Angeles. By 1847 San Francisco had only 800 people. However, that quickly changed when gold was found.

Gold was found in California not long before the treaty with Mexico was signed. In January 1848 James Marshall and several other workers were building a waterwheel for John Sutter's new sawmill along the American River near present-day Sacramento. Suddenly, something was seen glittering in the water. No one is sure who first laid eyes on or picked up the stone that was half the size of a pea, but James Marshall said that he was the one.

This painting shows people digging for gold during the California gold rush. Looking for gold was hard work.

408 ■ Unit 5

"It made my heart thump, for I was certain it was gold," he remembered.

The finding of gold in California set off a **gold rush**, a sudden rush of new people to an area where gold has been found. Within a year, more than 80,000 gold seekers arrived in California. They came from Europe and Asia as well as from other parts of the United States.

The gold seekers began calling themselves **forty-niners** because they had arrived in the year 1849. Many forty-niners made their way west on the Oregon Trail, cutting south on the Old Spanish Trail across the Nevada desert and through the passes of the Sierra Nevada. This trip often took three months or longer. Others traveled to California by sailing around Cape Horn

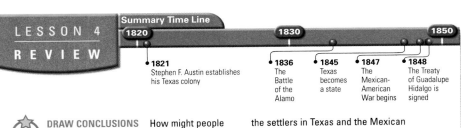

The discovery of gold brought many people to California.

at the southern tip of South America and then north along the Pacific coast. That journey often took six to eight months. Clipper ships, the fastest ships of the time, could make the same trip in just three to four months. However, travel by clipper ship cost too much for most forty-niners.

A few lucky forty-niners struck it rich, but most did not. While some returned home empty-handed, many stayed and settled in California. It is estimated that California's population grew by 100,000 people by the end of 1849. In 1850, only two years after Marshall's discovery of gold at Sutter's Mill, California became a state.

REVIEW Why did gold seekers in California call themselves forty-niners?
because they had arrived in the year 1849

LESSON 4 REVIEW

Summary Time Line

1820 — 1830 — 1850

• 1821 Stephen F. Austin establishes his Texas colony

• 1836 The Battle of the Alamo
• 1845 Texas becomes a state
• 1847 The Mexican-American War begins
• 1848 The Treaty of Guadalupe Hidalgo is signed

 DRAW CONCLUSIONS How might people traveling west influence the kinds of items that were manufactured?

❶ **BIG IDEA** How did the United States expand its borders in the 1800s?

❷ **VOCABULARY** Make a word web that shows how **gold rush** and **forty-niner** are related.

❸ **TIME LINE** What happened in 1836?

❹ **HISTORY** What caused the conflicts between the settlers in Texas and the Mexican government?

❺ **CRITICAL THINKING—Hypothesize** What might have happened if gold had not been discovered in California?

PERFORMANCE—Write a List Imagine that you are going to travel on the Oregon Trail. Make a list of items that you will take on your journey.

Chapter 11 ■ 409

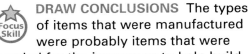

OBJECTIVES

- **Identify borders on a map.**
- **Apply critical thinking skills to organize and use information from maps.**
- **Use historical maps to collect data about the past.**

1 Motivate

Why It Matters

Explain to students that historical maps can help them learn how places have changed over time. Emphasize the importance of being able to correctly identify borders on a map. Point out that the borders of countries all over the world have changed many times throughout history and that historical maps can be used to see those changes.

· SKILLS ·

MAP AND GLOBE

Identify Changing Borders

➡ WHY IT MATTERS

Historical maps give important information about places as they were in the past. By studying a historical map, you can see how a place and its borders have changed over time. Seeing those changes on a historical map can help you better understand the changes and how they came about.

➡ WHAT YOU NEED TO KNOW

In this chapter you read about the United States and the different countries that have controlled lands west of the Mississippi River. You also read about events that changed borders in the continental United States over time. The map on page 411 uses different colors to show how those borders changed over nearly 70 years. It uses labels to identify the different regions and to give the year in which each one became a part of the United States.

➡ PRACTICE THE SKILL

Use the historical map on page 411 to answer the following questions.

1. What color shows land that was acquired by the United States in 1803?
2. In what year did the United States win control of the Oregon Territory?
3. When did the United States get the land where the states of California and Nevada are now?

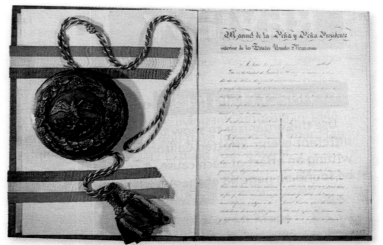

The Treaty of Guadalupe Hidalgo ended the Mexican-American War. Mexico agreed to give up the lands that came to be called the Mexican Cession, and, in return, the United States agreed to pay Mexico $15 million.

MAKE IT RELEVANT

In Your Community Invite a local historian to talk with students. Ask him or her to talk about the history of your community and, if possible, show a historical map. Have students prepare in advance several questions to ask the historian about the community.

REACH ALL LEARNERS

Advanced Learners For students who are interested in learning more about the history of their state, have them research and present an oral report. They can use local library resources or the Internet to find a historical map of their state. Have students describe the state as it once was and tell about some of the changes that have occurred over time.

MENTAL MAPPING

Regions of the United States Provide each student with a blank map of the United States. After students have had a chance to look closely at the map on page 411, ask them to re-create the map without looking at their books. Encourage them to look on the blank map for landmarks such as the Mississippi River to help them identify the regions.

The Growth of the United States

RUSSIA

ALASKA PURCHASE 1867

CANADA

0 200 400 Miles
0 400 Kilometers

PACIFIC OCEAN

CANADA

TREATY WITH BRITAIN 1842

—— Present-day border

0 200 400 Miles
0 200 400 Kilometers
Albers Equal-Area Projection

TREATY WITH BRITAIN 1818

OREGON TERRITORY 1846

Lake Superior

Lake Huron

Lake Michigan

Lake Ontario
Lake Erie

40°N

LOUISIANA PURCHASE 1803

40°N

MEXICAN CESSION 1848

UNITED STATES 1783

ATLANTIC OCEAN

70°W

PACIFIC OCEAN

40°N

30°N

GADSDEN PURCHASE 1853

TEXAS ANNEXATION 1845

1810

1812

1813

FLORIDA 1819

30°N

120°W

HAWAII ANNEXATION 1898

PACIFIC OCEAN

MEXICO

Gulf of Mexico

90°W

80°W

N
W E
S

0 100 Miles
0 100 Kilometers

❹ What area did the United States get in 1842 as the result of a treaty with Britain?

❺ In what year did the Gadsden Purchase become part of the United States?

❻ In what year did the Texas Annexation take place?

❼ When did Alaska become part of the United States?

➡ APPLY WHAT YOU LEARNED

The map on this page lets you identify the changing borders of the United States. You can also see changes by comparing two maps. On a sheet of paper, draw a map showing the borders of the United States in 1803. Then draw another map showing the borders of the United States in 1848. Find the information in this chapter that explains the difference between the two maps.

Practice your map and globe skills with the **GeoSkills CD-ROM.**

Chapter 11 ■ 411

MAP AND GLOBE SKILLS

---

2 Teach

What You Need to Know

Have students look at the map key to identify how the map uses colors. Explain that the colors show how the borders of the United States have changed over time. Encourage students to find on the map the region their state belongs to. Ask students to determine what year this region became a part of the United States.

Practice the Skill—Answers

❶ yellow
❷ 1846
❸ 1848
❹ the northern part of what is now Maine
❺ 1853
❻ 1845
❼ 1867

3 Close

Apply What You Learned

Students should draw two separate maps, one showing the borders of the United States in 1803 and another showing the borders in 1848. Students should compare their two maps and note the differences.

OBJECTIVES

■ Analyze the changes in the United States brought about by the Industrial Revolution.

■ Analyze how the transportation of goods changed during the nineteenth century.

■ Analyze how mass production and interchangeable parts affected the economy of the United States.

Draw Conclusions pp. 383, 412, 416, 419, 420

Vocabulary

SEE READING AND VOCABULARY TRANSPARENCY 5-12 OR THE WORD CARDS ON PP. V65–V68.

industrial revolution p. 412	**mass production** p. 418
investor p. 414	**supply** p. 418
textile p. 416	**cotton gin** p. 418
interchangeable parts p. 418	**demand** p. 418
	patent p. 419

 When Minutes Count

Ask students to skim the lesson to find the names of two inventions.

Quick Summary

This lesson examines the new technologies that were developed during the Industrial Revolution.

 Motivate

Set the Purpose

Big Idea Make sure students understand the term *technology*.

Access Prior Knowledge

Ask students how products were manufactured in the early United States.

DRAW CONCLUSIONS

As you read, draw conclusions about how new technologies caused changes.

BIG IDEA

The development of new technology changed life in the United States in the first half of the 1800s.

VOCABULARY

industrial revolution
investor
textile
interchangeable parts
mass production
supply
cotton gin
demand
patent

412 ■ Unit 5

An Industrial Revolution

| 1780 | 1800 | 1820 | 1840 | 1860 |

1810–1850

The first half of the 1800s saw a rush of new things and a feeling of confidence in the United States. The country seemed to have met its "manifest destiny," as it now stretched from sea to sea. Nothing seemed too difficult as Americans overcame one problem after another. As the country continued to grow, other important changes were taking place. New inventions changed the way goods were made. People began using machines instead of hand tools. This industrial revolution changed the way people in the United States lived, traveled, and worked.

New Roads

Americans badly needed good roads in the early 1800s. Most roads were dirt paths full of tree stumps and holes. When it rained, these roads sometimes turned into "rivers."

Just before Ohio became a state in 1803, Congress voted to build a road to Ohio. The road would be used to transport goods and help settlers reach the new state. This route became known as the National Road. It was the nation's first important highway joining the eastern United States and places west of the Appalachian Mountains.

The National Road was built using the best technology of the day. It was level, and it was paved with stones and tar. The first part of the National Road opened in 1818. It ran from

This mile marker once guided people on the National Road in Maryland.

BACKGROUND

Industrial Revolution Explain to students that the Industrial Revolution started in Great Britain in the last part of the 1700s. It then spread to other parts of Europe and to the United States in the 1800s. However, it did not reach parts of Asia and the Pacific Rim until the twentieth century. Industrialization continues to spread to new areas of the world today, particularly to developing countries.

REACH ALL LEARNERS

English as a Second Language Request that students who are acquiring English add the lesson vocabulary to their vocabulary notebooks. Have students list and define each vocabulary term as well as use each term in a sentence. Practice the pronunciation of each term with students.

Maryland to present-day West Virginia. By 1841 the National Road was open through Ohio. It ended in Vandalia, Illinois.

By 1860 there were more than 88,000 miles (about 142,000 km) of roads in the United States. Traveling by road, however, still cost a lot and took a long time. Most wagons could carry only small amounts of goods and travelers often had to make several trips to carry their loads.

REVIEW Why was the National Road important? It linked the eastern United States to places west of the Appalachian Mountains.

Canal Building

Because road travel cost so much and took so much time, people turned to canals. Traveling on canals, boats or barges could carry larger loads at less cost than wagons could on land. One of the most important canals built during these years was the Erie Canal in New York.

People living near the Great Lakes, however, still had to transport products to and from cities in the eastern United States by wagon. Goods could not be moved on boats because the Appalachian Mountains separated rivers flowing into the Great Lakes from rivers flowing into the Atlantic Ocean. Only one river, the St. Lawrence, flowed from the Great Lakes into the Atlantic Ocean. However, rapids and shallows kept boats from sailing its whole length.

In 1817 the state of New York voted to build a "Grand Canal" to Lake Erie.

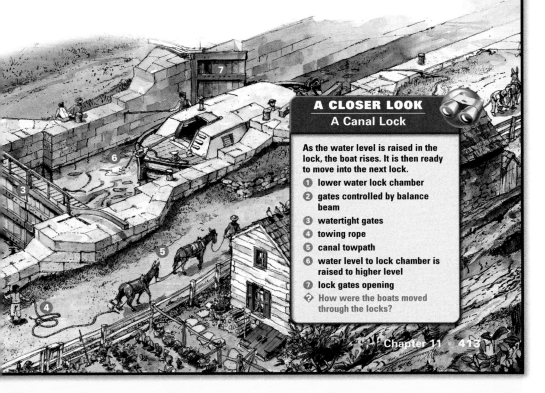

A CLOSER LOOK
A Canal Lock

As the water level is raised in the lock, the boat rises. It is then ready to move into the next lock.

1. lower water lock chamber
2. gates controlled by balance beam
3. watertight gates
4. towing rope
5. canal towpath
6. water level to lock chamber is raised to higher level
7. lock gates opening

◆ How were the boats moved through the locks?

Chapter 11 413

Study Questions Have students use these questions as guides for their reading.

1. How did canals affect travel?
2. How did mass production affect the cost of goods?

● USE READING AND VOCABULARY TRANSPARENCY 5-12.

5-12
TRANSPARENCY

2 Teach

New Roads

Read and Respond

Geography Inform students that the National Road is now part of U.S. Highway 40. Consider why this road is used primarily for local travel today. Travelers can save time by using interstate highways.

Canal Building

Read and Respond

Economics Discuss with students why it cost less money to transport goods by boat than by wagon. Point out that although roads were improving, they were still difficult to travel.

A CLOSER LOOK
A Canal Lock

Have students examine the diagram and trace with their fingers the path a boat follows as it travels through the lock. Ask them to explain each step that is illustrated. CAPTION ANSWER: by raising and lowering the water level

STUDY/RESEARCH SKILLS

Graphic Organizer Tell students that a graphic organizer can help them organize information and see how it is related. Encourage each student to make an idea map using information from the lesson. The center of the map should be "Industrial Revolution." Remind students to connect the circles in their idea maps to show that two events are related.

INTEGRATE MATHEMATICS

Computation Ask students to calculate how many years passed between the opening of the National Road and the completion of the National Road. 1841 – 1818 = 23 years

Read and Respond

Link Civics and Government with Economics Point out to students that the state government in New York voted to build the Erie Canal, but it used private money to do so. Lead a discussion about how government projects are funded today. Students should respond that money from taxpayers is used to build roads, buildings, schools, and bridges.

Q **What is an example of a building or other project in the community that was built with money from taxpayers?**

A Responses might include government buildings, post offices, interstates, and schools built with government funds.

Geography Have students locate the Erie Canal on a map. Ask them to draw conclusions about why the Erie Canal was built so that it ended at the Hudson River. because people could use the Hudson River to ship goods the rest of the way to New York City

History Explain that the Erie Canal was begun in 1817 and finished in 1825—two years earlier than planned. A celebration was held to commemorate the joining of Lake Erie and the Atlantic Ocean.

Steamboats and Railroads

Read and Respond

Culture and Society Point out that steamboats were used not only to carry goods but also to carry passengers. Explain that many steamboats also made excursion trips. Point out that steamboat excursions were part of people's social lives at the time.

It would start at the Hudson River and be 363 miles (584 km) long. To pay for building it, the governor of New York, DeWitt Clinton, asked investors to buy stock in the canal. An **investor** is a person who uses money to buy or make something that will yield a profit. By the summer of 1817, Clinton had enough investors to pay for the digging of the canal.

Most of the Erie Canal was dug by about 3,000 Irish immigrants who used only hand tools. The Irish came to the United States to get jobs working on the canal. Workers were paid 80 cents a day and were given meals and housing. These wages were three times what the immigrants could earn in Ireland.

After eight years of hard work, the Erie Canal opened in 1825. It cut the price of shipping goods between New York City and Buffalo on Lake Erie from $100 a ton to less than $10 a ton. It also helped make New York City the leading center of trade

This decorative hat box shows a scene on the Erie Canal.

in the United States at the time. The success of the Erie Canal set off a canal-building boom. By the 1830s, canals were being dug all over the country. Pennsylvania developed a system of canals connecting Philadelphia to other parts of the state. Ohio and Indiana built canals joining the Great Lakes and the Ohio River.

REVIEW Why was the Erie Canal built? to provide a less costly way to transport products between places near the Great Lakes and eastern cities

Steamboats and Railroads

Canal building lasted only a short time in the United States. New and faster methods of carrying goods and people soon took over. Steamboats quickly became the main form of river travel, and railroads changed the way people and goods moved on land.

The steam engine was invented in Britain by Thomas Newcomen in the

The Tom Thumb was made famous in a race with a horse. The locomotive was small, but powerful for its day. The first locomotives went about 10 miles (16 km) per hour.

414 ▪ Unit 5

early 1700s. It used the steam produced by boiling water to power its moving parts. Over the years the steam engine was improved and applied to various uses. Robert Fulton of New York used the steam engine to power a boat. In 1807 Fulton amazed people when his steamboat, the *Clermont*, chugged up the Hudson River from New York City to Albany. It was a 150-mile (241-km) trip, and it took 32 hours. Until this time, boats had not been able to travel easily upstream, or against the flow of the river.

Steamboat builders soon wanted to outdo each other as the new boats grew in popularity. Builders began to build bigger and faster boats. Greater speed meant that more cargo and passengers could be delivered in a shorter amount of time. This meant a bigger profit for cargo companies and their customers.

Soon steamboats were being used in other parts of the country, especially on the Ohio and Mississippi Rivers. By 1860 there were more than 1,000 great paddle-wheel steamboats in the United States. They traveled on most of the country's large rivers and lakes.

About the same time that steam engines were being used to power steamboats, they were also being used to power locomotives, or railroad engines. The first locomotive made in the United States was the *Tom Thumb*. A manufacturer named Peter Cooper built it in 1830 for the Baltimore and Ohio Railroad.

The company had been using railroad cars pulled by horses for its route.

 GEOGRAPHY THEME

Movement These maps show major transportation links that had been built by 1850.

⬥ Why do you think few links had been built west of the Mississippi River?

Transportation in the East, 1850

Major road

Major canal

Major railroad

Chapter 11 ▪ 415

Read and Respond

History Explain to students that the earliest railways were simply wooden planks laid on the ground. The planks were placed parallel to one another and as wide apart as wagon wheels. Explain that over time, the wooden planks developed into the rails we see on railroad tracks today.

Geography Have students discuss the changes brought about by the railroads in terms of the movement of people and goods.

Q How did railroads affect the movement of goods?

A Railroads made it easier and cheaper to move goods.

Economics Discuss with students the economic connection between manufacturing and transportation. Have them speculate on why improved transportation resulted in the growth of manufacturing.

Visual Learning

Map Explain to students that improvements in transportation encouraged people to travel. Invite students to locate towns that had a major road, a major canal, and a major railroad. Possible answers: New York City, Washington, D.C., Cleveland, Chicago, St. Louis, Richmond
CAPTION ANSWER: There were fewer towns west of the Mississippi River.

Experiment with Steam
Do the following simple experiment with students to show how steam power is produced. Boil a pot of water with the lid partly on. When you have a steady flow of steam coming from the uncovered part of the pot, place a pinwheel in the stream of steam. Watch the pinwheel spin. Ask students to hypothesize how this power could be used to move a train. CAUTION: Keep students away from the heat source, the boiling water, and steam.

Railroad Gauges The gauge of a railroad is the distance between the inner edges of the rails measured at a point 0.629 inch (1.6 cm) below the top of the railheads. Many countries have a standard gauge of 56.5 inches (143.51 cm). People have long speculated about how this number became the standard. The most likely reason is that early tramroads were built for wagons with 5-foot (1.5-m) axles. When edge rails were put on these plateways, the gauge was reduced to the present standard distance.

Growth in Manufacturing

Read and Respond

Economics Lead a discussion with students about why Britain did not want the rest of the world to find out about its textile machines. Point out to students that at that time, Britain was the only country that had machines for spinning and weaving cloth.

Q What would being the only source for machine-made cloth mean for Britain economically?

A Because Britain was the only source for machine-made cloth, its producers could charge high prices for it. People had no choice but to pay the exorbitant cost. Consequently Britain made a lot of money from cloth.

Culture and Society Discuss with students how the shift from working at home to working in factories affected American society. Point out that today many people work in office buildings or factories, but in early America many people farmed or manufactured goods by hand in their homes.

Q How do you think this change affected the daily lives of families?

A People moved to the city, family life restructured around factory hours, and time at home became limited.

Civics and Government Remind students that Francis Cabot Lowell treated his workers well. Inform them that this was not true of most factory owners. Explain that in 1800 in the United States, the average work-day was 14 hours for both men and women and sometimes for children as well. Compare an adult's workweek now with a workweek of the 1800s. Most adults today work five 8-hour days, or 40 hours per week, compared with the 60-hour or the 72-hour workweek of 1800s.

To prove that a locomotive could pull a heavy load faster than a horse, Cooper raced his *Tom Thumb* against a railroad car pulled by a horse. The locomotive broke down before the finish line and lost the race. Even so, it was clear that the steam-powered locomotive had better pulling power than a horse.

The number of railroads grew quickly after 1830. By 1850 about 9,000 miles (about 14,500 km) of track crossed the nation, mostly joining cities in the East. Railroads made it easier and cheaper to move heavy loads of raw materials and manufactured goods to all regions of the country. As the railroads grew, so did manufacturing in the United States.

REVIEW How did steam engines affect transportation methods in the United States?

DRAW CONCLUSIONS Steam engines were used to power steamboats and locomotives.

Growth in Manufacturing

In the late 1700s Britain was the only country in the world that had machines that spun thread and wove **textiles**, or cloth. People in Britain did not want the rest of the world to find out about these machines. Neither the machines nor the plans for building them were allowed out of the country. Even the textile workers were not allowed to leave. Samuel Slater, however, carefully studied the machines in the British cotton mill where he worked. He memorized how each iron gear and wooden spool worked.

Wearing a disguise and using a different name, Slater left Britain and took what he knew to the United States. With money from an investor named Moses Brown, Slater built from memory machines like the ones he had used in Britain.

In 1790 Slater and Brown started the first American spinning mill in Pawtucket, Rhode Island. This mill marked the beginning of large-scale manufacturing in the United States.

Early mills, like Slater's, were all built next to rushing rivers. These mills used the water to turn waterwheels, which in turn powered the machines connected to them. Later, steam engines were used to power machines. Steam engines were more reliable than water power, so they allowed production to expand. A steam-powered machine called a spinning jenny wove thread into fabric. At textile mills these machines spun up to 120 threads at a time from wool or cotton.

Instead of working at home, as most people had done in the past, more people began to go to work in factories. These workers did not need the same skills as workers who made goods by hand. Factories needed workers who could be trained to run the machines. Many of these workers were women, children, and immigrants. They worked first in the mills and then later in other industries.

Francis Cabot Lowell of Massachusetts developed a new system of organizing factories. Lowell put the entire process of turning cotton into cloth under one roof at his factory in Waltham, Massachusetts. Before that time, factory workers made the thread, but other workers used hand looms in their homes to weave the thread into cloth. Lowell's system, known as the Waltham system, was also different because it provided boardinghouses for its workers. Lowell provided good living conditions for his workers. However, not all factory owners followed his lead.

INTEGRATE ART

Weave Gather supplies for students to do a small weaving project, such as a potholder. Explain to students that patterns in cloth are made by weaving the strands of material together. Challenge students to choose colors and design a pattern. If you cannot obtain weaving supplies, students could also weave using strips of colored paper.

READING SKILL
Focus Skill

Draw Conclusions Have students use the following graphic organizer to draw conclusions about events and inventions from the Industrial Revolution.

Transportation of Goods	Manufacturing of Goods
the National Road steamboats railroads canals	mass production interchangeable parts patents cotton gin

A CLOSER LOOK
A Textile Mill

Early textile mills used water power to run their machines. The water of a rushing river or waterfall turned the waterwheel. The waterwheel turned gears connected to belts that made the machines run.

❶ river turns water wheel and gears

❷ spinning cotton fibers into yarn

❸ warping, or lining up side by side, the strands of yarn to prepare them for weaving

❹ weaving the yarn into cloth

◆ How does the waterwheel make the machines in the mill run?

Chapter 11 ■ 417

A CLOSER LOOK
A Textile Mill

Encourage students to trace the path of energy from the water, to the water wheel, to the gears and belts connecting them. Ask students what they notice about the wheel size as the distance between the water and the gears and belts increases. the wheels become smaller
CAPTION ANSWER: The falling water turns the water wheel, which in turn moves gears, belts, and other wheels connected to it.

Read and Respond

Economics Discuss with students how mass production reduces the cost of the goods manufactured. Point out that in mass production, many jobs are done by machines instead of by people. Ask students what happens to people whose jobs are done by machine. Unemployment rates rise; people learn to operate the machines or find another line of work.

BACKGROUND

The Changing Workweek In the 1820s workers fought for shorter hours, but at the time of the Civil War, a 72-hour workweek was common. At the end of the 1800's, pressure from workers led to the 60-hour workweek and a 10-hour workday. The Fair Labor Standards Act of 1938 limited the workweek for most workers in the United States to 40 hours.

Inventions Bring Change

Read and Respond

Economics Review with students the effects of supply and demand on a business. Then have students evaluate how supply and demand affected resource allocation in the South. Student responses may indicate that more money and effort were directed toward cotton plantations.

Culture and Society Explain to students that inventions such as the cotton gin affected people in different ways. Because it made the preparation of more cotton possible, it also meant that more cotton was grown and picked by hand. Ask students how the cotton gin may have affected the number of Africans purchased by cotton farmers. Students may respond that the cotton gin increased the need for more slaves.

• SCIENCE AND TECHNOLOGY •

Cast-Steel Plow

Discuss with students how the invention of the cast-steel plow affected farming. Ask students to suggest what economic effect the cast-steel plow had. Farmers could grow more crops.

3 Close

Summarize Key Content

- The National Road was built to transport goods between the East Coast and Ohio.
- The Erie Canal was built to connect Lake Erie to the Hudson River and the Atlantic Ocean.
- Steamboats and railroads were widely used in the 1800s.
- Manufacturing in the United States changed dramatically because of mass production and interchangeable parts.
- The number of patents in the United States increased greatly in the 1800s.

Another idea also had changed American manufacturing. In 1800 Eli Whitney developed a new system of interchangeable parts to make guns. **Interchangeable parts** were parts that were exactly alike. If one part of a gun was damaged, another part of the same kind could be put in its place. In the past, skilled workers were needed to make most products. Now anyone could put together machine-made parts and do it faster than a craftworker.

Eli Whitney invented the cotton gin (bottom), a machine that removed seeds from cotton fibers.

This idea made **mass production** possible. This is a system of producing large amounts of goods at one time. Over time many goods were made this way.

Because of mass production, the supply of manufactured goods rose sharply. In business, the **supply** is the amount of a good or service available for sale. When the supply of a product is high, prices generally fall. As a result, more expensive handmade goods were quickly replaced by cheaper ones made by machine.

REVIEW How was Lowell's system of organizing factories different from other systems? Lowell put the entire process of converting cotton into cloth under one roof at his factory.

Inventions Bring Change

In 1793 Eli Whitney developed a machine called the cotton gin, or engine. The **cotton gin** removed the seeds from cotton fibers much faster than workers could by hand. With the cotton gin, cotton could be prepared for market in less time. This made it possible for plantations to grow more cotton. Because of the cotton gin, more slaves were needed to work in the fields and harvest the cotton. In turn, planters in the southern states could supply more cotton to textile mills in the northern states and in Europe. Worldwide demand for cotton increased.

In business, a **demand** is the need or the want for a good or service by people who are willing to pay for it. When the demand for a product is high, its price usually goes up. When the price of a product goes up, people usually want to use their resources to make more of it. That means the supply of a good usually rises or falls to meet the demand.

BACKGROUND

Jo Anderson In 1831 while Cyrus McCormick worked to complete his mechanical reaper he was assisted by an African American slave named Jo Anderson. The reaper was designed, built, and tested within six weeks. By assisting McCormick in his Virginia workshop, Anderson contributed to one of the most important inventions of the 1800s.

EXTEND AND ENRICH

Research Suggest that students work in small groups to research other inventions from the Industrial Revolution that dramatically changed life in America. Encourage them to use the Internet and other reference sources to find information. Request that each group choose one invention in particular to research and give a short presentation to the class about that invention.

· SCIENCE AND TECHNOLOGY ·

Cast-Steel Plow

As a blacksmith in Grand Detour, Illinois, John Deere was always repairing the wooden and cast-iron plows of farmers. The heavy, damp prairie soil stuck to these plows, and farmers had to stop and clean them every few minutes. Deere and his partner, Major Leonard Andrus, designed a plow that could easily cut through the soil. The blade of the new plow was made of cast steel. The moldboard, or the part of the plow used for lifting and turning the soil, was made of wrought iron. Both parts were then polished so smooth that the damp prairie soil could not stick to them.

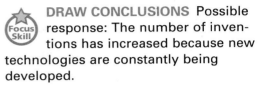

Other useful inventions also made farming on a large scale possible in the United States. In 1832 Cyrus McCormick invented a mechanical reaper for harvesting grain. With this invention farmers could cut as much wheat in one day as they had been able to cut in two weeks using hand tools. In 1837 John Deere developed the first cast-steel plow in the United States. This plow made tilling the soil easier.

As the need for finding new ways of solving problems arose, the number of inventions increased. In 1800 there were 309 **patents**, or licenses to make, use, or sell new inventions, registered with the United States Patent Office. By 1860 there were more than 40,000 patents.

REVIEW How did Cyrus McCormick's mechanical reaper help farmers? With the mechanical reaper, farmers could now harvest in one day what once took them two weeks.

LESSON 5 REVIEW

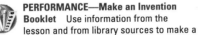

Summary Time Line

1810	1830	1850
• 1818 The National Road opens	• 1825 The Erie Canal opens	• 1830 The *Tom Thumb* is built • 1850 Many eastern cities now linked by railroads

 DRAW CONCLUSIONS Do you think the number of inventions has grown or decreased since 1860? Explain.

1 BIG IDEA How did new technologies change life in the United States?

2 VOCABULARY How are **supply** and **demand** related?

3 TIME LINE When did the Erie Canal open?

4 ECONOMICS How did the mass production of goods affect the price of many goods?

5 CRITICAL THINKING—Evaluate Evaluate the effects of supply and demand on plantations.

 PERFORMANCE—Make an Invention Booklet Use information from the lesson and from library sources to make a booklet about the items that were invented in the 1800s. Share your booklet with the class.

Chapter 11 ■ 419

RETEACH THE LESSON

Graphic Organizer Direct students to complete the following graphic organizer. Remind students that there may be more than one effect.

Cause	Effect
The National Road is opened.	Goods and people can be transported from the East Coast to Ohio.
The Erie Canal is opened.	It becomes less expensive to ship goods to and from New York City; more canals are built.
The steam engine is invented.	Steamboats and railroads become the main means of transporting goods.
Mass production begins.	Goods become less expensive.

READING SOCIAL STUDIES

Study Questions Encourage students to supply answers to the study questions.

1. Traveling on canals, boats or barges could carry larger loads at less cost than wagons on land.

2. Mass production increased supplies of manufactured goods, so the cost of those goods fell.

● USE READING AND VOCABULARY TRANSPARENCY 5-12.

5-12 TRANSPARENCY

Assess

Lesson 5 Review—Answers

DRAW CONCLUSIONS Possible response: The number of inventions has increased because new technologies are constantly being developed.

1 BIG IDEA New technologies led to a growth in manufacturing and changes in transportation.

2 VOCABULARY **Supply** is the amount of a product or service available, and **demand** is the need or wish for that product or service.

3 TIME LINE in 1825

4 ECONOMICS Mass production reduced the price of many goods.

5 CRITICAL THINKING—Evaluate Demand for cotton caused plantations to grow more cotton.

Performance Assessment Guidelines Students' invention booklets should include at least three inventions. Students should identify each invention and explain what it does.

ACTIVITY BOOK

Use ACTIVITY BOOK, p.109, to reinforce and extend student learning.

DRAW CONCLUSIONS

Students may use the graphic organizer that appears on page 110 of the Activity Book. Answers appear in the Activity Book, Teacher's Edition.

Think & Write

Write a Journal Entry Students' journal entries should include accurate descriptions of the mountain environment encountered by the Lewis and Clark expedition. Journal entries might describe the search for mountain passes or the discovery of new plant and animal species.

Write a Persuasive Letter Students' letters should be clearly phrased and explain why the potential investor should provide money for the textile factory. Students' arguments should be logical, with adequate support provided to convince the investor that providing funds would be worthwhile. In addition, students should explain how the textile factory will return a profit to the investor.

ACTIVITY BOOK

A copy of the graphic organizer appears in the ACTIVITY BOOK on page 110.

TRANSPARENCY

This graphic organizer appears on READING AND VOCABULARY TRANSPARENCY 5-13.

---

11 Review and Test Preparation

Summary Time Line
1800

- **1801** Thomas Jefferson elected President of the United States
- **1803** The Louisiana Purchase
- **1805** Lewis and Cl the Pacific O

Draw Conclusions

Copy the following graphic organizer onto a separate sheet of paper. Use the information you have learned to draw conclusions about the Industrial Revolution.

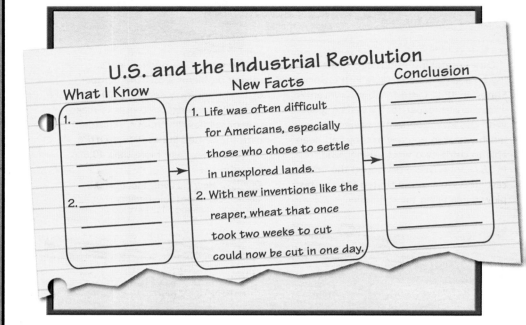

U.S. and the Industrial Revolution

What I Know
1. _____
2. _____

New Facts
1. Life was often difficult for Americans, especially those who chose to settle in unexplored lands.
2. With new inventions like the reaper, wheat that once took two weeks to cut could now be cut in one day.

Conclusion
_____

THINK & WRITE

Write a Journal Entry During the Lewis and Clark expedition, many members of the expedition kept journals. Imagine you are a member of the expedition and are journeying through the Rocky Mountains. Write a journal entry describing your environment.

Write a Persuasive Letter Imagine the year is 1820 and you are trying to raise money to open a textile factory. Write a persuasive letter to a potential investor, explaining why that person should consider investing in your factory.

TEST PREPARATION

Review these tips with students:

- Read the directions before reading the questions.
- Read each question twice, focusing the second time on all the possible answers.
- Take the time to think about all the possible answers before deciding on an answer.
- Move past questions that give you trouble, and answer the ones you know. Then return to the difficult items.

UNIT PROJECT

Progress Check Have students refer to their charts and select key events in the economic and territorial growth of the United States through the 1800s. As students begin to organize these selected events for their time lines, remind them that time line entries are usually written in the present tense. Also, point out that years on the time line should be evenly spaced.

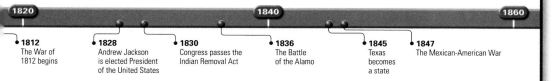

1820   1840   1860

1812
The War of
1812 begins

1828
Andrew Jackson
is elected President
of the United States

1830
Congress passes the
Indian Removal Act

1836
The Battle
of the Alamo

1845
Texas
becomes
a state

1847
The Mexican-American War

USE THE TIME LINE

Use the chapter summary time line to answer these questions.

1 How many years after the Louisiana Purchase did Lewis and Clark reach the Pacific Ocean?

2 Was Andrew Jackson elected President before or after Texas became a state?

USE VOCABULARY

Use a term from this list to complete each of the sentences that follow.

| inaugurated (p. 384) |
| siege (p. 393) |
| annexed (p. 394) |
| dictator (p. 402) |
| investors (p. 414) |

3 After the War of 1812 the United States _____ West Florida.

4 Andrew Jackson's soldiers survived a ten-day _____ during the Battle of New Orleans.

5 To pay for the Erie Canal, DeWitt Clinton brought in _____ from Europe.

6 In 1801 Thomas Jefferson was _____ as President.

7 Antonio López de Santa Anna made himself _____ of Mexico in 1834.

RECALL FACTS

Answer these questions.

8 What event caused the United States to double in size in 1803?

9 Why did many Americans want to go to war with the British in 1812?

10 How did John Deere's cast-steel plow help prairie farmers?

Write the letter of the best choice.

11 The Lewis and Clark expedition was helped by a Shoshone Indian guide named —
A Dakota.
B Mandan.
C Metacomet.
D Sacagawea.

12 Samuel Slater and Moses Brown helped begin the American—
F steel industry.
G railroad industry.
H textile industry.
J banking industry.

THINK CRITICALLY

13 Why do you think the United States did not surrender to the British after they invaded Washington, D.C., during the War of 1812?

14 What kind of compromise could Andrew Jackson have negotiated with Native American tribes instead of forcing them to leave their homelands?

15 Do you think many Americans welcomed the changes brought about by the Industrial Revolution? Why or why not?

APPLY SKILLS

Identify Changing Borders
Study the map on page 411. Then answer the following questions.

16 What color shows land that was acquired by the United States in 1846?

17 What present-day states would form the western border of the United States if the nation had not expanded after 1788?

Chapter 11 ■ 421

Think Critically

13 Students might observe that the attack on the capital city increased citizens' patriotic drive.

14 Students might suggest sharing the land or even restoring it to the Native American tribes.

15 Those who think Americans welcomed the Industrial Revolution may cite the increase in production and profits it offered. Those who feel Americans did not welcome it may point out that work became tedious, hours became longer, and working conditions grew more dangerous.

Apply Skills

Identify Changing Borders

16 purple

17 Minnesota, Wisconsin, Illinois, Kentucky, Tennessee, and Mississippi

ACTIVITY BOOK

Use the CHAPTER 11 TEST PREPARATION on page 111 of the Activity Book.

ASSESSMENT

Use the CHAPTER 11 TEST on pages 81–84 of the Assessment Program.

Use the Time Line
1 two years
2 before

Use Vocabulary
3 annexed
4 siege
5 investors
6 inaugurated
7 dictator

Recall Facts
8 the Louisiana Purchase (p. 385)
9 The British were aiding the Indians who were attacking American settlers; in addition, the British navy impressed American sailors into service on British ships. (p. 389)
10 John Deere's plow made tilling the soil easier. (p. 419)
11 D (pp. 386–387)
12 H (p. 416)

Old Ironsides

OBJECTIVES

- Identify key events in the War of 1812.
- Use visual material to acquire historical information about the United States.

Summary

"Old Ironsides," the USS *Constitution*, is the world's oldest commissioned warship. Today it is a floating museum in Boston Harbor.

 Motivate

Get Ready

Inform students that the USS *Constitution* gained fame in the War of 1812. Many visitors to Boston visit this historic ship every year. Ask students whether any of them have visited a historic ship. Encourage them to tell the class about their experiences.

2 Teach

What to See

Have students look at the photographs and read the captions beneath them. Ask students the following questions:

- *What are the sailors on the ship wearing? What are they doing?*
- *How do you think the USS* Constitution's *location adds to a visitor's experience?*
- *Why do you think attaching the sailors' beds by rope is helpful?*

VISIT OLD IRONSIDES

GET READY

WHAT TO SEE

The USS *Constitution*, built in the 1790s, has a new life as a floating museum in Boston Harbor. Shipbuilders working with the original plans of designer Joshua Humphreys have restored "Old Ironsides" to like-new condition.

When you step aboard the old sailing vessel, you will be stepping back in history. Members of the United States Navy, dressed as sailors of the early 1800s, will take you on a tour. As the ship sways on the ocean's waves, you will feel what it was like to be a sailor during the war of 1812.

LOCATE IT

Boston
MASSACHUSETTS

422 Unit 5

BACKGROUND

Annual Turnaround Cruise
Once a year the USS *Constitution* is towed into Boston Harbor and returned to its dock facing the opposite direction. This is done to prevent the masts from being damaged by the effects of the sun and wind.

INTEGRATE MATHEMATICS

Computation Remind students that the USS *Constitution* was christened on October 21, 1797. Ask students to compute the following:

How old was the ship in 1812?
1812 – 1797 = 15 years

How old was the ship when it began a 30-month voyage around the world in 1844?
1844 – 1797 = 47 years

The USS *Constitution* earned the nickname Old Ironsides during battle. Astonished sailors noticed that cannon balls could not break through the ship's sturdy sides.

Dressed in a historic uniform, the captain of the USS *Constitution* welcomes visitors aboard.

Navy officers aboard the ship slept in beds like these. The beds are attached to the ceiling by ropes so that they move with the swaying of the ship.

TAKE A FIELD TRIP

GO ONLINE
A VIRTUAL TOUR
Visit The Learning Site at **www.harcourtschool.com** to take virtual tours of other historical museums.

CNN Turner Le@rning
A VIDEO TOUR
Check your media center or classroom library for a videotape tour of the USS *Constitution*.

Unit 5 **423**

Take a Field Trip

Instruct students to research one of the battles the USS *Constitution* fought in during the War of 1812. Ask students to find out whom the battle was against, how it ended, and what role the ship had in the battle.

A Virtual Tour Depending on the availability of computers, have students work individually, in pairs, or in small groups to view the virtual tours. Suggest that they research the events of the War of 1812 as they explore the Web sites. Remind students to use what they learn on their virtual tours as background information for the Unit Project.

GO ONLINE **INTERNET RESOURCES**

THE LEARNING SITE
Go to **www.harcourtschool.com** for a listing of Web sites focusing on historical museums in the United States.

A Video Tour Ask students to write down three interesting or important facts about the USS *Constitution* as they watch the CNN video tour of the ship. Then ask for volunteers to read the facts they have written. Make a class list on the board of all the facts that students recorded while watching the videotape.

VIDEO

Use the CNN/Turner Learning TAKE A FIELD TRIP videotape of the USS *Constitution*.

REACH ALL LEARNERS

Advanced Learners
Encourage advanced learners to research the construction of the USS *Constitution*. Challenge them to find out what materials were used, how long it took to build, and how it was constructed. Suggest that they write brief reports about their findings.

EXTEND AND ENRICH

Write A Letter Have students imagine they are about to visit the USS *Constitution* in Boston. Request that they write letters to friends or relatives and describe what they plan to see. Ask them to include specific details about the ship and their plans.

Unit 5 Review and Test Preparation

Visual Summary

Students' news stories should describe the chosen event and how the event affected the country.

- **The signing of the Constitution**   The signing on September 17, 1787, set forth plans for a stronger government. The document outlined the three branches of government and incorporated a system of checks and balances.

- **The Bill of Rights becomes part of the Constitution**   The first ten amendments to the Constitution, known as the Bill of Rights, were added in 1791. They outlined personal freedoms such as freedom of speech, freedom of the press, and freedom of religion.

- **The Corps of Discovery departs** This group of about 30 explorers, led by Meriwether Lewis and George Rogers Clark, explored the land acquired in the Louisiana Purchase. The information they collected was used later by settlers moving west.

- **The Battle of the Alamo** The Alamo, a Spanish mission in San Antonio, Texas, was attacked by Santa Anna's forces on February 23, 1836.

- **The Mexican-American War begins**   The Mexican-American War began when Mexican soldiers crossed the Rio Grande in 1846. The river was a boundary in a border dispute between Mexico and the United States.

- **The California gold rush begins** Gold was discovered in California in January 1848. Soon more than 80,000 people went to California in search of gold.

· UNIT ·
5 Review and Test Preparation

VISUAL SUMMARY

Write a Paragraph Study the pictures and captions below to help you review Unit 5. Then choose one of the events shown. Write a news story about that event and how it affected the country.

USE VOCABULARY

Identify the term that correctly matches each definition.

arsenal (p. 348)	
census (p. 359)	
due process of law (p. 372)	
doctrine (p. 394)	
patent (p. 419)	

1. a population count
2. a government plan of action
3. a building used for storing weapons
4. a person's right to a fair public trial
5. a license to make, use, or sell new inventions

RECALL FACTS

Answer these questions.

6. What was Shays's Rebellion?
7. Who was Benjamin Banneker?
8. How did Dolley Madison assist her country during the War of 1812?

Write the letter of the best choice.

9. The Constitutional Convention delegate who actually wrote the Constitution was—
   A Roger Sherman.
   B Benjamin Franklin.
   C Elbridge Gerry.
   D Gouverneur Morris.

10. The term *manifest destiny* referred to a belief that the United States should—
   F stretch from the Atlantic Ocean to the Pacific Ocean.
   G avoid involvement in all foreign conflicts.
   H close the Western Hemisphere.
   J ratify the Constitution.

Visual Summary

1780   1800   182(

1787 The signing of the Constitution p. 366

1791 The Bill of Rights becomes part of the Constitution p. 370

1804 The Corps of Discovery departs p. 386

Use Vocabulary

1. census
2. doctrine
3. arsenal
4. due process of law
5. patent

Recall Facts

6. It was an event at which farmers and their supporters interrupted court proceedings to draw attention to their economic plight. (pp. 347–348)

7. He assisted in the surveying of Washington, D.C. (p. 376)

8. She preserved important papers and artworks. (p. 392)

9. D (p. 358)

10. F (p. 402)

Think Critically

11. The economic difficulties of the individual states probably would have worsened, and they may have remained vulnerable to attack.

THINK CRITICALLY

11 What do you think might have happened if the United States had decided to keep the Articles of Confederation?

12 Do you think the United States could have avoided war with Britain in 1812? Explain your answer.

13 How do you think Americans viewed the Monroe Doctrine? How do you think Europeans viewed the Monroe Doctrine?

14 Why do you think the Cherokee nation chose to fight for its homeland in the courts instead of on a battlefield?

15 How do you think the introduction of factory work changed family life in the United States?

APPLY SKILLS

Identify Changing Borders
Use the historical map on this page to answer the following questions.

16 Was Austin's original colony in eastern or western Texas?

17 Was Austin's colony larger or smaller than the Republic of Texas?

18 What river forms part of the western border of the state of Texas?

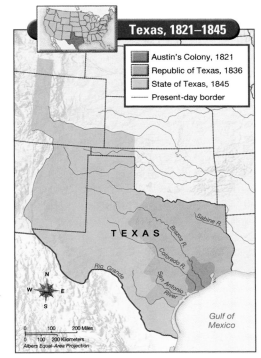

Texas, 1821–1845

- Austin's Colony, 1821
- Republic of Texas, 1836
- State of Texas, 1845
- ———— Present-day border

TEXAS

Sabine R.
Brazos R.
Colorado R.
Rio Grande
San Antonio River

Gulf of Mexico

0   100   200 Miles
0   100   200 Kilometers
Albers Equal-Area Projection

19 Was the Republic of Texas larger or smaller than the state of Texas today?

20 How did the state border of Texas change from 1845 to the present day?

336   **The Battle of the Alamo**
.403

1847   **The Mexican-American War**
begins   p. 407

1849   **The California Gold Rush**
begins   p. 409

1840

1860

425

12 Those who feel they could have avoided war may suggest that Americans could have made peace with the Native Americans and slowed westward expansion. They also may feel that they could have sent a naval force out to protect merchant ships, asked for foreign assistance from trade partners, or signed a truce with the British to preserve their trade.

13 Americans were probably happy because then they would not have to compete for lands. Europeans may have been angry at Monroe for not allowing any more colonization.

14 Students might suggest that the Cherokees decided that a legal resolution would be more lasting than any achieved in battle.

15 Families would no longer work together to earn a living. They would rely on family members who worked in factories.

Apply Skills

Identify Changing Borders

16 eastern

17 smaller

18 the Rio Grande

19 smaller

20 The northwestern part of Texas became parts of present-day states of Oklahoma, Kansas, Colorado, and New Mexico.

TEST PREPARATION

Review these tips with students:

- Read the directions before reading the questions.

- Read each question twice, focusing the second time on all the possible answers.

- Take the time to think about all the possible answers before deciding on an answer.

- Move past questions that give you trouble, and answer the ones you know. Then return to the difficult items.

ASSESSMENT

Use the UNIT 5 TEST on pages 85–93 of the Assessment Program.

Unit Activities

Produce a Speech

Assign each group one of these historical figures covered in the unit: James Madison, Benjamin Banneker, Sacagawea, or Davy Crockett. Explain that speeches should reflect the accomplishments and character of their assigned individual.

Performance Assessment Guidelines Check that students make relevant character references and use appropriate tones in their speeches. When students have finished, have them present their speeches to the class.

Create a Newspaper Front Page

To aid in the timely completion of the project, assign roles to each group member, including researcher, writer, designer, and artist. Explain that daily newspapers are organized in this way, with specialists handling particular duties.

Performance Assessment Guidelines Look for evidence that students understand the historic significance of their assigned event and that the art they select corresponds to their topic.

Complete the Unit Project

Remind groups that their time lines should display events in chronological order. Ask them to include a variety of events throughout the 1800s.

Performance Assessment Guidelines Check that students include the correct dates for the time period they covered and that these dates were properly sequenced. When the time lines are completed, display them on the wall.

Unit Activities

GO ONLINE Visit The Learning Site at www.harcourtschool.com for additional activities.

Produce a Speech

Work in a group to produce a speech that might have been given by one of these people: James Madison, Benjamin Banneker, Sacagawea, or Davy Crockett. Divide the work of researching, writing, and editing the speech. Then select a member of your group to deliver the completed speech before the class.

Create a Newspaper Front Page

Work in a group to create the front page of a newspaper that will cover one of the following events: the opening of the Erie Canal, the completion of the National Road, Robert Fulton's voyage on the *Clermont*, or the race between the *Tom Thumb* and a horse. First, research and write your story. Then, add pictures. Next, arrange your front page on a posterboard. Finally, present your completed front page to the class.

COMPLETE THE UNIT PROJECT

A Growing Nation Time Line Work with a group of classmates to finish the unit project—a time line that shows the economic and territorial growth of the United States through the 1800s. Illustrate the events that appear on your time line by using drawings or pictures printed from the Internet. Present your completed time line to the class. Then explain why your group selected the events that it did.

426 ▪ Unit 5

VISIT YOUR LIBRARY

■ *The Santa Fe Trail* by David Lavender. Holiday House.

■ *By the Dawn's Early Light: The Story of the Star-Spangled Banner* by Steven Kroll. Scholastic.

■ *Woman of Independence: The Life of Abigail Adams* by Susan Provost Beller. Shoe Tree Press.

Visit Your Library

Encourage independent reading after students' study of the development and expansion of the United States with these books or others of your choice. Additional books are listed on the Multimedia Resources, on page 339D of this Teacher's Edition.

Easy *The Santa Fe Trail* by David Lavender. Holiday House, 1995. The experiences of early traders on the Santa Fe Trail are described.

Average *By the Dawn's Early Light: The Story of the Star-Spangled Banner* by Steven Kroll. Scholastic, 1994. A historic account of the writing of our national anthem is presented.

Challenging *Woman of Independence: The Life of Abigail Adams* by Susan Provost Beller. Shoe Tree Press, 2000. The life of First Lady Abigail Adams is detailed.

Civil War Times

President Abraham
Lincoln's Hat

Unit 6 Planning Guide Civil War Times

Introduce	CONTENT	RESOURCES
pp. 427–433	**UNIT OPENER**, p. 427 **PREVIEW**, pp. 428–429 **START WITH A JOURNAL** "All for the Union," pp. 430–433	Unit 6 Audiotext Unit 6 School-to-Home Newsletter, p. S11 Reading and Vocabulary Transparency, 6-1 Time for Kids Readers Internet Resources

Chapter 12

The Nation Divided, pp. 434–473	**INTRODUCE THE CHAPTER**, pp. 434–435 **LESSON 1** Regional Disagreements, pp. 436–441 **READING SKILLS** Identify Frame of Reference, pp. 442–443 **LESSON 2** Slavery and Freedom, pp. 444–449 **LESSON 3** The Union Breaks Apart, pp. 450–455 **MAP AND GLOBE SKILLS** Compare Maps with Different Scales, pp. 456–457 **LESSON 4** Civil War, pp. 458–464 **LESSON 5** The Road to Union Victory, pp. 465–471 **CHAPTER REVIEW AND TEST PREPARATION**, pp. 472–473	Activity Book, pp. 112–121 Assessment Program, Chapter 12, pp. 95–98 Reading and Vocabulary Transparencies, 6-2, 6-3, 6-4, 6-5, 6-6, 6-7 Skills Transparencies 6-1, 6-2A, 6-2B Internet Resources GeoSkills CD-ROM

Chapter 13

The Nation Reunited, pp. 474–509	**INTRODUCE THE CHAPTER**, pp. 474–475 **LESSON 1** Reconstruction, pp. 476–480 **LESSON 2** The South After the War, pp. 481–485 **LESSON 3** Settling the Last Frontier, pp. 486–491 **CHART AND GRAPH SKILLS** Use a Climograph, pp. 492–493 **LESSON 4** The Rise of New Industries, pp. 494–499 **EXAMINE PRIMARY SOURCES** Edison's Inventions, pp. 500–501 **LESSON 5** A Changing People, pp. 502–507 **CHAPTER REVIEW AND TEST PREPARATION**, pp. 508–509	Activity Book, pp. 122–131 Assessment Program, Chapter 13, pp. 99–102 Reading and Vocabulary Transparencies, 6-8, 6-9, 6-10, 6-11, 6-12, 6-13 Skills Transparencies 6-3A, 6-3B Internet Resources

Wrap Up

pp. 510–514	**VISIT** The Gettysburg National Military Park, pp. 510–511 **UNIT REVIEW AND TEST PREPARATION**, pp. 512–514	Internet Resources The Learning Site: Virtual Tours Take a Field Trip Video Assessment Program, Unit 6, pp. 103–111

4 WEEKS

WEEK 1	WEEK 2	WEEK 3	WEEK 4
Introduce the Unit	Chapter 12	Chapter 13	Wrap Up the Unit

Unit 6 Skills Path

Unit 6 features the reading skills of categorizing, determining point of view, and identifying frame of reference. It also highlights the social studies skills of comparing maps with different scales and using a climograph.

FOCUS SKILLS

CHAPTER 12 READING SKILL

 CATEGORIZE

- INTRODUCE p. 435
- APPLY pp. 438, 441, 444, 449, 450, 452, 455, 458, 460, 464, 465, 466, 471, 472

CHAPTER 13 READING SKILL

 POINT OF VIEW

- INTRODUCE p. 475
- APPLY pp. 475, 476, 479, 480, 481, 484, 485, 490, 491, 494, 498, 499, 502, 505, 507

READING SOCIAL STUDIES

- Anticipation Guide, pp. 437, 441, 459, 464, 487, 491
- K-W-L Chart, pp. 445, 449, 503, 507
- Study Questions, pp. 451, 455, 482, 485
- Graphic Organizer, pp. 430, 432, 466, 471, 477, 480
- Paraphrase, p. 470
- Personal Response, pp. 495, 499
- Summarize, pp. 467, 482

MAP AND GLOBE SKILLS

COMPARE MAPS WITH DIFFERENT SCALES

- INTRODUCE pp. 456–457
- APPLY p. 473

CHART AND GRAPH SKILLS

USE A CLIMOGRAPH

- INTRODUCE pp. 492–493
- APPLY p. 509

READING SKILL

IDENTIFY FRAME OF REFERENCE

- INTRODUCE pp. 442–443
- APPLY p. 473

STUDY AND RESEARCH SKILLS

- Note Taking, pp. 439, 502
- Outlining, pp. 444, 486
- Using Reference Sources, p. 454
- Summarizing Information, p. 465
- Skimming and Scanning, p. 476

Multimedia Resources

The Multimedia Resources can be used in a variety of ways. They can supplement core instruction in the classroom or extend and enrich student learning at home.

Independent Reading

Easy

Harness, Cheryl. ***Abe Lincoln Goes To Washington.***  National Geographic Society, 1997. Story of Abraham Lincoln beginning with his service as a young lawyer and covering his family life and political career through the Civil War.

Hest, Amy. ***When Jessie Came Across the Sea.*** Candlewick Press, 1997. The story of an orphan girl who immigrates to New York and works to save enough money to bring her grandmother to the United States.

Vaughan, Marcia K. ***Secret to Freedom.*** Lee & Low Books, Inc., 2001. Underground Railroad story of two young slaves who help others to freedom by communicating secret messages made from quilt patterns.

Average

Connell, Kate. ***Tales from the Underground Railroad.*** Steck Vaughn, 1993. Stories highlighting the network of people who comprised the Underground Railroad and helped thousands of African Americans escape slavery.

Haskins, Jim. ***Blue, Black, and Gray: African Americans in the Civil War.*** Simon  & Schuster Children's, 1998. Vintage photos and excerpts from letters help tell the story of African American soldiers who served in the Civil War.

Osborne, Mary Pope. ***My Brother's Keeper: Virginia's Diary, Gettysburg, PA 1863.*** Scholastic, Inc., 2000. Nine-year-old Virginia, a Gettysburg resident, records the events she witnesses before, during, and after the Battle as well as Lincoln's famous address.

Challenging

Reeder, Carolyn. ***Across the Lines.*** Simon & Schuster, 1997. Edward, the son of a Southern plantation owner, and Simon, a slave and Edward's lifelong 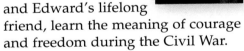 friend, learn the meaning of courage and freedom during the Civil War.

Adair, Gene. ***Thomas Alva Edison: Oxford Portraits in Science.*** Oxford University Children's Press, 1997. Story of Edison's adventures and inventions, beginning as a child of 12 and spanning his career.

Taylor, Mildred D. ***The Land.*** Phyllis Fogelman Books, 2001. Examines the struggles of an African American family in the South during and after the Civil War. Prequel to *Roll of Thunder, Hear My Cry.*

Computer Software

American Civil War. 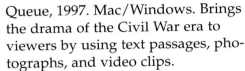 Queue, 1997. Mac/Windows. Brings the drama of the Civil War era to viewers by using text passages, photographs, and video clips.

His Name Was Lincoln. Sunburst, 1996. Mac/Windows. Multidisciplinary approach to Lincoln's life covered in two CDs: *Peace*, which covers his early life up to the presidency, and *War*, which explores Lincoln during the Civil War.

Videos and DVDs

Civil War Journal: Commanders. A&E, 2001. Civil War commanders who helped determine the course of the war, includes profiles of Stonewall Jackson and Robert E. Lee.

Heroes of Today and Yesterday: Harriet Tubman. Sunburst, 1998. Escaped slave Harriet Tubman, a "conductor" on the Underground Railroad, helps over 300 slaves to freedom.

Additional books also are recommended at point of use throughout the unit.
Note that information, while correct at time of publication, is subject to change.

ISBNs and other publisher information can be found at **www.harcourtschool.com**

The Learning Site: Social Studies Center

The Learning Site at www.harcourtschool.com offers a special Social Studies Center. The center provides a wide variety of activities, Internet links, and online references.

Here are just some of the HARCOURT Internet resources you'll find!

Multimedia Biographies

www.harcourtschool.com

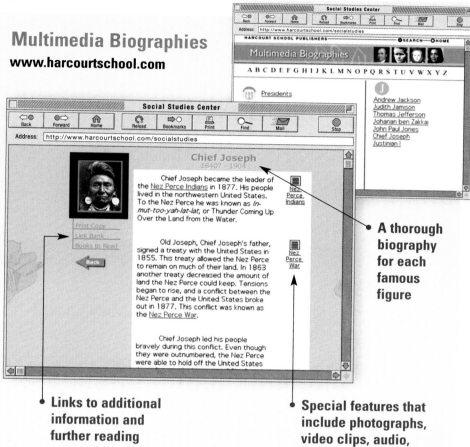

A thorough biography for each famous figure

Links to additional information and further reading

Special features that include photographs, video clips, audio, and additional text

INTERNET RESOURCES

Find all this at
The Learning Site at
www.harcourtschool.com

- Activities and Games
- Content Updates
- Current Events
- Free and Inexpensive Materials
- Multimedia Biographies
- Online Atlas
- Primary Sources
- Video Updates
- Virtual Tours
- Your State

and more!

Free and Inexpensive Materials

- Addresses to write for free and inexpensive products
- Links to unit-related materials
- Internet maps
- Internet references

www.harcourtschool.com

Primary Sources

- Artwork
- Clothing
- Diaries
- Government Documents
- Historical Documents
- Maps
- Tools

and more!

www.harcourtschool.com

Virtual Tours

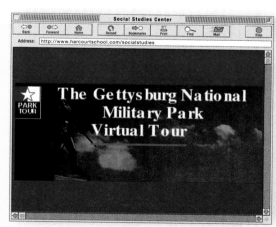

- Capitols and Government Buildings
- Cities
- Countries
- Historical Sites
- Museums
- Parks and Scenic Areas

and more!

www.harcourtschool.com

Integrate Learning Across the Curriculum

Use these topics to help you integrate social studies into your daily planning.
See the page numbers indicated for more information about each topic.

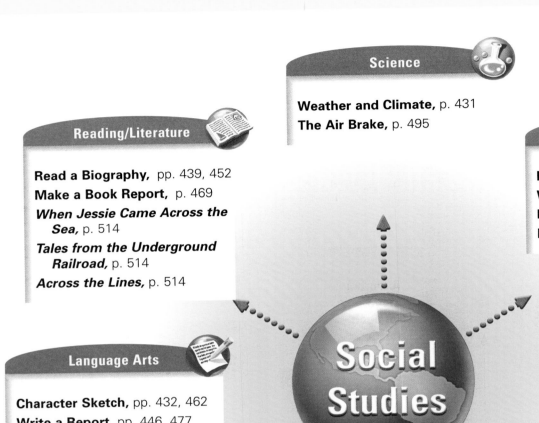

Science
Weather and Climate, p. 431
The Air Brake, p. 495

Reading/Literature
Read a Biography, pp. 439, 452
Make a Book Report, p. 469
When Jessie Came Across the Sea, p. 514
Tales from the Underground Railroad, p. 514
Across the Lines, p. 514

Art
Drawing, p. 448
Watercolor, p. 454
Make a Banner, p. 460
Design a Monument, p. 510

Health
First Aid, p. 462
Learn More About Illnesses, p. 468

Language Arts
Character Sketch, pp. 432, 462
Write a Report, pp. 446, 477
Create a Multimedia Presentation, p. 451
Informative Writing, p. 452
Write a Personal Narrative, p. 482
Compare and Contrast, p. 497

Languages
Americanisms, p. 483
Learn About Chinese, p. 504

Music
"God Bless America," p. 503

Technology
GeoSkills CD-ROM, p. 457
Go Online, pp. 433, 439, 452, 467, 490, 501, 511
CNN Video, p. 511

Mathematics
Total States and Territories, p. 428
Percents, p. 437
Measurement, p. 456
Computation, pp. 461, 488

Reach All Learners

Use these activities to help individualize your instruction. Each activity has been developed to address a different level or type of learner.

English as a Second Language

Materials
- index cards
- textbook
- pens or pencils

WRITE A VOCABULARY QUIZ Have pairs of students who are learning English write fill-in-the-blank questions using vocabulary terms from Unit 6.

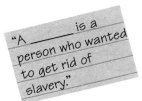

- Assign a lesson from the unit to each pair of students.
- Direct students to review the lesson's vocabulary terms and their definitions.
- Ask students to write original sentences for half of the lesson's vocabulary. Have students copy their sentences on to the front of an index card, leaving a blank where the vocabulary word would appear. Students should write the answer on the back of the card.
- Invite students to exchange cards and guess the answers.

Below-Level Learners

Materials
- posterboard
- pens or markers
- textbook

Two Points of View on Secession

IDENTIFY POINTS OF VIEW Have students work in groups to research and explain differing points of view on an issue or event discussed in Unit 6.

- Allow students to form groups of four. Ask each group to find a key issue or an event from the unit.
- Challenge students to consider the groups or individuals that had different points of view on the issue or event.
- Have students review the material in their textbook to find evidence to support their ideas.
- Instruct students to write a paragraph summarizing the two points of view. Ask each group to present its summary to the class.

Advanced Learners

Materials
- paper
- pen or pencil
- textbook

ANSWER "WHAT IF?" QUESTION Have advanced learners hypothesize about the possible effects of different historic outcomes.

- Ask students to identify a historic outcome discussed in Unit 6, such as the defeat of the Confederacy or the assassination of Abraham Lincoln.
- Challenge students to consider what would have happened if the event had not happened or had happened differently.
- Have students write a short "What If?" paragraph in which they hypothesize about how history would have been changed if events had gone differently. Challenge students to be creative but logical in their responses.

Assessment Options

The Assessment Program gives all learners many opportunities to show what they know and can do. It also provides ongoing information about each student's understanding of social studies.

Formal Assessment

- **LESSON REVIEWS,** at ends of lessons
- **CHAPTER REVIEWS AND TEST PREPARATION,** pp. 472–473, pp. 508–509
- **CHAPTER TESTS**
  Assessment Program, pp. 95–98, pp. 99–102
- **UNIT REVIEW AND TEST PREPARATION,** pp. 512–513
- **UNIT ASSESSMENT**
  STANDARD TEST,
  Assessment Program, pp. 103–109
  INDIVIDUAL PERFORMANCE TASK,
  Assessment Program, p. 110
  GROUP PERFORMANCE TASK,
  Assessment Program, p. 111

Student Self-Evaluation

- **ANALYZE PRIMARY SOURCES AND VISUALS** within lessons of Pupil Book
- **GEOGRAPHY THEME QUESTIONS** within lessons of Pupil Book
- **INDIVIDUAL END-OF-PROJECT SUMMARY** Assessment Program, p. viii
- **GROUP END-OF-PROJECT CHECKLIST** Assessment Program, p. ix
- **INDIVIDUAL END-OF-UNIT CHECKLIST** Assessment Program, p. x

Informal Assessment

- **ANALYZE THE LITERATURE,** p. 433
- **REVIEW QUESTIONS,** throughout lessons
- **EXAMINE PRIMARY SOURCES,** pp. 500–501
- **SOCIAL STUDIES SKILLS CHECKLIST** Assessment Program, p. iv–vii

- **SKILLS**
  Practice the Skill, pp. 443, 457, 493
  Apply What You Learned, pp. 443, 457, 493

Performance Assessment

- **PERFORMANCE ACTIVITY** in Lesson Reviews
- **UNIT ACTIVITIES** p. 514
- **COMPLETE THE UNIT PROJECT,** p. 514
- **INDIVIDUAL PERFORMANCE TASK** Assessment Program, p. 110
- **GROUP PERFORMANCE TASK** Assessment Program, p. 111

Portfolio Assessment

STUDENT-SELECTED ITEMS MAY INCLUDE:
- **THINK AND WRITE,** p. 472, p. 508
- **UNIT ACTIVITIES,** p. 514
- **COMPLETE THE UNIT PROJECT,** p. 514

TEACHER-SELECTED ITEMS MAY INCLUDE:
- **UNIT ASSESSMENT** Assessment Program, pp. 103–111
- **PORTFOLIO SUMMARY** Assessment Program, p. xv
- **GROUP END-OF-PROJECT CHECKLIST** Assessment Program, p. ix
- **INDIVIDUAL END-OF-UNIT CHECKLIST** Assessment Program, p. x

Unit 6 Test

·UNIT·

Name _____ Date _____

6 Test

Part One: Test Your Understanding

MULTIPLE CHOICE (2 points each)

Directions Circle the letter of the best answer.

1 Under the agreement known as the Missouri Compromise—
A California joined the Union as a free state.
B lands gained from Mexico became the Utah and New Mexico territories.
C people in Kansas and Nebraska decided for themselves whether they wanted slavery.
(D) Maine joined the Union as a free state.

2 In his campaign for the United States Senate, Abraham Lincoln conducted a series of famous debates with—
F John Breckinridge of Kentucky.
(G) Senator Stephen A. Douglas.
H Senator Jefferson Davis.
J abolitionist William Lloyd Garrison.

3 The first major battle of the Civil War was fought at—
A Vicksburg, Mississippi.
B Antietam Creek, Maryland.
C Chancellorsville, Virginia.
(D) Manassas Junction, Virginia.

4 The Union's plan to cripple the South's economy was called—
F the Dred Scott decision.
(G) the Anaconda Plan.
H the Missouri Compromise.
J Reconstruction.

5 The Confederate Army was led by—
A Thomas "Stonewall" Jackson.
B Ulysses S. Grant.
C Jefferson Davis.
(D) Robert E. Lee.

6 President Lincoln issued an order freeing slaves in the Confederate states that were still fighting the Union—
F when the Civil War began.
G as soon as he was elected.
(H) more than a year after the Civil War started.
J after the South was defeated.

7 Pickett's Charge was an unsuccessful Confederate attack during—
A the siege of Vicksburg.
(B) the Battle of Gettysburg.
C the Battle of Bull Run.
D the capture of Atlanta.

(continued)

Unit 6 Test   Assessment Program ■ 103

Name _____ Date _____

8 Most enslaved Africans worked—
F as miners.
G in factories.
(H) in plantation fields.
J as housekeepers.

9 One well-known conductor on the Underground Railroad was—
(A) Harriet Tubman.
B Elizabeth Cady Stanton.
C Harriet Beecher Stowe.
D Sojourner Truth.

10 Which of the following describes President Andrew Johnson's plan for Reconstruction of the South?
F Southern states that passed the Fourteenth Amendment could rejoin the Union.
G Southern states could enter the Union after passing laws called black codes.
H Southern states could enter the Union after agreeing to military rule.
(J) Southern states that passed the Thirteenth Amendment could rejoin the Union.

11 A person who farms in exchange for part of the final crop is called—
(A) a sharecropper.
B a scalawag.
C a carpetbagger.
D a freedman.

12 Andrew Carnegie made his fortune by—
F inventing the Bessemer process.
G completing the transcontinental railroad.
(H) developing a steel business.
J controlling the nation's oil refineries.

13 John D. Rockefeller's Standard Oil Company—
(A) drove many other companies out of the oil business.
B produced the world's best barrels and pipelines.
C developed a process to make kerosene from oil.
D discovered oil in Titusville, Pennsylvania.

14 A strong, unfair feeling against someone is called—
F a tenement.
(G) prejudice.
H emancipation.
J a regulation.

(continued)

104 ■ Assessment Program   Unit 6 Test

Name _____ Date _____

FILL IN THE BLANK (3 points each)

Directions Fill in each blank space with the correct word or words from the list below.

15 Troops in an army may _____ retreat _____, or fall back, in fierce fighting.

16 Delaware, Kentucky, Maryland, and Missouri were _____ border states _____ that permitted slavery but did not secede from the Union.

17 Many enslaved Africans escaped to freedom with the help of the _____ Underground Railroad _____.

18 A voting method that does not allow anyone to know how a person voted is called a _____ secret ballot _____.

19 Both the Union and Confederate armies suffered many _____ casualties _____ during the Civil War.

> border states
> secret ballot
> Underground Railroad
> retreat
> casualties

(continued)

Unit 6 Test   Assessment Program ■ 105

Name _____ Date _____

SHORT ANSWER (3 points each)

Directions Complete each sentence in the space provided.

20 The loyalty people from the North and the South felt for their region of the country was known as _____ sectionalism _____ and often led to disagreements.

21 People who fought to do away with slavery in the United States, such as Harriet Beecher Stowe and William Lloyd Garrison, were known as _____ abolitionists _____.

22 During the Civil War, General Sherman's army burned houses and destroyed crops in a march that became known as _____ the March to the Sea _____.

23 The Battle of Gettysburg was a turning point in the war for the South because _____ Possible responses: the South suffered many casualties, the South _____ retreated, the South could not launch another major attack _____

24 Northerners who moved south after the Civil War to work in Reconstruction governments were often called _____ carpetbaggers _____, a name that referred to their suitcases.

25 _____ Range wars _____ developed between farmers and ranchers as they competed for open lands on the Great Plains.

26 Between 1915 and 1930, thousands of African Americans left farms in the South to move to Northern cities in a movement known as _____ the Great Migration _____

(continued)

106 ■ Assessment Program   Unit 6 Test

Unit 6 Test

Name _____ Date _____

Part Two: Test Your Skills
COMPARE MAPS WITH DIFFERENT SCALES (16 points)

Directions Map A and Map B both show sites important to the Battle of Gettysburg. Use the maps to answer the following questions.

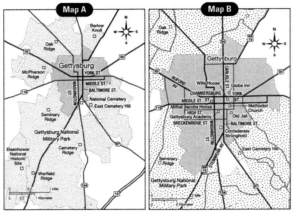

27 Which map would you use to find Cemetery Ridge? _____ Map A

28 Which map shows the intersection of York and Baltimore street? _____ either Map A or Map B

29 On which map would you find the Globe Inn, near the intersection of York Street and Baltimore Street? _____ Map B; the Wills House

30 Which map would be more helpful to a person trying to drive to the city of Gettysburg? _____ Map A because it shows roads leading to the city.

(continued)

Name _____ Date _____

Part Three: Apply What You Have Learned
31 MAIN IDEA AND DETAILS (10 points)

Listed below are states that either wanted to be admitted to the Union or wanted to secede from it. Put the name of each state in the correct column below. Then provide details about that state's position toward the Union.

List of States and Territories

- South Carolina
- Missouri
- Kansas
- Virginia

States That Wanted to Be Admitted to the Union	States That Wanted to Secede from the Union
Missouri	South Carolina
Details:	Details:
Possible responses: Missouri wanted to be admitted to the Union, but as a slave state. Admitting Missouri to the Union would have changed the balance of slave and free states; admission to the Union required Missouri Compromise.	Possible responses: It was the first state to secede after Lincoln's election; John C. Calhoun of South Carolina argued that states' rights were more important than federal union.
Kansas	Virginia
Details:	Details:
Possible responses: The Kansas-Nebraska Act allowed people in Kansas to decide whether they wanted to have slaves or not; fighting broke out as many people moved to Kansas just so	Possible responses: It seceded after the fall of Fort Sumter; Richmond, Virginia, was the site of the Confederate capital.

(continued)

Name _____ Date _____

32 ESSAY (10 points)

After the Civil War, the United States developed lands in the West. Write a paragraph that compares the growth of the United States before the Civil War and after. Be sure to describe inventions, industries, and discoveries that helped make development in the western United States possible.

Possible response: Before the Civil War, there was conflict as to whether territories would be admitted to the Union as free or slave states. People passed through territories in the center of the United States on their way to California and Oregon, but they did not stay. After the Civil War the discovery of minerals, such as gold and silver, drew many people to western lands. Improved means of transportation, such as the transcontinental railroad, helped people move more easily. Improved communication was possible because of developments in the telegraph. After the Civil War the steel, oil, and cattle industries experienced great growth, which also contributed to the West's development.

NOTES

_____
_____
_____
_____
_____
_____
_____
_____
_____
_____
_____
_____
_____
_____
_____
_____
_____
_____

Name _____ Date _____

Individual Performance Task

Job Description

Write a job description for one of the jobs listed below. Your description should tell what special skills the job will require, what type of education is needed, where the work will be performed, and what type of pay, if any, might be expected.

- Conducting people on the Underground Railroad
- Working as a reporter on an abolitionist newspaper
- Working as nurse's assistant to Clara Barton or Sally Tompkins
- Moving cattle to a Kansas railroad town
- Laying tracks for the transcontinental railroad
- Making steel in one of Andrew Carnegie's steel plants
- Helping to drill oil wells in Pennsylvania and Ohio
- Working as an assistant to Thomas Edison at his laboratory in Menlo Park

To write your job description, you will need to look in your school's library or on the Internet for more information about the type of work you want to describe. Try to include factual information about the types of equipment people would have used at these jobs and the type of environment in which they would have worked. If you find illustrations in your research, be sure to include these in your job description.

© Harcourt

Name _____ Date _____

Group Performance Task

Wartime Meeting

Working in groups of five to six people, stage an emergency wartime meeting that includes some of the Civil War's most important people. First decide whether the group will be on the side of the Union or the Confederacy. Then decide what issue you will explore. For example, Confederate leaders could decide how they would respond to the Emancipation Proclamation, or Union leaders could discuss how they would respond to the Confederate victory at Chancellorsville. Your meeting should also include input from nurses, foot soldiers, abolitionists, and slaves from the period.

Before you begin your wartime meeting, you may want to find more information about people your group has chosen by using the school library or the Internet. Make sure that each person in the group contributes information from his or her unique perspective.

© Harcourt

RUBRICS FOR SCORING

SCORING RUBRICS The rubrics below list the criteria for evaluating the tasks above. They also describe different levels of success in meeting those criteria.

INDIVIDUAL PERFORMANCE TASK

SCORE 4	SCORE 3	SCORE 2	SCORE 1
• Rich description is provided. • Details fit historical period strongly. • Description is well researched. • Description is well organized.	• Some description is provided. • Details fit historical period. • Description is fairly well researched. • Description is somewhat organized.	• Little description is provided. • Details fit historical period weakly. • Description is minimally researched. • Description is poorly organized.	• No description is provided. • Details do not fit the historical period. • Description is not researched. • Description is not organized.

GROUP PERFORMANCE TASK

SCORE 4	SCORE 3	SCORE 2	SCORE 1
• Performance shows excellent creativity. • Characters presented are relevant to topic. • Script is historically accurate.	• Performance shows some creativity. • Characters presented are mostly relevant to topic. • Script is mostly historically accurate.	• Performance shows little creativity. • Characters presented are minimally relevant to topic. • Script is partially historically accurate.	• Performance shows no creativity. • Characters presented are not relevant to topic. • Script is not historically accurate.

Introduce the Unit

OBJECTIVES

- Use artifacts and primary sources to acquire information about the United States.
- Interpret information in visuals.

Access Prior Knowledge

Invite students to tell what they know about previous issues that arose between Northern and Southern states. Lead the class in brainstorming a list of conflicts and compromises related to this period in United States history. Record suggestions in a chart.

Issues Between the North and the South

Conflicts	Compromises
counting slaves in population when deciding representation	bicameral legislature the three-fifths compromise
too much government activity takes place in the north	relocation of capital to Washington, D.C

The Lincoln Memorial, Washington, D.C.

BACKGROUND

Lincoln's Hat Abraham Lincoln wore this hat to Ford's Theater on April 14, 1865, the night John Wilkes Booth assassinated him. Hats were a frequent part of Lincoln's wardrobe. It has even been said that he used his hats, once removed, to temporarily store items, such as letters or other documents given to him in meetings. Lincoln referenced this habit in a letter he wrote in 1850.

Abraham Lincoln At the time of the Republican National Convention in 1858, Abraham Lincoln had developed a strong following of supporters—in the North. However, he had yet to develop much of a reputation beyond those areas.

BACKGROUND

The Civil War As students read books about this period in history, they may see the terms *War Between the States*, *War of Rebellion*, or *War for Southern Independence*. Inform students that these terms all refer to the same historical event, the Civil War.

·UNIT·6

Civil War Times

"A house divided against itself cannot stand."

—Abraham Lincoln, Republican
State Convention, Springfield, Illinois, June 16, 1858

Preview the Content

Scan the unit and read the chapter and lesson titles. Use what you have read to make a unit outline. Once you have finished, write down any questions you may have about the Civil War.

Preview the Vocabulary

Compound Words   A compound word is a combination of two or more words that form a new word when put together. For each term listed below, use the meanings of the smaller words to figure out the meaning of the compound word. Then look up each word in the Glossary to check its meaning.

SMALLER WORD		SMALLER WORD		COMPOUND WORD	POSSIBLE MEANING
under	+	ground	=	underground	
rail	+	road	=	railroad	
share	+	cropping	=	sharecropping	
carpet	+	bagger	=	carpetbagger	

Unit 6 ■ 427

Visual Learning

Picture The background image is of the Lincoln Memorial in Washington, D.C. Tell students that the 36 columns represent the states of the Union at the time of his death. Lincoln's second inaugural address appears on the north wall, the Gettysburg Address is on the south wall, and above his statue are the words, "In this Temple, as in the hearts of the people for whom he saved the Union, the memory of Abraham Lincoln is enshrined forever."

Analyze Primary Sources

Abraham Lincoln's Hat Have students take a close look at Abraham Lincoln's hat and describe what they see. Ask them why they think this image was selected to open a unit about the Civil War.

Quotation Have a volunteer read aloud the quotation from the Republican State Convention.

Q **What does Lincoln mean when he says, "A house divided against itself cannot stand"?**

A Students may respond that Lincoln believed that the United States could not survive a split in the Union.

AUDIOTEXT

Use the Unit 6 AUDIOTEXT for a reading of the Unit narrative.

·Unit 6·

Preview the Content
Students' outlines should resemble the one below.

I. The Nation Divided
   A. Regional Disagreements
   B. Slavery and Freedom
   C. The Union Breaks Apart
   D. Civil War
   E. The Road to Union Victory
II. The Nation Reunited
   A. Reconstruction
   B. The South After the War
   C. Settling the Last Frontier
   D. The Rise of New Industries
   E. A Changing People

Preview the Vocabulary
Once students have checked the definitions in the glossary, ask them to use each word in a sentence.

Preview the Unit

PAGES 428–429

OBJECTIVES

- Interpret information in databases and visuals.
- Use appropriate mathematical skills to interpret social studies information such as maps and graphs.

Access Prior Knowledge

Have students describe what they have already learned about differences over slavery in the North and the South.

Visual Learning

Map Direct students' attention to the map and map key. Explain that the map shows how the United States was divided in the beginning of the Civil War.

Q Which states were Confederate states?

A Texas, Arkansas, Louisiana, Mississippi, Alabama, Tennessee, Georgia, Florida, South Carolina, North Carolina, and Virginia

Time Line To help students prepare for their reading, have them work in pairs to ask and answer questions about the time line.

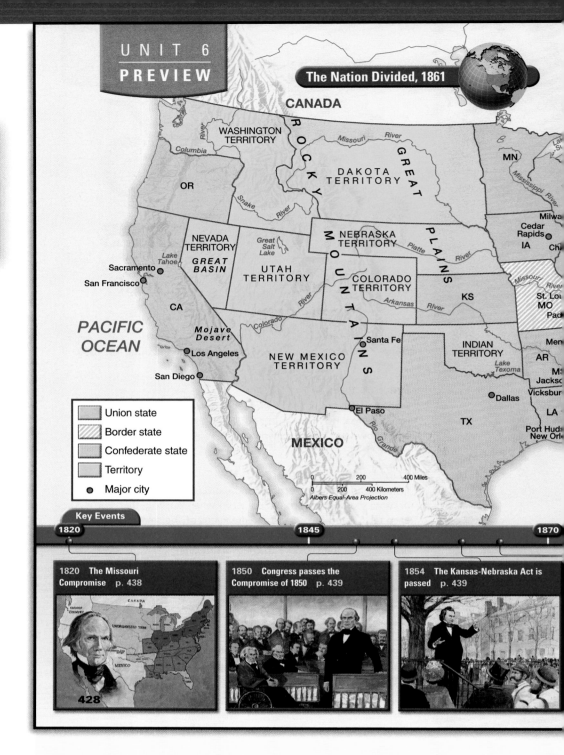

UNIT 6 PREVIEW

The Nation Divided, 1861

Union state
Border state
Confederate state
Territory
● Major city

Key Events

1820
1845
1870

1820 The Missouri Compromise p. 438

1850 Congress passes the Compromise of 1850 p. 439

1854 The Kansas-Nebraska Act is passed p. 439

428

INTEGRATE MATHEMATICS

Total States and Territories Have students examine the map and map key to determine the distribution of Union states, Confederate states, border states, and territories at this time. Confederate states: 11; Union states: 19, border states: 5, territories: 8 Then have students write a paragraph describing their observations about the totals.

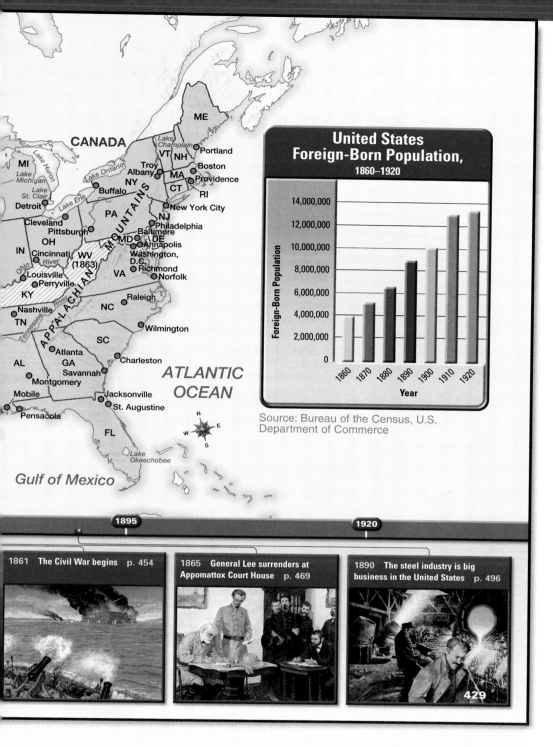

United States Foreign-Born Population, 1860–1920

Source: Bureau of the Census, U.S. Department of Commerce

1895

1920

| 1861 | The Civil War begins | p. 454 |

| 1865 | General Lee surrenders at Appomattox Court House | p. 469 |

| 1890 | The steel industry is big business in the United States | p. 496 |

429

SCHOOL TO HOME

Use the Unit 6 SCHOOL-TO-HOME NEWSLETTER on pages S11–S12 to introduce the unit to family members and suggest activities they can do at home.

Time Line Illustrations Ask students to speculate about the significance of the events shown on the time line.

- Henry Clay persuaded Congress to agree to the Missouri Compromise which kept a balance of free states and slave states.
- Henry Clay's Compromise of 1850 divided the lands gained from Mexico into two new territories. It also brought California into the Union as a free state.
- The Kansas-Nebraska Act allowed people in Kansas and Nebraska to decide by voting whether they would be free or slave territories.
- During the Civil War thousands of people in both the North and the South joined the war effort.
- Robert E. Lee surrendered his Confederate forces to Union General Ulysses S. Grant.
- As people found new uses for steel, more steel mills were built in the United States.

Visual Learning

Bar Graph Have students examine the bar graph. Pose such questions as the following:

- *What does this bar graph show?* It shows the number of foreign-born people in the United States between 1860 and 1920.
- *How much did the foreign-born population increase between 1860 and 1920?* by about 9,500,000 people

Make Connections

Link Map and Time Line Have students examine the map and the events shown on the time line. Then have them identify which events are related to the United States being divided. the Missouri Compromise, the Compromise of 1850, The Kansas-Nebraska Act, the Civil War, and General Lee's surrender

Start with a Journal

PAGES 430–433

OBJECTIVES

- Use first-hand accounts of historical events to gather information about history.
- Describe major events of the Civil War, such as the Battle of Gettysburg.

Summary

The Battle of Gettysburg was the bloodiest battle of the Civil War. The diary and letters of Elisha Hunt Rhodes describe the battle and how it was fought.

1 Motivate

Set the Purpose

Soldiers often wrote letters to their families during the Civil War that described the battles they had fought. These letters and diaries can teach us about the Civil War.

Access Prior Knowledge

Ask students to tell what they know about the Battle of Gettysburg.

READING SOCIAL STUDIES

Graphic Organizer Ask students to create a flow chart of the events of the Battle at Gettysburg. Encourage them to write two to three events in their flow chart from each day of the journal. Emphasize that their chart will focus on the journal author's experiences.

● USE READING AND VOCABULARY TRANSPARENCY 6-1.

6-1 TRANSPARENCY

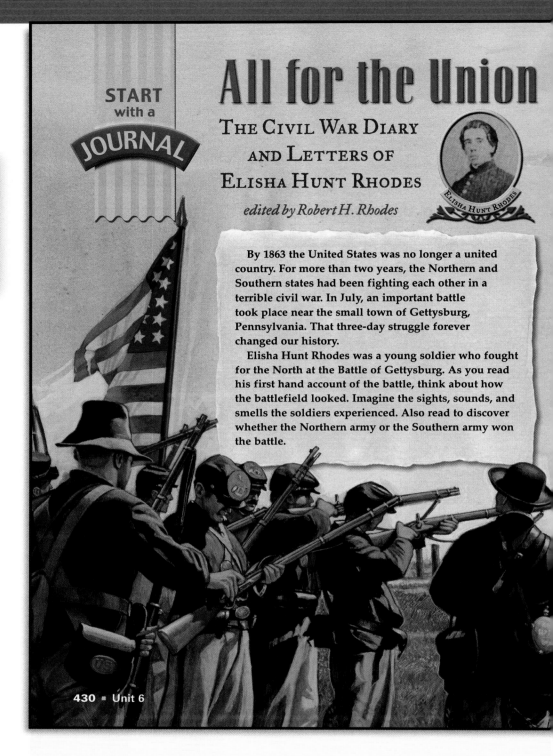

START with a JOURNAL

All for the Union
THE CIVIL WAR DIARY AND LETTERS OF ELISHA HUNT RHODES

edited by Robert H. Rhodes

By 1863 the United States was no longer a united country. For more than two years, the Northern and Southern states had been fighting each other in a terrible civil war. In July, an important battle took place near the small town of Gettysburg, Pennsylvania. That three-day struggle forever changed our history.

Elisha Hunt Rhodes was a young soldier who fought for the North at the Battle of Gettysburg. As you read his first hand account of the battle, think about how the battlefield looked. Imagine the sights, sounds, and smells the soldiers experienced. Also read to discover whether the Northern army or the Southern army won the battle.

430 ▪ Unit 6

WORD WORK

Historical Context Several terms that may be unfamiliar to students are defined at the bottom of the pupil pages. Other words may be unfamiliar to students. Have students make a table listing each unfamiliar word along with what they think it means from the context. Have students verify the correct definitions.

Word	Context Definition	Dictionary Definition

BACKGROUND

Elisha Hunt Rhodes Elisha Hunt Rhodes was only nineteen years old when he entered the Union army as a private in 1861. By the end of the war, he had reached the rank of lieutenant colonel. Parts of his diaries were used in a television series called "The Civil War." Robert Hunt Rhodes, the editor of the diaries, is the great-grandson of Elisha Hunt Rhodes.

July 3rd 1863—This morning the troops were under arms before light and ready for the great battle that we knew must be fought. The firing began, and our <u>Brigade</u> was hurried to the right of the line to reinforce it. While not in the front line yet we were constantly exposed to the fire of the <u>Rebel</u> Artillery, while bullets fell around us. We moved from point to point, wherever danger to be <u>imminent</u> until noon when we were ordered to report to the line held by Gen. Birney. Our Brigade marched down the road until we reached the house used by General Meade as Headquarters. The road ran between ledges of rocks while the fields were strewn with boulders. To our left was a hill on which we had many <u>batteries</u> posted. Just as we reached Gen. Meade's Headquarters, a shell burst over our heads, and it was immediately followed by showers of iron. More than two hundred guns were belching forth their thunder, and most of the shells that came over the hill struck in the road on which our Brigade was moving. Solid shot would strike the large rocks and split them as if exploded by gunpowder. The flying iron and pieces of stone struck men down in every direction. It is said that this fire continued for about two hours, but I have no idea of the time. We could not see the enemy, and we could only cover ourselves the best we could behind rocks and trees. About 30 men of our Brigade were killed or wounded by this fire. Soon the Rebel yell was heard, and we have found since that the Rebel General Pickett made a charge with his Division and was <u>repulsed</u> after reaching some of our batteries. Our lines of Infantry in front of us rose up and poured in a terrible fire. As we were only a few yards in rear of our lines we saw all the fight. The firing gradually died away, and but for an occasional shot all was still. But what a scene it was. Oh the dead and the dying on this bloody field. The 2nd <u>R.I.</u> lost only one man killed and five wounded. One of the latter belonged to my Co. "B". Again night came upon us and again we slept amid the dead and dying.

Brigade a large body of troops
Rebel the Southern army or a Southern soldier
imminent ready to take place

batteries groupings of big guns
repulsed driven back
R.I. Rhode Island

Unit 6   431

English as a Second Language Pair students who are acquiring English with English speakers in the class. Have them read the journal together by taking turns reading aloud. Ask them to stop when they find an unfamiliar word and try to figure out the meaning of the word together. Have them add the words to their vocabulary chart. After they have finished the journal, have them write three or four sentences that summarize the journal.

Weather and Climate Have students research the weather and climate of Gettysburg, Pennsylvania. Ask students to write a summary of the type of weather in the area in early July. Discuss with students how this weather may have affected the soldiers during the Battle of Gettysburg.

2 Teach

Read and Respond

Understand the Journal Ask students to imagine they are a soldier during the Civil War. Ask for volunteers to describe some of the feelings they might have before, during, and after the Battle of Gettysburg.

Q How do you think soldiers felt before going into battle in the Civil War?

A They probably felt frightened and nervous.

Geography Help students locate Gettysburg on a map of Pennsylvania. Show them how to look up the population of a city in an atlas and help them find the current population of Gettysburg.

Visual Learning

Illustration Ask students to look closely at the illustrations on pages 430–433. Ask the following questions:

- What are the soldiers wearing?
- What kinds of weapons do they have?

AUDIOTEXT

Text of these journal entries can be found on the Unit 6 AUDIOTEXT.

Read and Respond

Understand the Journal Ask students to think about how Elisha Hunt Rhodes's view of the Battle of Gettysburg would have been different if he had fought for the Confederate army.

Culture and Society Tell students that many Civil War battles that lasted for more than one day paused at night so soldiers could sleep.

Q How are Civil War battles different from the battles fought by the military today?

A Today, most battles are fought with airplanes and tanks. The equipment the military uses has changed how battles are fought.

 **Close**

Summarize the Reading

- Elisha Hunt Rhodes was a soldier for the Union army who kept a diary about what happened at the Battle of Gettysburg.
- The Union army defeated the Confederate army at the Battle of Gettysburg, but many soldiers from both armies were killed.

READING SOCIAL STUDIES

Graphic Organizer Have students use their graphic organizers to write a summary about the Battle of Gettysburg.

> soldiers prepare for battle
>
> ↓
>
> the battle
>
> ↓
>
> Union soldiers learn the Confederates had fallen back
>
> ↓
>
> Union troops win the battle

● USE READING AND VOCABULARY TRANSPARENCY 6-1.

6-1 TRANSPARENCY

July 4, 1863— Was ever the Nation's Birthday celebrated in such a way before. This morning the 2nd R.I. was sent out to the front and found that during the night General Lee and his Rebel Army had fallen back. It was impossible to march across the field without stepping upon dead or wounded men, while horses and broken Artillery lay on every side. We advanced to a sunken road (Emmitsburg Road) where we deployed as skirmishers and lay down behind a bank of earth. Berdan's Sharpshooters joined us, and we passed the day in firing upon any Rebels that showed themselves. At 12 M. a National Salute with shotted guns was fired from several of our Batteries, and the shells passed over our heads toward the Rebel lines. At night we were relieved and went to the rear for a little rest and sleep.

skirmishers scouts

432 ■ Unit 6

INTEGRATE LANGUAGE ARTS

Character Sketch
Challenge students to use information from the journal to write a character sketch of Elisha Hunt Rhodes. Help get students started by asking the following questions: *Do you think he was a brave soldier? Was he frightened in the battle? Was he loyal to the Union?*

July 5th 1863— Glorious news! We have won the victory, thank God, and the Rebel Army is fleeing to Virginia. We have news that Vicksburg has fallen. We have thousands of prisoners, and they seem to be <u>stupified</u> with the news. This morning our Corps (the 6th) started in pursuit of Lee's Army. We have had rain and the roads are bad, so we move slow. Every house we see is a hospital, and the road is covered with the arms and equipments thrown away by the Rebels.

stupified stunned

Analyze the Literature

1. What brigade did Elisha Hunt Rhodes belong to?

2. Where did the Southern army flee after losing the Battle of Gettysburg?

3. How can reading a first hand account of a historical event help you better understand it?

READ A BOOK

START THE UNIT PROJECT

The Hall of Fame With your classmates, create a Hall of Fame about the key people in the unit. As you read take notes on the contributions key people made. Your notes will help you create your Hall of Fame.

USE TECHNOLOGY

Visit The Learning Site at **www.harcourtschool.com** for additional activities, primary sources, and other resources to use in this unit.

Unit 6 ▪ **433**

Read a Book

Students may enjoy reading these leveled Independent Readers. Additional books are listed on p. 427D of this Teacher's Edition.

Easy *Freedom Quilts* by Carolyn Jackson. Students learn how these quilts were used to navigate the Underground Railroad.

Average *The Golden Spike* by Renee Skelton. Students read about the construction of the transcontinental railroad and its ceremonial completion in 1869.

Challenging *The Secrets of the Hunley* by Allen Mogol. Students learn about scholarly and scientific efforts to discover why the *Hunley*, a Confederate submarine whose remains were located in 1995, sank in 1864.

Start the Unit Project

Hint Encourage students to use a chart to help them keep track of information about key people of the Civil War.

Key People	Contributions

Use Technology

Analyze the Literature
Answers

1. Elisha Hunt Rhodes belonged to the Second Rhode Island Brigade.

2. The Southern army fled to Virginia after losing the Battle of Gettysburg.

3. When you read a first-hand account of a historical event, you feel more like you are there. You are better able to imagine what actually happened.

Chapter 12 Planning Guide The Nation Divided

Introducing the Chapter, pp. 434–435

LESSON	PACING	OBJECTIVES	VOCABULARY
Introduce the Chapter pp. 434–435	1 Day	■ Describe causes and effects of the Civil War. ■ Apply geographic tools to interpret visuals, including maps.	**Word Work:** Preview Vocabulary, p. 435
1 Regional Disagreements pp. 436–441	1 Day	■ Analyze events leading to the Civil War. ■ Describe legislative acts that dealt with slavery, such as the Missouri Compromise and the Kansas–Nebraska Act. ■ Explain how the Kansas–Nebraska Act led to conflict. ■ Analyze how the Dred Scott decision affected the United States.	sectionalism tariff states' rights free state slave state
READING SKILLS **Identify Frame of Reference** pp. 442–443	1 Day	■ Analyze quotations and written accounts of events to identify frame of reference. ■ Apply critical thinking skills to analyze information from primary references.	frame of reference
2 Slavery and Freedom pp. 444–449	1 Day	■ Describe the importance of slavery to the Southern economy. ■ Analyze laws pertaining to slavery. ■ Describe the purpose of the Underground Railroad and how it worked. ■ Analyze the contributions of women to the antislavery movement. ■ Identify important abolitionists and how they worked to end slavery.	emancipation resist code fugitive underground abolitionist equality **Word Work:** Use Reference Sources, p. 444

Categorize, p. 435

 Categorize, p. 436

Reading Social Studies:
Anticipation Guide, p. 437

Reading Social Studies:
Anticipation Guide Responses, p. 441

Mathematics
Percents, p. 437

Reading
Read a Biography, p. 439

Auditory Learners, p. 438

Extend and Enrich, p. 440

Reteach the Lesson, p. 441

Activity Book, p. 112

Reading and Vocabulary Transparency, 6-2

Internet Resources

Below-Level Learners,
p. 442

Extend and Enrich, p. 443

Reteach the Skill, p. 443

Activity Book, p. 113

Skill Transparency, 6-1

Reading Social Studies:
K-W-L Chart, p. 445

Reading Social Studies:
K-W-L Chart Responses,
p. 449

Language Arts
Write a Report, p. 446

Art
Drawing, p. 448

Below-Level Learners,
p. 445

Tactile Learners, p. 446

Extend and Enrich, p. 448

Reteach the Lesson, p. 449

Activity Book, p. 114

Reading and Vocabulary Transparency, 6-3

Chapter 12 Planning Guide The Nation Divided

LESSON	PACING	OBJECTIVES	VOCABULARY
3 The Union Breaks Apart pp. 450–455	1 Day	■ Describe Abraham Lincoln's political career. ■ Identify the states that made up the Confederate States of America. ■ Analyze the dynamics of the election of 1860. ■ Identify reasons that some Southern states left the Union. ■ Describe the events at Fort Sumter that marked the beginning of the Civil War.	**secede** **Confederacy**
MAP AND GLOBE SKILLS **Compare Maps with Different Scales** pp. 456–457	1 Day	■ Apply critical thinking skills to organize and use information from maps. ■ Use map scales to find distances on a map.	
4 Civil War pp. 458–464	2 Days	■ Analyze early battles of the Civil War. ■ Describe actions President Lincoln took during the Civil War. ■ Compare the resources and battle strategies of the United States and the Confederacy. ■ Explain the Emancipation Proclamation, and describe its effects. ■ Analyze how different groups of Americans contributed to the Civil War effort.	**retreat** **border state** **strategy** **casualty**
5 The Road to Union Victory pp. 465–471	1 Day	■ Identify major battles of the Civil War and their results. ■ Describe actions President Lincoln took during the Civil War. ■ Analyze the Gettysburg Address and its impact on the Civil War. ■ Describe the surrender of General Lee to General Grant at Appomattox.	**address** **Word Work:** Words with Multiple Meanings, p. 468
Chapter Review and Test Preparation pp. 472–473	1 Day		

READING	INTEGRATE LEARNING	REACH ALL LEARNERS	RESOURCES
Reading Social Studies: Study Questions, p. 451 **Reading Social Studies:** Study Question Responses, p. 455	Language Arts **Create a Multimedia Presentation,** p. 451 Language Arts **Informative Writing,** p. 452 Reading **Read a Biography,** p. 452 Art **Watercolor,** p. 454	**Auditory Learners,** p. 451 **Advanced Learners,** p. 453 **Extend and Enrich,** p. 455 **Reteach the Lesson,** p. 455	**Activity Book,** p. 115 **Reading and Vocabulary Transparency, 6-4** Internet Resources
	Mathematics **Measurement,** p. 456	**Extend and Enrich,** p. 457 **Reteach the Skill,** p. 457	**Activity Book,** pp. 116–117 **Skill Transparencies, 6-2A and 6-2B** **GeoSkills CD-ROM**
Reading Social Studies: Anticipation Guide, p. 459 **Reading Social Studies:** Anticipation Guide Responses, p. 464	Art **Make a Banner,** p. 460 Mathematics **Computation,** p. 461 Language Arts **Character Sketch,** p. 462 Health **First Aid,** p. 462	**Advanced Learners,** p. 459 **Extend and Enrich,** p. 464 **Reteach the Lesson,** p. 464	**Activity Book,** p. 118 **Reading and Vocabulary Transparency, 6-5** Internet Resources
Reading Social Studies: Graphic Organizer, p. 466 **Reading Social Studies:** Summarize, p. 467 **Reading Social Studies:** Paraphrase, p. 470 **Reading Social Studies:** Graphic Organizer Responses, p. 471	Health **Learn More About Illnesses,** p. 468 Reading **Make a Book Report,** p. 469	**English as a Second Language,** p. 465 **Extend and Enrich,** p. 470 **Reteach the Lesson,** p. 471	**Activity Book,** p. 119 **Reading and Vocabulary Transparency, 6-6** Internet Resources
		Test Preparation, p. 472	**Activity Book,** pp. 120–121 **Reading and Vocabulary Transparency, 6-7** **Assessment Program, Chapter 12 Test,** pp. 95–98

Activity Book

LESSON 1

Name _____ Date _____

Regional Disagreements

Directions Read the passage below. Then fill in the chart that follows, showing the differences between the North and South.

The North and the South could not come to an agreement about slavery. Northerners did not think that slavery should be allowed to spread to the western territories, while Southerners thought they had the right to take their enslaved workers west with them—just as they would take their other property.

The Northern economy relied on manufacturing and shipping, not agriculture, so the North did not need laborers as the South did. Also, many Northerners thought that slavery was wrong and should be abolished, or done away with. Those Northerners were called abolitionists, and they wanted all people to be free. Even Northerners who were not abolitionists did not want more slave states added to the country.

However, the economy of the South depended on laborers. Plantation owners were able to harvest more cotton, indigo, and tobacco by using slaves to work in the fields. Those Southerners believed that individual states had the right to decide whether people could have slaves.

	North	South
Economy based on	manufacturing and shipping	farming
Viewed slavery as	wrong	a necessity to work the fields
Ideas about extending slavery	No more slave states should come into the nation.	States had the right to decide whether people could own slaves.

Directions Use the passage and chart above to answer the questions.

❶ What were Northerners called who did not agree with slavery? Why were they called that? <u>abolitionists; the word *abolition* means "the act of doing away with," so abolitionists wanted to do away with slavery.</u>

❷ Where did most Northerners believe slavery should not be allowed to spread? <u>the western territories</u>

Use after reading Chapter 12, Lesson 1, pages 436–441.

SKILL PRACTICE

Name _____ Date _____

 READING SKILLS

Identify Frame of Reference

Directions Read the material below and then answer the questions.

Henry Clay

When Missouri asked to be a state in 1819, Henry Clay was a congress member from Kentucky. Although Clay owned slaves, he did not want slavery to divide the country. He worked very hard to find a solution that would make both the North and the South happy. While other members of Congress were arguing for their region of the country, Clay said, "I know no South, no North, no East, no West, to which I owe any allegiance [loyalty]." His solution was called the Missouri Compromise.

John Quincy Adams

John Quincy Adams, a Northerner, was the secretary of state at the time. Adams kept a diary, and in February 1820 he wrote about what he thought the future might bring, ". . . if the dissolution [breaking apart] of the Union should result from the slave question, it is as obvious as anything. . . that it must shortly afterwards be followed by the universal emancipation [freeing] of the slaves. . ."

❶ What viewpoint did Henry Clay have about the Union? How do you know?

<u>Clay thought that the Union was more important than any one region of the country. He said he was not loyal to any one section of the country.</u>

❷ What did John Quincy Adams think would happen if the Union broke apart?

<u>Shortly afterwards, all slaves would be freed.</u>

Use after reading Chapter 12, Skill Lesson, pages 442–443. **Activity Book ■ 113**

LESSON 2

Name _____ Date _____

Slavery and Freedom

Directions On the blanks provided, write the word or name that best completes each sentence. Some letters in your answers will have numbers under them. Write these letters in the appropriate boxes below, and you will find the name of the most famous conductor of the Underground Railroad.

❶ A man named <u>N a t   T u r n e r</u> led the first slave rebellion.
  (7 under the r)

❷ Something done in secret is done <u>u n d e r g r o u n d</u>.
  (3 under the d)

❸ A person who is running away is a <u>f u g i t i v e</u>.
  (9 under the e)

❹ To act against slavery is to <u>r e s i s t</u> it.
  (4 under the s)

❺ The Virginia legislature debated the <u>e m a n c i p a t i o n</u>, or freeing, of slaves.
  (11 under the m, 2 under the a)

❻ Sets of laws, known as slave <u>c o d e s</u>, ruled the lives of slaves.
  (6 under the e)

❼ Harriet Beecher Stowe wrote a book titled <u>U n c l e   T o m ' s   C a b i n</u>.
  (8 under the m, 13 under the n)

❽ The newspaper *Freedom's Journal* called for <u>e q u a l i t y</u>, or equal rights for all people.
  (12 under the t)

❾ Someone who wanted to end slavery was called an <u>a b o l i t i o n i s t</u>.
  (10 under the i, 5 under the i)

❿ A former slave named <u>S o j o u r n e r   T r u t h</u> traveled the country to speak out against slavery.
  (1 under the S)

H	a	r	r	i	e	t		T	u	b	m	a	n
1	2	3	4	5	6	7		8	9	10	11	12	13

Use after reading Chapter 12, Lesson 2, pages 444–449.

LESSON 3

Name _____ Date _____

The Union Breaks Apart

Directions Read the passage below. Then read each statement that follows. If the statement is true, write *T* in the blank. If the statement is false, write *F* in the blank.

Abraham Lincoln had barely a year of formal schooling, but he learned to read and write. He was very intelligent and read everything he could. Growing up, Lincoln had many jobs such as a rail-splitter, riverboat man, store clerk, and postmaster. After studying very hard on his own, he finally became a lawyer.

About five years later, in 1842, Abe Lincoln married Mary Todd. Soon after, they purchased a home in Springfield, Illinois. The Lincolns had four sons, but only one lived past the age of 19.

In 1846, Lincoln was elected to the United States Congress, where he served one term in the House of Representatives. Fourteen years later, he was elected President of the United States. Lincoln is the only President to own a patent for an invention. In 1849 he patented a device for lifting boats up over shallow places in rivers. Lincoln was also presented with several honorary degrees during the time of the Civil War.

As respected and honored as President Lincoln was, Mrs. Lincoln was not very popular in Washington. She came from a Southern family, and four of her brothers were in the Confederate army. Some people feared Mary Lincoln was a Confederate spy.

<u>T</u> ❶ The Lincolns had four children.

<u>F</u> ❷ Mrs. Lincoln was well liked in Washington.

<u>T</u> ❸ Mrs. Lincoln had brothers in the Confederate army.

<u>F</u> ❹ Lincoln never owned a home of his own.

<u>T</u> ❺ Lincoln received several honorary degrees.

<u>F</u> ❻ Many presidents had inventions that they patented.

<u>F</u> ❼ Lincoln went to school for many years.

<u>F</u> ❽ Lincoln was elected to the United States Senate.

Use after reading Chapter 12, Lesson 3, pages 450–455. **Activity Book ■ 115**

SKILL PRACTICE

Name _____ Date _____

 MAP AND GLOBE SKILLS

Compare Maps with Different Scales

Directions Look at the maps below, and then answer the questions on the facing page.

Map A: The Missouri Compromise, 1820

Map B: The Missouri Compromise, 1820

(continued)

116 ■ Activity Book   Use after reading Chapter 12, Skill Lesson, pages 456–457.

SKILL PRACTICE

Name _____ Date _____

Directions Use the maps on page 116 to answer the questions below.

1 Which map would be used to compare the size of Missouri to the size of Maine?
Map A

2 Which map would be used to determine the length of the border between Missouri and Kentucky? Map B

3 How many slave states were there at the time of the Missouri Compromise?
11

4 Was there more free territory or slave territory reserved?
free territory

5 Which state entered the Union at the same time as Missouri?
Maine

6 How many free states were there at the time of the Missouri Compromise?
11

Directions Compare the two maps. Write *A* in the answer blank if Map A is more useful, and *B* if Map B is more useful.

___B___ **7** Determine the length of the part of the Mississippi River that forms a Missouri border.

___A___ **8** Determine whether the free or slave states had the largest land area.

___B___ **9** Determine the length of the part of the Missouri River that flows from the eastern border to the western border of Missouri.

___A___ **10** Determine the number of miles of border separating the free states and the slave states.

Use after reading Chapter 12, Skill Lesson, pages 456–457.   **Activity Book ■ 117**

LESSON 4

Name _____ Date _____

Civil War

Directions In the box provided, write a brief paragraph to explain why each item on the left was important to the Civil War.
Student responses will vary. Possible responses are given.

EVENT	IMPORTANT BECAUSE
The Battle of Bull Run 	The Battle of Bull Run was the first major battle fought between the Union and Confederacy. The Confederates won the battle, proving to the Northerners that the South was more powerful than they thought.
Anaconda Plan	The purpose of the Union plan was to win control of the Mississippi River and blockade Confederate ports so that the South could not ship its cotton or bring in goods. With the South unable to sell cash crops, it would not have money to buy supplies for its army.
The Battle of Antietam 	Although the fighting at Antietam ended in nearly a tie, as a result of the battle President Lincoln announced his decision to issue an order freeing the slaves in areas that were still fighting against the Union.
The Emancipation Proclamation	The presidential order said that all slaves living in those parts of the South still fighting against the Union would be freed. The Emancipation Proclamation also hurt the South's chances of getting help from Britain and France.

118 ■ Activity Book   Use after reading Chapter 12, Lesson 4, pages 458–464.

LESSON 5

Name _____ Date _____

The Road to Union Victory

Directions Place the Civil War events in chronological order by numbering the dates on the time line.

1 Much of Atlanta burns to the ground after being captured by the Union army.

2 The Confederate army wins the Battle of Chancellorsville, and heads north towards Gettysburg.

3 The Union victory at the Battle of Gettysburg cripples the Confederate army.

4 General Robert E. Lee surrenders at Appomattox Court House, Virginia.

5 Lincoln gives the Gettysburg Address to inspire the nation and Union soldiers.

Civil War Events

May, 1863	May, 1864	May, 1865

July, 1863	Spring, 1864	April, 1865
3	1	4

May, 1863	November, 1863
2	5

Use after reading Chapter 12, Lesson 5, pages 465–471.   **Activity Book ■ 119**

Name _____ Date _____

Important Leaders and Battles of the Civil War

Directions Complete this graphic organizer by categorizing important leaders and battles of the Civil War.

UNION ARMY

IMPORTANT LEADERS
1. **Abraham Lincoln**
2. Ulysses S. Grant
3. William Tecumseh Sherman

IMPORTANT VICTORIES
1. **Battle of Gettysburg**
2. Battle of Vicksburg
3. Sherman's capture of Atlanta

CONFEDERATE ARMY

IMPORTANT LEADERS
1. **Jefferson Davis**
2. Robert E. Lee
3. Thomas "Stonewall" Jackson

IMPORTANT VICTORIES
1. **Victory at Fort Sumter**
2. Battle of Bull Run
3. Battle of Chancellorsville

© Harcourt

Use after reading Chapter 12, pages 435–471.

CHAPTER

Name _____ Date _____

12 Test Preparation

Directions Read each question and choose the best answer. Then fill in the circle for the answer you have chosen. Be sure to fill in the circle completely.

1. Who was one of the men who persuaded Congress to accept the Missouri Compromise?
   - Ⓐ John Calhoun
   - Ⓑ Daniel Webster
   - Ⓒ Henry Clay
   - Ⓓ Abraham Lincoln

2. Who defended the rights of both slaves and women?
   - Ⓕ Elizabeth Cady Stanton
   - Ⓖ Harriet Beecher Stowe
   - Ⓗ Clara Barton
   - Ⓙ Mary Todd Lincoln

3. Abraham Lincoln became well known through his debates with—
   - Ⓐ Henry Clay.
   - Ⓑ Stephen Douglas.
   - Ⓒ Jefferson Davis.
   - Ⓓ Major Robert Anderson.

4. The Union strategy to win the war by weakening the South was called the—
   - Ⓕ Join or Die Plan.
   - Ⓖ slash and burn policy.
   - Ⓗ King Cotton policy.
   - Ⓙ Anaconda Plan.

5. How did Abraham Lincoln honor the dead at Gettysburg?
   - Ⓐ He set up a memorial fund.
   - Ⓑ He had a monument built at the cemetery.
   - Ⓒ He gave a speech at the cemetery.
   - Ⓓ He sent the Vice President to the battlefield.

© Harcourt

COMMUNITY RESOURCES

Historical Societies
_____
_____
_____
_____
_____

Museums
_____
_____
_____
_____
_____

Experts on the Civil War
_____
_____
_____
_____
_____

Historical Sites
_____
_____
_____
_____
_____

Chapter 12 Assessment

CHAPTER

Name _____ Date _____

12 Test

Part One: Test Your Understanding

MULTIPLE CHOICE (4 points each)

Directions Circle the letter of the best answer.

1 The 1828 tax on imported goods mainly benefited—
A the South.
B the North.
C the West.
D Europe.

2 Andrew Jackson believed that—
F the Bank of the United States was good for the country.
G South Carolina should leave the Union.
H the federal government should have authority over states.
J regional loyalty was more important than the federal Union.

3 Maine joined the United States as a free state—
A before the Louisiana Purchase was made.
B to balance Missouri, a slave state.
C many years after Missouri entered the Union.
D at the same time South Carolina left the Union.

4 Which man was known as the Great Compromiser?
F John C. Calhoun
G Andrew Jackson
H Roger B. Taney
J Henry Clay

5 Dred Scott argued that he should be free because—
A his owner had died.
B he had moved often from one area to another.
C he had once lived in a free state.
D the Missouri Compromise kept people from owning property.

6 *Uncle Tom's Cabin* was—
F a stop on the Underground Railroad.
G a best-selling novel that opposed slavery.
H the first newspaper owned and written by African Americans.
J a newspaper published by abolitionist William Lloyd Garrison.

(continued)

Chapter 12 Test

Name _____ Date _____

7 The Civil War began when—
A Texas joined the Confederacy.
B South Carolina seceded from the Union.
C Abraham Lincoln was elected President.
D Confederate troops fired on Fort Sumter.

8 The Union's first plan for defeating the South—
F blocked goods from going into and out of Southern ports.
G worked to capture Richmond.
H gained the support of France and Britain.
J called for the invasion of manufacturing areas in the South.

9 The Emancipation Proclamation—
A immediately freed all slaves.
B ensured that Britain and France would help the South.
C allowed free slaves to serve in the military.
D freed slaves in those parts of the South that were still fighting against the Union.

10 The Battle of Gettysburg was a turning point in the Civil War because—
F it gave the South confidence to try invading the North.
G the South lost a major manufacturing city.
H the South could no longer control the Mississippi River.
J the weakened Southern army could no longer try to invade the North.

MATCHING (4 points each)

Directions Match terms and definitions by writing the correct letter in the space provided.

11 _E_ kept balance between slave and free states

12 _D_ regional loyalty

13 _A_ tax on imported goods

14 _C_ ruled that slavery was legal

15 _B_ the freeing of slaves

A. tariff

B. emancipation

C. Dred Scott decision

D. sectionalism

E. Missouri Compromise

(continued)

Chapter 12 Test

Name _____ Date _____

Part Two: Test Your Skills

IDENTIFY FRAME OF REFERENCE (5 points each)

Directions Read the quotation, and answer the questions that follow.

Frederick Douglass, former slave: "My first experience of life, as I now remember it, began in the family of my grandmother and grandfather, Betsey and Isaac Bailey. . .

. . . Whether because she [Grandmother Betsey] was too old for field service, or because she had so faithfully done the duties of her station in early life, I know not, but she enjoyed the special right of living in a cabin separate from the other cabins, having given her only the charge of the young children and the burden of her support. . . . The practice of separating mothers from their children and hiring them out at distances too great to allow their meeting, except after long periods of time, was a marked feature of the cruelty and hardness of the slave system. . . .

. . . My grandmother's five daughters were hired out. . . and my only recollections of my own mother are of a few hasty visits made in the night on foot, after the daily tasks were over, and when she had to return in time to answer the driver's call to the field in the early morning. These little glimpses of my mother under such conditions and against such odds, meager as they were, are permanently stamped upon my memory. She was tall and had dark, glossy skin with regular features, and amongst the slaves was remarkably sedate and dignified."

16 What was Frederick Douglass's opinion of slavery? Possible response: Douglass thought slavery was a cruel, hard system because it often separated mothers from their children.

17 Why do you think Douglass's meetings with his mother were "permanently stamped" on his memory? Possible response: Since Douglass only saw his mother a few times he wanted to remember everything he could about her.

18 Do you think Douglass's view of slavery was different from that of most slaveowners? Why or why not? Possible response: Yes. His view of slavery was different from that of most slaveowners because he had grown up as a slave and had been separated from his family.

(continued)

Chapter 12 Test

Name _____ Date _____

Part Three: Apply What You Have Learned

20 **CATEGORIZE** (10 points)

In the boxes below, write the names of two important Confederate victories and two important Union victories. List two important details about each battle.

Confederate Victories	Union Victories
Possible responses: The Battle of Manassas (Battle of Bull Run): Confederates were led by General Stonewall Jackson; the defeat shocked the Union; both armies were untrained. Chancellorsville: Confederates defeated a much larger Union army; General Jackson was accidentally killed in battle; the victory gave Confederates confidence to invade the North.	Possible responses: Vicksburg: The battle determined who would control the Mississippi River; the Union army held a siege around the city; the city of Vicksburg ran out of supplies. Gettysburg: Union forces stopped the Confederate invasion of the North. The Confederate army was greatly weakened and was never again able to enter Northern territory.

21 **ESSAY** (10 points)

The Civil War began as a war over the rights of individual states rather than as a war over slavery. However, by 1863 the North was fighting both to preserve the Union and to end slavery. Write a paragraph that describes the importance of slavery to the Civil War.

Possible response: Tensions between the North and South arose over issues of slave ownership, and conflict was narrowly avoided through the Missouri Compromise. In an attempt to enlarge the war's purpose, Abraham Lincoln issued the Emancipation Proclamation, which freed slaves in the Confederacy. Freed slaves also helped the Union by fighting in the Union army.

Chapter 12 Test

Introduce the Chapter

PAGES 434–435

OBJECTIVES

- Describe causes and effects of the Civil War.
- Apply geographic tools to interpret visuals, including maps.

Access Prior Knowledge

Ask students to think about whether they have ever had a conflict with a friend or family member. What was the cause of the conflict? How was the problem resolved? Have students discuss the most effective ways for settling disputes.

Visual Learning

Picture Have students examine the photograph. As a class, discuss what this image reveals about the focus of the chapter.

Locate It Map The Antietam National Battlefield covers more than 3,000 acres and commemorates the Civil War Battle of Antietam, also called the Battle of Sharpsburg. The battle was fought near Sharpsburg, Maryland, on Antietam Creek.

ANTIETAM NATIONAL BATTLEFIELD

The Battle of Antietam claimed more American lives in a single day than any other one day battle in United States history. Nearly 4,700 Union and Confederate soldiers were lost on September 17, 1862. Visitors to Antietam National Battlefield can tour over 90 monuments built to honor those fallen soldiers.

LOCATE IT

MARYLAND

Antietam National Battlefield

434 ▪ Unit 6

BACKGROUND

Picture The Union Army halted the first Confederate invasion of the North at the Battle of Antietam. General Robert E. Lee tried to establish a Confederate presence in Union territory by marching into Maryland in 1862. Union General McClellan halted Lee's advance at Sharpsburg, and the Confederate troops retreated.

BACKGROUND

Quotation Many popular tunes were written in response to the Civil War. Songwriters in both the North and South expressed feelings about the war through music. George Frederick Root (1820–1895) composed one of the North's most popular songs, *The Battle Cry of Freedom*. The song was even popular with Confederate troops.

12

The Nation Divided

" Yes, we'll rally 'round the flag, boys, we'll rally once again, Shouting the battle cry of freedom. "

—George Frederick Root,
The Battle Cry of Freedom, 1863

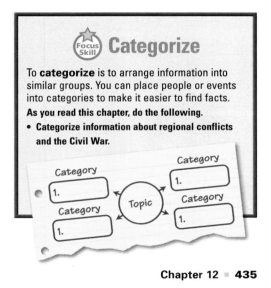

Categorize

To **categorize** is to arrange information into similar groups. You can place people or events into categories to make it easier to find facts.

As you read this chapter, do the following.

- Categorize information about regional conflicts and the Civil War.

Chapter 12 ■ **435**

Read and Respond

Ask a volunteer to read the chapter title aloud. Ask students what they think the title means. Have them think about different ways a nation can become divided.

Quotation Read the quotation aloud to the class.

Q How might patriotic music be important during a war?

A Students might suggest that music helps unite people and lift their spirits during hard times.

The Confederate victory at Fort Sumter marked the start of the Civil War. Union troops recaptured the fort in 1865 and played *The Battle Cry of Freedom* as they raised the Union flag.

Categorize

As students read the chapter, have them categorize information about the Union and Confederate armies in a graphic organizer.

- A blank graphic organizer for categorizing appears on page 120 of the Activity Book.

- Explain to students that categorizing is a way to organize information, and that it can help them interpret and remember facts.

- A completed graphic organizer can be found on page 120 of the Activity Book, Teacher's Edition.

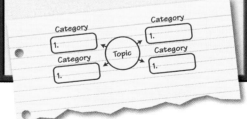

WORD WORK

Preview Vocabulary Have students skim the chapter to determine the meaning of the lesson vocabulary. Ask students to organize terms into two categories, the North and the South. Not all words will apply to these categories. Some terms may fall under both categories.

MAKE IT RELEVANT

Discussion Topics Use these topics to generate discussion as students read the chapter. The topics are meant to help students relate the information they are learning to contemporary issues.

- Why do countries fight civil wars today?

- What effect does a civil war have on a nation?

OBJECTIVES

- Analyze events leading to the Civil War.
- Describe legislative acts that dealt with slavery, such as the Missouri Compromise and the Kansas–Nebraska Act.
- Explain how the Kansas–Nebraska Act led to conflict.
- Analyze how the Dred Scott decision affected the United States.

Categorize pp. 435, 436, 438, 441, 472

Vocabulary

SEE READING AND VOCABULARY TRANSPARENCY 6-2 OR THE WORD CARDS ON PP. V69–V70.

sectionalism p. 436

tariff p. 436

states' rights p. 436

free state p. 437

slave state p. 437

 ### When Minutes Count

Organize the class into five groups. Have each group study a different subsection in the lesson. Then ask a volunteer from each group to share a summary of what they learned.

Quick Summary

This lesson discusses the tension between the North and the South over states' rights, tariffs, and slavery.

 **Motivate**

Set the Purpose

Big Idea Make sure students understand *regional differences* as used in the Big Idea statement. Discuss differences that might cause people living in different regions to disagree.

 CATEGORIZE
As you read, categorize the beliefs and actions of Americans by regions.

BIG IDEA
Regional differences caused conflict between Northern and Southern states.

VOCABULARY

sectionalism
tariff
states' rights
free state
slave state

People in the South used money from the cash crops they sold to buy goods from Europe.

Regional Disagreements

1820–1860

As the United States expanded its borders in the first half of the 1800s, strong differences developed among the various regions. Because of those differences, it was difficult for Americans to agree on many issues. In Congress, representatives from the North, South, and West often made decisions based on helping their own section, or region, rather than the country as a whole. This regional loyalty is called **sectionalism** (SEK•shuhn•uh•lih•zuhm), and the disagreements it caused threatened to tear the country apart.

Debate over State Authority

Sectionalism in the United States became a serious problem in 1828, when Congress set a high **tariff**, or tax, on some imports. The tariff made goods from Europe cost more than goods made in the United States. This protected factory owners and workers in the United States from foreign competition and made it easier for factories to sell their products.

The tariff helped the North because most of the nation's factories were located there. However, it did little to help the South, which remained mostly an agricultural region. People in the South sold many of their cash crops to businesses in Europe. In return, they bought many European manufactured goods. Southerners generally opposed the tariff because they did not like having to pay higher prices for those goods.

In 1829 Andrew Jackson became President, and John C. Calhoun of South Carolina became Vice President. Calhoun argued against the tariff. He believed in **states' rights**, or the idea that the states, not the federal government, should have the final authority over their own affairs. Calhoun believed

436

BACKGROUND

Sectionalism Even in the earliest days of the United States, George Washington was concerned about sectionalism. He confided in Thomas Jefferson that he was apprehensive about the tendency of the North and the South to be split on political matters. He felt that this split eventually might lead to the dissolution of the United States.

READING SKILL

Categorize Remind students that it is often helpful to categorize information. There are many opportunities for practicing this skill in this lesson. Ask students to categorize the following as they read: free states, slave states, and conflicts between the North and the South.

---

that states had the right to refuse to accept a law passed by Congress.

Although President Jackson was known to support states' rights, he still believed that the federal government had the constitutional right to collect the tariff, even if South Carolina thought it was too high. President Jackson made his feelings clear when he spoke at a dinner honoring the memory of former President Thomas Jefferson. Jackson, looking straight at Calhoun, firmly said, "Our Federal Union—It must and shall be preserved!" Calhoun, who was just as determined, answered, "The Union, next to our liberty most dear. May we all remember that it can be preserved only by respecting the rights of the states."

The debate over states' rights continued after Congress passed another tariff in 1832. Sectionalism grew stronger, and it further divided the people of the United States.

REVIEW Why did most people in the South oppose tariffs?

Division over Slavery

Another issue that had long divided the nation was slavery. Northern and Southern states had argued about it since the writing of the Constitution. The Mason-Dixon Line—roughly the border between Pennsylvania and Maryland—was seen as the dividing line between states that allowed slavery and those that did not. As settlers moved west, however, the arguments about slavery flared up again. Many settlers from the South wanted to bring their enslaved workers to the western territories.

Settlers from the North did not want slavery in the new western lands. Most

For political advice Jackson sometimes relied on a group of unofficial advisers, whom many referred to as Jackson's "Kitchen Cabinet."

Northerners thought that slavery should go no farther than where it already was—in the South. Most Southern slave owners believed that they had the right to take their slaves wherever they wanted. As the new western territories grew, settlers there asked to join the Union as new states. In each case, the same question arose. Would the new state be a free state or a slave state? A **free state** did not allow slavery. A **slave state** did.

For a time there were as many free states as slave states. This kept a balance between the North and the South in the Senate. Then, in 1819, settlers in the Missouri Territory, a part of the Louisiana Purchase, asked to join the Union as a slave state. If this happened, slave states would outnumber free states for the first time since the founding of the country.

The tariffs caused people in the South to pay a higher price for goods manufactured in Europe.

Chapter 12 ■ 437

Read and Respond

Civics and Government Lead a discussion with students about why keeping a balance of free states and slave states in the Union was of great concern. Remind students that each state automatically receives two seats in the Senate and a number of seats in the House of Representatives based on the population of the state. Ask students to think about how the passage of new laws would be affected if there were an imbalance of slave states and free states. Laws passed would favor the states with the majority of votes.

Visual Learning

Map Direct students' attention to the map on page 438. Ask them to locate the Mason-Dixon line and to identify the states directly next to the line. CAPTION ANSWER: Missouri and Maine

A New Compromise

Read and Respond

Geography Ask students to research which six states were admitted to the Union in the time between the Missouri Compromise and the Compromise of 1850. Then ask students to find each of the states on a map. Have students list in the following graphic organizer which of the states were free states and which were slave states according to the Missouri Compromise.

Free	Slave
Iowa	Texas
Wisconsin	Florida
Michigan	Arkansas

Make sure students understand that if California was admitted as a free state, there would be more free states than slave states.

The Missouri Compromise, 1820

Free state
Free territory
Admitted as a free state
Slave state
Slave territory
Admitted as a slave state
Missouri Compromise line
Mason-Dixon Line

0 200 400 Miles
0 200 400 Kilometers
Albers Equal-Area Projection

Regions The Missouri Compromise line divided lands that could join the Union as free states from lands that could join as slave states.

◆ Which two states were admitted to the Union as part of the compromise?

The Missouri question was debated in Congress for months. Henry Clay, a member of Congress from Kentucky, found himself in the middle of these heated arguments about slavery. Clay himself owned slaves, but he did not want to see the issue of slavery divide the country. He worked day and night to help solve the problem. Finally, in 1820, Clay persuaded Congress to agree to a plan known as the Missouri Compromise.

Under this plan Missouri would be allowed to join the Union as a slave state. Maine, which had also asked to become a state, would join as a free state. This would keep the balance between free states and slave states. Then a line would be drawn on a map of the rest of the lands gained in the Louisiana Purchase. Slavery would be allowed in places south of the line. It would not be allowed in places north of the line.

REVIEW How did the Missouri Compromise keep the balance between free states and slave states? CATEGORIZE It allowed Missouri to join the Union as a slave state and Maine to join the Union as a free state.

Henry Clay became known as the Great Compromiser because of his work to settle differences between the North and the South.

A New Compromise

The Missouri Compromise kept the peace for nearly 30 years. During this time six new states joined the Union. The number of free states and slave states remained equal. Then, in 1848, the United States gained new lands after winning the war with Mexico. Settlers in California, a part of these new lands, asked to join the Union as a free state. Once again arguments about the spread of slavery broke out. The Missouri Compromise did not apply to lands outside of the Louisiana Purchase.

Henry Clay again worked toward a compromise—the Compromise of 1850. Under this compromise, California joined the Union as a free state. The rest of the lands gained from Mexico were divided into two territories—New Mexico and Utah. The people in those territories would decide for themselves whether to allow slavery.

Henry Clay, who became known as the Great Compromiser, died in 1852. He never gave up hope that the country would find a peaceful way to settle its differences. On his grave marker in Lexington, Kentucky, are the words *I know no North—no South—no East— no West.* Two years after Clay's death, however, bad feelings between free states and slave states turned to violence.

REVIEW **Who became known as the Great Compromiser?** Henry Clay

Bleeding Kansas

In 1854 Congress passed the Kansas–Nebraska Act, which changed the rules of the Missouri Compromise. Under the Missouri Compromise, slavery would not have been allowed in the territories of Kansas and Nebraska. Under the Kansas–Nebraska Act, however, people in those territories were given the opportunity to decide for themselves whether to allow slavery. They would decide by voting.

The Kansas Territory quickly became the center of attention in the nation. People for and against slavery rushed into the territory. They hoped to help decide the outcome by casting their votes.

Compromise of 1850

Free state
Free territory
Slave state
Indian territory
Decision on slavery left to territory

GEOGRAPHY THEME

Regions Henry Clay's compromise brought California into the Union as a free state.

◆ What states were later formed from the Utah territory?

Chapter 12 ■ 439

Read and Respond

History Inform students that another important measure of the Compromise of 1850 was the Fugitive Slave Act, which required all runaway slaves to be returned to their owners. Discuss the implications this law may have had for escaped slaves. If slaves were returned to owners, escaping would be much more difficult.

Visual Learning

Map Ask students to compare the slave states and free states on the map on page 438 with those on the map on page 439.
CAPTION ANSWER: Nevada and Utah.

Analyze Primary Sources

Quotation Have students read Clay's epitaph on page 439. What do these words convey about Clay's hope for the Union? Clay hoped the North and the South would reconcile their political differences.

GO ONLINE Students might enjoy researching information about other monuments and tombstones. Have them visit The Learning Site at **www.harcourtschool.com**.

Bleeding Kansas

Read and Respond

History Point out to students that the war between proslavery and antislavery settlers in Kansas continued on and off for almost four years. Explain also that Kansas had many territorial legislatures and had voted on a constitution more than once before finally being admitted to the Union on January 29, 1861, as a free state.

Q **What issue did Congress allow the territories of Nebraska and Kansas to decide for themselves?**

A whether or not slavery would be allowed there

Analyze Primary Sources

Poster Have students study the poster carefully. Encourage them to read the document to find the date and reason for the meeting.

CAPTION ANSWER: to show that people support the free states

Visual Learning

Map Have students locate the Kansas and Nebraska Territories.

CAPTION ANSWER: four territories—Kansas, Nebraska, Utah, and New Mexico

The Dred Scott Decision

Read and Respond

Culture and Society Discuss with students how the Dred Scott decision increased tensions between the North and the South.

Q How were both the North and the South affected by the decision?

A Possible response: It highlighted their differences and made the problem worse.

3 Close

Summarize Key Content

- The debate over tariffs and states' rights divided the people of the United States.
- The Missouri Compromise kept the number of slave states and free states balanced for 30 years.
- The Compromise of 1850 admitted California into the Union as a free state and allowed the new territories of Utah and New Mexico to decide whether to allow slavery.
- The Kansas–Nebraska Act changed the Missouri Compromise and allowed people in the territories to vote on slavery.
- The Supreme Court denied Dred Scott freedom, which led to increased tension between the North and the South.

Kansas–Nebraska Act

Analyze Primary Sources

This poster was used to announce a meeting of those who supported the Kansas–Nebraska Act.

❶ The headline states what type of meeting was being held.

❷ The date shows when the meeting was held.

❸ The phrase indicates that many people were to attend the meeting.

◆ Why do you think quotations are included on the poster?

"UNION IS STRENGTH."

FREE STATE CONVENTION!

All who are favorable to union

BIG SPRING, THIRD DISTRICT,

On Wednesday, September 5th,

Mass Meeting

"United we stand; divided we fall."

It was not long before fighting broke out between the two sides. More than 200 people were killed in the bitter conflict that is known as "Bleeding Kansas."

Kansas eventually joined the Union as a free state, but the bloodshed there was a sign of things to come. Many people on both sides of the slavery issue no longer saw compromise as a possible solution. Some in the South began to speak of leaving the Union.

REVIEW What did the Kansas–Nebraska Act do? It gave the people in these territories the opportunity to decide for themselves whether to allow slavery.

The Dred Scott Decision

In 1857 the United States Supreme Court decided the case of an enslaved African American named Dred Scott. Scott had asked the Court for his freedom. The Court said no.

Scott was the slave of an army doctor. His owner moved often and always took Scott with him. For a time they lived in Illinois, a free state. Then they lived in

GEOGRAPHY THEME Regions The Kansas–Nebraska Act allowed people in the Kansas and Nebraska territories to decide by voting whether they would be free or slave territories.

◆ How many territories could now decide for themselves whether to allow slavery?

Free state
Free territory
Slave state
Indian territory
Decision on slavery left to territory

BACKGROUND

Dred Scott Dred Scott eventually gained his freedom on May 26, 1857, when he and his family were bought and freed by the sons of his first owner. Scott died only a few months later on February 17, 1858.

EXTEND AND ENRICH

Debate the Issues Divide the class into four groups, and assign each group one of these topics: the Missouri Compromise, the Compromise of 1850, the Kansas–Nebraska Act, the Dred Scott Case. Have each group prepare and present a five-minute debate that gives both sides of each issue. Ask each group to summarize how the disagreements over its particular issue were settled.

Wisconsin, a free territory under the Missouri Compromise.

After his owner died, Scott took his case to court. He argued that he should be free because he had once lived on free land. The case moved up through the federal court system until it reached the Supreme Court. There, Chief Justice Roger B. Taney (TAH•nee) said that because Scott was a slave, he had "none of the rights and privileges" of an American citizen. Having lived in a free territory did not change that.

Taney also declared that Congress had no right to forbid slavery in the Wisconsin Territory. He felt that the United States Constitution protected the right of people to own slaves. Slaves, he wrote, were property. He believed that the Missouri Compromise was keeping people from owning property. This, Taney wrote, was unconstitutional.

In 1857 the Supreme Court decided that Dred Scott should not be given his freedom.

Many people had hoped the Dred Scott decision would finally settle the disagreements among sections of the country over slavery once and for all. Instead, it made the problem worse.

REVIEW Why did the Supreme Court deny freedom to Dred Scott? because Scott was a slave and he had none of the rights and privileges of an American citizen

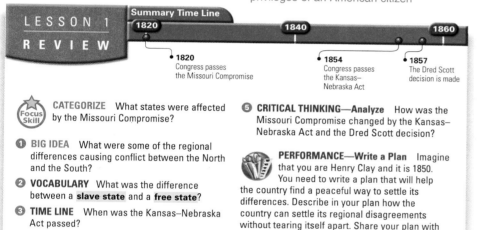

LESSON 1 REVIEW

Summary Time Line

- **1820** Congress passes the Missouri Compromise
- **1854** Congress passes the Kansas–Nebraska Act
- **1857** The Dred Scott decision is made

(Focus Skill) **CATEGORIZE** What states were affected by the Missouri Compromise?

1 **BIG IDEA** What were some of the regional differences causing conflict between the North and the South?

2 **VOCABULARY** What was the difference between a **slave state** and a **free state**?

3 **TIME LINE** When was the Kansas–Nebraska Act passed?

4 **GEOGRAPHY** In what region of the country were tariffs helpful?

5 **CRITICAL THINKING—Analyze** How was the Missouri Compromise changed by the Kansas–Nebraska Act and the Dred Scott decision?

PERFORMANCE—Write a Plan Imagine that you are Henry Clay and it is 1850. You need to write a plan that will help the country find a peaceful way to settle its differences. Describe in your plan how the country can settle its regional disagreements without tearing itself apart. Share your plan with the rest of the class.

Chapter 12 ■ 441

Assess

Lesson 1 Review—Answers

 CATEGORIZE Missouri and Maine were affected by the Missouri Compromise.

1 **BIG IDEA** The North and the South were divided over tariffs, states' rights, and slavery.

2 **VOCABULARY** A **free state** did not allow slavery, and a **slave state** did.

3 **TIME LINE** in 1854

4 **GEOGRAPHY** Tariffs were most helpful in the North.

5 **CRITICAL THINKING—Analyze** The Kansas–Nebraska Act changed the rules of the Missouri Compromise, allowing people in the territories to determine whether to allow slavery or not. Hostilities between the two sides grew after the decision in the Dred Scott case.

 Performance Assessment Guidelines Students' plans should include ways to solve the tariff and slavery issues in a peaceful manner.

ACTIVITY BOOK

Use ACTIVITY BOOK, p. 112, to reinforce and extend student learning.

RETEACH THE LESSON

Graphic Organizer Have students fill in the following graphic organizer with the opinions of most people in the North and the South regarding the issues that divided the country before the Civil War.

Issue	North	South
states' rights	The Union comes first.	States should have final authority.
tariffs	in favor of tariffs	against tariffs
slavery	against the spread of slavery	supported the spread of slavery

Skill Lesson

PAGES 442–443

OBJECTIVES

- Analyze quotations and written accounts of events to identify frames of reference.
- Apply critical thinking skills to analyze information from primary references.

Vocabulary

frame of reference p. 442

WORD CARDS

See pp. V69–V70.

1 Motivate

Why It Matters

Explain to students that people often see things differently. A person's frame of reference can influence how he or she describes an event and his or her opinion of it. Emphasize that historians must identify frames of reference to help them understand how events actually happened and what feelings people had about the event.

SKILLS · READING

Identify Frame of Reference

VOCABULARY

frame of reference

▶ WHY IT MATTERS

When you read something that people have written about an event or listen to them tell about it, you need to consider their **frame of reference**—where they were when the event happened or what role they played in it. A person's frame of reference can influence how he or she sees an event or feels about it. It can also influence how a person describes an event. Considering a person's frame of reference as you read or listen can help you better understand what happened.

▶ WHAT YOU NEED TO KNOW

In the 1800s, people's opinions about slavery and other issues were often influenced by where they lived. People who lived in the South, North, and West all had different frames of reference.

SENATOR JAMES HENRY HAMMOND, South Carolina, 1858

❝ The greatest strength of the South arises from the harmony of her political and social institutions. This harmony gives her a frame of society, the best in the world, and an extent of political freedom, combined with entire security, such as no other people ever enjoyed upon the face of the earth. . . . In all social systems there must be a class to do the menial [unskilled] duties. ❞

442 ▪ Unit 6

REACH ALL LEARNERS

Below-Level Learners
Ask students to give their opinion about whether recess should be shorter, longer, or the same length of time it is now. Most students will reply "longer" to this question. Next, ask them to give reasons they feel the way they do. Help them understand that their frame of reference influences the way they feel. Since they are students, they would most likely prefer a longer recess.

BACKGROUND

William Seward After he served as a United States senator, William Seward was secretary of state for President Abraham Lincoln and President Andrew Johnson. He was integral in keeping Europe from becoming involved in the Civil War. He is probably most remembered for securing the purchase of Alaska from Russia in 1867 for $7,200,000. Many people thought it was an unwise purchase and called it Seward's Folly.

The statements on these pages were made in 1858 by Senator James Henry Hammond of South Carolina and Senator William Seward of New York. Senator Hammond owned a cotton plantation and had served as governor of South Carolina in 1842. Senator Seward was born, raised, and educated in New York State. He served as governor of New York from 1839 to 1843 and established a strong antislavery stand.

As you read the statements, consider how each senator's frame of reference might have affected what he said.

➡ PRACTICE THE SKILL

Answer these questions.

❶ What was Senator Hammond's position on slavery? How might his frame of reference have affected it?

❷ How was Senator Seward's position on slavery different from the one held by Senator Hammond? In what way was Seward's frame of reference different?

❸ How might a Southerner's opinion of Senator Seward's description of the "slave system" be different from that of a person from the North? of a person from the West?

➡ APPLY WHAT YOU LEARNED

Think about a present-day example of how frames of reference cause differences in opinions and beliefs. Write a paragraph that describes this present-day example and explains why the people involved may think the way they do. Share your paragraph with a classmate.

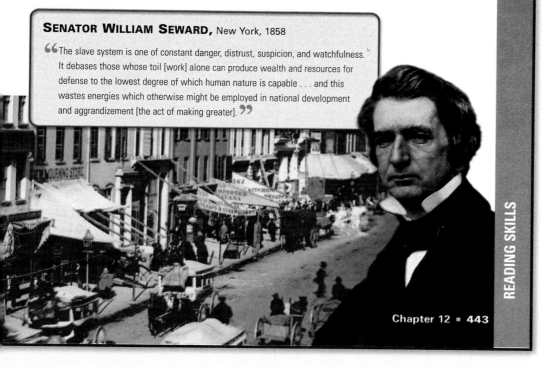

SENATOR WILLIAM SEWARD, New York, 1858

❝The slave system is one of constant danger, distrust, suspicion, and watchfulness. It debases those whose toil [work] alone can produce wealth and resources for defense to the lowest degree of which human nature is capable . . . and this wastes energies which otherwise might be employed in national development and aggrandizement [the act of making greater].❞

READING SKILLS

Chapter 12 ■ 443

---

2 Teach

What You Need to Know

Have students read the quotations from Senator Hammond and Senator Seward. Ask students to think about how the states in which the senators lived influenced their frames of reference. Remind students that people often feel connected to their home states or communities.

Practice the Skill—Answers

❶ Senator Hammond supported slavery. He was from the South, where slavery was important to the economy.

❷ Senator Seward opposed slavery. He was from the North, where slavery had been abolished.

❸ A Southerner would probably disagree with Senator Seward's description, whereas a Northerner would probably agree. A person from the West would probably agree, but it might depend on whether he or she first came from a slave state.

3 Close

Apply What You Learned

Students' paragraphs should describe an example in which at least two people have different opinions or beliefs because they have different frames of reference. Students should include reasons for each person's frame of reference. Have students share their paragraphs with classmates.

ACTIVITY BOOK

Use ACTIVITY BOOK, p. 113, to give students additional practice using this skill.

EXTEND AND ENRICH

Research Encourage students to go online to research more about Senator Hammond and Senator Seward. Ask them to find more information that enables them to determine each man's frame of reference. Have students share their findings with the class.

TRANSPARENCY

Use SKILL TRANSPARENCY 6-1.

RETEACH THE SKILL

Write Questions Have students work in groups to develop questions that could be asked to help determine people's frames of reference. Suggest questions such as "Where do they live?" "What is their job?" "Are they involved in politics?" "Do they own a business?" Compile the groups' questions into a classroom guide for determining frame of reference.

Categorize pp. 435, 444, 449, 472

Vocabulary

SEE READING AND VOCABULARY TRANSPARENCY 6-3 OR THE WORD CARDS ON PP. V69–V72.

emancipation p. 445	**underground** p. 446
resist p. 445	**abolitionist** p. 448
code p. 445	**equality** p. 448
fugitive p. 445	

When Minutes Count

Ask students to write the vocabulary terms and definitions. Then read aloud the Big Idea statement. Ask volunteers to explain how each term relates to the Big Idea.

Quick Summary

This lesson examines proslavery legislation and the work of abolitionists before the Civil War.

1 Motivate

Set the Purpose

Big Idea Discuss with students the kinds of things they think people did to try to end slavery.

· LESSON ·

2

CATEGORIZE

As you read, categorize examples of differing views of slavery by regions.

BIG IDEA

Some people worked to try to end slavery.

VOCABULARY

emancipation
resist
code
fugitive
underground
abolitionist
equality

Slavery and Freedom

1820	1870	1920

1820–1860

By 1860 there were nearly 4 million slaves in the United States, an increase from 900,000 in 1800. This growth of slavery was due chiefly to the growing importance of cotton as a cash crop in the South. Cotton became such an important part of the Southern economy that it was called "King Cotton." The demand for cotton created a demand for more enslaved workers.

The Slave Economy

Slavery had been a part of American life since colonial days. Some people thought that slavery was wrong. Other people could not make money using enslaved workers. The cost of feeding, clothing, and housing slaves was too great.

In the South, however, slavery continued because owners had come to depend on the work of enslaved people. Slaves were made to work as miners, carpenters, factory workers, and house servants. Some, however, were taken to large plantations. There they raised many acres of cotton and other cash crops, such as rice, tobacco, and sugarcane.

Many slaves had to wear identification badges (above). This scene (right) shows a plantation on the Mississippi River.

444 ■ Unit 6

While wealthy planters owned more than half the slaves in the South, most white Southerners owned no slaves at all. By 1860 one of every four white Southern families owned slaves.

REVIEW In which region of the United States was slavery most important? Why?

Slavery and the Law

Until the 1820s most people in the South thought slavery was wrong but necessary. In 1832, members of the Virginia legislature even debated **emancipation** (ih•man•suh•PAY•shuhn), or the freeing of slaves, in their state.

The debate started because many Virginians had been frightened by a slave rebellion the year before. The rebellion took place in Southampton County, Virginia. A slave named Nat Turner led an attack that killed more than 50 people, among them his owner. In turn, slave owners trying to end the rebellion killed more than 100 slaves.

Most slaves never took part in such rebellions, but they did whatever they

could to **resist**, or act against, slavery. They broke tools, pretended to be sick, or acted as if they did not understand what they had been told. Such actions were dangerous, however, and slaves had to be careful to avoid punishment.

The Virginia legislature voted not to end slavery. To prevent future uprisings, Virginia joined with other slave states who had passed laws that put more controls on slaves. These laws were called slave codes. Under these **codes**, or sets of laws, slaves were not allowed to leave their owners' land, to meet in groups, or to buy or sell goods. Most slaves were not allowed to learn to read or write, and speaking against slavery became a crime.

The federal government also passed laws about slavery. One of these laws was called the Fugitive Slave Act. A **fugitive** is a person who is running away from something. Under this law, anyone caught helping a slave escape could be punished. People who found runaway slaves had to return them to the South.

REVIEW What were slave codes? sets of laws that put more controls on slaves

Analyze Graphs   Many people did not own slaves.
◆ What percent of Southerners owned no slaves?

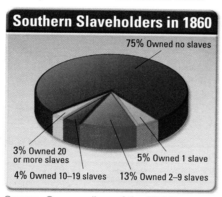

Southern Slaveholders in 1860

75% Owned no slaves
3% Owned 20 or more slaves
4% Owned 10–19 slaves
5% Owned 1 slave
13% Owned 2–9 slaves

Source: Compendium of the Eighth Census, 1860

Chapter 12 ■ 445

Access Prior Knowledge

Review with students what they know about slavery in the United States.

READING SOCIAL STUDIES

K-W-L Chart Have students fill in the "What I Know" and "What I Want to Know" sections of the K-W-L chart before they read the lesson.

What I Know	What I Want to Know	What I Learned
Many slaves worked on plantations in the South.	What was the Underground Railroad?	
Few Northerners had slaves.	What did people do to stop slavery?	

● USE READING AND VOCABULARY TRANSPARENCY 6-3.

2 Teach

The Slave Economy

Read and Respond

Economics Discuss with students the economic importance of slaves to Southern plantation owners. Ask students to hypothesize how planters came to depend on slavery. Students may respond that at that time many people were needed to work in the fields. The planters could not have made as much money from their crops if they had paid the slaves for their work.

Q **What were some of the jobs of enslaved persons?**

A mining, carpentry, factory work, fieldwork, housework

Visual Learning

Graph Direct students' attention to the graph on page 445. Have them speculate about the reasons people owned slaves.

CAPTION ANSWER: 75 percent

Slavery and the Law

Read and Respond

Civics and Government Inform students that the Fugitive Slave Act appointed federal marshals to help capture runaway slaves.

Q Why did the government pass a law requiring slaves to be returned to their owners?

A Southerners thought that slaves were private property and should be returned to their owners.

The Underground Railroad

Read and Respond

Culture and Society Lead a discussion with students about how slaves were treated. Ask students to think about the reasons slaves might have chosen to run away. Remind students that many enslaved people risked their lives when they ran away.

Visual Learning

Map Point out the various routes that could be taken to escape to free states.
CAPTION ANSWER: the Mississippi, Ohio, and Missouri Rivers

The Underground Railroad

By 1860 there were more than 500,000 free African Americans living in the United States. Some had been born to parents who were free. Some had bought their freedom or had been freed by their owners. Others had escaped slavery by running away.

Over the years thousands of slaves tried to gain their freedom by running away. Some ran away alone. Others tried to escape with their families or friends.

Once away from their owners' land, runaway slaves had to find safe places to hide. Many slaves helped each other along the way. Native American groups helped slaves by giving them shelter. Some slaves hid in forests, swamps, or mountains, sometimes for years.

Many runaway slaves continued moving for months until they reached Canada or Mexico or free states in the North. Some found helpers who led the way— the brave men and women of the Underground Railroad. The word **underground** is often used to describe something done in secret.

The Underground Railroad was a system of secret escape routes leading to free

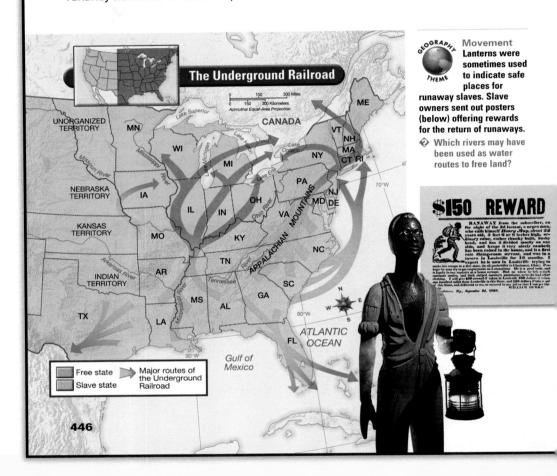

The Underground Railroad

Movement Lanterns were sometimes used to indicate safe places for runaway slaves. Slave owners sent out posters (below) offering rewards for the return of runaways.

◈ Which rivers may have been used as water routes to free land?

$150 REWARD

Free state
Slave state
Major routes of the Underground Railroad

446

---

lands. Most routes led from the South to free states in the North or to Canada. Some led to Mexico and to islands in the Caribbean Sea.

Working mostly at night, conductors, or helpers along the Underground Railroad, led runaway slaves from one hiding place to the next along the routes. These hiding places—barns, attics, storage rooms—were called stations. There the runaways could rest and eat, preparing for the journey to the next station.

Most conductors were free African Americans and white Northerners who opposed slavery. Harriet Tubman, an African American who had escaped from slavery herself, was one of the best-known conductors of the Underground Railroad. During the 1850s Tubman returned to the South 20 times and guided about 300 people to freedom. She proudly claimed, "I never lost a single passenger."

REVIEW What was the Underground Railroad? 🌐 CATEGORIZE
a secret system of escape routes that helped slaves get to free lands

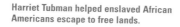
Harriet Tubman helped enslaved African Americans escape to free lands.

Women Work for Change

Many of the people who worked to free slaves were themselves not entirely free. White women, many of whom spoke out against slavery, were generally not accepted as men's equals. They could not vote, hold public office, or sit on juries.

In 1840, a group of American women went as delegates to a world anti-slavery convention in London, England. They were denied the right to participate and could only watch the proceedings from the balcony.

One of the women who took part in the convention in London also played an important role at another convention eight years later. Elizabeth Cady Stanton, a defender of the rights of both women and slaves, participated at the first women's rights convention, held in Seneca Falls, New York. Stanton wrote a statement listing women's grievances.

This mural by Hames Michael Newell shows runaway slaves on the Underground Railroad.

Harriet Tubman Harriet Tubman began her trips for the Underground Railroad in 1850. On her first trip, she took her sister and two nieces north. The following year she rescued her brother, and in 1857 she took her parents to freedom. She often disguised herself to avoid suspicion when she traveled in slave states. She usually began her escapes on a Saturday night because many slaves did not work on Sunday and it was less likely that they would be missed by their owners on a Sunday.

Harriet Beecher Stowe The daughter of a New England minister, Stowe saw for herself the mistreatment of enslaved people when she traveled in Kentucky. *Uncle Tom's Cabin* was first published in a newspaper and then as a two-volume book. In one year it sold more than 300,000 copies and was translated into many foreign languages. In addition to her interest in the abolitionist movement, Stowe was active in the fight for women's suffrage.

Read and Respond

History Tell students that it is unknown how many slaves followed the Underground Railroad to freedom, but despite the professional slave catchers and the officials looking for escaped slaves, thousands did escape.

Q What might conductors on the Underground Railroad have done to protect themselves and those they were helping to free?

A Answers will vary but may include resting during the day; traveling at night; providing food, water, and clothing.

Visual Learning

Mural Have students study the mural shown on page 447. Explain that the painting shows slaves on their way to freedom while staying at Brockett Farm, a stop on the Underground Railroad near Dolgeville, New York. The mural was commissioned in 1940 to be displayed in the Dolgeville post office.

Women Work for Change

Read and Respond

Link Culture and Society with Civics and Government Point out that Elizabeth Cady Stanton was one of many nineteenth-century women who worked for women's rights. Explain that these women demanded the same political, social, and economic rights as men. However, women continued to be denied equal rights for many years after the struggle for women's rights began. Have students speculate on the risks these women took to speak out.

Q Where was the first women's rights convention held?

A Seneca Falls, New York

Culture and Society Discuss with students the impact Harriet Beecher Stowe's book, *Uncle Tom's Cabin*, had in helping to turn people against slavery.

Abolitionists

Read and Respond

Culture and Society Discuss with students why media such as newspapers were integral in spreading the antislavery messages of abolitionists. Ask students to think about why two free African Americans would publish a newspaper. They thought it was time to speak up on their own behalf.

Visual Learning

Bar Graph Direct students' attention to the graph on page 448. Have students speculate about what might have caused the number of enslaved African Americans to rise. CAPTION ANSWER: The number of enslaved African Americans rose dramatically from 1800 to 1860, while the number of free African Americans increased only slightly.

Analyze Primary Sources

Quotation Explain that many abolitionists had very strong views about slavery. Direct students' attention to the words of William Lloyd Garrison. Ask students why the final portion of the quotation is in capital letters. for emphasis

 **Close**

Summarize Key Content

- Slavery continued in the South because owners depended on slaves to work in the fields.
- The Fugitive Slave Act was passed as part of the Compromise of 1850.
- The Underground Railroad helped runaway slaves reach freedom.
- Elizabeth Cady Stanton spoke out against slavery and worked for women's rights.
- Abolitionists had been working to end slavery since the 1680s.

In her statement, she demanded that women "have immediate admission to all the rights and privileges which belong to them as citizens of the United States."

In 1852 Harriet Beecher Stowe worked for change by publishing a novel that turned many people against slavery. The book, *Uncle Tom's Cabin*, told the heartbreaking story of slaves being mistreated by a cruel overseer. The book quickly became a best-seller and was made into a play.

Many of the same people who fought for equal rights for women also fought to end slavery. They often united antislavery and women's rights to form a double crusade for freedom.

REVIEW What book turned many people against slavery? *Uncle Tom's Cabin*

Abolitionists

People who opposed slavery worked to abolish, or end, it. Those who wanted to abolish slavery were called **abolitionists** (a•buh•LIH•shuhn•ists). Among the first to speak out, as early as the 1680s, were members of the Society of Friends, commonly known as the Quakers. In

Millions of people read Stowe's novel, *Uncle Tom's Cabin.*

448 ▪ Unit 6

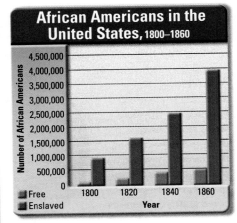

African Americans in the United States, 1800–1860

Analyze Graphs **This graph shows the numbers of free and enslaved African Americans in the United States.**

What trend does this graph show?

1775, Quakers formed the first organized group to work against slavery.

In 1827 two free African Americans, Samuel Cornish and John Russwurm, started a newspaper that called for **equality**, or equal rights, for all Americans. The newspaper, *Freedom's Journal*, was the first to be owned and written by African Americans. In it Cornish and Russwurm wrote, "Too long have others spoken for us."

A few years later another abolitionist, William Lloyd Garrison, a white Northerner, founded a newspaper called *The Liberator*. Garrison called for a complete end to slavery, saying, "On this subject I do not wish to think, or speak, or write with moderation. I am earnest . . . I will not excuse. I will not retreat a single inch—AND I WILL BE HEARD."

In Congress, Horace Mann and others gave speeches against slavery. Other

---

INTEGRATE ART

Drawing Tell students to imagine that they are abolitionists working to have slavery abolished. Have them design posters or brochures aimed at persuading others to help in their efforts to abolish slavery.

EXTEND AND ENRICH

Research Have each student do further research on Horace Mann, Preston Brooks, Sojourner Truth, or Frederick Douglass. Encourage students to use the Internet and other reference sources to find out about that person's life. Request that they write a paragraph about what they have learned. Ask for volunteers to share their paragraphs with the class.

abolitionists gave speeches at crowds. One well-known abolitionist speaker was Frederick Douglass, a runaway slave. In 1841 Douglass attended a convention of the Massachusetts Antislavery Society. He often told his audiences, "I appear this evening as a thief and a robber. I stole this head, these limbs, this body from my master [slave owner], and ran off with them."

Like Douglass, another former slave named Isabella Van Wagener (WAI•guh•nur) traveled the country speaking out against slavery. Van Wagener believed that God had called her to "travel up and down the land" to preach. She changed her name to reflect her path. She chose *Sojourner*, which means "traveler," for her first name and *Truth* as her last name.

Frederick Douglass was a runaway slave and an abolitionist.

Sojourner Truth believed that slavery could be ended peacefully. On the night of October 16, 1859, John Brown led a group to seize a government storehouse at Harpers Ferry, in what is now West Virginia. The storehouse was filled with guns. Brown planned to give the guns to slaves so they could fight for freedom. He was soon caught, put on trial, and hanged for his actions.

Violence also broke out in Congress. Preston Brooks, a representative from South Carolina, attacked a senator from Massachusetts while he was giving an anti-slavery speech. It was clear that the North and South were going to be divided by civil war.

REVIEW Who were abolitionists? people who wanted to abolish, or end, slavery

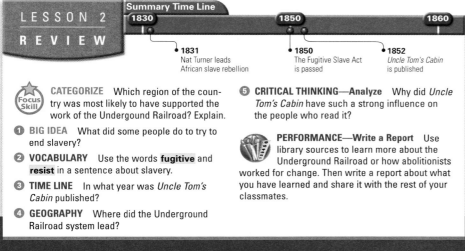

LESSON 2 REVIEW

Summary Time Line

1830	1850	1860

1831 Nat Turner leads African slave rebellion

1850 The Fugitive Slave Act is passed

1852 *Uncle Tom's Cabin* is published

CATEGORIZE Which region of the country was most likely to have supported the work of the Undergound Railroad? Explain.

①BIG IDEA What did some people do to try to end slavery?

②VOCABULARY Use the words **fugitive** and **resist** in a sentence about slavery.

③TIME LINE In what year was *Uncle Tom's Cabin* published?

④GEOGRAPHY Where did the Underground Railroad system lead?

⑤CRITICAL THINKING—Analyze Why did *Uncle Tom's Cabin* have such a strong influence on the people who read it?

 PERFORMANCE—Write a Report Use library sources to learn more about the Underground Railroad or how abolitionists worked for change. Then write a report about what you have learned and share it with the rest of your classmates.

Chapter 12 ▪ 449

OBJECTIVES

- **Describe Abraham Lincoln's political career.**
- **Identify the states that made up the Confederate States of America.**
- **Analyze the dynamics of the election of 1860.**
- **Identify reasons that some Southern states left the Union.**
- **Describe the events at Fort Sumter that marked the beginning of the Civil War.**

 Categorize pp. 435, 450, 452, 455, 472

Vocabulary

SEE READING AND VOCABULARY TRANSPARENCY 6-4 OR THE WORD CARDS ON PP. V71–V72.

secede p. 453   **Confederacy** p. 453

 When Minutes Count

Have students read pages 454–455. Then invite them to tell in their own words what happened at Fort Sumter.

Quick Summary

This lesson examines how the election of 1860 led to the dissolution of the Union. It also describes some parts of Abraham Lincoln's life.

 Motivate

Set the Purpose

Big Idea Remind students that the election of 1860 was a presidential election.

Access Prior Knowledge

Ask students to tell what they know about Abraham Lincoln. What was his background?

· LESSON ·

3

 CATEGORIZE

As you read, categorize the positions different people took on the issue of slavery.

BIG IDEA
The election of 1860 further divided the United States.

VOCABULARY

secede
Confederacy

People today can visit a replica of Abraham Lincoln's boyhood home at the Lincoln Boyhood National Memorial near Little Pigeon Creek, Indiana.

The Union Breaks Apart

1820   1870   1920
1855–1865

In the 1850s, new national leaders, such as Abraham Lincoln, began to speak out on the slavery issue. Abraham Lincoln was not an abolitionist, but he was against the spread of slavery. He did not think that the federal government had the right to abolish slavery in the United States. Instead, he hoped that if slavery were not allowed to spread, it would one day die out.

Young Abe Lincoln

Abraham Lincoln was named for his grandfather, who had been a friend of Daniel Boone. Lincoln's grandfather had followed Boone to Kentucky, on the western frontier. He had a son named Thomas, who eventually married Nancy Hanks. They lived in a small log cabin with a dirt floor. Abraham Lincoln was born in that cabin in 1809.

The Lincolns left their home in Kentucky in 1816 and moved to the Indiana Territory. One reason they left Kentucky was that many people there owned slaves. Because slaves did most of the work, there were few paying jobs available. The Lincolns

LOCATE IT
INDIANA
Indianapolis
Lincoln Boyhood National Memorial

450 ▪ Unit 6

MAKE IT RELEVANT

In Your State Almost every state in the Union was affected by slavery in some way. Have students research the background of their state to find out how slavery affected it.

BACKGROUND

The Republican Party Abraham Lincoln was a member of the Republican party, which was formed in 1854 by combining the former members of the Whig, Free-Soil, and Know-Nothing parties and a few disenchanted Northern Democrats who were antislavery. One goal most Republicans shared was preventing the spread of slavery to the West.

Stephen Douglas and Abraham Lincoln held seven debates in 1858. This painting shows Lincoln (standing) and Douglas (to Lincoln's right) debating in Charleston, Illinois.

lived in Indiana for 14 years. By then, Indiana seemed crowded to them, so they moved to the Illinois Territory.

As a young man, Abraham Lincoln held several jobs. All the while, he studied law. In the 1830s he became a lawyer and opened a law office in Illinois.

In 1834 Abraham Lincoln entered public service. He served first in the Illinois legislature. Later, in 1846, he was elected to the United States Congress, where he served one term in the House of Representatives. After returning to Illinois, Lincoln became concerned about the spread of slavery to the West. He joined a new political party formed to fight the spread of slavery. This party was called the Republican party.

In 1858 Lincoln decided to run again for government office. On June 17, Lincoln was nominated, or chosen, by the Republican party to be its candidate for the United States Senate. In his acceptance speech, Lincoln used words from the Bible to explain his beliefs about the spread of slavery and the future of the United States. He said, "A house divided against itself cannot stand. I believe this government cannot endure permanently half slave and half free." Lincoln hoped that his strong stand would not cost him the election.

REVIEW **What newly formed political party did Abraham Lincoln join?** Republican party

Lincoln and Douglas

Abraham Lincoln ran against Senator Stephen A. Douglas, the person who had written the Kansas–Nebraska Act. Lincoln and Douglas were very different from each other. Abraham Lincoln was very tall and thin, while Stephen Douglas was heavy and a full foot shorter than Lincoln.

Chapter 12 ▪ 451

2 Teach

Young Abe Lincoln

Read and Respond

Geography Have students use a map to locate the states where the Lincoln family lived. Kentucky, Indiana, and Illinois Ask students to give the years the Lincoln family moved to Indiana and Illinois. Indiana–1816, Illinois–1830

Analyze Primary Sources

Quotation Ask a volunteer to read aloud the words Lincoln spoke in his acceptance speech following his nomination for the United States Senate. Explain that Lincoln believed very strongly that the future of the United States depended on the unity of the states on the issue of slavery.

Lincoln and Douglas

Read and Respond

Civics and Government Point out to students that Lincoln and Douglas first ran against each other for the office of United States senator from Illinois.

Q **Why might it have been difficult for a newcomer such as Lincoln to beat the incumbent in an election?**

A The incumbent was better known and had more experience.

CHAPTER 12 ▪ 451

Read and Respond

Culture and Society Discuss with students how newspapers helped the nation get to know Abraham Lincoln. Remind students that newspapers were the primary source of news and information at that time. Point out that newspapers printed the opinions of both Lincoln and Douglas. Ask students to complete the following graphic organizer about the differences between Lincoln and Douglas.

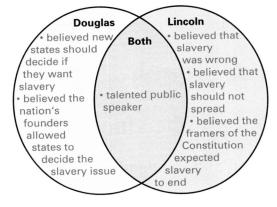

Douglas
• believed new states should decide if they want slavery
• believed the nation's founders allowed states to decide the slavery issue

Both
• talented public speaker

Lincoln
• believed that slavery was wrong
• believed that slavery should not spread
• believed the framers of the Constitution expected slavery to end

The Election of 1860

Read and Respond

Civics and Government Direct a discussion with students about how division within the Democratic party made Lincoln's election almost certain. Remind students that the Democratic party had two candidates. Help students realize that because two candidates split the votes of the Southern states, neither one of them had enough votes to beat Lincoln.

Analyze Primary Sources

Poster Direct students to read both posters on page 452. Note that political posters helped encourage support for a particular issue. Ask students to summarize the message of each poster.

Students might enjoy researching information about other historic posters. Have them visit The Learning Site at **www.harcourtschool.com.**

Because Douglas was already serving in the Senate, he was well known across the country. Few people in places other than Illinois had ever heard of Lincoln.

Despite their differences, Lincoln and Douglas were alike in one important way. Both were talented public speakers. In the summer of 1858, the two candidates traveled around the state of Illinois and debated questions that were important to voters. Huge crowds turned out to listen to them, and newspapers printed what each man had to say.

Stephen Douglas argued that each new state should decide the slavery question for itself. That was what the nation's founders had allowed, he said, and that was what the new Kansas–Nebraska Act allowed.

THE UNION, CONSTITUTION AND THE FLAG MUST AND SHALL BE UPHELD.

Posters in the North were made to show people's support for the Union.

Abraham Lincoln responded that "the framers of the Constitution intended and expected" slavery to end. The problem, Lincoln pointed out, was more than a question of what each state wanted. It was a question of right and wrong. Slavery should not spread to the West, Lincoln said, because slavery was wrong.

Although Stephen Douglas won reelection to the Senate for another term, people all over the country now knew who Lincoln was. Two years later, in 1860, the two men faced each other in another election. This one would decide the next President of the United States.

REVIEW How were the positions of Lincoln and Douglas on the spread of slavery different?

CATEGORIZE Douglas argued that each new state should decide the slavery question for itself, while Lincoln argued that slavery was wrong and should end everywhere.

The Election of 1860

In the 1860 election for the presidency Abraham Lincoln represented the Republican party, which firmly opposed the spread of slavery. The Democratic party was divided in its views. Some members of the party supported Stephen Douglas, who continued to argue that western settlers should decide for themselves whether to allow slavery. Other

CHARLESTON MERCURY EXTRA: THE UNION DISSOLVED!

The first notice of South Carolina's secession was printed in the *Charleston Mercury*. Jefferson Davis (left) was elected president of the Confederacy.

---

members, mostly Southerners, backed John Breckinridge of Kentucky. Breckinridge thought that the federal government should allow slavery everywhere in the West.

The division within the Democratic party made Lincoln's election almost certain. Although Lincoln promised not to abolish slavery in the South, he said he hoped it would end there one day. Many Southerners feared that Lincoln was attacking their whole way of life. Some leaders in the South said that their states would **secede** from, or leave, the Union if Lincoln became President. Like most Southerners, they believed that states could freely leave the Union since the states had created the Union in the first place.

On Election Day in November 1860, Lincoln did not win a single state in the South. However, he won enough states in the North and the West to win the presidency. Southern leaders did not wait long before carrying out their threat to secede. On December 20, South Carolina seceded from the Union.

Five other states—Alabama, Florida, Georgia, Louisiana, and Mississippi—soon followed. Together these six states formed their own government at Montgomery, Alabama, early in February 1861. They called themselves the Confederate States of America, or the **Confederacy**. Jefferson Davis, a United States senator from Mississippi, was elected president. Alexander Stephens of Georgia became vice president. That month Texas seceded and later joined the Confederacy.

REVIEW What did seven Southern states do after Lincoln was elected President?
They seceded from the Union.

POINTS OF VIEW
Union or Secession

JOHN C. CALHOUN, a senator from South Carolina

❝ What is the cause of this discontent? It will be found in the belief in the people of the Southern States . . . that they can not remain, as things are now. . . . If you who represent the stronger portion [the North], can not agree to settle [these differences] on the broad principle of justice and duty, say so; and let the states we both represent agree to separate and part in peace. ❞

SAM HOUSTON, the governor of Texas

❝ I tell you that, while I believe with you in the doctrine of State's Rights, the North is determined to preserve this Union. They are not a fiery, impulsive people as you are, for they live in colder climates. But when they begin to move in a certain direction. . . they move with the steady momentum and perseverance of a mighty avalanche. ❞

Analyze the Viewpoints

1. What views about secession did each Southerner hold?
2. What other viewpoints might Southerners have held on the matter of secession?
3. **Make It Relevant** Look at the Letters to the Editor section of your newspaper. Find two letters that express different viewpoints about the same issue, and summarize the viewpoints of each letter.

Chapter 12 ■ 453

Read and Respond

Link Geography and History Remind students that South Carolina was the first state to secede from the Union. Tell them that the next state to secede was Mississippi, followed by Florida, Alabama, Georgia, and Louisiana. Ask students to locate each of these states on a map of the United States.

Q Why did the seceding states think they had the freedom to leave the Union?

A The seceding states thought that because the Union had been formed freely and all had joined freely, they could leave at any time.

POINTS OF VIEW
Union or Secession?

Encourage students to analyze the two viewpoints and to identify differences. Explain that often the place where one lives and works influences one's thinking.

Analyze the Viewpoints—Answers

1. Calhoun believed that the states should be allowed to part in peace. Houston believed that the North was determined to preserve the Union and would persevere until that end was achieved.
2. Other Southerners might have believed that the South should secede from the Union no matter what happened.
3. Ask volunteers to read the letters they found and their summary of each viewpoint.

A CLOSER LOOK
Fort Sumter Prior to the War

Encourage students to study the diagram of Fort Sumter and locate each of the places identified.

CAPTION ANSWER: Cannons on every side meant that the fort was prepared for an attack on all sides.

Crisis at Fort Sumter

Analyze Primary Sources

Quotation Discuss with students what President Lincoln meant when he said that a state could not leave the Union on its own mere action. Ask students to think about how the federal government works and what would happen if a state wanted to leave the Union.

Read and Respond

Economics Explain to students that President Lincoln had promised to hold all property that belonged to the United States government, not only to deter the Southern states from seceding but also to maintain the nation's economic stability.

 **Close**

Summarize Key Content

- Abraham Lincoln served in the Illinois legislature and the United States House of Representatives before joining the Republican Party to fight the spread of slavery.
- Abraham Lincoln lost an 1858 United States Senate election to Stephen Douglas.
- Soon after Abraham Lincoln was elected President in 1860, six Southern states seceded.
- President Lincoln called on Americans to join an army after the fall of Fort Sumter marked the beginning of the Civil War.

A CLOSER LOOK
Fort Sumter Prior to the War

Fort Sumter was one of many forts built by the United States after the War of 1812.
1. stair tower
2. soldiers' barracks
3. officers' quarters
4. wall facing Charleston
5. fort lantern
6. mess hall
7. cannons
8. wharf

◆ Why do you think cannons were placed on nearly every side of the fort?

Crisis at Fort Sumter

On March 4, 1861, Abraham Lincoln took the oath of office as President of the United States. In his inauguration speech, he declared, "I have no purpose directly or indirectly to interfere with the institution of slavery in the states where it exists." Yet he firmly stated, "No state, upon its own mere action, can lawfully get out of the Union." Like many Northerners, Lincoln believed the United States could not be divided.

For one month after Lincoln's inauguration, the tension built. Americans everywhere wondered what Lincoln would do about the seceding states. Some people thought he should let them go. Others said that he should accept the Southern position on the slavery question and hope that the Southern states would return. Still others felt that Lincoln should use the army to end the revolt. The country's fate was soon determined at Fort Sumter, which is located on an island off the coast of South Carolina.

When the Southern states seceded, they had taken over post offices, forts, and other federal government property within their borders. Fort Sumter was one of the few forts in the South that remained

under Union control. By April 1861, however, supplies at the fort were running out. The fort's commander, Major Robert Anderson, feared that if more supplies were not sent soon, he would have to surrender the fort to the Confederacy.

Lincoln had promised to hold on to all property that belonged to the United States. He sent supply ships to the fort and waited to see how the Confederate leaders would react. On April 12, 1861, Confederate leaders demanded that Union forces surrender. When Major Anderson refused, Confederate troops fired their cannons on the fort. They bombarded the fort for the next 34 hours, until the Union troops surrendered.

Learning of the fall of Fort Sumter, President Lincoln called for 75,000 Americans to join an army to stop the Southern rebellion and preserve the United States. Four more states—Arkansas, North Carolina, Tennessee, and Virginia—seceded and joined the

454 ▪ Unit 6

READING SOCIAL STUDIES

Study Questions Have students work with a partner to check their answers to the study questions.

1. He believed that because slavery was wrong, it should not be allowed to spread.

2. South Carolina seceded from the United States.

3. Jefferson Davis

● USE READING AND VOCABULARY TRANSPARENCY 6-4.

6-4
TRANSPARENCY

Confederacy. This brought the number of Confederate states to 11. Tensions between the Union and the Confederate States—the North and the South—had reached their breaking point. The Civil War had begun.

REVIEW Who was in command of Fort Sumter when it was fired upon?
Major Robert Anderson

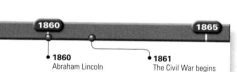

Summary Time Line

1855 ———————— 1860 ———————— 1865

• 1860
Abraham Lincoln is elected President

• 1861
The Civil War begins

LESSON 3 REVIEW

CATEGORIZE What states made up the Confederacy?

1 BIG IDEA Why did many Southerners fear Lincoln's election?

2 VOCABULARY Use the words **Confederacy** and **secede** in a sentence.

3 TIME LINE When did the Civil War begin?

4 HISTORY What event led South Carolina's leaders to secede from the Union?

5 GEOGRAPHY How many states in the South did Lincoln win in the election of 1860?

6 CRITICAL THINKING—Analyze Why do you think Fort Sumter was important to both Abraham Lincoln and Jefferson Davis?

PERFORMANCE—Write a Newspaper Headline Write two newspaper headlines, one from a Northern newspaper and one from a Southern newspaper, as they would have appeared the day after the election of 1860. Think about what each paper might have printed as a headline.

Chapter 12 ■ 455

Assess

Lesson 3 Review—Answers

 CATEGORIZE South Carolina, Alabama, Florida, Georgia, Louisiana, Mississippi, Texas, Arkansas, North Carolina, Tennessee, and Virginia

❶ **BIG IDEA** slavery

❷ **VOCABULARY** Eleven states **seceded** from the Union to form the **Confederacy**.

❸ **TIME LINE** in 1861

❹ **HISTORY** the election of Lincoln

❺ **GEOGRAPHY** none

❻ **CRITICAL THINKING—Analyze** Fort Sumter was important because it was one of the few forts in the South that was under Union control.

 Performance Assessment Guidelines Students' headlines should reflect the reactions of the North and South to the results of the election of 1860.

ACTIVITY BOOK

Use ACTIVITY BOOK, p. 115, to reinforce and extend student learning.

EXTEND AND ENRICH

Make a Map Have students draw maps of the Confederate States of America. Ask them to label each state. Students should also include a map key and a compass rose on their maps.

RETEACH THE LESSON

Graphic Organizer Ask students to complete the following graphic organizer.

The Civil War

Who fought?
Union
Confederacy

What event marked the war's beginning?
the attack on Fort Sumter

OBJECTIVES

■ Apply critical thinking skills to organize and use information from maps.

■ Use map scales to find distances on a map.

1 Motivate

Why It Matters

Remind students that thousands of maps exist of thousands of places in the world. Explain that without map scales people would not be able to find the distance between two places on a map. Discuss with students why it may be helpful to look at two different maps of the same area. Emphasize the importance of their understanding map scales so they can correctly measure distances on maps and choose the most appropriate maps for their needs.

· SKILLS ·
MAP AND GLOBE

Compare Maps with Different Scales

➤ WHY IT MATTERS

Have you ever helped your family plan a trip? You may have wanted to know how far you had to travel.

A map scale helps you find out how far one place is from another. The map scale compares a distance on a map to a distance in the real world. Map scales are different depending on how much area is shown. This means that different maps are drawn to different scales. Knowing about map scales can help you choose the best map for gathering the information you need.

➤ WHAT YOU NEED TO KNOW

Look at the map below and the map on page 457. They both show Fort Sumter and the surrounding area, but with different scales. On Map A, Fort Sumter looks larger. For that reason the scale is said to be larger. When the map scale is larger, more details can be shown. On Map B, Fort Sumter appears smaller, and the scale is said to be smaller.

Although they have different scales, Maps A and B can both be used to measure the distance between the same two places.

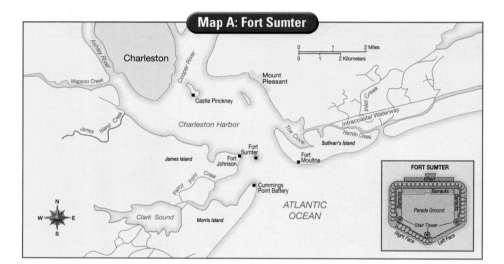

Map A: Fort Sumter

INTEGRATE MATHEMATICS

Measurement To help students understand how to use a map scale to find actual distance, work out the following problem with them.

If the distance on a map between City A and City B is 4.5 inches and the map scale is 1 inch = 50 miles, how many miles is it from City A to City B?

4.5 × 50 = 225 miles

Have students find the answer to the following problem.

Laura lives halfway between Uptown and Downtown. Uptown and Downtown are 5 inches apart on a map on which 1 inch = 0.5 km. How far would you travel from Uptown toward Downtown to reach Laura's house?

5 × 0.5 ÷ 2 = 1.25 km

PRACTICE THE SKILL

On April 12, 1861, Confederate troops opened fire on Fort Sumter from Fort Moultrie, Fort Johnson, Castle Pinckney, and various batteries around Charleston Harbor. This act signaled the beginning of the Civil War.

Use the maps below to find the real distance in miles between Fort Sumter and Castle Pinckney.

1 On Map A, use a ruler to measure the exact length of the scale, or use a pencil to mark off the length on a sheet of paper. How long is the line that stands for one mile?

2 Still using Map A, find Fort Sumter and Castle Pinckney. Using the ruler or the sheet of paper you marked, measure the distance between these two places. What is the real distance in miles between Fort Sumter and Castle Pinckney?

3 Now go through the same steps for Map B. How long is the scale length that stands for one mile? Use that scale length to measure the distance between Fort Sumter and Castle Pinckney on the map. What is the real distance in miles? Are the real distances you found on the two maps the same? You should see that even when map scales are different the real distances shown on the maps are the same.

APPLY WHAT YOU LEARNED

Find two maps with different scales—perhaps a map of your state and a map of a large city within your state. Compare the real distances between two places that are on both maps.

 Practice your map and globe skills with the **GeoSkills CD-ROM.**

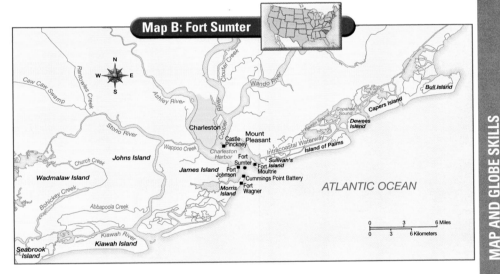

Map B: Fort Sumter

ATLANTIC OCEAN

Chapter 12 ■ 457

2 Teach

What You Need to Know

Direct students to Map A. Ask them to measure the map scale with a ruler. Next, have them measure the map scale for Map B. Ask students to compare the scales from the two maps. Have one-half of the class determine the distance between two points on Map A and the other half of the class determine the distance between the same two points on Map B. The distances should be identical.

Practice the Skill—Answers

1 $\frac{1}{2}$ inch (1.3 cm)

2 2.75 miles

3 $\frac{1}{6}$ inch (0.4 cm); 2.75 miles; yes

3 Close

Apply What You Learned

Students should find two maps to compare. The actual distances between two places that are on both maps should be the same.

You may wish to help students draw a map of their school and a map of the classroom, using two different scales.

> **ACTIVITY BOOK**
>
> Use ACTIVITY BOOK, pp. 116–117, to give students additional practice using this skill.

> **TRANSPARENCY**
>
> Use SKILL TRANSPARENCIES 6-2A and 6-2B.

> **EXTEND AND ENRICH**
>
> **Write a Paragraph** Ask students to look at the two maps they chose for *Apply What You Learned*. Have them write one paragraph comparing and contrasting the two maps. Tell students to write about specific things on the maps, such as scales.

> **CD-ROM**
>
> Explore GEOSKILLS CD-ROM to learn more about map and globe skills.

> **RETEACH THE SKILL**
>
> **Make a Map** Have students make maps of their city or state or of a historic building in their area. Remind students to make map scales for their maps. Then have students write questions about the distance between two places on their maps. Ask students to trade maps with a partner and answer each other's questions.

CHAPTER 12 ■ 457

Lesson 4

OBJECTIVES

- Analyze early battles of the Civil War.
- Describe the actions President Lincoln took during the Civil War.
- Compare the resources and battle strategies of the United States and the Confederacy.
- Explain the Emancipation Proclamation, and describe its effects.
- Analyze how different groups of Americans contributed to the Civil War effort.

 Categorize pp. 435, 458, 460, 464, 472

Vocabulary

SEE READING AND VOCABULARY TRANSPARENCY 6-5 OR THE WORD CARDS ON PP. V71–V72.

retreat p. 458	**strategy** p. 459
border state p. 459	**casualty** p. 461

 When Minutes Count

Have students examine the illustrations and captions. Ask them to tell which illustrations belong in the categories: the Union, the Confederacy, or the Union and the Confederacy.

Quick Summary

This lesson describes major events in the early years of the Civil War.

1 Motivate

Set the Purpose

Big Idea Remind students that key events are major events that have a great impact.

Access Prior Knowledge

Ask students to make a list of the main causes of the Civil War.

· LESSON · 4

 CATEGORIZE

As you read, categorize events that affected the North and South during the Civil War.

BIG IDEA

Several key events happened in the early years of the Civil War.

VOCABULARY

retreat
border state
strategy
casualty

Civil War

1820   1870   1920
1861–1863

After Confederate troops fired on Fort Sumter, hopes for peace between the North and the South ended. Both the Union and the Confederacy prepared for war. Men and boys eagerly joined regiments made up of their neighbors and friends.

The Fighting Begins

The first of the major battles between the Union and the Confederacy was fought in July 1861. The battle took place at Bull Run, a stream near the town of Manassas Junction, Virginia. On the day of the battle, crowds of enthusiastic sight-seers came in carriages from nearby Washington, D.C. They brought picnic lunches as if to watch a sporting event. A Union soldier said, "We thought it wasn't a bad idea to have the great men from Washington come out to see us thrash the Rebs [Confederate troops]."

At Bull Run two untrained armies clashed in a confusing battle. At first it appeared that the Union army would win. Then, as the Confederate army started to **retreat**, or fall back, new troops arrived. At their head was Thomas Jackson, a skilled Confederate general from Virginia. Jackson managed to stop the retreat. "There's Jackson standing like a stone wall," shouted another general as the Confederates turned and again

General Thomas Jackson

FAST FACT The Union named battles after the nearest streams, and the Confederates named battles after the nearest towns. That is why the Battle of Manassas (shown here) is also known as the Battle of Bull Run.

QUESTIONS KIDS ASK

Q How could people watch a battle without getting hurt?

A Battles during the Civil War were usually well contained on the battlefields. This is because the armies marched in a line with soldiers shoulder to shoulder. They also went slowly so no one was left behind. This made it difficult for sightseers some distance away to be affected directly by the battle.

BACKGROUND

Civil War Troops When the Civil War began, the troops in both the Confederate and the Union armies had come from the state militias. Then civilians began to volunteer in large numbers. However, as the war continued, both sides resorted to drafting men into the armies because the number of volunteers was less than the number of casualties on the battlefields.

Northern soldiers wore blue uniforms.

Advantages in the Civil War

NORTHERN ADVANTAGES
Advanced industry

Advanced railroad system

Strong navy

SOUTHERN ADVANTAGES
Large number of military leaders

Troops experienced in outdoor living

Familiar with the environment of the South

Analyze Graphs **This graph compares the advantages of the North and South.**

◆ What advantages did the North have?

Southern soldiers wore gray uniforms.

attacked the Union army. From that day on, General Jackson was known as Stonewall Jackson.

The Confederates won the Battle of Manassas, also called the Battle of Bull Run. The defeat shocked the Union. The South had proved more powerful than most Northerners had expected. Americans came to realize that this war would last far longer than they had first believed.

Most Northerners supported the Union, while most white Southerners supported the Confederacy. For some Americans, however, the choice between the Union and the Confederacy was not an easy one. The war had deeply divided people in all regions. People in the **border states**—Delaware, Kentucky, Maryland, and Missouri—were especially torn between the two sides. These states, which were located between the North and the South, permitted slavery but had not seceded.

REVIEW Where did the first major battle of the Civil War take place? ⊕ **CATEGORIZE**
Manassas Junction, Virginia

Battle Plans

The Union **strategy**, or long-range plan, for winning the war was first to weaken the South and then to invade it. To weaken the South, Lincoln and his advisers came up with a strategy that some people called the Anaconda (a•nuh•KAHN•duh) Plan. An anaconda is a large snake that squeezes its prey to death. The Union would squeeze the South by not letting it ship its cotton or bring in goods. If the South could not sell its cash crops, it would not have the money to buy supplies for its army.

The purpose of the plan was to block all imports from reaching the South. The plan called for winning control of the Mississippi River and for establishing a naval blockade of Confederate ports. Not everyone in the North liked the idea of a blockade, however. Many people thought it would take too long to set up. They wanted the Union army to invade the South. "On to Richmond!" they shouted.

2 Teach

The Fighting Begins

Read and Respond

Discuss with students the casual attitude people had toward the first major battle of the Civil War. Ask students to predict whether people's attitudes changed as the war continued.

Battle Plans

Visual Learning

Chart Direct students' attention to the chart on page 459. Explain to students that the North had more factories and railroads than the South did because the North had a more industrial economy while the South had a largely agricultural economy.
CAPTION ANSWER: The North had advanced industry, an advanced railroad system, and a strong navy.

Read and Respond

Economics Point out to students that the Anaconda Plan—cutting off trading and shipping to and from the South—was economically devastating to the region.

Read and Respond

Economics Explore the importance of Southern cotton to markets in France and Britain. Have students analyze why the South needed to continue to trade in order to fight the war.

History Explain to students that the war strategies of the Confederacy and the Union contrasted significantly because their goals were different. The South wanted independence and approached the war with the idea of defending the new nation. The North sought to restore the Union, which meant bringing the Southern states to submission.

Visual Learning

Map Remind students that the border states were located between the North and the South. Those states permitted slavery but did not secede. However, as a condition of statehood, West Virginia made provisions for ending slavery there.

CAPTION ANSWER: Delaware, Maryland, West Virginia, Kentucky, and Missouri

Q Were there more states in the Union or in the Confederacy?

A in the Union

The Battle at Antietam

Read and Respond

Culture and Society Ask students how both the strategy of the North and the strategy of the South began to affect life in each region by 1862, a year after the war had begun.

Students may respond that life in the North was not as devastated by the war as life in the South was because the supply lines to the North were not destroyed as those in the South were.

Explain that in the North people were also becoming discouraged. They had not yet seen results of all their sacrifices.

The Union and the Confederacy

Union state
Border state
Confederate state
Territory

Regions The Civil War had divided the nation. In western Virginia, feelings for the Union were so strong that the people voted to break away from Virginia. West Virginia joined the Union in 1863.

 Which states were border states?

The Union army's strategy was to weaken the South by blocking all trade routes. Richmond, Virginia, had become the capital of the Confederacy by this time.

At first the most important strategy of the Confederate states was simply to protect their lands. This strategy was based on the belief that Britain and France would help the South. Both countries depended on Southern cotton to keep their textile mills going. The South also hoped that the North would tire of the war. Many Southerners, however, were impatient. Cries of "On to Washington!" were soon answered with plans to invade the North.

REVIEW How did the battle plans of the North and South differ? **CATEGORIZE**

The Battle at Antietam

As the Civil War dragged on into 1862, the Anaconda Plan seemed to be working. The blockade brought trade in the South to a halt, and supplies there ran

This cannon was used in the Battle of Antietam.

460 ■ Unit 6

INTEGRATE ART

Make a Banner Remind students that many people did not have the patience for a long war. They supported one side or the other, hoping the war would end soon. Have one-half of the class make a banner that says "On to Richmond" and the other half of the class make a banner that says "On to Washington." Have the members of each group list the reasons why the side they represent wants to invade the other side's land and capture its capital.

BACKGROUND

The Confederate Capital In 1861 Richmond, Virginia, was chosen as the capital city of the new Confederacy. Situated on the James River and only 110 miles (177 km) from the Union capital of Washington, D.C., Richmond was a symbol of the pride of the South. It was a medical and manufacturing center and quickly became the center for supplies sent to Confederate troops.

very low. This made life increasingly difficult for Southern troops, who became poorly equipped, fed, and clothed. Even so, many Northerners became discouraged by the long lists of war casualties. A **casualty** is a person who has been killed or wounded in a war.

Then, in September 1862, the Union and the Confederates fought a major battle at Antietam (an•TEE•tuhm) Creek, near Sharpsburg, Maryland. By that time Robert E. Lee was Confederate commander of the Army of Northern Virginia. General Lee had led his army from Virginia into Maryland, intending to reach Harrisburg, Pennsylvania. There, Lee planned to cut off railroad communication between the states in the East and those in the West. Lee also hoped to find in Pennsylvania supplies that his troops badly needed.

At Antietam Creek, Lee's army was stopped by Union troops. The battle that followed resulted in the highest number of casualties in one day of the whole war. Union casualties numbered more than 2,000 killed and 9,500 wounded. Confederate casualties totaled 2,700 killed and over 9,000 wounded. "Never before or after in all the war were so many men shot on one day," historian Bruce Catton wrote. Having lost one-fourth of his army, Lee retreated to Virginia.

Although the battle at Antietam was really a draw, or tie, it had an important result. Five days later, on September 22, 1862, President Lincoln announced his decision to issue an order freeing the slaves in areas that were still fighting against the Union.

REVIEW Why was General Lee leading his army to Pennsylvania? so he could cut off railroad communication between the states in the East and the states in the West and to find supplies

The Emancipation Proclamation

To President Lincoln, the purpose of the war had been to keep the country together—to save the Union. It had not been to abolish slavery. In 1862 President Lincoln wrote a letter explaining his view to Horace Greeley, publisher of the *New York Tribune*. "My [main] object in this struggle is to save the Union, and is not either to save or destroy slavery.

• BIOGRAPHY •

Robert E. Lee   1807–1870
Character Trait: Loyalty

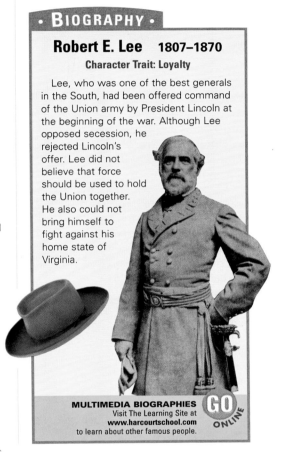

Lee, who was one of the best generals in the South, had been offered command of the Union army by President Lincoln at the beginning of the war. Although Lee opposed secession, he rejected Lincoln's offer. Lee did not believe that force should be used to hold the Union together. He also could not bring himself to fight against his home state of Virginia.

MULTIMEDIA BIOGRAPHIES
Visit The Learning Site at
www.harcourtschool.com
to learn about other famous people.

Read and Respond

Civics and Government Tell students that President Lincoln did not have the power to abolish slavery in states that remained loyal to the Union. The Constitution protected their right to have slaves. Slavery could only be completely abolished by an amendment to the Constitution.

Q What was Lincoln's primary goal in issuing the Emancipation Proclamation?

A to preserve the Union

Visual Learning

Art This painting, titled *The First Reading of the Emancipation Proclamation Before the Cabinet*, by Francis Carpenter, depicts Lincoln reading the proclamation's initial draft to his stunned Cabinet on July 22, 1862. Later, Lincoln showed them the completed painting in the White House. Some Cabinet members disliked it, but Lincoln pronounced the painting "absolutely perfect."

Read and Respond

Civics and Government Explain to students that among the reasons for emancipating the slaves was the conflict over slaves who had been running away from the South to join the armies of the North. Tell students that this was called self-emancipation. However, Union armies struggled with whether these slaves should be returned because of the Fugitive Slave Act. Point out that Lincoln's administration agreed with the policy of General Benjamin F. Butler, who decided he would not return slaves because they were property and it was legal in times of war to seize the enemy's property.

Q Why would a slave run away to become part of the Union army?

A Service in the Union army provided the best opportunity for emancipation and full citizenship.

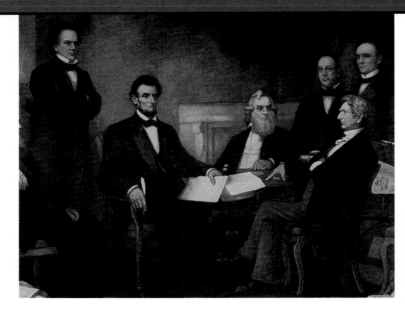

This painting shows Abraham Lincoln meeting with his cabinet to discuss the Emancipation Proclamation.

If I could save the Union without freeing any slave I would do it; and if I could save it by freeing all the slaves I would do it; and if I could save it by freeing some and leaving others alone I would also do that."

Early in the war Lincoln had felt that making emancipation the main goal of the war might divide the North. It might also turn people in the border states against the Union. However, the move to end slavery grew stronger. Finally, after the Battle of Antietam Creek, Lincoln decided the time had come for an emancipation order.

The Emancipation Proclamation, which Lincoln issued on January 1, 1863, said that all slaves living in those parts of the South that were still fighting against the Union would

be "then, thenceforward, and forever free." The proclamation did not give all enslaved people instant freedom. The order was meant only for the states that had left the Union, not for the border states or for areas that had already been won back by the Union.

The Emancipation Proclamation hurt the South's hopes of getting help from Britain and France. Now that the war had become a fight against slavery, most British and French citizens, who opposed slavery, gave their support to the Union. Confederate President Jefferson Davis called Lincoln's proclamation "the most execrable [terrible] measure recorded in the history of a guilty man."

To celebrate the proclamation, it was reprinted on this poster.

462 ▪ Unit 6

INTEGRATE LANGUAGE ARTS

Character Sketch Suggest that students reread the words on pages 461 and 462 that President Lincoln wrote in a letter to Horace Greeley. Ask them to use information about Lincoln that they have learned from the textbook to write one-paragraph character sketches of him. Encourage them to use specific adjectives to describe Lincoln.

INTEGRATE HEALTH

First Aid Ask each student to research the kind of aid provided for wounded soldiers in the Civil War. What were the medical capabilities at that time? What kinds of wounds were treatable? Have students summarize their findings in paragraphs. Ask volunteers to read their paragraphs to the class.

As the Union troops advanced farther and farther into the Confederacy, they carried out the Emancipation Proclamation. Thousands of enslaved people fled to freedom behind the Northern battle lines, where they worked as laborers or joined the Union army or navy. By allowing freed slaves to serve in the military, the Emancipation Proclamation helped ease the Union army's shortage of soldiers.

REVIEW What was the Emancipation Proclamation? an order by President Lincoln that freed all slaves in the Confederate states that were still fighting against the Union

Contributions from All

In both the North and the South, only men were allowed to join the army. Women, however, found many ways to help. They took over factory, business, and farm jobs that men left behind. They sent food to the troops, made bandages, and collected supplies. Many women, such as Clara Barton and Sally Tompkins, worked as nurses. Dorothea Dix worked as the supervisor of all nurses. A few women served as spies, and some even dressed as men and fought in battles.

About 180,000 African Americans eventually served in the Union army during the Civil War as well. They served in separate regiments, mostly under the command of white officers. At first they were not paid as much as white soldiers. They were also given poor equipment, and they often ran out of supplies. Despite these hardships, African American soldiers proved themselves on the battlefield. They led raids behind Confederate lines, served as spies and scouts, and fought in almost every major battle of the war.

The Union navy was open to African American men when the Civil War began. During the war the Union navy enlisted about 20,000 African American sailors. Among those who served was Robert Smalls. In 1862 Smalls and some other slaves took over a Confederate steamer in Charleston Harbor and surrendered it to Union forces.

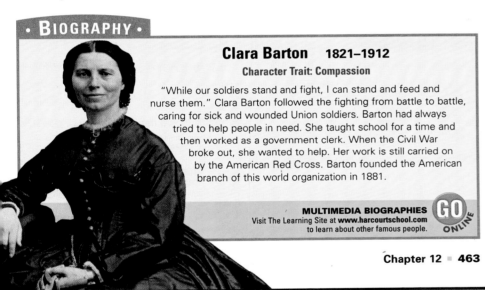

• BIOGRAPHY •

Clara Barton   1821–1912

Character Trait: Compassion

"While our soldiers stand and fight, I can stand and feed and nurse them." Clara Barton followed the fighting from battle to battle, caring for sick and wounded Union soldiers. Barton had always tried to help people in need. She taught school for a time and then worked as a government clerk. When the Civil War broke out, she wanted to help. Her work is still carried on by the American Red Cross. Barton founded the American branch of this world organization in 1881.

MULTIMEDIA BIOGRAPHIES
Visit The Learning Site at www.harcourtschool.com to learn about other famous people. **GO ONLINE**

Chapter 12 ■ 463

Contributions from All

Read and Respond

Culture and Society Lead a discussion with students about the roles women played during the Civil War.

Read and Respond

Civics and Government Tell students that after the Civil War, African Americans argued that they should have the right to vote and live as full citizens in American society. Explain to students that one of the main arguments in their favor was the fact that they had risked their lives for the Union in the Civil War.

3 Close

Summarize Key Content

- The first major battle of the Civil War took place at Bull Run, near Manassas Junction, Virginia, in July 1861.
- The Union strategy for winning the Civil War was to weaken the South. The South's strategy was to defend its territory.
- After the Battle of Antietam, President Lincoln issued the Emancipation Proclamation, which set free all slaves living in parts of the South that were still fighting against the Union on January 1, 1863.
- Many groups, including women, African Americans, and immigrants, contributed to the Civil War.

Anticipation Guide Have students check their predictions.

1. The Union's long-term strategy was to weaken the South and then invade it.

2. The Battle of Antietam resulted in the war's highest number of casualties in one day.

3. Some ~~All~~ slaves were freed by the Emancipation Proclamation.

● USE READING AND VOCABULARY TRANSPARENCY 6-5.

6-5
TRANSPARENCY

Assess

Lesson 4 Review—Answers

CATEGORIZE Delaware, Kentucky, Maryland, Missouri, and West Virginia

❶ **BIG IDEA** The South had won.

❷ **VOCABULARY** The troops decided to **retreat** before they suffered more losses.

❸ **TIME LINE** Bull Run

❹ **HISTORY** There was no clear winner of the Battle of Antietam. It caused Lincoln to decide to issue the Emancipation Proclamation.

❺ **HISTORY** Women helped by working in factories, in businesses, in farm jobs, and as nurses for the military.

❻ **CRITICAL THINKING—Evaluate** It hurt the South's hopes of getting help from Britain and France.

Performance Assessment Guidelines Students' letters should be clearly and creatively written.

ACTIVITY BOOK

Use Activity Book, p. 118, to reinforce and extend student learning.

African American troops (left) played a key role in support of the Union. Thousands of Hispanic Americans also took part in the war, with some fighting for the Union and others fighting for the Confederacy. Unlike African American soldiers, most Hispanic Americans served in regular army units.

European immigrants who came to this country for a better life marched off to preserve the Union, as well. There were Irishmen in the Fighting 69th, the Irish Zouaves, Irish Volunteers, and St. Patrick Brigade. Italians fought with the Garibaldi Guards and Italian Legion. Germans fought with the Steuben Volunteers, German Rifles, Turner Rifles, and DeKalb Regiment. In fact, the immigrant population in the Northern states helped the Union army replenish itself and eventually wear out a depleted Confederate army.

REVIEW How did African American soldiers help the Union during the war? by fighting in the Union army and navy, and by serving as spies and scouts

LESSON 4 REVIEW

Summary Time Line
1860 — 1865

● **1861** The Battle of Bull Run is fought

● **1862** The Battle of Antietam is fought

● **1863** President Lincoln issues the Emancipation Proclamation

CATEGORIZE Name the border states.

❶ **BIG IDEA** Why did the first major battle of the Civil War shock the Union?

❷ **VOCABULARY** Use the word **retreat** in a sentence.

❸ **TIME LINE** What Civil War battle occurred first, Antietam or Bull Run?

❹ **HISTORY** What were the results of the Battle of Antietam?

❺ **HISTORY** How did women in both the North and South help the troops?

❻ **CRITICAL THINKING—Evaluate** How did the Emancipation Proclamation affect the Confederates' strategy?

PERFORMANCE—Write a Letter Imagine that you are living in the South during the Civil War. Write a letter to a friend describing how the Union's blockade is changing your life. Then share your letter with a classmate.

464 ▪ Unit 6

EXTEND AND ENRICH

Research Ask each student to choose a battle of the Civil War to research. Suggest that students use primary and secondary sources as well as the Internet to find information about the battle. Encourage them to look for information such as how the terrain or the weather affected the fighting, how the battle was fought, how long it lasted, and what effect it had on the outcome of the war.

RETEACH THE LESSON

Graphic Organizer Ask students to complete the following flow chart to review the lesson.

| Battle of Bull Run |
| Battle of Antietam |
| The Emancipation Proclamation is issued. |
| Slaves join the Union army. |

The Road to Union Victory

1820   1870   1920

1863–1865

The Emancipation Proclamation gave new hope to enslaved people and new spirit to the North. In the months that followed, the Union won several key battles and seemed to be winning the war. Across the South, very young men joined the army to replace soldiers who had been killed or wounded. In southern cities such as Richmond, Virginia, there was so little food that there were bread riots. Huge groups of people ran through the streets demanding bread.

Vicksburg and Chancellorsville

By May 1863 the Union army finally had a general as effective as Confederate General Robert E. Lee. His name was Ulysses S. Grant. One of Grant's first important battles began in May at Vicksburg, Mississippi, the Confederate headquarters on the Mississippi River.

Grant laid siege to the city. The Union guns pounded Vicksburg, and the Union army cut off all supplies to the city. The trapped Confederates, both soldiers and townspeople, soon ran out of food. Conditions were so bad that they had to tear down houses for firewood and dig caves in hillsides for shelter. Yet the people of Vicksburg were determined to endure whatever Grant had in store for them. One Vicksburg woman wrote, "We'll just burrow into these hills and let them batter away as hard as they please."

Ulysses S. Grant (right) used this box to carry his saddle and other field equipment.

 CATEGORIZE
As you read, categorize key events as Union or Confederate victories.

BIG IDEA
Several key battles led to a Union victory.

VOCABULARY
address

OBJECTIVES

- **Identify major battles of the Civil War and their results.**
- **Describe actions President Lincoln took during the Civil War.**
- **Analyze the Gettysburg Address and its impact on the Civil War.**
- **Describe the surrender of General Lee to General Grant at Appomattox.**

 Categorize pp. 435, 465, 466, 471, 472

Vocabulary

SEE READING AND VOCABULARY TRANSPARENCY 6-6 OR THE WORD CARDS ON PP. V71–V72.

address p. 467

When Minutes Count

Model for students how to turn headings into questions.

Heading–Vicksburg and Chancellorsville

Question–What happened at Vicksburg and Chancellorsville?

Then have pairs of students work together to write questions and answer them.

Quick Summary

This lesson describes major events in the final two years of the Civil War.

 Motivate

Set the Purpose

Big Idea Ask students to speculate how the Union was eventually able to win the Civil War.

Access Prior Knowledge

Discuss with students what they know about the first two years of the Civil War. Ask who seemed to be winning the war.

Graphic Organizer Have students complete the following graphic organizer as they read.

Battle	Who Won?	What Was Gained?
Vicksburg		
Chancell-orsville		
Gettys-burg		

● USE READING AND VOCABULARY TRANSPARENCY 6-6.

6-6 TRANSPARENCY

2 Teach

Vicksburg and Chancellorsville

Read and Respond

Geography Have students locate Vicksburg on the map on page 470. Ask them why Vicksburg's location was strategically important in helping the Union defeat the Confederacy.

It gave the Union control of the Mississippi River, which cut the Confederacy into two parts.

• SCIENCE AND TECHNOLOGY •

The *H. L. Hunley*

Explain to students that the design of the submarine *H. L. Hunley* was about 50 years ahead of its time. It sank the *Housatonic*, which was almost $5\frac{1}{2}$ times longer and almost 10 times wider.

The Battle of Gettysburg

Read and Respond

Geography Have students locate Gettysburg on the map on page 470. Discuss the movement of troops from the North and the South to the battle-grounds at Gettysburg.

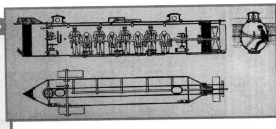

• SCIENCE AND TECHNOLOGY •

The *H. L. Hunley*

In 1864 the *H. L. Hunley* became the first submarine to sink an enemy ship during wartime. Measuring just over 39 feet (12 m) long and just under 4 feet (1 m) wide, the *Hunley* was powered by crew members who cranked a propeller by hand. The submarine was built to ram a torpedo into a target and then back away, causing a trip line to set off the explosion. The design of the *Hunley* proved to be successful when it sank the Union warship *Housatonic*.

The diagram (above right) shows the inside of the Hunley (below).

However, by July 4, 1863, the people of Vicksburg could hold out no longer. They finally surrendered.

Vicksburg proved to be a key victory. Its location gave the Union control of the Mississippi River. This, in turn, cut the Confederacy into two parts. The western states of the Confederacy were no longer able to communicate easily with the states to the east or to supply many reinforcements to them.

At about the same time that Grant started to lay siege to Vicksburg, General Lee and his army defeated a Union army at Chancellorsville, Virginia. In winning, however, Lee lost one of the South's best

generals. In the confusion of battle, Stonewall Jackson was accidentally shot by one of his own troops and later died.

Despite Jackson's death, the victory at Chancellorsville gave the Confederacy confidence to try again to invade the North. The Confederates' goal was to win a victory on Northern soil.

If they could do so, the Confederates hoped people in the North would demand an end to the war. In June 1863, General Lee's troops headed north. They reached the small town of Gettysburg, Pennsylvania, on July 1.

REVIEW Did the Union or the Confederacy win at Vicksburg? at Chancellorsville?

⬡ **CATEGORIZE** the Union won at Vicksburg; the Confederacy won at Chancellorsville

The Battle of Gettysburg

General Robert E. Lee believed that victory at Gettysburg might turn the war in favor of the Confederacy. However, after two days of fighting, victory did not seem possible. In a final attempt on July 3, 1863, Lee ordered General George Pickett's entire division—15,000 soldiers—to make a direct attack. They were to charge across open country toward a stone fence at the Union army's center.

Marching shoulder to shoulder, Pickett's troops formed a line half a mile (0.8 km) wide. Steadily, the wall of soldiers in what came to be called Pickett's Charge

---

H. L. Hunley The night the *H. L. Hunley* made history by sinking a ship in battle was the last time the submarine was seen afloat. A watchman saw the *H. L. Hunley* signal victory, that all were safe and they were on their way in. But the crew of the *H. L. Hunley* was never seen again. It was not until 1995 that a team of underwater divers discovered the sunken *H. L. Hunley* after a 15-year search. The submarine was raised intact in August 2000.

Geography Request that students locate Vicksburg, Mississippi, on a map. Next, ask students to determine which Confederate states were on the east side of the Mississippi River and which were on the west. East—Virginia, North Carolina, South Carolina, Georgia, Florida, Alabama, Mississippi, and Tennessee; West—Arkansas, Louisiana, and Texas

the Confederate attack at Gettysburg in which 15,000 soldiers charged across an open field to attack the Union army. This pin was worn on the hats of Civil War soldiers to indicate that they were foot soldiers.

moved forward. As the Confederates moved closer, they were met by the fire of Union guns, which controlled the higher ground of the battlefield. "Men were falling all around us, and cannon and muskets were raining death upon us," remembered a Confederate officer. "Still on and up the slope toward the stone fence our men steadily swept."

Pickett's soldiers reached the fence but were stopped there in fierce fighting. The charge had failed, and Pickett's men retreated, leaving behind half their number dead or wounded.

The Battle of Gettysburg was one of the deadliest battles of the Civil War. In fighting between July 1 and 3, 1863, more than 3,000 Union soldiers and nearly 4,000 Confederates were killed. More than 20,000 on each side were wounded or reported missing.

The fate of the Fourteenth Tennessee Regiment tells the story. When the battle began, there were 365 men in the unit. When the battle ended, there were only 3.

The Union victory at Gettysburg marked a turning point in the war. After the battle, General Lee's army retreated to Virginia. It would never again be able to launch a major attack against the Union.

REVIEW What was Pickett's Charge?

The Gettysburg Address

On November 19, 1863, President Lincoln went to Gettysburg to dedicate a cemetery for the Union soldiers who had died in the battle. A crowd of nearly 6,000 people gathered for the ceremony.

Lincoln gave a short speech, or **address**, that day. In fact, he spoke for less than three minutes. Lincoln's Gettysburg Address was so short that many people in the crowd were disappointed. Soon, however, people realized that this short speech was one of the most inspiring speeches ever given by a United States President.

In his address, Lincoln spoke to the heart of the war-weary North.

This scene, painted by James Walker, shows the battle at Gettysburg.

READING SOCIAL STUDIES

Summarize There are opportunities on Pupil Edition pages 467–468 for students to summarize what they read. Ask students to summarize Lincoln's message in the Gettysburg Address. Then ask them to summarize the results of the address.

BACKGROUND

The Gettysburg Address A popular belief is that President Lincoln wrote the Gettysburg Address on the back of an envelope. In reality, he wrote two drafts of the speech but may have also changed some text as he spoke. He later made copies of the address as he had presented it.

Read and Respond

History Explain to students that in the Civil War, soldiers moved together in lines instead of splitting up in battle. Tell students that one reason soldiers stayed close together was so their officers could control their actions. Explain that it was difficult to hear commands in battle, so soldiers watched the other soldiers around them to know what to do.

Visual Learning

Fine Art Have students look at the painting on page 467. Ask them if they think the painting accurately portrays the Battle of Gettysburg.

GO ONLINE Students might enjoy researching information about other historic sites in the United States. Have them visit The Learning Site at **www.harcourtschool.com**.

The Gettysburg Address

Read and Respond

History Tell students that before President Lincoln gave his address, Edward Everett, a famous speaker at that time, spoke for two hours. Explain to students that the next day's newspapers put Everett's remarks on the front page and Lincoln's on an inside page. Point out, however, that Everett wrote Lincoln a note the next day saying that he wished he could have said in two hours what it took Lincoln only two minutes to say.

Analyze Primary Sources

Speech Ask for volunteers to read aloud to the class different sections of the Gettysburg Address on page 468. Help students use context clues to unlock the meanings of words, and be sure they understand what Lincoln meant when he asked Americans to "resolve that these dead shall not have died in vain." Tell students that a score equals 20 of something—in this case, years.

Q To what event is Lincoln referring when he says "four score and seven years ago"?

A the United States' Declaration of Independence: 1863 – 87 = 1776

Read and Respond

Culture and Society Remind students that people in the North as well as in the South were growing tired of the war. Lead a discussion with students about how the Gettysburg Address inspired people to continue the fight to keep the Union together.

Q What does the phrase "these dead shall not have died in vain" mean?

A To preserve the Union would mean that the soldiers who died at Gettysburg had not died without a purpose.

The Road to Appomattox

Read and Respond

History Explain that General Ulysses S. Grant planned to march to Richmond, and General William Tecumseh Sherman was to march to Atlanta. Tell students that the Confederate army attempted to stop the Union army. After an initial Confederate success, the Union troops pushed through and attacked Atlanta. Confederate losses were heavy, as many as one-fourth of the 40,000 men.

Q Why did Sherman destroy railroad tracks?

A to cut Southern supply lines

THE GETTYSBURG ADDRESS

Four score and seven years ago our fathers brought forth on this continent a new nation, conceived in Liberty, and dedicated to the proposition that all men are created equal.

Now we are engaged in a great civil war, testing whether that nation or any nation so conceived and so dedicated, can long endure. We are met on a great battlefield of that war. We have come to dedicate a portion of that field, as a final resting place for those who here gave their lives that that nation might live. It is altogether fitting and proper that we should do this.

But, in a larger sense, we can not dedicate—we can not consecrate—we can not hallow—this ground. The brave men, living and dead, who struggled here, have consecrated it, far above our poor power to add or detract. The world will little note nor long remember what we say here, but it can never forget what they did here. It is for us the living, rather, to be dedicated here to the unfinished work which they who fought here have thus far so nobly advanced. It is rather for us to be here dedicated to the great task remaining before us—that from these honored dead we take increased devotion to that cause for which they gave the last full measure of devotion—that we here highly resolve that these dead shall not have died in vain—that this nation, under God, shall have a new birth of freedom—and that government of the people, by the people, for the people, shall not perish from the earth.

He spoke of the ideals of liberty and equality on which the nation had been founded. He honored the many soldiers who had died defending those ideals. He also called on the people of the Union to try even harder to win the struggle those soldiers had died for—to save the "government of the people, by the people, for the people" so that the Union would be preserved.

REVIEW Why did Lincoln give the Gettysburg Address?
to dedicate a cemetery for the Union soldiers who died in the Battle of Gettysburg

The Road to Appomattox

In March 1864 Lincoln gave command of all the Union armies to General Ulysses S. Grant. Grant soon devised a plan to invade the South and destroy its will to fight. The plan called for an army under Grant's command to march to Richmond, the Confederate capital. At the same time a second army under General William Tecumseh Sherman was to march from Chattanooga, Tennessee, to Atlanta, Georgia.

WORD WORK

Words with Multiple Meanings Remind students that the word *address* has many meanings. Ask students to give as many definitions for *address* as they can. Discuss with students how they can find out which definition is correct by looking at the context of the word in a sentence.

INTEGRATE HEALTH

Learn More About Illnesses Inform students that about two-thirds of the soldiers who died in the Civil War died from illnesses. Arrange students into groups, and have each group research living conditions, lack of medicine and doctors, or other circumstances that would have favored the spread of disease.

As Sherman captured Atlanta, much of the city burned to the ground. The destruction of Atlanta, a manufacturing center and junction of several railroads, was a great loss for the Confederacy.

From Atlanta, Sherman's army of 62,000 men headed toward Savannah in a march that has become known as the March to the Sea. The army cut a path of destruction 60 miles (97 km) wide and 300 miles (483 km) long. Union soldiers burned homes and stores, destroyed crops, wrecked bridges, and tore up railroad tracks. When Sherman reached Savannah on December 22, 1864, he sent a message to President Lincoln. He wrote, "I beg to present you as a Christmas gift the city of Savannah."

From Georgia, Sherman turned north and marched through South Carolina, destroying even more than he had in Georgia. At the same time, General Grant moved south into Virginia. In his pursuit of General Lee's army, Grant cut off Lee's supply lines and kept pushing the Confederates in retreat. In early April 1865, Richmond was evacuated and set on fire by retreating Confederates. More than 900 buildings were destroyed and hundreds more were badly damaged. Union troops took control of the city.

General Lee's army moved west, with General Grant in constant pursuit. Lee's men were starving, and they were now outnumbered by 10 to 1. Lee could retreat no farther, nor could he continue to fight. Lee said, "There is nothing left for me to do but to go and see General Grant, and I would rather die a thousand deaths."

On the afternoon of April 9, 1865, Lee surrendered to Grant at Appomattox (a•puh•MA•tuhks) Court House, Virginia.

This painting shows General Lee (seated at left) surrendering to General Grant (seated at right) at the home of Wilmer McLean.

BACKGROUND

Battle of Mobile Bay While Sherman was marching through the South, the Union army fought important battles in other areas, too. In the Gulf of Mexico Confederate blockade runners often managed to smuggle news and supplies past the Union ships. In August of 1864 a fleet of 18 Union ships moved in to end blockade running in Mobile Bay, Alabama. Although the city of Mobile was not captured, the Union forces soon won control of the bay.

Read and Respond

Link Geography and Economics
Help students trace Sherman's March to the Sea on a map. Ask students to locate Atlanta. Then have them follow southeast toward Savannah. Discuss with students the reason for the destruction. Explain that once the South had lost the ability to manufacture and transport goods, its economy was broken. Without funds, the Confederacy was beaten. General Lee surrendered to General Grant at Appomattox Courthouse, Virginia, on April 9, 1865.

Visual Learning

Painting Point out to students the painting on page 469. Draw students' attention to the number and placement of the people depicted. Ask students to explain why more Union officers are shown. Possible response: General Lee is surrendering to General Grant. The number of Union officers shows the strength of the Union in comparison with the Confederacy.

Read and Respond

Link History and Economics Explain to students that the South suffered great economic losses. Tell students that between 1860 and 1870, the wealth of the South had decreased by 60 percent. In contrast, the North's wealth increased by 50 percent. Ask students how this was possible. Most of the fighting was in the South, and many railroads and industries were destroyed. There was little fighting in the North, so industries were still intact.

Visual Learning

Map Encourage students to use the map scale to calculate the miles covered by Union armies on the march from Atlanta to Savannah.
about 300 miles
CAPTION ANSWER: Union victories at New Orleans and Mobile Bay severely limited the flow of supplies to the South.

• HERITAGE •

Memorial Day

Inform students that Memorial Day was first observed to honor those who died in the Civil War. Have students describe the significance of Memorial Day today. Students may respond that Memorial Day is now observed to honor those who have died in all the wars in which the United States has been involved.

3 Close

Summarize Key Content

- General Ulysses S. Grant led the Union to victory in the Battle of Vicksburg.
- General Robert E. Lee defeated the Union army at Chancellorsville, Virginia.
- The Battle of Gettysburg was one of the deadliest of the Civil War.
- President Lincoln gave his Gettysburg Address at the dedication of a cemetery for Union soldiers who had died at Gettysburg.
- In the March to the Sea, General Sherman's army destroyed almost everything in a path 60 miles (97 km) wide and 300 miles (483 km) long.
- General Lee surrendered to General Grant at Appomattox Courthouse on April 9, 1865.

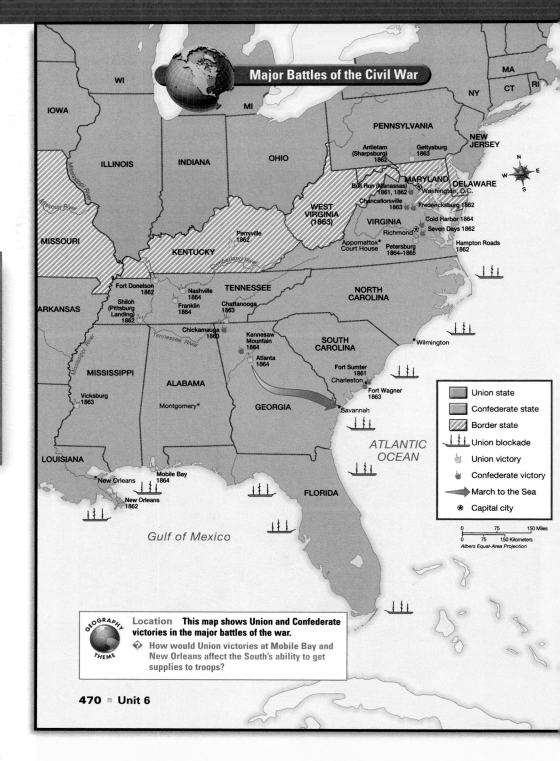

Major Battles of the Civil War

Union state
Confederate state
Border state
Union blockade
Union victory
Confederate victory
March to the Sea
Capital city

0   75   150 Miles
0   75   150 Kilometers
Albers Equal-Area Projection

Location This map shows Union and Confederate victories in the major battles of the war.
How would Union victories at Mobile Bay and New Orleans affect the South's ability to get supplies to troops?

470 ■ Unit 6

READING SOCIAL STUDIES

Paraphrase Remind students that to paraphrase is to restate in one's own words something they have read. Encourage students to paraphrase the information in the lesson to include in their charts. Ask students to reread the Heritage section about Memorial Day. Then ask students to paraphrase in writing what they have read.

EXTEND AND ENRICH

Compose a Story Suggest that students compose short stories about a soldier in one of the battles of the Civil War. Encourage them to be creative but to include accurate details about the battle.

Memorial Day

On May 5, 1866, people in Waterloo, New York, honored those who died in the Civil War. The people closed businesses for the day and decorated soldiers' graves with flowers. This was the beginning of the holiday known as Memorial Day, or Decoration Day. On this day Americans remember those who gave their lives for their country in all wars. Today most states observe Memorial Day on the last Monday in May.

People often celebrate this holiday by holding parades.

In a meeting at the home of Wilmer McLean, the two generals agreed to the terms of the Confederate army's surrender. After signing the surrender, Lee mounted his horse Traveller and rode back to his men.

In the next few weeks, as word of General Lee's surrender reached them, other Confederate generals surrendered, too. After four years of bloodshed the Civil War was over. The Union had been preserved, but at a horrible cost.

More than 600,000 soldiers had died during the war. Many died as a result of battle. Others, however, had died from disease. Thousands of soldiers also returned home wounded, scarred both physically and emotionally from the terrible devastation the war had brought.

REVIEW Why did Lee surrender to Grant?
Lee could not retreat any farther, nor could he continue to fight.

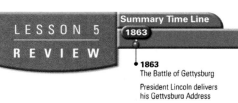

LESSON 5 REVIEW

Summary Time Line

1863 — 1865

● **1863**
The Battle of Gettysburg
President Lincoln delivers his Gettysburg Address

● **1865**
The Civil War ends

 CATEGORIZE On what holiday do Americans remember those who gave their lives for their country in wars?

❶ **BIG IDEA** What key battles led to a Union victory in the Civil War?

❷ **VOCABULARY** Use the word **address** in a sentence about Abraham Lincoln.

❸ **TIME LINE** Did Lincoln give his Gettysburg Address before or after the Civil War ended?

❹ **HISTORY** What was the purpose of General Sherman's March to the Sea?

❺ **CRITICAL THINKING—Evaluate** Why do you think people today still find meaning in the words of Lincoln's Gettysburg Address?

 PERFORMANCE—Make a Diorama Make a diorama of one of the events described in the lesson. Then share your diorama with your classmates.

RETEACH THE LESSON

Graphic Organizer Ask students to complete the following graphic organizer. Remind them to use the textbook to find or check information.

The Civil War

What were the major battles?	Who won?	How did it end?
List any major battles.	the Union	Lee surrendered.

READING SOCIAL STUDIES

Graphic Organizer Check to make sure students have correctly filled in their graphic organizers.

Battle	Who Won?	What Was Gained?
Vicksburg	Union	control of the Mississippi River
Chancellorsville	Confederacy	renewed confidence
Gettysburg	Union	severely weakened the Confederate army

● **USE READING AND VOCABULARY TRANSPARENCY 6-6.** **6-6** TRANSPARENCY

Assess

Lesson 5 Review—Answers

 CATEGORIZE Memorial Day

❶ **BIG IDEA** victories at the Battle of Vicksburg and the Battle of Gettysburg and Sherman's March to the Sea

❷ **VOCABULARY** Abraham Lincoln gave an **address** at Gettysburg.

❸ **TIME LINE** before

❹ **HISTORY** to crush the South and end the war

❺ **CRITICAL THINKING—Evaluate** The words of the Gettysburg Address are true for all time and inspire hope in times of national stress.

Performance Assessment Guidelines Students should create a diorama that illustrates one of the events described in the lesson.

ACTIVITY BOOK

Use Activity Book, p. 119, to reinforce and extend student learning.

CATEGORIZE

Students may use the graphic organizer that appears on page 120 of the Activity Book. Answers appear in the Activity Book, Teacher's Edition.

Think & Write

Write a List of Questions Students' lists should demonstrate their knowledge of the events that President Lincoln was involved in or that took place during his presidency.

Write a Song Students' songs should accurately commemorate an event from the Civil War. They may refer to such battles as Fort Sumter or Gettysburg, or to the surrender at Appomattox Courthouse.

ACTIVITY BOOK

A copy of the graphic organizer appears in the ACTIVITY BOOK on page 120.

TRANSPARENCY

The graphic organizer appears on READING AND VOCABULARY TRANSPARENCY 6–7.

12 Review and Test Preparation

Summary Time Line
1820

1820 Congress passes the Missouri Compromise

Categorize

Copy the following graphic organizer onto a separate sheet of paper. Use the information you have learned to categorize important leaders and battles of the Civil War.

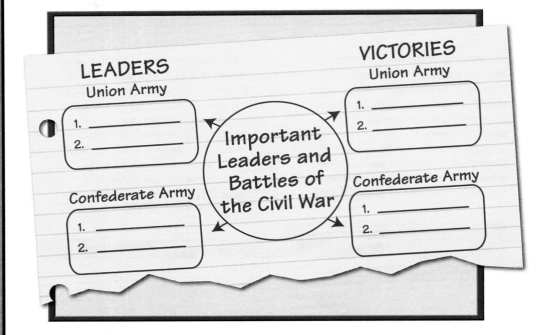

THINK & WRITE

Write a List of Questions Imagine you are a newspaper reporter in 1863. You have the opportunity to interview President Lincoln at the White House. Write a list of questions you would like to ask the President.

Write a Song The Civil War inspired the writing of many patriotic American songs, such as "The Battle Hymn of the Republic." Write a song to honor the soldiers who fought in the Civil War.

472 ▪ **Chapter 12**

TEST PREPARATION

Review these tips with students:

- Read the directions before reading the questions.
- Read each question twice, focusing the second time on all the possible answers.
- Take the time to think about all the possible answers before deciding on an answer.
- Move past questions that give you trouble, and answer the ones you know. Then return to the difficult items.

UNIT PROJECT

Progress Check Suggest that students make a web diagram for each key person who is discussed in the chapter. Students can use these diagrams to make notes on key details of each person's life.

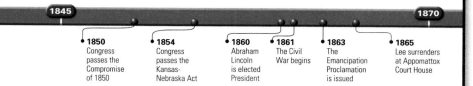

1850 Congress passes the Compromise of 1850

1854 Congress passes the Kansas-Nebraska Act

1860 Abraham Lincoln is elected President

1861 The Civil War begins

1863 The Emancipation Proclamation is issued

1865 Lee surrenders at Appomattox Court House

USE THE TIME LINE

Use the chapter summary time line to answer these questions.

1 In what year did the Civil War end?

2 How many years after the Missouri Compromise did the Civil War begin?

USE VOCABULARY

Use these terms to write a story about life in the United States during the Civil War.

states' rights (p. 436)

abolitionist (p. 448)

equality (p. 448)

secede (p. 453)

Confederacy (p. 453)

RECALL FACTS

Answer these questions.

3 What effect did the Kansas-Nebraska Act have on life in the Kansas Territory?

4 How did Harriet Tubman contribute to the abolitionist cause?

5 What were some of the causes of the Civil War?

Write the letter of the best choice.

6 One effect of the worldwide demand for Southern cotton was that —
A it made Southern planters want to end slavery.
B many new public schools were built in the South.
C it created a need for more enslaved workers.
D many new factories were built in the South.

7 During the Civil War, many European immigrants helped preserve the Union by—
F serving as members of Congress.
G working as Union spies.
H donating money to the war effort.
J serving in the Union army.

THINK CRITICALLY

8 How did changes brought about by the Industrial Revolution lead to conflicts between different regions in the United States?

9 Why do you think the North and South were not able to reach a compromise over slavery in 1861?

10 What do you think would have happened if Abraham Lincoln had waited until after the Civil War to issue the Emancipation Proclamation?

APPLY SKILLS

Identify Frame of Reference

11 The debate over states' rights was one of the issues that led to the Civil War. Explain how a Southern politician's view of states' rights might have been different from a Northern politician's.

Compare Maps with Different Scales

Study the two maps of Fort Sumter on pages 456 and 457. Then answer the following question.

12 Which map would you use if you wanted to see a more detailed view of Fort Sumter and the surrounding area? Explain.

Chapter 12 ■ 473

Think Critically

8 The factories in the North did not rely on slave labor, and abolitionists worked to end slavery. The South relied heavily on slavery to meet demands for its cash crops and it relied on the North and Europe for manufactured goods.

9 because the Southern economy was dependent on slavery

10 Answers may vary but may reflect the fact that Britain and France could have come into the war and supported the South.

Apply Skills

Identify Frame of Reference

11 Students' responses should reflect the fact that a Southern politician may have favored states' rights but a Northern politician may have opposed the idea.

Compare Maps with Different Scales

12 Map A; the scale is larger and shows more detail.

ACTIVITY BOOK

Use the CHAPTER 12 TEST PREPARATION on page 121 of the Activity Book.

ASSESSMENT

Use the CHAPTER 12 TEST on pages 95–98 of the Assessment Program.

Use the Time Line

1 in 1865

2 41

Use Vocabulary

Responses will vary but may include: The North went to war to preserve the Union; the South went to war to preserve **states' rights**. Many Northerners were **abolitionists** and believed in **equality** among people. Southerners decided to **secede** from the Union and formed the **Confederacy**.

Recall Facts

3 People rushed to the territory to vote either for or against slavery and fighting broke out. (pp. 439–440)

4 She guided about 300 people to freedom. (p. 447)

5 states' rights, secession, slavery, the crisis at Fort Sumter (pp. 452–454)

6 C (p. 444)

7 J (p. 464)

LESSON	PACING	OBJECTIVES	VOCABULARY
Introduce the Chapter pp. 474–475	1 Day	■ Describe nineteenth-century political and social changes. ■ Identify how technological developments affected the economy. ■ Use critical thinking skills to analyze primary sources.	**Word Work:** Preview Vocabulary, p. 475
1 Reconstruction pp. 476–480	1 Day	■ Describe the events surrounding President Lincoln's death. ■ Analyze plans for the Reconstruction of the United States. ■ Analyze the reactions of both Southerners and Northerners to Reconstruction efforts. ■ Identify problems with Reconstruction governments.	**Reconstruction** **assassinate** **black codes** **acquittal** **Word Work:** Preview Vocabulary, p. 476
2 The South After the War pp. 481–485	1 Day	■ Identify challenges facing the South after the Civil War. ■ Analyze Reconstruction efforts to help freed slaves. ■ Describe carpetbaggers and scalawags and their roles in Reconstruction. ■ Analyze segregation and how it affected the lives of African Americans.	**freedmen** **sharecropping** **carpetbagger** **scalawag** **secret ballot** **segregation**
3 Settling the Last Frontier pp. 486–491	2 Days	■ Explain the reasons people settled the West. ■ Analyze the Homestead Act of 1862 and how it affected settlement in the West. ■ Analyze conflicts between Native Americans and settlers.	**boom** **refinery** **prospector** **bust** **long drive** **homesteader** **open range** **reservation**

READING	INTEGRATE LEARNING	REACH ALL LEARNERS	RESOURCES
Point of View, p. 475			
Reading Social Studies: **Graphic Organizer,** p. 477 Reading Social Studies: **Graphic Organizer Responses,** p. 480	Language Arts **Write a Report,** p. 477	**Advanced Learners,** p. 478 **Extend and Enrich,** p. 480 **Reteach the Lesson,** p. 480	**Activity Book,** p. 122 **Reading and Vocabulary Transparency, 6-8** Internet Resources
Reading Social Studies: **Study Questions,** p. 482 Reading Social Studies: **Summarize,** p. 482 Reading Social Studies: **Study Question Responses,** p. 485	Language Arts **Write a Personal Narrative,** p. 482 Languages **Americanisms,** p. 483	**English as a Second Language,** p. 481 **Extend and Enrich,** p. 484 **Reteach the Lesson,** p. 485	**Activity Book,** p. 123 **Reading and Vocabulary Transparency, 6-9**
Reading Social Studies: **Anticipation Guide,** p. 487 **Point of View,** p. 490 Reading Social Studies: **Anticipation Guide Responses,** p. 491	Mathematics **Computation,** p. 488	**Extend and Enrich,** p. 490 **Reteach the Lesson,** p. 491	**Activity Book,** pp. 124–125 **Reading and Vocabulary Transparency, 6-10** Internet Resources

Chapter 13 Planning Guide The Nation Reunited

LESSON	PACING	OBJECTIVES	VOCABULARY
CHART AND GRAPH SKILLS **Use a Climograph** pp. 492–493	**1 Day**	■ Use climographs to obtain information about precipitation and temperature of a specific place. ■ Apply critical thinking skills to analyze information from climographs. ■ Compare climographs of different places.	**climograph**
4 The Rise of New Industries pp. 494–499	**1 Day**	■ Analyze how new industries, including the transcontinental railroad, led to economic growth in the late 1800s. ■ Describe the contributions of entrepreneurs to the economy. ■ Analyze the effect of Thomas Edison's inventions on life in the United States.	**free enterprise** **transcontinental railroad** **entrepreneur** **petroleum** **capital** **human resource**
EXAMINE PRIMARY SOURCES **Edison's Inventions** pp. 500–501	**1 Day**	■ Identify Thomas Edison as one of America's most important inventors. ■ Explain the importance of some of Edison's inventions.	
5 A Changing People pp. 502–507	**1 Day**	■ Analyze how the population grew and changed after the Civil War. ■ Compare new and old immigrants and describe the challenges they both faced. ■ Explain how prejudice against immigrants led to regulations on immigration. ■ Analyze the Great Migration of African Americans to the North in the early 1900s.	**old immigration** **new immigration** **advertisement** **tenement** **prejudice** **regulation**
Chapter Review and Test Preparation pp. 508–509	**1 Day**		

READING	INTEGRATE LEARNING	REACH ALL LEARNERS	RESOURCES
		Extend and Enrich, p. 493 **Reteach the Skill,** p. 493	**Activity Book,** pp. 126–127 Skill Transparencies, 6-3A and 6-3B
Reading Social Studies: **Personal Response,** p. 495 Reading Social Studies: **Personal Response,** p. 499	Science **The Air Brake,** p. 495 Language Arts **Compare and Contrast,** p. 497	**Advanced Learners,** p. 498 **Extend and Enrich,** p. 498 **Reteach the Lesson,** p. 499	**Activity Book,** p. 128 Reading and Vocabulary Transparency, 6-11
		Extend and Enrich, p. 501 **Reteach the Lesson,** p. 501	Internet Resources
Reading Social Studies: **K-W-L Chart,** p. 503 (Focus Skill) **Point of View,** p. 505 Reading Social Studies: **K-W-L Chart Responses,** p. 507	Music **Study "God Bless America,"** p. 503 Languages **Learn About Chinese,** p. 504	**Tactile Learners,** p. 506 **Extend and Enrich,** p. 506 **Reteach the Lesson,** p. 507	**Activity Book,** p. 129 Reading and Vocabulary Transparency, 6-12 Internet Resources
		Test Preparation, p. 508	**Activity Book,** pp. 130–131 Reading and Vocabulary Transparency, 6-13 Assessment Program, Chapter 13 Test, pp. 99–102

Activity Book

Name _____ Date _____

Reconstruction

Directions Read the time line of events surrounding Reconstruction below. Then answer the questions that follow.

Reconstruction 1865–1870

1865 1866 1867 1868 1869 1870

March 4, 1865 Lincoln gives his second inaugural address

February 1866 Freedmen's Bureau is established

March 1867 South comes under military rule

February 1868 President Andrew Johnson is impeached

March 1870 Fifteenth Amendment is ratified

December 1865 Thirteenth Amendment is ratified

April 14, 1865 Lincoln is assassinated

June 1866 Fourteenth Amendment is ratified

1. Was the Thirteenth Amendment ratified before or after President Lincoln gave his second inaugural address? _after_

2. What happened to President Abraham Lincoln on April 14, 1865?
   He was assassinated.

3. How many years passed between President Lincoln's assassination and President Johnson's impeachment? _three_

4. What two events shown on the time line both happened in the month of february? _The Freedmen's Bureau was established and President Johnson was impeached._

5. Was the Freedmen's Bureau established before or after the South came under military rule? _before_

6. How many constitutional amendments were passed between 1865 and 1870?
   three

Name _____ Date _____

The South After the War

Directions Match each vocabulary word with its definition. Then use the vocabulary words to fill in the blanks of the sentences below.

_D_ 1. former slaves

_B_ 2. government agency

_F_ 3. the practice of paying farm workers in harvested crops

_E_ 4. Northerners who went South during Reconstruction

_C_ 5. a method of voting in which no one knows for whom you voted

_A_ 6. separation of people based on race

A. segregation
B. bureau
C. secret ballot
D. freedmen
E. carpetbaggers
F. sharecropping

7. The ____secret ballot____ is one of the most important parts of a fair election.

8. There are still many ____bureaus____ in the United States government.

9. Life was hard for the ____freedmen____ after the Civil War since few of them had enough money to buy their own land.

10. ____carpetbaggers____ were given their name because of the suitcases many of them used to carry their belongings.

11. The practice of ____segregation____ kept people apart in most public places.

12. Under the ____sharecropping____ system most farmworkers found it difficult to make a living.

Name _____ Date _____

Settling the Last Frontier

Directions Study the map below.

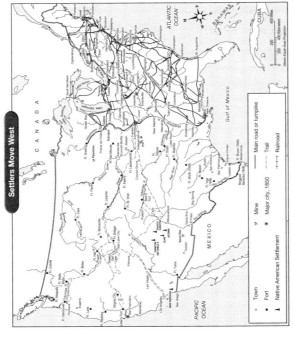

Settlers Move West

Main road or turnpike
Trail
Railroad

× Mine
● Major city, 1850

■ Town
● Fort
▲ Native American Settlement

(continued)

Name _____ Date _____

Directions Use the map and key on the preceding page to help you answer the questions. Write your answers in the blanks provided.

1. In what part of the country were most railroads located? _northeast_

2. What Texas fort was the farthest west? _Ft. Inge_

3. In what parts of the country were most forts located? _in the West and Midwest_

4. Could you travel by railroad from St. Louis, Missouri, to Salt Lake City?
   _no_

5. How might you travel from Norfolk, Virginia to Wilmington, North Carolina?
   railroad, main road

6. Find the area that represents your state on the map. How settled was it? What might life have been like for the settlers who lived there?
   Answers will vary.

SKILL PRACTICE

Name _____ Date _____

CHART AND GRAPH SKILLS

Use a Climograph

Directions Look at the climograph of Austin, Texas, below. Then answer the questions on the blanks provided.

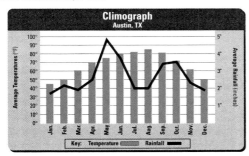

(continued)

126 ▪ Activity Book   Use after reading Chapter 13, Skill Lesson, pages 492–493.

SKILL PRACTICE

Name _____ Date _____

❶ What is the average temperature in Austin in July? about 85 degrees

❷ What is the average rainfall in October? about 3.5 inches

❸ Which three months are the driest? January, March, December

❹ Which month is the coolest month? January

❺ Which month is the warmest month? August

❻ Which month gets the most precipitation? May

❼ What do you observe about the months of July and August?

They are nearly the same in both average temperature and rainfall.

❽ If you were driving cattle, what months do you think would be hardest on

people and cattle? What hardships might you face during the drive?

Answers will vary but may include the wettest months, driest months, hottest

months, and coldest months. Hardships may include unexpected rainstorms,

drought, and extreme heat or cold.

_____

Use after reading Chapter 13, Skill Lesson, pages 492–493.   **Activity Book** ▪ 127

LESSON 4

Name _____ Date _____

The Rise of New Industries

Directions Read the passages below, and answer the questions that follow.

In the 1800s the United States government made land grants to several railroad companies. More than 130 million acres were given to the Union Pacific, the Santa Fe, the Central and Southern Pacific, and the Northern Pacific railroads. In addition, western states gave the railroads 49 million acres. These land grants allowed the railroad industry to open new markets in the West for goods produced in the East.

One effect of the railroad boom was the need for stronger track. When the railroads were first built, the rails were made of iron. With the arrival of bigger and faster locomotives, however, these iron rails were not strong enough to withstand the weight of the new trains. A man named Henry Bessemer invented a way to make steel tracks strong enough for the larger locomotives. As a result, many companies were able to ship their products throughout the United States at a faster pace.

One company that used the new, faster trains to its advantage was Standard Oil. Founded by John D. Rockefeller in 1867, Standard Oil used the trains to ship oil all over the country. By 1882 Standard Oil controlled almost all of the oil refining and distribution in the United States.

❶ Where did the railroad companies get the land on which to build the lines?

The United States government and western states made land grants.

❷ What effect did replacing iron rails with steel rails have on how U.S. companies

could ship their products? Many U.S. companies could now ship their products

at a faster pace.

❸ What company did John D. Rockafeller found in 1867? Standard Oil

❹ What role do you think the railroads played in the growth of Standard Oil?

Standard Oil used the railroads to ship oil all over the United States. As a result,

by 1882, the company controlled most of the oil distribution in the United States.

128 ▪ Activity Book   Use after reading Chapter 13, Lesson 4, pages 494–499.

LESSON 5

Name _____ Date _____

A Changing People

Directions Read the passage below and answer the questions that follow.

Irving Berlin's father was a cantor, a person who sings at religious services in Jewish synagogues. Perhaps it was his father's music that caused Berlin to be interested in writing songs. When he was in the army during World War I, Berlin wrote a musical show. He later won both the United States Army's award of Merit and a Congressional Medal for his songs. One of his most popular songs is "God Bless America."

Although Sophia Alice Callahan lived to be only 26 years old, she wrote an important novel. *Wynema: A Child of the Forest* is thought to be the first novel written by a Native American woman. Callahan's father was one-eighth Creek Indian. The novel has two major characters, Wynema and a Methodist teacher named Genevieve, who try to overcome prejudice against both Indians and women in the late nineteenth century.

Hiram Fong graduated from Harvard Law School before he returned to his native Hawaii to practice law. Hawaii at that time was still a territory. Fong served in the territorial legislature from 1938 to 1954. When Hawaii became a state, he was elected to the United States Senate. He served in the Senate from 1959 until 1977.

African American artist Jacob Lawrence did a 63-painting series on the lives of Harriet Tubman and Frederick Douglass. He studied painting in the Harlem section of New York City. During the Depression, Lawrence worked for a federal project. This gave him enough money to be able to paint *Migration*, a series of 60 panels showing the movement of African Americans from the South to the North.

❶ Explain what all the people in the passage have in common.

All were members of minority groups. Berlin was Jewish, Callahan was a

Native American woman, Fong was from a territory far from the mainland and

Lawrence was African American.

❷ Who might have influenced Irving Berlin's interested in music? his father, who

was a cantor in a Jewish synagogue

❸ How did Hiram Fong serve his homeland? He was part of the territorial legislature

and a member of the Senate after Hawaii became a state.

❹ What two series of paintings were created by Jacob Lawrence? a series on

Harriet Tubman and Frederick Douglass and a series titled *Migration* showing

the movement of African Americans from the south to the north

Use after reading Chapter 13, Lesson 5, pages 502–507.   **Activity Book** ▪ 129

Name _____ Date _____

Abraham Lincoln and Reconstruction

Directions Complete this graphic organizer by describing different points of view about Reconstruction.

WHO SAID IT	WHAT WAS SAID	WHY IT WAS SAID	POINT OF VIEW
Abraham Lincoln ____ ____ ____ ____	"With malice toward none, with charity for all, with firmness in the right as God gives us to see the right, let us strive on to finish the work we are in, to bind up the nation's wounds…"	Because the country had been torn apart by the Civil War	Lincoln believed the South should not be punished for the Civil War and that the country should be brought back together peacefully and quickly.

WHO SAID IT	WHAT WAS SAID	WHY IT WAS SAID	POINT OF VIEW
Mary Chesnut	"Lincoln—old Abe Lincoln— killed… I know this foul murder will bring down miseries on us."	In response to Abraham Lincoln's assassination ____ ____ ____	Chesnut feared that, with the President gone, the South would now be held responsible for the Civil War and Lincoln's murder.

© Harcourt

Use after reading Chapter 13, pages 475–507.

· CHAPTER ·

Name _____ Date _____

13   Test Preparation

Directions Read each question and choose the best answer. Then fill in the circle for the answer you have chosen. Be sure to fill in the circle completely.

1 Which of the following was **not** a condition for a Southern state's readmission to the Union?
- Ⓐ rewriting the state constitution
- ● giving slaves some of the land
- Ⓒ ratifying the Thirteenth Amendment
- Ⓓ ratifying the Fifteenth Amendment

2 The most important work of the Freedmen's Bureau was—
- ● education.
- Ⓖ running the courts.
- Ⓗ helping people farm.
- Ⓙ rebuilding homes.

3 Which of the following was **not** a problem for homesteaders?
- Ⓐ drought
- Ⓑ range wars
- Ⓒ bitter cold and snow
- ● land costs

4 The last of the transcontinental railroad was laid in—
- Ⓕ Spokane, Washington.
- ● Promontory, Utah.
- Ⓗ Erie, Pennsylvania.
- Ⓙ St. Louis, Missouri.

5 The term "new immigration" refers to—
- Ⓐ people coming from Britain, Germany, and Ireland.
- Ⓑ African Americans coming north.
- ● people coming from Italy, Russia, and Greece.
- Ⓓ people coming from South America.

© Harcourt

Use after reading Chapter 13, pages 476–507.

Historical Societies
_____
_____
_____
_____
_____

Museums
_____
_____
_____
_____
_____

Experts on Reconstruction
_____
_____
_____
_____
_____

Historic Sites
_____
_____
_____
_____
_____

Chapter 13 Assessment

·CHAPTER·

Name _____ Date _____

13 Test

Part One: Test Your Understanding

MULTIPLE CHOICE (4 points each)

Directions Circle the letter of the best answer.

1 The Thirteenth Amendment to the Constitution—
A freed slaves in the Confederacy.
B freed all slaves in the United States and its territories.
C was written by Abraham Lincoln.
D states that all people born in the United States are citizens, except Native Americans.

2 Black codes were designed to—
F acquit President Andrew Johnson.
G protect the rights of all citizens.
H extend and enforce voting rights
J limit the rights of former slaves.

3 The Freedmen's Bureau helped former slaves by—
A finding them sharecropping jobs.
B building schools to help them learn to read.
C giving them land to farm.
D increasing their wages.

4 After 1858, Colorado's Pikes Peak was the site of what business activity?
F homesteading
G wheat farming
H mining
J cattle ranching

5 Which of the following cities grew up at the end of a cattle trail?
A Cheyenne, Wyoming
B Galveston, Texas
C Shreveport, Louisiana
D Promontory, Utah

6 A steel plow was important on the Great Plains—
F to help build sod houses.
G because Russian wheat was difficult to plant.
H because the tough sod was hard to turn over.
J to locate water deep underground.

(continued)

Chapter 13 Test

Name _____ Date _____

7 At the Little Bighorn River, General George Custer encountered—
A the Sioux.
B the Nez Perce.
C the French.
D the Iroquois.

8 The transcontinental railroad stretched—
F to the new territory of Alaska.
G from the Atlantic to the Pacific Oceans.
H to the borders of both Canada and Mexico.
J from Florida to Maine.

9 George Westinghouse aided railroads by—
A creating refrigerated cars.
B inventing air brakes.
C building bridges across valleys.
D developing a telegraph system.

10 During the Great Migration—
F only a small number of people could come to the United States from Japan.
G Chinese people had difficulty getting state jobs.
H many African Americans moved to the North.
J most immigrants came from northern and western Europe.

TRUE OR FALSE (4 points each)

Directions Indicate whether the following statements are true or false by writing **T** or **F** in the spaces provided.

11 __T__ The House of Representatives acquitted President Andrew Johnson of a crime.

12 __F__ Abraham Lincoln was assassinated before Robert E. Lee surrendered at the end of the Civil War.

13 __F__ A sharecropper is paid in cash rather than with a part of the crop.

14 __F__ The Bessemer process is important for the production of oil.

15 __T__ John Rockefeller's Standard Oil Company once controlled most of the oil refining in the United States.

(continued)

Chapter 13 Test

Name _____ Date _____

Part Two: Test Your Skills

USE A CLIMOGRAPH (5 points each)

Directions Use the climographs to answer the following questions.

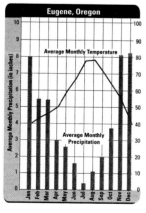

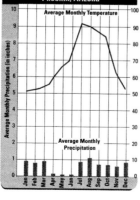

16 What is the wettest month in Eugene, Oregon? _____ December _____

17 What is the average temperature in January for each place?
_____ 40°F in Eugene and 51°F in Phoenix _____

18 About how much precipitation falls in January in each place? __about eight inches__ __in Eugene and about one inch in Phoenix__

19 In which months does each city receive less than one inch of precipitation?
__In July Eugene averages less than one inch of precipitation. Phoenix averages less__
__than one inch of precipitation in every month except August.__

(continued)

Chapter 13 Test

Name _____ Date _____

Part Three: Apply What You Have Learned

20 **ACTIONS AND REACTIONS** (10 points)

The movement of people into the western United States had many impacts. Listed below on the left are actions that happened in the West after the Civil War. Fill in each box on the right with a reaction to that action.

Action	Reaction(s)
Gold is discovered.	Possible response: Many people move to areas such as California, Colorado, Idaho, Montana, and Alaska. Mining areas experience an economic boom.
Cities in the East grow and demand for beef increases.	Possible response: Prices for cattle in the East rise. Ranchers begin to drive their cattle to railroads in order to get higher prices for their cattle.
Congress passes the Homestead Act in 1862.	Possible response: Thousands of settlers move to the Great Plains.
Some farmers and ranchers fence their land for different reasons.	Possible response: Range wars develop as farmers and ranchers cut each other's fences.
Settlers in the West take lands away from Native Americans.	Possible response: Native Americans are forced to move to reservations.

21 **ESSAY** (10 points)

Abraham Lincoln developed a plan to bring the country back together after the Civil War. Write a paragraph explaining how that plan changed after Lincoln's death.

Possible response: Lincoln's plan focused on helping the nation heal after the war, and President Andrew Johnson attempted to carry out that plan. Johnson wanted to readmit Confederate states to the Union after they ratified the Thirteenth Amendment. Congress, however, wanted to do more to punish the South, and it impeached President Johnson. As a result of these tensions, the South was occupied by Union troops. As Southern governments were re-established, they passed laws that prevented African Americans from voting.

Chapter 13 Test

Introduce the Chapter

PAGES 474–475

OBJECTIVES

- Describe nineteenth-century political and social changes.
- Identify how technological developments affected the economy.
- Use critical thinking skills to analyze primary sources.

Access Prior Knowledge

Have students recall a time when they may have played the role of peacemaker between people at odds.

Visual Learning

Picture Have students examine the photograph and the Locate It map. How do these images indicate what the chapter will be about?

Locate It Map Drayton Hall is in Charleston, South Carolina. The house was completed in 1742, and it is the oldest preserved house in the United States.

BACKGROUND

Picture Ask students to describe their impressions of Drayton Hall and to discuss what kind of people might have lived there. Point out that it is a large house situated on more than 600 acres of land, which means that many people were needed to tend to the building and grounds. Drayton Hall was completed in 1742 and has been owned by seven generations of the Drayton family. The main house is in nearly its original condition and is still without running water, electricity, or central heating. Drayton Hall was built in the Georgian style of architecture, which was popular in England in the early 1700s. Today the house is a National Trust Historic Site.

BACKGROUND

Quotation Generals Ulysses S. Grant and Robert E. Lee were a study in contrasts when they met at Appomattox Court House, Virginia, to negotiate the South's surrender on April 9, 1865. Grant was in a dirty uniform that barely showed his rank as general, while Lee came formally dressed, bearing his sword. Lee gratefully accepted Grant's generous terms.

· CHAPTER ·

13

The Nation Reunited

" The war is over—the rebels are our countrymen again. "

—Ulysses S. Grant, April 9, 1865, silencing his cheering troops after Robert E. Lee surrendered

(Focus Skill) Point of View

When you determine someone's **point of view** on a subject, you identify that person's way of looking at it.

As you read this chapter, be sure to do the following.

• Determine different people's points of view about Reconstruction, industrial growth, and immigration.

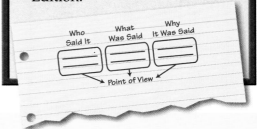

Who Said It | What Was Said | Why It Was Said

Point of View

Read and Respond

Have students consider what the title of the chapter suggests about the aftermath of the Civil War.

Quotation Have a volunteer read the quotation aloud.

Q **What do Grant's words and his efforts to quiet his troops reveal about his attitude about the war?**

A Students' responses should indicate that Grant believed the war was over and the process of healing had begun.

The quotation shows that Grant wanted to reunite the country by bridging the gap between the armies.

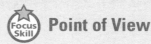

(Focus Skill) Point of View

Have students construct graphic organizers showing points of view about chapter topics.

• A blank point-of-view graphic organizer appears on page 130 of the Activity Book.

• A completed graphic organizer can be found on page 130 of the Activity Book, Teacher's Edition.

Who Said It | What Was Said | Why It Was Said

Point of View

WORD WORK

Preview Vocabulary Have students review the lesson vocabulary by reading through the chapter to find out what the words mean. Students should write definitions for the vocabulary based on the historical context in which the word is used. They may use a chart to record their work.

Word	Historical Definition

MAKE IT RELEVANT

Discussion Topics Ask students these questions as they read the chapter.

■ What industrial or technological advances have been most important to the growth of the country in your lifetime?

■ Why are people interested in immigrating to the United States today?

■ Why is "Reconstruction" an appropriate term for describing the period after the Civil War?

Lesson 1
PAGES 476–480

OBJECTIVES

- Describe the events surrounding President Lincoln's death.
- Analyze plans for the Reconstruction of the United States.
- Analyze the reactions of both Southerners and Northerners to Reconstruction efforts.
- Identify problems with Reconstruction governments.

 Point of View pp. 475, 476, 479, 480, 508

Vocabulary

SEE READING AND VOCABULARY TRANSPARENCY 6-8 OR THE WORD CARDS ON PP. V73–V74.

Reconstruction p. 476	**black codes** p. 478
assassinate p. 477	**acquittal** p. 479

 When Minutes Count

Direct students to the illustration on page 476. Use the illustration as a springboard to discuss Lincoln's death.

Quick Summary

This lesson describes President Lincoln's death and Reconstruction plans after the Civil War.

1 Motivate

Set the Purpose

Big Idea Help students understand how the United States government helped rebuild the South after the Civil War.

Access Prior Knowledge

Encourage students to think about what would need rebuilding after the Civil War.

· LESSON ·

1

 POINT OF VIEW
As you read, look for different points of view about the rebuilding of the South.

BIG IDEA
The United States government tried to rebuild the South after the Civil War.

VOCABULARY
Reconstruction
assassinate
black codes
acquittal

Reconstruction

1820 — 1870 — 1920
1865–1870

The end of the Civil War brought the Confederacy to its end. Now it was time to try to bring the country back together. This time of rebuilding, called Reconstruction, had two distinct parts. The first part was the President's plan for Reconstruction. The second part was Congress's Reconstruction plan. Before Reconstruction could begin, however, one more tragedy would add to the country's pain.

One More Tragic Death

Before the Civil War ended, Abraham Lincoln was inaugurated for a second term as President. He realized he would face a challenging task in rebuilding the country. Lincoln, however, believed the South should not be punished for the war. He wanted to bring the country back together peacefully and as quickly as possible. Lincoln spoke of his plans for Reconstruction in his second inaugural address on March 4, 1865.

> With malice toward none, with charity for all, with firmness in the right as God gives us to see the right, let us strive on to finish the work we are in, to bind up the nation's wounds. . . .

This poster announces Lincoln's plans to attend Ford's Theatre. Below are the glasses he wore that night.

FAST FACT After shooting the President, John Wilkes Booth jumped onto the stage and cried out, "Sic semper tyrannis!," which means "Thus ever for tyrants" in Latin.

476

WORD WORK

Preview Vocabulary Read each vocabulary term aloud. Ensure that students can pronounce the terms correctly. Ask students to define the terms they know and use them in sentences. Have students look up any terms that they do not understand in the Glossary of the Pupil Edition.

STUDY/RESEARCH SKILLS

Skimming and Scanning
Remind students that when they are looking for specific information it is helpful to skim and scan the lesson. Ask students to scan the lesson and to find the page that features information about the Thirteenth Amendment.

Following Lincoln's death, Andrew Johnson (above) was sworn in as the nation's seventeenth President. Johnson supported passage of the Thirteenth Amendment (right).

The President's plans were tragically cut short. On April 14, 1865, just five days after Lee's surrender, Lincoln went with Mary Todd Lincoln, his wife, to watch a play at Ford's Theatre in Washington, D.C. There he was **assassinated**—murdered in a sudden or secret attack—by John Wilkes Booth. Booth, an actor at Ford's Theatre, supported the Confederate cause.

Lincoln's death shocked the nation. Northerners had lost the leader who had saved the Union. Southerners had lost the leader who had promised an easy peace between the North and the South. Mary Chesnut, a Southerner, feared the worst. When she learned of Lincoln's death, Chesnut wrote in her diary, "Lincoln—old Abe Lincoln—killed. . . . I know this foul murder will bring down worse miseries on us."

REVIEW Why might many Southerners be upset by Lincoln's death? He had promised an easy peace between the North and the South.

The President's Plan

After Lincoln's death, the Vice President, Andrew Johnson, became President. Johnson returned the rights of citizenship to most Confederates who pledged loyalty to the United States. Their states then held elections, and state governments went back to work.

Johnson also said that the former Confederate states had to abolish slavery before they could rejoin the Union. To that end, the Thirteenth Amendment to the Constitution was ratified in December 1865. It ended slavery in the United States and its territories.

Such easy terms for rejoining the Union made many Northerners angry. They felt the Confederates were not being punished for their part in the war. White Southerners were again being elected to office and running state governments.

Chapter 13 ■ 477

Read and Respond

Culture and Society Lead a discussion with students about how black codes affected African Americans. Then have students complete the following graphic organizer.

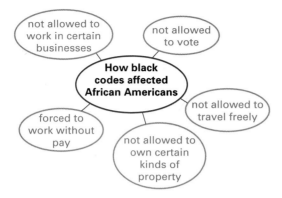

How black codes affected African Americans

- not allowed to work in certain businesses
- not allowed to vote
- forced to work without pay
- not allowed to own certain kinds of property
- not allowed to travel freely

Congress's Plan

Read and Respond

Civics and Government Inform students that after the congressional election of 1866, Republicans were the majority in Congress. They worked together to replace Johnson's plan with their own.

Q **What were the requirements Congress made of the Southern states?**

A Civil governments were replaced with military government, states had to adopt a new constitution giving all men the right to vote, and states had to pass the Fourteenth Amendment.

Q **Explain the reasons for the Fourteenth Amendment.**

A Congress wanted all people born in the United States, except Native Americans, to be citizens of their state and country.

History After students read the description of President Johnson's impeachment on page 479, inform them that Johnson was charged at his impeachment with violating the Tenure of Office Act. This act required the President to get the approval of Congress before firing an official that had been approved by the Senate. Another charge was that he had attempted to undermine Congress.

However, few people talked about the rights of the former slaves.

It was not long before the newly elected state legislatures in the South passed laws to limit the rights of former slaves. These laws, called **black codes**, differed from state to state. In most states, however, former slaves were not allowed to vote. In some they were not allowed to travel freely. They could not own certain kinds of property or work in certain businesses. They could be forced to work without pay if they could not find other jobs.

REVIEW **Why was the Thirteenth Amendment to the Constitution ratified?** to end slavery in the United States and its territories

Congress's Plan

Congress was upset about what was happening in the South. As a result, Congress replaced the President's Reconstruction plan with one of its own.

As part of its plan, Congress did away with the new state governments and put the Southern states under military rule. Union soldiers kept order, and army officers were appointed to be governors. Before any Southern state could reestablish its state government, it had to write a new state constitution giving all men, both black and white, the right to vote.

Under its plan for Reconstruction, Congress sent Union troops to the Southern states. The troops in the photograph below are standing in front of a house in Atlanta, Georgia.

REACH ALL LEARNERS

Advanced Learners
Have students compare the conditions for African Americans under the black codes with those under slavery. Have students draw conclusions about the intentions of the black codes.

BACKGROUND

Impeachment Articles of impeachment are brought about by the House of Representatives, and an impeachment trial takes place in the Senate. A two-thirds majority vote in the Senate is needed for a conviction. Only two Presidents, Andrew Johnson and Bill Clinton, have been impeached. Neither was convicted.

Johnson was the first President to be impeached. His trial in the Senate (above) drew large crowds of people.

A state also had to approve the Fourteenth Amendment. The Fourteenth Amendment states that all persons born in the United States, except Native Americans, and those who later become citizens are citizens of the United States and of the state in which they live. The amendment also protects the rights of all citizens.

President Johnson was very angry about this plan and about other laws Congress had passed to limit his authority as President. After Johnson fired a popular member of his cabinet in 1868, the House of Representatives voted to impeach him. The Senate put Johnson on trial. By just one vote, the Senate failed to get the two-thirds majority needed to remove Johnson from office. The final and deciding vote for **acquittal**, or a verdict of not guilty, was cast by Senator Edmund G. Ross of Kansas. Although Andrew Johnson stayed in office, he was no longer respected as a strong leader. In 1868 war hero Ulysses S. Grant was elected President instead.

REVIEW **What was Johnson's point of view about Congress's plan?** POINT OF VIEW
he was angry about the plan

Reconstruction Governments

As the Southern states began to write new state constitutions and approve the Fourteenth Amendment, new elections were held. For the first time African Americans, such as Blanche K. Bruce and Hiram R. Revels of Mississippi, were elected to the United States Congress.

Many African Americans also served in the new Reconstruction governments in the Southern states. Jonathan C. Gibbs became secretary of state in Florida and helped set up Florida's public school system. Before this time, most schools in the South were privately run. Francis L. Cardozo, another African American, was secretary of state and, later, state treasurer in South Carolina.

Most Confederates accepted their defeat and the abolition of slavery.

Chapter 13 ■ 479

Reconstruction Governments

Read and Respond

Link Civics and Government with Culture and Society Discuss how the Fifteenth Amendment affected black codes. Point out that states could no longer deny African Americans the right to vote.

Q Why was the Fifteenth Amendment passed?

A The Fifteenth Amendment was passed to guarantee that no citizen shall be denied the right to vote based on "race, color, or previous condition of servitude."

3 Close

Summarize Key Content

- President Lincoln was assassinated on April 14, 1865.
- President Andrew Johnson's Reconstruction plan included the Thirteenth Amendment, which abolished slavery.
- Congress put Southern states under military rule and made them grant the right to vote to all men and also ratify the Fourteenth Amendment, which granted citizenship to all people born in the United States.
- The Fifteenth Amendment, which affirmed the right of former slaves to vote, was passed despite widespread Southern opposition to Reconstruction.

Graphic Organizer Have students check their graphic organizers.

Amendment	Provisions
Thirteenth	It ended slavery in the United States.
Fourteenth	All persons born in the United States, except Native Americans, are citizens of the United States and the state in which they live.
Fifteenth	No citizen shall be denied the right to vote because of race, color, or previous condition of servitude.

 USE READING AND VOCABULARY TRANSPARENCY 6-8.

6-8 TRANSPARENCY

Assess

Lesson 1 Review—Answers

 POINT OF VIEW Lincoln thought the South should be treated fairly.

❶ **BIG IDEA** by passing amendments and putting Southern states under military rule.

❷ **VOCABULARY** **Black codes** took away many of the rights provided during **Reconstruction**.

❸ **TIME LINE** 1870

❹ **HISTORY** The Thirteenth Amendment ended slavery.

❺ **CRITICAL THINKING—Evaluate** Many Southerners did not want African Americans to have equal rights.

 Performance Assessment Guidelines Students should prepare their interviews from the appropriate point of view.

ACTIVITY BOOK

Use ACTIVITY BOOK, p. 122, to reinforce and extend student learning.

This poster (left) celebrates the passage of the Fifteenth Amendment (above).

However, many were against equal rights for African Americans. They did not want African Americans to vote or to hold office, and they opposed the Reconstruction governments.

Congress then proposed the Fifteenth Amendment to the Constitution. It states that no citizen shall be denied the right to vote because of "race, color, or previous condition of servitude." This amendment, which was ratified in 1870, was designed to extend voting rights and to enforce them by law.

REVIEW What is the Fifteenth Amendment?
It states that no citizen shall be denied the right to vote because of "race, color, or previous condition of servitude."

 **LESSON 1 REVIEW**

Summary Time Line
1865 — 1870

- **1865** Abraham Lincoln is assassinated
  The Thirteenth Amendment is ratified
- **1868** The Fourteenth Amendment is approved
- **1870** The Fifteenth Amendment is ratified

 POINT OF VIEW How did President Lincoln think the South should be treated after the Civil War ended?

❶ **BIG IDEA** How did the United States government try to rebuild the South after the Civil War?

❷ **VOCABULARY** Use the words **Reconstruction** and **black codes** in a sentence about the South after the Civil War.

❸ **TIME LINE** When did the Fifteenth Amendment become part of the Constitution?

❹ **HISTORY** Which amendment ended slavery in the United States?

❺ **CRITICAL THINKING—Evaluate** Why did many white Southerners oppose the new Reconstruction governments?

 PERFORMANCE—Conduct an Interview Imagine that you are a news reporter. Write an interview with President Andrew Johnson, a senator who supports Congress's plan for Reconstruction, or an African American elected to serve in a Reconstruction government in the South. Provide both questions and answers. Then share your interview with classmates.

EXTEND AND ENRICH

Write to Compare and Contrast Have students write one to two paragraphs comparing Congress's plan for Reconstruction and Southerners' views on Reconstruction. Encourage students to use compare-and-contrast words and phrases in their paragraphs.

RETEACH THE LESSON

Write Questions Request that each student write one question for each subsection of the lesson. Then have students exchange papers and answer each other's questions.

The South After the War

1820   1870   1920
1865–1877

When the Civil War ended, much of the South was in ruins. The money issued by the Confederacy was worthless, and most Confederate banks were closed. Entire cities had been burned, and many railroads, bridges, plantations, and farms had been destroyed. As one Southerner remembered, "All the talk was of burning homes, houses knocked to pieces, . . . famine, murder, desolation."

The years following the war were hard ones for all people in the South. For the more than 4 million former slaves living there, however, those years also brought new hope.

The Freedmen's Bureau

In March 1865, even before the war ended, the United States Congress set up the Bureau of Refugees, Freedmen, and Abandoned Lands—the Freedmen's Bureau, as it was called. It aided all needy people in the South, although freedmen—men, women, and children who had been slaves—were its main concern.

Many former slaves, like those shown outside this Freedmen's Bureau school (below), were eager to learn to read and write. Many of the teachers in those schools were Northern women.

481

 POINT OF VIEW
As you read, determine different points of view held by Southern citizens after the war ended.

BIG IDEA
The South faced many challenges after the war.

VOCABULARY
freedmen
sharecropping
carpetbagger
scalawag
secret ballot
segregation

OBJECTIVES
- Identify challenges facing the South after the Civil War.
- Analyze Reconstruction efforts to help freed slaves.
- Describe carpetbaggers and scalawags and their roles in Reconstruction.
- Analyze segregation and how it affected the lives of African Americans.

 Point of View pp. 475, 481, 484, 485, 508

Vocabulary
SEE READING AND VOCABULARY TRANSPARENCY 6-9 OR THE WORD CARDS ON PP. V73–V74.

freedmen p. 481	**scalawag** p. 484
sharecropping p. 483	**secret ballot** p. 484
carpetbagger p. 483	**segregation** p. 484

 ## When Minutes Count

Read aloud the Big Idea statement. Then ask students to examine the illustrations and identify how each one relates to the Big Idea.

Quick Summary

This lesson examines challenges facing African Americans and white Southerners during Reconstruction.

1 Motivate

Set the Purpose

Big Idea Ask students to list some of the challenges the South faced after the Civil War.

Access Prior Knowledge

Encourage students to think about the difficulties African Americans faced after the Civil War.

REACH ALL LEARNERS

English as a Second Language Have students who are acquiring English add the lesson vocabulary to their vocabulary notebooks. Ask them to list and define each vocabulary word and write each word in a sentence to help them remember the word's meaning.

BACKGROUND

The Freedmen's Bureau The Freedmen's Bureau controlled about 800,000 acres of land after the Civil War. This land was originally intended to be given to former slaves in lots not bigger than 40 acres. If this plan had been followed, about 20,000 plots of land would have been given to former slaves.

Study Questions Invite students to use these questions as guides for their reading:

1. What was the Freedmen's Bureau?

2. How did landowners benefit from sharecropping?

3. What is segregation?

● USE READING AND VOCABULARY TRANSPARENCY 6-9.

2 Teach

The Freedmen's Bureau

Read and Respond

Link History with Civics and Government Explain to students that the Freedmen's Bureau was originally intended to operate for only one year, but that period was extended in 1866. Most of the activities of the Freedmen's Bureau stopped in 1869. The education program, however, continued until 1872.

Q Why was educating newly freed slaves an important goal?

A Education would help them start a new life as free citizens.

• HERITAGE •

Juneteenth

Have students read the Heritage section on page 482. Ask any students who have participated in Juneteenth celebrations to describe them to the class. Discuss how Juneteenth has become a part of African American heritage.

---

to aid needy people in the South, but especially to teach former slaves to read and write

Many former slaves were wandering through the country looking for the means to start a new life. The Freedmen's Bureau gave food and supplies to these people. It also helped some white farmers rebuild their farms. The most important work of the Freedmen's Bureau, however, was education. Newly freed slaves were eager to learn to read and write. To help meet this need, the Freedmen's Bureau built more than 4,000 schools and hired thousands of teachers.

The Freedmen's Bureau also wanted to help former slaves earn a living by providing them with land to farm, but this plan did not work. The land was to have come from the plantations taken or abandoned during the war, but the federal government decided to give those plantations back to their original owners. In the end, most former slaves were not given any land. Without money to buy land of their own, they had to find work where they could.

REVIEW Why was the Freedmen's Bureau set up?

This photograph (left) shows people going to an early Juneteenth celebration. Many people, such as those participating in this parade in Austin, Texas (below), celebrate Juneteenth.

• HERITAGE •

Juneteenth

Abraham Lincoln had issued the Emancipation Proclamation on January 1, 1863. But because Union troops did not control Texas at the time, the order had little effect there. On June 19, 1865, Union soldiers landed in Galveston, Texas. On that day Union General Gordon Granger read an order declaring that all slaves in Texas were free. Today people in Texas and across the country celebrate June 19, or Juneteenth, as a day of freedom. It is a holiday marked by picnics, parades, and family gatherings.

482 ▪ Unit 6

Summarize Emphasize to students that it is helpful to summarize important details about a topic. Remind them that reviewing summaries they have written is a good way to study a lesson. Have students write a summary for this subsection.

Write a Personal Narrative Remind students that by the time sharecroppers paid rent for the land, there was little money left for them to get ahead. Ask students to imagine that they are sharecroppers and to write how they feel about sharecropping compared with slavery, including their hope or lack of hope for the future.

Sharecropping

In their search for jobs, many former slaves went back to work on plantations. Planters welcomed them. Fields needed to be plowed, and crops needed to be planted. Now, however, planters had to pay the former slaves for their work.

Because there was not much money available in the years following the war, many landowners paid workers in shares of crops rather than in cash. Under this system, known as **sharecropping**, a landowner gave a worker a cabin, mules, tools, and seed. The worker, called a sharecropper, or tenant farmer, then farmed the land. At harvesttime the landowner took a share of the crops to cover the cost of the worker's housing. What was left was the worker's share.

Sharecropping gave landowners the help they needed to work the fields. It also gave former slaves work for pay. Yet few people got ahead through sharecropping. When crops failed, both landowners and workers suffered. Even in good times, most workers' shares were very little, if anything at all.

REVIEW How were workers paid in a sharecropping system?

Carpetbaggers and Scalawags

To rebuild bridges, buildings, and railroads, the South's Reconstruction governments had to increase taxes. In Louisiana, for example, taxes almost doubled. Mississippi's taxes were 14 times higher than they had been. White Southerners blamed the higher taxes on African American state legislators and on

Using tools like this plow, many former slaves worked as sharecroppers in the years following the Civil War.

other state government leaders they called carpetbaggers and scalawags.

Carpetbaggers were people from the North who moved to the South to take part in Reconstruction governments. They were called carpetbaggers because many of them carried their belongings in suitcases made of carpet material. Some of them truly wanted to help. Others were looking for an opportunity for personal gain.

At harvesttime the landowner took a share of the crops plus enough to cover the worker's housing and supplies. The rest was the worker's share.

Chapter 13 ■ **483**

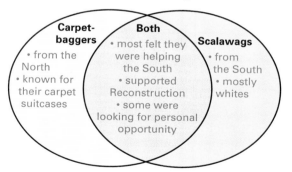

Read and Respond

Economics Discuss with students how building factories in the South might have affected the region's economy. Remind students that the North's factories had given it an advantage during the Civil War. Ask students whether they think James Longstreet's ideas would have had a positive or a negative effect on the South.

Reconstruction Ends

Read and Respond

History Remind students that the Fifteenth Amendment made it illegal to deny citizens the right to vote based on race. In response, many Southern states made it difficult for African Americans to vote. Some laws required them to pay a tax or pass a literacy test before they could vote.

Q Why might passing a literacy test be difficult for many African Americans?

A Most African Americans could not read because teaching a slave to read and write had been illegal.

 **3 Close**

Summarize Key Content

- The South faced many challenges after the Civil War.
- The Freedmen's Bureau was set up to help people in the South, particularly freed slaves.
- Many former slaves became sharecroppers.
- White Southerners blamed carpetbaggers and scalawags for high taxes in the South after the Civil War.
- The end of Reconstruction was followed by the beginning of segregation.

James Longstreet believed that building factories would help the South rebuild its economy.

A **scalawag** (SKA•lih•wag) is a rascal, someone who supports a cause for his or her own gain. Many scalawags were white Southerners who had opposed the Confederacy. Some were thinking only of themselves. Others felt they were doing what was best for the South.

Among the most famous of the scalawags was James Longstreet, a former Confederate general. Longstreet believed that the South needed to cooperate with the North in order to prosper. He and other leading business people wanted to build factories to lessen the South's dependence on agriculture.

REVIEW Why did Southerners blame higher taxes on state legislators and other state government leaders? **POINT OF VIEW** because the South Reconstruction government had to increase taxes

484 ■ Unit 6

Reconstruction Ends

Many white Southerners did not want their way of life to change. Burdened by heavy taxes and a changing society, they began to organize to regain their authority. One way to do so was to control the way people voted.

In the 1860s there was no secret ballot, as there is today. A **secret ballot** is a voting method that does not allow anyone to know how a person has voted. Before the secret ballot was used, the names of voters and how they voted were published in newspapers.

Secret societies were formed to keep African Americans from voting or to make sure they voted only in certain ways. Those who joined the secret societies included white Southerners who resented the fact that African Americans were now considered their equals. Members of one secret society, the Ku Klux Klan, used violence to keep African Americans from voting or to make sure they voted as they were told.

Over time, white Southerners once again took control of their state governments and society. Despite the Fifteenth Amendment, new state laws were passed that made it very difficult, if not impossible, for African Americans to vote. African Americans also were required to go to separate schools and churches and to sit in separate railroad cars. Laws such as these led to **segregation**, or the

Many carpetbaggers who came to the South during Reconstruction carried their belongings in bags made of carpet material.

The Fifteenth Amendment guaranteed African Americans the right to vote, as seen in this illustration. With the end of Reconstruction, however, that right was again denied to most African Americans living in the South.

practice of keeping people in separate groups based on their race or culture.

Reconstruction was over by 1877. In that year the last of the Union troops left the South. The rights and freedoms that African Americans had won were again being taken away in the South. By 1900 African Americans in many of the Southern states were not allowed to vote, and few held public office.

REVIEW How did white Southerners take back control of their state governments and society? They formed secret societies to keep African Americans from voting or to make sure they voted only in certain ways.

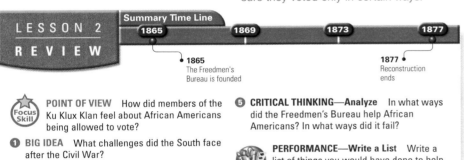

LESSON 2 REVIEW

Summary Time Line

1865 — 1869 — 1873 — 1877

- 1865 The Freedmen's Bureau is founded
- 1877 Reconstruction ends

 POINT OF VIEW How did members of the Ku Klux Klan feel about African Americans being allowed to vote?

1 BIG IDEA What challenges did the South face after the Civil War?

2 VOCABULARY Use the words **carpetbagger** and **scalawag** in a sentence about the South after the Civil War.

3 TIME LINE When did Reconstruction end?

4 ECONOMICS Why was it difficult for sharecroppers to get ahead?

5 CRITICAL THINKING—Analyze In what ways did the Freedmen's Bureau help African Americans? In what ways did it fail?

 PERFORMANCE—Write a List Write a list of things you would have done to help rebuild the South after the Civil War. Be sure to include ways in which you would have helped the newly freed slaves, as well as the economies of the Southern states. Share your list with the rest of the class.

Chapter 13 ■ 485

RETEACH THE LESSON

Graphic Organizer Ask students to complete the following graphic organizer to review the lesson. Students should categorize the challenges the South faced after the war as economic, social, or political problems.

Economic Problems	Social Problems	Political Problems
Money was worthless; banks had closed; railroads, bridges, and homes had been burned.	White people did not want African Americans to have equal rights; white people did not want African Americans to vote.	Taxes had to be increased; some carpetbaggers and scalawags took advantage; Reconstruction governments were in place.

READING SOCIAL STUDIES

Study Questions Invite students to check their answers to the study questions.

1. The Freedmen's Bureau was an organization set up by Congress to help people in the South, particularly freed slaves.

2. Landowners received help working the fields through sharecropping.

3. the separation of people because of race or culture

● **USE READING AND VOCABULARY TRANSPARENCY 6-9.** 6-9 TRANSPARENCY

Assess

Lesson 2 Review—Answers

 POINT OF VIEW Members of the Ku Klux Klan strongly opposed African Americans being allowed to vote.

1 BIG IDEA The money in the South was worthless. Cities, railroads, bridges, plantations, and farms had been destroyed.

2 VOCABULARY Southerners blamed **carpetbaggers** and **scalawags** for higher taxes after the war.

3 TIME LINE in 1877

4 ECONOMICS Most workers' share of crops was very small.

5 CRITICAL THINKING—Analyze The Freedmen's Bureau provided food, supplies, and education. It did not provide land or jobs to many former slaves.

Performance Assessment Guidelines Lists should include ways to help the economy and the freed slaves.

ACTIVITY BOOK

Use ACTIVITY BOOK, p. 123, to reinforce and extend student learning.

OBJECTIVES

- Explain the reasons people settled the West.
- Analyze the Homestead Act of 1862 and how it affected settlement in the West.
- Analyze conflicts between Native Americans and settlers.

Point of View pp. 475, 486, 490, 491, 508

Vocabulary

SEE READING AND VOCABULARY TRANSPARENCY 6-10 OR THE WORD CARDS ON PP. V73–V76.

boom p. 486   **homesteader**
refinery p. 487   p. 488
prospector   **open range**
  p. 487   p. 489
bust p. 487   **reservation**
long drive p. 487   p. 490

 When Minutes Count

Have students scan the lesson to find out about prospectors and homesteaders.

Quick Summary

This lesson describes the settlement of the western frontier and the conflicts this caused with Native Americans.

 1 Motivate

Set the Purpose

Big Idea Ask students to describe the geography of the western United States. Have students predict what challenges new settlers might face.

Access Prior Knowledge

Challenge students to recall why California's population grew quickly in the late 1840s.

· LESSON ·

3

 POINT OF VIEW
As you read, identify the points of view that different settlers and explorers had about the West.

BIG IDEA
Many people decided to move to the West after the Civil War.

VOCABULARY
boom
refinery
prospector
bust
long drive
homesteader
open range
reservation

Settling the Last Frontier

| 1820 | | 1870 | | 1920 |

1850–1890

After the Civil War, many Americans moved to the Great Plains, the Rocky Mountains, and the Great Basin. Among those settlers were soldiers who had fought in the war and freed African Americans. They believed this last frontier would provide them with new opportunities.

Miners

After the California gold rush of 1849, new discoveries of gold and silver brought more miners to the West and supplied new sources of mineral wealth for the nation. Thousands of miners hurried to Colorado after gold was found near Pikes Peak in 1858. The next year, news of huge deposits of silver in the area known as the Comstock Lode drew thousands to what is now Nevada. Between 1862 and 1868, other finds in present-day Arizona, Idaho, Montana, and Alaska added to the West's **boom**, or time of fast economic or population growth.

When gold or silver was discovered in a place, miners moved into the area hoping to strike it rich. They claimed

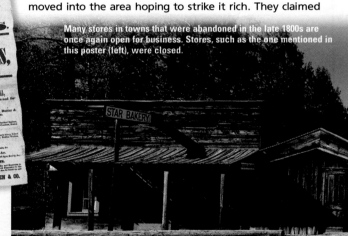

Many stores in towns that were abandoned in the late 1800s are once again open for business. Stores, such as the one mentioned in this poster (left), were closed.

486 ■ Unit 6

STUDY/RESEARCH SKILLS

Outlining As they read, students can make an outline of the lesson to help them understand how events and people are related. Give them the three following topics to begin the outline.

I. Miners
II. Ranchers
III. Homesteaders

BACKGROUND

New Settlements After the end of the Civil War many people wanted to start a new life. Some Union soldiers did not want to return to their homes in the North, and some Confederate soldiers' homes had been destroyed. Many of these people traveled out into the frontier. So did freed African Americans who were unhappy with the sharecropping system in the South. Some started new townships, such as Langston, Oklahoma.

land and set up camps, which often grew into towns. Some towns sprang up almost overnight as people quickly started businesses and farms and built refineries. A **refinery** is a factory where metals, fuels, and other materials are cleaned and made into usable products.

Fights often broke out among the **prospectors**, or those searching for gold, silver, and other mineral resources. The towns had no sheriffs, and law and order did not exist. "Street fights were frequent," one writer reported, "and . . . everyone was on his guard against a random shot." As mining towns grew, families began to arrive. Many mining towns set up governments and started schools, hospitals, and churches.

In most places all of the gold or silver was mined in just a few years. When that happened, the miners left to look for new claims and the mining town was often abandoned. Just as quickly as a boom built a town, a **bust**, or time of fast economic decline, left a town lifeless. Some of these abandoned towns, called ghost towns, can still be seen in the West today.

REVIEW What brought miners to the West?
the discovery of gold and silver

Ranchers

Settlers had many resources available to them in the West. The Pacific Ocean made trade with China easier. Settlers trapped wild animals for the fur trade and built fisheries along the coast. One of the most plentiful natural resources was the grassland. The West's vast grasslands attracted many ranchers to the region. Large-scale cattle ranching had begun in Texas in the early 1800s. After the Civil War, however, as cities in the East grew, the demand for beef increased. Ranchers could make more money if they could get their cattle to eastern markets.

At first Texas ranchers drove, or herded, their cattle to port cities, such as Galveston, Texas, for shipment to New Orleans and to cities in the East. In the late 1860s, a cheaper, faster method became available as railroads were built out West. Between 1867 and 1890, ranchers drove about 10 million head of cattle north to the railroads on **long drives**.

The long drives followed cattle trails such as the Sedalia Trail, which went from Texas to Sedalia, Missouri.

Chapter 13 • 487

BACKGROUND

The Pony Express Many changes in communication took place as the frontier expanded. At first settlers in California could only get mail delivered by boat or stagecoach. It took more than three weeks to get a letter from friends or family on the East coast. In 1860 and 1861, however, a company of horseback riders called the Pony Express delivered letters on horseback. In March 1861, Pony Express riders delivered a copy of one of Abraham Lincoln's speeches to Sacramento, California, in less than 8 days.

MENTAL MAPPING

State Location Challenge students to name all of the states surrounding Texas without looking at a map. New Mexico, Oklahoma, Arkansas, Louisiana Then ask students to name the country south of Texas. Mexico

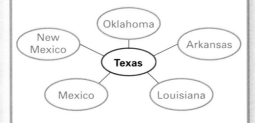

READING SOCIAL STUDIES

Anticipation Guide Ask students to predict which of the following are true and which are false. Students may correct their predictions as they read.

1. A bust is a time of fast economic growth. FALSE

2. The Homestead Act allowed any head of a household over 18 to acquire land. FALSE

3. Conflicts arose in the West between settlers and Native Americans. TRUE

● USE READING AND VOCABULARY TRANSPARENCY 6-10.

2 Teach

Miners

Analyze Primary Sources

Advertisement Have students study the flier on page 486.

Q How might the flier have encouraged people to move west?

A The offer of cheap supplies may have persuaded readers that they could afford to begin a new life in the West.

Read and Respond

Economics Explain to students that the new frontier offered many opportunities for economic gain. Point out that, in addition to natural resources such as furs and fisheries, people on the frontier could also benefit from trade with China. This trade was easier because the West coast provided access to the Pacific Ocean.

Ranchers

Read and Respond

Economics Ask students why it was better for ranchers to move their livestock to market by railroad instead of by cattle drives.

Read and Respond

Economics Explain that the price of an item may differ from one market to another, and have students speculate on why this happens. Have students discuss the reasons why people in northern cities would have to pay more for beef.

Visual Learning

Map Point out the four trails used for driving cattle. Be sure to note that cattle drives were replaced by the railroad, which made transporting livestock easier. Ask students to name the four trails used for driving cattle.
Goodnight-Loving Trail, Western Trail, Chisholm Trail, Sedalia Trail
CAPTION ANSWER: Chisholm Trail

Homesteaders

Read and Respond

History Explain to students that many politicians who pushed for the Homestead Act thought undeveloped land was worthless. Ask students to compare and contrast this view of the land with the view held by the Plains Indians.

Economics Explain to students that the land homesteaders claimed was not entirely free. Homesteaders had to pay various fees before being allowed to claim the land.

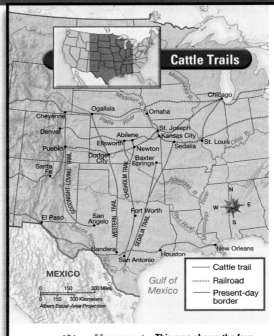

Cattle Trails

Movement **This map shows the four major cattle trails used by ranchers in the 1880s.**
❷ **Which trail led to both Abilene and Ellsworth?**

Other trails—the Chisholm, the Western, and the Goodnight-Loving—led to other "cow towns" along the railroads. Abilene, Kansas; Ogallala, Nebraska; and Cheyenne, Wyoming, were towns that grew at the end of cattle trails. At each town the cattle were loaded onto railroad cars and sent to Chicago. There the animals were prepared for market. The meat was then sent in refrigerated freight cars to markets in the East.

REVIEW How were railroads important to Texas ranchers?

Barbed wire was used to build fences on the Great Plains.

488

Saddles and hats like these were used by ranchers on long drives.

Homesteaders

In 1862 Congress passed the Homestead Act. This law opened the Great Plains to settlers by giving 160 acres of land to any head of a family who was over 21 years of age and who would live on the land for five years. Thousands of Americans, as well as about 100,000 immigrants from Europe, rushed to claim those plots of land called homesteads. The people who settled them were known as **homesteaders**.

Living on the Great Plains was very difficult. There were few streams for water or trees for wood. Many settlers used sod to build their houses, but sod houses were difficult to keep clean. Dirt often fell from the sod ceiling onto the furniture. Drought, dust storms, and floods were common in the summer, and homesteaders worried about prairie fires. In winter, snow and bitterly cold temperatures froze the region. Insects, too, were a problem. In 1874, grasshoppers came by the millions, turning the sky black and eating anything that was green.

Many homesteaders saw the Great Plains as a "treeless wasteland." They

Railroads provided a cheaper, faster method for the ranchers to transport their cattle.

---

believed that the tough sod and dry soil were unsuited for farming, and they left. Those who stayed used new technologies to solve some of the challenges the land presented. They used an improved steel plow, invented by James Oliver of Indiana, to cut through the thick sod. They used new models of windmills to pump water from the ground. They planted Russian wheat, which needed less water, and used reapers to harvest it.

Relations with ranchers posed another problem for farmers. It was difficult to grow crops in the same area where cattle ranchers kept their herds. To keep the cattle out of their fields, farmers began using wire with steel points, known as barbed wire, to build fences. Some ranchers also built fences to keep their cattle from wandering off the ranches.

Fences often kept farmers from reaching the water they needed for their crops and kept ranchers from reaching the water they needed for their cattle. Fences also blocked some cattle from reaching the millions of acres of government land that ranchers used as **open range**, or free grazing land.

GEOGRAPHY THEME

Movement This map shows the areas of the United States that were settled by 1870 and 1890. Among the settlers was this Nebraska family (right), who used sod to build their home.

◆ What happened to the frontier as settlers moved west?

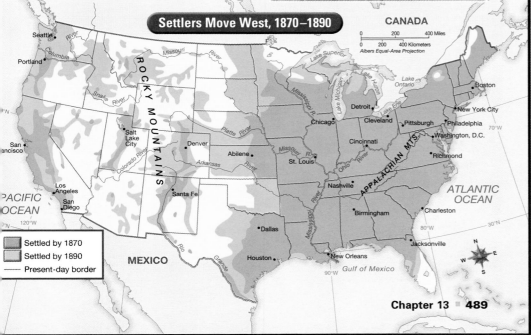

Settlers Move West, 1870–1890

- Settled by 1870
- Settled by 1890
- Present-day border

Chapter 13 ■ 489

STUDY/RESEARCH SKILLS

Using the Internet Explain to students that Frederic Remington was a famous artist who painted the lands and people of the West. Encourage students to use the Internet to research Remington's paintings or sculptures, such as *The Bronco Buster*. Have students share their findings with the class.

BACKGROUND

The Homestead Act The Homestead Act remained in effect until 1976. However, homesteading continued in Alaska until 1986. The Taylor Grazing Act, which was passed in 1934 to provide for the leasing of public land for grazing, decreased the amount of land available for homesteading significantly.

Read and Respond

Civics and Government Remind students that homesteaders had to live on the land for five years, build homes, and begin farming before the land could become theirs. Tell students that once homesteaders had done this, they needed to complete final forms stating the improvements they had made to the land. In addition, they had to find two friends or neighbors who would vouch for their honesty about the improvements and sign the forms.

Culture and Society The building of fences caused conflicts between farmers and ranchers. Have students compare how farmers and ranchers may have viewed the use of fences.

	Advantages of Fences	Disadvantages of Fences
Farmers	Fences kept the cattle out of their fields.	Fences kept farmers from reaching their water sources for their crops.
Ranchers	Fences helped keep the cattle from wandering off the ranches.	Ranchers sometimes could not get their cattle to water. Fences blocked cattle from reaching the open range.

Visual Learning

Map Point out the number of years that it took for the West to be settled. Tell students that natural resources had a great deal to do with this. Places along major bodies of water were settled more quickly than were dry or rocky regions.

Q Why might farmers move from one region to another?

A better cropland, more water resources, or better climate

CAPTION ANSWER: The West became more settled and populated.

Conflict in the West

Read and Respond

Civics and Government Explain to students that the conflict between Native Americans and settlers increased as railroad lines and mail service developed. One of the final blows occurred when gold was discovered in the Black Hills reservation.

Q Why did the Native Americans not want settlers on the Black Hills reservation?

A The land was set aside for use by Native Americans.

 Students might enjoy researching information about other national monuments. Have them visit The Learning Site at **www.harcourtschool.com.**

• GEOGRAPHY •

Little Bighorn Battlefield

Understanding Places and Regions The Little Bighorn Battlefield National Monument was once called the Custer Battlefield National Monument. The name was changed in 1991. The cemetery is known as Custer National Cemetery.

3 Close

Summarize Key Content

- New discoveries of gold and silver brought many miners to the West.
- The grasslands of the West appealed to ranchers, who used railroads to ship their cattle east.
- The Homestead Act of 1862 opened up the Great Plains to settlers by giving 160 acres of land to any head of a family who was over 21 years of age.
- Conflict arose between farmers and ranchers over fences; Native Americans were forced onto reservations.

Farmers and ranchers began cutting one another's fences. Some people even started shooting one another. These fights, called range wars, went on through the 1880s until ranchers were told they had to move their cattle off government land.

In spite of these problems, about 5 million homesteaders had migrated to the Great Plains by 1890. So many people had moved there and to lands farther west, in the Rocky Mountains and the Great Basin, that in 1890 the Census Bureau declared the last frontier "closed."

REVIEW How did many homesteaders view the Great Plains? ⊚ POINT OF VIEW
little rainfall, few trees, harsh weather, insects, dry soil, and range wars

Conflict in the West

Many of the Native American groups on the Great Plains had long depended on the buffalo for their needs. As railroads were built and settlers began using the land for farming and ranching, the buffalo began to die out. By 1880 fewer than 1,000 were left on the Great Plains.

With fewer buffalo and the loss of their hunting lands, many Plains Indian leaders

signed treaties with the United States. Those treaties set up reservations for the Indians. A **reservation** is an area of land set aside by the government for use only by Native Americans.

Sometimes Indian groups were forced onto the reservations. In the 1860s members of the Sioux Nation continued to roam the Black Hills region of present-day

• GEOGRAPHY •

Little Bighorn Battlefield

Understanding Places and Regions

Two of the Sioux chiefs at the Little Bighorn Battlefield were named Sitting Bull and Crazy Horse. They led the attack that killed hundreds of soldiers, including five members of the Custer family. The Little Bighorn Battlefield was made a national military cemetery in 1879, and in 1946 it was designated a national monument.

490 ▪ Unit 6

![Focus Skill]
READING SKILL

Point of View This lesson provides the opportunity for students to compare and contrast the points of view of ranchers and homesteaders. Have students make the following comparisons.

1. Which group, farmers or ranchers, benefitted most from building fences?

2. Which group was more likely to support open ranges?

EXTEND AND ENRICH

Compose a Story Challenge students to imagine they are a Native American of the Sioux Nation. Have them write a treaty with the United States. The treaty might include provisions for land boundaries, ways to trade with United States citizens, and a call for peace.

South Dakota and Wyoming. After gold was discovered in the Black Hills, the United States sent soldiers to move all the Sioux to reservations.

In June 1876 Lieutenant Colonel George Custer led an attack against the Sioux and their Cheyenne allies at the Little Bighorn River. As many as 2,000 Indian warriors surrounded Custer and his men. In the battle that followed, about 225 soldiers were killed, but the Sioux were later defeated. The fighting ended in 1880 when hundreds of Sioux were killed at the Battle of Wounded Knee in South Dakota.

In 1877 the United States government also ordered the Nez Perce (NES PERS) Indians in Eastern Oregon to move to a reservation in Idaho. The Nez Perce leader, Chief Joseph, led a group of 800 in an attempt to escape to Canada. They

Chief Joseph

were stopped and surrendered without a fight. Chief Joseph told his people, "I am tired of fighting."

Other groups did not give up as easily. In the Southwest, an Apache chief named Geronimo led a series of attacks against the United States army. During the 1870s and 1880s Geronimo and his warriors won many battles. In spite of his efforts, though, he was eventually forced to surrender and move to a reservation. By 1880 almost all Native Americans in the United States had been moved onto reservations. In 1924 Congress granted citizenship to all Native Americans. In 1934 it gave Indians on reservations the right to govern themselves.

REVIEW Why did Custer attack the Sioux?
to take back the land the government had given them

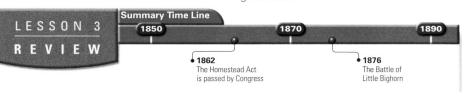

LESSON 3 REVIEW

Summary Time Line

1850   1870   1890

• 1862
The Homestead Act
is passed by Congress

• 1876
The Battle of
Little Bighorn

 POINT OF VIEW How did ranchers and farmers think differently about cattle ranching?

1 BIG IDEA Why did settlers migrate to the West after the Civil War?

2 VOCABULARY How did **prospectors** cause **booms** in some areas?

3 TIME LINE When was the Homestead Act passed?

4 ECONOMICS What were the main ways that settlers in the West earned their living?

5 CRITICAL THINKING—Analyze How do you think the destruction of the buffalo affected Native Americans?

 PERFORMANCE—Write a List of Questions Imagine that it is 1870 and that you are going to move out West to become a homesteader. Write a list of questions that you would want to ask a homesteader or cattle rancher that will make your journey easier and help you live in an unfamiliar land.

Chapter 13 ■ 491

RETEACH THE LESSON

Graphic Organizer Review the lesson with students by helping them complete the following graphic organizer. Draw the web on the board, and ask students to fill in who settled the West and for what reasons.

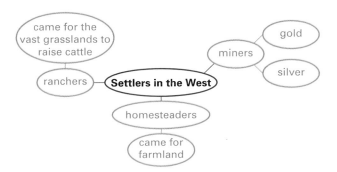

came for the vast grasslands to raise cattle — ranchers — **Settlers in the West** — miners — gold, silver — homesteaders — came for farmland

READING SOCIAL STUDIES

Anticipation Guide Have students check their responses to the Anticipation Guide at the start of the lesson.

1. A bust is a time of ~~fast~~ economic growth. slow

2. The Homestead Act allowed any head of a household over ~~18~~ to acquire land. 21

3. Conflicts arose in the West between settlers and Native Americans.

● USE READING AND VOCABULARY TRANSPARENCY 6-10.

 6-10 TRANSPARENCY

Assess

Lesson 3 Review—Answers

 POINT OF VIEW Ranchers used the plains as a grazing ground for their cattle. Farmers did not like the cattle trampling and eating their crops.

1 BIG IDEA Settlers migrated to the West to prospect for gold, become cattle ranchers, or farm.

2 VOCABULARY Prospectors moved to an area and caused fast economic growth, or **booms**, there.

3 TIME LINE 1862

4 ECONOMICS mining, farming, ranching

5 CRITICAL THINKING—Analyze Native Americans depended on buffalo for many important resources. The destruction of buffalo made it difficult for Native Americans to get these resources.

 Performance Assessment Guidelines Students' questions should be ones that will help them learn about the West.

ACTIVITY BOOK

Use ACTIVITY BOOK, pp. 124–125, to reinforce and extend student learning.

Skill Lesson

OBJECTIVES

- Use climographs to obtain information about precipitation and temperature of a specific place.
- Apply critical thinking skills to analyze information from climographs.
- Compare climographs of different places.

Vocabulary

climograph p. 492

WORD CARDS

See pp. V75–V76.

1 Motivate

Why It Matters

Ask students to consider how the weather affects their daily lives. Students might respond that it affects what they wear, what they do, and whether they spend time inside or outside. Stress that weather affects many aspects of people's lives. Point out that scientists use climographs to learn about the climate in different places.

·SKILLS· Use a Climograph

CHART AND GRAPH

VOCABULARY
climograph

➡ WHY IT MATTERS

In the late 1800s many Americans who moved from eastern cities to the Great Plains were surprised by much of what they found there. However, probably nothing surprised them more than the extremes of temperature and precipitation.

If you and your family were moving to another place, you would want to know more about its climate before you moved there. One way to learn about the climate of a place is to study a climograph, or climate graph. A **climograph** shows on one graph the average monthly temperature and the average monthly precipitation for a place. Comparing climographs can help you understand differences in climates.

➡ WHAT YOU NEED TO KNOW

The climographs on page 493 show the average monthly temperature and precipitation for Omaha, Nebraska, and Philadelphia, Pennsylvania. The temperatures are shown as a line graph. The amounts of precipitation are shown as a bar graph. The months are listed along the bottom of each climograph, from January to December.

Along the left-hand side of each climograph is a Fahrenheit scale for temperature. A point is shown on the climograph for the average temperature for each month. These points are connected with a red line. By studying the line, you can see which months are usually warm and which are usually cold.

Along the right-hand side of each climograph is a scale for precipitation. The average monthly amounts of precipitation are shown in inches. By studying the heights of the blue bars, you can see which months are usually dry and which are usually wet.

Pioneers who settled on the Great Plains sometimes experienced ice storms. These storms covered fences, plants, and the ground with a layer of ice.

492 ■ Unit 6

BACKGROUND

Climatology Climatology is the study of everyday weather conditions over a period of time. Climatologists use climographs to help people prepare for droughts or heavy rainfall. Climatologists can help answer such questions as: How often does drought occur in a region? How long do droughts usually last?

BACKGROUND

The Donner Party Climate changes were a matter of life and death to many early settlers in the West. In the spring of 1846 a large group of families set off on a journey to California. Along the way, a group of 87 people took a shortcut across the Sierra Nevada. However, they were surprised by a blizzard and the resulting winter was so cold that the party was trapped in the mountains for five months. More than 40 people died because the Donner party did not know the climate of the Sierra Nevada.

Climograph
Omaha, Nebraska

Source: The World Almanac

Climograph
Philadelphia, Pennsylvania

Source: The World Almanac

➡ PRACTICE THE SKILL

Use the climographs above to answer the following questions.

❶ Which is the warmest month in each of these cities? Which is the coolest?

❷ What is the wettest month in each city?

❸ What is the driest month in each city?

❹ Which city receives more precipitation during the year?

❺ What is the average temperature for each place in January?

❻ How much precipitation falls during January in each place?

➡ APPLY WHAT YOU LEARNED

Use an almanac, an encyclopedia, or the Internet to create a climograph for your city or for a city close to where you live. Compare your climograph with the ones shown on this page. Which place shows the greatest changes in temperature and precipitation? Share your findings with a family member or friend. Then discuss why people might need to know this kind of information.

Chapter 13 ▪ 493

CHART AND GRAPH SKILLS

2 Teach

What You Need to Know

Explain to students that precipitation and temperature are the main factors used to determine the climate of a place. Remind them that they can see both temperature and precipitation at the same time on a climograph. Ask students to find the average temperature for March in the climographs on page 493. What is the average precipitation for both places in March? Omaha: almost 2 inches; Philadelphia: almost 4 inches

Practice the Skill—Answers

❶ In Omaha, the warmest month is July and the coldest month is January. In Philadelphia, the warmest month is July and the coldest month is January.

❷ Omaha, May; Philadelphia, August

❸ Omaha, December; Philadelphia, October

❹ Philadelphia, Pennsylvania

❺ In January the average temperature in Omaha is 18°F; in Philadelphia the average temperature is 32°F.

❻ Omaha receives 1 inch of rain in January, but Philadelphia receives 3 inches.

3 Close

Apply What You Learned

Students should use real data to make their climographs. Point out that they can use a Celsius scale for temperature if they choose. Discuss with the class when the information on a climograph might be useful.

ACTIVITY BOOK

Use ACTIVITY BOOK, pp. 126–127, to give students additional practice in using this skill.

EXTEND AND ENRICH

Research Point out to students that states may be part of one, two, or even three climate zones. Ask students to research their state online and find out how the climate or climates of their state are described. Encourage them to try to find a climograph for their state or city.

RETEACH THE SKILL

Write Questions Have students write three questions that can be answered by the climographs they made. Encourage them to ask questions that make full use of the climographs.

TRANSPARENCY

Use SKILL TRANSPARENCIES 6-3A–6-3B.

OBJECTIVES

■ Analyze how new industries, including the transcontinental railroad, led to economic growth in the late 1800s.

■ Describe the contributions of entrepreneurs to the economy.

■ Analyze the effect of Thomas Edison's inventions on life in the United States.

 Point of View pp. 475, 494, 498, 499, 508

Vocabulary

SEE READING AND VOCABULARY TRANSPARENCY 6-11 OR THE WORD CARDS ON PP. V75–V78.

free enterprise p. 494	**petroleum** p. 497
transcontinental railroad p. 494	**capital** p. 497
entrepreneur p. 495	**human resource** p. 499

When Minutes Count

Have students examine the map on page 498. Use the map as a springboard to discuss the Big Idea of the lesson.

Quick Summary

This lesson examines the rise of the railroad, steel, and oil industries in the late 1800s, as well as Thomas Edison's inventions.

1 Motivate

Set the Purpose

Big Idea Check to make sure students understand the word *economy*.

Access Prior Knowledge

Have students make a list of the types of industries in the United States during the late 1800s.

 · LESSON ·

4

 POINT OF VIEW
As you read, determine ways in which points of view changed as businesses and cities grew.

BIG IDEA
The United States economy grew and changed in the late 1800s.

VOCABULARY
free enterprise
transcontinental railroad
entrepreneur
petroleum
capital
human resource

 **FAST FACT** A train trip from New York to California on the transcontinental railroad typically took from 10 to 12 days. For $100, people could sit on plush seats in fancy cars. For $40, they had to sit on hard benches in plain cars.

494

The Rise of New Industries

1820　　　1870　　　1920
1860–1900

After the Civil War great changes took place in the American economy. Inventors developed new technologies that made it easier for people to travel and communicate with one another. It was an important time for free enterprise—an economic system in which people are able to start and run businesses with little control by the government.

The Transcontinental Railroad

From 1860 to 1900, the railroad network in the United States grew rapidly. Railroads were used for travel and to move raw materials to factories and finished products to market. The people who owned the railroads made millions of dollars. They became known as tycoons, or powerful businesspeople. By 1900 a **transcontinental railroad** crossed the entire continent of North America. The transcontinental railroad was actually made

MAKE IT RELEVANT

In Your Country Remind students that in a free enterprise economy, people can run their own businesses. Have students trace the development of the free enterprise economy through the colonial period, the growth of factories and mills in the 1700s, and the rise of new industries in the 1800s.

BACKGROUND

Transatlantic Cable One new technology that made it easier for people to communicate with one another was transatlantic cable. In 1854 an American businessman named Cyrus W. Fields began the process of running a telegraph cable across the Atlantic Ocean. For 12 years he and his employees worked to run cable along the ocean floor. Finally, in 1866, the project succeeded. Telegraph messages could then be sent between Europe and the United States.

up of a number of different lines, including the Union Pacific Railroad and the Central Pacific Railroad. Together they linked the Atlantic and Pacific coasts and opened the nation's vast interior to people who wanted to settle there. They also made trade between different parts of the country easier, which caused the economy to grow.

One reason for the growth of railroads was the development of new inventions that improved rail transportation. George Westinghouse's air brake made trains safer by stopping not only the locomotive but also each car. Granville T. Woods improved the air brake and also developed a telegraph system that allowed trains and stations to communicate.

The transcontinental railroad crossed both the Rocky Mountains and the Sierra Nevada. Workers had to build bridges across valleys, cut ledges on mountainsides, and blast tunnels through mountains. At Promontory, Utah, on May 10, 1869, workers laid the last of the transcontinental railroad. A ceremonial golden spike was driven into place.

REVIEW How did the transcontinental railroad help the economy grow? by making trade between different parts of the country easier

The Steel Industry

Railroads needed strong, long-lasting tracks. At first, iron rails were used. With bigger and heavier locomotives, however, iron rails were no longer strong enough. Steel rails would be harder and last longer than iron, but steel was much more expensive to make.

In 1872 Andrew Carnegie, an entrepreneur (ahn•truh•pruh•NER) from Pittsburgh, Pennsylvania, visited Britain. An **entrepreneur** is a person who sets up and runs a business. In Britain, Carnegie saw a new process for making steel. Invented by Henry Bessemer, this process melted iron ore and other metals and materials together in a new kind of coal-fired furnace, called a blast furnace.

A CLOSER LOOK
Transcontinental Railroad

To complete the transcontinental railroad, workers often worked long hours in dangerous conditions. Most of the workers were Chinese and Irish immigrants.

❶ Workers used tools, such as pickaxes and shovels, to clear tunnels.

❷ A small locomotive powered machines that hauled dirt and rock to the surface.

❸ Explosives were used to blast through rock.

❹ Workers stayed behind a protective wall during tunnel blasting.

❺ Workers on the transcontinental railroad laid more than 1,776 miles (2,858 km) of track.

◆ What kinds of work did immigrant workers have to do to build the transcontinental railroad?

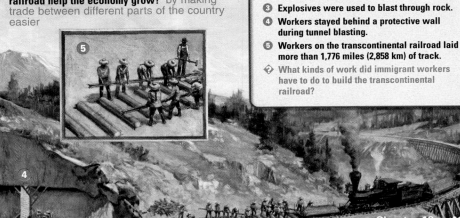

Chapter 13   495

INTEGRATE SCIENCE

The Air Brake Have students work in small groups to research more information about the air brake invented by George Westinghouse. Then ask them to write a report that includes what they learned. Encourage students to include information about how the air brake works and the changes it brought about in the United States.

BACKGROUND

Railroad Tycoons The people who ran the transcontinental railroads often became very wealthy. As a result, they gained a great deal of political power, too. Although some tycoons were honest, others bribed government officials and even used force to add to their wealth and power. Powerful railroad tycoons soon had a great deal of influence over the United States government.

READING SOCIAL STUDIES

Personal Response Encourage students to think about the following question as they read the lesson.

How has life today been affected by changes in industry in the late 1800s?

● USE READING AND VOCABULARY TRANSPARENCY 6-11.

6-11
TRANSPARENCY

2 Teach

The Transcontinental Railroad

Read and Respond

Economics Discuss with students the importance of trade between regions to the nation's economy. Point out that resources come from all over the country. When a process such as shipping goods becomes easier, prices drop, which leads to more people buying goods, causing the economy to grow.

Q How would the transcontinental railroad benefit society?

A People would be able to travel more easily, goods could be shipped more cheaply, and the economy could grow.

A CLOSER LOOK
Transcontinental Railroad

The completion of the transcontinental railroad sparked a railroad boom in the United States.
CAPTION ANSWER: clear tunnels, blast rock, and lay tracks

The Steel Industry

Read and Respond

History Discuss why heavier trains require stronger tracks. Explain that the iron rails used in early railroads weighed less than 13 lb/ft (20 kg/m). The first steel rails weighed about 20 lb/ft (30 kg/m).

Read and Respond

Economics Emphasize to students that entrepreneurs set up and run a business, but they do not need to own the money to start the business. Explain that Andrew Carnegie got the money to start his steel company from investors. Discuss with students how the investors profited when Carnegie's business did well.

Q **Why would some people want investors in their company even though they could fund it themselves?**

A Investors share in economic losses as well as gains.

Culture and Society Inform students that once Andrew Carnegie was making $50,000 a year, at the age of 33, he decided he never needed to earn more than that amount and anything more he did earn should be given to charity. Tell students that Carnegie donated money to over 2,800 libraries around the world and that he has been honored all over the world for his generous contributions.

Visual Learning

Graph Have students examine the graph of steel production.

Q **Why was there such a sharp increase in steel production in the late 1880s?**

A By that time other industries, including William Jenney's type of skyscraper construction, had found uses for steel.

CAPTION ANSWER: between 1895 and 1900

It was called a blast furnace because blasts of air were forced through the molten metal to burn out the impurities. This process made the steel stronger.

Back in Pennsylvania, Carnegie found investors to help him build a steel mill. By the early 1870s, Carnegie's steel business was so successful that he built more steel mills and bought coal and iron mines to supply them. Then he bought ships to carry these natural resources to his mills. With his mines and ships, he could make a greater supply of steel at a lower cost than other mills could.

By the 1890s Andrew Carnegie had become one of the wealthiest people in the world. Some people called Carnegie and other rich entrepreneurs "robber barons" because they had become so wealthy from their businesses. However, Carnegie also gave much of his wealth to build libraries and schools.

Other industries quickly discovered new uses for steel. In the 1880s William Jenney used steel frames to build taller buildings. People called these tall buildings skyscrapers because they seemed to scrape the sky.

John Roebling, a German immigrant, used steel cables and beams to build suspended bridges. One of his bridges, the Brooklyn Bridge, still links Manhattan with Brooklyn, in New York City.

As the demand for steel increased, more steel mills were built. In the late 1800s, large deposits of iron ore were discovered in the Mesabi Range, west of Lake Superior. To be nearer to those resources, the steel industry spread to cities along the Great Lakes, such as Cleveland, Ohio, and Chicago, Illinois.

Analyze Graphs Building projects, such as the Brooklyn Bridge (left), contributed to an increase in steel production in the United States.
◆ Between which years did steel production increase the most?

496 ■ Unit 6

QUESTIONS KIDS ASK

Q **How could air burn out impurities from molten metal?**

A The temperature of the air was not as important as the oxygen in the air. The oxygen combined chemically with the impurities in the metal. The air created a chemical burning, not a burning because of temperature.

BACKGROUND

Business Risk When Andrew Carnegie built his first steel mill, he took a risk that his business would fail. Any entrepreneur who starts a business risks losing the money that he or she has invested. Some businesses have a higher business risk than others. Each entrepreneur must evaluate those risks to make sure that the new business is worth starting.

Ships and railroads carried raw materials to steel mills and carried steel to factories and cities across the nation.

REVIEW Why did the steel industry spread to cities along the Great Lakes? New deposits of iron ore were discovered in the Mesabi Range, west of Lake Superior.

The Oil Industry

For years people had been aware of the **petroleum**, or oil, that gathered on ponds in western Pennsylvania and other places. Then, in the 1840s, a Canadian scientist named Abraham Gesner discovered that petroleum burned well. When kerosene, a fuel made from petroleum, became widely used for lighting lamps, the demand for petroleum increased. This caused its price to rise.

In 1859 Edwin Drake drilled an oil well in Titusville, Pennsylvania. When the well began producing large amounts of oil, an oil boom took place. Oil towns soon sprang up all over western Pennsylvania and eastern Ohio.

John D. Rockefeller was 23 years old in 1863 when he invested money to build an oil refinery near Cleveland. The money needed to set up or improve a business is called **capital**. Rockefeller steadily invested more capital, buying up some of the other 30 refineries in the Cleveland area. In 1867 he combined his refineries into one business, which he called the Standard Oil Company.

To cut costs and be more efficient, Rockefeller bought other businesses. His company built its own barrels, pipelines, warehouses, and tank cars. As a result, it could produce and distribute oil products at the lowest prices. Other companies could no longer compete and were driven out of the oil business.

Oil Production, 1865–1900

= 5,000,000 barrels

Year: 1865 1870 1875 1880 1885 1890 1895 1900

Analyze Graphs Drake's oil well (right) produced large amounts of oil. Such discoveries led to increases in oil production in the United States.

◈ About how many barrels of oil were produced in 1900?

Source: Historical Statistics of the United States

Chapter 13 ▪ 497

Read and Respond

Geography Have students locate the Mesabi Iron Range on a map of the United States. Then ask them to locate Chicago, Illinois, and Cleveland, Ohio. Have students trace the route that ships followed from Lake Superior to Chicago and Cleveland.

The Oil Industry

Read and Respond

Economics Tell students that John D. Rockefeller saved money by having his company make its own barrels, tanks, and pipelines. Explain that a company has to pay for the raw materials to make a product and for the process of making the product, which includes paying workers. If the company wants to make a profit, it must add those costs to the price of the product.

Q How was Rockefeller able to save money?

A He did not need to pay another company for barrels, tanks, and pipelines because he used his own.

History Tell students that before Edwin Drake drilled an oil well, oil was collected as ground seepage. Wells that had been drilled for water and salt occasionally had petroleum in them also. This convinced Drake that it was possible to get oil in large quantities by drilling.

Visual Learning

Graph Encourage students to examine the graph of oil production.

Q Between which years did oil production increase the most?

A 1885 and 1890

CAPTION ANSWER: about 65 million barrels

Visual Learning

Map Encourage students to examine the map of industries in the United States in the 1890s.

Q In which states was copper mined?

A Montana, Utah, Arizona, New Mexico, and Michigan
CAPTION ANSWER: in the Northeast

Thomas Alva Edison

Read and Respond

Culture and Society Discuss with students how Thomas Edison's inventions changed everyday life. Have students complete the following graphic organizer about Edison's inventions.

Invention	Effects
electrical vote recorder	less time spent counting votes
a new telegraph system	telegraph companies saved money by sending more messages over fewer wires
the electric lightbulb	better light in homes and businesses
power stations	made electricity available to many people

3 Close

Summarize Key Content

- The transcontinental railroad opened up trade and travel between different parts of the United States.
- Andrew Carnegie was important in developing the steel industry.
- John D. Rockefeller started the Standard Oil Company, which controlled almost all oil refining and distribution in the United States by 1882.
- Thomas Edison's contributions include the invention of the electric lightbulb and the creation of power plants.

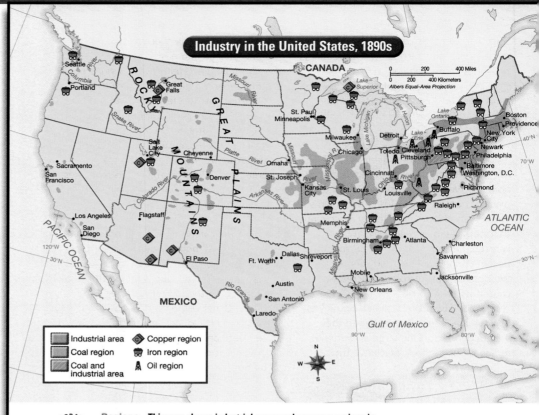

Industry in the United States, 1890s

Industrial area	Copper region
Coal region	Iron region
Coal and industrial area	Oil region

Regions This map shows industrial areas and resource regions in the United States about 1890.

◆ In which part of the United States were most industrial areas found?

by buying businesses and having his company build its own barrels, pipelines, warehouses, and tank cars.

By 1882 the Standard Oil Company controlled almost all of the oil refining and distribution in the United States and much of the world's oil trade as well. After the gasoline engine was invented and automobiles came into use, Rockefeller's oil refineries turned to producing gasoline and engine oil.

REVIEW How did John D. Rockefeller believe he could make his company more profitable?
POINT OF VIEW

Thomas Alva Edison

One of the most important inventors and industrial leaders in the United States was Thomas Alva Edison. Growing up, Edison had learned about the telegraph. Samuel Morse's telegraph, patented in the 1840s, was the nineteenth century's equivalent of the World Wide Web.

While studying the telegraph, Edison learned some of the practical uses of electricity. This knowledge led to his first

---

REACH ALL LEARNERS

Advanced Learners
Challenge advanced learners to invent their own products. Have them make posters showing their products and what they do. Ask students to present their products to the class and describe how they work and how they are useful.

EXTEND AND ENRICH

Research an Invention Ask students to use the Internet and other reference sources to research inventions of their choice. Suggest that they choose something that they use in their everyday lives, such as an electric toothbrush or a toaster. Have students present to the class what they have learned about the history of the inventions.

serious invention in 1869, an electrical vote recorder for the Massachusetts State Legislature. Two years later, in 1871, Edison started a laboratory in Newark, New Jersey. At the time, Newark was known for its many fine machinists. Those machinists were just the kind of **human resources**—the workers and the ideas and skills they bring to their jobs—that Edison needed.

In 1874 Edison's laboratory developed a telegraph system that could send more than one message over a single wire. With the money he earned from selling that telegraph system, Edison opened a laboratory in Menlo Park, New Jersey, in 1876. That

laboratory averaged one patented invention every five days. The best known was the first practical electric lightbulb. Among the others was an improved telephone, an invention that Alexander Graham Bell had patented in 1876.

In 1882 Edison set up the first central power station in New York City. It made electricity available to large parts of the city. Less than 10 years later, hundreds of communities all over the United States had Edison power stations. With Edison's help, electricity soon became an important source of power for American homes, offices, and industries.

REVIEW What was Edison's best-known patented invention at Menlo Park?
the first practical electric lightbulb

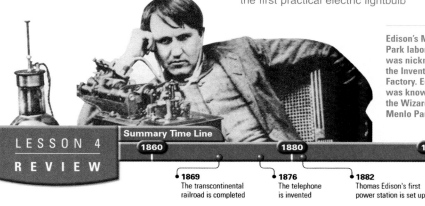

Edison's Menlo Park laboratory was nicknamed the Invention Factory. Edison was known as the Wizard of Menlo Park.

LESSON 4 REVIEW

Summary Time Line

1860	1880	1900
● 1869 The transcontinental railroad is completed	● 1876 The telephone is invented	● 1882 Thomas Edison's first power station is set up

 POINT OF VIEW How do you think John D. Rockefeller felt about the benefits of the free enterprise system?

❶ **BIG IDEA** How did the United States economy change in the years after the Civil War?

❷ **VOCABULARY** Use the word **entrepreneur** in a sentence about **free enterprise**.

❸ **TIME LINE** When was the transcontinental railroad completed?

❹ **ECONOMICS** How did the discovery of oil help the United States economy grow?

❺ **CRITICAL THINKING—Analyze** How did Andrew Carnegie contribute to the growth of cities?

PERFORMANCE—Write "Who Am I" Questions Write a list of "Who Am I" questions about some of the people you read about in this lesson. Ask your classmates the "Who Am I" questions and see if they can identify who you are.

Chapter 13 ■ 499

CHAPTER 13 ■ **499**

Examine Primary Sources

OBJECTIVES

- Identify Thomas Edison as one of America's most important inventors.
- Explain the importance of some of Edison's inventions.

1 Motivate

Set the Purpose

Thomas Edison was one of America's greatest inventors. By studying some of his inventions, students can understand how Edison affected the lives of people around the world.

Access Prior Knowledge

Review with students some of the inventors about whom they have learned. Ask them to identify inventions that have helped simplify their lives.

2 Teach

Read and Respond

Have a volunteer read aloud the opening paragraph on page 500. Explain that a patent is a legal guarantee that, for a certain number of years, an inventor will be the only one allowed to make or sell his or her invention. Have students draw conclusions about Thomas Edison based on his number of patents. Students may indicate that he was a prolific inventor.

Ask students to use the captions to identify the inventions on these pages. Have students rank the inventions in order of importance to their lives today.

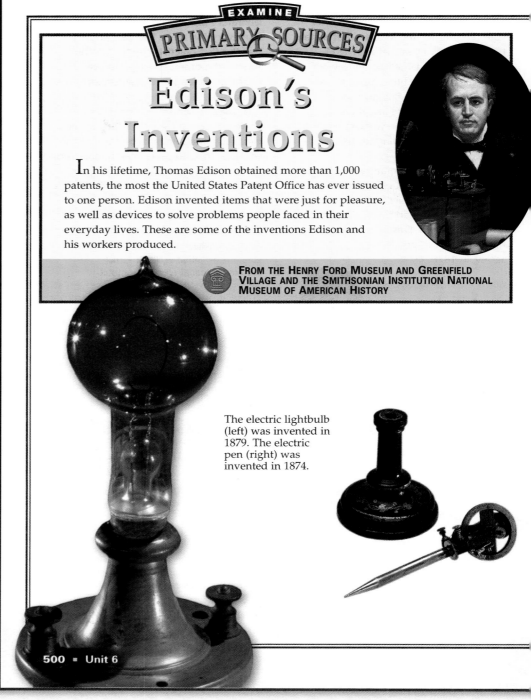

EXAMINE PRIMARY SOURCES

Edison's Inventions

In his lifetime, Thomas Edison obtained more than 1,000 patents, the most the United States Patent Office has ever issued to one person. Edison invented items that were just for pleasure, as well as devices to solve problems people faced in their everyday lives. These are some of the inventions Edison and his workers produced.

FROM THE HENRY FORD MUSEUM AND GREENFIELD VILLAGE AND THE SMITHSONIAN INSTITUTION NATIONAL MUSEUM OF AMERICAN HISTORY

The electric lightbulb (left) was invented in 1879. The electric pen (right) was invented in 1874.

500 ■ Unit 6

BACKGROUND

More About the Owner The Henry Ford Museum and Greenfield Village, which holds several artifacts pictured on pages 500–501, was the idea of Henry Ford, the founder of Ford Motor Company. Greenfield Village is a collection of about 100 historic structures that together help tell the story of America's industrialization. Today the Henry Ford Museum and Greenfield Village is the largest indoor-outdoor museum complex in the nation. Its exhibits attract more than 1 million visitors a year.

The Kinetoscope, invented in 1892, was a machine that showed motion pictures.

Analyze the Primary Source

❶ Which of these inventions looks familiar to you?

❷ Identify the purpose of each invention. Which inventions do you think made people's lives easier?

❸ Explain how one or more of Edison's inventions might work.

The phonograph (left), patented in 1878, is still thought of as Edison's most original invention. The electronic stock ticker (below) was used to print out stock information.

ACTIVITY

Think Critically Make a list of tasks or jobs that you do often. Beside each item on your list, name the tools or appliances that you use to help make the task easier. Do you think you would be able to do the same tasks if the tools or appliances had not been invented?

RESEARCH

Visit The Learning Site at **www.harcourtschool.com** to research other primary sources.

Chapter 13 ▪ 501

Analyze the Primary Source
Answers

❶ Students may say that the lightbulb on page 500 and the kinetoscope on page 501 look familiar, although their designs have changed over time.

❷ Answers will vary; some students may say that the electric lightbulb made people's lives easier, because it allowed them to see at night.

❸ Answers may vary, but may indicate the principles behind these inventions.

3 Close

Activity

Think Critically Ask students to determine the function of Edison's inventions on pages 500–501. Discuss with students which invention they consider to be most useful.

Research

Students will find a variety of Edison's inventions at The Learning Site at **www.harcourtschool.com**.

Ask students to research one of Edison's inventions and determine its use.

INTERNET RESOURCES

THE LEARNING SITE
Go to **www.harcourtschool.com** for a DIRECTORY OF PRIMARY SOURCES.

EXTEND AND ENRICH

Create a Prototype Organize students into small groups, and have each group brainstorm ideas about items that might be invented in the future. Have group members predict which invention would most benefit them. Ask each group to illustrate its invention, either by drawing it, building it, or writing a description of it. Have groups share their prototypes with the class.

RETEACH

Make a Table Ask students to make a three-column table with the headings *Lightbulb, Movie Projector,* and *Record Player.* Encourage students to research how these devices have changed over time and what devices have replaced these items. Students should place the items that are now in use or the new items in the appropriate column.

Lesson 5
PAGES 502–507

OBJECTIVES

■ Analyze how the population grew and changed after the Civil War.

■ Compare new and old immigrants and describe the challenges they both faced.

■ Explain how prejudice against immigrants led to regulations on immigration.

■ Analyze the Great Migration of African Americans to the North in the early 1900s.

 Point of View pp. 475, 502, 505, 507, 508

Vocabulary

SEE READING AND VOCABULARY TRANSPARENCY 6-12 OR THE WORD CARDS ON PP. V77–V78.

old immigration p. 502	**tenement** p. 503
new immigration p. 503	**prejudice** p. 504
advertisement p. 503	**regulation** p. 505

 When Minutes Count

Have students scan the lesson to find the meaning of each lesson vocabulary term. Then ask them to use the terms in sentences.

Quick Summary

This lesson explores immigration to the United States after 1890, the reasons immigrants came, and the hardships they faced.

 **Motivate**

Set the Purpose

Big Idea Ask students to predict some of the problems immigrants may have faced.

· LESSON ·

5

 POINT OF VIEW
As you read, determine how points of view about immigration differed.

BIG IDEA
Immigrants to the United States faced problems in the past.

VOCABULARY
old immigration
new immigration
advertisement
tenement
prejudice
regulation

A Changing People

1820   1870   1920
1880–1920

Like its economy, the population of the United States grew and changed after the Civil War. Between 1860 and 1910, about 23 million immigrants arrived on our shores. Those from Europe settled mostly in the cities of the East and Middle West. Those from Asia, Mexico, and parts of Central America and South America settled mostly in the West. Immigrants from all over the world played an important part in the growth of industry and agriculture in the United States.

Immigrants Old and New

European immigrants were by far the largest group to come to the United States. Before 1890 most immigrants from Europe came from northern and western Europe. They were part of the **old immigration**. That is, they came from the same parts of the world as earlier immigrants. The largest groups were from Britain, Germany, and Ireland. Others came from countries such

Between 1890 and 1920, nearly 16 million immigrants from Europe arrived in the United States. The passport below belonged to the Flinck family, from Sweden.

502

STUDY/RESEARCH SKILLS

Note Taking Remind students that it is helpful to take notes on the lesson as they read. Explain that notes they take can be used to study or to help them find information in the lesson. Encourage them to write notes for each subsection of the lesson as they read.

BACKGROUND

Ellis Island Congress created the Immigration and Naturalization Service (INS) in 1891. In 1892 the INS opened the immigrant screening station at Ellis Island. About 12 million immigrants had entered the United States through the Ellis Island station by the time it closed in 1954.

Irving Berlin (left) was one of the millions of immigrants who came to the United States. As a result of immigration, many cities, like New York City (above), grew very quickly.

as Denmark, Norway, and Sweden. These were the immigrants who helped build the Erie Canal and transcontinental railroad and who took part in settling the West.

Beginning about 1890, a period of **new immigration** began. People still came from the countries of northern and western Europe, but now most came from countries in southern and eastern Europe and from other parts of the world. Those from Europe came from countries such as Austria, Hungary, Italy, Greece, Poland, and Russia.

Most of the new immigrants from Europe were poor, and they had few opportunities in their homelands. They came to the United States hoping to find a better life. Many of them learned about jobs in the United States through advertisements. An **advertisement** is a public announcement that tells people about a product or an opportunity. Railroad, coal, and steel companies in the United States placed advertisements in other countries to attract new workers.

Most of the new immigrants settled in cities. They tended to live among people from their own country, with whom they shared a common language and familiar customs. Many lived with relatives, crowded together in poorly built apartment buildings called **tenements**. Wages were so low that everyone in the family—even young children—had to work to earn enough money for food.

In spite of the difficult conditions, many new immigrants succeeded. One of these people was Irving Berlin. He and his family moved to New York City from Russia in 1893. While Berlin was a boy, his father died. To help support his family, Berlin performed as a street singer and singing waiter. He began to write song lyrics and published his first song in 1907. During his life, Berlin wrote more than 800 songs, including "God Bless America," perhaps his most famous song.

REVIEW How did many immigrants learn about jobs in the United States?
through advertisements

Chapter 13 ■ 503

Ask students to name some of the countries that early immigrants came from. Why did those immigrants come to the United States?

READING SOCIAL STUDIES

K-W-L Chart Have students fill in the first two columns of a K-W-L chart before they read the lesson. Encourage them to fill in the third column as they read.

K	W	L
Early immigrants came from Britain. African Americans came from Africa as part of the slave trade.	When did Asians start coming to the United States? How did the United States control immigration?	

● USE READING AND VOCABULARY TRANSPARENCY 6-12.

2 Teach

Immigrants Old and New

Read and Respond

Culture and Society Discuss with students why new immigrants tended to live among people from their own countries. Point out that many of them had not yet learned English.

Economics Explain to students that many immigrants in northern cities worked for low wages in factories.

Q How did immigrants affect the economic development and growth of the United States?

A Since many immigrants worked for low wages businesses were able to build more factories and produce more goods. This, in turn, helped the economy grow.

INTEGRATE MUSIC

Study "God Bless America" Give students a copy of the lyrics to Irving Berlin's "God Bless America." Read the lyrics aloud with students. Play the song for students, and then have them sing along as you play the music a second time. Ask them to tell how the words and the music make them feel about the United States.

MENTAL MAPPING

Country Location Challenge students to name the countries of Western and Eastern Europe where old and new immigrants came from. Give them a blank map of Europe, and have them fill in the names of the countries that are discussed in the lesson.

Graph Encourage students to study the immigration bar graph.

Q What places might be included in the bars for "Other countries"?

A countries in Asia, Africa, Australia, and South America

CAPTION ANSWER: 1891–1900

Immigrants from Asia

Read and Respond

Link History and Economics Tell students that many Asian immigrants who came to the United States already had an agreement to work for an American employer. Their employers often paid for their transportation from their homelands.

Q What job opportunities were available to immigrants from Japan?

A jobs in agriculture

Reaction to Immigrants

Read and Respond

Culture and Society Discuss with students why Americans discriminated against immigrants in the past.

Q Why did some Americans not want immigrants to live in the United States?

A They were worried that the immigrants would take jobs away from American workers, and that the immigrants would not understand a democracy.

Culture and Society Ask students to identify similarities and differences that may exist between an Asian immigrant from China and an Asian immigrant from Japan. Students' responses should include that although both immigrants are of the same race, they have different cultures, and speak different languages.

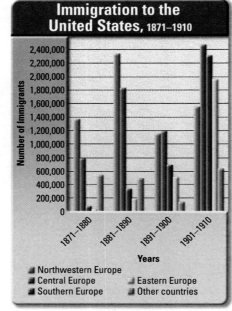

Immigration to the United States, 1871–1910

Number of Immigrants

2,400,000
2,200,000
2,000,000
1,800,000
1,600,000
1,400,000
1,200,000
1,000,000
800,000
600,000
400,000
200,000
0

1871–1880   1881–1890   1891–1900   1901–1910

Years

■ Northwestern Europe
■ Central Europe   ■ Eastern Europe
■ Southern Europe   ■ Other countries

Analyze Graphs This graph compares the number of immigrants for different periods of time.

❖ When did the number of immigrants from central Europe first become larger than the number from northwestern Europe?

Immigrants from Asia

Immigrants from China first came to the United States in large numbers after the California gold rush. By 1852 about 25,000 Chinese were working in the goldfields.

As less and less gold was found, some Chinese immigrants returned home. But most stayed and looked for other kinds of work. They often worked for low wages because above all they wanted to stay in the United States. In the 1860s Chinese workers played an important part in building the transcontinental railroad. Some Chinese immigrants set up businesses in California or other parts of the West.

504 ■ Unit 6

Immigrants from Japan and other countries in Asia also began to enter the United States and find opportunities in the West. Most found jobs in agriculture, mainly in California. Some bought their own land.

Over time, thousands of immigrants came to the United States from Asia. However, the number of Asian immigrants remained small when compared to the number of immigrants who came from Europe.

REVIEW Why did large numbers of Chinese people first come to the United States? They took part in the California gold rush.

Reaction to Immigrants

Many people born in the United States reacted harshly to the immigrants. Some Americans felt that because many of the immigrants had little education, they were not qualified to take part in a democracy. Others worried that the newcomers would take jobs away from American workers. As a result, many immigrants faced prejudice. **Prejudice** is an unfair feeling of hate or dislike for

These three children and their families came to the United States from Asia. Most immigrants were searching for new opportunities and a better life.

Immigrants Tell students that less than 10 percent of all the immigrants who have come to the United States have come for political reasons. The majority have come for economic reasons. Lead a discussion about reasons why a family might decide to move to the United States. Encourage students to imagine the family members' feelings about the move.

Learn About Chinese Explain to students that Chinese is written differently from European languages— with characters instead of letters. Tell students that the characters represent words or ideas. Ask students to go online to investigate Chinese characters. Have them try to reproduce a character of their choice. Ask them to show it to the class and explain what it means.

members of a certain group because of their background, race, or religion.

Immigrants were sometimes taunted and called unkind names. They were denied jobs by many businesses, and certain businesses even posted signs that said things such as "Irish need not apply." Jewish immigrants were denied access to the better universities and often found it difficult to get jobs. Some immigrants also suffered physical attacks, and many were ridiculed for their religious beliefs. These anti-immigrant feelings led to the formation of groups that pressured Congress to pass laws that would limit the number of immigrants who could enter the country.

In the West there had been opposition to Asian immigrants for a long time. Their language, appearance, and customs were unfamiliar to most native-born Americans. As feelings against the Chinese grew, numerous **regulations**, or controls, were set up. Some states in the West passed laws that made life harder for the Chinese. Chinese people could not

· BIOGRAPHY ·

Hiram L. Fong   1906–
Character Trait: Perseverance

Hiram Fong's parents left China to work on sugarcane plantations in Hawaii, where Hiram Fong was born. To earn money, young Hiram shined shoes and sold newspapers. He worked hard to earn enough to attend school. In time he graduated from law school. He dedicated himself to public service and was elected to Hawaii's legislature. Later he served four terms in the United States Congress as the nation's first Chinese American senator.

MULTIMEDIA BIOGRAPHIES
Visit The Learning Site at
www.harcourtschool.com
to learn about other famous people.
GO ONLINE

get state jobs, and their lawsuits would not be heard by state courts.

In 1882 the United States Congress passed the Chinese Exclusion Act. This act excluded, or kept out, all new Chinese workers. It prevented any Chinese workers from coming to the United States for ten years. By the early 1900s many Americans were calling for a stop to all immigration from Asia. Instead of passing such laws, however, the United States government persuaded Asian countries such as Japan to allow only a small number of its people to come to the United States.

REVIEW Why did many Americans react harshly to immigrants? **POINT OF VIEW**
They felt immigrants were not qualified to take part in a democracy and that they would take jobs needed by American workers.

Chapter 13 ■ 505

Focus Skill   **READING SKILL**

Point of View Students can use the information on pages 504 and 505 to practice determining point of view. Have them answer the following questions about point of view:

1. How did Americans feel about Asian immigrants? **They felt immigrants were not qualified to take part in democracy and that they would take jobs needed by Americans.**

2. What did many immigrants think about the United States? **They thought the United States offered them new opportunities.**

Read and Respond

Link History with Civics and Government Tell students that discrimination against Chinese immigrants continued in the United States during World War II. Tell them that China was an ally of the United States. Explain that the cooperation between China and the United States led to the repealing of the Chinese Exclusion Act in 1943. The United States also allowed first-generation Chinese immigrants to apply for citizenship.

Q How did regulations restrict the Chinese?

A Chinese people could not get state jobs and their lawsuits would not be heard by state courts.

· BIOGRAPHY ·

Hiram L. Fong

Perseverance Ask students to think about how Hiram Fong exemplifies the trait of perseverance. Students might mention that even though he was born poor, he became wealthy and a United States senator. Point out that he earned enough money to put himself through law school.

Culture and Society Remind students that many immigrants lived in tenement housing under terrible conditions. Tell them that in 1890 an American journalist and photographer named Jacob Riis published a book named "How the Other Half Lives." This famous book included photos and stories about the terrible conditions poor immigrants faced in New York City.

Q Why did so many immigrants have to live in tenement housing?

A They often came to the United States without jobs and had to work for very low wages

African Americans on the Move

Read and Respond

Culture and Society Have students consider whether as many African Americans would have migrated to the North if they had had better opportunities open to them in the South.

Economics Remind students that the main reason that African Americans moved north was that they were unable to make a living in the South. Discuss with students why there were more economic opportunities for African Americans in the North. Remind them that the South was still recovering from the Civil War.

Q **Why did African Americans think the move to the North was a good economic choice?**

A Floods and the boll weevil had destroyed crops at the same time jobs began opening up in the North.

 **3** **Close**

Summarize Key Content

- Old immigrants came to the United States from northern and western Europe, and new immigrants came from southern and eastern Europe and from other parts of the world.
- Asian immigrants began coming to the United States at the time of the California gold rush.
- New immigrants faced prejudice from Americans, which led to immigration regulations.
- As many as 500,000 African Americans moved north in the Great Migration.

African Americans on the Move

Even as immigrants were moving to the United States from other countries, people within the United States were moving from place to place. This was true of many different groups of Americans, including African Americans. Many African Americans were looking for new places to live and work.

Many African Americans migrated from the South to the West. There they started farms or found job opportunities they did not have in the South. Some African Americans who had fought in the Civil War stayed in the Army and became part of units formed to fight against Native Americans in the West. The Indians gave the African American troops the name buffalo soldiers because they saw the same fighting spirit in the soldiers that they saw in the buffalo.

Most African Americans who did not move after the end of the Civil War found jobs in the South, often as sharecroppers. Few African Americans moved to the cities because they could not find work there. That changed between 1915 and 1930, when many African Americans moved north. This movement of people came to be known as the Great Migration.

One of the main reasons for the Great Migration was that many African Americans working on farms in the South were going through hard times. Floods had damaged many farms, and year after year an insect called the boll weevil had

This painting by artist Jacob Lawrence depicts the Great Migration. In it African Americans are shown leaving the South for cities in the North.

REACH ALL LEARNERS

Tactile Learners Help tactile learners understand the Great Migration by having them find Boston, Chicago, Cleveland, Detroit, New York, Pittsburgh, and St. Louis on a map of the United States. Explain that thousands of African Americans moved to each of these cities. Have students put self-stick notes on the map showing the percentage of African Americans in the North and the South before and after the Civil War.

EXTEND AND ENRICH

Describe a Painting Ask students to examine Jacob Lawrence's painting shown on this page. Then have them write a conversation that could have taken place among the people shown in the painting. Have students present their conversations to the class and explain what the painting illustrates in the story of the Great Migration.

destroyed the cotton crop. At the same time, jobs began to open up in the North.

Many African Americans found factory jobs in large cities such as Boston, Chicago, Cleveland, Detroit, New York, Pittsburgh, Cincinnati, and St. Louis. Newspapers owned by African Americans in those cities actively encouraged this migration. "Get out of the South," advised the *Chicago Defender*. "Come north." As many as 500,000 people did.

Before the early 1900s nearly 90 percent of African Americans lived in the South. Because of the Great Migration, more than half of all African Americans now live in the North and in the Middle West. Most have parents, grandparents, or great-grandparents who were part of the huge movement north.

Jacob Lawrence's parents moved to the North in the early 1900s as part of the Great Migration.

Jacob Lawrence's parents moved north in the early 1900s. Lawrence went to art school in New York City and became a painter. He wrote in his book *The Great Migration*, "Life in the North brought many challenges, but the migrants' lives had changed for the better. The children were able to go to school, and their parents gained the freedom to vote. And the migrants kept coming. Theirs is a story of African-American strength and courage. I share it now as my parents told it to me, because their struggles and triumph ring true today. People all over the world are still on the move, trying to build better lives for themselves and for their families."

REVIEW What was the Great Migration?
the movement north of many African Americans between 1915 and 1930

LESSON 5 REVIEW

Summary Time Line

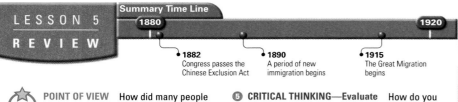

1880

1882 Congress passes the Chinese Exclusion Act

1890 A period of new immigration begins

1915 The Great Migration begins

1920

POINT OF VIEW How did many people born in the United States feel about immigrants?

1 BIG IDEA What were some of the problems immigrants to the United States faced?

2 VOCABULARY How did **prejudice** lead to the **regulation** of some immigrants?

3 TIME LINE In what year did Congress pass the Chinese Exclusion Act?

4 GEOGRAPHY Where did most people come from during the old immigration?

5 CRITICAL THINKING—Evaluate How do you think African Americans felt about the Great Migration?

PERFORMANCE—Write an Advertisement Imagine that you are the owner of a railroad company in 1890. Write an advertisement to attract immigrant workers to your company. Share your advertisement with your classmates.

Chapter 13 ■ 507

K-W-L Chart Ask students to complete the last column of their K-W-L charts.

K	W	L
Early immigrants came from Britain. African Americans came from Africa as part of the slave trade.	When did Asians start coming to the United States? How did the United States control immigration?	Asian immigrants started coming in 1849. The United States set up regulations that controlled immigration.

● USE READING AND VOCABULARY TRANSPARENCY 6-12.

 6-12 TRANSPARENCY

Assess

Lesson 5 Review—Answers

POINT OF VIEW Many people born in the United States did not like immigrants because they were afraid newcomers would take their jobs.

1 BIG IDEA prejudice, regulations, and exclusion

2 VOCABULARY Because people were **prejudiced** against immigrants, laws were passed that **regulated** immigrants coming to the United States.

3 TIME LINE in 1882

4 GEOGRAPHY northern and western European countries

5 CRITICAL THINKING—Evaluate African Americans probably felt that the Great Migration gave them the chance to live better lives than they could in the South.

Performance Assessment Guidelines Students' advertisements should include information about the jobs available and the pay workers would receive.

ACTIVITY BOOK

Use ACTIVITY BOOK, p. 129, to reinforce and extend student learning.

RETEACH

Graphic Organizer Ask students to fill in the following graphic organizer about immigration and migration in the United States. Give students the causes and have them fill in the effects.

Causes	Effects
Poor economic conditions existed in their original countries.	Many people came to the United States.
Americans reacted harshly to the immigrants.	Numerous immigration regulations were set up.
African Americans faced hardships in the South.	Up to 500,000 African Americans moved north.

Chapter 13 Review

 POINT OF VIEW

Students may use the graphic organizer that appears on page 130 of the Activity Book. Answers appear in the Activity Book, Teacher's Edition.

Think & Write

Write a Folktale Students should include in their folktales accurate details about the lives of miners and business owners. Students might mention details such as the importance of the railroad to daily life, the tools and supplies needed for mining life, and the influence of immigrants.

Write a Letter Students' letters should show an understanding of the difficulties faced by immigrants in the 1800s. They may describe details such as their reasons for coming, their living situation, and support they received from people in their new community.

ACTIVITY BOOK

A copy of the graphic organizer appears in the ACTIVITY BOOK on page 130.

TRANSPARENCY

The graphic organizer appears on READING AND VOCABULARY TRANSPARENCY 6-13.

· CHAPTER ·

13 Review and Test Preparation

Summary Time Line

1860

- **1862** The Homestead Act is passed
- **1869** The Transcontinental Railroad is completed
- **1870** The Fifteenth Amendment becomes law
- **1877** Recon ends

 Point of View

Copy the following graphic organizer onto a separate sheet of paper. Use the information you have learned to describe different points of view about Abraham Lincoln and Reconstruction.

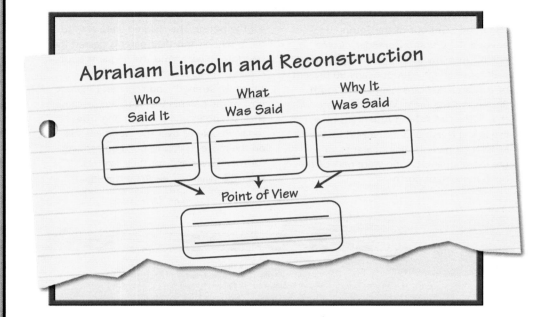

THINK & WRITE

Write a Folktale Many American folktales grew out of the nation's western experience. Imagine you are hiking in the west when you come upon a ghost town. Write a folktale about your discovery and the miners and business owners who once lived there.

Write a Letter Immigrants to the United States have always been presented with both opportunities and challenges. Imagine you are a nineteenth-century immigrant trying to adjust to your new home. Write a letter to a friend describing your situation and hopes for the future.

508 ■ Chapter 13

TEST PREPARATION

Review these tips with students:

- Read the directions before reading the questions.
- Read each question twice, focusing the second time on all the possible answers.
- Take the time to think about all the possible answers before deciding on an answer.
- Move past questions that give you trouble, and answer the ones you know. Then return to the difficult items.

UNIT PROJECT

Progress Check By now students should have web diagrams for each major figure covered in this unit. Suggest that each student select one figure he or she wishes to include in the group's project. Have students compare diagrams to ensure that they have collected all the key aspects of their chosen figure's life. Then have them discuss the design of their poster.

1915
The Great
Migration
begins

USE THE TIME LINE

Use the chapter summary time line to answer these questions.

1 When was the Transcontinental Railroad completed?

2 Did Reconstruction end before or after the Fifteenth Amendment was passed?

USE VOCABULARY

For each pair of terms, write a sentence that explains how the terms are related.

3 **freedmen** (p. 481), **segregation** (p. 484)

4 **long drive** (p. 487), **open range** (p. 489)

5 **entrepreneur** (p. 495), **capital** (p. 497)

6 **new immigration** (p. 503), **tenement** (p. 503)

RECALL FACTS

Answer these questions.

7 Why was the Fifteenth Amendment passed?

8 What challenges did Native Americans face in the years after the Civil War?

9 What was the main reason for the Great Migration?

Write the letter of the best choice.

10 The Fourteenth Amendment was passed to—
 A end slavery in the United States.
 B establish the Freedmen's Bureau.
 C give citizenship to all people born in the United States—including former slaves.
 D give every United States citizen the right to vote regardless of his or her race.

11 The most important work of the Freedmen's Bureau was—
 F to ensure voting rights for all African American males.
 G to promote African American political candidates.
 H to decide whether President Johnson should be removed from office.
 J to educate newly freed slaves.

12 The main reason oil production greatly increased in the late nineteenth century was because—
 A ranchers often traded their herds for oil.
 B people used kerosene to light their lamps.
 C homesteaders used petroleum to kill insects.
 D oil was used to fuel trains.

THINK CRITICALLY

13 Why do you think Southern state legislatures passed black codes after the Civil War?

14 How do you think the Great Migration affected the economy of the United States?

15 Why do you think many homesteaders chose to move west despite all the difficulties?

APPLY SKILLS

Use a Climograph
Study the climographs on page 493. Then answer the following questions.

16 What is the average temperature for each city in August?

17 How much precipitation falls during August in each city?

Chapter 13 ▪ 509

9 Many African Americans living on farms in the South were going through hard times. At the same time, more jobs were becoming available in the factories of Northern cities. As a result, many African Americans soon moved to the North to work at those factory jobs. (p. 506)

10 C (p. 479)

11 J (p. 482)

12 B (p. 497)

Think Critically

13 Some people in the South wanted to limit the rights of former slaves and did not want them to have a say in electing leaders. (p. 478)

14 Some may feel that it helped the economy by bringing in many new workers.

15 They wanted a chance for better lives.

Apply Skills

Use a Climograph

16 The average temperature in August in Omaha is 74°F; in Philadelphia it is 75°F.

17 The average precipitation in August in Omaha is 4 inches and in Philadelphia is 4 inches.

ACTIVITY BOOK

Use the CHAPTER 13 TEST PREPARATION on page 131 of the Activity Book.

ASSESSMENT

Use the CHAPTER 13 TEST on pages 99–102 of the Assessment Program.

Use the Time Line

1 in 1869

2 after

Use Vocabulary

3 After emancipation, **freedmen** still experienced the effects of **segregation**.

4 The **long drives** followed trails north across the **open range** to the railroads.

5 **Entrepreneurs**, such as Andrew Carnegie, invested **capital** in their new businesses.

6 **New immigrants** often could only afford to live in **tenements**.

Recall Facts

7 to ensure voting rights for African Americans (p. 480)

8 starvation, disease, wars, being driven off their land (pp. 490–491)

The Gettysburg National Military Park

PAGES 510–511

OBJECTIVES

■ Identify major events of the Civil War.

■ Use visual material to acquire historical information about the United States.

Summary

The Gettysburg National Military Park memorializes the armies who fought in the Battle of Gettysburg.

1 Motivate

Get Ready

Point out that Gettysburg is a small Pennsylvania town located about 50 miles northwest of Baltimore, Maryland. Tell students that many people visit the park to see its monuments and memorials and to learn about the Civil War. Discuss with students what they can learn from memorials and monuments.

2 Teach

What to See

Direct students' attention to the photographs and captions on pages 510 and 511. Ask students the following questions:

• *Who do you think is buried at the Gettysburg National Cemetery?*

• *How are the people who are reenacting Civil War battles dressed?*

• *What kinds of weapons were used at the Battle of Gettysburg?*

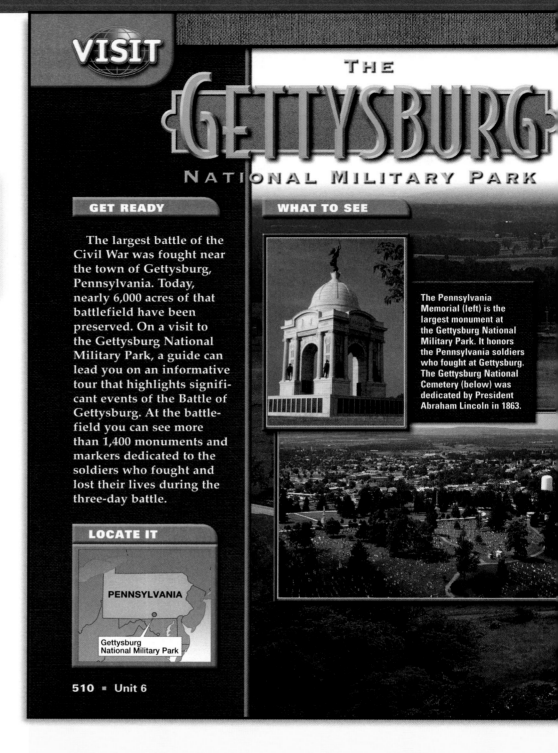

VISIT THE GETTYSBURG

NATIONAL MILITARY PARK

GET READY

The largest battle of the Civil War was fought near the town of Gettysburg, Pennsylvania. Today, nearly 6,000 acres of that battlefield have been preserved. On a visit to the Gettysburg National Military Park, a guide can lead you on an informative tour that highlights significant events of the Battle of Gettysburg. At the battlefield you can see more than 1,400 monuments and markers dedicated to the soldiers who fought and lost their lives during the three-day battle.

LOCATE IT

PENNSYLVANIA

Gettysburg National Military Park

WHAT TO SEE

The Pennsylvania Memorial (left) is the largest monument at the Gettysburg National Military Park. It honors the Pennsylvania soldiers who fought at Gettysburg. The Gettysburg National Cemetery (below) was dedicated by President Abraham Lincoln in 1863.

510 ■ Unit 6

BACKGROUND

The Gettysburg National Cemetery The Gettysburg National Cemetery was designed by William Saunders, a landscape gardener. There is a central site where the Soldiers' Monument stands. In a semi-circular pattern around the monument are cemetery plots arranged by state. The soldiers are buried in their state's plot. More than 7,000 people are buried at the cemetery. Over 3,500 of them fought in the Civil War.

INTEGRATE ART

Design a Monument Challenge students to design monuments to honor military veterans in their state. Students can choose a particular war if they wish. Encourage them to use reference sources and the Internet to research other monuments.

Actors dressed as Union and Confederate soldiers reenact Civil War battles at the Gettysburg National Military Park.

Unit 6 ▪ 511

Take a Field Trip

Direct students to research the commanders of the Union and Confederate armies during the Battle of Gettysburg. Students may be interested in learning more about how the decisions the commanders made affected the outcome of the battle.

A Virtual Tour Depending on the availability of computers, have students work individually, with partners, or in small groups to view the virtual tour. Encourage them to research events of the Civil War as they explore the Web sites. Remind students to use what they learn on their virtual tours as background information for the Unit Project.

A Video Tour View the CNN video tour of the Gettysburg National Military Park with students. After viewing the video, have them work together in small groups to create activities, such as crossword puzzles or matching exercises, using information they learned from the videotape. Have groups exchange activities. Show the videotape a second time, and have students complete the activities.

VIDEO

Use the CNN/Turner Learning TAKE A FIELD TRIP videotape of the Gettysburg National Military Park.

MAKE IT RELEVANT

In Your State Have students work in small groups to research a state or national cemetery in their state. Ask them to find out who is buried there, when the cemetery was established, and why.

EXTEND AND ENRICH

Create a Time Line Invite students to create timelines of the Battle of Gettysburg. Remind them that the battle lasted three days. Suggest that they use information from their virtual tour and other reference sources to create time lines that include at least two events on each day of the battle.

Unit 6 Review and Test Preparation

PAGES 512–514

Visual Summary

Students' letters should correctly describe the chosen event and how the event will change the country.

- **The Missouri Compromise** In 1820 Congress signed an agreement that maintained the balance of free and slave states and territories. This compromise kept the peace for nearly 30 years.

- **The Compromise of 1850** Under this compromise California joined the Union as a free state and the rest of the lands gained from Mexico were divided into New Mexico and Utah, where the people would decide whether to allow slavery.

- **The Kansas-Nebraska Act** Congress passed this act in 1854, which allowed Kansans and Nebraskans to vote on slavery. As people flocked to Kansas hoping to influence the vote, the conflict became violent and was known as "Bleeding Kansas."

- **The Civil War begins** On April 12, 1861, Confederate soldiers fired on Fort Sumter. As a result, Lincoln called for more troops to stop the Southern rebellion and four more states seceded.

- **Lee surrenders at Appomattox Court House** Union forces overtook Confederate holdings and interrupted supply lines, resulting in Lee's surrender and the war's end on April 9, 1865.

- **By 1890 the steel industry is a big business in the United States** Steel was needed to make strong, long-lasting railroad tracks. Many other uses for steel were discovered, and entrepreneurs became rich.

Use Vocabulary

1. acquittal
2. tariffs
3. homesteaders

·UNIT·

6 Review and Test Preparation

VISUAL SUMMARY

Write a Letter Study the pictures and captions below to help you review Unit 6. Then choose one of the events shown. Write an informative letter to a friend describing the event and how you think it will change the country.

USE VOCABULARY

Use a term from this list to complete each of the following sentences.

tariffs (p. 436)

acquittal (p. 479)

homesteaders (p. 488)

1. Senator Edmund G. Ross cast the deciding vote for the _____ of Andrew Johnson.

2. Before the Civil War, the North and South disagreed on the issue of _____.

3. Nearly 100,000 European immigrants became _____ on the Great Plains.

RECALL FACTS

Answer these questions.

4. How did enslaved people resist slavery?

5. What is the free enterprise system?

Write the letter of the best choice.

6. The conflict that started the Civil War took place at—
   A Williamsburg, Virginia.
   B Fort Sumter, South Carolina.
   C Gettysburg, Pennsylvania.
   D Antietam Creek, Maryland.

7. One major effect of the Civil War was that—
   F the United States never again admitted a new state to the Union.
   G Northerners were not allowed to settle in the South.
   H Southerners were not allowed to vote.
   J the Southern economy suffered many hardships.

Visual Summary

1820

1845

1870

1820 The Missouri Compromise p. 438

1850 Congress passes the Compromise of 1850 p. 439

1854 The Kansas–Nebraska Act is passed p. 439

512

Recall Facts

4. rebellion, breaking tools, pretending to be sick, acting as if they did not understand what they were told, and running away (p. 445)

5. an economic system in which people are able to start and run businesses with little control by the government (p. 494)

6. B (p. 454)

7. J (p. 481)

8. C (p. 478)

Think Critically

9. Many people in the South thought Lincoln was trying to end their way of life.

10. The South could have won the war.

11. The growth of railroads expanded the steel industry, improving the economy. It also gave people and industries a means to travel west.

12. economic opportunity

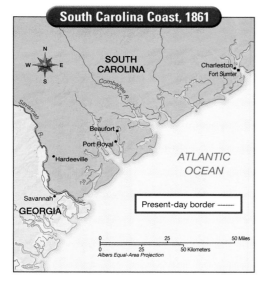

South Carolina Coast, 1861

SOUTH CAROLINA

Charleston
Fort Sumter

Combahee R.

Savannah R.

Beaufort
Port Royal

Hardeeville

ATLANTIC OCEAN

Savannah
GEORGIA

Present-day border ------

0   25   50 Miles
0   25   50 Kilometers
Albers Equal-Area Projection

8 During Reconstruction the Southern states were under military rule because—
A the Fourteenth Amendment to the Constitution allowed Congress to do so.
B Abraham Lincoln's assassination angered many Northerners.
C legislators began to pass laws limiting the rights of former slaves.
D it was a way to return the rights of American citizenship to most Confederates.

THINK CRITICALLY

9 Lincoln once was called "the miserable tool of traitors and rebels." Today he is thought of as a great leader. Why might someone at the time have been so critical of him?

10 What do you think would have happened if the South had won the Battle of Gettysburg?

11 How did the growth of railroads in the United States play an important role in the growth of the country? Explain your answer.

12 Why did many immigrants come to the United States?

APPLY SKILLS

Compare Maps with Different Scales

Use the map on this page and the maps on pages 456–457 to answer the following questions.

13 Compare the map on this page to Map B on page 457. Which map would you use to find the distance between Fort Sumter and the city of Charleston, South Carolina?

14 Compare the map on this page to Map A on page 456. Which map would you use to find the South Carolina–Georgia border?

1895   1920

1861   The Civil War begins   p. 454

1865   General Lee surrenders at Appomattox Court House   p. 469

1890   The steel industry is a big business in the United States   p. 496

513

TEST PREPARATION

Review these tips with students:

■ Read the directions before reading the questions.

■ Read each question twice, focusing the second time on all the possible answers.

■ Take the time to think about all the possible answers before deciding on an answer.

■ Move past questions that give you trouble, and answer the ones you know. Then return to the difficult items.

ASSESSMENT

Use the UNIT 6 TEST on pages 103–111 of the Assessment Program.

Unit Activities

Draw a Map

Have students work together to draw their outline maps. Encourage them to use reference materials when drawing the maps.

 Performance Assessment Guidelines Check to make sure that students' maps have accurately depicted the states and territories of the United States at the time of the Civil War. Colors and shading should also correctly reflect the loyalties of each state.

Make a Chart

Suggest that group members divide the work according to different sections of the chart. They may wish to have each member complete a separate section. Then have all members check each section for accuracy.

 Performance Assessment Guidelines Look for evidence that students understand the ways that African Americans were affected by the new laws; check that they have addressed the difference in the ways that Northern and Southern people were affected.

Complete the Unit Project

Organize the class into groups with each member performing a different role in the group. Roles include researcher, writer, and artist. Encourage students to use biographies in their research and to keep a list of the reference materials they used.

 Performance Assessment Guidelines Check to make sure that students understand the significance of their chosen people and that their posters accurately and creatively represent it.

Unit Activities

 Draw a Map

Work together to draw a map of the United States at the time of the Civil War. Use different colors for the states of the Union, the states of the Confederacy and the border states. Write the date on which each Southern state seceded. Draw diagonal lines on the border states. Label the capitals of the North and the South and the major battle sites. Use your map to tell your classmates about the Civil War.

 Make a Chart

Work together in a group to make a chart titled *How New Laws Affected the Lives of Americans After the Civil War.* The first section of your chart should show how new national and state laws affected African Americans. The second section should show how new laws affected Southerners. The third section should show how new laws affected Northerners. Present your completed chart to your classmates.

 GO ONLINE Visit The Learning Site at **www.harcourtschool.com** for additional activities.

VISIT YOUR LIBRARY

- *When Jessie Came Across the Sea* by Amy Hest. Candlewick Press.

 - *Tales from the Underground Railroad* by Kate Connell. Steck-Vaughn.

- *Across the Lines* by Carolyn Reeder. Simon & Schuster.

COMPLETE THE UNIT PROJECT

Hall of Fame Work with a group of your classmates to finish the unit project—a hall of fame honoring individuals who showed strength and bravery before, during, or after the Civil War. Your group should choose five people from this unit to include in your hall of fame. Then design a poster that includes short biographies as well as drawings or pictures of the people you have chosen. Display your group's finished poster together with those of your classmates.

514 ■ Unit 6

Visit Your Library

Encourage independent reading after students' study of the 1800s with these books or books of your choice. Additional books are listed on the Multimedia Resources, on page 427D of this Teacher's Edition.

Easy *When Jessie Came Across the Sea* by Amy Hest. Candlewick, 1997. Jessie, a young orphan, immigrates to New York and after three years, she has saved enough money to bring her grandmother to the United States.

Average *Tales from the Underground Railroad* by Kate Connell. Steck Vaughn, 1993. Students will read about the network of people who comprised the Underground Railroad and helped many African Americans escape slavery.

Challenging *Across the Lines* by Carolyn Reeder. Simon & Schuster, 1997. Edward, the son of a Southern plantation owner, and Simon, a slave and lifelong friend of his, come to understand the meaning of courage and freedom during the Civil War.

The Twentieth Century

Apollo 11 mission patch

Unit 7 Planning Guide The Twentieth Century

Introduce	CONTENT	RESOURCES

pp. 515–521	**UNIT OPENER**, p. 515
	PREVIEW, pp. 516–517
	START WITH A STORY *The Eagle Has Landed*, pp. 518–521
		Unit 7 Audiotext
		Unit 7 School-to-Home
		  Newsletter, p. S13
		🔊 Reading and Vocabulary
		  Transparency 7-1
		Time for Kids Readers
		💻 Internet Resources

Chapter 14

| Becoming a World Power, pp. 522–551 | **INTRODUCE THE CHAPTER**, pp. 522–523
LESSON 1 Building an American Empire, pp. 524–529
MAP AND GLOBE SKILLS Compare Map Projections, pp. 530–531
LESSON 2 Progressives and Reform, pp. 532–536
LESSON 3 The Great War, pp. 537–541
LESSON 4 Good Times and Hard Times, pp. 542–549
CHAPTER REVIEW AND TEST PREPARATION, pp. 550–551 | ✔ Activity Book, pp. 132–140
✔ Assessment Program,
  Chapter 14, pp. 113–116
🔊 Reading and Vocabulary
  Transparencies, 7-2, 7-3, 7-4,
  7-5, 7-6
🔊 Skills Transparencies, 7-1A, 7-1B
💻 Internet Resources
💿 GeoSkills CD-ROM |

Chapter 15

| Global Conflict, pp. 552–577 | **INTRODUCE THE CHAPTER**, pp. 552–553
LESSON 1 World War II Begins, pp. 554–558
READING SKILLS Predict a Historical Outcome, p. 559
LESSON 2 Americans and the War, pp. 560–563
CITIZENSHIP SKILLS Make Economic Choices, p. 564
LESSON 3 Winning the War, pp. 565–569
CHART AND GRAPH SKILLS Read Parallel Time Lines, pp. 570–571
LESSON 4 The Effects of the War, pp. 572–575
CHAPTER REVIEW AND TEST PREPARATION, pp. 576–577 | ✔ Activity Book, pp. 141–149
✔ Assessment Program,
  Chapter 15, pp. 117–120
🔊 Reading and Vocabulary
  Transparencies, 7-7, 7-8, 7-9,
  7-10, 7-11
🔊 Skills Transparencies, 7-2, 7-3,
  7-4
💻 Internet Resources |

Chapter 16

| Into Modern Times, pp. 578–605 | **INTRODUCE THE CHAPTER**, pp. 578–579
LESSON 1 The Early Years of the Cold War, pp. 580–584
LESSON 2 Working for Equal Rights, pp. 585–589
LESSON 3 The Cold War Continues, pp. 590–593
EXAMINE PRIMARY SOURCES Editorial Cartoons, pp. 594–595
LESSON 4 A World of Change, pp. 596–601
MAP AND GLOBE SKILLS Read a Population Map, pp. 602–603
CHAPTER REVIEW AND TEST PREPARATION, pp. 604–605 | ✔ Activity Book, pp. 150–159
✔ Assessment Program,
  Chapter 16, pp. 121–124
🔊 Reading and Vocabulary
  Transparencies, 7-12, 7-13,
  7-14, 7-15, 7-16
🔊 Skills Transparency, 7-5
💻 Internet Resources
💿 GeoSkills CD-ROM |

Wrap Up

| pp. 606–610 | **VISIT** The Birmingham Civil Rights Institute, pp. 606–607
UNIT REVIEW AND TEST PREPARATION, pp. 608–610 | 💻 Internet Resources
The Learning Site: Virtual Tours
Take a Field Trip Video
✔ Assessment Program, Unit 7,
  pp. 125–133 |

5 WEEKS	WEEK 1	WEEK 2	WEEK 3	WEEK 4	WEEK 5
	Introduce the Unit	Chapter 14	Chapter 15	Chapter 16	Wrap Up the Unit

Unit 7 Skills Path

Unit 7 features the reading skills of making inferences, identifying cause and effect, predicting an outcome. It also highlights the social studies skills of comparing map projections, reading a population map, making economic choices, and reading parallel time lines.

FOCUS SKILLS

CHAPTER 14 READING SKILL

 MAKE INFERENCES

- INTRODUCE p. 523
- APPLY pp. 504, 525, 526, 529, 534, 536, 539, 541, 542, 546, 549, 550

CHAPTER 15 READING SKILL

 CAUSE AND EFFECT

- INTRODUCE p. 553
- APPLY pp. 557, 558, 561, 563, 568, 569, 573, 574, 575

CHAPTER 16 READING SKILL

 PREDICT AN OUTCOME

- INTRODUCE p. 579
- APPLY pp. 583, 584, 586, 587, 589, 592, 593, 601

READING SOCIAL STUDIES

- Personal Response, pp. 518, 520, 525, 528, 586, 589
- Read Aloud, p. 519
- Study Questions, pp. 533, 536, 561, 563
- Anticipation Guide, pp. 538, 541, 566, 568, 597, 601
- K-W-L Chart, pp. 543, 549, 555, 558, 591, 593
- Reread to Clarify, p. 547
- Graphic Organizer, pp. 573, 575, 581, 584, 591

MAP AND GLOBE SKILLS

COMPARE MAP PROJECTIONS

- INTRODUCE pp. 530–531
- APPLY p. 551

READ A POPULATION MAP

- INTRODUCE pp. 602–603
- APPLY p. 605

CITIZENSHIP SKILLS

MAKE ECONOMIC CHOICES

- INTRODUCE p. 564
- APPLY p. 577

CHART AND GRAPH SKILLS

READ PARALLEL TIME LINES

- INTRODUCE pp. 570–571
- APPLY p. 577

READING SKILL

PREDICT A HISTORICAL OUTCOME

- INTRODUCE p. 559
- APPLY p. 577

STUDY AND RESEARCH SKILLS

- Using Periodicals and Newspapers, p. 534
- Using Maps, pp. 539, 545
- Outlining, pp. 556, 596
- Skimming and Scanning, p. 560
- Summarizing, p. 580

Multimedia Resources

The Multimedia Resources can be used in a variety of ways. They can supplement core instruction in the classroom or extend and enrich student learning at home.

Independent Reading

Easy

Fritz, Jean. **You Want Women to Vote, Lizzie Stanton?** Penguin Putnam Books for Young Readers, 1999. Known as a radical in her time, Elizabeth Cady Stanton worked as a women's rights activist in the suffragist movement.

McKissack, Patricia C. **Goin' Someplace Special.** Atheneum, 2001. Story of a young girl's visit to the only non-segregated place in her neighborhood, the library.

Mochizuki, Ken. **Passage to Freedom: The Sugihara Story.** Lee & Low Books, 1997. In 1940, a Japanese diplomat stationed in Lithuania goes against the wishes of his government and grants visas to Jews fleeing the Nazis.

Average

Currie, Stephen. **We Have Marched Together.** Lerner Publishing, 1997. The plight of child labor leads to a protest march in 1903, led by Mother Jones and child workers. The protesters marched from Philadelphia to New York City in order to see President Theodore Roosevelt.

Hunter, Sara Hoagland. **The Unbreakable Code.** Northland Publishing, 1996. John, a young Navajo, hears the story of how the Navajo Code Talkers helped the United States during World War II.

Lowry, Lois. **Number the Stars.** Laureleaf, 1998. When the Nazis put out word that Jews living in Denmark will be sent to concentration camps, ten-year-old Annemarie must help her best friend's family out of the country.

Challenging

Ambrose, Stephen E. **The Good Fight: How World War II Was Won.** Simon & Schuster Children's, 2001. Story of the origins of World War II, its major battles and events, and the effect it had on the lives of people everywhere.

Fremon, David K. **The Watergate Scandal in American History.** Enslow Publishers, 1998. Follows the events as they were reported in the story of this infamous political scandal.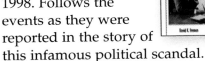

King, Martin Luther. **The Words of Martin Luther King, Jr.** Selected by Coretta Scott King. Newmarket Press, 1987. Offers samples of Martin Luther King, Jr.'s writings and ideas.

Computer Software

American Memory Primary Sources: Culture. Library of Congress, 2000. Cultural perspective of the United States over the first half of the 20th century.

African-American History: Heroism, Struggle, and Hope: Part 2. Clearvue, 1995. Mac/Windows. Story of African Americans including key leaders such as Booker T. Washington, W.E.B. Du Bois, Rosa Parks, and Martin Luther King, Jr.

Videos and DVDs

America: The Living Dream: WWI, Prohibition, Roaring Twenties, Great Depression, WWII, & the Cold War. TMW Media Group, 1998. Documentary that examines major events and developments of the early and mid-twentieth century.

The Industrial Revolution. Clearvue, 1994. Live-action historical reenactments that examine the events and inventions that spurred the Industrial Revolution.

Additional books also are recommended at point of use throughout the unit.
Note that information, while correct at time of publication, is subject to change.

ISBNs and other publisher information can be found at www.harcourtschool.com

The Learning Site: Social Studies Center

The Learning Site at www.harcourtschool.com offers a special Social Studies Center. The center provides a wide variety of activities, Internet links, and online references.

Find all this at The Learning Site at www.harcourtschool.com

- Activities and Games
- Content Updates
- Current Events
- Free and Inexpensive Materials
- Multimedia Biographies
- Online Atlas
- Primary Sources
- Video Updates
- Virtual Tours
- Your State

and more!

Here are just some of the HARCOURT Internet resources you'll find!

Multimedia Biographies
www.harcourtschool.com

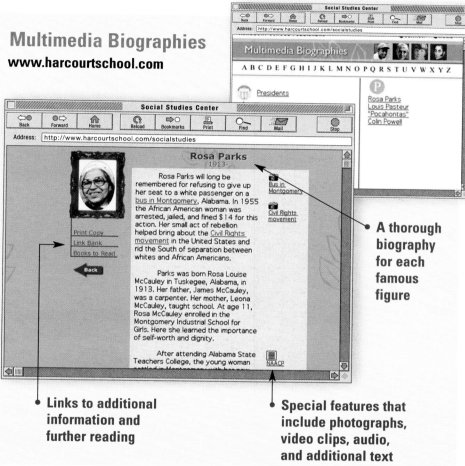

A thorough biography for each famous figure

Links to additional information and further reading

Special features that include photographs, video clips, audio, and additional text

Free and Inexpensive Materials
- Addresses to write for free and inexpensive products
- Links to unit-related materials
- Internet maps
- Internet references

www.harcourtschool.com

Primary Sources
- Artwork
- Clothing
- Diaries
- Government Documents
- Historical Documents
- Maps
- Tools

and more!
www.harcourtschool.com

Virtual Tours
- Capitols and Government Buildings
- Cities
- Countries
- Historical Sites
- Museums
- Parks and Scenic Areas

and more!
www.harcourtschool.com

Integrate Learning Across the Curriculum

Use these topics to help you integrate social studies into your daily planning.
See the page numbers indicated for more information about each topic.

Reading/Literature

The Eagle Has Landed, pp. 518–521
Read a Biography, p. 544
Read About People, p. 573
The Words of Martin Luther King, Jr., p. 610
The Unbreakable Code, p. 610
Goin' Someplace Special, p. 610

Science

Learn About the Moon, p. 520
Technology, p. 530
Report on Technology, p. 555

Music

Sing a Song, p. 535
Listen to Jazz, p. 542
Interpret Lyrics, p. 585

Language Arts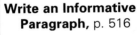

Write an Informative Paragraph, p. 516
Persuasive Writing, p. 526
Speaking, p. 532
News Writing, p. 545
Expressive Writing, p. 548
Write a Summary, p. 566
Write a News Report, p. 570
Expository Writing, p. 597
Write a Poem, p. 607

Social Studies

Art

Draw a Picture, p. 518
Make a Poster, p. 534
Paint a Picture, p. 543
Draw a Poster, p. 586
Make a Collage, p. 592

Mathematics

Compute Totals, p. 524
Computation, p. 540
Compute Measurement, p. 581

Languages

Learn Hawaiian, p. 525
Vietnamese, p. 591

Technology

GeoSkills CD-ROM, pp. 531, 603
Go Online, pp. 521, 544, 555, 595, 599, 607
CNN Video, p. 607

Health

Learn More About Diseases, p. 528

Reach All Learners

Use these activities to help individualize your instruction. Each activity has been developed to address a different level or type of learner.

English as a Second Language

Materials
- notebook paper
- textbook
- pens or pencils

MAKE TIME LINES Have students who are acquiring English work with proficient English speakers to generate time lines of the lessons in Unit 7.

- Assign each pair a lesson from the unit.
- While one member of the pair skims the lesson, the other makes a time line sequencing the events described.
- Then have the second student skim the same passage for key events while the first checks the time line that has been created.
- Have pairs discuss difficult words and phrases.

Time line of Lesson 1

Below-Level Learners

Materials
- notebook paper
- pens or markers
- textbook

Lesson 3:
—Winning the War
—D day and the bomb end the war for the United States.

WRITE SUBTITLES Have students write subtitles for the lessons in Unit 7 and generate an annotated table of contents.

- Explain that a subtitle is a phrase or short sentence that follows the main title of a book, chapter, or lesson, giving more specific information about it.
- Assign each student a lesson and challenge him or her to write a subtitle that explains the lesson's main idea.
- Have students share their subtitles. Then lead the class in generating an expanded table of contents for the unit. Ask a volunteer to write the lesson titles and subtitles on the chalkboard.

Advanced Learners

Materials
- pens or markers
- textbook
- posterboard or overhead transparency

IDENTIFY CAUSES AND EFFECTS Have advanced learners work in pairs to identify the causes and effects of a historic event discussed in Unit 7.

- Identify important events in the unit.
- Have pairs choose an important event in the unit. Ask pairs to analyze the causes and effects of the event.
- Have pairs research causes and effects in addition to the ones discussed in the textbook. One student should focus on the causes, and the other on the effects.
- Ask students to create a poster or an overhead transparency with a graphic organizer that shows the causes and effects of the event.
- Have students share their visuals with the class.

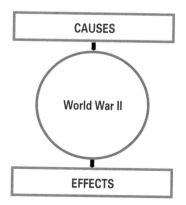

CAUSES

World War II

EFFECTS

Assessment Options

The Assessment Program gives all learners many opportunities to show what they know and can do. It also provides ongoing information about each student's understanding of social studies.

Formal Assessment

- **LESSON REVIEWS,** at ends of lessons
- **CHAPTER REVIEWS AND TEST PREPARATION,** pp. 550–551, pp. 576–577, pp. 604–605
- **CHAPTER TESTS**
  Assessment Program, pp. 113–116, pp. 117–120, pp. 121–124
- **UNIT REVIEW AND TEST PREPARATION,** pp. 608–609
- **UNIT ASSESSMENT**
  STANDARD TEST,
  Assessment Program, pp. 125–131
  INDIVIDUAL PERFORMANCE TASK,
  Assessment Program, p. 132
  GROUP PERFORMANCE TASK,
  Assessment Program, p. 133

Student Self-Evaluation

- **ANALYZE PRIMARY SOURCES AND VISUALS** within lessons of Pupil Book
- **GEOGRAPHY THEME QUESTIONS** within lessons of Pupil Book
- **INDIVIDUAL END-OF-PROJECT SUMMARY** Assessment Program, p. vi
- **GROUP END-OF-PROJECT CHECKLIST** Assessment Program, p. vii
- **INDIVIDUAL END-OF-UNIT CHECKLIST** Assessment Program, p. viii

Informal Assessment

- **ANALYZE THE LITERATURE,** p. 521
- **REVIEW QUESTIONS,** throughout lessons
- **EXAMINE PRIMARY SOURCES,** pp. 594–595
- **SOCIAL STUDIES SKILLS CHECKLIST** Assessment Program, p. iv

- **SKILLS**
  Practice the Skill, pp. 531, 559, 564, 570, 603
  Apply What You Learned, pp. 531, 559, 564, 571, 603

Performance Assessment

- **PERFORMANCE ACTIVITY** in Lesson Reviews
- **UNIT ACTIVITIES** p. 610
- **COMPLETE THE UNIT PROJECT,** p. 610
- **INDIVIDUAL PERFORMANCE TASK** Assessment Program, p. 132
- **GROUP PERFORMANCE TASK** Assessment Program, p. 133

Portfolio Assessment

STUDENT-SELECTED ITEMS MAY INCLUDE:
- **THINK AND WRITE,** pp. 550, 576, 604
- **UNIT ACTIVITIES,** p. 610
- **COMPLETE THE UNIT PROJECT,** p. 610

TEACHER-SELECTED ITEMS MAY INCLUDE:
- **UNIT ASSESSMENT** Assessment Program, pp. 125–133
- **PORTFOLIO SUMMARY** Assessment Program, p. xiii
- **INDIVIDUAL END-OF-UNIT CHECKLIST** Assessment Program, p. viii
- **GROUP END-OF-PROJECT CHECKLIST** Assessment Program, p. vii

Unit 7 Test

·UNIT·

7 Test

Name _____ Date _____

Part One: Test Your Understanding
MULTIPLE CHOICE (2 points each)

Directions Circle the letter of the best answer.

1 The United States' purchase of Alaska—
A was widely praised at the time.
B occurred only after gold was discovered in Canada.
(C) brought the nation many natural resources.
D cost a great deal of money per acre.

2 Which of the following events happened first?
F The United States annexed Hawaii.
G The Spanish-American War began.
(H) The United States purchased Alaska.
J World War I began.

3 The Panama Canal was built to—
(A) link American ports on the Atlantic coast with those on the Pacific coast.
B replace the Erie Canal.
C link Washington, D.C., to New York City.
D replace the Great Wagon Road.

4 Which United States President began the Panama Canal?
F Franklin Roosevelt
(G) Theodore Roosevelt
H Woodrow Wilson
J Herbert Hoover

5 Which event prompted the United States to enter World War I?
A Pearl Harbor was bombed.
B Archduke Francis Ferdinand was assassinated.
C Germany invaded Poland.
(D) German U-boats sank three United States merchant ships.

6 During World War I, American soldiers—
(F) fought in trenches.
G took part in the D day invasion.
H fought in Africa.
J battled the Empire of Japan.

(continued)

Unit 7 Test   Assessment Program ■ 125

Name _____ Date _____

7 George Washington Carver—
A began the Harlem Renaissance.
B created a new method of freezing foods.
(C) developed many new food products using peanuts.
D was the first person to fly nonstop across the Atlantic Ocean.

8 The New Deal program that produced large amounts of electricity was the—
(F) Tennessee Valley Authority.
G Works Progress Administration.
H Civilian Conservation Corps.
J merit system.

9 The German economy developed problems after World War I because—
A Germany did not join the League of Nations.
B Berlin was divided.
C the United States did not join the League of Nations.
(D) Germany had to pay other countries for war damages.

10 What country invaded the United States in World War II?
F Italy
(G) Japan
H Russia
J Germany

11 The Soviet Union joined the Allied forces after—
A Japan bombed Pearl Harbor.
B Germany invaded Poland.
(C) Germany invaded the Soviet Union.
D Japan took over Manchuria.

12 The Soviet Union tried to force the Western Allies out of West Berlin with—
F an airlift.
G trench warfare.
H an invasion.
(J) a blockade.

13 A temporary end to a conflict is called—
(A) a cease-fire.
B an armistice.
C a surrender.
D an arms race.

14 A bus boycott in Montgomery, Alabama, began when—
F Linda Brown wanted to change laws that segregated schools.
(G) Rosa Parks refused to move to a different seat.
H Thurgood Marshall argued a case before the Supreme Court.
J Malcolm X called for strict racial separation.

(continued)

126 ■ Assessment Program   Unit 7 Test

Name _____ Date _____

MATCHING (3 points each)

Directions Match the description on the left with the correct name on the right. Write the correct letter in the space provided.

15 _E_ leader of the D day invasion

16 _D_ a leader in the Civil Rights movement of the 1950s and 1960s

17 _B_ Secretary of State who helped purchase Alaska

18 _A_ dictator of Italy during World War II

19 _C_ founder of the National Association for the Advancement of Colored People (NAACP)

A. Benito Mussolini

B. William Seward

C. W.E.B. DuBois

D. Martin Luther King, Jr.

E. Dwight D. Eisenhower

(continued)

Unit 7 Test   Assessment Program ■ 127

Name _____ Date _____

SHORT ANSWER (3 points each)

Directions Complete each statement in the space provided.

20 Hull House was a ____settlement house____ where immigrants and working people learned new skills.

21 W.E.B. DuBois helped found the ____National Association for the Advancement of Colored People, or NAACP____, which worked to increase civil rights for African Americans.

22 President Woodrow Wilson developed the idea of a ____League of Nations____, which would find peaceful methods of solving conflicts between countries.

23 The 1920s period when African American artists, musicians, and writers flourished is called the ____Harlem Renaissance____.

24 Henry Ford's system of building automobiles used a moving ____assembly line____ that produced cars faster and cheaper than before.

25 Because of anger against Japan after the bombing of Pearl Harbor, many Japanese Americans were forced to move to ____relocation camps____ during World War II.

26 World War II ended when the United States dropped two ____atom bombs____ on Japan.

27 During the Cold War, the United States and the Soviet Union competed in an ____arms race____ in which both counties built many weapons for protection.

28 Martin Luther King, Jr., believed in using ____Possible answers: nonviolence, peaceful ways____ to end segregation in the United States.

(continued)

128 ■ Assessment Program   Unit 7 Test

Unit 7 Test

STANDARD TEST

Name _____ Date _____

Part Two: Test Your Skills
READ A POPULATION MAP (10 points)

Directions The map below shows the population of the state of New York. Use it to answer the questions that follow.

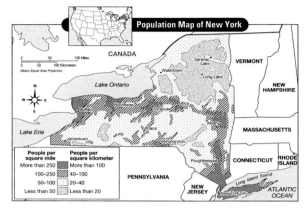

Population Map of New York

CANADA

VERMONT

NEW HAMPSHIRE

Lake Ontario

Saranac Lake

Long Lake

Watertown

Lake Erie

Jamestown

Ithaca

MASSACHUSETTS

Poughkeepsie

CONNECTICUT

RHODE ISLAND

PENNSYLVANIA

NEW JERSEY

Long Island Sound

ATLANTIC OCEAN

People per square mile	People per square kilometer
More than 250	More than 100
100–250	40–100
50–100	20–40
Less than 50	Less than 20

29 Which city has a smaller population, Rochester or Ithaca? _____Ithaca_____

30 What is the city with the smallest population? _____Long Lake_____

31 Which city is located in an area with higher population density, Albany or Jamestown? _____Albany_____

32 What area of New York is the most densely populated overall—northern or southern New York? _____southern New York_____

(continued)

STANDARD TEST

Name _____ Date _____

Part Three: Apply What You Have Learned
33 **CATEGORIZE KEY EVENTS** (10 points)

During the Cold War, the Soviet Union had an important impact on events in a number of foreign countries. Describe the Soviet Union's actions in each of the cities or countries listed below.

Berlin	North Korea	Cuba
Possible responses: The Soviet Union controlled East Berlin. At one time, the Soviets blockaded part of the city and eventually built a wall around the area. The German people tore down the Berlin Wall in 1989.	Possible response: The Soviet Union trained and equipped the communist North Korean army to help it invade South Korea.	Possible responses: The Soviet Union supported the government of Fidel Castro and built missile sites in Cuba.

(continued)

STANDARD TEST

Name _____ Date _____

34 **ESSAY** (10 points)

The United States participated in two global wars in the twentieth century, World War I and World War II. Write a paragraph that compares the two conflicts. Compare the nations that were involved, the types of combat that took place, and the effects of each war.

Possible response: In both wars, the United States, Great Britain, and France fought against Germany and its allies, including Italy. In World War II, the conflict was fought on two fronts, since the Allies also fought against Japan in the Pacific. World War I was fought using trench warfare, with soldiers using tanks to protect themselves against powerful new machine guns. In trench warfare, soldiers advanced and retreated slowly. In World War II, the development of airplanes allowed troops to move faster, and that conflict covered much more territory than the previous war. World War I ended by punishing Germany in a way that damaged its economy and led to further conflict. World War II ended without resolving the tensions between the Soviet Union and the West, setting up the conflicts of the Cold War.

NOTES

Name _____ Date _____

Individual Performance Task

Travel Brochure

Choose one of the sites listed below, and write a travel brochure for the area. Make a brochure that might have been created during an important time in that area's history.

- Harlem, New York City
- Kitty Hawk, North Carolina
- Grand Canyon National Park
- Cape Canaveral, Florida
- Alaska
- The Panama Canal

Scan Unit 7 for information that is given about the site. You may find additional information in magazines, in encyclopedias, or on the Internet. You will want to include details about the following topics in your travel brochure:

- The area's environment
- The area's people and culture
- The area's landmarks

You may want to write a brochure that looks at events in the present time. However, you may also write travel guides as they might have appeared in the past. For example, you could create a brochure that invites people to visit the new territory of Alaska, or one that celebrates the opening of the Panama Canal. Be sure to illustrate your brochure with photographs or other illustrations you find during your research.

© Harcourt

132 ▪ Assessment Program   Unit 7 Test

Name _____ Date _____

Group Performance Task

Interviews

Choose a situation below and act out a conversation that might have taken place if the people listed had met. In each of the situations, the historical characters might have different opinions about an idea or topic. Find out as much as you can about these historical figures from your textbook, your library, or the Internet. Then write questions that an interviewer can ask the characters, as well as the answers that the characters might have given. The characters interviewed might want to ask one another questions, as well. Your interviews should last about 10 minutes.

▶ **SITUATION 1**   **Progressive Reformers:** Carrie Lane Chapman Catt worked hard to help women gain the right to vote. Jane Addams established settlement houses to help educate needy people. Find out what Catt and Addams thought were the most important issues facing Americans at the beginning of the twentieth century, and how they each thought the country should have dealt with its problems.

▶ **SITUATION 2**   **The League of Nations:** Interview President Woodrow Wilson and a United States senator who opposes the League of Nations. Find out why each person feels the way he does about the League. Also, find out what each believes will happen if the United States joins the League.

▶ **SITUATION 3**   **The Great Depression:** Presidents Herbert Hoover and Franklin Roosevelt both held office during times of economic difficulty. Have both Presidents talk about their plans for helping the nation overcome poverty and unemployment. Ask them how they might have wanted their programs to work differently or what changes they might have made to their programs during their time in office.

▶ **SITUATION 4**   **Civil Rights:** W.E.B. DuBois, Thurgood Marshall, Malcolm X, and Martin Luther King, Jr., were all important figures in the Civil Rights movement. Find out if they agreed or disagreed about the best way to bring about positive changes for African Americans.

© Harcourt

Unit 7 Test   **Assessment Program** ▪ **133**

RUBRICS FOR SCORING

SCORING RUBRICS The rubrics below list the criteria for evaluating the tasks above. They also describe different levels of success in meeting those criteria.

INDIVIDUAL PERFORMANCE TASK

SCORE **4**	SCORE **3**	SCORE **2**	SCORE **1**
• Rich description is provided. • Details fit historical period strongly. • Brochures are well organized. • Topic is very well researched.	• Some description is provided. • Details fit historical period. • Brochures are somewhat organized. • Topic is somewhat well researched.	• Little description is provided. • Details fit historical period weakly. • Brochures are poorly organized. • Topic is poorly researched.	• No description is provided. • Details do not fit historical period. • Brochures are not organized. • Topic is not researched.

GROUP PERFORMANCE TASK

SCORE **4**	SCORE **3**	SCORE **2**	SCORE **1**
• Performance shows excellent creativity. • Script is historically accurate. • Discussion of issue is very balanced.	• Performance shows some creativity. • Script is mostly historically accurate. • Discussion of issue is somewhat balanced.	• Performance shows little creativity. • Script is partially historically accurate. • Discussion of issue is poorly balanced.	• Performance shows no creativity. • Script is not historically accurate. • Discussion of issue is unbalanced.

Introduce the Unit

John F. Kennedy Space Center, Cape Canaveral, Florida

OBJECTIVES

- Use artifacts and primary sources to acquire information about the United States.
- Interpret information in visuals.

Access Prior Knowledge

Invite students to tell what they know about the beginning of the twentieth century. Lead the class in brainstorming a list of people, places, and events related to this period in history. Record suggestions in a web diagram.

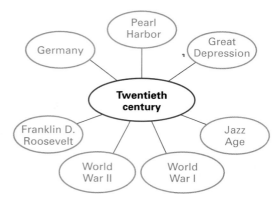

BACKGROUND

The Outer Space Treaty Two years before the United States landed the first man on the moon, it signed a space peace treaty with the Soviet Union, Britain, and fifty-seven other countries. In this treaty, which received approval in the Senate, the nations agreed to peacefully explore space. It banned nuclear weapons, military bases, and the testing of weapons in space.

Neil Armstrong Neil Armstrong earned his pilot's license by the age of 16 and became an air cadet in the navy the following year. He continued to pursue his interest in flight throughout his career, earning three medals for his flying in the Korean War. He then worked for the National Advisory Committee for Aeronautics, eventually joining NASA. In 1962, at the age of 32, he became an astronaut.

BACKGROUND

The *Apollo 11* Mission The *Apollo 11* mission was the world's first moon landing and return. During the eight-day mission the crew, Neil Armstrong, Michael Collins, and Edwin E. Aldrin, Jr. made seven television transmissions. The first transmission was made on the surface of the moon and lasted for 29 minutes.

7

The Twentieth Century

66 That's one small step for [a] man, one giant leap for mankind. 99

—Neil Armstrong, from the
Eagle moon lander, July 20, 1969

Preview the Content

Read the lesson titles. Then fill in the first two columns of the chart with information about the twentieth century. After you have read the unit, fill in the last column.

K (What I Know)	W (What I Want to Know)	L (What I Have Learned)

Preview the Vocabulary

Related Words Words that are related have meanings that are connected in some way. Using the vocabulary words **reform**, **isolation**, **aviation**, and **ration**, make a chart of words that are related to each vocabulary word.

Unit 7 ▪ 515

Visual Learning

Picture The background image is of the Rocket Garden at the John F. Kennedy Space Center in Cape Canaveral, Florida. Tell students that the rockets in this outdoor exhibit were launched at different times in history.

Analyze Primary Sources

Patch from Apollo II Mission Have students take a close look at the pictured item and describe what they see. Students should notice that the eagle is landing on the moon.

Quotation Have a volunteer read aloud the quotation from Neil Armstrong.

Q **What do you think Armstrong meant by this quotation?**

A Students may say that his footstep represented a big step in human progress and technological development.

AUDIOTEXT

Use the Unit 7 AUDIOTEXT for a reading of the Unit narrative.

1

2

3

4

5

6

7

8

· Unit 7 ·

Preview the Content
Students' charts should be similar to the one below.

K	W	L
the economy boomed before it went into a depression	Why did the depression happen?	
America and its allies won World War II	How did they win the war?	
The United States put a man on the moon	Why was the United States in a space race?	

Preview the Vocabulary
Make sure students' responses resemble the one below.

reform	reformer, change, fix
isolation	isolationism, alone, by yourself
aviation	aviator, flying, airplanes
ration	rationing, dole out, conserve

Preview the Unit

PAGES 516–517

OBJECTIVES

- Interpret information in data-bases and visuals.
- Use appropriate mathematical skills to interpret social studies information such as maps and graphs.

Access Prior Knowledge

Have students describe what they have already learned about the United States as a world power.

Visual Learning

Map Have students examine the map and its key and share their observations. Then as a class, discuss what the relationship is between the elements in the key as they are depicted on the map. Students may notice that interstate highways tend to connect large cities.

Time Line To help students prepare for their reading, have them work in pairs to ask and answer questions about the time line. For example, a student might ask: *What wars were fought in the twentieth century?* World War I, World War II, and the Vietnam War

Time Line Illustrations Ask students to speculate about the significance of the events shown on the time line.

- The United States provided the rein-forcements needed by the Allies to defeat the German army in World War I.
- The stock market crash led to an economic depression.
- The attack on Pearl Harbor caused the United States to enter World War II.
- The Civil Rights Act led to more opportunities for more Americans.
- Americans were divided about the Vietnam War.
- The United States pulls ahead of the Soviet Union in the space race.

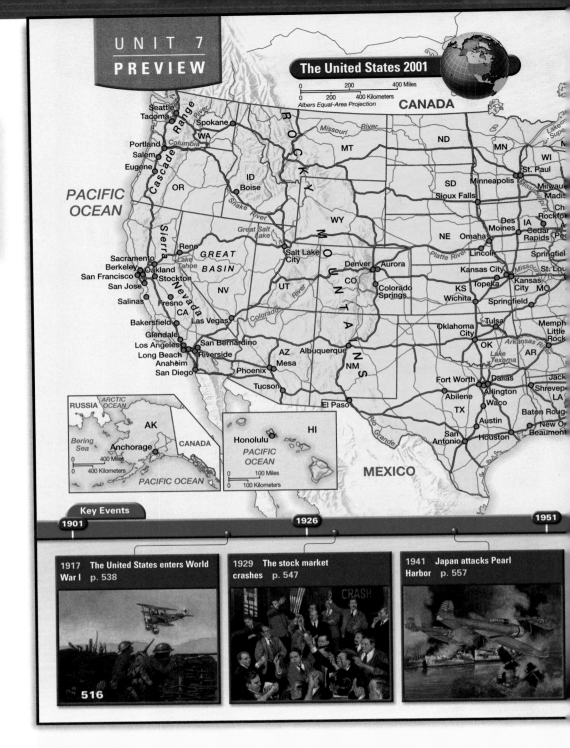

UNIT 7 PREVIEW

The United States 2001

Albers Equal-Area Projection

Key Events

1901

1926

1951

1917 The United States enters World War I   p. 538

1929 The stock market crashes   p. 547

1941 Japan attacks Pearl Harbor   p. 557

516

INTEGRATE LANGUAGE ARTS

Write an Informative Paragraph Ask students to describe one of the graphic elements in pages 516–517. They can choose the map, the time line, or the bar graph. Instruct students to describe the graphic information using sentences and paragraphs. Students can share their informative writing with a classmate.

REACH ALL LEARNERS

Beginning and English as a Second Language Learners Pair these learners up with a student who has mastered the information presented on these pages. Have them take turns sharing observations with each other. Encourage the advanced learners to explain to their partners how they arrived at their observations. This will assist beginning learners and English as a second language learners to make accurate observations of their own.

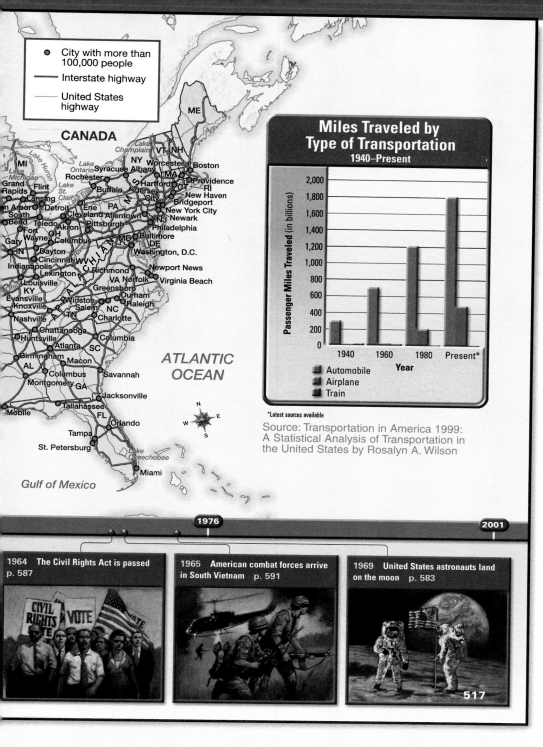

Miles Traveled by Type of Transportation
1940–Present

Passenger Miles Traveled (in billions)

	Automobile	Airplane	Train
1940	~300		
1960	~680		
1980	~1,200	~200	
Present*	~1,780	~450	

*Latest sources available

Source: Transportation in America 1999: A Statistical Analysis of Transportation in the United States by Rosalyn A. Wilson

1964 The Civil Rights Act is passed p. 587

1965 American combat forces arrive in South Vietnam p. 591

1969 United States astronauts land on the moon p. 583

517

Visual Learning

Bar Graph Work with students to interpret the data presented in the bar graph. To help students understand the information, you may want to ask such questions as:

- *What does this bar graph show?* the number of miles traveled within the United States by type of transportation
- *Which vehicle was used to travel the most miles in each period of time?* Automobile

Make Connections

Link Bar Graph and Map Ask students to use the information presented in the bar graph and the map to make observations and draw conclusions about the relationship between the development of the American highway system and the amount of people who traveled by automobile.

SCHOOL TO HOME

Use the Unit 7 SCHOOL-TO-HOME NEWSLETTER on pages S13–S14 to introduce the unit to family members and suggest activities they can do at home.

OBJECTIVES

- Identify major events of the twentieth century.
- Describe the first landing of a person on the moon.

Summary

The United States sent the first astronauts to the moon in July 1969. Neil Armstrong and Buzz Aldrin were the first astronauts to walk on the moon.

1 Motivate

Set the Purpose

In the 1960s, space exploration was reaching new heights. In only seven years, the United States went from putting an astronaut in orbit around Earth to putting astronauts on the moon.

Access Prior Knowledge

Ask students to tell what they know about the first moon landing. How many astronauts walked on the moon? What did they see?

READING SOCIAL STUDIES

Personal Response As students read the selection, ask them to provide responses to the following questions.

1. What do you think Neil Armstrong meant when he said, "That's one small step for man, one giant leap for mankind"?

2. Why do you think the astronauts left behind a plaque and a United States flag?

3. What would it be like to travel in space?

● USE READING AND VOCABULARY TRANSPARENCY 7-1.   **7-1** TRANSPARENCY

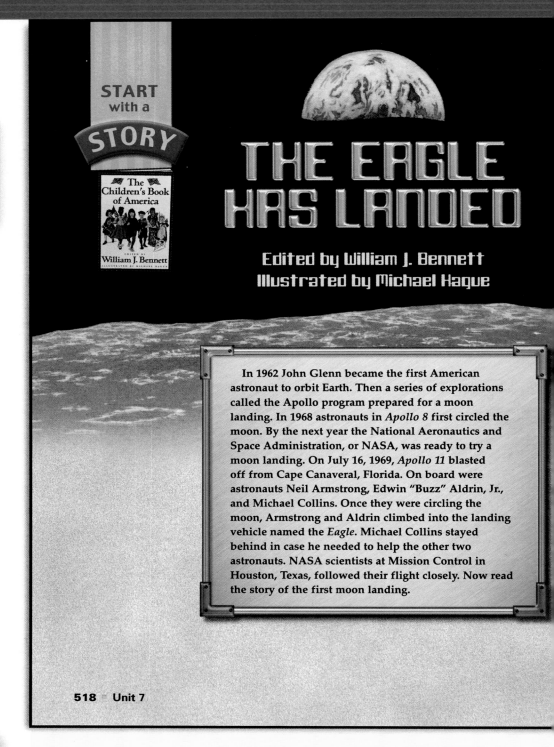

START with a STORY

The Children's Book of America
Edited by William J. Bennett

THE EAGLE HAS LANDED

Edited by William J. Bennett
Illustrated by Michael Hague

In 1962 John Glenn became the first American astronaut to orbit Earth. Then a series of explorations called the Apollo program prepared for a moon landing. In 1968 astronauts in *Apollo 8* first circled the moon. By the next year the National Aeronautics and Space Administration, or NASA, was ready to try a moon landing. On July 16, 1969, *Apollo 11* blasted off from Cape Canaveral, Florida. On board were astronauts Neil Armstrong, Edwin "Buzz" Aldrin, Jr., and Michael Collins. Once they were circling the moon, Armstrong and Aldrin climbed into the landing vehicle named the *Eagle*. Michael Collins stayed behind in case he needed to help the other two astronauts. NASA scientists at Mission Control in Houston, Texas, followed their flight closely. Now read the story of the first moon landing.

518 ◾ Unit 7

BACKGROUND

Mission to the Moon In a speech to Congress on May 25, 1961, President John F. Kennedy challenged the United States to land a crewed mission on the moon and return it safely to Earth before the end of the decade.

INTEGRATE ART

Draw a Picture Encourage students to research more information about the moon and then draw a picture of the moon's surface. Ask volunteers to share their pictures with the class.

"*Eagle*, you are go for landing. Go!"

The spacecraft continued downward.

Armstrong turned to the window to look for their landing zone. He did not like what he saw. They were not where they were supposed to be.

The computer was programmed to steer the ship to a flat, smooth place for a landing. But it had overshot its target. They were plunging straight toward an area littered with deadly rocks and craters.

A light blinked on the control panel. They were running out of landing fuel.

There was no time to waste. Armstrong gripped the hand controller and took command from the computer. He had to find a place where they could set down, fast, or they would have to fire their rockets and return to space.

Gently he brought the *Eagle* under his control. The lander hovered as Armstrong searched the ground below for a level spot.

"Sixty seconds," the voice from Mission Control warned.

Sixty seconds of fuel left.

Balanced on a cone of fire, the *Eagle* scooted over rocky ridges and yawning craters.

There was no place to land!

"Thirty seconds!"

Unit 7   519

Read and Respond

Understand the Story Lead a discussion with students about why people wanted to explore the moon.

Civics and Government Explain that the United States and the former Soviet Union were in competition to explore space. That competition was called "the space race" by many.

Q What do you think the United States wanted to prove by sending the first astronaut to the moon?

A The United States wanted to prove that its technology was superior to that of the Soviet Union.

AUDIOTEXT

Text of this story can be found on the Unit 7 AUDIOTEXT.

READING SOCIAL STUDIES

Read Aloud Organize students in pairs, and have them read the story aloud to each other. Encourage one student to read the story with very little feeling or emotion. Then suggest that the second student read the story with a great deal of emotion. Discuss how the differences in reading styles may affect listeners' interpretations of the text.

REACH ALL LEARNERS

Advanced Learners Encourage advanced learners to research items such as rocks and soil brought from the moon to Earth by astronauts. Suggest that students use the Internet and other reference materials to find out what experiments were done on these items and what scientists learned from them.

Read and Respond

Understand the Story Explain that in the weeks and months preceding a mission, astronauts undergo a series of tests and simulations that determine their fitness.

Q **How do you think the astronauts felt when they first stepped on the moon?**

A Answers should reflect that the astronauts probably were excited and happy but nervous.

Visual Learning

Illustration Direct students' attention to the illustration on page 520. Ask students to carefully examine the American flag.

Q **Why do you think the flag is not waving on the moon?**

A It is not waving because on the moon there is no atmosphere or air to blow it.

 **Close**

Summarize the Reading

- *Apollo 11* blasted off on July 16, 1969, carrying astronauts to the moon.
- Neil Armstrong and Buzz Aldrin became the first humans to walk on the moon.

READING SOCIAL STUDIES

Personal Response Have students share their answers.

1. Armstrong meant that he was taking one small step off the ladder onto the moon's surface, but the human race was taking an enormous step off the Earth, the first step in space exploration.

2. The astronauts left artifacts behind to indicate that they had landed on the moon.

3. Students may say that space travel would be fun, exciting, scary, or difficult.

● USE READING AND VOCABULARY TRANSPARENCY 7-1.

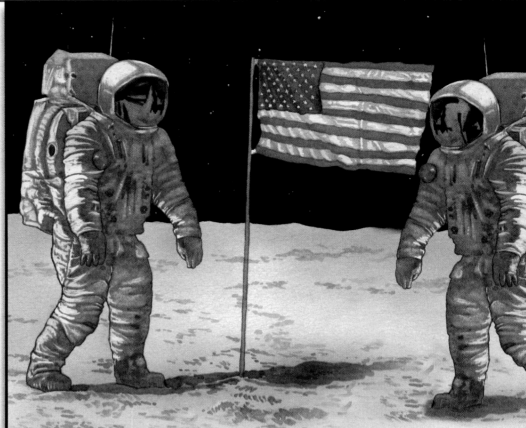

Now there was no turning back. If the engines gulped the last of the landing fuel, there would be no time to fire the rockets that could take them back into orbit. They would crash.

The landing craft swooped across boulder fields as its pilot hunted, judged, and committed. Flames shot down as the *Eagle* dropped the last few feet. Dust that had lain still for a billion years flew up and swallowed the craft.

Back on Earth, millions of people held their breaths and waited. They prayed and listened.

Then Neil Armstrong's faint voice came crackling across the gulf of space.

"Houston, Tranquillity Base here. The *Eagle* has landed."

In a short while a hatch on the lander opened. A man in a bulky space suit backed down nine rungs of a ladder and placed his foot on the gray lunar soil. People all over the world watched the fuzzy black-and-white images on their television screens. They leaned toward their sets to catch the first words spoken by Neil Armstrong from the surface of the moon.

"That's one small step for man, one giant leap for mankind."

520 Unit 7

INTEGRATE SCIENCE

Learn About the Moon
Explain that an atmosphere is a mixture of gases surrounding a planet or a moon. Ask which gas enables life to exist on Earth. oxygen Inform students that the gases in the atmosphere are what create wind and weather. Explain that the moon's gravity is too weak to keep gases from escaping into space. As a result, the moon does not have an atmosphere that is capable of sustaining life.

A few minutes later Buzz Aldrin crawled out of the *Eagle* to join his comrade. Together the astronauts planted a flag. It would never flap in a breeze on the airless moon, so a stiff wire held it out from its pole. Aldrin stepped back and saluted the Stars and Stripes.

America had made the age-old dream come true. When they departed, our astronauts left behind a plaque that will always remain. Its words proclaim:

HERE MEN FROM THE PLANET EARTH
FIRST SET FOOT UPON THE MOON
JULY, 1969 A.D.
WE CAME IN PEACE FOR ALL MANKIND

Analyze the Literature

❶ Why did Neil Armstrong take control of the *Eagle*?

❷ What kinds of problems do you think the scientists at NASA had to solve in building a spacecraft to carry people to the moon?

READ A BOOK

START THE UNIT PROJECT

A Class Newspaper With your classmates, create a newspaper about the 20th century. As you read the unit, make a list of key people, places, and events. This list will help you decide which people, places, and events to feature in articles in your newspaper.

USE TECHNOLOGY

GO ONLINE Visit The Learning Site at **www.harcourtschool.com** for additional activities, primary sources, and other resources to use in this unit.

Read a Book

Students may enjoy reading these leveled Independent Readers. Additional books are listed on pp. 515D–515E of this Teacher's Edition

Easy *A Certain Courage* by Renee Skelton. Students learn how students, with the help of federal marshals, integrated Central High School in Little Rock, Arkansas.

Average *The Berlin Airlift* by Heather Miller. This book explains how the United States dropped supplies into the blockaded city of West Berlin following World War II.

Challenging *The Surprising Mr. Birdseye* by Roberta Ann Cruise. Students can read about Clarence Birdseye, the man best known for inventing frozen foods.

Start the Unit Project

Hint Suggest that students use a graphic organizer to list people, places, and events of the twentieth century. Encourage students to put a star next to the items they would like to feature in their newspaper.

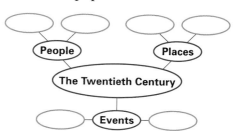

Use Technology

GO ONLINE INTERNET RESOURCES

THE LEARNING SITE Go to **www.harcourtschool.com** to view Internet resources for this unit.

TIME FOR KIDS Go to **www.harcourtschool.com** for the latest news in a student-friendly format.

Analyze the Literature
Answers

❶ Because the onboard computer had overshot its target landing spot, Neil Armstrong had to land the *Eagle* before it ran out of fuel.

❷ Possible response: NASA had to solve many problems, including what the astronauts ate, where they slept, how they landed, how they survived outside the ship, and how they returned to Earth.

LESSON	PACING	OBJECTIVES	VOCABULARY
Introduce the Chapter pp. 522–523	1 Day	■ Interpret information in visuals. ■ Use critical thinking skills to organize and analyze information.	**Word Work:** Preview Vocabulary, p. 523
1 Building an American Empire pp. 524–529	1 Day	■ Analyze the growth of the United States in the late 1800s and early 1900s. ■ Describe the purchase of Alaska and list its advantages. ■ Explain how Hawaii came to be part of the United States. ■ Analyze imperialism and how it affects people. ■ Describe the events of the Spanish-American War. ■ Identify reasons for building the Panama Canal.	**imperialism** **armistice**
MAP AND GLOBE SKILLS **Compare Map Projections** pp. 530–531	1 Day	■ Analyze map projections and their distortions. ■ Apply critical thinking skills to compare information from different map projections.	**projection** **distortion**
2 Progressives and Reform pp. 532–536	1 Day	■ Analyze political and social reforms of the early 1900s. ■ Identify and describe reform groups of the early 1900s. ■ Identify influential progressives and their contributions.	**reform** **progressive** **commission** **conservation** **merit system** **political boss** **settlement house** **civil rights** **suffrage** **Word Work:** Categorize Vocabulary, p. 533

READING	INTEGRATE LEARNING	REACH ALL LEARNERS	RESOURCES
Make Inferences, p. 523			
Reading Social Studies: **Personal Response,** p. 525 **Make Inferences,** p. 526 Reading Social Studies: **Personal Response,** p. 528	Mathematics **Compute Totals,** p. 524 Languages **Learn Hawaiian,** p. 525 Language Arts **Persuasive Writing,** p. 526 Health **Learn More About Diseases,** p. 528	**Advanced Learners,** p. 524 **Extend and Enrich,** p. 528 **Reteach the Lesson,** p. 529	**Activity Book,** pp. 132–133 **Reading and Vocabulary Transparency, 7-2**
	Science **Technology,** p. 530	**Tactile Learners,** p. 530 **Extend and Enrich,** p. 531 **Reteach the Skill,** p. 531	**Activity Book,** pp. 134–135 **Skill Transparencies, 7-1A and 7-1B** **GeoSkills CD-ROM**
Reading Social Studies: **Study Questions,** p. 533 Reading Social Studies: **Study Question Responses,** p. 536	Language Arts **Speaking,** p. 532 Art **Make a Poster,** p. 534 Music **Sing a Song,** p. 535	**Below-Level Learners,** p. 532 **Extend and Enrich,** p. 536 **Reteach the Lesson,** p. 536	**Activity Book,** p. 136 **Reading and Vocabulary Transparency, 7-3**

Chapter 14 Planning Guide Becoming a World Power

LESSON	PACING	OBJECTIVES	VOCABULARY
3 The Great War pp. 537–541	1 Day	■ Identify the causes of World War I and the countries that fought on each side. ■ Explain the reasons the United States entered World War I. ■ Analyze how the United States built up its military to fight in World War I. ■ Describe the economic and social changes in the United States during World War I. ■ Describe the end of World War I and the creation of the League of Nations.	military draft no-man's-land isolation
4 Good Times and Hard Times pp. 542–549	1 Day	■ Identify new forms of artistic and musical expression in the 1920s. ■ Analyze the changes industries brought in the 1920s. ■ Analyze the stock market crash of 1929 and the economic changes it caused. ■ Identify New Deal programs and describe their effects.	consumer good assembly line division of labor industrialization urbanization mechanization of agriculture stock market depression bureaucracy unemployment **Word Work:** Suffixes, p. 546
Chapter Review and Test Preparation pp. 550–551	1 Day		

READING	INTEGRATE LEARNING	REACH ALL LEARNERS	RESOURCES
Reading Social Studies: **Anticipation Guide,** p. 538 **Reading Social Studies:** **Anticipation Guide Responses,** p. 541	**Mathematics** **Computation,** p. 540	**Tactile Learners,** p. 537 **Extend and Enrich,** p. 541 **Reteach the Lesson,** p. 541	**Activity Book,** p. 137 **Reading and Vocabulary Transparency, 7-4**
Reading Social Studies: **K-W-L Chart,** p. 543 **Reading Social Studies:** **Reread to Clarify,** p. 547 **Reading Social Studies:** **K-W-L Chart Responses,** p. 549	**Music** **Listen to Jazz,** p. 542 **Art** **Paint a Picture,** p. 543 **Reading** **Read a Biography,** p. 544 **Language Arts** **News Writing,** p. 545 **Language Arts** **Expressive Writing,** p. 548	**English as a Second Language,** p. 543 **Extend and Enrich,** p. 549 **Reteach the Lesson,** p. 549	**Activity Book,** p. 138 **Reading and Vocabulary Transparency, 7-5** **Internet Resources**
		Test Preparation, p. 550	**Activity Book,** pp. 139–140 **Reading and Vocabulary Transparency, 7-6** **Assessment Program, Chapter 14 Test,** pp. 113–116

Activity Book

Name _____ Date _____

Building an American Empire

Directions Use the information below to complete the chart.

- Americans set up a republic in 1893. The United States annexes the territory in 1898.
- source of fish, timber, coal, copper, and gold.
- Secretary of State William Seward buys the land from Russia in 1867.
- For producing cattle and sugar.
- To link American ports on the Atlantic coast on the Pacific coast.
- The United States supports a revolution against Colombia. In 1904, the United States begins a major building project.

Territory	How and When Territory Was Added	Reason for Acquiring Territory
Alaska	Secretary of State William Seward buys the land from Russia in 1867.	source of fish, timber, coal, copper, and gold
Hawaii	Americans set up a republic in 1893. The United States annexes the territory in 1898.	For producing cattle and sugars
Panama Canal Zone	The United States supports a revolution against Colombia. In 1904, the United States begins a major building project.	To link American ports on the Atlantic coast with those on the Pacific coast.

(continued)

© Harcourt

Name _____ Date _____

Directions Use the information from the table on the previous page to write a paragraph trying to convince someone that Alaska, Hawaii, or the Panama Canal Zone should be added to the United States.

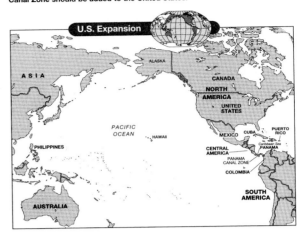

U.S. Expansion

Students' arguments should include the reasons from the chart on the facing page.

For Hawaii students also might mention that the islands provide a useful American

outpost in the Pacific, halfway between the continental United States and the

Philippines. For the Panama Canal Zone, students also might mention that the

Canal dramatically shortens the ocean journey from the Atlantic coast of the United

States to the Pacific coast.

_____

_____

© Harcourt

SKILL PRACTICE

Name _____ Date _____

MAP AND GLOBE SKILLS

Compare Map Projections

Map A: Europe, 1914

Map B: Europe, 1914

(continued)

© Harcourt

SKILL PRACTICE

Name _____ Date _____

Directions Study the conformal projection and equal-area projection maps. For each statement below, put a check mark in the column for which the statement is true. Some statements will be true for both projections. All statements will be true for at least one projection.

Conformal Projection	Equal-Area Projection	
✓	✓	❶ Shows the nations of Europe in 1914
	✓	❷ Shows the curved feature of Earth
✓		❸ Uses straight lines for all lines of latitude and longitude
✓		❹ Shows all lines of latitude and longitude at right angles to each other
✓	✓	❺ Shows national borders
	✓	❻ Shows most of the Ottoman Empire
✓		❼ Uses a straight line for the prime meridian
✓		❽ Shows directions correctly
✓	✓	❾ Shows parallels *not* intersecting
	✓	❿ Shows correctly the sizes of nations compared with one another
✓		⓫ Shows lines of latitude farther apart at the poles
	✓	⓬ Uses curved lines to show latitude
✓		⓭ Uses straight lines to show longitude
	✓	⓮ Shows lines of longitude closer together toward the north pole
✓		⓯ Shows all meridians parallel
	✓	⓰ Changes the shapes of nations

© Harcourt

Name _____ Date _____

Progressives and Reform

Directions Write each word or phrase from the list below in the correct section of the chart.

end boss rule	National Association for the Advancement of Colored People	national parks	Square Deal
Interstate Commerce Commission		National Urban League	support for injured workers
limit child labor	National League of Women Voters	Pure Food and Drug Act	ten-hour workday
merit system		settlement houses	women's suffrage
			Wisconsin Idea

Federal

Interstate Commerce Commission, national parks, Pure Food and Drug Act, Square Deal

State and Local

end boss rule, limit child labor, merit system, support for injured workers, ten-hour workday, Wisconsin Idea

Individual

National Association for the Advancement of Colored People, National League of Women Voters, National Urban League, settlement houses, women's suffrage

© Harcourt

Use after reading Chapter 14, Lesson 2, pages 532–536.

Name _____ Date _____

The Great War

Directions Write a short story about an American family during World War I. Some topics that you may want to feature in your story include worries about German U-boats, concerns about the draft, fighting to make the world "safe for democracy," and thoughts about a family member serving overseas. You may also want to describe how the war has changed the lives of women and African Americans.

_____
_____
_____
_____
_____
_____
_____
_____
_____
_____
_____
_____
_____
_____
_____
_____
_____
_____

© Harcourt

Use after reading Chapter 14, Lesson 3, pages 537–541.

Name _____ Date _____

Good Times and Hard Times

Directions Each event listed below occurred either before or after the stock market crash on October 29, 1929. Write the number of each event on the correct side of the time line below.

Before 1929

2
4
5
7
8
11

After 1929

1
3
6
9
10
12

❶ The size of the federal government is greatly increased.

❷ African American artists, musicians, and writers launch the Harlem Renaissance.

❸ Americans elect Franklin Roosevelt for his first term as President.

❹ Automobiles become affordable and popular.

❺ Charles Lindbergh flies across the Atlantic in the *Spirit of St. Louis.*

❻ Congress sets up the Tennessee Valley Authority.

❼ For the first time in United States history, more people live in cities than on farms.

❽ Moviegoers see the first "talkies."

❾ President Roosevelt announces the New Deal.

❿ The number of United States commercial radio stations tops 800.

⓫ Jazz becomes a popular form of music.

⓬ American farmers are hurt by low crop prices.

© Harcourt

Use after reading Chapter 14, Lesson 4, pages 542–549.

Name _____ Date _____

The Great Depression

Directions Complete this graphic organizer by making inferences about the Great Depression.

FACT

On October 29, 1929, the stock market crashed.

FACT

Because of the crash, many businesses failed.

INFERENCE

Because of the stock market crash, the economy did not grow and many people lost their jobs.

FACT

Because people lost their jobs, they had no money to spend.

FACT

Manufacturers could not sell their goods because people had no money to buy them.

INFERENCE

Because manufacturers could not sell their products, factories shut down and more people lost their jobs.

© Harcourt

Use after reading Chapter 14, pages 522–549.

CHAPTER

Name _____ Date _____

14 Test Preparation

Directions Read each question and choose the best answer. Then fill in the circle for the answer you have chosen. Be sure to fill in the circle completely.

1. Which area did the United States gain as a result of the Spanish-American War?
   Ⓐ Alaska
   Ⓑ Hawaii
   ● Puerto Rico
   Ⓓ Panama Canal

2. One of the main goals of the progressives was to —
   Ⓕ make peace with Germany.
   Ⓖ overcome the Great Depression.
   ● improve state and local government.
   Ⓙ expand the territory of the United States.

3. Which best describes the Great Migration?
   Ⓐ Many Germans moved to the United States during the 1920s, after World War I.
   ● Many African Americans moved to northern cities, especially during World War I.
   Ⓒ Many immigrants left cities to find work in the suburbs during the Great Depression.
   Ⓓ Many workers left the United States after losing their jobs during the Great Depression.

4. Langston Hughes was a —
   Ⓕ scientist who helped southern farmers.
   Ⓖ United States military leader during World War I.
   Ⓗ government official who purchased Alaska.
   ● well-known poet of the Harlem Renaissance.

5. The New Deal was Franklin Roosevelt's plan to —
   Ⓐ help immigrants adjust to life in the United States.
   Ⓑ organize the United States effort to build the Panama Canal.
   Ⓒ support the Allies against the Central Powers in World War I.
   ● put Americans back to work and end the Great Depression.

© Harcourt

Use after reading Chapter 14, pages 522–551.

COMMUNITY RESOURCES

Historical Societies

_____
_____
_____
_____
_____

Museums

_____
_____
_____
_____
_____

Experts on the Depression

_____
_____
_____
_____

Historical Sites

_____
_____
_____
_____

Chapter 14 Assessment

· CHAPTER ·

Name _____ Date _____

14 Test

Part One: Test Your Understanding

MULTIPLE CHOICE (4 points each)

Directions Circle the letter of the best answer.

1 Christian missionaries were among the first Americans to arrive in—
A Canada.
B Alaska.
C Russia.
D Hawaii.

2 The Spanish-American War began after the battleship *Maine* exploded in waters near—
F Guam.
G Cuba.
H the Philippines.
J Puerto Rico.

3 Most deaths during the Spanish-American War occurred—
A on the *Maine*.
B during the siege of Santiago.
C because of disease.
D in the Philippines.

4 Which of the following illustrates Theodore Roosevelt's ideas about conservation?
F the Interstate Commerce Commission
G the Pure Food and Drug Act
H the Meat Inspection Act
J Grand Canyon National Park

5 To make sure that government jobs were filled with qualified people, the governor of Wisconsin started a—
A settlement house.
B commission.
C merit system.
D Square Deal program.

6 Austria-Hungary declared war on Serbia because—
F a Serb rebel had killed members of Austria-Hungary's royal family.
G Serbia already was at war with the Central Powers.
H the Allied Powers wanted to form a Serbian homeland.
J France was a member of the Central Powers.

(continued)

Chapter 14 Test

Name _____ Date _____

7 At the beginning of World War I, President Woodrow Wilson wanted the United States to—
A join the Central Powers.
B remain neutral.
C join the Allied Powers.
D sink German U-boats.

8 The League of Nations was an organization that proposed—
F forming alliances within Europe.
G weakening Germany.
H helping avoid future wars.
J maintaining the isolation of the United States.

9 Which of the following pairs of artists were jazz musicians?
A Claude McKay and Countee Cullen
B Duke Ellington and Louis Armstrong
C Frank Lloyd Wright and Georgia O'Keeffe
D Charlie Chaplin and Mary Pickford

10 A time when there is little economic growth is called—
F a depression.
G a Jazz Age.
H a New Deal.
J a division of labor.

FILL IN THE BLANK (5 points each)

Directions Fill in the blank with the correct word or words from the list below.

11 An agreement to stop fighting a war is called a(n) _____armistice_____.

12 The _____Rough Riders_____ were a group of soldiers, led by Theodore Roosevelt, who fought in the Spanish-American War.

13 Theodore Roosevelt's progressive program was called the _____Square Deal_____.

14 The Selective Service Act began a(n) _____military draft_____ to bring men aged 21 to 30 into military service.

15 The Civilian Conservation Corps and the Works Progress Administration were programs in the _____New Deal_____, President Franklin D. Roosevelt's plan to put people back to work.

Square Deal
military draft
armistice
New Deal
Rough Riders

(continued)

Chapter 14 Test

Name _____ Date _____

Part Two: Test Your Skills

COMPARE MAP PROJECTIONS (5 points each)

Directions Use the two maps below to answer the questions that follow.

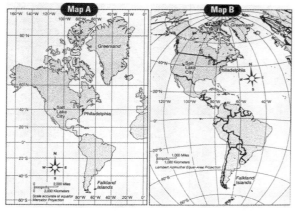

16 If a person wanted to compare the size of the Caribbean Islands with the size of islands in the Arctic Ocean, which map would be more accurate? Map A

17 What area of the Western Hemisphere appears most alike on both maps?
Possible responses: Central America; the center of the maps

18 On Map B, the 60th meridian runs from the Falkland Islands in the south to Greenland in the north. In North America, Salt Lake City and Philadelphia both lie near the 40th parallel, which runs east and west. Are the sizes of the landforms on Map B more accurate along the 60th meridian or along the 40th parallel? The landforms are more accurate from east to west, along the 40th parallel.

(continued)

Chapter 14 Test

Name _____ Date _____

Part Three: Apply What You Have Learned

19 **MAIN IDEA AND SUPPORTING DETAILS** (10 points)

The 1920s saw both economic prosperity and economic hardship. In the boxes below, list two details each about the good times, the hard times, and the New Deal's attempts to help the United States economy.

Economic Prosperity	Economic Hardship	Economic Help from New Deal
Possible responses: More consumer goods were available for people who had electricity in their homes; development of the assembly line allowed growth of the automobile industry and related industries, such as steel and oil; industrialization grew; agriculture became mechanized.	Possible responses: The stock market crashed; there was little economic growth; many people had to spend their savings; banks closed.	Possible responses: More authority was given to the federal government; Civilian Conservation Corps hired young men to build bridges and other projects; Works Progress Administration hired workers to create public buildings and record life; Tennessee Valley Authority created hydroelectric dams.

20 **ESSAY** (10 points)

The United States continued to expand its territory in the 1800s and early 1900s. Write a paragraph describing how the United States grew during this time and why this growth was important.

Possible response: The United States grew by purchasing land (Alaska), by acquiring territory through wars (Cuba, Puerto Rico, Guam, and the Philippines), and by taking over countries that were important for business or trade reasons (Hawaii and Panama). America's acquired lands were important because they provided new sources of raw materials, increased United States trade, and helped make the United States a world power.

Chapter 14 Test

Introduce the Chapter

PAGES 522–523

OBJECTIVES

- Interpret information in visuals.
- Use critical thinking skills to organize and analyze information.

Access Prior Knowledge

Ask students what they think of when they hear the phrase *world power*. What kinds of responsibilities do students associate with being a powerful country? Discuss with students how in the last century the United States has emerged as a powerful country.

Visual Learning

Picture As students examine the photograph, ask them to determine how a strong military would boost a country's status as a world power. Students may suggest that countries with strong militaries are more likely to be powerful.

Locate It Map The battleship *USS Texas* is docked in the Houston Ship Channel at San Jacinto State Historical Park, near Houston in Texas.

SAN JACINTO STATE HISTORICAL PARK

The *USS Texas* is the only American battleship from World War I still in existence. The *Texas* was commissioned in 1914 and remained part of the United States Navy until 1948. Today, visitors to San Jacinto State Historical Park can explore many different parts of this historic vessel.

LOCATE IT

TEXAS

San Jacinto State Historical Park

522 ▪ Unit 7

BACKGROUND

Picture The San Jacinto State Historical Park is the resting place of the battleship *USS Texas*. During World War I battleships like the *USS Texas* were the United States Navy's most powerful ships. Unlike aircraft carriers, battleships do not carry airplanes, but are used to attack enemy ships and protect the coastline. The *USS Texas* was decommissioned from the United States Navy on April 21, 1948, and given to the state of Texas. There it became the first battleship memorial museum in the United States. Its engines were named National Engineering Landmarks in 1975, and the ship itself was designated a National Historic Landmark in 1977. The Texas Parks and Wildlife Department, which maintains the *USS Texas,* helped fund an extensive restoration of the ship in the late 1980s.

BACKGROUND

Quotation A distinguished admiral, prolific writer, and leading expert on naval strategy, Alfred Thayer Mahan (1840–1914), helped shape United States international policy. His books and articles on the importance of a strong Navy influenced leaders in the United States and Europe.

· CHAPTER ·

14

Becoming a World Power

❝ **Whether they will or no, Americans must now begin to look outward.** ❞

—Alfred T. Mahan, *The United States Looking Outward,* 1890

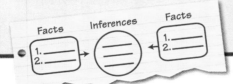 **Make Inferences**

When you make an **inference,** you use facts and your experiences to come to a conclusion about something.

As you read this chapter, be sure to do the following.
• **List the facts about the United States' expanding role in world affairs.**
• **List information from your own experiences.**
• **Use the facts to make inferences about the United States becoming a world power.**

Chapter 14 ■ 523

Read and Respond

Direct students' attention to the title of the chapter. Ask them to predict what the chapter might be about and how a country becomes one of the world's most powerful nations.

Quotation Have a volunteer read the quotation aloud.

Q What does the phrase "to look outward" mean in this quotation?

A Students' responses should reflect that looking outward would mean that a country is involved in world affairs.

 Make Inferences

Students can use the graphic organizer to help them make inferences about the United States' involvement in world affairs.

• Students will find a blank graphic organizer on page 139 of the Activity Book.

• A completed graphic organizer can be found on page 139 of the Activity Book, Teacher's Edition.

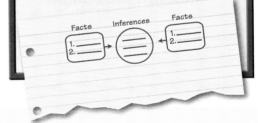

WORD WORK

Preview Vocabulary Have students work in groups to complete a vocabulary chart, which they can revise as necessary as they read the chapter.

Term	Definition	Sentence

MAKE IT RELEVANT

Discussion Topics As you teach this chapter, you might enjoy using these topics to generate discussion with your students. The topics help relate what the students are learning to today's world.

■ How does the United States influence world events today?

■ How can citizens express their opinions about the role the country takes in international affairs?

■ What would you like to see the United States do today as a world power?

Lesson 1

PAGES 524–529

OBJECTIVES

- Analyze the growth of the United States in the late 1800s and early 1900s.
- Describe the purchase of Alaska and list its advantages.
- Explain how Hawaii came to be part of the United States.
- Analyze imperialism and how it affected people.
- Describe the events of the Spanish-American War.
- Identify reasons for building the Panama Canal.

 Make Inferences pp. 523, 524, 525, 526, 529, 534, 536, 539, 541, 542, 546, 549, 550

Vocabulary

SEE READING AND VOCABULARY TRANSPARENCY 7-2 OR THE WORD CARDS ON PP. V79–V80.

imperialism p. 526   **armistice** p. 527

 When Minutes Count

Have students examine the map on page 526. Use the map as a springboard to discuss the Big Idea.

Quick Summary

This lesson examines how the United States expanded its territory and became a world power.

 Motivate

Set the Purpose

Big Idea Discuss how adding to a country's territory can increase its power.

Access Prior Knowledge

Ask students what two territories on the Pacific coast became states before Alaska was purchased in 1867.
California and Oregon

524 ■ UNIT 7

LESSON

1

 MAKE INFERENCES

As you read, make inferences about how stretching its borders helped the United States become a world power.

BIG IDEA
The United States added to its land area and increased its power at the end of the 1800s.

VOCABULARY
imperialism
armistice

Building an American Empire

| 1850 | 1900 | 1950 |

1860–1920

By the late 1800s, the western frontier had been settled and the United States was a world leader in industry and agriculture. Yet many Americans were ready to find new frontiers. They believed that setting up colonies in other parts of the world would bring the country both new sources of raw materials and new markets for its goods. The time seemed right for the United States to become a world power.

Alaska

In 1867 the United States bought Alaska from Russia for $7.2 million—about two cents an acre! At that time few Americans knew about Alaska or its peoples. Many thought it was foolish of the United States to buy land so far north. All across the country, newspapers criticized Secretary of State William

The April 1898 cover of the *Klondike News,* (left) illustrates the life of Alaskan miners, which included trekking through Klondike Valley (below).

FAST FACT Alaska is today the largest state in the United States. It is 488 times as large as Rhode Island, and two and a half times as large as Texas.

524   Unit 7

REACH ALL LEARNERS

Advanced Learners
Invite advanced learners to create tourist brochures for Alaska by hand or on a computer. Suggest that they do research on the Internet to find out about some of Alaska's tourist destinations. Encourage them to share their brochures with the class.

INTEGRATE MATHEMATICS

Compute Totals Explain to students that each person traveling into the Klondike was required to have enough supplies to last a year—about 1,000 pounds worth. The Chilkoot Indians profited from the gold rush by helping miners carry supplies over the Chilkoot Pass for a fee of $5 to $15 per 100 pounds. Ask students to compute the total fee charged for 500 pounds of supplies at $12 per hundred pounds. $60

King Kalakaua (left), and later his sister Queen Liliuokalani (right), were the last monarchs of the Hawaiian Islands (above).

Seward for agreeing to the deal. People even started calling Alaska Seward's Folly or the Polar Bear Garden.

In 1896 many people changed their opinions about Alaska after gold was found in the Klondike River valley in Canada, near Alaska. The discovery started a gold rush in the valley. From 1897 to 1899 more than 100,000 people raced to Alaska, hoping to get rich.

Most of the people who traveled to Alaska did not find gold. However, Alaska brought new wealth to the United States in other ways. Alaska was rich in natural resources, such as fish, timber, coal, and copper.

REVIEW Why did the discovery of gold change people's opinions about Alaska?
MAKE INFERENCES
It made people realize that Alaska had rich natural resources.

The Hawaiian Islands

In the late 1800s, Americans also, looked to the Hawaiian Islands as a place to get more new lands. This chain of 8 major islands and 124 smaller ones lies in the Pacific Ocean about 2,400 miles (3,862 km) southwest of California. During the eighth century, Polynesian people migrated to Hawaii from other islands in the Pacific. They set up a monarchy ruled by a royal family.

Christian missionaries were among the first Americans to arrive in Hawaii. Later, American businesspeople started cattle ranches and sugar plantations on the islands. By the 1870s those Americans controlled much of the land in Hawaii.

When the Hawaiian king, Kalakaua (kah•lah•KAH•ooh•ah), tried to keep the Americans from taking over the islands in 1887, they decided to take away the king's authority. They made him sign a new constitution that left the Hawaiian monarchy without authority. In 1893 the king's sister Queen Liliuokalani (lih•lee•uh•woh•kuh•LAH•nee), tried to regain power. But the Americans took over the government and set up a republic. The United States annexed Hawaii in 1898.

REVIEW How did Hawaii become part of the United States? It was annexed in 1898.

Chapter 14 ▪ 525

Read and Respond

Link History with Civics and Government Explain to students that in January 1893 Queen Liliuokalani was removed from her throne. The government was taken over by wealthy American sugar growers who controlled the economy and wanted Hawaii to be annexed by the United States. Ask students why they think Hawaii was so important to the United States. Hawaii was a good place for cattle ranches and sugar plantations.

Visual Learning

Map Ask students to point out each of the new United States possessions on the map.
CAPTION ANSWER: the Pacific Ocean

War with Spain

Read and Respond

History Remind students that Christopher Columbus claimed Cuba for Spain in 1492. By the 1800s Cubans wanted their independence from Spain, but they were divided over whether they wanted complete independence for Cuba or for Cuba to be annexed to the United States. Cuba became independent in 1902.

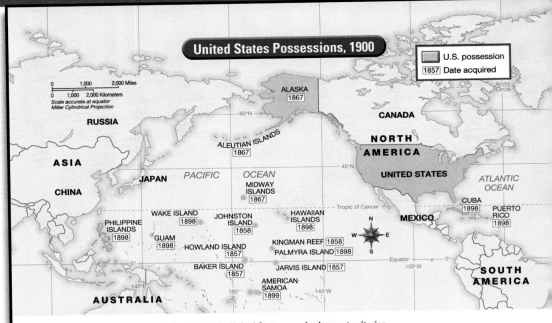

United States Possessions, 1900

U.S. possession
1857 Date acquired

Location In the late 1800s the United States acquired many territories around the world.

◈ In what part of the world did the United States gain most of its new land?

War with Spain

Some people now accused the country's leaders of **imperialism**, or empire building. They believed that extending the nation's borders would cause conflict between the United States and European nations—especially Spain.

At the end of the 1800s, Spain still had two colonies—the Philippine Islands and Guam—in the Eastern Hemisphere. In the Western Hemisphere, Spain controlled Puerto Rico and Cuba. However, many Cubans wanted their island to become independent. Twice, in 1868 and again in 1895, they had rebelled against Spanish rule, but the rebellions had failed.

People in the United States watched as the conflict between Spain and Cuba continued. Many Americans, including those who had moved there to start businesses, supported the Cubans' fight for independence. Newspapers in the United States were full of stories about Spain's harsh rule of the island. Some of these stories were true, but others were not.

In 1898 President William McKinley ordered the battleship *Maine* to Havana, Cuba, to protect Americans living there. Just three weeks after the *Maine* arrived, it exploded in Havana's harbor. More than 260 sailors were killed. It was not clear why the ship blew up, but the United States blamed Spain. "Remember the *Maine*!" Americans cried, calling for action. On April 25, the United States declared war on Spain.

526 ■ Unit 7

Focus Skill **READING SKILL**

Make Inferences Ask students to answer the following questions after they have read about the annexation of Hawaii.

■ How do you think most native Hawaiians felt when the Americans took control of Hawaii?

■ Why were the Americans able to take control of Hawaii so easily?

INTEGRATE LANGUAGE ARTS

Persuasive Writing Invite students to write persuasive letters to members of Congress in 1898, urging war with Spain. Ask them to support their requests with reasons.

The first battles of the Spanish-American War were fought in the Philippine Islands. Led by Commodore George Dewey, the United States Navy destroyed the Spanish fleet there and captured Manila Bay. The fighting then shifted to Cuba.

Thousands of Americans volunteered to fight in the war. Among them was Theodore Roosevelt. He had been assistant secretary of the navy when the war started, but he quit that job to form a fighting company made up mostly of cowhands and college athletes. In Cuba, the Rough Riders, as they were called, took part in the Battle of San Juan Hill and the siege of Santiago.

On August 12, 1898, after a number of defeats, Spain signed an armistice (AHR•muh•stuhs). An **armistice** is an

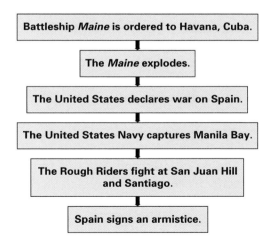
This canteen was carried by a Rough Rider in Cuba.

agreement to stop fighting a war. The Spanish-American War lasted less than four months, but more than 5,000 American soldiers died. Most of them died from diseases such as malaria and yellow fever.

As a result of the Spanish-American War, the United States became a world power. Spain agreed to give the United States control of Cuba, Puerto Rico, Guam, and the Philippine Islands. Cuba and the Philippine Islands later became independent countries, but Puerto Rico and Guam remain part of the United States today.

REVIEW What lands did the United States gain as a result of the Spanish-American War?
Cuba, Puerto Rico, Guam, and the Philippine Islands; Puerto Rico and Guam remain part of the United States

This painting shows Roosevelt and the Rough Riders charging San Juan Hill. However, the charge was really made on foot.

Chapter 14 ■ 527

Culture and Society Explain to students that before the Spanish-American War many newspapers printed sensational stories about Spain's treatment of people in Cuba. The sensational tactics practiced by these newspapers came to be called "yellow journalism."

Analyze Primary Sources

Painting Explain that although this group of 1,000 soldiers was nicknamed the Rough Riders, in Cuba they battled mainly on foot. Ask students why the painter may have chosen to depict the soldiers on horses rather than on foot. Horses lend action and emotion to this dramatic charge; the name Rough Riders gives the impression that they did ride on horseback.

Read and Respond

History Tell students that tensions were so high between Spain and the United States that even a small event could have triggered the war. The explosion of the *Maine* did just that. Have students create a flow chart similar to the one below, highlighting the events of the war.

Battleship *Maine* is ordered to Havana, Cuba.

↓

The *Maine* explodes.

↓

The United States declares war on Spain.

↓

The United States Navy captures Manila Bay.

↓

The Rough Riders fight at San Juan Hill and Santiago.

↓

Spain signs an armistice.

History Tell students that an armistice ended the fighting in the Spanish-American War, also known as the War of 1898. The end of the war also marked the end of the long-lasting Spanish Empire.

The Spanish-American War

The peace treaty between the United States and Spain stated that Spain would withdraw from Cuba, leaving it temporarily under United States rule. Spain still remained responsible for Cuba's debt. Puerto Rico, Guam, and the Philippines were ceded to the United States; however, the United States gave Spain $20 million for these lands.

Q Why didn't Cuba and the Philippines become part of the United States?

A The Teller Amendment, which was passed when the United States declared war on Spain, prohibited the United States from taking over Cuba. In the Philippines the people waged war with the United States for two years before becoming an independent country.

The Panama Canal

Read and Respond

Economics Discuss with students how the Panama Canal helped the United States economy grow.

Q Why is it better to transport some goods by ship than by train?

A Some goods are too large or heavy for trains, and it may be cheaper to ship the goods by boat.

Visual Learning

Map Point out that the trade route from New York to San Francisco through the Panama Canal is much shorter than the route around South America.

CAPTION ANSWER: about 45 miles in length and 10 miles in width

3 Close

Summarize Key Content

- Alaska was purchased from Russia in 1867 bringing the United States a wealth of natural resources.
- The United States annexed Hawaii in 1898, after Americans had taken over the government.
- As a result of the Spanish-American War, the United States gained control of Cuba, Puerto Rico, Guam, and the Philippine Islands.
- The United States supported a revolution to end Colombian rule in Panama and then built the Panama Canal to connect the Atlantic and Pacific Oceans.

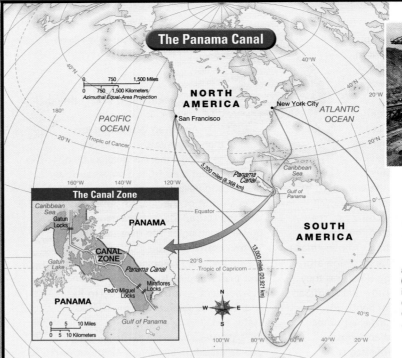

The Panama Canal

The Canal Zone

GEOGRAPHY THEME Human-Environment Interactions People used large machines and heavy equipment (above) to clear the land in Central America and construct the locks (above) of the Panama Canal.

◆ How many miles of land did the canal zone cover?

The Panama Canal

Soon after Theodore Roosevelt came back from Cuba, he was elected governor of New York. Two years later he was elected Vice President of the United States, serving under President William McKinley. On September 6, 1901, President McKinley was shot by a person who was angry with the government. McKinley died eight days later, and Roosevelt became President.

One of President Roosevelt's main goals was to build a canal across the Isthmus of Panama, in Central America. The canal would link the Atlantic Ocean and the Pacific Ocean. This, in turn, would link American ports on the Atlantic coast with those on the Pacific coast. "I wish to see the United States the dominant power on the shores of the Pacific Ocean," Roosevelt said.

In 1902 Congress voted to build the canal. However, the Isthmus of Panama did not belong to the United States. It belonged to Colombia. The United States offered Colombia $10 million for the right to build a canal, but Colombia rejected the offer.

Roosevelt then spread the word that he would welcome a revolution in Panama to end Colombian rule. He sent the United States Navy to protect the isthmus. If a revolution began, the navy was to keep Colombian troops from landing on shore. Within three months a revolution took place, and the people of Panama formed a new nation. Panama's

528 ■ Unit 7

INTEGRATE HEALTH

Learn More About Diseases Remind students that fighting disease was one of the biggest challenges to building the Panama Canal. Ask students to research malaria and yellow fever to find out exactly how those diseases are transmitted and where in the world they still exist today.

EXTEND AND ENRICH

Write to Compare and Contrast Ask students to write a few paragraphs discussing the different ways the United States acquired each of the following lands: Alaska, Hawaii, Guam, and Puerto Rico.

leaders then gave the United States the right to build the canal. The United States would control the canal and an area 5 miles (8 km) wide on each side of it.

Work on the canal began in 1904. Workers guided huge machines to cut down the trees and thick jungle growth.

Engineers designed huge canal locks to help ships move through the waterway.

Unlike the French who had first tried to build the canal in the 1880s, American workers stayed healthy. Doctors now knew that malaria and yellow fever, the diseases that had stopped the French, were carried by mosquitoes. The Americans learned to control the mosquitoes by using insecticides and draining the swamps where the insects lived.

Building the canal took ten years and cost about $380 million. After it opened, goods could be shipped between ports on the Atlantic coast and ports on the Pacific coast in about one month. Just as the transcontinental railroad had done, the canal helped the United States economy grow. Today the canal, which is under Panama's control, continues to help move people and goods around the world.

REVIEW **Why did the United States want to build the Panama Canal?** because it would link American ports on the Atlantic coast with those on the Pacific coast

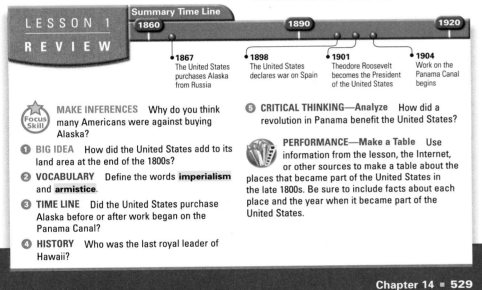

LESSON 1 REVIEW

Summary Time Line

1860 — 1890 — 1920

- **1867** The United States purchases Alaska from Russia
- **1898** The United States declares war on Spain
- **1901** Theodore Roosevelt becomes the President of the United States
- **1904** Work on the Panama Canal begins

MAKE INFERENCES Why do you think many Americans were against buying Alaska?

❶ **BIG IDEA** How did the United States add to its land area at the end of the 1800s?

❷ **VOCABULARY** Define the words **imperialism** and **armistice**.

❸ **TIME LINE** Did the United States purchase Alaska before or after work began on the Panama Canal?

❹ **HISTORY** Who was the last royal leader of Hawaii?

❺ **CRITICAL THINKING—Analyze** How did a revolution in Panama benefit the United States?

PERFORMANCE—Make a Table Use information from the lesson, the Internet, or other sources to make a table about the places that became part of the United States in the late 1800s. Be sure to include facts about each place and the year when it became part of the United States.

Chapter 14 ▪ 529

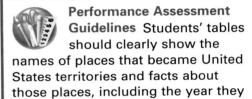

Skill Lesson

OBJECTIVES

- Analyze map projections and their distortions.
- Apply critical thinking skills to compare information from different map projections.

Vocabulary

projection   **distortion** p. 530
p. 530

WORD CARDS

See pp. V79–V80.

1 Motivate

Why It Matters

Explain that different map projections are used in different ways. With students, list reasons to use a map: to compare land areas, to locate places, or to find distances. Point out that the more area a map covers, the more distorted parts of the map become. Tell students that it is important to use a map that will give them the most accurate information.

·SKILLS· Compare Map Projections

MAP AND GLOBE

VOCABULARY

projections

distortions

➡ WHY IT MATTERS

Because the Earth is round and maps are flat, maps cannot represent the Earth's shape exactly. As a result, cartographers have different ways of showing the Earth on flat paper. These different views are called **projections**. All projections have **distortions**, or areas that are not accurate. But different kinds of projections have different kinds of distortions. Identifying areas on a map that are distorted will help you understand how different maps can best be used.

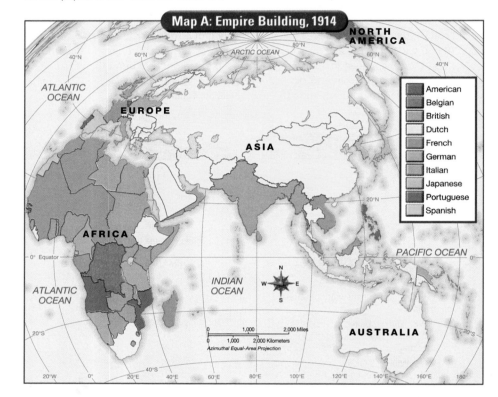

Map A: Empire Building, 1914

Legend:
- American
- Belgian
- British
- Dutch
- French
- German
- Italian
- Japanese
- Portuguese
- Spanish

Azimuthal Equal-Area Projection

INTEGRATE SCIENCE

Technology Inform students that technological advances have improved mapmaking since World War II. Aerial and satellite photography are used regularly to take pictures. Discuss the difference between pictures obtained by aerial photography and those obtained by satellite photography. Tell students that computers have also improved mapmaking because computer programs allow a person to make a more accurate drawing than one done by hand.

REACH ALL LEARNERS

Tactile Learners To help students understand the difficulty in making flat maps of the world, have them attempt to make their own maps. Suggest that students lay sheets of paper over the globe and trace the continents. Have them number or letter their sheets of paper so they know how they should go together. Then have them lay their sheets of paper out flat. Discuss with students that distances between places on their maps will be distorted.

▶ WHAT YOU NEED TO KNOW

Map A and Map B show the same area, but they use different kinds of projections. Map A is an azimuthal (a•zuh•MUH•thuhl) equal-area projection. Equal-area projections show the sizes of regions in correct relation to one another, but they distort, or change, their shapes.

Map B is a Miller cylindrical projection. It is just one example of a conformal projection. Notice that the meridians on Map B are all an equal distance apart. Notice also that the parallels closer to the North and South Poles are farther apart than those near the equator. Conformal projections, like the one used on Map B, show directions correctly, but they distort sizes, especially of the places near the poles.

▶ PRACTICE THE SKILL

Use Map A and Map B to answer the following questions.

❶ On which parts of Maps A and B do the shapes of the land areas appear to be the same?

❷ On which map does Africa appear to be larger? On which map is the size of Africa more accurate?

▶ APPLY WHAT YOU LEARNED

Look at the maps in the Atlas on pages A4–A17 to see other map projections. Write a paragraph about the advantages and disadvantages of using equal-area and conformal projections.

 Practice your map and globe skills with the **GeoSkills CD-ROM.**

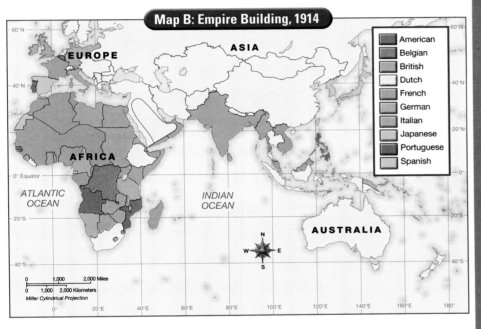

Map B: Empire Building, 1914

Legend:
- American
- Belgian
- British
- Dutch
- French
- German
- Italian
- Japanese
- Portuguese
- Spanish

EUROPE · ASIA · AFRICA · AUSTRALIA · ATLANTIC OCEAN · INDIAN OCEAN

0 1,000 2,000 Miles
0 1,000 2,000 Kilometers
Miller Cylindrical Projection

MAP AND GLOBE SKILLS

Chapter 14 ▪ 531

2 Teach

What You Need to Know

Discuss with students the best use of Map A. Students should note that it would be helpful when comparing the areas of different countries. Ask students when they would use Map B. Students should respond that Map B would be helpful when it is important to know correct direction.

Practice the Skill—Answers

❶ the center of the maps: India, the Middle East, central Asia

❷ Africa appears larger on Map A. Its size is more accurate on Map A.

3 Close

Apply What You Learned

Students' paragraphs should clearly list the advantages and disadvantages of both equal-area and conformal projection maps.

ACTIVITY BOOK

Use ACTIVITY BOOK, pp. 134–135, to give students additional practice using this skill.

TRANSPARENCY

Use SKILL TRANSPARENCIES 7-1A and 7-1B.

EXTEND AND ENRICH

Write to Compare and Contrast Encourage each student to describe in writing the similarities and differences he or she sees between Map A and Map B.

CD-ROM

Explore GEOSKILLS CD-ROM to learn more about map and globe skills.

RETEACH

Research Map Projections Have students work in small groups to find world maps in this textbook as well as in atlases and encyclopedias. Have students compare the maps they find with those in the lesson. How many equal-area and conformal maps did they find? For what purposes are these two kinds of map projections used in the textbook and in reference books?

Lesson 2

PAGES 532–536

OBJECTIVES

- Analyze political and social reforms of the early 1900s.
- Identify and describe reform groups of the early 1900s.
- Identify influential progressives and their contributions.

 Make Inferences pp. 523, 524, 525, 526, 529, 534, 536, 539, 541, 542, 546, 549, 550

Vocabulary

SEE READING AND VOCABULARY TRANSPARENCY 7-3 OR THE WORD CARDS ON PP. V79–V82.

reform p. 532

progressive p. 532

commission p. 532

conservation p. 533

merit system p. 533

political boss p. 534

settlement house p. 535

civil rights p. 535

suffrage p. 535

When Minutes Count

Have students skim the lesson to find the meanings of the vocabulary words. Ask them to tell how each word relates to the Big Idea.

Quick Summary

This lesson describes the progressives and the reforms they supported.

1 Motivate

Set the Purpose

Big Idea Ask students to list aspects of life in the 1900s that people may have wanted to improve.

Access Prior Knowledge

Ask students to think about how the government helps people in the United States today.

532 ■ UNIT 7

· LESSON ·

2

 MAKE INFERENCES
As you read, make inferences about how changes in the early 1900s helped improve life in the United States.

BIG IDEA
People worked to improve life in the United States in the early 1900s.

VOCABULARY
reform
progressive
commission
conservation
merit system
political boss
settlement house
civil rights
suffrage

Progressives and Reform

1900–1920

The growing power of the United States made many Americans hopeful. But they also saw the need to **reform**, or change for the better, some parts of life in the United States. This was especially true in America's cities, which continued to grow as more and more people moved into them to work in industries.

Federal Reforms

Among those who saw the need for reform was President Theodore Roosevelt. Because Roosevelt and his followers wanted to improve government and make life better for people, they came to be called **progressives**.

Roosevelt started a program called the Square Deal. As part of this program, Roosevelt wanted the federal government to make rules for businesses to follow. To do this, he set up or supported efforts to increase the authority of special government boards called **commissions**. One of these was the Interstate Commerce Commission. New laws gave it more authority to regulate some industries doing business across state lines and to set "just and reasonable" railroad fares.

President Roosevelt (left) set up commissions to regulate businesses. The Interstate Commerce Commission was given the authority to set some railroad fares (right).

532 ▪ Unit 7

• HERITAGE •

Labor Day

In New York City on September 5, 1882, Americans held the first Labor Day parade. Matthew Maguire, a machine worker, and Peter McGuire, a carpenter, came up with the idea of Labor Day. It is a day to honor working people and to recognize their importance to the United States. In 1894 Congress made Labor Day a legal holiday. Today, the United States and Canada celebrate Labor Day on the first Monday in September. Many other countries also honor workers with labor celebrations.

Not all people supported these changes, however. They worried that the federal government would become too powerful.

Roosevelt also wanted the federal government to make sure that foods and medicines were safe. In 1906 Congress passed the Pure Food and Drug Act. The act said that all foods and medicines had to meet government safety standards. Congress also passed the Meat Inspection Act. This act said that government-paid inspectors would visit every plant that packaged meat to make sure the meat was handled safely.

Roosevelt was also interested in conservation. **Conservation** is the protection and wise use of natural resources. Roosevelt asked Congress to set aside millions of acres of land in different parts of the country as national parks. Among these were the Grand Canyon, Mesa Verde, and Glacier national parks.

REVIEW **What did progressives want to do?**
They wanted to improve government and make life better for people.

State and Local Reforms

Progressives also worked to reform state governments. In Wisconsin, Governor Robert La Follette made so many reforms that President Roosevelt called the state, a "laboratory of democracy."

Officials in many states had been giving government jobs to people who did favors for them. To keep this from happening in Wisconsin, La Follette started a **merit system** to make sure that people were qualified for their jobs. Each person applying for a government job was given a test. The person who scored the highest on the test got the job.

Wisconsin also passed laws to help other workers. One said that a workday could be no more than ten hours. Others listed jobs for which children could not be hired and said that the state would pay workers who were hurt while working at their jobs.

Chapter 14 ■ 533

WORD WORK

Categorize Vocabulary Ask students to review the vocabulary and to place each term into the appropriate category. Some terms may fall into both categories.

Government	Reforms
reform	reform
progressive	progressive
commission	settlement house
conservation	civil rights
merit system	suffrage
political boss	

BACKGROUND

The Jungle Tell students that in 1906 Upton Sinclair published *The Jungle,* a book detailing the unsanitary conditions of meatpacking plants. Sinclair's book enraged the public and encouraged the legislation that became the Pure Food and Drug Act and the Meat Inspection Act. Sinclair was one of the journalists President Theodore Roosevelt labeled a muckraker. Muckrakers used investigative journalism to expose political bosses, unfair working conditions, and various other injustices.

Study Questions Suggest that students use these questions as guides for their reading:

1. What did the NAACP work to achieve?
2. What did the Nineteenth Amendment do?

● USE READING AND VOCABULARY TRANSPARENCY 7-3.

7-3 TRANSPARENCY

2 Teach

Federal Reforms

• HERITAGE •

Labor Day

Discuss the meaning of Labor Day with students. Ask volunteers to describe the origin of Labor Day and to share with the class how they celebrate this holiday.

Read and Respond

Geography Have students locate these national parks on a United States map: Grand Canyon, Mesa Verde, and Glacier. Ask students to look at a map of their state and locate any national parks.

State and Local Reforms

Read and Respond

History Tell students that children often had to work to help feed their families in the early 1800s. At the time, one-third of factory workers were children ages 7 to 12. By 1853 many states had prohibited children from working more than ten hours a day. Compare the number of hours students spend in school today with a ten-hour workday. Ask students to consider what life was like for those children.

Analyze Primary Sources

Political Cartoon Remind students that editorial cartoons express opinions, usually about politics or government. Encourage students to use what they know from the caption to interpret the cartoon. The caption to the cartoon suggests that money is the reason for the victory. The fancy suit and the size of the man imply that money is powerful.

More Reforms

Read and Respond

Culture and Society Tell students that Hull House in Chicago became one of the largest settlement houses in the United States. It had a nursery, a gymnasium, recreation and meeting rooms, classrooms for arts and crafts, a music school, a social service center, and a theater. Tell students that it was privately funded, and ask them the following question.

Q Why do you think people gave money to help the immigrants and the poor?

A It was beneficial for all of society if all citizens were skilled and productive.

Culture and Society Discuss with students how society today is shaped by the social services begun in the early 1900s. Ask students to complete the graphic organizer of progressive organizations and the groups who were primarily served by them.

Organization	Who Benefited?
Hull House and other settlement houses	Immigrants and poor workers
NAACP	African Americans
National Urban League	African Americans
National American Woman Suffrage Association	women
National League of Women Voters	women

THE "BRAINS."
THAT ACHIEVED THE TAMMANY VICTORY AT THE ROCHESTER DEMOCRATIC CONVENTION.

This political cartoon drawn by illustrator Thomas Nast suggests that money was used to influence political decision making in New York City.

People in other states called what La Follette was doing the Wisconsin Idea. Many states soon copied his changes.

Progressive reforms also affected city governments. At the time, many large cities were controlled by powerful leaders. These leaders—often the mayors—were called **political bosses**. People who worked for them sometimes gave money to voters so they would vote for the boss.

Some cheated in elections by counting the votes of people who were not citizens or who did not vote. In this way, political bosses often were elected many times.

One of the best-known political bosses was New York City's George Plunkitt. In 1905 a journalist wrote a book based on interviews with Plunkitt. In the book, Plunkitt described how he did favors for people. Those favors, however, were always done in exchange for votes.

Progressives wanted to end boss rule. One way to do this was to change the form of city government. To keep the mayor from having all the authority, some cities set up commissions made up of several people. Each commission member oversaw a city department.

REVIEW Why did progressives want to stop political bosses? **MAKE INFERENCES**
These powerful leaders were not always fairly elected; they often had too much authority.

More Reforms

Progressives were often ordinary people trying to improve their lives or the lives of others. Jane Addams was one of these people. In 1889 Addams and Ellen Gates Starr opened a settlement house named Hull House in one of the poorest areas of Chicago.

Jane Addams (right with child) founded Hull House (below) in a poor Chicago neighborhood. It became the model for community centers throughout the country.

534 ▪ Unit 7

Janie Porter Barrett worked to educate African American children living in Virginia.

W.E.B. Du Bois worked for racial equality and was a founder of the NAACP.

A **settlement house** was a community center where immigrants and poor working people could learn new skills.

Hull House became a model for other community centers. In 1890 African American teacher Janie Porter Barrett founded a settlement house in Hampton, Virginia. Five years later, Lillian Wald started the Henry Street Settlement in New York City. By 1900 almost 100 settlement houses had opened across the country.

African American leaders also used progressive ideas to try to fight prejudice. Booker T. Washington, a former slave, led an effort to provide African Americans with more opportunities for education. In 1881 he helped found Tuskegee Institute, a trade school for African Americans, in Alabama.

In 1909 W.E.B. Du Bois (doo•BOYS) and other leaders formed the National Association for the Advancement of Colored People, or NAACP. The NAACP worked to change state laws that denied full civil rights to African Americans. **Civil rights** are the rights guaranteed to all citizens by the Constitution.

The National Urban League, founded in 1910, also worked to help African Americans. It helped the many African Americans who were moving to cities at the time find jobs and homes.

Another group of progressives, the National American Woman Suffrage Association, led the fight for women's rights. **Suffrage** refers to the right to vote. The president of the association from 1900 to 1904, and from 1915 to 1920, was Carrie Lane Chapman Catt. She had first became politically active in her home state of Iowa in the 1880s.

Due to Catt and other progressives, many states responded to women's demand. By 1915, most of the states permitted women to vote in certain elections, such as for members of school boards.

Chapter 14 ▪ 535

Read and Respond

History Explain to students that the NAACP was founded on February 12, 1909, the one hundredth anniversary of the birth of Abraham Lincoln. Point out that the founders included white Americans as well as African Americans.

• BIOGRAPHY •

Carrie Lane Chapman Catt

Citizenship Ask students how the trait of citizenship relates to Carrie Lane Chapman Catt, who is featured in the Biography on p. 536. She fought to get women the right to vote and founded the League of Women Voters.

3 Close

Summarize Key Content

- President Theodore Roosevelt encouraged Congress to pass the Pure Food and Drug Act and the Meat Inspection Act and to set aside millions of acres of land for national parks.
- Progressives worked to reform state and local governments.
- Progressive groups worked for the rights of African Americans and women.

BACKGROUND

The Suffrage Movement From 1848 to 1920 many men and women of all social classes worked to gain the right for women to vote. The constitutional amendment was voted on just in time for the 1920 election. Illinois and Wisconsin hurried to be the first state to ratify the amendment, and Georgia and Alabama competed to be the first state to reject it. Tennessee was the tiebreaker state, and the amendment was passed.

INTEGRATE MUSIC

Sing a Song Tell students that members of the suffrage movement sometimes sang songs that supported women's suffrage. This song, entitled "The New America," was sung at the National American Woman Suffrage Convention in 1891. Sing the song to the tune of "America" ("My Country, 'Tis of Thee"):

Our country, now from thee, Claim we our liberty, In freedom's name.

Guarding home's altar fires, Daughters of patriot sires, Their zeal our own inspires, Justice to claim.

Women in every age, For this great heritage, Tribute have paid.

Our birth-right claim we now, Longer refuse to bow, On freedom's altar now, Our hand is laid.

Assess

Lesson 2 Review—Answers

 MAKE INFERENCES Roosevelt strongly supported conservation.

❶ **BIG IDEA** People reformed government, started settlement houses, and worked for civil rights and women's suffrage.

❷ **VOCABULARY** A **political boss** was a powerful elected official, often a mayor, who controlled a city's government.

❸ **TIME LINE** 1920

❹ **HISTORY** Catt helped women gain the right to vote and founded the National League of Women Voters, now called the League of Women Voters.

❺ **CRITICAL THINKING—Evaluate** Possible responses: schools, neighborhoods, the government, the environment

 Performance Assessment Guidelines Speeches should be well written and clearly spoken with convincing reasons for people to celebrate Labor Day.

Almost a dozen states, most of them in the West, had given women full voting rights in state elections. In 1920 the Nineteenth Amendment to the United States Constitution was ratified, giving all American women the right to vote. That same year Catt founded a group called the National League of Women Voters, now called the League of Women Voters.

REVIEW What group led the fight for women's suffrage? the National American Woman Suffrage Association

LESSON 2 REVIEW

Summary Time Line
1900 ——— 1910 ——— 1920

• 1909
The NAACP is founded

• 1920
The Nineteenth Amendment is ratified

 MAKE INFERENCES Why do you think President Roosevelt set aside certain areas to serve as national parks?

❶ **BIG IDEA** What were some of the things people did to improve life in the United States in the early 1900s?

❷ **VOCABULARY** Write a description of a **political boss**.

❸ **TIME LINE** What year was the Nineteenth Amendment ratified?

❹ **HISTORY** What did Carrie Lane Chapman Catt accomplish?

❺ **CRITICAL THINKING—Evaluate** The progressives of the early 1900s worked to improve many different things. What kinds of things are people trying to improve today?

 PERFORMANCE—Deliver a Speech Imagine that you are taking part in the first Labor Day parade. Write a speech about why people should participate in this national celebration.

The Great War

1901   **1951**   **2001**

1914–1918

In 1914 ongoing conflicts in Europe exploded into war. At first, most Americans saw the war as a European problem. In time, however, our nation was drawn into what was then known as the Great War. It would later be called World War I.

Causes of the War

Nations across Europe had formed alliances. The members of each alliance promised to help one another if they were attacked. Europeans hoped that these alliances would prevent war, but they had the opposite effect.

Serbia, a country in southern Europe, bordered Austria-Hungary. Many Serbs, however, lived in the southern part of Austria-Hungary, and they longed to be a part of their Serbian homeland. On June 28, 1914, a Serb rebel shot and killed two members of Austria-Hungary's royal family. As a result, Austria-Hungary declared war on Serbia.

Serbia and Austria-Hungary were both members of alliances, so other European nations were quickly drawn into the conflict. On one side were the Allied Powers, or Allies.

· LESSON ·

3

 MAKE INFERENCES

As you read, make inferences about how World War I threatened democracy and world peace.

BIG IDEA
The United States entered World War I.

VOCABULARY
military draft
no-man's-land
isolation

The assassination of Archduke Ferdinand and his wife led to war.

The New York Times.

HEIR TO AUSTRIA'S THRONE IS SLAIN WITH HIS WIFE BY A BOSNIAN YOUTH TO AVENGE SEIZURE OF HIS COUNTRY

537

Lesson 3
PAGES 537–541

OBJECTIVES

- Identify the causes of World War I and the countries that fought on each side.
- Explain the reasons the United States entered World War I.
- Analyze how the United States built up its military to fight in World War I.
- Describe the economic and social changes in the United States during World War I.
- Describe the end of World War I and the creation of the League of Nations.

 Make Inferences pp. 523, 537, 539, 541, 550

Vocabulary
SEE READING AND VOCABULARY TRANSPARENCY 7-4 OR THE WORD CARDS ON PP. V81–V82.

military draft p. 538
no-man's-land p. 539
isolation p. 541

 When Minutes Count

Direct students to examine the illustrations and predict what they think the Big Idea is. Encourage them to read the lesson to find out.

Quick Summary

This lesson examines the causes of World War I and the role played by the United States.

 Motivate

Set the Purpose

Big Idea Review with students the common causes of war.

Access Prior Knowledge

Ask students to tell what they know about World War I.

REACH ALL LEARNERS

Tactile Learners Assist tactile learners in understanding the location of the events of World War I. As they go through the lesson, have students use a map to trace these locations on paper.

BACKGROUND

Francis Ferdinand The archduke of Austria, Francis Ferdinand, and his wife, Sophie Chotek, were the members of Austria-Hungary's royal family who were assassinated on June 28, 1914. Francis Ferdinand was heir to the Austro-Hungarian crown at the time of his death.

Anticipation Guide Ask students to predict which of the following statements are true and which are false. Students may correct their predictions as they read.

1. The United States joined the Central Powers in the Great War. FALSE

2. The Selective Service Act provided for a military draft. TRUE

● USE READING AND VOCABULARY TRANSPARENCY 7-4.

7-4
TRANSPARENCY

2 Teach

Causes of the War

Read and Respond

History Explain to students that in World War I the major European nations formed two opposing alliances—the Allied Powers and the Central Powers. These alliances caused the war to become a world conflict. Although the United States tried to remain neutral, Americans became angry when the Germans sank the British ship *Lusitania*.

The United States Enters the War

Read and Respond

History Inform students that events finally caused President Wilson to change his mind about the United States joining the war. In 1917 President Wilson asked for a declaration of war, saying that though the United States had no quarrel with the Germans, it could not allow these hostile actions to continue. "The world must be made safe for democracy," said Wilson. Four days later Congress passed the War Resolution.

They included Britain, Russia, France, Italy, and Serbia. On the other side were the Central Powers—Germany, Austria-Hungary, the Ottoman Empire, and Bulgaria.

Many Americans, including President Woodrow Wilson, wanted the United States to be neutral in the war. However, that proved to be difficult. Patrolling the seas were German submarines, called *Unterseeboots*, or U-boats. On May 7, 1915, a U-boat sank the British passenger ship *Lusitania*. Almost 1,200 people were killed, including 128 Americans.

People in the United States were angry at Germany. Some began to believe the United States should enter the war on the side of the Allies. However, President Wilson still hoped to keep the United States neutral. In 1916 he was reelected President. His campaign slogan was "He kept us out of war."

REVIEW Why were many European countries drawn into World War I? because of the alliances they had formed

---

The United States Enters the War

In early 1917, German leaders said that U-boats would begin to attack all ships, including American ships, found in British waters. U-boats soon sank three American ships. On April 2, 1917, President Wilson asked Congress to declare war on Germany, saying,

❝ The world must be made safe for democracy. ❞

Four days later, the United States joined the Allied Powers.

The United States was not prepared for war. Its army was small, and it did not have many weapons. To make the army larger, Congress passed the Selective Service Act. This new law provided for a **military draft**, a way to bring people into military

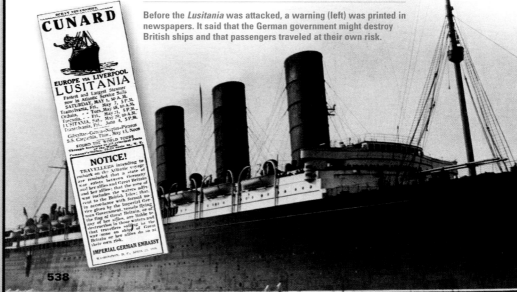

Before the *Lusitania* was attacked, a warning (left) was printed in newspapers. It said that the German government might destroy British ships and that passengers traveled at their own risk.

538

Q **Why did Germany want to attack American ships?**

A Germany wanted to attack any ships that were trying to get to Britain. Their goal was to cut off Britain from trading with other countries. They hoped that this would cripple Britain's economy.

Lusitania The RMA *Lusitania* was a luxury ocean liner owned by a British company. In the early part of the twentieth century, the only way to cross the Atlantic was by ocean liner. Launched in the summer of 1906, the RMA *Lusitania* was a grand ship. At 785 feet (239 m) long and 31,550 gross tons, the ship took the title of the largest liner on the Atlantic at the time. When attacked by German U-boats in 1915, the *Lusitania* sank in 18 minutes, claiming almost 1,200 lives.

World War I

Allied Powers
Central Powers
Neutral countries
👆 Major battle

ATLANTIC OCEAN

North Sea

RUSSIA
• Moscow

IRELAND (BRITAIN) BRITAIN DENMARK
London • NETHERLANDS • Berlin
Paris • BELGIUM GERMANY Tannenberg •
Versailles • LUXEMBOURG
Château- Argonne
Thierry Forest Vienna •
FRANCE SWITZERLAND AUSTRIA-HUNGARY
ITALY Caporetto
Lisbon • • Madrid Corsica MONTENEGRO SERBIA ROMANIA
PORTUGAL Sarajevo • BULGARIA Black Sea
SPAIN • Rome ALBANIA
Sardinia GREECE • Constantinople
Sicily Gallipoli
MOROCCO ALGERIA TUNISIA • Malta OTTOMAN EMPIRE ASIA
(FRANCE) (FRANCE) (FRANCE) Mediterranean Crete Cyprus
SPANISH SAHARA AFRICA Sea

Aral Sea
Caspian Sea

0   250   500 Miles
0   250   500 Kilometers
Azimuthal Equal-Area Projection

GEOGRAPHY THEME

Regions This map shows how the war had divided Europe.
🌐 What problems do you think Germany had because of Allied Powers on both its eastern and western borders?

service. It required all men between the ages of 21 and 30 to sign up with draft boards. Members of the draft boards then used the lists of names to choose who would serve in the military.

Most American soldiers who arrived in Europe in 1917 were sent to France, where much of the fighting took place. Soldiers fought one another from trenches, or ditches, dug in the ground. The trenches of the two opposing sides were separated by a **no-man's-land**. This land was not controlled by either side and was filled with barbed wire and bombs buried in the ground.

Soldiers faced terrible new weapons. The Germans had developed machine guns that fired hundreds of bullets each minute. To fight against these guns, the British built tanks with steel walls. Machine gun bullets could not pass through the tank walls. The most feared of the weapons was poison gas. It killed soldiers—even those in tanks—by making them unable to breathe.

REVIEW Why did the United States decide to enter the war? 🌐 **MAKE INFERENCES**
because American ships were attacked and the world had to be made safe for democracy **Chapter 14 ▪ 539**

Visual Learning

Map Point out to students that this map shows the regions controlled by the Central Powers, the Allied Powers, and the neutral countries in Europe during World War I.
CAPTION ANSWER: Protecting both fronts would divide and weaken Germany's forces.

Read and Respond

History Tell students that in addition to ground weapons, airplanes and hot-air balloons were also used in World War I. Explain that airplanes and balloons were used in the war to observe and bomb enemy troops. Point out that the number of people in the American Air Service, as it was called, was about 1,200 at the beginning of the war and about 200,000 at the end of the war.

Q **What advantage would air strikes have over ground strikes?**

A Enemy troops were easier to spot from the air, and pilots could bomb enemy troops while avoiding much of their fire from the ground.

Changes at Home

Read and Respond

Economics Discuss how people at home supported the war effort. Ask students why these activities were necessary and how they affected the economy. The war required the manufacture of certain supplies and caused the shortage of others, which had to be rationed. The shortage of workers meant jobs for women and African Americans and increased wages for some workers.

The End of the War

Read and Respond

Civics and Government Explain that President Wilson devised a plan to maintain a lasting peace after the war, which he presented to other world leaders gathered in Paris. Tell students that President Wilson described what he called his Fourteen Points for a fair peace in Europe. One of these points called for the creation of an "association of nations." Ask students what this association came to be. the League of Nations

 Close

Summarize Key Content

- World War I began when a Serb rebel killed two members of Austria-Hungary's royal family.
- The United States entered World War I after Germany attacked three American merchant ships.
- World War I offered new roles in factories, offices, and the military for African Americans and women.
- World War I ended when the Germans surrendered and the Treaty of Versailles was signed.

Changes at Home

Building an army and supplying it in a hurry were huge tasks. Goods had to be moved quickly from farms and factories to ports, where they could be shipped to Europe. To help do this, President Wilson set up the War Industries Board to oversee the production and distribution of goods. He also placed all the nation's railroads under government management.

As more and more men left their jobs to go fight in the war, there were fewer and fewer workers at home. Because of this shortage, wages generally rose, and many workers had opportunities to find better jobs. The need for workers especially helped African Americans. Between 1914 and 1919, as part of the Great Migration, half a million African Americans moved to northern cities to find jobs in the war plants there.

Thousands of women also found jobs in factories and offices. They could not have hoped to get such jobs before the war started. Some women became mechanics or worked in weapons factories.

Some went to Europe as nurses or ambulance drivers. Thousands more joined the army or navy as clerks or telegraph operators. Women, however, were not drafted or allowed to fight in the war.

REVIEW **What groups of people found new job opportunities during the war?** Women and African Americans both found new job opportunities.

The End of the War

American efforts made an important difference in World War I. Working together, the Americans and the other Allies began to push back the German army. Finally, on November 11, 1918, the Germans surrendered and signed an armistice that ended the fighting. Before the fighting ended, however, about 53,000 Americans had been killed. Another 230,000 had been wounded.

Allied leaders gathered in Paris, France, to make peace terms. President Wilson did not want Germany or any of its allies to be punished too harshly. However, the other Allied leaders wanted to weaken Germany so it could never again wage war.

During the war, women and African Americans filled jobs left by men who went overseas to serve in the military.

540 ▪ Unit 7

INTEGRATE MATHEMATICS

Computation Ask students to determine how many months the United States fought in World War I.

April 1917 through December 1917 = 9 months

January 1918 to November 1918 = 11 months

9 months + 11 months = 20 months

BACKGROUND

The League of Nations The League of Nations existed from 1920 to 1946. Although the United States supported the league by attending meetings, it did not join the League of Nations. The last meeting of the League of Nations was held on April 8, 1946. At that time the United Nations, which the United States did join, became the primary international organization of nations.

World leaders met at the Palace of Versailles (ver•SY), near Paris, to sign the treaty that officially ended World War I. All together, more than 8 million people died in the war.

During these talks Wilson described his idea for a League of Nations. He hoped this organization would help avoid future wars by finding peaceful ways to solve nations' conflicts. The Treaty of Versailles (ver•SY), which officially ended the war, set up the League of Nations. The United States, however, did not join. The Senate refused to approve the treaty. Many senators believed that membership in the League would involve the United States in other nations' wars. Some wanted the nation to return to a policy of **isolation**—remaining separate from other countries. Twenty years later this policy would again be challenged.

REVIEW What happened when the United States did not approve the Treaty of Versailles?
The United States did not join the League of Nations.

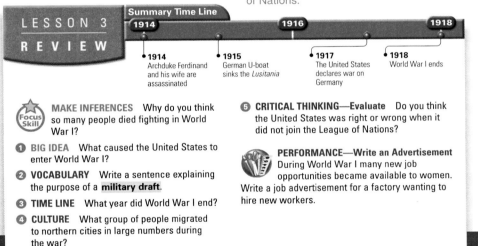

LESSON 3 REVIEW

Summary Time Line

1914 — 1916 — 1918

- **1914** Archduke Ferdinand and his wife are assassinated
- **1915** German U-boat sinks the *Lusitania*
- **1917** The United States declares war on Germany
- **1918** World War I ends

 MAKE INFERENCES Why do you think so many people died fighting in World War I?

1 **BIG IDEA** What caused the United States to enter World War I?

2 **VOCABULARY** Write a sentence explaining the purpose of a **military draft**.

3 **TIME LINE** What year did World War I end?

4 **CULTURE** What group of people migrated to northern cities in large numbers during the war?

5 **CRITICAL THINKING—Evaluate** Do you think the United States was right or wrong when it did not join the League of Nations?

PERFORMANCE—Write an Advertisement During World War I many new job opportunities became available to women. Write a job advertisement for a factory wanting to hire new workers.

Chapter 14 ■ 541

READING SOCIAL STUDIES

Anticipation Guide Have students check their responses to the Anticipation Guide.

1. The United States joined the ~~Central Powers~~ in the Great War.
Allied Powers

2. The Selective Service Act provided for a military draft.

● USE READING AND VOCABULARY TRANSPARENCY 7-4. **7-4** TRANSPARENCY

Assess

Lesson 3 Review—Answers

MAKE INFERENCES The war caused many fatalities because of new machine guns, tanks, and poison gas.

1 **BIG IDEA** The United States entered World War I because German U-boats sank American ships.

2 **VOCABULARY** A **military draft** is designed to bring people into the armed forces.

3 **TIME LINE** 1918

4 **CULTURE** African Americans

5 **CRITICAL THINKING—Evaluate** Students should support their opinions with valid reasons.

 Performance Assessment Guidelines Students' advertisements should be directed toward women. Students should include specific information about the factory and the kind of jobs available.

ACTIVITY BOOK

Use ACTIVITY BOOK, p. 137, to reinforce and extend student learning.

EXTEND AND ENRICH

Simulation Divide the class into two groups with one group representing the United States and the other group representing the other Allied Powers. Give students time to prepare and then simulate a debate that might have taken place between the countries at the peace talks in Paris.

RETEACH THE LESSON

Make a Time Line Divide the class into small groups. Challenge each group to make a time line of the main events of World War I. Have the groups share and discuss their completed time lines.

Lesson 4
PAGES 542–549

OBJECTIVES

- Identify new forms of artistic and musical expression in the 1920s.
- Analyze the changes industries brought in the 1920s.
- Analyze the stock market crash of 1929 and the economic changes it caused.
- Identify New Deal programs and describe their effects.

 Make Inferences pp. 523, 524, 525, 526, 529, 534, 536, 539, 541, 542, 546, 549, 550

Vocabulary

SEE READING AND VOCABULARY TRANSPARENCY 7-5 OR THE WORD CARDS ON PP. V81–V84.

consumer good p. 544	**mechanization of agriculture** p. 546
assembly line p. 544	**stock market** p. 547
division of labor p. 544	**depression** p. 547
industrialization p. 545	**bureaucracy** p. 549
urbanization p. 546	**unemployment** p. 549

When Minutes Count

Have pairs of students work together to find the answers to the review questions.

Quick Summary

This lesson compares the opportunities of the 1920s with the hardships of the 1930s.

 Motivate

Set the Purpose

Big Idea Point out that life in the United States changed dramatically during the 1920s and 1930s.

 ·LESSON·

4

 MAKE INFERENCES

As you read, make inferences about how life changed as the good times of the 1920s were replaced by the hard times of the 1930s.

BIG IDEA

Life in the United States during the 1920s was very different than life during the 1930s.

VOCABULARY

consumer good
assembly line
division of labor
industrialization
urbanization
mechanization of agriculture
stock market
depression
bureaucracy
unemployment

Good Times and Hard Times

1901   1951   2001
1900–1930

The early 1920s were good times for many Americans. People looked forward to new opportunities and wanted to enjoy themselves. For this reason, the 1920s are often called the Roaring Twenties. Many Americans thought these good times would go on forever. By the end of the decade, however, Americans again faced hard times.

New Forms of Expression

Many people in the 1920s were looking for new ways to express themselves. This new spirit of artistic freedom influenced many art forms during the Roaring Twenties. Among them was a new kind of music called jazz.

Jazz grew out of the African American musical heritage made up of music brought from West Africa and spirituals that enslaved people had sung in the United States. In the 1920s

Louis Armstrong

FAST FACT Jazz was so popular among Americans that some have called the 1920s the Jazz Age.

542 ■ Unit 7

INTEGRATE MUSIC

Listen to Jazz Play some of Duke Ellington's or Louis Armstrong's jazz music from the 1920s for students. Check with your local library for recordings. Discuss with students what they think about jazz music.

Nipper, the dog on RCA Victor's label, first appeared on phonographs and records in 1901. Charlie Chaplin (right) was the most popular comic actor of the time.

This is the great picture upon which the famous comedian has worked a whole year.

6 reels of Joy.

Charles Chaplin IN "THE KID"

Written and directed by Charles Chaplin

A First National Attraction

jazz musicians such as Duke Ellington and Louis Armstrong helped make this form of music popular.

Both Ellington and Armstrong often performed in the New York City neighborhood of Harlem. So many African American musicians, artists, and writers lived and worked in Harlem during the 1920s that this time came to be known as the Harlem Renaissance.

One of the best-known writers of the Harlem Renaissance was the poet Langston Hughes. He described Harlem during the 1920s as a magnet for African Americans from across the country. Writers such as Claude McKay, Countee Cullen, and Zora Neale Hurston went to Harlem to share their talents.

This time of artistic freedom also encouraged other Americans to create new ways of doing things. Frank Lloyd Wright, for example, used new designs to create unique buildings. Painter Georgia O'Keeffe created paintings about city life.

New forms of entertainment gave Americans new ways to spend their free time. The first commercial radio stations began broadcasting in the 1920s. By 1929 more than 800 stations were reaching about 10 million families. By listening to the radio, Americans could follow news and sporting events from around the country.

Another popular pastime was attending the movies. The movie business, based in Hollywood, California, started making silent films before World War I. By the late 1920s, many movies were talkies—they were made with sound.

REVIEW What forms of entertainment were popular in the 1920s? listening to jazz music, listening to the radio, and watching movies

Industries Bring More Changes

When World War I ended, there was no longer a demand for factories to produce weapons and other war supplies. Factories started to make products such as vacuum cleaners, washing machines, refrigerators, toasters, radios, and other new electric appliances for the home.

Chapter 14 ▪ 543

Access Prior Knowledge

Ask volunteers to describe what they know about the Roaring Twenties and the Great Depression.

READING SOCIAL STUDIES

K-W-L Chart Have students complete the first two columns of a K-W-L chart about the 1920s and 1930s. Encourage students to look for the answers in the lesson.

What I Know	What I Want to Know	What I Learned
Cars became popular in the 1920s.	What other kinds of products were made in the 1920s?	
Many people had no money or jobs during the Great Depression.	What caused the Great Depression?	

● USE READING AND VOCABULARY TRANSPARENCY 7-5.

 7-5 TRANSPARENCY

2 Teach

New Forms of Expression

Read and Respond

Link History with Culture and Society Emphasize that the Harlem Renaissance brought about new interest in civil rights. African Americans returned from World War I proud and determined to secure their rights as Americans.

Culture and Society Point out that after the war, Americans began focusing on themselves. This focus led to greater individualism and artistic expression, which took form in the clothing, music, and art of the 1920s.

Industries Bring More Changes

Read and Respond

Economics Review the concepts of supply and demand with students. Ask students to describe how the laws of supply and demand helped Henry Ford's company grow. Have students fill in the following flow chart, detailing the growth of Ford's company.

> **Ford developed mass production using the assembly line.**
>
> ↓
>
> **Employees each performed one task on the assembly line.**
>
> ↓
>
> **Automobiles were produced faster and for less money.**
>
> ↓
>
> **More people wanted automobiles because they were cheaper to buy.**
>
> ↓
>
> **Ford's company grew by selling more automobiles.**

A CLOSER LOOK
Ford's Factory

Direct students' attention to the illustration on pages 544–545. Point out that the assembly line method enabled workers to produce cars much faster than before. Ask students what other products they think could be produced easily on an assembly line.

CAPTION ANSWER: Assembly lines could produce more cars in less time for less money.

Students might enjoy researching information about other factories. Have them visit The Learning Site at **www.harcourtschool.com**.

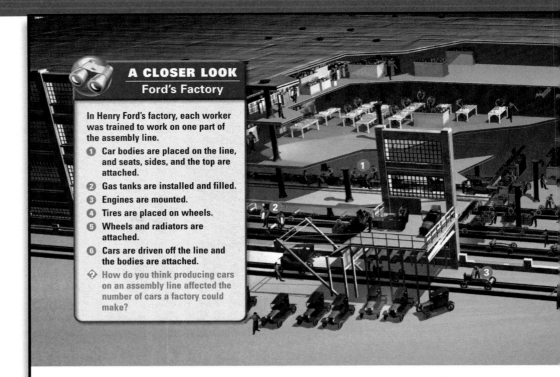

A CLOSER LOOK
Ford's Factory

In Henry Ford's factory, each worker was trained to work on one part of the assembly line.

1. Car bodies are placed on the line, and seats, sides, and the top are attached.
2. Gas tanks are installed and filled.
3. Engines are mounted.
4. Tires are placed on wheels.
5. Wheels and radiators are attached.
6. Cars are driven off the line and the bodies are attached.

◇ How do you think producing cars on an assembly line affected the number of cars a factory could make?

These **consumer goods**—the name given to products made for personal use— were possible because more people had electricity in their homes.

Americans had a variety of consumer goods to choose from, but perhaps the most important were automobiles. The first successful gasoline-powered automobile had been built in the 1890s. By the time the United States entered World War I, companies were producing about 1 million cars a year. By 1923 they were making more than 3 million.

One of the reasons for this dramatic growth in the automobile industry was the work of a man from Michigan, named Henry Ford. Ford had developed a system of mass production that relied on a moving **assembly line**. Instead of being built one at a time, Ford's cars were assembled, or put together, as they moved past a line of workers.

Each worker at Ford's factory was trained to do only one task, such as putting in headlights or seats. Other workers along the assembly line did other tasks until the car was finished. Dividing work so that each worker does only part of a larger job is called **division of labor**. By using an assembly line and dividing the labor among his workers, Ford could produce automobiles faster and cheaper and still afford to pay his workers well. By 1925 a person could buy one of Ford's cars for about $260.

Once automobiles became more affordable, the demand for them rose sharply. This demand also affected the growth of

544 ■ Unit 7

BACKGROUND

Robber Barons From the 1880s into the early twentieth century, the growth of industry brought great wealth to entrepreneurs. During the 1920s, however, some people compared the great industrialists to early English barons who had gained great riches by exploiting their workers. In 1934 Matthew Josephson argued this point in a book named *The Robber Barons*. The term "robber baron" soon became popular with people who did not like the great industialists.

INTEGRATE READING

Read a Biography
Encourage students to choose from this lesson a famous figure of the 1920s, such as Charles Lindbergh, Clarence Birdseye, Henry Ford, the Wright brothers, George Washington Carver, Duke Ellington, Louis Armstrong, Langston Hughes, Frank Lloyd Wright, Georgia O'Keeffe, or Charlie Chaplin. Have each student locate and read a biography of the person he or she chooses and write a short summary about the person to be presented in class.

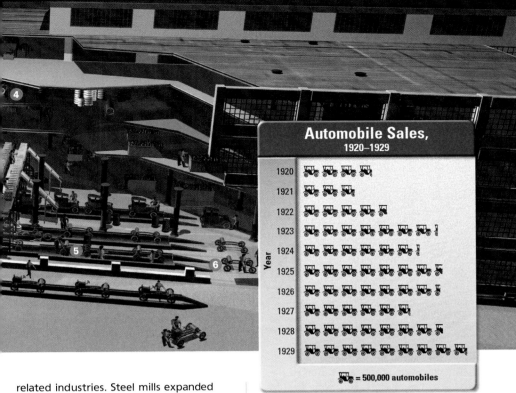

Automobile Sales,
1920–1929

Year	
1920	🚗 🚗 🚗
1921	🚗 🚗 🚗
1922	🚗 🚗 🚗 🚗
1923	🚗 🚗 🚗 🚗 🚗 ⅰ
1924	🚗 🚗 🚗 🚗 🚗 ⅰ
1925	🚗 🚗 🚗 🚗 🚗 🚗 ⅰ
1926	🚗 🚗 🚗 🚗 🚗 🚗 ⅰ
1927	🚗 🚗 🚗 🚗 🚗
1928	🚗 🚗 🚗 🚗 🚗 🚗 ⅰ
1929	🚗 🚗 🚗 🚗 🚗 🚗 🚗 🚗

🚗 = 500,000 automobiles

Source: Historical Statistics of the United States

Analyze Graphs Henry Ford's idea of producing cars on an assembly line helped increase sales of automobiles.

◈ About how many cars were sold in 1929?

related industries. Steel mills expanded so that they could supply more steel for making automobiles. More tires, oil, and gas were needed, too. The demand for these products increased as farmers began to use gasoline-powered tractors.

Air transportation also contributed to the nation's **industrialization** (in•duhs•tree•uh•luh•ZAY•shuhn), or the growth of industries. Two brothers, Orville and Wilbur Wright, had made the first flight in 1903 at Kitty Hawk, North Carolina. Over the years, the airplane was improved, but very few people traveled by plane.

Then, on May 20, 1927, Charles Lindbergh, an American airmail pilot, took off from New York in a small plane named the *Spirit of St. Louis*. His goal was

to be the first person to fly nonstop across the Atlantic Ocean. About 34 hours after leaving New York, Lindbergh finally arrived in Paris, France. Lindbergh's flight helped make people more interested in air travel, and soon commercial airlines were making flights.

Advances in technology in the 1920s changed American eating habits, too. George Washington Carver was an African American scientist and teacher who worked at the Tuskegee Institute.

Chapter 14 ■ 545

The Growth of Cities

Read and Respond

Civics and Government Explain to students that many people who lived in cities in the late 1800s lived in poverty. The large numbers of people moving into cities strained local governments.

Q **What services does your local government provide? What would happen if your city stopped collecting garbage?**

A Possible responses: clean water, garbage collection, and wastewater systems. My city or town would get dirty and unpleasant.

Emphasize that this kind of problem happened regularly in many growing cities in the late 1800s and the early 1900s.

Economics Review with students the definition of *surplus*. Lead students to understand how surpluses forced many people to leave their farms. Have students complete the graphic organizer about the effects of mechanization of agriculture. List the causes for them, and have them fill in the effects.

Causes	Effects
Machines were used to plant and harvest crops.	Farmers could farm more land.
Farmers could plant more crops.	There was a surplus of crops.
The prices paid for crops dropped.	Farmers moved to the city to look for work.

Culture and Society Tell students that labor unions argued for laws to protect workers. Ask students why unions wanted a minimum wage and a maximum number of working hours. Possible response: to prevent employers from mistreating their workers.

He became well known for his work with peanuts and ways to improve farming. Carver and his students developed hundreds of new food products from peanuts, sweet potatoes, and soybeans. His advice to southern farmers to grow peanuts as a cash crop helped the region's economy.

Clarence Birdseye developed a method of freezing foods that helped preserve their original taste. His quick-frozen foods, which he sold in small packages, were an immediate success and helped change the way Americans ate.

REVIEW How did the growth of the automobile industry affect related industries?
Steel mills expanded, more oil and gas was needed.

The Growth of Cities

The continuing industrialization of the United States also affected where people lived in the 1920s. For the first time in the nation's history, more people in the United States lived in urban areas than on farms. In fact, the population of many cities doubled during the 1920s.

As a result of this **urbanization** (ur•buh•nuh•ZAY•shuhn), or movement of people to cities, cities changed in other ways. Skyscrapers and large apartment buildings became part of many city skylines. Downtown streets became crowded with cars and buses.

As cities grew, the suburbs around them also grew. Cars and buses made it possible for more people to work in cities and live in suburbs outside them.

While the population of the cities increased, the number of Americans

546 ■ **Unit 7**

Fewer workers were needed due to **Clarence Birdseye** the mechanization of agriculture, so workers left.

living in farming communities decreased. During the 1920s more of the equipment that farmers used to prepare their fields and to plant and harvest crops became mechanized (MEH•kuh•nizd), or powered by machines. As a result of this **mechanization of agriculture**, farmers could plant more land than they could when work had to be done by hand or when equipment was powered by horses or mules. Improved farming equipment increased the amount of crops that were grown on American farms. However, the surplus drove down the prices of many crops, forcing people to sell their farms.

As a result of the change, fewer farm workers were needed. Many workers left farms and sought jobs in cities. Some of these workers joined labor unions. A labor union is a group of workers who join together to improve their pay and working conditions.

REVIEW Why did so many people leave farming communities in the 1920s?
MAKE INFERENCES

Many skyscrapers and apartment buildings were built in New York City as a result of urbanization.

WORD WORK

Suffixes Draw students' attention to the vocabulary terms on pages 545 and 546—*industrialization, urbanization,* and *mechanization of agriculture*. Ask students what the words have in common. the suffix *-tion* Review with students that the suffix *-tion* changes a verb into a noun. Ask students what the verb is in each of the three vocabulary terms. industrialize, urbanize, and mechanize

BACKGROUND

Labor Unions The first national labor group to remain active for an extended period was the Noble Order of the Knights of Labor, established in 1869. In 1886 this group was reorganized as the American Federation of Labor, or AFL. At first the AFL and other unions worked for widespread social reform, but by the early 1900s most union leaders were concentrating on higher wages and fewer working hours.

The Great Depression

People can make money in many ways. For example, they can buy real estate or bonds. When a person buys a bond, they get the money back with interest after several years.

During the 1920s, many Americans chose a riskier way to make money. They invested money in the stock market. The **stock market** is a place where people can buy or sell stocks, or shares in businesses. If more people want to sell than buy, the price goes down. During the 1920s the prices on stocks kept rising. People even borrowed sums of money to invest.

Beginning in the fall of 1929, some people decided to take their money out of the stock market. This caused stock prices to fall. As prices fell, many investors decided to sell, too. Soon panicked stockholders were trying to sell all their stocks. On October 29, 1929, the stock market crashed. Nearly everyone who owned stocks lost money.

The crash of the stock market ended the good times of the Roaring Twenties. Soon people everywhere were facing hard times as businesses failed and an economic depression gripped the nation and the rest of the world. A **depression** is a time of little economic growth when there are few jobs and people have little money. This depression, which continued through the 1930s, was so bad that it became known as the Great Depression.

After the stock market crash, many people needed to spend their savings in order to live. Large numbers of them tried to take money out of the banks.

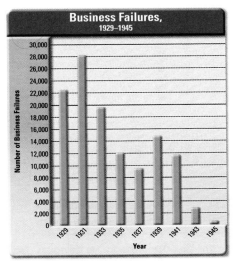

Analyze Graphs **This graph shows the number of companies that went out of business from 1929 to 1945.**

◆ About how many companies went out of business in 1931?

Source: Historical Statistics of the United States

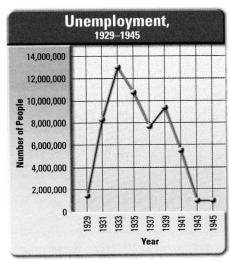

Analyze Graphs **This line graph shows the number of people who lost their jobs from 1929 to 1945.**

◆ How did the number of unemployed people change over time?

The Great Depression

Read and Respond

Economics Discuss with students the danger in buying stocks with borrowed money. Point out that when you borrow money, you have to pay back the money you have borrowed plus the interest on that money. Write the following example on the board as you explain it to students: Paul borrows $100 from a bank to buy $100 worth of stocks. Paul must pay back the bank $100 plus $10 of interest within 1 year. If Paul's stock falls and is worth only $40, not only has he lost $60, but he still owes the bank $110.

Economics Emphasize that when you put your money in a bank, it does not sit in a vault. The bank uses it. Explain that banks take money that has been deposited and use it to give other people loans.

Economics Explain to students that people take risks in the hope that their money will increase in value. Some options are riskier than others, but they may cause money to increase in value much faster. Investing in real estate or bonds is often less risky than investing in the stock market. However, money invested in stocks could double or triple in value in a single day.

Visual Learning

Bar Graph Direct students to the bar graph on page 547. Work with the students to interpret the data presented.
CAPTION ANSWER: About 28,000 companies

Line Graph Direct students to the line graph on page 547. Have students speculate about what caused the decline in unemployment between 1933 and 1937.
CAPTION ANSWER: Unemployment rose sharply in the beginning of Great Depression and then began to fall steadily.

Dust Bowl Region

Understanding Environment and Society Help students locate the Dust Bowl region on the map. Discuss with students the effect that the severe droughts had on farmers and the economy.

The New Deal

Read and Respond

Link Civics and Government with Economics Ask students to describe how President Franklin Roosevelt's New Deal programs helped workers. Students should respond that the programs created jobs for workers who were unemployed. Discuss how providing more jobs can stimulate the economy. Explain that if people have jobs, they have more money to spend.

Culture and Society Ask students to consider what effect new roads, airports, and public buildings had on society. Possible response: They gave people hope that the economy would improve.

3 Close

Summarize Key Content

- Many new forms of artistic expression appeared in the 1920s.
- As a result of industrialization and urbanization, many cities doubled in size during the 1920s.
- The mechanization of agriculture allowed farmers to produce more crops by using fewer people, which led to many people leaving farms.
- During the Great Depression many people lost their savings and their jobs.
- President Franklin D. Roosevelt's New Deal set up programs to give people jobs building roads, bridges, and airports.

Dust Bowl Region
Understanding Environment and Society

The Dust Bowl was the name given to a section of the southern Great Plains that suffered a series of severe droughts, or periods with little or no rain, through the 1930s. The Dust Bowl region was spread out over parts of Colorado, Kansas, Texas, Oklahoma, and New Mexico. The dust storms that developed in this area were known as "black blizzards" because the swirling dirt often blocked the sun. The storms forced thousands of farm families to leave their homes.

A father and son in Oklahoma raise the fence on their property to keep it from being buried by soil.

Many banks closed. People who had money in them lost all their savings.

Because people had little money to spend, manufacturers could not sell what they had made. Factory workers then lost their jobs and could not pay what they owed to banks and businesses. So more banks and businesses failed. More farmers lost their farms.

President Herbert Hoover, who was elected in 1928, tried to give everyone hope. "Prosperity," he said, "is just around the corner." But it was not. By 1932 thousands of businesses had closed. One of every four American workers was without a job. Hungry people stood in line for bread or free meals.

REVIEW How did the Great Depression affect both manufacturers and workers?
Manufacturers could not sell what they made, which caused workers to lose their jobs.

The New Deal

In 1932 the American people elected Franklin D. Roosevelt as President. Roosevelt believed that to end the Great Depression, the federal government needed to take bold, new action. On his inauguration day, he told Americans,

> 66 The only thing we have to fear is fear itself. 99

Roosevelt's words gave people hope that things would improve. He quickly developed a plan to combat the effects of the Great Depression. He called his plan the New Deal. Its goal was to get people back to work.

The New Deal gave the federal government more authority. It also made it

---

Expressive Writing
Ask students to imagine they lived in the Dust Bowl during the droughts in the 1930s. Have students write descriptions of how their homes and fields looked the morning after a huge dust storm. Ask students to read their descriptions to the class.

Hoover Dam President Hoover supported many public works programs during the Depression. In 1928, the federal government designed and supervised the construction of a new dam on the Colorado River in Arizona. The project cost $385 million and provided employment for many Americans. Hoover Dam, as the structure was later named, is one of the world's highest concrete dams.

larger. This growing number of government workers formed a bureaucracy. A **bureaucracy** (byu•RAH•kruh•see) is the many workers and groups that are needed to run government programs.

One New Deal program was called the Civilian Conservation Corps, or CCC. The CCC hired thousands of young men to build bridges, plant trees, and do other helpful things. Another program, the Works Progress Administration, or WPA, hired workers to build roads, airports, and public buildings. The WPA also hired writers and artists to record life during the Great Depression.

To further growth, Congress set up the Tennessee Valley Authority, or TVA. The purpose of the TVA was to control flooding on the Tennessee River system and produce electricity with hydroelectric dams. The government would then sell the electricity at low rates to users.

President Roosevelt had high hopes for his New Deal programs.

Even with all of President Roosevelt's new programs, **unemployment**, or the number of people without jobs, remained high. But at least unemployment did not get worse.

REVIEW What was the New Deal?
A plan that gave the government more authority and made it larger so it could run government programs.

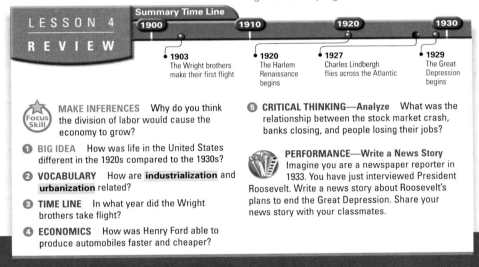

LESSON 4 REVIEW

Summary Time Line

1900	1910	1920	1930

- **1903** The Wright brothers make their first flight
- **1920** The Harlem Renaissance begins
- **1927** Charles Lindbergh flies across the Atlantic
- **1929** The Great Depression begins

 MAKE INFERENCES Why do you think the division of labor would cause the economy to grow?

1 BIG IDEA How was life in the United States different in the 1920s compared to the 1930s?

2 VOCABULARY How are **industrialization** and **urbanization** related?

3 TIME LINE In what year did the Wright brothers take flight?

4 ECONOMICS How was Henry Ford able to produce automobiles faster and cheaper?

5 CRITICAL THINKING—Analyze What was the relationship between the stock market crash, banks closing, and people losing their jobs?

PERFORMANCE—Write a News Story Imagine you are a newspaper reporter in 1933. You have just interviewed President Roosevelt. Write a news story about Roosevelt's plans to end the Great Depression. Share your news story with your classmates.

Chapter 14 ■ 549

READING SOCIAL STUDIES

K-W-L Chart Have students complete their K-W-L charts.

What I Know	What I Want to Know	What I Learned
Cars became popular in the 1920s.	What other kinds of products were made in the 1920s?	vacuum cleaners, washing machines, and other consumer goods
Many people had no money or jobs during the Great Depression.	What caused the Great Depression?	The Great Depression was caused by the stock market crashing.

● USE READING AND VOCABULARY TRANSPARENCY 7-5.

 7-5 TRANSPARENCY

Assess

Lesson 4 Review—Answers

 MAKE INFERENCES Products were produced faster and cheaper. People could afford more, so they bought more.

1 BIG IDEA In the 1920s people had jobs and industries were growing. In the 1930s the economy went into a depression.

2 VOCABULARY Industrialization caused **urbanization** by turning towns into cities.

3 TIME LINE in 1903

4 ECONOMICS He used an assembly line.

5 CRITICAL THINKING—Analyze The crash caused many people to withdraw their savings, and banks closed. With very few people buying products, factories closed and people lost their jobs.

Performance Assessment Guidelines News stories should be well written and contain facts about Roosevelt's plan to end the Great Depression.

ACTIVITY BOOK

Use ACTIVITY BOOK, p. 138, to reinforce and extend student learning.

EXTEND AND ENRICH

Compose a Story Ask students to imagine that they were successful bankers who lost all of their money in the stock market crash of 1929. Ask them to write short stories about what they did after they lost all of their money. Have the students share their stories with the class.

RETEACH THE LESSON

Write Questions Organize the class into five groups. Assign each group a subsection of the lesson. Ask each group to write five questions that can be answered with information from the subsection. Have each group ask its questions of the class. Make sure the questions are all answered correctly.

Chapter 14 Review

 MAKE INFERENCES

Students may use the graphic organizer that appears on page 139 of the Activity Book. Answers appear in the Activity Book, Teacher's Edition.

Think & Write

Write an Informative Letter
Students' letters should include accurate references to the different points of view concerning Hawaiian annexation. Some points of view they might consider are those of the Hawaiian people, the royal family, Christian missionaries, American businesspeople, and American politicians.

Write a Packing List
Students' lists should display an understanding of the change in way of living that occurred when moving from a farming community to the city in the early 1900s. Items to bring may include clothes and furniture. Items to sell may include farm tools, land, and animals. Items to purchase may include tools for work.

ACTIVITY BOOK

A copy of the graphic organizer appears in the ACTIVITY BOOK on page 139.

TRANSPARENCY

The graphic organizer appears on READING AND VOCABULARY TRANSPARENCY 7-6.

· CHAPTER ·

14 Review and Test Preparation

Summary Time Line
1880

 Make Inferences

Copy the following graphic organizer onto a separate sheet of paper. Use the information you have learned to make inferences about the Great Depression.

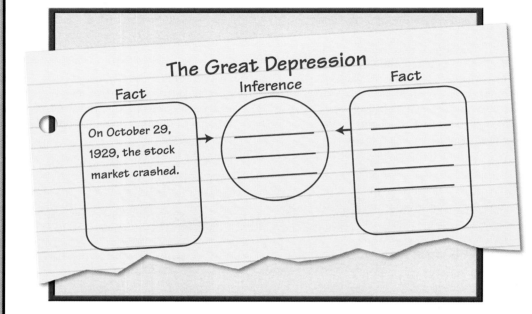

Write an Informative Letter Imagine you are living in the Hawaiian Islands during the late nineteenth century. Write a letter to a friend explaining why some people want the United States to annex Hawaii and other people do not.

Write a Packing List Imagine your family has decided to move from a small farming community to a large city. Write a list of items to pack for your journey and a list of things you might have to purchase when you arrive in the city.

550 ■ Chapter 14

TEST PREPARATION

Review these tips with students:

- Read the directions before reading the questions.

- Read each question twice, focusing the second time on all the possible answers.

- Take the time to think about all the possible answers before deciding on an answer.

- Move past questions that give you trouble, and answer the ones you know. Then return to the difficult items.

UNIT PROJECT

Progress Check Remind students that the notes they take now will be useful to them as they prepare for the Unit Project. Suggest that students begin an outline with the headings of *Key People, Events,* and *Places of the Twentieth Century.*

1920   1940

1906
Congress passes
the Pure Food
and Drug Act

1915
The *Lusitania*
is sunk

1917
The United
States enters
World War I

1920
The Nineteenth
Amendment
is passed

1929
The Great
Depression
begins

1933
President
Roosevelt
introduces
the New Deal

USE THE TIME LINE

Use the chapter summary time line to answer these questions.

1 When was the Nineteenth Amendment passed?

2 How many years after the Great Depression began was the New Deal introduced?

USE VOCABULARY

Identify the term that correctly matches each definition.

suffrage (p. 535)

isolation (p. 541)

unemployment (p. 549)

3 remaining separate from other countries

4 the number of people without jobs

5 the right to vote

RECALL FACTS

Answer these questions.

6 What event led to the start of World War I?

7 Why did people start to celebrate Labor Day?

8 How did Carrie Chapman Catt work for greater democracy in the United States?

Write the letter of the best choice.

9 One of the results of increased urbanization was that—
 A wheat production in the United States greatly decreased.
 B fewer people worked on farms.
 C the United States had to import much of its food from Europe.
 D political bosses lost all of their power.

10 George Washington Carver and Clarence Birdseye helped change—
 F corrupt city governments.
 G national voting laws.
 H the way Americans traveled.
 J the way Americans eat.

11 One event that started the Great Depression was—
 A the United States' entry into World War I.
 B the stock market crash of 1929.
 C the building of the Panama Canal.
 D the destruction of the battleship *Maine*.

THINK CRITICALLY

12 How did the Spanish-American War help make the United States a world power?

13 Why do you think Jane Addams chose to become involved in her community?

14 How do you think farm life in the 1920s was different from farm life in the 1820s?

15 What effect do you think the Great Depression may have had on other countries?

APPLY SKILLS

Compare Map Projections
Study the maps on pages 530–531. Then answer the following questions.

16 On which map are all the meridians an equal distance apart?

17 On which map does Australia appear to be larger? On which map is the size of Australia more accurate?

Chapter 14 ■ 551

Think Critically

12 The United States was able to increase its land holdings as a result of the war.

13 Students may suggest that she felt that by improving the lives of those in her community, she also would improve her life.

14 Due to advances in technology, work was done for profit more than just subsistence.

15 It probably hurt their economies as the United States' demand for their goods declined.

Apply Skills
Compare Map Projections

16 map B

17 map A; map B

ACTIVITY BOOK

Use the CHAPTER 14 TEST PREPARATION on page 140 of the Activity Book.

ASSESSMENT

Use the CHAPTER 14 TEST on pages 113–116 of the Assessment Program.

Use the Time Line

1 in 1920

2 four

Use Vocabulary

3 isolation (p. 541)

4 unemployment (p. 549)

5 suffrage (p. 535)

Recall Facts

6 the assassination of members of Austria-Hungary's royal family (p. 537)

7 to honor the working people and to recognize their importance to the United States (p. 533)

8 She worked for women's suffrage. (pp. 535–536)

9 B (p. 546)

10 J (pp. 545–546)

11 B (p. 547)

Chapter 15 Planning Guide Global Conflict

Introducing the Chapter, pp. 552–553

LESSON	PACING	OBJECTIVES	VOCABULARY
Introduce the Chapter pp. 552–553	1 Day	■ Identify causes and effects of World War II. ■ Use critical thinking skills to predict outcomes.	**Word Work:** Preview Vocabulary, p. 553
1 World War II Begins pp. 554–558	1 Day	■ Analyze how the aftermath of World War I affected countries worldwide. ■ Analyze the beginning of World War II in Europe. ■ Examine how the United States responded to the beginning of World War II. ■ Discuss what effect Japan's attack on Pearl Harbor had on the United States.	**concentration camp** **dictatorship** **civilian**
READING SKILLS **Predict a Historical Outcome** p. 559	1 Day	■ Analyze information by making predictions. ■ Apply critical thinking skills to analyze and evaluate predictions.	**prediction**
2 Americans and the War pp. 560–563	1 Day	■ Identify how World War II affected the economy of the United States. ■ Discuss how World War II affected American women. ■ Describe and evaluate how World War II affected Japanese Americans.	**rationing** **recycle** **interest** **relocation camp** **Word Work:** Prefixes and Suffixes, p. 560
CITIZENSHIP SKILLS **Make Economic Choices** p. 564	1 Day	■ Identify economic terms and concepts. ■ Understand how economic choices affect people.	**trade-off** **opportunity cost**

READING	INTEGRATE LEARNING	REACH ALL LEARNERS	RESOURCES
(Focus Skill) **Cause and Effect**, p. 553			
Reading Social Studies: **K-W-L Chart**, p. 555 Reading Social Studies: **K-W-L Chart Responses,** p. 558	Science **Report on Technology,** p. 555	**Advanced Learners**, p. 554 **Extend and Enrich**, p. 558 **Reteach the Lesson**, p. 558	**Activity Book**, p. 141 🌐 **Reading and Vocabulary Transparency**, 7-7 💻 Internet Resources
		Extend and Enrich, p. 559 **Reteach the Skill**, p. 559	**Activity Book**, p. 142 🌐 **Skill Transparency**, 7-2
Reading Social Studies: **Study Questions**, p. 561 (Focus Skill) **Cause and Effect**, p. 561 Reading Social Studies: **Study Question Responses**, p. 563		**Extend and Enrich**, p. 563 **Reteach the Lesson**, p. 563	**Activity Book**, p. 143 🌐 **Reading and Vocabulary Transparency**, 7-8
		Extend and Enrich, p. 564 **Reteach the Skill**, p. 564	**Activity Book**, p. 144 🌐 **Skill Transparency**, 7-3

Chapter 15 Planning Guide Global Conflict

LESSON	PACING	OBJECTIVES	VOCABULARY
3 **Winning the War** pp. 565–569	**1 Day**	■ Analyze the importance of the fighting in Africa, Europe, and the Pacific during World War II. ■ Analyze how the war continued in the Pacific after the Allied victory in Europe. ■ Identify the causes and effects of dropping atom bombs on Japan. ■ Identify how the actions of Dwight D. Eisenhower and Harry S. Truman affected society.	**front** **D day** **island-hopping** **Word Work:** Historical Context, p. 565
CHART AND GRAPH SKILLS **Read Parallel Time Lines** pp. 570–571	**1 Day**	■ Interpret information in time lines. ■ Organize information in time lines.	**parallel time line**
4 **The Effects of the War** pp. 572–575	**1 Day**	■ Identify changes that occurred in countries after World War II. ■ Examine the creation of the United Nations and the United States' relationship to other nations in the fight against communism.	**Holocaust** **refugee** **communism** **free world** **cold war** **Word Work:** Categorize Vocabulary, p. 572
Chapter Review and Test Preparation pp. 576–577	**1 Day**		

READING	INTEGRATE LEARNING	REACH ALL LEARNERS	RESOURCES
Reading Social Studies: **Anticipation Guide,** p. 566 Reading Social Studies: **Anticipation Guide Responses,** p. 568	Language Arts **Write a Summary,** p. 566	**Extend and Enrich,** p. 569 **Reteach the Lesson,** p. 569	**Activity Book,** p. 145 🌐 **Reading and Vocabulary Transparency, 7-9**
	Language Arts **Write a News Report,** p. 570	**Extend and Enrich,** p. 571 **Reteach the Skill,** p. 571	**Activity Book,** p. 146 🌐 **Skill Transparency, 7-4**
Reading Social Studies: **Graphic Organizer,** p. 573 (Focus Skill) **Cause and Effect,** p. 573 Reading Social Studies: **Graphic Organizer Responses,** p. 575	Reading **Read About People,** p. 573	**English as a Second Language,** p. 572 **Extend and Enrich,** p. 575 **Reteach the Lesson,** p. 575	**Activity Book,** p. 147 🌐 **Reading and Vocabulary Transparency, 7-10**
		Test Preparation, p. 576	**Activity Book,** pp. 148–149 🌐 **Reading and Vocabulary Transparency, 7-11** ✓ **Assessment Program, Chapter 15 Test,** pp. 117–120

Activity Book

LESSON 1

Name _____ Date _____

World War II Begins

Directions Below is a list of causes and effects related to World War II. Write each cause and effect in the appropriate place on the chart.

❶ Germany invades Poland in 1939.

❷ Dictators rise to power in Germany, Italy, Spain, and the Soviet Union.

❸ Japan attacks Pearl Harbor.

❹ The Soviet Union joins with Britain and France to fight the Axis Powers.

CAUSE ➡	EFFECT
World War I and the economic depression of the 1930s bring hard times to many countries around the world.	2. Dictators rise to power in Germany, Italy, Spain, and the Soviet Union.
3. Japan attacks Pearl Harbor.	The United States declares war on Japan.
1. Germany invades Poland in 1939.	France and Britain declare war on Germany, and World War II begins.
Germany invades the Soviet Union.	4. The Soviet Union joins with Britain and France to fight the Axis Powers.

Use after reading Chapter 15, Lesson 1, pages 554–558.

Activity Book ■ 141

SKILL PRACTICE

Name _____ Date _____

READING SKILLS

Predict a Historical Outcome

Directions The flow chart below lists the steps for predicting a likely outcome. Follow the steps to predict the effects of the end of World War II on the United States economy.

THINK ABOUT WHAT YOU ALREADY KNOW.
At the end of World War I, the United States economy prospered. In the years that followed, new consumer products appeared on the market, and new forms of entertainment became part of American life.

REVIEW NEW INFORMATION YOU HAVE LEARNED.
During World War II, most Americans were able to find good jobs and contribute to the economy.

MAKE A PREDICTION.
The United States economy might also have prospered following World War II.

READ OR GATHER MORE INFORMATION.
Does the new information support my prediction?
Do I need to change my prediction?

GO THROUGH THE STEPS AGAIN IF NECESSARY.

142 ■ Activity Book

Use after reading Chapter 15, Skill Lesson, page 559.

LESSON 2

Name _____ Date _____

Americans and the War

Directions During World War II Americans at home were told to "Use it up, wear it out, make it do, or do without." Write a paragraph that explains the meaning of this motto and the reasons Americans were encouraged to do this during the war.

Students should note that the motto refers to Americans' behavior as consumers during World War II. Food, metals, fuel, and consumer goods were in short supply. The motto encouraged Americans to support rationing, to conserve the goods and resources that they had, and to recycle. This allowed more goods and resources to be devoted to the war effort.

Use after reading Chapter 15, Lesson 2, pages 560–563.

Activity Book ■ 143

SKILL PRACTICE

Name _____ Date _____

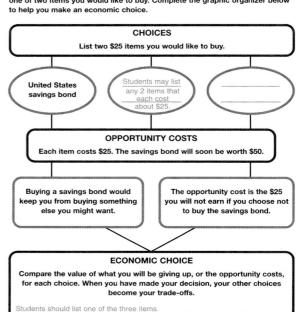

CITIZENSHIP SKILLS

Make Economic Choices

Directions Imagine you have $25 to spend. You must choose between a savings bond which will increase in value after a certain number of years or one of two items you would like to buy. Complete the graphic organizer below to help you make an economic choice.

CHOICES
List two $25 items you would like to buy.

United States savings bond

Students may list any 2 items that each cost about $25.

OPPORTUNITY COSTS
Each item costs $25. The savings bond will soon be worth $50.

Buying a savings bond would keep you from buying something else you might want.

The opportunity cost is the $25 you will not earn if you choose not to buy the savings bond.

ECONOMIC CHOICE
Compare the value of what you will be giving up, or the opportunity costs, for each choice. When you have made your decision, your other choices become your trade-offs.

Students should list one of the three items.

144 ■ Activity Book

Use after reading Chapter 15, Skill Lesson, page 564.

552E ■ CHAPTER 15 ORGANIZER

Name _____ Date _____

Winning the War

Directions Use the terms below to solve the crossword puzzle.

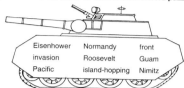

Eisenhower	Normandy	front
invasion	Roosevelt	Guam
Pacific	island-hopping	Nimitz

Across
3 Ocean that surrounds Hawaii
4 D day landing site
7 Allies' plan for defeating Japan

Down
1 Action taken by Allies on D day
2 Commander of Allied troops in Europe

4 American admiral in the Pacific
5 President of the United States during most of World War II
6 Battle line
8 Important Pacific island captured by Allied troops

(Crossword solution)
Across: 3 PACIFIC, 4 NORMANDY, 7 ISLAND-HOPPING
Down: 1 INVASION, 2 EISENHOWER, 5 ROOSEVELT, 6 FRONT, 8 GUAM

Use after reading Chapter 15, Lesson 3, pages 565–569.

Activity Book ■ 145

Name _____ Date _____

CHART AND GRAPH SKILLS
Read Parallel Time Lines

Directions Find the year each of the following events took place. Write the year in the space provided. Then, if the event occurred in the United States, write the letter of the event at the appropriate date below the *Events at Home* time line. Write the letters of all the events that occurred outside the United States at the appropriate date below the *Events Overseas* time line.

1943 A. Allies push Germany out of North Africa.
1940 B. Japan invades Indochina.
1944 C. American troops capture Rome.
1945 D. President Roosevelt dies.
1941 E. President Roosevelt gives the "Date of Infamy" speech.
1943 F. American factories produce almost 86,000 aircraft.

1945 G. Germany surrenders.
1939 H. Germany invades Poland.
1942 I. Japanese Americans are forced to move to relocation camps.
1944 J. Allies launch D-day invasion.
1944 K. Americans elect Franklin Roosevelt for a fourth term as President.
1945 L. Japan surrenders.

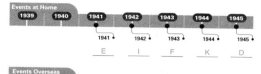

Events at Home
1939 1940 1941 1942 1943 1944 1945
1941 E   1942 I   1943 F   1944 K   1945 D

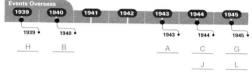

Events Overseas
1939 1940 1941 1942 1943 1944 1945
1939 H   1940 B   1943 A   1944 C   1945 G
                              1944 J   1945 L

146 ■ Activity Book

Use after reading Chapter 15, Skill Lesson, pages 570–571.

Name _____ Date _____

The Effects of War

Directions Write each effect of World War II in the appropriate column of the table below.

• Germany is divided between Britain, France, the Soviet Union, and the United States.
• Nazi leaders are tried for their crimes at Nuremberg.
• More than 12 million people die in Nazi concentration camps; about half are European Jews.
• The Cold War begins.

• Europe and Japan begin rebuilding cities destroyed in the war.
• Representatives from 50 countries form the United Nations.
• The Soviet Union sets up communist governments in Eastern Europe.
• The United States introduces the Marshall Plan.

Effects of World War II		
The Holocaust	**Plans for Peace**	**A Changed World**
More than 12 million people die in Nazi concentration camps; about half are European Jews.	Europe and Japan begin rebuilding cities destroyed in the war.	The Soviet Union sets up communist governments in Eastern Europe.
Nazi leaders are tried for their crimes at Nuremberg.	Germany is divided between Britain, France, the Soviet Union, and the United States.	The United States introduces the Marshall Plan.
	Representatives from 50 countries form the United Nations.	The Cold War begins.

Use after reading Chapter 15, Lesson 4, pages 572–575.

Activity Book ■ 147

Name _____ Date _____

World War II and the United States

Directions Complete this graphic organizer by determining the causes and effects of the involvement of the United States in World War II.

CAUSE
The Japanese attacked Pearl Harbor.

EFFECT
19 American ships are sunk or damaged and 150 planes are destroyed.

EFFECT
The United States enters World War II.

EFFECT
2,000 sailors and soldiers are killed in the attack.

CAUSE
The United States joins the Allied forces.

EFFECT
15 million Americans serve in the armed forces during the war.

EFFECT
Food, fuel, and metals are rationed and the production of many consumer goods is stopped.

EFFECT
Because of the need for large amounts of wartime materials, many people now have jobs.

148 ■ Activity Book

Use after reading Chapter 15, pages 553–575.

TEST PREPARATION

· CHAPTER ·

Name _____ Date _____

15   Test Preparation

Directions Read each question and choose the best answer. Then fill in the circle for the answer you have chosen. Be sure to fill in the circle completely.

1 Who became dictator of the Soviet Union in 1928?
  Ⓐ Adolf Hitler
  Ⓑ Joseph Stalin
  Ⓒ Francisco Franco
  Ⓓ Benito Mussolini

2 By the end of 1941, Germany had taken over—
  Ⓕ Pearl Harbor.
  Ⓖ much of China.
  Ⓗ much of Europe.
  Ⓙ Britain and Canada.

3 During World War II, many American women held jobs as—
  Ⓐ fighter pilots.
  Ⓑ wheat farmers.
  Ⓒ factory workers.
  Ⓓ cattle ranchers.

4 What strategy did the Allies use to defeat Japan in the Pacific?
  Ⓕ the Marshall Plan
  Ⓖ *Blitzkrieg*
  Ⓗ relocation
  Ⓙ island-hopping

5 Why did the Soviet Union join the Allies?
  Ⓐ Germany attempted an invasion of the Soviet Union.
  Ⓑ Japan launched a surprise attack against the Soviet Union.
  Ⓒ The Soviet Union wanted to support other communist nations.
  Ⓓ The Allies offered the Soviet Union aid from the Marshall Plan.

© Harcourt

Use after reading Chapter 15, pages 552–577.

Activity Book ▪ 149

NOTES

COMMUNITY RESOURCES

Historical Societies

Museums

Experts on World War II

Veterans of World War II

Chapter 15 Assessment

•CHAPTER•

Name _____ Date _____

15 Test

Part One: Test Your Understanding

MULTIPLE CHOICE (4 points each)

Directions Circle the letter of the best answer.

1 Germany started World War II when it invaded—?
A Russia.
B Britain.
(C) Poland.
D France.

2 Japan invaded countries in Asia and the Pacific in order to—
F retain the power it had in ancient times.
G pay for damages it caused in World War I.
H begin a revolution.
(J) get resources for its industries.

3 Before the United States entered World War II, the country—
(A) sent food and war supplies to Britain.
B supported Japan's invasion of China.
C signed a peace and defense treaty with France.
D reduced its supply of valuable goods.

4 Americans paid for the cost of waging World War II by buying—
F victory gardens.
G large amounts of meat, butter, and sugar.
(H) war bonds.
J goods from other countries.

5 On D day, June 6, 1944, the Allied forces—
A forced German leaders to surrender in Berlin.
(B) staged the largest water-to-land invasion in history.
C first gained control of the Mediterranean Sea.
D controlled almost all of Europe and North Africa.

6 Which of these events occurred closest to the date of the Japanese surrender in World War II?
F About 100,000 Japanese soldiers died at Okinawa.
G Harry S. Truman became President of the United States.
(H) The United States bombed Nagasaki.
J The Allies developed a battle plan called "island-hopping."

(continued)

Chapter 15 Test   **Assessment Program ■ 117**

CONTENT / VOCABULARY

Name _____ Date _____

7 The largest number of people killed in Nazi concentration camps were—
(A) Jewish people.
B Allied soldiers.
C Germans unable to work.
D political leaders.

8 After World War II the United Nations was formed in order to—
F help settle war refugees in their original homes.
(G) keep world peace and promote cooperation.
H bring Nazi leaders to trial.
J regulate the Nazi party in Germany.

9 The United States helped rebuild Europe by—
(A) providing military and economic aid under the Marshall Plan.
B providing information about the dangers of communism.
C forcing Germany to pay for the damages it caused.
D dividing Germany into four parts.

10 A cold war is fought with—
F Allied groups of nations.
G aircraft.
(H) propaganda and money.
J nuclear weapons.

FILL IN THE BLANK (4 points each)

Directions Fill in the blank with the correct word or words from the list below.

11 During World War II Germany's Nazi government created prisons called ___concentration camps___.

12 The United States government ___rationed___ or limited, the supply of gasoline, meat, and sugar during wartime.

13 In February 1942 about 110,000 Japanese Americans were ordered to move to ___relocation camps___ in several states, including California, Arizona, and Wyoming.

14 The murder of more than 6 million European Jews has come to be known as the ___Holocaust___.

15 In a ___communist___ economic system, all land and industries are owned by the government.

rationed
communist
concentration camps
relocation camps
Holocaust

(continued)

118 ■ Assessment Program   Chapter 15 Test

Name _____ Date _____

Part Two: Test Your Skills

READ PARALLEL TIME LINES (5 points each)

Directions Study the parallel time lines below, and answer the questions that follow.

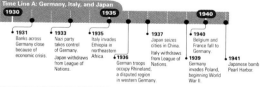

Time Line A: Germany, Italy, and Japan
1930 — 1935 — 1940

1931 Banks across Germany close because of economic crisis.
1933 Nazi party takes control of Germany. Japan withdraws from League of Nations.
1935 Italy invades Ethiopia in northeastern Africa.
1936 German troops occupy Rhineland, a disputed region in western Germany.
1937 Japan seizes cities in China.
1939 Germany invades Poland, beginning World War II.
1940 Belgium and France fall to Germany.
1941 Japanese bomb Pearl Harbor.

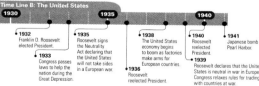

Time Line B: The United States
1930 — 1935 — 1940

1932 Franklin D. Roosevelt elected President.
1933 Congress passes laws to help the nation during the Great Depression.
1935 Roosevelt signs the Neutrality Act declaring that the United States will not take sides in a European war.
1936 Roosevelt reelected President.
1938 The United States economy begins to boom as factories make arms for European countries.
1939 Roosevelt declares that the United States is neutral in war in Europe. Congress relaxes rules for trading with countries at war.
1940 Roosevelt reelected President.
1941 Japanese bomb Pearl Harbor.

16 Which event took place first, the Italian invasion of Ethiopia or the decision of Congress to relax rules for trading with countries at war?
the Italian invasion of Ethiopia

17 Did President Roosevelt sign the Neutrality Act before or after Germany invaded Poland? before

18 Why do you think the event *Japanese bomb Pearl Harbor* is on both time lines?
Possible response: The bombing of Pearl Harbor was a key event for both Japan and the United States.

19 What important event in the United States happened in the year that France and Belgium fell to Germany? Roosevelt was reelected President.

(continued)

Chapter 15 Test   **Assessment Program ■ 119**

Name _____ Date _____

Part Three: Apply What You Have Learned

20 ACTIONS AND REACTIONS (10 points)

Directions Fill in the boxes on the right with the reactions to actions during World War II.

Area	Action	Reaction(s)
European Front	Germany invades Poland.	Possible responses: Allies declare war on Germany; the United States sends supplies to Britain.
Pacific Front	Japan bombs Pearl Harbor.	Possible response: The United States declares war on Japan.
Home Front	Many goods are sent overseas to supply the military, creating shortages at home.	Possible responses: Some goods are rationed; people grow "victory gardens" to make more of their own food.

22 ESSAY (10 points)

Write a paragraph describing how economic problems in Asia and Europe after World War I contributed to World War II, and explain how World War II affected the economy of the United States.

Possible response: Germany suffered terrible inflation after World War I. The country did not have enough money to pay its debt for damages it caused in World War I. Japan did not have the resources it needed for its industries, so it invaded other Asian nations to acquire their resources. The United States was suffering from the Great Depression, but wartime industry helped its economy and put many people back to work. Farmers received good prices for their crops, and many people worked in shipyards and aircraft plants.

120 ■ Assessment Program   Chapter 15 Test

Introduce the Chapter

OBJECTIVES

■ Identify causes and effects of World War II.

■ Use critical thinking skills to predict outcomes.

Access Prior Knowledge

Encourage students to think about the beginnings of the Revolutionary War, the Civil War, and World War I. Have students discuss the causes of each war. How were they similar? How were they different?

Visual Learning

Photograph Ask students to examine the photograph and have them describe the *USS Arizona* Memorial. How does this photograph connect to the topic of global conflict?

Locate It Map Pearl Harbor is a harbor on the Hawaiian Island of Oahu. The Pearl Harbor Naval Base covers more than 20,000 acres and is the center of all the United States Navy's Pacific operations. The *USS Arizona* Memorial is located in Pearl Harbor, just west of Honolulu.

ARIZONA MEMORIAL

The *USS Arizona* Memorial is anchored at Pearl Harbor. It was built to honor the 1,177 sailors who lost their lives on December 7, 1941. The memorial is positioned above the sunken battleship that still lies on the ocean floor. President Dwight D. Eisenhower approved the creation of the memorial, which was dedicated in 1962.

LOCATE IT

HAWAII

USS Arizona Memorial, Pearl Harbor

BACKGROUND

Picture Inform students that the *USS Arizona* Memorial serves to commemorate those sailors who lost their lives on December 7, 1941. On that day, Japanese bombers destroyed or damaged twenty-one United States naval vessels. The single biggest loss was the *USS Arizona*, which sank in less than nine minutes. More than half of the total fatalities in the Pearl Harbor bombing were sailors on the *USS Arizona*.

BACKGROUND

Quotation President Roosevelt was the first and only President to be elected to four terms. He led the country through many difficult times, including the Great Depression and World War II. His actions and words affected world leaders and world events. His speech to Congress on December 8, 1941, reflected the outrage and determination of the American people.

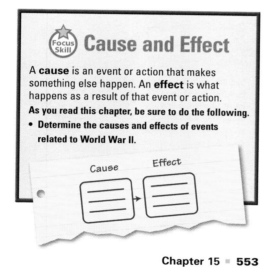

15

Global Conflict

 Yesterday, December 7, 1941—a date which will live in infamy—

—Franklin D. Roosevelt, December 8, 1941, in a message to Congress

Cause and Effect

A **cause** is an event or action that makes something else happen. An **effect** is what happens as a result of that event or action.

As you read this chapter, be sure to do the following.

- Determine the causes and effects of events related to World War II.

Cause   Effect

Read and Respond

Have students discuss the connection between the chapter title and the quotation.

Quotation Have a volunteer read the quotation aloud.

Q What do you think the word "infamy" means?

A Explain that *infamy* means to be known as criminal, shocking, or disgraceful.

Cause and Effect

Have students complete a graphic organizer to show the causes and effects of the war. Point out that words like *because, therefore, so,* and *since* often signal cause-and-effect relationships.

- A blank cause-and-effect graphic organizer can be found on page 148 of the Activity Book.

- A completed graphic organizer can be found on page 148 of the Activity Book, Teacher's Edition.

Cause   Effect

WORD WORK

Preview Vocabulary Have students make a list of the vocabulary terms in this chapter. Then have students read through the lessons and write brief definitions of the terms. Ask students to concentrate on the words that could have multiple meanings. Students should list the alternate meanings of these words next to the definitions from the chapter.

MAKE IT RELEVANT

Discussion Topics Students might enjoy discussing these topics as they read the chapter.

- Why do you think advances in science and technology sometimes occur during times of war?

- How can citizens help their country during a war?

- If a similar situation arose today, do you think people in the United States today would make the same kinds of sacrifices they did during World War II?

Lesson 1

OBJECTIVES

- Analyze how the aftermath of World War I affected countries worldwide.
- Analyze the beginning of World War II in Europe.
- Examine how the United States responded to the beginning of World War II.
- Discuss what effect Japan's attack on Pearl Harbor had on the United States.

 Cause and Effect pp. 553, 554, 557, 558, 576

Vocabulary

SEE READING AND VOCABULARY TRANSPARENCY 7-7 OR THE WORD CARDS ON PP. V85–V86.

concentration camp p. 555

dictatorship p. 555

civilian p. 557

 When Minutes Count

Ask students to examine the photographs and captions in this lesson. Then have them write a brief summary that describes the Big Idea of the lesson.

Quick Summary

This lesson explains how World War II began and how countries around the world became involved.

 Motivate

Set the Purpose

Big Idea Make sure students understand why the conflict was called a world war.

Access Prior Knowledge

Have students discuss what they learned about World War I. How might World War II be similar?

LESSON 1

 CAUSE AND EFFECT

As you read, look for the causes and effects of World War II.

BIG IDEA
World War II began and the United States became involved.

VOCABULARY

concentration camp
dictatorship
civilian

German leader Adolf Hitler addresses German soldiers at Nuremberg, Germany, in 1937.

World War II Begins

1901   1951   2001
1921–1941

Franklin D. Roosevelt was reelected President in 1936. His New Deal programs had raised many people's spirits, but the worldwide depression continued. Many Europeans, still rebuilding their countries after World War I, had a hard time finding jobs to support their families. In Asia, some countries were running out of the resources needed to make their economies grow. Powerful new leaders in some European and Asian nations now promised to solve their countries' problems by force.

Worldwide Troubles

The treaty that ended World War I required Germany to pay other European countries for war damages. Germany, however, did not have enough money to pay this debt. As a result, its economy suffered. By 1923 inflation was so bad that a suitcase full of money could barely buy a loaf of bread.

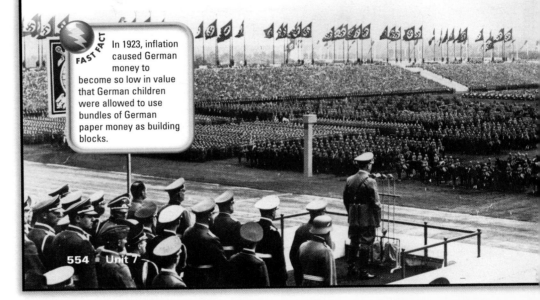

FAST FACT In 1923, inflation caused German money to become so low in value that German children were allowed to use bundles of German paper money as building blocks.

554 • Unit 7

REACH ALL LEARNERS

Advanced Learners As they read the chapter, have students list the countries involved in World War II. Encourage them to note the changes in those countries during the war. Have them use research materials to find out what happened in those countries after the war.

---

554 ▪ **UNIT 7**

Hirohito, emperor of Japan, salutes as he inspects a group of Japanese troops. The hat (above) was worn by a Japanese officer in World War II.

Beginning in the 1920s a German World War I veteran named Adolf Hitler started giving speeches that said that Germany had not been treated fairly after the war. Hitler also said that Germans were better than all other peoples of the world. His words, however, did not apply to all Germans. He blamed the Jewish people in Germany for many of the country's problems.

Hitler became the leader of a political party in Germany called the National Socialists, or Nazis. The Nazi party promised to make Germany a powerful nation once again. It grew in power and set up a private army. Its soldiers, called storm troopers, used force to crush anyone who disagreed with them. Later, they put many of these people in terrible prisons called **concentration camps**.

In 1933 the Nazi party took control of Germany, and Hitler began ruling as a dictator. Hitler rebuilt the nation's economy by preparing for another war. He dreamed that Germany would one day rule over all other nations.

Dictators rose to power in several other European countries, too. In Italy, Benito Mussolini (buh•NEE•toh moo•suh•LEE•nee) seized power in 1922. He wanted Italy to regain the power and glory it had in ancient times, when it was the center of the Roman Empire. With help from Hitler and Mussolini, Francisco Franco also set up a **dictatorship**—a country ruled by a dictator—in Spain. In 1924 Joseph Stalin took control of the Soviet Union, which had been formed following a revolution in Russia in 1917.

Dictators also ruled Japan, in Asia. The Japanese emperor, Hirohito (hir•oh•HEE•toh), had little authority after military officers seized the government. To get the resources Japan's industries needed, these military leaders decided to conquer other nations in Asia and the Pacific.

In the 1930s the nations of Japan, Italy, and Germany began taking over other countries. In 1931 Japan invaded Manchuria, a part of China. Then, in 1935 Italy took over the African country of Ethiopia.

Chapter 15 ■ 555

K-W-L Chart Ask students to fill in the first two columns of the following chart about World War II.

What I Know	What I Want to Know	What I Learned
Germany and the United States were both involved in World War II.	What started World War II?	

● USE READING AND VOCABULARY TRANSPARENCY 7-7.

7-7 TRANSPARENCY

2 Teach

Worldwide Troubles

Read and Respond

History Have students identify the reasons for Adolf Hitler's rise to power in Germany and analyze his treatment of the Jewish people there.

Q How do you think the Germans felt about losing World War I?

A They may have felt angry and resentful.

Students might enjoy researching information about historic clothing. Have them visit The Learning Site at **www.harcourtschool.com.**

Read and Respond

Economics Emphasize that economic distress was a chief contributor to the rise of dictatorships in Germany, Italy, and Japan. Many people turned to political groups that promised to end their countries' economic problems.

Germany's Neighbors Point out that Germany lies roughly in the center of Europe. Explain that Germany took advantage of its geographical position to conquer other countries. Have students arrange the following countries in relation to Germany.

Germany	Poland
France	Czechoslovakia
	Austria

Report on Technology Have a small group of students research and prepare an oral report about the changes in warfare technology from World War I to World War II. Ask them to make illustrations to accompany their reports. The illustrations could show new military weapons, airplanes, submarines, ships, and land vehicles.

The War Begins

Analyze Primary Sources

Newspaper Ask students what they can infer about the significance of the Nazi invasion of Poland from the newspapers pictured on page 556. The article is the top story on the front page of an American newspaper. Although the war was happening on another continent, it was important to Americans.

Read and Respond

Culture and Society Explain that Americans who opposed the United States' entry into World War II were called *isolationists*. These people did not want the government helping countries that were at war. Another group, *interventionists*, wanted the United States to help its allies in Europe. Have students fill in the following chart as they consider the advantages and disadvantages of each position.

Isolationist		Interventionist	
Pros	**Cons**	**Pros**	**Cons**
The United States would not have to risk its people or resources.	Germany, Japan, and Italy would be able to take over more countries.	The United States would be able to protect people around the world.	The United States would have to send troops to fight in the war.

German soldiers (above) march to the Polish border during Germany's invasion of Poland in 1939. American newspapers (right) announce the news.

Two years later, in 1937, Japan started a war against the rest of China. In 1938, Germany took over Czechoslovakia (chehk•uh•sloh•VAHK•ee•uh) and Austria, in Europe.

Because of painful memories of World War I, other countries, including the United States, did little to stop these aggressive acts. Most people hoped war could be avoided.

REVIEW What countries were ruled by dictators before World War II? Germany, Italy, Spain, and the Soviet Union

The War Begins

On September 1, 1939, German forces, numbering nearly 2 million, invaded Poland. They attacked with tanks on land and planes in the air, quickly defeating their neighbor. The Germans called this fighting style *blitzkrieg*, or "lightning war." Two days later Poland's allies,

Britain and France, responded to this attack by declaring war on Germany. World War II had begun.

German forces stormed across Europe with incredible speed. By the end of 1941, much of the continent was under German control. The only countries that remained free were Britain, Russia, and a few small neutral nations. In France, rebel armies fought to weaken Germany's grip. In the skies over Britain, German bombers continued their attacks, but Britain bravely fought on.

Germany's invasions shocked and angered most Americans. However, few Americans wanted the United States to become involved in another foreign war.

In 1940 President Roosevelt was elected to a third term. He promised to keep the United States out of the war, but he wanted the country to be prepared in case it was attacked. A military draft was

---

Outlining Provide students with the following statements. Have them create an outline of the key events of World War II.

I Germany invades Poland.
II Japan invades Indochina.
III Japan attacks Pearl Harbor.
IV The United States enters the war.

The German and British Air War The fight between German bombers and the British Royal Air Force (RAF) during the 1940s is called the Battle of Britain. The RAF successfully defended the country against a massive German air assault. Winston Churchill, Britain's Prime Minister during the war, said, "Never in the field of human conflict was so much owed by so many to so few." Churchill meant that the relatively small group of pilots helped all British people by protecting the country.

begun, and the United States started making airplanes, tanks, and other war supplies. It also began to send food and war supplies to help Britain. To meet the growing demands for these goods, many businesses reopened and new ones started. Once again people were able to find jobs. The Great Depression was clearly coming to an end.

In 1940 Japanese troops invaded French Indochina, which is now made up of the countries of Laos, Cambodia, and Vietnam. Many American leaders feared that Japan would soon threaten the Philippines and other places in the Pacific. They were right.

REVIEW What action by Germany started World War II? CAUSE AND EFFECT
the invasion of Poland

The United States Enters the War

At 7:55 A.M. on Sunday, December 7, 1941, the roar of Japanese planes shattered the early morning calm over the Hawaiian Islands. The planes dropped bombs on American ships docked at Pearl Harbor, an American naval base. World War II had come to the United States.

In less than two hours, 19 warships were sunk or damaged in the harbor. In addition, about 150 planes were destroyed at nearby Hickam Airfield. More than 2,000 sailors and soldiers and 68 civilians were killed. A **civilian** is a person who is not in the military.

The Japanese attack on Pearl Harbor caused terrible damage and loss of life.

LOCATE IT

HAWAII

USS Arizona Memorial, Pearl Harbor

Dorie Miller There were fewer than 5,000 African Americans in the United States military at the beginning of World War II. They served in segregated units, and could not become members of the Army Air Corps or the Marine Corps. However, one of the first heroes of World War II was Dorie Miller, an African American naval mess attendant who worked in the kitchen of the battleship *West Virginia*. On December 7, 1941, Miller heard the exploding bombs. When he rushed up on deck, he saw Japanese aircraft dropping bombs and his captain lying wounded. After moving the captain to safety, Miller grabbed a machine gun and shot down four Japanese planes. He received the Navy Cross for his bravery.

The United States Enters the War

Read and Respond

Culture The attack on the United States Pacific fleet shocked the nation and temporarily prevented the navy from blocking Japanese aggression in the Pacific.

Q How do you think Americans reacted to the Japanese attack on Pearl Harbor?

A They were angry, and their opposition ended to Roosevelt's policies about war preparations.

Visual Learning

Map and Picture Direct students' attention to the map and picture on page 557. Reinforce that both Japan and the Hawaiian Islands are in the Pacific Ocean.

Q Why might Japan have wanted to destroy American warships and planes stationed in Hawaii?

A Japanese leaders wanted to cripple United States military strength in the Pacific because they realized the United States Navy could stop Japan's plans to control East Asia.

3 Close

Summarize Key Content

- Many dictators, including Adolf Hitler, came to power after World War I.
- World War II began when Germany invaded Poland. Although Germany took control of most European countries, Britain and Russia fought on.
- The United States entered the war when the Japanese bombed Pearl Harbor.

Assess

Lesson 1 Review—Answers

 CAUSE AND EFFECT The war ended the Great Depression because it caused a demand to produce war-related goods.

❶ **BIG IDEA** Germany's invasion of Poland

❷ **VOCABULARY** A **dictator** rules a country with absolute authority.

❸ **TIME LINE** Germany invaded Poland before Pearl Harbor was attacked.

❹ **HISTORY** Allied Powers: Britain, France, Soviet Union, United States. Axis Powers: Germany, Italy, Japan.

❺ **CRITICAL THINKING—Analyze** Dictators continued to take over countries, and eventually nations opposed to this aggression joined forces to stop it.

 Performance Assessment Guidelines Memorials should recognize that the attack caused the United States to become involved in a war.

ACTIVITY BOOK

Use ACTIVITY BOOK, p. 141, to reinforce and extend student learning.

Americans were outraged by the attack on Pearl Harbor. President Roosevelt went before Congress the next day to ask that war be declared on Japan. He said,

> ❝Yesterday, December 7, 1941, a date which will live in infamy— the United States of America was suddenly and deliberately attacked by naval and air forces of the Empire of Japan. . . . I ask that the Congress declare that since the . . . attack by Japan . . . a state of war has existed between the United States and the Japanese Empire.❞

Three days later, Germany and Italy declared war on the United States, and Congress recognized a state of war with them, too. Germany, Italy, and Japan were known as the Axis Powers. The United States joined with the Allies, which included Britain, France, and the Soviet

President Franklin D. Roosevelt asks Congress for a declaration of war on Japan.

Union. The Soviet Union had joined the Allies after Germany invaded it in the summer of 1941.

REVIEW **What event led the United States to enter the war?** the Japanese attack on Pearl Harbor

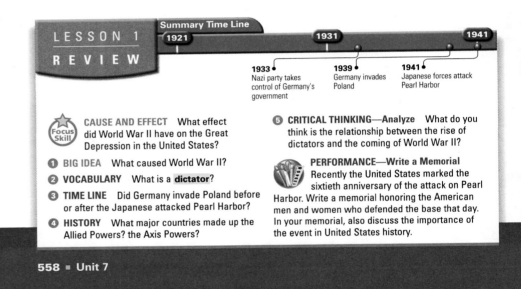

LESSON 1 REVIEW

Summary Time Line

1921	1931	1941

1933 Nazi party takes control of Germany's government

1939 Germany invades Poland

1941 Japanese forces attack Pearl Harbor

CAUSE AND EFFECT What effect did World War II have on the Great Depression in the United States?

❶ **BIG IDEA** What caused World War II?

❷ **VOCABULARY** What is a **dictator**?

❸ **TIME LINE** Did Germany invade Poland before or after the Japanese attacked Pearl Harbor?

❹ **HISTORY** What major countries made up the Allied Powers? the Axis Powers?

❺ **CRITICAL THINKING—Analyze** What do you think is the relationship between the rise of dictators and the coming of World War II?

PERFORMANCE—Write a Memorial Recently the United States marked the sixtieth anniversary of the attack on Pearl Harbor. Write a memorial honoring the American men and women who defended the base that day. In your memorial, also discuss the importance of the event in United States history.

558 ■ Unit 7

·SKILLS· READING

Predict a Historical Outcome

VOCABULARY
prediction

➡ WHY IT MATTERS

People often make **predictions**. This means they look at the way things are and decide what they think will most likely happen next. When people make predictions, they are not just guessing about what will happen in the future. They are using information and past experiences to predict a probable, or likely, outcome.

➡ WHAT YOU NEED TO KNOW

You have read about how many women worked in factories during World War I. When World War II began, American factories were again in need of many workers.

➡ PRACTICE THE SKILL

Use the following steps to predict what groups of people were employed in large numbers by American factories during World War II.

This photograph shows women working in a factory during World War II.

Step 1 Think about what you already know about the number of women who worked in American factories during World War I.

Step 2 Review the new information you learned about the beginning of World War II.

Step 3 Make a prediction about what group of people American factories began employing in large numbers during World War II.

Step 4 As you read or gather more information, ask yourself whether you still think your prediction is correct.

Step 5 If necessary, go through the steps again to form a new prediction.

After going through these steps, you should have been able to predict that factories employed many women.

➡ APPLY WHAT YOU LEARNED

Think about a prediction you made at school this week. What steps did you follow? Do you think that your prediction was a correct one?

READING SKILLS

Chapter 15 ■ 559

OBJECTIVES

■ Analyze information by making predictions.

■ Apply critical thinking skills to analyze and evaluate predictions.

Vocabulary

prediction p. 559

WORD CARDS

See pp. V85–V86.

1 Motivate

Why It Matters

Help students realize that they make predictions when they read.

2 Teach

What You Need to Know

Remind students that World War II renewed the need for many goods.

Practice the Skill—Answers

Students should predict that many women worked in factories during World War II.

3 Close

Apply What You Learned

Students should identify the steps they used to make their predictions.

ACTIVITY BOOK

Use ACTIVITY BOOK, p. 142, to give students additional practice using this skill.

EXTEND AND ENRICH

Discussion Lead a discussion about why it seemed unusual for women to be employed in large numbers during the war.

TRANSPARENCY

Use SKILL TRANSPARENCY 7-2.

RETEACH THE SKILL

Make a Chart Ask students to complete the chart to make a prediction about the events in the next lesson.

Step 1: Consider what you know.	World War II began.
Step 2: Gather new information.	World War II lasted for several years.
Step 3: Make a prediction.	The next lesson will be about what happened during the war.
Step 4: Evaluate the prediction.	The next lesson is called "Americans and the War," which confirms my prediction.
Step 5: Repeat the steps.	

OBJECTIVES

- Identify how World War II affected the economy of the United States.
- Discuss how World War II affected American women.
- Describe and evaluate how World War II affected Japanese Americans.

Cause and Effect pp. 553, 560, 561, 563, 576

Vocabulary

SEE READING AND VOCABULARY TRANSPARENCY 7-8 OR THE WORD CARDS ON PP. V85–V86.

rationing p. 561   **relocation camp**
recycle p. 562   p. 563
interest p. 562

When Minutes Count

Have students scan the lesson to find out what effect World War II had on Japanese Americans.

Quick Summary

This lesson explains how industries changed as a result of the war and how people helped the war effort. It also examines how Japanese Americans were treated after the bombing of Pearl Harbor.

1 Motivate

Set the Purpose

Big Idea Have students suggest ways Americans might have been challenged during the war.

Access Prior Knowledge

Have students discuss how American citizens reacted to World War I.

· LESSON ·

2

CAUSE AND EFFECT

As you read, look for ways in which World War II had long-lasting effects on the American people.

BIG IDEA
World War II brought new challenges to the American people.

VOCABULARY
rationing
recycle
interest
relocation camp

Americans and the War

1901   1951   2001

1941–1943

Supplying war materials to the Allies had already helped prepare the United States for war. After the bombing of Pearl Harbor, however, the United States suddenly had to produce even more airplanes, tanks, and other war supplies. This work provided jobs for many more Americans. Now instead of not enough jobs, there were not enough workers.

Wartime Industries

Fighting World War II led to the further growth of the federal government's authority. To produce enough war supplies, the government took control of many businesses. It set both the prices that businesses could charge for their products and the wages that they could pay their workers. The government also stopped the production of many consumer goods. Manufacturers who had produced these goods before the war were now told to make weapons or other war materials.

To produce these wartime goods, hundreds of thousands of new workers were needed. Across the country people went to

Posters (left) encouraged Americans to help with the war effort. The photograph (below) shows American soldiers transporting war supplies.

560   Unit 7

WORD WORK

Prefixes and Suffixes Ask students to read the lesson vocabulary. Then have them place words that have prefixes or suffixes in the appropriate column in the chart. Invite volunteers to identify the meanings of prefixes and suffixes.

Prefixes	Suffixes
recycle	rationing
relocation	relocation

STUDY/RESEARCH SKILLS

Skimming and Scanning Have students skim the lesson to find out what jobs Americans did during the war.

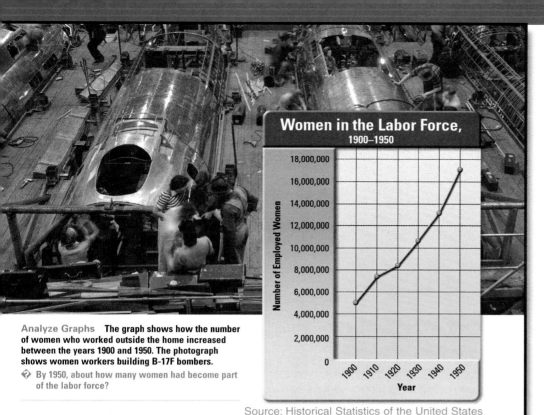

Women in the Labor Force,
1900–1950

(y-axis) Number of Employed Women: 0; 2,000,000; 4,000,000; 6,000,000; 8,000,000; 10,000,000; 12,000,000; 14,000,000; 16,000,000; 18,000,000

(x-axis) Year: 1900, 1910, 1920, 1930, 1940, 1950

Source: Historical Statistics of the United States

Analyze Graphs The graph shows how the number of women who worked outside the home increased between the years 1900 and 1950. The photograph shows women workers building B-17F bombers.

◆ By 1950, about how many women had become part of the labor force?

work in factories, steel mills, shipyards, and aircraft plants. Many of these workers were women. As they had done in World War I, women took over jobs that previously had been held only by men.

Working around the clock, American workers were able to produce huge amounts of war materials at record speed. At the beginning of the war, President Roosevelt challenged American industries to produce as many as 60,000 aircraft a year. Many people believed this was an impossible goal, but in 1943 alone, American workers built almost 86,000 aircraft!

REVIEW How did the government get businesses to produce enough war supplies?
CAUSE AND EFFECT
It stopped the production of many consumer goods and got manufacturers who had produced these goods to make weapons or other war materials.

The Home Front

More than 15 million Americans served in the armed forces during World War II, including about 338,000 women. Many women in the armed forces made maps, drove ambulances, and worked as mechanics, clerks, or nurses.

To help feed the thousands of people serving in the military, farmers planted more crops and raised more livestock. This demand for food brought about prosperous times for farmers.

The war often caused shortages of goods. To make sure there were enough goods to supply soldiers, new government rules called for **rationing**, or limiting, what civilians could purchase.

Chapter 15 ■ 561

2 Teach

Wartime Industries

Read and Respond

Economics Ask students to explain how President Roosevelt's challenge to American industries to produce 60,000 aircraft would help the military. It would provide the military with the aircraft it needed to help defend the Allied forces.

Visual Learning

Line Graph Explain that factories depended on women workers during the war.
CAPTION ANSWER: about 17 million

The Home Front

Read and Respond

Civics and Government Have students discuss the reasons for the shortages of goods caused by the war.

Q How did the government control the rationing of food and other goods?

A by issuing coupon books, which citizens had to use to buy the rationed items

Japanese Americans

Read and Respond

History Tell students that about 800 of the Japanese Americans who volunteered to serve in the United States armed forces during the war came from the relocation camps.

3 Close

Summarize Key Content

- The federal government asserted more control over industries in order to produce more war supplies.
- American workers, including large numbers of women, produced huge amounts of war materials very quickly.
- Civilians endured rationing, paid higher taxes, and bought war bonds to help pay for the war.
- Japanese Americans were put in camps after Japan bombed Pearl Harbor.

To purchase certain items, such as butter, sugar, meat, and gasoline, people had to have government coupons. They could buy only the amount that the coupons allowed. That way the government could control how much of a product was sold at home, so more of it would be available to send to the soldiers who were fighting overseas.

Civilians helped in other ways, too. They collected pots and tin cans for metal drives. They also collected old tires or anything else that could be **recycled**, or reused, to make war supplies.

Many Americans helped pay for the war by buying war bonds. A war bond was a paper showing that the buyer had loaned money to the government to help pay the cost of a war. When people bought war bonds, they were letting the government use their money for a certain amount of time. After the time was up, people could turn in their bonds and get their money back with interest. **Interest**

Relocated Japanese Americans had to wear identification tags like this one.

WAR RELOCATION AUTHORITY
JAMES KAWAMINAMI
14967

is the money a bank or borrower pays for the use of money.

REVIEW How did Americans help pay for the war? Americans bought war bonds.

Japanese Americans

The war changed people's lives. It also led to terrible problems for Japanese Americans. At the time of the attack on Pearl Harbor, about 125,000 Japanese Americans lived in the United States. Most had been born there and were citizens. The attack on Pearl Harbor had shocked them as much as anyone else.

After Pearl Harbor, however, anger against Japanese Americans grew. Some United States military officials believed that Japanese Americans might even help Japan invade the United States.

In February 1942, President Roosevelt ordered the army to put about 110,000

• SCIENCE AND TECHNOLOGY •

Blood Storage

Charles Drew

Before World War II, scientists were unable to store donated blood for long periods of time. As a result, injured people who had lost too much blood usually died. Charles Drew, an African American doctor, helped change this. Drew discovered that the plasma, or the liquid part of blood, could be separated from the red blood cells. The two could then be frozen separately and stored for long periods. When an injured or sick person needed a blood transfusion, the two parts could be combined again. During the war, Drew helped found the American Red Cross Blood Program, which saved the lives of thousands of wounded soldiers.

562 ■ Unit 7

Many of the soldiers in the 442nd Regimental Combat Team were Japanese Americans. They fought in Italy and Germany and received many service awards like the medal shown here.

Japanese Americans in what were called **relocation camps**. Japanese Americans had to wear identification tags, and they had to sell their homes, businesses, and belongings. They were moved to relocation camps in California, Arizona, Wyoming, Arkansas, and Idaho.

While their families and friends were in the relocation camps, more than 17,000 Japanese Americans served in the army. Most became members of the 442nd Regimental Combat Team.

REVIEW Why were many Japanese Americans sent to relocation camps? because some United States military officials believed that Japanese Americans might help Japan invade the United States

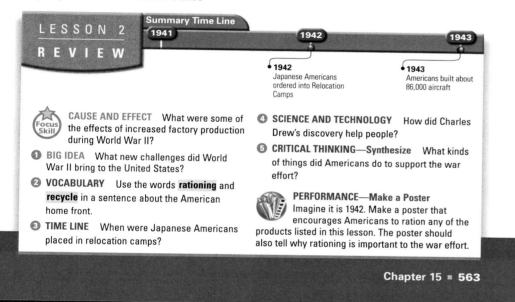

LESSON 2 REVIEW

Summary Time Line

1941 — 1942 — 1943

• 1942
Japanese Americans ordered into Relocation Camps

• 1943
Americans built about 86,000 aircraft

 CAUSE AND EFFECT What were some of the effects of increased factory production during World War II?

❶ **BIG IDEA** What new challenges did World War II bring to the United States?

❷ **VOCABULARY** Use the words **rationing** and **recycle** in a sentence about the American home front.

❸ **TIME LINE** When were Japanese Americans placed in relocation camps?

❹ **SCIENCE AND TECHNOLOGY** How did Charles Drew's discovery help people?

❺ **CRITICAL THINKING—Synthesize** What kinds of things did Americans do to support the war effort?

PERFORMANCE—Make a Poster
Imagine it is 1942. Make a poster that encourages Americans to ration any of the products listed in this lesson. The poster should also tell why rationing is important to the war effort.

Chapter 15 ▪ 563

READING SOCIAL STUDIES

Study Questions Have students provide answers to the study questions.

1. The government set prices and wages and decided which goods would be produced.

2. Women made maps, drove ambulances, and worked as mechanics, clerks, and nurses.

3. The military feared Japanese Americans might help Japan invade the United States.

● USE READING AND VOCABULARY TRANSPARENCY 7-8. **7-8** TRANSPARENCY

Assess

Lesson 2 Review—Answers

CAUSE AND EFFECT Many workers, including women, were now employed, and incomes rose.

❶ **BIG IDEA** Industries were reorganized; citizens made sacrifices; Japanese Americans endured internment.

❷ **VOCABULARY** During the war Americans endured **rationing** of goods and collected items to **recycle** into war materials.

❸ **TIME LINE** in 1942

❹ **SCIENCE AND TECHNOLOGY** Drew's discovery allowed more people to receive transfusions.

❺ **CRITICAL THINKING—Synthesize** Americans used ration books to buy products, collected items for recycling, grew some of their own food, paid higher taxes, and bought war bonds.

Performance Assessment Guidelines Posters should identify a product and give reasons for rationing it.

ACTIVITY BOOK

Use ACTIVITY BOOK, p. 143, to reinforce and extend student learning.

EXTEND AND ENRICH

Write a Description Divide the class into three groups. Assign one of these roles to each group: a factory worker, a civilian at home, a Japanese American. Have the groups write brief descriptions about life during the war from their characters' perspectives. Each group should elect a member to read its description aloud.

RETEACH THE LESSON

Graphic Organizer Use a web diagram to help students recall things American civilians did during the war. Write the topic in the middle circle, and have students make the remaining connections.

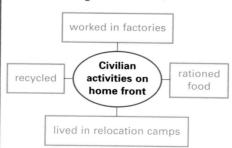

worked in factories

recycled — **Civilian activities on home front** — rationed food

lived in relocation camps

Skill Lesson

OBJECTIVES

- Identify economic terms and concepts.
- Understand how economic choices affect people.

Vocabulary

trade-off p. 564
opportunity cost p. 564

WORD CARDS

See pp. V85–V86.

1 Motivate

Why It Matters

Illustrate the idea of trade-offs.

2 Teach

What You Need to Know

Explain that about $36 billion in bonds were sold during World War II.

Practice the Skill—Answers

1 helping the country's war effort now; waiting until later for interest on bonds

2 not buying new work clothes

3 Close

Apply What You Learned

Explanations should indicate an understanding of trade-offs and opportunity costs.

ACTIVITY BOOK

Use ACTIVITY BOOK, p. 144, to give students additional practice using this skill.

· SKILLS · CITIZENSHIP

Make Economic Choices

VOCABULARY
trade-off
opportunity cost

► WHY IT MATTERS

When you buy something at a store or restaurant, you are making an economic choice. Your choice may differ from other people's choices based on what is most important to you. Although you benefit from what you buy, you must spend money that you cannot use in the future. This is called a **trade-off**. What you give up is the **opportunity cost** of what you get. Understanding trade-offs and opportunity costs can help you make more thoughtful economic choices.

► WHAT YOU NEED TO KNOW

You have read that during World War II, Americans showed their support for the war effort in a number of ways. One way was by buying war bonds. Buying war bonds helped support the war effort. At the same time, the war bonds paid interest to their owners.

CITIZENSHIP SKILLS

564 ■ Unit 7

► PRACTICE THE SKILL

Imagine that you are an American factory worker in 1944. After paying your bills you have some money left over. You could use it to buy something you want now, like new work clothes or you could use it to buy war bonds.

1 Think about the trade-offs. You could use the work clothes, but you would not get any money back from this purchase. By buying war bonds, you are helping the war effort, but you would have to wait a while to earn interest on your bonds. What are the trade-offs of buying war bonds?

2 Think of the opportunity costs. You do not have enough money to buy both work clothes and war bonds, so you have to give up one. If you buy war bonds, you would be giving up something you want now, to earn money later. What are the opportunity costs of buying war bonds?

► APPLY WHAT YOU LEARNED

Imagine that you want to buy a book and rent a movie, but you do not have enough money for both. Explain to a partner the trade-offs and the opportunity costs of your choices.

People lined up to buy war bonds in New York in 1945.

EXTEND AND ENRICH

Write an Explanation Ask students to write paragraphs about why they think Americans bought so many war bonds.

RETEACH THE SKILL

Write Definitions Have students write brief definitions of **trade-off** and **opportunity cost**. Tell them to share their definitions by discussing war bonds.

TRANSPARENCY

Use SKILL TRANSPARENCY 7-3.

Winning the War

1942–1945

World War II was a new kind of war. Instead of fighting from trenches, as had been done in World War I, soldiers used tanks, ships, and airplanes to quickly move from battle to battle. Bombs dropped from larger, faster airplanes destroyed whole cities.

World War II was also fought over a much larger area than any other war—almost half the world. It was fought on two major **fronts**, or battle lines, at the same time. The first was in Africa and Europe. The second was in the Pacific. Victory on both fronts would be needed to win the war.

The Fighting in Africa and Europe

To defeat the Axis Powers in Europe, the Allies decided that they should first gain control of the Mediterranean Sea. To do that, they knew that they would have to defeat the German and Italian forces in North Africa and then invade Italy. By 1942 Adolf Hitler controlled almost all of Europe and most of North Africa.

In 1942 President Roosevelt put General Dwight D. Eisenhower (EYE•zin•how•er) in command of all the American troops in Europe. A respected leader and skilled military planner, Eisenhower led the Americans as they joined in the attack against Axis forces in North Africa. After several months of fighting, the Allies won North Africa in May 1943. They then pushed north through Italy. Although the Italian government surrendered in September 1943, heavy fighting continued in Italy until the Americans captured Rome the next year.

While the Allies were fighting in Italy, they were planning another invasion of Europe, this time on the northern coast of France. On June 6, 1944, the date known as **D day**, the Allies began the largest water-to-land invasion in history.

LESSON 3

CAUSE AND EFFECT

As you read, identify events that caused the United States to win the war.

BIG IDEA
The Allies defeated the Axis Powers.

VOCABULARY
front
D day
island-hopping

General Dwight D. Eisenhower was commander of all the American troops in Europe.

Chapter 15 ■ **565**

Lesson 3
PAGES 565–569

OBJECTIVES

- Analyze the importance of the fighting in Africa, Europe, and the Pacific during World War II.
- Analyze how the war continued in the Pacific after the Allied victory in Europe.
- Identify the causes and effects of dropping atom bombs on Japan.
- Identify how the actions of Dwight D. Eisenhower and Harry S. Truman affected society.

Cause and Effect pp. 553, 565, 568, 569, 576

Vocabulary

SEE READING AND VOCABULARY TRANSPARENCY 7-9 OR THE WORD CARDS ON PP. V85–V88.

front p. 565   **island-hopping**
D day p. 565   p. 567

When Minutes Count

Have students read the Big Idea of the lesson. Then have them read the lesson and find at least one sentence that supports the Big Idea.

Quick Summary

This lesson explains events leading up to Germany's surrender. It also follows the war in the Pacific, which ended when atom bombs were dropped on Japan.

1 Motivate

Set the Purpose

Big Idea Explain that students will read about two Axis defeats: first in Europe and then in Asia.

Access Prior Knowledge

Have students list resources a country might need to win a war.

WORD WORK

Historical Context Point out that the lesson vocabulary contains common terms that have special meanings in the context of World War II. Instruct students to look through the lesson and find the definitions of the vocabulary terms. Have students list the terms and their definitions based on historical context.

MENTAL MAPPING

Locate the Mediterranean Sea
Remind students that Europe, North Africa, and the Mediterranean Sea were important battlegrounds during the war. Ask students to think about where these places are in relation to each other.

> Europe

> Mediterranean Sea

> North Africa

Anticipation Guide Have students predict which statements below are true and which are false. Students may change their answers as they read.

1. The Allies won victory in Europe when they captured Rome. FALSE

2. When the war in Europe ended, Allied forces fought on in the Pacific. TRUE

3. The Japanese surrendered after the United States dropped one atom bomb on Japan. FALSE

● USE READING AND VOCABULARY TRANSPARENCY 7-9.

7-9 TRANSPARENCY

2 Teach

The Fighting in Africa and Europe

Analyze Primary Sources

Quotation Read General Eisenhower's quote. Ask students to discuss how his words might have helped motivate Allied troops. Explain that General Eisenhower eventually became President Eisenhower—twice. He won the 1952 and 1956 elections.

Read and Respond

Geography Explain that the Germans believed that any invasion from England would land at Calais, France, since Calais is only 26 miles (42 km) from England across the English Channel. Instead, the Allies launched the invasion toward the Normandy beaches west of Calais. At about 90 miles (145 km), this channel crossing took considerably longer.

the Allied invasion of northern France that was the largest water-to-land invasion in history

General Eisenhower, who earlier that year had become the commander of all Allied forces in Europe, led the D day invasion. On the morning of June 6, he told his troops,

> 66 You are about to embark upon the great crusade. . . . The hopes and prayers of liberty-loving people everywhere march with you. 99

On D day about 2,700 ships sailed across the English Channel from Britain. On board were more than 175,000 troops from the United States, Britain, and Canada. The troops landed on the beaches of Normandy, in France, where German forces met them with heavy gunfire.

Many soldiers gave their lives on D day, but the invasion was successful. The Allies broke through the German lines and began moving inland from the west. By the end of June, there were

about 1 million Allied troops in France. They slowly pushed the enemy back toward Germany. At the same time, forces from the Soviet Union were pushing back the German armies from the east. The Allied troops met near Berlin, Germany's capital, in April 1945. There they learned that Hitler had killed himself.

Berlin fell to the Soviets on May 2, 1945, and the German military leaders asked to surrender. On May 8 the Allies accepted Germany's surrender. This day was called V-E Day, or Victory in Europe Day. It marked the end of the war in Europe.

REVIEW What was the D day invasion?

FAST FACT During World War II, battleships were named after states, submarines after fish and marine animals, cruisers after cities or territories, and destroyers after military heroes.

566 ■ Unit 7

Write a Summary One famous airplane of World War II was the B-17 bomber, called the "Flying Fortress." It could fly at high altitudes, carry a heavy load of bombs, and hit its targets very accurately. The plane also carried thirteen machine guns and a ten-man crew. Ask students to research other World War II airplanes and choose one about which to write a short report describing its capabilities. Encourage students to present their reports to the class.

The Normandy Invasion The Allied invasion of France was scheduled for June 5 but was delayed because of bad weather. The first troops were loaded onto their ships and moved out into the English Channel on June 3. Stormy weather blew in, obscuring visibility, and the operation was postponed. On June 5, in spite of persistent rough weather, Eisenhower made the decision to set the date for June 6.

The Pacific Front

Although the war was over in Europe, it raged on in the Pacific. The battle plan there called for the Allies to defeat Japan by forcing its troops back from the islands they had conquered. This plan of **island-hopping** meant that Allied troops would take back the islands one at a time until they reached Tokyo, Japan's capital. At the same time, the Allies would bomb Japan from the air. The first of these attacks took place in 1942, when a surprise bombing raid was led against Tokyo and other Japanese cities.

The Japanese controlled thousands of small islands in the Pacific. The Allies decided to take back only the most important ones. Still, Allied leaders knew that island-hopping would be costly. Early battles, such as the one on the island of Guadalcanal (gwah•duhl•kuh•NAL), proved this to be true. More than 1,600 Allied troops were killed.

The Allies, under the command of Americans, General Douglas MacArthur and Admiral Chester W. Nimitz, pressed on, capturing island after island. As the Allies got closer to Japan, however, the losses grew. At Iwo Jima (EE•woh JEE•muh), an island 750 miles (1,207 km) from Tokyo, more than 4,000 American soldiers lost their lives. More than 20,000 Japanese soldiers died. At Okinawa (oh•kuh•NAH•wah), about 11,000 Americans died. The Japanese lost more than 100,000 people. The Japanese were not going to give up easily.

REVIEW Who commanded the Allied forces in the Pacific? General Douglas MacArthur and Admiral Chester W. Nimitz

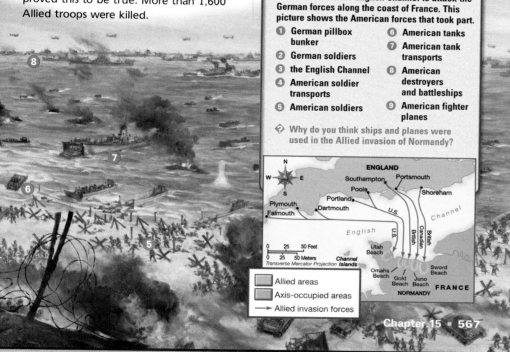

A CLOSER LOOK
D day Invasion at Normandy

Ships carried American, British, and Canadian soldiers across the English Channel to attack the German forces along the coast of France. This picture shows the American forces that took part.

1. German pillbox bunker
2. German soldiers
3. the English Channel
4. American soldier transports
5. American soldiers
6. American tanks
7. American tank transports
8. American destroyers and battleships
9. American fighter planes

◈ Why do you think ships and planes were used in the Allied invasion of Normandy?

Map: ENGLAND — Southampton, Portsmouth, Poole, Shoreham, Portland, Plymouth, Dartmouth, Falmouth, English Channel, U.S., Canadian, British, Utah Beach, Omaha Beach, Gold Beach, Juno Beach, Sword Beach, NORMANDY, FRANCE, Channel Islands

0 25 50 Feet
0 25 50 Meters
Transverse Mercator Projection

- Allied areas
- Axis-occupied areas
→ Allied invasion forces

QUESTIONS KIDS ASK

Q Is the bombing of Tokyo connected to the bombing of Japan that ended the war?

A No. The surprise raid on Tokyo took place much earlier in the war, in 1942. The United States was reacting to Japan's attack on Pearl Harbor. The airplanes, which carried conventional bombs, took off from an aircraft carrier. The atom bombs, used to force Japan's surrender, were dropped in 1945.

A CLOSER LOOK
D Day Invasion at Normandy

Point out that the illustration shows only the American portion of the Allied forces that invaded Normandy. The United States forces and the British forces, which included Canadians, attacked separate beaches. Supply students with reference materials that describe the United States military ships and aircraft that participated in the Normandy invasion. Ask students to provide brief oral descriptions of each.

CAPTION ANSWER: Some ships carried landing craft and soldiers. Battleships fired onto the beaches. Planes dropped paratroopers behind German lines to capture bridges and railroad tracks.

The Pacific Front

Read and Respond

History Remind students that the Allies moved across the Pacific, capturing islands in sequence. When they had control of one island, they used it as a base of operations to invade the next designated island. Tell students that the strategy of attacking only certain islands held by the Japanese was called island-hopping.

Q Why was island-hopping a sensible strategy?

A The military could concentrate its time, energy, resources, and personnel on fewer islands.

The War Ends

Visual Learning

Map Have students study the map of Allied and Axis Powers.

CAPTION ANSWER: Centrally located between Europe and Japan, the United States could launch military operations from the Pacific coast and Hawaii for the Pacific front and from the Atlantic coast for the European front.

 **Close**

Summarize Key Content

- As the Allies approached from the west and the Soviets advanced from the east, Germany surrendered in May 1945.
- The battle for control of Pacific islands continued even after the Allied victory in Europe and led to great loss of life on both sides.
- President Harry S. Truman decided to drop atom bombs on Japan, thus ending World War II.

READING SOCIAL STUDIES

Anticipation Guide Have students check their answers to the Anticipation Guide.

1. The Allies won victory in Europe when they captured ~~Rome~~. Berlin

2. When the war in Europe ended, Allied forces fought on in the Pacific.

3. The Japanese surrendered after the United States dropped ~~one atom bomb~~ on Japan. two atom bombs

● USE READING AND VOCABULARY TRANSPARENCY 7-9.

7-9 TRANSPARENCY

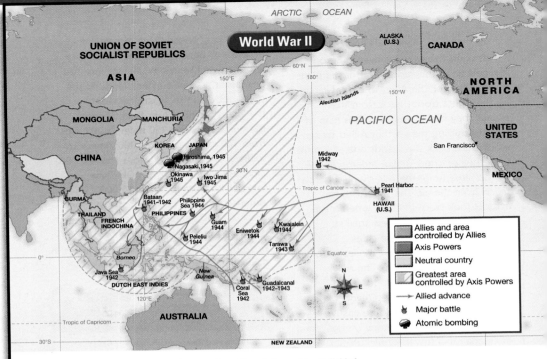

World War II

Legend:
- Allies and area controlled by Allies
- Axis Powers
- Neutral country
- Greatest area controlled by Axis Powers
- Allied advance
- Major battle
- Atomic bombing

GEOGRAPHY THEME

Location During the war, almost the whole world was divided between the Allies and the Axis Powers.

◆ Why was the location of the United States helpful?

The War Ends

President Franklin D. Roosevelt, who had been elected to a fourth term in 1944, did not live to see the end of the war. He died on April 12, 1945. Vice President Harry S. Truman became President.

Truman soon learned that the United States was developing the most powerful bomb the world had ever known—the atom bomb. By the summer of 1945, this new weapon was ready to be used. President Truman made the difficult decision to drop the atom bomb on Japan. He wanted to end the war quickly.

On August 6, 1945, the American bomber *Enola Gay* flew over the city of Hiroshima (hir•uh•SHEE•muh), Japan. A single bomb was dropped. There was a flash like an exploding sun. The bomb flattened and burned a huge area of Hiroshima and killed more than 75,000 people.

As terrible as the atom bomb attack was, Japan did not surrender. On August 9, the United States dropped an atom bomb on Nagasaki (nah•guh•SAH•kee). Then Japan agreed to surrender. On August 15, Americans celebrated V-J Day, or Victory over Japan Day. World War II was over.

REVIEW Why did the Japanese finally surrender? CAUSE AND EFFECT
They finally surrendered after the United States dropped an atom bomb on Nagasaki.

568 ■ Unit 7

BACKGROUND

After the Atom Bombs The atom bombs entirely destroyed about five square miles in the centers of Hiroshima and Nagasaki. Since the end of the war, both cities have been rebuilt. The Peace Memorial Park was built in Hiroshima to honor the victims, and a building damaged in the blast was left standing as a symbol of peace.

BACKGROUND

Navajo Code Talkers Tell students that Navajos served as code talkers in the Marines during World War II, transmitting information about war tactics and troop movements, orders, and other battlefield information. Philip Johnston, the son of a Navajo missionary, spoke Navajo fluently. Johnston knew that the language could be used as an unbreakable code because it is unwritten and complex. Navajos were respected for their speed and accuracy in transmitting messages during the war.

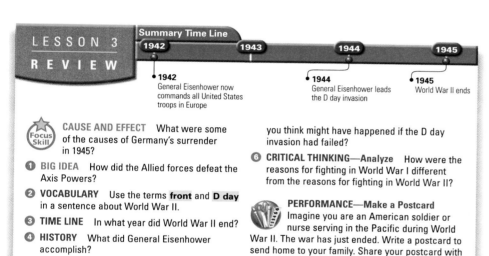

LESSON 3 REVIEW

Summary Time Line

1942 — 1943 — 1944 — 1945

1942
General Eisenhower now commands all United States troops in Europe

1944
General Eisenhower leads the D day invasion

1945
World War II ends

CAUSE AND EFFECT What were some of the causes of Germany's surrender in 1945?

1 BIG IDEA How did the Allied forces defeat the Axis Powers?

2 VOCABULARY Use the terms **front** and **D day** in a sentence about World War II.

3 TIME LINE In what year did World War II end?

4 HISTORY What did General Eisenhower accomplish?

5 CRITICAL THINKING—Hypothesize What do you think might have happened if the D day invasion had failed?

6 CRITICAL THINKING—Analyze How were the reasons for fighting in World War I different from the reasons for fighting in World War II?

PERFORMANCE—Make a Postcard Imagine you are an American soldier or nurse serving in the Pacific during World War II. The war has just ended. Write a postcard to send home to your family. Share your postcard with a classmate.

Chapter 15 ■ 569

EXTEND AND ENRICH

Research Have small groups of students use primary and secondary sources to research key figures in World War II. Then have students write short biographies about one of the key figures. Ask volunteers to share their biographies with the class.

RETEACH THE LESSON

Map Have students complete these two graphic organizers to show the movement of Allied forces on the two fronts.

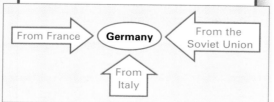

Assess

Lesson 3 Review—Answers

CAUSE AND EFFECT Allied troops reached Germany from the west and east, Hitler was dead, and Berlin was captured.

1 BIG IDEA The Allies captured Berlin, forced the Germans to surrender, and then defeated Japan.

2 VOCABULARY The **D day** invasion of Normandy was a crucial battle on the European **front** of World War II.

3 TIME LINE in 1945

4 HISTORY Under Eisenhower's leadership, American troops helped take control of North Africa and Rome. As Allied commander, Eisenhower led the successful D day invasion.

5 CRITICAL THINKING—Hypothesize Germany might have continued to dominate Europe, and the war might not have ended.

6 CRITICAL THINKING—Analyze In World War I the United States was not directly attacked. The United States fought in World War II because its own land was attacked.

Performance Assessment Guidelines Students' postcards should mention details about where they are and what they see and hear. Students also should express their emotions regarding the war's end.

ACTIVITY BOOK

Use ACTIVITY BOOK, p. 145, to reinforce and extend student learning.

Skill Lesson
PAGES 570–571

OBJECTIVES

- Interpret information in time lines.
- Organize information in time lines.

Vocabulary

parallel time line p. 570

WORD CARDS

See pp. V87–V88.

1 Motivate

Why It Matters

Remind the class that the final year of World War II was both a sad and a joyful time for Americans. People around the world were dying in the war, but major events were bringing the war closer to an end. Some of those events occurred in Europe, others in the Pacific. Parallel time lines can help students understand how battles in those two locations were related in time.

·SKILLS· Read Parallel Time Lines

CHART AND GRAPH

VOCABULARY
parallel time line

▶ WHY IT MATTERS

When there are many events happening at the same time in different places, it can be difficult to put them in order on one time line. Parallel time lines can help. **Parallel time lines** are two or more time lines that show the same period of time. Parallel time lines can also show events that happened in different places.

▶ WHAT YOU NEED TO KNOW

The parallel time lines on this page show events that took place in 1945, the last year of World War II. Time Line A shows the important events that affected the European front. Time Line B shows the important events that affected the Pacific front. You can use these parallel time lines to compare when different events in different places happened.

▶ PRACTICE THE SKILL

1. Which event took place first, the Pearl Harbor attack or the declaration of war on Germany and Italy?

2. Did the Allies capture Guam before or after they captured North Africa?

3. Why do you think the label *Truman becomes President* is on both lines?

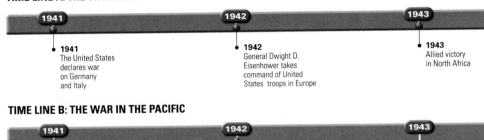

TIME LINE A: THE WAR IN EUROPE

1941	1942	1943
1941 The United States declares war on Germany and Italy	**1942** General Dwight D. Eisenhower takes command of United States troops in Europe	**1943** Allied victory in North Africa

TIME LINE B: THE WAR IN THE PACIFIC

1941	1942	1943
1941 Japanese forces attack Pearl Harbor, Hawaii	**1942** United States forces strike Tokyo, Japan	

570 ▪ Unit 7

INTEGRATE LANGUAGE ARTS

Write a News Report
Have students use the information from the time lines on pages 570–571 to write news reports about World War II. Encourage students to include transitions when switching between the war in Europe and the war in the Pacific. Ask students to deliver their reports as if they were radio broadcasters during World War II.

MAKE IT RELEVANT

In Your State and Community
Organize students into groups and assign one of the following decades to each group: 1950s, 1960s, 1970s, 1980s, or 1990s. Have groups make parallel time lines of their decade, one for their state and one for their community. Ask volunteers to share their time lines with the class.

4 What happened in the Pacific the year that Dwight D. Eisenhower arrived to command United States forces in Europe?

➡ APPLY WHAT YOU LEARNED

Create parallel time lines of events that have happened in your lifetime. Use one time line to show the important events in your life, beginning with the

The *Enola Gay* sits on a runway on Tinian Island in the Pacific after dropping an atom bomb on Hiroshima, Japan.

year you were born and ending with the present year. Use the other time line to show important events that have taken place in the United States during these same years.

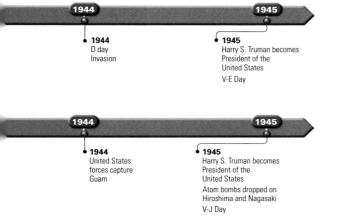

1944
1945

1944
D day
Invasion

1945
Harry S. Truman becomes
President of the
United States
V-E Day

1944
1945

1944
United States
forces capture
Guam

1945
Harry S. Truman becomes
President of the
United States
Atom bombs dropped on
Hiroshima and Nagasaki
V-J Day

CHART AND GRAPH SKILLS

Chapter 15 ■ 571

---

2 Teach

What You Need to Know

Suggest that students use two different strategies to read the parallel time lines. Have them read each line across to get a sense of the sequence of the events that occurred on each front. Make sure students understand that the time lines cover the same period of time but different geographic areas.

Practice the Skill—Answers

1 Both events occurred in 1941.

2 The Allies captured Guam after they captured North Africa.

3 It is on both time lines because both fronts were affected when Truman became President.

4 The United States forces raided Tokyo.

3 Close

Apply What You Learned

Students should create time lines that show certain dates in their lives and specific events that occurred on those dates. The second time lines should display accurate information about events that happened in the United States.

ACTIVITY BOOK

Use ACTIVITY BOOK, p. 146, to give students additional practice using this skill.

TRANSPARENCY

Use SKILL TRANSPARENCY 7-4.

Lesson 4

PAGES 572–575

OBJECTIVES

- Identify changes that occurred in countries after World War II.

- Examine the creation of the United Nations and the relationship of the United States to other nations in the fight against communism.

 Cause and Effect pp. 553, 572, 573, 574, 575, 576

Vocabulary

SEE READING AND VOCABULARY TRANSPARENCY 7-10 OR THE WORD CARDS ON PP. V87–V88.

Holocaust p. 573

refugee p. 573

communism p. 574

free world p. 575

cold war p. 575

 When Minutes Count

Invite pairs of students to examine the illustrations in the lesson. Then have them come up with one question they think will be answered by reading the lesson. Encourage students to read the lesson to find the answers to their questions.

Quick Summary

This lesson examines the effects of World War II, including how Germany was divided, how the United States became a world leader, and how the Cold War began.

 Motivate

Set the Purpose

Big Idea Lead a discussion about what a threat to democracy might be.

Access Prior Knowledge

Have students discuss what they have learned about why countries have conflicts with each other.

 · L E S S O N ·

4

CAUSE AND EFFECT

As you read, look for the events that caused two major powers to emerge from the war.

BIG IDEA

The end of the war brought about another threat to democracy.

VOCABULARY

Holocaust
refugee
communism
free world
cold war

The Effects of the War

1901   1951   2001

1945–1948

World War II caused more death and destruction than any other war in history. About 17 million soldiers died as a result of the war, including more than 400,000 American soldiers. No one knows for certain how many civilians were killed, but the number was in the millions. The end of the war also focused the world's attention on another horror—what had happened in the Nazis' concentration camps.

The Holocaust

Not until the war in Europe was over did people discover everything that Hitler and the Nazis had done. As Allied troops marched across central Europe toward Berlin, they freed people in the Nazis' concentration camps. The Allies learned that more than 6 million men, women, and children had been murdered in those camps. One of the largest of them was at Auschwitz (OWSH•vits), in Poland. About one and a half million people were killed at this concentration camp.

The photograph below shows the harsh, barbed-wire fence that surrounded the concentration camp at Auschwitz.

572 Unit 7

REACH ALL LEARNERS

English as a Second Language Have students write these words: *abolish, illegal, delegates, disabled,* and *propaganda.* Have them try to write a definition of each word, without using a dictionary, as they find the word in the lesson. If they cannot figure out a word's meaning from context, then have them use a dictionary to define the term.

WORD WORK

Categorize Vocabulary Have students read the definitions of the vocabulary terms found in the chapter. Then ask them to categorize the terms based on whether they refer to politics and government or to personal hardship.

Politics and Government	Personal Hardship
communism	Holocaust
free world	refugee
cold war	

Many Nazi leaders were tried for their crimes in a court in Nuremberg, Germany.

The Nazis killed people for many reasons. Many were killed for their religious and political beliefs. Others were killed because they were ill or disabled and could not work. The largest group of victims were Jews, the people Hitler blamed for Germany's problems.

During the war more than 6 million Jewish people were murdered on Hitler's orders. This terrible mass murder of more than two-thirds of all European Jews came to be known as the **Holocaust** (HOH•luh•kawst). Hitler had called it the "final solution to the Jewish question." It was a planned attempt to destroy an entire people.

Beginning in 1945, Nazi leaders accused of committing these deeds were brought to trial by the Allies. The most important trials were held in the German city of Nuremberg. Many of the Nazi leaders were convicted and sentenced to death for their crimes.

REVIEW **What was the Holocaust?** It was the terrible mass murder of more than two-thirds of all European Jews.

Plans for Peace

When World War II ended, cities and towns across Europe and in Japan and other places where the fighting had taken place were in ruins. In some cities more than 9 of every 10 buildings were too badly damaged to be used. Many people had no homes, no jobs, and often nothing to eat. They became **refugees**— people who seek shelter and safety elsewhere. They traveled from place to place in search of food and a safe place to live.

The United States came out of World War II as the strongest nation in the world. Americans used this strength to help feed and clothe war refugees and rebuild war-torn countries. The United States worked with other nations to create agencies that supplied food, clothing, shelter, and medical care to millions of people around the world. Much of the money spent by these agencies came from people in the United States.

Chapter 15 ■ 573

2 Teach

The Holocaust

Read and Respond

History Even before World War II, the term *holocaust* was applied to any great or widespread destruction. When the magnitude of Hitler's crimes became known, it seemed appropriate to apply the term *holocaust* to them.

Q What was one of the largest concentration camps?

A Auschwitz, in Poland

Plans for Peace

Read and Respond

Civics and Government Have students recall the League of Nations and identify the similarities between the League of Nations and the United Nations.

Q Why do you think the United States joined the United Nations even though it had not joined the League of Nations?

A United States leaders realized that it was not possible to be isolated from the rest of the world. After the war, the United States, as one of the strongest nations in the world, wanted to work for peace.

Visual Learning

Map Have students study the map of Europe during the Cold War.

CAPTION ANSWER The map shows how Germany was under the control of other countries.

Read and Respond

History Explain that Japan was also occupied by American troops after the war. Like Germany, Japan was forced to dismantle its military structure. Discuss with students why the Allies would want to disarm Germany and Japan.

A Changed World

Read and Respond

Link History and Geography
Bulgaria, Romania, Hungary, Poland, Czechoslovakia, Albania, and Yugoslavia all became communist countries in the 1940s. Have students find these countries on a map and discuss why they were important to the Soviet Union. Because they either bordered the Soviet Union or a waterway that Soviets may have used.

 **Close**

Summarize Key Content

- On Hitler's orders, more than 6 million Jewish people were murdered in Nazi concentration camps.
- After the war the United States helped feed and clothe refugees in Europe.
- The Soviet Union began to spread communism, and the free world fought against it.
- The conflict between communist countries and the free world was called the Cold War.

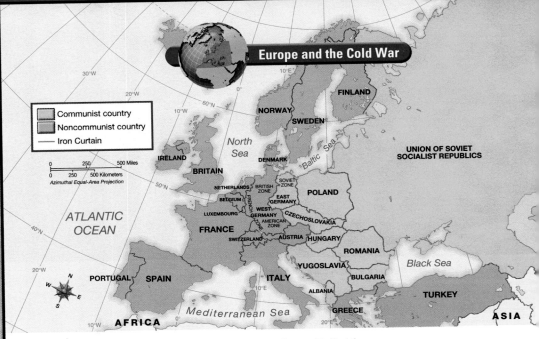

Europe and the Cold War

- ▢ Communist country
- ▢ Noncommunist country
- — Iron Curtain

0 250 500 Miles
0 250 500 Kilometers
Azimuthal Equal-Area Projection

FINLAND
NORWAY
SWEDEN
UNION OF SOVIET SOCIALIST REPUBLICS
North Sea
Baltic Sea
IRELAND
BRITAIN
DENMARK
SOVIET ZONE
NETHERLANDS BRITISH ZONE
BELGIUM EAST GERMANY
POLAND
ATLANTIC OCEAN
LUXEMBOURG FRENCH WEST GERMANY ZONE
AMERICAN ZONE
CZECHOSLOVAKIA
FRANCE
SWITZERLAND AUSTRIA HUNGARY
ROMANIA
YUGOSLAVIA
Black Sea
PORTUGAL SPAIN
ITALY
BULGARIA
ALBANIA
TURKEY
GREECE
Mediterranean Sea
AFRICA
ASIA

Place World War II changed Europe in ways that would affect the world for years to come.

◈ What does this map show about changes that took place in Germany after World War II?

Even before the fighting ended, the United States and the other Allies had begun to make plans for peace. They decided to abolish Germany's armed forces and make the Nazi party illegal. They also decided to take some land away from Germany and divide the country into four parts. Each of the major Allies—the United States, Britain, France, and the Soviet Union—took control of one part.

Just as they had after World War I, world leaders again turned to the idea of an organization of nations. This time the United States supported the idea. In April 1945, delegates from 50 countries met in San Francisco to form the United Nations,

or UN. Today, the UN is located in New York City. The purpose of the UN is to keep world peace and promote cooperation among nations.

REVIEW How did the Allies' plans for peace affect Germany? ◉ CAUSE AND EFFECT the plans changed Germany's armed forces, government, and land distribution

A Changed World

Even as plans for peace were being made, new conflicts were beginning. The United States and the Soviet Union had been allies during World War II. But that changed quickly once the war ended. The Soviet Union was a communist nation. **Communism** is a social and economic system in which all land and industries are

574 ■ Unit 7

owned by the government. Individuals have few rights and little freedom.

When the war ended, the Soviet Union began setting up communist governments in the eastern European countries it had invaded during the war. The **free world**—the United States and its allies in the fight against communism—saw this as a threat to freedom.

At the urging of President Truman and other leaders, such as Secretary of State George C. Marshall, the United States began to help countries fight communism by giving them military and economic aid. In 1948 the United States Congress passed the European Recovery Act, also known as the Marshall Plan. It provided $13 billion to help European countries rebuild their economies. President Truman believed that an economically healthy Europe would have little interest in communism.

Hostility, or unfriendliness, soon developed between the free world and the

President Harry S. Truman (left) meets with Secretary of State George C. Marshall (right).

communist nations. This hostility became known as the Cold War. A **cold war** is fought mostly with propaganda and money rather than with soldiers and weapons. For much of the second half of the twentieth century, the Cold War shaped many world events.

REVIEW How did the United States help countries fight communism? by giving them military and economic aid

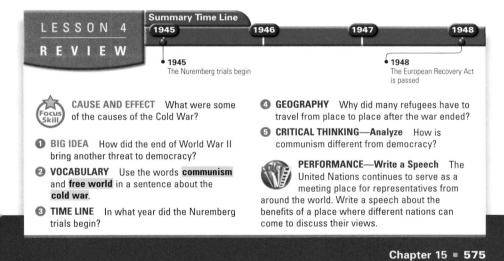

LESSON 4 REVIEW

Summary Time Line
1945 — 1946 — 1947 — 1948

1945
The Nuremberg trials begin

1948
The European Recovery Act is passed

CAUSE AND EFFECT What were some of the causes of the Cold War?

❶ **BIG IDEA** How did the end of World War II bring another threat to democracy?

❷ **VOCABULARY** Use the words **communism** and **free world** in a sentence about the **cold war**.

❸ **TIME LINE** In what year did the Nuremberg trials begin?

❹ **GEOGRAPHY** Why did many refugees have to travel from place to place after the war ended?

❺ **CRITICAL THINKING—Analyze** How is communism different from democracy?

 PERFORMANCE—Write a Speech The United Nations continues to serve as a meeting place for representatives from around the world. Write a speech about the benefits of a place where different nations can come to discuss their views.

Chapter 15 ■ 575

Chapter 15 Review

 CAUSE AND EFFECT

Students may use the graphic organizer that appears on page 148 of the Activity Book. Answers appear in the Activity Book, Teacher's Edition.

Think & Write

Write a Conversation Students' conversations should display an awareness of the events surrounding the decision to launch the D day invasion and the strategy employed in it. They should mention the victories in North Africa and Italy as well as the details about the planned invasion.

Write a Diary Entry Students' diary entries should reflect an understanding of how World War II affected the availability of certain goods and services. Diaries may discuss the types and quantities of products a family could buy. Some students may relate how they helped with the war effort by recycling products or buying war bonds. The tone and style of the entry should reflect that of a personal diary.

ACTIVITY BOOK

A copy of the graphic organizer appears in the ACTIVITY BOOK on page 148.

TRANSPARENCY

The graphic organizer appears on READING AND VOCABULARY TRANSPARENCY 7-11.

· CHAPTER ·

15 Review and Test Preparation

Summary Time Line
1920

 Cause and Effect

Copy the following graphic organizer onto a separate sheet of paper. Use the information you have learned to determine the causes and effects of the involvement of the United States in World War II.

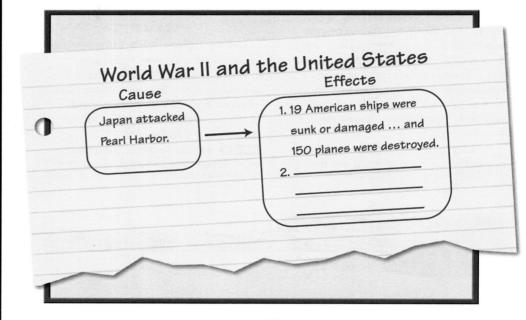

World War II and the United States

Cause

Japan attacked Pearl Harbor.

Effects

1. 19 American ships were sunk or damaged ... and 150 planes were destroyed.

2. _____

THINK & WRITE

Write a Conversation Write a conversation that could have taken place between Dwight D. Eisenhower and some of his advisers the night before the D day invasion. The individuals should discuss how important it is for the operation to succeed.

Write a Diary Entry Imagine that you are living during World War II. Write a diary entry about going shopping with your family. Describe the ways the war has affected what you can buy. Also describe other ways the war has affected your family.

576 ■ Chapter 15

TEST PREPARATION

Review these tips with students:

■ Read the directions before reading the questions.

■ Read each question twice, focusing the second time on all the possible answers.

■ Take the time to think about all the possible answers before deciding on an answer.

■ Move past questions that give you trouble, and answer the ones you know. Then return to the difficult items.

UNIT PROJECT

Class Newspaper Inform students that they should continue adding headings to their outlines. Suggest to students that they begin to include a level of details about each person, event, and place they have used as a heading.

1939
World War II begins as German forces invade Poland

1941
The United States enters World War II

1942
Japanese Americans ordered into relocation camps

1944
The D day invasion takes place

1945
World War II ends

1948
The European Recovery Act is passed

USE THE TIME LINE

Use the chapter summary time line to answer these questions.

1 When did World War II begin?

2 How many years after the D day invasion was the European Recovery Act passed?

USE VOCABULARY

Use each term in a complete sentence that will help explain its meaning.

3 concentration camp (p. 555)

4 civilian (p. 557)

5 interest (p. 562)

6 D day (p. 565)

7 Holocaust (p. 573)

RECALL FACTS

Answer these questions.

8 How did the United States help Great Britain even before American forces entered World War II?

9 Why did the federal government set up a rationing program during World War II?

10 What was V-J day?

Write the letter of the best choice.

11 One major effect of the D day invasion was that—
  A it caused Germany to surrender.
  B it helped the Allies move into France.
  C it caused Japan to surrender.
  D it helped the Allies gain control of Italy.

12 After World War II, world leaders came together to form—
  F the United Nations.
  G the League of Nations.
  H the Red Cross.
  J the Works Progress Administration.

THINK CRITICALLY

13 What do you think was Franklin D. Roosevelt's greatest accomplishment?

14 What do you think was Dwight D. Eisenhower's greatest contribution to the war effort?

15 How did World War II change the world?

APPLY SKILLS

Predict a Historical Outcome
Review the information on page 559. Then answer the following question.

16 What do you predict happened to relations between the United States and the Soviet Union in the decades after World War II? Explain how you arrived at your answer.

Make Economic Choices
Review the information on page 564. Then answer the following question.

17 Describe a time when you had to think about the trade-off and opportunity cost before you made a purchase.

Read Parallel Time Lines
Review the time lines on pages 570–571. Then answer the following question.

18 Did the D day invasion occur before or after Harry S. Truman became President?

Chapter 15 ▪ 577

Think Critically

13 Student responses may include Roosevelt's New Deal programs or his decision for the United States to enter into World War II.

14 Students' responses should reflect that Eisenhower led the successful D day invasion in France.

15 It led to the formation of several new alliances and the founding of the United Nations.

Apply Skills

16 **Predict a Historical Outcome**
Students may indicate that relations between the two countries would grow more tense in the years following World War II. Students should cite the prediction steps listed on page 559 as evidence of how they arrived at their answers.

17 **Make Economic Choices**
Students' responses should correctly discuss the terms **trade-off** and **opportunity cost**.

18 **Read Parallel Time Lines** before Truman became the President

ACTIVITY BOOK

Use the CHAPTER 15 TEST PREPARATION, page 149, of the Activity Book.

ASSESSMENT

Use the CHAPTER 15 TEST pages 117–120 of the Assessment Program.

Use the Time Line

1 in 1939

2 four

Use Vocabulary

3 Germans placed millions of people in **concentration camps**.

4 A **civilian** is a person who is not in the military.

5 When people cash in bonds, they receive their money back plus **interest**.

6 **D day** was the largest water-to-land invasion in history.

7 The mass murder of more than two-thirds of all European Jews is known as the **Holocaust**.

Recall Facts

8 They supplied war materials to the Allies, including Great Britain. (p. 557)

9 to preserve necessary items in support of the war effort (p. 561)

10 Victory over Japan Day (p. 568)

11 F (p. 566)

12 A (p. 574)

Chapter 16 Planning Guide Into Modern Times

Introducing the Chapter, pp. 578–579

LESSON	PACING	OBJECTIVES	VOCABULARY
Introduce the Chapter pp. 578–579	1 Day	■ Interpret information in visuals. ■ Use critical thinking skills to organize and analyze information.	**Word Work:** Preview Vocabulary, p. 579
1 The Early Years of the Cold War pp. 580–584	1 Day	■ Analyze the division of Germany and Korea into separate nations following the end of World War II. ■ Describe how the Cold War led to an arms race and a space race between the United States and Soviet Union. ■ Analyze the factors behind the missile crisis in Cuba.	superpower airlift cease-fire arms race satellite
2 Working for Equal Rights pp. 585–589	1 Day	■ Identify the reasons behind the struggle for civil rights. ■ Identify the achievements of individuals who contributed to the struggle for civil rights. ■ Describe and evaluate the struggles of various groups to gain equal rights.	nonviolence integration migrant worker **Word Work:** Structural Clues, p. 585
3 The Cold War Continues pp. 590–593	1 Day	■ Discuss causes and effects of American involvement in the Vietnam War. ■ Examine the changing relationship between the United States and its Cold War adversaries. ■ Describe the contributions of President Lyndon Johnson. ■ Summarize the Watergate scandal and the resolution to end the war in Vietnam.	arms control détente scandal **Word Work:** Preview Vocabulary, p. 590

Predict an Outcome, p. 579

READING	INTEGRATE LEARNING	REACH ALL LEARNERS	RESOURCES
Reading Social Studies: **Graphic Organizer,** p. 581 **Reading Social Studies:** **Graphic Organizer Responses,** p. 584	**Mathematics** **Compute Measurement,** p. 581	**Tactile Learners,** p. 580 **Extend and Enrich,** p. 584 **Reteach the Lesson,** p. 584	**Activity Book,** pp. 150–151 **Reading and Vocabulary Transparency, 7-12**
Reading Social Studies: **Personal Response,** p. 586 **Predict an Outcome,** p. 587 **Reading Social Studies:** **Personal Response,** p. 589	**Music** **Interpret Lyrics,** p. 585 **Art** **Draw a Poster,** p. 586	**Extend and Enrich,** p. 589 **Reteach the Lesson,** p. 589	**Activity Book,** p. 152 **Reading and Vocabulary Transparency, 7-13**
Reading Social Studies: **K-W-L Chart,** p. 591 **Reading Social Studies:** **Graphic Organizer,** p. 591 **Reading Social Studies:** **K-W-L Chart Responses,** p. 593	**Languages** **Vietnamese,** p. 591 **Art** **Make a Collage,** p. 592	**Advanced Learners,** p. 590 **Extend and Enrich,** p. 593 **Reteach the Lesson,** p. 593	**Activity Book,** p. 153 **Reading and Vocabulary Transparency, 7-14** Internet Resources

Chapter 16 Planning Guide Into Modern Times

LESSON	PACING	OBJECTIVES	VOCABULARY
EXAMINE PRIMARY SOURCES **Editorial Cartoons** pp. 594–595	1 Day	■ Identify editorial cartoons as expressions of opinions regarding politics or government. ■ Identify the points of view illustrated by historical editorial cartoons.	
4 A World of Change pp. 596–601	2 Days	■ Discuss the causes and effects of the Iran hostage crisis. ■ Examine how American international relations changed when the Cold War ended. ■ Describe the contributions of national leaders such as Jimmy Carter, Ronald Reagan, George Bush, and Bill Clinton. ■ Explain how terrorism has affected the United States.	terrorism deficit hijack **Word Work:** Related Words, p. 596
MAP AND GLOBE SKILLS **Read a Population Map** pp. 602–603	1 Day	■ Apply geographic tools, including keys, to interpret maps. ■ Organize and interpret information from maps.	population density
Chapter Review and Test Preparation pp. 604–605	1 Day		

READING	INTEGRATE LEARNING	REACH ALL LEARNERS	RESOURCES
		Extend and Enrich, p. 595 **Reteach,** p. 595	Internet Resources
Reading Social Studies: **Anticipation Guide,** p. 597 Reading Social Studies: **Anticipation Guide Responses,** p. 601	Language Arts **Expository Writing,** p. 597	**Below-Level Learners,** p. 598 **Extend and Enrich,** p. 601 **Reteach the Lesson,** p. 601	**Activity Book,** pp. 154–155 **Reading and Vocabulary Transparency,** 7-15 Internet Resources
		Reteach the Skill, p. 602 **Extend and Enrich,** p. 603	**Activity Book,** pp. 156–157 **Skill Transparency,** 7-5 **GeoSkills CD-ROM**
		Test Preparation, p. 604	**Activity Book,** pp. 158–159 **Reading and Vocabulary Transparency,** 7-16 **Assessment Program, Chapter 16 Test,** pp. 121–124

Activity Book

Name _____ Date _____

The Early Years of the Cold War

Directions In the space provided, write the year each of the following events took place. Then write the number of each event in the appropriate place on the time line.

1 __1952__ Americans elect Dwight D. Eisenhower as President.

2 __1949__ China becomes a communist country.

3 __1958__ Congress sets up NASA.

4 __1959__ Cuba becomes a communist country.

5 __1961__ East Germany builds a wall to stop its citizens from leaving.

6 __1963__ Lyndon Johnson becomes President of the United States.

7 __1950__ North Korea invades South Korea.

8 __1963__ President Kennedy is assassinated.

9 __1948__ South Korea becomes a republic; North Korea becomes a communist country.

10 __1948__ The Soviet Union cuts Berlin off from West Germany.

11 __1957__ The Soviet Union launches *Sputnik,* the first space satellite.

12 __1962__ The United States blockades Cuba to force it to remove Soviet missiles.

13 __1969__ United States astronaut Neil Armstrong becomes the first human to walk on the moon.

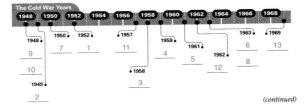

The Cold War Years
1948 1950 1952 1954 1956 1958 1960 1962 1964 1966 1968

1948   1950 1952   1957   1959   1963   1969
9   7   1   11   4   1961   6   13
10   1962   8
1949   1958   5   12
2   3

(continued)

150 ■ Activity Book   Use after reading Chapter 16, Lesson 1, pages 580–584.

Name _____ Date _____

Directions Use the information from the time line on the previous page to decide whether each statement below is true or false. If the statement is true, write a *T* next to the statement. If the statement is false, write an *F* and explain why the statement is false.

__F__ **14** North Korea became a communist country by following the example set by Cuba. North Korea became a communist country 11 years before Cuba did.

__F__ **15** Congress set up NASA in response to the Soviet blockade of Berlin. The Berlin blockade occurred ten years before Congress set up NASA. Congress acted in response to the launch of *Sputnik.*

__F__ **16** President Johnson tried to stop China from becoming a communist country. By the time Johnson became president in 1963, China had been a communist nation for 14 years.

__T__ **17** The United States was the first nation to land a person on the moon.

__F__ **18** The Soviet Union launched *Sputnik* to force President Kennedy to back down during the Cuban Missile Crisis. The Soviet Union launched *Sputnik* five years before the Cuban Missile Crisis.

Use after reading Chapter 16, Lesson 1, pages 580–584.   **Activity Book ■ 151**

Name _____ Date _____

Working for Equal Rights

Directions Use the information below to complete the chart.

- Thurgood Marshall
- This person's refusal to give up a seat on a segregated bus led the United States Supreme Court to rule that public transportation could no longer be segregated.
- This leader fought for the rights of migrant farm workers and helped start a group that became the United Farm Workers.

- Malcolm X
- Cesar Chavez
- This winner of the Nobel Peace Prize helped lead the Montgomery Bus Boycott, encouraged people to use nonviolent ways to end segregation, and led a famous civil rights march in Washington, D.C.

Civil Rights Activist	Notable Ideas/Accomplishments
Cesar Chavez	This leader led a nationwide boycott of California grapes to convince grape growers to improve the pay and conditions for migrant workers.
Dolores Huerta	This leader fought for the rights of migrant farm workers and helped start a group that became the United Farm Workers.
Martin Luther King, Jr.	This winner of the Nobel Peace Prize helped lead the Montgomery Bus Boycott, encouraged people to use nonviolent ways to end segregation, and led a famous civil rights march in Washington, D.C.
Thurgood Marshall	This lawyer argued and won the case *Brown v. Board of Education of Topeka,* which resulted in a United States Supreme Court ruling that public schools could no longer be segregated.
Rosa Parks	This person's refusal to give up a seat on a segregated bus led the United States Supreme Court to rule that public transportation could no longer be segregated.
Malcolm X	This civil rights leader at first spoke in favor of segregation, but later talked about racial cooperation.

152 ■ Activity Book   Use after reading Chapter 16, Lesson 2, pages 585–589.

Name _____ Date _____

The Cold War Continues

Directions Below is a list of causes and effects related to the Vietnam War. Write each item from the list in the appropriate box on the cause-and-effect chart.

Bombing does not stop North Vietnam from supporting Vietcong

President Nixon signs cease-fire

President Johnson orders bombing of North Vietnam

United States economy suffers

United States wants to stop spread of communism

President Nixon wants to withdraw from Vietnam, but does not want communists to take over South Vietnam

South Vietnam surrenders

United States blockades North Vietnam and increases bombing

CAUSE → **EFFECT**

CAUSE	EFFECT
United States wants to stop spread of communism.	United States supports South Vietnam
North Vietnam torpedoes United States Navy Ship	President Johnson orders bombing of North Vietnam
Bombing does not stop North Vietnam from supporting Vietcong	United States sends hundreds of thousands of soldiers to help South Vietnam
United States government raises taxes and borrows money	United States economy suffers
President Nixon wants to withdraw from Vietnam, but does not want communists to take over South Vietnam	United States begins bringing troops home but also sends some troops to Cambodia to destroy North Vietnam's war supplies
North Vietnam starts large-scale attack on South Vietnam	United States blockades North Vietnam and increases bombing
President Nixon signs cease-fire	United States troops come home
North Vietnam attacks South Vietnam again	South Vietnam surrenders

Use after reading Chapter 16, Lesson 3, pages 590–593.   **Activity Book ■ 153**

LESSON 4

Name _____ Date _____

A World of Change

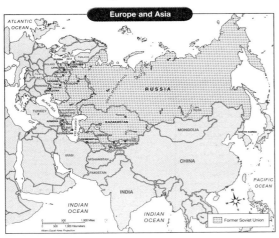

Europe and Asia

Use after reading Chapter 16, Lesson 4, pages 596–601.

(continued)

LESSON 4

Name _____ Date _____

Directions Study the map on the facing and answer the questions below.

1 When the Soviet Union broke up, how many independent countries were formed? 15

2 Which of these independent countries is the largest? Russia

3 Which of these independent countries are landlocked? Armenia, Azerbaijan, Belarus, Kazakhstan, Kyrgyzstan, Moldova, Tajikistan, Turkmenistan, Uzbekistan

4 Which of these independent countries share a border with China?
Kazakhstan, Kyrgyzstan, Russia, Tajikistan

5 Which of these independent countries share a border with Afghanistan?
Turkmenistan, Uzbekistan, Tajikistan

6 Which of these independent countries have access to the Black Sea?
Georgia, Russia, Ukraine

7 Which body of water is at the southern end of the Volga River?
the Caspian Sea

8 What is the capital of Uzbekistan? Tashkent

9 Of the countries that were formerly part of the Soviet Union, which has the northernmost capital? Estonia

10 Which mountains are on the northern border of the Republic of Georgia?
the Caucasus Mountains

SKILL PRACTICE

Name _____ Date _____

 MAP AND GLOBE SKILLS
Read a Population Map

Directions Study the map, and answer the questions below.

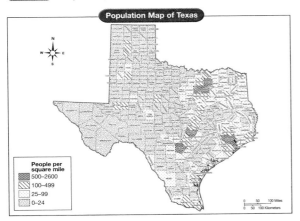

Population Map of Texas

People per square mile
500–2600
100–499
25–99
0–24

1 About how many people per square mile live in El Paso?
between 100 and 500

2 About how many people per square mile live in Corpus Christi?
between 100 and 500

3 Do more people live in Plano or in Dallas? Dallas

4 Which is more populated, East Texas or West Texas? East Texas

(continued)

Use after reading Chapter 16, Skill Lesson, pages 602–603.

SKILL PRACTICE

Name _____ Date _____

Population density is the number of people per unit of area, such as "100 people per square mile." Population density describes how crowded an area is. To calculate population density, divide the total number of people by the total area of land. For example, the United States has a population of 272,639,608 and is 3,717,796 square miles in area.

Population ÷ Area = Population Density
272,639,608 ÷ 3,717,796 = about 73 people per square mile

To do this on a calculator:

enter 272639608   press ÷   enter 3717796   press =

Directions Calculate the population densities of the nations listed below.

5 Australia's population is 18,783,551 people, and its area is 2,967,900 square miles.

$$\frac{18,783,551}{(population)} \div \frac{2,967,900}{(area)} = \frac{about\ 6}{(population\ density)}$$ people per square mile

6 United Kingdom's population is 59,113,439 people, and its area is 94,500 square miles.

$$\frac{59,113,439}{(population)} \div \frac{94,500}{(area)} = \frac{about\ 626}{(population\ density)}$$ people per square mile

7 Russia's population is 146,393,569 people, and its area is 6,592,800 square miles.

$$\frac{146,393,569}{(population)} \div \frac{6,592,800}{(area)} = \frac{about\ 22}{(population\ density)}$$ people per square mile

8 Japan's population is 126,182,077 people, and its area is 145,882 square miles.

$$\frac{126,182,077}{(population)} \div \frac{145,882}{(area)} = \frac{about\ 865}{(population\ density)}$$ people per square mile

Name _____ Date _____

The Cold War and the End of the Soviet Union

Directions Complete this graphic organizer by filling in facts and outcomes about the Cold War.

EVENT	FACTS	OUTCOME
The Cuban Missile Crisis	The Soviet Union places nuclear missiles in Cuba, less than one hundred miles from the coast of the United States. →	The U.S. sets up a blockade. Eventually the missiles are removed. _____ _____

EVENT	FACTS	OUTCOME
Mikhail Gorbachev becomes the leader of the Soviet Union.	As leader, Gorbachev introduces reforms that give the Soviet people more freedoms. →	The reforms introduced by Gorbachev lead to the end of the Soviet Union. _____ _____

© Harcourt

· CHAPTER · Name _____ Date _____

16 Test Preparation

Directions Read each question and choose the best answer. then fill in the circle for the answer you have chosen. be sure to fill in the circle completely.

1 In an arms race, nations compete to —
Ⓐ sell the most weapons.
Ⓑ use the most weapons.
● build the most weapons.
Ⓓ destroy the most weapons.

2 In the case *Brown v. Board of Education of Topeka* the United States Supreme Court decided that —
Ⓕ all cities must set up public school systems.
Ⓖ segregation on school buses is unconstitutional.
● segregated schools cannot offer an equal education.
Ⓙ all teachers must receive equal pay, no matter what their race is.

3 Sandra Day O'Connor was the first woman to —
Ⓐ orbit the Earth and walk on the moon.
Ⓑ run for President of the United States.
● serve as a United States Supreme Court justice.
Ⓓ fight for the rights of migrant workers.

4 What was the Great Society?
Ⓕ an organization that fought for civil rights for African Americans
● President Johnson's plan to improve the lives of Americans
Ⓗ the United States strategy to force Cuba to get rid of its Soviet missiles
Ⓙ an organization that encouraged people to visit the United States

5 How did President George Bush respond when Irac invaded Kuwait?
Ⓐ He pulled all United States troops out of Vietnam.
● He convinced the leaders of Egypt and Israel to sign a peace treaty.
Ⓒ He called Iraq "an evil empire."
Ⓓ He organized Operation Desert Storm.

© Harcourt

COMMUNITY RESOURCES

Historical Societies
_____
_____
_____
_____
_____

Museums
_____
_____
_____
_____
_____

Experts on the Cold War
_____
_____
_____
_____

Historical Sites
_____
_____
_____
_____

Chapter 16 Assessment

CONTENT / VOCABULARY

·CHAPTER·

Name _____ Date _____

16 Test

Part One: Test Your Understanding

MULTIPLE CHOICE (4 points each)

Directions Circle the letter of the best answer.

1 After World War II, East Germany and North Korea were both—
- **A** rebuilt by Britain, France, and the United States.
- **B** blockaded by the Soviet Union.
- **C** invaded by Soviet troops.
- **(D)** led by communist governments.

2 One of the greatest successes of the United States' Apollo space program was—
- **F** creating the world's first satellite.
- **G** launching *Sputnik*.
- **(H)** putting an astronaut on the moon.
- **J** developing the National Aeronautics and Space Administration.

3 The Cuban missile crisis ended when—
- **(A)** the Soviet Union removed all its missiles from Cuba.
- **B** the United States blockaded Cuba.
- **C** Soviet leader Nikita Khrushchev resigned.
- **D** President John F. Kennedy was assassinated.

4 Which of the following people received a Nobel Peace Prize?
- **F** Thurgood Marshall
- **G** Cesar Chavez
- **H** Sandra Day O'Connor
- **(J)** Dr. Martin Luther King, Jr.

5 Dr. Martin Luther King, Jr. believed in—
- **A** strict racial separation.
- **(B)** change through nonviolent means.
- **C** limiting the power of the federal government.
- **D** protesting the Supreme Court's ruling in *Brown v. Board of Education of Topeka*.

6 The Civil Rights Act of 1964—
- **F** ended segregation in public schools.
- **G** improved the lives of farm workers.
- **(H)** made segregation in all public places illegal.
- **J** allowed Native American tribes to run their own businesses.

(continued)

Chapter 16 Test

Assessment Program ■ **121**

CONTENT / VOCABULARY

Name _____ Date _____

7 President Lyndon Johnson's Great Society programs included plans to—
- **(A)** provide medical care for older people.
- **B** reduce the size of the federal government.
- **C** withdraw troops from Vietnam.
- **D** decrease tariffs on imported goods.

8 President Richard Nixon resigned from office because he had—
- **F** promoted trade with the Soviet Union.
- **G** visited China.
- **(H)** covered up illegal acts.
- **J** called for better training of South Vietnamese troops.

9 The removal of the Berlin Wall symbolized—
- **A** the removal of trade barriers throughout the world.
- **B** the end of the Vietnam War.
- **C** the reduction of nuclear arms through treaties.
- **(D)** new freedoms for communist nations in Europe.

10 The explosion of a bomb in a federal building in Oklahoma City was—
- **F** a result of *perestroika*.
- **G** the last battle of the Cold War.
- **(H)** an act of terrorism.
- **J** a result of the Iranian hostage crisis.

MATCHING (4 points each)

Directions Match the descriptions on the left with the terms on the right. Write the correct letter in the space provided.

11 __D__ competing countries build more weapons to protect themselves from one another

12 __C__ occurs when the government spends more money than it takes in

13 __E__ the world's first space satellite

14 __B__ bringing together people of all races in education, housing, and jobs

15 __A__ an easing of tensions between nations

- **A.** détente
- **B.** integration
- **C.** deficit
- **D.** arms race
- **E.** *Sputnik*

(continued)

122 ■ Assessment Program

Chapter 16 Test

SKILLS

Name _____ Date _____

Part Two: Test Your Skills

READ A POPULATION MAP (5 points each)

Directions Use the population map of Texas to answer the following questions.

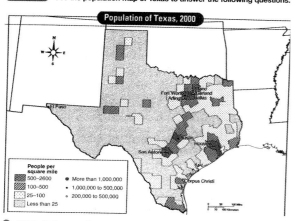

Population of Texas, 2000

People per square mile
- 500–2600 — More than 1,000,000
- 100–500 — 1,000,000 to 500,000
- 25–100 — 200,000 to 500,000
- Less than 25

16 Which city has a smaller population, Fort Worth or Arlington?
Arlington

17 What are the three cities with the greatest populations? Houston, Dallas, and San Antonio

18 Which city is located in an area with higher population density, El Paso or Corpus Christi? Corpus Christi

19 What area of Texas is the most densely populated overall—northern, southern, eastern, or western Texas? eastern Texas

(continued)

Chapter 16 Test

Assessment Program ■ **123**

APPLICATION / WRITING

Name _____ Date _____

Part Three: Apply What You Have Learned

20 **MAIN IDEA AND SUPPORTING DETAILS** (10 points)

Look at the main ideas and supporting details listed in the organizer below. Write missing details in the blanks provided.

> The Cold War was a time of unrest in the United States and around the world.

The Korean War
- Korea divided
- communist North Korea invades South Korea
- Possible responses: United Nations troops,
- 1952 presidential election, cease-fire

Race into Space
- Apollo program
- NASA
- Possible responses: *Sputnik*; satellite; John Glenn; orbit the Earth; walk on the moon

The Vietnam War
- spread of communism
- increased taxes to pay for costs of war
- Possible responses: Vietcong; antiwar protests in United States

21 **ESSAY** (10 points)

From 1945 to 1991 the world's two superpowers competed in many areas around the globe. Write a paragraph describing the events in one country where the United States and the Soviet Union struggled for control, and explain the importance of this power struggle.

Responses may discuss the missile crisis in Cuba, the Berlin airlift, or the Korean or Vietnam wars. Students should explain the importance of the chosen event to the overall Cold War.

124 ■ Assessment Program

Chapter 16 Test

Introduce the Chapter

PAGES 578–579

OBJECTIVES

- Interpret information in visuals.
- Use critical thinking skills to organize and analyze information.

Access Prior Knowledge

Ask students to think about why conflicts arise between countries. Have them discuss the issues that could lead countries to be in conflict with each other.

Visual Learning

Picture As students look over the photograph, ask them how the library represents President Reagan and his presidency.

Locate It Map Home of the Reagan Presidential Library, the Simi Valley in California lies at the western end of the San Fernando Valley roughly 30 miles (48 km) from the center of Los Angeles.

RONALD REAGAN PRESIDENTIAL LIBRARY

The Ronald Reagan Presidential Library is one of ten presidential libraries. In this photograph taken outside the library, a piece of the Berlin Wall is displayed. The original wall was 96 miles (154 km) long and divided Germany for almost 30 years. Helping bring down the wall was one of President Reagan's greatest accomplishments.

LOCATE IT

CALIFORNIA

Ronald Reagan Presidential Library

578 ▪ Unit 7

BACKGROUND

Picture Point out that a presidential library is devoted to housing papers, records, documents, and other items associated with a President during his time in office. Many presidential libraries also include personal objects, such as desks, that belonged to the President.

The Ronald Reagan Presidential Library, which opened in 1991, contains numerous collections and archives. Copies of Reagan's major speeches; collections of photographs; written and audiovisual material; and biographical information all can be found at the library.

BACKGROUND

Quotation The Berlin Wall was one of the most powerful symbols of the Cold War. It was built in the 1960s by East Germany with the help of the Soviet Union because supporters of communism wanted to separate the communist section of Berlin from the rest of the city. Citizens of East Berlin were kept behind the wall, and the rest of the world was kept out of East Berlin. The wall stood until 1989.

16

Into Modern Times

" **Mr. Gorbachev, tear down this wall.** "

—Ronald Reagan, June 12, 1987,
in a speech at the Berlin Wall

 Predict an Outcome

When people make **predictions**, they use information and past experiences to determine what will happen next.

As you read this chapter, make predictions about outcomes for events that affected the United States in the second half of the twentieth century.

• List facts about events, people, or places.

• Use your list to make predictions.

Chapter 16 ■ 579

Read and Respond

Have a volunteer read the title aloud, then ask students what the title suggests about the chapter.

Quotation Explain that President Reagan worked closely with Soviet leader Mikhail Gorbachev to bring about the end of the Cold War.

Q **How did the cooperation between Gorbachev and Reagan influence world affairs?**

A The conversation started by President Reagan and Mikhail Gorbachev led the East Germans to open, and then tear down, the Berlin Wall.

 Predict an Outcome

Have students use a graphic organizer to make predictions about how certain events affected the history of the United States.

• Students will find a blank graphic organizer on page 158 of the Activity Book.

• A completed graphic organizer can be found on page 158 of the Activity Book, Teacher's Edition.

WORD WORK

Preview Vocabulary Have students work in pairs and read through the terms in the lesson vocabulary lists. Ask students to pick out and define the compound words on the lists. Remind students that a compound word is one word made by joining two words.

Compound Word	Definition

MAKE IT RELEVANT

Discussion Topics Use these topics to generate discussion as you teach the chapter.

■ Do you think a government should be allowed to keep its people from leaving the country?

■ Why would a government want to have a great amount of control over the lives of the citizens?

■ What skills do you need if you are going to talk to people who think differently from you?

OBJECTIVES

- Analyze the division of Germany and Korea into separate nations following the end of World War II.
- Describe how the Cold War led to an arms race and a space race between the United States and the Soviet Union.
- Analyze the factors behind the missile crisis in Cuba.

Predict an Outcome
pp. 579, 580, 583, 584, 604

Vocabulary

SEE READING AND VOCABULARY TRANSPARENCY 7-12 OR THE WORD CARDS ON PP. V89–V90.

superpower p. 580

airlift p. 581

cease-fire p. 582

arms race p. 582

satellite p. 583

When Minutes Count

Have students skim the lesson to find out the meaning of *arms race* and which two countries were involved in one.

Quick Summary

This lesson examines the early years of the Cold War between the United States and the Soviet Union. It explains how conflicts such as the Korean War and the Cuban missile crisis were conflicts between the superpowers.

1 Motivate

Set the Purpose

Big Idea Explain that tense relations between the free world and communist countries led to conflicts.

Access Prior Knowledge

Have students discuss the two countries involved in the Cold War.

· LESSON ·

1

PREDICT AN OUTCOME

As you read, predict the effects of the conflict between the United States and the Soviet Union.

BIG IDEA

The Cold War affected relations between the free world and communist nations.

VOCABULARY

superpower
airlift
cease-fire
arms race
satellite

FAST FACT American and British pilots made more than 272,000 flights over East Germany during the Berlin Airlift.

The Early Years of the Cold War

1901   1951   2001

1950–1970

The Cold War years were a frightening time for many people. The United States and the Soviet Union had become the world's most powerful nations, and conflicts developed between them. Because of the roles each country played in world events at that time, they were called superpowers. Even though the conflicts between these two superpowers were fought mostly with words and economic weapons, the threat of a real war was always present.

A Crisis in Berlin

The United States, Britain, and France worked to rebuild the economy of West Germany after World War II. West Germany was made up of the areas that these Western Allies had controlled since the war ended. They wanted to see West Germany become a democracy. East Germany, the area held by the Soviet Union, had a communist government.

STUDY/RESEARCH SKILLS

Summarizing Ask students to select and research a topic from one of the subsections of the lesson. Encourage students to use a variety of reference sources, including the Internet. Have students write brief summaries of their findings and present them orally to the class.

REACH ALL LEARNERS

Tactile Learners Ask students to trace or photocopy an outline map of the world and locate places mentioned in the lesson, such as the United States, the Soviet Union, Berlin, North Korea, South Korea, and Cuba. Have students outline each place with a colored marker to illustrate the global nature of the Cold War.

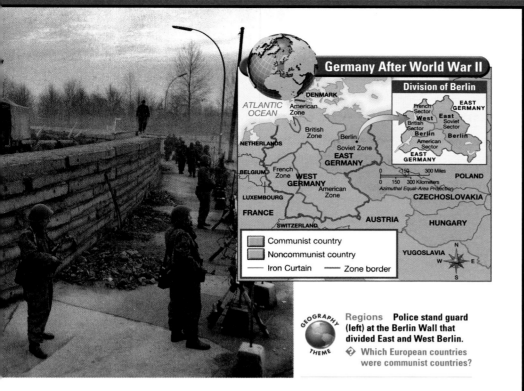

Germany After World War II

ATLANTIC OCEAN

DENMARK

American Zone

British Zone

NETHERLANDS

BELGIUM

French Zone

LUXEMBOURG

FRANCE

SWITZERLAND

Berlin

Soviet Zone

EAST GERMANY

WEST GERMANY

American Zone

AUSTRIA

POLAND

CZECHOSLOVAKIA

HUNGARY

YUGOSLAVIA

0   150   300 Miles
0   150   300 Kilometers
Azimuthal Equal-Area Projection

Division of Berlin

EAST GERMANY

French Sector

West Berlin

British Sector

American Sector

East Berlin

Soviet Sector

EAST GERMANY

Legend:
- Communist country
- Noncommunist country
- Iron Curtain
- Zone border

Regions Police stand guard (left) at the Berlin Wall that divided East and West Berlin.
◆ **Which European countries were communist countries?**

Berlin, the capital of Germany, had also been divided after the war. The Western Allies controlled the areas that made up West Berlin, while the Soviets controlled East Berlin.

In June 1948 the Soviet Union blocked all travel between Berlin and West Germany. The Soviets hoped this would force the Western Allies out of West Berlin. The Allies, however, refused to leave.

To get around the blockade, the Allies started the Berlin Airlift. An **airlift** is a system of moving supplies by airplane. American and British pilots carried more than 2 million tons of supplies to West Berlin. In May 1949, the Soviets lifted the blockade.

The situation in Berlin remained tense even after the blockade ended, and many people tried to leave East Berlin to escape communist rule. In 1961 the East German government, with Soviet help, built a fence to keep its people from leaving. East Germany later replaced the fence with a concrete wall. The Berlin Wall, as it came to be known, was guarded by soldiers ready to shoot those who tried to cross it.

REVIEW **What was the Soviet Union's goal in blockading Berlin?** Its goal was to force the Western Allies out of West Berlin.

The Korean War

Like Germany, the Asian country of Korea was divided after World War II. Soviet troops occupied North Korea, and American troops occupied South Korea.

Chapter 16 ■ 581

2 Teach

A Crisis in Berlin

Read and Respond

Culture and Society Ask students why the East German government tried to contain its citizens in East Berlin. Remind students that East Germany was a communist country. Students may respond that people living under communist rule generally have restricted personal freedoms.

Visual Learning

Map Encourage students to examine the map on page 581.

Q Which countries controlled zones in East and West Germany?

A France, Britain, United States, Soviet Union

CAPTION ANSWER: East Germany, Poland, Czechoslovakia, and Hungary

The Korean War

Read and Respond

History Explain that China and the Soviet Union, both communist countries, aided North Korea in the Korean War. The United States provided most of the troops, equipment and supplies sent to South Korea.

Read and Respond

History Have students analyze why the United States would get involved in another war thousands of miles from its shores.

Visual Learning

Map Direct students' attention to the map on page 582. Ask students to locate the capitals of North Korea and South Korea. Pyongyang and Seoul

Q About how far away was the capital of South Korea from the prewar boundary line?

A about 30 miles (50 km)
CAPTION ANSWER: at the 38th parallel

Read and Respond

History Explain that by 1952 the casualty rate among United States soldiers was so high that presidential candidate Dwight D. Eisenhower made ending the war a key promise in his campaign.

Q Why did Dwight D. Eisenhower include a promise to end the Korean War in his presidential campaign?

A Answers may vary but should reflect that Dwight D. Eisenhower believed if he were President he could end the war.

The Arms Race

Read and Respond

History Inform students that over time a series of treaties has led to the elimination of many kinds of missiles and other weapons in the United States and Russia.

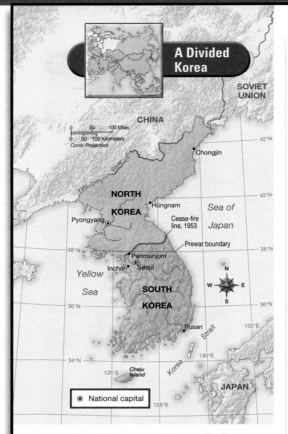

A Divided Korea

Movement **The cease-fire line changed the northern boundary of South Korea.**

❖ Where was the pre-war boundary?

In 1948 North Korea formed a communist government, and South Korea formed a republic.

In 1950 the North Korean army, which had been trained and equipped by the Soviet Union, invaded South Korea. North Korea wanted to make all of Korea communist.

President Truman sent more soldiers to South Korea to stop the invasion. The United Nations also sent troops. In all,

about 15 countries were now fighting the Korean War.

The Korean War became a major issue in the 1952 presidential election. Dwight D. Eisenhower promised to end the war if he were elected. Soon after his election he kept his promise. By 1953 the North Korean troops had been pushed back into North Korea. A **cease-fire**, or a temporary end to the conflict, was declared and an armistice was signed. South Korea remained a republic.

REVIEW **What started the Korean War?**
The North Korean army invaded South Korea in 1950.

The Arms Race

The Cold War started an arms race between the two superpowers. In an **arms race** one country builds weapons to protect itself against another country. The other country then builds more weapons to protect itself. Both the United States and the Soviet Union believed that having the strongest weapons would keep their people safe.

Soon after the United States built the first atom bombs, the Soviet Union built its own atom bombs. In response, the United States created an even more powerful bomb—the hydrogen bomb, or the H-bomb. By the 1960s both of the superpowers had also developed missiles that could carry the new H-bombs to targets that were halfway around the world.

REVIEW How was the arms race dangerous for Americans? 🔮 PREDICT AN OUTCOME

The Race into Space

The two superpowers also took the Cold War into space. In 1957 the Soviet Union surprised the United States by launching *Sputnik* (SPUT•nik). *Sputnik* was the world's first space **satellite**, an object that orbits Earth. Because of *Sputnik*, the United States sped its own efforts to explore space. In 1958 the National Aeronautics (air•uh•NAW•tiks) and Space Administration, or NASA, was set up to develop the nation's space program.

In 1961 John F. Kennedy became President of the United States. At his inauguration, Kennedy tried to inspire Americans to work for the good of their country. He said,

> 66 Ask not what your country can do for you; ask what you can do for your country. 99

President Kennedy soon set a new goal for the United States—to put a person on the moon by the end of the decade.

In 1962 John Glenn became the first American astronaut to orbit Earth. A series of explorations called the Apollo program then prepared for a moon landing. On July 16, 1969, *Apollo 11* blasted off from Cape Canaveral, Florida. On board were astronauts Neil Armstrong, Edwin "Buzz" Aldrin, Jr., and Michael Collins. Four days later, on July 20, Armstrong became the first person to walk on the moon. President Kennedy's goal had been met.

America's interest in space exploration, however, did not end with the first moon landing. Scientists and astronomers such as Carl Sagan continued to draw people's attention with their work. In the 1960s, Sagan worked at a space observatory. There, he participated in a project trying to find signs of life on other planets. Later, Sagan helped NASA plan several crewless missions to explore and take pictures of the solar system.

REVIEW What was the Apollo program? a series of space explorations that included a moon landing

Apollo II (far left) took astronauts into space. The plaque (above) is a replica of the plaque Armstrong and Aldrin left on the surface of the moon (left).
because the United States and the Soviet Union kept building bigger and more powerful weapons that could be used against each other

Chapter 16 ■ 583

The Race into Space

Read and Respond

Culture and Society Emphasize to students that the United States and the Soviet Union also were rivals in areas of science and engineering. Explain that this competition resulted in the race into space.

A Crisis in Cuba

Read and Respond

History Encourage students to complete the following chart comparing the Soviet blockade of West Berlin with the United States blockade of Cuba in 1962.

	Soviet blockade of West Berlin	United States blockade of Cuba
Purpose	to force Allies out of West Berlin	to stop Soviets from sending missiles to Cuba
Duration	11 months	13 days
Outcome	the Berlin airlift	Soviets stopped sending missiles to Cuba

3 Close

Summarize Key Content

- Tensions between East Germany and West Germany led to the construction of the Berlin Wall in 1961.
- The United States supported South Korea against communist North Korea in the Korean War.
- Tensions from the Cold War led the United States and the Soviet Union to develop powerful weapons and to explore space.
- President Kennedy averted war in 1962 by stopping the Soviet Union's shipment of missiles to Cuba.

Graphic Organizer Have students compare their charts to the one below.

Soviet Union	Conflict	United States
blocked West Berlin	Berlin crisis	airlifted supplies to West Berlin
helped invade South Korea	Korean War	supported South Korea
sent missiles to Cuba	Cuban missile crisis	blockaded Cuba

 USE READING AND VOCABULARY TRANSPARENCY 7-12.

7-12 TRANSPARENCY

Assess

Lesson 1 Review—Answers

 PREDICT AN OUTCOME The United States might have gone to war with the Soviet Union.

❶ **BIG IDEA** It led to conflicts.

❷ **VOCABULARY** **Cease** means "stop," and **fire** refers to military attacks.

❸ **TIME** in 1969

❹ **SCIENCE AND TECHNOLOGY** Neil Armstrong described the moon, and Carl Sagan helped take pictures of other parts of the solar system.

❺ **CRITICAL THINKING—Analyze** South Korea wanted to drive out the communists and preserve its democratic government.

 Performance Assessment Guidelines Reports should provide information about the moon landing. Have students include a list of sources they used to prepare their reports.

ACTIVITY BOOK

Use ACTIVITY BOOK, pp. 150–151, to reinforce and extend student learning.

The Soviet Union agreed to stop sending missiles to Cuba and remove the missiles already there.

A Crisis in Cuba

Soon after President Kennedy took office, Cold War problems began to take up much of his time. In October 1962 Kennedy learned that the Soviet Union had built launch sites for missiles in Cuba, just 90 miles (145 km) off the southern tip of Florida. Fidel Castro had taken control of Cuba in 1959. With the help of the Soviet Union, he had formed a communist government there.

Kennedy knew that the Soviets could use the missiles in Cuba to attack the United States, so he ordered a blockade of Cuba. The United States Navy would keep Soviet ships that were carrying missiles from reaching Cuba. Americans worried as they listened to the news.

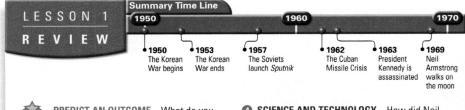

John F. Kennedy

What if the ships refused to stop? Would there be war?

Thirteen days later, the Soviet Union agreed to stop sending missiles to Cuba and to remove all the missiles that were already there. In response, the United States agreed to end the blockade and to remove American missiles from near the Soviet Union. War had been avoided.

On November 22, 1963, President Kennedy and Jacqueline, his wife, visited Dallas, Texas, to meet with supporters there. As their car drove through the streets, several shots rang out. President Kennedy was killed. A few hours later, Vice President Lyndon B. Johnson took the oath of office as the new President.

REVIEW How was the crisis in Cuba ended?

LESSON 1 REVIEW

Summary Time Line

1950 — 1960 — 1970

- **1950** The Korean War begins
- **1953** The Korean War ends
- **1957** The Soviets launch *Sputnik*
- **1962** The Cuban Missile Crisis
- **1963** President Kennedy is assassinated
- **1969** Neil Armstrong walks on the moon

 PREDICT AN OUTCOME What do you think might have happened if the Soviet Union had not agreed to remove its nuclear missiles from Cuba?

❶ **BIG IDEA** How did the Cold War affect relations between the free world and communist nations?

❷ **VOCABULARY** What do you think each word part of **cease-fire** means?

❸ **TIME LINE** What year did the United States first land a person on the moon?

❹ **SCIENCE AND TECHNOLOGY** How did Neil Armstrong and Carl Sagan contribute to people's knowledge of space?

❺ **CRITICAL THINKING—Analyze** How did the Korean War become a fight for democracy?

 PERFORMANCE—Present a News Report Imagine you are a news reporter. Write a news report on the moon landing. Then read your report to the class.

584 ■ Unit 7

EXTEND AND ENRICH

Write a Paragraph Provide students with the following quotation from President Kennedy's 1961 inauguration speech:

"Let every nation know, whether it wishes us well or ill, that we shall pay any price, bear any burden, meet any hardship, support any friend, oppose any foe to assure the survival and the success of liberty."

Have students write a paragraph about how Kennedy's remarks related to the Cold War.

RETEACH THE LESSON

Graphic Organizer Ask students to complete the web by filling in three places where conflict occurred between the United States and the Soviet Union during the Cold War. Then have students write a few sentences describing each conflict.

Cuba — West Berlin — **Cold War Conflicts** — South Korea

---

584 ■ **UNIT 7**

Working for Equal Rights

1901   1951   2001

1960–1980

Working to maintain peace was not the only struggle that Americans faced after World War II. Many people across the United States continued to struggle for equal rights.

A Supreme Court Ruling

Seven-year-old Linda Brown of Topeka, Kansas, did not understand why laws in her state made African American children attend separate schools from whites. Federal laws also allowed this segregation as long as the separate schools were equal. In most cases they really were not.

In the early 1950s, Linda Brown's family and 12 other African American families decided to try to get these laws changed. The NAACP agreed to help them. One of its lawyers, Thurgood Marshall, presented their case before the United States Supreme Court.

Thurgood Marshall (below left) argued against school segregation so that students, like Linda Brown (below), could get an equal education.

Chapter 16 ■ 585

· LESSON ·

2

PREDICT AN OUTCOME

As you read, predict how the struggle for equal rights would affect the United States.

BIG IDEA

Individuals and groups in the United States worked to gain equal rights.

VOCABULARY

nonviolence
integration
migrant worker

Lesson 2

PAGES 585–589

OBJECTIVES

- Identify the reasons behind the struggle for civil rights.
- Identify the achievements of individuals who contributed to the struggle for equal rights.
- Describe and evaluate the struggles of various groups to gain equal rights.

 Predict an Outcome
pp. 579, 585, 586, 587, 589, 604

Vocabulary

SEE READING AND VOCABULARY TRANSPARENCY 7-13 OR THE WORD CARDS ON PP. V89–V90.

nonviolence
p. 587

integration
p. 587

migrant worker
p. 588

When Minutes Count

Read aloud the Big Idea statement at the beginning of the lesson. Then ask students to examine the photographs and captions in the lesson and identify how each one relates to the Big Idea.

Quick Summary

This lesson describes the struggle for equal rights in the United States. It explains the means different groups used to gain equal rights.

1 Motivate

Set the Purpose

Big Idea Have students list ways that individuals and groups might try to gain equal rights.

Access Prior Knowledge

Ask students to give examples of how people in their community have worked together to improve their city.

WORD WORK

Structural Clues Ask students to identify the root word in each vocabulary term. Have them write the prefixes and/or suffixes attached to the roots.

Word	Root	Prefix/Suffix
nonviolence	violent	non–, –ence
integration	integrate	–ion
migrant	migrate	–ant

INTEGRATE MUSIC

Interpret Lyrics Provide students with copies of the lyrics to "We Shall Overcome" and to the spiritual "Free at Last." Have students read and analyze the lyrics. Then have them discuss the reasons songs such as these helped give African Americans a sense of unity and the courage to continue their struggle for equal rights.

CHAPTER 16 ■ 585

2 Teach

A Supreme Court Ruling

Read and Respond

Civics and Government Inform students that the "separate but equal" doctrine came from an 1896 Supreme Court ruling. Lead students to understand that over time some laws can become outdated and may need to be revisited by courts.

A Boycott in Montgomery

Read and Respond

Economics Explain that a boycott is a refusal to do business with an individual, company, group, or country. Protesters hope that by boycotting a business it will be hurt financially and may change as a result.

Q Is a boycott an effective means of protest? Why or why not?

A Students' answers will vary but should reflect that a boycott can be an effective form of protest.

Q What role did Rosa Parks play in the struggle for civil rights?

A Her refusal to give up her bus seat led to a bus boycott and the eventual end of segregation on public transportation.

Rosa Parks is fingerprinted after her arrest for refusing to move to the back of the bus.

In this case, known as *Brown v. Board of Education of Topeka*, Marshall argued that separate schools did not provide an equal education.

In 1954 the Supreme Court made a decision that supported Marshall's argument. Chief Justice Earl Warren said, "In the field of education the doctrine [idea] of 'separate but equal' has no place." The Court ordered an end to segregation in public schools. However, many states were slow to obey that order. Their schools and many other public places remained segregated.

REVIEW Who was Thurgood Marshall?
a lawyer from the NAACP who argued that separate schools did not provide equal education

A Boycott in Montgomery

On December 1, 1955, Rosa Parks got on a city bus in Montgomery, Alabama, and sat in the middle section. Under Alabama law, African Americans could sit in the middle section only if the seats were not needed for white passengers. As the bus filled up, the driver told Rosa Parks to move to the back. When she

586 ▪ Unit 7

refused, the driver called the police, and Parks was arrested.

African Americans were angry when they heard what had happened. They knew the bus company needed the money it earned from them. So they passed the word—"Don't take the bus on Monday." A bus boycott began.

One of the leaders of the boycott was Martin Luther King, Jr., a young minister in Montgomery. For almost a year, King and other African Americans boycotted the buses. King said that by working together they could bring about change peacefully. Finally, in November 1956, the Supreme Court ruled that all public transportation companies had to end segregation.

REVIEW What were the effects of Rosa Parks's actions? ⊜ PREDICT AN OUTCOME

The Struggle for Justice

Many African Americans looked to Martin Luther King, Jr., as their leader in the fight for civil rights. King believed

People boycotted buses and the Supreme Court eventually ruled to end all segregation on public transportation.

in using **nonviolence**, or peaceful ways, to bring about change. He said that nonviolence would change people's minds and hearts, while violence would only make matters worse.

Across the country, African Americans protested segregation. They held sit-ins at lunch counters, and at other public places. These were protests at which African Americans would not move from their seats at places that were segregated. African Americans also held marches to protest segregation and support **integration**, or the bringing together of people of all races.

In 1963 about 250,000 people gathered for a march in Washington, D.C. The marchers were there to show their support for a new civil rights law that Congress was debating. Martin Luther King, Jr., spoke to the marchers about his hopes for the future. He said, "I have a dream that one day on the red hills of

Georgia the sons of former slaves and the sons of former slaveowners will be able to sit down together at the table of brotherhood. . . ."

In 1964 Congress passed the Civil Rights Act of 1964, which made segregation in public places illegal. It also said that people of all races should have equal job opportunities.

REVIEW How did Martin Luther King, Jr., work for civil rights? He led people in using nonviolent ways to change people's minds and hearts about segregation.

Other Ideas

In 1964 Martin Luther King, Jr., won the Nobel Peace Prize for his peaceful efforts to bring about social change. However, some African American leaders disagreed with King's belief in nonviolent protest. Malcolm X was one of them. He was a member of the Nation of Islam, or the Black Muslims. He wanted change to happen faster.

Martin Luther King, Jr., (shown at center) marched in support of a new civil rights law.

Chapter 16 ▪ 587

The Struggle for Justice

Read and Respond

Culture and Society Ask students to explain what Martin Luther King, Jr., meant when he said nonviolence would change people's minds and hearts. How might a nonviolent struggle such as that advocated by King make an impact not only on a cause but also on society? A nonviolent protest might bring attention to a problem and attract sympathy for victims of injustice.

Q **How did King's work impact politics in the United States?**

A Supporting the marchers in Washington, D.C., helped show support for the civil rights law that Congress was debating.

Other Ideas

Read and Respond

Geography Inform students that Mecca is a city near the Red Sea in western Saudi Arabia. Explain that it is the holiest city of Islam and that Muhammad, the prophet of Islam, was born there. Ask students why Malcolm X's trip to Mecca might have changed his philosophy of separation to one of cooperation. He learned more about the peaceful ways of Muslims.

Focus Skill
READING SKILL

Predict an Outcome Lead a discussion in which students predict likely outcomes to these situations. What might have happened if:

- the Supreme Court had not ruled that school segregation was illegal?
- Martin Luther King, Jr., and Malcolm X had not protested against racial discrimination?

QUESTIONS KIDS ASK

Q **Is the Nation of Islam the same as the religion of Islam?**

A The religion of Islam originated in the Middle East and is practiced around the world. The Nation of Islam, an organization of African Americans, was founded in 1930 and is based in the United States. The Nation of Islam is not strictly a religious group. Its political positions have been combined with some aspects of traditional Islamic religion.

BACKGROUND

Hispanic Americans and Civil Rights The effort by Hispanic Americans to achieve equal rights has a long history. In 1929 the League of United Latin American Citizens, or LULAC, was formed to help Hispanic Americans gain equal rights in economics, politics, housing, and education. Many of its early Presidents, such as Ben Garza, were Mexican Americans. In the 1960s the United Farm Workers and the National Council of La Raza brought awareness of the struggles of Hispanic Americans to the entire nation.

DEMOCRATIC VALUES
Individual Rights

Encourage students to consider how the Civil Rights Act and the Voting Rights Act changed society. Point out that an increased number of African American voters meant more African Americans would be elected to public office.

Analyze the Value—Answers

❶ It prohibited segregation in public places and created the Equal Employment Opportunity Commission (EEOC).

❷ **Make It Relevant** Students' paragraphs should be supported by facts.

Civil Rights for Other Groups

Read and Respond

Culture and Society Explain that Cesar Chavez did much to improve migrants' working conditions.

Q **How was Cesar Chavez's situation similar to that of Rosa Parks?**

A Both were important figures in boycotts that led to civil rights improvements.

3 Close

Summarize Key Content

- The Supreme Court declared that segregated schools do not provide an equal education.
- A bus boycott by African Americans in Alabama led to a Supreme Court decision that public transportation could not be segregated.
- Martin Luther King, Jr., led a peaceful attempt to gain equal civil rights for African Americans.
- Malcolm X initially opposed using nonviolent forms of protest to end racial discrimination.
- Over time American Indians, Mexican Americans, and women all worked to increase their civil rights.

CITIZENSHIP

DEMOCRATIC VALUES
Individual Rights

When Lyndon Johnson became President, he worked hard to help ensure that the Civil Rights Act of 1964 became law. The law prohibited segregation in public places, and it created the Equal Employment Opportunity Commission (EEOC). In 1965 Johnson outlawed unfair voting rules, which led to a large increase in the number of registered African American voters.

Analyze the Value

❶ What did the Civil Rights Act of 1964 do?

❷ **Make It Relevant** Write a paragraph about why it is important that everyone is treated equally.

Malcolm X was named Malcolm Little but he changed his last name to X to stand for the unknown African name his family had lost through slavery. In his early speeches Malcolm X called for a strict separation between white people and African Americans. Only in this way, he said, could African Americans truly be free. Later, after a trip to the Islamic holy city of Mecca in 1964, he talked less about separation and more about cooperation among groups.

Malcolm X had little time to act on his new ideas. He was assassinated in 1965. Three years later, in April 1968, Martin Luther King, Jr., also was assassinated. Even though African Americans had lost two important leaders, they kept working for justice.

REVIEW How did Malcolm X's ideas change?

Cesar Chavez
At first he spoke in favor of segregation, but he later talked about racial cooperation.

Civil Rights for Other Groups

Following the lead of the African American Civil Rights movement, other groups worked for equal rights. American Indians, for example, formed groups to work for the rights that they had been promised in earlier treaties with the federal government. In many cases those treaties had not been honored. Then, in 1975, Congress passed the Indian Self-Determination and Educational Assistance Act. For the first time, Indian tribes could run their own businesses and health and education programs.

To help improve the lives of farm workers, Cesar Chavez, Dolores Huerta (HWAIR•tah), and others organized a group that would become the United Farm Workers (UFW). Most of its members were Mexican American migrant workers. A **migrant worker** is someone who moves from place to place with the seasons, harvesting crops.

Cesar Chavez called for nonviolent action to solve problems. In 1965 he organized a strike by California grape

---

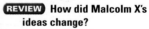

MAKE IT RELEVANT

In Your Community Since the civil rights struggles of the 1960s and 1970s, women have found more employment for higher pay in a wider variety of jobs. Ask students to discover how women are being employed in their community. Have students research how many women hold positions in the local government. Ask students to present their findings to the class.

BACKGROUND

Obstacles to Voting To prevent African Americans, Hispanic Americans, and other groups from voting, many Southern states had passed poll taxes and established white-only primaries. A poll tax was a tax that had to be paid before a person could vote, which effectively deprived poor people of their voting rights. Other laws required potential voters to pass literacy tests. Those literacy tests were not applied fairly—the members of minority groups were asked harder questions than white voters were asked. The Voting Rights Act of 1965 made all of these obstacles illegal.

pickers and started a nationwide boycott of grapes. His goal was to get better wages and improve working conditions for farm workers. He met this goal in 1970.

Like other groups, women organized to work for change. The Civil Rights Act of 1964 said that all people should have equal job opportunities, but many jobs were still not open to women. When men and women did have the same kind of jobs, women were often paid less than men. By the 1970s new laws had been passed saying that employers must treat men and women equally. Jobs now had to be open to both men or women.

As a result, more women began careers in jobs that were once held only by men. Some women won elections and became mayors, governors, and members of Congress. In 1981 Sandra Day O'Connor became the first woman appointed to the United States Supreme Court. In 1984 Geraldine Ferraro became the first

Source: Historical Statistics of the United States

Women in the Labor Force, 1950–2000

Analyze Graphs The number of women in the labor force increased from 1950 to 2000.

 About how many women were employed in 2000?

woman nominated for Vice President by a major political party.

REVIEW What did Cesar Chavez accomplish?
He got better wages and improved working conditions for farm workers.

LESSON 2 REVIEW

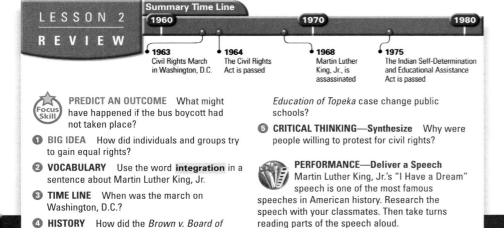

Summary Time Line

| 1960 | | 1970 | 1980 |

- **1963** Civil Rights March in Washington, D.C.
- **1964** The Civil Rights Act is passed
- **1968** Martin Luther King, Jr., is assassinated
- **1975** The Indian Self-Determination and Educational Assistance Act is passed

PREDICT AN OUTCOME What might have happened if the bus boycott had not taken place?

1 **BIG IDEA** How did individuals and groups try to gain equal rights?

2 **VOCABULARY** Use the word **integration** in a sentence about Martin Luther King, Jr.

3 **TIME LINE** When was the march on Washington, D.C.?

4 **HISTORY** How did the *Brown v. Board of Education of Topeka* case change public schools?

5 **CRITICAL THINKING—Synthesize** Why were people willing to protest for civil rights?

PERFORMANCE—Deliver a Speech Martin Luther King, Jr.'s "I Have a Dream" speech is one of the most famous speeches in American history. Research the speech with your classmates. Then take turns reading parts of the speech aloud.

Chapter 16 ▪ 589

EXTEND AND ENRICH

Write a Biographical Sketch Assign each student a leader or achiever who worked for equal rights. Examples include Rosa Parks, Martin Luther King, Jr., Thurgood Marshall, Chief Justice Earl Warren, President John Kennedy, President Lyndon Johnson, Malcolm X, Cesar Chavez, Betty Friedan, Sandra Day O'Connor, Barbara Jordan, and Shirley Chisholm. Ask students to use library resources to write and illustrate a biographical sketch about the person, focusing on his or her contribution to the struggle for equal rights.

RETEACH THE LESSON

Graphic Organizer Ask students to create a web diagram that identifies a group of people that worked for equal rights, details the methods they used, and describes the gains they made.

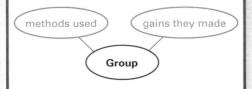

methods used — gains they made — **Group**

Visual Learning

Graph Direct students' attention to the graph on page 589. Ask students to draw a conclusion about the number of women in the workforce over the past fifty years. It has increased dramatically.
CAPTION ANSWER: about 67 million women

Assess

Lesson 2 Review—Answers

PREDICT AN OUTCOME The bus company probably would have continued with segregated seating.

1 **BIG IDEA** Individuals and groups used nonviolent protests, such as boycotts and sit-ins, as well as the legal system to gain equal rights.

2 **VOCABULARY** Martin Luther King, Jr., participated in the bus boycott that led to the **integration** of public transportation systems.

3 **TIME LINE** in 1963

4 **HISTORY** It made segregation in public schools illegal.

5 **CRITICAL THINKING—Synthesize** They believed that all Americans should be treated equally in society and under the law.

 Performance Assessment Guidelines Students should locate copies of the speech and read it with appropriate expression.

Predict an Outcome
pp. 579, 590, 592, 593, 604

Vocabulary

SEE READING AND VOCABULARY TRANSPARENCY 7-14 OR THE WORD CARDS ON PP. V89–V90.

arms control p. 592

détente p. 592

scandal p. 593

When Minutes Count

Have students read about the Vietnam War on pages 590–591. Then invite them to tell in their own words what they just read.

Quick Summary

This lesson explores the Vietnam War and how public opinion pressured the government to bring United States troops home.

Motivate

Set the Purpose

Big Idea Ask students what might cause the United States to enter into a foreign war.

Access Prior Knowledge

Have students review times in American history when the people and the government have disagreed about an issue or a policy.

PREDICT AN OUTCOME
As you read, predict how the Cold War continued to affect the United States.

BIG IDEA
There were many causes and effects of the Vietnam War.

VOCABULARY
arms control
détente
scandal

The Cold War Continues

| 1901 | 1951 | 2001 |

1955–1975

While many groups in the 1960s were working for equal rights, President Lyndon B. Johnson was working on new government programs that he believed would improve life for all Americans. These programs were all part of Johnson's plans for what he called the Great Society. They included medical care for older people, money to rebuild cities, and help with education, housing, and jobs for those who needed it. At the same time, the United States was becoming deeply involved in another war in Southeast Asia. This war—the Vietnam War—sharply divided the American people.

The Vietnam War

FAST FACT Approximately 12,000 helicopters were used by American troops in the Vietnam War.

Like Korea, Vietnam was divided into two countries after World War II. North Vietnam became a communist country, and South Vietnam became a republic. In the late 1950s, South Vietnamese communists, called the Vietcong, tried to take over South Vietnam's government. They were helped by North Vietnam. As part of its Cold War plan to stop the spread of communism, the United States sent money, war supplies, and

590 ▪ Unit 7

WORD WORK

Preview Vocabulary Have students make a list of the lesson vocabulary words. Instruct them to write definitions of the words as they read them in the lesson.

Word	Definition
arms control	limiting a nation's number of weapons
détente	an easing of tensions
scandal	an action that brings disgrace

REACH ALL LEARNERS

Advanced Learners Have students use research materials such as a periodicals database to find out how newspapers reported on the Vietnam War during the 1960s and 1970s. Ask students to summarize at least two news articles. Encourage students to list their sources and share them with the class.

advisers to help South Vietnam fight the Vietcong. China and the Soviet Union sent help to North Vietnam.

By the time Johnson became President in 1963, the Vietcong were winning the war. President Johnson ordered air strikes against North Vietnam. He hoped the bombing would end the war by stopping the flow of supplies from North Vietnam. But the fighting continued.

The first American ground combat forces arrived in South Vietnam in 1965. By 1968 more than 500,000 United States soldiers were serving there. The Vietnam War was now costing the United States billions of dollars each year—and thousands of lives. To pay for both the Vietnam War and the Great Society programs, the government had to raise taxes

This photograph shows President Johnson and some of his Cabinet discussing the war.

and borrow a lot of money. The country's economy began to suffer.

As the number of Americans killed in Vietnam continued to climb, more and more people began to oppose the war. Antiwar protests and marches took place all over the country.

In 1968 President Johnson shocked the nation when he suddenly announced that he would not run for reelection. Later that year, the American people elected a new President—Richard M. Nixon. Nixon called for better training for the South Vietnamese army and for the gradual withdrawal of the American troops. That withdrawal began in 1969.

The next year, however, President Nixon sent American soldiers into neighboring Cambodia to destroy war supplies that the North Vietnamese had stored there. When North Vietnam launched a major attack on South Vietnam in 1972, Nixon ordered a naval blockade of North Vietnam and an increase in the bombing.

REVIEW Why did the United States become involved in Vietnam? to stop the spread of communism

Analyze Graphs This graph shows how the rate of inflation has changed over time.

❖ How was the rate of inflation related to the country's changing role in the war?

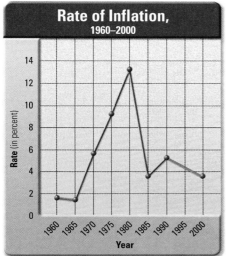

Source: Historical Statistics of the United States

Chapter 16 ▪ 591

2 Teach

The Vietnam War

Read and Respond

Economics Write a list on the board as students volunteer examples of war costs. Write a second list that shows students examples of Great Society programs, such as Medicare, housing aid, aid for education, and aid to improve living standards for the poor. Explain to students that Johnson believed that the United States could afford both the cost of the war and the Great Society programs.

Visual Learning

Graph Direct students to the graph on page 591. Ask how inflation changed between 1985 and 2000. It remained virtually the same.

CAPTION ANSWER: As the United States became more involved in the war, the rate of inflation increased.

Improved Relations

Read and Respond

History Explain that President Nixon's talks with China and the Soviet Union represented a shift in Cold War policy. Ask students why he would want open relations with these countries. to reduce the threat of war and to increase trade options

Visual Learning

Map Ask students to examine the map on page 592 and identify the capitals of North Vietnam and South Vietnam. Hanoi and Saigon
CAPTION ANSWER: They were not involved in the war.

Nixon Resigns and the Vietnam War Ends

Read and Respond

Civics and Government Explain that Nixon's resignation came after a judicial committee recommended his impeachment. Remind students that impeachment occurs when an elected official is charged with serious misconduct while in office. If the person is a federal official, the House of Representatives decides what charges are brought, and the Senate decides whether the official is guilty.

3 Close

Summarize Key Content

- The United States became involved in the Vietnam War to help South Vietnam battle communist forces.
- The United States and the Soviet Union agreed to a plan for arms control.
- President Nixon gradually withdrew American troops from Vietnam.
- President Nixon tried to cover up the illegal acts that took place at the Watergate complex and then resigned from office.

A Divided Vietnam

Movement **The Ho Chi Minh Trail was a supply route from North Vietnam to South Vietnam.**
◆ **Why did the trail go through Laos and Cambodia?**

Improved Relations

While the Vietnam War raged on, President Nixon worked to reduce Cold War tensions between the countries of the free world and the communist nations. He became the first American President to visit both China and the Soviet Union.

In 1972 Nixon accepted an invitation from China's leader, Mao Zedong (MOW zeh•DOONG), to visit China. As a result of his

592 ■ Unit 7

visit, the two nations agreed to trade with each other and to allow visits from each other's scientific and cultural groups.

Three months after visiting China, Nixon flew to Moscow to meet with Soviet leader Leonid Brezhnev (BREZH•nef). The two nations agreed to increase trade and to work together on scientific and cultural projects. They also agreed on a plan for **arms control**, or limiting the number of weapons that each nation could have. This was the first of several important arms control treaties between the two nations. These agreements marked the beginning of a period of **détente** (day•TAHNT), or an easing of tensions, between the United States and the Soviet Union.

REVIEW Why did President Nixon work to ease tensions with China and the Soviet Union?
PREDICT AN OUTCOME in order to allow trade and to allow the exchange of scientific and cultural projects

Nixon Resigns and the Vietnam War Ends

In 1972 Nixon was reelected President. The next year he agreed to a cease-fire in Vietnam. He also agreed to bring the remaining American soldiers back from Vietnam. The last ground troops left Vietnam in March 1973.

During the election campaign, some people working to help Nixon, who was a Republican, had done some things that were against the law. One thing that they did was to break into an office of the Democratic party in the Watergate complex. It was later shown that when Nixon learned about this illegal act, he tried to cover it up.

A Vietnam service medal

President Nixon announces his plan to resign from office.

The Watergate scandal ended Nixon's presidency. A **scandal** is an action that brings disgrace. On August 9, 1974, Nixon became the first American President to resign. On that same day, Vice President Gerald Ford became President.

Soon after the last American ground troops had left Vietnam, fighting had broken out again. Without the support of American troops, however, South Vietnam could not continue to fight.

Then, on April 30, 1975, South Vietnam surrendered. The war was over.

On Veterans Day in 1982, the Vietnam Veterans Memorial in Washington, D.C., was opened. Part of the memorial is a large wall of black stone. The wall lists the names of more than 58,000 American men and women who fought for their country and died or were reported missing during the Vietnam War.

REVIEW What scandal ended Nixon's presidency? the Watergate scandal

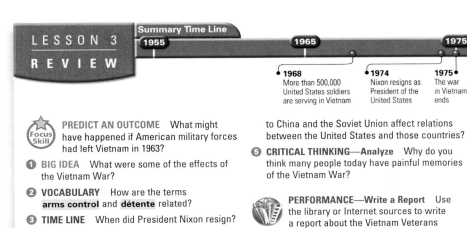

LESSON 3 REVIEW

Summary Time Line

1955 — 1965 — 1975

1968 More than 500,000 United States soldiers are serving in Vietnam

1974 Nixon resigns as President of the United States

1975 The war in Vietnam ends

 PREDICT AN OUTCOME What might have happened if American military forces had left Vietnam in 1963?

1 BIG IDEA What were some of the effects of the Vietnam War?

2 VOCABULARY How are the terms **arms control** and **détente** related?

3 TIME LINE When did President Nixon resign?

4 HISTORY How did President Nixon's trips to China and the Soviet Union affect relations between the United States and those countries?

5 CRITICAL THINKING—Analyze Why do you think many people today have painful memories of the Vietnam War?

 PERFORMANCE—Write a Report Use the library or Internet sources to write a report about the Vietnam Veterans Memorial. Share your report with your class.

Chapter 16 ■ 593

Examine Primary Sources

PAGES 594–595

OBJECTIVES

- Identify editorial cartoons as expressions of opinions regarding politics or government.
- Identify the points of view illustrated by historical editorial cartoons.

1 Motivate

Set the Purpose

Editorial cartoons express how people feel about certain issues. By studying these cartoons, students will realize that not all people agreed with the government's policies regarding Vietnam.

Access Prior Knowledge

Ask students to identify types of cartoons they are familiar with. Explain that editorial cartoons are similar to other cartoons, but that their subject matter often deals with politics or government.

2 Teach

Read and Respond

Have students identify the time in United States history during which these cartoons were drawn. during the Vietnam War

Remind students that the Vietnam conflict spanned several presidencies. Display pictures of Presidents Kennedy, Johnson, and Nixon. Which President is characterized in these cartoons? Johnson How can students tell? The features in the cartoons resemble the features in the picture of President Johnson.

Editorial Cartoons

Cartoons that express opinions about politics or about government are called editorial cartoons. Since the middle 1700s, editorial cartoons have been appearing in magazines and newspapers. Researchers and students can study editorial cartoons to learn more about historical events of the past. The Vietnam War is an example of an event that stirred the opinions of editorial cartoonists. In the cartoon to the right, cartoonist John Riedell expressed his political opinions about President Lyndon B. Johnson's handling of the war.

AAEC EDITORIAL CARTOON DIGITAL COLLECTION AT THE UNIVERSITY OF SOUTHERN MISSISSIPPI

These editorial cartoons (above and right) drawn by Eddie Germano reflect his views. They reveal the difficulty that President Johnson faced as he worked to resolve the conflict in Vietnam.

594 ■ Unit 7

BACKGROUND

More About the Artist Eddie Germano first sold one of his cartoons to his hometown weekly newspaper. Germano began cartooning professionally in 1948. Over the years, he has won several national awards for his cartoons.

More About the Time Although President Johnson is mainly remembered for the Vietnam War, other important events occurred during his presidency. He signed into law both the Civil Rights Act and the Voting Rights Act, which helped end discrimination in the workplace and at the polls.

The photograph shows Eddie Germano (below) at work in his studio in the late 1960s. His editorial cartoon (left) is called Flicker of Hope.

ACTIVITY

Express an Opinion Think of an issue on which you have an opinion. Make an editorial cartoon that expresses your opinion. Write a caption to help explain the meaning of your cartoon.

RESEARCH

 Visit The Learning Site at **www.harcourtschool.com** to research other primary sources.

595

Analyze the Primary Source
Answers

1. Short phrases explain the subjects of the cartoons.

2. On page 594: Americans are cutting the mast from which Johnson is leading the United States; Johnson is juggling a grenade labeled "Vietnam"; Johnson and Uncle Sam are navigating the "Road to Peace." On page 595: Johnson is walking through the jungle carrying a candle.

3. On page 594: the American public disagrees with Johnson's Vietnam policies and is trying to get rid of him; Johnson is uncertain what to do about the Vietnam situation; the road to peace in Vietnam is not clear; Johnson is participating in talks on Cambodia, which the artist viewed as a positive sign.

4. Supporters of the United States' participation in the Vietnam War might have disagreed with the cartoons' messages.

3 Close

Activity

Express an Opinion Have students find other issues in this unit that might have prompted editorial cartoons.

Research

Students will find a variety of editorial cartoons at The Learning Site at **www.harcourtschool.com**.

Ask each student to choose one of the editorial cartoons at the site and identify the issue addressed in it.

INTERNET RESOURCES

THE LEARNING SITE

Go to **www.harcourtschool.com** for a DIRECTORY OF PRIMARY SOURCES.

EXTEND AND ENRICH

Identify Points of View
Organize students into small groups, and supply each group with a recent newspaper. Ask students on what page they would expect to find an editorial cartoon. the editorial page Point out that the editorial page also contains letters expressing points of view. Ask each group to choose a letter and identify the issue and the author's point of view. Have the groups share their findings with the class.

RETEACH

Write a Title
Point out to students that the editorial cartoon on page 595 has a title. It is called "Flicker of Hope." Now direct students' attention to the editorial cartoons on page 594, and ask them to write an appropriate title for each. Ask volunteers to share their titles with the class, as other students guess the cartoon described by each title.

Lesson 4

PAGES 596–601

OBJECTIVES

- Discuss the causes and effects of the Iran hostage crisis.
- Examine how American international relations changed when the Cold War ended.
- Describe the contributions of national leaders such as Jimmy Carter, Ronald Reagan, George Bush, and Bill Clinton.
- Explain how terrorism has affected the United States.

Predict an Outcome
pp. 579, 596, 601, 604

Vocabulary

SEE READING AND VOCABULARY TRANSPARENCY 7-15 OR THE WORD CARDS ON PP. V89–V92.

terrorism p. 596 **hijack** p. 600
deficit p. 597

When Minutes Count

Have the class scan the lesson to find the meanings of the lesson vocabulary terms. Then ask students to use the terms in sentences.

Quick Summary

This lesson examines the events leading to the end of the Cold War. It also explains the many new challenges facing the United States today.

1 Motivate

Set the Purpose

Big Idea Ask students to predict what effects the end of the Cold War would have on the rest of the world.

Access Prior Knowledge

Have students discuss what they know about the Cold War and speculate about what influence its end might have on world relations.

· LESSON ·

4

PREDICT AN OUTCOME

As you read, predict the outcome of the end of the Cold War.

BIG IDEA

After many years, the Cold War finally ended, but the United States faced new challenges.

VOCABULARY

terrorism
deficit
hijack

A World of Change

1901   1951   2001

1971–2001

President Nixon had helped reduce tensions between the free world and communist nations, but the Cold War was not over. Americans continued to deal with troubling conflicts around the world. They also experienced **terrorism**, the deliberate use of violence to promote a cause.

Tensions at Home and Abroad

In 1976 Georgia Governor Jimmy Carter was elected President. Two years later, he earned worldwide praise for helping bring about a peace agreement between Israel, in Southwest Asia, and Egypt, in Northeast Africa. Those two nations had long been enemies.

Together, Southwest Asia and Northeast Africa are often called the Middle East. For centuries people in this region have been divided by religious, cultural, and political differences. In 1979, while Carter was President, a revolution took place in the Middle Eastern nation of Iran. Supporters of the revolution were angry at the United States for its support of Iran's previous leader. They attacked the United States embassy in Tehran, Iran's capital, and took 53 Americans as hostages.

For more than a year, President Carter tried, but failed, to win the release of the hostages. At the same time, the nation's economy slowed and unemployment rose.

President Carter (center) is shown shaking hands with President Sadat (suh•DAHT) of Egypt (left) and Prime Minister Begin (BAY•guhn) of Israel at the signing of their peace agreement.

596 ▪ Unit 7

WORD WORK

Related Words Instruct students to skim the lesson for the definitions of the vocabulary terms. Have them consider which two words might be related. Students should write the related words in the graphic organizer and suggest how they might relate to each other.

> terrorism
> hijack
> → To hijack a vehicle is an act of terrorism.

STUDY/RESEARCH SKILLS

Outlining Have students construct brief outlines of major events in the presidencies of Jimmy Carter, Ronald Reagan, George Bush, Bill Clinton, and George W. Bush. Students should use a standard outline format and complete it as they read the lesson.

Ronald Reagan   1911–2004

Character Trait: Individualism

Because of his ability to hold an audience's attention, Ronald Reagan was often referred to as the Great Communicator. Reagan developed his speaking skills by working first as a radio sportscaster and later as a movie actor. Twice, in 1980 and 1984, he was elected President. In his first inaugural address, he stressed the importance of individual achievement. Reagan has always believed in the promise of the United States, once saying, "Every promise, every opportunity is still golden in this land."

MULTIMEDIA BIOGRAPHIES
Visit The Learning Site at
www.harcourtschool.com
to learn about other famous people.

Inflation remained very high, and there were fuel shortages. In many cities, lines formed at filling stations as Americans tried to buy gasoline for their cars.

Many people blamed Carter for the Iran crisis and the nation's troubles. He ran again for President in 1980 but lost the election to former California Governor Ronald Reagan. The day that Reagan became President, the Iranians finally released the hostages.

Before President Reagan took office, the future looked dim to many Americans. But Reagan helped change that. His positive attitude and strong sense of patriotism appealed to many people.

Reagan quickly won approval from Congress for large tax cuts. The economy grew stronger, and high inflation ended. At the same time, however, the government's budget **deficit**, or shortage, increased. When there is a deficit, the government spends more money than it takes in each year in taxes and other income.

 REVIEW How did the nation's economy change after Ronald Reagan was elected President? *It grew stronger.*

The Cold War Ends

"Peace through strength" was Ronald Reagan's motto. As President, he increased defense spending. He called the Soviet Union "an evil empire" and said that the Cold War was a "struggle between right and wrong, good and evil."

The Soviet Union continued to build more weapons, too, and it helped communist governments and rebels all over the world. Then, in 1985, a new leader named Mikhail Gorbachev (mee•kah•EEL gawr•buh•CHAWF) came to power in the Soviet Union. Nothing would be the same again.

Chapter 16 ■ 597

BACKGROUND

Jimmy Carter (1924–) In the 1980s Jimmy Carter and his wife, Rosalynn, opened the Carter Presidential Center in Atlanta and also began building houses for low-income families. He has been a key diplomat, working to ensure peace with nations such as Nicaragua, Panama, Ethiopia, North Korea, and Haiti. In 1999 Jimmy and Rosalynn Carter were awarded the Presidential Medal of Freedom, the nation's highest civilian honor.

INTEGRATE LANGUAGE ARTS

Expository Writing President Reagan's motto "peace through strength" was accompanied by an increase in defense spending in the early 1980s. Instruct students to write paragraphs in which they explain this phrase in relation to the Cold War. What connection was Reagan making between military strength and the quest for peace? *To ensure peace, a country must be able to defend itself.*

READING SOCIAL STUDIES

Anticipation Guide Ask students to predict whether each statement below is true or false.

1. The economy improved before Ronald Reagan became President. FALSE
2. Soviet tanks brought down the Berlin Wall. FALSE
3. President Clinton helped reduce the stockpile of nuclear weapons. TRUE

● USE READING AND VOCABULARY TRANSPARENCY 7-15.   **7-15 TRANSPARENCY**

2 Teach

Tensions at Home and Abroad

Read and Respond

Economics Inform students that as a function of supply and demand, prices often rise in times of shortage. Ask students to predict what would happen if a product shortage occurred during a time of inflation, as it did with gasoline during the 1970s. *The product's price would rise, and people could not afford to buy as much of it as before.*

• BIOGRAPHY •

Ronald Reagan

Individualism Ask students how Reagan's words on individualism applied to his own life. *Reagan's many achievements range from his days as a sportscaster and movie actor to a long political career.*

The Cold War Ends

Read and Respond

History Have students conclude why President Reagan welcomed the chance to meet with Mikhail Gorbachev and agreed to more arms treaties.

Read and Respond

History Explain that during his tenure, President Gorbachev implemented many reforms, including a policy of *glasnost,* or openness, that had not existed previously in the Soviet Union. Inform students that under glasnost, people and institutions received additional freedoms.

Q What effect did President Gorbachev's reforms have on the Cold War?

A The reforms led to increased personal freedoms and the eventual end of the Cold War.

New Challenges

Read and Respond

Culture and Society Ask students to consider the phrase "new world order" and to answer these questions.

Q What conflicts would be ended by the "new world order"?

A Cold War conflicts

Q How might the end of the Cold War change culture and society?

A There would be more interaction and cooperation between countries that once had been enemies.

President George Bush (seated in chair on the right) meets with his advisers, including General Colin Powell (far left and below). During the Gulf War, burning oil fields (above) were a common sight.

President Reagan said he would welcome the chance to meet the new Soviet leader in the "cause of world peace." In April 1985 Gorbachev agreed to a meeting. He said that better relations between the two nations were "necessary—and possible." This meeting marked the beginning of a real thaw in the Cold War. The two countries soon agreed to more arms control treaties.

In the Soviet Union, Gorbachev was already changing many of the old ways of doing things. He called for reforms that gave the Soviet people more of the freedoms they wanted.

Changes in the Soviet Union led to changes in other communist nations, too. People in Czechoslovakia, Poland, and Hungary also gained new freedoms. In East Germany, leaders opened the gates of the Berlin Wall. Then, in 1989, the German people tore down the Berlin Wall. The next year they reunited their country.

In 1989 the new President of the United States, George Bush, met with Mikhail Gorbachev. The two leaders talked about the many changes taking place in Europe and the Soviet Union. The Cold War was finally ending.

REVIEW How did relations between the United States and the Soviet Union change during the 1980s? The leaders of the United States and the Soviet Union began to meet and agree to more arms control treaties.

New Challenges

Talking about the idea of a world without the Cold War, President Bush said, "Now we can see . . . the very real prospect of a new world order." By "a new world order," Bush meant a world without the conflicts of the past. Despite his hopes, new conflicts soon developed.

In August 1990 the Middle Eastern nation of Iraq, led by its dictator Saddam

598 Unit 7

Hussein (hoo•SAYN), invaded the small country of Kuwait (koo•WAYT). The Iraqi army quickly took over Kuwait, a major producer of oil in the Middle East. When Iraq refused to withdraw, allied forces from 27 countries, including the United States, attacked Iraq. The United States led this attack, known as Operation Desert Storm.

Among President Bush's advisers during Operation Desert Storm, also known as the Gulf War, was General Colin L. Powell. He was Chairman of the Joint Chiefs of Staff—the leaders of all the different branches of the military. Having commanded troops in South Korea and in the Vietnam War, General Powell used his military experience and leadership qualities to help the allied forces defeat the Iraqis and return Kuwait's leaders to power within seven months. Powell won fame during the Gulf War and became a national hero. In 2001 he became the United States secretary of state.

The early 1990s also marked the end of communism in eastern Europe. In 1991 the Soviet Union itself broke up into several independent countries, with Russia being the largest. Many countries in eastern Europe began fighting one another for power and the right to self-government. Some of the worst fighting occurred in the country once known as Yugoslavia. The civil war there has claimed thousands of lives.

REVIEW What caused the Gulf War to happen?
Iraq invaded Kuwait.

Toward a New Century

George Bush led the United States and its allies to victory in the Gulf War, but he lost the 1992 presidential election to Arkansas Governor Bill Clinton. As President, Clinton oversaw one of the greatest periods of economic growth in the nation's history. In the 1990s businesses created millions of new jobs, and unemployment dropped to its lowest level in decades. Working together, President Clinton and members of Congress also helped end the government's budget deficit and achieve a balanced budget.

Clinton also worked with Boris Yeltsin, the new president of Russia, to further reduce the number of nuclear weapons. In his 1995 State of the Union Address, Clinton said, "Tonight . . . is the first State of the Union Address ever delivered since the beginning of the Cold War when not a single Russian missile is pointed at . . . America."

President Clinton worked with Congress to achieve a balanced budget.

599

Visual Learning

Picture Direct students' attention to the picture of General Colin L. Powell on page 598. Point out that Powell was the first African American to become the Chairman of the Joint Chiefs of Staff. Inform students that in 2001 Powell achieved another first when he became the first African American secretary of state.

Q **What was Colin Powell's contribution to the Persian Gulf War?**

A He used his military experience and leadership to help the Allied forces defeat the Iraqis.

Students might be interested in learning more about Colin L. Powell and the Persian Gulf War. Have them visit The Learning Site at **www.harcourtschool.com.**

Read and Respond

History Inform students that the Persian Gulf War lasted about six weeks. It began on January 15, 1991, with air strikes on Iraqi targets and culminated in a cease-fire agreement on February 28.

Toward a New Century

Read and Respond

Civics and Government Remind students that Bill Clinton's tenure as President featured both accomplishments and controversies. In the 1990s Clinton oversaw one of the greatest periods of economic growth in United States history. In 1999 he became the second American President to be impeached.

Facing New Dangers

Read and Respond

Civics and Government Explain that a global war on terrorism began in October 2001 with air strikes against the country of Afghanistan.

History Discuss with students the terrorist attacks of September 11, 2001. Point out that while other acts of terrorism have occurred in the United States, this was the worst attack in United States history. Since that time new laws have been made to strengthen the nation's security.

3 | Close

Summarize Key Content

- President Carter helped negotiate a landmark peace treaty between Egypt and Israel.
- President Reagan and Soviet leader Mikhail Gorbachev worked to end the Cold War.
- As the Cold War ended, the United States entered a new battle in the Persian Gulf.
- Under President Clinton, the United States enjoyed a thriving economy.
- The United States and its allies responded to terrorist acts by waging a global war on terrorism.

President Clinton achieved many successes, but he also experienced controversy. In 1999 he became only the second American President to be impeached. Clinton's 37-day trial for obstructing justice and lying under oath could have resulted in his removal from office. As a result of the Senate vote, however, he was able to finish his term.

> **REVIEW** How did economic growth in the 1990s affect unemployment? Unemployment
> 🔮 **PREDICT AN OUTCOME**
> dropped to its lowest level in decades.

DEMOCRATIC VALUES
Citizen Participation

In the 2000 election, the importance of every citizen's vote became clear. About 106 million Americans voted in 2000. Most of them voted for Al Gore, a Democrat, or George W. Bush, a Republican. The election was so close, however, that it took five weeks for the winner to be announced. Bush's lead of about 550 votes in Florida helped decide the election in his favor. In the 2004 election, about 120 million Americans voted—the largest number ever. Bush received about 60 million votes, while John Kerry received about 57 million.

Analyze the Value
Why is it important for people to vote?

Facing New Dangers

At the end of the twentieth century, the United States faced new dangers outside its borders. The nation's military continued to defend democratic values around the world. The nation also experienced acts of terrorism as bombs exploded at two United States embassies in Africa and next to a United States navy ship in the Middle East.

Acts of terrorism occurred inside the United States, too. In the early 1990s, a bomb rocked the World Trade Center in New York City. Then, in 1995, an American citizen who was angry with the government set off a bomb near the federal office building in Oklahoma City, Oklahoma. The blast killed 168 people.

However, the worst act of terrorism in the nation's history occurred on September 11, 2001. That morning, terrorists **hijacked**, or illegally took control of, four American airplanes. Two of the hijacked planes were flown directly into the twin towers of the World Trade Center, causing them to catch on fire and then collapse. The third plane was flown into the side of the Pentagon, the nation's military headquarters, near Washington, D.C. The fourth plane crashed in an empty field in Pennsylvania. Thousands of Americans died on that tragic day, which became known as 9/11.

Americans could not understand why the terrorists had such hatred for the United States. President George W. Bush declared that the United States would lead a war against terrorism. Government leaders soon learned that many of the 9/11 terrorists

George W. Bush takes the oath of office.

BACKGROUND

The Heroes of Flight 93 On September 11, 2001, passengers aboard Flight 93 learned they were being hijacked. They knew that a few minutes earlier the World Trade Center towers had been hit by hijacked planes. At least four passengers—Todd Beamer, Mark Bingham, Tom Burnett, and Jeremy Glick—tried to take the plane from the hijackers. The plane crashed into an empty field in Pennsylvania, killing all aboard but injuring no one on the ground. Some believe that until the plane was diverted, it had been headed for one of the government buildings in Washington, D.C.

had links to the Taliban government in Afghanistan. Because of this, the United States and its allies overthrew the Taliban in late 2001.

In 2003 President Bush declared that Saddam Hussein, the Iraqi leader, was also a danger to the world. Along with some of its allies, the United States defeated Hussein's government. With the help of the United States and other countries, the Iraqi people are now working to form a new government.

REVIEW In what ways has terrorism affected the United States? Terrorism has caused the loss of many people's lives in the United States, and the nation has pledged to lead the world in a war against terrorism.

After the attacks, the World Trade Towers caught fire (top left). Firefighters (above) stand among the ruins and raise an American flag as a symbol of patriotism.

LESSON 4 REVIEW

Summary Time Line

1971	1981	1991	2001
• 1979 The Iran hostage crisis	• 1989 The Berlin Wall is torn down	• 1990 The Gulf War	• 2001 Terrorists attack sites in the United States

 PREDICT AN OUTCOME What do you think might have happened if the United States had not organized Operation Desert Storm?

❶ **BIG IDEA** How did the Cold War finally end?

❷ **VOCABULARY** What is a **deficit**?

❸ **TIME LINE** In what year was the Berlin Wall torn down?

❹ **HISTORY** What was Colin Powell's role in the Gulf War?

❺ **CRITICAL THINKING—Analyze** Why did the breakup of the Soviet Union cause confusion in many eastern European countries?

PERFORMANCE—Create a Time Line The Cold War between the United States and the Soviet Union lasted almost 50 years. Create a time line that shows the major events of the Cold War.

Chapter 16 ▪ 601

Skill Lesson

OBJECTIVES

■ **Apply geographic tools, including keys, to interpret maps.**

■ **Organize and interpret information from maps.**

Vocabulary

population density p. 602

WORD CARDS

See pp. V91–V92.

1 Motivate

Why It Matters

Explain that population maps are especially useful for showing the relative populations of cities or regions. Even if a map does not show exact population counts, much information about an area can be gained by comparing the population density of one area with the population density of another area.

·SKILLS· Read a Population Map

MAP AND GLOBE

VOCABULARY
population density

➡ WHY IT MATTERS

Like most other geographic information, population can be shown on maps in many different ways. One way is with color. Knowing how to read a population map can make it easier for you to find out the number of people who live in different areas.

➡ WHAT YOU NEED TO KNOW

Look at the key on the population map of the United States on page 603. The key tells you that the colors on the map stand for different population densities. **Population density** is the number of people who live in 1 square mile or 1 square kilometer of land. A square mile is a square piece of land. Each of its four sides is 1 mile long. A square kilometer is a square piece of land with sides that are each 1 kilometer long.

Many people today live in crowded cities (left), while others live in small, rural communities (below).

602 ▪ Unit 7

MAKE IT RELEVANT

In Your State Have students make a population map for their state. They should include a key indicating the colors being used for the state's population densities.

BACKGROUND

Population Trends in the United States Urban areas, which include cities and their suburbs as well as smaller towns, cover a small percentage of the land in the United States. Yet these areas contain a majority of the nation's people. The Northeast and Midwest long have had the largest urban populations. But since the mid-1900s, areas in the West, South, Southeast, and Southwest have drawn large numbers of new residents.

RETEACH THE SKILL

Write a Summary Instruct students to summarize in writing the information they learned from the map. Summaries should include descriptions of the most and least populated areas and references to the largest and smallest cities.

United States: Population Density

People per square mile
- More than 500
- 250–500
- 50–250
- 10–50
- Less than 10

People per square kilometer
- More than 200
- 100–200
- 20–100
- 4–20
- Less than 4

On the map, the tan color stands for the least crowded areas. Red stands for the most crowded areas. Read the map key to find the parts of the United States that have more than 500 people per square mile or less than 10 people per square mile.

➡ PRACTICE THE SKILL

Use the map to answer the following questions.

❶ Find New York City on the map. What is the population density of the area in which it is located?

❷ Find the dots for the cities of Jackson, Mississippi, and Toledo, Ohio. Which city has more people?

❸ Which city has fewer people, Miami, Florida, or Carson City, Nevada?

➡ APPLY WHAT YOU LEARNED

Study the population information given on the map. Then show some of the same information by using a chart, graph, or table. You might make a bar graph comparing the different population sizes of cities in the United States or a table showing the five states with the largest populations.

 Practice your map and globe skills with the **GeoSkills CD-ROM**.

Chapter 16 ■ **603**

2 Teach

What You Need to Know

Have students look at the colors on the key and on the map. Lead students to understand that the red areas of the map show the northeastern part of the country, and that it is more populated than the southern part of the country. Have students locate another region that is more densely populated than the South. parts of the Midwest

Practice the Skill—Answers

❶ The population density of New York City is more than 500 people per square mile.

❷ Toledo, Ohio, has more people than does Jackson, Mississippi.

❸ Carson City, Nevada, has fewer people than does Miami, Florida.

3 Close

Apply What You Learned

Students should present information that is clearly drawn and labeled. Information presented in the chart, graph, or table should accurately reflect the information on the map.

ACTIVITY BOOK

Use ACTIVITY BOOK, pp. 156–157, to give students additional practice using this skill.

TRANSPARENCY

Use SKILL TRANSPARENCY 7-5.

CD-ROM

Explore GEOSKILLS CD-ROM to learn more about map and globe skills.

EXTEND AND ENRICH

Calculate Population Density Provide students with the following data they can use to calculate each state's average population density.

State	Population	Land Area	Density
California	33,871,648	155,973 sq mi (403,940 sq km)	217 persons per sq mi (84 persons per sq km)
Texas	20,851,820	261,914 sq mi (678,305 sq km)	80 persons per sq mi (31 persons per sq km)
New York	18,976,457	47,224 sq mi (122,300 sq km)	402 persons per sq mi (155 persons per sq km)
Florida	15,982,378	54,153 sq mi (140,245 sq km)	295 persons per sq mi (114 persons per sq km)

⭐ Focus Skill PREDICT AN OUTCOME

Students may use the graphic organizer that appears on page 158 of the Activity Book. Answers appear in the Activity Book, Teacher's Edition.

Think & Write

Write a Radio News Report
Students' news reports should include accurate references to the ways in which the Allies shipped supplies to West Berlin. Students should write their reports in present tense, using active verbs.

Write Your Opinion Students' opinions should be clearly stated and factually supported. They may refer to the tensions that existed between the United States and the Soviet Union throughout the time of the space race.

ACTIVITY BOOK

A copy of the graphic organizer appears in the ACTIVITY BOOK on page 158.

TRANSPARENCY

The graphic organizer appears on READING AND VOCABULARY TRANSPARENCY 7-16.

· CHAPTER ·

16 **Review and Test Preparation**

Summary Time Line
1940

• **1948**
The Berlin Airlift begins

• **1950**
The Korean War begins

 Focus Skill Predict an Outcome

Copy the following graphic organizer onto a separate sheet of paper. Use the information you have learned to fill in facts and outcomes about the Cold War.

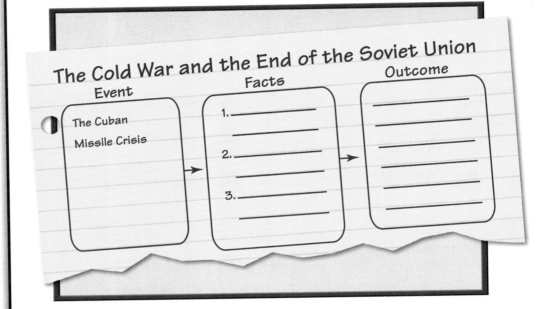

The Cold War and the End of the Soviet Union

Event	Facts	Outcome
The Cuban Missile Crisis	1. _____ 2. _____ 3. _____	

THINK & WRITE

Write a Radio News Report Imagine that you are living in West Berlin. The radio station you work for has asked you to report on the Berlin Airlift. Think about the situation. Then write what you will say about how the Allies are getting supplies to West Berlin.

Write Your Opinion The astronauts aboard *Apollo 11* faced many dangers during their trip to the moon, but they also made history. Write a paragraph describing why you would or would not have wanted to be an astronaut on board that historic flight.

604 ■ Chapter 16

TEST PREPARATION

Review these tips with students:

■ Read the directions before reading the questions.

■ Read each question twice, focusing the second time on all the possible answers.

■ Take time to think about all the possible answers before deciding on an answer.

■ Move past questions that give you trouble, and answer the ones you know. Then return to the difficult items.

UNIT PROJECT

Progress Check Instruct groups to select the key people, events, and places that they wish to focus on in their newspapers. Suggest that students work as a group to decide the focus of their articles and then work in pairs to conduct research and write the articles. Pairs of students can exchange articles and edit each other's work.

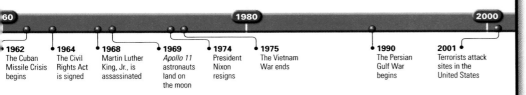

1962 The Cuban Missile Crisis begins

1964 The Civil Rights Act is signed

1968 Martin Luther King, Jr., is assassinated

1969 *Apollo 11* astronauts land on the moon

1974 President Nixon resigns

1975 The Vietnam War ends

1990 The Persian Gulf War begins

2001 Terrorists attack sites in the United States

USE THE TIME LINE

Use the chapter summary time line to answer these questions.

1 When did the Gulf War begin?

2 Did President Nixon resign before or after the end of the Vietnam War?

USE VOCABULARY

Use a term from this list to complete each of the sentences that follow.

superpowers (p. 580)
cease-fire (p. 582)
nonviolence (p. 587)
scandal (p. 593)
terrorism (p. 596)
deficit (p. 597)

3 Working for change by using ____ was important to Martin Luther King, Jr.

4 The United States has faced ____ both inside and outside its borders.

5 A ____ brought an end to the Korean War.

6 After World War II, the United States and the Soviet Union became the world's two ____.

7 During the 1980s the federal government's budget ____ increased.

8 A ____ forced President Nixon to resign.

RECALL FACTS

Answer these questions.

9 How did Carl Sagan contribute to Americans' understanding of space?

10 How did Rosa Parks help the Civil Rights movement?

11 How did Colin Powell contribute to the United States' victory in the Gulf War?

Write the letter of the best choice.

12 In 1958 Congress set up NASA to—
A increase the nation's arms supply.
B protect South Korea from North Korea.
C protect West Berlin from East Berlin.
D develop the nation's space program.

13 The Civil Rights Act of 1964 helped change life in the United States by—
F giving African Americans the right to vote.
G creating thousands of jobs for unemployed people.
H making segregation in public places illegal.
J calling for the building of hundreds of new schools.

THINK CRITICALLY

14 Why do you think winning the space race was important to the United States?

15 What do you think was Martin Luther King, Jr.'s greatest contribution to the Civil Rights movement?

16 Why do you think so many nations supported the United States during the Gulf War?

APPLY SKILLS

Read a Population Map
Review the map on page 603. Then answer the following questions.

17 Which city has more people—Houston or Louisville?

18 Which city has fewer people—Denver or Philadelphia?

Chapter 16 ■ **605**

Think Critically

14 The United States wanted to win the space race so that it could have the most knowledge about space.

15 Students' responses will vary but may include his leadership and commitment to nonviolence.

16 Many countries wanted to prevent Iraq from taking over any other countries.

Apply Skills

Read a Population Map
17 Houston
18 Denver

ACTIVITY BOOK

Use the CHAPTER 16 TEST PREPARATION on page 159 of the Activity Book.

ASSESSMENT

Use the CHAPTER 16 TEST on pages 121–124 of the Assessment Program.

Use the Time Line
1 in 1990
2 before

Use Vocabulary
3 nonviolence (p. 587)
4 terrorism (p. 596)
5 cease-fire (p. 582)
6 superpowers (p. 580)
7 deficit (p. 597)
8 scandal (p. 593)

Recall Facts
9 through his work at an observatory and on a NASA project (p. 583)
10 Her arrest for refusing to sit in the back of the bus caused many African Americans in Alabama to boycott the buses. (p. 586)
11 He contributed his military experience and leadership in helping the allied forces defeat the Iraqis. (p. 599)
12 D (p. 583)
13 H (p. 587)

Visit the Birmingham Civil Rights Institute

PAGES 606–607

OBJECTIVES

- Identify important events of the Civil Rights movement.
- Describe segregation faced by African Americans in the 1950s and 1960s.

Summary

The Birmingham Civil Rights Institute honors the courage of the men and women who fought for equal rights for African Americans.

1 Motivate

Get Ready

Point out that many important events in the Civil Rights movement happened in Alabama. Tell students that many people visit the Institute to learn more about the Civil Rights movement. Ask whether any students have visited a civil rights museum. If any have, ask them to share their experiences with the class.

2 Teach

What to See

Have students look carefully at the photographs on page 607. Ask students the following questions:

- *What is happening in the lunch counter exhibit on page 607?*
- *Why do you think the museum chose to use life-size figures in the exhibits rather than showing only photographs and other images?*

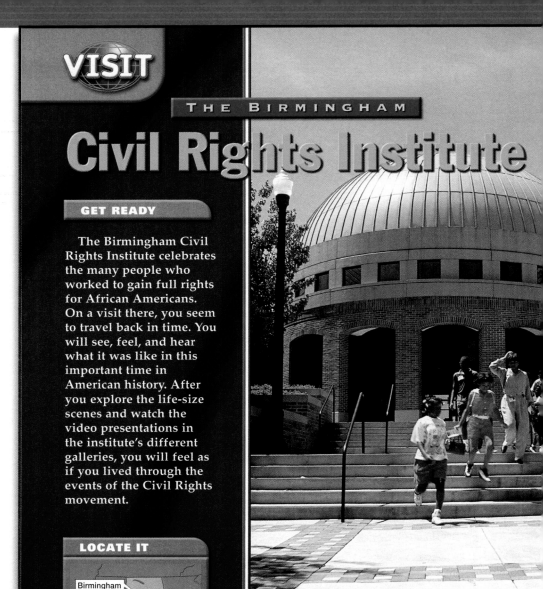

VISIT

THE BIRMINGHAM
Civil Rights Institute

GET READY

The Birmingham Civil Rights Institute celebrates the many people who worked to gain full rights for African Americans. On a visit there, you seem to travel back in time. You will see, feel, and hear what it was like in this important time in American history. After you explore the life-size scenes and watch the video presentations in the institute's different galleries, you will feel as if you lived through the events of the Civil Rights movement.

LOCATE IT

Birmingham

ALABAMA

606 ▪ Unit 7

BACKGROUND

Birmingham, Alabama
Birmingham was the site of several major events in the Civil Rights movement. Martin Luther King, Jr., outlined his commitment to nonviolent protest in a letter he wrote while being held in Birmingham's jail in April 1963. In September 1963 the nation was shocked when members of the Ku Klux Klan bombed the Sixteenth Street Baptist Church, killing four children attending Sunday school.

REACH ALL LEARNERS

Tactile Learners Ask these learners to research a famous event of the Civil Rights movement, such as King's "I Have a Dream" speech. Have these students make a sketch that depicts the event. Encourage students to present their sketches and describe what is happening to their classmates.

Life-size figures and a time line walk you through important events of the Civil Rights movement.

The lunch counter exhibit at the Birmingham Civil Rights Institute illustrates a time of segregation.

TAKE A FIELD TRIP

GO ONLINE

A VIRTUAL TOUR
Visit The Learning Site at
www.harcourtschool.com
to take virtual tours of other
historic sites in the United States.

CNN Turner Le@rning

A VIDEO TOUR
Check your media
center or classroom library
for a videotape tour of the
Birmingham Civil Rights Institute.

Unit 7 ■ 607

INTEGRATE LANGUAGE ARTS

Write a Poem Ask students to imagine that they are fighting for civil rights in the 1960s. Challenge them to write short poems about their experiences or about a civil rights issue. Inform them that Maya Angelou, a famous African American poet and writer, has written many poems about strong and courageous African American women. Encourage them to locate one of her poems and use it as a model.

EXTEND AND ENRICH

Write a Contrast Essay Ask students to look at the picture of the lunch counter exhibit closely. Have them write paragraphs describing how African Americans are being treated at the lunch counter. Ask for volunteers to read their paragraphs to the class.

3 Close

Take a Field Trip

Direct students to research one important event or person from the Civil Rights movement. Students may wish to learn more about the exhibits that can be found at the Birmingham Civil Rights Institute.

A Virtual Tour Depending on the availability of computers, have students work individually, in pairs, or in small groups to view the virtual tour. Encourage them to research events of the Civil Rights movement as they explore the Web sites. Remind students to use what they learn on their virtual tours as background information for the Unit Project.

GO ONLINE **INTERNET RESOURCES**

THE LEARNING SITE
Go to
www.harcourtschool.com
for a listing of Web sites
focusing on historical sites in
the United States.

Video Tour Before students watch the CNN video tour of the Birmingham Civil Rights Institute, have them write down three questions about the institute. Invite them to answer the questions as they watch the videotape. Ask for volunteers to share their questions and answers with the class.

VIDEO

Use the CNN/Turner Learning TAKE A FIELD TRIP videotape of the Birmingham Civil Rights Institute.

Unit 7 Review and Test Preparation

PAGES 608–610

Visual Summary

Students' writings should describe the event and tell why it remains important to Americans today.

- **The United States enters World War I** The United States entered the war after German U-boats sank three American ships.

- **The stock market crashes** Nearly everyone who owned stocks lost money when the stock market crashed in 1929.

- **Japan attacks Pearl Harbor** Soon after Japan bombed ships docked at Pearl Harbor, the United States entered World War II.

- **The Civil Rights Act is signed into law** The Civil Rights Act of 1964 made segregation in public places illegal and said that people of all races should have equal job opportunities.

- **The United States enters the Vietnam War** American troops were sent to fight in Vietnam after the South Vietnamese communists tried to take over South Vietnam's government.

- **United States astronauts land on the moon** In 1969 Neil Armstrong became the first person to walk on the moon.

Use Vocabulary

Stories should display an awareness of the significance of the following terms: *military draft*, *stock market*, *D day*, *refugees*, and *arms race*.

·UNIT·

7 Review and Test Preparation

VISUAL SUMMARY

Write a Description   Study the pictures and captions below to help you review Unit 7. Then choose one of the events shown. Write a description of the event, and tell why it remains important to Americans today.

USE VOCABULARY

Use the following terms to write a story about life during the twentieth century.

| military draft (p. 538) |
| stock market (p. 547) |
| D day (p. 565) |
| refugees (p. 573) |
| arms race (p. 582) |

RECALL FACTS

Answer these questions.

❶ On what fronts did World War II take place?

❷ What democratic means did Cesar Chavez use to improve the lives of migrant workers?

Write the letter of the best choice.

❸ The United States declared war on Germany in 1917 because—
  A members of Austria-Hungary's royal family had been killed.
  B Germany invaded Poland.
  C 260 sailors were killed when the *Maine* exploded and sank.
  D German U-boats attacked American ships.

❹ The New Deal changed the federal government by—
  F shifting much of its power to state governments.
  G allowing the President to raise taxes without the approval of Congress.
  H rewriting the Constitution.
  J giving it more authority and more employees.

Visual Summary

| 1901 | 1926 | 1951 |

1917 The United States enters World War I   p. 538

1929 The stock market crashes   p. 547

1941 Japan attacks Pearl Harbor   p. 557

608

Recall Facts

❶ Europe and the Pacific (pp. 565–568)

❷ organizing unions and boycotting (pp. 588–589)

❸ D (p. 538)

❹ J (pp. 548–549)

❺ B (p. 556)

Think Critically

❻ Goods were produced faster and more cheaply. This meant lower prices and more variety for consumers, larger profits for business owners, and increased wages for many workers.

❼ Germany may have won the war, or the United States might have entered the war sooner than it did.

❽ It has brought more Americans equal rights and opportunities.

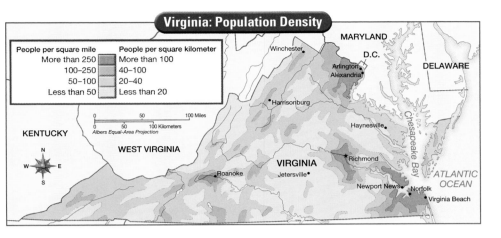

Virginia: Population Density

People per square mile
More than 250
100–250
50–100
Less than 50

People per square kilometer
More than 100
40–100
20–40
Less than 20

0   50   100 Miles
0   50   100 Kilometers
Albers Equal-Area Projection

MARYLAND
D.C.
DELAWARE

Winchester
Arlington
Alexandria

Harrisonburg
Haynesville
Chesapeake Bay

KENTUCKY
WEST VIRGINIA
VIRGINIA
Richmond
Roanoke   Jetersville
Newport News   Norfolk
Virginia Beach

ATLANTIC OCEAN

N W E S

5 World War II began in Europe when—
  A Italy took over Ethiopia.
  B Germany invaded Poland.
  C Japan invaded Manchuria.
  D Germany attacked France.

THINK CRITICALLY

6 How did mass production change the economy in the twentieth century?

7 What do you think would have happened if Germany had taken control of Britain before the United States entered World War II?

8 In what ways has the Civil Rights movement changed the United States?

APPLY SKILLS

Read a Population Map
Use the map on this page to answer the following questions.

9 Which city has a higher population density—Winchester or Virginia Beach?

10 Which city has a lower population density—Norfolk or Harrisonburg?

1976   2001

1964 The Civil Rights Act is passed   p. 587

1965 American combat forces arrive in South Vietnam   p. 591

1969 United States astronauts land on the moon   p. 583

609

Apply Skills
Read a Population Map
9 Virginia Beach
10 Harrisonburg

TEST PREPARATION

Review these tips with students:

- Read the directions before reading the questions.
- Read each question twice, focusing the second time on all the possible answers.
- Take the time to think about all the possible answers before deciding on an answer.
- Move past questions that give you trouble, and answer the ones you know. Then return to the difficult items.

ASSESSMENT

Use the UNIT 7 TEST on pages 125–133 of the Assessment Program.

Unit Activities

Give a Presidential Speech

Have students work with a partner who has chosen the same President as they have. Partners can perform research together and share the facts that they found.

 Performance Assessment Guidelines Make sure that students understand their chosen President's historical significance. Check that they have the facts about his accomplishments correct.

Complete the Unit Project

Organize the class into groups to complete the unit project.

 Performance Assessment Guidelines Look for evidence that students understand the significance of the key events, people, and places that they covered in their newspapers.

Visit Your Library

Encourage independent reading after students' study of the United States in the twentieth century with these books or books of your choice. Additional books are listed on the Multimedia Resources, on page 515D of this Teacher's Edition.

Easy *Goin' Someplace Special* by Patricia C. McKissack. Atheneum, 2001. This is the story of a young girl's visit to the only non-segregated place in her neighborhood, the library.

Average *The Unbreakable Code* by Sara Hoagland Hunter. Northland Publishing, 1996. John, a young Navajo, hears the story of how the Navajo Code Talkers helped the United States during World War II.

Challenging *The Words of Martin Luther King, Jr.*, by Coretta Scott King. Newmarket Press, 1987. This book offers samples of Martin Luther King, Jr.'s writings and ideas.

Unit Activities

 Visit The Learning Site at **www.harcourtschool.com** for additional activities.

 Give a Presidential Speech

Work as a group to write, edit, and deliver a Presidential State of the Union speech. Choose a President discussed in this unit. Then research that President and the important events that occurred during his time in office. Next, write and edit a speech to the American people, describing the state of the union and outlining goals for the upcoming year. Finally, select a member of your group to deliver your speech to the class.

COMPLETE THE UNIT PROJECT

Class Newspaper Work with a group of your classmates to finish the unit project—a newspaper about the twentieth century. Review your list of key people, places, and events of the twentieth century. Then decide which of those people, places, and events you wish to feature in your newspaper. Research and write articles on the subjects you have chosen. Then draw or find pictures to go along with your articles. Arrange your articles and pictures on a posterboard. Finally, present your newspaper to the class, and discuss the subjects you featured.

VISIT YOUR LIBRARY

 ■ *Goin' Someplace Special* by Patricia C. McKissack. Atheneum.

 ■ *The Unbreakable Code* by Sara Hoagland Hunter. Northland Publishing.

 ■ *The Words of Martin Luther King, Jr.* Selected by Coretta Scott King. Newmarket Press.

610 Unit 7

The United States and the World

Patriotic folk art

Unit 8 Planning Guide The United States and the World

Introduce	CONTENT	RESOURCES
pp. 611–617	**UNIT OPENER**, p. 611 **PREVIEW**, pp. 612–613 **START WITH A STORY** *Dia's Story Cloth*, pp. 614–617	Unit 8 Audiotext Unit 8 School-to-Home Newsletter, p. S15 Reading and Vocabulary Transparency 8-1 Time for Kids Readers Internet Resources

Chapter 17		
The United States Today, pp. 618–649	**INTRODUCE THE CHAPTER**, pp. 618–619 **LESSON 1** The American People Today, pp. 620–625 **CHART AND GRAPH SKILLS** Use a Cartogram, pp. 626–627 **LESSON 2** The Challenges of Growth, pp. 628–631 **LESSON 3** The American Economy, pp. 632–637 **LESSON 4** Government and the People, pp. 638–643 **CITIZENSHIP SKILLS** Identify Political Symbols, pp. 644–645 **EXAMINE PRIMARY SOURCES** Political Buttons, pp. 646–647 **CHAPTER REVIEW AND TEST PREPARATION**, pp. 648–649	Activity Book, pp. 160–169 Assessment Program, Chapter 17, pp. 135–138 Reading and Vocabulary Transparencies, 8-2, 8-3, 8-4, 8-5, 8-6 Skills Transparencies, 8-1A, 8-1B, 8-2 Internet Resources GeoSkills CD-ROM

Chapter 18		
Partners in the Hemisphere, pp. 650–677	**INTRODUCE THE CHAPTER**, pp. 650–651 **LESSON 1** Mexico, pp. 652–656 **LESSON 2** Central America and the Caribbean, pp. 657–661 **CHART AND GRAPH SKILLS** Read Population Pyramids, pp. 662–663 **LESSON 3** South America, pp. 664–668 **LESSON 4** Canada, pp. 669–673 **MAP AND GLOBE SKILLS** Use a Time Zone Map, pp. 674–675 **CHAPTER REVIEW AND TEST PREPARATION**, pp. 676–677	Activity Book, pp. 170–179 Assessment Program, Chapter 18, pp. 139–142 Reading and Vocabulary Transparencies, 8-7, 8-8, 8-9, 8-10, 8-11 Skills Transparencies, 8-3, 8-4 Internet Resources GeoSkills CD-ROM

Wrap Up		
pp. 678–682	**VISIT** Washington, D.C., pp. 678–679 **UNIT REVIEW AND TEST PREPARATION**, pp. 680–682	Internet Resources The Learning Site: Virtual Tours Take a Field Trip Video Assessment Program, Unit 8, pp. 143–151

4	WEEK 1	WEEK 2	WEEK 3	WEEK 4
WEEKS	Introduce the Unit	Chapter 17	Chapter 18	Wrap Up the Unit

Unit 8 Skills Path

Unit 8 features the reading skills of telling fact from opinion and comparing and contrasting. It also highlights the social studies skills of using a cartogram, reading population pyramids, identifying political symbols, and using a time zone map.

FOCUS SKILLS

CHAPTER 17 READING SKILL

 FACT AND OPINION

- INTRODUCE p. 619
- APPLY pp. 620, 622, 625, 630, 631, 634, 637, 638, 643

CHAPTER 18 READING SKILL

COMPARE AND CONTRAST

- INTRODUCE p. 651
- APPLY pp. 652, 653, 656, 659, 661, 664, 667, 668, 669, 670, 673

READING SOCIAL STUDIES

- Personal Response, pp. 614, 616
- Predictions, pp. 621, 625
- Summarize, pp. 623, 670, 673
- Graphic Organizer, pp. 629, 630, 654, 658, 661
- Create Mental Images, p. 629
- Study Questions, pp. 633, 636, 665, 668
- Read Aloud, p. 633
- K-W-L Chart, pp. 639, 643
- Anticipation Guide, pp. 653, 656
- Time Line, p. 654
- Reread to Clarify, p. 660

CHART AND GRAPH SKILLS

USE A CARTOGRAM

- INTRODUCE pp. 626–627
- APPLY p. 649

READ POPULATION PYRAMIDS

- INTRODUCE pp. 662–663
- APPLY p. 677

CITIZENSHIP SKILLS

IDENTIFY POLITICAL SYMBOLS

- INTRODUCE pp. 644–645
- APPLY p. 649

MAP AND GLOBE SKILLS

USE A TIME ZONE MAP

- INTRODUCE pp. 674–675
- APPLY p. 677

STUDY AND RESEARCH SKILLS

- Note Taking, p. 634
- Using Reference Sources, p. 664
- Outlining, p. 666

Multimedia Resources

The Multimedia Resources can be used in a variety of ways. They can supplement core instruction in the classroom or extend and enrich student learning at home.

Independent Reading

Easy

Cherry, Lynne. ***The Great Kapok Tree: A Tale of the Amazon Rainforest.***  Voyager Picture Book, 2000. Modern fable of a man who is sent to the rainforest to cut down a kapok tree and is visited in a dream by animals who plead with him not to destroy their home.

Halperin, Wendy Anderson. ***Once Upon A Company...: A True Story.*** Orchard Books, 1998. Three young children become entrepreneurs in this story that provides an introduction to business.

Johnston, Tony. ***My Mexico-México Mío.*** G. P. Putnam's Sons, 1996. Slice-of-life poems about Mexico in both English and Spanish.

Average

Jordan, Martin and Tanis. ***Angel Falls: A South American Journey.*** Kingfisher, 1995. Follow two travelers on an expedition that highlights the unique geographic wonders of South America.

Krull, Kathleen. ***A Kids' Guide to America's Bill of Rights: Curfews, Censorship, and the 100-Pound Giant.*** Avon Books, 1999. Overview of the Bill of Rights and how it affects the daily life of every American, including children.

Lesinski, Jeanne M. ***Bill Gates.*** Lerner Publishing Group, 2000. Biography of software pioneer who founded Microsoft, a multi-billion dollar company.

Challenging

Creeden, Sharon. ***Fair is Fair.*** August House Publishers, Inc., 1997. Thirty international folktales relating to law and justice that illuminate today's legal issues. Many stories followed by commentary on current legal debates and court cases.

Isler, Claudia: ***Volunteering to Help in Your Neighborhood.*** Children's Press, 2000. Provides students with advice on volunteerism and what to expect in a service-learning program.

Pandell, Karen. ***Journey Through the Northern Rainforest.*** Penguin Putnam Books for Young Readers, 1999. Chronicles the changes taking place in the rainforest region.

Computer Software

Inspirer: International Inspirer. Tom Snyder Productions, 1997. Mac/Windows. Students learn about international issues such as alliances, economics, and geographic and economic ties countries have to one another.

Videos and DVDs

My America: Becoming an Active Citizen. Sunburst, 1997. Provides students with an understanding of what the role of an active citizen should be.

Symbols and Ceremonies: Celebrating America. Sunburst, 1999. Provides students with information about the origin and meanings of symbols and ceremonies such as the flag, the Pledge of Allegiance, The Great Seal, and Statue of Liberty.

Additional books also are recommended at point of use throughout the unit.
Note that information, while correct at time of publication, is subject to change.

ISBNs and other publisher information can be found at
www.harcourtschool.com

The Learning Site: Social Studies Center

The Learning Site at www.harcourtschool.com offers a special Social Studies Center. The center provides a wide variety of activities, Internet links, and online references.

Here are just some of the HARCOURT Internet resources you'll find!

Multimedia Biographies
www.harcourtschool.com

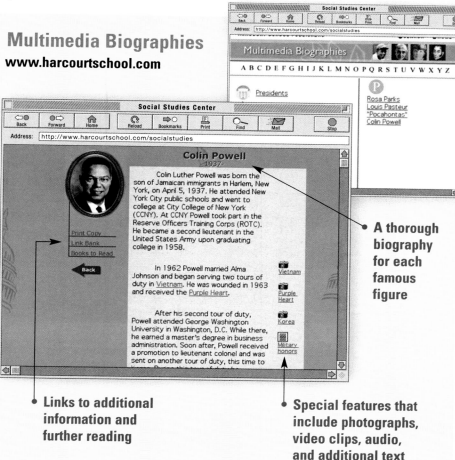

A thorough biography for each famous figure

Links to additional information and further reading

Special features that include photographs, video clips, audio, and additional text

INTERNET RESOURCES

Find all this at
The Learning Site at
www.harcourtschool.com
- Activities and Games
- Content Updates
- Current Events
- Free and Inexpensive Materials
- Multimedia Biographies
- Online Atlas
- Primary Sources
- Video Updates
- Virtual Tours
- Your State

and more!

Free and Inexpensive Materials
- Addresses to write for free and inexpensive products
- Links to unit-related materials
- Internet maps
- Internet references

www.harcourtschool.com

Primary Sources
- Artwork
- Clothing
- Diaries
- Government Documents
- Historical Documents
- Maps
- Tools

and more!
www.harcourtschool.com

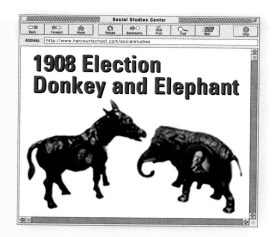

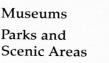

Virtual Tours
- Capitols and Government Buildings
- Cities
- Countries
- Historical Sites
- Museums
- Parks and Scenic Areas

and more!
www.harcourtschool.com

Integrate Learning Across the Curriculum

Use these topics to help you integrate social studies into your daily planning.
See the page numbers indicated for more information about each topic.

Mathematics

Figuring Percentages, p. 622
Figuring Exchange Rates,
p. 655

Art

Sketch a Story Cloth, p. 616
Make a Symbol, p. 644

Language Arts

Prepare a Book Report, p. 612
Descriptive Writing, p. 623
Write a Persuasive Paper,
p. 630
Expressive Writing, p. 646
Informative Writing, p. 655
Write a Scientific Summary,
p. 662

Music

Canadian Music, p. 672

Science

Hurricanes, p. 659
Identify Unique Species, p. 665

Technology

Discussion, p. 624
GeoSkills CD-ROM, pp. 627,
675
Go Online, pp. 617, 622, 647,
665, 670, 679
CNN Video, p. 679

Languages

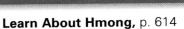

Learn About Hmong, p. 614

Reading/Literature

Dia's Story Cloth, pp. 614–617
Discussing the National News,
p. 641
My Mexico-México Mío, p. 682
*Angel Falls: A South American
Journey,* p. 682
*Journey Through the Northern
Rainforest,* p. 682

Social Studies

8

Reach All Learners

Use these activities to help individualize your instruction. Each activity has been developed to address a different level or type of learner.

English as a Second Language

15 minutes a day

Materials
- notebook paper
- textbook
- pens or pencils

WRITE PERSONAL RESPONSES Have students who are acquiring English write personal responses to the issues discussed in Unit 8.

- Prepare students by asking them to set aside a few pages in a notebook for personal responses to Unit 8.
- Have students read or review the lessons of the unit and take notes on issues that relate in some way to their own experiences.
- Invite students to write a paragraph explaining their responses to one of the issues they selected. Challenge them to use vocabulary from the unit.
- Allow students to meet with a partner to proofread each other's writing.
- Prompt volunteers to share their responses with the class.

Below-Level Learners

30 minutes for 3 days

Materials
- paper
- pencils
- scissors
- sample newspaper front page

PREPARE A FRONT PAGE Have students work in groups to prepare the front page of a newspaper, based on the issues in Unit 8.

- Organize students into groups, and ask them to identify key issues in the unit.
- Direct each student in the group to prepare a short news article, complete with a headline and an illustration with a caption, about one of the issues in the unit.
- When students have written their articles, provide students with a sample newspaper front page. Have the group lay out their own newspaper front page, using their articles and images. Encourage students to name their newspaper.
- Ask students to share their completed pages with the class.

Advanced Learners

45 minutes for 2 days

Materials
- notebook paper
- pens or markers
- textbook

ACT OUT A SUMMIT MEETING Have students work in groups to role play a meeting in which they discuss issues raised in Unit 8.

- Organize students into groups of three. Assign one person in each group to represent the United States, Mexico, or Canada.
- Have students who represent the same country leave their original groups and meet together. Instruct them to review Unit 8 for information about the country they represent.
- Direct students to return to their original groups and to participate in a round-table discussion of the problems their country faces.
- Ask each group to summarize its discussion for the class.

Assessment Options

The Assessment Program gives all learners many opportunities to show what they know and can do. It also provides ongoing information about each student's understanding of social studies.

Formal Assessment

- **LESSON REVIEWS,** at ends of lessons
- **CHAPTER REVIEWS AND TEST PREPARATION,** pp. 648–649, pp. 676–677
- **CHAPTER TESTS** Assessment Program, pp. 135–138, pp. 139–142
- **UNIT REVIEW AND TEST PREPARATION,** pp. 680–681
- **UNIT ASSESSMENT** **STANDARD TEST,** Assessment Program, pp. 143–149 **INDIVIDUAL PERFORMANCE TASK,** Assessment Program, p. 150 **GROUP PERFORMANCE TASK,** Assessment Program, p. 151

Student Self-Evaluation

- **ANALYZE PRIMARY SOURCES AND VISUALS** within lessons of Pupil Book
- **GEOGRAPHY THEME QUESTIONS** within lessons of Pupil Book
- **INDIVIDUAL END-OF-PROJECT SUMMARY** Assessment Program, p. vi
- **GROUP END-OF-PROJECT CHECKLIST** Assessment Program, p. vii
- **INDIVIDUAL END-OF-UNIT CHECKLIST** Assessment Program, p. viii

Informal Assessment

- **ANALYZE THE LITERATURE,** p. 617
- **REVIEW QUESTIONS,** throughout lessons
- **EXAMINE PRIMARY SOURCES,** pp. 646–647
- **SOCIAL STUDIES SKILLS CHECKLIST** Assessment Program, p. iv

- **SKILLS** Practice the Skill, pp. 627, 645, 663, 674 Apply What You Learned, pp. 627, 645, 663, 675

Performance Assessment

- **PERFORMANCE ACTIVITY** in Lesson Reviews
- **UNIT ACTIVITIES,** p. 682
- **COMPLETE THE UNIT PROJECT,** p. 682
- **INDIVIDUAL PERFORMANCE TASK** Assessment Program, p. 150
- **GROUP PERFORMANCE TASK** Assessment Program, p. 151

Portfolio Assessment

STUDENT-SELECTED ITEMS MAY INCLUDE:

- **THINK AND WRITE,** p. 648, 676
- **UNIT ACTIVITIES,** p. 682
- **COMPLETE THE UNIT PROJECT,** p. 682

TEACHER-SELECTED ITEMS MAY INCLUDE:

- **UNIT ASSESSMENT** Assessment Program, pp. 143–149
- **PORTFOLIO SUMMARY** Assessment Program, p. xiii
- **INDIVIDUAL END-OF-UNIT CHECKLIST** Assessment Program, p. viii
- **GROUP END-OF-PROJECT CHECKLIST** Assessment Program, p. vii

Unit 8 Test

·UNIT·

Name _____ Date _____

8 Test

Part One: Test Your Understanding

MULTIPLE CHOICE (2 points each)

Directions Circle the letter of the best answer.

1 Today most immigrants into the United States come from countries in—
A Europe and Asia.
B Latin America and Europe.
C Asia and Australia.
(D) Latin America and Asia.

2 Today most immigrants enter the United States through—
F a train station.
(G) an airport.
H a ship's dock.
J a bus depot.

3 In recent years the number of people in the United States over the age of 65 has—
(A) grown steadily.
B fallen sharply.
C stayed about the same.
D declined only slightly.

4 Computers were first developed—
(F) during World War II.
G after the creation of the World Wide Web.
H before the development of air conditioning.
J during World War I.

5 The Internet was first developed for—
A research needs.
(B) military communication.
C personal shopping.
D financial transactions.

6 Why would a community want to find methods to reduce urban growth?
F to limit shopping opportunities for consumers
(G) to protect farmland from being sold and developed
H to provide more housing for workers in new industries
J to encourage the development of modern highway systems

7 States that received more seats in Congress because their populations grew between 1990 and 2000 were located—
A in the Northeast.
(B) in the Sun Belt.
C in the Northwest.
D in the Great Plains.

(continued)

Name _____ Date _____

8 One result of responsible conservation in the United States is—
F the extinction of some types of wildlife.
G the presence of chemicals in the water supply.
H the creation of large amounts of trash.
(J) the increase of the American bald eagle population.

9 A person who works in a service job might—
(A) repair appliances or automobiles.
B build electronic equipment.
C work on a farm.
D work in a factory.

10 The first Native American to be elected president of Mexico was—
F Porfirio Díaz.
G Vicente Fox.
(H) Benito Juárez.
J Father Miguel Hidalgo.

11 For more than 70 years, the Partido Revolucionario (PRI) controlled—
A which people were elected to the Mexican Congress.
B railroads and factories in Mexico.
C Mexican farming and agriculture.
(D) which people were elected president of Mexico.

12 Which Mexican city is surrounded by the Federal District?
(F) Mexico City
G Monterrey
H Puebla
J the Sierra Madre

13 Except for El Salvador, every country in Central America has—
A a border on the Pacific Ocean.
(B) a border on the Caribbean Sea.
C active volcanoes.
D set aside 25 percent of its land for nature preserves.

14 Canada is located—
F west of the United States.
G east of the United States.
(H) north of the United States.
J south of the United States.

(continued)

Name _____ Date _____

FILL IN THE BLANK (3 points each)

Directions Complete each sentence in the space provided.

15 A meeting that links people through electronic equipment is called a _____teleconference_____

16 An automobile with a _____Global Positioning System_____ uses receiver satellites to determine the vehicle's location.

17 The development of the _____microchip_____ allowed computers to become smaller and less expensive.

18 The United States produces more _____manufactured_____ goods than any other nation in the world.

19 The states that we today call _____Texas, Arizona, California, Colorado, New Mexico, and Utah_____ were once a part of Mexico.

(continued)

Name _____ Date _____

SHORT ANSWER (3 points each)

Directions Complete each statement in the space provided.

20 An invention that made life more comfortable and spurred population growth in the Sun Belt was _____air conditioning_____

21 A(n) _____ethnic group_____ is a collection of people who share the same country, race, or culture.

22 When urban areas spread into land that was once used for farming, the result is called _____urban growth_____.

23 Countries that have a _____free-trade agreement_____, such as Canada, the United States, and Mexico, charge no taxes on goods they sell to each other.

24 Mexico City, located in the Mexican Plateau, is the world's largest _____metropolitan area_____.

25 Central America contains fertile land on which crops such as _____Possible responses: bananas, sugarcane, coffee, corn, cotton, beans_____ are grown.

26 Nations such as Puerto Rico and Canada are called _____commonwealth nations_____ because they are united with another country.

27 Some scientists worry that the greenhouse effect could lead to _____Possible responses: rising temperatures, melting polar ice caps, flooding_____.

28 Cuba has had a _____communist_____ government since 1959.

(continued)

Unit 8 Test

Name _____ Date _____

Part Two: Test Your Skills
USE A TIME ZONE MAP (10 points)

Directions Use the time zone map to answer the following questions.

Time Zone Map of North and Central America

Midnight 1 A.M. 2 A.M. 3 A.M. 4 A.M. 5 A.M. 6 A.M. 7 A.M. 8 A.M. 9 A.M. 10 A.M. 11 A.M. Noon

CANADA

ALASKA

Vancouver

UNITED STATES OF AMERICA

Boston

PACIFIC OCEAN

MEXICO

Mexico City

ATLANTIC OCEAN

COSTA RICA

29 When it is 11 A.M. in Saskatchewan, what time is it in Costa Rica?
The time would be the same, 11 A.M.

30 Find Alaska and Mexico City on the map. At 8 A.M. in Alaska, what time is it in Mexico City? 11 A.M.

31 Name two countries that lie in more than one time zone.
Possible responses: Mexico, Canada, and the United States

32 What is the time difference between Mexico City and Boston? In which city is it later? 1 hour; Boston

33 What generalization can you make about how time changes when a person travels from south to north? The time does not change when a person travels from south to north. It changes only when a person travels east or west.

(continued)

Unit 8 Test   **Assessment Program ■ 147**

Name _____ Date _____

Part Three: Apply What You Have Learned
34 CATEGORIZE AND DESCRIBE (10 points)

Some countries in North America, Central America and the Caribbean, and South America have had many types of government. Look at the types of government, the examples, and the details that are already shown in the chart. Choose the correct terms from the list below and write them in the blanks to complete the chart.

Governments in North America			
Type	**Democracy**	Commonwealth	**Communist Government**
Example	Haiti	Canada	Cuba
Details	a. has a history of military takeovers b. in 1990 elected Jean-Bertrand Aristide in a free election	a. has local self-government b. government headed by a prime minister	a. has been governed by both Spain and the United States b. government headed by Fidel Castro since 1959
	Costa Rica	**Puerto Rico**	
	a. government structure similar to the United States b. has three branches of government and a president elected for a four-year term	a. is a territory of the United States b. citizens hold United States citizenship	

Terms:
- is a territory of the United States
- government structure similar to the United States
- government headed by a prime minister
- has a history of military takeovers
- government headed by Fidel Castro since 1959
- Commonwealth
- Cuba
- Haiti

(continued)

148 ■ Assessment Program   Unit 8 Test

Name _____ Date _____

35 ESSAY (10 points)

British, French, and Native American traditions have brought both diversity and conflict to Canada's government. Write a paragraph that describes the Canadian model of self-government and compare it to the other examples of government you have read about in Unit 8.

Possible response: Canada, like other countries in North America, was once governed entirely by European nations. Unlike countries such as the United States and Mexico, Canada did not have a revolution to change its government. Canada is politically independent, but it still has political ties to Great Britain. Quebec attempted to secede from Canada. The territory of Nunavut was created in 1999 and will be governed by the Inuit tradition of consensus.

Unit 8 Test   **Assessment Program ■ 149**

Name _____ Date _____

Individual Performance Task

Advertisement

Write an advertisement for one of the types of companies described below. Your advertisement should contain information about why people should be interested in the company or service.

- A business that makes silicon chips for computers
- A company that sells farm equipment over the Internet
- An eye clinic that performs laser surgery to correct people's vision
- A company that teaches businesses how to set up teleconferences
- A bank that specializes in international trade.

Before you begin to create your advertisement, you may need more information about the type of company you will be promoting. You can look in the library or on the Internet for this information. Make up a creative name for your company and include eye-catching illustrations or design. Be sure that you provide factual information about the kind of product or service such a business would offer.

© Harcourt

Name _____ Date _____

Group Performance Task

Round-Table Discussion

Hold a round-table discussion with any historical figures you have read about in Unit 8. Choose six to eight historical people who worked to shape their country and who played an important role in their government. Be sure to have a broad selection of governments represented, with characters such as Father Miguel Hidalgo and Simón Bolívar. Find information about your character in your textbook, in the school library, or on the Internet. Then help write questions that a moderator can use to direct your discussion. Your round-table discussion should take 10 to 15 minutes.

© Harcourt

RUBRICS FOR SCORING

SCORING RUBRICS The rubrics below list the criteria for evaluating the tasks above. They also describe different levels of success in meeting those criteria.

INDIVIDUAL PERFORMANCE TASK

SCORE **4**	SCORE **3**	SCORE **2**	SCORE **1**
• Rich description is provided.	• Some description is provided.	• Little description is provided.	• No description is provided.
• Advertisement is well organized.	• Advertisement is somewhat well organized.	• Advertisement is poorly organized.	• Advertisement is not organized.
• Advertisement includes excellent designs or illustrations.	• Advertisement includes average designs or illustrations.	• Advertisement includes poor designs or illustrations.	• Advertisement includes designs or illustrations.
• Topic is very well researched.	• Topic is fairly well researched.	• Topic is minimally researched.	• Topic is not researched.

GROUP PERFORMANCE TASK

SCORE **4**	SCORE **3**	SCORE **2**	SCORE **1**
• Peformance shows excellent creativity.	• Performance shows some creativity.	• Performance shows little creativity.	• Performance shows no creativity.
• Characters chosen are very relevant to discussion.	• Characters chosen are somewhat relevant to discussion.	• Characters chosen are minimally relevant to discussion.	• Characters chosen are not relevant to discussion.
• Discussion is historically accurate.	• Discussion is mostly historically accurate.	• Discussion is partially historically accurate.	• Discussion is not historically accurate.

Introduce the Unit

Statue of Liberty, Liberty Island,
New York

- Use artifacts and primary sources to acquire information about the United States.
- Interpret information in visuals.

Access Prior Knowledge

Lead the class in a discussion about the changing global relations during the Cold War. Have students think about how those relations have changed over time.

BACKGROUND

The Statue of Liberty The Statue of Liberty is one of the largest statues in the world. Lady Liberty, as it is sometimes called, holds in her left hand a tablet inscribed with the date of the Declaration of Independence. At her feet a broken shackle symbolizes the overthrow of tyranny. The statue was erected on Liberty Island in 1886.

BACKGROUND

The United States With the collapse of the Soviet Union in 1989, the United States became the world's sole remaining superpower. As such, the United States maintains an active role in foreign relations throughout the world.

8

·UNIT· 8

The United States and the World

❝ History and destiny have made America the leader of the world that would be free. ❞

—Colin Powell, Chairman of the United States Joint Chiefs of Staff, in a speech, September 28, 1993

Preview the Content

Read the title and the Big Idea for each lesson. Then write a short paragraph for each lesson, telling what you think it is about.

Preview the Vocabulary

Suffixes A suffix is a part of a word that is added to the end of a root word. Use the root words and suffixes in the chart below to learn the meaning of each vocabulary word.

SUFFIX	ROOT WORD	VOCABULARY WORD	POSSIBLE MEANING
-ity	responsible	**responsibility**	
-ism	patriot	**patriotism**	

Unit 8 ◼ 611

Visual Learning

Picture Tell students that the Statue of Liberty was a gift to the United States from France.

Q **Why is the Statue of Liberty often considered a patriotic symbol?**

A Because it is a symbol of freedom and justice.

Analyze Primary Sources

Patriotic Folk Art Have students take a close look at the artifact and describe what they see. Students should notice that the star is painted like the United States flag.

Quotation Have a volunteer read aloud the quotation from Colin Powell's speech.

Q **How does Colin Powell's statement reflect America's position in global relations?**

A Students may say that Colin Powell regards the United States as the leader of the free world.

AUDIOTEXT

Use the Unit 8 AUDIOTEXT for a reading of the Unit narrative.

· Unit 8 ·

Preview the Content
Students' paragraphs should reflect an understanding of the changing relationship among countries around the world. Global interdependence has increased and this has changed the way people learn, transfer information, work, and lead nations.

Preview the Vocabulary
Make sure students identify the root word. Then have students check the definitions of each word.

Preview the Unit

PAGES 612–613

OBJECTIVES

- Interpret information in data-bases and visuals.
- Use appropriate mathematical skills to interpret social studies information such as maps and graphs.

Access Prior Knowledge

Have students describe what they have already learned about global relations in the twentieth century.

Visual Learning

Map Have students examine the map and locate the United States, Canada, and Mexico.

Q **What are the capitals of the United States, Canada, and Mexico?**

A Washington, D.C.; Ottawa; and Mexico City

Time Line To help students prepare for their reading, have them work in pairs to ask and answer questions about the time line. For example, a student might ask: *What industry employs more people than any other?* the service industry

Time Line Illustrations Ask students to speculate about the significance of the events shown on the time line.

- The United States is home to people from all over the world.
- Today more people in the United States work in the service industry than any other field.
- In the twenty-first century, Mexico City became one of the largest metropolitan areas in the world.
- Jean-Bertrand Aristide becomes Haiti's first elected president.
- South American General Simón Bolívar fought for independence for many Latin American countries.
- The St. Lawrence Seaway allows ships to travel from the Atlantic Ocean to the Great Lakes.

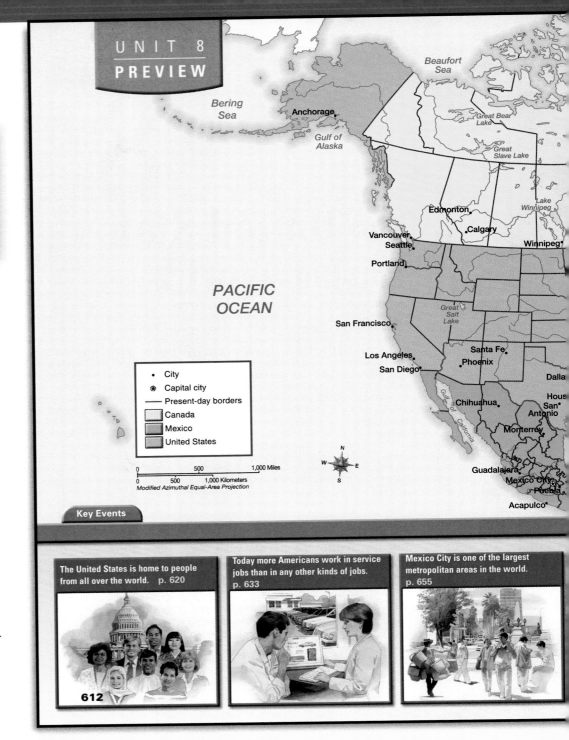

UNIT 8
PREVIEW

Beaufort Sea
Bering Sea
Anchorage
Gulf of Alaska
Great Bear Lake
Great Slave Lake
Edmonton
Lake Winnipeg
Calgary
Vancouver
Seattle
Winnipeg
Portland

PACIFIC OCEAN

San Francisco
Great Salt Lake
Los Angeles
Santa Fe
Phoenix
San Diego
Dalla
Hous
San Antonio
Gulf of California
Chihuahua
Monterrey
Guadalajara
Mexico City
Puebla
Acapulco

- • City
- ⊛ Capital city
- — Present-day borders
- Canada
- Mexico
- United States

0 500 1,000 Miles
0 500 1,000 Kilometers
Modified Azimuthal Equal-Area Projection

N E S W

Key Events

The United States is home to people from all over the world. p. 620

612

Today more Americans work in service jobs than in any other kinds of jobs. p. 633

Mexico City is one of the largest metropolitan areas in the world. p. 655

INTEGRATE LANGUAGE ARTS

Prepare a Book Report
Suggest that each student select and read a nonfiction book about an event shown. Students can use the information gathered to write a short report that focuses on changes that occurred in the United States, Canada, or Mexico.

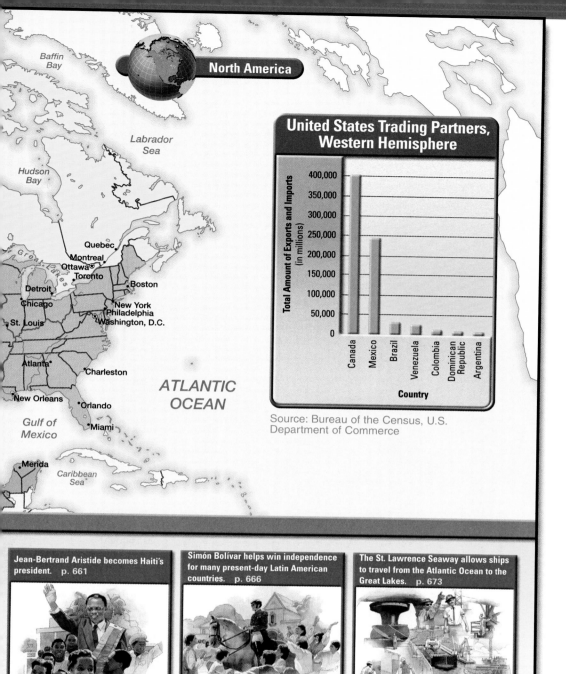

United States Trading Partners, Western Hemisphere

Total Amount of Exports and Imports (in millions)

| 400,000 |
| 350,000 |
| 300,000 |
| 250,000 |
| 200,000 |
| 150,000 |
| 100,000 |
| 50,000 |
| 0 |

Canada, Mexico, Brazil, Venezuela, Colombia, Dominican Republic, Argentina

Country

Source: Bureau of the Census, U.S. Department of Commerce

Jean-Bertrand Aristide becomes Haiti's president. p. 661

Simón Bolívar helps win independence for many present-day Latin American countries. p. 666

The St. Lawrence Seaway allows ships to travel from the Atlantic Ocean to the Great Lakes. p. 673

613

Visual Learning

Bar Graph Have students examine the bar graph. Pose such questions as the following:

- *What does this bar graph show?* It shows the United States' trading partners in the Western Hemisphere.
- *According to the graph, which country is America's most important trading partner?* Canada

Make Connections

Link Bar Graph and Map Ask students to use the information presented in the bar graph and map to draw conclusions about physical proximity and trade relationship.

Link Map and Key Events Have students identify the countries that were affected by each of the key events.

- People from all over the world have come to live in the United States. United States
- The service industry employs more people in the United States than does any other industry. United States
- Mexico City is now one of the largest metropolitan areas in the world. Mexico
- The St. Lawrence Seaway allows ships to travel between the Great Lakes and the Atlantic Ocean. Canada, United States
- Simón Bolívar won independence for the present-day countries in Latin America. Latin America
- Jean-Bertrand Aristide was elected as Haiti's president. Haiti

Start with a Story

PAGES 614–617

OBJECTIVES

- Gather information about history from pictures, photographs, and art.
- Learn about people who have immigrated to the United States.

Summary

Many Hmong people have come to the United States from Asia. The embroidered story cloths tell the story of Dia Cha, who immigrated to the United States when she was fifteen years old.

1 Motivate

Set the Purpose

People have different ways of recording their history. For the Hmong, story cloths show important things in their history and culture.

Access Prior Knowledge

Ask students to share what they know about the countries in Asia.

READING SOCIAL STUDIES

Personal Response Encourage students to ask questions about the text. After they have read the text, have them write one question about something in the text they did not understand or were curious about. As a class, work together to answer the students' questions.

● USE READING AND VOCABULARY TRANSPARENCY 8-1.

8-1
TRANSPARENCY

START with a STORY

Dia's Story Cloth

The Hmong People's Journey of Freedom

by Dia Cha
stitched by Chue and Nhia Thao Cha

This hand-embroidered story cloth tells the story of the Hmong and their long journey from Laos to the United States. The name *Hmong* means "free people."

People from all over the world have come to live in the United States, and the freedoms and economic opportunities offered by our country continue to attract newcomers. Many immigrants today tell stories of how they came to the United States. Some tell their stories in letters. Others tell their stories in poems and songs. This immigrant story was inspired by a Hmong [MONG] hand-sewn story cloth. Hmong needleworkers sew pictures on cloth, using no patterns or measurements, to remember their past. The story cloth on these pages tells the story of how Dia Cha [DEE·ah CHAY] and her family left Asia, to come to the United States in 1979.

614 ■ Unit 8

WORD WORK

Vocabulary Chart Ask students to make a list of unfamiliar words as they read. Encourage students to write down what they think the words mean based on the context. When they have finished reading, have them look up the definitions of the words in the dictionary, correcting their definitions if necessary.

Vocabulary Chart	
Word	**Definition**

INTEGRATE LANGUAGES

Learn About Hmong
Explain to students that the Hmong language has eight different tones. The tones indicate the meaning of a word. Tell students that the very last letter of a word tells what tone the word has.

614 ■ **UNIT 8**

8

Only 15 years old when she arrived in the United States, Dia Cha found life in America very different from life in Laos.

When my people first arrived in America, most didn't speak or write English. Many families had sponsors, who picked us up at the airport.

Everything about life in America was different for the Hmong.

I was 15 years old when I came to this country. I'd never been to school, so I had to start everything from scratch. They wanted to put me in high school, but I didn't know anything. Then they wanted to put me in adult school, but the teachers said I was too young.

Shoulder baskets (left) are made in adult and child sizes for carrying crops and other items. The stool, gourd water jar, and bamboo table (right) are like those found in many Hmong households.

2 Teach

Read and Respond

Understand the Story Challenge students to imagine that they have immigrated to a country where they do not speak the language. Ask students to describe their feelings. Some students in the class may be immigrants to the United States and may have gone through this experience. Encourage them to share their stories with the class.

Q What are some of the challenges new immigrants face in the United States?

A They may not speak English. They need to find jobs and a place to live. They may have very little money.

Visual Learning

Illustration Explain to students that the story cloth made by Chue and Nhia Thao Cha is shown in its entirety on page 614. Sections of the story cloth are on pages 615–616. Ask students to study the scene shown on page 615. Use the following question to begin a discussion about the story cloth.

• How did Dia Cha's family get to the United States? by airplane

AUDIOTEXT

Text of this story can be found on the Unit 8 AUDIOTEXT.

BACKGROUND

The Hmong The Hmong are an Asian ethnic group that live mostly in China and Southeast Asia. Only 300,000 to 600,000 live in the countries of Vietnam, Laos, and Thailand, whereas 8 million live in southern China. Hmong immigrants have settled in Australia, Canada, France, and the United States.

Read and Respond

Understand the Story Ask students to think about how Dia Cha's story may inspire other immigrants.

Civics and Government Explain to students that most of the Hmong that immigrated to the United States were refugees from the Vietnam War. They were displaced from their homes during the war and the United States became a new home to more than 110,000 of them. They settled primarily in California, Minnesota, and Wisconsin.

Visual Learning

Illustration Ask students to examine the scene shown on page 616. Discuss with students what it shows about life in Laos. Ask students to list some of the differences between life in Laos and life in the United States.

 **Close**

Summarize the Reading

- The Hmong people use story cloths to tell about their history and culture.
- Dia Cha is an immigrant from Laos who came to the United States.

READING SOCIAL STUDIES

Personal Response Have students use reference materials to help answer the questions. Then ask them to write a summary about what they learned.

● USE READING AND VOCABULARY TRANSPARENCY 8-1.

 8-1 TRANSPARENCY

The Hmong are known for their beautiful needlework, which is called *pa'ndau* (pan•DOW), or "flower cloth." Each design follows a theme. Those shown above, from left to right, are called "lightning", "snail house," and "frog legs."

Finally, I started high school. Thirteen years later, I received my master's degree from Northern Arizona University. I went back to Laos as an anthropologist in 1992 to work with Hmong and Lao women in the refugee camps in Thailand.

This story cloth reminds me of the history of my family and of my people. Some of the memories it brings are good, and some are bad. But it is important for me to remember everything the Hmong have been through.

Dia Cha believes that each memory sewn into the story cloth is important. This part of the story cloth shows Cha's home in Laos.

616 ■ Unit 8

INTEGRATE ART

Sketch a Story Cloth
Ask students to draw a story cloth depicting some event or events in their life. Suggest they choose a special event. Tell them to study the story cloths in the lesson for ideas. Then have them draw their story on a piece of paper. Ask for volunteers to show their story cloths to the class.

The Hmong's heavily embroidered clothes set them apart from neighboring peoples in Asia. Hmong clothes sometimes combine green, pink, black, dark blue, and white, as seen in the child's jacket and sash above.

Hmong women in America continue to stitch new story cloths. We all have vivid memories about our lives and culture and history. The story cloth is a bridge to all the generations before us. When I show the story cloth to my niece and nephew, who were both born here in the United States, I point to different pictures and tell them that this is what it was like.

Analyze the Literature

❶ What is the purpose of a Hmong story cloth?

❷ Why do you think many people feel it is important to remember their past?

READ A BOOK

START THE UNIT PROJECT

A Cultural Fair With your classmates, hold a cultural fair. As you read the unit, take notes about the different cultures discussed. Your notes will help you decide what to include in your cultural fair.

USE TECHNOLOGY

GO ONLINE Visit The Learning Site at **www.harcourtschool.com** for additional activities, primary sources, and other resources to use in this unit.

Unit 8 ◼ 617

Read a Book

Students may enjoy reading these leveled Independent Readers. Additional books are listed on pages 611D–611E of this Teacher's Edition.

Easy *The Pride of Puerto Ricans* by Rebecca Gomez. Students learn about Felisa Rincón de Gautier and Sila Maria Calderon, two women who are important to the history and government of Puerto Rico.

Average *Visit Vancouver* by Joy Dickerson. This book visits the largest city in the Canadian province of British Columbia.

Challenging *Election 2000* by Elaine Israel. Students can read about the electoral process and the events of the 2000 election.

Start the Unit Project

Hint Suggest that students use an outline to help them organize their notes about the different cultures in the unit.

Use Technology

INTERNET RESOURCES

THE LEARNING SITE Go to **www.harcourtschool.com** to view Internet resources for this unit.

TIME FOR KIDS Go to **www.harcourtschool.com** for the latest news in a student-friendly format.

Analyze the Literature
Answers

❶ Hmong story cloths tell stories of the past.

❷ People feel it is important to remember their past because they want to stay connected to their family, culture, and history.

LESSON	PACING	OBJECTIVES	VOCABULARY
Introduce the Chapter pp. 618–619	1 Day	■ Interpret information in visuals. ■ Use critical-thinking skills to organize and analyze information.	**Word Work:** Preview Vocabulary, p. 619
1 The American People Today pp. 620–625	2 Days	■ Explain the reasons for population growth in the United States. ■ Analyze cultural and ethnic diversity within the United States. ■ Explain how cultural differences affect life in the United States. ■ Describe the influence of technology on the way people in the United States live and work.	**Sun Belt** **ethnic group** **Internet** **teleconference** **Word Work:** Prefixes, p. 620
CHART AND GRAPH SKILLS **Use a Cartogram** pp. 626–627	1 Day	■ Use diagrams and maps to collect, analyze, and interpret data. ■ Apply critical thinking skills to organize and use information from diagrams and maps.	**cartogram** **Word Work:** Word Origins, p. 626
2 The Challenges of Growth pp. 628–631	1 Day	■ Analyze the effects of the growth of the American population. ■ Analyze environmental challenges that result from population growth in the United States.	**rapid-transit system**
3 The American Economy pp. 632–637	2 Days	■ Identify how the American economy has changed in recent years. ■ Explain how international trade has affected the United States. ■ Describe how the free enterprise system works in the United States	**diverse economy** **high-tech** **Information Age** **e-commerce** **interdependent** **international trade** **free-trade agreement** **global economy** **Word Work:** Historical Context, p. 632

Fact and Opinion,
p. 619

 Fact and Opinion,
p. 620

Reading Social Studies:
Prediction, p. 621

Reading Social Studies:
Summarize, p. 623

Reading Social Studies:
Prediction Responses,
p. 625

Mathematics
Figuring Percentages, p. 622

Language Arts
Descriptive Writing, p. 623

Technology
Discussion, p. 624

Advanced Learners, p. 621
Extend and Enrich, p. 624
Reteach the Lesson, p. 625

Activity Book,
pp. 160–161

**Reading and Vocabulary
Transparency, 8-2**

Internet Resources

Extend and Enrich, p. 627
Reteach the Skill, p. 627

Activity Book,
pp. 162–163

**Skill Transparencies, 8-1A
and 8-1B**

GeoSkills CD-ROM

Reading Social Studies:
Graphic Organizer, p. 629

Reading Social Studies:
Create Mental Images,
p. 629

Reading Social Studies:
**Graphic Organizer
Responses,** p. 630

Language Arts
Write a Persuasive Paper,
p. 630

**English as a Second
Language,** p. 628
Extend and Enrich, p. 631
Reteach the Lesson, p. 631

Activity Book, p. 164

**Reading and Vocabulary
Transparency, 8-3**

Reading Social Studies:
Study Questions, p. 633

Reading Social Studies:
Read Aloud, p. 633

Reading Social Studies:
**Study Question
Responses,** p. 636

Below-Level Learners,
p. 632
Advanced Learners, p. 635
Extend and Enrich, p. 636
Reteach the Lesson, p. 637

Activity Book, p. 165

**Reading and Vocabulary
Transparency, 8-4**

Chapter 17 Planning Guide The United States Today

LESSON	PACING	OBJECTIVES	VOCABULARY
4 **Government and the People** pp. 638–643	2 Days	■ Identify the roles of the federal government. ■ Compare and contrast the responsibilities of state and federal governments. ■ Describe the duties and responsibilities of citizens. ■ Explain the importance of patriotism and good citizenship.	**responsibility** **register** **informed citizen** **jury** **volunteers** **patriotism** **Word Work:** Suffixes, p. 638
CITIZENSHIP SKILLS **Identify Political Symbols** pp. 644–645	1 Day	■ Identify important political symbols that represent American beliefs and principles. ■ Explain how political symbols contribute to our national identity.	
EXAMINE PRIMARY SOURCES **Political Buttons** pp. 646–647	1 Day	■ Identify political buttons as an effective campaigning technique. ■ Compare and contrast the effectiveness of examples of political memorabilia from our nation's past.	
Chapter Review and Test Preparation pp. 648–649	1 Day		

READING	INTEGRATE LEARNING	REACH ALL LEARNERS	RESOURCES
Reading Social Studies: **K-W-L Chart,** p. 639 Reading Social Studies: **K-W-L Chart Responses,** p. 643	Reading **Discussing the National News,** p. 641	**English as a Second Language,** p. 638 **Advanced Learners,** p. 639 **Kinesthetic Learners,** p. 640 **Extend and Enrich,** p. 642 **Reteach the Lesson,** p. 643	**Activity Book,** p. 166 🌐 **Reading and Vocabulary Transparency, 8-5**
	Art **Make a Symbol,** p. 644	**Extend and Enrich,** p. 645 **Reteach the Skill,** p. 645	**Activity Book,** p. 167 🌐 **Skill Transparency, 8-2**
	Language Arts **Expressive Writing,** p. 646	**Extend and Enrich,** p. 647 **Reteach,** p. 647	💻 Internet Resources
		Test Preparation, p. 648	**Activity Book,** pp. 168–169 🌐 **Reading and Vocabulary Transparency, 8-6** ✔ **Assessment Program, Chapter 17 Test,** pp. 135–138

Activity Book

LESSON 1

Name _____ Date _____

The American People Today

Directions Choose two of the items shown. Write a paragraph explaining the effect that each item has had on life in the United States. Describe what life might be like without the item. *Students' answers may vary; possible answers are given.*

Cellular telephone—Effect: helps people stay connected; makes communications/ businesses move faster. Without: would be harder to reach people when they were away from home or office. Personal computer—Effect: allows people to complete many tasks, even run businesses from home; allows people to connect via Internet and World Wide Web to sources of information around the world; allows instant sharing of documents, images, and sounds via e-mail. Without: would have to physically travel to accomplish many tasks (shopping, banking, researching); sharing information would take longer. Air conditioner—Effect: spurred population and economic growth and environmental change in the Sun Belt by making life there more comfortable. Without: population of South would probably be much smaller; population of West would probably not be fastest-growing in the United States.

(continued)

LESSON 1

Name _____ Date _____

Directions Use the clues to complete the word puzzle. The letters in the outlined box will spell a word that describes a characteristic of the United States population.

Clues

❶ Many people who come to live in the United States are looking for _____ and opportunity.

❷ More than 1 million _____ came to the United States during the 1990s.

❸ The United States population grows when more people are born and when more people _____ to this country.

❹ The Sun _____ stretches across the southern United States.

❺ Texas and _____ have the largest Hispanic populations.

❻ Currently most people who come to live in the United States are from Latin American or _____ countries.

❼ Of the 20 percent of United States school children who do not speak English at home, most speak _____.

❽ A group of people from the same country, of the same race, or who share the same culture is called a(n) _____ group.

❾ A decade is a period of ten _____.

```
¹F  R  E  E  D [O] M
       ²I  M  M [I] G  R  A  N  T  S
          ³M  O  [V] E
             ⁴B  [E] L  T
⁵C  A  L  I  F  O  R  N  I  A
             ⁶A  S  I  A  N
       ⁷S  P  A  N  I  S  H
             ⁸E  T  H  N  I  C
                ⁹Y  E  A  R  S
```

SKILL PRACTICE

Name _____ Date _____

 CHART AND GRAPH SKILLS

Use a Cartogram

The cartogram below shows the population of North America.

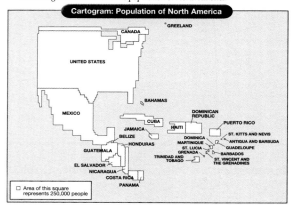

Cartogram: Population of North America

Directions Write a brief paragraph that defines the term *population cartogram*, and discusses appropriate and inappropriate uses of a population cartogram.

Definition: The size of each geographical area represents the size of the population of the area rather than the physical size of the area.

Appropriate: to compare populations of various locations

Inappropriate: to determine distances between locations

(continued)

SKILL PRACTICE

Name _____ Date _____

Directions Use the population cartogram of North America on the previous page and a political map of North America to answer the following questions. Remember that Puerto Rico is a territory of the United States.

❶ Which country has the largest population? United States

❷ What is the approximate population of Costa Rica? 3 million

❸ Which country has the greatest land area? Canada

❹ Which country has the smallest population? Panama

❺ Which is larger: the population of Canada or the population of Mexico?
Mexico

❻ Which country has the least land area? Costa Rica (Puerto Rico is not a country.)

❼ Which countries have the largest populations?
United States and Mexico

❽ What is the approximate population of the United States?
280 million

❾ What does the size of Canada on the cartogram and on the map tell you about the population of Canada?
that Canada does not have a very large population

LESSON 2

Name _____ Date _____

The Challenges of Growth

Directions The table shows six challenges that face a growing population. Write each solution from the list below in the appropriate box in the table. Some challenges will have more than one solution. Some solutions may help solve more than one challenge.

Solutions

add more bus routes

adjust number of seats in Congress to match current state populations

build rapid-transit systems

pass laws to protect endangered species

improve public transportation

prevent building on some land

recycle glass, metal, plastic, and paper

use electronic highway signs

use computer-controlled traffic lights

pass laws to stop land and water pollution

improve technology

Challenges	Solutions
❶ Damage to wildlife	pass laws to protect endangered species; pass laws to stop land and water pollution; prevent building on some land
❷ Large amounts of trash	recycle glass, metal, plastic, and paper
❸ Demands on natural resources	pass laws to stop land and water pollution; recycle glass, metal, plastic, and paper; improve technology
❹ Keeping government fair	adjust number of seats in Congress to match current state populations
❺ Roads jammed with cars and trucks	add more bus routes; build rapid-transit systems; use computer-controlled traffic lights; use electronic highway signs; improve public transportation

---

LESSON 3

Name _____ Date _____

The American Economy

Directions Use the terms from the lesson to solve the crossword puzzle.

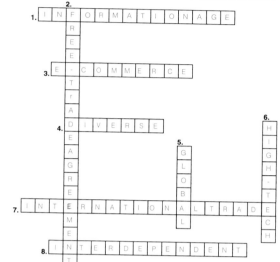

Crossword answers:
1. INFORMATION AGE
3. E-COMMERCE
4. DIVERSE
7. INTERNATIONAL TRADE
8. INTERDEPENDENT
Down 2. FREE TRADE AGREEMENT
5. GLOBAL
6. HIGH-TECH

Across
❶ A period when people can find and share rapidly-growing knowledge
❸ Buying products on the Internet
❹ An economy that is not based on just one kind of industry
❼ Buying and selling between companies in more than one country
❽ Businesses that rely on each other for resources, products, or services

Down
❷ A promise between nations not to tax the products that they buy from or sell to each other
❺ An economy that includes businesses from around the world
❻ Businesses that design, produce, or use electronic equipment

---

LESSON 4

Name _____ Date _____

Government and the People

Directions Complete the Web page below by filling in certain responsibilities of United States citizens. The home page on the left lists some constitutional rights. Use the items below to fill in the pop-up windows with citizens' matching responsibilities.

- Stay informed about local, state, and national events; respect the views of others
- Register and take part in local, state, and national elections
- Treat others fairly
- Be willing to serve on a jury

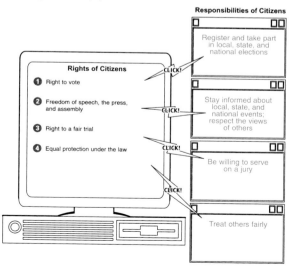

Responsibilities of Citizens

Register and take part in local, state, and national elections

Stay informed about local, state, and national events; respect the views of others

Be willing to serve on a jury

Treat others fairly

Rights of Citizens
❶ Right to vote
❷ Freedom of speech, the press, and assembly
❸ Right to a fair trial
❹ Equal protection under the law

CLICK!

SKILL PRACTICE

Name _____ Date _____

CITIZENSHIP SKILLS
Identify Political Symbols

Directions Match each symbol below with the appropriate description. Write the letter of the description on the line next to the symbol. Some descriptions will be used more than once.

a. United States government
b. Democratic party
c. United States Congress
d. Republican party
e. President of the United States
f. The United States of America
g. freedom

❶   e

❷  a

❸  d   ❻   b

❹   f   ❼  c

❺  f   ❽   g

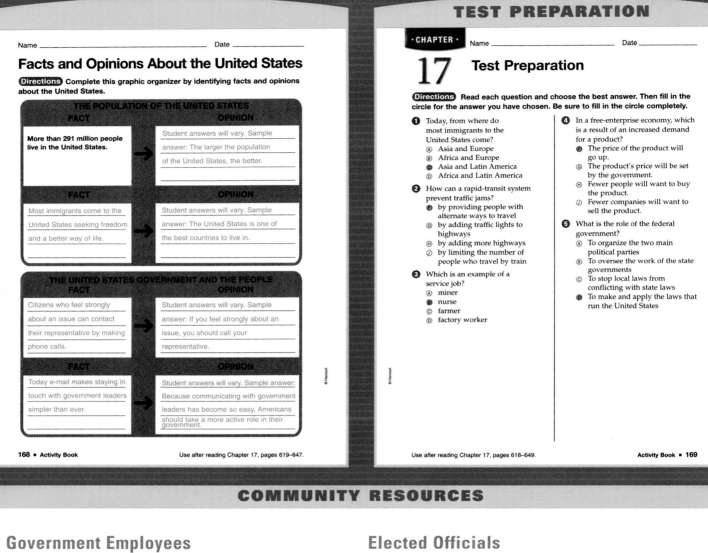

Name _____ **Date** _____

Facts and Opinions About the United States

Directions Complete this graphic organizer by identifying facts and opinions about the United States.

THE POPULATION OF THE UNITED STATES

FACT	OPINION
More than 291 million people live in the United States.	Student answers will vary. Sample answer: The larger the population of the United States, the better.
Most immigrants come to the United States seeking freedom and a better way of life.	Student answers will vary. Sample answer: The United States is one of the best countries to live in.

THE UNITED STATES GOVERNMENT AND THE PEOPLE

FACT	OPINION
Citizens who feel strongly about an issue can contact their representative by making phone calls.	Student answers will vary. Sample answer: If you feel strongly about an issue, you should call your representative.
Today e-mail makes staying in touch with government leaders simpler than ever.	Student answers will vary. Sample answer: Because communicating with government leaders has become so easy, Americans should take a more active role in their government.

© Harcourt

· CHAPTER · **Name** _____ **Date** _____

17 Test Preparation

Directions Read each question and choose the best answer. Then fill in the circle for the answer you have chosen. Be sure to fill in the circle completely.

1 Today, from where do most immigrants to the United States come?
- Ⓐ Asia and Europe
- Ⓑ Africa and Europe
- Ⓒ Asia and Latin America
- Ⓓ Africa and Latin America

2 How can a rapid-transit system prevent traffic jams?
- Ⓕ by providing people with alternate ways to travel
- Ⓖ by adding traffic lights to highways
- Ⓗ by adding more highways
- Ⓙ by limiting the number of people who travel by train

3 Which is an example of a service job?
- Ⓐ miner
- Ⓑ nurse
- Ⓒ farmer
- Ⓓ factory worker

4 In a free-enterprise economy, which is a result of an increased demand for a product?
- Ⓕ The price of the product will go up.
- Ⓖ The product's price will be set by the government.
- Ⓗ Fewer people will want to buy the product.
- Ⓙ Fewer companies will want to sell the product.

5 What is the role of the federal government?
- Ⓐ To organize the two main political parties
- Ⓑ To oversee the work of the state governments
- Ⓒ To stop local laws from conflicting with state laws
- Ⓓ To make and apply the laws that run the United States

© Harcourt

COMMUNITY RESOURCES

Government Employees
_____
_____
_____
_____
_____

Elected Officials
_____
_____
_____
_____
_____

Experts in Economics
_____
_____
_____
_____

Experts in Political Science
_____
_____
_____
_____

Chapter 17 Assessment

·CHAPTER·
Name _____ Date _____

17 Test

Part One: Test Your Understanding
MULTIPLE CHOICE (4 points each)

Directions Circle the letter of the best answer.

1 Four of every five people in the United States live in—
A the Sun Belt.
B metropolitan areas.
C New York and Pennsylvania.
D California and Texas.

2 The state that has the highest percentage of Hispanic residents is—
F Texas.
G Florida.
H California.
J New Mexico.

3 Why was the Internet created?
A The University of Washington wanted to develop a database to keep better records of its students.
B The Department of Defense established a computer network for military communications.
C The Library of Congress needed a database to track its library collection.
D The Department of Commerce wanted a computer program to help banks record credit card purchases.

4 A passenger transportation system that uses elevated or underground trains is called—
F urban growth.
G land use.
H a rapid-transit system.
J a rush-hour system.

5 Reusing old materials to create new products is called—
A reducing materials.
B recycling materials.
C naturalizing materials.
D rebranding materials.

6 Most residents of the United States today work in what kinds of jobs?
F construction jobs
G farming jobs
H service jobs
J factory jobs

(continued)

Chapter 17 Test

Name _____ Date _____

7 People in high-tech industries—
A make up about four of every five workers.
B work in banks or insurance companies.
C are mainly government or transportation workers.
D invent or build computers or electronic equipment.

8 Two countries that are interdependent—
F trade very few products.
G rely on each other for products or resources.
H have unstable economic systems.
J have similar natural resources.

9 Which of the following documents set up the federal system of government and protects the rights and freedoms of United States citizens?
A the Declaration of Independence
B the Articles of Confederation
C the Constitution
D the Emancipation Proclamation

10 In order to vote, United States citizens must—
F pass a reading and citizenship test.
G register to show they live where the voting is taking place.
H serve on a jury at least two times.
J volunteer to serve on an election campaign.

TRUE OR FALSE (4 points each)

Directions Indicate whether the following statements are true or false by writing *T* or *F* in the spaces provided.

11 __T__ People who belong to the same ethnic group share the same race, country, or culture.

12 __F__ Almost no schoolchildren in the United States today speak a language other than English.

13 __F__ People must usually travel great distances to attend teleconferences.

14 __F__ E-commerce has greatly decreased the number of goods and services available to American consumers.

15 __T__ The Speaker of the House of Representatives is always a member of the majority party.

(continued)

Chapter 17 Test

Name _____ Date _____

Part Two: Test Your Skills
IDENTIFY POLITICAL SYMBOLS (4 points each)

Directions Look at the image below to answer the following questions.

16 Does this image represent a small part of government or does it represent a larger government? The United States flag represents the entire United States government, not just a particular branch of the government.

17 Where have you seen this symbol? Possible responses: Flags are flown by individuals and federal buildings, such as post offices. Flags are also reproduced on coins, paper money, and official documents.

18 During what holidays would you be most likely to see this symbol displayed? Possible response: Independence Day, Veterans Day, Flag Day, and Memorial Day

19 What do the 13 stripes on the flag represent? What do the 50 stars represent? The stripes represent the 13 original colonies. The stars represent the 50 states.

20 Why do you think the flag is a good representation of the United States? Possible response: The 13 stripes represent the country's history. The pattern of stars shows that all the states come together in one national government.

(continued)

Chapter 17 Test

Name _____ Date _____

Part Three: Apply What You Have Learned
21 **PROBLEMS AND SOLUTIONS** (10 points)

Describe the cause of each problem listed below, and write a solution that has been used to help solve the problem. One cause is provided.

Problems of Growth	Cause	Solution
traffic jams	too many vehicles on highways and streets	Possible response: improved public transportation
environmental pollution	Possible response: Chemicals have gotten into the water supply.	Possible response: Harmful chemicals can be limited or banned to stop pollution.
too much trash	Possible response: Communities do not have enough space to dispose of garbage.	Possible response: recycling materials

22 **ESSAY** (10 points)

Today, the United States is part of a global economy in which countries trade goods around the world. Write a paragraph describing factors that increase trade among countries.

Possible response: Global trade is made possible by modern communication and transportation systems. Governments also must agree to allow the passage of goods between countries. Free-trade agreements that limit tariffs and taxes encourage international trade. Because resources can be unevenly divided, supply and demand can set up conditions that encourage trade between countries.

Chapter 17 Test

Introduce the Chapter

PAGES 618–619

OBJECTIVES

- Interpret information in visuals.
- Use critical thinking skills to organize and analyze information.

Access Prior Knowledge

Ask students if they have ever seen the residence of a famous person or national leader on television. What did these places tell them about the people who live there?

Visual Learning

Picture Have students look at the picture of the White House and describe what they see. Why has this image become a national symbol? Answers may vary, but should reflect that the White House is the center of American government.

Locate It Map Washington, D.C., is located on the eastern bank of the Potomac River and is bordered by Maryland and Virginia.

THE WHITE HOUSE

For over two hundred years, the White House has symbolized the executive branch. In 1800, President John Adams and his wife Abigail became the White House's first residents. Since then, the building has been home to 41 United States Presidents. On average, the White House receives nearly 5,000 visitors a day.

LOCATE IT

MARYLAND

Washington, D.C.

VIRGINIA

White House

618 ▪ Unit 8

BACKGROUND

Picture In 1800, the United States government moved to Washington, D.C., from Philadelphia. President John Adams and his family moved into the unfinished mansion just a few months before leaving office. At the time the White House was a spectacular building in an isolated setting. Today the White House is surrounded by a bustling, developed area. The Adamses made the best of living in the new executive mansion, although it was difficult at first to host official social functions with only a handful of finished rooms.

BACKGROUND

Quotation After serving under George Washington as Vice President, John Adams (1735–1826) became the second President of the United States in 1797. His term ended in 1801, not long after he and his family had become the first occupants of the White House. Letters written between Adams and his wife, Abigail, have become important historical documents, revealing much about life and politics in the late 1700s.

17
The United States Today

> **❝I pray Heaven to bestow the best of blessings on this house and all that shall hereafter inhabit it. ❞**
> —John Adams, letter to Abigail Adams, November 2, 1800

 Fact and Opinion

A **fact** is a statement that can be proved. An **opinion** is a statement tht tells what a person thinks or believes. It cannot be proved.

As you read this chapter, identify facts and opinions about the United States.

• Identify the facts by asking, *Can the idea be proved true by testing?*

• Look for phrases and words such as *think, feel, worst,* and *best* to identify opinions.

Chapter 17 ▪ 619

Read and Respond

Read aloud the title and the quotation. Have students discuss how the quotation from 1800 is connected to the title of this chapter.

Quotation Have a volunteer read the quotation aloud.

Q What does John Adams mean by wishing for "blessings" on the White House?

A Students might suggest that Adams wishes success for the nation and its leaders.

 Fact and Opinion

Have students complete a graphic organizer to show facts and opinions related to the topic of the chapter.

• A graphic organizer can be found on page 168 of the Activity Book.

• Remind students to read carefully.

• A completed graphic organizer appears on page 168 of the Activity Book, Teacher's Edition.

WORD WORK

Preview Vocabulary Have students use a three-column chart to list and define the lesson vocabulary terms. They can list the terms and definitions in the first two columns. Students should use the last column to make notes that will help them remember what the terms mean.

Term	Definition	Notes

MAKE IT RELEVANT

Discussion Topics You and your students might enjoy discussing these topics about the image of the United States in today's world.

■ What feature or characteristic of the United States is most impressive to you?

■ When people visit the United States for the first time, what impressions might they have of it?

Lesson 1
PAGES 620–625

OBJECTIVES

- Explain the reasons for population growth in the United States.
- Analyze cultural and ethnic diversity within the United States.
- Explain how cultural differences affect life in the United States.
- Describe the influence of technology on the way people in the United States live and work.

 Fact and Opinion pp. 619, 620, 622, 625, 648

Vocabulary

SEE READING AND VOCABULARY TRANSPARENCY 8-2 OR THE WORD CARDS ON PP. V93–V94.

Sun Belt p. 621   **Internet** p. 624
ethnic group   **teleconference**
p. 622   p. 625

 When Minutes Count

Have students read about the microchip on page 624. Then invite them to state one fact and one opinion about what they just read.

Quick Summary

This lesson discusses the growth and diversity of the population of the United States and explains how technology affects the way Americans live and work.

1 Motivate

Set the Purpose

Big Idea Make sure that students understand the meaning of the word *diversity* as used in the Big Idea statement.

Access Prior Knowledge

Have students discuss what they have learned about why people came to the United States in the past.

620 ■ UNIT 8

· LESSON ·

1

 FACT AND OPINION

As you read, find facts and opinions about how people in the United States live and work today.

BIG IDEA
Technology and diversity have affected the way people in the United States live and work.

VOCABULARY
Sun Belt
ethnic group
Internet
teleconference

 FAST FACT Today about one of every ten people in the United States was born in another country.

The American People Today

People have been coming to the Americas since before history was recorded. Over time, the United States has become a nation of many cultures. The nation has changed in other ways, too.

A Growing Nation

More than 281 million people live in the United States today, and that number is rising fast. During the 1990s alone, the population of the United States grew by almost 33 million people—the largest ten-year increase in the country's history.

The population of the United States is growing as more people are born and more immigrants arrive. People who are born in the United States or who have at least one parent who is a United States citizen are called "natural born" citizens. They are automatically given citizenship at birth.

Many immigrants have become naturalized citizens. To become a naturalized citizen, a person must have lived in the United States for at least five years (or three if married to a citizen). Then that person must apply for citizenship and pass a test to show that he or she understands United States history and government. Finally, the person must take part in a ceremony in which he or she promises to be loyal to the United States.

Many immigrants become citizens of the United States each year.

WORD WORK

Prefixes Instruct students to look through the lesson for vocabulary terms highlighted in yellow. After students locate the terms and read their definitions, have them identify the vocabulary terms that contain prefixes. Internet, teleconference Allow students to work in pairs to identify the meanings of the prefixes. Encourage them to predict the meanings before confirming them in a dictionary.

READING SKILL

Fact and Opinion Remind students that a fact is a statement that can be proven true. Explain that statements that include numbers or statistics are usually facts. Ask them to identify at least one fact on page 620. Possible facts: More than 281 million people live in the United States; during the 1990s, the population increased by almost 33 million people; and the 33 million increase was the largest 10-year increase in the United States ever.

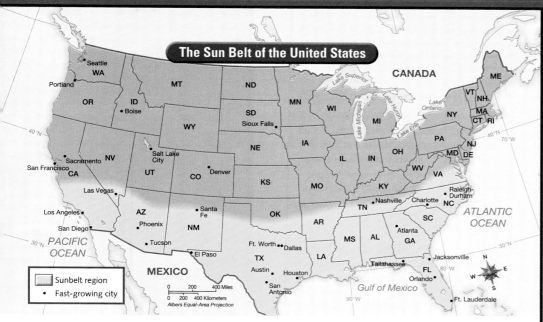

The Sun Belt of the United States

Sunbelt region
• Fast-growing city

GEOGRAPHY THEME

Regions Many Americans are attracted to the warm and sunny weather of the Sun Belt.

◈ What cities in Texas are growing fast?

In the past, most immigrants came to the United States from Europe. Today, most immigrants come from countries in Asia and Latin America. Like immigrants in the past, they come seeking freedom and new opportunities for a better life. Many seek refuge from war, weak economies, and poor living conditions in their homelands.

Most new immigrants, like most other Americans, live in metropolitan areas. In fact, about four of every five people in the United States live in metropolitan areas. About one-third of all Americans live in metropolitan areas of more than 5 million people.

More than half of the American people live in the ten states with the greatest populations—California, Texas, New York, Florida, Illinois, Pennsylvania, Ohio, Michigan, New Jersey, and Georgia. However, the population of every state is growing.

Although the population of every region of the United States is growing, different regions are growing at different rates. Much of the nation's growth has taken place in the **Sun Belt**, a wide area of the southern United States that has a mild climate all year. The Sun Belt stretches from the Atlantic coast to the Pacific coast. Places in the Sun Belt region began growing during World War II. One reason for this growth was the development of air conditioning.

Air conditioning was introduced in the early twentieth century. It was first used in movie theaters and railroad cars.

Chapter 17 ▪ 621

2 Teach

A Growing Nation

Visual Learning

Photograph Inform students that the photograph on page 620 shows a citizenship ceremony in which immigrants become citizens of the United States. Similar ceremonies happen regularly throughout the United States.

Map Have students study the map and identify fast-growing cities. Ask them to name challenges a fast-growing city might face.
CAPTION ANSWER: Austin, Dallas, Ft. Worth, Houston, San Antonio, and El Paso

Read and Respond

Link Geography and Economics
Have volunteers identify the ten states with the greatest populations.
California, Texas, New York, Florida, Illinois, Pennsylvania, Ohio, Michigan, New Jersey, and Georgia

Q **What development in technology enabled people to live more comfortably in the Sun Belt?**

A air conditioning

A Diverse Nation

Read and Respond

Culture and Society Point out that almost all people in the United States are descended from immigrants. Ask students to name ways that each ethnic group has contributed to the culture of the United States.

Q Why do you think most Hispanics in the United States live in the South or the West?

A Many Hispanic people lived in the South or the West before those regions became part of the United States. Recent Hispanic immigrants to the United States often settle in the South or the West partly because they may have family there.

Culture and Society Using the information on page 622, ask students to make a bar graph that shows the breakdown of people in the United States. Ask students to rank the populations from largest to smallest based on ethnic background.

Students might enjoy researching information about different areas of the United States. Have them visit The Learning Site at **www.harcourtschool.com.**

Culture and Society Explain to students that people who have moved to the United States from a country in Latin America are sometimes called Latinos. Then challenge them to explain the similarities and differences that may exist between Latinos from Brazil and Latinos from Costa Rica. Latinos from Brazil would speak Portuguese, and Latinos from Costa Rica would speak Spanish. Both may speak English.

Immigrants who share a culture sometimes choose to settle in the same neighborhood. One example of this is Chinatown in San Francisco, California.

In the 1920s, the first fully air-conditioned office building, the Milam Building in San Antonio, Texas, was constructed. As air conditioning spread across the Sun Belt in the 1950s, it helped make living there more comfortable. Millions of people moved to the region, built homes and started businesses, and forever changed the environment.

The Sun Belt stretches across parts of both the South and the West. In recent years, both of these regions have grown faster than other regions of the United States. The West is the fastest-growing region of the United States, but the South has the largest population of any region. Almost 100 million people live in states in the South.

REVIEW How did the use of air-conditioning change the Sun Belt?

FACT AND OPINION Millions of people moved to the region and built homes and businesses.

A Diverse Nation

The population of the United States is growing quickly. At the same time, the United States is becoming a more diverse nation. In fact, the United States has one of the world's most diverse populations in terms of ancestry. Today about 210 million Americans are of European background. Almost 35 million are African Americans, and more than 10 million are of Asian background. About two and a half million people in the United States are Native Americans.

Hispanic Americans make up the fastest-growing ethnic group in the

622 Unit 8

---

nation. An **ethnic group** is a group of people from the same country, of the same race, or with a shared culture. A little more than 1 in 10 Americans, or about 35 million people, are of Hispanic descent. More than three-fourths of them live in the South or West. California and Texas have the largest Hispanic populations, but the state with the highest percentage of Hispanic residents is New Mexico. In New Mexico more than 4 of every 10 people are of Hispanic background.

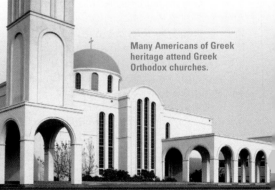

Many Americans of Greek heritage attend Greek Orthodox churches.

MAKE IT RELEVANT

In Your Community Talk with students about the ethnic diversity in their community. What ethnic groups are represented? Have a volunteer make a list of the groups mentioned in discussion. Encourage students to interview members of their families or neighbors for anecdotes that answer the questions "What ethnic groups are in our community?" and "What customs did they bring with them?"

INTEGRATE MATHEMATICS

Figuring Percentages Use the population information on page 622, and review with students how to figure percentages. Ask students to find the percentage of the United States population that is descended from European Americans, Asian Americans, Hispanic Americans, African Americans, and Native Americans. 72%, 3%, 12%, 12%, and 1%, respectively

Most people in the United States are either immigrants or descendants of immigrants. Some people's families have been living in the United States for hundreds of years. Others have come to live in this country only recently. Instead of arriving on ships, as immigrants often did in the past, most immigrants today arrive by plane at one of the nation's international airports.

Some people who have immigrated to this country still speak the language of the country in which they were born. So do some of their descendants. In fact, about one-fifth of all schoolchildren in the United States today speak a language other than English at home. Most of them speak Spanish.

Many Americans continue to take part in the customs and traditions that are unique to their culture. Some Native American peoples still live by the laws and customs of their tribal governments. Cultural differences among Americans in the style of dress some people wear, the different customs and traditions people have, the kinds of foods people eat and music they listen to, and the religious groups they belong to

can also be seen in the foods they eat and the religious groups they belong to.

Having so many different cultures has made the United States a more diverse place. At the same time, it has given Americans a richer life. Over the years, people from each culture have contributed to American life. Cultural differences help explain why people in the United States often seem so different from one another in so many ways.

Although Americans are different from one another, they also have much in common. Americans share a deep belief in individual rights. Most Americans support the government, which is based on representation and the consent of the people. Americans also value our economic system, which supports free enterprise and the ideas of competition, open opportunity, and private property. These common beliefs help unite Americans.

REVIEW In what ways can one see cultural differences among Americans?

• HERITAGE •

Epiphany

For many Hispanic families in the United States, the Christmas season does not end on December 25. It continues with Epiphany, or Three Kings Day, which is celebrated on January 6. According to tradition, 12 days after the birth of Jesus, the Three Kings, or Wise Men, arrived to present the newborn child with gifts. The night before Epiphany, many Hispanic children leave snacks out for the Kings. The children hope to find candy and presents waiting for them the next day. Other Epiphany traditions include eating special ring-shaped cakes called roscones and attending Three Kings Day parades.

Chapter 17 ■ 623

Read and Respond

Culture and Society Point out to students that the United States celebrates its diversity as one of its great strengths. The tragedy of the World Trade Center attack in September 2001 reminded many Americans that we are of every race, religion, and ethnicity. In a speech Mayor Rudolph Giuliani of New York City said, "Our diversity has always been our greatest source of strength. It's the thing that renews us and revives us in every generation— our openness to new people from all over the world. . . We are defined as Americans by our beliefs—not by our ethnic origins, our race or our religion."

Q What beliefs do most Americans share?

A beliefs in individual rights, representative government, and economic freedom

• HERITAGE •

Epiphany

Discuss Epiphany with students. Ask students to describe special holidays or events they celebrate in the month of December. Point out that some December celebrations, such as Christmas, Hanukkah, and Kwanzaa, are celebrated primarily by people of a certain religious or ethnic background. Encourage students to describe holiday traditions, customs, and celebrations that are unique to their cultural background.

INTEGRATE LANGUAGE ARTS

Descriptive Writing
Invite students to research or to take part in an event that involves people from different ethnic groups, and to write about their experience. Students might attend an event at a cultural center or attend a heritage parade. They should take notes and then use them to write descriptions of the event and their experiences.

READING SOCIAL STUDIES

Summarizing Remind students that a summary includes only the main ideas or key points of a passage. Have students work in pairs to identify the main idea of each paragraph in the section and to use the main ideas to write a summary. Challenge students to use their own words.

Changing Ways of Life

Read and Respond

Culture and Society Ask students to list the kinds of technology that are available to people every day. cellular phones, personal computers, handheld computers, and the Internet In discussion, ask students to explain how improvements made in the field of communication have benefited individuals and society.

Read and Respond

Economics Point out that the Internet helps businesses, customers, and ordinary people communicate in new ways. Challenge students to identify other communications technologies that influenced economic activity in the United States in the past.

3 Close

Summarize Key Content

- The population of the United States has grown substantially, in part because of immigration.
- The United States population is becoming more diverse.
- Technology has changed the way Americans live, communicate, and work.

Changing Ways of Life

The United States is also changing in other ways. Advances in technology, such as computers and cellular telephones, affect how people live and work. In many high paying jobs, employees must know how to use computers and other machines. Many people choose to get an education that teaches them about new technologies. These skills can increase their productivity and success at work.

Computers first came into widespread use after World War II. At that time computers were so big that just one would fill an entire room. Then, in 1958, scientists working independently in Texas and California each invented the silicon chip. This tiny device can now store millions of bits of computer information. Silicon chips have allowed businesses to make smaller, faster, and cheaper computers.

Today millions of computers are used in businesses and in homes and schools throughout the world. Many people even run their own businesses from their homes with the use of the Internet. The **Internet** is a network that links computers around the world for the exchange of information.

The United States Department of Defense set up a computer network in the late 1960s for military communications. The network changed and grew over the years. In 1992, the World Wide Web came into use. It allows millions of people to send and receive electronic mail, or e-mail, as well as electronic documents, pictures, and sounds.

• SCIENCE AND TECHNOLOGY •
The Microchip

The integrated circuit, or microchip, was one of the twentieth century's greatest inventions. Introduced in 1959, the microchip helped reduce the size of all types of electronic machines. It did so by letting hundreds of electronic parts be put on a single silicon chip half the size of a paper clip. Starting in the early 1970s, microchips were used to run handheld calculators. Over the years, microchips grew more and more powerful. Today they are used in everything from personal computers to space satellites.

Today many computers like the one above are very compact. Early computers, however, were bulky machines (below). They often filled an entire room.

624 ■ Unit 8

Using the Internet, people can shop for clothing, cars, or any other item online. They can check on bank accounts, transfer money, pay bills, make reservations, and do many other tasks. They can also reach government agencies, libraries, and other online sites to research almost any subject.

Another change in people's lives is the ability to travel much faster from one place to another. Each year more than 700 million people travel on jet airplanes. In just a few hours they can travel from city to city or halfway around the world to visit family members. People also travel to attend business meetings. However, people do not have to travel at all to communicate directly with others. They can hold a **teleconference**—a conference, or meeting, that uses electronic machines to connect people. Having a teleconference allows people from all over the world to

Satellites such as this one make it possible for people around the world to communicate with one another instantly.

communicate directly with one another by turning on a computer or dialing a telephone. Advances in technology have changed people's lives in other ways, too. Doctors can use tiny video cameras attached to plastic tubes to see inside a person. Eye doctors now use laser beams to help correct eye problems. The way some automobile drivers find out how to get where they want to go has changed, too. Today, automobiles can be equipped with a Global Positioning System (GPS) receiver. These receivers use satellites to help find a driver's location anywhere on Earth. Drivers can also receive directions through the GPS.

REVIEW What is the Internet? A network that links computers around the world for the exchange of information.

LESSON 1 REVIEW

 FACT AND OPINION The United States has one of the world's most diverse populations in terms of ancestry. Is this statement a fact or an opinion? How do you know?

1 BIG IDEA How have technology and diversity affected the way Americans live and work?

2 VOCABULARY Write a description of the **Sun Belt**.

3 SCIENCE AND TECHNOLOGY How have advances in technology helped people?

4 CRITICAL THINKING—Analyze Compare and contrast today's immigrant groups and immigrant groups from 100 years ago.

 PERFORMANCE—Write a Report Use library or Internet sources to research information about different cultures in the United States. Then write a report about the similarities and differences among the cultures you researched.

Chapter 17 ■ 625

RETEACH THE LESSON

Graphic Organizer Offer students the following chart. Have students fill in each section with one fact or idea that they learned in each subsection. Remind students that they may use the book to find or confirm information.

A Growing Nation (p. 620)	A Diverse Nation (p. 622)	Changing Ways of Life (p. 624)
Much of America's population growth is in the Sun Belt.	The United States has a diverse ethnic population.	New technology has affected the way Americans communicate and do their work.

READING SOCIAL STUDIES

Prediction Invite students to check their written predictions. Then ask students to make general statements about the immigrant experience.

● USE READING AND VOCABULARY TRANSPARENCY 8-2.

8-2 TRANSPARENCY

Assess

Lesson 1 Review—Answers

 FACT AND OPINION Fact; official figures about the population can confirm the statement.

1 BIG IDEA Diversity has given Americans a richer life as different cultures merge with American culture. Technology has made it easier to communicate, travel, and work.

2 VOCABULARY The **Sun Belt** is a wide area of the southern United States, from the Atlantic coast to the Pacific coast, which is rapidly growing.

3 SCIENCE AND TECHNOLOGY Advances in technology have improved communication and made many kinds of work easier.

4 CRITICAL THINKING—Analyze One hundred years ago most immigrants arrived by boat; today most arrive on airplanes. As in the past, many of today's immigrants come to the United States to find freedom and start a new life.

Performance Assessment Guidelines Students' reports should include specific examples of similarities and differences among the cultures they researched.

ACTIVITY BOOK

Use ACTIVITY BOOK, pp. 160–161, to reinforce and extend student learning.

Skill Lesson
PAGES 626–627

OBJECTIVES

- Use diagrams and maps to collect, analyze, and interpret data.
- Apply critical thinking skills to organize and use information from diagrams and maps.

Vocabulary

cartogram p. 626

WORD CARDS

See pp. V93–V94.

1 Motivate

Why It Matters

Explain to students that a cartogram is one of many special tools that geographers use to present information about a place. Ask students what other visual tools they could use to show population. a table, a circle graph, a bar graph

·SKILLS· CHART AND GRAPH

Use a Cartogram

VOCABULARY

cartogram

➡ WHY IT MATTERS

One way to show the population of different places is to use a cartogram. A **cartogram** is a diagram that gives information about places by the size shown for each place. Knowing how to read a cartogram can help you quickly compare information about different places.

➡ WHAT YOU NEED TO KNOW

Some maps of the United States base the size of each state on its land area. With a cartogram, a state's size is based on a geographical statistic. On the cartogram on page 627, size is based on population.

A population cartogram shows the states as their sizes would be if each

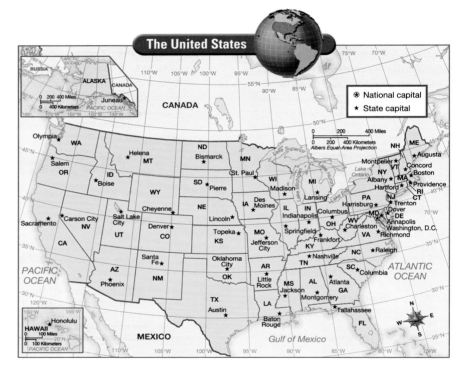

The United States

626 ▪ Unit 8

WORD WORK

Word Origins The term *cartogram* is of French origin. The first part, *cart-*, comes from the French *carte*, meaning "card or map." The ending *-gram* traces its origins to the Greek *gramma*, meaning "letter or writing." It is also the root of the modern English words *grammar* and *gram*. Taken together, *cartogram* literally means "writing in map form." Ask students to think of other words that use these word parts. cartographer, diagram, telegram

MAKE IT RELEVANT

At School Lead the class in a discussion about statistical information they could gather about their class. Suggest statistics such as height, number of members in students' households, and travel time to school each day. Choose three types of statistics, and gather the data with the class using a survey or a show of hands. Record the data on the board. Have students make maps of the classroom. Then have students make cartograms based on the data recorded on the board.

Population Cartogram of the United States

One square equals 500,000 people

---

person had the same amount of land. A state with many people would be much bigger than a state with few people. When states are shown this way, you can quickly compare populations around the country.

➡ **PRACTICE THE SKILL**

The map on page 626 is a political map of the United States. The size of each state is based on its land area. Compare the size of New Jersey with the size of South Dakota. South Dakota is larger in land area. The cartogram on this page is a population cartogram. The size of each state is based on population. Compare the sizes of New Jersey and South Dakota again. Although New Jersey has a smaller land area than South Dakota, it is shown larger than South Dakota on the cartogram because it has more people.

Continue to compare land area and population to answer these questions.

1 Which state has more land area, Pennsylvania or Montana?

2 Which of those states is shown larger on the cartogram? Why is it shown larger?

3 What does the cartogram tell about Alaska when you compare its size on the political map?

➡ **APPLY WHAT YOU LEARNED**

With a partner, brainstorm other ideas for cartograms. What other statistics could be shown in this way to help people compare and contrast states? Make a cartogram of the United States that is based on other statistics besides population statistics. Then prepare a list of questions that could be answered by looking at your cartogram.

Chapter 17 ■ 627

CHART AND GRAPH SKILLS

---

2 Teach

What You Need to Know

Have students compare the sizes of states in the map and on the cartogram. Encourage students to analyze the data by combining prior knowledge with the new information presented. Use this data to make inferences and draw conclusions about the populations of states.

Practice the Skill—Answers

Briefly discuss the advantages of using a cartogram. Then have students answer the questions in this section.

1 Montana

2 Pennsylvania, because it has a larger population

3 Alaska has a large area of land and a small population.

3 Close

Apply What You Learned

Students should research statistics and create cartograms based on the data they collect. Prompt students to use several different question formats on their quizzes, such as multiple choice, fill-in-the blank, and critical thinking questions.

ACTIVITY BOOK

Use ACTIVITY BOOK, pp. 162–163, to give students additional practice using this skill.

TRANSPARENCY

Use SKILL TRANSPARENCIES 8-1A and 8-1B.

CD-ROM

Explore GEOSKILLS CD-ROM to learn more about map and globe skills.

EXTEND AND ENRICH

Make Historical Cartograms
Have students use an almanac or the Internet to research the populations of their own state and the states bordering it for each decade over the last fifty years. Then have students make 5 population cartograms, one for each decade. Ask students to compare the cartograms and discuss how the population of the region has changed.

RETEACH THE SKILL

Write a Paragraph Have students write a paragraph that describes how cartograms show information and why cartograms are useful. Encourage students to share their paragraphs with a classmate.

CHAPTER 17 ■ 627

Lesson 2

PAGES 628–631

OBJECTIVES

- Analyze the effects of the growth of the American population.

- Analyze environmental challenges that result from population growth in the United States.

 Fact and Opinion pp. 619, 628, 630, 631, 648

Vocabulary

SEE READING AND VOCABULARY TRANSPARENCY 8-3 OR THE WORD CARDS ON PP. V93–V94.

 p. 629

When Minutes Count

Ask students to skim the lesson to find at least one way that growth has affected the United States.

Quick Summary

This lesson examines the effects of the dramatic population growth of the United States and of efforts to conserve and repair natural resources.

1 Motivate

Set the Purpose

Big Idea Help students understand that a significant event, such as population growth, presents challenges as well as benefits for the people of the United States.

Access Prior Knowledge

Have students discuss what they have learned about the growth and changes in the population of the United States. What benefits do they see as a result of the growth? What drawbacks do they see in their own lives?

 LESSON

2

FACT AND OPINION

As you read, identify different facts and opinions about the growing population of the United States.

BIG IDEA

Growth has affected the United States and its natural resources.

VOCABULARY

rapid-transit system

About eight out of every ten people live in or near large cities. Areas that were once undeveloped, such as this Florida neighborhood, are now home to large communities.

The Challenges of Growth

In 1790 the first census of the United States counted 3,929,214 people living in the country. Today more than 281 million people live in the United States. By the year 2050, experts estimate the nation's population will be more than 400 million. With this growth have come challenges.

The Effects of Growth

Since that first census more than two hundred years ago, the population of the United States has continued to grow. Over time, quiet towns with small populations and a handful of buildings have grown into large cities. As those cities and the suburbs around them continue to grow, they often spread out over larger and larger areas. Land that was once used for farming is now used for houses, stores, office buildings, and highways.

Across the country many communities are choosing to manage urban growth by passing laws to control it. These laws not only limit where buildings may go, but what kinds of buildings may be built in an area. The laws set aside areas of land to be used only for homes, offices, or businesses, such as shopping centers. In some cases, the laws say the land cannot be used for buildings.

628

REACH ALL LEARNERS

English as a Second Language Stress to students the difference between causes and effects. Work with students to reinforce the idea that a cause is an event that makes something happen. An effect is the result of an event or a cause. Also, point out the difference between the words *effect* and *affect*. Ask students to identify causes and effects discussed in the lesson.

BACKGROUND

Taxation and Growth The United States government helps individual communities and states meet the challenges of growth. Money from federal income taxes is used to provide basic services for the growing population, such as health care, public education, and the national defense. Federal tax money is also given to states to construct highways, mass transit systems, and airports.

As the population grows and the spread of urban areas continues, the need for more services, such as fire protection, also increases.

Some people disagree with placing limits on how land can be used. They believe that it is unfair to restrict use of land that has valuable resources. Some believe that private ownership of land also can help to conserve it. This is because the land's owner usually wants to protect his or her land and use its resources wisely so it will remain valuable in the future.

Rapid population growth has presented many other challenges for the American people. As the nation's population has grown, so has the number of vehicles on its highways and city streets. In many places roads are often jammed with cars, trucks, and buses. This is especially true during rush hour, the time when people are going to work or going home. To help keep traffic

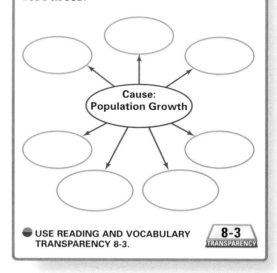

Directing traffic helps keep city streets from jamming up.

moving, some cities now use computers to control traffic lights. Others use electronic highway signs to warn drivers of problems and to suggest other routes they can take.

To help reduce the number of vehicles on their streets, many cities have worked to improve their public transportation systems. These cities have added more bus lines and built rapid-transit systems. A **rapid-transit system** is a passenger transportation system that uses elevated or underground trains or both.

A growing population means growth in the amount of services that are needed. For example, more electricity is needed for people to run their homes and businesses. More people also means that increases are needed in other services.

Chapter 17 ■ 629

Graphic Organizer Provide students with the following cause-and-effect graphic organizer. Ask them to fill in the organizer as they read about the effects of population growth on cities and on natural resources.

Cause: Population Growth

● USE READING AND VOCABULARY TRANSPARENCY 8-3.

8-3
TRANSPARENCY

2 Teach

The Effects of Growth

Read and Respond

Culture and Society Discuss with students how cities work to enforce traffic safety laws. For example, the driver of a car must wear a seatbelt and obey the legal speed limit. Explain that traffic safety applies to both drivers and pedestrians. Ask students to discuss pedestrian safety rules. Answers will vary, but should show an awareness of traffic safety.

Economics Explain to students that urban growth brings with it challenges such as changing property values, increased crime, the need for new roads and sewers, and the need for higher taxes to pay for schools, parks, and municipal buildings.

Q How is land mostly modified in growing urban areas?

A Most of the land is used for buildings and streets.

In Your State Direct students to look at a map of their state and to identify the major highways and railroad lines. Ask students to make a generalization, based on the map, about how easy it is for people to travel from place to place within the state and out of state.

Create Mental Images Direct students to jot down mental images that come to mind as they read the subsection. Then ask volunteers to share the images with the class. Challenge students to create a complete picture by identifying sounds, smells, and other sensations that appeal to the senses.

Challenges for the Environment

Read and Respond

Culture and Society Challenge students to analyze how scientific discoveries and technological innovations have changed the environment. Students may respond that the discoveries and innovations have helped people develop new uses for resources, allowed people to use resources more efficiently, and have helped in the development of new sources of energy.

3 Close

Summarize Key Content

- Population growth has led to the growth of urban areas, causing heavy traffic, the need for more public services, and changes in government.
- Population growth has also benefited the United States through the increase in new ideas from the growing number of people and the improvement of transportation and communication systems.
- People and the government have taken steps to preserve natural resources.

Water, garbage collection, education, health care, and police and fire protection must meet the demands of a growing population.

Changes in population mean changes in government. An increase in population can affect a state's representation in Congress. When a state's population changes, the number of seats it has in the House of Representatives can change also.

Population growth also has its benefits. Having more people helps increase the number of new ideas that can lead to new inventions and new and better ways of doing things. Population growth can also help businesses grow by increasing the market for many goods and services. Having more people also encourages improvements in transportation and communication systems.

REVIEW How have many cities reduced the number of vehicles on their streets?

FACT AND OPINION

Challenges for the Environment

As the population continues to grow, so does a greater need for natural resources. As a nation it is our responsibility to use our natural resources wisely. Over the years some people's actions have damaged the country's natural resources. Water, land, and even wildlife have been affected.

However, through conservation efforts, some of the damage has been repaired. For example, at one time the American bald eagle was on the endangered species

This slide is made of recycled materials. Many everyday products can be made from recycled materials.

They have worked to improve their public transportation system by adding more bus lines and building rapid-transit systems.

630 ■ Unit 8

list. There were only about 417 pairs of the eagles left in the United States.

To help save the endangered birds, laws were passed banning a chemical that was getting into the water supply. This chemical poisoned the fish eaten by the eagles. By 1998 there were more than 5,000 pairs of American bald eagles in the United States.

Another way to help preserve natural resources is to recycle. Countries with large populations, such as the United States, produce large amounts of trash. To solve this problem, many communities across the nation recycle.

Trash containing materials such as metal, glass, plastic, and paper is used to make new products. Many factories use recycled materials instead of new natural resources to make their products. Everyday items such as videocassettes, playground equipment, and clothing, can be made from recycled materials.

As in the past, Americans continue to rely on natural resources to meet their

National preserves, such as this one in Alabama, help to protect natural resources.

wants and needs. Today, however, most people understand the need to help protect the nation's natural resources for future Americans and to make sensible plans about how those natural resources are used.

REVIEW **How do many communities try to solve their trash problems?** by recycling

---

LESSON 2 REVIEW

 FACT AND OPINION In the lesson, find examples of one statement that is fact and one that is opinion.

1 BIG IDEA How has the growth of the United States population affected the land and its natural resources?

2 VOCABULARY What are the benefits of using a **rapid-transit system**?

3 HISTORY What helped save the American bald eagle?

4 GEOGRAPHY Why do some people disagree with placing limits on how land can be used?

5 CRITICAL THINKING—Hypothesize By the year 2050 over 400 million people may be living in the United States. What new problems do you think Americans will have in that time? How might the increase in population benefit Americans?

 PERFORMANCE—Interview a Person Interview a parent, a grandparent, or someone else older than you to find out what your city or town was like when he or she was your age. Have your questions ready before the interview. Write down the answers and present them to your class.

Lesson 2 Review—Answers

 FACT AND OPINION Possible answer: Fact: more than 281 million people live in the United States; Opinion: it is unfair to restrict use of land that has valuable resources.

1 BIG IDEA Population growth has increased the use of land and natural resources.

2 VOCABULARY A **rapid-transit system** decreases pollution and traffic congestion.

3 HISTORY banning a dangerous chemical

4 GEOGRAPHY Some people believe that private owners will make the best decisions about how to protect land.

5 CRITICAL THINKING—Hypothesize Possible answer: The limited resources of land and water may be a challenge. The population increase may result in new ideas about how to solve these problems.

 Performance Assessment Guidelines Students' interviews should include their own questions as well as their subject's answers. Suggest that students work in pairs to proofread each other's interviews before submitting them.

ACTIVITY BOOK

Use ACTIVITY BOOK, p. 164, to reinforce and extend student learning.

EXTEND AND ENRICH

Roundtable Discussion Arrange students into two teams. One team should research and form ideas about the benefits of urban growth. The other should research and generate ideas about the need for protecting the environment. Then have students from each team meet with those of the opposing view to discuss how urban growth can be accomplished without harming the environment.

RETEACH THE LESSON

Oral Exercise Conduct an oral exercise in which you guide students through all the causes and effects discussed in the lesson. Start by asking, "What is one effect of urban growth?" Call on one student and repeat his or her answer. Then ask, "Did this effect cause something else?" (For example, traffic is an effect of urban growth and is the cause of improved public transportation.) If there is no answer, then continue the exercise by asking, "What is another effect of urban growth?"

Lesson 3
PAGES 632–637

OBJECTIVES

- Identify how the American economy has changed in recent years.
- Explain how international trade has affected the United States.
- Describe how the free enterprise system works in the United States.

 Fact and Opinion pp. 619, 632, 634, 637, 648

Vocabulary

SEE READING AND VOCABULARY TRANSPARENCY 8-4 OR THE WORD CARDS ON PP. V93–V96.

diverse economy p. 632

high-tech p. 633

Information Age p. 633

e-commerce p. 634

interdependent p. 635

international trade p. 635

free-trade agreement p. 636

global economy p. 636

 When Minutes Count

Have students tell how each vocabulary term relates to the Big Idea.

Quick Summary

This lesson describes the American economy and free enterprise.

 **Motivate**

Set the Purpose

Big Idea Be sure that students understand the word *economy*.

Access Prior Knowledge

Have students discuss what they have learned about the diversity of the American population.

 · LESSON ·

3

The American Economy

FACT AND OPINION
As you read, identify facts and opinions about our nation's diverse economy.

BIG IDEA
The economy of the United States has changed in recent years.

VOCABULARY
diverse economy
high-tech
Information Age
e-commerce
interdependent
international trade
free-trade agreement
global economy

Just as the people of the United States have become more and more diverse over time, so has the nation's economy. A **diverse economy** is one that is based on many kinds of industries. Our nation's diverse economy has created many new kinds of jobs for American workers. It has also changed the kinds of jobs that most of them do to earn a living.

A Changing Economy

Many American workers continue to do the traditional jobs that they have always done. Some people farm the land, fish the waters, cut down trees, and mine the earth for mineral resources. Others construct highways and buildings. Many others—more than 18 million—work in factories, where together they produce more manufactured goods than any other nation in the world.

While all of those jobs remain important parts of the American economy today, more Americans now work in

While some people continue to work in traditional jobs, advances in technology have increased the number of high-tech jobs available to Americans.

632 Unit 8

WORD WORK

Historical Context Explain that most of the vocabulary terms in this lesson are relatively recent in origin. Instruct students to skim the lesson to find the vocabulary terms and their definitions. Then ask students to make a generalization about the terms. Students should suggest that most of the terms are compound words and several refer to computers and technology.

REACH ALL LEARNERS

Below-Level Learners Encourage these students to make flash cards to help them understand the vocabulary in this lesson. Students may draw pictures, use illustrations from newspapers or magazines, or write detailed notes on the backs of their flash cards. Allow students to work with partners to discuss and determine the meanings of unfamiliar ideas.

Analyze Graphs The graph shows the number of Americans who work in different kinds of industries. Today more Americans, such as this doctor (below), work in the service industry than in any other kind of industry.

◆ About how many more Americans work in the service industry than in the trade and transportation industry?

Source: Bureau of Labor Statistics

Occupations in the United States by Industry

Industry (vertical axis): Manufacturing, Mining & Construction, Transportation & Trade, Service, Government, Banking, Insurance, and Real Estate

Total Number Employed (in millions): 0 5 10 15 20 25 30 35 40 45

service jobs than in any other kinds of jobs. In fact, about one-third of all workers have service jobs, such as working in restaurants, repairing cars and appliances, or providing health care. If other groups of workers who provide services are included, such as government and transportation workers and people who work in stores, banks, and insurance companies, then about four of every five workers in the United States hold service jobs.

Many of the changes in the kinds of jobs that people do have come about because of advances in technology. In recent years, high-technology, or high-tech, industries have been of growing importance to the American economy. **High-tech** industries are those that invent, build, or use computers and other kinds of electronic equipment. These new devices have made it easier for businesspeople to communicate, travel, trade goods and services, and organize information.

The early 1970s marked the beginning of the **Information Age**. This period in history has been defined by the growing amount of information available to people. In fact, most of what is known about the human body has been learned in the past 40 years.

Today, organizing and storing information and getting the information to people when they need it is a major industry.

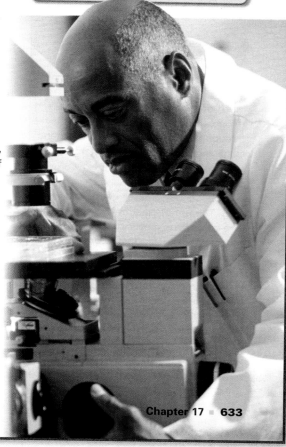

Chapter 17 ■ 633

2 Teach

A Changing Economy

Read and Respond

Read and Respond

Culture and Society Ask students to speculate on the effects of advanced medical care on the size of the population in the United States.

Q What kind of new jobs might advances in medicine create?

A Jobs for researchers to develop new technology and products, workers at companies to make the new products, and an increased number of health care professionals to provide more kinds of care.

Economics Ask whether any student or an adult in his or her family has researched products on the Internet or purchased anything online. Ask students how online shopping might affect business at local stores. Then discuss with them how a greater number of choices available on the Internet might affect consumers.

Visual Learning

Photograph Ask students to study the photographs and read the caption. Point out that many of the new high-tech jobs require education in very specific fields. Ask students how the availability of education might affect the development of new technologies and economic growth.

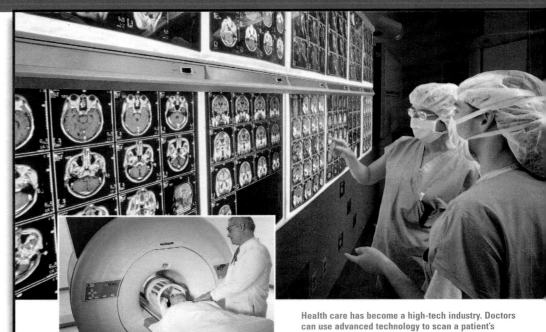

Health care has become a high-tech industry. Doctors can use advanced technology to scan a patient's brain to find out what may be wrong with the patient.

Much of this work is done electronically, through private computer networks or through public Web sites. Setting up and managing these computer systems is a growing field for workers.

New technologies are also changing the way people buy and sell goods and services. The rise of electronic commerce, or **e-commerce**, means that companies can market their products worldwide. E-commerce has allowed thousands of Americans to run businesses from their homes. American businesses and individual consumers spend billions of dollars on e-commerce purchases each year. Most of the e-commerce purchases are made up of business-to-business sales, or businesses selling things to one another. Businesses and individual consumers often choose to use credit for e-commerce. Credit allows people to buy goods without exchanging money until a later time.

New technologies are also changing the part of the American economy that relates to medicine and science. High-tech advances in the field of medicine have already changed the way doctors treat disease. For example, the use of lasers in surgery has helped millions of people.

As technology and knowledge advance, the possibility of additional scientific discoveries increases. Scientific discoveries will likely change the American economy even more in time. Technology used in the area of space exploration has already given the United States many new pictures of different parts of space.

REVIEW How have new technologies changed people's lives?

FACT AND OPINION

by changing the work people do, the way doctors treat disease, and the way people buy and sell goods and services

634 ■ Unit 8

Q How do people use credit to buy goods?

A Credit allows people to buy goods or services and pay for them later. One form of consumer credit is a credit card, which can be used to charge purchases at restaurants, businesses, or online. Another type of consumer credit is an installment plan, which allows the buyer to make small payments over a period of time. Many people use installment plans to buy furniture or large household appliances.

Note Taking Offer students some guidance on taking notes on each section of the lesson. Remind students to include the heading of each subsection as well as boldfaced vocabulary terms and their definitions. Students may also jot down key words and phrases. Finally, they should write and answer the Review question at the end of each subsection. Students' answers should include the key words they wrote in their notes.

A Global Economy

Each day, people in different states and in different regions of the United States exchange natural resources, finished products, and services. That is because no one state or region has all the natural resources that people and businesses there may need or want. And no one state or region can produce all the goods and services that people may need or want.

North Carolina, for example, grows too little cotton to supply all of its textile mills, so mill owners there buy cotton grown in other states, such as California and Texas. In turn, farmers in those states may buy products such as cotton blankets, towels, and clothing made by workers in mills and factories in North Carolina. In this way people in different states and regions are **interdependent**— they depend on one another for natural resources, finished products, and services.

The United States and other countries are also interdependent. Modern transportation and communication systems have made it easier for people in one country to trade with people in other countries. Goods from the United States are exported to places all over the world. At the same time, the United States imports many goods from other countries. This **international trade**, or trade among nations, allows people in the United States and in other countries to buy goods that their own countries do not make or grow. The United States' most important international trading partners are Canada, China, Britain, Germany, Japan, and Mexico.

This man is working on an American brand of automobile in a factory in Beijing, China. Below, cars in Japan await shipment overseas.

A Global Economy

Read and Respond

Geography Ask students to consider the natural resources in their region of the country. What resources does their region provide? Then invite students to name products that their region does not produce. Guide students to see that without regional and global trade, people in their region would not have all the things they need.

Visual Learning

Photograph Ask students how the photographs demonstrate the importance of transportation for global trade. Point out that the cars might be shipped to a port in the United States. Have students speculate how cars made in other countries reach their town to be sold locally.

Read and Respond

History Ask a volunteer to describe the triangular trade routes which flourished when the United States was a colony of Britain. Ask students to describe similarities and differences between that trading system and today's global economy.

Economics Remind students that the government is part of the nation's economic system. Government agencies purchase goods and services from contractors. The government's policies also affect competitive markets. Ask students to discuss how government policies about international trade could impact American business owners.

BACKGROUND

Not-for-Profit Most businesses are meant to earn a profit. However, there are also many organizations that are not-for-profit. A not-for-profit organization usually works for the public good. The employees of these organizations still earn a living, but the business does not make money. Some not-for-profit organizations have religious, scientific, or educational purposes.

REACH ALL LEARNERS

Advanced Learners Invite students to explore trends in international trade over the last decade. Students may consult books, newspapers, periodicals, or the Internet to discover which countries are the United States' most important trading partners and what is traded most often. Challenge students to find exact information regarding the amount and the total value of the goods traded. Ask students to present their information to the class.

A Free Enterprise Economy

Read and Respond

Culture and Society Lead a discussion in which students consider what products and services are most in demand by Americans today.

3 Close

Summarize Key Content

- In recent years, high-tech and service jobs have become more important in the American economy.
- Scientific and technological advances have made trade and communications with other countries easier.
- In a free enterprise economy, people own and run their own businesses and produce goods or services that are in demand.

READING SOCIAL STUDIES

Study Questions Have students check their answers to the Study Questions.

1. farming, logging, mining, manufacturing, service jobs, and high-tech jobs

2. Technology has increased choices for consumers, improved medical care, and helped businesses communicate more quickly and easily.

3. International trade allows the United States to exchange needed goods with other countries.

4. The free enterprise system is a system that is based on consumers' demands for goods.

● USE READING AND VOCABULARY
TRANSPARENCY 8-4.

8-4

TRANSPARENCY

To increase international trade, many countries, including the United States, have signed free-trade agreements. A **free-trade agreement** is a treaty in which countries agree not to charge tariffs, or taxes, on goods they buy from and sell to each other. Such an agreement gives industries in each of the trading nations the chance to compete better. In 1994, Mexico, Canada, and the United States put the North American Free Trade Agreement, or NAFTA, into effect. One of NAFTA's goals has been to assist the movement of goods and services across national borders. As a result, the number of goods and services available to people in all three nations has increased.

International trade adds much to the economy of the United States. The United

a treaty in which countries agree not to charge tariffs on goods they buy from and sell to each other

636 ■ Unit 8

States also interacts with other countries in other ways. Many companies in the United States have offices and factories in other countries. Many companies from other countries also have businesses in the United States. Almost 5 million people in the United States work in businesses owned by people in other countries. This means that the nations of the world are now part of a **global economy**, the world market in which companies from different countries buy and sell goods and services.

REVIEW What is a free-trade agreement?

A Free Enterprise Economy

A free enterprise system, such as that of the United States, is made up mainly of producers and consumers. In this market economy, consumers are free to choose between different goods and services. Producers, such as business firms, sell goods and services in exchange for money. The money that one person spends becomes another person's income. Government agencies can also affect the economy by buying and selling goods and services.

Price affects demand and demand affects price. For example, few people would want to buy a computer game that cost $1,000. If the price of the game is $10, many people will want to buy it. Demand for the product will be high, so the company will produce many games.

In a free enterprise economy, people own and run their own businesses. In other kinds of economies, the government owns businesses. It tells factory

Many people in the United States, such as this Virginia couple, run their businesses from their homes.

BACKGROUND

Consumer Rights All consumers have rights. These rights include the right to know the costs of loans, credit cards, and charge cards; to accurate information about what businesses are selling; to a variety of choices in products and to fair selling prices for these products; to expect that products they use have been tested for safety and are safe to use; and to complain if they are dissatisfied with products.

EXTEND AND ENRICH

Research Challenge students to research the free enterprise economy in the United States. Tell them to include the importance of credit in the buying of goods and services. Explain to students that credit allows consumers to obtain goods and services while borrowing money from a lender. This may include credit card purchases at a store, homes, cars, medical needs, and a vacation. Banks and other lenders earn interest from borrowers as payment for using their money. Lead a class discussion in which students discuss what they read.

Under the free enterprise system, Americans can open a wide variety of businesses, such as this store in Waitsfield, Vermont.

managers what goods to produce and how to produce them. In the United States, these decisions are made by business owners, or entrepreneurs. Government policies can also affect how these decisions are made.

In a competitive market such as that of the United States, entrepreneurs first need to decide what good or service to produce. Then they decide who will produce it and how. This freedom has led to the creation of many new products. For example, some of today's largest computer companies began in people's homes. The owners designed their product any way they wished. As a result, consumers have more choices.

Another benefit of a free enterprise economy is that anyone, even a young person, can start a business. Some of the many businesses young people have started include everything from dog-walking services to Web site design companies.

REVIEW In what kind of economy are people allowed to own and run their own businesses?
a free enterprise economy

LESSON 3 REVIEW

 FACT AND OPINION Price affects demand, and demand affects price. Is this statement a fact or an opinion? Explain.

❶ **BIG IDEA** How has the economy of the United States changed in recent years?

❷ **VOCABULARY** Explain how **e-commerce** is a part of the nation's **diverse economy**.

❸ **HISTORY** When did the Information Age begin?

❹ **ECONOMICS** In what ways is the United States part of a global economy?

❺ **CRITICAL THINKING—Analyze** How do the federal government's policies affect American businesses?

 PERFORMANCE—Conduct a Survey Survey your classmates and ask them what kind of job they would like to have when they are older. Find out how many of your classmates want to have traditional jobs and compare that to how many of your classmates want to have either high-tech or service jobs.

Chapter 17 ■ 637

Assess

Lesson 3 Review—Answers

 FACT AND OPINION Fact: the sentence can be proven true

❶ **BIG IDEA** The economy of the United States has become more diverse, creating new kinds of jobs for American workers.

❷ **VOCABULARY** Possible answer: **E-commerce** allows many companies to compete for business in today's **diverse economy**.

❸ in the early 1970s

❹ **ECONOMICS** The United States exports and imports products to and from places all over the world.

❺ **CRITICAL THINKING—Analyze** E-commerce has allowed businesses to expand their services without having to build more factories or offices. Businesses can buy and sell materials quickly and efficiently. E-commerce also gives businesses access to more customers.

 Performance Assessment Guidelines Students' surveys should mention how many students were polled and list their answers without revealing who said what. Suggest that students make a chart of the careers mentioned by their classmates. Students may also present the information in different ways. For example, they might show what careers girls and boys preferred.

ACTIVITY BOOK

Use ACTIVITY BOOK, p. 165, to reinforce and extend student learning.

RETEACH THE LESSON

Graphic Organizer Have students complete the following graphic organizer. Allow them to read through the lesson to check or confirm information.

What is the free enterprise system?
The free enterprise system means anybody can begin a business if he or she can supply a product or a service that consumers want to buy.

The American Economy

How has it changed?
More people in America work in service jobs than any other kind of job.

Why is it global?
A global economy is helpful as it brings in natural resources from other places.

Lesson 4

PAGES 638–643

OBJECTIVES

- Identify the roles of the federal government.
- Compare and contrast the responsibilities of state and federal governments.
- Describe the duties and responsibilities of citizens.
- Explain the importance of patriotism and good citizenship.

 Fact and Opinion pp. 619, 638, 643, 648

Vocabulary

SEE READING AND VOCABULARY TRANSPARENCY 8-5 OR THE WORD CARDS ON PP. V95–V96.

responsibility p. 640

register p. 641

informed citizen p. 641

jury p. 641

volunteer p. 642

patriotism p. 643

 When Minutes Count

Have pairs of students work together to find the answers to the subsection review questions.

Quick Summary

This lesson discusses the roles, structure, and powers of the government. It also focuses on the responsibilities and duties of American citizens.

1 Motivate

Set the Purpose

Big Idea Make sure students understand the word *citizens* as it is used in the Big Idea statement.

Access Prior Knowledge

Have students discuss the ways in which government, rules, and laws were necessary for the nation's growth.

 FACT AND OPINION

As you read, identify facts and opinions about government and citizens in the United States.

BIG IDEA

It is important to know the role of government and the main rights and responsibilities of American citizens.

VOCABULARY

responsibility
register
informed citizen
jury
volunteer
patriotism

4 Government and the People

The Constitution of the United States of America, which became law in 1788, set up the government for the nation. More than 200 years later, government leaders still look to the Constitution to help guide their actions. Without the rules and laws of our system of government, the American people would not have the freedoms they enjoy today.

The Federal System

The federal system created by the Constitution divides political power between the national, or federal, government and the state governments. The federal government is the country's largest government system.

From the national capital in Washington, D.C., the federal government affects the lives of all Americans. It runs programs to help the poor, aged, or disabled. It tests foods and drugs for safety, conducts research, and controls pollution. It deals

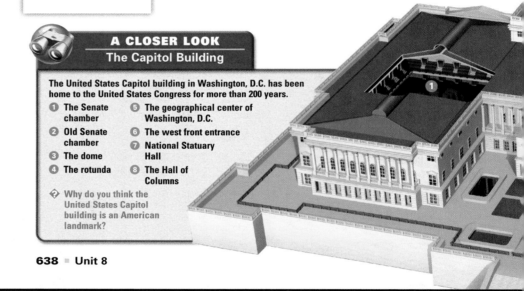

A CLOSER LOOK
The Capitol Building

The United States Capitol building in Washington, D.C. has been home to the United States Congress for more than 200 years.

1. The Senate chamber
2. Old Senate chamber
3. The dome
4. The rotunda
5. The geographical center of Washington, D.C.
6. The west front entrance
7. National Statuary Hall
8. The Hall of Columns

❖ Why do you think the United States Capitol building is an American landmark?

638 ■ Unit 8

 **REACH ALL LEARNERS**

English as a Second Language Allow students to work in pairs and to spend extra time on the details of the federal system. Also, consider displaying photographs of the landmarks mentioned on page 639.

WORD WORK

Suffixes Point out that some of the vocabulary terms in this lesson have suffixes. Work with students to identify the suffixes and to create a list with the suffixes and their definitions. Challenge students to think of other words that have the suffixes –*ity* and –*ism*.

with the governments of other nations, and it sets trade rules with them. The federal government is also in charge of space exploration, air travel safety, national parks and historic sites, and the federal highway system. It also oversees a military force to defend the nation.

Many famous landmarks across the country are associated with the federal government. These include the Statue of Liberty, the White House, and Mount Rushmore. These patriotic symbols remind Americans of the things that unite them as people.

Many Americans of different backgrounds are also united by the political party to which they belong. The two main political parties are the Republican and Democratic parties. In Congress, the party with the most members in each house is known as the majority party. The party with fewer members is called the minority party.

The most powerful officer of the House of Representatives is the Speaker of the House. No member of the House may speak until called upon by the Speaker. The Speaker is always a member of the majority party and has usually served in Congress for many years.

The most powerful officers of the Senate are the majority leader and the minority leader. These people help direct the actions of their party in the Senate.

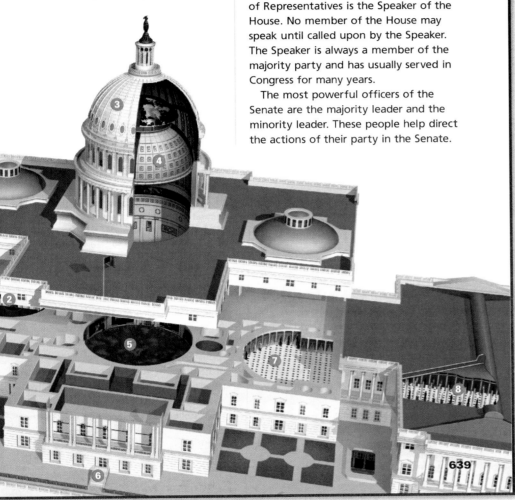

639

2 Teach

The Federal System

Read and Respond

Civics and Government Remind students that each state sends two senators to the Senate and a certain number of representatives to the House of Representatives. The number of representatives per state is based on that state's population. Ask students how many representatives their state sends to Washington, D.C., and to identify the political party of each representative. Responses will vary.

Uncle Sam

Ask students to think of places where they have seen depictions of the character of Uncle Sam. Point out that the symbol was used in serious campaigns during World War I and World War II to get volunteers for the armed forces.

Read and Respond

Government Inform students that there are about 3 million civilians employed by the federal government, more than 4 million by state governments, and more than 11 million by local governments. Illustrate the information by using the following circle graph.

Government Employees

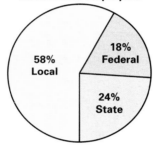

58% Local

18% Federal

24% State

Civic Affairs

Read and Respond

Civics and Government Explain to students that all local and state governments form, debate, and carry out public policy. Although local governments are created by state governments, they still have their own powers. Some small town governments work together with other local governments to provide basic services. Ask students to discuss why state and local governments are important.

Civics and Government Inform students that large groups of lobbyists are called interest groups. Interest groups may work to protect the environment, provide for the homeless, or improve healthcare.

Uncle Sam

American history is filled with heroes, but only a few of them have been preserved as cartoons. During the War of 1812, Samuel Wilson, owner of a New York meat-packing business, helped supply the United States Army with beef. Wilson's supply wagons were marked with the initials *U.S.* It was reported that U.S. stood for "Uncle Sam" Wilson. In fact, the letters stood for *United States*. In 1868 Thomas Nast created the first Uncle Sam cartoon. In 1961 Congress passed a resolution honoring Samuel Wilson.

These offices also exist at the state level. Like the federal government, each state government has three branches.

Each state has its own constitution and laws to help determine public policy. The powers of the state and local governments are distributed, shared, and limited by each state's constitution. However, state laws and activities must not conflict with the United States Constitution. In turn, the activities of local governments must not conflict with state and national laws. For example, the mayor of a city does not have as much authority as the governor of a state.

640 ▪ Unit 8

Federal, state, and local governments have the right to tax and to spend and borrow money. State and local governments place taxes on property, including land. Officials use the tax money to pay for services such as transportation and recycling.

All the government offices at the local, state, and federal levels are part of our constitutional democracy. A democracy depends on the justice, equality, and honesty of its citizens and officials. Federal, state, and local officials work to govern the nation. Some, such as state representatives to Congress, are elected by voters. Others, such as federal judges, are chosen by a governing body. For example, Hillary Rodham Clinton was elected to the United States Senate by the voters of New York. Supreme Court Justice Sandra Day O'Connor was nominated by the President of the United States.

REVIEW What are some powers that the federal and state governments share?

FACT AND OPINION
the rights to tax and to spend and borrow money

Civic Affairs

The Constitution says that citizens who meet the age requirements have the right to vote and the right to hold public office. All residents in the United States—including noncitizens—have freedom of speech, freedom of the press, freedom of religion, freedom to own property, and freedom to gather in groups. They also have the right to lobby, or work to convince government leaders to change the law. Some citizens form interest groups to lobby public officials.

Elected Officials The President of the United States is George W. Bush, and the Vice President is Richard "Dick" Cheney. Florida's senators are Bill Nelson, a Democrat, and Mel Martinez, a Republican. Florida's members of Congress are Michael Bilirakis, Allen Boyd, Corrine Brown, Ginny Brown-Waite, Ander Crenshaw, Jim Davis, Lincoln Diaz-Balart, Mario Diaz-Balart, Tom Feeney, Mark Foley, Katherine Harris, Alcee Hastings, Ric Keller, Connie Mack IV, John Mica, Kendrick Meek, Jeff Miller, Adam Putnam, Ileana Ros-Lehtinen, E. Clay Shaw, Jr., Cliff Stearns, Dave Weldon, Robert Wexler, C.W. Bill Young, and Debbie Wasserman Schultz.

Kinesthetic Learners Allow students to work in small groups to act out scenes that show the responsibilities of citizens. For example, students might act out the process of sitting on a jury or voting on election day. As the groups perform these scenes, ask students in the audience to identify the activities.

With these rights come responsibilities. A **responsibility** is a duty—something that a person is expected to do. With the right to vote, for example, comes the responsibility of voting. Most citizens who want to take part in an election must **register** to vote, or show that he or she lives where the voting takes place. Voting is a responsibility because every vote matters in an election. In the 2000 Presidential election a few hundred votes made the difference in George W. Bush's win over Al Gore.

With freedom of speech, each person becomes individually responsible for being an informed and active citizen. An **informed citizen** is one who knows what is happening in the community, the state, the nation, and the world. An informed citizen is more likely to understand why things happen and to see other people's points of view.

Citizens who feel strongly about an issue can always contact their representatives by writing letters or making phone calls. Today e-mail makes staying in touch with government leaders simpler than ever.

The responsibilities of citizens are not written in the Constitution, but they follow naturally from what is written there. For example, the Constitution says that every person charged with a crime will be judged by a jury. A **jury** is a group of citizens who decide a case in court. Citizens must be willing to be members of a jury if called upon to serve. The Constitution gives Congress the authority to raise money to run the nation. Citizens must be willing to pay taxes if the nation is to run smoothly.

Besides voting, obeying the laws, defending the nation, serving on a jury, and paying taxes, some citizens take a more active part in the government. One way citizens take action is by taking part in political campaigns.

Volunteers (right) help to register voters before the 2000 Presidential election. Other volunteers (below) work in the campaign office of California Representative Loretta Sanchez.

Chapter 17 ■ 641

Read and Respond

Economics Direct students' attention to the discussion about state and local taxes on page 640. Ask students to discuss why state and local taxes are important.

Culture and Society Remind students that basic rights are important in American society. Stress that the belief in human rights, or fundamental rights, lies at the heart of the United States citizenship and enables people to worship as they wish, speak freely, and read and write what they choose.

Civics and Government Have students explain why the right to lobby is an important right of United States citizens. Citizens who are not members of the government can still influence the nation's laws and policies.

Inform students that in the 2000 Presidential election between Governor George W. Bush and Vice President Al Gore there was a 327-vote difference out of 6 million votes cast in Florida. Emphasize to students that was an incredibly close margin! That would be about equivalent to a 1-vote margin in an election with 18,000 votes cast.

Q Why is it important that all citizens vote in elections?

A Every vote cast makes a difference in who is elected. And the person elected makes a difference in each citizen's life.

Visual Learning

Photograph Inform students that many people who work on campaigns and help register voters are volunteers. By performing these services, the volunteers are participating in the government.

Read and Respond

Civics and Government Have students explain how people participate in political parties. They can be chosen to serve as delegates to their party's national convention. They can also vote on who their party will nominate as its Presidential candidate.

Working Together

Read and Respond

Culture and Society Lead students in a discussion of what they think it means to be an American. Have students give examples of how they might show their patriotism.

• HERITAGE •

Pledge of Allegiance

Inform students that the wording of the Pledge of Allegiance has been changed twice over the years. For nearly forty years, students pledged only to "my flag." In 1923, Congress made the change to "the flag of the United States of America." Thirty years later, the words "under God" were added. Have students recite and explain the meaning of the Pledge of Allegiance.

---

3 Close

Summarize Key Content

- The federal government conducts thousands of activities that affect the lives of Americans.
- State governments are similar to the federal government but they have different powers.
- Citizens have many rights but have a responsibility to vote, become informed, and serve on juries.
- By working together to support the nation and by being good citizens, Americans uphold the work of the original founders of the nation.

Some citizens go from door to door, handing out information on their candidates or on issues. Other citizens telephone voters to remind them to go to the polls on election day. Most campaign workers are **volunteers**, or people who work without pay.

The most common way citizens take part in politics is by joining a political party. Most registered voters are members of either the Republican or Democratic party. However, a growing number of voters are choosing to register as independents. These voters are not connected to any organized party.

Members of organized parties can be chosen to serve as delegates to their party's national convention. These conventions, which take place every four years, are where presidential candidates are selected. Every state sends a certain number of delegates to each convention. The greater the state's population, the more delegates it can send. These delegates then vote on who their party will nominate as its Presidential candidate.

Citizens can also be candidates themselves. One person who decided to take an active part in government is Patty Murray. As a parent volunteer, she lobbied for more money for education. In 1992 she ran for office and won, becoming the first woman to represent the state of Washington in the United States Senate.

REVIEW How are political campaigns important to American citizens? it gives citizens the opportunity to participate in politics by writing letters, sending e-mail, or making phone calls

Working Together

The writers of the United States Constitution were not sure their government would last. No other nation had ever had a government quite like the one described by the Constitution. No other people had ever had all of the rights that

Elected officials and local citizens hold a city council meeting in Gloucester, Massachusetts.

642 ▪ Unit 8

EXTEND AND ENRICH

Prepare a Citizenship Pamphlet Have students work in small groups to prepare a pamphlet that explains the responsibilities and duties of a good citizen. Students may use the information in this chapter as well as other sources. Encourage students to use clip art and graphics that will help make their points.

BACKGROUND

Flag Etiquette The United States Flag Code describes how the nation's flag should be properly displayed and honored. For example, no flags of other nations or states should fly higher than the American flag. The flag should also be displayed only between sunrise and sunset, and if it is flown at night it must be illuminated. To show respect for the flag, citizens stand tall and place their right hands over their hearts. Members of the military give a formal salute.

American citizens enjoyed. But would the people be able to keep their government going and protect their freedoms over time? The country would need good citizens—citizens who would work for the common good.

Past republics, like that of ancient Rome, broke up partly because the people grew greedy and selfish. To keep the nation strong, Americans would have to keep the spirit that had given the nation its independence and its Constitution. They would need to show **patriotism**, or love of country. Patriotism is more than simply waving the American flag at special times. The writers of the Constitution knew that Americans would have to be good citizens all the time.

REVIEW What are good citizens?

citizens who work for the common good of the country

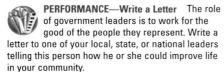

**LESSON 4
REVIEW**

Focus Skill **FACT AND OPINION** The most powerful officer of the House of Representatives is the Speaker of the House. Is this statement a fact or an opinion? Explain.

❶ **BIG IDEA** What are the roles of government and citizens in the United States?

❷ **VOCABULARY** Use the word **register** in a sentence about voting.

❸ **CIVICS AND GOVERNMENT** What are some of the responsibilities that come with the rights of United States residents?

❹ **CRITICAL THINKING—Analyze** In what ways can citizens organize and shape government at local and state levels?

PERFORMANCE—Write a Letter The role of government leaders is to work for the good of the people they represent. Write a letter to one of your local, state, or national leaders telling this person how he or she could improve life in your community.

Chapter 17 ■ 643

Assess

Lesson 4 Review—Answers

Focus Skill **FACT AND OPINION** Fact: the statement can be proven true.

❶ **BIG IDEA** The government's role is to protect and govern citizens; citizens pay taxes and obey the laws of the land.

❷ **VOCABULARY** Once you **register**, you may vote in elections.

❸ **CIVICS AND GOVERNMENT** by being an informed citizen, voting, obeying laws, taking part in political campaigns

❹ **CRITICAL THINKING—Analyze** The Pledge of Allegiance is a statement of loyalty to the United States.

Performance Assessment Guidelines Students' letters should mention at least one specific concern that students have.

RETEACH THE LESSON

Graphic Organizer Ask students to complete the following Venn diagram to reinforce the lesson.

State
• deals with local governments
• funds state parks, forests, historic sites, and museums
• builds and maintains roads, schools, and public buildings
• maintains state military reserves

Both
• provide aid to poor, aged, disabled
• set standards for pollution control

Federal
• maintains Federal branches of military
• maintains national parks, forests, historic sites, and museums
• deals with foreign governments
• conducts research
• tests food and drugs
• space travel

OBJECTIVES

- Identify important political symbols that represent American beliefs and principles.
- Explain how political symbols contribute to our national identity.

1 Motivate

Why It Matters

Explain to students that political symbols have been used for centuries to identify governments, armies, and rulers. Today, political symbols are often used to show allegiance or to convey information quickly.

2 Teach

What You Need to Know

Have students study the description of political symbols. Ask students to identify places where they see political symbols. If students have difficulty, ask them to visualize a dollar bill and name some of the symbols printed there.

INTEGRATE ART

Make a Symbol

Organize students into small groups. Encourage students to generate ideas for symbols of their classroom or school. Have students design a school symbol, using pens and markers. Display school symbols in the classroom.

· SKILLS · Identify Political Symbols

CITIZENSHIP

➡ WHY IT MATTERS

People often recognize sports teams, clubs, and other organizations by their symbols. The same is true for political parties, the President, Congress, the Supreme Court, and even voters. Being able to identify political symbols and what they stand for can help you better understand news reports, political cartoons, and other sources of information.

➡ WHAT YOU NEED TO KNOW

Two of the country's most famous political symbols are animals. The donkey represents the Democratic party. The elephant represents the Republican party. The donkey was probably first used to represent President Andrew Jackson, a Democrat, in the 1830s. Later the donkey became a symbol for the entire party. Cartoonist Thomas Nast introduced the elephant as a symbol of the Republican party in 1874. Both of these symbols are still used today.

One of the symbols for the national government is Uncle Sam. The bald eagle and the Statue of Liberty are other symbols for our government. Buildings are often used as political symbols. The White House is a symbol for the President, and the United States Capitol is a symbol for Congress.

644 ■ Unit 8

BACKGROUND

Thomas Nast Born in Germany, Nast came to the United States in 1846 when he was six years old. He studied art at the National Academy of Design and began his career at 15 as a draftsman for an illustrated newspaper. By age 18, Nast was working at *Harper's Weekly*, one of the most influential publications of the Gilded Age. Soon his pro-Union, pro-abolitionist cartoons on Civil War activities were being published regularly in *Harper's Weekly*. Nast popularized the Democratic party's donkey and created the elephant for the Republican party. His political cartoons criticizing New York City's corrupt "Boss" Tweed during the 1870s eventually led to Tweed's arrest.

➡ PRACTICE THE SKILL

When you see a political symbol, answer the following questions to help you understand its meaning.

❶ Do you recognize the symbol? Does it stand for the whole national government or only part of the national government? Does it stand for a person or group that is involved in government, such as a political party or organization?

❷ Where did you see the symbol? If it appeared in a magazine, did the writer give you any clues about its meaning?

❸ Does it include any captions or other words that help explain what the symbol means? A symbol labeled

"To Protect and Serve," for example, might tell you that it stands for the police.

❹ Why do you think the symbol is a good representation of the person or group it stands for?

❺ When do you think you are most likely to see the symbol?

➡ APPLY WHAT YOU LEARNED

Look through current news-magazines, in the editorial pages of newspapers, or on the Internet. Cut or print out an example of a political symbol and paste it on a sheet of paper. Below the symbol, write a brief description of what it stands for.

The elephant (left) is the symbol of the Republican party. The donkey (below) is the symbol of the Democratic party.

Chapter 17 ▪ **645**

Practice the Skill—Answers

Have the students work through the questions listed in Practice the Skill. Choose a symbol from a current publication and use it to model the questions.

 **Close**

Apply What You Learned

Have students search current publications for examples of political symbols. Students may also wish to search the Internet for the Web sites of political parties and action groups for more political symbols. When students have written descriptions for their examples, display their work in the classroom.

ACTIVITY BOOK

Use ACTIVITY BOOK, p. 167, to give students additional practice using this skill.

TRANSPARENCY

Use SKILL TRANSPARENCY 8-2.

EXTEND AND ENRICH

Research State Symbols Tell students that each state has its own political symbols. Have students do research to identify the state seal, flag, bird, and tree and other symbols of their own state. Encourage students to research the symbols of a nearby state.

RETEACH THE SKILL

Evaluate Symbols Organize students into groups. Have each group choose two symbols of the United States and discuss them. Have groups consider when and where they are most likely to see the symbols. Ask them to use critical thinking skills to evaluate why their choices are fitting symbols of the United States.

Examine Primary Sources

OBJECTIVES

- Identify political buttons as an effective campaigning technique.
- Compare and contrast the effectiveness of examples of political memorabilia from our nation's past.

1 Motivate

Set the Purpose

Political buttons are one way in which candidates rally support from voters. By studying these political buttons, students will determine symbols and phrases candidates used to gain support.

Access Prior Knowledge

Ask students if they have ever owned a button on which appeared a funny or wise saying. Point out that politicians also use buttons to spread their political messages.

2 Teach

Read and Respond

Tell students that some of the earliest political buttons to appear in this country appeared with the first United States President—George Washington. These early buttons were actually brass clothing buttons that had been engraved. How do political buttons today differ from buttons used on clothing? Students may say that instead of being permanently sewn on, political buttons are temporarily pinned to clothes.

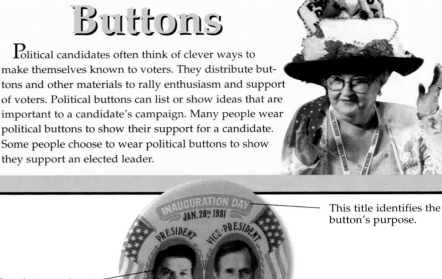

EXAMINE PRIMARY SOURCES

Political Buttons

Political candidates often think of clever ways to make themselves known to voters. They distribute buttons and other materials to rally enthusiasm and support of voters. Political buttons can list or show ideas that are important to a candidate's campaign. Many people wear political buttons to show their support for a candidate. Some people choose to wear political buttons to show they support an elected leader.

This title identifies the button's purpose.

The photographs on this button show who was elected.

The eagle is a patriotic symbol of the United States.

The elephant is a political symbol of the Republican party.

Red, white, and blue are the colors of the American Flag.

646 ▪ Unit 8

BACKGROUND

More About the Time Each President of the United States has sworn the same oath upon entering office. That oath, which is set forth in Article II, Section 1 of the Constitution of the United States, reads as follows:

"I do solemnly swear (or affirm) that I will faithfully execute the office of President of the United States, and will, to the best of my ability, preserve, protect, and defend the Constitution of the United States."

INTEGRATE LANGUAGE ARTS

Expressive Writing Ask small groups of students to use newspapers, magazines, and other reference materials to research the current President. Their assignment is to determine what kind of political button would reflect one of this President's beliefs or policies. Once the group has chosen a topic, have members work together to think of a clever way it could be phrased on a political button. Have group representatives share each group's 'button text' with the class.

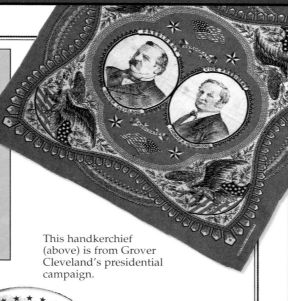

This handkerchief (above) is from Grover Cleveland's presidential campaign.

Analyze the Primary Source

1. How do you think a voter wearing a political button can help a candidate become better known? Why would a candidate or elected official want to picture their face on a political button?

2. Can you think of other campaign items a candidate might use?

3. List the patriotic symbols you see on the political buttons and campaign items.

OUR CHOICE

Political buttons show a variety of information. The postcard (left) is from William Taft's presidential campaign.

ACTIVITY

Write to Explain Imagine you are running for an elected office. Design a political button for your supporters to wear. Write a paragraph that explains the information on your button.

RESEARCH

Visit The Learning Site at **www.harcourtschool.com** to research other primary sources.

Analyze the Primary Source
Answers

1. A political button worn by a supporter indicates that someone strongly favors a particular candidate; political buttons worn by supporters can make a face more familiar to other voters.

2. In addition to the handkerchief and postcard shown here, students may list items such as calendars, business cards, and embossed pencils.

3. Flags, ribbons, eagles, an elephant, a donkey, World War II poster, and the colors red, white, and blue.

3 Close

Activity

Write to Explain Have students actually create the political button they have designed by cutting out a circle of paper on which the design is replicated. Each student should then pin the finished 'button' to his or her clothes with a safety pin.

Research

Students will find a variety of political artifacts at The Learning Site at **www.harcourtschool.com.**

Ask each student to choose one of the political artifacts at the site and then identify what the political artifact symbolizes.

GO ONLINE INTERNET RESOURCES

THE LEARNING SITE
Go to **www.harcourtschool.com** for a DIRECTORY OF PRIMARY SOURCES.

EXTEND AND ENRICH

Write a Report Ask each student to choose one of the public figures pictured on these political buttons. Tell students to research and write reports on the persons that they have chosen. Explain that their reports should answer these questions: *When might the button have been used? Did the person win or lose the election? In what year(s) did the person run for office?* Ask volunteers to read aloud their completed reports to the class.

RETEACH

Compare and Contrast Have each student choose two of the political buttons pictured. Tell students to write paragraphs comparing and contrasting the figures, symbols, and colors used by each button. Ask them to determine which political button made a more favorable impression on them as future voters. Have volunteers read aloud their paragraphs to the class.

FACT AND OPINION

Students may use the graphic organizer that appears on page 168 of the Activity Book. Answers appear in the Activity Book, Teacher's Edition.

Think & Write

Write a List of Questions Students' lists of questions will vary based on the students' interests and concerns. They may include immigration, new technologies, the environment, the economy, or the President's views on responsible citizenship.

Write a Poem Students' poems will vary, depending upon their opinions regarding the qualities of the United States that make it a great nation. Topics may range from the opportunities offered to its citizens to the assistance it provides to other nations.

ACTIVITY BOOK

A copy of the graphic organizer appears in the ACTIVITY BOOK on page 168.

TRANSPARENCY

The graphic organizer appears on READING AND VOCABULARY TRANSPARENCY 8-6.

· CHAPTER ·

17 Review and Test Preparation

 Fact and Opinion

Copy the following graphic organizer onto a separate sheet of paper. Use the information you have learned to identify facts and opinions about the United States.

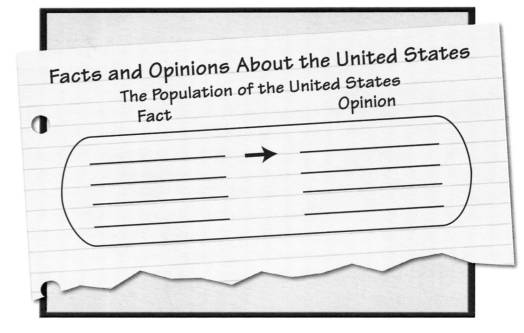

Facts and Opinions About the United States
The Population of the United States
Fact   Opinion

THINK & WRITE

Write a List of Questions Imagine that the President of the United States has scheduled a trip to visit your school and to spend time with your class. Write a list of questions you would like to ask the President.

Write a Poem Many patriotic poems have been written about the United States over the course of its history. Think of the things that make the United States a great nation, and then write a poem that honors the country.

648 ■ Chapter 17

TEST PREPARATION

Review these tips with students:

- Read the directions before reading the questions.

- Read each question twice, focusing the second time on all the possible answers.

- Take the time to think about all the possible answers before deciding on an answer.

- Move past questions that give you trouble, and answer the ones you know. Then return to the difficult items.

UNIT PROJECT

Progress Check Students may wish to make a chart listing countries people have come from, reason they have come to the United States, and contributions groups have made to the United States.

CHAPTER 17 ▪ 649

USE VOCABULARY

For each pair of terms, write a sentence that explains how the terms are related.

1 Internet (p. 624), **teleconference** (p. 625)

2 interdependent (p. 635), **global economy** (p. 636)

3 register (p. 641), **informed citizen** (p. 641)

RECALL FACTS

Answer these questions.

4 In what ways can people contact their representatives?

5 Why was the Pledge of Allegiance written?

Write the letter of the best choice.

6 Today most new immigrants to the United States come from countries in—
A Europe and South America.
B Asia and Europe.
C Asia and Latin America.
D Africa and South America.

7 Under a free enterprise system—
F people can own and run their own businesses.
G the government owns most businesses.
H most people work in agriculture.
J the government tells businesses what to charge for goods and services.

8 The two main political parties in the United States today are the—
A Republican and Federalist parties.
B Federalist and Democratic parties.
C Republican and Democratic parties.
D Democratic and Whig parties.

9 The most common way American citizens take part in politics is by—
F running for office.
G volunteering as campaign workers.
H joining a political party.
J serving on a jury.

THINK CRITICALLY

10 How does immigration continue to shape the United States today?

11 What do you think might happen if cities did not try to manage urban growth?

12 How have American jobs changed over the last 100 years?

13 Why do you think the United States has remained a strong nation for so long?

APPLY SKILLS

Use a Cartogram
Review the map and the cartogram in the skill on pages 626–627. Then answer the following questions.

14 Why is New Jersey shown larger than Maine on the cartogram?

15 Which West Coast state has the smallest population?

Identify Political Symbols

16 Write down the names of the last five United States Presidents. Then use the Almanac in the back of your textbook to find out their political parties. Decide which party symbol would be used to represent each President.

Chapter 17 ▪ **649**

Think Critically

10 People come from many different countries, bringing with them customs and traditions that diversify the culture of the United States.

11 They may risk becoming overcrowded.

12 More Americans work in foreign-owned companies, and many people rely upon new technologies and other innovations, such as the microchip and the Internet, to do their work.

13 The framers of the Constitution created a document that provided a strong enough balance of structure and flexibility to suit the nation's changing needs.

Apply Skills

Use a Cartogram

14 because it has more people

15 Oregon

Identify Political Symbols

16 Students should correctly identify the last five Presidents and their parties, using appropriate symbols to represent each one's party.

ACTIVITY BOOK

Use the CHAPTER 17 TEST PREPARATION on page 169 of the Activity Book.

ASSESSMENT

Use the CHAPTER 17 TEST on pages 135–138 of the Assessment Program.

Use Vocabulary

1 Innovations such as the **Internet** and **teleconferencing** allow people to communicate without having to travel.

2 **Interdependence** among nations has led to the development of a larger **global economy**.

3 An **informed citizen** who is **registered** to vote is able to take part in the political process.

Recall Facts

4 letter, phone call, and e-mail (p. 641)

5 for students to recite on Columbus Day (p. 643)

6 C (p. 621)

7 F (p. 636)

8 C (p. 642)

9 H (p. 642)

Chapter 18 Planning Guide Partners in the Hemisphere

Introducing the Chapter, pp. 650–651

LESSON	PACING	OBJECTIVES	VOCABULARY
Introduce the Chapter pp. 650–651	1 Day	■ Interpret information in visuals. ■ Use critical thinking skills to organize and analyze information.	**Word Work:** Preview Vocabulary, p. 651
1 Mexico pp. 652–656	1 Day	■ Describe the geography and cultural heritage of Mexico. ■ Identify changes over time in Mexico's government, from its days as a republic to its current status as a democratic nation. ■ Identify leaders in Mexico's government, such as Vicente Fox. ■ Analyze the relationship between the growth of Mexico's cities and the growth of the middle class.	**middle class** **interest rate** **Word Work:** Compound Terms, p. 652
2 Central America and the Caribbean pp. 657–661	1 Day	■ Describe the geography and people of Central America and the Caribbean. ■ Identify the challenges of living in a tropical climate. ■ Describe the governments of Central America and the Caribbean.	**commonwealth** **embargo** **free election** **Word Work:** Word Origins, p. 657
CHART AND GRAPH SKILLS **Read Population Pyramids** pp. 662–663	1 Day	■ Interpret information in a population pyramid. ■ Gather and organize information using a population pyramid.	**population pyramid** **life expectancy** **median age**

650A ■ **CHAPTER 18 ORGANIZER**

READING	INTEGRATE LEARNING	REACH ALL LEARNERS	RESOURCES

 Compare and Contrast, p. 651

Reading Social Studies:
  Anticipation Guide, p. 653

 Compare and Contrast, p. 653

Reading Social Studies:
  Graphic Organizer, p. 654

Reading Social Studies:
  Anticipation Guide Responses, p. 656

Language Arts
Informative Writing, p. 655

Mathematics
Figuring Exchange Rates, p. 655

Auditory Learners, p. 654

Extend and Enrich, p. 656

Reteach the Lesson, p. 656

Activity Book, p. 170

🌐 **Reading and Vocabulary Transparency,** 8-7

Reading Social Studies:
  Graphic Organizer, p. 658

Reading Social Studies:
  Reread to Clarify, p. 660

Reading Social Studies:
  Graphic Organizer Responses, p. 661

Science
Hurricanes, p. 659

Extend and Enrich, p. 661

Reteach the Lesson, p. 661

Activity Book, p. 171

🌐 **Reading and Vocabulary Transparency,** 8-8

💻 Internet Resources

Language Arts
Write a Scientific Summary, p. 662

Extend and Enrich, p. 663

Reteach the Skill, p. 663

Activity Book, pp. 172–173

🌐 **Skill Transparency,** 8-3

Chapter 18 Planning Guide Partners in the Hemisphere

LESSON	PACING	OBJECTIVES	VOCABULARY
3 South America pp. 664–668	**1 Day**	■ Describe the geography and people of South America. ■ Describe how South American countries gained their independence and some of the problems that came with it. ■ Identify new challenges facing South America.	**standard of living** **liberate** **deforestation**
4 Canada pp. 669–673	**1 Day**	■ Identify the geography of Canada. ■ Describe Canada's history, from first settlement to self-government. ■ Explain why some citizens want to secede from Canada. ■ Identify Canada's role in the world economy.	**province** **separatist** **Word Work**: Preview Vocabulary, p. 669
MAP AND GLOBE SKILLS **Use a Time Zone Map** pp. 674–675	**1 Day**	■ Analyze and interpret a time zone map. ■ Compare time in different parts of the United States.	**time zone**
Chapter Review and Test Preparation pp. 676–677	**1 Day**		

READING	INTEGRATE LEARNING	REACH ALL LEARNERS	RESOURCES
Reading Social Studies: **Study Questions,** p. 665 Reading Social Studies: **Study Question Responses,** p. 668	Science **Identify Unique Species,** p. 665	**Kinesthetic Learners,** p. 666 **Below-Level Learners,** p. 667 **Extend and Enrich,** p. 668 **Reteach the Lesson,** p. 668	**Activity Book,** p. 174 **Reading and Vocabulary Transparency, 8-9** Internet Resources
Reading Social Studies: **Summarize,** p. 670 Reading Social Studies: **Summarize Responses,** p. 673	Music **Canadian Music,** p. 672	**Below-Level Learners,** p. 669 **Auditory Learners,** p. 671 **Extend and Enrich,** p. 673 **Reteach the Lesson,** p. 673	**Activity Book,** p. 175 **Reading and Vocabulary Transparency, 8-10**
		Extend and Enrich, p. 675 **Reteach the Skill,** p. 675	**Activity Book,** pp. 176–177 **Skill Transparency, 8-4** **GeoSkills CD-ROM**
		Test Preparation, p. 676	**Activity Book,** pp. 178–179 **Reading and Vocabulary Transparency, 8-11** **Assessment Program, Chapter 18 Test,** pp. 139–142

Activity Book

Name _____ Date _____

Mexico

Directions Write the letter next to each event listed below in the appropriate place on the time line.

a. In the early 1900s, Mexican leaders wrote a new constitution that included land for farmers and a six-year limit on presidents' terms.

b. Soon after the Mexico economy starts to recover, Mexico elects its first president from the Partido Acción Nacional (PAN), Vicente Fox.

c. United States President George W. Bush meets with Mexican President Vicente Fox to show the importance of ties between the two nations.

d. In the late 1900s Mexico, Canada, and the United States sign the North American Free Trade Agreement (NAFTA).

e. In the 1820s part of Spain's army helps Mexico win its independence.

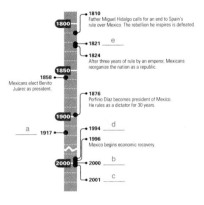

1800
1810 Father Miguel Hidalgo calls for an end to Spain's rule over Mexico. The rebellion he inspires is defeated.

1821 e

1824 After three years of rule by an emperor, Mexicans reorganize the nation as a republic.

1850
1858 Mexicans elect Benito Juárez as president.

1876 Porfirio Díaz becomes president of Mexico. He rules as a dictator for 30 years.

1900
a **1917**

1994 d

1996 Mexico begins economic recovery.

2000
2000 b

2001 c

170 ■ Activity Book   Use after reading Chapter 18, Lesson 1, pages 652–656.

Name _____ Date _____

Central America and the Caribbean

Directions Answer the questions below.

❶ What seven countries make up Central America? Belize, Guatemala, Honduras, El Salvador, Nicaragua, Costa Rica, Panama

❷ What crops are grown in the countries of Central America? bananas, beans, coffee, corn, cotton, and sugarcane

❸ Which natural events challenge the residents of islands in the Caribbean? volcanic eruptions, earthquakes, tropical storms, hurricanes, droughts, heavy rains, mudslides, and flooding

❹ What kind of government does Cuba have? a communist dictatorship

❺ Which Caribbean islands are part of the United States? Puerto Rico, the Virgin Islands

❻ How is the government of Costa Rica similar to the government of the United States? It is a democracy with three branches of government and a president elected to a four-year term

Use after reading Chapter 18, Lesson 2, pages 657–661.   Activity Book ■ 171

Name _____ Date _____

CHART AND GRAPH SKILLS
How to Read Population Pyramids

Directions Study the population pyramid of Costa Rica below. Then write a paragraph that explains to another student what the pyramid reveals about the population of Costa Rica. As you write, try to answer these questions:

❶ What is a population pyramid?

❷ Which part of the pyramid is the largest? What does this mean?

❸ Which part of the pyramid is the smallest? What does this mean?

❹ Does the pyramid show any differences between females and males?

❺ About how many Costa Ricans are in your age group?

Costa Rica
MALE   FEMALE
Source: U.S. Census Bureau, International Data Base.

Students' paragraphs should include the following:

1) A population pyramid shows the division of a country's population by age and sex.   2) The largest part is males aged 10–14. There are more people in this group than in any other group in Costa Rica.   3) The smallest part is males aged 80 and above. This is the smallest population group in Costa Rica.

4) There are more young men than young women in Costa Rica, about the same number of middle-aged men and women, and slightly more older women than men.   5) For 10-year olds: more than 400,000 people in age group; for 9-year olds: about 400,000 people in age group

(continued)

172 ■ Activity Book   Use after reading Chapter 18, Skill Lesson, pages 662–663.

Name _____ Date _____

Directions The population pyramid on the left represents the population of Mexico in 1980. The population pyramid on the right illustrates what the Mexican population might look like in 2030. Use the information from the two pyramids to answer the questions below.

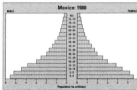
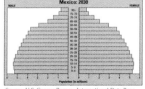

Mexico: 1980
MALE   FEMALE
Source: U.S. Census Bureau, International Data Base.

Mexico: 2030
MALE   FEMALE
Source: U.S. Census Bureau, International Data Base.

❻ About how many people were 20–24 years old in 1980? about 6 million
in 2030? about 10 million

❼ Which gender/age group was the smallest in 1980? males 80+ years old
in 2030? males 80+ years old

❽ Which gender/age-group is the largest in 1980? males 0–4 years old
in 2030? males 10–14 years old

❾ What is the predicted approximate increase in the number of people 50–54 years old between 1980 and 2030? about 7 million

❿ Do any gender/age groups show a predicted decrease between 1980 and 2030? yes
If so, which one(s)? males and females 0–4 years old

⓫ About how many people were less than 15 years old in 1980? about 30 million

Use after reading Chapter 18, Skill Lesson, pages 662–663.   Activity Book ■ 173

LESSON 3

Name _____ Date _____

South America

Directions Read each statement below. If the statement is true, write *T* in the blank. If the statement is false, write *F* in the blank.

1 __F__ Most of South America is covered in tropical rain forest.

2 __T__ Scientists feel that it is important to preserve the rain forests of South America because of their potential medical benefits.

3 __F__ At one time Spain controlled all of South America.

4 __F__ All *mestizos* come from South America.

5 __T__ The American and French revolutions encouraged people in South American colonies to fight for their independence.

6 __T__ Simón Bolívar was one of the leaders of the efforts to free South American colonies.

7 __F__ Simón Bolívar believed that the former South American colonies had so much in common that they could join together as a single nation.

8 __T__ In the new, independent countries of South America, dictators or armies often took control of the political process.

9 __T__ Reformers in South America have worked to help small farmers own their land.

LESSON 4

Name _____ Date _____

Canada

Directions Circle the letter of the best answer.

1 Which best represents the flag of Canada?

A.    B.   (C.)    D.

2 Which is a prairie province of Canada?
(F.) Alberta   H. Ontario
G. Quebec   J. Nunavut

3 Which ocean does **not** border Canada?
A. Arctic   C. Pacific
(B.) Indian   D. Atlantic

4 Which best describes the relationship between Canada and Great Britain right after the North America Act of 1867?
F. Independent nation   H. Commonwealth partner
G. Conquered territory   (J.) Representative government

5 Who is the official leader of the executive branch of the Canadian government?
A. The Parliament   (C.) The British monarch
B. The Prime Minister   D. The governor-general

6 Who runs the executive branch of the Canadian government on a day-to-day basis?
F. The Parliament   H. The British monarch
(G.) The Prime Minister   J. The governor-general

7 Which nation buys the majority of Canada's exports?
A. France   C. Great Britain
B. Australia   (D.) the United States

SKILL PRACTICE

Name _____ Date _____

 MAP AND GLOBE SKILLS

Use a Time Zone Map

Directions Use the time zone map below to answer the questions.

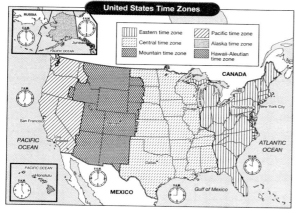

1 How many time zones cover the 50 states? 6

2 Which of these cities are in the Central time zone: Chicago, Dallas, Denver?

Chicago, Dallas

3 When it is 8:00 A.M. in New York City, what time is it in Los Angeles?

5:00 A.M.

4 When it is 3:30 P.M. in Chicago, what time is it in Honolulu?

11:30 A.M.

(continued)

SKILL PRACTICE

Name _____ Date _____

Directions Use the time zone map to complete the chart below.

When the time is . . .	The time is . . .
5 2:00 A.M. in Buenos Aires	11:00 P.M. in Chicago
6 1:00 P.M. in São Paulo	11:00 A.M. in La Paz
7 6:30 A.M. in Los Angeles	9:30 A.M. in Lima
8 3:45 P.M. in Houston	4:45 P.M. in Bogotá
9 2:00 P.M. in Rio de Janeiro	11:00 A.M. in Phoenix
10 11:30 A.M. in Managua	11:30 A.M. in Mexico City
11 9:15 P.M. in Caracas	8:15 P.M. in Washington, D.C.

Name _____ Date _____

The United States, Canada, and Mexico

THE UNITED STATES AND CANADA		THE UNITED STATES AND MEXICO	
↙	↘	↙	↘
SIMILARITIES	**DIFFERENCES**	**SIMILARITIES**	**DIFFERENCES**
Both Canada and the United States were once under British Rule.	Today, Canada's Executive is still Branch headed by Britain's Monarch while the United States govern-ment is fully independent.	Mexico and the United States each have democratic governments.	The President of Mexico can only serve one six-year term while the President of the United States can serve two four-year terms.

© Harcourt

· CHAPTER · Name _____ Date _____

18   Test Preparation

Directions Read each question and choose the best answer. then fill in the circle for the answer you have chosen. be sure to fill in the circle completely.

1 Which two civilizations have created the cultural heritage of Mexico?
- Ⓐ PRI and PAN
- Ⓑ *Mestizo* and French
- Ⓒ Native American and Spanish
- Ⓓ North American and South American

2 Which do many of the Central American and Caribbean nations have in common?
- Ⓕ Land area
- Ⓖ Population size
- Ⓗ Threat of hurricanes
- Ⓙ Communist governments

3 Which word best describes the political history of Haiti?
- Ⓐ Isolated
- Ⓑ Unstable
- Ⓒ Communist
- Ⓓ Democratic

4 Which person led the efforts to free parts of South America from colonial rule?
- Ⓕ Fidel Castro
- Ⓖ Simón Bolívar
- Ⓗ Jean-Bertrand Aristide
- Ⓙ Father Miguel Hidalgo

5 Which two nations in the Western Hemisphere share a border of more than 5,000 miles?
- Ⓐ Colombia and Brazil
- Ⓑ Colombia and Panama
- Ⓒ United States and Mexico
- Ⓓ United States and Canada

© Harcourt

COMMUNITY RESOURCES

Experts on International Relations
_____
_____
_____
_____
_____

Experts on Mexico
_____
_____
_____
_____
_____

Experts on Canada
_____
_____
_____
_____
_____

Experts on South America
_____
_____
_____
_____
_____

Chapter 18 Assessment

·CHAPTER·   Name _____ Date _____

18 Test

Part One: Test Your Understanding
MULTIPLE CHOICE (4 points each)

Directions Circle the letter of the best answer.

1 What two cultures does a mestizo heritage blend?
A Native American and French
B French and Austrian
C Spanish and French
D Native American and Spanish *(circled)*

2 Which of the following rulers governed Mexico for more than 30 years?
F an Austrian prince
G dictator Porfirio Díaz *(circled)*
H Father Miguel Hidalgo
J President Benito Juárez

3 Mexico's 1917 constitution ensured that—
A only PAN candidates could be elected as president.
B the PRI party would have to share power.
C presidents could serve for only six years. *(circled)*
D people's political choices would increase.

4 Many cities in northern Mexico grew during the twentieth century because—
F they were located in a federal district.
G they encouraged people to move from cities to farms.
H interest rates increased greatly.
J many factories were built there. *(circled)*

5 What is the main language of most Central American countries?
A English
B Spanish *(circled)*
C French
D African languages

6 Which Central American country has three branches of government like those of the United States?
F Cuba
G Haiti
H Puerto Rico
J Costa Rica *(circled)*

Chapter 18 Test

Assessment Program ■ 139

(continued)

Name _____ Date _____

7 In the late 1700s and early 1800s, people in South America wanted—
A to colonize Central America.
B independence from European countries. *(circled)*
C goods from North America.
D economic freedom.

8 Simón Bolívar and José de San Martín were important figures in South America because they—
F established sugarcane and coffee plantations.
G supported the French Revolution.
H worked to make South American colonies independent. *(circled)*
J helped settle the area for the Dutch.

9 The Quebec Act of 1774—
A included a Charter of Rights and Freedoms.
B made Canada and New Zealand partner nations in the British Commonwealth.
C created Nova Scotia, Quebec, and the Dominion of Canada.
D allowed French settlers in Canada to maintain their laws, language, and religion. *(circled)*

10 Canada's strongest economic partnership is with—
F Mexico.
G the United States. *(circled)*
H France.
J Britain.

MATCHING (4 points each)

Directions Match the descriptions on the left with the terms on the right. Then write the correct letter in the space provided.

11 _C_ when one nation refuses to trade with another

12 _A_ a type of Canadian political region

13 _E_ a percentage amount banks charge when they loan money

14 _D_ when many trees in an area are cut down

15 _B_ a kind of territory that governs itself

A province
B commonwealth
C embargo
D deforestation
E interest rate

140 ■ Assessment Program

Chapter 18 Test

(continued)

Name _____ Date _____

Part Two: Test Your Skills
READ A POPULATION PYRAMID (5 points each)

Directions Use the population pyramid to answer the following questions.

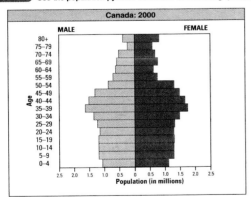

Canada: 2000

Source: U.S. Census Bureau, International Data Base.

16 In the year 2000 what age group had the largest number of people in Canada?
The largest group was people aged 35–39 years.

17 In the year 2000 what age group had the smallest number of people in Canada?
The group of people aged 75–79 was the smallest.

18 In which age groups are there more females than males? all but ages 60–64

19 What general statement can you make about Canada's population from this pyramid? Possible response: The largest group of Canadian citizens is between the ages of 30 and 49.

Chapter 18 Test

Assessment Program ■ 141

(continued)

Name _____ Date _____

Part Three: Apply What You Have Learned

20 SEQUENCING (10 points)

The list below describes some of the many governments that have ruled in Mexico. Put this list of governments in order on the time line below.

Governments in Mexico

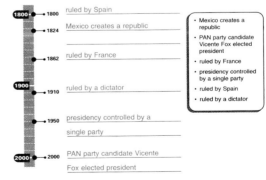

- Mexico creates a republic
- PAN party candidate Vicente Fox elected president
- ruled by France
- presidency controlled by a single party
- ruled by Spain
- ruled by a dictator

21 ESSAY (10 points)

Many people in Central America, South America, and Canada have struggled to attain self-government. Write a paragraph that describes one region discussed in the chapter and explains how people there have changed the way that their area is ruled.

Possible responses: Many countries were European colonies for a long time.
Simón Bolívar and José de San Martín led many South American countries to
gain independence from Spain. Canada gradually gained more independence
from Great Britain. Haiti has had problems maintaining a stable democracy.

142 ■ Assessment Program

Chapter 18 Test

Introduce the Chapter

PAGES 650–651

OBJECTIVES

- Interpret information in visuals.
- Use critical thinking skills to organize and analyze information.

Access Prior Knowledge

Ask students to share experiences they have had with their neighbors. Why is it important to maintain good relations with neighbors?

Visual Learning

Picture Have students examine the photograph. As a class, discuss how these images suggest the content of this chapter.

Locate It Map Washington, D.C. is located on the Potomac River. The city of Washington, D.C., is on federal land, and is not part of any state.

ORGANIZATION OF AMERICAN STATES FLAG GARDEN

The Organization of American States, or OAS, was formed in 1890. It is the world's oldest regional organization. Today, the OAS is made up of 35 Western Hemisphere nations. It has four official languages—English, Spanish, French, and Portuguese.

LOCATE IT

MARYLAND

Washington, D.C.

VIRGINIA

Organization of American States Flag Garden

650 ■ Unit 8

BACKGROUND

Picture The flags in the picture represent the countries that are part of the Organization of American States (OAS). Countries as large as Canada and as small as Trinidad are among the organization's members. With its headquarters in Washington, D.C., the OAS promotes social justice, supports international law, and believes that an attack against a member nation is an attack against all OAS members. The OAS works to settle disputes peacefully.

BACKGROUND

Quotation President George W. Bush, elected in November 2000, is the son of George Bush, who was President of the United States from 1989–1993. Not since John Adams (1796) and his son, John Quincy Adams (1824), were each elected President have both a father and son been Presidents of the United States. President George W. Bush's State Department speech was one of his first speeches as President.

 · CHAPTER ·

18

Partners in the Hemisphere

66 Our future cannot be
separated from the future
of our neighbors. 99

—George W. Bush, State Department speech,
February 15, 2001

Read and Respond

As students read the title, ask them
in which hemisphere they live.
The Western Hemisphere includes
Greenland, Canada, the United States,
Mexico, Central America, South
America, and the Caribbean islands.

Quotation Have a volunteer read the
quotation aloud.

**Q To whom does the word
"neighbors" refer?**

A Answers will vary, but should reflect
that President Bush is referring to
neighboring countries. He considers
our country to be part of a global
community.

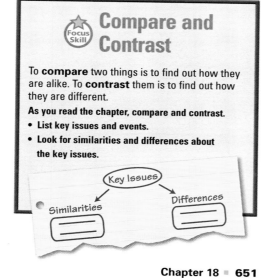

(Focus Skill) **Compare and Contrast**

To **compare** two things is to find out how they
are alike. To **contrast** them is to find out how
they are different.

As you read the chapter, compare and contrast.

• List key issues and events.

• Look for similarities and differences about
the key issues.

Key Issues

Similarities   Differences

Chapter 18 ▪ 651

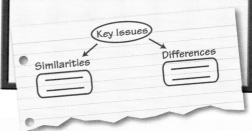

(Focus Skill) **Compare and Contrast**

Have students use a graphic
organizer to illustrate the similarities and differences they identify
about key topics in the chapter.

• Students will find a compare-
and-contrast organizer on page
178 of the Activity Book.

• A completed organizer can be
found on page 178 of the Activity
Book, Teacher's Edition.

Key Issues

Similarities   Differences

WORD WORK

Preview Vocabulary Have students list the vocabulary terms from
each lesson of the chapter and
write what they already know about
each term in a chart like the one
shown. Then have students read
the chapter, and record the definitions in the third column.

Term	What I Know about the Term	Definition

MAKE IT RELEVANT

Discussion Topics As you teach the chapter, generate discussion with
students using these topics. The topics encourage students to think
beyond the borders of the United States.

■ What other countries have you visited in the Western Hemisphere?
How were they the same as or different from the United States?

■ What makes a "good" neighbor—either in your community or in the
global community?

■ Who are the United States' closest neighbors?

Compare and Contrast
pp. 651, 652, 653, 656, 676

Vocabulary

SEE READING AND VOCABULARY TRANSPARENCY 8-7 OR THE WORD CARDS ON PP. V97–V98.

middle class	interest rate
p. 656	p. 656

 When Minutes Count

Have students examine the map of Mexico on page 653. Use the map to discuss the Big Idea of the lesson.

Quick Summary

This lesson describes the geography, history, economy, and people of Mexico.

 **Motivate**

Set the Purpose

Big Idea Explain to students that Mexico is a collection of states with diverse lands, people, and histories.

Access Prior Knowledge

Ask students to review what they know about the war between Mexico and the United States.

· LESSON ·

1 Mexico

1800	1900	PRESENT

COMPARE AND CONTRAST
As you read, compare and contrast different regions and cultures in Mexico.

BIG IDEA
Learn about the land, people, history, and economy of Mexico.

VOCABULARY
middle class
interest rate

In 1521 the Spanish conquistador Hernando Cortés conquered the Aztec Empire and claimed Mexico for Spain. For the next 300 years, Mexico remained under Spanish rule. Then, in 1821, a revolution ended Spain's rule, and Mexico became an independent country.

Independence, however, did not immediately bring peace. For many years afterward, the people of Mexico struggled to build an orderly society. The Mexican Constitution of 1917 reorganized the country's government and led to closer ties with the United States. Today, the two countries are major trading partners.

The Land and People of Mexico

Mexico is a land with many mountains. Two mountain ranges, the Sierra Madre Occidental on the west and the Sierra Madre Oriental on the east, stretch along Mexico's coast. Between these mountains lies the Mexican Plateau, a region of rich

FAST FACT Two states in Mexico share part of their names with a state in the United States—California.

652 ▪ Unit 8

WORD WORK

Compound Terms Point out that the vocabulary terms for this lesson are compound terms and that the words *middle, class, interest,* and *rate* have several different meanings by themselves. Invite students to work in groups to prepare sentences that show the many different meanings of the individual words as well as the compound terms *middle class* and *interest rate*.

BACKGROUND

Mexico Today About 100 million people live in Mexico today, the vast majority of them in urban areas such as Mexico City. Mexico's wealth of natural resources has led to the growth of industries such as silver mining and oil production. Tourism is one of Mexico's fastest-growing industries and its most important after oil.

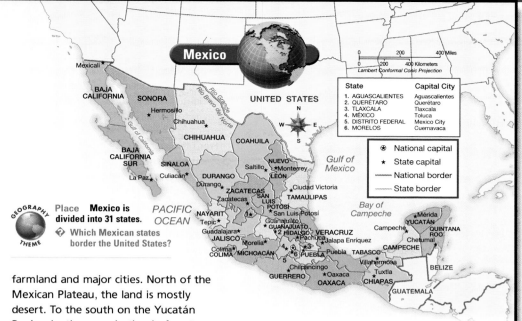

Mexico

State	Capital City
1. AGUASCALIENTES	Aguascalientes
2. QUERÉTARO	Querétaro
3. TLAXCALA	Tlaxcala
4. MÉXICO	Toluca
5. DISTRITO FEDERAL	Mexico City
6. MORELOS	Cuernavaca

⊛ National capital
★ State capital
—— National border
—— State border

GEOGRAPHY THEME
Place Mexico is divided into 31 states.
❖ Which Mexican states border the United States?

farmland and major cities. North of the Mexican Plateau, the land is mostly desert. To the south on the Yucatán Peninsula, there are both rain forests and grassy plains.

Most people in Mexico today trace their cultural heritage to two main groups—Native American and Spanish. In fact, more than 60 percent of the people are mestizos, people of mixed Indian and Spanish ancestry. Mexicans continue to honor the contributions of both groups with public history displays and celebrations. *Native American and Spanish*

REVIEW What two groups have mainly influenced Mexico's culture and people?
🔲 COMPARE AND CONTRAST

These hikers (left) are in the rugged desert of Mexico's Baja Peninsula.

Mexico, a Republic

Most of the wealth and power in colonial Mexico belonged to people of pure Spanish ancestry. Other Mexicans had few opportunities. In September 1810, Father Miguel Hidalgo (mee•GAYL ee•DAHL•goh) gave a speech in his church calling for a revolution against Spain. Hidalgo's rebel army was later defeated, but his actions were not forgotten. The revolution continued, and in 1821 Mexico gained its independence.

In time, Mexico became a republic. The Mexican people, however, had little experience with self-government. Presidents were no sooner elected than they were forced out of office by their enemies. During those same years, Mexico lost most of its northern lands to the United States. Texas, which won its independence from Mexico in 1836, became part of the United States in 1845.

Chapter 18 ▪ **653**

Focus Skill
READING SKILL

Compare and Contrast Ask students to compare the struggles of the Mexican people to establish a republic to that of the British colonists in America in the 1770s. Encourage students to research both movements and to report their findings in brief summaries.

READING SOCIAL STUDIES

Anticipation Guide Ask students to predict which of the following statements are true and which are false. Students may correct their predictions as they read.

1. The people of Mexico trace their heritage to three main groups. FALSE

2. Mexico lost the land that is now Texas as a result of a war with the United States. TRUE

3. Mexico's trade with Canada nearly tripled after the signing of the North American Free Trade Agreement in 1994. FALSE

● USE READING AND VOCABULARY TRANSPARENCY 8-7.

8-7
TRANSPARENCY

2 Teach

The Land and People of Mexico

Read and Respond

Geography Reinforce to students that the majority of Mexico is highlands or mountains, with very little suitable farming land.

Visual Learning

Map Help students locate the state of Mexico on the map on page 653. Explain that Mexico is both the name of the country and the name of a member state.
CAPTION ANSWER: Baja California, Sonora, Chihuahua, Coahuila, Nuevo León, and Tamaulipas

Mexico, a Republic

Read and Respond

History Explain that in the years following Mexico's independence, the country was run by a series of select groups seeking personal gains. As a result, there was inefficiency in Mexico's government.

Read and Respond

Culture and Society Explain that the Mexican Revolution began in response to dissatisfaction with Díaz's policies. Inform students that the revolution lasted for a decade and involved struggles among various factions for control of the country. Explain that many of the reforms sought during the revolution were realized in the Constitution of 1917, such as workers' rights and limits on a president's tenure.

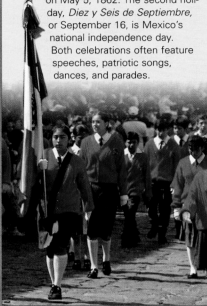

• HERITAGE •

Fiestas Patrias

Each year the Mexican people celebrate two national holidays known as the *Fiestas Patrias*, or festivals of the country. The first of these holidays, *Cinco de Mayo*, or May 5, honors Mexico's victory over the French at Puebla on May 5, 1862. The second holiday, *Diez y Seis de Septiembre*, or September 16, is Mexico's national independence day. Both celebrations often feature speeches, patriotic songs, dances, and parades.

Three years later, following a war with the United States, Mexico agreed to give up most of its remaining northern lands to the United States. These lands included present-day California, Utah, and Nevada and parts of New Mexico, Arizona, Colorado, and Wyoming. In return, the United States paid Mexico $15 million. Mexico later sold

654 ■ Unit 8

the southern parts of present-day Arizona and New Mexico to the United States.

In 1861 Benito Juárez (HWAHR•ays), a Zapotec Indian, became president. As president, Juárez helped bring about many reforms, including the private ownership of land.

From the start, Juárez had enemies who wanted him out of office. Those enemies looked to France for help. On May 5, 1862, French soldiers invaded Mexico and attacked the city of Puebla. Though greatly outnumbered, the Mexicans at Puebla defeated the French.

Despite their loss at Puebla, the French eventually took control of Mexico and removed Juárez from office. Within a few years, however, the Mexican people rebelled. Juárez became president again.

After Juárez died, the dictator Porfirio Díaz (pour•FEER•yoh DEE•ahs) ruled for more than 30 years. Díaz ordered railroads built and factories enlarged. Díaz brought economic growth to Mexico, but problems remained. Many poor farmers lost their land. When Díaz took control, 20 percent of the people owned land. Thirty years later, only 2 percent of the people owned land.

In 1910 many Mexican farmers and other groups fought against the dictatorship. Díaz resigned, but the fighting continued in Mexico. When the fighting ended, the leaders of the revolution took control of Mexico. They wrote a new constitution that limited the time a president could serve to a six-year term.

Benito Juárez

Mexico City, like all large cities, has crowded streets. Air pollution from automobile exhaust is often a problem in the city.

LOCATE IT

Mexico City

MEXICO

Many government-owned farms were divided among farm families.

While more people owned land, they still had few political choices. For more than 70 years, a single party controlled the presidency. Candidates from other political parties were elected to the Mexican Congress, but only those from the Partido Revolucionario Institucional (PRI) became president.

The election of July 2000 changed everything. Mexicans chose Vicente Fox, from the Partido Acción Nacional (PAN), as their new president. When asked how difficult his job as president would be, Fox replied, "The challenge is gigantic, but so are our resources. In Mexico we have a saying, 'Every newborn child comes with a gift.' Democracy will bring us lots of benefits and hope."

REVIEW **How does the Mexican constitution limit a president's power?** A president can serve only a six-year term.

A Growing Middle Class

Mexico is divided into 31 states and one federal district. The federal district contains Mexico City, Mexico's capital. About 9 million people live in Mexico City. About 9 million more people live in its metropolitan area, making Mexico City one of the world's most populated metropolitan areas.

Mexico City is just one of the large cities that lie on the Mexican Plateau. In fact, more than half of Mexico's population lives in this region. Other large cities on the Mexican Plateau include Monterrey, Guadalajara, and Puebla. Each of these cities has more than a million people.

Many cities in Mexico have grown as people have moved from rural areas to cities to find new jobs and better wages. In recent years, many new factories have been built in northern Mexico.

Chapter 18 ■ 655

A Growing Middle Class

Read and Respond

Civics and Government Explain that the Federal District in Mexico City is equivalent to the District of Columbia in the United States. Inform students that both areas are seats of national government.

Visual Learning

Photograph Direct students' attention to the picture of Mexican president Vicente Fox and United States President George W. Bush on page 656. Explain that both leaders have worked closely with political parties other than their own to pass legislation.

Q **What leadership qualities do both President Fox and President Bush share?**

A Answers may vary, but should reflect that both leaders share the leadership quality of cooperation.

3 Close

Summarize Key Content

- Mexico is a land of mountains, plateaus, deserts, and rain forests.
- Mexico's people trace their heritage to two main groups, Native Americans and the Spanish.
- Mexico struggled for many years to become a republic and succeeded in the year 2000, when Vicente Fox was elected president.
- Mexico has become a nation of major cities in which people work largely in manufacturing and other related industries.

INTEGRATE MATHEMATICS

Figuring Exchange Rates Tell students that American travelers in Mexico must exchange their dollars for Mexican pesos. Exchange rates may change daily. In September, 2003, one United States dollar was worth the following units:

    11.04 Mexican pesos
    1.34 Canadian dollars
    1600 Venezuelan bolivars

Ask students to use these figures to find the worth of 100 United States dollars in all three currencies.

INTEGRATE LANGUAGE ARTS

Informative Writing Ask students to research and write short reports explaining the causes and effects of Mexican people moving to cities. Students may focus on the economic, cultural, or political impacts that such a move would bring. Encourage students to use reference sources, including encyclopedias and the Internet, in their research.

Anticipation Guide Have students check their responses to the Anticipation Guide.

1. The people of Mexico trace their heritage to ~~three~~ main groups. two

2. Mexico lost the land that is now Texas as a result of a war with the United States.

3. Mexico's trade with Canada nearly ~~tripled~~ after the signing of the North American Free Trade Agreement in 1994. doubled

● USE READING AND VOCABULARY TRANSPARENCY 8-7. **8-7** TRANSPARENCY

Assess

Lesson 1 Review—Answers

COMPARE AND CONTRAST The land in northern Mexico is mostly desert; the land in the Yucatán includes rain forests and grassy plains.

❶ **BIG IDEA** in the Mexican Plateau

❷ **VOCABULARY** The growth of manufacturing in Mexico has led to the growth of a **middle class**.

❸ **TIME LINE** in 1821

❹ **HISTORY** It wanted to remove Benito Juárez from office.

❺ **CRITICAL THINKING—Analyze** Challenges might include overcrowding, pollution, and poverty.

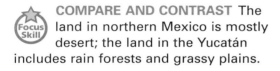

Performance Assessment Guidelines Check students' bar graphs. Then ask students to research data for the current year and add it to their graphs.

ACTIVITY BOOK

Use ACTIVITY BOOK, p. 170, to reinforce and extend student learning.

George W. Bush's first international trip as President of the United States was to visit with Mexican president Vicente Fox. The trip emphasized the strong ties between the two nations.

As a result, Ciudad Juárez, Matamoros, Tijuana, and other cities near the United States border have all grown quickly.

The growth of manufacturing and other industries in Mexico also led to the growth of a large **middle class**, an economic level between the poor and the wealthy. Today, Mexico's middle class is one of the largest in the Americas.

In 1994, however, even middle-class families found buying most products difficult. The value of the peso, Mexico's basic unit of money, suddenly dropped because of inflation and the government's need to pay its debts. That caused prices in Mexico to rise sharply. Some doubled. Others tripled. **Interest rates**, the amounts that banks charge to loan money, rose as high as 80 percent. To help stabilize the Mexican economy, the United States arranged $52 billion in loans to Mexico. Had the Mexican economy collapsed, it would have had a terrible effect on the world economy.

Another major economic change occurred in 1994 when Canada, Mexico, and the United States put the North American Free Trade Agreement into effect. The year before NAFTA began, trade between the United States and Mexico totaled $80 billion a year. By 2000 that figure was $230 billion.

REVIEW Why did Mexico's middle class grow larger? because of the growth in manufacturing and other industries

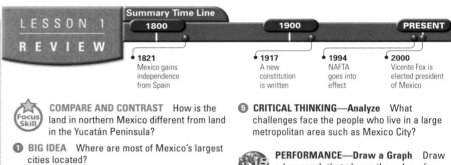

LESSON 1 REVIEW

Summary Time Line

1800 — 1900 — PRESENT

● **1821** Mexico gains independence from Spain

● **1917** A new constitution is written

● **1994** NAFTA goes into effect

● **2000** Vicente Fox is elected president of Mexico

COMPARE AND CONTRAST How is the land in northern Mexico different from land in the Yucatán Peninsula?

❶ **BIG IDEA** Where are most of Mexico's largest cities located?

❷ **VOCABULARY** Write a sentence using the term **middle class**.

❸ **TIME LINE** When did Mexico gain its independence from Spain?

❹ **HISTORY** Why did France invade Mexico in 1862?

❺ **CRITICAL THINKING—Analyze** What challenges face the people who live in a large metropolitan area such as Mexico City?

PERFORMANCE—Draw a Graph Draw a bar graph that shows the value of trade between Mexico and the United States in 1993, the year before NAFTA went into effect, and in 2000. Compare your graph with those of classmates.

EXTEND AND ENRICH

Research Ask students to research the relations between Mexico and the United States before, during, and after the Mexican-American War. Students may report their findings in a round-table discussion.

RETEACH THE LESSON

Graphic Organizer Have students fill in the graphic organizer with facts from each subsection. Remind students that they may use the text to find or confirm information. Direct students to identify on their own the main topics covered in the lesson.

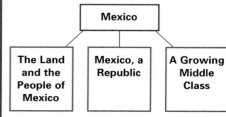

Mexico

| The Land and the People of Mexico | Mexico, a Republic | A Growing Middle Class |

Central America and the Caribbean

COMPARE AND CONTRAST

As you read, compare and contrast parts of Central America and the Caribbean.

1880 — 1940 — PRESENT

Like the United States, many nations in Central America and the Caribbean have a history of democracy. Costa Rica has a long democratic tradition. So does Puerto Rico, with its ties to the United States. In some places in the region, however, people continue to struggle for democracy and economic security.

BIG IDEA
Central American and Caribbean countries have various regions and common heritages, and face similar challenges.

The Land and People

The geography of the nations of Central America and the Caribbean is as varied as the backgrounds of the people who live there. Towering mountains, sandy beaches, dense forests, and remote islands are just some of the features that mark these two regions.

VOCABULARY
commonwealth
embargo
free election

On the outskirts of Guatemala City, a large volcano looms.

LOCATE IT

MEXICO

GUATEMALA

Guatemala City

Chapter 18 ■ 657

OBJECTIVES

- Describe the geography and people of Central America and the Caribbean.
- Identify the challenges of living in a tropical climate.
- Describe the governments of Central America and the Caribbean.

Compare and Contrast
pp. 651, 657, 659, 661, 676

Vocabulary

SEE READING AND VOCABULARY TRANSPARENCY 8-8 OR THE WORD CARDS ON PP. V97–V98.

commonwealth
p. 660

free election
p. 661

embargo p. 660

When Minutes Count

Read aloud the Big Idea statement at the beginning of the lesson. Then ask students to examine the photographs and captions in the lesson and identify how each one relates to the Big Idea.

Quick Summary

This lesson describes the various features and people of Central America and the Caribbean.

1 Motivate

Set the Purpose

Big Idea Explain that Central American and Caribbean countries share common heritages and face similar challenges.

Access Prior Knowledge

Have students discuss what they know about life in Central America and the Caribbean. How is life there similar to life in the United States? How is it different?

WORD WORK

Word Origins Write the word *commonwealth* on the board, and ask students to break the word into two parts, *common* and *wealth*. Explain that the word dates to the Middle Ages, when *commun welthe* referred to a community's general well-being. Explain that today the word may refer to a group of people or a state, such as the Commonwealth of Massachusetts, or to a specific political body, such as the Commonwealth of Independent States.

BACKGROUND

The United States in Central America The United States became involved in the development of Central America at the start of the 1900s, when Panama declared its independence and invited the United States to build a canal that would connect the Pacific and Atlantic oceans. The Panama Canal took ten years to complete and was considered a significant engineering achievement. The United States controlled the canal until 2000 when the rights reverted to Panama.

Graphic Organizer Suggest that students work in pairs to make web diagrams about Central America and the Caribbean. As students read, they should build web diagrams by writing key words, phrases, or concepts that relate to their region. After reading, students should compare their diagrams.

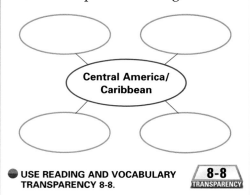

Central America/ Caribbean

● USE READING AND VOCABULARY TRANSPARENCY 8-8.

8-8
TRANSPARENCY

2 Teach

The Land and People

Read and Respond

Geography Explain that Central America is essentially a land bridge that unites the ecosystems of North America and South America. Inform students that as a result, Central America features a mixture of plant and animal species from both continents.

Visual Learning

Map Direct student's attention to the map on page 658. Explain that the Caribbean Sea separates Central America from the Caribbean countries.

◑ Which Central American countries border both the Caribbean Sea and the Pacific Ocean?

A Guatemala, Honduras, Nicaragua, Costa Rica, and Panama

CAPTION ANSWER: the Bahamas

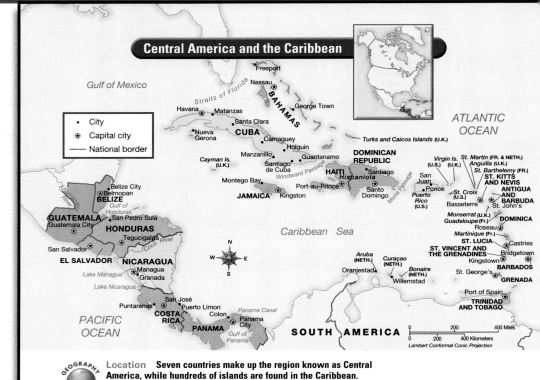

Central America and the Caribbean

- • City
- ⊛ Capital city
- —— National border

Gulf of Mexico

ATLANTIC OCEAN

Caribbean Sea

PACIFIC OCEAN

SOUTH AMERICA

200   400 Miles
0   200   400 Kilometers
Lambert Conformal Conic Projection

Location   Seven countries make up the region known as Central America, while hundreds of islands are found in the Caribbean.

Which Caribbean country lies farthest north?

Traveling south from Mexico, a visitor would pass through Belize (buh•LEEZ), Guatemala (gwah•tuh•MAH•luh), Honduras, El Salvador, Nicaragua (nih•kuh•RAH•gwah), Costa Rica, and Panama. These seven countries form the 202,000 square miles (523,180 sq km) called Central America. Almost all the Central American countries have mountains. Volcanoes, some still active, formed the mountains. Ash from the volcanoes made the surrounding land fertile.

The Pacific Ocean forms the western borders of all the Central American countries except Belize. The Caribbean Sea, which is part of the Atlantic Ocean, forms

the eastern borders of all the Central American countries except El Salvador.

Rain forests brighten the landscapes of Guatemala and Costa Rica. Costa Rica especially wants to preserve its rain forests' rich variety of plant and animal life. About 25 percent of Costa Rica's land has been set aside as nature preserves.

The fertile land of Central America is farmed to produce crops such as bananas, sugarcane, coffee, corn, cotton, and beans. Fishing is an important industry in Belize. Some countries, such as Guatemala and Panama, also have mineral resources.

People who live on islands in the Caribbean grow many of the same kinds

658 ▪ Unit 8

MENTAL MAPPING

Mapping Central America
Ask students to picture in their minds the arrangement of countries in Central America. Have students work in groups to make a map showing the order and placement of the countries.

of crops as people in Central America, and they earn their livings in similar ways. Among the hundreds of islands in the Caribbean are Cuba, Puerto Rico, the Bahamas, Jamaica, and Hispaniola.

European explorers first visited these islands in the late 1400s and early 1500s. The beauty of the tropical islands and the rich land impressed the explorers. Today, visitors come for the islands' lovely beaches and warm climates.

Despite the beauty and the rich land, places in the Caribbean and Central America face special challenges. Earthquakes are common in Central America, and tropical storms often bring heavy rains to both regions. Hurricane Georges, for example, hit the eastern Caribbean, Haiti, and the Dominican Republic in September 1998. The storm caused more then $1.5 billion in damages.

One month later, Hurricane Mitch roared into the western Caribbean, with winds that reached 180 miles (290 km) per hour. The storm then came ashore in Honduras, where its heavy rains caused mudslides in Central America. The storm killed more than 10,000 people and injured about 13,000.

Many of the people who live in Central America and the Caribbean are of Spanish and Native American descent. Many people of African descent also live in the regions. Their ancestors were brought from Africa as slaves. The main language in most of the countries is Spanish, but in some countries most people speak either English, French, or Dutch.

REVIEW What are two major challenges to living in Central America and the Caribbean?

🌐 COMPARE AND CONTRAST earthquakes and tropical storms

In 1998 Hurricane Mitch (below) hit the Caribbean island of Guanaja (right), destroying most buildings and boat docks.

155 mph   PRESSURE: 923 MB   CUBA

(YUCATAN)

JAMAICA

Chapter 18   659

Visual Learning

Photograph Explain that hurricane season lasts from June to November and that during that time, hurricanes are a threat to many people and places. Central America is one of the two regions in the world with the highest recorded hurricane activity each year.

Q **Where is the hurricane located in the satellite photograph?**

A Students should indicate that the hurricane is located in between Jamaica and Mexico.

Read and Respond

Culture and Society Many forms of popular music come from the Caribbean Islands. The merengue began in the Dominican Republic and is based on both Spanish and African musical styles. Calypso music, which is based on West African work songs, began in Trinidad during the 1800s. It is music of celebration, but it also tells of social and political problems. Another type of Latin American music called salsa began in Cuba and Puerto Rico. Salsa combines the rhythm of African drums with brass instruments.

Culture and Society Inform students that languages and cultures vary not only among islands, but sometimes within them. Explain that the island of Saint Martin is shared by two governments, the French and the Dutch. Explain that the Dutch control the southern one-third of the island which is known for sandy beaches and thriving tourism. The French control the northern two-thirds of the island, known for its abundant fishing.

Q **How is the island of Saint Martin organized?**

A Saint Martin is divided into two nations—the Dutch part, known for tourism, and the French part, renowned for its fishing.

Government in the Regions

Read and Respond

Civics and Government Explain to students that in a capitalist country like the United States, people own land and businesses. Inform students that in a communist country such as Cuba, the government owns the land and businesses.

Q **What are some advantages of a capitalist government?**

A People can own their own land and businesses.

• SCIENCE AND TECHNOLOGY •

The Arecibo Observatory

Explain that until the 1940s, most of the world's observatories were in the Northern Hemisphere. Inform students that after World War II, scientists realized they lacked information about the skies over the Southern Hemisphere. Soon observatories were built in Chile and Australia as well as in Puerto Rico. Help students find star charts that show constellations from both the Northern and Southern hemispheres.

 **Close**

Summarize Key Content

- Central America and the Caribbean have features such as mountains, beaches, dense forests, and remote islands, as well as tropical climates that present many challenges.
- All nations in Central America and the Caribbean, except for Cuba, have democratic governments, but many have achieved democracy only recently.

Fidel Castro has ruled Cuba since 1959.

Government in the Regions

For the first time in recent history, almost all the nations in Central America and the Caribbean have some form of democratic government. Cuba, which is a communist dictatorship, is the exception.

Both Puerto Rico and Cuba came under United States control in 1898, after the Spanish-American War. Puerto Rico was made a United States territory, but Cuba became an independent country in 1902. In 1952 Puerto Rico became a **commonwealth**, a kind of territory that governs itself. As citizens of a territory, Puerto Ricans hold United States citizenship. The United States Virgin Islands is another United States territory in the Caribbean.

Since 1959 Fidel Castro has ruled Cuba as a communist dictator. In an effort to end communism in Cuba, the United States government set up an economic embargo against the nation in 1960. An **embargo** is one nation's refusal to trade goods with another. Cuba's economy has been weakened by the embargo, but Cuba still remains a communist nation. Meanwhile, many Cuban Americans in the United States continue to hope that Cuba will become a democracy.

At Castro's request, Pope John Paul II visited Cuba in January 1998. Although

• SCIENCE AND TECHNOLOGY •

The Arecibo Observatory

In the late 1950s, American scientist William E. Gordon was searching for a site to build a space observatory. Because of what Gordon wished to study, the observatory had to be able to see a certain part of the sky, near the equator. The site finally chosen was Arecibo (ah•rah•SEE•boh) in northwest Puerto Rico. Today, the Arecibo Observatory has the world's largest single-dish radio telescope. The dish has a 1000-foot (305 m) diameter and covers 20 acres. The telescope has helped locate planets outside our solar system.

BACKGROUND

Puerto Rico In 1898, as a result of the Spanish-American War, Puerto Rico became part of the United States. In 1952 Puerto Rico drafted its own constitution and became a United States commonwealth. Today, Puerto Rico has a governor and a local government that operates in much the same way that a state's does. Over time, citizens of Puerto Rico have discussed statehood.

READING SOCIAL STUDIES

Reread to Clarify To ensure understanding of the text, ask students to write brief summaries of each subsection. Then have students reread each subsection to confirm their summaries.

the Roman Catholic Church is not out-lawed, its members cannot join the Communist party, which controls housing and jobs. In honor of the Pope's visit, Castro allowed Christmas to be celebrated in public for the first time in many years.

Many democratic governments in Central America and the Caribbean have struggled to survive. Costa Rica has been the most stable democracy. Like the United States, Costa Rica has three branches of government.

Despite being the second-oldest republic in the Western Hemisphere, after the United States, Haiti has had a history of military takeovers of its government. For much of its history, Haiti was ruled by dictators.

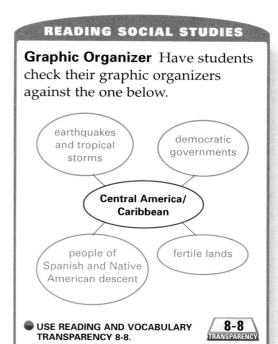

Former president of Haiti, Jean-Bertrand Aristide

At other times, however, the people of Haiti have freely elected their leaders. In 1990 Haiti held a **free election**—one that offers a choice of candidates, instead of a single candidate. Jean-Bertrand Aristide (air•ih•STEED) was elected, but military leaders soon took over. Aristide escaped to the United States. To help end military rule and return Aristide to office, the United States sent troops to Haiti in 1994. Soon Aristide returned to office.

Since that time, Haiti has held other free elections. Most people in Haiti are hopeful that their government will remain a democracy.

REVIEW What nation in the Caribbean continues to be a communist country? Cuba

LESSON 2 REVIEW

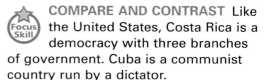

Summary Time Line

1880	1940	PRESENT

- **1898** Cuba, the Philippines, and Puerto Rico are under United States control
- **1952** Puerto Rico becomes a United States commonwealth
- **1990** Haiti holds free elections
- **1998** Pope John Paul II visits Cuba

COMPARE AND CONTRAST How are the governments of Costa Rica and Cuba different?

1 BIG IDEA What do all the countries in Central America and the Caribbean, except Cuba, have in common?

2 VOCABULARY What is a **commonwealth**?

3 TIME LINE When did Puerto Rico become a commonwealth?

4 HISTORY Why did the United States send troops to Haiti in 1994?

5 CRITICAL THINKING—Analyze How might an embargo affect a country?

PERFORMANCE—Make a Mobile Make a mobile about the land and the people of Central America and the Caribbean. Include pictures that represent the regions' physical features and products. Use your mobile to describe the regions to other students.

Chapter 18 ■ 661

Assess

Lesson 2 Review—Answers

COMPARE AND CONTRAST Like the United States, Costa Rica is a democracy with three branches of government. Cuba is a communist country run by a dictator.

1 BIG IDEA They all are democracies.

2 VOCABULARY A **commonwealth** is a kind of territory that governs itself.

3 TIME LINE in 1952

4 HISTORY to help return President Jean-Bertrand Aristide to office

5 CRITICAL THINKING—Analyze It could weaken a nation's economy.

Performance Assessment Guidelines Students' mobiles should show a variety of products and physical features from the region.

OBJECTIVES

- Interpret information in a population pyramid.
- Gather and organize information using a population pyramid.

Vocabulary

population pyramid p. 662

median age p. 662

life expectancy p. 662

WORD CARDS

See pp. V97–V98.

1 Motivate

Why It Matters

Explain that population pyramids can provide valuable information about a country or society. Inform students that scientists can use data from different countries to draw conclusions about factors such as birth rates, death rates, and the general health of the people.

INTEGRATE LANGUAGE ARTS

Write a Scientific Summary Ask students to review the population pyramid of Puerto Rico on page 663. Have students interpret the major findings of the pyramids and use them to write brief outlines. From these outlines, ask students to write short summaries about Puerto Rico's population.

· SKILLS · CHART AND GRAPH

Read Population Pyramids

VOCABULARY

population pyramid
life expectancy
median age

➡ WHY IT MATTERS

A graph that shows the division of a country's population by age is called a **population pyramid**. Each side of the graph is divided by age. One side of the graph shows the female population. The other side of the graph shows the male population.

Two factors affect the shape of the population pyramid—a country's birth rate and its death rate. The birth rate is the number of children born each year for every 1,000 people in the country. The death rate is the number of people who die each year for every 1,000 people in the country.

A population pyramid also gives a picture of a country's **life expectancy**, the number of years people can expect to live. This number varies from country to country. It tells in general how long people in a country live, but it does not say how long any one person will live.

A population pyramid also shows the country's median age. The word *median* means "middle." Half the people in the country are older than the **median age**, and half are younger.

Four generations of the same family can be seen in this photograph.

662 ▪ Unit 8

BACKGROUND

Life Expectancy The life expectancy for Americans has steadily risen over the last century to its current average of 77 years. In 1900 the average was 47 years. The increase in life span has come as factors such as childhood diseases and poor sanitation have been reduced through scientific and public-health advances. Scientists cite those improvements along with a history of good health, a healthful diet, and regular exercise as keys to living long and productive lives. Many scientists believe that life expectancy may be further extended, but probably not much beyond an ultimate age of 120.

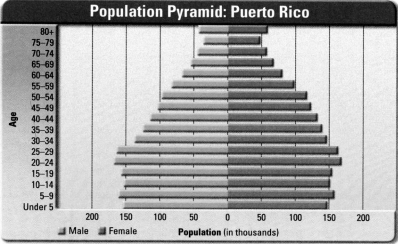

Population Pyramid: Puerto Rico

Age: 80+, 75–79, 70–74, 65–69, 60–64, 55–59, 50–54, 45–49, 40–44, 35–39, 30–34, 25–29, 20–24, 15–19, 10–14, 5–9, Under 5

200 150 100 50 0 50 100 150 200

■ Male ■ Female **Population** (in thousands)

Source: U.S. Census Bureau, International Database

▶ WHAT YOU NEED TO KNOW

The population pyramid shown above gives the population of Puerto Rico. Notice how it is divided into age groups, with the youngest at the bottom and the oldest at the top. The left side of the population pyramid shows the number of males in each age group. The right side shows the number of females. If you want to know the number that a whole age group represents, add together the number of males and the number of females in that age group. For example, in the 10–14 age group, there are about 152,000 males and about 150,000 females. So there are about 302,000 persons age 10–14 in Puerto Rico.

The pyramid's shape indicates how rapidly Puerto Rico's population is growing. The very wide parts of the pyramid show that the greatest number of people are under 29 years of age. The top of the pyramid indicates that fewer people are over 70 years of age.

▶ PRACTICE THE SKILL

Use the population pyramid to answer the following questions.

❶ Find your age group on the population pyramid. About how many boys in Puerto Rico are in that age group? About how many girls?

❷ In which age groups are there more females than males?

❸ Which age group is the largest?

❹ About how many people in Puerto Rico have lived 80 years or longer?

❺ What general statement can you make about Puerto Rico's population from this pyramid?

▶ APPLY WHAT YOU LEARNED

Think about the ages of people in your own family or in your class at school. Draw a population pyramid that shows the number of people of different ages in your family or class.

Chapter 18 ■ 663

CHART AND GRAPH SKILLS

2 Teach

What You Need to Know

Direct students' attention to the population pyramid. Ask students why the number of people decreases in the higher age groups. As people age, many die. Have students compare the number of males in the pyramid with the number of females. There are more males at lower age levels but more females at higher age levels.

Practice the Skill—Answers

❶ about 152,000 boys and about 151,000 girls

❷ 30–34, 35–39, 40–44, 45–49, 50–54, 55–59, 60–64, 65–69, 70–74, 75–79, 80+

❸ 20–24

❹ about 100,000

❺ Females in Puerto Rico tend to live longer than do males.

3 Close

Apply What You Learned

Check to ensure that students' pyramids are constructed with younger people at the bottom of the pyramid and older people at the top.

ACTIVITY BOOK

Use ACTIVITY BOOK, pp. 172–173, to give students additional practice using this skill.

TRANSPARENCY

Use SKILL TRANSPARENCY 8-3.

EXTEND AND ENRICH

Compare and Contrast Ask students to research and locate population maps of two areas, states, or countries and to draw conclusions about the information in them. Have students write brief summaries based on their conclusions. Ask volunteers to share their summaries with the class.

RETEACH THE SKILL

Make a Population Pyramid Organize students into groups and ask them to locate and use information from the 2000 census to construct a population pyramid of their state. Encourage students to use calculators to convert numbers into percentages.

South America

OBJECTIVES

- Describe the geography and people of South America.

- Describe how South American countries gained their independence and some of the problems that came with it.

- Identify new challenges facing South America.

(Focus Skill) **Compare and Contrast**
pp. 651, 664, 667, 668, 676

Vocabulary

SEE READING AND VOCABULARY TRANSPARENCY 8-9 OR THE WORD CARDS ON PP. V97–V98.

standard of living p. 664

liberate p. 666

deforestation p. 668

 When Minutes Count

Organize the class into three groups. Have each group study a different subsection in the lesson. Then ask a volunteer from each group to share a summary of what they learned.

Quick Summary

This lesson describes the geography, history, and development of South America.

1 Motivate

Set the Purpose

Big Idea Inform students that South America's many climatic and geographic differences led its countries to develop on their own rather than as one nation.

Access Prior Knowledge

Ask students to state what they know about the British colonies' quest for independence from Britain.

(Focus Skill) **COMPARE AND CONTRAST**
As you read, compare and contrast regions and cultures in South America.

BIG IDEA
Learn about the land and people of South America and how countries there gained independence.

VOCABULARY
standard of living
liberate
deforestation

1800   1900   PRESENT

South America's diversity can be seen in its lands, climates, and resources. Across the continent, landforms range from towering mountains to broad plateaus and plains. Climates range from tropical in the north to arid and desert in the south. The continent has abundant natural resources, but some of them have not yet been fully developed. Since the countries of South America differ in their economic development, their standards of living also vary widely. A **standard of living** is a measure of how well people in a country live.

South America and Its People

South America, the fourth largest continent, covers more than twice the area of the continental United States. Only Africa has a less indented coastline than South America. Because of this, there are few good harbors along most of South America's coasts.

The Andes Mountains extend 4,500 miles (7,250 km) along the western side of South

LOCATE IT

Caracas
VENEZUELA

Angel Falls

664 ▪ Unit 8

STUDY/RESEARCH SKILLS

Using Reference Sources

Organize students in groups and assign each group a South American country to research. Have groups answer the following questions:

- How large is the country, and how many people live in it?

- What is the country's capital?

- What are the main industries in the country's economy?

Ask groups to orally present their findings to the class.

America, from the Caribbean in the north to the continent's southern tip. East of the Andes are areas of plateaus and plains, including the Guiana Highlands in the north and the Pampus and Patagonia to the south. Three major river systems—the Río de la Plata, the Orinoco (ohr•ee•NOH•koh), and the Amazon—run like veins through the continent's lowlands. Many of these lowlands lie in the tropics. Rain forests, with unique animals and plants, cover much of the land along the Amazon and along many of the other rivers in the region.

While much of South America is hot and humid, some areas are dry and cold. West of the snowcapped Andes, along the coast of northern Chile, is the Atacama Desert. It is the world's driest desert. So little rain falls there that people have found ways to capture moisture from the early morning fogs. The southern part of the continent is cold for much of the year.

Native peoples lived in South America for thousands of years. Then, in the 1500s, Spain, Portugal, and other European countries began to build colonies there.

Location There are 13 countries on the continent of South America. Of those 13, Brazil is the largest.

◆ How are Bolivia and Paraguay different from the other countries of South America?

FAST FACT South America has the world's highest waterfall, longest mountain range, and largest river by volume of water. Angel Falls, the Andes Mountains, and the Amazon River are three A's to remember!

The Valley of the Moon is an arid region in Chile. Angel Falls (left), in Venezuela, is the world's highest waterfall.

Chapter 18 ■ 665

READING SOCIAL STUDIES

Study Questions Ask students to use these questions as guides for their reading.

1. Why did South American countries develop independently instead of as a union?

2. What problems do many South American nations face?

3. What may be the result of deforestation in South America?

● USE READING AND VOCABULARY TRANSPARENCY 8-9.

8-9 TRANSPARENCY

2 Teach

South America and Its People

Read and Respond

Geography Explain that although part of South America extends north of the equator, it also extends farther south than any other continent except Antarctica. Inform students that this results in vast climatic and ecological differences across the continent.

GO ONLINE Students might be interested in learning more about the countries of South America. Have them visit The Learning Site at **www.harcourtschool.com.**

Visual Learning

Map Ask students to study the map on page 665. Explain that Brazil covers an area of 3,300,171 square miles (8,546,783 sq km), or roughly half the total area of South America.

Q Which nations border Brazil?

A French Guiana, Suriname, Guyana, Venezuela, Colombia, Peru, Bolivia, Paraguay, Uruguay, and Argentina

CAPTION ANSWER: They are landlocked.

BACKGROUND

The Amazon River The Amazon is among the world's longest and most powerful rivers. It runs for about 4,000 miles (6,400 km) from the mountains of Peru to Brazil's Atlantic coast—roughly the distance from New York City to Rome. The Amazon is the world's largest drainage basin, carrying about 20 percent of the world's total water supply.

INTEGRATE SCIENCE

Identify Unique Species Invite students to research the ecosystem of the Amazon River. Encourage them to find information about a particular species of animal or plant that is unique to the Amazon. Ask students to present their findings to the class.

Simón Bolívar

Leadership Discuss with students how the character trait of leadership applied to Simón Bolívar. Ask students how Bolívar's leadership led the countries of South America to gain their independence. *Bolívar's leadership inspired the people of South America to take back their homeland.* Remind students that Bolívar's nickname, *El Libertador,* refers to the effect he had on South America.

Visual Learning

Picture Direct students' attention to the statue of José de San Martín. Inform students that San Martín was a Spanish officer for twenty years before switching his allegiance and leading revolutions against Spanish rule in Argentina, Chile, and Peru.

Old Problems in New Countries

Read and Respond

Civics and Government Inform students that despite the Spanish colonies' close cooperation during the revolutionary period, they did not take Bolívar's advice and become a confederacy. Explain that for reasons of geography and poor communications the countries developed independently. Point out that as a result, many countries were run by dictatorships and that wealth and power were concentrated in the hands of a few people.

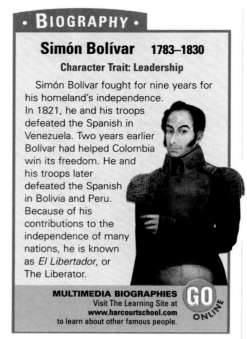

Simón Bolívar   1783–1830

Character Trait: Leadership

Simón Bolívar fought for nine years for his homeland's independence. In 1821, he and his troops defeated the Spanish in Venezuela. Two years earlier Bolívar had helped Colombia win its freedom. He and his troops later defeated the Spanish in Bolivia and Peru. Because of his contributions to the independence of many nations, he is known as *El Libertador,* or The Liberator.

MULTIMEDIA BIOGRAPHIES
Visit The Learning Site at
www.harcourtschool.com
to learn about other famous people.
GO ONLINE

Europeans soon ruled most of the continent.

During the late 1700s and early 1800s, political independence became a goal for many people in South America. They had observed the success of the 13 British colonies in North America in breaking free of British rule and forming the United States. In the early 1800s, colony after colony in South America declared its independence—usually through revolution.

Simón Bolívar (see•MOHN boh•LEE•var) in Venezuela and José de San Martín

666 ▪ Unit 8

(sahn mar•TEEN) in Argentina were key figures in the struggle to **liberate**, or set free, these colonies. By 1828 all of Spain's and Portugal's colonies in South America had become independent. By the mid-1800s most parts of South America had been liberated.

Bolívar hoped for a single nation in South America but knew how unlikely that would be. "[South] America is separated by climatic differences, geographical diversity, conflicting interests, and dissimilar characteristics," he said. Each country developed on its own, often fighting over borders with its neighbors.

REVIEW What was the goal of many people in South America in the early 1800s?
political independence

Old Problems in New Countries

Even after independence, most of the people in South America had little say in government. Wealth was concentrated in the hands of a few landowners, and political matters were in the hands of dictators or armies. The people lacked the education necessary to make changes. They were also unschooled in the ways of self-government.

Various reformers throughout South America began working to solve these problems.

This statue of José de San Martín is in Cordoba, Argentina.

Outlining Invite students to work together and outline on a sheet of paper the problems mentioned on pages 666–668. Have students organize the outlines in two categories, Old Problems and New Problems. Using their outlines as a guide, students should then write paragraphs comparing and contrasting the types of problems facing South America.

Kinesthetic Learners Encourage students to learn the geography of South America by having them draw maps of the continent. Ask students to show countries and key cities, such as capitals, as well as landforms such as mountain ranges and major rivers.

One solution was to redistribute the land so that individuals could own small farms. During the colonial period large haciendas, which were similar to plantations in the southern United States, were common. Since the 1960s, land reform supporters have enjoyed some victories, but many farmers still do not own the land on which they work.

REVIEW What were some problems the newly independent countries shared?

COMPARE AND CONTRAST little experience in democracy, little education, and wealth and land in the hands of a few people

New Problems for All Countries

Many South American countries continue to face the problems of poverty, unemployment, and keeping their democracies. Land use has once again become a major issue. In some places, Indian tribes have protested land development, which

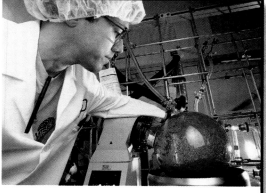
Many scientists are working to solve problems related to the destruction of the rain forests.

they believe disturbs centuries-old patterns of life. These tribes are beginning to take legal measures to regain their ancestral lands.

In addition, many scientists are concerned over the destruction of the rain forests in some areas of South America.

• GEOGRAPHY •

Galápagos Islands

Understanding Places and Regions

Six hundred miles (966 km) west of Ecuador in the Pacific Ocean are the 19 islands called the Galápagos. They were once called the Enchanted Isles, and pirates were known to bury treasure there. Today, the islands are best known for the bird and animal species that are found nowhere else. Among these are 13 species of finches, large lizards, and huge land turtles. The Spanish word for these turtles, *galápagos*, gave the islands their name.

GALÁPAGOS ISLANDS

Isla Pinta
Isla Marchena
Isla Genovesa
Isla Fernandina
Isla San Salvador
Isla Santa Cruz
Isla San Cristóbal
Isla Isabela
Baquerizo Moreno
Isla Santa Maria
Isla Española
PACIFIC OCEAN
0   20   40 Miles
0   20   40 Kilometers

Chapter 18 ▪ 667

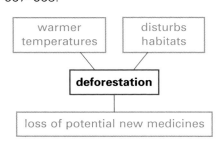

Study Questions Encourage students to supply answers to the study questions.

1. Differences in geography, climate, and people led South American countries to develop independently.

2. They face problems of poverty, unemployment, deforestation, and maintaining stable democracies.

3. Some scientists believe that deforestation can result in a greenhouse effect, or warmer temperatures worldwide.

● USE READING AND VOCABULARY TRANSPARENCY 8-9.

8-9
TRANSPARENCY

Assess

Lesson 3 Review—Answers

 COMPARE AND CONTRAST The climate along the Amazon is tropical, while the climate of southern South America is cold for much of the year.

❶ **BIG IDEA** Simón Bolívar and José de San Martín helped most South American countries fight for independence.

❷ **VOCABULARY** Simón Bolívar helped **liberate** the people of South America from Spanish rule.

❸ **TIME LINE** by 1828

❹ **HISTORY** They were key figures in the struggle to liberate South America from Spanish rule.

❺ **CRITICAL THINKING—Analyze** If farmers own the land, they likely will have an incentive to produce more crops.

 Performance Assessment Guidelines Students' lists should reflect the varied climates and geography.

ACTIVITY BOOK

Use ACTIVITY BOOK, p. 174, to reinforce and extend student learning.

Hikers journey toward the Upsala Glacier in *Los Glaciares* National Park, Argentina. The Upsala Glacier is the largest glacier in South America.

Across South America, rain forests are cleared for their valuable wood or to build new farms, towns, and roads. As the forests are cut down, and burned, carbon dioxide is released into the atmosphere and there are fewer trees to absorb it. Some scientists believe that having more carbon dioxide in the atmosphere leads to warmer temperatures, which scientists term the *greenhouse effect*.

Scientists have begun to explore the use of rain forest plants for medicine. Although less than 1 percent of the plants in the rain forest have been tested for medical benefits, about 25 percent of western medicines come from rain forest plants. Destroying these plants may prevent new medicines from being discovered.

Brazil has worked to slow this **deforestation**, or the widespread cutting down of forests. Not only has the rate of cutting slowed, but lands have been set aside for protection. The Amazon region now has several plant and animal reserves, national parks, and national forests.

REVIEW What kinds of lands have been set aside for protection in the Amazon region? *plant and animal reserves, national parks, and national forests*

LESSON 3 REVIEW

Summary Time Line
1800 — 1900 — PRESENT

• **1828** All of Spain's and Portugal's South American colonies are independent

 COMPARE AND CONTRAST How is the climate of southern South America different from the climate along the Amazon?

❶ **BIG IDEA** How did most countries in South America gain independence?

❷ **VOCABULARY** Use the word **liberate** in a sentence that explains its meaning.

❸ **TIME LINE** When did the last of Spain's and Portugal's South American colonies gain independence?

❹ **HISTORY** Who were Simón Bolívar and José de San Martín?

❺ **CRITICAL THINKING—Analyze** Why might production increase if farmers own small plots of land, rather than having the government own all the land?

 PERFORMANCE—Write a Packing List The climate and geography of parts of South America are very different. Imagine that you will be taking a trip across the continent. Tell where you will visit, and write a packing list of the clothes and supplies you might need there.

EXTEND AND ENRICH

Research Organize students in teams and provide each team with a country to research. Ask each team to research that country's quest for independence and make a time line showing the course of events leading to its independence. Then ask each team to present its time line to the class.

RETEACH THE LESSON

Cloze Sentences Have students complete the following sentences.

1. _____ helped free, or _____, many South American countries in the 1800s. *Simón Bolívar or José de San Martín, liberate*

2. The _____ of South American rain forests may lead to _____ temperatures. *deforestation, warmer*

3. South America is the fourth-largest _____ in the world. *continent*

Canada

Canada's red and white maple leaf flag is a familiar symbol to many Americans. Canada and the United States share one of the longest borders in the world, and about two-thirds of all Canadians live within 100 miles of the United States border. Geography, however, is just one reason why the two nations have such strong ties to each other.

A Varied Landscape

In land area, Canada is the second-largest country in the world. It covers more than 40 percent of North America. Canada, like the United States, stretches from the Atlantic Ocean to the Pacific Ocean, and from a 3,987-mile (6,416-km) southern border shared with the continental United States to islands in the Arctic Ocean. Canada's people may live near mountains, lakes, forests, prairies, or tundra.

A wide variety of climates and landforms can be found in Canada. Cattle graze on fertile prairie land. This glacier (inset) is in northern Alberta.

Chapter 18 ■ 669

· LESSON ·

4

 COMPARE AND CONTRAST

As you read, compare and contrast regions and cultures in Canada.

BIG IDEA

Canada is a land of great variety and has strong ties to the United States.

VOCABULARY

province
separatist

Lesson 4
PAGES 669–673

OBJECTIVES

- Describe the geography of Canada.
- Describe Canada's history, from first settlement to self-government.
- Explain why some citizens want to secede from Canada.
- Identify Canada's role in the world economy.

 Compare and Contrast
pp. 651, 669, 670, 673, 676

Vocabulary

SEE READING AND VOCABULARY TRANSPARENCY 8-10 OR THE WORD CARDS ON PP. V97–V100.

province p. 670   **separatist** p. 672

When Minutes Count

Direct students to examine the illustrations in the lesson. Have them predict what they think the Big Idea of the lesson is. Encourage them to read the lesson to find out if they were correct

Quick Summary

This lesson describes Canada's geography and history and its place in today's world economy.

1 Motivate

Set the Purpose

Big Idea Discuss with students the long history that Canada shares with the United States.

Access Prior Knowledge

Have students review what they learned about European colonization of North America in the 1600s. Why did Europeans come to North America? What did they hope to gain?

REACH ALL LEARNERS

Below-Level Learners
Ask students for words or phrases that they associate with Canada. Write their responses on the board. After students have read the lesson, return to the list to correct or confirm items on it.

WORD WORK

Preview Vocabulary Ask students to preview each vocabulary word and its definition. Then have each student use both words in a sentence. Many citizens of the **province** of Quebec are **separatists** who favor seceding from Canada.

CHAPTER 18 ■ **669**

Summarize Ask students as they read the lesson to use the following chart to summarize characteristics of Canada.

Land	• _____
	• _____
Government	• _____
	• _____
Economy	• _____
	• _____

● USE READING AND VOCABULARY TRANSPARENCY 8-10.

8-10
TRANSPARENCY

2 Teach

A Varied Landscape

Read and Respond

Civics and Government Point out that Canada's first provinces were founded in 1867.

Students might be interested in learning more about the provinces and territories of Canada. Have them visit The Learning Site at **www.harcourtschool.com**.

Culture and Society Inform students that although Canada has the second-largest land area of any country in the world, its population is only as large as California's.

Visual Learning

Map Explain that like the United States, Canada has one national capital. It also has many provincial capitals that are like state capitals in the United States.

Q What is Canada's capital?

A Ottawa

CAPTION ANSWER: Quebec is the largest province and Nunavut is the largest territory.

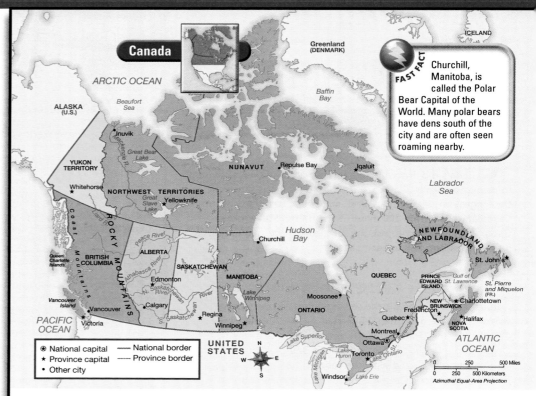

Canada

National capital — National border
★ **Province capital** ---- Province border
• **Other city**

0   250   500 Miles
0   250   500 Kilometers
Azimuthal Equal-Area Projection

Regions This map shows the 10 provinces and 3 territories of Canada.
◆ Which Canadian province is the largest? Which territory is the largest?

Canada is a land of variety. The low Coast Mountains extend along the Pacific coast, while farther inland are the towering Rockies. The Interior Plains cover the central part of Canada. To the northeast is the Canadian Shield, a huge region of poor, rocky soil. Southeast of the Canadian Shield is the St. Lawrence Lowlands. This region has most of Canada's people and industries. The Appalachian Mountains extend into southeastern Canada.

Canada has many rivers and lakes that provide beauty and natural resources for the country. Four of the five Great Lakes help define its southern border.

Canada has 10 provinces and 3 territories. A **province** is a political region similar to a state in the United States. Each province has its own government, and it can take many actions without the approval of the national government.

REVIEW How is western Canada different from central Canada?
◆ COMPARE AND CONTRAST
Western Canada has mountains, while central Canada has plains.

670 ■ Unit 8

Journey to Self-Government

Thousands of years ago, Canada's first settlers entered the region, probably over a land bridge from Asia. Many of the descendants of these early settlers still live in Canada today. They are known as the First Nation peoples.

Canada's flag

The Vikings first explored what is now eastern Canada around A.D. 1000, but other European explorers did not reach Canada until about 500 years later. Both Britain and France wanted to control Canada's vast lands, and each nation sent explorers to claim land. After wars in Europe and North America, France lost its Canadian holdings to Britain. In the Quebec Act of 1774, Britain agreed that French settlers in Canada could keep their own laws, language, and religion.

In 1867 the British Parliament passed the British North American Act. This act, which united all of Canada into one nation, also served as Canada's first constitution. It gave Canada a representative government, but Britain held the final word in Canadian affairs.

In 1931 the British Parliament passed the Statute of Westminister. It allowed Canada to conduct its own foreign affairs, but Canada still remained partly under British rule. Canada also became a partner in the British Commonwealth of Nations, the name given to territories that give allegiance to the British crown.

Canadians wanted more control over their own government and decisions. A new constitution in 1982 permitted constitutional amendments without approval from the British Parliament.

LOCATE IT

Members of the Canadian Senate (inset) meet inside the Parliament Building, in Ottawa.

Journey to Self-Government

Read and Respond

Culture and Society Inform students that the first inhabitants of Canada had developed complex societies well before the first Europeans landed there in the 1200s. Explain that the word *canada* comes from an Iroquois word meaning "village" or "community."

Culture and Society Explain that by the mid-1700s, there were about 1.5 million British colonists living in North America. Ask students to consider ways in which the British influence continues to be felt today in Canada. Most citizens of Canada speak English, and the national government includes features modeled after the British system of government.

Visual Learning

Picture Direct students to the picture of the national flag of Canada on page 671. Point out that the flag, featuring a red maple leaf on a white background, was officially adopted in 1964. Explain that the maple leaf has historically been a Canadian symbol and that red and white have been Canada's official colors since 1921.

New Solutions to Old Problems

Read and Respond

Civics and Government Discuss advantages and disadvantages of becoming an independent country.

POINTS OF VIEW

Should Quebec Secede?

Encourage students to analyze the two viewpoints.

Analyze the Viewpoints— Answers

❶ Marc-Andre Bedard believes that Quebec's identity deserves sovereign standing. Pierre Trudeau believes that Quebec's secession would hurt the confederation of Canada.

❷ Encourage students to ask at least five people for their views on the subject.

A World Partner

Read and Respond

Geography Point out that the St. Lawrence Seaway was the final link in a waterway that extends about 2,340 miles (3,766 km) from Duluth, Minnesota, to the Atlantic Ocean.

3 Close

Summarize Key Content

- Canada's geographical features include mountains, lakes, forests, prairies, and tundra.
- Canada was settled by Europeans hundreds of years ago.
- Some citizens of Quebec hope to preserve their culture by forming their own country.
- Canada has a history of cooperation with the United States.

POINTS OF VIEW

Should Quebec Secede?

Almost since Britain won control of New France in 1763, Quebec has struggled to hold on to its French heritage. Some French Canadians of Quebec have tried to win Quebec's independence from Canada.

MARC-ANDRE BEDARD, a leader of the separatist movement

"Are we a people or are we not? If we are, we should be sovereign. We should be at the table with the international community."

PIERRE TRUDEAU, former Canadian prime minister

"It would be disastrous. . . . It would mean a major setback in the course of history. And the burden would lie with those who would like to break up one of history's greatest achievements—the Canadian federation."

Analyze the Viewpoints

❶ What views does each person hold?

❷ **Make it Relevant** Choose an issue about which the people in your class or community have different views. Find out what people think about the issue.

In Montreal (below), signs such as this one are in both French and English.

672 ■ Unit 8

The constitution also included a Charter of Rights and Freedoms, similar to the United States Bill of Rights. Canada's independence was complete.

Canada's executive branch is still headed by Britain's monarch, who appoints a representative, the governor-general. Daily governmental affairs, however, are handled by the prime minister. He or she is a member of the ruling majority party of the House of Commons. Along with the Senate, the House of Commons makes up the Canadian Parliament.

REVIEW What did the Constitution of 1982 do? It allowed constitutional amendments without approval from Britain and made Canada independent.

New Solutions to Old Problems

For a long time, many Quebec citizens, called **separatists**, have wanted to form a separate country in order to preserve their French culture. In 1998, a vote to secede from Canada failed. The Canadian Supreme Court then ruled that Quebec could not secede unless the rest of Canada agreed.

Like the people of Quebec, the native peoples of Canada want to preserve their culture. In 1999 Nunavut, part of the Northwest Territories, became Canada's third territory. Most of the people who live in Nunavut are Inuit. They plan to govern the territory of Nunavut according to the traditional means of consensus, or the agreement of the community.

REVIEW Why do separatists want to secede from Canada? They wish to preserve their French culture.

BACKGROUND

Canadian Imports and Exports Manufactured goods comprise the bulk of Canada's imports. Important Canadian exports include newsprint, lumber, wheat, machinery, natural gas, and telecommunications equipment.

INTEGRATE MUSIC

Canadian Music Explain to students that Canada has a rich tradition of music. Invite students to find examples of both traditional and modern Canadian music that reflect the country's cultural heritages. Ask students to play recordings or to perform the songs themselves before commenting on the music.

A World Partner

Canada has economic partnerships with many countries, but it has the greatest cooperation with the United States. The United States and Canada are major trading partners. In 1987 the two countries signed a free trade agreement that was a forerunner to NAFTA. Today, more than 80 percent of Canada's exports go to the United States, and Canada gets about 70 percent of its imports from the United States.

One of the greatest examples of cooperation between the two neighbors was the construction of the St. Lawrence Seaway. The St. Lawrence River flows nearly 800 miles (1,287 km) from Lake Ontario to the Atlantic Ocean, but parts of the river are not deep enough for large ships to navigate. The St. Lawrence Seaway also includes the Welland Ship Canal, built between Lake Ontario and Lake Erie to bypass Niagara Falls. Construction of the St. Lawrence Seaway

This photograph shows the first ship to enter the locks of the St. Lawrence Seaway in April of 1959.

was completed in 1959. This allowed large ships to reach the Great Lakes from the Atlantic Ocean.

REVIEW What is one example of cooperation between Canada and the United States?
trade; building the St. Lawrence Seaway

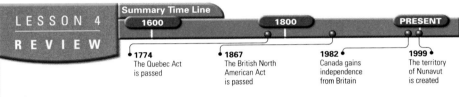

LESSON 4 REVIEW

Summary Time Line

1600		1800		PRESENT

• **1774** The Quebec Act is passed

• **1867** The British North American Act is passed

1982 Canada gains independence from Britain

1999 The territory of Nunavut is created

 COMPARE AND CONTRAST Compare and contrast the residents of Quebec and the residents of Nunavut.

❶ **BIG IDEA** Why does Canada have strong ties to the United States?

❷ **VOCABULARY** What is a **province**?

❸ **TIME LINE** Which occurred first, the Quebec Act or the British North American Act?

❹ **GEOGRAPHY** What are the three main mountain ranges in Canada?

❺ **CRITICAL THINKING—Analyze** Why do you think Canada and the United States cooperated to build the St. Lawrence Seaway?

PERFORMANCE—Draw a Map Use your textbook, library books, and the Internet to draw a map of Canada. Find the location of each of Canada's major landforms, and label them on your map. Also show each of Canada's provinces and territories.

Chapter 18 ■ 673

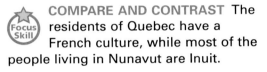

Use a Time Zone Map

VOCABULARY

time zone

OBJECTIVES

- ■ Analyze and interpret a time zone map.
- ■ Compare time in different parts of the United States.

Vocabulary

time zone p. 674

WORD CARDS

See pp. V99–V100.

1 Motivate

Why It Matters

Ask volunteers if they have ever made telephone calls to friends or family members who live in a different region from them. Explain that with these calls, they may have had to take into account a time difference. For example, explain that calls made late in the evening in the West could wake people living in the East where it is several hours later. Emphasize that all parts of a single time zone observe the same time.

➡ **WHY IT MATTERS**

"What time is it?" The answer depends on where you are. That is because people who live in different parts of the world set their clocks at different times.

For centuries people used the sun to determine time. When the sun was at its highest point in the sky, it was noon. However, the sun cannot be at its highest point all around the Earth at the same time. As the Earth rotates, the sun is directly overhead in different places at different times. The sun is past its highest point at places east of where you are, and it has not yet reached its highest point at places west of you.

In the 1800s Charles Dowd of the United States and Sandford Fleming of

Canada developed the idea of dividing the Earth into time zones. A **time zone** is a region in which a single time is used. To figure out the time in a place, you can use a time zone map like the one on page 675.

➡ **WHAT YOU NEED TO KNOW**

Dowd and Fleming divided the Earth into 24 time zones. A new time zone begins every fifteenth meridian, starting at the prime meridian. In each new time zone to the west, the time is one hour earlier than in the time zone before it.

The map on page 675 shows the time zones in the Western Hemisphere. Find Dallas, in the central time zone. Now find New York City. It is in the eastern time zone, which is just east of the central time zone. The time in the central time zone is one hour earlier than the time in the eastern time zone. If it is 5:00 P.M. in the central time zone, it is 6:00 P.M. in the eastern time zone.

➡ **PRACTICE THE SKILL**

Use the time zone map of the Western Hemisphere to answer these questions.

❶ In which time zone is Los Angeles?

❷ If it is 10:00 A.M. in Los Angeles, what time is it in San Antonio?

❸ In which time zone is Puerto Rico?

While the sun sets in Honolua Bay, Hawaii, it is already dark in other places in the United States.

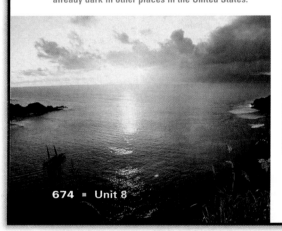

674 ■ Unit 8

MAKE IT RELEVANT

At Home Encourage students to ask their families to help them make lists of cities and towns in other states or countries in which relatives or friends live. Ask students to figure what time it is in these places if it is 6 P.M. in their community.

BACKGROUND

Daylight Saving Time The idea for a daylight saving time was first put forth by Benjamin Franklin, who wrote about it in a 1784 essay. Years later during World War II, several countries, including Australia, Britain, and the United States, adopted summer daylight saving time to conserve fuel for the war effort. Today, we still use this system. On the first Sunday in April, clocks are set ahead one hour so that it gets dark "later" and people can work longer without turning on lights. On the last Sunday in October, clocks are set back to standard time so that it gets light "earlier," and fewer people have to get up in the dark. The saying "Spring forward, fall back" reminds us which way to turn our clocks. Three states—Arizona, Hawaii, and most of Indiana—do not currently use daylight saving time.

Time Zones of the Western Hemisphere

1 P.M.   2 P.M.   3 P.M.   4 P.M.   5 P.M.   6 P.M.   7 P.M.   8 P.M.

GREENLAND

CANADA

NORTH AMERICA

Vancouver

Toronto · Montreal
Chicago · Ottawa
· Detroit · New York City
Philadelphia
UNITED STATES · Washington, D.C.

Los Angeles
· Phoenix · Dallas
San Diego
San Antonio · Houston
MEXICO

International Date Line

Prime Meridian

BAHAMAS   TURKS & CAICOS
CAYMAN   DOMINICAN REPUBLIC
ISLANDS   VIRGIN ISLANDS   ANTIGUA
CUBA   BARBUDA
BELIZE   HAITI   GUADELOUPE
JAMAICA PUERTO   DOMINICA
GUATEMALA   RICO   MARTINIQUE
EL SALVADOR   ARUBA   ST. LUCIA
HONDURAS   NICARAGUA   BARBADOS
COSTA RICA   GRENADA
PANAMA   VENEZUELA TRINIDAD AND TOBAGO
COLOMBIA   GUYANA
ECUADOR   SURINAME
      FRENCH GUIANA

SOUTH AMERICA

PERU   BRAZIL

BOLIVIA

Line Islands

Marquesas Islands 2:30

Society Islands
Cook Islands
(NEW ZEALAND)   Tuamoto Archipelago   Pitcairn Island 3:30   Easter Island (CHILE)

CHILE   PARAGUAY

URUGUAY

ARGENTINA

Falkland Islands   South Georgia

N   W E   S

0   750   1,500 Miles
0   750 1,500 Kilometers
Miller Projection

Legend:
- Hawaii-Aleutian time zone
- Alaska time zone
- Pacific time zone
- Mountain time zone
- Central time zone
- Eastern time zone
- Atlantic time zone
- Greenland time zone
- Non-standard time zone
- Area not in the Western Hemisphere

❹ If it is 3:00 P.M. in Puerto Rico, what time is it in Philadelphia? in Houston?

❺ If it is 6:00 A.M. in San Diego, what time is it in Toronto?

❻ Imagine that you are in Honduras. Is the time earlier than, later than, or the same as in Chicago?

▶ **APPLY WHAT YOU LEARNED**

Record the current time where you live. Now figure out the time in Montreal, Canada; Vancouver, Canada; Venezuela; and Argentina. Explain why it might be useful to know the time in different places.

Practice your map and globe skills with the **GeoSkills CD-ROM.**

Chapter 18 ■ 675

MAP AND GLOBE SKILLS

2 Teach

What You Need to Know

Encourage students to examine the time zones on page 675. Ask them why Charles Dowd and Sandford Fleming decided to organize time zones.

Practice the Skill—Answers

❶ the Pacific Time Zone

❷ 12:00 P.M.

❸ the Atlantic Time Zone

❹ 2 P.M.; 1 P.M.

❺ 9 A.M.

❻ the same

3 Close

Apply What You Learned

Students' answers will vary depending on their location. Check to make sure students are correctly figuring time by subtracting when moving east to west and adding when moving west to east.

ACTIVITY BOOK

Use ACTIVITY BOOK, pp. 176–177, to give students additional practice using this skill.

TRANSPARENCY

Use SKILL TRANSPARENCY 8-4.

CD-ROM

Explore GEOSKILLS CD-ROM to learn more about map and globe skills.

EXTEND AND ENRICH

Determine Time in the Eastern Hemisphere Encourage students to locate a time zone map of the Eastern Hemisphere and use it to find time in cities such as Moscow; Beijing; Sydney, Australia; and Calcutta, India. Advise students to work their way east on the map to find the times.

RETEACH THE SKILL

Reset Clocks Have students imagine that they are traveling by car from Los Angeles. Ask students whether they should reset their clocks when they arrive at each of the following cities.

Phoenix yes	Chicago yes
San Antonio yes	Detroit yes
Dallas yes	Philadelphia yes

Ask students whether they would be resetting their watches ahead or back as they travel across the country. ahead

COMPARE AND CONTRAST

Students may use the graphic organizer that appears on page 178 of the Activity Book. Answers appear in the Activity Book, Teacher's Edition.

Think & Write

Write a Postcard Students' postcards should display accurate references to the diversity of South America's land, resources, climate, and people. They may wish to depict the lowlands of the tropics or the snowcapped mountains of the Andes.

Write a Wise Saying Students' sayings should display their understanding of the benefits that can be derived from maintaining peaceful and supportive relationships with our neighbors. They may wish to reference the economic benefits offered through trade relations or the mutual protection that can be derived through alliances.

ACTIVITY BOOK

A copy of the graphic organizer appears in the ACTIVITY BOOK on page 178.

TRANSPARENCY

The graphic organizer appears on READING AND VOCABULARY TRANSPARENCY 8-11.

 Compare and Contrast

Copy the following graphic organizer onto a separate sheet of paper. Use the information you have learned to compare and contrast the United States, Canada, and Mexico.

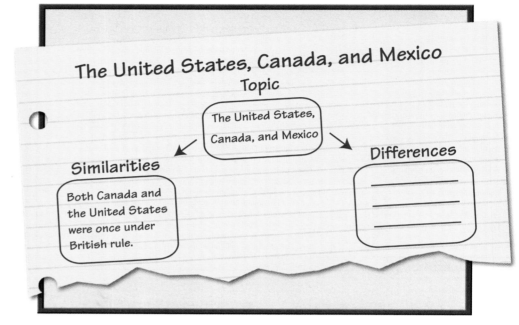

The United States, Canada, and Mexico
Topic

The United States, Canada, and Mexico

Similarities

Both Canada and the United States were once under British rule.

Differences

 THINK & WRITE

Write a Postcard Imagine you are traveling through South America on a family vacation. Write a postcard to a friend describing the natural wonders you have seen. Be sure to mention where these places are located.

Write a Wise Saying Having a good relationship with one's neighbors is important for both people and nations. Write a wise saying about the importance of the United States maintaining good relations with its neighbors.

676 ▪ Chapter 18

TEST PREPARATION

Review these tips with students:

- Read the directions before reading the questions.
- Read each question twice, focusing the second time on all the possible answers.
- Take the time to think about all the possible answers before deciding on an answer.
- Move past questions that give you trouble, and answer the ones you know. Then return to the difficult items.

UNIT PROJECT

Progress Check Encourage students to complete their charts. Then have them select what they would like to show or make for their cultural fair.

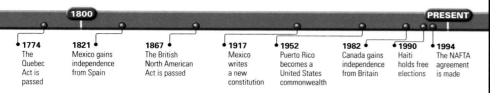

1800 | PRESENT

1774 The Quebec Act is passed

1821 Mexico gains independence from Spain

1867 The British North American Act is passed

1917 Mexico writes a new constitution

1952 Puerto Rico becomes a United States commonwealth

1982 Canada gains independence from Britain

1990 Haiti holds free elections

1994 The NAFTA agreement is made

USE VOCABULARY

Identify the term that correctly matches each definition.

middle class (p. 656)

interest rate (p. 656)

free election (p. 661)

province (p. 670)

❶ the amount that banks charge to loan money

❷ a political region

❸ people who are economically between the rich and the poor

❹ a political race that offers a choice of candidates

RECALL FACTS

Answer these questions.

❺ Why are *Fiestas Patrias* important for many Mexican Americans?

❻ How is the province of Nunavut different from other Canadian provinces?

Write the letter of the best choice.

❼ The purpose of NAFTA is to—
A protect French Canadian culture.
B continue an embargo on exports from Cuba.
C increase trade among the United States, Canada, and Mexico.
D bring democracy to all the nations of Central America and the Caribbean.

❽ Benito Juárez was the first Native American president of—
F Mexico.
G Bolivia.
H El Salvador.
J Costa Rica.

❾ Which of the following Canadian provinces has stated a wish to secede?
A Alberta
B New Brunswick
C Quebec
D British Columbia

THINK CRITICALLY

❿ Why is immigration such an important issue for the United States and Mexico?

⓫ Why do you think some Latin American countries have had difficulty forming stable governments?

⓬ What might happen if Quebec decides to secede from Canada?

APPLY SKILLS

Read Population Pyramids
Review the population pyramid on page 663. Then answer the following questions.

⓭ What age group makes up the smallest part of the population?

⓮ In which age groups are there more males than females?

Use a Time Zone Map
Find the Bahamas on the time zone map on page 675. Then answer the following questions.

⓯ If it is 9:00 A.M. in the Bahamas, what time is it in Dallas?

⓰ If it is 12:00 P.M. in the Bahamas, what time is it in Vancouver?

Chapter 18 ■ 677

Apply Skills

Read Population Pyramids
⓭ 75–79
⓮ under 5, 5–9, 10–14, 15–19, 20–24, 25–29

Use a Time Zone Map
⓯ 8:00 A.M.
⓰ 9:00 A.M.

ACTIVITY BOOK

Use the CHAPTER 18 TEST PREPARATION on page 179 of the Activity Book.

ASSESSMENT

Use the CHAPTER 18 TEST on pages 139–142 of the Assessment Program.

Use Vocabulary
❶ interest rate (p. 656)
❷ province (p. 670)
❸ middle class (p. 656)
❹ free election (p. 661)

Recall Facts
❺ It honors their victory over the French in 1862 and their national independence. (p. 654)
❻ Most of the population is Inuit, and they plan to govern themselves in the traditional way. (p. 672)

❼ C (p. 673)
❽ F (p. 654)
❾ C (p. 672)

Think Critically
❿ It has a large impact on each country's economy and culture.
⓫ Students may observe that people continue to fight for control of some of the countries, and the people cannot elect leaders.
⓬ People may fight to keep Quebec a part of Canada.

Washington, D.C.

PAGES 678–679

OBJECTIVES

- Locate major centers of government in the United States.
- Use visual material to learn about the history of the United States.

Summary

Washington, D.C., home of the national government, has many museums, memorials, and buildings that honor the history of the United States.

1 Motivate

Get Ready

Point out that Washington, D.C., is not part of any state. It was established to house the federal government. Many people visit Washington, D.C., every year to see its many monuments and memorials. Ask whether any students have visited Washington, D.C. Encourage them to share their experiences with the class.

2 Teach

What to See

Direct students to the photographs of sites in Washington, D.C. Ask students the following questions:

- *Which sites shown in the photographs house part of the government?*
- *Where can you learn about the history of space travel?*
- *What other kinds of items might be on display at the National Archives?*

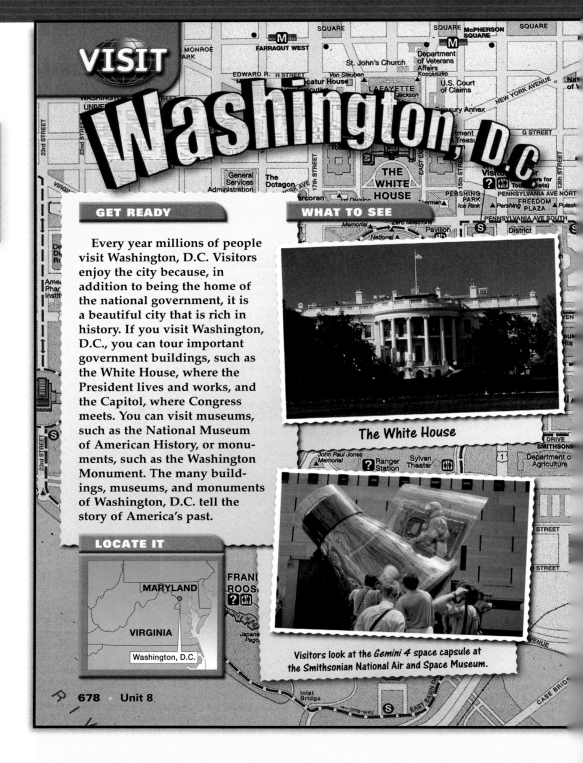

VISIT Washington, D.C

GET READY

WHAT TO SEE

Every year millions of people visit Washington, D.C. Visitors enjoy the city because, in addition to being the home of the national government, it is a beautiful city that is rich in history. If you visit Washington, D.C., you can tour important government buildings, such as the White House, where the President lives and works, and the Capitol, where Congress meets. You can visit museums, such as the National Museum of American History, or monuments, such as the Washington Monument. The many buildings, museums, and monuments of Washington, D.C. tell the story of America's past.

LOCATE IT

MARYLAND

VIRGINIA

Washington, D.C.

The White House

Visitors look at the *Gemini 4* space capsule at the Smithsonian National Air and Space Museum.

678 • Unit 8

MAKE IT RELEVANT

In Your Community Ask students to identify a memorial or monument in their community. Have them write short reports on the memorial or monument, including when it was built and whom or what it honors. Invite volunteers to read their reports to the class.

REACH ALL LEARNERS

English as a Second Language Pair students who are acquiring English with English-speaking classmates. Have partners study the feature together. Tell partners to discuss the reading and summarize the information in their own words.

The Capitol

The Washington Monument

The Declaration of Independence is displayed at the National Archives.

The United States Botanic Garden has more than 10,000 varieties of plants.

TAKE A FIELD TRIP

GO ONLINE **A VIRTUAL TOUR** Visit The Learning Site at www.harcourtschool.com to take virtual tours of places of interest in the United States.

CNN Turner Le@rning **A VIDEO TOUR** Check your media center or classroom library for a videotape tour of Washington, D.C.

Unit 8 679

3 Close

Take a Field Trip

Direct students to research one memorial or museum that can be found in Washington, D.C. Students may want to learn more about the Washington or Lincoln memorials, the Smithsonian, or the Capitol building.

A Virtual Tour Depending on the availability of computers, suggest that students work individually, in pairs, or in small groups to view the virtual tour. Encourage them to research monuments throughout the United States as they explore the Web sites. Students may use what they learn on their virtual tours as background information for the Unit Project.

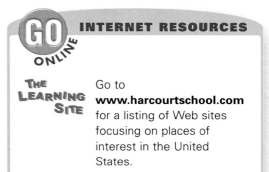

GO ONLINE **INTERNET RESOURCES**

THE LEARNING SITE

Go to **www.harcourtschool.com** for a listing of Web sites focusing on places of interest in the United States.

A Video Tour Ask students to jot down three questions that can be answered by the CNN video tour of Washington, D.C., as they are watching it. Then have students exchange questions with a partner. Partners should answer each other's questions. Ask students to make sure that their partners arrived at the correct answers.

VIDEO

Use the CNN/Turner Learning TAKE A FIELD TRIP videotape of Washington, D.C.

BACKGROUND

The Washington Monument
This monument, honoring George Washington, is the tallest structure in Washington, D.C. It stands 555 feet $5\frac{1}{2}$ inches tall (about 169 m). People can travel by elevator from the lobby to the observation deck, 500 feet up (152 m). The walls in the lobby are 15 feet (5 m) thick. The thickness of the walls decreases as you go up and the walls are only 18 inches (46 cm) thick at the observation level.

EXTEND AND ENRICH

Make a Brochure Challenge students to create travel brochures for Washington, D.C. Tell them to include at least four major sites in their brochures. Encourage them to be creative and to share their brochures with their classmates.

Unit 8 Review and Test Preparation

PAGES 680–682

Visual Summary

Students' newspaper headlines should clearly describe the pictures.

- **The United States is home to people from all over the world** Because people of many different cultures have come to live in the United States, it is a diverse nation.

- **Today more Americans work in service jobs than in any other kinds of jobs** About one-third of all workers in the United States have jobs in the service industry.

- **Mexico City is one of the largest metropolitan areas in the world** More than half of Mexico's population lives in or near Mexico City.

- **Jean-Bertrand Aristide becomes Haiti's president** In 1990 Aristide was elected.

- **Simón Bolívar helps win independence for many present-day Latin American countries** Bolívar is known as *El Libertador*.

- **The St. Lawrence Seaway allows ships to travel from the Atlantic Ocean to the Great Lakes** The Seaway was built by people in the United States and Canada.

Use Vocabulary

1. rapid-transit system
2. register
3. Sun Belt
4. embargo

·UNIT·

8 Review and Test Preparation

VISUAL SUMMARY

Write a Newspaper Headline Study the pictures and captions below to help you review Unit 8. Then choose one of the pictures. Write a newspaper headline that goes along with the picture you have chosen.

USE VOCABULARY

Use a term from this list to complete each of the sentences that follow.

| Sun Belt (p. 621) |
| rapid-transit system (p. 629) |
| register (p. 641) |
| embargo (p. 660) |

1. A ____ moves passengers on an underground train.

2. Before a citizen can vote, that person must ____.

3. Much of the recent growth in the United States has taken place in the ____.

4. An ____ occurs when one nation refuses to trade goods with another.

RECALL FACTS

Answer these questions.

5. How has the Information Age affected science?

6. How has NAFTA affected trade between the United States, Canada, and Mexico?

Write the letter of the best choice.

7. The fastest-growing ethnic group in the United States today is—
   A Hispanic Americans.
   B African Americans.
   C Asian Americans.
   D Irish Americans.

8. About one-third of all American workers have jobs in the—
   F federal government.
   G banking, insurance, and real estate industry.
   H service industry.
   J medical profession.

Visual Summary

The United States is home to people from all over the world. p. 620

Today more Americans work in service jobs than in any other kinds of jobs. p. 633

Mexico City is one of the largest metropolitan areas in the world. p. 655

680

Recall Facts

5. It has greatly increased knowledge about the human body. (p. 633)

6. It has increased the number of goods and services available to people in all three nations. (p. 636)

7. A (p. 622)

8. H (p. 633)

Think Critically

9. Students may suggest that it makes their opinion heard or that it helps leaders know which party's policies are backed by the most citizens, helping them to better serve the nation's needs.

10. Students may observe that the Mexican people may have been ready for a change and they wanted to find out how another party would improve life in Mexico.

11. Students' answers will vary.

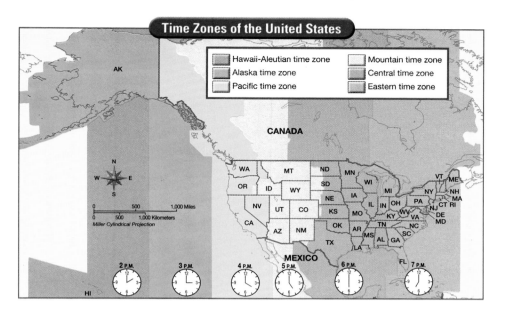

Time Zones of the United States

Hawaii-Aleutian time zone	Mountain time zone
Alaska time zone	Central time zone
Pacific time zone	Eastern time zone

CANADA

WA MT ND MN WI MI VT ME
OR ID WY SD NY NH MA
NV UT CO NE IA IL IN OH PA CT RI
CA AZ NM KS MO KY WV VA NJ DE MD
OK AR TN NC
TX MS AL GA SC
LA FL

MEXICO

2 P.M. 3 P.M. 4 P.M. 5 P.M. 6 P.M. 7 P.M.

HI

THINK CRITICALLY

9 Why is voting an important part of a citizen's responsibility?

10 Why do you think the Mexican people chose to elect Vicente Fox as president in 2000?

11 What might happen if Quebec decides to secede from Canada?

APPLY SKILLS

Use a Time Zone Map
Use the map to answer the following questions.

MAP AND GLOBE SKILLS

12 What is the time difference between New Jersey and New Mexico?

13 What is the time difference between Oklahoma and Montana?

Jean-Bertrand Aristide becomes Haiti's president. p. 661

Simón Bolívar helps win independence for many present-day Latin American countries. p. 666

The St. Lawrence Seaway allows ships to travel from the Atlantic Ocean to the Great Lakes. p. 673

681

Apply Skills

Use a Time Zone Map

12 two hours

13 one hour

TEST PREPARATION

Review these tips with students:

- Read the directions before reading the questions.

- Read each question twice, focusing the second time on all the possible answers.

- Take the time to think about all the possible answers before deciding on an answer.

- Move past questions that give you trouble, and answer the ones you know. Then return to the difficult items.

ASSESSMENT

Use the UNIT 8 TEST on pages 143–151 of the Assessment Program.

Unit Activities

Make a Mural

Assign each group one of the following monuments: the Washington Monument, the Lincoln Memorial, the Statue of Liberty, or Mount Rushmore. Explain that their mural should include a label as well as a description of the features of their assigned monument.

 Performance Assessment Guidelines Look for evidence that students understand their monument's features and its historic significance and that they have clearly and creatively communicated them through their mural.

Prepare a Newscast

Suggest that students use material presented in this unit in their newscasts. They may also wish to enhance the information provided in the text by performing outside research in newspapers and other periodicals.

 Performance Assessment Guidelines Make sure that students have based their newscasts on facts they read about in this unit or in current periodicals that they have used in their research.

Complete the Unit Project

Suggest that each group make a contribution to the cultural fair. Students may wish to invite students from other classes to attend.

 Performance Assessment Guidelines Check to make sure that students have selected symbols, colors, foods, and traditions from their selected cultures.

Unit Activities

GO ONLINE Visit The Learning Site at www.harcourtschool.com for additional activities.

 Make a Mural

Work with a group of your classmates to create a mural of famous United States monuments. First, decide which monuments you want to show on your mural. Some examples include the Washington Monument, the Lincoln Memorial, the Statue of Liberty, and Mount Rushmore. After choosing the monuments you wish to show, draw or paint them on a posterboard. Remember to label each monument. Finally, display your mural with those of your classmates.

 Prepare a Newscast

Work in a group to prepare a newscast on a meeting between the President of the United States and a leader of a Western Hemisphere nation. Each member of your group should have a job, such as researcher, writer, reporter, or anchorperson. When planning your newscast, include information about the other nation and its relationship with the United States. When you are finished, present your newscast to your class.

682 ■ Unit 8

VISIT YOUR LIBRARY

- *My Mexico— México Mío* by Tony Johnston. G. P. Putnam's Sons.

- *Angel Falls: A South American Journey* by Martin and Tanis Jordan. Kingfisher.

- *Journey Through the Northern Rainforest* by Karen Pandell. Penguin Putnam Books for Young Readers.

COMPLETE THE UNIT PROJECT

A Cultural Fair Work with a group of your classmates to finish the unit project—presenting a cultural fair. Look over your notes describing the different cultures discussed in this unit. Use these notes to decide what to include in your cultural fair. Your fair may feature posters representing different art forms or styles of dress. You may also wish to feature different kinds of foods or music. Finally, hold your cultural fair.

Visit Your Library

Encourage independent reading after students' study of the issues and challenges facing the United States today with these books or books of your choice. Additional books are listed on the Multimedia Resources, on page 611D of this Teacher's Edition.

Easy *My Mexico-México mío* by Tony Johnston. G. P. Putnam's Sons, 1996. This book offers poems about Mexico in both English and Spanish.

Average *Angel Falls: A South American Journey* by Martin and Tanis Jordan. Kingfisher, 1995. This story explores the wonder of the rainforest.

Challenging *Journey Through the Northern Rainforest* by Karen Pandell. Penguin Putnam Books for Young Readers, 1999. In this book students will read about the changes taking place in the rainforest.

For Your Reference

Almanac

Facts About the States

State Flag	State	Year of Statehood	Population*	Area (sq. mi.)	Capital	Origin of State Name
	Alabama	1819	4,486,508	50,750	Montgomery	Choctaw, *alba ayamule*, "one who clears land and gathers food from it"
	Alaska	1959	643,786	570,374	Juneau	Aleut, *alayeska*, "great land"
	Arizona	1912	5,456,453	113,642	Phoenix	Papago, *arizonac*, "place of the small spring"
	Arkansas	1836	2,710,079	52,075	Little Rock	Quapaw, "the downstream people"
	California	1850	35,116,033	155,973	Sacramento	Spanish, a fictional island
	Colorado	1876	4,506,542	103,730	Denver	Spanish, "red land" or "red earth"
	Connecticut	1788	3,460,503	4,845	Hartford	Mohican, *quinnitukqut*, "at the long tidal river"
	Delaware	1787	807,385	1,955	Dover	Named for Lord de la Warr
	Florida	1845	16,713,149	54,153	Tallahassee	Spanish, "filled with flowers"
	Georgia	1788	8,560,310	57,919	Atlanta	Named for King George II of England
	Hawaii	1959	1,244,898	6,450	Honolulu	Polynesian, *hawaiki* or *owykee*, "homeland"
	Idaho	1890	1,341,131	82,751	Boise	Invented name with unknown meaning

State Flag	State	Year of Statehood	Population*	Area (sq. mi.)	Capital	Origin of State Name
	Illinois	1818	12,600,620	55,593	Springfield	Algonquin, *iliniwek*, "men" or "warriors"
	Indiana	1816	6,159,068	35,870	Indianapolis	*Indian + a*, "land of the Indians"
	Iowa	1846	2,936,760	55,875	Des Moines	Dakota, *ayuba*, "beautiful land"
	Kansas	1861	2,715,884	81,823	Topeka	Sioux, "land of the south wind people"
	Kentucky	1792	4,092,891	39,732	Frankfort	Iroquoian, *ken-tah-ten*, "land of tomorrow"
	Louisiana	1812	4,482,646	43,566	Baton Rouge	Named for King Louis XIV of France
	Maine	1820	1,294,464	30,865	Augusta	Named after a French province
	Maryland	1788	5,458,137	9,775	Annapolis	Named for Henrietta Maria, Queen Consort of Charles I of England
	Massachusetts	1788	6,427,801	7,838	Boston	Massachusett tribe of Native Americans, "at the big hill" or "place of the big hill"
	Michigan	1837	10,050,446	56,809	Lansing	Ojibwa, "large lake"
	Minnesota	1858	5,019,720	79,617	St. Paul	Dakota Sioux, "sky-blue water"
	Mississippi	1817	2,871,782	46,914	Jackson	Indian word meaning "great waters" or "father of waters"
	Missouri	1821	5,672,579	68,898	Jefferson City	Named after the Missouri Indian tribe. *Missouri* means "town of the large canoes."

* latest available population figures

Almanac ▪ R3

State Flag	State	Year of Statehood	Population*	Area (sq. mi.)	Capital	Origin of State Name
	Montana	1889	909,453	145,566	Helena	Spanish, "mountainous"
	Nebraska	1867	1,729,180	76,878	Lincoln	From an Oto Indian word meaning "flat water"
	Nevada	1864	2,173,491	109,806	Carson City	Spanish, "snowy" or "snowed upon"
	New Hampshire	1788	1,275,056	8,969	Concord	Named for Hampshire County, England
	New Jersey	1787	8,590,300	7,419	Trenton	Named for the Isle of Jersey
	New Mexico	1912	1,855,059	121,365	Santa Fe	Named by Spanish explorers from Mexico
	New York	1788	19,157,532	47,224	Albany	Named after the Duke of York
	North Carolina	1789	8,320,146	48,718	Raleigh	Named after King Charles II of England
	North Dakota	1889	634,110	70,704	Bismarck	Sioux, *dakota*, "friend" or "ally"
	Ohio	1803	11,421,267	40,953	Columbus	Iroquois, *oheo*, "great water"
	Oklahoma	1907	3,493,714	68,679	Oklahoma City	Choctaw, "red people"
	Oregon	1859	3,521,515	96,003	Salem	Unknown; generally accepted that it was taken from the writings of Maj. Robert Rogers, an English army officer
	Pennsylvania	1787	12,335,091	44,820	Harrisburg	*Penn + sylvania*, meaning "Penn's woods"

State Flag	State	Year of Statehood	Population*	Area (sq. mi.)	Capital	Origin of State Name
	Rhode Island	1790	1,069,725	1,045	Providence	From the Greek island of Rhodes
	South Carolina	1788	4,107,183	30,111	Columbia	Named after King Charles II of England
	South Dakota	1889	761,063	75,898	Pierre	Sioux, *dakota*, "friend" or "ally"
	Tennessee	1796	5,797,289	41,220	Nashville	Name of a Cherokee village
	Texas	1845	21,779,893	261,914	Austin	Native American, *tejas*, "friend" or "ally"
	Utah	1896	2,316,256	82,168	Salt Lake City	From the Ute tribe, meaning "people of the mountains"
	Vermont	1791	616,592	9,249	Montpelier	French, *vert*, "green," and *mont*, "mountain"
	Virginia	1788	7,293,542	39,598	Richmond	Named after Queen Elizabeth I of England
	Washington	1889	6,068,996	66,582	Olympia	Named for George Washington
	West Virginia	1863	1,801,873	24,087	Charleston	From the English-named state of Virginia
	Wisconsin	1848	5,441,196	54,314	Madison	Possibly Algonquian, "the place where we live"
	Wyoming	1890	498,703	97,105	Cheyenne	From Delaware Indian word meaning "land of vast plains"
	District of Columbia		570,898	67		Named after Christopher Columbus

* latest available population figures

Almanac

Facts About the Western Hemisphere

Country	Population*	Area (sq. mi.)	Capital	Origin of Country Name
North America				
Antigua and Barbuda	67,897	171	St. Johns	Named for the Church of Santa María la Antigua in Seville, Spain
Bahamas	297,477	5,382	Nassau	Spanish, *bajamar*, "shallow water"
Barbados	277,264	166	Bridgetown	Means "bearded"—probably referring to the beard like vines early explorers found on its trees
Belize	266,440	8,867	Belmopan	Mayan, "muddy water"
Canada	32,207,113	3,851,788	Ottawa	Huron-Iroquois, *kanata*, "village" or "community"
Costa Rica	3,896,092	19,730	San José	Spanish, "rich coast"
Cuba	11,263,429	42,803	Havana	Origin unknown
Dominica	69,655	291	Roseau	Latin, *dies dominica*, "Day of the Lord"
Dominican Republic	8,715,602	18,815	Santo Domingo	Named after the capital city
El Salvador	6,470,379	8,124	San Salvador	Spanish, "the Savior"
Grenada	89,258	133	St. George's	Origin unknown
Guatemala	13,309,384	42,042	Guatemala City	Indian, "land of trees"
Haiti	7,527,817	10,714	Port-au-Prince	Indian, "land of mountains"
Honduras	6,669,789	43,278	Tegucigalpa	Spanish, "profundities" —probably referring to the depth of offshore waters
Jamaica	2,695,867	4,244	Kingston	Arawak, *xamayca*, "land of wood and water"
Mexico	104,907,991	761,602	Mexico City	Aztec, *mexliapan*, "lake of the moon"
Nicaragua	5,128,517	49,998	Managua	from *Nicarao*, the name of an Indian chief

Country	Population*	Area (sq. mi.)	Capital	Origin of Country Name
Panama	2,960,784	30,193	Panama City	From an Indian village's name
Saint Kitts and Nevis	38,763	101	Basseterre	Named by Christopher Columbus—Kitts for St. Christopher, a Catholic saint; Nevis, for a cloud-topped peak that looked like *las nieves*, "the snows"
Saint Lucia	162,157	239	Castries	Named by Christopher Columbus for a Catholic saint
Saint Vincent and the Grenadines	116,812	150	Kingstown	May have been named by Christopher Columbus for a Catholic saint
Trinidad and Tobago	1,104,209	1,980	Port-of-Spain	Trinidad, from the Spanish word for "trinity"; Tobago, named for tobacco because the island has the shape of a person smoking a pipe
United States of America	290,342,554	3,794,083	Washington, D.C.	Named after the explorer Amerigo Vespucci

South America

Country	Population*	Area (sq. mi.)	Capital	Origin of Country Name
Argentina	38,740,807	1,068,296	Buenos Aires	Latin, *argentum*, "silver"
Bolivia	8,586,443	424,162	La Paz/Sucre	Named after Simón Bolívar, the famed liberator
Brazil	182,032,604	3,286,470	Brasília	Named after a native tree that the Portuguese called "bresel wood"
Chile	15,665,216	292,258	Santiago	Indian, *chilli*, "where the land ends"
Colombia	41,662,073	439,733	Bogotá	Named after Christopher Columbus
Ecuador	13,710,234	109,483	Quito	From the Spanish word for *equator*, referring to the country's location
Guyana	702,100	83,000	Georgetown	Indian, "land of waters"
Paraguay	6,036,900	157,046	Asunción	Named after the Paraguay River, which flows through it
Peru	28,409,897	496,223	Lima	Quechua, "land of abundance"
Suriname	435,449	63,039	Paramaribo	From an Indian word, *surinen*
Uruguay	3,413,329	68,039	Montevideo	Named after the Uruguay River, which flows through it
Venezuela	24,654,694	352,143	Caracas	Spanish, "Little Venice"

* latest available population figures

Almanac

Facts About the Presidents

1 George Washington

1732–1799
Birthplace:
Westmoreland County, VA
Home State: *VA*
Political Party: *None*
Age at Inauguration: *57*
Served: *1789–1797*
Vice President:
John Adams

2 John Adams

1735–1826
Birthplace: *Braintree, MA*
Home State: *MA*
Political Party: *Federalist*
Age at Inauguration: *61*
Served: *1797–1801*
Vice President:
Thomas Jefferson

3 Thomas Jefferson

1743–1826
Birthplace:
Albemarle County, VA
Home State: *VA*
Political Party:
Democratic-Republican
Age at Inauguration: *57*
Served: *1801–1809*
Vice Presidents:
Aaron Burr,
George Clinton

4 James Madison

1751–1836
Birthplace:
Port Conway, VA
Home State: *VA*
Political Party:
Democratic-Republican
Age at Inauguration: *57*
Served: *1809–1817*
Vice Presidents:
George Clinton,
Elbridge Gerry

5 James Monroe

1758–1831
Birthplace:
Westmoreland County, VA
Home State: *VA*
Political Party:
Democratic-Republican
Age at Inauguration: *58*
Served: *1817–1825*
Vice President:
Daniel D. Tompkins

6 John Quincy Adams

1767–1848
Birthplace: *Braintree, MA*
Home State: *MA*
Political Party:
Democratic-Republican
Age at Inauguration: *57*
Served: *1825–1829*
Vice President:
John C. Calhoun

7 Andrew Jackson

1767–1845
Birthplace:
Waxhaw settlement, SC
Home State: *TN*
Political Party:
Democratic
Age at Inauguration: *61*
Served: *1829–1837*
Vice Presidents:
John C. Calhoun,
Martin Van Buren

8 Martin Van Buren

1782–1862
Birthplace: *Kinderhook,*
NY
Home State: *NY*
Political Party:
Democratic
Age at Inauguration: *54*
Served: *1837–1841*
Vice President:
Richard M. Johnson

9 William H. Harrison

1773–1841
Birthplace: *Berkeley, VA*
Home State: *OH*
Political Party: *Whig*
Age at Inauguration: *68*
Served: *1841*
Vice President:
John Tyler

10 John Tyler

1790–1862
Birthplace: *Greenway, VA*
Home State: *VA*
Political Party: *Whig*
Age at Inauguration: *51*
Served: *1841–1845*
Vice President: *none*

11 James K. Polk

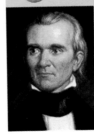

1795–1849
Birthplace:
near Pineville, NC
Home State: *TN*
Political Party:
Democratic
Age at Inauguration: *49*
Served: *1845–1849*
Vice President:
George M. Dallas

12 Zachary Taylor

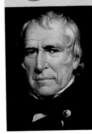

1784–1850
Birthplace:
Orange County, VA
Home State: *LA*
Political Party: *Whig*
Age at Inauguration: *64*
Served: *1849–1850*
Vice President:
Millard Fillmore

13 Millard Fillmore

1800–1874
Birthplace: *Locke, NY*
Home State: *NY*
Political Party: *Whig*
Age at Inauguration: *50*
Served: *1850–1853*
Vice President: *none*

Home State refers to the state of residence when elected.

14 Franklin Pierce

1804–1869
Birthplace: *Hillsboro, NH*
Home State: *NH*
Political Party: *Democratic*
Age at Inauguration: *48*
Served: *1853–1857*
Vice President: *William R. King*

15 James Buchanan

1791–1868
Birthplace: *near Mercersburg, PA*
Home State: *PA*
Political Party: *Democratic*
Age at Inauguration: *65*
Served: *1857–1861*
Vice President: *John C. Breckinridge*

16 Abraham Lincoln

1809–1865
Birthplace: *near Hodgenville, KY*
Home State: *IL*
Political Party: *Republican*
Age at Inauguration: *52*
Served: *1861–1865*
Vice Presidents: *Hannibal Hamlin, Andrew Johnson*

17 Andrew Johnson

1808–1875
Birthplace: *Raleigh, NC*
Home State: *TN*
Political Party: *National Union*
Age at Inauguration: *56*
Served: *1865–1869*
Vice President: *none*

18 Ulysses S. Grant

1822–1885
Birthplace: *Point Pleasant, OH*
Home State: *IL*
Political Party: *Republican*
Age at Inauguration: *46*
Served: *1869–1877*
Vice Presidents: *Schuyler Colfax, Henry Wilson*

19 Rutherford B. Hayes

1822–1893
Birthplace: *near Delaware, OH*
Home State: *OH*
Political Party: *Republican*
Age at Inauguration: *54*
Served: *1877–1881*
Vice President: *William A. Wheeler*

20 James A. Garfield

1831–1881
Birthplace: *Orange, OH*
Home State: *OH*
Political Party: *Republican*
Age at Inauguration: *49*
Served: *1881*
Vice President: *Chester A. Arthur*

21 Chester A. Arthur

1829–1886
Birthplace: *Fairfield, VT*
Home State: *NY*
Political Party: *Republican*
Age at Inauguration: *51*
Served: *1881–1885*
Vice President: *none*

22 Grover Cleveland

1837–1908
Birthplace: *Caldwell, NJ*
Home State: *NY*
Political Party: *Democratic*
Age at Inauguration: *47*
Served: *1885–1889*
Vice President: *Thomas A. Hendricks*

23 Benjamin Harrison

1833–1901
Birthplace: *North Bend, OH*
Home State: *IN*
Political Party: *Republican*
Age at Inauguration: *55*
Served: *1889–1893*
Vice President: *Levi P. Morton*

24 Grover Cleveland

1837–1908
Birthplace: *Caldwell, NJ*
Home State: *NY*
Political Party: *Democratic*
Age at Inauguration: *55*
Served: *1893–1897*
Vice President: *Adlai E. Stevenson*

25 William McKinley

1843–1901
Birthplace: *Niles, OH*
Home State: *OH*
Political Party: *Republican*
Age at Inauguration: *54*
Served: *1897–1901*
Vice Presidents: *Garret A. Hobart, Theodore Roosevelt*

26 Theodore Roosevelt

1858–1919
Birthplace: *New York, NY*
Home State: *NY*
Political Party: *Republican*
Age at Inauguration: *42*
Served: *1901–1909*
Vice President: *Charles W. Fairbanks*

27 William H. Taft

1857–1930
Birthplace: *Cincinnati, OH*
Home State: *OH*
Political Party: *Republican*
Age at Inauguration: *51*
Served: *1909–1913*
Vice President: *James S. Sherman*

28 Woodrow Wilson

1856–1924
Birthplace: *Staunton, VA*
Home State: *NJ*
Political Party: *Democratic*
Age at Inauguration: *56*
Served: *1913–1921*
Vice President: *Thomas R. Marshall*

(29) Warren G. Harding

1865–1923
Birthplace:
Blooming Grove, OH
Home State: *OH*
Political Party:
Republican
Age at Inauguration: *55*
Served: *1921–1923*
Vice President:
Calvin Coolidge

(30) Calvin Coolidge

1872–1933
Birthplace:
Plymouth Notch, VT
Home State: *MA*
Political Party:
Republican
Age at Inauguration: *51*
Served: *1923–1929*
Vice President:
Charles G. Dawes

(31) Herbert Hoover

1874–1964
Birthplace: *West Branch, IA*
Home State: *CA*
Political Party:
Republican
Age at Inauguration: *54*
Served: *1929–1933*
Vice President:
Charles Curtis

(32) Franklin D. Roosevelt

1882–1945
Birthplace: *Hyde Park, NY*
Home State: *NY*
Political Party:
Democratic
Age at Inauguration: *51*
Served: *1933–1945*
Vice Presidents:
John N. Garner,
Henry A. Wallace,
Harry S. Truman

(33) Harry S. Truman

1884–1972
Birthplace: *Lamar, MO*
Home State: *MO*
Political Party:
Democratic
Age at Inauguration: *60*
Served: *1945–1953*
Vice President:
Alben W. Barkley

(34) Dwight D. Eisenhower

1890-1969
Birthplace: *Denison, TX*
Home State: *NY*
Political Party:
Republican
Age at Inauguration: *62*
Served: *1953–1961*
Vice President:
Richard M. Nixon

(35) John F. Kennedy

1917–1963
Birthplace: *Brookline, MA*
Home State: *MA*
Political Party:
Democratic
Age at Inauguration: *43*
Served: *1961–1963*
Vice President:
Lyndon B. Johnson

(36) Lyndon B. Johnson

1908–1973
Birthplace:
near Stonewall, TX
Home State: *TX*
Political Party:
Democratic
Age at Inauguration: *55*
Served: *1963–1969*
Vice President:
Hubert H. Humphrey

(37) Richard M. Nixon

1913–1994
Birthplace: *Yorba Linda, CA*
Home State: *NY*
Political Party:
Republican
Age at Inauguration: *56*
Served: *1969–1974*
Vice Presidents:
Spiro T. Agnew,
Gerald R. Ford

(38) Gerald R. Ford

1913–
Birthplace: *Omaha, NE*
Home State: *MI*
Political Party:
Republican
Age at Inauguration: *61*
Served: *1974–1977*
Vice President:
Nelson A. Rockefeller

(39) Jimmy Carter

1924–
Birthplace: *Plains, GA*
Home State: *GA*
Political Party:
Democratic
Age at Inauguration: *52*
Served: *1977–1981*
Vice President:
Walter F. Mondale

(40) Ronald W. Reagan

1911–2004
Birthplace: *Tampico, IL*
Home State: *CA*
Political Party:
Republican
Age at Inauguration: *69*
Served: *1981–1989*
Vice President:
George Bush

(41) George Bush

1924–
Birthplace: *Milton, MA*
Home State: *TX*
Political Party:
Republican
Age at Inauguration: *64*
Served: *1989–1993*
Vice President:
Dan Quayle

(42) William Clinton

1946–
Birthplace: *Hope, AR*
Home State: *AR*
Political Party:
Democratic
Age at Inauguration: *46*
Served: *1993–2001*
Vice President:
Albert Gore

(43) George W. Bush

1946–
Birthplace: *New Haven, CT*
Home State: *TX*
Political Party:
Republican
Age at Inauguration: *54*
Served: *2001–*
Vice President:
Richard Cheney

R10 ▪ **Reference**

American Documents

THE DECLARATION OF INDEPENDENCE

**In Congress, July 4, 1776.
The unanimous Declaration of the
thirteen United States of America,**

When in the Course of human events it becomes necessary for one people to dissolve the political bands which have connected them with another, and to assume among the powers of the earth, the separate and equal station to which the Laws of Nature and of Nature's God entitle them, a decent respect to the opinions of mankind requires that they should declare the causes which impel them to the separation.

We hold these truths to be self-evident, that all men are created equal, that they are endowed by their Creator with certain unalienable Rights, that among these are Life, Liberty and the pursuit of Happiness.

That to secure these rights, Governments are instituted among Men, deriving their just powers from the consent of the governed,

That whenever any Form of Government becomes destructive of these ends, it is the Right of the People to alter or to abolish it, and to institute new Government, laying its foundation on such principles and organizing its powers in such form, as to them shall seem most likely to effect their Safety and Happiness. Prudence, indeed, will dictate that Governments long established should not be changed for light and transient causes; and accordingly all experience hath shown, that mankind are more disposed to suffer, while evils are sufferable, than to right themselves by abolishing the forms to which they are accustomed. But when a long train of abuses and usurpations, pursuing invariably the same Object evinces a design to reduce them under absolute Despotism, it is their right, it is their duty, to throw off such Government, and to provide new Guards for their future security.

Such has been the patient sufferance of these Colonies; and such is now the necessity which constrains them to alter their former Systems of Government. The history of the present King of Great Britain is a history of repeated injuries and usurpations, all having in direct object the establishment of an absolute Tyranny over these States. To prove this, let Facts be submitted to a candid world.

He has refused his Assent to Laws, the most wholesome and necessary for the public good.

He has forbidden his Governors to pass Laws of immediate and pressing importance, unless suspended in their operation till his Assent should be obtained; and when so suspended, he has utterly neglected to attend to them.

Preamble
The Preamble tells why the Declaration was written. It states that the members of the Continental Congress believed the colonies had the right to break away from Britain and become a free nation.

A Statement of Rights
The opening part of the Declaration tells what rights the members of the Continental Congress believed that all people have. All people are equal in having the rights to life, liberty, and the pursuit of happiness. The main purpose of a government is to protect the rights of the people who consent to be governed by it. These rights cannot be taken away. When a government tries to take these rights away from the people, the people have the right to change the government or do away with it. The people can then form a new government that respects these rights.

Charges Against the King
The Declaration lists more than 25 charges against the king. He was mistreating the colonists, the Declaration says, in order to gain total control over the colonies.

The king rejected many laws passed by colonial legislatures.

He has refused to pass other Laws for the accommodation of large districts of people, unless those people would relinquish the right of Representation in the Legislature, a right inestimable to them and formidable to tyrants only.

The king made the colonial legislatures meet at unusual times and places.

He has called together legislative bodies at places unusual, uncomfortable, and distant from the depository of their public Records, for the sole purpose of fatiguing them into compliance with his measures.

The king and the king's governors often dissolved colonial legislatures for disobeying their orders.

He has dissolved Representative Houses repeatedly, for opposing with manly firmness his invasions on the rights of the people.

He has refused for a long time, after such dissolutions, to cause others to be elected; whereby the Legislative powers, incapable of Annihilation, have returned to the People at large for their exercise; the State remaining in the mean time exposed to all the dangers of invasion from without, and convulsions within.

The king stopped people from moving to the colonies and into the western lands.

He has endeavored to prevent the population of these States; for that purpose obstructing the Laws for Naturalization of Foreigners; refusing to pass others to encourage their migrations hither, and raising the conditions of new Appropriations of Lands.

The king prevented the colonists from choosing their own judges. The king chose the judges, and they served only as long as the king was satisfied with them.

He has obstructed the Administration of Justice, by refusing his Assent to Laws for establishing Judiciary powers.

He has made Judges dependent on his Will alone, for the tenure of their offices, and the amount and payment of their salaries.

The king hired people to help collect taxes in the colonies.

He has erected a multitude of New Offices, and sent hither swarms of Officers to harass our people, and eat out their substance.

The king appointed General Thomas Gage, commander of Britain's military forces in the Americas, as governor of Massachusetts.

He has kept among us, in times of peace, Standing Armies without the Consent of our legislatures.

He has affected to render the Military independent of and superior to the Civil power.

He has combined with others to subject us to a jurisdiction foreign to our constitution, and unacknowledged by our laws; giving his Assent to their Acts of pretended Legislation:

For quartering large bodies of armed troops among us:

The king expected the colonists to provide housing and supplies for the British soldiers in the colonies.

For protecting them, by a mock Trial, from punishment for any Murders which they should commit on the Inhabitants of these States:

For cutting off our Trade with all parts of the world:

The king and Parliament demanded that colonists pay many taxes, even though the colonists did not agree to pay them.

For imposing Taxes on us without our Consent:

Colonists were tried by British naval courts, which had no juries.

For depriving us in many cases, of the benefits of Trial by Jury:

Colonists accused of treason were sent to Britain to be tried.

For transporting us beyond Seas to be tried for pretended offenses:

For abolishing the free System of English Laws in a neighboring Province, establishing therein an Arbitrary government, and enlarging its Boundaries so as to render it at once an example and fit instrument for introducing the same absolute rule into these Colonies:

For taking away our Charters, abolishing our most valuable Laws, and altering fundamentally the Forms of our Governments:

For suspending our own Legislatures, and declaring themselves invested with power to legislate for us in all cases whatsoever.

He has abdicated Government here, by declaring us out of his Protection and waging War against us.

He has plundered our seas, ravaged our Coasts, burnt our towns, and destroyed the lives of our people.

He is at this time transporting large Armies of foreign Mercenaries to complete the works of death, desolation and tyranny, already begun with circumstances of Cruelty & perfidy scarcely paralleled in the most barbarous ages, and totally unworthy the Head of a civilized nation.

He has constrained our fellow Citizens taken Captive on the high Seas to bear Arms against their Country, to become the executioners of their friends and Brethren, or to fall themselves by their Hands.

He has excited domestic insurrections amongst us, and has endeavored to bring on the inhabitants of our frontiers, the merciless Indian Savages, whose known rule of warfare, is an undistinguished destruction of all ages, sexes and conditions.

In every stage of these Oppressions We have Petitioned for Redress in the most humble terms: Our repeated Petitions have been answered only by repeated injury. A Prince, whose character is thus marked by every act which may define a Tyrant, is unfit to be the ruler of a free people.

Nor have We been wanting in attentions to our British brethren. We have warned them from time to time of attempts by their legislature to extend an unwarrantable jurisdiction over us. We have reminded them of the circumstances of our emigration and settlement here. We have appealed to their native justice and magnanimity, and we have conjured them by the ties of our common kindred to disavow these usurpations, which, would inevitably interrupt our connections and correspondence. They too have been deaf to the voice of justice and of consanguinity. We must, therefore, acquiesce in the necessity, which denounces our Separation, and hold them, as we hold the rest of mankind, Enemies in War, in Peace Friends.

We, therefore, the Representatives of the united States of America, in General Congress, Assembled, appealing to the Supreme Judge of the world for the rectitude of our intentions, do, in the Name, and by Authority of the good People of these Colonies, solemnly publish and declare, That these United Colonies are, and of Right ought to be Free and Independent States; that they are Absolved from all Allegiance to the British Crown, and that all political connection between them and the State of Great Britain, is and ought to be totally dissolved; and that as Free and Independent States, they have full Power to levy War, conclude Peace, contract Alliances, establish Commerce, and to do all other Acts and Things which Independent States may of right do.

The king allowed General Gage to take military action to enforce British laws in the colonies.

The king hired Hessian mercenaries and sent them to fight the colonists.

The king's governor in Virginia promised freedom to all enslaved people who joined the British forces. The British also planned to use Indians to fight the colonists.

The Declaration explained the efforts of the colonists to avoid separation from Britain. But the colonists said that the king had ignored their protests. Because of the many charges against the king, the writers of the Declaration concluded that he was not fit to rule free people.

A Statement of Independence The writers declared that the colonies were now free and independent states. All ties with Britain were broken. As free and independent states, they had the right to make war and peace, to trade, and to do all the things free countries could do.

To support the Declaration, the signers promised one another their lives, their fortunes, and their honor.

And for the support of this Declaration, with a firm reliance on the protection of divine Providence, we mutually pledge to each other our Lives, our Fortunes and our sacred Honor.

John Hancock

NEW HAMPSHIRE
Josiah Bartlett
William Whipple
Matthew Thornton

MASSACHUSETTS
John Adams
Samuel Adams
Robert Treat Paine
Elbridge Gerry

NEW YORK
William Floyd
Philip Livingston
Francis Lewis
Lewis Morris

RHODE ISLAND
Stephen Hopkins
William Ellery

NEW JERSEY
Richard Stockton
John Witherspoon
Francis Hopkinson
John Hart
Abraham Clark

PENNSYLVANIA
Robert Morris
Benjamin Rush
Benjamin Franklin
John Morton
George Clymer
James Smith
George Taylor
James Wilson
George Ross

DELAWARE
Caesar Rodney
George Read
Thomas McKean

MARYLAND
Samuel Chase
William Paca
Thomas Stone
Charles Carroll of Carrollton

NORTH CAROLINA
William Hopper
Joseph Hewes
John Penn

VIRGINIA
George Wythe
Richard Henry Lee
Thomas Jefferson
Benjamin Harrison
Thomas Nelson, Jr.
Francis Lightfoot Lee
Carter Braxton

SOUTH CAROLINA
Edward Rutledge
Thomas Heyward, Jr.
Thomas Lynch, Jr.
Arthur Middleton

CONNECTICUT
Roger Sherman
Samuel Huntington
William Williams
Oliver Wolcott

GEORGIA
Button Gwinnett
Lyman Hall
George Walton

Members of the Continental Congress stated that copies of the Declaration should be sent to all Committees of Correspondence and to commanders of the troops and that it should be read in every state.

Resolved, That copies of the Declaration be sent to the several assemblies, conventions, and committees, or councils of safety, and to the several commanding officers of the continental troops; that it be proclaimed in each of the United States, at the head of the army.

THE CONSTITUTION OF
THE UNITED STATES OF AMERICA

Preamble*

We the people of the United States, in order to form a more perfect Union, establish justice, insure domestic tranquillity, provide for the common defense, promote the general welfare, and secure the blessings of liberty to ourselves and our posterity, do ordain and establish this Constitution for the United States of America.

ARTICLE I
THE LEGISLATIVE BRANCH

SECTION 1. CONGRESS

All legislative powers herein granted shall be vested in a Congress of the United States, which shall consist of a Senate and House of Representatives.

SECTION 2. THE HOUSE OF REPRESENTATIVES

(1) The House of Representatives shall be composed of members chosen every second year by the people of the several states, and the electors in each state shall have the qualifications requisite for electors of the most numerous branch of the state legislature.

(2) No person shall be a Representative who shall not have attained to the age of twenty-five years, and been seven years a citizen of the United States, and who shall not, when elected, be an inhabitant of that state in which he shall be chosen.

(3) Representatives [*and direct taxes*]** shall be apportioned among the several states which may be included within this Union, according to their respective numbers [*which shall be determined by adding to the whole number of free persons, including those bound to service for a term of years, and excluding Indians not taxed, three-fifths of all other persons*]. The actual enumeration shall be made within three years after the first meeting of the Congress of the United States, and within every subsequent term of ten years, in such manner as they shall by law direct. The number of Representatives shall not exceed one for every 30,000, but each state shall have at least one Representative [*; and until such enumeration shall be made, the State of New Hampshire shall be entitled to choose three; Massachusetts eight; Rhode Island and Providence Plantations one; Connecticut five; New York six; New Jersey four; Pennsylvania eight; Delaware one; Maryland six; Virginia ten; North Carolina five; South Carolina five; and Georgia three*].

*Titles have been added to make the Constitution easier to read. They did not appear in the original document.

**The parts of the Constitution that no longer apply are printed in italics within brackets [ ]. These portions have been changed or set aside by later amendments.

Preamble
The introduction to the Constitution states the purposes and principles for writing it. The writers wanted to set up a fairer form of government and to secure peace and freedom for themselves and for future generations.

Congress
Congress has the authority to make laws. Congress is made up of two groups of lawmakers: the Senate and the House of Representatives.

(1) Election and Term of Members
Qualified voters are to elect members of the House of Representatives every two years. Each member of the House of Representatives must meet certain requirements.

(2) Qualifications
Members of the House of Representatives must be at least 25 years old. They must have been citizens of the United States for at least seven years. They must live in the state that they will represent.

(3) Determining Apportionment
The number of representatives a state may have depends on the number of people living in each state. Every ten years the federal government must take a census, or count, of the population in every state. Every state will have at least one representative.

(4) Filling Vacancies
If there is a vacancy in representation in Congress, the governor of the state involved must call a special election to fill it.

(4) When vacancies happen in the representation from any state, the executive authority thereof shall issue writs of election to fill such vacancies.

(5) Special Authority
The House of Representatives chooses a Speaker as its presiding officer. It also chooses other officers as appropriate. The House is the only government branch that may impeach, or charge, an official in the executive branch or a judge of the federal courts for failing to carry out his or her duties. These cases are tried in the Senate.

(5) The House of Representatives shall choose their Speaker and other officers; and shall have the sole power of impeachment.

(1) Number, Term, and Selection of Members
Each state is represented by two senators. Until Amendment 17 was passed, state legislatures chose the senators for their states. Each senator serves a six-year term and has one vote in Congress.

SECTION 3. THE SENATE
(1) The Senate of the United States shall be composed of two Senators from each state [*chosen by the legislature thereof*], for six years, and each Senator shall have one vote.

(2) Overlapping Terms and Filling Vacancies
One-third of the senators are elected every two years for a six-year term. This grouping allows at least two-thirds of the experienced senators to remain in the Senate after each election. Amendment 17 permits state governors to appoint a replacement to fill a vacancy until the next election is held.

(2) [*Immediately after they shall be assembled in consequence of the first election, they shall be divided as equally as may be into three classes. The seats of the Senators of the first class shall be vacated at the expiration of the second year, of the second class at the expiration of the fourth year, and of the third class at the expiration of the sixth year, so that one-third may be chosen every second year; and if vacancies happen by resignation, or otherwise, during the recess of the legislature of any state, the executive thereof may make temporary appointments until the next meeting of the legislature, which shall then fill such vacancies.*]

(3) Qualifications
Senators must be at least 30 years old. They must have been citizens of the United States for at least nine years. They must live in the state that they will represent.

(3) No person shall be a Senator who shall not have attained to the age of thirty years, and been nine years a citizen of the United States, and who shall not, when elected, be an inhabitant of that state for which he shall be chosen.

(4) President of the Senate
The Vice President acts as chief officer of the Senate but does not vote unless there is a tie.

(4) The Vice President of the United States shall be President of the Senate, but shall have no vote, unless they be equally divided.

(5) Other Officers
The Senate chooses its other officers and a president pro tempore, who serves if the Vice President is not present or if the Vice President becomes President. *Pro tempore* is a Latin term meaning "for the time being."

(5) The Senate shall choose their other officers, and also a President *pro tempore*, in the absence of the Vice President, or when he shall exercise the office of the President of the United States.

(6) The Senate shall have the sole power to try all impeachments. When sitting for that purpose, they shall be on oath or affirmation. When the President of the United States is tried, the Chief Justice shall preside; and no person shall be convicted without the concurrence of two-thirds of the members present.

(7) Judgment in cases of impeachment shall not extend further than to removal from office, and disqualification to hold and enjoy any office of honor, trust, or profit under the United States; but the party convicted shall nevertheless be liable and subject to indictment, trial, judgment and punishment, according to law.

SECTION 4. ELECTIONS AND MEETINGS

(1) The times, places, and manner of holding elections for Senators and Representatives shall be prescribed in each state by the legislature thereof; but the Congress may at any time by law make or alter such regulations, [*except as to the places of choosing Senators*].

(2) The Congress shall assemble at least once in every year, [*and such meeting shall be on the first Monday in December, unless they shall by law appoint a different day*].

SECTION 5. RULES OF PROCEDURE

(1) Each house shall be the judge of the elections, returns and qualifications of its own members, and a majority of each shall constitute a quorum to do business; but a smaller number may adjourn from day to day, and may be authorized to compel the attendance of absent members, in such manner and under such penalties as each house may provide.

(2) Each house may determine the rules of its proceedings, punish its members for disorderly behavior, and, with the concurrence of two-thirds, expel a member.

(3) Each house shall keep a journal of its proceedings, and from time to time publish the same, excepting such parts as may in their judgment require secrecy; and the yeas and nays of the members of either house on any question shall, at the desire of one-fifth of those present, be entered on the journal.

(6) Impeachment Trials
If the House of Representatives votes articles of impeachment, the Senate holds a trial. A two-thirds vote is required to convict a person who has been impeached.

(7) Penalty for Conviction
If convicted in an impeachment case, an official is removed from office and may never hold office in the United States government again. The convicted person may also be tried in a regular court of law for any crimes.

(1) Holding Elections
Each state makes its own rules about electing senators and representatives. However, Congress may change these rules at any time. Today congressional elections are held on the Tuesday after the first Monday in November, in even-numbered years.

(2) Meetings
The Constitution requires Congress to meet at least once a year. That day is the first Monday in December, unless Congress sets a different day. Amendment 20 changed this date to January 3.

(1) Organization
Each house of Congress may decide if its members have been elected fairly and are able to hold office. Each house may do business only when a quorum—a majority of its members—is present. By less than a majority vote, each house may compel absent members to attend.

(2) Rules
Each house may decide its own rules for doing business, punish its members, and expel a member from office if two-thirds of the members agree.

(3) Journal
The Constitution requires each house to keep records of its activities and to publish these records from time to time. The House Journal and the Senate Journal are published at the end of each session. How each member voted must be recorded if one-fifth of the members ask for this to be done.

(4) Adjournment
When Congress is in session, neither house may take a recess for more than three days without the consent of the other.

(1) Pay and Privileges
Members of Congress set their own salaries, which are to be paid by the federal government. Members cannot be arrested or sued for anything they say while Congress is in session. This privilege is called congressional immunity. Members of Congress may be arrested while Congress is in session only if they commit a crime.

(2) Restrictions
Members of Congress may not hold any other federal office while serving in Congress. A member may not resign from office and then take a government position created during that member's term of office or for which the pay has been increased during that member's term of office.

(1) Money-Raising Bills
All money-raising bills must be introduced first in the House of Representatives, but the Senate may suggest changes.

(2) How a Bill Becomes a Law
After a bill has been passed by both the House of Representatives and the Senate, it must be sent to the President. If the President approves and signs the bill, it becomes law. The President can also veto, or refuse to sign, the bill. Congress can override a veto by passing the bill again by a two-thirds majority. If the President does not act within ten days, two things may happen. If Congress is still in session, the bill becomes a law. If Congress ends its session within that same ten-day period, the bill does not become a law.

(3) Orders and Resolutions
Congress can pass orders and resolutions, some of which have the same effect as a law. Congress may decide on its own when to end the session. Other such acts must be signed or vetoed by the President.

(4) Neither house, during the session of Congress, shall, without the consent of the other, adjourn for more than three days, nor to any other place than that in which the two houses shall be sitting.

SECTION 6. PRIVILEGES AND RESTRICTIONS

(1) The Senators and Representatives shall receive a compensation for their services, to be ascertained by law and paid out of the Treasury of the United States. They shall in all cases, except treason, felony, and breach of the peace, be privileged from arrest during their attendance at the session of their respective houses, and in going to and returning from the same; and for any speech or debate in either house, they shall not be questioned in any other place.

(2) No Senator or Representative shall, during the time for which he was elected, be appointed to any civil office under the authority of the United States, which shall have been created, or the emoluments whereof shall have been increased, during such time; and no person holding any office under the United States shall be a member of either house during his continuance in office.

SECTION 7. MAKING LAWS

(1) All bills for raising revenue shall originate in the House of Representatives; but the Senate may propose or concur with amendments as on other bills.

(2) Every bill which shall have passed the House of Representatives and the Senate shall, before it become a law, be presented to the President of the United States; if he approve, he shall sign it, but if not, he shall return it, with his objections, to that house in which it shall have originated, who shall enter the objections at large on their journal, and proceed to reconsider it. If after such reconsideration two-thirds of that house shall agree to pass the bill, it shall be sent, together with the objections, to the other house, by which it shall likewise be reconsidered, and, if approved by two-thirds of that house, it shall become a law. But in all such cases the votes of both houses shall be determined by yeas and nays, and the names of the persons voting for and against the bill shall be entered on the journal of each house respectively. If any bill shall not be returned by the President within ten days (Sundays excepted) after it shall have been presented to him, the same bill shall be a law, in like manner as if he had signed it, unless the Congress by their adjournment prevent its return, in which case it shall not be a law.

(3) Every order, resolution, or vote to which the concurrence of the Senate and House of Representatives may be necessary (except on a question of adjournment) shall be presented to the President of the United States; and before the same shall take effect, shall be approved by him, or being disapproved by him, shall be repassed by two-thirds of the Senate and House of Representatives, according to the rules and limitations prescribed in the case of a bill.

SECTION 8. POWERS DELEGATED TO CONGRESS

The Congress shall have power

(1) To lay and collect taxes, duties, imposts and excises, to pay the debts and provide for the common defense and general welfare of the United States; but all duties, imposts and excises shall be uniform throughout the United States;

(2) To borrow money on the credit of the United States;

(3) To regulate commerce with foreign nations, and among the several states and with the Indian tribes;

(4) To establish an uniform rule of naturalization, and uniform laws on the subject of bankruptcies throughout the United States;

(5) To coin money, regulate the value thereof, and of foreign coin, and fix the standard of weights and measures;

(6) To provide for the punishment of counterfeiting the securities and current coin of the United States;

(7) To establish post offices and post roads;

(8) To promote the progress of science and useful arts by securing for limited times to authors and inventors the exclusive right to their respective writings and discoveries;

(9) To constitute tribunals inferior to the Supreme Court;

(10) To define and punish piracies and felonies committed on the high seas and offenses against the law of nations;

---

(1) Taxation
Only Congress has the authority to raise money to pay debts, defend the United States, and provide services for its people by collecting taxes or tariffs on foreign goods. All taxes must be applied equally in all states.

(2) Borrowing Money
Congress may borrow money for national use. This is usually done by selling government bonds.

(3) Commerce
Congress can control trade with other countries and between states.

(4) Naturalization and Bankruptcy
Congress decides what requirements people from other countries must meet to become United States citizens. Congress can also pass laws to protect people who are bankrupt, or cannot pay their debts.

(5) Coins, Weights, and Measures
Congress can coin money and decide its value. Congress also decides on the system of weights and measures to be used throughout the nation.

(6) Counterfeiting
Congress may pass laws to punish people who make fake money, bonds, or stamps.

(7) Postal Service
Congress can build post offices and make rules about the postal system and the roads used for mail delivery.

(8) Copyrights and Patents
Congress can issue patents and copyrights to inventors and authors to protect the ownership of their works.

(9) Federal Courts
Congress can establish a system of federal courts under the Supreme Court.

(10) Crimes at Sea
Congress can pass laws to punish people for crimes committed at sea. Congress may also punish United States citizens for breaking international law.

(11) Declaring War
Only Congress can declare war.

(11) To declare war, grant letters of marque and reprisal, and make rules concerning captures on land and water;

(12) The Army
Congress can establish an army, but it cannot vote enough money to support it for more than two years. This part of the Constitution was written to keep the army under civilian control.

(12) To raise and support armies, but no appropriation of money to that use shall be for a longer term than two years;

(13) The Navy
Congress can establish a navy and vote enough money to support it for as long as necessary. No time limit was set because people thought the navy was less of a threat to people's liberty than the army was.

(13) To provide and maintain a navy;

(14) Military Regulations
Congress makes the rules that guide and govern all the armed forces.

(14) To make rules for the government and regulation of the land and naval forces;

(15) The Militia
Each state has its own militia, now known as the National Guard. The National Guard can be called into federal service by the President, as authorized by Congress, to enforce laws, to stop uprisings against the government, or to protect the people in case of floods, earthquakes, and other disasters.

(15) To provide for calling forth the militia to execute the laws of the Union, suppress insurrections and repel invasions;

(16) Control of the Militia
Congress helps each state support the National Guard. Each state may appoint its own officers and train its own guard according to rules set by Congress.

(16) To provide for organizing, arming, and disciplining the militia, and for governing such part of them as may be employed in the service of the United States, reserving to the states, respectively, the appointment of the officers, and the authority of training the militia according to the discipline prescribed by Congress;

(17) National Capital and Other Property
Congress may pass laws to govern the nation's capital (Washington, D.C.) and any land owned by the government.

(17) To exercise exclusive legislation in all cases whatsoever, over such district (not exceeding ten miles square) as may, by cession of particular states, and the acceptance of Congress, become the seat of government of the United States, and to exercise like authority over all places purchased by the consent of the legislature of the state in which the same shall be, for the erection of forts, magazines, arsenals, dock-yards, and other needful buildings; —and

(18) Other Necessary Laws
The Constitution allows Congress to make laws that are necessary to enforce the powers listed in Article I. This clause has two conflicting interpretations. One is that Congress can only do what is absolutely necessary to carry out the powers listed in Article I. The other is that Congress may stretch its authority in order to carry out these powers, but not beyond limits established by the Constitution.

(18) To make all laws which shall be necessary and proper for carrying into execution the foregoing powers, and all other powers vested by this Constitution in the government of the United States, or in any department or officer thereof.

SECTION 9. POWERS DENIED TO CONGRESS

(1) [*The migration or importation of such persons as any of the states now existing shall think proper to admit shall not be prohibited by the Congress prior to the year 1808; but a tax or duty may be imposed on such importation, not exceeding 10 dollars for each person.*]

(2) The privilege of the writ of habeas corpus shall not be suspended, unless when in cases of rebellion or invasion the public safety may require it.

(3) No bill of attainder or ex post facto law shall be passed.

(4) [*No capitation or other direct tax shall be laid, unless in proportion to the census or enumeration herein before directed to be taken.*]

(5) No tax or duty shall be laid on articles exported from any state.

(6) No preference shall be given by any regulation of commerce or revenue to the ports of one state over those of another; nor shall vessels bound to, or from, one state, be obliged to enter, clear, or pay duties in another.

(7) No money shall be drawn from the Treasury, but in consequence of appropriations made by law; and a regular statement and account of the receipts and expenditures of all public money shall be published from time to time.

(1) Slave Trade
Some authority is not given to Congress. Congress could not prevent the slave trade until 1808, but it could put a tax of ten dollars on each slave brought into the United States. After 1808, when a law was passed to stop slaves from being brought into the United States, this section no longer applied.

(2) Habeas Corpus
A writ of habeas corpus is a privilege that entitles a person to a hearing before a judge. The judge must then decide if there is good reason for that person to have been arrested. If not, that person must be released. The government is not allowed to take this privilege away except during a national emergency, such as an invasion or a rebellion.

(3) Special Laws
Congress cannot pass laws that impose punishment on a named individual or group, except in cases of treason. Article III sets limits to punishments for treason. Congress also cannot pass laws that punish a person for an action that was legal when it was done.

(4) Direct Taxes
Congress cannot set a direct tax on people, unless it is in proportion to the total population. Amendment 16, which provides for the income tax, is an exception.

(5) Export Taxes
Congress cannot tax goods sent from one state to another or from a state to another country.

(6) Ports
When making trade laws, Congress cannot favor one state over another. Congress cannot require ships from one state to pay a duty to enter another state.

(7) Public Money
The government cannot spend money from the treasury unless Congress passes a law allowing it to do so. A written record must be kept of all money spent by the government.

American Documents ■ **R21**

(8) Titles of Nobility and Gifts
The United States government cannot grant titles of nobility. Government officials cannot accept gifts from other countries without the permission of Congress. This clause was intended to prevent government officials from being bribed by other nations.

(1) Complete Restrictions
The Constitution does not allow states to act as if they were individual countries. No state government may make a treaty with other countries. No state can print its own money.

(2) Partial Restrictions
No state government can tax imported goods or exported goods without the consent of Congress. States may charge a fee to inspect these goods, but profits must be given to the United States Treasury.

(3) Other Restrictions
No state government may tax ships entering its ports unless Congress approves. No state may keep an army or navy during times of peace other than the National Guard. No state can enter into agreements called compacts with other states without the consent of Congress.

(1) Term of Office
The President has the authority to carry out our nation's laws. The term of office for both the President and the Vice President is four years.

(2) The Electoral College
This group of people is to be chosen by the voters of each state to elect the President and Vice President. The number of electors in each state is equal to the number of senators and representatives that state has in Congress.

(3) Election Process
This clause describes in detail how the electors were to choose the President and Vice President. In 1804 Amendment 12 changed the process for electing the President and the Vice President.

---

(8) No title of nobility shall be granted by the United States; and no person holding any office of profit or trust under them, shall, without the consent of the Congress, accept of any present, emolument, office, or title, of any kind whatever, from any king, prince, or foreign state.

SECTION 10. POWERS DENIED TO THE STATES

(1) No state shall enter into any treaty, alliance, or confederation; grant letters of marque and reprisal; coin money; emit bills of credit; make anything but gold and silver coin a tender in payment of debts; pass any bill of attainder, ex post facto law, or law impairing the obligation of contracts, or grant any title of nobility.

(2) No state shall, without the consent of the Congress, lay any imposts or duties on imports or exports, except what may be absolutely necessary for executing its inspection laws; and the net produce of all duties and imposts, laid by any state on imports or exports, shall be for the use of the Treasury of the United States; and all such laws shall be subject to the revision and control of the Congress.

(3) No state shall, without the consent of Congress, lay any duty of tonnage, keep troops, or ships of war in time of peace, enter into any agreement or compact with another state, or with a foreign power, or engage in war, unless actually invaded, or in such imminent danger as will not admit of delay.

ARTICLE II
THE EXECUTIVE BRANCH
SECTION 1. PRESIDENT AND VICE PRESIDENT

(1) The executive power shall be vested in a President of the United States of America. He shall hold his office during the term of four years, and together with the Vice President, chosen for the same term, be elected as follows:

(2) Each state shall appoint, in such manner as the legislature thereof may direct, a number of electors, equal to the whole number of Senators and Representatives to which the state may be entitled in the Congress; but no Senator or Representative, or person holding an office of trust or profit under the United States, shall be appointed an elector.

(3) [*The electors shall meet in their respective states, and vote by ballot for two persons, of whom one at least shall not be an inhabitant of the same state with themselves. And they shall make a list of all the persons voted for, and of the number of votes for each; which list they shall sign and certify, and transmit sealed to the seat of the government of the United States, directed to the president of the Senate. The president of the Senate shall, in the presence of the Senate and House of Representatives, open all the certificates, and the votes shall then be counted. The person having the greatest number of votes shall be the President, if such number be a majority of the whole number of electors appointed; and if there be more than one who have such majority, and have an equal number of votes, then the House of Representatives shall immediately choose by ballot one of them for President; and if no person have*]

a majority, then from the five highest on the list the said House shall in like manner choose the President. But in choosing the President the votes shall be taken by states, the representation from each state having one vote: A quorum for this purpose shall consist of a member or members from two-thirds of the states, and a majority of all the states shall be necessary to a choice. In every case, after the choice of the President, the person having the greatest number of votes of the electors shall be the Vice President. But if there should remain two or more who have equal votes, the Senate shall choose from them by ballot the Vice President.]

(4) The Congress may determine the time of choosing the electors, and the day on which they shall give their votes; which day shall be the same throughout the United States.

(5) No person except a natural-born citizen [*or a citizen of the United States, at the time of the adoption of this Constitution,*] shall be eligible to the office of the President; neither shall any person be eligible to that office who shall not have attained to the age of thirty-five years, and been fourteen years a resident within the United States.

(6) [*In case of the removal of the President from office, or of his death, resignation, or inability to discharge the powers and duties of the said office, the same shall devolve on the Vice President, and the Congress may by law provide for the case of removal, death, resignation or inability, both of the President and Vice President, declaring what officer shall then act as President, and such officer shall act accordingly, until the disability be removed, or a President shall be elected.*]

(7) The President shall, at stated times, receive for his services, a compensation, which shall neither be increased nor diminished during the period for which he shall have been elected, and he shall not receive within that period any other emolument from the United States, or any of them.

(8) Before he enter on the execution of his office, he shall take the following oath or affirmation:—"I do solemnly swear (or affirm) that I will faithfully execute the office of President of the United States, and will to the best of my ability, preserve, protect, and defend the Constitution of the United States."

SECTION 2. POWERS OF THE PRESIDENT
(1) The President shall be Commander in Chief of the Army and Navy of the United States, and of the militia of the several states, when called into the actual service of the United States; he may require the opinion, in writing, of the principal officer in each of the executive departments, upon any subject relating to the duties of their respective offices, and he shall have power to grant reprieves and pardons for offenses against the United States, except in cases of impeachment.

(4) Time of Elections
Congress decides the day the electors are to be elected and the day they are to vote.

(5) Qualifications
The President must be at least 35 years old, be a citizen of the United States by birth, and have been living in the United States for 14 years or more.

(6) Vacancies
If the President dies, resigns, or is removed from office, the Vice President becomes President.

(7) Salary
The President receives a salary that cannot be raised or lowered during a term of office. The President may not be paid any additional salary by the federal government or any state or local government. Today the President's salary is $400,000 a year, plus expenses for things such as housing, travel, and entertainment.

(8) Oath of Office
Before taking office, the President must promise to perform the duties faithfully and to protect the country's form of government. Usually the Chief Justice of the Supreme Court administers the oath of office.

(1) The President's Leadership
The President is the commander of the nation's armed forces and of the National Guard when it is in service of the nation. All government officials of the executive branch must report their actions to the President when asked. The President can excuse people from punishment for crimes committed.

(2) Treaties and Appointments
The President has the authority to make treaties, but they must be approved by a two-thirds vote of the Senate. The President nominates justices to the Supreme Court, ambassadors to other countries, and other federal officials with the Senate's approval.

(3) Filling Vacancies
If a government official's position becomes vacant when Congress is not in session, the President can make a temporary appointment.

Duties
The President must report to Congress on the condition of the country. This report is now presented in the annual State of the Union message.

Impeachment
The President, the Vice President, or any government official will be removed from office if impeached, or accused, and then found guilty of treason, bribery, or other serious crimes. The Constitution protects government officials from being impeached for unimportant reasons.

Federal Courts
The authority to decide legal cases is granted to a Supreme Court and to a system of lower courts established by Congress. The Supreme Court is the highest court in the land. Justices and judges are in their offices for life, subject to good behavior.

(1) General Authority
Federal courts have the authority to decide cases that arise under the Constitution, laws, and treaties of the United States. They also have the authority to settle disagreements among states and among citizens of different states.

(2) He shall have power, by and with the advice and consent of the Senate, to make treaties, provided two-thirds of the senators present concur; and he shall nominate, and by and with the advice and consent of the Senate, shall appoint ambassadors, other public ministers and consuls, judges of the Supreme Court, and all other officers of the United States, whose appointments are not herein otherwise provided for, and which shall be established by law; but the Congress may by law vest the appointment of such inferior officers, as they think proper, in the President alone, in the courts of law, or in the heads of departments.

(3) The President shall have power to fill up all vacancies that may happen during the recess of the Senate, by granting commissions which shall expire at the end of their next session.

SECTION 3. DUTIES OF THE PRESIDENT
He shall from time to time give to the Congress information of the state of the Union, and recommend to their consideration such measures as he shall judge necessary and expedient; he may, on extraordinary occasions, convene both houses, or either of them, and in case of disagreement between them, with respect to the time of adjournment, he may adjourn them to such time as he shall think proper; he shall receive ambassadors and other public ministers; he shall take care that the laws be faithfully executed, and shall commission all the officers of the United States.

SECTION 4. IMPEACHMENT
The President, Vice President and all civil officers of the United States, shall be removed from office on impeachment for, and conviction of, treason, bribery, or other high crimes and misdemeanors.

ARTICLE III
THE JUDICIAL BRANCH
SECTION 1. FEDERAL COURTS
The judicial power of the United States shall be vested in one Supreme Court, and in such inferior courts as the Congress may from time to time ordain and establish. The judges, both of the supreme and inferior courts, shall hold their offices during good behavior, and shall, at stated times, receive for their services a compensation, which shall not be diminished during their continuance in office.

SECTION 2. AUTHORITY OF THE FEDERAL COURTS
(1) The judicial power shall extend to all cases, in law and equity, arising under this Constitution, the laws of the United States, and treaties made or which shall be made, under their authority; to all cases affecting ambassadors, other public ministers and consuls; to all cases of admiralty and maritime jurisdiction; to controversies to which the United States shall be a party; to controversies between two or more states; [*between a state and citizens of another state;*] between citizens of different states; —between citizens of the same state claiming lands under grants of different states, [*and between a state or the citizens thereof, and foreign states, citizens, or subjects.*]

(2) In all cases affecting ambassadors, other public ministers and consuls, and those in which a state shall be party, the Supreme Court shall have original jurisdiction. In all the other cases before mentioned, the Supreme Court shall have appellate jurisdiction, both as to law and fact, with such exceptions, and under such regulations as the Congress shall make.

(3) The trial of all crimes, except in cases of impeachment, shall be by jury; and such trial shall be held in the state where the said crimes shall have been committed; but when not committed within any state, the trial shall be at such place or places as the Congress may by law have directed.

SECTION 3. TREASON
(1) Treason against the United States shall consist only in levying war against them, or in adhering to their enemies, giving them aid and comfort. No person shall be convicted of treason unless on the testimony of two witnesses to the same overt act, or on confession in open court.

(2) The Congress shall have power to declare the punishment of treason, but no attainder of treason shall work corruption of blood, or forfeiture except during the life of the person attainted.

ARTICLE IV
RELATIONS AMONG STATES
SECTION 1. OFFICIAL RECORDS
Full faith and credit shall be given in each state to the public acts, records, and judicial proceedings of every other state. And the Congress may by general laws prescribe the manner in which such acts, records, and proceedings shall be proved, and the effect thereof.

SECTION 2. PRIVILEGES OF THE CITIZENS
(1) The citizens of each state shall be entitled to all privileges and immunities of citizens in the several states.

(2) A person charged in any state with treason, felony, or other crime, who shall flee from justice, and be found in another state, shall on demand of the executive authority of the state from which he fled, be delivered up, to be removed to the state having jurisdiction of the crime.

(3) [*No person held to service or labor in one state, under the laws thereof, escaping into another, shall in consequence of any law or regulation therein, be discharged from such service or labor, but shall be delivered up on claim of the party to whom such service or labor may be due.*]

---

(2) Supreme Court
The Supreme Court can decide certain cases being tried for the first time. It can review cases that have already been tried in a lower court if the decision has been appealed, or questioned, by one side.

(3) Trial by Jury
The Constitution guarantees a trial by jury for every person charged with a federal crime. Amendments 5, 6, and 7 extend and clarify a person's right to a trial by jury.

(1) Definition of Treason
Acts that may be considered treason are making war against the United States or helping its enemies. A person cannot be convicted of attempting to overthrow the government unless there are two witnesses to the act or the person confesses in court to treason.

(2) Punishment for Treason
Congress can decide the punishment for treason, within certain limits.

Official Records
Each state must honor the official records and judicial decisions of other states.

(1) Privileges
A citizen moving from one state to another has the same rights as other citizens living in that person's new state of residence. In some cases, such as voting, people may be required to live in their new state for a certain length of time before obtaining the same privileges as citizens there.

(2) Extradition
At the governor's request, a person who is charged with a crime and who tries to escape justice by crossing into another state may be returned to the state in which the crime was committed.

(3) Fugitive Slaves
The original Constitution required that runaway slaves be returned to their owners. Amendment 13 abolished slavery, eliminating the need for this clause.

American Documents ■ R25

(1) Admission of New States
Congress has the authority to admit new states to the Union. All new states have the same rights as existing states.

(2) Federal Property
The Constitution allows Congress to make or change laws governing federal property. This applies to territories and federally owned land within states, such as national parks.

Guarantees to the States
The federal government guarantees that every state have a republican form of government. The United States must also protect the states against invasion and help the states deal with rebellion or local violence.

Amending the Constitution
Changes to the Constitution may be proposed by a two-thirds vote of both the House of Representatives and the Senate or by a national convention called by Congress when asked by two-thirds of the states. For an amendment to become law, the legislatures or conventions in three-fourths of the states must approve it.

(1) Public Debt
Any debt owed by the United States before the Constitution went into effect was to be honored.

(2) Federal Supremacy
This clause declares that the Constitution and federal laws are the highest in the nation. Whenever a state law and a federal law are found to disagree, the federal law must be obeyed so long as it is constitutional.

(3) Oaths of Office
All federal and state officials must promise to follow and enforce the Constitution. These officials, however, cannot be required to follow a particular religion or satisfy any religious test.

SECTION 3. NEW STATES AND TERRITORIES

(1) New states may be admitted by the Congress into this Union; but no new state shall be formed or erected within the jurisdiction of any other state; nor any state be formed by the junction of two or more states, or parts of states, without the consent of the legislatures of the states concerned as well as of the Congress.

(2) The Congress shall have power to dispose of and make all needful rules and regulations respecting the territory or other property belonging to the United States; and nothing in this Constitution shall be so construed as to prejudice any claims of the United States, or of any particular state.

SECTION 4. GUARANTEES TO THE STATES

The United States shall guarantee to every state in this Union a republican form of government, and shall protect each of them against invasion; and on application of the legislature, or of the executive (when the legislature cannot be convened) against domestic violence.

ARTICLE V
AMENDING THE CONSTITUTION

The Congress, whenever two-thirds of both houses shall deem it necessary, shall propose amendments to this Constitution, or, on the application of the legislatures of two-thirds of the several states, shall call a convention for proposing amendments, which, in either case, shall be valid to all intents and purposes, as part of this Constitution, when ratified by the legislatures of three-fourths of the several states, or by conventions in three-fourths thereof, as the one or the other mode of ratification may be proposed by the Congress; provided that [*no amendment which may be made prior to the year 1808 shall in any manner affect the first and fourth clauses in the Ninth Section of the First Article; and that*] no state, without its consent, shall be deprived of its equal suffrage in the Senate.

ARTICLE VI
GENERAL PROVISIONS

(1) All debts contracted and engagements entered into, before the adoption of this Constitution, shall be as valid against the United States under this Constitution, as under the Confederation.

(2) This Constitution, and the laws of the United States which shall be made in pursuance thereof, and all treaties made, or which shall be made, under the authority of the United States, shall be the supreme law of the land; and the judges in every state shall be bound thereby, anything in the Constitution or laws of any state to the contrary notwithstanding.

(3) The Senators and Representatives before mentioned, and the members of the several state legislatures, and all executive and judicial officers, both of the United States and of the several states, shall be bound by oath or affirmation, to support this Constitution; but no religious test shall ever be required as a qualification to any office or public trust under the United States.

ARTICLE VII
RATIFICATION

The ratification of the conventions of nine states, shall be sufficient for the establishment of this Constitution between the states so ratifying the same.

Done in convention by the unanimous consent of the states present the seventeenth day of September in the year of our Lord one thousand seven hundred and eighty seven and of the independence of the United States of America the Twelfth. In witness whereof we have hereunto subscribed our names.

George Washington—President and deputy from Virginia

DELAWARE
George Read
Gunning Bedford, Jr.
John Dickinson
Richard Bassett
Jacob Broom

MARYLAND
James McHenry
Daniel of St. Thomas Jenifer
Daniel Carroll

VIRGINIA
John Blair
James Madison, Jr.

NORTH CAROLINA
William Blount
Richard Dobbs Spaight
Hugh Williamson

SOUTH CAROLINA
John Rutledge
Charles Cotesworth Pinckney
Charles Pinckney
Pierce Butler

GEORGIA
William Few
Abraham Baldwin

NEW HAMPSHIRE
John Langdon
Nicholas Gilman

MASSACHUSETTS
Nathaniel Gorham
Rufus King

CONNECTICUT
William Samuel Johnson
Roger Sherman

NEW YORK
Alexander Hamilton

NEW JERSEY
William Livingston
David Brearley
William Paterson
Jonathan Dayton

PENNSYLVANIA
Benjamin Franklin
Thomas Mifflin
Robert Morris
George Clymer
Thomas FitzSimons
Jared Ingersoll
James Wilson
Gouverneur Morris

ATTEST: William Jackson, secretary

Ratification
In order for the Constitution to become law, 9 of the 13 states had to approve it. Special conventions were held for this purpose. The process took 9 months to complete.

Basic Freedoms
The Constitution guarantees our five basic freedoms of expression. It provides for the freedoms of religion, speech, the press, peaceable assembly, and petition for redress of grievances.

Weapons and the Militia
This amendment protects the right of the state governments and the people to maintain militias to guard against threats to their public order, safety, and liberty. In connection with that state right, the federal government may not take away the right of the people to have and use weapons.

Housing Soldiers
The federal government cannot force people to house soldiers in their homes during peacetime. However, Congress may pass laws allowing this during wartime.

Searches and Seizures
This amendment protects people's privacy and safety. Subject to certain exceptions, a law officer cannot search a person or a person's home and belongings unless a judge has issued a valid search warrant. There must be good reason for the search. The warrant must describe the place to be searched and the people or things to be seized, or taken.

Rights of Accused Persons
If a person is accused of a crime that is punishable by death or of any other crime that is very serious, a grand jury must decide if there is enough evidence to hold a trial. People cannot be tried twice for the same crime, nor can they be forced to testify against themselves. No person shall be fined, jailed, or executed by the government unless the person has been given a fair trial. The government cannot take a person's property for public use unless fair payment is made.

AMENDMENT 1 (1791)***
BASIC FREEDOMS

Congress shall make no law respecting an establishment of religion, or prohibiting the free exercise thereof; or abridging the freedom of speech, or of the press; or the right of the people peaceably to assemble, and to petition the government for a redress of grievances.

AMENDMENT 2 (1791)
WEAPONS AND THE MILITIA

A well-regulated militia, being necessary to the security of a free state, the right of the people to keep and bear arms shall not be infringed.

AMENDMENT 3 (1791)
HOUSING SOLDIERS

No soldier shall, in time of peace, be quartered in any house, without the consent of the owner; nor in time of war, but in a manner to be prescribed by law.

AMENDMENT 4 (1791)
SEARCHES AND SEIZURES

The right of the people to be secure in their persons, houses, papers, and effects, against unreasonable searches and seizures, shall not be violated; and no warrants shall issue but upon probable cause, supported by oath or affirmation, and particularly describing the place to be searched, and the persons or things to be seized.

AMENDMENT 5 (1791)
RIGHTS OF ACCUSED PERSONS

No person shall be held to answer for a capital, or otherwise infamous crime, unless on a presentment or indictment of a grand jury, except in cases arising in the land or naval forces, or in the militia, when in actual service in time of war or public danger; nor shall any person be subject for the same offense to be twice put in jeopardy of life or limb; nor shall be compelled in any criminal case to be a witness against himself; nor be deprived of life, liberty, or property, without due process of law; nor shall private property be taken for public use without just compensation.

*** The date beside each amendment is the year that the amendment was ratified and became part of the Constitution.

AMENDMENT 6 (1791)
RIGHT TO A FAIR TRIAL

In all criminal prosecutions, the accused shall enjoy the right to a speedy and public trial, by an impartial jury of the state and district wherein the crime shall have been committed, which district shall have been previously ascertained by law, and to be informed of the nature and cause of the accusation; to be confronted with the witnesses against him; to have compulsory process for obtaining witnesses in his favor, and to have the assistance of counsel for his defense.

AMENDMENT 7 (1791)
JURY TRIAL IN CIVIL CASES

In suits at common law, where the value in controversy shall exceed 20 dollars, the right of trial by jury shall be preserved, and no fact tried by a jury shall be otherwise re-examined in any court of the United States, than according to the rules of the common law.

AMENDMENT 8 (1791)
BAIL AND PUNISHMENT

Excessive bail shall not be required, nor excessive fines imposed, nor cruel and unusual punishments inflicted.

AMENDMENT 9 (1791)
RIGHTS OF THE PEOPLE

The enumeration in the Constitution, of certain rights, shall not be construed to deny or disparage others retained by the people.

AMENDMENT 10 (1791)
POWERS OF THE STATES AND THE PEOPLE

The powers not delegated to the United States by the Constitution, nor prohibited by it to the states, are reserved to the states respectively, or to the people.

AMENDMENT 11 (1798)
SUITS AGAINST STATES

The judicial power of the United States shall not be construed to extend to any suit in law or equity, commenced or prosecuted against one of the United States or citizens of another state, or by citizens or subjects of any foreign state.

Right to a Fair Trial
A person accused of a crime has the right to a public trial by an impartial jury, locally chosen. The trial must be held within a reasonable amount of time. The accused person must be told of all charges and has the right to see, hear, and question any witnesses. The federal government must provide a lawyer free of charge to a person who is accused of a serious crime and who is unable to pay for legal services.

Jury Trial in Civil Cases
In most federal civil cases involving more than 20 dollars, a jury trial is guaranteed. Civil cases are those disputes between two or more people over money, property, personal injury, or legal rights. Usually civil cases are not tried in federal courts unless much larger sums of money are involved or unless federal courts are given the authority to decide a certain type of case.

Bail and Punishment
Courts cannot treat harshly people accused of crimes or punish them in unusual or cruel ways. Bail is money put up as a guarantee that an accused person will appear for trial. In certain cases bail can be denied altogether.

Rights of the People
The federal government must respect all natural rights, whether or not they are listed in the Constitution.

Powers of the States and the People
Any powers not clearly given to the federal government or denied to the states belong to the states or to the people.

Suits Against States
A citizen of one state cannot sue another state in federal court.

AMERICAN DOCUMENTS

Election of President and Vice President
This amendment replaces the part of Article II, Section 1, that originally explained the process of electing the President and Vice President. Amendment 12 was an important step in the development of the two-party system. It allows a party to nominate its own candidates for both President and Vice President.

AMENDMENT 12 (1804)
ELECTION OF PRESIDENT AND VICE PRESIDENT

The electors shall meet in their respective states, and vote by ballot for President and Vice President, one of whom, at least, shall not be an inhabitant of the same state with themselves; they shall name in their ballots the person voted for as President, and in distinct ballots the person voted for as Vice President, and they shall make distinct lists of all persons voted for as President, and of all persons voted for as Vice President, and of the number of votes for each, which lists they shall sign and certify, and transmit, sealed, to the seat of government of the United States, directed to the President of the Senate; the President of the Senate shall, in the presence of the Senate and House of Representatives, open all the certificates, and the votes shall then be counted; the person having the greatest number of votes for President shall be the President, if such a number be a majority of the whole number of electors appointed; and if no person have such majority; then from the persons having the highest numbers not exceeding three on the list of those voted for as President, the House of Representatives shall choose immediately, by ballot, the President. But in choosing the President, the votes shall be taken by states, the representation from each state having one vote; a quorum for this purpose shall consist of a member or members from two thirds of the states, and a majority of all the states shall be necessary to a choice. [And *if the House of Representatives shall not choose a President whenever the right of choice shall devolve upon them, before the fourth day of March next following, then the Vice President shall act as President, as in the case of the death or other constitutional disability of the President.*] The person having the greatest number of votes as Vice President, shall be the Vice President, if such number be a majority of the whole number of electors appointed, and if no person have a majority, then, from the two highest numbers on the list the Senate shall choose the Vice President; a quorum for the purpose shall consist of two thirds of the whole number of Senators, and a majority of the whole number shall be necessary to a choice. But no person constitutionally ineligible to the office of President shall be eligible to that of Vice President of the United States.

End of Slavery
People cannot be forced to work against their will unless they have been tried for and convicted of a crime for which this means of punishment is ordered. Congress may enforce this by law.

AMENDMENT 13 (1865)
END OF SLAVERY

SECTION 1. ABOLITION

Neither slavery nor involuntary servitude, except as a punishment for crime whereof the party shall have been duly convicted, shall exist within the United States, or any place subject to their jurisdiction.

SECTION 2. ENFORCEMENT

Congress shall have power to enforce this article by appropriate legislation.

Citizenship
All persons born or naturalized in the United States are citizens of the United States and of the state in which they live. State governments may not deny any citizen the full rights of citizenship. This amendment also guarantees due process of law. According to due process of law, no state may take away the rights of a citizen. All citizens must be protected equally under law.

AMENDMENT 14 (1868)
RIGHTS OF CITIZENS

SECTION 1. CITIZENSHIP

All persons born or naturalized in the United States and subject to the jurisdiction thereof, are citizens of the United States and of the state wherein they reside. No state shall make or enforce any law which shall abridge the privileges or immunities of citizens of the United States, nor shall any state deprive any person of life, liberty, or property, without due process of law; nor deny to any person within its jurisdiction the equal protection of the laws.

SECTION 2. NUMBER OF REPRESENTATIVES

Representatives shall be apportioned among the several states according to their respective numbers, counting the whole number of persons in each state, [*excluding Indians not taxed*]. But when the right to vote at any election for the choice of electors for President and Vice President of the United States, representatives in Congress, the executive and judicial officers of a state, or the members of the legislature thereof, is denied to any of the [*male*] inhabitants of such state, being [*twenty-one years of age and*] citizens of the United States, or in any way abridged, except for participation in rebellion or other crime, the basis of representation therein shall be reduced in the proportion which the number of such [*male*] citizens shall bear to the whole number of [*male*] citizens [*twenty-one years of age*] in such state.

SECTION 3. PENALTY FOR REBELLION

No person shall be a Senator or Representative in Congress, or elector of President and Vice President, or hold any office, civil or military, under the United States, or under any state, who, having previously taken an oath, as a member of Congress, or as an officer of the United States, or as a member of any state legislature, or as an executive or judicial officer of any state, to support the Constitution of the United States, shall have engaged in insurrection or rebellion against the same, or given aid or comfort to the enemies thereof. But Congress may, by a vote of two thirds of each house, remove such disability.

SECTION 4. GOVERNMENT DEBT

The validity of the public debt of the United States, authorized by law, including debts incurred for payment of pensions and bounties for services in suppressing insurrection or rebellion, shall not be questioned. But neither the United States nor any state shall assume or pay any debt or obligation incurred in aid of insurrection or rebellion against the United States, [*or any claim for the loss or emancipation of any slave;*] but all such debts, obligations, and claims shall be held illegal and void.

SECTION 5. ENFORCEMENT

The Congress shall have power to enforce, by appropriate legislation, the provisions of this article.

AMENDMENT 15 (1870)
VOTING RIGHTS

SECTION 1. RIGHT TO VOTE

The right of citizens of the United States to vote shall not be denied or abridged by the United States or by any state on account of race, color, or previous condition of servitude.

SECTION 2. ENFORCEMENT

The Congress shall have power to enforce this article by appropriate legislation.

AMENDMENT 16 (1913)
INCOME TAX

The Congress shall have power to lay and collect taxes on incomes, from whatever source derived, without apportionment among the several states, and without regard to any census or enumeration.

Number of Representatives
Each state's representation in Congress is based on its total population. Any state denying eligible citizens the right to vote will have its representation in Congress decreased. This clause abolished the Three-fifths Compromise in Article I, Section 2. Later amendments granted women the right to vote and lowered the voting age to 18.

Penalty for Rebellion
No person who has rebelled against the United States may hold federal office. This clause was originally added to punish the leaders of the Confederacy for failing to support the Constitution of the United States.

Government Debt
The federal government is responsible for all public debts. It is not responsible, however, for Confederate debts or for debts that result from any rebellion against the United States.

Enforcement
Congress may enforce these provisions by law.

Right to Vote
No state may prevent a citizen from voting simply because of race or color or condition of previous servitude. This amendment was designed to extend voting rights to enforce this by law.

Income Tax
Congress has the power to collect taxes on its citizens, based on their personal incomes rather than on the number of people living in a state.

Direct Election of Senators
Originally, state legislatures elected senators. This amendment allows the people of each state to elect their own senators directly. The idea is to make senators more responsible to the people they represent.

AMENDMENT 17 (1913)
DIRECT ELECTION OF SENATORS
SECTION 1. METHOD OF ELECTION
The Senate of the United States shall be composed of two Senators from each state, elected by the people thereof, for six years; and each Senator shall have one vote. The electors in each state shall have the qualifications requisite for electors of the most numerous branch of the state legislatures.
SECTION 2. VACANCIES
When vacancies happen in the representation of any state in the Senate, the executive authority of such state shall issue writs of election to fill such vacancies: *Provided,* that the legislature of any state may empower the executive thereof to make temporary appointments until the people fill the vacancies by election as the legislature may direct.
SECTION 3. EXCEPTION
[*This amendment shall not be so construed as to affect the election or term of any Senator chosen before it becomes valid as part of the Constitution.*]

Prohibition
This amendment made it illegal to make, sell, or transport liquor within the United States or to transport it out of the United States or its territories. Amendment 18 was the first to include a time limit for approval. If not ratified within seven years, it would be repealed, or canceled. Many later amendments have included similar time limits.

AMENDMENT 18 (1919)
BAN ON ALCOHOLIC DRINKS
SECTION 1. PROHIBITION
[*After one year from the ratification of this article the manufacture, sale, or transportation of intoxicating liquors within, the importation thereof into, or the exportation thereof from the United States and all territory subject to the jurisdiction thereof for beverage purposes is hereby prohibited.*]
SECTION 2. ENFORCEMENT
[*The Congress and the several states shall have concurrent power to enforce this article by appropriate legislation.*]
SECTION 3. RATIFICATION
[*This article shall be inoperative unless it shall have been ratified as an amendment to the Constitution by the legislatures of the several states as provided in the Constitution, within seven years from the date of the submission hereof to the states by the Congress.*]

Women's Voting Rights
This amendment protected the right of women throughout the United States to vote.

AMENDMENT 19 (1920)
WOMEN'S VOTING RIGHTS
SECTION 1. RIGHT TO VOTE
The right of citizens of the United States to vote shall not be denied or abridged by the United States or by any state on account of sex.
SECTION 2. ENFORCEMENT
Congress shall have power to enforce this article by appropriate legislation.

Terms of Office
The terms of the President and the Vice President begin on January 20, in the year following their election. Members of Congress take office on January 3. Before this amendment newly elected members of Congress did not begin their terms until March 4. This meant that those who had run for reelection and been defeated remained in office for four months.

AMENDMENT 20 (1933)
TERMS OF OFFICE
SECTION 1. BEGINNING OF TERMS
The terms of the President and Vice President shall end at noon on the 20th day of January, and the terms of Senators and Representatives at noon on the 3rd day of January, of the years in which such terms would have ended if this article had not been ratified; and the terms of their successors shall then begin.

SECTION 2. SESSIONS OF CONGRESS

The Congress shall assemble at least once in every year, and such meeting shall begin at noon on the 3rd day of January, unless they shall by law appoint a different day.

SECTION 3. PRESIDENTIAL SUCCESSION

If, at the time fixed for the beginning of the term of the President, the President-elect shall have died, the Vice President-elect shall become President. If a President shall not have been chosen before the time fixed for the beginning of his term, or if the President-elect shall have failed to qualify, then the Vice President-elect shall act as President until a President shall have qualified; and the Congress may by law provide for the case wherein neither a President-elect nor a Vice President-elect shall have qualified, declaring who shall then act as President, or the manner in which one who is to act shall be selected and such person shall act accordingly until a President or Vice President shall be qualified.

SECTION 4. ELECTIONS DECIDED BY CONGRESS

The Congress may by law provide for the case of the death of any of the persons from whom the House of Representatives may choose a President whenever the right of choice shall have devolved upon them, and for the case of the death of any of the persons from whom the Senate may choose a Vice President whenever the right of choice shall have devolved upon them.

SECTION 5. EFFECTIVE DATE

[*Sections 1 and 2 shall take effect on the 15th day of October following the ratification of this article.*]

SECTION 6. RATIFICATION

[*This article shall be inoperative unless it shall have been ratified as an amendment to the Constitution by the legislatures of three fourths of the several states within seven years from the date of its submission.*]

AMENDMENT 21 (1933)
END OF PROHIBITION

SECTION 1. REPEAL OF AMENDMENT 18

The eighteenth article of amendment to the Constitution of the United States is hereby repealed.

SECTION 2. STATE LAWS

The transportation or importation into any state, territory, or possession of the United States for delivery or use therein of intoxicating liquors, in violation of the laws thereof, is hereby prohibited.

SECTION 3. RATIFICATION

[*This article shall be inoperative unless it shall have been ratified as an amendment to the Constitution by conventions in the several states, as provided in the Constitution within seven years from the date of the submission hereof to the states by Congress.*]

Sessions of Congress
Congress meets at least once a year, beginning at noon on January 3. Congress had previously met at least once a year beginning on the first Monday of December.

Presidential Succession
If the newly elected President dies before January 20, the newly elected Vice President becomes President on that date. If a President has not been chosen by January 20 or does not meet the requirements for being President, the newly elected Vice President becomes President. If neither the newly elected President nor the newly elected Vice President meets the requirements for office, Congress decides who will serve as President until a qualified President or Vice President is chosen.

End of Prohibition
This amendment repealed Amendment 18. This is the only amendment to be ratified by state conventions instead of by state legislatures. Congress felt that this would give people's opinions about prohibition a better chance to be heard.

Two-Term limit for Presidents
A President may not serve more than two full terms in office. Any President who serves less than two years of a previous President's term may be elected for two more terms.

Presidential Electors for District of Columbia
This amendment grants three electoral votes to the national capital.

Ban on Poll Taxes
No United States citizen may be prevented from voting in a federal election because of failing to pay a tax to vote. Poll taxes had been used in some states to prevent African Americans from voting.

Presidential Vacancy
If the President is removed from office or resigns from or dies while in office, the Vice President becomes President.

AMENDMENT 22 (1951)
TWO-TERM LIMIT FOR PRESIDENTS
SECTION 1. TWO-TERM LIMIT
No person shall be elected to the office of the President more than twice, and no person who has held the office of President, or acted as President, for more than two years of a term to which some other person was elected President shall be elected to the office of the President more than once. [*But this article shall not apply to any person holding the office of President when this article was proposed by the Congress, and shall not prevent any person who may be holding the office of President, or acting as President, during the term within which this article becomes operative from holding the office of President, or acting as President, during the remainder of such term.*]
SECTION 2. RATIFICATION
[*This article shall be inoperative unless it shall have been ratified as an amendment to the Constitution by the legislatures of three-fourths of the several states within seven years from the date of its submission to the states by the Congress.*]

AMENDMENT 23 (1961)
PRESIDENTIAL ELECTORS FOR DISTRICT OF COLUMBIA
SECTION 1. NUMBER OF ELECTORS
The District constituting the seat of Government of the United States shall appoint in such manner as Congress may direct:

A number of electors of President and Vice President equal to the whole number of Senators and Representatives in Congress to which the District would be entitled if it were a state, but in no event more than the least populous state; they shall be in addition to those appointed by the states, but they shall be considered, for the purposes of the election of President and Vice President, to be electors appointed by a state, and they shall meet in the District and perform such duties as provided by the twelfth article of amendment.
SECTION 2. ENFORCEMENT
The Congress shall have power to enforce this article by appropriate legislation.

AMENDMENT 24 (1964)
BAN ON POLL TAXES
SECTION 1. POLL TAX ILLEGAL
The right of citizens of the United States to vote in any primary or other election for President or Vice President, for electors for President or Vice President, or for Senator or Representative in Congress, shall not be denied or abridged by the United States or any state by reason of failure to pay any poll tax or other tax.
SECTION 2. ENFORCEMENT
The Congress shall have power to enforce this article by appropriate legislation.

AMENDMENT 25 (1967)
PRESIDENTIAL SUCCESSION
SECTION 1. PRESIDENTIAL VACANCY
In case of the removal of the President from office or of his death or resignation, the Vice President shall become President.

SECTION 2. VICE PRESIDENTIAL VACANCY

Whenever there is a vacancy in the office of the Vice President, the President shall nominate a Vice President who shall take the office upon confirmation by a majority vote of both houses of Congress.

SECTION 3. PRESIDENTIAL DISABILITY

Whenever the President transmits to the President pro tempore of the Senate and the Speaker of the House of Representatives his written declaration that he is unable to discharge the powers and duties of his office, and until he transmits to them a written declaration to the contrary, such powers and duties shall be discharged by the Vice President as Acting President.

SECTION 4. DETERMINING PRESIDENTIAL DISABILITY

Whenever the Vice President and a majority of either the principal officers of the executive departments or of such other body as Congress may by law provide, transmit to the President pro tempore of the Senate and the Speaker of the House of Representatives their written declaration that the President is unable to discharge the powers and duties of his office, the Vice President shall immediately assume the powers and duties of the office as Acting President.

Thereafter, when the President transmits to the President pro tempore of the Senate and the Speaker of the House of Representatives his written declaration that no inability exists, he shall resume the powers and duties of his office unless the Vice President and a majority of either the principal officers of the executive department or of such other body as Congress may by law provide, transmit within four days to the President pro tempore of the Senate and the Speaker of the House of Representatives their written declaration that the President is unable to discharge the powers and duties of his office. Thereupon Congress shall decide the issue, assembling within 48 hours for that purpose if not in session. If the Congress, within 21 days after receipt of the latter written declaration, or, if Congress is not in session, within 21 days after Congress is required to assemble, determines by two-thirds vote of both houses that the President is unable to discharge the powers and duties of his office, the Vice President shall continue to discharge the same as Acting President; otherwise the President shall resume the powers and duties of his office.

AMENDMENT 26 (1971)
VOTING AGE

SECTION 1. RIGHT TO VOTE

The right of citizens of the United States, who are 18 years of age or older, to vote shall not be denied or abridged by the United States or any state on account of age.

SECTION 2. ENFORCEMENT

The Congress shall have the power to enforce this article by appropriate legislation.

AMENDMENT 27 (1992)
CONGRESSIONAL PAY

No law, varying the compensation for the services of the Senators and Representatives, shall take effect, until an election of Representatives shall have intervened.

Vice Presidential Vacancy
If the office of the Vice President becomes open, the President names someone to assume that office and that person becomes Vice President if both houses of Congress approve by a majority vote.

Presidential Disability
This section explains in detail what happens if the President cannot continue in office because of sickness or any other reason. The Vice President takes over as acting President until the President is able to resume office.

Determining Presidential Disability
If the Vice President and a majority of the Cabinet inform the Speaker of the House and the president pro tempore of the Senate that the President cannot carry out his or her duties, the Vice President then serves as acting President. To regain the office, the President has to inform the Speaker and the president pro tempore in writing that he or she is again able to serve. But, if the Vice President and a majority of the Cabinet disagree with the President and inform the Speaker and the president pro tempore that the President is still unable to serve, then Congress decides who will hold the office of President.

Voting Age
All citizens 18 years or older have the right to vote. Formerly, the voting age was 21 in most states.

Congressional Pay
A law raising or lowering the salaries for members of Congress cannot be passed for that session of Congress.

"The Star-Spangled Banner" was written by Francis Scott Key in September 1814 and adopted as the national anthem in March 1931. The army and navy had recognized it as such long before Congress approved it.

During the War of 1812, Francis Scott Key spent a night aboard a British warship in the Chesapeake Bay while trying to arrange for the release of an American prisoner. The battle raged throughout the night, while the Americans were held on the ship. The next morning, when the smoke from the cannons finally cleared, Francis Scott Key was thrilled to see the American flag still waving proudly above Fort McHenry. It symbolized the victory of the Americans.

There are four verses to the national anthem. In these four verses, Key wrote about how he felt when he saw the flag still waving over Fort McHenry. He wrote that the flag was a symbol of the freedom for which the people had fought so hard. Key also told about the pride he had in his country and the great hopes he had for the future of the United States.

THE NATIONAL ANTHEM

The Star-Spangled Banner

(1)

Oh, say can you see by the dawn's early light
What so proudly we hail'd at the twilight's last gleaming,
Whose broad stripes and bright stars through the perilous fight
O'er the ramparts we watch'd were so gallantly streaming?
And the rockets' red glare, the bombs bursting in air,
Gave proof through the night that our flag was still there.
Oh, say does that star-spangled banner yet wave
O'er the land of the free and the home of the brave?

(2)

On the shore dimly seen through the mists of the deep,
Where the foe's haughty host in dread silence reposes,
What is that which the breeze, o'er the towering steep,
As it fitfully blows, half conceals, half discloses?
Now it catches the gleam of the morning's first beam,
In full glory reflected now shines in the stream.
'Tis the star-spangled banner, oh, long may it wave
O'er the land of the free and the home of the brave!

(3)

And where is that band who so vauntingly swore
That the havoc of war and the battle's confusion
A home and a country should leave us no more?
Their blood has wash'd out their foul footstep's pollution.
No refuge could save the hireling and slave
From the terror of flight or the gloom of the grave,
And the star-spangled banner in triumph doth wave
O'er the land of the free and the home of the brave.

(4)

Oh, thus be it ever when freemen shall stand
Between their lov'd home and the war's desolation!
Blest with vict'ry and peace may the heav'n-rescued land
Praise the power that hath made and preserv'd us a nation!
Then conquer we must, when our cause it is just,
And this be our motto, "In God is our Trust,"
And the star-spangled banner in triumph shall wave
O'er the land of the free and the home of the brave.

THE PLEDGE OF ALLEGIANCE

I pledge allegiance to the Flag
of the United States of America,
and to the Republic
for which it stands,
one Nation under God, indivisible,
with liberty and justice for all.

The flag is a symbol of the United States of America. The Pledge of Allegiance says that the people of the United States promise to stand up for the flag, their country, and the basic beliefs of freedom and fairness upon which the country was established.

Biographical Dictionary

The Biographical Dictionary lists many of the important people introduced in this book. The page number tells where the main discussion of each person starts. See the Index for other page references.

A

Adams, Abigail *1744–1818* Patriot who wrote about women's rights in letters to John Adams, her husband. p. 311

Adams, John *1735–1826* 2nd U.S. President and one of the writers of the Declaration of Independence. pp. 303, 306, 353, 377, 379

Adams, Samuel *1722–1803* American Revolutionary leader who set up a Committee of Correspondence in Boston and helped form the Sons of Liberty. pp. 281, 289, 353, 369

Addams, Jane *1860–1935* American reformer who brought the idea of settlement houses from Britain to the United States. With Ellen Gates Starr, she founded Hull House in Chicago. p. 534

Aldrin, Edwin, Jr. *1930–* American astronaut who was one of the first people to set foot on the moon. p. 583

Ali, Sunni *1400s* Ruler of African empire of Songhay from 1464 to 1492. p. 111

Allen, Ethan *1738–1789* American Patriot from Vermont who led the Green Mountain Boys. p. 318

Anderson, Robert *1805–1871* Union commander of Fort Sumter who was forced to surrender to the Confederacy. p. 454

Aristide, Jean-Bertrand (air•ih•STEED, ZHAHN bair•TRAHN) *1953–* Freely elected president of Haiti who was overthrown in 1991 but was returned to office in 1994. p. 661

Armstrong, Louis *1901–1971* Noted jazz trumpeter who helped make jazz popular in the 1920s. p. 543

Armstrong, Neil *1930–* American astronaut who was the first person to set foot on the moon. p. 583

Arnold, Benedict *1741–1801* Continental Army officer who became a traitor and worked for the British army. p. 323

Atahuallpa (ah•tah•WAHL•pah) *1502?–1533* Inca ruler who was killed in the Spanish conquest of the Incas. p. 133

Attucks, Crispus (A•tuhks) *1723?–1770* Patriot and former slave who was killed during the Boston Massacre. p. 285

Austin, Moses *1761–1821* American pioneer who wanted to start an American colony in Texas. p. 402

Austin, Stephen F. *1793–1836* Moses Austin's son. He carried out his father's dream of starting an American colony in Texas. p. 402

B

Bache, Sarah Franklin *1700s* Daughter of Benjamin Franklin; took over Philadelphia Association when Esther Reed died. p. 311

Balboa, Vasco Núñez de (bahl•BOH•uh, NOON•yays day) *1475–1519* Spanish explorer who, in 1513, became the first European to reach the western coast of the Americas—proving to Europeans that the Americas were separate from Asia. p. 123

Banneker, Benjamin *1731–1806* African American who helped survey the land for the new capital of the United States. p. 376

Barrett, Janie Porter *1865–1948* African American teacher who founded a settlement house in Hampton, Virginia. p. 535

Barton, Clara *1821–1912* Civil War nurse and founder of the American Red Cross. p. 463

Bates, Katharine Lee *1859–1929* American educator and poet. p. 17

Becknell, William *1796?–1865* American pioneer from Missouri who opened the Santa Fe Trail. p. 404

Bellamy, Francis *1800s* Writer of patriotic oath that came to be called the Pledge of Allegiance. p. 643

Berlin, Irving *1888–1989* American songwriter who moved to New York City from Russia in 1893. p. 503

Bessemer, Henry *1813–1898* British inventor of a way to produce steel more easily and cheaply than before. p. 495

Bienville, Jean-Baptiste Le Moyne, Sieur de (bee•EN•vil, ZHAHN ba•TEEST luh•MWAHN) *1680–1747* French explorer who—with his brother, Pierre Le Moyne, Sieur d'Iberville—started an early settlement at the mouth of the Mississippi River. p. 154

Birdseye, Clarence *1886–1956* American scientist who developed methods of quick-freezing foods to preserve freshness. p. 546

Black Hawk *1767–1838* Leader of Sauk and Fox Indians; led fight against U.S. troops and Illinois militia. p. 398

Bolívar, Simón (boh•LEE•var, see•MOHN) *1783–1830* Leader of independence movements in Bolivia, Colombia, Ecuador, Peru, and Venezuela. p. 666

Bonaparte, Napoleon (BOH•nuh•part, nuh•POH•lee•uhn) *1769–1821* French leader who sold all of the Louisiana region to the United States. p. 385

Boone, Daniel *1734–1820* American who was one of the first pioneers to cross the Appalachians. pp. 225, 276

Booth, John Wilkes *1838–1865* Actor who assassinated President Abraham Lincoln. p. 477

Bowie, James *1796–1836* American soldier killed at the Alamo. p. 403

Braddock, Edward *1695–1755* Commander in chief of British forces in French and Indian War; defeated in surprise attack. p. 271

Bradford, William *1590–1657* Governor of Plymouth Colony. p. 168

Breckinridge, John *1821–1875* Democrat from Kentucky who ran against Abraham Lincoln in the 1860 presidential election. p. 453

Brezhnev, Leonid (BREZH•nef) *1906–1982* Leader of the Communist Party of the Soviet Union from 1964 until his death in 1982. President Nixon's 1972 visit with him in the Soviet Union led to arms control and began a period of détente. p. 592

Brown, John *1800–1859* American abolitionist who seized a weapons storehouse to help slaves rebel. He was caught and hanged. p. 449

Brown, Linda *1943–* African American student whose family was among a group that challenged public-school segregation. p. 585

Brown, Moses *1738–1836* Textile pioneer who built the first textile mill in the United States, using Samuel Slater's plans. p. 416

Bruce, Blanche K. *1841–1898* Former slave who became U.S. senator from Mississippi. p. 479

Bruchac, Joseph Author of Native American folktales and legends. p. 14

Burgoyne, John (ber•GOYN) *1722–1792* British general who lost a battle to the Continental Army on October 17, 1777, at Saratoga, New York. p. 316

Burnet, David G. *1788–1870* First president of the Republic of Texas, when it was formed in 1836. p. 403

Bush, George *1924–* 41st U.S. President. He was President at the end of the Cold War and during Operation Desert Storm. pp. 598-599

Bush, George W. *1946–* 43rd U.S. President; son of George Bush, he won the closest election in history. pp. 600, 641, 651

C

Cabeza de Vaca, Álvar Núñez (kah•BAY•sah day VAH•kah) *1490?–1560?* Spanish explorer who went to Mexico City and told stories of the Seven Cities of Gold. p. 131

Caboto, Giovanni (kah•BOH•toh) *1450?–1499?* Italian explorer who in 1497 sailed from England and landed in what is now Newfoundland, though he thought he had landed in Asia. The English gave him the name John Cabot. p. 123

Calhoun, John C. *1782–1850* Vice President under John Quincy Adams and Andrew Jackson. He was a strong believer in states' rights. pp. 437, 453

Calvert, Cecilius *1605–1675* First proprietor of the Maryland colony; appointed his brother Leonard Calvert as governor of Maryland. p. 233

Calvert, George *1580?–1632* Member of Virginia Company and the first Lord Baltimore; bought land in Newfoundland, but found it too cold; moved to Chesapeake Bay area; father of Cecilius Calvert. p. 232

Cardozo, Francis L. *1800s* African American who became secretary of state and state treasurer in South Carolina. p. 479

Carnegie, Andrew *1835–1919* Entrepreneur who helped the steel industry grow in the United States. pp. 495, 496

Carter, Jimmy *1924–* 39th U.S. President. He brought about a peace agreement between Israel and Egypt. p. 596

Carteret, Sir George *c.1610–1680* Proprietor with Lord John Berkeley of territory between the Hudson and Delaware Rivers; named the state of New Jersey for his birthplace. p. 213

Cartier, Jacques (kar•TYAY, ZHAHK) *1491–1557* French explorer who sailed up the St. Lawrence River and began a fur-trading business with the Hurons. p. 137

Carver, George Washington *c.1864–1943* African American scientist who developed hundreds of new uses for peanuts, sweet potatoes, and soybeans. p. 545

Castro, Fidel *1926–* Leader who took over Cuba in 1959 and made it a communist nation. pp. 584, 660

Catt, Carrie Chapman *1859–1947* President of National American Woman Suffrage Association. pp. 535–536

Cavelier, René-Robert (ka•vuhl•YAY) *See* La Salle.

Champlain, Samuel de (sham•PLAYN) *1567?–1635* French explorer who founded the first settlement at Quebec. p. 151

Charles I *1500–1558* King of Spain. p. 145

Charles I *1600–1649* British king who chartered the colonies of Massachusetts and Maryland. pp. 188, 233

Charles II *1630–1685* British king who granted charters for the New Hampshire Colony and the Carolina Colony. Son of Charles I and Henrietta Maria. pp. 197, 234

Chavez, Cesar *1927–1993* Labor leader and organizer of the United Farm Workers. p. 588

Clark, George Rogers *1752–1818* American Revolutionary frontiersman who helped protect western lands and settlers. p. 319

Clark, William *1770–1838* American explorer who aided Meriwether Lewis in an expedition through the Louisiana Purchase. p. 386

Clay, Henry *1777–1852* Representative from Kentucky who worked for compromises on the slavery issue. pp. 390, 438

Clemens, Samuel Langhorne *1835–1910* American writer and steamboat pilot; he wrote under the pen name Mark Twain. p. 30

Clinton, DeWitt *1769–1828* Governor of New York who found European investors to pay for building of Erie Canal. p. 414

Clinton, George *1739–1812* American politician who helped form the Democratic-Republican party. p. 367

Clinton, Hillary Rodham *1947–* Wife of William Clinton; senator of New York. p. 640

Clinton, William *1946–* 42nd U.S. President. pp. 599–600

Collins, Michael *1930–* American astronaut who remained in the lunar orbiter during the *Apollo 11* moon landing. p. 583

Columbus, Christopher *1451–1506* Italian-born Spanish explorer who in 1492 sailed west from Spain and thought he had reached Asia but had actually reached islands near the Americas, lands that were unknown to Europeans. pp. 106, 121

Cooper, Peter *1791–1883* American manufacturer who built *Tom Thumb*, one of the first locomotives made in the United States. p. 415

Cornish, Samuel *1795–1858* African American who in 1827 helped John Russwurm found an abolitionist newspaper called *Freedom's Journal*. p. 448

Cornwallis, Charles *1738–1805* British general who surrendered at the Battle of Yorktown, resulting in victory for the Americans in the Revolutionary War. p. 324

Coronado, Francisco Vásquez de (kawr•oh•NAH•doh) *1510?–1554* Spanish explorer who led an expedition from Mexico City into what is now the southwestern United States in search of the Seven Cities of Gold. p. 131

Cortés, Hernando (kawr•TEZ) *1485–1547* Spanish conquistador who conquered the Aztec Empire. pp. 128–130, 652

Crazy Horse *1842?–1877* Sioux leader who fought against General George Custer. p. 490

Crockett, Davy *1786–1836* American pioneer who was killed at the Alamo. pp. 395, 403

Custer, George *1839–1876* U.S. Army general who led an attack against Sioux and Cheyenne Indians. Custer and all of his men were killed in the battle. p. 491

D

da Gama, Vasco (dah GA•muh) *1460?–1524* Portuguese navigator who sailed from Europe, around the southern tip of Africa, and on to Asia between 1497 and 1499. p. 118

Davis, Jefferson *1808–1889* United States senator from Mississippi who became president of the Confederacy. p. 453

Dawes, William *1745–1799* American who, along with Paul Revere, warned the Patriots that the British were marching toward Concord. p. 291

Deere, John *1804–1886* American industrialist who created steel plows for use on the Great Plains. p. 419

Deganawida (deh•gahn•uh•WIH•duh) *1500s* Legendary Iroquois holy man who called for an end to the fighting among the Iroquois, a view that led to the formation of the Iroquois League. p. 90

de Narváez, Pánfilo *1500s* Spanish explorer who hoped to conquer lands along the Gulf of Mexico but failed. p. 130

de Soto, Hernando (day SOH•toh) *1496?–1542* Spanish explorer who led an expedition into what is today the southeastern United States. p. 132

Dewey, George *1837–1917* American naval commander who destroyed the Spanish fleet and captured Manila Bay in the Spanish-American War. p. 527

Dias, Bartolomeu (DEE•ahsh) *1450?–1500* Portuguese navigator who in 1488 became the first European to sail around the southern tip of Africa. p. 118

Díaz, Porfirio *1830–1915* Mexican dictator. p. 654

Dickinson, John *1732–1808* Member of the Continental Congress who wrote most of the Articles of Confederation, adopted in 1781. pp. 283, 293, 306

Dinwiddie, Robert *1693–1770* British Lieutenant Governor of Virginia; sent George Washington to defend Ohio Valley from seizure by the French. p. 269

Douglas, Stephen A. *1813–1861* American legislator who wrote the Kansas-Nebraska Act and debated Abraham Lincoln in a race for a Senate seat from Illinois. p. 452

Douglass, Frederick *1817–1895* Abolitionist speaker and writer who had escaped from slavery. p. 449

Drake, Edwin *1819–1880* American pioneer in oil industry; became first to tap petroleum at its source. p. 497

Drake, Francis *1543–1596* English explorer who sailed around the world. p. 157

Drew, Charles *1904–1950* American physician who developed an efficient way to store blood plasma in blood banks. p. 562

Du Bois, W. E. B. (doo•BOYS) *1868–1963* African American teacher, writer, and leader who helped form the National Association for the Advancement of Colored People (NAACP). p. 535

E

Edison, Thomas *1847–1931* American who invented the phonograph and the electric lightbulb; he also built the first power station to supply electricity to New York City. pp. 498–499, 500–501

Eisenhower, Dwight D. *1890–1969* 34th U.S. President and, earlier, American general who led the D day invasion. pp. 565–566, 582

Elizabeth I *1533–1603* Queen of England from 1558 to 1603. p. 156

Ellington, Edward Kennedy (Duke) *1899–1974* Band leader who became well-known playing jazz during the 1920s. p. 543

Emerson, Ralph Waldo *1803–1882* American poet who wrote "Concord Hymn." pp. 267, 292

Endecott, John *1588–1665* Member of New England Company who sailed to New England in 1628 and settled at Salem. p. 188

Equiano, Olaudah (ek•wee•AHN•oh, OHL•uh•dah) *1750?–1797* African who was kidnapped from his village and sold into slavery. He later wrote a book describing his experiences. p. 244

Esteban (ehs•TAY•bahn) *1500–1539* African explorer who went with Cabeza de Vaca to Mexico City and told stories of the Seven Cities of Gold. Esteban was killed on a later expedition, the purpose of which was to find out whether the stories were true. p. 131

F

Farragut, Jorge (FAIR•uh•guht, HAWR•hay) *1755–1817* Spanish-born man who fought in the Continental Army and the navy. p. 318

Ferdinand II *1452–1516* King of Spain who—with Queen Isabella, his wife—sent Christopher Columbus on his voyage to find a western route to Asia. p. 121

Ferraro, Geraldine *1935–* First woman to be nominated as a major party's candidate for Vice President of the United States. p. 589

Finley, John Fur trader who helped Daniel Boone find the way across the Appalachian Mountains to Kentucky. p. 277

Fong, Hiram L. *1906–* Chinese immigrant who settled in Hawaii; became first Chinese American senator. p. 505

Ford, Gerald *1913–* 38th U.S. President. The Vietnam War ended during his term. p. 593

Ford, Henry *1863–1947* American automobile manufacturer who mass-produced cars at low cost by using assembly lines. p. 544

Fox, Vicente *1942–* Elected president of Mexico in 2000. p. 655

Frame, Richard *1600s* Colonist and writer. p. 209

Franco, Francisco *1892–1975* Spanish dictator. p. 555

BIOGRAPHICAL DICTIONARY

Franklin, Benjamin *1706–1790* American leader who was sent to Britain to ask Parliament for representation. He was a writer of the Declaration of Independence, a delegate to the Constitutional Convention, and a respected scientist and business leader. pp. 221, 271, 283, 303, 318, 352, 366

Frontenac, Louis de Buade, Count de (FRAHN•tuh•nak) *1622–1698* French leader who was appointed governor-general of New France. p. 152

Fulton, Robert *1765–1815* American engineer and inventor who created the first commercial steamboat. p. 415

G

Gadsden, James *1788–1858* U.S. minister to Mexico who arranged to buy parts of present-day New Mexico and Arizona from Mexico—known as the Gadsden Purchase. p. 407

Gage, Thomas *1721–1787* Head of the British army in North America and colonial governor. pp. 291, 294

Gálvez, Bernardo de (GAHL•ves) *1746–1786* Spanish governor of Louisiana who sent supplies to the Patriots in the Revolutionary War and led his own soldiers in taking a British fort in Florida. p. 318

Garrison, William Lloyd *1805–1879* American abolitionist who started a newspaper called *The Liberator*. p. 448

Gates, Horatio *1728–1806* American general who defeated the British in 1777 at Saratoga, New York. p. 316

George II *1683–1760* British king who chartered the Georgia Colony. p. 236

George III *1738–1820* King of England during the Revolutionary War. pp. 276, 296

Gerry, Elbridge *1744–1814* Massachusetts delegate to the Constitutional Convention. p. 366

Gibbs, Jonathan C. *1800s* African American who became secretary of state in Florida; helped set up public school system. p. 479

Glenn, John H., Jr. *1921–* American astronaut who was the first American to orbit the Earth. Former U.S. senator. p. 583

Gorbachev, Mikhail (gawr•buh•CHAWF, mee•kuh•EEL) *1931–* Leader of the Soviet Union from 1985 to 1991. He improved relations with the United States and expanded freedom in the Soviet Union. pp. 597-598

Gordon, William E. *1918–* American scientist who established the Arecibo Observatory in Puerto Rico. p. 660

Gore, Albert *1948–* Vice President under President Bill Clinton. Defeated by George W. Bush in the 2000 election—the closest election in history. pp. 600, 641

Granger, Gordon Union general who read the order declaring all slaves in Texas to be free. p. 482

Grant, Ulysses S. *1822–1885* 18th U.S. President and, earlier, commander of the Union army in the Civil War. pp. 465, 468, 469, 471, 475

Greeley, Horace *1811–1872* American journalist and political leader; publisher of a newspaper called the *New York Tribune*. p. 461

Greene, Nathanael *1742–1786* Commander of the Continental Army in the Southern Colonies; forced British out of Georgia and the Carolinas. p. 322

Grenville, George *1712–1770* British prime minister who passed the Stamp Act in 1765. p. 280

Gutenberg, Johannes *1390–1468* German inventor; invented movable type. p. 109

H

Hale, Nathan *1755–1776* American Revolutionary hero who was hanged by the British for spying for the Patriots. p. 319

Hamilton, Alexander *1755–1804* American leader in calling for the Constitutional Convention and winning support for it. He favored a strong national government. pp. 368, 375, 377

Hammond, James Henry *1807–1864* Senator from South Carolina. p. 442

Hancock, John *1737–1793* Leader of the Sons of Liberty in the Massachusetts Colony. pp. 306, 353, 369

Harrison, William Henry *1773–1841* 9th U.S. President. Earlier he directed U.S. forces against the Indians at the Battle of Tippecanoe and was a commander in the War of 1812. p. 390

He, Zheng *1400s* Chinese admiral who made seven voyages between 1405 and 1433. p. 109

Henrietta Maria *1609–1669* Queen of Charles I of England. The Maryland Colony was named in her honor. p. 233

Henry *1394–1460* Henry the Navigator, prince of Portugal, who set up the first European school for training sailors in navigation. p. 115

Henry IV *1553–1610* King of France. p. 150

Henry, Patrick *1736–1799* American colonist who spoke out in the Virginia legislature against paying British taxes. His views became widely known, and Loyalists accused him of treason. pp. 282, 290, 350, 353, 367, 378

Hiawatha (hy•uh•WAH•thuh) *1500s* Mohawk chief who persuaded other Iroquois tribes to form the Iroquois League. p. 90

Hidalgo, Miguel *1753–1811* Mexican priest who called for a revolution against Spain in 1810. p. 653

Hirohito *1901–1989* Emperor of Japan from 1926 until his death. p. 555

Hitler, Adolf *1889–1945* Nazi dictator of Germany. His actions led to World War II and the killing of millions of people. p. 555

Hooker, Thomas *1586?–1647* Minister who helped form the Connecticut Colony. His democratic ideas were adopted in the Fundamental Orders. p. 196

Hoover, Herbert *1874–1964* 31st U.S. President. When the depression began, he thought that the economy was healthy and conditions would improve. p. 548

Houston, Sam *1793–1863* President of the Republic of Texas and, later, governor of the state of Texas. pp. 403, 453

Howard, Martin *1700s* Rhode Island colonist who defended Britain's right to tax the colonists. p. 280

Hudson, Henry *?–1611* Explorer who sailed up the Hudson River, giving the Dutch a claim to the area. p. 138

Huerta, Dolores *1900s* Labor leader and organizer, along with Cesar Chavez, of the United Farm Workers. p. 588

Hughes, Langston *1902–1967* African American poet and one of the best-known Harlem writers. p. 543

Hurston, Zora Neale *1903–1960* African American novelist and one of the best-known Harlem writers. p. 543

Hussein, Saddam *1937–* Leader of Iraq. p. 598

Hutchinson, Anne Marbury *1591–1643* English-born woman who left Massachusetts because of her religious beliefs. She settled near Providence, which joined with other settlements to form the Rhode Island Colony. p. 195

Iberville, Pierre Le Moyne, Sieur d' (ee•ber•VEEL) *1661–1706* French explorer who—with his brother, Jean-Baptiste Le Moyne, Sieur de Bienville—started an early settlement at the mouth of the Mississippi River. p. 154

Ibn Majid, Ahmad *1432–1500* Great contributor to study of navigation; born in what is today United Arab Emirates. p. 118

Isabella I *1451–1504* Queen of Spain who—with King Ferdinand, her husband—sent Columbus on his voyage to find a western route to Asia. p. 121

Jackson, Andrew *1767–1845* 7th U.S. President and, earlier, commander who won the final battle in the War of 1812. As President he favored a strong Union and ordered the removal of Native Americans from their lands. pp. 393, 396–398, 437

Jackson, Thomas (Stonewall) *1824–1863* Confederate general. pp. 458, 466

James I *1566–1625* King of England in the early 1600s. The James River and Jamestown were named after him. pp. 160, 164

Jay, John *1745–1829* American leader who wrote letters to newspapers, defending the Constitution. He became the first chief justice of the Supreme Court. pp. 368, 375

Jefferson, Thomas *1743–1826* 3rd U.S. President and the main writer of the Declaration of Independence. pp. 303–305, 353, 368, 371, 375, 376, 377, 384

Jenney, William *1832–1907* American engineer who developed the use of steel frames to build tall buildings. p. 496

John I *1357–1433* King of Portugal during a time of great exploration. Father of Prince Henry, who set up a school of navigation. p. 115

Johnson, Andrew *1808–1875* 17th U.S. President. Differences with Congress about Reconstruction led to his being impeached, though he was found not guilty. pp. 477, 479

Johnson, Lyndon B. *1908–1973* 36th U.S. President. He started Great Society programs and expanded U.S. involvement in the Vietnam War. pp. 584, 588, 590, 591

Joliet, Louis (zhohl•YAY, loo•EE) *1645–1700* French fur trader who explored lakes and rivers for France, with Jacques Marquette and five others. p. 152

Jones, John Paul *1747–1792* American naval officer who defeated bigger and better-equipped British ships during Revolutionary War. p. 319

Joseph *1840?–1904* Nez Perce chief who tried to lead his people to Canada after they were told to move onto a reservation. p. 491

Josephy, Alvin M., Jr. *1915–* Historian and author of books about Native Americans and the United States westward movement. p. 55

Juárez, Benito *1806–1872* Served twice as president of Mexico; made many reforms. p. 654

Kalakaua (kah•lah•KAH•ooh•ah) *1836–1891* Hawaiian king who tried but failed to keep Americans from taking over the Hawaiian Islands. p. 525

Kennedy, John F. *1917–1963* 35th U.S. President. He helped propose the Civil Rights Act. pp. 583–584

Key, Francis Scott *1779–1843* American lawyer and poet who wrote the words to "The Star-Spangled Banner." pp. 392–393

King, Martin Luther, Jr. *1929–1968* African American civil rights leader who worked for integration in nonviolent ways. King won the Nobel Peace Prize in 1964. pp. 586, 587

Knox, Henry *1750–1806* Secretary of war in the first government under the Constitution. pp. 375, 377

Kosciuszko, Thaddeus (kawsh•CHUSH•koh) *1746–1817* Polish officer who helped the Patriots in the Revolutionary War. He later returned to Poland and led a revolution there. p. 317

Kublai Khan (KOO•bluh KAHN) *1215–1294* Ruler of China who was visited by Marco Polo. p. 109

La Follette, Robert *1855–1925* Wisconsin governor who began many reforms in his state, including a merit system for government jobs. p. 533

La Salle, René-Robert Cavelier, Sieur de (luh•SAL) *1643–1687* French explorer who found the mouth of the Mississippi River and claimed the whole Mississippi Valley for France. p. 153

Lafayette, Marquis de (lah•fee•ET) *1757–1834* French noble who fought alongside the Americans in the Revolutionary War. p. 317

Las Casas, Bartolomé de (lahs KAH•sahs, bar•toh•loh•MAY day) *1474–1566* Spanish missionary who spent much of his life trying to help Native Americans. p. 145

Law, John *1671–1729* Scottish banker who was appointed proprietor of the Louisiana region in 1717. p. 155

Lawrence, Jacob *1900s* African American artist; his parents took part in the Great Migration. p. 507

Le Moyne, Jean-Baptiste *See* Bienville.

Le Moyne, Pierre *See* Iberville.

Lee, Richard Henry *1732–1794* American Revolutionary leader who said to the Continental Congress that the colonies should become independent from Britain. p. 303

Lee, Robert E. *1807–1870* United States army colonel who gave up his post to become commander of the Confederate army in the Civil War. pp. 461, 466, 471

L'Enfant, Pierre Charles *1754–1825* French-born American engineer who planned the buildings and streets of the new capital of the United States. p. 377

Lewis, Meriwether *1774–1809* American explorer chosen by Thomas Jefferson to be a pathfinder in the territory of the Louisiana Purchase. p. 386

Liliuokalani, Lydia (lih•lee•uh•woh•kuh•LAH•nee) *1838–1917* Hawaiian queen who tried but failed to bring back the Hawaiian monarchy's authority. p. 525

Lincoln, Abraham *1809–1865* 16th U.S. President, leader of the Union in the Civil War, and signer of the Emancipation Proclamation. pp. 450–455, 461, 462, 467, 468, 476–477

Lincoln, Mary Todd *1818–1882* Wife of Abraham Lincoln. p. 477

Lindbergh, Charles *1902–1974* Airplane pilot who was the first to fly solo between the United States and Europe. p. 545

Livingston, Robert R. *1746–1813* One of the writers of the Declaration of Independence. p. 303

Longstreet, James *1821–1904* Former Confederate general who wanted the South to build more factories; considered a scalawag. p. 484

Louis XIV *1638–1715* King of France. pp. 152, 153

Lowell, Francis Cabot *1775–1817* Textile pioneer who set up an American mill in which several processes were completed under one roof. p. 416

M

MacArthur, Douglas *1880–1964* Commanded Allied forces in the Pacific during World War II. p. 567

Madison, Dolley *1768–1849* James Madison's wife and First Lady during the War of 1812. p. 392

Madison, James *1751–1836* 4th U.S. President. He was a leader in calling for the Constitutional Convention, writing the Constitution, and winning support for it. pp. 350, 352, 360, 368, 371, 378, 390

Magellan, Ferdinand (muh•JEH•luhn) *1480?–1521* Portuguese explorer who in 1519 led a fleet of ships from Spain westward to Asia. He died on the voyage, but one of the ships made it back to Spain, completing the first trip around the world. p. 124

Maguire, Matthew *1800s* Machine worker who, along with Peter McGuire, came up with the idea for Labor Day. p. 533

Mahan, Alfred T. *1840–1914* American naval officer and historian. p. 523

Malcolm X *1925–1965* African American leader who disagreed with the views of Martin Luther King, Jr., on nonviolence and integration. p. 587

Malintzin (mah•LINT•suhn) *1501?–1550* Aztec princess who interpreted for Hernando Cortés and helped him in other ways to conquer Mexico. p. 128

Mao Zedong (MOW zeh•DOONG) *1893–1976* Leader of China from 1949 until his death. President Nixon's 1972 visit with him in China led to trade and cultural exchange with the United States. p. 592

Marion, Francis *1732?–1795* Known as the Swamp Fox, he led Continental soldiers through the swamps of South Carolina on daring raids against the British. p. 319

Marquette, Jacques (mar•KET, ZHAHK) *1637–1675* Catholic missionary who knew several American Indian languages. With Louis Joliet, he explored lakes and rivers for France. p. 152

Marshall, George C. *1880–1959* U.S. Secretary of State who developed the European Recovery Program, also known as the Marshall Plan, after World War II. p. 575

Marshall, James *1810–1885* Carpenter who found gold at John Sutter's sawmill near Sacramento, California, leading to the California gold rush of 1849. p. 408

Marshall, John *1755–1835* Chief Justice of the Supreme Court in 1832; Marshall ruled that the United States should protect the Cherokees and their lands in Georgia. p. 398

Marshall, Thurgood *1908–1993* NAACP lawyer who argued the school segregation case that the Supreme Court ruled on in 1954 and, later, was the first African American to serve on the Supreme Court. p. 585

Mason, George *1725–1792* Virginia delegate to the Constitutional Convention who argued for an end to the slave trade. pp. 366, 370

Massasoit (ma•suh•SOYT) *?–1661* Chief of the Wampanoags, who lived in peace with the Pilgrims. p. 169

Mather, Cotton *1663–1728* Member of well-known family of American Congregational clergymen; published over 400 works on religious, historical, scientific, and moral subjects. p. 187

McCauley, Mary Ludwig Hays *1754?–1832* Known as Molly Pitcher, she carried water to American soldiers during the Battle of Monmouth; when her husband fell during the battle, she began firing his cannon. p. 319

McCormick, Cyrus *1809–1884* Inventor of a reaping machine for harvesting wheat. p. 419

McGuire, Peter *1800s* Carpenter who, along with Matthew Maguire, came up with the idea for Labor Day. p. 533

McKinley, William *1843–1901* 25th U.S. President. The Spanish-American War was fought during his term. pp. 526, 528

Menéndez de Avilés, Pedro (may•NAYN•days day ah•vee•LAYS) *1519–1574* Spanish leader of settlers in St. Augustine, Florida, the first permanent European settlement in what is now the United States. p. 146

Metacomet *1639?–1676* Called King Philip by the English. Son of Massasoit; leader of Wampanoags; made war upon New England settlers—called King Philip's War. p. 198

Minuit, Peter *1580–1638* A director of the New Netherland Colony who purchased Manhattan Island from the Manhattan Indians for $24. p. 211

Mongoulacha (mahn•goo•LAY•chah) *1700s* Indian leader who helped Bienville and Iberville. p. 154

BIOGRAPHICAL DICTIONARY

Monroe, James *1758–1831* 5th U.S. President. He established the Monroe Doctrine, which said that the United States would stop any European nation from expanding its American empire. p. 394

Morgan, Daniel *1736–1802* American general who defeated the British at Cowpens in the Revolutionary War. p. 322

Morris, Gouverneur (guh•ver•NIR) *1752–1816* American leader who was in charge of the final wording of the United States Constitution. pp. 358-359

Motecuhzoma (maw•tay•kwah•SOH•mah) *1466–1520* Emperor of the Aztecs when they were conquered by the Spanish. He is also known as Montezuma. p. 129

Muhlenberg, John Peter *1746–1807* Young minister, son of the colonies' Lutheran leader, who became a Patriot militia officer. p. 309

Mussolini, Benito (moo•suh•LEE•nee, buh•NEE•toh) *1883–1945* Ruler of Italy from 1922 until 1943, most of that time as dictator. p. 555

Nast, Thomas *1840–1902* American cartoonist who created the "Uncle Sam" character. p. 640

Newcomen, Thomas *1663–1729* English blacksmith and inventor who invented the steam engine. p. 414

Nimitz, Chester W. *1885–1966* Commander of U.S. Pacific fleet during World War II. p. 567

Nixon, Richard M. *1913–1994* 37th U.S. President. He tried to end the Vietnam War, he reduced tensions with communist nations, and he resigned the presidency because of the Watergate scandal. pp. 591–593

Niza, Marcos de (day NEE•sah) *1495–1558* Spanish priest who was sent with Esteban to confirm stories of the Seven Cities of Gold. When he returned to Mexico City, he said he had seen a golden city. p. 131

O'Connor, Sandra Day *1930–* First woman to be appointed to the United States Supreme Court. pp. 589, 640

Oglethorpe, James *1696–1785* English settler who was given a charter to settle Georgia. He wanted to bring in debtors from England to help settle it. p. 236

O'Keeffe, Georgia *1887–1986* American painter who developed her own style showing abstract studies of color and light. p. 543

Osceola *1804–1838* Leader of the Seminoles in Florida. p. 398

Otis, James *1725–1783* Massachusetts colonist who spoke out against British taxes and called for "no taxation without representation." pp. 280, 282, 283

Paine, Thomas *1737–1809* Author of a widely read pamphlet called *Common Sense*, in which he attacked King George III and called for a revolution to make the colonies independent. p. 302

Parks, Rosa *1913–* African American woman whose refusal to give up her seat on a Montgomery, Alabama, bus started a year-long bus boycott. p. 586

Paterson, William *1745–1806* Constitutional delegate from New Jersey who submitted the New Jersey Plan, under which each state would have one vote, regardless of population. p. 355

Penn, William *1644–1718* Proprietor of Pennsylvania under a charter from King Charles II of Britain. Penn was a Quaker who made Pennsylvania a refuge for settlers who wanted religious freedom. p. 213

Perry, Oliver Hazard *1785–1819* American naval commander who won an important battle in the War of 1812. p. 390

Philip IV *1605–1665* King of Spain from 1621 to 1665. p. 143

Pickett, George *1825–1875* Confederate general who led the charge against Gettysburg; forced to retreat. p. 466

Pike, Zebulon *1779–1813* American who led an expedition down the Arkansas River to explore the southwestern part of the Louisiana Purchase. pp. 19, 388

Pinckney, Eliza Lucas *1722?–1793* South Carolina settler who experimented with indigo plants. She gave away seeds, and indigo then became an important cash crop in the colonies. p. 236

Pitt, William *1708–1778* British leader of Parliament who helped Britain win battles against the French. p. 273

Pizarro, Francisco (pee•ZAR•oh) *1475?–1541* Spanish conquistador who conquered the Inca Empire. p. 133

Plunkitt, George *1800–1900s* Political boss in New York City. p. 534

Pocahontas (poh•kuh•HAHN•tuhs) *1595–1617* Indian chief Powhatan's daughter. p. 162

Polk, James K. *1795–1849* 11th U.S. President. He gained land for the United States by setting a northern boundary in 1846 and winning a war with Mexico in 1848. pp. 405, 407

Polo, Maffeo Trader from Venice; uncle of Marco Polo. p. 109

Polo, Marco *1254–1324* Explorer from Venice who spent many years in Asia in the late 1200s. He wrote a book about his travels that gave Europeans information about Asia. pp. 109, 112

Polo, Nicolò Trader from Venice; father of Marco Polo. p. 109

Ponce de León, Juan (POHN•say day lay•OHN) *1460–1521* Spanish explorer who landed on the North American mainland in 1513, near what is now St. Augustine, Florida. p. 127

Pontiac *c.1720–1769* Ottawa Indian chief who led a rebellion against the British to stop the loss of Indian hunting lands. p. 275

Powell, Colin L. *1937–* Chairman of the Joint Chiefs of Staff during the Gulf War; became U.S. secretary of state in 2001. p. 599

Powhatan (pow•uh•TAN) *1550?–1618* Chief of a federation of Indian tribes that lived in the Virginia territory. Pocahontas was his daughter. p. 162

Prescott, Samuel *1751–1777?* American who, along with Paul Revere, warned the Patriots that the British were marching toward Concord. p. 291

Ptolemy, Claudius (TAH•luh•mee) *100s* Astronomer in ancient Egypt. p. 123

Pulaski, Casimir (puh•LAS•kee) *1747–1779* Polish noble who came to the British colonies to help the Patriots in the Revolutionary War. p. 317

Putnam, Israel *1718–1790* American Revolutionary commander who fought at the Battle of Bunker Hill. p. 295

R

Raleigh, Sir Walter (RAH•lee) *1554–1618* English explorer who used his own money to set up England's first colony in North America, on Roanoke Island near North Carolina. p. 158

Randolph, Edmund *1753–1813* Virginia delegate to the Constitutional Convention who wrote the Virginia Plan, which stated that the number of representatives a state would have in Congress should be based on the population of the state. pp. 355, 366, 375

Read, George *1733–1798* Delaware delegate to the Constitutional Convention who thought the states should be done away with in favor of a strong national government. p. 354

Reagan, Ronald *1911–2004* 40th U.S. President. His meetings with Soviet leader Mikhail Gorbachev led to a thaw in the Cold War, including advances in arms control. pp. 579, 597–598

Reed, Esther *1700s* American who, in 1780, started the Philadelphia Association to help the Continental Army. p. 311

Revels, Hiram R. *1822–1901* First African American elected to U.S. Senate. p. 479

Revere, Paul *1735–1818* American who warned the Patriots that the British were marching toward Concord, where Patriot weapons were stored. pp. 285, 291

Rockefeller, John D. *1839–1937* American oil entrepreneur who joined many refineries into one business, called the Standard Oil Company. pp. 497-498

Roebling, John *1806–1869* Engineer and industrialist who designed suspension bridges. p. 496

Rolfe, John *1585–1622* English colonist of the Jamestown colony whose discovery of a method of drying tobacco led to great profits. p. 163

Roosevelt, Franklin Delano *1882–1945* 32nd U.S. President. He began New Deal programs to help the nation out of the depression, and he was the nation's leader during World War II. pp. 548-549, 553, 556, 558, 568

Roosevelt, Theodore *1858–1919* 26th U.S. President. He showed the world America's strength, made it possible to build the Panama Canal, and worked for progressive reforms and conservation. pp. 527–528, 532–533

Root, George Frederick *1820–1895* American composer and teacher. p. 435

Ross, Edmund G. *1826–1907* Senator from Kansas who voted to acquit President Johnson. p. 479

Ross, John *1790–1866* Chief of the Cherokee nation. He fought in United States courts to prevent the loss of the Cherokees' lands in Georgia. Though he won the legal battle, he still had to lead his people along the Trail of Tears to what is now Oklahoma. p. 398

Russwurm, John *1799–1851* Helped Samuel Cornish found an abolitionist newspaper called *Freedom's Journal* in 1827. p. 448

S

Sacagawea (sa•kuh•juh•WEE•uh) *1786?–1812?* Shoshone woman who acted as an interpreter for the Lewis and Clark expedition. p. 386

Sagan, Carl *1934–1996* American astronomer who worked to find life on other planets and helped NASA plan missions to explore the solar system. p. 583

Salem, Peter *1750?–1816* African who fought with the Minutemen at Concord and at the Battle of Bunker Hill. p. 310

Salomon, Haym *1740–1785* Polish banker who spied for the Patriots and helped fund the Revolution. p. 317

Samoset *1590?–1653?* Native American chief who spoke English and who helped the settlers at Plymouth. p. 169

San Martín, José de (sahn mar•TEEN) *1778–1850* Leader of an independence movement in Argentina. p. 666

Santa Anna, Antonio López de *1794–1876* Dictator of Mexico; defeated Texans at the Alamo. pp. 402–403

Scott, Dred *1795?–1858* Enslaved African who took his case for freedom to the Supreme Court and lost. p. 440

Scott, Winfield *1786–1866* American general in the war with Mexico. p. 407

Serra, Junípero *1713–1784* Spanish missionary who helped build a string of missions in California. pp. 148, 174

Seward, William H. *1801–1872* Secretary of state in the cabinet of Abraham Lincoln. p. 443

Shays, Daniel *1747?–1825* Leader of Shays's Rebellion, which showed the weakness of the government under the Articles of Confederation. pp. 347, 352

Sherman, Roger *1721–1793* One of the writers of the Declaration of Independence. Connecticut delegate to the Constitutional Convention who worked out the compromise in which Congress would have two houses—one based on state population and one with two members from each state. pp. 303, 356

Sherman, William Tecumseh *1820–1891* Union general who, after defeating Confederate forces in Atlanta, led the March to the Sea, on which his troops caused great destruction. pp. 468–469

Sitting Bull *1831–1890* Sioux leader who fought against General George Custer. p. 490

Slater, Samuel *1768–1835* Textile pioneer who helped bring the Industrial Revolution to the United States by providing plans for a new spinning machine. p. 416

Slocomb, Mary *1700s* North Carolina colonist who fought in the Revolutionary War. p. 319

BIOGRAPHICAL
DICTIONARY

Smalls, Robert *1839–1915* African American who delivered a Confederate steamer to the Union forces. p. 463

Smith, John *1580–1631* English explorer who, as leader of the Jamestown settlement, saved its people from starvation. pp. 161, 231

Smith, Joseph *1805–1844* Mormon leader who settled his people in Illinois and was killed there. p. 406

Soule, John B. L. *1815–1891* Editor of the Terre Haute (Indiana) *Express* in the mid-1800s. p. 383

Squanto *See* Tisquantum.

Stalin, Joseph *1879–1953* Dictator of the Soviet Union from 1924 until his death. p. 555

Standish, Miles *1584?–1656* Captain who sailed with Pilgrims to America aboard the *Mayflower*. p. 167

Stanton, Elizabeth Cady *1815–1902* American reformer who organized the first convention for women's rights. p. 447

Starr, Ellen Gates *1860–1940* Reformer who, with Jane Addams, founded Hull House in Chicago. p. 534

Steuben, Friedrich, Baron von (vahn SHTOY•buhn) *1730–1794* German soldier who helped train Patriot troops in the Revolutionary War. p. 317

Stowe, Harriet Beecher *1811–1896* American abolitionist who in 1852 wrote the book *Uncle Tom's Cabin*. p. 448

Stuyvesant, Peter (STY•vuh•suhnt) *1610?–1672* Last governor of the Dutch colony of New Netherland. p. 212

Sutter, John *1803–1880* American pioneer who owned the sawmill where gold was discovered, leading to the California gold rush. p. 408

T

Taney, Roger B. (TAH•nee) *1777–1864* Supreme Court chief justice who wrote the ruling against Dred Scott. p. 441

Tapahonso, Luci *1953–* Navajo poet and author. p. 72

Tecumseh (tuh•KUHM•suh) *1768–1813* Shawnee leader of Indians in the Northwest Territory. He wanted to stop Americans from settling on Indian lands. p. 390

Thayendanegea (thay•en•da•NEG•ah) *1742–1807* Known as Joseph Brant; Mohawk leader who befriended a British general, became a Christian, and worked as a missionary. p. 312

Tisquantum *1585?–1622* Native American who spoke English and who helped the Plymouth Colony. p. 169

Tompkins, Sally *1833–1916* Civil War nurse who eventually ran her own private hospital in Richmond, Virginia. She was a captain in the Confederate army, the only woman to achieve such an honor. p. 463

Tonti, Henri de (TOHN•tee, ahn•REE duh) *1650–1704* French explorer with La Salle. p. 154

Travis, William B. *1809–1836* Commander of the Texas force at the Alamo, where he was killed. p. 403

Truman, Harry S. *1884–1972* 33rd U.S. President. He ordered the atom bomb to be dropped on Japan to end World War II; he later sent American soldiers to support South Korea in 1950. pp. 568, 575, 582

Truth, Sojourner *1797?–1883* Abolitionist and former slave who became a leading preacher against slavery. p. 449

Tubman, Harriet *1820–1913* Abolitionist and former slave who became a conductor on the Underground Railroad. She led about 300 slaves to freedom. p. 447

Turner, Nat *1800–1831* Enslaved African who led a rebellion against slavery. p. 445

Tuscalusa (tuhs•kuh•LOO•suh) *1500s* Leader of the Mobile people when they battled with Spanish troops led by Hernando de Soto. p. 132

V

Verrazano, Giovanni da (ver•uh•ZAH•noh) *1485?–1528?* Italian navigator who discovered New York Bay while searching for a water route linking the Atlantic and Pacific Oceans. p. 136

Vespucci, Amerigo (veh•SPOO•chee, uh•MAIR•ih•goh) *1454–1512* Italian explorer who made several voyages from Europe to what many people thought was Asia. He determined that he had landed on another continent, which was later called America in his honor. pp. 123–124

W

Wald, Lillian *1867–1940* Reformer who started the Henry Street Settlement in New York City. p. 535

Waldseemüller, Martin (VAHLT•zay•mool•er) *1470–1518?* German cartographer who published a map in 1507 that first showed a continent named America. p. 123

Warren, Earl *1891–1974* Chief justice of the Supreme Court who wrote the 1954 decision against school segregation. p. 586

Warren, Mercy Otis *1728–1814* Massachusetts colonist who wrote poems and plays supporting the Patriot cause. p. 311

Washington, Booker T. *1856–1915* African American who founded Tuskegee Institute in Alabama. p. 535

Washington, George *1732–1799* 1st U.S. President, leader of the Continental army during the Revolutionary War, and president of the Constitutional Convention. pp. 269, 270, 293, 314, 327, 328, 352, 374

Westinghouse, George *1846–1914* American inventor who designed an air brake for stopping trains. p. 495

Wheatley, Phillis *1753?–1784* American poet who wrote poems that praised the Revolution. p. 296

White, John *?–1593?* English painter and cartographer who led the second group that settled on Roanoke Island. p. 158

Whitman, Narcissa *1808–1847* American missionary and pioneer in the Oregon Country. p. 404

Whitney, Eli *1765–1825* American inventor who was most famous for his invention of the cotton gin and his idea of interchangeable parts, which made mass production possible. p. 418

Williams, Roger *1603?–1683* Founder of Providence in what is now Rhode Island. He had been forced to leave Massachusetts because of his views. p. 194

Wilson, Samuel *1766–1854* American meat packer who inspired the "Uncle Sam" national symbol. p. 640

Wilson, Woodrow *1856–1924* 28th U.S. President. He brought the country into World War I after trying to stay neutral. He favored the League of Nations, but the Senate rejected U.S. membership in the league. pp. 538, 541

Winthrop, John *1588–1649* Puritan leader who served several times as governor of the Massachusetts Bay Colony. Helped form confederation among people of New England and served as its first president. p. 189

Woods, Granville T. *1856–1910* African American who improved the air brake and developed a telegraph system for trains. p. 495

Wright, Frank Lloyd *1867–1959* American architect known for producing unusual buildings. p. 543

Wright, Orville *1871–1948* Pioneer in American aviation who—with his brother, Wilbur—made and flew the first successful airplane, at Kitty Hawk, North Carolina. p. 545

Wright, Wilbur *1867–1912* Pioneer in American aviation who—with his brother, Orville—made and flew the first successful airplane, at Kitty Hawk, North Carolina. p. 545

York *1800s* Enslaved African whose hunting and fishing skills contributed to the Lewis and Clark expedition. p. 386

Young, Brigham *1801–1877* Mormon leader who came after Joseph Smith. He moved his people west to the Great Salt Lake valley. p. 406

Yzquierdo, Pedro *1400s* Member of Columbus's first expedition to America. p. 105

Gazetteer

The Gazetteer is a geographical dictionary that will help you locate places discussed in this book. The page number tells where each place appears on a map.

A

Abilene A city in central Kansas on the Smoky Hill River; a major railroad town. (39°N, 97°W) p. 488

Adena (uh•DEE•nuh) An ancient settlement of the Mound Builders; located in southern Ohio. (40°N, 81°W) p. 65

Adirondack Mountains (a•duh•RAHN•dak) A mountain range in northeastern New York. p. 89

Africa Second-largest continent on Earth. p. 27

Alamo A mission in San Antonio, Texas; located in the southeastern part of the state; used as a fort during the Texas Revolution. (29°N, 98°W) p. 404

Alaska Range A mountain range in central Alaska. p. 20

Albany The capital of New York; located in the eastern part of the state, on the Hudson River. (43°N, 74°W) p. 212

Alberta One of Canada's ten provinces; located in western Canada. p. 670

Aleutian Islands (uh•LOO•shuhn) A chain of volcanic islands; located between the North Pacific Ocean and the Bering Sea, extending west from the Alaska Peninsula. pp. 20, 526

Alexandria Seaport on the northern coast of Egypt. (31°N, 29°E) p. 108

Allegheny River (a•luh•GAY•nee) A river in the northeastern United States; flows southwest to join the Monongahela River in Pennsylvania, forming the Ohio River. p. 341

Altamaha River (AWL•tuh•muh•haw) A river that begins in southeastern Georgia and flows into the Atlantic Ocean. p. 234

Amazon River The longest river in South America, flowing from the Andes Mountains across Brazil and into the Atlantic Ocean. p. 665

American Samoa (suh•MOH•uh) A United States territory in the Pacific Ocean. p. 526

Andes Mountains (AN•deez) The longest chain of mountains in the world; located along the entire western coast of South America. p. 665

Annapolis (uh•NA•puh•luhs) The capital of Maryland; located on Chesapeake Bay; home of the United States Naval Academy. (39°N, 76°W) p. 234

Antarctica One of Earth's seven continents. p. 27

Antietam (an•TEE•tuhm) A creek near Sharpsburg in north central Maryland; site of a Civil War battle in 1862. (39°N, 78°W) p. 470

Antigua An island in the eastern part of the Leeward Islands, in the eastern West Indies. p. 658

Appalachian Mountains (a•puh•LAY•chuhn) A mountain system of eastern North America; extends from southeastern Quebec, Canada, to central Alabama. pp. 20, 225

Appomattox (a•puh•MA•tuhks) A village in central Virginia; site of the battle that ended the Civil War in 1865; once known as Appomattox Courthouse. (37°N, 79°W) p. 470

Arctic Ocean One of Earth's four oceans; located north of the Arctic Circle. p. 27

Arkansas River A tributary of the Mississippi River, beginning in central Colorado and ending in southeastern Arkansas. pp. 29, 153

Asia Largest continent on Earth. p. 27

Atlanta Georgia's capital and largest city; located in the northwest central part of the state; site of a Civil War battle in 1864. (33°N, 84°W) pp. 470, 621

Atlantic Ocean Second-largest ocean; separates North and South America from Europe and Africa. p. 27

Austin Capital of Texas; located in south central Texas. (30°N, 97°W) p. 621

Australia A country; smallest continent on Earth. p. 27

B

Baghdad Capital of Iraq; located on the Tigris River in central Iraq. (33°N, 44°E) p. 108

Bahamas An island group in the North Atlantic Ocean; located southeast of Florida and north of Cuba. p. 658

Baja California A peninsula in northwestern Mexico extending south-southeast between the Pacific Ocean and the Gulf of California. p. 653

Baltimore A major seaport in Maryland; located on the upper end of Chesapeake Bay. (39°N, 77°W) pp. 47, 234

Barbados An island in the Lesser Antilles, West Indies; located east of the central Windward Islands. p. 658

Barbuda A flat coral island in the eastern West Indies. p. 658

Baxter Springs A city in the southeastern corner of Kansas. (37°N, 94°W) p. 488

Beaufort Sea (BOH•fert) That part of the Arctic Ocean between northeastern Alaska and the Canadian Arctic Islands. p. 20

Beijing (bay•JING) The capital of China; located on a large plain in northeastern China; once known as Khanbalik. (40°N, 116°E) p. 108

Belmopan A town in Central America; capital of Belize. (17°N, 88°W) p. 658

Benin (buh•NEEN) A former kingdom in West Africa; located along the Gulf of Guinea; present-day southern Nigeria. p. 108

Bennington A town in the southwestern corner of Vermont; site of a major Revolutionary War battle in 1777. (43°N, 73°W) p. 323

Bering Strait A narrow strip of water; separates Asia from North America. p. 57

Beringia (buh•RIN•gee•uh) An ancient land bridge that once connected Asia and North America. p. 57

Black Sea A large inland sea between Europe and Asia. p. 113

Bogotá A city in South America located on the plateau of the Andes; capital of Colombia. (4°N, 74°W) p. 665

R48 ■ Reference

Boise (BOY•zee) Idaho's capital and largest city; located in the southwestern part of the state. (44°N, 116°W) p. 621

Bonampak An ancient settlement of the Mayan civilization; located in present-day southeastern Mexico. (16°N, 91°W) p. 65

Boston The capital and largest city of Massachusetts; a port city located on Massachusetts Bay. (42°N, 71°W) p. 291

Boston Harbor The western section of Massachusetts Bay; located in eastern Massachusetts; the city of Boston is located at its western end. p. 291

Brandywine A battlefield on Brandywine Creek in southeastern Pennsylvania; site of a major Revolutionary War battle in 1777. (40°N, 76°W) p. 323

Brasília A city in South America on the Tocantins River; capital of Brazil. (15°S, 48°W) p. 665

Brazos River (BRAH•zuhs) A river in central Texas; flows southeast into the Gulf of Mexico. p. 404

British Columbia One of Canada's ten provinces; located on the west coast of Canada and bordered by the Yukon Territory, the Northwest Territories, Alberta, the United States, and the Pacific Ocean. p. 670

Brookline A town in eastern Massachusetts; west-southwest of Boston. (42°N, 71°W) p. 291

Brooks Range A mountain range crossing northern Alaska; forms the northwestern end of the Rocky Mountains. p. 20

Buenos Aires A city in South America; the capital of Argentina. (34°S, 58°W) p. 665

Bull Run A stream in northeastern Virginia; flows toward the Potomac River; site of Civil War battles in 1861 and in 1862. p. 470

C

Cahokia (kuh•HOH•kee•uh) A village in southwestern Illinois; site of an ancient settlement of the Mound Builders. (39°N, 90°W) pp. 65, 108

Calgary A city in southern Alberta, Canada; located on the Bow River. (51°N, 114°W) p. 670

Calicut (KA•lih•kuht) A city in southwestern India; located on the Malabar Coast. (11°N, 76°E) p. 108

Cambridge A city in northeastern Massachusetts; located near Boston. (42°N, 71°W) p. 291

Camden A city in north central South Carolina, near the Wateree River; site of a major Revolutionary War battle in 1780. (34°N, 81°W) p. 323

Canal Zone A strip of territory in Panama. p. 528

Canary Islands An island group in the Atlantic Ocean off the northwest coast of Africa. (28°N, 16°W) p. 122

Canton A port city in southeastern China; located on the Canton River; known in China as Guangzhou. (23°N, 113°E) p. 108

Canyon de Chelly An ancient settlement of the Anasazi; located in present-day northeastern Arizona. p. 65

Cape Cod A peninsula of southeastern Massachusetts, extending into the Atlantic Ocean and enclosing Cape Cod Bay. (42°N, 70°W) p. 197

Cape Fear A cape at the southern end of Smith Island; located off the coast of North Carolina, at the mouth of the Cape Fear River. (34°N, 78°W) p. 234

Cape Fear River A river in central and southeastern North Carolina; formed by the Deep and Haw Rivers; flows southeast into the Atlantic Ocean. p. 234

Cape Hatteras (HA•tuh•ruhs) A cape on southeastern Hatteras Island; located off the coast of North Carolina. (35°N, 75°W) p. 234

Cape of Good Hope A cape located on the southernmost tip of Africa. (34°S, 18°E) p. 119

Cape Verde Islands (verd) A group of volcanic islands off the western coast of Africa. (16°N, 24°W) p. 119

Caracas A city in northern Venezuela; capital of Venezuela. (10°N, 67°W) p. 665

Caribbean Sea A part of the Atlantic Ocean between the West Indies and Central and South America. p. 658

Cascade Range A mountain range in the western United States; a continuation of the Sierra Nevada; extends north from California to Washington. p. 20

Cayenne A city on the northwestern coast of Cayenne Island, in northern South America; capital of French Guiana. (5°N, 52°W) p. 665

Chaco Canyon (CHAH•koh) An ancient settlement of the Anasazi; located in present-day northwestern New Mexico. (37°N, 108°W) p. 65

Chancellorsville (CHAN•suh•lerz•vil) A location in northeastern Virginia, just west of Fredericksburg; site of a Civil War battle in 1863. (38°N, 78°W) p. 470

Charles River A river in eastern Massachusetts; separates Boston from Cambridge; flows into Boston Bay. p. 291

Charleston A city in southeastern South Carolina; a major port on the Atlantic Ocean; once known as Charles Towne. (33°N, 80°W) pp. 234, 249, 323, 470

Charlestown A city in Massachusetts; located on Boston Harbor between the mouths of the Charles and Mystic Rivers. p. 291

Charlotte The largest city in North Carolina; located in the south central part of the state. (35°N, 81°W) p. 621

Charlottetown The capital of Prince Edward Island, Canada; located in the central part of the island. (46°N, 63°W) p. 670

Chattanooga (cha•tuh•NOO•guh) A city in southeastern Tennessee; located on the Tennessee River; site of a Civil War battle in 1863. (35°N, 85°W) p. 470

Cherokee Nation (CHAIR•uh•kee) A Native American nation located in present-day northern Georgia, eastern Alabama, southern Tennessee, and western North Carolina. p. 398

Chesapeake Bay An inlet of the Atlantic Ocean; surrounded by Virginia and Maryland. pp. 29, 233

Cheyenne (shy•AN) The capital of Wyoming; located in the southeastern part of the state. (41°N, 105°W) p. 488

Chicago A city in Illinois; located on Lake Michigan; the third-largest city in the United States. (42°N, 88°W) p. 488

Chickamauga (chik•uh•MAW•guh) A city in northwestern Georgia; site of a Civil War battle in 1863. (35°N, 85°W) p. 470

Chihuahua A city and state in northern Mexico. (28°N, 85°W) p. 653

Cincinnati (sin•suh•NA•tee) A large city in southwestern Ohio; located on the Ohio River. (39°N, 84°W) p. 47

GAZETTEER

Coast Mountains A mountain range in western British Columbia and southern Alaska; a continuation of the Cascade Range. p. 20

Coast Ranges Mountains along the Pacific coast of North America, extending from Alaska to Baja California. p. 20

Coastal Plain Low, mostly flat land that stretches inland from the Atlantic Ocean and the Gulf of Mexico. p. 20

Cold Harbor A location in east central Virginia, north of the Chickahominy River; site of Civil War battles in 1862 and in 1864. (38°N, 77°W) p. 470

Colorado River A river in the southwestern United States; its basin extends from the Rocky Mountains to the Sierra Nevada; flows into the Gulf of California. p. 29

Columbia River A river that begins in the Rocky Mountains in southwestern Canada, forms the Washington–Oregon border, and empties into the Pacific Ocean below Portland; supplies much of that area's hydroelectricity. pp. 29, 385

Compostela (kahm•poh•STEH•lah) A city in west central Mexico. (21°N, 105°W) p. 129

Concord A town in northeastern Massachusetts, near Boston; site of a major Revolutionary War battle in 1775. (42°N, 71°W) pp. 291, 323

Concord River A river in northeastern Massachusetts; formed by the junction of the Sudbury and Assabet Rivers; flows north into the Merrimack River at Lowell. p. 291

Connecticut River The longest river in New England; begins in New Hampshire, and empties into Long Island Sound, New York. p. 197

Constantinople (kahn•stant•uhn•OH•puhl) A port city in northwestern Turkey. (41°N, 29°E) p. 108

Copán (koh•PAHN) An ancient settlement of the Mayan civilization; located in present-day Honduras, in northern Central America. (15°N, 89°W) p. 65

Cowpens A town in northwestern South Carolina; located near the site of a major Revolutionary War battle in 1781. (35°N, 82°W) p. 323

Crab Orchard An ancient settlement of the Mound Builders; located in present-day southern Illinois. (38°N, 89°W) p. 65

Cuba An island country in the Caribbean; the largest island of the West Indies. (22°N, 79°W) pp. 129, 526, 658

Cuzco (KOOS•koh) The ancient capital of the Inca Empire; a city located in present-day Peru, in western South America. (14°S, 72°W) pp. 108, 133

D

Dallas A city in northeastern Texas; located on the Trinity River. (33°N, 97°W) p. 621

Damascus (duh•MAS•kuhs) The capital of Syria; located in southwest Syria. p. 108

Deerfield A town in northwestern Massachusetts. (43°N, 73°W) p. 197

Delaware Bay An inlet of the Atlantic Ocean; located between southern New Jersey and Delaware. p. 212

Delaware River A river in the northeastern United States; begins in southern New York and flows into the Atlantic Ocean at Delaware Bay. p. 89

Denver Colorado's capital and largest city. (40°N, 105°W) pp. 488, 621

Des Moines (dih•MOYN) Iowa's capital and largest city. (42°N, 94°W) p. A3

Dickson An ancient settlement of the Mound Builders; located in present-day central Illinois. p. 65

Dodge City A city in southern Kansas; located on the Arkansas River; once a major railroad center on the Santa Fe Trail. (38°N, 100°W) p. 488

Dominica (dah•muh•NEE•kuh) An island and a republic in the West Indies; located in the center of the Lesser Antilles between Guadeloupe and Martinique. p. 658

Dominican Republic A country in the West Indies, occupying the eastern part of Hispaniola. p. 658

Dover (DE) The capital of Delaware; located in the central part of the state. (39°N, 76°W) p. 212

Dover (NH) A city in southeastern New Hampshire. (43°N, 71°W) p. 197

Durango A city and state in northwestern central Mexico. (24°N, 104°W) p. 653

E

Edenton (EE•duhn•tuhn) A town in northeastern North Carolina; located on Albemarle Sound, near the mouth of the Chowan River. (36°N, 77°W) p. 234

Edmonton The capital of Alberta, Canada; located in the south central part of the province on both banks of the North Saskatchewan River. (53°N, 113°W) p. 670

El Paso A city at the western tip of Texas; located on the Rio Grande. (32°N, 106°W) p. 621

Ellsworth A city in central Kansas. p. 488

Emerald Mound An ancient settlement of the Mound Builders; located in present-day southwestern Mississippi. (32°N, 91°W) p. 65

Equator Great circle of Earth that is equal distance from the North and South Poles and divides the surface into Northern and Southern Hemispheres. p. 50

Erie Canal The longest canal in the world; located in New York; connects Buffalo (on Lake Erie) with Troy (on the Hudson River). p. 415

Europe One of Earth's seven continents. p. 27

F

Falkland Islands A British colony in the Atlantic Ocean; located east of the Strait of Magellan. p. 665

Falmouth (FAL•muhth) A town in southwestern Maine. (44°N, 70°W) p. 197

Fort Atkinson A fort in southern Kansas; located on the Sante Fe Trail. (43°N, 89°W) p. 406

Fort Boise (BOY•zee) A fort in eastern Oregon; located on the Snake River and on the Oregon Trail. p. 406

Fort Bridger A present-day village in southwestern Wyoming; once an important station on the Oregon Trail. (41°N, 110°W) p. 406

Fort Christina A Swedish fort; located in present-day Wilmington, Delaware. p. 211

Fort Crèvecoeur (KREEV•ker) A fort in central Illinois; located on the Illinois River; built by La Salle in 1680. (41°N, 90°W) p. 153

Fort Crown Point A French fort; located in northeastern New York, on the shore of Lake Champlain. p. 274

Fort Cumberland A British fort located in northeastern West Virginia, on its border with Maryland. p. 274

Fort Dearborn A fort in northeastern Illinois; built in 1803; eventually became part of Chicago; site of a major battle in the War of 1812. (42°N, 88°W) p. 391

Fort Donelson A fort located in northwestern Tennessee; site of a major Civil War battle in 1862. p. 470

Fort Duquesne (doo•KAYN) A French fort in present-day Pittsburgh, Pennsylvania; captured by the British and new fort built and named Fort Pitt. (40°N, 80°W) p. 274

Fort Edward A British fort in New York, on the Hudson River; a present-day village. (43°N, 74°W) p. 274

Fort Frontenac (FRAHN•tuh•nak) A French fort once located on the site of present-day Kingston, Ontario, in southeastern Canada; destroyed by the British in 1758. (44°N, 76°W) pp. 153, 274

Fort Gibson A fort in eastern Oklahoma; end of the Trail of Tears. (36°N, 95°W) p. 398

Fort Hall A fort in southeastern Idaho; located on the Snake River, at a junction on the Oregon Trail. p. 406

Fort Laramie A fort in southeastern Wyoming; located on the Oregon Trail. (42°N, 105°W) p. 406

Fort Lauderdale A city in southeast Florida along the Atlantic coast. p. 621

Fort Ligonier (lig•uh•NIR) A British fort; located in southern Pennsylvania near the Ohio River. p. 274

Fort Louisbourg (LOO•is•berg) A French fort; located in eastern Canada on the coast of the Atlantic Ocean. (46°N, 60°W) p. 274

Fort Mackinac A fort located on the tip of present-day northern Michigan; site of a major battle in the War of 1812. (46°N, 85°W) p. 391

Fort Mandan A fort in present-day central North Dakota, on the Missouri River; site of a winter camp for the Lewis and Clark expedition. (48°N, 104°W) p. 385

Fort McHenry A fort in central Maryland; located on the harbor in Baltimore; site of a major battle in the War of 1812. (39°N, 77°W) p. 391

Fort Miamis A French fort located on the southern shore of Lake Michigan, in present-day southwestern Michigan. p. 153

Fort Necessity A British fort located in southwestern Pennsylvania; located in present-day Great Meadows. (38°N, 80°W) p. 274

Fort Niagara A fort located in western New York, at the mouth of the Niagara River. (43°N, 79°W) p. 274

Fort Oswego A British fort; located in western New York, on the coast of Lake Ontario. (43°N, 77°W) p. 274

Fort Sumter A fort on a human-made island, off the coast of South Carolina, in Charleston Harbor; site of the first Civil War battle in 1861. (33°N, 80°W) p. 470

Fort Ticonderoga (ty•kahn•der•OH•gah) A historic fort on Lake Champlain, in northeastern New York. (44°N, 73°W) p. 274

Fort Vancouver A fort in southwestern Washington, on the Columbia River; the western end of the Oregon Trail; present-day Vancouver. (45°N, 123°W) p. 406

Fort Wagner A fort near Charleston, South Carolina; site of a Civil War battle in 1863. p. 470

Fort Walla Walla A fort in southeastern Washington; located on the Oregon Trail. (46°N, 118°W) p. 406

Fort William Henry A British fort located in eastern New York. (43°N, 74°W) p. 274

Fort Worth A city in northern Texas; located on the Trinity River. (33°N, 97°W) p. 621

Fox River Located in southeast central Wisconsin; flows southwest toward the Wisconsin River, and then flows northeast and empties into Green Bay. p. 153

Franklin A city in central Tennessee; site of a major Civil War battle in 1864. (36°N, 87°W) p. 470

Fredericksburg A city in northeastern Virginia; located on the Rappahannock River; site of a Civil War battle in 1862. (38°N, 77°W) p. 470

Fredericton The capital of New Brunswick, Canada; located in the southwestern part of the province. (46°N, 66°W) p. 670

Frenchtown A town in present-day eastern Michigan; site of a major battle in the War of 1812. (42°N, 83°W) p. 391

G

Galápagos Islands Nineteen islands off the coast of Ecuador; home to many unique bird and animal species. p. 667

Gatun Lake (gah•TOON) A lake in Panama; part of the Panama Canal system. p. 528

Georgetown A city in South America; located at the mouth of the Demerara River; capital of Guyana. (6°N, 58°W) p. 665

Germantown A residential section of present-day Philadelphia, on Wissahickon Creek, in southeastern Pennsylvania; site of a major Revolutionary War battle in 1777. (40°N, 75°W) p. 323

Gettysburg A town in southern Pennsylvania; site of a Civil War battle in 1863. (40°N, 77°W) pp. 470, 510

Golconda (gahl•KAHN•duh) A city in the southeastern corner of Illinois; a point on the Trail of Tears. (37°N, 88°W) p. 398

Gonzales (gohn•ZAH•lays) A city in south central Texas; site of the first battle of the Texas Revolution. (30°N, 97°W) p. 404

Great Basin One of the driest parts of the United States; located in Nevada, Utah, California, Idaho, Wyoming, and Oregon; includes the Great Salt Lake Desert, the Mojave Desert, and Death Valley. pp. 20, 406

Great Lakes A chain of five lakes; located in central North America; the largest group of freshwater lakes in the world. p. 29

Great Plains A continental slope in western North America; borders the eastern base of the Rocky Mountains from Canada to New Mexico and Texas. pp. 20, 406

Great Salt Lake The largest lake in the Great Basin; located in northwestern Utah. pp. 29, 406

GAZETTEER

Great Wagon Road A former route used in the mid-1700s by colonists moving to settle in the backcountry. p. 225

Greenland The largest island on Earth; located in the northern Atlantic Ocean, east of Canada. p. 20

Grenada (grah•NAY•duh) An island in the West Indies; the southernmost of the Windward Islands. p. 658

Groton (GRAH•tuhn) A town in southeastern Connecticut; located on Long Island Sound. (41°N, 72°W) p. 197

Guadalajara A city in western central Mexico; capital of Jalisco state. (20°N, 103°W) p. 653

Guam (GWAHM) United States territory in the Pacific Ocean; largest of the Mariana Islands. p. 526

Guatemala City Capital of Guatemala; largest city in Central America. (14°N, 90°W) p. 658

Guiana Highlands Highland area in northern South America. p. 665

Guilford Courthouse (GIL•ferd) A location in north central North Carolina, near Greensboro; site of a major Revolutionary War battle in 1781. (36°N, 80°W) p. 323

Gulf of Alaska A northern inlet of the Pacific Ocean; located between the Alaska Peninsula and the southwestern coast of Canada. p. 29

Gulf of California An inlet of the Pacific Ocean; located between Baja California and the northwestern coast of Mexico. p. 20

Gulf of Mexico An inlet of the Atlantic Ocean; located on the southeastern coast of North America; surrounded by the United States, Cuba, and Mexico. pp. 29, 153

Gulf of Panama A large inlet of the Pacific Ocean; located on the southern coast of Panama. p. 528

Haiti A country in the West Indies; occupies the western part of the island of Hispaniola. p. 658

Halifax The capital of the province of Nova Scotia, Canada; a major port on the Atlantic Ocean; remains free of ice all year. (44°N, 63°W) p. 670

Hampton Roads A channel in southeastern Virginia that flows into Chesapeake Bay; site of a Civil War naval battle in 1862 between two ironclad ships, the *Monitor* and the *Merrimack*. p. 470

Hartford The capital of Connecticut. (42°N, 73°W) p. 197

Havana The capital of Cuba; located on the northwestern coast of the country. (23°N, 82°W) p. 129

Hawaiian Islands A state; a chain of volcanic and coral islands; located in the north central Pacific Ocean. p. 526

Hawikuh (hah•wee•KOO) A former village in southwestern North America; located on the route of the Spanish explorer Coronado in present-day northwestern New Mexico. p. 129

Hiroshima Japanese city upon which first atom bomb was dropped in World War II. p. 568

Hispaniola (ees•pah•NYOH•lah) An island in the West Indies made up of Haiti and the Dominican Republic; located in the Caribbean Sea between Cuba and Puerto Rico. pp. 129, 658

Honolulu (hahn•nuh•LOO•loo) Hawaii's capital and largest city; located on Oahu. (21°N, 158°W) p. A2

Hopewell An ancient settlement of the Mound Builders; located in present-day southern Ohio. (39°N, 83°W) p. 65

Horseshoe Bend A location in eastern Alabama; site of a battle in the War of 1812; a present-day national military park. p. 391

Houston A city in southeastern Texas; third-largest port in the United States; leading industrial center in Texas. (30°N, 95°W) p. 621

Hudson Bay An inland sea in east central Canada surrounded by the Northwest Territories, Manitoba, Ontario, and Quebec. p. 138

Hudson River A river in the northeastern United States beginning in upper New York and flowing into the Atlantic Ocean; named for the explorer Henry Hudson. p. 89

Iceland An island country in the northern Atlantic Ocean; between Greenland and Norway. p. 569

Illinois River A river in western and central Illinois; flows southwest into the Mississippi River. pp. 29, 153

Independence A city in western Missouri; the starting point of the Oregon and Santa Fe Trails. (39°N, 94°W) p. 406

Indian Ocean One of Earth's four oceans; located east of Africa, south of Asia, west of Australia, and north of Antarctica. p. 27

Iqaluit The capital of Nunavut Territory, Canada; located on the eastern coast. p. 670

Isthmus of Panama (IS•muhs) A narrow strip of land that connects North America and South America. p. 125

Iwo Jima Japanese island; site of major battles during World War II. p. 568

Jacksonville A city in northeastern Florida; located near the mouth of the St. Johns River. (30°N, 82°W) p. 621

Jamaica (juh•MAY•kuh) An island country in the West Indies; south of Cuba. pp. 129, 658

Jamestown The first permanent English settlement in the Americas; located in eastern Virginia, on the shore of the James River. (37°N, 76°W) p. 234

Jerusalem The capital of Israel; located in the central part of the country. (32°N, 35°E) p. 108

Kahoolawe (kah•hoh•uh•LAY•vay) One of the eight main islands of Hawaii; located west of Maui. p. A14

Kaskaskia (ka•SKAS•kee•uh) A village in southwestern Illinois; site of a major Revolutionary War battle in 1778. (38°N, 90°W) p. 323

Kauai (kah•WAH•ee) The fourth-largest of the eight main islands of Hawaii. p. A14

Kennebec River (KEN•uh•bek) A river in west central and southern Maine; flows south from Moosehead Lake to the Atlantic Ocean. p. 197

Kennesaw Mountain (KEN•uh•saw) An isolated peak in northwestern Georgia, near Atlanta; site of a Civil War battle in 1864. p. 470

Kings Mountain A ridge in northern South Carolina and southern North Carolina; site of a Revolutionary War battle in 1780. p. 323

Kingston A commercial seaport in the West Indies; capital of Jamaica. (18°N, 76°W) p. 658

La Paz A city in South America; capital of Bolivia. (16°S, 68°W) p. 665

La Venta An ancient settlement of the Olmecs; located in present-day southern Mexico, on an island near the Tonalá River. (18°N, 94°W) p. 65

Labrador A peninsula in northeastern North America; once known as Markland. p. 20

Labrador Sea Located south of Greenland and northeast of North America. p. 20

Lake Champlain (sham•PLAYN) A lake between New York and Vermont. p. 89

Lake Erie The fourth-largest of the Great Lakes; borders Canada and the United States. p. 29

Lake Huron The second-largest of the Great Lakes; borders Canada and the United States. p. 29

Lake Michigan The third-largest of the Great Lakes; borders Michigan, Illinois, Indiana, and Wisconsin. pp. 29, 153

Lake Okeechobee (oh•kuh•CHOH•bee) A large lake in south Florida. p. 29

Lake Ontario The smallest of the Great Lakes; borders Canada and the United States. pp. 29, 89

Lake Superior The largest of the Great Lakes; borders Canada and the United States. p. 29

Lake Tahoe A lake on the California-Nevada border. p. 29

Lanai (luh•NY) One of the eight main islands of Hawaii. p. A14

Lancaster A city in southeastern Pennsylvania. (40°N, 76°W) p. 212

Las Vegas (lahs VAY•guhs) A city in southeastern Nevada. (36°N, 115°W) p. 621

Lexington A town in northeastern Massachusetts; site of the first battle of the Revolutionary War in 1775. (42°N, 71°W) pp. 291, 323

Lima (LEE•mah) The capital of Peru; located on the Rímac River. (12°S, 77°W) p. 665

Lisbon The capital of Portugal; a port city located in the western part of the country. (39°N, 9°W) pp. 108, 119

Little Bighorn A location near the Little Bighorn River in southern Montana; site of a fierce battle in 1876 between Sioux and Cheyenne Indians and United States Army soldiers led by General George Armstrong Custer. p. 490

London A city located in the southern part of England; capital of present-day Britain. (52°N, 0°) p. 108

Long Island An island located east of New York City and south of Connecticut; lies between Long Island Sound and the Atlantic Ocean. p. 323

Los Adaes Site of a mission of New Spain; located in present-day eastern Texas. p. 149

Los Angeles The largest city in California; second-largest city in the United States; located in the southern part of the state. (34°N, 118°W) p. 621

Louisiana Purchase A territory in the west central United States; it doubled the size of the nation when it was purchased from France in 1803; extended from the Mississippi River to the Rocky Mountains, and from the Gulf of Mexico to Canada. p. 385

M

Machu Picchu (MAH•choo PEEK•choo) The site of an ancient Inca city on a mountain in the Andes, northwest of Cuzco, Peru. (13°S, 73°W) p. 133

Macon (MAY•kuhn) A city in central Georgia; located on the Ocmulgee River. (33°N, 84°W) p. 415

Madeira (mah•DAIR•uh) An island group in the eastern Atlantic Ocean, off the coast of Morocco. p. 122

Managua A city in Central America; capital of Nicaragua; located on the south shore of Lake Managua. (12°N, 86°W) p. 658

Manitoba (ma•nuh•TOH•buh) A province in central Canada; bordered by the territory of Nunavut, Hudson Bay, Ontario, the United States, and Saskatchewan; located on the Interior Plains of Canada. p. 670

Marshall Gold Discovery State Historic Park A historical park in eastern California located at the site where James Marshall discovered gold in 1848; setting of the California gold rush of 1849. p. 408

Massachusetts Bay An inlet of the Atlantic Ocean; on the eastern coast of Massachusetts; extends from Cape Ann to Cape Cod. p. 189

Maui (MOW•ee) The second-largest island in Hawaii. p. A14

Mecca A city in western Saudi Arabia; a holy city and chief pilgrimage destination of Islam. p. 108

Medford A city in northeastern Massachusetts, north of Boston. (42°N, 71°W) p. 291

Mediterranean Sea (meh•duh•tuh•RAY•nee•uhn) An inland sea, enclosed by Europe on the west and north, Asia on the east, and Africa on the south. p. 113

Menotomy Located in northeastern Massachusetts. p. 291

Mérida A city in southeastern Mexico; capital of Yucatán state. (21°N, 89°W) p. 653

Merrimack River A river in southern New Hampshire and northeastern Massachusetts; empties into the Atlantic Ocean. p. 197

Mesa Verde (MAY•suh VAIR•day) An ancient settlement of the Anasazi; located in present-day southwestern Colorado. (37°N, 108°W) p. 65

Mexico City A city on the southern edge of the Central Plateau of Mexico; the present-day capital of Mexico. (19°N, 99°W) pp. 149, 653

Midway Islands A United States territory in the central Pacific Ocean. p. 526

Minneapolis The largest city in Minnesota; located in the southeast central part of the state, on the Mississippi River; twin city with St. Paul. (45°N, 93°W) p. 498

Mississippi River The longest river in the United States; located centrally, its source is Lake Itasca in Minnesota; flows south into the Gulf of Mexico. pp. 29, 153

Missouri River A tributary of the Mississippi River; located centrally, it begins in Montana and ends at St. Louis, Missouri. pp. 29, 385

Mobile Bay An inlet of the Gulf of Mexico; located off the coast of southern Alabama; the site of a Civil War naval battle in 1864. p. 470

Mohawk River A river in central New York that flows east to the Hudson River. p. 89

Molokai (mah•luh•KY) One of the eight main islands of Hawaii. p. A14

Monterrey A city in northeastern Mexico; capital of Nuevo León state. (25°N, 100°W) p. 653

Montevideo A seaport city located in the southern part of the north shore of La Plata estuary; capital of Uruguay. (35°S, 56°W) p. 665

Montreal The second-largest city in present-day Canada; located in southern Quebec, on Montreal Island on the north bank of the St. Lawrence River. (46°N, 73°W) p. 274

Morristown A town in northern New Jersey; located west-northwest of Newark. (41°N, 74°W) p. 212

Moscow The capital and largest city of Russia; located in the western part of the country. (56°N, 38°E) p. 108

Moundville An ancient settlement of the Mound Builders; located in present-day central Alabama. (33°N, 88°W) p. 65

Murfreesboro A city in central Tennessee; located on the west fork of the Stones River; a site on the Trail of Tears. (36°N, 86°W) p. 398

Mystic River A short river rising in the Mystic Lakes; located in northeastern Massachusetts; flows southeast into Boston Harbor north of Charlestown. p. 291

N

Nagasaki Japanese city upon which the second atom bomb was dropped, resulting in an end to World War II. p. 568

Narragansett Bay An inlet of the Atlantic Ocean in southeastern Rhode Island. (41°N, 71°W) p. 197

Nashville The capital of Tennessee; site of a Civil War battle in 1864. (36°N, 87°W) pp. 470, 621

Nassau A city on the northeastern coast of New Providence Island; capital of the Bahamas. (25°N, 77°W) p. 658

Natchitoches (NAH•kuh•tuhsh) The first settlement in present-day Louisiana; located in the northwest central part of the state. (32°N, 93°W) p. 385

Nauvoo (naw•VOO) A city in western Illinois; located on the Mississippi River; beginning of the Mormon Trail. (41°N, 91°W) p. 406

New Amsterdam A Dutch city on Manhattan Island; later became New York City. (41°N, 74°W) p. 211

New Bern A city and port in southeastern North Carolina. (35°N, 77°W) p. 234

New Brunswick One of Canada's ten provinces; bordered by Quebec, the Gulf of St. Lawrence, Northumberland Strait, the Bay of Fundy, the United States, and Nova Scotia. p. 670

New Echota (ih•KOHT•uh) A Native American town in northwestern Georgia; chosen as the capital of the Cherokee Nation in 1819. (34°N, 85°W) p. 398

New France The possessions of France in North America from 1534 to 1763; included Canada, the Great Lakes region, and Louisiana. p. 269

New Guinea (GIH•nee) An island of the eastern Malay Archipelago; located in the western Pacific Ocean, north of Australia. p. 568

New Haven A city in southern Connecticut; located on New Haven Harbor. (41°N, 73°W) p. 197

New London A city in southeastern Connecticut; located on Long Island Sound at the mouth of the Thames River. (41°N, 72°W) p. 247

New Orleans The largest city in Louisiana; a major port located between the Mississippi River and Lake Pontchartrain. (30°N, 90°W) pp. 391, 470

New Spain The former Spanish possessions from 1535 to 1821; included the southwestern United States, Mexico, Central America north of Panama, the West Indies, and the Philippines. p. 269

New York City The largest city in the United States; located in southeastern New York at the mouth of the Hudson River. (41°N, 74°W) p. 603

Newark A port in northeastern New Jersey; located on the Passaic River and Newark Bay. (41°N, 74°W) p. 212

Newfoundland (NOO•fuhn•luhnd) One of Canada's ten provinces; bordered by Quebec and the Atlantic Ocean. p. 670

Newport A city on the southern end of Rhode Island; located at the mouth of Narragansett Bay. (41°N, 71°W) p. 197

Newton A city in south central Kansas. (38°N, 97°W) p. 488

Niihau (NEE•how) One of the eight main islands of Hawaii. p. A14

Norfolk (NAWR•fawk) A city in southeastern Virginia; located on the Elizabeth River. (37°N, 76°W) p. 234

Normandy Region of northwest France; site of Allied D day invasion on June 6, 1944. p. 569

North America One of Earth's seven continents. p. 27

North Pole The northernmost point on Earth. p. 50

Northwest Territories One of Canada's three territories; located in northern Canada. p. 670

Nova Scotia (NOH•vuh SKOH•shuh) A province of Canada; located in eastern Canada on a peninsula. pp. 151, 670

Nueces River (noo•AY•says) A river in southern Texas; flows into Nueces Bay, at the head of Corpus Christi Bay. p. 404

Nunavut One of Canada's three territories; formed in 1999 and inhabited mostly by Inuit peoples. p. 670

O

Oahu (oh•AH•hoo) The third-largest of the eight main islands of Hawaii; Honolulu is located there. p. A14

Oaxaca (wuh•HAH•kuh) A city and state in southern Mexico. (17°N, 96°W) p. 653

Ocmulgee (ohk•MUHL•gee) An ancient settlement of the Mound Builders; located in present-day central Georgia. p. 65

Ocmulgee River (ohk•MUHL•gee) A river in central Georgia; formed by the junction of the Yellow and South Rivers; flows south to join the Altamaha River. p. 234

Oconee River (oh•KOH•nee) A river in central Georgia; flows south and southeast to join the Ocmulgee and form the Altamaha River. p. 234

Ogallala (oh•guh•LAHL•uh) A city in western Nebraska on the South Platte River. (41°N, 102°W) p. 488

Ohio River A tributary of the Mississippi River, beginning in Pittsburgh, Pennsylvania, and ending at Cairo, Illinois. p. 29

Old Spanish Trail Part of the Santa Fe Trail that linked Santa Fe to Los Angeles. p. 406

Omaha (OH•muh•hah) The largest city in Nebraska; located in the eastern part of the state, on the Missouri River. (41°N, 96°W) p. 406

Ontario (ahn•TAIR•ee•oh) One of Canada's ten provinces; located between Quebec and Manitoba. p. 670

Oregon Country A former region in western North America; located between the Pacific coast and the Rocky Mountains, from the northern border of California to Alaska. p. 385

Oregon Trail A former route to the Oregon Country; extended from the Missouri River northwest to the Columbia River in Oregon. p. 406

Orinoco River A river in Venezuela in northern South America. p. 665

Orlando A city in central Florida. (28°N, 81°W) p. 621

Ottawa (AH•tuh•wuh) The capital of Canada; located in Ontario on the St. Lawrence Lowlands. (45°N, 75°W) p. 670

P

Pacific Ocean Largest body of water on Earth; extends from Arctic Circle to Antarctic Regions, separating North and South America from Australia and Asia. p. 27

Pagan Ruined Asian town; capital of a powerful dynasty during the 11th–13th centuries. p. 113

Palenque (pah•LENG•kay) An ancient settlement of the Mayan civilization; located in present-day Chiapas, in southern Mexico. (18°N, 92°W) p. 65

Palmyra Island (pal•MY•ruh) One of the northernmost of the Line Islands; located in the central Pacific Ocean. p. 526

Pampas Plains of South America; located in southern part of the continent, extending for nearly 1,000 miles. p. 665

Panama Canal A canal across the Isthmus of Panama; extends from the Caribbean Sea to the Gulf of Panama. p. 528

Panama City The capital of Panama; located in Central America. (9°N, 80°W) p. 658

Paramaribo A seaport city located on the Suriname River; capital of Suriname. (5°N, 55°W) p. 665

Paraná River A river in southeast central South America; formed by the joining of the Rio Grande and the Paranaíba River in south central Brazil. p. 665

Patagonia A barren tableland in South America between the Andes and the Atlantic Ocean. p. 665

Pearl Harbor An inlet on the southern coast of Oahu, Hawaii; the Japanese attacked an American naval base there on December 7, 1941. p. 557

Pecos River (PAY•kohs) A river in eastern New Mexico and western Texas; empties into the Rio Grande. p. 488

Pee Dee River A river in North Carolina and South Carolina; forms where the Yadkin and Uharie Rivers meet; empties into Winyah Bay. p. 234

Perryville A city in east central Kentucky; site of a major Civil War battle in 1862. (38°N, 90°W) p. 470

Perth Amboy A port city in central New Jersey; located on Raritan Bay. (40°N, 74°W) p. 212

Petersburg A port city in southeastern Virginia; located on the Appomattox River; site of a series of Civil War battles from 1864 to 1865. (37°N, 77°W) p. 470

Philadelphia A city in southeastern Pennsylvania, on the Delaware River; a major United States port. (40°N, 75°W) p. 219

Philippine Islands A group of more than 7,000 islands off the coast of southeastern Asia, making up the country of the Philippines. pp. 125, 526

Phoenix Capital and largest city of Arizona; located in south central Arizona. p. 621

Piedmont Area of high land on the eastern side of the Appalachian Mountains. p. 20

Pikes Peak A mountain in east central Colorado; part of the Rocky Mountains. p. 385

Pittsburgh The second-largest city in Pennsylvania; located in the southwestern part of the state, on the Ohio River. (40°N, 80°W) p. 47

Platte River (PLAT) A river in central Nebraska; flows east into the Missouri River below Omaha. p. 406

Plattsburgh A city in northeastern New York; located on the western shore of Lake Champlain; site of a major battle in the War of 1812. (45°N, 73°W) p. 391

Plymouth A town in southeastern Massachusetts, on Plymouth Bay; site of the first settlement built by the Pilgrims, who sailed on the *Mayflower*. (42°N, 71°W) p. 189

Port Royal A town in western Nova Scotia, Canada; name changed to Annapolis Royal in honor of Queen Anne; capital of Nova Scotia until 1749. (45°N, 66°W) p. 151

Port-au-Prince A seaport located on Hispaniola Island, in the West Indies, on the southeastern shore of the Gulf of Gonâve; capital of Haiti. (18°N, 72°W) p. 658

Portland (ME) A port city in southwestern Maine; located on Casco Bay. (44°N, 70°W) p. 353

Portland (OR) Oregon's largest city and principal port; located in the northwestern part of the state on the Willamette River. (46°N, 123°W) p. 621

Port of Spain A seaport in the northwestern part of the island of Trinidad; capital of Trinidad and Tobago. (10°N, 61°W) p. 658

Portsmouth (NH) (PAWRT•smuhth) A port city in southeastern New Hampshire; located at the mouth of the Piscataqua River. (43°N, 71°W) p. 197

Portsmouth (RI) A town in southeastern Rhode Island; located on the Sakonnet River. (42°N, 71°W) p. 197

Potomac River (puh•TOH•muhk) A river on the Coastal Plain of the United States; begins in West Virginia and flows into Chesapeake Bay; Washington, D.C., is located on this river. p. 233

Prince Edward Island One of Canada's ten provinces; located in the Gulf of St. Lawrence. p. 670

Princeton A borough in west central New Jersey; site of a major Revolutionary War battle. (40°N, 75°W) p. 323

Providence Rhode Island's capital and largest city; located in the northern part of the state, at the head of the Providence River. (42°N, 71°W) p. 197

Puebla A city and state in southeastern central Mexico. (19°N, 98°W) p. 653

Pueblo (PWEH•bloh) A city in Colorado. p. 488

Pueblo Bonito (PWEH•bloh boh•NEE•toh) Largest of the prehistoric pueblo ruins; located in Chaco Canyon National Monument, New Mexico. p. 65

Puerto Rico An island of the West Indies; located southeast of Florida; a commonwealth of the United States. pp. 129, 526

Put-in-Bay A bay on South Bass Island, north of Ohio in Lake Erie; site of a major battle in the War of 1812. (42°N, 83°W) p. 391

Q

Quebec (kwih•BEK) The capital of the province of Quebec, Canada; located on the northern side of the St. Lawrence River; the first successful French settlement in the Americas; established in 1608. (47°N, 71°W) pp. 151, 670

R

Raleigh (RAW•lee) The capital of North Carolina; located in the east central part of the state. (36°N, 79°W) p. 621

Red River A tributary of the Mississippi River; rises in eastern New Mexico, flows across Louisiana and into the Mississippi River; forms much of the Texas–Oklahoma border. pp. 29, 385

Regina (rih•JY•nuh) The capital of Saskatchewan, Canada; located in the southern part of the province. (50°N, 104°W) p. 670

Richmond The capital of Virginia; a port city located in the east central part of the state, on the James River; capital of the Confederacy. (38°N, 77°W) p. 470

Rio de Janeiro A commercial seaport in southeastern Brazil on the southwestern shore of Guanabara Bay. (23°S, 43°W) p. 665

Río de la Plata A river on the southeastern coast of South America. p. 665

Rio Grande A river in southwestern North America; it begins in Colorado and flows into the Gulf of Mexico; forms the border between Texas and Mexico. pp. 29, 385

Roanoke River A river in southern Virginia and northeastern North Carolina; flows east and southeast across the North Carolina border and into Albemarle Sound. p. 234

Rocky Mountains A range of mountains in the western United States and Canada, extending from Alaska to New Mexico; these mountains divide rivers that flow east from those that flow west. pp. 20, 385

Roxbury A residential district in southern Boston, Massachusetts; formerly a city, but became part of Boston in 1868; founded in 1630. (42°N, 71°W) p. 291

S

Sabine River (suh•BEEN) A river in eastern Texas and western Louisiana; flows southeast to the Gulf of Mexico. p. 404

Sacramento The capital of California; located in the north central part of the state, on the Sacramento River. (39°N, 121°W) p. 621

Sacramento River A river in northwestern California; rises near Mt. Shasta and flows south into Suisun Bay. p. 406

Salem A city on the northeastern coast of Massachusetts. (43°N, 71°W) p. 189

Salt Lake City Utah's capital and largest city; located in the northern part of the state, on the Jordan River. (41°N, 112°W) pp. 406, 621

San Antonio A city in south central Texas; located on the San Antonio River; site of the Alamo. (29°N, 98°W) pp. 404, 621

San Antonio River A river in southern Texas; flows southeast and empties into San Antonio Bay. p. 404

San Diego A large port city in southern California; located on San Diego Bay. (33°N, 117°W) pp. 149, 174, 621

San Francisco The second-largest city in California; located in the northern part of the state, on San Francisco Bay. (38°N, 123°W) pp. 149, 621

San Jacinto (hah•SEEN•toh) A location in southeastern Texas; site of a battle in the Texas Revolution in 1836. (31°N, 95°W) p. 404

San José A city in Central America; capital of Costa Rica. (10°N, 84°W) p. 658

San Juan (san WAHN) Puerto Rico's capital and largest city. (18°N, 66°W) p. 658

San Lorenzo An ancient settlement of the Olmecs; located in present-day southern Mexico. (29°N, 113°W) p. 65

San Salvador One of the islands in the southern Bahamas; Christopher Columbus landed there in 1492. p. 122

Santa Fe (SAN•tah FAY) The capital of New Mexico; located in the north central part of the state. (36°N, 106°W) pp. 149, 406, 621

Santa Fe Trail A former commercial route to the western United States; extended from western Missouri to Santa Fe, in central New Mexico. p. 406

Santee River A river in southeast central South Carolina; formed by the junction of the Congaree and Wateree Rivers; flows southeast into the Atlantic Ocean. p. 234

Santo Domingo The capital of the Dominican Republic. (18°N, 70°W) p. 658

São Francisco River A river in eastern Brazil; flows north, northeast, and east into the Atlantic Ocean. p. 665

São Paulo A city in southeastern Brazil; capital of São Paulo state. p. 665

Saratoga A village on the western bank of the Hudson River in eastern New York; site of a major Revolutionary War battle in 1777; present-day Schuylerville. (43°N, 74°W) p. 323

Saskatchewan (suh•SKA•chuh•wahn) One of Canada's ten provinces; located between Alberta and Manitoba. p. 670

Savannah The oldest city and a principal seaport in southeast Georgia; located in the southeastern part of the state, at the mouth of the Savannah River. (32°N, 81°W) pp. 234, 470

Savannah River A river that forms the border between Georgia and South Carolina; flows into the Atlantic Ocean at Savannah, Georgia. p. 234

Schenectady (skuh•NEK•tuh•dee) A city in eastern New York; located on the Mohawk River. (43°N, 74°W) p. 212

Seattle The largest city in Washington; a port city located in the west central part of the state, on Puget Sound. (48°N, 122°W) p. 621

Sedalia (suh•DAYL•yuh) A city in west central Missouri. (39°N, 93°W) p. 488

Serpent Mound An ancient settlement of the Mound Builders; located in present-day southern Ohio. (39°N, 83°W) p. 65

Shiloh (SHY•loh) A location in southwestern Tennessee; site of a major Civil War battle in 1862; also known as Pittsburg Landing. (35°N, 88°W) p. 470

Sierra Madre Occidental (see•AIR•ah MAH•dray ahk•sih•den•TAHL) A mountain range in western Mexico, running parallel to the Pacific coast. p. 20

Sierra Madre Oriental (awr•ee•en•TAHL) A mountain range in eastern Mexico, running parallel to the coast along the Gulf of Mexico. p. 20

Sierra Nevada A mountain range in eastern California that runs parallel to the Coast Ranges. p. 20

Snake River A river that begins in the Rocky Mountains and flows west into the Pacific Ocean; part of the Oregon Trail ran along this river. p. 385

South America One of Earth's seven continents. p. 27

South Pass A pass in southwestern Wyoming; crosses the Continental Divide; part of the Oregon Trail. p. 406

South Pole The southernmost point on Earth. p. 50

Spiro An ancient settlement of the Mound Builders; located in eastern Oklahoma. (35°N, 95°W) p. 65

Springfield (MA) A city in southwestern Massachusetts; located on the Connecticut River. (42°N, 73°W) p. 197

Springfield (MO) A city in southwestern Missouri; a point on the Trail of Tears. (37°N, 93°W) p. 398

St. Augustine (AW•guh•steen) A city on the coast of northeastern Florida; the oldest city founded by Europeans in the United States. (30°N, 81°W) pp. 129, 149

St. Croix (KROY) A city on the border of Maine and New Brunswick, Canada. (45°N, 67°W) p. 151

St. Ignace (IG•nuhs) A city in Michigan; located on the southeastern side of Michigan's upper peninsula. (46°N, 85°W) p. 153

St. John's A city on the southeastern coast of Canada, on the Atlantic Ocean; the capital of Newfoundland. (47°N, 52°W) p. 670

St. Joseph A city in northwestern Missouri on the Missouri River. (40°N, 95°W) p. 488

St. Lawrence River A river in northeastern North America; begins at Lake Ontario and flows into the Atlantic Ocean; forms part of the border between the United States and Canada. p. 151

St. Louis A major port city in east central Missouri; known as the Gateway to the West. (38°N, 90°W) pp. 47, 385

St. Lucia An island and an independent state of the Windward Islands; located in the eastern West Indies, south of Martinique and north of St. Vincent. p. 658

St. Marys A village in southern Maryland; the capital until 1694; present-day St. Marys City. (38°N, 76°W) p. 233

St. Paul The capital of Minnesota; located in the eastern part of the state, on the Mississippi River. (45°N, 93°W) p. 498

Strait of Magellan (muh•JEH•luhn) The narrow waterway between the southern tip of South America and Tierra del Fuego; links the Atlantic Ocean with the Pacific Ocean. p. 125

Sucre A city in Bolivia, South America. (19°S, 65°W) p. 665

Sudbury River A river in western Massachusetts; connects with the Concord River. p. 291

Suriname A country in north central South America. p. 665

Susquehanna River (suhs•kwuh•HA•nuh) A river in Maryland, Pennsylvania, and central New York; rises in Otsego Lake, New York, and empties into northern Chesapeake Bay. p. 89

T

Tallahassee Capital of Florida; located in the state's panhandle. (34°N, 84°W) p. 621

Tegucigalpa A city in Central America; capital of Honduras. (14°N, 87°W) p. 658

Tenochtitlán (tay•nohch•teet•LAHN) The ancient capital of the Aztec Empire, on the islands of Lake Texcoco; location of present-day Mexico City, in southern Mexico. (19°N, 99°W) p. 108

Tikal (tih•KAHL) An ancient settlement of the Mayan civilization; located in present-day Guatemala, in Central America. (17°N, 89°W) p. 65

Timbuktu A town in Mali; located in western Africa, near the Niger River. (17°N, 3°W) p. 108

Toledo (tuh•LEE•doh) A port city in northwestern Ohio located at the southwestern corner of Lake Erie. (42°N, 84°W) p. 498

Toronto The capital of the province of Ontario, Canada; located near the northwestern end of Lake Ontario; largest city in Canada. (43°N, 79°W) p. 670

Trail of Tears A trail that was the result of the Indian Removal Act of 1830; extended from the Cherokee Nation to Fort Gibson, in the Indian Territory. p. 398

Trenton The capital of New Jersey; located in the west central part of the state; site of a major Revolutionary War battle in 1776. (40°N, 75°W) p. 323

Tres Zapotes (TRAYS sah•POH•tays) An ancient settlement of the Olmecs; located in southern Mexico. (18°N, 95°W) p. 65

Trinidad and Tobago An independent republic made up of the islands of Trinidad and Tobago; located in the Atlantic Ocean off the northeastern coast of Venezuela. p. 658

Tucson (TOO•sahn) A city in southern Arizona; located on the Santa Cruz River. (32°N, 111°W) p. 621

Turtle Mound An ancient settlement of the Mound Builders; located on the present-day east central coast of Florida. (29°N, 81°W) p. 65

Valley Forge A location in southeastern Pennsylvania, on the Schuylkill River; site of General George Washington's winter headquarters during the Revolutionary War. (40°N, 77°W) p. 323

Vancouver Canada's eighth-largest city; located where the northern arm of the Fraser River empties into the Pacific Ocean. (49°N, 123°W) p. 670

Vandalia (van•DAYL•yuh) A city in south central Illinois. (39°N, 89°W) p. 415

Venice A port city in northeastern Italy; located on 118 islands in the Lagoon of Venice. (45°N, 12°E) pp. 108, 113

Veracruz (veh•rah•KROOZ) A state in Mexico; located in the eastern part of the country, on the Gulf of Mexico. (19°N, 96°W) p. 653

Vicksburg A city in western Mississippi; located on the Mississippi River; site of a major Civil War battle in 1863. (32°N, 91°W) p. 470

Victoria The capital of British Columbia, Canada; located on Vancouver Island. (48°N, 123°W) p. 670

Vincennes (vihn•SENZ) A town in southwestern Indiana; site of a Revolutionary War battle in 1779. (39°N, 88°W) p. 323

W

Wabash River (WAW•bash) A river in western Ohio and Indiana; flows west and south to the Ohio River, to form part of the Indiana–Illinois border. p. 323

Wake Island A United States territory in the Pacific Ocean. p. 526

Washington, D.C. The capital of the United States; located between Maryland and Virginia, on the Potomac River in a special district that is not part of any state. (39°N, 77°W) pp. 25, 391

West Indies The islands enclosing the Caribbean Sea, stretching from Florida in North America to Venezuela in South America. p. 202

West Point A United States military post since the Revolutionary War; located in southeastern New York on the western bank of the Hudson River. p. 323

Whitehorse The capital of the Yukon Territory, Canada; located on the southern bank of the Yukon River. (60°N, 135°W) p. 670

Whitman Mission Site of a Native American mission, established in 1836 by Marcus and Narcissa Whitman; located in present-day southeastern Washington. p. 406

Williamsburg A city in southeastern Virginia; located on a peninsula between the James and York Rivers; capital of the Virginia Colony. pp. 234, 254

Wilmington A coastal city in southeastern North Carolina; located along the Cape Fear River. p. 234

Winchester A city in northern Virginia; located in the Shenandoah Valley. (39°N, 78°W) p. 353

Winnipeg The capital of the province of Manitoba, Canada; located on the Red River. (50°N, 97°W) p. 670

Wisconsin River A river located in central Wisconsin that flows south and southeast to the Mississippi River. p. 153

Y

Yellowknife Capital of the Northwest Territories in Canada; located on the northwestern shore of Great Slave Lake at the mouth of the Yellowknife River. (62°N, 114°W) p. 670

Yellowstone River A river in northwestern Wyoming, southeastern Montana, and northwestern North Dakota; flows northeast to the Missouri River. p. 385

York Former name of Toronto, Canada; located near the northwestern end of Lake Ontario; site of a major battle in the War of 1812. p. 391

Yorktown A small town in southeastern Virginia; located on Chesapeake Bay; site of the last major Revolutionary War battle in 1781. (37°N, 76°W) p. 323

Yucatán Peninsula (yoo•kah•TAN) A peninsula in southeastern Mexico and northeastern Central America. p. 20

Yukon Territory One of Canada's three territories; bordered by the Arctic Ocean, the Northwest Territories, British Columbia, and Alaska. p. 670

Glossary

The Glossary contains important social studies words and their definitions. Each word is respelled as it would be in a dictionary. When you see this mark ´ after a syllable, pronounce that syllable with more force than the other syllables. The page number at the end of the definition tells where to find the word in your book.

add, āce, câre, pälm; end, ēqual; it, īce; odd, ōpen, ôrder; to͝ok, po͞ol; up, bûrn; yo͞o as *u* in *fuse*;
oil; pout; ə as *a* in *above*, *e* in *sicken*, *i* in *possible*, *o* in *melon*, *u* in *circus*; check; ring; thin; this;
zh as in *vision*

A

abolitionist (a•bə•li´shən•ist) A person who wanted to end slavery. p. 448

absolute location (ab´sə•lo͞ot lō•kā´shən) The exact location of a place on Earth, either a postal location or its lines of latitude and longitude. p. 50

acquittal (ə•kwi´təl) A verdict of not guilty. p. 479

adapt (ə•dapt´) To adjust ways of living to land and resources. pp. 6, 70

address (ə•dres´) A formal speech. p. 467

advertisement (ad•vər•tīz´mənt) A public announcement that tells people about a product or an opportunity. p. 503

agriculture (a´grə•kul•chər) Farming. p. 64

airlift (âr´lift) A system of moving supplies by airplane. p. 581

allegiance (ə•lē´jəns) Loyalty. p. 303

alliance (ə•lī´əns) A formal agreement among nations, states, or individuals to cooperate. p. 270

ally (a´lī) A partner in an alliance; a friend, especially in times of war. p. 270

almanac (ôl´mə•nak) A yearly calendar and weather forecast that helps farmers know when to plant crops. p. 222

amendment (ə•mend´mənt) An addition or change to the Constitution. p. 370

analyze (a´nəl•īz) To look closely at how the parts of an event connect with one another and how the event is connected to other events. p. 3

ancestor (an´ses•tər) An early family member. p. 59

annex (ə•neks´) To add on. p. 394

Anti-Federalist (an´tī•fe´də•rə•list) A citizen who was against ratification of the Constitution. p. 368

apprentice (ə•pren´təs) A person who learns a trade by living with the family of a skilled worker and training for several years. p. 249

archaeologist (är•kē•o´lə•jist) A scientist who studies the culture of people who lived long ago. p. 57

arid (ar´əd) Dry. p. 36

armada (är•mä´də) A Spanish fleet of warships. p. 159

armistice (är´mə•stəs) An agreement to stop fighting a war. p. 527

arms control (ärmz kən•trōl´) A limiting of the number of weapons that each nation may have. p. 592

arms race (ärmz rās) A situation in which two or more countries build weapons to protect themselves against each other. p. 582

arsenal (är´sə•nəl) A place used for storing weapons. p. 348

artifact (är´tə•fakt) An object made by early people. p. 58

assassinate (ə•sa´sən•āt) To murder a leader by sudden or secret attack. p. 477

assembly line (ə•sem´blē līn) A system of mass production in which parts of a product, such as a car, are put together as they move past a line of workers. p. 544

astrolabe (as´tra•lāb) An instrument formerly used to calculate one's position compared to the sun, moon, and stars. p. 116

auction (ôk´shən) A public sale. p. 243

authority (ə•thôr´ə•tē) The right to control and make decisions. p. 164

B

backcountry (bak´kən•trē) The land between the Coastal Plain and the Appalachian Mountains. p. 224

barter (bär´tər) To exchange goods usually without using money. p. 77

basin (bā´sən) Low, bowl-shaped land with higher ground all around it. p. 22

bias (bī´əs) An opinion or feeling for or against someone or something. p. 286

bill (bil) An idea for a new law. p. 356

bill of rights (bil uv rīts) A list of freedoms. p. 276

black codes (blak kōdz) Laws limiting the rights of former slaves in the South. p. 478

blockade (blä•kād´) To use warships to prevent other ships from entering or leaving a harbor. p. 289

boom (bo͞om) A time of fast economic growth. p. 486

border state (bôr´dər stāt) During the Civil War, a state—Delaware, Kentucky, Maryland, or Missouri—between the North and the South that was unsure of which side to support. p. 459

borderlands (bôr´dər•landz) Areas of land on or near the borders between countries, colonies, or regions that serve as barriers. p. 146

boycott (boi´kät) To refuse to buy or use goods or services. p. 282

broker (brō´kər) A person who is paid to buy and sell for someone else. p. 241

budget (bu´jət) A plan for spending money. p. 280

buffer zone (bu´fər zōn) An area of land that serves as a barrier. p. 146

bureaucracy (byo͞o•rä´krə•sē) A system of organizing the many workers and groups that are needed to run government programs. p. 549

burgess (bûr´jəs) A representative in the legislature of colonial Virginia or Maryland. p. 163

bust (bust) A time of quick economic decline. p. 487

C

Cabinet (kab´ə•nit) A group of the President's most important advisers. p. 375

candidate (kan´də•dāt) A person running for office. p. 378

capital (ka´pə•təl) The money needed to set up or improve a business. p. 497

caravel (kâr´ə•vel) A ship that used square or triangular sails to travel long distances swiftly. p. 116

cardinal direction (kä rd´nal də•rek´shən) One of the main directions: north, south, east, or west. p. A3

carpetbagger (kär´pət•ba•gər) A Northerner who moved to the South to take part in Reconstruction governments. p. 483

cartogram (kär´tə•gram) A diagram that gives information about places based on the size shown for each place. p. 626

cartographer (kä r•tä´grə•fər) A person who makes maps. p. 115

cash crop (kash krop) A crop that people raise to sell rather than to use themselves. p. 163

casualty (ka´zhəl•tē) A person who has been killed or wounded in a war. p. 461

cause (kôz) An event or action that makes something else happen. p. 120

cease-fire (sēs•fīr´) A temporary end to a conflict. p. 582

census (sen´səs) An official population count. p. 359

century (sen´chə•rē) A period of 100 years. p. 60

ceremony (ser´ə•mō•nē) A series of actions performed during a special event. p. 72

cession (se´shən) Something given up, such as land. p. 407

charter (chär´tər) An official paper in which certain rights are given by a government to a person, group, or business. p. 188

checks and balances (cheks and ba´lən•səz) A system that gives each branch of government different powers so that each branch can watch over the authority of the others. p. 363

chronology (krə•nä´lə•jē) Time order. p. 2

circle graph (sûr´kəl graf) A round chart that can be divided into pieces, or parts; often referred to as a pie graph. p. 223

city-state (si´tē•stāt) A city and the surrounding area that stands as an independent state. p. 111

civic participation (si´vik pär•ti•sə•pā´shən) Being concerned with and involved in issues related to the community, state, country, or world. p. 9

civics (si´viks) The study of citizenship. p. 9

civil rights (si´vəl rīts) Rights guaranteed to all citizens by the Constitution. p. 535

civil war (si´vəl wôr) A war between two groups in the same country. p. 151

civilian (sə•vil´yən) A person who is not in the military. p. 557

civilization (si•və•lə•zā´shən) A culture that usually has cities with well-developed forms of government, religion, and learning. p. 65

claim (klām) To declare that a person or a country owns something. p. 121

clan (klan) A group of families that are related to one another. p. 78

class (klas) A group of people who are alike in some way. Classes are treated with different amounts of respect in a society. p. 65

classify (kla´sə•fī) To group. p. 171

climate (klī´mət) The kind of weather a place has most often, year after year. p. 33

climograph (klī´mə•graf) A chart that shows the average monthly temperature and the average monthly precipitation for a place. p. 492

code (kōd) A set of laws. p. 445

cold war (kōld wôr) Hostilities in which opposing nations attack each other by using propaganda and money rather than soldiers and weapons. p. 575

colonist (kä´lə•nist) A person who lives in a land ruled by a distant country. p. 144

colony (kä´lə•nē) A land ruled by a distant country. p. 144

commander in chief (kə•man´dər in chēf´) A person who is in control of all the armed forces of a nation. p. 294

commerce (kä´mərs) Trade. p. 351

commission (kə•mi´shən) A special committee that is set up to study something. p. 532

common (kä´mən) An open area where sheep and cattle graze; village green. p. 190

commonwealth (kä´mən•welth) A nation that governs itself but is a territory of another country. p. 660

communism (kä m´yə•ni•zəm) A social and economic system in which all land and industries are owned by the government, and individuals have few rights and little freedom. p. 574

compact (kä m´pakt) An agreement. p. 167

company (kum´pə•nē) A business. p. 138

compass (kum´pəs) An instrument used to find direction. p. 109

compass rose (kum´pəs rōz) A circular direction marker on a map. p. A3

compromise (kä m´prə•mīz) An agreement in which each side in a conflict gives up some of what it wants in order to get some of what it wants. p. 91

concentration camp (kon•sən•trā´shən kamp) A guarded camp built by the German National Socialist party, or Nazis, where prisoners were held. p. 555

Confederacy (kən•fe´də•rə•sē) The group of eleven states that left the Union, also called the Confederate States of America. p. 453

confederation (kən•fe•də•rā´shən) A loosely united group of governments working together. p. 89

congress (kän´grəs) A formal meeting of government representatives who have the authority to make laws. p. 270

conquistador (kä n•kēs´tə•dôr) Any of the Spanish conquerors in the Americas during the early 1500s. p. 127

consent (kən•sent´) Agreement. p. 195

consequence (kä n´sə•kwens) Something that happens because of an action. p. 313

conservation (kä n•sər•vā´shən) The protection and wise use of natural resources. p. 533

constitution (kä n•stə•tōō´shən) A written plan of government. p. 235

consumer good (kən•sōō´mər gŏŏd) A product made for personal use. p. 544

contour line (kä n´tōōr līn) A line on a drawing or map that connects all points of equal elevation. p. 24

convention (kən•ven´shən) An important meeting. p. 351

cotton gin (kä´tən jin) A machine that removed seeds and hulls from cotton fibers much more quickly than workers could by hand. p. 418

council (koun´səl) A group that makes laws. p. 90

county (koun´tē) The large part of a colony or a state. p. 250

county seat (koun´tē sēt) The main town of a county. p. 250

crossroads (krôs´rōdz) A place that connects people, goods, and ideas. p. 46

cultural region (kul´chə•rəl rē´jən) An area in which people share some ways of life. p. 45

culture (kul´chər) A way of life. p. 10

current (kûr´ənt) The part of a body of water flowing in a certain direction. p. 26

D

D day (dē dā) June 6, 1944, a day on which Allied forces during World War II worked together in the largest water-to-land invasion in history. p. 565

debtor (de´tər) A person who was put in prison for owning money. p. 236

decade (de´kād) A period of ten years. p. 60

declaration (de•klə•rā´shən) An official statement. p. 283

deficit (de´fə•sət) A shortage. p. 597

deforestation (dē•fôr•ə•stā´shən) The cutting down of most or all trees in an area. p. 668

delegate (de´li•gət) A representative. p. 271

demand (di•mand´) The need or want for a product or service by people who are willing to pay for it. p. 418

demarcation (dē•mä r•kā´shən) A line that marks a boundary. p. 126

democracy (di•mä´krə•sē) A form of government in which the people have power to make choices about their lives and government, either directly or through representation. p. 395

depression (di•pre´shən) A time of little economic growth when there are few jobs and people have little money. p. 547

descendant (di•sen´dənt) A person's child, grand-child, and so on. p. 58

desertion (di•zûr´shən) Leaving one's duties, such as military service, without permission. p. 132

détente (dā•tä nt´) An easing of tensions, especially between countries. p. 592

dictator (dik´tā•tər) A leader who has complete control of the government. p. 402

dictatorship (dik´tā•tər•ship) A form of government where a leader has complete control of the government. p. 555

distortion (di•stôr´shən) An area that is not accurate on a map. p. 530

diverse economy (də•vûrs´ i•kä´nə•mē) An economy that is based on many kinds of industries. p. 632

division of labor (də•vi´zhən uv lā´bər) Work that is divided so that each worker does a small part of a larger job. p. 544

doctrine (däk´trən) A government plan of action. p. 394

drainage basin (drā´nij bā´sən) Land drained by a river system. p. 31

drought (drout) A long period with little or no rain. p. 36

due process of law (dōō prä´ses uv lô) The principle that guarantees the right to a fair public trial. p. 372

dugout (dug´out) A boat made from a large, hollowed-out log. p. 76

E

earthwork (ûrth´wərk) A wall made of dirt or stone. p. 294

e-commerce (ē•kä´mərs) The buying and selling of goods and services through computer connections. p. 634

economic region (e•kə•nä´mik rē´jən) An area
defined by the kind of work people do or the
products they produce. p. 45

economics (e•kə•nä´miks) The study of how people
use resources to meet their needs. p. 8

economy (i•kä´nə•mē) The way people of a state,
region, or country use resources to meet their needs.
p. 8

effect (i•fekt´) The result of an event or action. p. 120

electoral college (i•lek´tə•rəl kä´lij) A group of officials
chosen by citizens to vote for the President and Vice
President. p. 360

elevation (e•lə•vā´shən) The height of land in relation
to sea level. p. 24

emancipation (i•man•sə•pā´shən) The freeing of
enslaved peoples. p. 445

embargo (im•bär´gō) The refusal of one nation to
trade goods and services with another. p. 660

empire (em´pīr) The conquered lands of many people
and places governed by one ruler. p. 106

encounter (in•koun´tər) A meeting. p. 106

enlist (in•list´) To join. p. 315

entrepreneur (än•trə•prə•nûr´) A person who sets up
and runs a business. p. 495

equality (i•kwä´lə•tē) Equal rights. p. 448

erosion (i•rō´zhən) The wearing down of Earth's
surface, usually by wind or water. p. 42

estuary (es´chə•wer•ē) The wide mouth of a river
where ocean tides flow in. p. 137

ethnic group (eth´nik grōōp) A group of people from
the same country, of the same race, or with a shared
way of life. p. 622

expedition (ek•spə•di´shən) A journey. p. 118

expel (ik•spel´) To force to leave. p. 195

export (ek´spôrt) A product that leaves a country.
p. 201

extinct (ik•stingt´) No longer in existence. p. 64

F

fact (fakt) A statement that can be checked and proved
to be true. p. 240

fall line (fôl līn) A place where the elevation of the
land drops sharply, causing rivers to form waterfalls
or rapids. p. 31

farm produce (fä rm prō´dōōs) Grains, fruits, and
vegetables for sale. p. 215

federal system (fe´də•rəl sis´təm) A system of
government in which the authority to govern is
shared by the central and state governments. p. 354

Federalist (fe´də•rə•list) After the American
Revolution, a citizen who wanted a strong national
government and was in favor of ratifying the
Constitution. p. 368

fertilizer (fûr´təl•ī•zər) Matter added to the soil to
make it produce more crops. p. 41

flow chart (flō chärt) A diagram that shows the order
in which things happen. p. 364

fork (fôrk) A place in which a river divides. p. 269

forty-niner (fôr•tē•nī´nər) A gold seeker who arrived
in California in 1849. p. 409

frame of reference (frām uv ref´rəns) A set of
ideas that determine how a person understands
something. pp. 3, 442

free election (frē i•lek´shən) An election that offers a
choice of candidates. p. 661

free enterprise (frē en´tər•prīz) An economic system
in which people are able to start and run their own
businesses with little control by the government.
p. 494

free state (frē´ stāt) A state that did not allow slavery
before the Civil War. p. 437

free world (frē wûrld´) The United States and its
allies. p. 575

freedmen (frēd´mən) Men, women, and children who
had once been slaves. p. 481

free-trade agreement (frē•trād´ ə•grē´mənt) A treaty
in which countries agree to charge no tariffs, or
taxes, on goods they buy from and sell to each
other. p. 636

front (frənt) A battle line. p. 565

frontier (frən•tir´) The land that lies beyond settled
areas. p. 199

fugitive (fyōō´jə•tiv) A person who is running away
from something. p. 445

fundamental (fən•də•men´təl) Basic. p. 197

G

gap (gap) An opening or a low place between
mountains. p. 277

generalization (jen•ə•rə•lə•zā´shən) A statement
based on facts, used to summarize groups of facts
and to show relationships between them. p. 68

geography (jē•ä´grə•fē) The study of Earth's surface
and the way people use it. p. 6

glacier (glā´shər) A huge, slow-moving mass of ice
covering land. p. 56

global economy (glō´bəl i•kä´nə•mē) The world
market in which companies from different countries
buy and sell goods and services. p. 636

gold rush (gōld´ rush) A sudden rush of new people
to an area where gold has been found. p. 409

government (gu´vərn•mənt) A system by which
people of a community, state, or nation use leaders
and laws to help people live together. p. 9

grant (grant) A sum of money or other payment given
for a particular purpose. p. 127

Great Awakening (grāt ə•wā´kən•ing) A religious
movement started by a Dutch minister in the
Middle Atlantic Colonies that called for greater
freedom of choice in religion. p. 215

GLOSSARY

grid system (grid sis´təm) An arrangement of lines that divide something, such as a map, into squares. p. A3

grievance (grē´vəns) A complaint. p. 305

hacienda (ä•sē•en´dä) A large estate where cattle and sheep are raised. p. 147

harpoon (här•pōōn´) A long spear with a sharp shell point. p. 79

hatch lines (hach līnz) A pattern of stripes used on historical maps to show areas claimed by two or more countries. p. 278

heritage (her´ə•tij) Culture that has come from the past and continues today. p. 10

high-tech (hī•tek´) The term used to describe industries that invent, build, or use computers and other kinds of electronic equipment. p. 633

hijack (hī jak´) A person who illegally takes control of something. p. 600

historical empathy (hi•stôr´i•kəl em´pə•thē) An understanding of the thoughts and feelings people of the past had about events in their time. p. 3

historical map (hi•stôr´i•kəl map) A map that provides information about a place as it was in the past. p. 112

history (hi´stə•rē) Events of the past. p. 2

hogan (hō´gä n) A cone-shaped Navajo shelter built by covering a log frame with bark and mud. p. 72

Holocaust (hō´lə•kôst) The mass murder of European Jews, during World War II. p. 573

homesteader (hōm´sted•ər) A person living on land granted by the government. p. 488

human feature (hyōō´mən fē´chər) Something created by humans, such as a building or road, that alters the land. p. 6

human resource (hyōō´mən rē´sôrs) A worker who brings his or her own ideas and skills to a job. p. 499

humidity (hyōō•mi´də•tē) The amount of moisture in the air. p. 36

immigrant (i´mi•grənt) A person who comes into a country to make a new home. p. 219

impeach (im•pēch´) To accuse a government official, such as the President, of "treason, bribery, or other high crimes and misdemeanors." p. 361

imperialism (im•pir´ē•ə•liz•əm) Empire building. p. 526

import (im´pôrt) A product brought into a country. p. 201

impressment (im•pres´mənt) The taking of workers against their will. p. 389

inauguration (i•nô•gyə•rā´shən) A ceremony in which a leader takes office. p. 384

indentured servant (in•den´chərd sûr´vənt) A person who agreed to work for another person without pay for a certain length of time in exchange for passage to North America. p. 234

independence (in•də•pen´dəns) The freedom to govern on one's own. p. 302

indigo (in´di•gō) A plant from which a blue dye can be made. p. 235

industrial revolution (in•dus´trē•əl re•və•lōō´shən) The period of time during the 1700s and 1800s in which machines took the place of hand tools to manufacture goods. p. 412

industrialization (in•dəs•trē•ə•lə•zā´shən) The growth of industry. p. 545

industry (in´dəs•trē) All the businesses that make one kind of product or provide one kind of service. p. 200

inflation (in•flā´shən) An economic condition in which more money is needed to buy goods and services than was needed earlier. p. 347

Information Age (in•fər•mā´shən āj) The period in history that began in the second half of the twentieth century and is marked by the growing amount of information people can get. p. 633

informed citizen (in•fôrmd´ si´tə•zən) A citizen who knows what is happening in the community, the state, the nation, and the world. p. 641

inlet (in´let) An area of water extending into the land from a larger body of water. p. 27

inset map (in´set map) A smaller map within a larger one. p. A3

integration (in•tə•grā´shən) The bringing together of people of all races in education, jobs, and housing. p. 587

interchangeable parts (in•tər•chān´jə•bəl pä rts) Identical copies of parts made by machines so that if one part breaks, an identical one can be installed. p. 418

interdependent (in•tər•di•pen´dənt) Depending on each other. p. 635

interest (in´trəst) The fee a borrower pays for the use of money. p. 562

interest rate (in´trəst rāt) The amount a bank charges to lend money. p. 656

intermediate direction (in•tər•mē´dē•it də•rek´shən) One of the in-between directions: northeast, northwest, southeast, southwest. p. A3

international trade (in•tər•na´shə•nəl trād) Trade among nations. p. 635

Internet (in´tər•net) The system that joins computers around the world for the exchange of information. p. 624

intolerable (in•tä l´ər•ə•bəl) Unacceptable. p. 289

investor (in•ves´tər) A person who uses money to buy or make something that will yield a profit. p. 414

irrigation (i•rə•gā´shən) The use of canals, ditches, or pipes to move water to dry areas. p. 41

island-hopping (ī´lənd•hä´ping) The process of the Allies capturing island after island as they advanced toward Japan during World War II. p. 567

isolation (ī•sə•lā´shən) The policy of remaining separate from other countries. p. 541

isthmus (is´məs) A narrow strip of land that connects two larger land areas. p. 123

jury (jûr´ē) A group of citizens who decide a case in court. p. 641

justice (jus´təs) A Supreme Court judge. p. 361

justice (jus´təs) Fairness. p. 214

land use (land yoos) The way in which most of the land in a place is used. p. 43

landform (land´fôrm) A physical feature, such as a plain, mountain, hill, valley, or plateau, on the Earth's surface. p. 18

legislature (le´jəs•lā•chər) The lawmaking branch of government. p. 163

liberate (li´bə•rāt) To set free. p. 666

liberty (li´bər•tē) The freedom of people to make their own laws. p. 285

life expectancy (līf ik•spek´tən•sē) The average number of years a person can expect to live. p. 662

line graph (līn graf) A chart that uses one or more lines to show changes over time. p. 205

lines of latitude (līnz uv la´tə•tood) Lines on a map or globe that run east and west; also called parallels. p. 50

lines of longitude (līnz uv lon´jə•tood) Lines on a map or globe that run north and south; also called meridians. p. 50

location (lō•kā´shən) The place where something can be found. p. 6

locator (lō´kā•tər) A small map or picture of a globe that shows where an area on the main map is found in a state, on a continent, or in the world. p. A3

lodge (läj) A circular house of the Plains Indians. p. 82

loft (lôft) The part of a house located between the ceiling and the roof. p. 226

long drive (lông drīv) A trip made by ranchers to lead cattle to the market or the railroads. p. 487

longhouse (lông´hous) A long wooden building in which several related Iroquois families lived together. p. 89

Loyalist (loi´ə•list) A person who supported the British government during the American Revolution. p. 308

Magna Carta (mag´nə kär´tə) The English charter granted in 1215 by King John. It lists the rights of the royal class and limits the rights of the king. p. 370

majority rule (mə•jôr´ə•tē rool) The political idea that the majority of an organized group should have the power to make decisions for the whole group. p. 168

manifest destiny (ma´nə•fest des´tə•nē) The belief, shared by many Americans, that the United States should one day stretch from the Atlantic Ocean to the Pacific Ocean. p. 402

map key (map kē) A part of a map that explains what the symbols on a map stand for. p. A2

map scale (map skāl) A part of a map that compares a distance on the map to a distance in the real world. p. A3

map title (map tī´təl) Words on a map that tell the subject of the map. p. A2

mass production (mas prə•duk´shən) A system of producing large amounts of goods at one time. p. 418

mechanization of agriculture (me•kə•nə•zā´shən uv a´grə•kul•chər) The use of machines to plant and harvest crops. p. 546

median age (mē´dē•ən āj) The average age of all the people in a country. p. 662

mercenary (mûr´sən•er•ē) A soldier who serves for pay in the military of a foreign nation. p. 296

meridian (mə•ri´dē•ən) A line of longitude that runs from the North Pole to the South Pole. p. 50

merit system (mer´ət sis´təm) A way of making sure that the most qualified people get government jobs. p. 533

metropolitan area (me•trə•pä´lə•tən ar´ē•ə) A large city and the suburbs that surround it. p. 47

middle class (mi´dəl klas) The group of people who are economically between the rich and the poor. p. 656

migrant worker (mī´grənt wûr´kər) Someone who moves from place to place with the seasons to harvest crops. p. 588

migration (mī•grā´shən) The movement of people. p. 57

military draft (mil´ə•ter•ē draft) A way to bring people into military service. p. 538

militia (mə•li´shə) A volunteer army. p. 221

millennium (mə•le´nē•əm) A period of 1,000 years. p. 60

mission (mi´shən) A small religious settlement. p. 148

missionary (mi´shə•ner•ē) A person sent out by a church to spread its religion. p. 148

modify (mä´də•fī) To change. pp. 6, 40

monarch (mä´närk) A king or queen. p. 108

monopoly (mə•noʹpə•lē) The complete control of a product or service. p. 288

mountain range (mounʹtən rānj) A group of connected mountains. p. 19

mutiny (myo͞oʹtə•nē) Rebellion against the leader of one's group. p. 138

N

national anthem (naʹshə•nəl anʹthəm) A song of praise for a country that is recognized as the official song of that country. p. 393

nationalism (naʹshə•nəl•i•zəm) Pride in one's country. p. 394

natural resource (naʹchə•rəl rēʹsôrs) Something found in nature that people can use. p. 40

natural vegetation (naʹchə•rəl ve•jə•tāʹshən) The plant life that grows naturally in a place. p. 33

naval store (nāʹvəl stōr) A product that is used to build and repair a ship. p. 203

navigation (na•və•gāʹshən) The method of planning and controlling the course of a ship. p. 115

negotiate (ni•gōʹshē•āt) To talk with another to work out an agreement. p. 327

neutral (no͞oʹtrəl) Not taking a side in a disagreement. p. 309

new immigration (no͞o i•mə•grāʹshən) After 1890, the large group of people who came from southern and central Europe and other parts of the world to settle in North America. p. 503

nomad (nōʹmad) A wanderer who has no settled home. p. 63

no-man's-land (nōʹmanz•land) In a war, land that is not held by either side but is filled with obstacles such as barbed wire and land mines. p. 539

nonrenewable (nä n•ri•no͞oʹə•bəl) Not able to be made again quickly by nature or people. p. 41

nonviolence (nä n•vīʹə•ləns) The use of peaceful ways to bring about change. p. 587

Northwest Passage (nôrthʹwest paʹsij) A waterway in North America thought to connect the Atlantic Ocean and the Pacific Ocean. p. 136

O

old immigration (ōld i•mə•grāʹshən) Before 1890, people who came from northern and western Europe to settle in North America. p. 502

olive branch (äʹliv branch) An ancient symbol of peace. p. 296

open range (ōʹpən rānj) Land on which animals can graze freely. p. 489

opinion (ə•pinʹyən) A statement that tells what a person thinks or believes. p. 240

opportunity cost (ä•pər•to͞oʹnə•tē kôst) the value of the thing a person gives up in order to get something else. p. 564

oral history (ôrʹəl hisʹtə•rē) Stories, events, or experiences told aloud by a person who did not have a written language or who did not write down what happened. p. 2

ordinance (ôrʹdən•əns) A law or set of laws. p. 349

origin story (ôrʹə•jən stōrʹē) A story or set of stories by Native American people that tell about their beginnings and how the world came to be. p. 59

overseer (ōʹvər•sē•ər) A hired person who watched field slaves as they worked. p. 243

P

pacifist (paʹsə•fist) A believer in the peaceful settlement of differences. p. 310

palisade (pa•lə•sādʹ) A wall made of sharpened tree trunks to protect a village from enemies or wild animals. p. 87

parallel (parʹə•lel) A line of latitude. It is called this because parallels are always the same distance from one another. p. 50

parallel time line (parʹə•lel tīm līn) Two or more time lines that show the same period of time. p. 570

Parliament (pä rʹlə•mənt) The lawmaking body of the British government. p. 271

patent (paʹtənt) A license to make, use, or sell a new invention. p. 419

pathfinder (pathʹfīn•dər) Someone who finds a way through an unknown region. p. 387

Patriot (pāʹtrē•ət) A colonist who was against British rule and supported the rebel cause in the American Colonies. p. 308

patriotism (pāʹtrē•ə•ti•zəm) Love of one's country. p. 643

permanent (pûrʹmə•nənt) Long-lasting. p. 144

petition (pə•tiʹshən) A signed request made to an official person or organization. p. 290

petroleum (pə•trōʹlē•əm) Oil. p. 497

physical feature (fiʹzi•kəl fēʹchər) A land feature that has been made by nature. p. 6

piedmont (pēdʹmä nt) An area at or near the foot of a mountain. p. 19

pilgrim (pilʹgrəm) A person who makes a journey for religious reasons. p. 166

pioneer (pī•ə•nirʹ) A person who is first to settle a new place. p. 276

pit house (pit hous) A house that was partially built over a hole in the earth so some rooms could be underground. p. 78

plantation (plan•tāʹshən) A huge farm. p. 155

planter (planʹtər) A plantation owner. p. 241

plateau (pla•tōʹ) A broad area of high, mostly flat land. p. 21

point of view (point uv vyo͞o) A person's perspective. pp. 3, 286

political boss (pə•li´ti•kəl bôs) A powerful, often corrupt leader who has many dishonest employees and who is able to control the government. p. 534

political party (pə•li´ti•kəl pär´tē) A group whose members seek to elect government officials who share the group's points of view about many issues. p. 377

political region (pə•li´ti•kəl rē´jən) An area that shares a government and leaders. p. 45

population density (po•pyə•lā´shən den´sə•tē) The number of people who live within 1 square mile or 1 square kilometer of land. p. 602

population pyramid (po•pyə•lā´shən pir´ə•mid) A graph that shows the division of a country's population by age. p. 662

population region (po•pyə•lā´shən rē´jən) An area based on where people live. p. 45

potlatch (pät´lach) A special Native American gathering or celebration with feasting and dancing. p. 78

prairie (prer´ē) An area of flat or rolling land covered mostly by grasses and wildflowers. p. 38

preamble (prē´am•bəl) An introduction; first part. p. 304

prediction (pri•dik´shən) A decision about what may happen next, based on the way things are. p. 559

prejudice (pre´jə•dəs) An unfair feeling of hate or dislike for members of a certain group because of their background, race, or religion. p. 504

presidio (prā•sē´dē•ō) A Spanish fort. p. 146

primary source (prī´mer•ē sôrs) A record of an event made by a person who saw or took part in it. p. 4

prime meridian (prīm mə•ri´dē•ən) The meridian marked 0 degrees and that runs north and south through Greenwich, England. p. 50

principle (prin´sə•pəl) A rule that is used in deciding how to behave. p. 329

proclamation (prä•klə•mā´shən) An order from a leader to the citizens. p. 276

profit (prä´fət) The money left over after all expenses have been paid. p. 115

progressive (prə•gre´siv) A person who wants to improve government and make life better. p. 532

projection (prə•jek´shən) A way of showing Earth on flat paper. p. 530

proprietary colony (prə•prī´ə•tər•e kä´lə•nē) A colony owned and ruled by one person who was chosen by a king or queen. p. 155

proprietor (prə•prī´ə•tər) An owner. p. 155

prospector (präs´pek•tər) A person who searches for silver, gold, and other mineral resources. p. 487

prosperity (präs•per´ə•tē) Economic success. p. 162

province (prä´vəns) A political region, similar to a state. p. 670

public office (pub´lik ô´fəs) A job a person is elected to do. p. 192

public opinion (pub´lik ə•pin´yən) The point of view held by the majority of people. p. 302

public service (pub´lik sûr´vəs) A job someone does to help the community or society as a whole. p. 245

pueblo (pwe´blō) A Spanish word for *village*. p. 66

Puritan (pyûr´ə•tən) A member of the Church of England who settled in North America to follow Christian beliefs in a more "pure" way. p. 188

quarter (kwôr´tər) To provide or pay for housing at no cost to another person. p. 289

rain shadow (rān sha´dō) The driest side of a mountain. p. 35

rapid (ra´pəd) The fast-moving, dangerous place in a river caused by a sudden drop in elevation. p. 138

rapid-transit system (ra´pəd tran´sət sis´təm) A passenger transportation system that uses elevated or underground trains or both. p. 629

ratify (ra´tə•fī) To approve. p. 366

rationing (rash´ən•ing) The limiting of a supply of something. p. 561

raw material (rô mə•tir´ē•əl) A resource that can be used to make a product. p. 158

Reconstruction (rē•kən•struk´shən) The time during which the South was rebuilt after the Civil War. p. 476

recycle (rē•sī´kəl) To reuse. p. 562

refinery (ri•fī´nə•rē) A factory in which materials, especially fuels, are cleaned and made into usable products. p. 487

reform (ri•fôrm´) To change for the better. p. 532

refuge (re´fyo͞oj) A safe place. p. 213

refugee (ref´yo͞o•jē) A person who leaves home to seek shelter and safety elsewhere. p. 573

regiment (re´jə•mənt) A large, organized group of soldiers. p. 310

region (rē´jən) An area of Earth in which many features are similar. p. 6

register (rej´ə•stər) To enroll as a voter. p. 641

regulation (re•gyə•lā´shən) A rule or an order. p. 505

relative location (re´lə•tiv lō•kā´shən) The position of one place in relation to another. p. 44

relocation camp (rē•lō•kā´shən kamp) A temporary settlement in which Japanese Americans were forced to live during World War II. p. 563

Renaissance (re´nə•säns) A French word meaning "rebirth," used to name a time of advances in thought, learning, art, and science. p. 109

renewable (ri•no͞o´ə•bəl) Able to be made or grown again by nature or people. p. 42

repeal (ri•pēl´) To cancel, or undo, a law. p. 283

GLOSSARY

representation (re•pri•zen•tā´shən) The act of speaking on behalf of someone else. p. 281

republic (ri•pub´lik) A form of government in which people elect representatives to govern the country. p. 346

reservation (re•zər•vā´shən) An area of land set aside by the government for use only by Native Americans. p. 490

reserved powers (ri•zûrvd´ pou´ərz) Authority that belongs to the states or to the people, not to the national government. p. 372

resist (ri•zist´) To act against. p. 445

resolution (re•zə•lōō´shən) A formal statement of the feelings of a group of people about an important topic. p. 303

resolve (ri•zälv´) To settle. p. 91

responsibility (ri•spä n•sə•bil´ə•tē) A duty. p. 640

retreat (ri•trēt´) To fall back. p. 458

revolution (re•və•lōō´shən) A sudden, great change, such as the overthrow of an established government. p. 268

royal colony (roi´əl kä´lə•nē) A colony ruled directly by a monarch. p. 152

ruling (rōō´ling) A decision. p. 398

rural (rûr´əl) Like or having to do with a place away from a city. p. 46

S

satellite (sa´tə•līt) An object in orbit around Earth. p. 583

savanna (sə•va´nə) A kind of grassland that has areas with a few scattered trees. p. 39

scalawag (ska´li•wag) A rascal; someone who supports something for his or her own gain. p. 484

scandal (skan´dəl) An action that brings disgrace. p. 593

sea dog (sē dôg) A commander of English warships that attacked Spanish ships carrying treasure. p. 156

sea level (sē le´vəl) The level of the surface of the ocean. p. 21

secede (si•sēd´) To leave. p. 453

secondary source (se´kən•der•ē sôrs) A record of an event written by someone who was not there at the time. p. 5

secret ballot (sē´kret ba´lət) A voting method in which no one knows how anyone else voted. p. 484

sectionalism (sek´shən•ə•li•zəm) Regional loyalty. p. 436

sedition (si•di´shən) Speech or behavior that causes other people to work against a government. p. 196

segregation (se•gri•gā´shən) The practice of keeping people in separate groups based on their race or culture. p. 484

self-rule (self•rōōl´) Control of one's own government. p. 168

self-sufficient (self•sə•fi´shənt) Able to provide for one's own needs without help. p. 147

separatist (se´pə•rə•tist) A citizen of Quebec who wants Quebec to be independent. p. 672

settlement house (se´təl•mənt hous) A community center. p. 535

sharecropping (sher´krä p•ing) A system of working the land in which the worker was paid with a "share" of the crop. p. 483

siege (sēj) A long-lasting attack. p. 393

slash-and-burn (slash•and•bûrn) A method of clearing land for farming that includes cutting and burning of trees. p. 87

slave state (slā v stā t) A state that allowed slavery before the Civil War. p. 437

slavery (slā´və•rē) The practice of holding people against their will and making them carry out orders. p. 66

society (sə•sī´ə•tē) A human group. p. 10

sod (sod) Earth cut into blocks or mats, held together by grass and its roots. p. 82

sound (sound) A long inlet often parallel to the coast. p. 28

specialize (spe´shə•līz) To work at one kind of job and do it well. p. 190

spiritual (spir´i•chə•wəl) A religious song based on Bible stories. p. 244

standard of living (stan´dərd uv li´ving) A measure of how well people in a country live. p. 664

staple (stā´pəl) Something, such as milk or bread, that is always needed and used. p. 71

states' rights (stā ts rīts) The idea that the states, rather than the federal government, should have the final authority over their own affairs. p. 436

stock (stä k) A share of ownership in a business. p. 161

stock market (stä k mä r´kət) A place where people can buy and sell shares of a business. p. 547

strategy (stra´tə•jē) A long-range plan. p. 459

suburban (sə•bûr´bən) Of or like the area of smaller cities or towns around a large city. p. 46

suffrage (su´frij) The right to vote. p. 535

Sun Belt (sun belt) A wide area of the southern United States that reaches from the Atlantic coast to the Pacific coast. p. 621

superpower (sōō´pər•pou•ər) A nation that is one of the most powerful in the world. p. 580

supply (sə•plī´) The amount of a product or service that is available. p. 418

surplus (sûr´pləs) An amount that is more than what is needed. p. 71

T

tariff (tar´əf) A tax on goods brought into a country. p. 436

GLOSSARY

technology (tek•nä´lə•jē) The use of scientific knowledge and tools to make or do something. p. 63

teleconference (te´li•kä n•frəns) A conference, or meeting, that uses electronic equipment to connect people. p. 625

tenement (te´nə•mənt) A poorly built apartment building. p. 503

tepee (tē´pē) A cone-shaped tent made from wooden poles and buffalo skins. p. 84

territory (ter´ə•tôr•ē) Land that belongs to a national government but is not a state. p. 349

terrorism (ter´ər•i•zəm) The use of violence to promote a cause. p. 596

textile (tek´stīl) Cloth. p. 416

theory (thē´ə•rē) A possible explanation. p. 57

tide (tīd) The regular rise and fall of the ocean and of the bodies of water connected to it. p. 27

tidewater (tīd´wô•tər) Low-lying land along a coast. p. 241

time line (tīm līn) A diagram that shows events that took place during a certain period of time. p. 60

time zone (tīm zōn) A geographic region in which the same time is used. p. 674

totem pole (tō´təm pōl) A tall wooden post carved with shapes of animals and people and representing a family's history and importance. p. 79

town meeting (toun mē´ting) An assembly in the New England Colonies in which male landowners could take part in government. p. 192

township (toun´ship) An area of land. p. 218

trade-off (trād´ôf) The giving up of one thing to get another. p. 564

traitor (trā´tər) One who works against one's own government. p. 323

transcontinental railroad (trans•kä n•tə•nen´təl rā l´rōd) The railway line that crossed North America. p. 494

travois (trə•voi´) A device made of two poles fastened to a dog's harness, used to carry possessions. p. 85

treason (trē´zən) The act of working against one's own government. p. 282

treaty (trē´tē) An agreement between nations about peace, trade, or other matters. p. 126

trespass (tres´pas) To go onto someone else's property without asking permission. p. 388

trial by jury (trī´əl bī jûr´ē) The right of a person accused of a crime to be tried by a jury, or group, of fellow citizens. p. 214

triangular trade route (trī•ang´gyə•lər trād rōōt) A shipping route that linked England, the English colonies in North America, and the west coast of Africa, forming an imaginary triangle in the Atlantic Ocean. p. 202

tribe (trīb) A group of people who share the same language, land, and leaders. p. 64

tributary (tri´byōō•ter•ē) A stream or river that flows into a larger stream or river. p. 30

tundra (tun´drə) A cold, dry region where trees cannot grow. p. 37

turning point (tûr´ning point) A single event that causes important and dramatic change. p. 316

underground (un´dûr•ground) Done in secret. p. 446

unemployment (un•im•ploi´mənt) The number of people without jobs. p. 549

urban (ûr´bən) Of or like a city. p. 45

urbanization (ûr•bə•nə•zā´shən) The movement of people into cities. p. 546

veto (vē´tō) To reject. p. 361

volcano (väl•kā´nō) An opening in Earth, often on a hill or mountain, through which hot lava, gases, ash, and rocks may pour out. p. 23

volunteer (vä•lən•tir´) A person who works without pay. p. 642

wampum (wäm´pəm) Beads made from cut and polished seashells used to keep records, send messages to other tribes, barter for goods, or give as gifts. p. 88

war hawk (wôr hôk) A member of Congress who wanted war with Britain before the War of 1812. p. 390

wigwam (wig´wäm) A round, bark-covered Native American shelter. p. 88

Index

Page references for illustrations are set in italic type. An italic *m* indicates a map. Page references set in boldface type indicate the pages on which vocabulary terms are defined.

INDEX

INDEX

INDEX

Y

Z

For permission to reprint copyrighted material, grateful acknowledgment is made to the following sources:

Atheneum Books for Young Readers, an imprint of Simon & Schuster Children's Publishing Division: Cover illustration from *Anasazi* by Leonard Everett Fisher. Copyright © 1997 by Leonard Everett Fisher. Cover illustration by Ronald Himler from *Squish! A Wetland Walk* by Nancy Luenn. Illustration copyright © 1994 by Ronald Himler. Cover illustration by Jerry Pinkney from *Goin' Someplace Special* by Patricia McKissack. Illustration copyright © 2001 by Jerry Pinkney.

Candlewick Press Inc., Cambridge, MA: Cover illustration by P. J. Lynch from *When Jessie Came Across the Sea* by Amy Hest. Illustration copyright © 1997 by P. J. Lynch.

Candlewick Press Inc., Cambridge, MA, on behalf of Walker Books Ltd., London: Cover illustration by Kevin Tweddell from *The History News: Explorers* by Michael Johnstone. Illustration copyright © 1997 by Walker Books Ltd.

Dutton Children's Books, an imprint of Penguin Books for Young Readers, a division of Penguin Putnam Inc: Cover photograph by Art Wolfe from *Journey Through the Northern Rainforest* by Karen Pandell. Photograph copyright © 1999 by Art Wolfe.

Jane Feder, on behalf of Julie Downing: Cover illustration by Julie Downing from *If You Were There in 1492* by Barbara Brenner. Illustration copyright © 1991 by Julie Downing.

Harcourt, Inc.: "If We Should Travel" from *Between Earth & Sky* by Joseph Bruchac. Text copyright © 1996 by Joseph Bruchac.

HarperCollins Publishers: Cover illustration by James Watling from *Finding Providence: The Story of Roger Williams* by Avi. Illustration copyright © 1997 by James Watling. From *Stranded at Plimoth Plantation 1626* by Gary Bowen. Copyright © 1994 by Gary Bowen. Cover illustration by Stephen Fieser from *The Silk Route: 7,000 Miles of History* by John S. Major. Illustration copyright © 1995 by Stephen Fieser. Cover illustration by Bert Dodson from *American Adventures: Thomas* by Bonnie Pryor. Illustration copyright © 1998 by Bert Dodson.

David Higham Associates Limited: Cover illustration by Martin Jordan from *Angel Falls: A South American Journey* by Martin and Tanis Jordan. Illustration copyright © 1995 by Martin Jordan. Published by Larousse Kingfisher Chambers Inc.

Holiday House, Inc.: Cover illustration by Peter Fiore from *The Boston Tea Party* by Steven Kroll. Illustration copyright 1998 by Peter Fiore.

Henry Holt and Company, LLC: From "San Salvador" by Jamake Highwater in *The World in 1492* by Jean Fritz, Katherine Paterson, Patricia and Fredrick McKissack, Margaret Mahy, and Jamake Highwater, cover illustration by Stefano Vitale. Text copyright © 1992 by The Native Land Foundation; cover illustration copyright © 1992 by Stefano Vitale.

Lee & Low Books, Inc., 95 Madison Avenue, New York, NY 10016: From *Dia's Story Cloth: The Hmong People's Journey to Freedom* by Dia Cha, illustrated by Chue and Nhia Thao Cha. Copyright © 1996 by Denver Museum of Natural History.

Robin Moore and BookStop Literary Agency: Cover illustration by Robin Moore from *Across the Lines* by Carolyn Reeder. Illustration copyright © 1997 by Robin Moore.

Northland Publishing Company: Cover illustration by Julia Miner from *The Unbreakable Code* by Sara Hoagland Hunter. Illustration copyright © 1996 by Julia Miner.

Orion Books, a division of Random House, Inc.: From *All for the Union* by Robert Hunt Rhodes. Text and photograph copyright © 1985 by Robert Hunt Rhodes.

G. P. Putnam's Sons, an imprint of Penguin Putnam Books for Young Readers, a division of Penguin Putnam Inc.: From *Shh! We're Writing the Constitution* by Jean Fritz, illustrated by Tomie dePaola. Text copyright © 1987 by Jean Fritz; illustrations copyright © 1987 by Whitebird, Inc. Cover illustration by F. John Sierra from *My Mexico—México mío* by Tony Johnston. Illustration copyright © 1996 by F. John Sierra.

Scholastic Inc.: Cover illustration by Mark Summers from *James Printer: A Novel of Rebellion* by Paul Samuel Jacobs. Illustration © 1997 by Mark Summers. Published by Scholastic Press, a division of Scholastic Inc. Cover illustration by Dan Andreasen from *By the Dawn's Early Light: The Story of the Star-Spangled Banner* by Steven Kroll. Illustration copyright © 1994 by Dan Andreasen.

Simon & Schuster Books for Young Readers, an imprint of Simon & Schuster Children's Publishing Division: Cover illustration from *The Story of William Penn* by Aliki. Copyright © 1964 by Aliki Brandenberg; copyright renewed © 1992 by Aliki Brandenberg. From "The *Eagle* Has Landed" in *The Children's Book of America*, edited by William J. Bennett, illustrated by Michael Hague. Text copyright © 1998 by William J. Bennett; illustrations copyright © 1998 by Michael Hague.

Steck-Vaughn Company: Cover illustration by Debbe Heller from *Tales from the Underground Railroad* by Kate Connell. Illustration copyright © 1993 by Dialogue Systems, Inc.

ILLUSTRATION CREDITS

Pages 12-13, Angus McBride; 13, Steve Weston; 14-15, Leland Klanderman; 28, 34, 35, Sebastian Quigley; 56-57, Tom McNeely; 62-63, Dennis Lyall; 71, Luigi Galante; 77, Inklink; 100-101, Uldis Klavins; 102-103, Dave Hendersch; 107, Steve Weston; 106-107, Studio Liddell; 116-117, Dennis Lyall; 160-161, Mike Lamble; 167, Bill Smith Studio; 180-181, Andrew Wheatcroft; 182-185, Nina Martin; 190-191, George Gaadt; 220, 226-227, Yuan Lee; 260-261, George Gaadt; 308-309, Vincent Wakerley; 324, Dennis Lyall; 324-325, Sebastian Quigley; 325, Dennis Lyall; 340-341, Gino D'Achille; 355, Vincent Wakerley; 376-377, Chuck Carter; 393, Bill Smith Studio; 412-413, Don Foley; 428-429, Cliff Spohn; 430-433, George Gaadt; 454-455, Luigi Galante; 468, Bill Smith Studio; 494-495, Dennis Lyall; 516-517, Bill Maughan; 544-545, Chuck Carter; 566-567, Dennis Lyall; 612-613, Rick Johnson; 638-639, Studio Liddell; 643, Bill Smith Studio; 644-645, Vincent Wakerley.

All maps by MapQuest.com

PHOTO CREDITS

Cover: Stephen Krasemann/DRK Photo (eagle); Roger Ressmeyer/Corbis (shuttle); The Image Bank (Mt. Rushmore); G. George Diebold/Corbis Stock Market (waves).

PLACEMENT KEY: (t) top; (b) bottom; (l) left; (c) center; (r) right; (bg) background; (i) inset

POSTER INSERT

Flag: Don Mason/Corbis Stock Market, eagle: Minden Pictures.

TITLE PAGE AND TABLE OF CONTENTS

(fg) Andria/Hendrickson; (bg) Doug Armand/Stone; iv, The Detroit Institute of Arts; v, National Maritime Museum Picture Library; vi, Historical Society of Pennsylvania, Silver Gorget, c. 1757 Artist: Joseph Richardson, Sr., S-8-120; vii, Lester Lefkowitz/Corbis Stock Market; viii, Independence National Historical Park; ix, Smithsonian Institution; x, NASA.

INTRODUCTION

1 (t) Andria/Hendrickson, (l) Doug Armand/Stone; 2 (t) Bob Daemmrich/Stock, Boston/PictureQuest; 2 (b) ChromoSohm/Sohm/Visions of America; 3 (t) Christie Parker/Houserstock, Inc.; 3 (b) Underwood & Underwood/Corbis; 4 National Park Service; 4 National Park Service; 4 National Park Service; 5 (br) John McGrail; 5 (tl) The Granger Collection, New York; 5 (inset) National Park Service; 7 (tl) Mattew Borkoski/Stock, Boston Inc./PictureQuest; 7 (tr) Andre Jenny/Focus Group/PictureQuest; 7 (cl) Peter Pearson/Stone; 7 (cr) Jeffrey Muir Hamilton/Stock, Boston Inc./PictureQuest; 7 (bl) Robert Hildebrand; 7 (br) David Young-Wolff/PhotoEdit/PictureQuest; 8 (l) Jeff Lepore/Panoramic Images; 8 (r) David Young-Wolff/PhotoEdit; 9 (bl) Joseph Sohm/Stock, Boston Inc./PictureQuest; 9 (br) Bill Bachman/PhotoEdit; 10 (t) David Young-Wolff/PhotoEdit/PictureQuest; 10 (b) Calumet Regional Archives, Indiana University Northwest.

UNIT 1

UNIT OPENER, (fg) The Detroit Institute of Arts; (bg) Tom & Susan Bean, Inc.; 11 (t) The Detroit Institute of Arts; (l) Tom & Susan Bean, Inc; 16-17 Robert Hildebrand Photography; 18-19 (b) Russ Finley; 19 (t) David Muench/Corbis; 21 (b) Dave G. Houser; 22 (b) Marc Muench/David Muench Photography, Inc.; 23 (t) David Muench; 26 (b) Stocktrek/Corbis Stock Market; 30 (t) Greg Ryan/Sally Beyer/Positive Reflections; 30 (inset) Bettmann/Corbis; 31 (br) Stock Barrow; 32 (t) David Muench; 33 (b) Mark E. Gibson Photography; 37 California Stock Photography; 39 Tom & Susan Bean; 40 Ted Streshinsky/Corbis; 41 Mark E. Gibson Photography; 43 (t) Charles Gupton/Corbis Stock Market; 44 Henry T. Kaiser/Stock Connection/PictureQuest; 46-47 (b) Mark E. Gibson Photography; 48 Place Stock Photo; 54-55 David Muench Photography; 58 (b) John Maier, Jr./JB Pictures; 58 (inset) Mercyhurst Archaeological Institute; 59 Lawrence Migdale; 63 (t) Courtesy of Arizona State Museum, AZ/Jerry Jacka Photography; 64 (tl) Harald Sund/The Image Bank; 64 (tr) Zion National Park; 65 (br) Werner Forman/Art Resource; 66-67 (t) Michael Hampshire/Cahokia Mounds Historic Site; 67 (tr) Richard A. Cooke/Corbis; 68 American Hurrah; 70 Place Stock Photo; 72-73 (b) James Cowlin/Adstock; 72 (inset) Monty Roessel; 73 (t) Fifth Generation Traders, Farmington, N.M./Jerry Jacka Photography; 74 (t) Stephen Trimble; 74 (b) Smithsonian Institution; 75 (t) Aldo Tutino/ Art Resource, NY; 75 (c) John Bigelow Taylor/Art Resource, NY; 75 (b) Gift of

of the Massachusetts Historical Society; 297 (c) Peabody Essex Museum, Salem, MA. Photo by Mark Sexton; 297 (tr) Jamestown-Yorktown Foundation; 300-301 Morristown National Park; 302 (bc) Hulton/Archive; 302 The Granger Collection; 303 (b) Smithsonian Institution; 303 (tr) Independence National Historical Park; 305 Francis G. Mayer/Corbis; 306 (br) Lee Snider Photo Images; 306 (bkgd) Scott Barrow; 307 Historical Society of Pennsylvania; 308 (bl) Courtesy of the Massachusetts Historical Society; 309 (br) Martin Art Gallery, Muhlenberg College, Allentown, Pennsylvania; 310 (b) Valentine Museum, Richmond History Center; 310 (inset) Tracey W. McGregor Library/University of Virginia; 311 (tl) Bequest of Winslow Warren/Courtesy, Museum of Fine Arts, Boston; 311 (tr) Bettmann/Corbis; 311 (tlc) Detroit Publishing Co. Photograph Collection/Library of Congress; 311 (trc) Richard Walker/New York Historical Association, Cooperstown; 312 Independence National Historical Park; 314 (br) Eliot Cohen/Janelco Photographers; 314 (bl) Russ Finley; 315 (t) Fort Ticonderoga Museum; 315 (bl) Russ Finley; 315 (inset) The Granger Collection; 316 (t) The Valley Forge Historical Society; 317 (t) Bettmann/Corbis; 317 (b) Jewish-American Hall of Fame; 318 (b) Bettmann/Corbis; 318 (tl) Hulton/Archive Photos; 318 (tc) Hulton/Archive Photos; 318 (tr) Independence National Historical Park Collection; 319 Edifice/Corbis; 320-321 American Museum of American History/Smithsonian Institution. Trans. no. 76-3259; 322 (b) David Muench Photography; 325 (br) Roy Andersen/National Geographic Society; 326 (b) Yorktown Victory Center; 326 (t) a detail, John Trumbull "The Surrender of Lord Cornwallis at Yorktown, 19 October 1781", Yale University Art Gallery, Trumbull Collection; 327 (b) Courtesy, Winterthur Museum; 328 (t) Hulton/Archive Photos; 330 (b) Royal Geographical Society, London/The Bridgeman Art Library International; 330 (inset) American Antiquarian Society; 334 (t) Peter Southwick/Stock, Boston; 334 (bc) Michael Dwyer/Stock Boston; 334 (bg) Gibson Stock Photography; 335 (br) Danilo G. Donadoni/ Bruce Coleman; 335 (tr) Tibor Bognar/Corbis Stock Market; 335 (tc) Susan Cole Kelly; 335 (cl) Dave G. Houser/Corbis; 335 (tl) Ed Young/Corbis; 335 (bl) Richard Cummins/Corbis; 335 (cr) Dave G. Houser/Corbis.

UNIT 5
UNIT OPENER; (fg) Independence National Historical Park; (bg) Independence National Historical Park; 339 (t) Independence National Historical Park; (l) Independence National Historical Park; 344-345 Johnathan Wallen Photography; 346 Roman Soumar/Corbis; 347 (tc) From the Robert H. Gore Jr. Numismatic Collection; 347 (tr) American Antiquarian Society; 348 (bl) The Granger Collection; 348 (br) The New-York Historical Society; 350 Library of Congress; 351 (bl) The Granger Collection; 351 (br) The Granger Collection; 352 Bettmann/Corbis; 355 (tl) The Library of Virginia; 355 (tc) Ralph Earl Roger Sherman (1721-1793) M. G. (Hon.) 1786 Yale University Art Gallery/Gift of Roger Sherman White, BA. 1899, L. L. B. 1902; 355 (tr) Princeton University; 356 Emmet Collection, Rare Books and Manuscripts Division, The New York Public Library, Astor, Lennox, and Tilden Foundations; 357 (t) 'Residences and Slave Quarters of Mulbery

Plantation' by Thomas Coram, The Gibbes Museum of Art, Charleston, SC; 358 (b) Joseph Sohm/Stock, Boston/PictureQuest; 358 (inset) Northwind Picture Archives; 359 O and J Heaton/Stock, Boston; 360 (b) Dave G. Houser/Houserstock, Inc.; 361 Lee Snider Photo Images; 362 (bl) Dennis Brack/Black Star Publishing/PictureQuest; 362 (br) Richard W. Strauss/Smithsonian Institute/Supreme Court Historical Society; 363 Independence National Historical Park, Phil; 365 (l) James Foote/Photo Researchers; 365 (cr) James Foote/Photo Researchers; 366 Independence National Historical Park; 367 Virginia Museum of Fine Arts, Richmond. Gift of Edgar William and Bernice Chrysler Garbisich. Photo: Ron Jennings@Virginia Museum of Fine Arts.; 368 (bl) New York Historical/The Bridgeman Art Library International; 368 (br) Colonial Williamsburg Foundation; 370 National Archives and Records Administration; 371 (c) Culver Pictures; 371 (bl) Franklin Institute; 371 (br) The Granger Collection, New York; 372 Dover Publications; 373 (b) Courtesy, Winterthur Museum; 374 (b) LM Cooks Salute to General Washington in NY Harbor, Gift of Edgar Williams & Bernice Chrysler Garbisch Board of Trustees/National Gallery of Art, Washington; 374 (inset) Museum of the City of New York, Bequest of Mrs. J. Insley Blair in Memory of Mr. and Mrs. J. Insley Blair; 375 Courtesy of the John Carter Brown Library at Brown University; 376 (b) Maryland Historical Society; 378 White House Historical Assoc.; 379 The New-York Historical Society; 382-383 David Muench Photography; 384 C. Jean/Reunion des Musees Nationaux/Art Resource, NY; 386 (t) National Park Service; 386-387 (b) Amon Carter Museum; 386 (bl) Courtesy Independence National Historical Park; 387 (br) Courtesy Independence National Historical Park; 389 Bettmann/Corbis; 390 Bettmann/Corbis; 392 (t) Library of Congress; 392 (b) Collection of the New York Historical Society; 393 (br) Corbis; 394 Bettmann/Corbis; 395 (b) Burstein Collection/Corbis; 395 (inset) Lawrence County Historical Society; 396 (t) The Granger Collection, NY; 396 (b) Library of Congress; 397 Collection of The New York Historical Society; 399 Troy Anderson; 400 (bl) National Portrait Gallery/Smithsonian Institution/Art Resource, NY; 400 (br) Academy of Natural Sciences of Philadelphia/Corbis; 401 (t) Academy of Natural Sciences of Philadelphia/Corbis; 401 (c) North Carolina Museum; 401 (br) Academy of Natural Sciences of Philadelphia/Corbis; 401 (cl) Academy of Natural Sciences of Philadelphia/Corbis, Inc.; 402 The State Preservation Board, Austin Texas; 403 (b) Friends of the Governor's Mansion, Austin, Texas; 404 H. K. Barnett/Star of the Republic Museum, Jefferson, Texas; 405 (t) The Saint Louis Art Museum; 405 Whitman Mission National Historic Society; 406 Bettmann/Corbis; 407 The Granger Collection; 408 Smithsonian American Art Museum, Washington DC/Art Resource, NY; 409 Gill C. Kenny/The Image Bank; 410 National Archives; 412 Russ Poole Photography; 414 (t) Cooper Hewitt Museum; 414 B & O Railroad Museum; 418 (tl) Art Resource, NY; 418 (bl) Bettmann/Corbis; 419 (tr) Courtesy of the John Deere Company; 419 (inset) John Deere.

UNIT 6
UNIT OPENER; (fg) Smithsonian Institution; (bg) Peter Gridley/FPG International; 427 (t) Smithsonian Institution; (l) Peter Gridley/FPG International; 430 All for the Union; 434-435

David Muench Photography; 436 The American Clock and Watch Museum; 437 Stock Montage/Hulton Archive/Getty Images; 438 Bettmann/Corbis; 441 Missouri Historical Society; 442 (bl) Courtesy of the South Carolina Library; 442 (br) Courtesy of the South Carolina Library; 443 (br) Hulton-Deutsch Collection/Corbis; 443 (br) Bettmann/Corbis; 444 (br) Scala/Art Resource, NY; 444 (cl) The Charleston Museum; 446 Library of Congress; 447 (t) Hulton/Archive Photos; 447 (b) National Museum of American Art, Washington DC/Art Resource, NY; 448 (bl) National Portrait Gallery, Smithsonian Institution/Art Resource, NY; 448 (inset) Book cover slide of "Uncle Tom's Cabin" by Harriet Beecher Stowe. Courtesy of the Charles L. Blockson Afro-American Collection, Temple University; 449 (t) National Portrait Gallery, Smithsonian Institution/Art Resource, NY; 450 (b) Morton Beebe, S.F./Corbis; 451 Courtesy of the Illinois State Historical Library; 452 (bl) National Portrait Gallery, Smithsonian Institution/Art Resource, NY; 452 (bc) Corbis; 453 (t) National Portrait Gallery, Smithsonian Institution/Art Resource, NY; 453 (b) The Granger Collection; 458 (b) Brown Military Collection, Brown University; 458 (bl) National Portrait Gallery, Smithsonian Institution/Art Resource, NY; 460 James P. Rowan Photography; 461 Library of Congress; 462 (t) National Portrait Gallery; 462 (b) Library of Congress; 463 (b) Bettmann/Corbis; 464 Chicago Historical Society; 465 (bc) Salamander Books; 465 (br) National Portrait Gallery, Smithsonian Institution, Washington, D.C.; 466 (t) Courtesy of General Dynamics Corp., Electric Boat Div.; 466 (cl) Richmond, Virginia/Katherine Wetzel; 467 (b) New Hampshire Historical Society; 469 (b) Tom Lovell©National Geographic; 471 Tom Prettyman/PhotoEdit/PictureQuest; 476 (bl) Corbis; 476 (bc) Library of Congress; 477 (t) Hulton Archive/Getty Images; 477 (inset) Library of Congress; 478 Corbis; 479 (c) Library of Congress; 479 (tl) The Granger Collection, New York; 480 (tl) American Treasures of the Library of Congress; 480 (tr) Library of Congress; 481 (bl) Corbis; 481 (br) Southern Historical Collection; 482 (br) Bob Daemmrich Photography; 482 (cl) Bob Daemmrich Photography; 483 (t) The Metropolitan Museum of Art, Morris K. Jessup Fund; 483 (inset) Smithsonian Institution, Division of Agriculture; 484 (t) Hulton/Archive/Getty Images; 484 (b) Smithsonian Institute; 485 The Granger Collection; 486 (inset) The Bancroft Library; 486-487 Joseph Sohm/Visions of America/PictureQuest; 488 (b) Jeff Greenberg/PhotoEdit; 488 (tc) William Manns Photo/Zon International Publishing; 489 Solomon D. Butcher Collection, Nebraska State Historical Society; 490 Corbis; 491 Corbis; 492 Michael Forsberg; 496 Corbis; 497 Corbis; 499 From the Collections of Henry Ford Museum & Greenfield Village; 500 (t) Transfer from the National Museum of American Art; Gift of Dr. Eleanor A. Campbell to the Smithsonian Institution, 1942.; 500 (bl) Henry Ford Museum & Greenfield Village; 500 (br) History of Technology Division, National Museum of American History, photographed by John Tsantes/Smithsonian Institution; 501 (t) Henry Ford Museum & Greenfield Village; 501 (c) Science Museum, London, UK/The Bridgeman Art Library International; 501 (br) Alfred Harrell/Smithsonian Institution; 502 (inset) "By Courtesy of the Statue of Liberty National Monument"; 503 (tl) Corbis; 504-505 (b) Corbis;

Reading in the Content Area

Reading in the Content Area

Reading is an important part of social studies. The Reading in the Content Area copying masters help you integrate the use of reading skills into your social studies instruction. At the top of each copying master, a reading skill is modeled, using text from the pupil edition. At the bottom, additional pupil edition text is provided for students to practice the reading skill.

Contents

Main Idea and Supporting Details

> The **main idea** of a paragraph is what it is mostly about. The main idea may be stated in a sentence, or it may only be suggested. **Supporting details** give more information about the main idea.

Main Idea   The two largest mountain ranges in the United States are the Appalachian (ap•uh•LAY•chee•uhn) Mountains and the Rocky Mountains.   **page 19**

Supporting Details   A mountain range is a group of connected mountains. The Appalachians cover much of the eastern United States. They stretch all the way from central Alabama to southeastern Canada. The Rocky Mountains cover much of the western United States. They extend north from Mexico through Canada and into Alaska.

Directions: Circle the main idea of the paragraph. Underline the supporting details.   **page 43**

People use the Earth's surface in a variety of ways. They divide it into nations, states, and other government units. They build communities, transportation systems, and businesses on it. They also gather natural resources from it. Some of the land is owned by the public, and some of it belongs to private property owners. People buy and sell the land and make laws to decide how it can be used.

Compare and Contrast

When you **compare** information, you are showing how things are alike. When you **contrast** information, you are identifying how things are different.

Compare

To the peoples of the Southwest, the expression "up the ladder and down the ladder" meant "to enter a house." Like their Anasazi ancestors, many peoples of the Southwest lived in pueblos. To enter a home or to reach other levels of the pueblo, people went "up the ladder and down the ladder." In time all of the tribes who lived in pueblos, including the Hopis (HOH•peez), the Zunis (ZOO•neez), and others, became known as the Pueblo peoples.

page 70

What is being compared—Many peoples of the Southwest lived in pueblos as did their Anasazi ancestors.

Contrast

Other discoveries, in California and Peru, support the theory that the first Americans did not cross the land bridge at all. Instead, they may have traveled to the Americas in boats. Some may have actually crossed the Pacific Ocean. On San Miguel Island, about 25 miles (40 km) off the coast of California, archaeologists found evidence that people lived there about 13,000 years ago. Archaeologists know that these people used oceangoing boats because they ate fish that could be caught only far from shore. In Peru archaeologists found two 12,000-year-old sites whose residents also ate foods only found in the deep ocean.

page 58

What is being contrasted—Theories about when and how the first Americans arrived in the Americas.

Directions: Read the two paragraphs. Identify what is being compared and what is being contrasted.

pages 88–89

Each Algonquian tribe had anywhere from 1 to 20 villages. In most villages, 10 to 20 round, bark-covered shelters called wigwams were grouped around a village common. Most Algonquian tribes built their villages along the banks of rivers or streams. Some were built where two rivers or streams met. In wetland areas, villages were built on high ground to keep them safe from flooding.

Also like the Algonquians, the Iroquois tribes farmed and lived in villages. The Iroquois lived in dwellings called longhouses. A longhouse was a long wooden building in which several related Iroquois families lived together. It was made of elm bark and had a large entrance at each end.

Sequence

A **sequence** is the order in which one event comes after another. Words like *first, then, next, before, after*, and *later* can help you recognize a sequence.

Follow the sequence.   page 124

First   Magellan set sail from Spain in September 1519, in command of about 250 sailors on five ships.

Then   He sailed to what is now Brazil and then south along South America's eastern coast.

Next   For many months he sailed up rivers into the middle of the continent, hoping to find a river that would lead to the ocean on the other side. However, he never did, and each time he had to sail back down the rivers, to the coast.

Later   As the ships fought their way through huge, pounding waves and against howling winds, one ship and many of its crew were lost.

Finally   Finally, in the fall of 1520, the rest of Magellan's ships sailed through what is now called the Strait of Magellan, near the southern tip of South America.

Directions: Read the paragraphs. Determine the sequence. Underline words that help show sequence.   pages 138–139

    After Verrazano and Cartier, other Europeans continued to look for the Northwest Passage. Henry Hudson, an English sea captain, was one of them. In 1608, on his first expedition, he reached an island east of Greenland. He then sailed farther north by way of the Arctic Ocean but failed to find the Northwest Passage. The following year Hudson searched by way of the Barents Sea, an arm of the Arctic Ocean.

    For his third voyage, Hudson had been hired by the Dutch East India Company to find the Northwest Passage. The company, or business, gave him a ship, the *Half Moon,* and a crew of about 20 sailors. They set sail in 1609 for the Arctic Ocean, but his crew soon mutinied, or rebelled. Hudson was forced to head south along the North American coast.

Categorize

To **categorize** is to group information by category. You can sort facts into categories such as people, places, and events to make them easier to find.

At first very few Spanish people settled in New Spain. Many of those who did were conquistadors. After news spread of the discovery of gold, silver, and other treasures, however, many colonists came to seek their fortunes. The people who go to live in a colony are called colonists.

page 144

Many of the colonists worked in the gold and silver mines. Others brought oxen and plows to work the land and horses to ride. They brought cattle and sheep, fruit trees, grain, and vegetable seeds. Over time, the Spanish began to build cities, and tens of thousands more colonists came to live in them.

The Spanish colonists needed many workers to grow their crops, to mine gold and silver, and to build and provide services in their cities. So they made slaves of the American Indian peoples they had conquered.

The information can be sorted into these categories:

Events That Led to Colonization	People Who Lived in New Spain
• discovery of gold, silver, and other treasures • building of cities • need for workers	• conquistadors • colonists who worked in the gold and silver mines • colonists who brought oxen and plows to work the land • colonists who built and provided services in their cities • American Indians who were made slaves

Directions: Sort the information into the category given.

page 148

Spain's main interest in settling the borderlands was to protect its empire and to expand its economy. However, the Spanish king also said he wanted to "bring the people of that land to our Holy Catholic faith." To do this, missionaries were sent to turn the American Indians into Catholics as well as loyal Spanish subjects. A missionary is a person sent by a church to teach its religion.

Category

Reasons Spain Had for Settling the Borderlands
•

© Harcourt

Summarize

When you **summarize**, you tell just the important points of what you have read.

In 1631 Roger Williams and his family arrived in the Massachusetts Bay Colony from England. They settled in the village of Salem, where Roger Williams became a minister.

Williams was a popular minister because he and many people in Salem shared the same beliefs. They believed that their church should be separate from the colonial government and free from the rule of the Church of England. They also believed that people should not be punished if their beliefs were different from those of the Puritan leaders.

pages 194–195

Summary   Roger Williams was a popular minister in Salem because he and other people believed that their church should be separate from the government and that people should not be punished for beliefs that differed from those of the Puritan leaders.

Directions: Read the paragraph. Then write a summary of the paragraph.

page 200

Many coastal towns in New England Colonies prospered because of good fishing in the ocean waters. Because New Englanders could catch more fish than they needed, they had a surplus. The surplus catch could be dried and then sold or traded to people in Europe or to other English colonists in the West Indies.

Summary

Make Inferences

When you make an **inference**, you use facts and your experiences to come to a conclusion.

page 218

William Penn named his colony's chief city Philadelphia, a word meaning "brotherly love" in Greek. Like all of Pennsylvania, Philadelphia was founded on the idea that people of diverse backgrounds could get along with each other.

That idea was reflected in the layout of most of the colony's settlements. Penn wanted to divide his colony into townships. Each township, or area of land, would be 5,000 acres—a space large enough for ten families. Land belonging to individual families would be carved out of the township in giant pie-like slices. Penn wanted settlers to build their homes at the tips of the slices so that every family would be within walking distance of one another and of whatever church they chose to build.

Inference William Penn's belief in "brotherly love" caused him to create settlements that encouraged people to live together peacefully and to practice the religion of their own choosing.

Directions: Read the paragraph. Then make an inference about what you have read.

page 226

Most of the people who settled the backcountry lived simply. Their homes were log huts with chimneys made of sticks and mud. Most homes had one room with a dirt floor and no windows. Light came through the open door in the daytime and from the fireplace at night. Families burned wood in the fireplace to cook their food and to keep warm.

Inference

© Harcourt

Generalize

When you **generalize**, you summarize a group of facts and show the relationship between them.

Slaves were treated well or cruelly depending on their owners. Some planters took pride in being fair and kind to their slaves. There was little protection, however, for slaves who had cruel masters. Slave owners were free to beat, whip, or insult any slave as often as they chose to do so. These slaves looked only to escape or to resist their cruel treatment. "No day ever dawns for the slave, nor is it looked for," one enslaved African later wrote. "For the slave it is all night—all night, forever."

page 244

Generalizations
- Some slaves were treated well, but others were treated cruelly.
- Some slaves who had cruel masters tried to escape.
- Most slaves had little or no hope that the next day of their life would be better than the day before.

Directions: Read the paragraph. Then make generalizations about what you have read.

page 250

Wilmington's location on the Cape Fear River helped it prosper. The river is deep enough to be used by large ships, and it flows directly into the Atlantic Ocean. Immigrants also helped Wilmington grow and prosper. They came from other colonies and from many parts of Europe. Some of the town's earliest settlers came from northern Scotland. The first Africans to come to Wilmington were brought as slaves. Eventually, free Africans also lived there. Some were farmers. Others worked as painters, tailors, carpenters, and blacksmiths.

Generalizations

© Harcourt

Cause and Effect

A **cause** is an event or action that makes something else happen. An **effect** is what happens as a result of that event or action.

In Massachusetts the colonists responded to the Intolerable Acts by organizing special militia units. They were called Minutemen because they could be ready in a minute to defend Massachusetts.

page 291

Cause	Effects
Intolerable Acts	Special militia units were organized.

Directions: Read the paragraph. Then identify a cause and any effects of that cause.

page 296

In London, the Battle of Bunker Hill had further angered British leaders. Lord North advised King George III to think of the fighting in the colonies as a foreign war. On August 23 the king issued a proclamation of rebellion. In it, he promised to use every measure to crush the rebellion and "bring the traitors to justice." As a result, by the time the Olive Branch Petition reached British leaders in London on August 24, it was already a lost cause.

Cause	Effects

© Harcourt

Answer Key

Main Idea and Supporting Details

(People use the Earth's surface in a variety of ways.) They divide it into **page C1**
nations, states, and other government units. They build communities,
transportation systems, and businesses on it. They also gather natural
resources from it. Some of the land is owned by the public, and some of
it belongs to private property owners. People buy and sell the land and
make laws to decide how it can be used.

Compare and Contrast

What is being compared—The Algonquians and the Iroquois tribes **page C2**
farmed and lived in villages.

What is being contrasted—The Algonquians lived in bark-covered shelters called wigwams. The Iroquois lived in long wooden buildings called
longhouses.

Sequence

First   After Verrazano and Cartier, other Europeans continued to **page C3**
         look for the Northwest Passage. Henry Hudson, an English
         sea captain, was one of them. In 1608, on his first expedition,
         he reached an island east of Greenland.

Then   He then sailed farther north by way of the Arctic Ocean but
         failed to find the Northwest Passage.

Next   The following year Hudson searched by way of the Barents
         Sea, an arm of the Arctic Ocean.

Later   For his third voyage, Hudson had been hired by the Dutch
         East India Company to find the Northwest Passage. The
         company, or business, gave him a ship, the *Half Moon*, and a
         crew of about 20 sailors. They set sail in 1609 for the Arctic
         Ocean, but his crew soon mutinied, or rebelled. Hudson was
         forced to head south along the North American coast.

Categorize

Reasons Spain Had for Settling the Borderlands
• to protect the Spanish empire • to expand Spain's economy • to convert Native Americans to Christianity • to turn Native Americans into loyal Spanish subjects

page C4

Summarize

Possible response: Towns along the coast of New England prospered because of the abundance of fish that New Englanders were able to sell or trade to Europeans or other colonists.

page C5

Make Inferences

Possible response: People living in the backcountry had to make everything for themselves using available resources. Their homes were simple and they survived with very little.

page C6

Generalize

Possible response:

page C7

- Many southern ports prospered because they were near rivers.
- Immigrants have almost always helped areas to grow.
- Diverse populations usually have people who do different jobs.

Cause and Effect

Cause	Effects
The Battle of Bunker Hill angered British leaders. →	King George III issued a proclamation of rebellion in which he promised to use every measure to crush the rebellion and "bring the traitors to justice."
The Olive Branch Petition did not reach British leaders in London until August 24.	The Olive Branch Petition was unsuccessful.

page C8

Thinking Organizers

Thinking Organizers

Ideas and concepts may be organized in many different ways. The contents of the following pages are intended to act as guides for that organization. These copying masters may be used to help students organize the concepts in the lessons they have read. They may also help students complete the wide variety of activities that are assigned throughout the school year.

Contents

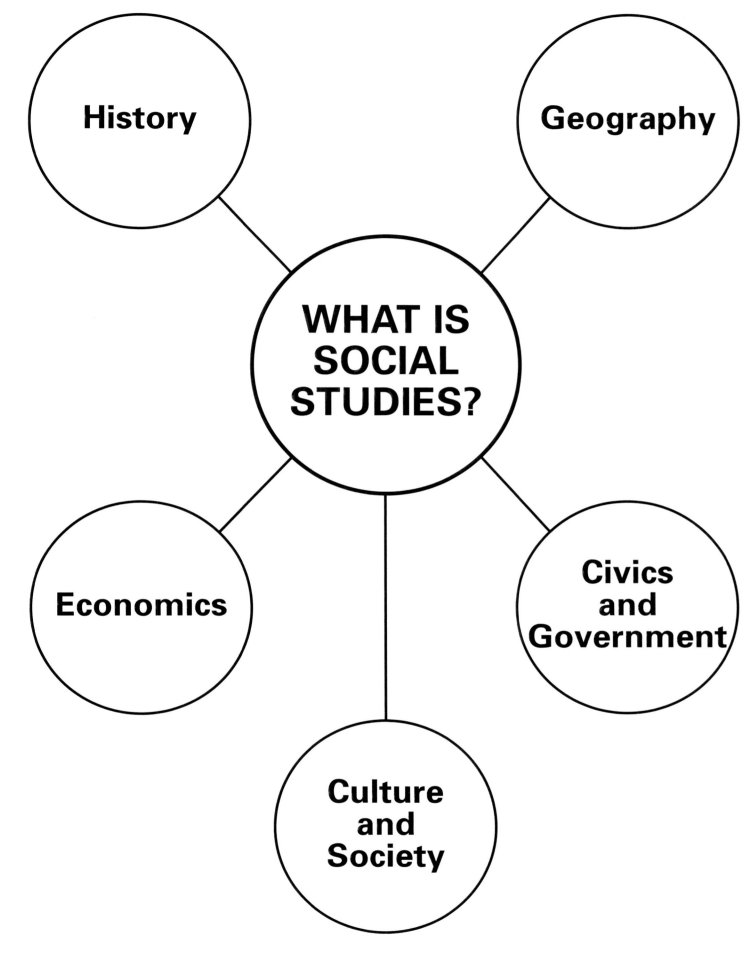

History

Geography

WHAT IS SOCIAL STUDIES?

Economics

Civics and Government

Culture and Society

Location

Where is the place located?

What is it near?

What direction is it from another place?

Why are certain features or places located where they are?

The Five Themes of Geography

Place

What is it like there?

What physical and human features does the place have?

Human-Environment Interactions

How are people's lives shaped by the place?

How has the place been shaped by people?

Regions

How is this place like other places?

What features set this place apart from other places?

Movement

How do people, products, and ideas get from one place to another?

Why do they make these movements?

© Harcourt

Essential Elements of Geography

The World in Spatial Terms

Why are things located where they are?

Human Systems

Where do people settle?

How do people earn their livings?

What laws do people make?

Places and Regions

What are the physical features of a region?

What are the human features?

Environment and Society

How do people affect the environment?

How does the environment affect people?

Physical Systems

How do wind, water, and precipitation affect Earth's surface?

How do living things create and change environments?

The Uses of Geography

What can I discover by looking at a map?

What kind of map should I use?

How can the map key help me?

© Harcourt

Reading About History

Ask yourself these questions as you read.

1. WHAT happened?

2. WHEN did it happen?

3. WHO took part in it?

4. HOW and WHY did it happen?

© Harcourt

Current Events

Summary of an important event:

WHO:

WHAT:

WHEN:

WHERE:

HOW:

Where did it take place? Draw a map.

Why?

What was the cause?   **What was the effect?**

Comparison

This event is similar to . . .

Prediction

What do I think will happen next?

Personal Reaction

My reaction to the event:

© Harcourt

Social Studies Journal

The single most important thing I learned was . . .

Something that confused me or that I did not understand was . . .

What surprised me the most was . . .

I would like to know more about . . .

Sources I can use to find answers to my questions . . .

The part that made the greatest impact on me was . . .

© Harcourt

Reading Guide

Questions I have before reading				New questions I have after reading
Question **1**	Question **2**	Question **3**	Question **4**	Question: Question:

Summary of what I learned after reading that answers my questions				Other interesting information I learned while reading
Question **1**	Question **2**	Question **3**	Question **4**	
General summary:				My reaction to what I read:

Visual Learning

Describe the artwork.

Explain what is happening in the artwork.

Explain what the artist is trying to show you.

Explain the mood set by the artwork.

Main Idea and Supporting Details

Supporting Detail

Supporting Detail

Main Idea

Supporting Detail

Supporting Detail

© Harcourt

Fact and Opinion

	Fact		Opinion	
✓	**Fact**	✗	**Opinion**	
✓	**Fact**	✗	**Opinion**	
✓	**Fact**	✗	**Opinion**	
✓	**Fact**	✗	**Opinion**	

Causes and Effects

What Caused the Event

Event

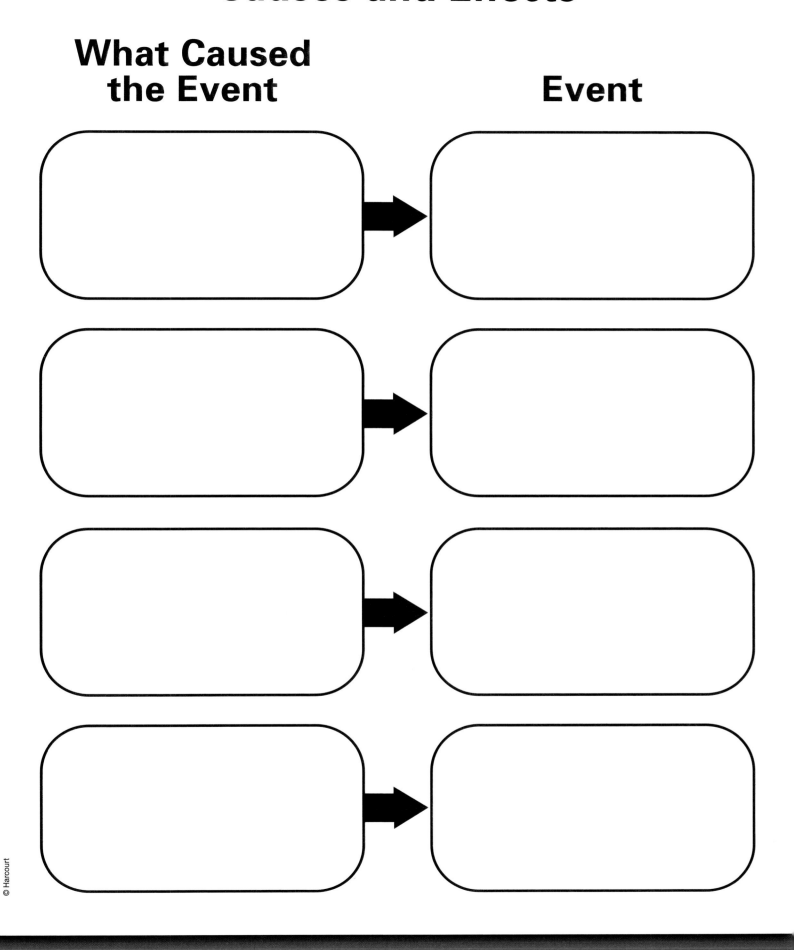

Compare and Contrast

Categorize

Sequence

Event

	Order
	◯

Event

	◯

Event

	◯

Event

	◯

Event

	◯

Summarize

Important Facts

SUMMARY

Important Facts

Make a Generalization

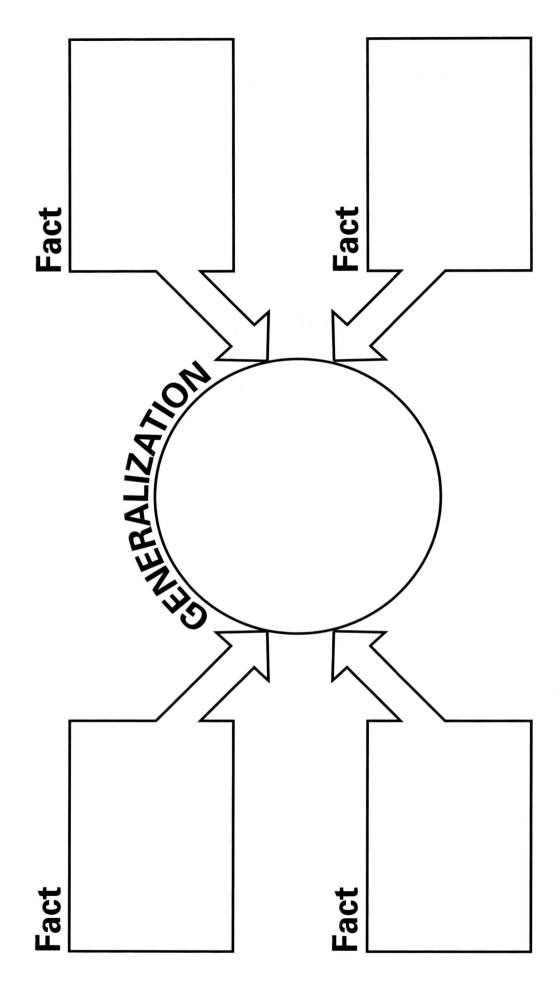

Fact

Fact

GENERALIZATION

Fact

Fact

Draw a Conclusion

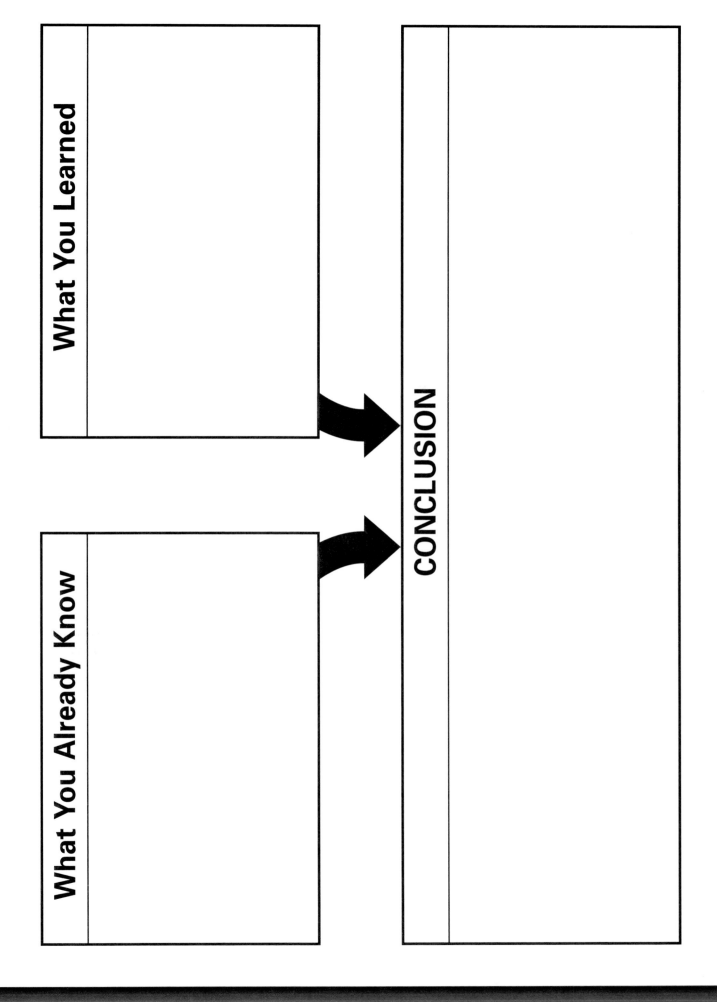

What You Learned

What You Already Know

CONCLUSION

© Harcourt

Point of View

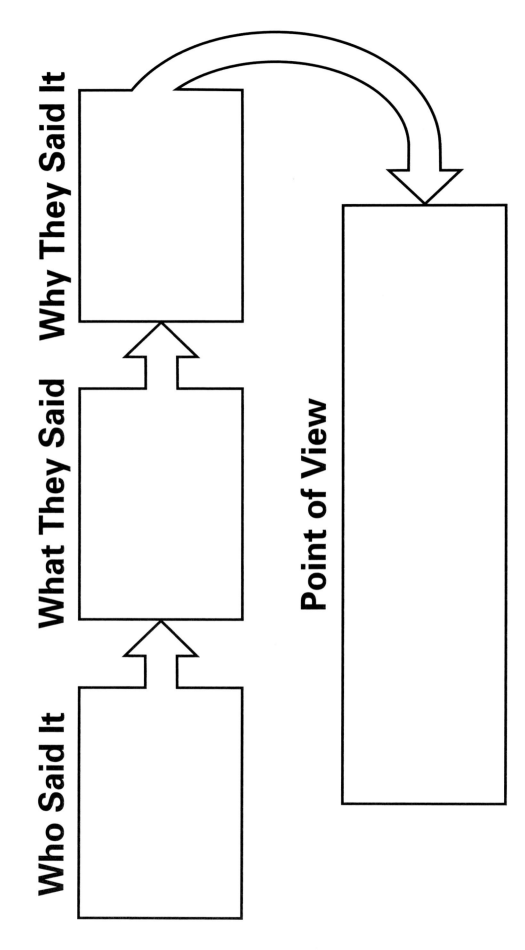

Who Said It

What They Said

Why They Said It

Point of View

Make Inferences

Make an Inference

[blank box]

$=$

Add Background Information and Your Own Opinions

[blank box]

$+$

Find Facts

[blank box]

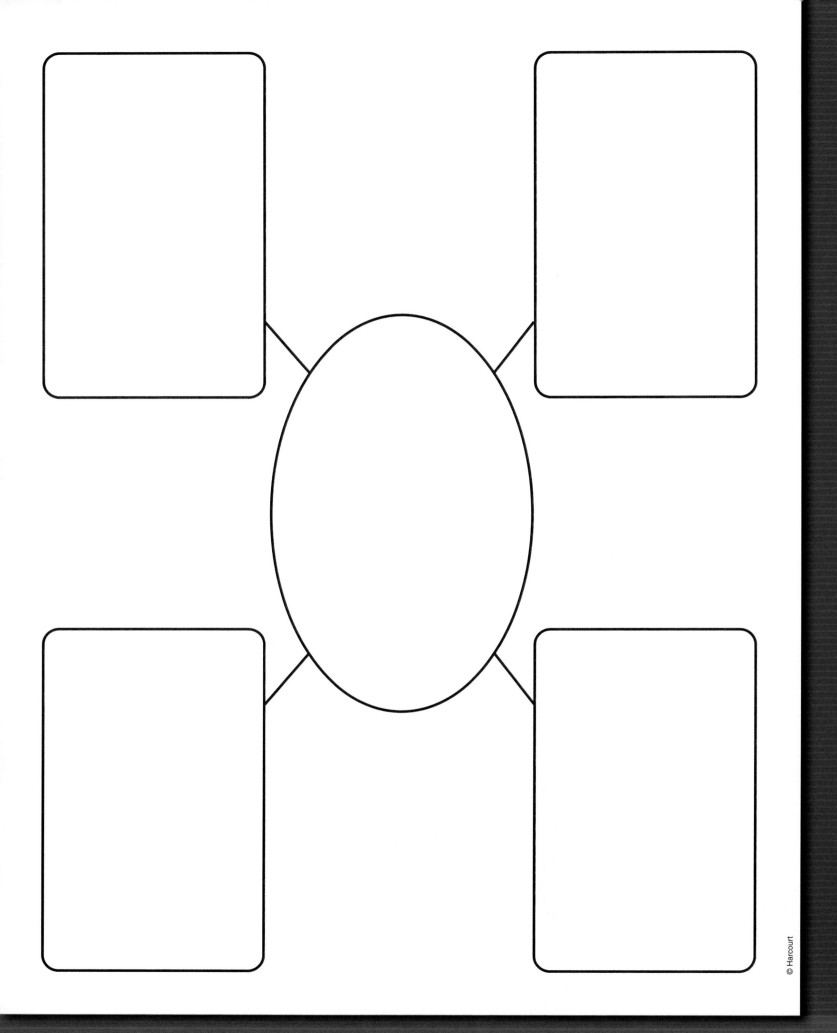

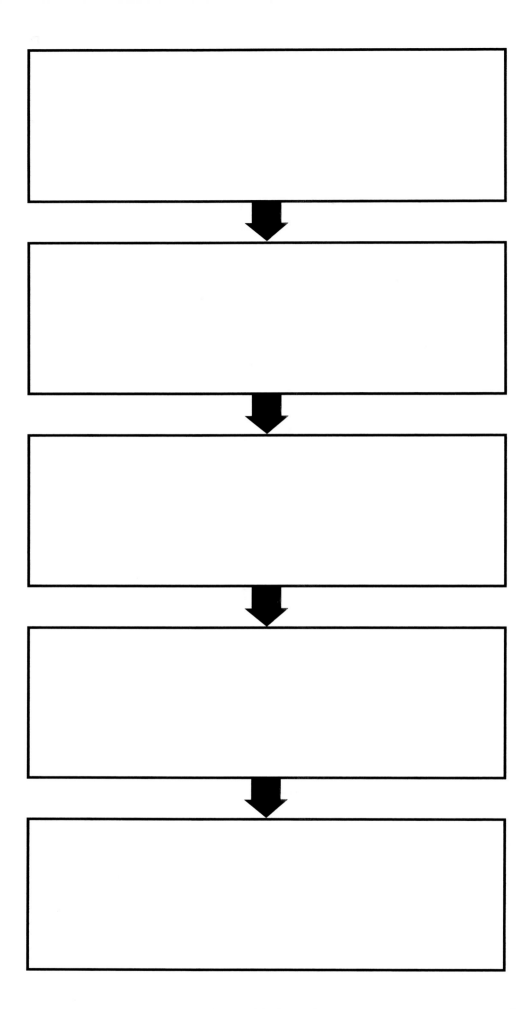

The United States

North America

The World

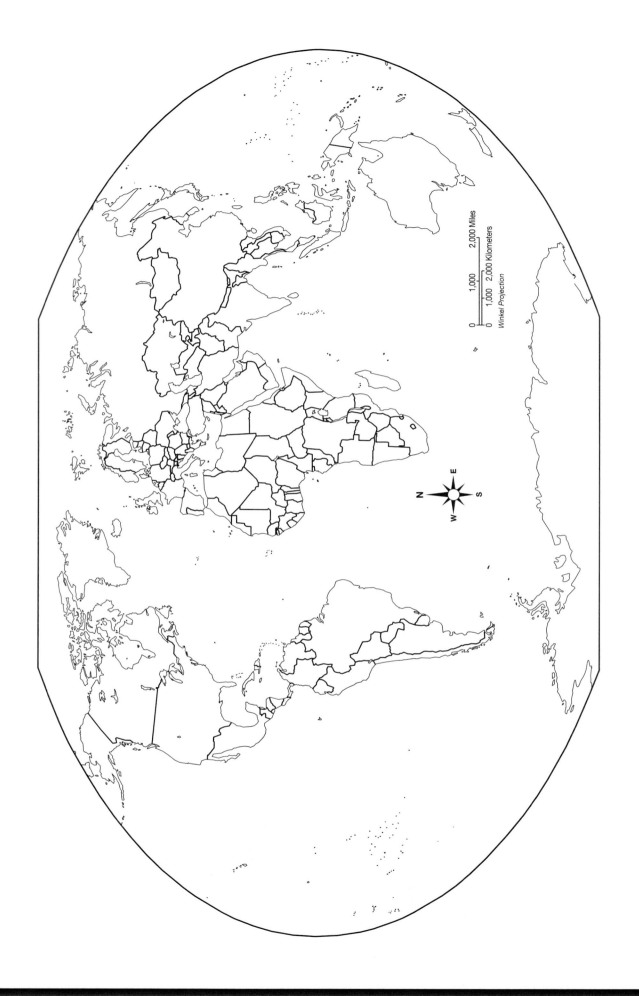

2,000 Miles

1,000

0

1,000   2,000 Kilometers

0   1,000   2,000 Kilometers

Winkel Projection

N
W   E
S

© Harcourt

Eastern Hemisphere

Western Hemisphere

Northern Hemisphere

Southern Hemisphere

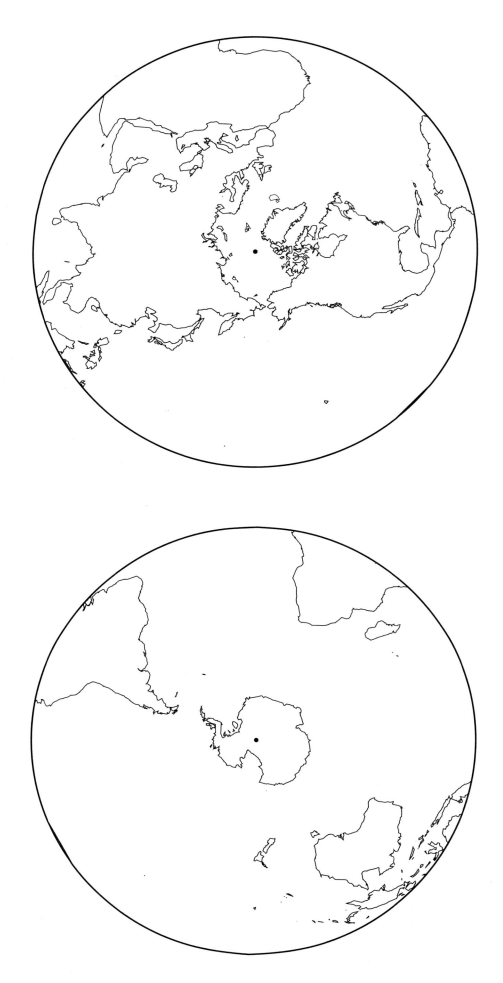

Holiday Activities

Holiday Activities

At appropriate times of the year, the holiday backgrounds and activities provided in this section can be used to introduce or reinforce concepts related to important holidays. The holiday activities explore a variety of individual and community celebrations. They can prompt discussion of the similarities and differences of the traditions and cultures found in the United States.

Contents

Labor Day

Labor Day

The first Monday in September marks the day dedicated to American workers— Labor Day. It signifies a national yearly tribute to the contributions workers have made to our country. The first Labor Day holiday was celebrated on September 5, 1882, in New York City. By 1885 many cities across the country had adopted this "workingman's holiday." In 1894, Congress passed an act making the first Monday in September a legal holiday.

- Today, Labor Day is celebrated with picnics and parades.
- To some, Labor Day marks the end of summer and the last three-day weekend of the year.

Risky Business

Have students poll their friends to find out which job or occupation they believe is the most dangerous. Then share with them information from the Census Bureau that lists some of the riskiest professions. Invite students to discuss those statistics.

Show Your Appreciation

Discuss how jobs can affect people's lives. Have students name jobs that impact their lives and think about the people who perform those jobs. Invite each student to select someone who does a job and to show that person his or her appreciation by creating a thank-you card.

Find a Job

1. Give each student a copy of the employment section of a newspaper.

2. Have students locate a job description.

3. Help students create a résumé that lists the skills needed to fill that job.

Career Fair

Have students invite people in different career fields to visit the class. Each career field can have a booth and handouts for more information. Or, have students research careers that they are interested in and set up career booths with handouts that tell others about their position and their job responsibilities. Invite other classes to visit these "experts" in their career fields.

Columbus Day

Columbus Day

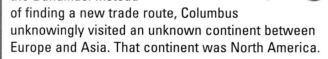

Christopher Columbus was an explorer for Spain who sailed across the Atlantic Ocean. He was looking for a shorter route to use in trading valuable goods with people in the Indies. Columbus landed on San Salvador, an island in what is now the Bahamas. Instead of finding a new trade route, Columbus unknowingly visited an unknown continent between Europe and Asia. That continent was North America.

About four hundred years after Christopher Columbus first arrived in the Americas, people in the United States held the first celebration in his honor. Today, Columbus Day is a national holiday celebrated on the second Monday in October. It is celebrated with parades and speeches. Government offices and many businesses are closed.

- Calendars traditionally show the second Monday in October as Columbus Day.

- When Columbus landed in the Americas, he believed that he had reached the Indies, so he called the people that he met *Indians*.

- On Columbus's first voyage, he sailed with three ships, the *Niña*, the *Pinta*, and the *Santa María*.

Map It Out

Provide students with world maps, and help them locate Spain and San Salvador. Ask students to label the continents and oceans. With a colored pencil or marker, have students map the approximate route Columbus followed to get to San Salvador. Students should show and label his three ships en route.

Log Book

There have been several biographies written about the life of Christopher Columbus and his voyages. Columbus also kept a detailed log book of the daily events that took place on his voyage. The log book included the sailors' actions and behaviors as well as how they reacted toward one another and toward the native peoples they met along the way.

Explain that a log book is very similar to a diary or a journal. Choose and read aloud to students a few translated selections from Columbus's log book. Then have students begin their own log book and write about what happens each day, how others react, and what their feelings are about it.

Convince the Queen

Remind students that Columbus needed support from Spain in order to pay for his voyage. He made many appeals to Queen Isabella to provide money, ships, and supplies for his voyage. Have students take the role of Columbus and prepare and present to the class a short speech to convince the queen of the merits of a voyage.

Veterans Day

Veterans Day

Veterans Day is a day for remembering those who fought for our country. It was originally called Armistice Day, for the armistice ending the fighting in World War I but later became known as Veterans Day. In 1971, President Nixon declared Veterans Day, the second Monday in November, a federal holiday. Veterans Day is a day to honor all who have served in the armed forces of the United States. It is also a day to remember the sacrifices that men and women made during all wars fought by the United States. Veterans march in parades, give speeches, and are recognized in ceremonies throughout the United States. These ceremonies are often held at national monuments or memorials, such as the Vietnam Veterans Memorial in Washington, D.C. It was built to honor soldiers from the Vietnam War. The names of those lost in the war are etched into a black granite wall.

- In 1921 an unknown soldier was buried at Arlington National Cemetery to honor all who have died serving their country.

- The armistice that ended the fighting in World War I was signed in 1918 at 11:00 on the eleventh day of the eleventh month.

Letters to Home

Ask students to imagine they are soldiers far from home. Have them write letters describing their thoughts about serving their country.

Dear Mom and Dad,
 I am sitting on the deck of our battleship. We are headed into enemy territory.
 I am proud to serve my country. I am ready to fight for our freedom.
 Keep me in your thoughts and prayers.
 I love you!
 Robert

War Time Line

Let students research and make a time line showing the dates of major wars since World War I, listing relevant facts about each.

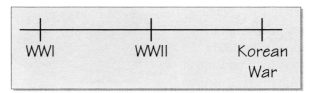

WWI   WWII   Korean War

God Bless America

Irving Berlin's patriotic song "God Bless America" was first sung on Armistice Day, November 11, 1938, at the New York World's Fair. Today, the song remains a very popular patriotic tribute to America. Berlin donated all of the royalties from the song to charity. Invite students to find out more about Irving Berlin. Then, sing "God Bless America" together.

GOD BLESS AMERICA
by Irving Berlin

God bless America.
Land that I love.
Stand beside her and guide her,
Thru the night with a light from above.
From the mountains to the prairies
To the oceans white with foam,
God bless America
My home sweet home.
God bless America
My home sweet home.

Thanksgiving

Thanksgiving Day

Thanksgiving is a holiday that celebrates a special harvest in America a long time ago. Many people left Europe in the 1600s looking for a new life in the Americas. One group, the Pilgrims, left England to find a place where they could worship as they wished. They sailed across the ocean on the *Mayflower* and landed in North America at a place they called Plymouth. There they worked to clear the land, build houses, and make a new life.

During the first winter in Plymouth, half of the settlers died. In the spring an Indian named Squanto helped those who survived plant crops. Their fall harvest was a success, so the Pilgrims held a feast to give thanks to God. The Pilgrims shared the feast with the Wampanoag Indians.

Today, families gather at Thanksgiving to share good things to eat and to give thanks for the good things in their lives.

- Turkey is a traditional Thanksgiving food. People at the first Thanksgiving feast may have eaten wild turkey, but they probably also enjoyed other meats including venison, duck, goose, lobster, and clams.

- President Abraham Lincoln made Thanksgiving a national holiday in 1863.

- Schools, banks, government offices, and most businesses are closed on Thanksgiving.

What's for Dinner?

Most people associate pumpkin pie and cranberry sauce with Thanksgiving dinner, when in fact, neither of these were served at the Pilgrims' first Thanksgiving celebration. Have students research foods eaten in the 1600s and collect data regarding period games and activities. Then make a mural showing the similarities and differences between the Pilgrims' first Thanksgiving and a present-day celebration.

Compare Plant Growth

Squanto showed the Pilgrims how to grow corn. To fertilize the soil, the Indians mixed in fish and fish parts before planting the corn seeds. Do a science experiment with fish fertilizer. (This is a product for household plants that can be purchased at a nursery.) Put soil in two pots. Mix fish fertilizer with the soil in one of the pots. Plant the same kinds of seeds in each pot. Observe the plants over the next few weeks. Record the observations on a chart or in a journal. What conclusions can be drawn from the experiment?

Do Not Tip the Mayflower

When the Pilgrims left for North America, they could not take all their belongings with them. Choices were made as to what they really needed for that long voyage. Let students work in small groups to make a list of items the Pilgrims would need and the approximate weight of each. Tell students that only 100 lbs per group may be taken on the ship. Have students work together to decide which items should be taken on the trip. Ask each group to defend their choices.

Christmas Day

Christmas Day

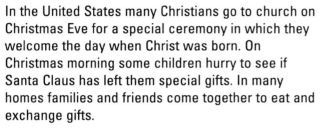

On December 25 many people celebrate Christmas. For many people Christmas is a religious holiday honoring the birth of Jesus Christ. Christmas customs vary from family to family and are often based on traditions brought by ancestors from other countries.

In the United States many Christians go to church on Christmas Eve for a special ceremony in which they welcome the day when Christ was born. On Christmas morning some children hurry to see if Santa Claus has left them special gifts. In many homes families and friends come together to eat and exchange gifts.

- Homes are often decorated with holly, ivy, and evergreen trees as reminders of the beauty of nature. Houses and stores may be trimmed with outdoor lights, and festive music may be played.

- Christmas is celebrated in many countries. The holiday signifies the spirit of peace and goodwill.

Caroling, Caroling

Take part in one of the most popular traditions of the holiday season—caroling. Many carols have origins in other countries. For example, "Bring a Torch, Jeanette, Isabella" is a French carol. "Deck the Halls" is a Welsh carol, and "O Christmas Tree" is a favorite in Germany. Sing "O Christmas Tree" in English and German.

> O Christmas Tree, O Christmas Tree,
> Your branches green delight us.
> They're green when summer days are bright:
> They're green when winter snow is white.
> O Christmas Tree, O Christmas Tree,
> Your branches green delight us.

> O Tannenbaum, o Tannenbaum,
> Wie treu sind deine Blätter.
> Du grünst nicht nur zur Sommerzeit,
> Nein, auch im Winter, wenn es schneit.
> O Tannenbaum, o Tannenbaum,
> Wie treu sind deine Blätter.

Symbols of the Season

Many symbols and traditions are associated with the Christmas season. Let students pick a symbol (example: candy cane, Christmas tree, mistletoe) and research its history and any other information available. Have students report on their findings and then compile the information in a class book.

Thinking of Others

You will need:

12" x 18" pieces of heavy cardboard
Gold, green, and red yarn
Scissors
Strips of cloth

The Christmas season is a time to think of others. Have students weave Christmas placemats to be taken and given to a local nursing facility or hospital for use during the holiday season.

To make the placemats, have students cut small slits at 1 inch intervals down both long sides of the cardboard. Have them wrap a long piece of gold yarn across the cardboard, connecting the slits. Then, using lengths of yarn and cloth strips, students can weave in and out of the gold yarn until the cardboard is covered.

New Year's Day

New Year's Day

Nearly everywhere in the world, people celebrate the end of the old year and the beginning of the new one.  New Year's Day in the United States is celebrated on January 1.

Many traditions are associated with New Year's Day. Perhaps the best-known tradition is to make New Year's resolutions. People make resolutions that will improve their lives, such as finding a new job. Another tradition is eating black-eyed peas, an idea thought to bring you good luck in the coming year. Celebrating the stroke of midnight is also very popular.

- January was named for the Roman god Janus, who had two faces. People believe one face looks forward and one looks back, just as we leave the old year behind and look forward to the new one.

New Year's Poem

> Fireworks
> Bright, colorful
> Boom, sparkle, explode
> Loud, exciting
> Celebration!

Have students brainstorm objects and images that are associated with New Year's Day celebrations. Then ask each student to choose one of the objects and create a New Year's Day poem about it. Have them use the poetic form known as cinquain. A cinquain poem has 5 lines and follows this format.

Line 1: 1 word title (noun)
Line 2: 2 adjectives that describe the title
Line 3: 3 verbs that relate to the title
Line 4: 2 adverbs that describe the verbs
Line 5: 1 noun that renames the title

Encourage volunteers to read their poems to the class.

Time Capsule

Have students make their own time capsule to be opened on a future date. Provide or have a student bring in a large coffee tin or cookie tin. Let students decorate the tin with paint or construction paper. Instruct students to put drawings of objects that are important to them now in the tin.  Seal the tin with tape, and tuck it away. Open it a few months from now, and have students determine if the same songs, games, clothes, and trends are still popular. Compare the current events now and then. Are they the same?

A Year in History

Invite students to reflect on events that have happened in the last year. They should think of events in history as well as events in their own lives. Begin a book "A Year in the Life of. . . ." Make a page for each event. This will serve as a reference of events in that particular year.

Old New Year

Sing a song of remembering old friendships and making new ones—"Auld Lang Syne." Explain that the title means "Old Long Since."

AULD LANG SYNE
by Robert Burns

*Should auld acquaintance be forgot
and never brought to mind?
Should auld acquaintance be forgot
and days of auld lang syne?
For auld lang syne, my dear,
for auld lang syne,
we'll take a cup of kindness yet,
for auld lang syne.*

Inauguration Day

Inauguration Day

The inauguration of a newly-elected President of the United States occurs every four years, following a presidential election. It is always on January 20 unless this is a Sunday, and then it would be on January 21. The swearing-in ceremony is the most important part of the day. This is when the President is given the oath of office. After the new President takes the oath of office, there is usually a parade down Pennsylvania Avenue from the United States Capitol to the White House.

■ Inauguration Day is considered a holiday only in Washington, D.C., two counties in Maryland, two counties in Virginia, and the cities of Alexandria and Falls Church, Virginia.

What It Takes

Have students research and list the qualifications for becoming President of the United States. Have students role-play using correct and incorrect information as the class decides if this person can be a candidate. (Example: I am 23 years old—No; I was born in the United States 50 years ago and have not been convicted of a felony—Yes.)

Design a New Seal

Show students a picture of the Seal of the President of the United States. Explain that it is the chief symbol of the presidency and is used to close envelopes containing messages or other documents from the President to the United States Congress. Have students study the objects shown on the seal. Explain that each symbol has its own meaning:

Eagle with shield—self-reliance
Olive branch—the desire for peace
Arrows—the ability to wage war
50 stars—the 50 states
Color *red*—hardiness and courage
Color *blue*—justice, vigilance, and perseverance
Color *white*—purity and innocence

Have students design a seal especially for a new President.

Dr. Martin Luther King, Jr., Day

Dr. Martin Luther King, Jr., Day

Dr. Martin Luther King, Jr., Day is one of our country's newest holidays. It honors a leader who was very important in helping Americans understand that everyone should be treated equally.

Dr. Martin Luther King, Jr., was born in Atlanta, Georgia, on January 15, 1929. While he was a minister in Montgomery, Alabama, an African American woman named Rosa Parks was arrested because she refused to give up her seat on a bus to a white man. Dr. King helped organize a bus boycott in Montgomery to protest the unfair treatment of African Americans. For 382 days, many people refused to ride the buses until the bus company finally agreed to change its rules. Dr. Martin Luther King, Jr., continued to speak out against the poor treatment of African Americans. He helped organize a historic march to Washington, D.C. There he gave a famous speech calling for freedom for all.

On April 4, 1968, Dr. King was assassinated. Today, Americans celebrate his birthday by remembering his fight for equal opportunity.

- On the third Monday in January each year, Americans honor Dr. King.
- Many cities celebrate Dr. Martin Luther King, Jr., Day with picnics, parades, and marches.

Time Line

Explain that we celebrate Dr. Martin Luther King, Jr., Day to honor a famous American who devoted his life to the struggle for equal rights for all people. Dr. King is particularly admired because he believed that people could and ought to peacefully protest against things that were unfair. Have students research Dr. King's life and illustrate the most important events in his life on a time line.

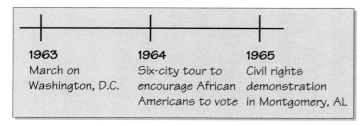

1963	1964	1965
March on Washington, D.C.	Six-city tour to encourage African Americans to vote	Civil rights demonstration in Montgomery, AL

"I have a dream...."

One of Dr. King's most famous speeches includes "I have a dream that my four little children will one day live in a nation where they will not be judged by the color of their skin but by the content of their character." Discuss the meaning of Dr. King's words. Then have students memorize and recite this thought-provoking sentence. Encourage them to add to King's speech, sharing their ideas for justice, fairness, or equality.

We Can Overcome

The song "We Shall Overcome" is associated with Dr. Martin Luther King, Jr., and the Civil Rights movement of the 1960s. Introduce the students to the version of the song that appears below. Read the first three verses aloud and talk about what the words mean. Then have the students sing the song with you. Challenge them to create their own verses for the song.

1. *We shall overcome*
    We shall overcome
    We shall overcome someday

Chorus: *Oh, deep in my heart*
            I do believe
            We shall overcome someday

2. *We'll walk hand in hand*
    We'll walk hand in hand
    We'll walk hand in hand someday

Chorus

3. *We shall all be free*
    We shall all be free
    We shall all be free someday

Chorus

Presidents' Day

Presidents' Day

Presidents' Day celebrates the works of two great Presidents of the United States—George Washington and Abraham Lincoln. Both Presidents were born in February, so people honor them on the third Monday in that month. The lives of the other Presidents are celebrated on this holiday, too.

George Washington is called the Father of Our Country. He led the Continental Army when our nation was trying to gain its freedom from Britain. The people of the United States elected him the first President. As President, he worked to make the nation strong. He helped keep the new nation out of war and worked to keep the states from fighting with each other.

Abraham Lincoln was born in a log cabin. His family was so poor that he could not go to school. Instead, he studied at home and became a lawyer. In his lifetime, he saw many slaves being treated poorly. As President, Lincoln preserved the Union during the Civil War and freed the slaves in areas of the South that were fighting against the United States.

- During the first public celebration of George Washington's birthday, soldiers who fought in the Revolutionary War with Washington held a drum and fife concert for him. Cannons were fired in his honor, too.

- On Presidents' Day, people often think about the history of the United States. Some people visit the Washington Monument and the Lincoln Memorial in Washington, D.C.

Landmarks

Mount Rushmore, in South Dakota, is a monument to the first 150 years of our nation's history. The faces of Presidents Washington, Jefferson, Roosevelt, and Lincoln are carved out of the mountain. Each bust is  60 feet (about 18 m) high; the entire monument took 400 workers about 14 years to complete. Invite students to sculpt a model of Mount Rushmore out of clay, papier-mâché, or foam.

Yankee Doodle

Talk with the students about George Washington's role as leader of the Continental Army when our nation was trying to gain its freedom from Britain. Explain that the song "Yankee Doodle" was originally sung by the British to make fun of the Americans, but the Americans made the song their own and added their own words. Sing this version of "Yankee Doodle" together.

YANKEE DOODLE

Father and I went down to camp,
Along with Captain Gooding;
And there we saw the men and boys,
As thick as hasty pudding.

Yankee doodle, keep it up,
Yankee doodle dandy;
Mind the music and the step,
And with the girls be handy.

Conduct an Interview

Most adults have lived long enough to see several different Presidents in office. Have the students compile a list of questions and then interview an adult about his or her favorite President. Set up  a mock TV station in the room, and let students share their reports with the classroom "audience."

Memorial Day

Memorial Day

Memorial Day is a day set aside to honor men and women who lost their lives while serving our country. What started in 1868 as citizens decorating the graves of Civil War veterans is now celebrated as the holiday that pays tribute to soldiers lost in later wars as well. Memorial Day is celebrated on the last Monday in May.

- Memorial Day was first called Decoration Day.

- Many people bring flowers or flags to the graves of those friends or family members who served in wars.

- People often observe Memorial Day with picnics, cookouts, and parades.

Memorial Day Essay

Share these lines, from Henry Wadsworth Longfellow, about soldiers who died in battle.

> *Your silent tents of green*
> *We deck with fragrant flowers;*
> *Yours has the suffering been,*
> *The memory shall be ours.*

Discuss the meaning of the poem with students and talk about why it is important to remember the men and women who died fighting for our country. Then ask students to write an essay about what Memorial Day means to them.

Family Memory Book

Memorial Day is the perfect time to start a family memory book. Have students think of family members who have died. Create one page for each person. Students should write facts and memories about the person and provide a picture, if possible.

Design a Badge

Memorial Day is sometimes called Decoration Day because people often decorate the graves of fallen soldiers. Decoration also refers to the decoration of a soldier with badges of honor or awards for bravery. Have students design a badge of honor for a soldier. Ask students to tell whom the badge was given to and what the badge was given for.

A Poppy to Remember

You will need:

Squares of red tissue paper
Craft wire

During World War I, soldiers fought many battles in Flanders in Belgium. Every spring the soldiers noticed red flowers blooming across the battlefields and on the graves of their friends who had been killed. Today, the poppy is worn to remind us of the many people killed in battle.

Have students make poppies by folding squares of red tissue paper back and forth like a fan. Twist a short section of craft wire to cinch the center of the folds. Then, unfold the "petals" of the flower. You can wrap the bottom of the flower with tape to hold it securely.

Flag Day

Flag Day

Our flag is more than just a cloth banner. It is a symbol of our country. In 1777 the Continental Congress adopted the Stars and Stripes pattern for our national flag. One hundred years later, in 1877, Flag Day was first celebrated. Many citizens and organizations wanted a national day to commemorate the United States flag. In 1949, President Harry Truman signed legislation making Flag Day a day of national observance.

- In 1983 the largest United States flag was displayed in Washington, D.C. The flag measured 411 feet (125 m) by 210 feet (64 m). Each star measured 13 feet (about 4 m) across.

- The United States flag has thirteen stripes, alternating red and white, with each stripe representing one of the thirteen original colonies.

- The United States flag has fifty stars, one for each state.

Create a Flag

Explain that George Washington's original pencil sketch for the flag indicated 6-pointed stars. Betsy Ross, however, recommended 5-pointed stars. At first, the Continental Congress protested that 5-pointed stars were too difficult to make, but the Congress eventually agreed to use them.

Ask students to work in groups and use the Internet or classroom reference books to research the history of the flag. Have each group create an original flag according to the specifications set out by the Continental Congress on June 14, 1777.

Our Flag

There are rules associated with our American flag. Discuss the guidelines for displaying a flag, the rules for folding the flag, and the proper disposal of an old flag.

1. The United States flag must never be lowered to any object or person while in a parade.

2. The flag should be raised quickly but lowered slowly.

3. The flag should never touch the ground.

4. The flag is customarily displayed from sunrise to sunset.

5. The flag should be folded lengthwise in half and then folded again. Then it is folded in a series of triangles starting with the stripes until only a blue field of stars is visible.

6. A worn-out flag should be burned.

Have students follow the guidelines for folding a flag. If possible, have a student be responsible for raising, lowering, and storing the flag that is displayed in front of your school.

The National Anthem

The national anthem of the United States is titled "The Star-Spangled Banner" and was written by Francis Scott Key. During the War of 1812, Key spent a night aboard a British warship in Chesapeake Bay while trying to arrange the release of an American prisoner. The next morning, Key saw that an American flag had survived the battle that had raged throughout the night. The flag inspired him to write the poem, which provides the words for our national anthem. Play a recording of the song, and have students sing the words of the song. The words appear on page R36 in the students' textbooks. Then divide the class into groups, with each group choosing a phrase from the song and explaining its meaning in their own words. Ask students to share their thoughts.

Independence Day

Independence Day

July 4, often called Independence Day, is a day Americans celebrate our country's freedom and independence. It is a legal holiday in all states. This date marks the anniversary of the day the Second Continental Congress adopted the Declaration of Independence in 1776. This document announced to the world that the 13 colonies were independent states and no longer belonged to Britain. Independence Day has become the most honored non-religious holiday in America.

- Firework displays have become a colorful tradition of this patriotic holiday.

- Independence Day is one of the few holidays that has not been moved to a Monday or a Friday to allow for a three-day weekend.

Famous Document

Ask students to fill in the missing words to the famous lines of this historic document:

The Declaration of Independence

We hold these truths to be self-evident,
that all _____ are created _____ ,
that they are endowed by their Creator
with certain unalienable _____ ,
that among these are Life, _____ ,
and the pursuit of Happiness.

Then, display and read a copy of the Declaration of Independence. Discuss what each line means. Have students copy the second paragraph onto a poster to display in the room.

Add Your "John Hancock"

Display a copy of the Declaration of Independence. Point out the signatures of each member of the Second Continental Congress. Challenge students to find the signature of the document's creator, Thomas Jefferson, and to look at John Hancock's signature. Invite students to speculate on the origin of the phrase "put your John Hancock here."

As American as Apple Pie

You will need:

    1 9-inch piecrust in an aluminum pan
    1 20-ounce can apple pie filling
    ½ cup sugar
    1 teaspoon cinnamon
    Spoons

Explain that having picnics and making apple pie are two traditions often associated with Independence Day celebrations. Ask students to share how they celebrate the holiday. Then, make an apple pie to celebrate Independence Day in the classroom.

1. Mix apples, sugar, and cinnamon.

2. Pour into a pie pan.

3. Bake as directed on the can of pie filling.

Vocabulary Cards

Vocabulary Cards

This reproducible section will help you create word cards for the vocabulary found at the beginning of each lesson in your Teacher's Edition. The cards may be used to preview the unit, build vocabulary notebooks, assist ESL students, and review vocabulary at the end of the unit. Use blank cards to add vocabulary to meet the special needs of your class.

Contents

map title	map key
Atlas	Atlas
compass rose	cardinal direction
Atlas	Atlas
intermediate direction	locator
Atlas	Atlas
map scale	inset map
Atlas	Atlas
grid system	history
Atlas	Introduction
chronology	oral history
Introduction	Introduction

© Harcourt

A part of a map that explains what the symbols on a map stand for.	Words on a map that tell the subject of the map.
One of the main directions: north, south, east, or west.	A circular direction marker on a map.
A small map or picture of a globe that shows where an area on the main map is found in a state, on a continent, or in the world.	One of the in-between directions: northeast, northwest, southeast, southwest.
A smaller map within a larger one.	A part of a map that compares a distance on the map to a distance in the real world.
Events of the past.	An arrangement of lines that divide something, such as a map, into squares.
Stories, events, or experiences told aloud by a person who did not have a written language or who did not write down what happened.	Time order.

point of view Introduction	**historical empathy** Introduction
frame of reference Introduction	**analyze** Introduction
primary source Introduction	**secondary source** Introduction
geography Introduction	**location** Introduction
physical feature Introduction	**human feature** Introduction
modify Introduction	**adapt** Introduction

© Harcourt

An understanding of the thoughts and feelings people of the past had about events in their time.	A person's perspective.
To look closely at how the parts of an event connect with one another and how the event is connected to other events.	A set of ideas that determine how a person understands something.
A record of an event written by someone who was not there at the time.	A record of an event made by a person who saw or took part in it.
The place where something can be found.	The study of Earth's surface and the way people use it.
Something created by humans, such as a building or road, that alters the land.	A land feature that has been made by nature.
To adjust ways of living to land and resources.	To change.

region Introduction	**economy** Introduction
economics Introduction	**civics** Introduction
civic participation Introduction	**government** Introduction
culture Introduction	**society** Introduction
heritage Introduction	

© Harcourt

The way people of a state, region, or country use resources to meet their needs.	An area of Earth in which many features are similar.
The study of citizenship.	The study of how people use resources to meet their needs.
A system by which people of a community, state, or nation use leaders and laws to help people live together.	Being concerned with and involved in issues related to the community, state, country, or world.
A human group.	A way of life.
	Culture that has come from the past and continues today.

landform	mountain range
Lesson 1	Lesson 1
piedmont	sea level
Lesson 1	Lesson 1
plateau	basin
Lesson 1	Lesson 1
volcano	elevation
Lesson 1	Skill 1
contour line	current
Skill 1	Lesson 2
tide	inlet
Lesson 2	Lesson 2

© Harcourt

A group of connected mountains.	A physical feature, such as a plain, mountain, hill, valley, or plateau, on the Earth's surface.
The level of the surface of the ocean.	An area at or near the foot of a mountain.
Low, bowl-shaped land with higher ground all around it.	A broad area of high, mostly flat land.
The height of land in relation to sea level.	An opening in Earth, often on a hill or mountain, through which hot lava, gases, ash, and rocks may pour out.
The part of a body of water flowing in a certain direction.	A line on a drawing or map that connects all points of equal elevation.
An area of water extending into the land from a larger body of water.	The regular rise and fall of the ocean and of the bodies of water connected to it.

sound Lesson 2	**tributary** Lesson 2
drainage basin Lesson 2	**fall line** Lesson 2
climate Lesson 3	**natural vegetation** Lesson 3
rain shadow Lesson 3	**humidity** Lesson 3
drought Lesson 3	**arid** Lesson 3
tundra Lesson 3	**prairie** Lesson 3

© Harcourt

A stream or river that flows into a larger stream or river.	A long inlet, often parallel to the coast.
A place where the elevation of the land drops sharply, causing rivers to form waterfalls or rapids.	Land drained by a river system.
The plant life that grows naturally in a place.	The kind of weather a place has most often, year after year.
The amount of moisture in the air.	The driest side of a mountain.
Dry.	A long period with little or no rain.
An area of flat or rolling land covered mostly by grasses and wildflowers.	A cold, dry region where trees cannot grow.

savanna	natural resource
Lesson 3	Lesson 4
modify	fertilizer
Lesson 4	Lesson 4
irrigation	nonrenewable
Lesson 4	Lesson 4
renewable	erosion
Lesson 4	Lesson 4
land use	relative location
Lesson 4	Lesson 5
political region	economic region
Lesson 5	Lesson 5

Something found in nature that people can use.	A kind of grassland that has areas with a few scattered trees.
Matter added to the soil to make it produce more crops.	To change.
Not able to be made again quickly by nature or people.	The use of canals, ditches, or pipes to move water to dry areas.
The wearing down of Earth's surface, usually by wind or water.	Able to be made or grown again by nature or people.
The position of one place in relation to another.	The way in which most of the land in a place is used.
An area defined by the kind of work people do or the products they produce.	An area that shares a government and leaders.

© Harcourt

cultural region	population region
Lesson 5	Lesson 5
urban	suburban
Lesson 5	Lesson 5
rural	crossroads
Lesson 5	Lesson 5
metropolitan area	absolute location
Lesson 5	Skill 2
lines of longitude	parallel
Skill 2	Skill 2
lines of latitude	meridian
Skill 2	Skill 2

© Harcourt

An area based on where people live.	An area in which people share some ways of life.
Of or like the area of smaller cities or towns around a large city.	Of or like a city.
A place that connects people, goods, and ideas.	Like or having to do with a place away from a city.
The exact location of a place on Earth, either a postal location or its lines of latitude and longitude.	A large city and the suburbs that surround it.
A line of latitude. It is called this because parallels are always the same distance from one another.	Lines on a map or globe that run north and south; also called meridians.
A line of longitude that runs from the North Pole to the South Pole.	Lines on a map or globe that run east and west; also called parallels.

© Harcourt

prime meridian

Skill 2

	The meridian marked 0 degrees that runs north and south through Greenwich, England.

glacier	migration
Lesson 1	Lesson 1
theory	archaeologist
Lesson 1	Lesson 1
artifact	descendant
Lesson 1	Lesson 1
origin story	ancestor
Lesson 1	Lesson 1
time line	decade
Skill 1	Skill 1
century	millennium
Skill 1	Skill 1

© Harcourt

The movement of people.	A huge, slow-moving mass of ice covering land.
A scientist who studies the culture of people who lived in the past.	A possible explanation.
A person's child, grandchild, and so on.	An object made by people.
An early family member.	A story or set of stories by Native American people that tells about their beginnings and how the world came to be.
A period of ten years.	A diagram that shows events that took place during a certain period of time.
A period of 1,000 years.	A period of 100 years.

nomad	technology
Lesson 2	Lesson 2
extinct	agriculture
Lesson 2	Lesson 2
tribe	civilization
Lesson 2	Lesson 2
class	slavery
Lesson 2	Lesson 2
pueblo	generalization
Lesson 2	Skill 2
adapt	staple
Lesson 3	Lesson 3

The use of scientific knowledge and tools to make or do something.	A wanderer who has no settled home.
Farming.	No longer in existence.
A culture that usually has cities with well-developed forms of government, religion, and learning.	A group of people who share the same language, land, and leaders.
The practice of holding people against their will and making them carry out orders.	A group of people who are alike in some way. Classes are treated with different amounts of respect in a society.
A statement based on facts, used to summarize groups of facts and to show relationships between them.	A Spanish word for *village*.
Something, such as milk or bread, that is always needed and used.	To adjust ways of living to land and resources.

surplus	ceremony
Lesson 3	Lesson 3
hogan	**dugout**
Lesson 3	Lesson 4
barter	**potlatch**
Lesson 4	Lesson 4
clan	**pit house**
Lesson 4	Lesson 4
harpoon	**totem pole**
Lesson 4	Lesson 4
lodge	**sod**
Lesson 5	Lesson 5

A series of actions performed during a special event.	An amount that is more than what is needed.
A boat made from a large, hollowed-out log.	A cone-shaped Navajo shelter built by covering a log frame with bark and mud.
A special Native American gathering or celebration with feasting and dancing.	To exchange goods usually without using money.
A house that was partially built over a hole in the earth so some rooms could be under ground.	A group of families that are related to one another.
A tall wooden post carved with shapes of animals and people and representing a family's history and importance.	A long spear with a sharp shell point.
Earth cut into blocks or mats, held together by grass and its roots.	A circular house of the Plains Indians.

tepee Lesson 5	**travois** Lesson 5
palisade Lesson 6	**slash and burn** Lesson 6
wigwam Lesson 6	**wampum** Lesson 6
longhouse Lesson 6	**confederation** Lesson 6
council Lesson 6	**compromise** Skill 3
resolve Skill 3	

A device made of two poles fastened to a dog's harness, used to carry possessions.	A cone-shaped tent made from wooden poles and buffalo skin.
A method of clearing land for farming that includes cutting and burning of trees.	A wall made of sharpened tree trunks to protect a village from enemies or wild animals.
Beads made from cut and polished seashells, used to keep records, send messages to other tribes, barter for goods, or to give as gifts.	A round, bark-covered Native American shelter.
A loosely united group of governments working together.	A long wooden building in which several related Iroquois families lived together.
An agreement in which each side in a conflict gives up some of what it wants in order to get some of what it wants.	A group that makes laws.
	To settle.

encounter Lesson 1	**empire** Lesson 1
monarch Lesson 1	**Renaissance** Lesson 1
compass Lesson 1	**city-state** Lesson 1
historical map Skill 1	**profit** Lesson 2
navigation Lesson 2	**cartographer** Lesson 2
astrolabe Lesson 2	**caravel** Lesson 2

© Harcourt

The conquered lands of many people and places governed by one ruler.	A meeting.
A French word meaning "rebirth," used to name a time of advances in thought, learning, art, and science.	A king or queen.
A city and the surrounding area that stand as an independent state.	An instrument used to find direction.
The money left over after all expenses have been paid.	A map that provides information about a place as it was in the past.
A person who makes maps.	The method of planning and controlling the course of a ship.
A ship that used square or triangular sails to travel long distances swiftly.	An instrument formerly used to calculate one's position compared to the sun, moon, and stars.

© Harcourt

expedition	cause
Lesson 2	Skill 2
effect	claim
Skill 2	Lesson 3
isthmus	demarcation
Lesson 3	Lesson 3
treaty	grant
Lesson 3	Lesson 4
conquistador	desertion
Lesson 4	Lesson 4
Northwest Passage	estuary
Lesson 5	Lesson 5

© Harcourt

An event or action that makes something else happen.	A journey.
To declare that a person or a country owns something.	The result of an event or action.
A line that marks a boundary.	A narrow strip of land that connects two larger land areas.
A sum of money or other payment given for a particular purpose.	An agreement between nations about peace, trade, or other matters.
Leaving one's duties, such as military service, without permission.	Any of the Spanish conquerors in the Americas during the early 1500s.
The wide mouth of a river where ocean tides flow in.	A waterway in North America thought to connect the Atlantic Ocean and the Pacific Ocean.

rapid	company
Lesson 5	Lesson 5
mutiny	
Lesson 5	

A business.	The fast moving, dangerous place in a river caused by a sudden drop in elevation.
	Rebellion against the leader of one's group.

© Harcourt

colony	colonist
<div align="right">Lesson 1</div>	<div align="right">Lesson 1</div>
buffer zone	**borderlands**
<div align="right">Lesson 1</div>	<div align="right">Lesson 1</div>
presidio	**permanent**
<div align="right">Lesson 1</div>	<div align="right">Lesson 1</div>
hacienda	**self-sufficient**
<div align="right">Lesson 1</div>	<div align="right">Lesson 1</div>
missionary	**mission**
<div align="right">Lesson 1</div>	<div align="right">Lesson 1</div>
civil war	**royal colony**
<div align="right">Lesson 2</div>	<div align="right">Lesson 2</div>

© Harcourt

A person who lives in a land ruled by a distant country.	A land ruled by a distant country.
Areas of land on or near the borders between countries, colonies, or regions that serve as barriers.	An area of land that serves as a barrier.
Long-lasting.	A Spanish fort.
Able to provide for one's own needs without help.	A large estate where cattle and sheep are raised.
A small religious settlement.	A person sent out by a church to spread its religion.
A colony ruled directly by a monarch.	A war between two groups in the same country.

proprietary colony Lesson 2	**proprietor** Lesson 2
plantation Lesson 2	**sea dog** Lesson 3
raw material Lesson 3	**Armada** Lesson 3
stock Lesson 4	**prosperity** Lesson 4
cash crop Lesson 4	**legislature** Lesson 4
burgess Lesson 4	**authority** Lesson 4

An owner.	A colony owned and ruled by one person who was chosen by a king or queen.
A commander of English warships that attacked Spanish ships carrying treasure.	A huge farm.
A Spanish fleet of warships.	A resource that can be used to make a product.
Economic success.	A share of ownership in a business.
The lawmaking branch of government.	A crop that people raise to sell rather than to use themselves.
The right to control and make decisions.	A representative in the legislature of colonial Virginia or Maryland.

pilgrim	compact
Lesson 5	Lesson 5
self-rule	majority rule
Lesson 5	Lesson 5
classify	
Skill 2	

© Harcourt

An agreement.	A person who makes a journey for religious reasons.
The political idea that the majority of an organized group should have the power to make decisions for the whole group.	Control of one's own government.
	To group.

Puritan	charter
Lesson 1	Lesson 1
common	specialize
Lesson 1	Lesson 1
town meeting	public office
Lesson 1	Lesson 1
expel	consent
Lesson 2	Lesson 2
sedition	fundamental
Lesson 2	Lesson 2
frontier	industry
Lesson 2	Lesson 3

© Harcourt

An official paper in which certain rights are given by a government to a person, group, or business.	A member of the Church of England who settled in North America to follow Christian beliefs in a more "pure" way.
To work at one kind of job and do it well.	An open area where sheep and cattle graze; village green.
A job a person is elected to do.	An assembly in the New England colonies in which male landowners could take part in government.
An agreement.	To force to leave.
Basic.	Speech or behavior that causes other people to work against a government.
All the businesses that make one kind of product or provide one kind of service.	The land that lies beyond settled areas.

export	import
Lesson 3	Lesson 3
triangular trade route	naval store
Lesson 3	Lesson 3
line graph	
Skill 1	

© Harcourt

A product brought into a country.	A product that leaves a country.
A product that is used to build and repair a ship.	A shipping route that linked England, the English colonies in North America, and the west coast of Africa, forming an imaginary triangle in the Atlantic Ocean.
	A chart that uses one or more lines to show changes over time.

refuge Lesson 1	**trial by jury** Lesson 1
justice Lesson 1	**farm produce** Lesson 1
Great Awakening Lesson 1	**township** Lesson 2
immigrant Lesson 2	**militia** Lesson 2
almanac Lesson 2	**circle graph** Skill 1
backcountry Lesson 3	**loft** Lesson 3

© Harcourt

The right of a person accused of a crime to be tried by a jury, or group, of fellow citizens.	A safe place.
Grains, fruits, and vegetables for sale.	Fairness.
An area of land.	A movement that called for a rebirth of religious ways of life.
A volunteer army.	A person who comes into a country to make a new home.
A round chart that can be divided into pieces, or parts; often referred to as a pie graph.	A yearly calendar and weather forecast that helps farmers know when to plant crops.
The part of a house located between the ceiling and the roof.	The land between the Coastal Plain and the Appalachian Mountains.

© Harcourt

indentured servant	constitution
Lesson 1	Lesson 1
indigo	debtor
Lesson 1	Lesson 1
fact	opinion
Skill 1	Skill 1
planter	tidewater
Lesson 2	Lesson 2
broker	auction
Lesson 2	Lesson 2
overseer	spiritual
Lesson 2	Lesson 2

A written plan of government.	A person who agreed to work for another person without pay for a certain length of time in exchange for passage to North America.
A person who was put in prison for owing money.	A plant from which a blue dye can be made.
A statement that tells what a person thinks or believes.	A statement that can be checked and proved to be true.
Low-lying land along a coast.	A plantation owner.
A public sale.	A person who is paid to buy and sell for someone else.
A religious song based on Bible stories.	A hired person who watched field slaves as they worked.

© Harcourt

public service	apprentice
Lesson 2	Lesson 3
county seat	county
Lesson 3	Lesson 3

A person who learns a trade by living with the family of a skilled worker and training for several years.	A job someone does to help the community or society as a whole.
A large part of a colony or a state.	The main town of a county.

revolution Lesson 1	**fork** Lesson 1
ally Lesson 1	**alliance** Lesson 1
congress Lesson 1	**delegate** Lesson 1
Parliament Lesson 1	**proclamation** Lesson 2
bill of rights Lesson 2	**pioneer** Lesson 2
gap Lesson 2	**hatch lines** Skill 1

© Harcourt

A place where two rivers join to form a third.	A sudden, complete change, such as the overthrow of an established government.
A formal agreement among nations, states, or individuals to cooperate.	A partner in an alliance; a friend, especially in times of war.
A representative.	A formal meeting of government representatives who have the authority to make laws.
An order from a country's leader to its citizens.	The lawmaking body of the British government.
A person who is one of the first to settle a new place.	A list of freedoms.
A pattern of stripes used on historical maps to show areas claimed by two or more countries.	An opening or a low place between mountains.

budget	representation
Lesson 3	Lesson 3
treason	boycott
Lesson 3	Lesson 3
declaration	repeal
Lesson 3	Lesson 3
liberty	point of view
Lesson 3	Skill 2
bias	monopoly
Skill 2	Lesson 4
blockade	quarter
Lesson 4	Lesson 4

The act of being represented.	A plan for spending money.
To refuse to buy or use goods or services.	To work against one's government.
To cancel, or undo, a law.	An official statement.
A person's perspective.	The freedom of people to make their own laws.
The complete control of a product or service.	When a person favors or opposes someone or something.
To provide or pay for housing at no cost to another person.	To use warships to prevent other ships from entering or leaving a harbor.

intolerable	petition
Lesson 4	Lesson 4
commander in chief	earthworks
Lesson 5	Lesson 5
olive branch	mercenary
Lesson 5	Lesson 5
public opinion	independence
Lesson 1	Lesson 1
allegiance	resolution
Lesson 1	Lesson 1
preamble	grievance
Lesson 1	Lesson 1

© Harcourt

A signed request made to an official person or organization.	Unacceptable.
Walls made of dirt or stone.	A person who is in control of all the armed forces of a nation.
A soldier who serves for pay in the military of a foreign nation.	An ancient symbol of peace.
The freedom to govern on one's own.	The point of view held by the majority of people.
A formal statement of the feelings of a group of people about an important topic.	Loyalty.
A complaint.	An introduction; first part.

Patriot	Loyalist
Lesson 2	Lesson 2
neutral	pacifist
Lesson 2	Lesson 2
regiment	consequence
Lesson 2	Skill 1

A person who supported the British government during the American Revolution.	A colonist who was against British rule and supported the rebel cause in the American Colonies.
A believer in the peaceful settlement of differences.	Not taking a side in a disagreement.
Something that happens because of an action.	A large, organized group of soldiers.

enlist	turning point
Lesson 3	Lesson 3
traitor	negotiate
Lesson 4	Lesson 4
principle	
Lesson 4	

A single event that causes important and dramatic change.	To join.
To talk with another to work out an agreement.	One who works against one's own government.
	A rule that is used in deciding how to behave.

© Harcourt

republic Lesson 1	**inflation** Lesson 1
arsenal Lesson 1	**territory** Lesson 1
ordinance Lesson 1	**convention** Lesson 2
commerce Lesson 2	**federal system** Lesson 2
bill Lesson 2	**census** Lesson 3
electoral college Lesson 3	**veto** Lesson 3

© Harcourt

An economic condition in which more money is needed to buy goods and services than was needed earlier.	A form of government in which people elect representatives to govern the country.
Land that belongs to a national government, but is not a state.	A place used for storing weapons.
An important meeting.	A law or set of laws.
A system of government in which the authority to govern is shared by the central and state governments.	Trade.
An official population count.	An idea for a new law.
To reject.	A group of officials chosen by citizens to vote for the President and Vice President.

impeach	justice
Lesson 3	Lesson 3
checks and balances	**flow chart**
Lesson 3	Skill 1
ratify	**Federalist**
Lesson 4	Lesson 4
Anti-Federalist	**amendment**
Lesson 4	Lesson 4
Magna Carta	**due process of law**
Lesson 4	Lesson 4
reserved powers	**Cabinet**
Lesson 4	Lesson 5

© Harcourt

A Supreme Court judge.	To accuse a government official, such as the President, of "treason, bribery, or other high crimes and misdemeanors."
A diagram that shows the order in which things happen.	A system that gives each branch of government different powers so that each branch can watch over the authority of the others.
A citizen who wanted a strong national government and was in favor of ratifying the Constitution.	To approve.
An addition or change to the Constitution.	A citizen who wanted a limited national government and was against ratification of the Constitution.
The principle that guarantees the right to a fair public trial.	The charter granted by the King of England in 1215. It listed the rights of the upper class and limited the rights of the king.
A group of the President's most important advisers.	Authority that belongs to the states or to the people, not to the national government.

© Harcourt

political party	candidate
Lesson 5	Lesson 5

© Harcourt

	A group whose members seek to elect government officials who share the group's points of view about many issues.
A person running for office.	

inauguration Lesson 1	**pathfinder** Lesson 1
trespass Lesson 1	**impressment** Lesson 2
War Hawk Lesson 2	**national anthem** Lesson 2
siege Lesson 2	**nationalism** Lesson 2
annex Lesson 2	**doctrine** Lesson 2
democracy Lesson 3	**ruling** Lesson 3

Someone who finds a way through an unknown region.	A ceremony in which a leader takes office.
The taking of workers against their will.	To go onto someone else's property without asking permission.
A song of praise for a country; it is recognized as the official song of that country.	A member of Congress who wanted war with Britain before the War of 1812.
Pride in one's country.	A long-lasting attack.
A government plan of action.	To add on.
A decision.	A form of government in which the people have power to make choices about their lives and government, either directly or through representation.

© Harcourt

manifest destiny Lesson 4	**dictator** Lesson 4
gold rush Lesson 4	**cession** Lesson 4
forty-niner Lesson 4	**Industrial Revolution** Lesson 5
textile Lesson 5	**investor** Lesson 5
mass production Lesson 5	**interchangeable parts** Lesson 5
cotton gin Lesson 5	**supply** Lesson 5

A leader who has complete control of the government.	The belief, shared by many Americans, that the United States should one day stretch from the Atlantic Ocean to the Pacific Ocean.
Something given up, such as land.	A sudden rush of new people to an area where gold has been found.
The period of time during the 1700s and 1800s in which machines took the place of hand tools to manufacture goods.	A gold seeker who arrived in California in 1849.
A person who uses money to buy or make something that will yield a profit.	Cloth.
Identical copies of parts made by machines so that if one part breaks, an identical one can be installed.	A system of producing large amounts of goods at one time.
The amount of a product or service that is available for sale.	A machine that removed seeds and hulls from cotton fibers much faster than workers could by hand.

demand	patent
Lesson 5	Lesson 5

A license to make, use, or sell a new invention.	The need or want for a product or service by people who are willing to pay for it.

sectionalism	tariff
Lesson 1	Lesson 1
states' rights	free state
Lesson 1	Lesson 1
slave state	frame of reference
Lesson 1	Skill 1
emancipation	resist
Lesson 2	Lesson 2
code	fugitive
Lesson 2	Lesson 2
underground	abolitionist
Lesson 2	Lesson 2

A tax on goods brought into a country.	Regional loyalty.
A state that did not allow slavery before the Civil War.	The idea that the states, rather than the federal government, should have the final authority over their own affairs.
A set of ideas that determine how a person understands something.	A state that allowed slavery before the Civil War.
To act against.	The freeing of enslaved peoples.
A person who is running away from something.	A set of laws.
A person who wanted to end slavery.	Done in secret.

equality	secede
Lesson 2	Lesson 3
Confederacy	**retreat**
Lesson 3	Lesson 4
border state	**strategy**
Lesson 4	Lesson 4
casualty	**address**
Lesson 4	Lesson 5

© Harcourt

To leave.	Equal rights.
To fall back.	The group of eleven states that left the Union, also called the Confederate States of America.
A careful plan.	During the Civil War, a state—Delaware, Kentucky, Maryland, Missouri—that was unsure which side to support.
A formal speech.	A person who has been killed or wounded.

© Harcourt

Reconstruction Lesson 1	**assassinate** Lesson 1
black codes Lesson 1	**acquittal** Lesson 1
freedmen Lesson 2	**sharecropping** Lesson 2
carpetbagger Lesson 2	**scalawag** Lesson 2
secret ballot Lesson 2	**segregation** Lesson 2
boom Lesson 3	**refinery** Lesson 3

© Harcourt

To murder a leader by sudden or secret attack.	The time during which the South was rebuilt after the Civil War.
A verdict of not guilty.	Laws limiting the rights of former slaves in the South.
A system of working the land in which the worker was paid with a "share" of the crop.	Men, women, and children who had once been slaves.
A rascal; someone who supports something for his or her own gain.	A Northerner who moved to the South to take part in Reconstruction governments.
The practice of keeping people in separate groups based on their race or culture.	A voting method in which no one knows how anyone else voted.
A factory in which minerals, especially fuels, are cleaned and made into usable products.	A time of fast economic growth.

prospector	bust
Lesson 3	Lesson 3
long drive	**homesteader**
Lesson 3	Lesson 3
open range	**reservation**
Lesson 3	Lesson 3
climograph	**free enterprise**
Skill 1	Lesson 4
transcontinental railroad	**entrepreneur**
Lesson 4	Lesson 4
petroleum	
Lesson 4	

A time of quick economic decline.	A person who searches for silver, gold, and other mineral resources.
A person living on land granted by the government.	A trip made by ranchers to lead cattle to the market or the railroads.
An area of land set aside by the government for use only by Native Americans.	Land on which animals can graze freely.
An economic system in which people are able to start and run their own businesses with little control by the government.	A chart that shows the average monthly temperature and the average monthly precipitation for a place.
A person who sets up and runs a business.	The railway line that crossed North America.
	Oil.

capital	human resource
Lesson 4	Lesson 4
old immigration	new immigration
Lesson 5	Lesson 5
advertisement	tenement
Lesson 5	Lesson 5
prejudice	regulation
Lesson 5	Lesson 5

A worker who brings his or her own ideas and skills to a job.	The money needed to set up or improve a business.
After 1890, people who came from southern and central Europe and other parts of the world to settle in North America.	Before 1890, people who came from northern and western Europe to settle in North America.
A poorly built apartment building.	A public announcement that tells people about a product or an opportunity.
A rule or an order.	An unfair feeling of hate or dislike for members of a certain group because of their background, race, or religion.

imperialism	**armistice**
<div align="right">Lesson 1</div>	<div align="right">Lesson 1</div>
projection	**distortion**
<div align="right">Skill 1</div>	<div align="right">Skill 1</div>
reform	**progressive**
<div align="right">Lesson 2</div>	<div align="right">Lesson 2</div>
commission	**conservation**
<div align="right">Lesson 2</div>	<div align="right">Lesson 2</div>
merit system	**political boss**
<div align="right">Lesson 2</div>	<div align="right">Lesson 2</div>
settlement house	**civil rights**
<div align="right">Lesson 2</div>	<div align="right">Lesson 2</div>

© Harcourt

An agreement to stop fighting a war.	Empire building.
An area that is not accurate on a map.	A way of showing Earth on flat paper.
A person who wants to improve government and make life better.	To change for the better.
The protection and wise use of natural resources.	A special committee that is set up to study something.
A powerful, often corrupt leader who held much political influence in the late 19th and early 20th centuries.	A way of making sure that the most qualified people get government jobs.
Rights guaranteed to all citizens by the Constitution.	A community center.

suffrage	military draft
Lesson 2	Lesson 3
no-man's-land	isolation
Lesson 3	Lesson 3
consumer good	assembly line
Lesson 4	Lesson 4
division of labor	industrialization
Lesson 4	Lesson 4
urbanization	mechanization of agriculture
Lesson 4	Lesson 4
stock market	depression
Lesson 4	Lesson 4

A way to bring people into military service.	The right to vote.
The policy of remaining separate from other countries.	In a war, land that is not held by either side but is filled with obstacles such as barbed wire and land mines.
A system of mass production in which parts of a product, such as a car, are put together as they move past a line of workers.	A product made for personal use.
The growth of industry.	Work that is divided so that each worker does a small part of a larger job.
The use of machines to plant and harvest crops.	The movement of people to cities.
A time of little economic growth when there are few jobs and people have little money.	A place where people can buy and sell stocks, or shares in businesses.

© Harcourt

bureaucracy	unemployment
Lesson 4	Lesson 4

© Harcourt

The number of people without jobs.	A system of organizing the many workers and groups that are needed to run government programs.

concentration camp Lesson 1	**dictatorship** Lesson 1
civilian Lesson 1	**prediction** Skill 1
rationing Lesson 2	**relocation camp** Lesson 2
interest Lesson 2	**recycle** Lesson 2
trade-off Skill 2	**opportunity cost** Skill 2
front Lesson 3	**D day** Lesson 3

© Harcourt

A form of government where a leader has complete control of the government.	A guarded camp built by the German National Socialist party, or Nazis, where prisoners were held.
A decision about what may happen next, based on the way things are.	A person who is not in the military.
A temporary settlement where Japanese Americans were ordered to live during World War II.	The limiting of the supply of something.
To reuse.	Money a bank or borrower pays for the use of money.
The value of the thing a person gives up in order to get something else.	The giving up of one thing to get another.
June 6, 1944, the day on which Allied forces in World War II worked together in the largest water-to-land invasion in history.	A battle line.

island-hopping	parallel time line
Lesson 3	Skill 3
Holocaust	**refugee**
Lesson 4	Lesson 4
communism	**free world**
Lesson 4	Lesson 4
cold war	
Lesson 4	

Two or more time lines that show the same period of time.	The process of the Allies capturing key islands in the Pacific as they advanced toward Japan during World War II.
A person who leaves home to seek shelter and safety elsewhere.	The mass murder of European Jews during World War II.
The United States and its allies.	A social and economic system in which all land and industries are owned by the government, and individuals have few rights and little freedom.
	Hostilities in which opposing nations attack each other by using propaganda and money rather than soldiers and weapons.

superpower Lesson 1	**airlift** Lesson 1
cease-fire Lesson 1	**arms race** Lesson 1
satellite Lesson 1	**nonviolence** Lesson 2
integration Lesson 2	**migrant worker** Lesson 2
arms control Lesson 3	**détente** Lesson 3
scandal Lesson 3	**terrorism** Lesson 4

© Harcourt

A system of moving supplies by airplane.	A nation that is one of the most powerful in the world.
A situation in which two or more countries build weapons to protect themselves against each other.	A temporary end to a conflict.
The use of peaceful ways to bring about change.	An object in orbit around the Earth.
Someone who moves from place to place with the seasons to harvest crops.	The bringing together of people of all races in education, jobs, and housing.
An easing of tensions, especially between countries.	A limiting of the number of weapons that each nation may have.
The use of violence to promote a cause.	An action that brings disgrace.

deficit	hijack
Lesson 4	Lesson 4
population density Skill 1	

© Harcourt

To illegally take control of an aircraft.	A shortage.
	The number of people who live within one square mile or one square kilometer of land.

© Harcourt

Sun Belt	ethnic group
Lesson 1	Lesson 1
Internet	**teleconference**
Lesson 1	Lesson 1
cartogram	**rapid-transit system**
Skill 1	Lesson 2
diverse economy	**high-tech**
Lesson 3	Lesson 3
Information Age	**e-commerce**
Lesson 3	Lesson 3
interdependent	**international trade**
Lesson 3	Lesson 3

A group of people from the same country, of the same race, or with a shared way of life.	A wide area of the southern United States that reaches from the Atlantic coast to the Pacific coast.
A conference, or meeting, that uses electronic equipment to connect people.	The system that joins computers around the world for the exchange of information.
A passenger transportation system that uses elevated or underground trains or both.	A diagram that gives information about places based on the size shown for each place.
The term used to describe industries that invent, build, or use computers and other kinds of electronic equipment.	An economy that is based on many kinds of industries.
The buying and selling of goods and services through computer connections.	The period in history that began in the second half of the twentieth century and has been marked by the growing amount of information available.
Trade among nations.	Depending on each other.

© Harcourt

free-trade agreement	global economy
Lesson 3	Lesson 3
responsibility	register
Lesson 4	Lesson 4
informed citizen	jury
Lesson 4	Lesson 4
volunteer	patriotism
Lesson 4	Lesson 4

The world market in which companies from different countries buy and sell goods and services.	A treaty in which countries agree to charge no tariffs, or taxes, on goods they buy from and sell to each other.
To enroll as a voter.	A duty.
A group of citizens who decide a case in court.	A citizen who knows what is happening in the community, state, nation, and world.
Love of one's country.	A person who works without pay.

middle class Lesson 1	**interest rate** Lesson 1
commonwealth Lesson 2	**embargo** Lesson 2
free election Lesson 2	**population pyramid** Skill 1
life expectancy Skill 1	**median age** Skill 1
standard of living Lesson 3	**liberate** Lesson 3
deforestation Lesson 3	**province** Lesson 4

© Harcourt

The amount a bank will charge to lend money.	The group of people who are economically between the rich and the poor.
The refusal of one nation to trade goods and services with another.	A nation that governs itself but is a territory of another country.
A graph that shows the division of a country's population by age.	An election that offers a choice of candidates.
The average age of all the people in a country.	The average number of years a person can expect to live.
To set free.	A measure of how well people in a country live.
A political region, similar to a state.	The cutting down of most or all trees in an area.

© Harcourt

separatist	time zone
Lesson 4	Skill 2

© Harcourt

A geographic region in which the same time is used.	A citizen of Quebec who wishes to separate from Canada.

School to Home Newsletter

School to Home Newsletters

These school to home newsletters offer a way of linking students' study of social studies to the students' family members. There is one newsletter, available in English and Spanish, for each unit. The newsletters include family activities as well as suggestions of books to read.

Contents

School to Home

Newsletter

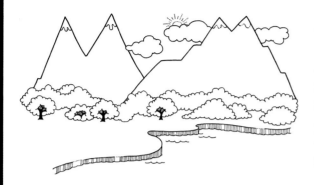

Books To Read

National Geographic Picture Atlas of Our Fifty States. National Geographic Society, 1991.

One Day in the Prairie by Jean Craighead George. HarperCollins, 1996.

Anasazi by Leonard Everett Fisher. Simon & Schuster, 1997.

The Pueblo by Charlotte and David Yue. Houghton Mifflin, 1986.

American Indian Children of the Past by Victoria Sherrow. Millbrook Press, 1997.

Content to Learn

Your child is about to begin studying the landforms and early people of the United States. Here are some of the topics that will be covered in the first unit, The Land and Early People:

- regions based on different landforms
- bodies of water and their importance to life in the United States
- climate and plant life and how they affect people in different regions
- how people use the land and its resources to meet their needs
- political, economic, cultural, and population regions
- where people settle and why they settle there
- how early people may have arrived in the Americas
- ancient Indian cultures and how they developed
- how environments in different regions of North America affected native peoples' ways of life

Activities to Try

- Look at an elevation map with your child. Discuss how the map shows how high or low the land is. Talk about how the area where you live is represented on the map. Then discuss what different regions of the country are like, based upon physical features such as mountains.

- Look at a map of the United States and point out where the largest cities are located. Talk with your child about why cities are located where they are.

- Choose an early Native American group, and visit the library with your child to learn more about that group. Draw a picture or build a model of a typical home or village.

Ideas to Discuss

- What kinds of landforms are found in the United States? near your community?

- How do people use land and water?

- Which Native American groups live in your state?

GO ONLINE Visit **The Learning Site** at www.harcourtschool.com/socialstudies for additional activities, primary sources, and other resources to use in this unit.

Carta para la casa

Boletín

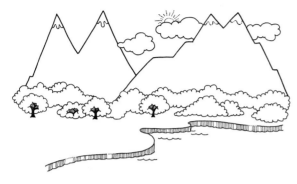

Tema de estudio

Su hijo comenzará a estudiar la geografía y los primeros pobladores de Estados Unidos. Éstos son algunos de los temas que cubrirá la primera unidad, Las Américas y sus primeros habitantes:

- regiones determinadas por sus características geográficas
- las masas de agua y su importancia para la vida en Estados Unidos
- el clima y la vida vegetal y cómo afectan a la población en las distintas regiones
- cómo la gente usa la tierra y sus recursos para satisfacer sus necesidades
- regiones políticas, económicas, culturales y demográficas
- dónde se asienta la gente y por qué se asienta allí
- cómo posiblemente llegaron a las Américas los primeros pobladores
- las antiguas culturas indígenas y su desarrollo
- cómo el medio ambiente de las distintas regiones de América del Norte influyó profundamente en el modo de vida de los pueblos indios

Actividades

- Mire con su hijo un mapa de altitudes. Hablen del modo en que el mapa muestra la elevación del terreno. Hablen de cómo se representa en el mapa el área donde viven. Vean qué regiones del país son similares, teniendo en cuenta rasgos geográficos como montañas, por ejemplo.

- Miren un mapa de Estados Unidos e indiquen dónde están las ciudades más grandes. Hable con su hijo de por qué las ciudades están situadas allí.

- Elijan un grupo indígena y visiten una biblioteca para aprender más sobre ese grupo. Hagan un dibujo o un modelo de una vivienda o aldea típica.

Ideas para comentar

- ¿Qué tipos de accidentes geográficos se hallan en Estados Unidos? ¿cerca de tu comunidad?

- ¿Cómo usa la gente la tierra y el agua?

- ¿Cuáles grupos indígeras viven en tu estado?

Libros

National Geographic Picture Atlas of Our Fifty States. National Geographic Society, 1991.

One Day in the Prairie por Jean Craighead George. HarperCollins, 1996.

Anasazi por Leonard Everett Fisher. Simon & Schuster, 1997.

The Pueblo por Charlotte y David Yue. Houghton Mifflin, 1986.

American Indian Children of the Past por Victoria Sherrow. Millbrook Press, 1997.

APRENDE en línea

Visiten The Learning Site en www.harcourtschool.com/socialstudies para obtener actividades adicionales, fuentes originales y otros recursos para usar en esta unidad.

School to Home

Books To Read

If You Were There in 1492 by Barbara Brenner. Bradbury Press, 1991.

Stranded at Plimoth Plantation, 1626 by Gary Bowen. HarperCollins, 1994.

Exploration and Conquest, The Americas After Columbus: 1500–1620 by Betsy and Giulio Maestro. Mulberry, 1997.

Ship by David Macaulay. Houghton Mifflin, 1993.

Jamestown Colony by Carter Smith. Silver Burdett, 1991.

Content to Learn

Your child is about to begin studying the age of exploration and early settlements by Europeans in the Americas. In the second unit, Time of Encounters, these are some of the topics that will be covered:

- the world in the 1400s
- the importance of Portugal's discovery of a water route to Asia
- how attempts to find a western route to Asia led Europeans to the Americas
- how further exploration of the Americas caused conflict between European explorers and Native Americans
- the search for the Northwest Passage
- early Spanish, French, and English settlements and their influences
- the settlements at Jamestown and Plymouth

Activities to Try

■ With your child, study one of the historic maps shown in this unit. Discuss how to use the map key to identify what colored arrows and other symbols represent. Then work together to identify what route each explorer took; whether the route was over land, water, or both; what cities, islands, or countries were visited; and when the expedition took place.

■ Work with your child to find places and bodies of water that are named for European explorers.

■ With your child, use an encyclopedia or the Internet to learn more about the settlements at either Jamestown or Plymouth. Together, make a fact sheet that explains how and why each colony was founded and what life was like for the colonists.

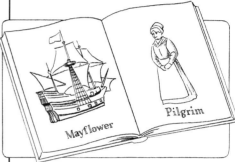

Mayflower   Pilgrim

Ideas to Discuss

■ Why was it so important for Europeans to find a route to Asia?

■ How did European explorers come to realize that the land they encountered when they sailed west was not Asia?

■ What Spanish, French, and English influences can still be seen today in the United States?

Visit **The Learning Site** at www.harcourtschool.com/socialstudies for additional activities, primary sources, and other resources to use in this unit.

© Harcourt

Carta para la casa

Boletín

Libros

If You Were There in 1492 por Barbara Brenner. Bradbury Press, 1991.

Stranded at Plimoth Plantation, 1626 por Gary Bowen. HarperCollins, 1994.

Exploration and Conquest, The Americas After Columbus: 1500–1620 por Betsy y Giulio Maestro. Mulberry, 1997.

Ship por David Macaulay. Houghton Mifflin, 1993.

Jamestown Colony por Carter Smith. Silver Burdett, 1991.

Tema de estudio

Su hijo comenzará a estudiar la época de la exploración y los primeros asentamientos por los europeos en las Américas. Éstos son algunos de los temas que cubrirá la segunda unidad, Una época de encuentros:

- el mundo en el siglo XV
- la importancia del descubrimiento portugués de una ruta marítima a Asia
- cómo los intentos de hallar una ruta marítima a Asia conducen a los europeos a las Américas
- cómo las nuevas exploraciones de las Américas provocaron conflictos entre los exploradores europeos y los indígenas
- la búsqueda del Paso del Noroeste
- primeros asentamientos españoles, franceses e ingleses y su influencia
- los asentamientos de Jamestown y Plymouth

✏ Actividades

- Con su hijo, estudie uno de los mapas históricos mostrados en esta unidad. Vean cómo usar la clare del mapa para identificar qué significan las flechas de color y otros símbolos. Luego identifiquen qué ruta siguió cada explorador, y si la expedición fue por tierra, por agua, o por ambas; por qué ciudades, islas o países

pasó, y cuándo tuvo lugar la expedición.

- Busque con su hijo lugares y masas de agua con nombres de exploradores europeos.

- Use con su hijo una enciclopedia o Internet para averiguar más sobre los asentamientos de Jamestown o Plymouth. Hagan juntos una hoja de datos que explique cómo y por qué fue fundada cada colonia y cómo era la vida allí.

Mayflower

Peregrino

Ideas para comentar

- ¿Por qué era tan importante para los europeos hallar una ruta a Asia?

- ¿Cómo se dieron cuenta los europeos de que navegando hacia el oeste no habían llegado a Asia?

- ¿Qué influencias españolas, francesas e inglesas siguen viéndose hoy en Estados Unidos?

APRENDE en línea

Visiten The Learning Site en <u>www.harcourtschool.com/socialstudies</u> para obtener actividades adicionales, fuentes originales y otros recursos para usar en esta unidad.

© Harcourt

School to Home

Harcourt Horizons • United States History, Unit 3

Newsletter

Content to Learn

Your child is about to begin studying the 13 English colonies. Here are some of the topics that will be covered in the third unit, The English Colonies:

- the Massachusetts Bay Colony and its influence on present-day government and education systems

- how some colonies expanded the ideas of freedom of speech and freedom of religion

- New England's economic success and its decreasing dependence on England

- why people of many cultures and religions settled in the Middle Atlantic Colonies

- Philadelphia's importance to the Pennsylvania Colony

- the challenges faced by settlers moving west

- the settlement of the Southern Colonies and the economic importance of cash crops

- development of plantations in the Southern Colonies

✏️ Activities to Try

- With your child, use an encyclopedia or the Internet to learn more about one of the colonists introduced in this unit, such as Roger Williams, Anne Hutchinson, William Penn, or James Oglethorpe. Make a fact sheet that includes details about this colonist's accomplishments.

- Imagine with your child that you live in one of the New England, Middle Atlantic, or Southern Colonies. Discuss what your life is like, including daily activities and how you earn a living.

- Work with your child to draw a map that shows the layout of a typical village in the Massachusetts Bay Colony or in a township in the Pennsylvania Colony. Create a map key to identify features on your map.

💡 Ideas to Discuss

- What are some ideas put into practice in the colonies, such as government systems and freedom of religion, that still influence our lives today?

- How did the English colonies come to be less dependent upon England?

- Why were there more towns and cities in the New England and Middle Atlantic Colonies than in the Southern Colonies?

Books To Read

Colonial People by Sarah Howarth. Millbrook, 1994.

Colonial Places by Sarah Howarth. Millbrook, 1994.

A Matter of Conscience: The Trial of Anne Hutchinson by Joan Kane Nichols. Steck-Vaughn, 1993.

What's the Big Idea, Ben Franklin? by Jean Fritz. Coward-McCann, 1976.

Visit **The Learning Site** at www.harcourtschool.com/socialstudies for additional activities, primary sources, and other resources to use in this unit.

© Harcourt

Carta para la casa

Boletín

Libros

Colonial People por Sarah Howarth. Millbrook, 1994.

Colonial Places por Sarah Howarth. Millbrook, 1994.

A Matter of Conscience: The Trial of Anne Hutchinson por Joan Kane Nichols. Steck-Vaughn, 1993.

What´s the Big Idea, Ben Franklin? por Jean Fritz. Coward-McCann, 1976.

Tema de estudio

Su hijo comenzará a estudiar las 13 colonias inglesas. Éstos son algunos de los tópicos que cubrirá la tercera unidad, Las colonias inglesas:

- la colonia de la bahía de Massachusetts y su influencia en los sistemas de gobierno y educación actuales
- cómo algunas de las colonias expandieron las ideas de libertad religiosa y libertad de expresión
- el éxito económico de Nueva Inglaterra y su decreciente dependencia de Inglaterra
- por qué colonos de distintas culturas y religiones se asentaron en las Colonias del Atlántico Medio
- la importancia de Philadelphia para la colonia de Pennsylvania
- los desafíos a los que se enfrentaron los colonos que iban al Oeste
- el asentamiento de las Colonias del Sur e importancia económica del cultivo comercial
- el desarrollo de las plantaciones en las Colonias del Sur

Actividades

- Con su hijo, usen una enciclopedia o Internet para averiguar más sobre alguno de los colonos presentados en esta unidad, como Roger Williams, Anne Hutchinson, William Penn o James Oglethorpe. Hagan una hoja de datos que incluya detalles sobre los logros de ese colono.
- Imaginen que viven en una de las colonias de Nueva Inglaterra, del Atlántico Medio o del Sur. Hablen de cómo es su vida, incluyendo las actividades diarias y cómo se ganan la vida.

- Con su hijo, hagan un mapa que muestre el esquema de una aldea típica en la colonia de la bahía de Massachusetts o de un municipio de Pennsylvania. Hagan una clare del mapa para identificar los detalles del mapa.

Ideas para comentar

- ¿Cuáles son algunas ideas puestas en práctica en las colonias, como los sistemas de gobierno y la libertad religiosa, que siguen influyendo hoy en nuestra vida?
- ¿Cómo llegaron las colonias inglesas a ser menos dependientes de Inglaterra?
- ¿Por qué había más pueblos y ciudades en Nueva Inglaterra y las colonias del Atlántico Medio que en las colonias del Sur?

APRENDE en línea

Visiten The Learning Site en www.harcourtschool.com/socialstudies para obtener actividades adicionales, fuentes originales y otros recursos para usar en esta unidad.

© Harcourt

School to Home

Books To Read

And Then What Happened, Paul Revere? by Jean Fritz. Putnam, 1996.

The American Revolution: How We Fought the War of Independence by Edward F. Dolan. Millbrook Press, 1995.

If You Were There in 1776 by Barbara Brenner. Macmillan, 1994.

The Secret Soldier by Ann McGovern. Scholastic, 1975.

Black Heroes of the American Revolution by Burke Davis. Harcourt, 1976.

The Boston Tea Party by Laurie A. O'Neill. Millbrook, 1996.

Content to Learn

Your child is about to begin studying major events leading up to and including the Revolutionary War. In the fourth unit, The American Revolution, these are some of the topics that will be covered:

- the French and Indian War and its outcome and effects
- why Britain's new tax laws angered the colonists
- how colonists worked together to respond to a growing British threat
- the Second Continental Congress and the actions it took to prepare for war with Britain
- the Declaration of Independence
- why Americans had different views about independence
- how the Continental Army overcame many obstacles to win the Revolutionary War

Activities to Try

- With your child, study a map of Boston and the areas surrounding it. Locate important battle sites of the Revolutionary War, and discuss the significance of each battle.

- Imagine with your child that you are witnesses to the Boston Tea Party. You are able to see events happening on the ships and ashore. Describe what you see. Talk about the importance of the event and why it is still so well known today.

- Work with your child to learn more about the Second Continental Congress and how it prepared for war. Then write a newspaper article to explain to the colonists the important decisions made by the Congress. Be sure to answer the questions *who?*, *what?*, *when?*, *where?*, and *why?*.

Ideas to Discuss

- What was the significance of the French and Indian War?

- Why were the colonists opposed to taxation without representation?

- Why is it significant that the colonists began to consider themselves Americans instead of British citizens?

Visit **The Learning Site** at www.harcourtschool.com/socialstudies for additional activities, primary sources, and other resources to use in this unit.

Carta para la casa

Boletín

Libros

And Then What Happened, Paul Revere? por Jean Fritz. Putnam, 1996.

The American Revolution: How We Fought the War of Independence por Edward F. Dolan. Millbrook Press, 1995.

If You Were There in 1776 por Barbara Brenner. Macmillan, 1994.

The Secret Soldier por Ann McGovern. Scholastic, 1975.

Black Heroes of the American Revolution por Burke Davis. Harcourt, 1976.

The Boston Tea Party por Laurie A. O'Neill. Millbrook, 1996.

Tema de estudio

Su hijo comenzará a estudiar la Guerra de la Independencia y los acontecimientos importantes que condujeron a ella. Éstos son algunos de los tópicos que cubrirá la cuarta unidad, La Revolución Americana:

■ los resultados y efectos de la guerra franco-indígena

■ por qué las nuevas leyes impositivas británicas indignaron a los colonos

■ cómo los colonos actuaron juntos para responder a la creciente amenaza británica

■ el Segundo Congreso Continental y las medidas inmediatas que tomaron para prepararse para la guerra con Gran Bretaña

■ la Declaración de la Independencia

■ por qué los americanos tenían ideas variadas sobre la independencia

■ cómo el Ejército Continental superó muchos obstáculos para ganar la Guerra de la Independencia

■ América obtuvo finalmente la independencia

Actividades

■ Con su hijo, estudien un mapa de Boston y sus alrededores. Ubiquen sitios de batallas trascendentes de la Guerra de la Independencia y hablen sobre la importancia de cada batalla.

■ Imaginen que usted y su hijo son testigos del Motín del Té de Boston. Pueden ver lo que ocurre en los barcos y en tierra. Describan lo que ven. Hablen sobre la importancia del hecho y digan por qué sigue siendo hoy tan conocido.

■ Juntos, busquen más información sobre el Segundo Congreso Continental y cómo se preparó para la guerra. Escriban luego un artículo periodístico para explicar a los colonos las importantes decisiones tomadas por el Congreso. Asegúrense de responder las preguntas ¿quién?, ¿qué?, ¿cuándo?, ¿dónde?, y ¿por qué?.

Ideas para comentar

■ ¿Cuál fue la importancia de la guerra franco-indígena?

■ ¿Por qué los colonos se oponían al sistema de impuestos sin tener representación?

■ ¿Por qué fue importante que los colonos empezaran a considerarse americanos en lugar de ciudadanos británicos?

Visiten The Learning Site en www.harcourtschool.com/socialstudies para obtener actividades adicionales, fuentes originales y otros recursos para usar en esta unidad.

© Harcourt

School to Home

Harcourt Horizons • United States History, Unit 5

Newsletter

Books To Read

A More Perfect Union: The Story of Our Constitution by Betsy and Giulio Maestro. Mulberry, 1987.

Dear Benjamin Banneker by Andrea Davis Pinkney. Harcourt, 1994.

Off the Map: The Journals of Lewis and Clark by Peter and Connie Roop. Walker and Company, 1993.

1787 by Joan Anderson. Harcourt, 1987.

Content to Learn

Your child is about to begin studying the years after the Revolutionary War. These are some of the topics that will be covered in unit five, A New Nation:

- the problems and successes of the first government of the United States and why compromises were critical in deciding on a new plan of government
- the United States Constitution
- the three branches of the United States government
- the Bill of Rights
- the Louisiana Purchase
- the War of 1812
- Andrew Jackson's presidency
- how the United States expanded to reach the Pacific Ocean
- how new technologies in the 1800s changed life in the United States

Activities to Try

- With your child, use print or online resources to learn more about the Lewis and Clark expedition. List the facts you learn.
- Together with your child, make a booklet to explain the different types of transportation that were used in the first half of the 1800s to transport goods and people. Draw an illustration of each mode of transportation and talk about what is shown and how and where it was used.

- Work with your child to create a time line that shows the major events discussed in this unit. Then discuss the time line together, talking about how each event was important.

Ideas to Discuss

- Why were compromises so important at the Constitutional Convention?
- How does the system of checks and balances work?
- How did the Industrial Revolution change the everyday lives of many people?

© Harcourt

Visit **The Learning Site** at www.harcourtschool.com/socialstudies for additional activities, primary sources, and other resources to use in this unit.

Carta para la casa

Boletín

Libros

A More Perfect Union: The Story of Our Constitution por Betsy y Giulio Maestro. Mulberry, 1987.

Dear Benjamin Banneker por Andrea Davis Pinkney. Harcourt, 1994.

Off the Map: The Journals of Lewis and Clark por Peter y Connie Roop. Walker and Company, 1993.

1787 por Joan Anderson. Harcourt, 1987.

Tema de estudio

Su hijo comenzará a estudiar los años después de la Revolución Americana. Éstos son algunos de los tópicos que cubrirá la quinta unidad, La nueva nación:

- los problemas y logros del primer gobierno de Estados Unidos y el porqué
- las negociaciones para llegar a un acuerdo fueron críticas al decidir un nuevo plan de gobierno
- la Constitución de Estados Unidos
- los tres poderes del gobierno de Estados Unidos
- la Declaración de Derechos y las libertades que la misma protege
- la compra de Louisiana
- la Guerra de 1812
- la presidencia de Andrew Jackson
- cómo los Estados Unidos se expandieron hasta alcanzar el océano Pacífico
- cómo en el siglo XIX, nuevos adelantos tecnológicos cambiaron la vida en Estados Unidos

Actividades

- Con su hijo, usen recursos impresos o de Internet para averiguar más sobre la expedición de Lewis y Clark. Anoten los datos que aprendan.

- Juntos, hagan un folleto para explicar qué medios de transporte se usaban en la primera mitad del siglo XIX para trasladar gente y mercaderías. Dibujen o copien una ilustración de cada medio de transporte y hablen sobre es que se muestra y cómo y dónde se usaba.

- Hagan juntos una línea cronológica que muestre los principales hechos tratados en esta unidad. Luego, comenten por qué fue importante cada uno de los hechos.

Ideas para comentar

- ¿Por qué las negociaciones para llegar a un acuerdo fueron tan importantes en la Convención Constituyente?

- ¿Cómo funciona el sistema de equilibrio de poderes?

- ¿Cómo cambió la vida cotidiana de mucha gente la Revolución Industrial?

Visiten The Learning Site en www.harcourtschool.com/socialstudies para obtener actividades adicionales, fuentes originales y otros recursos para usar en esta unidad.

© Harcourt

School to Home

Harcourt Horizons • United States History, Unit 6

Newsletter

Books To Read

Lincoln: A Photobiography by Russell Freedman. Clarion, 1987.

Lincoln in His Own Words by Milton Meltzer. Harcourt, 1993.

A House Divided: The Lives of Ulysses S. Grant and Robert E. Lee by Jules Archer. Scholastic, 1995.

Tales from the Underground Railroad by Kate Connell. Steck-Vaughn, 1993.

The Story of Thomas Alva Edison by Margaret Cousins. Random House Children's Publishing, 1997.

Immigrant Kids by Russell Freedman. Puffin Books, 1995.

Content to Learn

Your child is about to begin studying major events that occurred before, during, and after the Civil War. In the sixth unit, Civil War Times, these are some of the topics that will be covered:

- how regional differences caused conflict between the North and South

- the actions taken by some Americans to try to end slavery

- the effects of Lincoln's victory in the 1860 election

- the Civil War and Reconstruction

- the settlement of the West

- how industries and inventions changed life in the United States during the late 1800s

- opportunities and challenges faced by immigrants

Activities to Try

- Discuss with your child the concept of frame of reference— where someone was when an event happened and what role he or she played in it. Then talk about how a child's frame of reference during the Civil War—whether that child was from the North or the South— might have influenced how he or she felt about the war.

- Imagine with your child that you are a witness to one of the debates that took place between Abraham Lincoln and Stephen Douglas in the summer of 1858. Describe what you see and hear at the debate, such as how the candidates look and what they say.

- Talk to your child about how settlers who moved from the East Coast to the Great Plains would have had to adjust to a new environment with a new climate and new kinds of resources. Work with your child to write a series of diary entries describing the life of a settler on the Great Plains and how that settler's life has changed since arriving there.

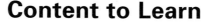

Ideas to Discuss

- Why did Lincoln's victory in the 1860 election eventually lead to the outbreak of the Civil War?

- How did Lincoln's death affect Reconstruction in the South?

- What were the main incentives that led to settlement of the West?

© Harcourt

GO ONLINE Visit **The Learning Site** at www.harcourtschool.com/socialstudies for additional activities, primary sources, and other resources to use in this unit.

Carta para la casa

Libros

Lincoln: A Photobiography por Russell Freedman. Clarion, 1987.

Lincoln In His Own Words por Milton Meltzer. Harcourt, 1993.

A House Divided: The Lives of Ulysses S. Grant and Robert E. Lee por Jules Archer. Scholastic, 1995.

Tales from the Underground Railroad por Kate Connell. Steck-Vaughn, 1993.

The Story of Thomas Alva Edison por Margaret Cousins. Random House Children's Publishing, 1997.

Immigrant Kids por Russell Freedman. Puffin Books, 1995.

Tema de estudio

Su hijo comenzará a estudiar grandes hechos que tuvieron lugar antes, durante y después de la Guerra Civil. Éstos son algunos de los tópicos que cubrirá la sexta unidad, La Guerra Civil:

- cómo las diferencias regionales provocaron conflictos entre el Norte y el Sur
- las acciones emprendidas por algunos americanos para tratar de terminar con la esclavitud
- los efectos de la victoria de Lincoln en las elecciones de 1860
- la Guerra Civil y la Reconstrucción
- la colonización del Oeste
- cómo nuevas industrias e inventos cambiaron la vida en Estados Unidos a fines del siglo XIX
- oportunidades y desafíos enfrentados por los inmigrantes

Actividades

- Hablen con su hijo sobre el concepto de marco de referencia—dónde estaba alguien cuando ocurrió un hecho y qué papel jugó en el mismo. Entonces hablen sobre cómo el marco de referencia de un niño durante la Guerra Civil—sea el niño del Norte o del Sur—podría haber influido en cómo se sentían acerca de la guerra.

- Con su hijo, imagine que presencia uno de los debates entre Abraham Lincoln y Stephen Douglas en el verano de 1858. Describan lo que ven y lo que escuchan en el debate, cómo el aspecto que tienen los candidatos y qué dicen.

- Hable con su hijo de cómo debieron adaptarse al nuevo ambiente, clima y nuevos tipos de recursos los colonos que se trasladaron de la costa este a las Grandes Llanuras. Ayude a su hijo a escribir una serie de anotaciones en un diario describiendo la vida de un colono en las Grandes Llanuras y de cómo cambia su vida al llegar allí.

Ideas para comentar

- ¿Por qué la victoria de Lincoln en las elecciones de 1860 condujo al estallido de la Guerra Civil?

- ¿Cómo afectó la muerte de Lincoln a la Reconstrucción en el Sur?

- ¿Cuáles fueron los principales incentivos que impulsaron la colonización del Oeste?

Visiten The Learning Site en www.harcourtschool.com/socialstudies para obtener actividades adicionales, fuentes originales y otros recursos para usar en esta unidad.

School to Home

Newsletter

Books To Read

Rosie the Riveter: Women Working on the Home Front During World War II by Penny Colman. Crown, 1995.

The Year They Walked: Rosa Parks and the Montgomery Bus Boycott by Beatrice Siegel. Macmillan, 1992.

Martin Luther King, Jr.: Free at Last by David A. Adler. Holiday House, 1986.

Content to Learn

Your child is about to begin studying life in the United States during the 1900s. These are some of the topics that will be covered in the seventh unit, The Twentieth Century:

- how the United States gained new territories and became a world power
- efforts to reform government and improve people's lives
- World War I
- the Roaring Twenties and the Great Depression
- the causes of World War II and America's entry into the war
- World War II and the events that led the Allies to defeat the Axis powers
- The Cold War and new threats to democracy
- the leaders and key events of the Civil Rights Movement
- the Vietnam War era
- the end of the Cold War and the successes and challenges faced by the United States in the final two decades of the twentieth century

Activities to Try

- With your child, look through print or online resources to find examples of music, art, and literature from the 1920s. Discuss how each example reflects life during the Roaring Twenties. Then talk about how current music, art, and literature reflect the culture we live in today.

- Imagine with your child that you are living during the time of World War II. Talk about the idea of rationing, why rationing is necessary, and how it affects your daily life.

- With your child, list some of the important events that happened during the 1990s that affected the United States. Then explain what you remember about these events and how you felt at the time. Compare and contrast these feelings with what people who lived through events early in the twentieth century probably felt.

Ideas to Discuss

- In what ways was World War II different from any other war?

- How did the Cold War affect the United States during the second half of the twentieth century?

GO ONLINE Visit **The Learning Site** at www.harcourtschool.com/socialstudies for additional activities, primary sources, and other resources to use in this unit.

Carta para la casa

Boletín

Libros

Rosie the Riveter: Women Working on the Home Front During World War II por Penny Colman. Crown, 1995.

The Year They Walked: Rosa Parks and the Montgomery Bus Boycott por Beatrice Siegel. Macmillan, 1992.

Martin Luther King, Jr.: Free at Last por David A. Adler. Holiday House, 1986.

Tema de estudio

Su hijo comenzará a estudiar la vida en Estados Unidos durante el siglo XX. Éstos son algunos de los tópicos que cubrirá la séptima unidad, El siglo XX:

- cómo Estados Unidos gana nuevos territorios y se convierte en una potencia mundial hacia fines del siglo diecinueve
- reformas para mejorar el gobierno y la vida de la gente
- la Primera Guerra Mundial
- la prosperidad de la década de 1920 y la Gran Depresión de los años treinta
- las causas de la Segunda Guerra Mundial y entrada de Estados Unidos en la guerra
- la Segunda Guerra Mundial y los hechos que condujeron a los aliados a derrotar a los poderes del Eje
- la Guerra Fría y nuevas amenazas a la democracia
- los líderes y los hechos clave del Movimiento por los Derechos Civiles
- la era de la Guerra de Vietnam
- el final de la Guerra Fría y los logros y desafíos enfrentados por Estados Unidos en las últimas dos décadas del siglo XX

Actividades

- Con su hijo, busque en material impreso o en Internet ejemplos de música, artes plásticas y literatura de la década de 1920. Hablen de cómo cada ejemplo refleja la vida durante los Años Locos. Discutan luego cómo la música, el arte y la literatura del presente reflejan la cultura de nuestros días.

- Juntos, imaginen estar viviendo en la época de la Segunda Guerra Mundial. Hablen sobre la idea de racionar por qué es importante y cómo afecta su vida cotidiana.

- Anoten juntos algunos de los hechos importantes ocurridos en la década de 1990 que afectaron a Estados Unidos. Expliquen luego qué recuerdan de esos hechos y cómo se sintieron entonces. Comparen esas sensaciones con las que probablemente sintió la gente que vivió los hechos de los primeros años del siglo XX.

Ideas para comentar

- ¿En qué sentidos la Segunda Guerra Mundial fue diferente de cualquier otra guerra?

- ¿Cómo afectó la Guerra Fría a Estados Unidos durante la segunda mitad del siglo XX?

Visiten The Learning Site en www.harcourtschool.com/socialstudies para obtener actividades adicionales, fuentes originales y otros recursos para usar en esta unidad.

© Harcourt

School to Home

Books To Read

Celebrate! In Central America by Diane and Joe Viesti. Lothrop, Lee & Shepard, 1997.

Canada Facts and Figures by Susan Levert. Chelsea House, 1992.

Chico Mendes: Defender of the Rain Forest by Joann Burch. Millbrook, 1994.

Content to Learn

Your child is about to begin studying the United States today, its relationship with other nations, and its neighbors in the Western Hemisphere. In the eighth unit, The United States and the World, these are some of the topics that will be covered:

- how technology and cultural diversity have affected Americans' way of life

- how population growth has presented new challenges for the United States

- how changes in the American economy have changed the way many people earn a living

- the role of government and the rights and responsibilities of citizens

- the history of Mexico and its relationship with the United States

- nations in the Caribbean and Central America

- South America and its past and present challenges

- the history of Canada and its relationship with the United States

Activities to Try

- Share with your child information about your family's culture and heritage. Use an encyclopedia or the Internet to learn more about the country where your family or your ancestors came from.

- Discuss with your child similarities and differences in your school experiences and those of your child. For example, contrast the way in which you gathered and wrote information for research reports with the way your child is able to gather and write information.

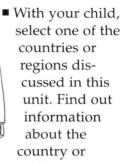

- With your child, select one of the countries or regions discussed in this unit. Find out information about the country or region, and create a travel brochure for it.

Ideas to Discuss

- How have new technologies and population growth affected people's daily lives?

- Why is the time in which we live called the Information Age?

- How is the United States interdependent with other countries?

Visit **The Learning Site** at www.harcourtschool.com/socialstudies for additional activities, primary sources, and other resources to use in this unit.

Carta para la casa

Boletín

Libros

Celebrate! In Central America por Diane y Joe Viesti. Lothrop, Lee & Shepard, 1997.

Canada Facts and Figures por Susan Levert. Chelsea House, 1992.

Chico Mendes: Defender of the Rain Forest por Joann Burch. Millbrook, 1994.

Tema de estudio

Su hijo comenzará a estudiar Estados Unidos hoy y su relación con otras naciones. Éstos son algunos de los tópicos que cubrirá la octava unidad, Estados Unidos y el mundo:

- los avances tecnológicos y la diversidad cultural han afectado el modo de vida de los estadounidenses
- el crecimiento de la población ha presentado nuevos desafíos para Estados Unidos
- los cambios en la economía americana han modificado el modo en que mucha se gana la vida
- el papel del gobierno y los derechos y responsabilidades del ciudadano
- la historia de México y su relación con Estados Unidos
- naciones del Caribe y América Central
- América del Sur y sus desafíos pasados y presentes
- la historia de Canadá y su relación con Estados Unidos

✏ Actividades

- Comparta con su hijo información sobre la cultura y la herencia de su familia. Usen una enciclopedia o Internet para buscar más información sobre el país del que provienen sus antepasados o su familia.

- Hablen sobre las similitudes y diferencias entre su propia experiencia escolar y la de su hijo. Por ejemplo, comparen la forma en que usted reunía y escribía la información y el modo en que lo hace su hijo.

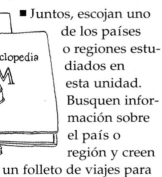

- Juntos, escojan uno de los países o regiones estudiados en esta unidad. Busquen información sobre el país o región y creen un folleto de viajes para ese sitio.

💡 Ideas para comentar

- ¿Cómo han afectado la vida cotidiana los adelantos tecnológicos y el aumento de la población?

- ¿Por qué este período en el cual vivimos la Era de la Información?

- ¿Es Estados Unidos interdependiente con otros países?

Visiten The Learning Site en www.harcourtschool.com/socialstudies para obtener actividades adicionales, fuentes originales y otros recursos para usar en esta unidad.

© Harcourt

Teacher's Edition
Index

Index

H

Health Activities, 81, 118, 151, 316, 407, 462, 468, 528

Heritage Features
Columbus Day, 123
Epiphany, 623
Family Heritage, 79
Fiestas Patrias, 654
French Quarter, The, 154
Independence Day, 306
Juneteenth, 482
Labor Day, 533
Memorial Day, 470
Pledge of Allegiance, 642
"Star-Spangled Banner, The," 392
Thanksgiving Day, 168
Uncle Sam, 640

History, 19, 20, 22, 28, 29, 38, 41, 47, 64, 82, 83, 107, 108, 109, 110, 116, 118, 124, 125, 129, 130, 131, 151, 153, 158, 161, 169, 190, 195, 198, 202, 213, 220, 221, 225, 233, 234, 235, 236, 242, 243, 269, 270, 271, 274, 275, 284, 290, 291, 294, 295, 303, 305, 309, 310, 315, 317, 318, 323, 324, 325, 326, 327, 348, 353, 354, 355, 356, 359, 360, 370, 371, 376, 378, 386, 390, 391, 392, 403, 404, 407, 414, 415, 439, 447, 453, 460, 461, 467, 468, 469, 477, 478, 482, 484, 488, 495, 497, 504, 505, 526, 527, 533, 535, 538, 539, 543, 545, 555, 562, 567, 573, 574, 581, 582, 583, 592, 597, 598, 599, 600, 635, 653

Holiday Activities (Tab Section), H1–H12

Holocaust Education, 572–573

I

Integrate, 11F, 12, 19, 20, 21, 24, 27, 29, 30, 34, 35, 40, 41, 42, 46, 48, 50, 57, 58, 60, 65, 78, 79, 81, 82, 83, 84, 87, 89, 94, 99F, 100, 102, 107, 108, 109, 116, 118, 122, 123, 125, 128, 129, 130, 131, 132, 137, 145, 146, 147, 148, 151, 156, 157, 162, 168, 174, 179F, 180, 183, 184, 190, 195, 197, 203, 211, 213, 214, 218, 220, 221, 233, 236, 238, 243, 246, 259F, 260, 262, 263, 270, 278, 280, 281, 283, 284, 286, 290, 291, 295, 296, 302, 303, 309, 315, 316, 317, 318, 326, 339F, 340, 348, 349, 353, 356, 359, 360, 362, 367, 368, 369, 370, 374, 376, 377, 385, 392, 393, 396, 397, 403, 406, 407, 413, 414, 415,

416, 422, 427F, 428, 431, 432, 437, 439, 446, 448, 451, 452, 454, 456, 460, 461, 462, 463, 468, 469, 477, 482, 483, 488, 495, 497, 503, 504, 510, 515F, 516, 518, 520, 524, 525, 526, 528, 530, 532, 534, 535, 540, 542, 543, 544, 545, 548, 555, 566, 570, 581, 585, 586, 591, 592, 597, 607, 611F, 612, 614, 616, 622, 623, 630, 641, 644, 646, 655, 659, 662, 665, 672
See also Art Activities; Health Activities; Language Arts Activities; Language (World) Activities; Mathematics Activities; Music Activities; Physical Education Activities; Reading Activities; Science Activities

Internet, 11E, 20, 58, 75, 83, 95, 99E, 103, 109, 117, 129, 135, 175, 179E, 185, 198, 217, 220, 255, 259E, 265, 269, 282, 291, 321, 339E, 343, 353, 370, 391, 401, 427E, 433, 452, 467, 488, 490, 501, 515E, 521, 544, 555, 595, 599, 607, 611E, 617, 622, 647, 665, 670, S1–S16

K

Kinesthetic Learners, 156, 196, 342, 367, 640, 666

L

Language Arts Activities, 12, 21, 29, 65, 82, 89, 94, 100, 107, 122, 130, 131, 132, 145, 146, 148, 156, 157, 190, 197, 214, 220, 238, 243, 246, 260, 270, 281, 284, 291, 296, 302, 309, 315, 318, 340, 360, 367, 369, 376, 385, 392, 432, 446, 451, 452, 462, 477, 482, 497, 516, 526, 532, 545, 548, 566, 597, 607, 612, 623, 630, 646, 655, 662

Language (World) Activities, 34, 50, 60, 102, 129, 137, 145, 211, 262, 278, 403, 483, 504, 525, 591, 614

Learning Site, The: Social Studies Center, 11E, 20, 47, 58, 75, 83, 95, 99E, 103, 109, 117, 129, 135, 175, 179E, 185, 198, 217, 220, 255, 259E, 265, 269, 282, 291, 321, 335, 339E, 343, 353, 370, 391, 401, 423, 427E, 433, 452, 467, 488, 490, 501, 511, 515E, 521, 544, 555, 595, 599, 607, 611E, 617, 622, 647, 665, 670, 679, S1–S16

Literature, 11D, 14–15, 98, 99D, 102–103, 178, 179D, 182–185, 258, 259D, 262–265, 338, 339D, 342–343, 426, 427D, 430–433, 514, 515D, 518–521, 610, 611D, 614–617, 682, S1–S16

M

Make It Relevant
Discussion Topics, 17, 55, 105, 143, 187, 209, 231, 267, 301, 345, 370, 383, 435, 475, 523, 553, 579, 619, 651
At Home, 20, 31, 226, 271, 327, 417, 561, 583, 674
At School, 70, 349, 354, 364, 626
In Your City, 354
In Your Community, 44, 47, 77, 95, 124, 150, 169, 250, 255, 288, 306, 354, 410, 494, 570, 588, 599, 622, 639, 678
In Your Country, 494
In Your State, 24, 44, 68, 88, 112, 163, 198, 243, 246, 282, 334, 359, 376, 450, 511, 570, 602, 624, 629

Map and Globe Skills, 68–69, 246–247, 278–279, 410–411, 456, 530–531, 602, 674–675

Mathematics Activities, 20, 24, 30, 41, 48, 123, 180, 195, 218, 283, 295, 317, 340, 348, 349, 353, 359, 397, 406, 413, 422, 428, 437, 456, 461, 488, 524, 540, 581, 622, 655

Mental Mapping, 13, 22, 45, 124, 131, 146, 153, 181, 189, 225, 234, 260, 269, 323, 326, 404, 410, 466, 487, 503, 539, 555, 565, 654, 658, 670

Multimedia Resources, 11D, 99D, 179D, 259D, 339D, 427D, 515D, 611D

Music Activities, 128, 147, 263, 290, 316, 362, 393, 414, 503, 535, 542, 585, 672

O

Objectives, 11L, 12, 16, 18, 24, 26, 33, 40, 44, 50, 54, 56, 60, 62, 68, 70, 74, 76, 81, 86, 91, 94, 99L, 100, 102, 104, 106, 112, 114, 120, 121, 127, 134, 136, 142, 144, 150, 156, 160, 165, 166, 171, 174, 179L, 180, 182, 186, 188, 194, 200, 205, 208, 210, 216, 218, 223, 224, 230, 232, 240, 241, 246, 248, 254, 259L, 260, 262, 266, 268, 273, 278, 280, 286, 288, 293, 300, 302, 308, 313, 314, 320, 322, 330, 339L, 340, 342, 344, 346, 351, 358, 364, 366, 373, 374, 382, 384, 389, 395, 400, 402, 410, 412, 427L, 428, 430, 434, 436, 442, 444, 450, 456, 458, 465, 474, 476, 481, 486, 492, 494, 500, 502, 515L, 516, 518, 522, 524, 530, 532, 537, 542, 552, 554, 559, 560, 564, 565, 570, 572, 578, 580,

585, 590, 594, 596, 602, 606, 611L, 612, 614, 618, 620, 626, 628, 632, 638, 644, 650, 652, 657, 662, 664, 669, 674

P

Performance Assessment
Lesson Performance, 23, 32, 39, 43, 49, 59, 67, 73, 80, 85, 90, 98, 111, 119, 126, 133, 139, 149, 155, 159, 170, 178, 193, 199, 204, 215, 222, 227, 239, 245, 251, 258, 272, 277, 285, 292, 297, 307, 312, 319, 329, 338, 350, 357, 363, 372, 379, 388, 394, 399, 409, 419, 426, 441, 449, 455, 464, 471, 480, 485, 491, 499, 507, 514, 529, 536, 541, 549, 558, 563, 569, 575, 584, 589, 593, 601, 610, 625, 631, 637, 643, 656, 661, 668, 673, 682
Unit Project, 15, 52, 92, 98, 103, 140, 172, 178, 185, 206, 228, 252, 258, 265, 298, 332, 338, 343, 380, 420, 426, 433, 472, 508, 514, 521, 550, 576, 604, 610, 617, 648, 676, 682

Physical Education Activities, 125
Planning Guides, 11B, 16A–16D, 54A–54D, 99B, 104A–104D, 142A–142D, 179B, 186A–186D, 208A–208D, 230A–230D, 259B, 266A–266D, 300A–300D, 339B, 344A–344D, 382A–382D, 427B, 434A–434D, 474A–474D, 515B, 522A–522D, 552A–552D, 578A–578D, 611B, 618A–618D, 650A–650D

Points of View Features
For or Against the Bill of Rights, 368
Should Quebec Secede?, 672
Taxes, 281
Union or Secession?, 453
Unknown Land, An, 124
Preview the Vocabulary, 11, 99, 179, 259, 339, 427, 515, 611
Primary Sources
See Analyze Primary Sources

Q

Questions Kids Ask, 8, 28, 42, 109, 138, 158, 161, 201, 211, 224, 242, 249, 274, 305, 328, 352, 361, 393, 458, 479, 496, 527, 538, 562, 567, 574, 582, 587, 634, 667, 671
Quotations, 17, 55, 105, 143, 187, 209, 231, 267, 300, 345, 383, 434, 435, 475, 523, 553, 579, 619, 651

R

Reach All Learners
Advanced Learners, 11G, 19, 38, 56, 99G, 101, 121, 151, 179G, 200, 221, 232, 259G, 295, 309, 314, 324, 330, 339G, 346, 348, 364, 368, 378, 387, 389, 404, 410, 423, 427G, 453, 459, 478, 498, 515G, 519, 524, 554, 590, 611G, 621, 635, 639
Auditory Learners, 70, 102, 137, 244, 291, 306, 310, 355, 358, 368, 375, 438, 451, 654, 671
Below-Level Learners, 11G, 64, 71, 99G, 160, 175, 179G, 188, 259G, 274, 289, 308, 339G, 347, 427G, 442, 445, 515G, 532, 598, 611G, 613, 632, 667, 669
English as a Second Language, 11G, 26, 99G, 117, 179G, 224, 254, 259G, 273, 334, 339G, 412, 427G, 431, 465, 481, 515G, 516, 543, 572, 611G, 628, 638, 678
Kinesthetic Learners, 156, 196, 342, 367, 640, 666
Tactile Learners, 28, 101, 127, 152, 237, 315, 369, 398, 446, 506, 537, 580, 606
Reading Activities, 174, 195, 214, 286, 296, 356, 368, 374, 396, 439, 452, 469, 544, 641
Reading in the Content Area (Tab Section), C1–C10
Reading Skills
Categorize, 143, 162, 435, 436
Cause and Effect, 120, 267, 275, 281, 553, 561, 573
Compare and Contrast, 55, 63, 76, 79, 83
Determine Point of View, 286–287, 475, 505
Draw Conclusions, 383, 403
Generalize, 231, 235, 242, 244
Identify Fact and Opinion, 240, 619, 620
Identify Frame of Reference, 442–443
Identify Primary and Secondary Sources, 4–5
Make Inferences, 209, 523, 526
Predict a Likely Outcome, 559, 579, 587
Sequence, 105, 110, 130, 301, 314
Summarize, 187, 191, 314, 345, 352, 366, 371
Reading Social Studies
Anticipation Guide, 27, 32, 63, 67, 71, 73, 115, 119, 157, 159, 201, 203, 249, 251, 274, 277, 294, 297, 323, 329, 352, 356, 437, 441, 459, 464, 487, 491, 538, 541, 566, 568, 597, 601, 653, 656
Create Mental Images, 87, 192, 219, 238, 264, 629

Graphic Organizer, 57, 59, 87, 90, 122, 126, 145, 149, 151, 155, 182, 184, 219, 222, 226, 289, 292, 347, 349, 359, 361, 363, 385, 388, 430, 432, 466, 471, 477, 480, 573, 575, 581, 584, 591, 629, 630, 658, 661
K-W-L Chart, 34, 39, 137, 139, 242, 245, 315, 319, 403, 409, 445, 503, 507, 543, 549, 555, 558, 591, 593, 639, 643
Paraphrase, 276, 470
Personal Response, 41, 43, 102, 103, 189, 193, 225, 227, 262, 264, 309, 312, 342, 343, 367, 495, 499, 518, 520, 525, 528, 586, 589, 614, 616
Predictions, 77, 80, 203, 317, 396, 399, 621, 625
Read Aloud, 519, 633
Reread to Clarify, 117, 237, 547, 660
Study Questions, 19, 23, 45, 48, 82, 84, 107, 111, 128, 161, 167, 195, 198, 211, 215, 233, 239, 269, 272, 281, 285, 303, 307, 375, 379, 390, 394, 413, 419, 451, 455, 482, 485, 533, 536, 561, 563, 633, 636, 665, 668
Summarize, 22, 304, 314, 467, 482, 623, 670, 673
Use Content to Confirm Meaning, 37
Use Text Structure and Format, 122
Reteach Activities, 23, 25, 32, 39, 43, 49, 51, 59, 61, 67, 69, 73, 75, 80, 85, 90, 91, 111, 113, 119, 120, 126, 133, 135, 139, 149, 155, 159, 165, 170, 171, 193, 199, 204, 205, 215, 217, 222, 223, 227, 239, 240, 245, 247, 251, 272, 277, 279, 285, 287, 292, 297, 307, 312, 313, 319, 321, 329, 331, 350, 357, 363, 365, 372, 373, 379, 388, 394, 399, 401, 409, 410, 411, 419, 441, 443, 449, 455, 457, 464, 471, 480, 485, 491, 493, 499, 501, 507, 529, 531, 536, 541, 549, 558, 559, 563, 564, 569, 571, 575, 584, 589, 593, 595, 601, 602, 625, 627, 631, 637, 643, 645, 647, 656, 661, 663, 668, 673, 675
Rubrics, 11K, 99K, 179K, 259K, 339K, 427K, 515K, 611K

S

School to Home Newsletter (Tab Section), S1–S16
Science Activities, 27, 35, 57, 84, 87, 108, 116, 213, 221, 233, 236, 377, 406, 415, 431, 495, 520, 530, 555, 659, 665
Science and Technology Features
Arecibo Observatory, The, 660
Blood Shortage, 562
Cast-Steel Plow, 418

H. L. Hunley, The, 466
Microchip, The, 624
Navigational Tools, 117
Skills Path, 11C, 99C, 179C, 259C, 339C, 427C, 515C, 611C
Social Studies Skills, A2–A3, 4–5, 24–25, 50–51, 60–61, 68–69, 91, 112–113, 120, 165, 171, 205, 223, 240, 246–247, 278–279, 286, 313, 330–331, 364–365, 373, 410–411, 442–443, 456–457, 492–493, 530–531, 559, 564, 570–571, 602–603, 626–627, 644–645, 662–663, 674–675
Study and Research Skills
Graphic Aids, Using, 325, 330
Graphic Organizers, Using, 391, 413
Internet, Using the, 311, 483, 489, 659
Maps, Using, 189, 248, 539, 545
Note Taking, 18, 77, 106, 234, 439, 502
Outlining, 44, 62, 81, 212, 304, 356, 444, 486, 556, 596, 666
Periodicals and Newspapers, Using, 318, 534
Reference Sources, Using, 200, 216, 384, 454, 664
Skimming and Scanning, 38, 150, 351, 476, 560
Summarizing Information, 127, 219, 241, 268, 465
Time Line, Make a, 322
Summarize Key Content, 38, 42, 48, 58, 66, 72, 79, 84, 89, 110, 118, 125, 132, 138, 148, 154, 158, 169, 192, 198, 203, 214, 221, 226, 238, 244, 250, 271, 276, 284, 291, 296, 306, 311, 319, 328, 349, 356, 362, 371, 378, 387, 393, 398, 408, 418, 440, 448, 454, 463, 470, 479, 484, 490, 498, 506, 528, 535, 540, 548, 557, 562, 568, 574, 583, 588, 592, 600, 624, 630, 636, 642, 655, 660, 667, 672
Summarize the Reading, 103, 184, 264, 343, 432, 520, 616

Tactile Learners, 28, 101, 127, 152, 237, 315, 369, 398, 446, 506, 537, 580, 606
Technology
GeoSkills CD-ROM, 25, 51, 69, 113, 247, 279, 411, 457, 531, 603, 675
Go Online, 11E, 20, 58, 75, 83, 95, 99E, 103, 109, 117, 129, 135, 175, 179E, 185, 198, 217, 220, 255, 259E, 265, 269, 282, 291, 321, 335, 339E, 343,

353, 370, 391, 401, 423, 427E, 433, 452, 467, 488, 490, 501, 511, 515E, 521, 544, 555, 595, 599, 607, 611E, 617, 622, 647, 665, 670, 679, S1–S16
The Learning Site: Social Studies Center, 11E, 20, 47, 58, 75, 83, 95, 99E, 103, 109, 117, 129, 135, 175, 179E, 185, 198, 217, 220, 255, 259E, 265, 269, 282, 291, 321, 335, 339E, 343, 353, 370, 391, 401, 423, 427E, 433, 452, 467, 488, 490, 501, 511, 515E, 521, 544, 555, 595, 599, 607, 611E, 617, 622, 647, 665, 670, 679, S1–S16
Test Preparation, 52, 92, 97, 140, 172, 177, 206, 228, 252, 257, 298, 332, 337, 380, 420, 425, 472, 508, 513, 550, 576, 604, 609, 648, 676, 681
Think & Write, 52, 92, 140, 172, 206, 228, 252, 298, 332, 380, 420, 472, 508, 550, 576, 604, 648, 676
Thinking Organizers (Tab Section), T1–T28
Time for Kids Readers, 15, 103, 185, 265, 343, 433, 521, 617
Time Lines, 12, 60–61, 100, 180, 260, 322, 340, 409, 428, 516, 541, 571, 612

Unit Project, 15, 52, 92, 98, 103, 140, 172, 178, 185, 206, 228, 252, 258, 265, 298, 332, 338, 343, 380, 420, 426, 433, 472, 508, 514, 521, 550, 576, 604, 610, 617, 648, 676, 682

Video, 11D, 99D, 179D, 259D, 339D, 427D, 515D, 611D
Take a Field Trip Video, 95, 175, 255, 335, 423, 511, 607, 679
Visual Learning
Art, 83, 88, 315, 462
Artifacts, 82, 87, 326, 386
Charts, 48, 101, 181, 353, 354, 459
Diagrams, 28, 35, 77, 146, 362
Documents, 234
Graphs, 261, 283, 341, 397, 429, 445, 448, 496, 497, 504, 517, 545, 547, 561, 589, 591, 613

Illustrations, 12, 100, 107, 109, 180, 183, 184, 235, 260, 263, 275, 340, 391, 431, 516, 520, 612, 616
Locate It Maps, 16, 54, 104, 142, 186, 209, 230, 266, 300, 345, 382, 434, 474, 522, 552, 578, 618, 650
Maps, 12, 20, 25, 27, 29, 36, 38, 42, 45, 51, 57, 65, 69, 89, 100, 108, 113, 118, 122, 125, 129, 138, 148, 151, 153, 154, 157, 162, 180, 189, 202, 211, 219, 225, 234, 238, 260, 269, 274, 291, 323, 329, 340, 353, 369, 385, 391, 398, 404, 406, 415, 428, 438, 439, 440, 446, 460, 470, 488, 489, 498, 516, 526, 528, 539, 552, 557, 568, 574, 581, 582, 592, 612, 621, 653, 658, 665, 670
Paintings, 82, 152, 305, 316, 317, 327, 469
Photographs, 58, 236, 552, 621, 634, 635, 641, 655, 659
Pictures, 11L, 16, 19, 21, 37, 54, 64, 79, 99L, 104, 142, 179, 186, 189, 208, 230, 259L, 266, 300, 339L, 344, 382, 434, 474, 477, 515, 522, 557, 578, 599, 611, 618, 650, 666, 671
Tables, 13
Time Lines, 12, 100, 180, 260, 340, 428, 516, 612
Vocabulary Cards (Tab Section), V1–V100

Word Work
Antonyms, 232
Categorize Vocabulary, 33, 86, 241, 308, 358, 533, 572
Compound Terms, 652
Context Clues, 302
Historical Context, 62, 182, 430, 565, 632
Multiple Meanings, 26, 262, 468
Prefixes, 40, 202, 560, 620
Preview Vocabulary, 17, 55, 105, 114, 136, 143, 144, 166, 187, 209, 210, 231, 248, 267, 293, 301, 345, 374, 383, 402, 435, 475, 476, 523, 553, 579, 590, 619, 620, 651, 669
Related Words, 6, 346, 596
Structural Clues, 585
Suffixes, 40, 282, 546, 560, 638
Synonyms, 232, 324
Use Reference Sources, 194, 286, 322, 444
Vocabulary Chart, 614
Word Origins, 58, 395, 626, 657